t DISTRIBUTION

Areas in Both Tails Combined for Student's *t* Distribution*

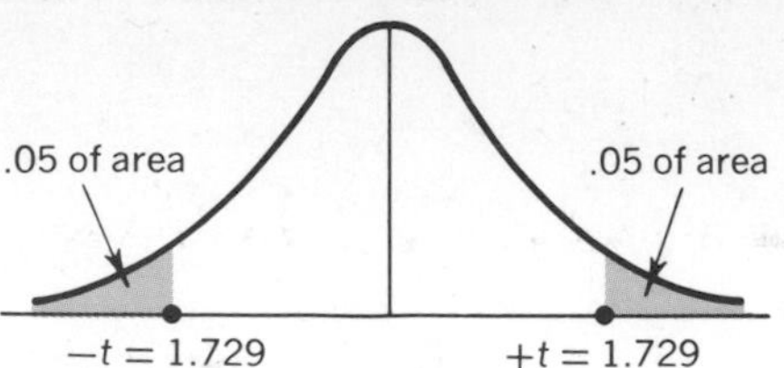

EXAMPLE: To find the value of *t* which corresponds to an area of .10 in both tails of the distribution combined, when there are 19 degrees of freedom, look under the .10 column, and proceed down to the 19 degrees of freedom row; the appropriate *t* value there is 1.729.

Degrees of freedom	Area in both tails combined			
	.10	.05	.02	.01
1	6.314	12.706	31.821	63.657
2	2.920	4.303	6.965	9.925
3	2.353	3.182	4.541	5.841
4	2.132	2.776	3.747	4.604
5	2.015	2.571	3.365	4.032
6	1.943	2.447	3.143	3.707
7	1.895	2.365	2.998	3.499
8	1.860	2.306	2.896	3.355
9	1.833	2.262	2.821	3.250
10	1.812	2.228	2.764	3.169
11	1.796	2.201	2.718	3.106
12	1.782	2.179	2.681	3.055
13	1.771	2.160	2.650	3.012
14	1.761	2.145	2.624	2.977
15	1.753	2.131	2.602	2.947
16	1.746	2.120	2.583	2.921
17	1.740	2.110	2.567	2.898
18	1.734	2.101	2.552	2.878
19	1.729	2.093	2.539	2.861
20	1.725	2.086	2.528	2.845
21	1.721	2.080	2.518	2.831
22	1.717	2.074	2.508	2.819
23	1.714	2.069	2.500	2.807
24	1.711	2.064	2.492	2.797
25	1.708	2.060	2.485	2.787
26	1.706	2.056	2.479	2.779
27	1.703	2.052	2.473	2.771
28	1.701	2.048	2.467	2.763
29	1.699	2.045	2.462	2.756
30	1.697	2.042	2.457	2.750
40	1.684	2.021	2.423	2.704
60	1.671	2.000	2.390	2.660
120	1.658	1.980	2.358	2.617
Normal Distribution	1.645	1.960	2.326	2.576

*Taken from Table III of Fisher and Yates, *Statistical Tables for Biological, Agricultural and Medical Research*, published by Longman Group Ltd., London (previously published by Oliver & Boyd, Edinburgh) and by permission of the authors and publishers.

THIRD EDITION

STATISTICS FOR MANAGEMENT

Richard I. Levin
The University of North Carolina, Chapel Hill

Prentice-Hall, Inc., Englewood Cliffs, New Jersey 07632

Library of Congress Cataloging in Publication Data

LEVIN, RICHARD I.
Statistics for management.

Bibliography: p.
Includes index.
1. Social sciences—Statistical methods. 2. Commercial statistics. 3. Management—Statistical methods.
I. Title.
HA29.L3887 1984 519.5 83-17790
ISBN 0-13-845248-2

CHAPTER OPENING PHOTO CREDITS
Chapter 2: Charlotte Public Service and Information Department *Chapter 3:* George Betancourt, Northeast Utilities *Chapter 4:* Van Bucher, Photo Researchers, Inc. *Chapter 5:* Resorts International Casino Hotel *Chapter 6:* Leviton Atlanta for Coca-Cola *Chapter 7:* Zenith Radio Corporation *Chapter 8:* Union Electric Company *Chapter 9:* The Houston Astrodome *Chapter 10:* Chrysler Corporation *Chapter 11:* Allied Corporation *Chapter 12:* Marc Anderson *Chapter 13:* United Nations *Chapter 14:* Bob Perry, Killington Photo *Chapter 15:* Bethlehem Steel *Chapter 16:* United Fresh Fruit and Vegetable Association

P-H International Series in Management

Editorial/production supervision: Sonia Meyer
Interior and cover design: Christine Gehring-Wolf
Cover photo: Paul Silverman
Photo researcher: Christine A. Pullo
Manufacturing buyer: Ed O'Dougherty

Printed in the United States of America
10 9 8 7 6 5 4 3 2 1

ISBN 0-13-845248-2

Prentice-Hall International, Inc., *London*
Prentice-Hall of Australia Pty. Limited, *Sydney*
Editora Prentice-Hall do Brasil, Ltda., *Rio de Janeiro*
Prentice-Hall Canada Inc., *Toronto*
Prentice-Hall of India Private Limited, *New Delhi*
Prentice-Hall of Japan, Inc., *Tokyo*
Prentice-Hall of Southeast Asia Pte. Ltd., *Singapore*
Whitehall Books Limited, *Wellington, New Zealand*

CONTENTS

Preface ix

CHAPTER 1

INTRODUCTION 2

1-1 Definitions 1-2 History 1-3 Subdivisions Within Statistics 1-4 Strategy, Assumptions, and Approach

CHAPTER 2

ARRANGING DATA TO CONVEY MEANING: TABLES AND GRAPHS 6

2-1 How Can We Arrange Data? 2-2 Examples of Raw Data 2-3 Arranging Data Using the Data Array and the Frequency Distribution 2-4 Constructing a Frequency Distribution 2-5 Graphing Frequency Distributions New Terms New Equations Review Exercises Concepts Test Conceptual Case Computer Data Base Exercises Flow Chart

CHAPTER 3

SUMMARY MEASURES OF FREQUENCY DISTRIBUTIONS 56

3-1 Beyond Tables and Graphs: Descriptive Measures of Frequency Distributions 3-2 A Measure of Central Tendency: The Arithmetic Mean 3-3 A Second Measure of Central Tendency: The Weighted Mean 3-4 A Third Measure of Central Tendency: The Geometric Mean 3-5 A Fourth Measure of Central Tendency: The Median 3-6 A Final Measure of Central Tendency: The Mode 3-7 Comparing the Mean, Median, and Mode

New Terms New Equations Review Exercises Concepts Test Conceptual Case Computer Data Base Exercise Flow Chart

CHAPTER 4

MEASURING VARIABILITY 104

4-1 Measures of Dispersion 4-2 Dispersion: Distance Measure 4-3 Dispersion: Average Deviation Measures 4-4 Relative Dispersion: The Coefficient of Variation 4-5 Exploratory Data Analysis New Terms New Equations Review Exercises Concepts Test Conceptual Case Computer Data Base Exercise Flow Chart

CHAPTER 5

PROBABILITY I: INTRODUCTORY IDEAS 142

5-1 History and Relevance of Probability Theory 5-2 Some Basic Concepts in Probability 5-3 Three Types of Probability 5-4 Probability Rules 5-5 Probabilities Under Conditions of Statistical Independence 5-6 Probabilities Under Conditions of Statistical Dependence 5-7 Revising Prior Estimates of Probabilities: Bayes' Theorem New Terms New Equations Review Exercises Concepts Test Conceptual Case Computer Data Base Exercise Flow Chart

CHAPTER 6

PROBABILITY II: DISTRIBUTIONS 198

6-1 Introduction to Probability Distributions 6-2 Random Variables 6-3 Use of Expected Value in Decision Making 6-4 The Binomial Distribution 6-5 The Poisson Distribution 6-6 The Normal Distribution: A Distribution of a Continuous Random Variable 6-7 Choosing the Correct Probability Distribution New Terms New Equations Review Exercises Concepts Test Conceptual Case Computer Data Base Exercise Flow Chart

CHAPTER 7

SAMPLING AND SAMPLING DISTRIBUTIONS 266

7-1 Introduction to Sampling 7-2 Random Sampling 7-3 Introduction to Sampling Distributions 7-4 Sampling Distributions in More Detail 7-5 An Operational Consideration in Sampling: The Relationship Between Sample Size and Standard Error 7-6 Design of Experiments New Terms New Equations Review Exercises Concepts Test Conceptual Case Computer Data Base Exercise Flow Chart

CHAPTER 8

ESTIMATION 310

8-1 Introduction 8-2 Point Estimates 8-3 Interval Estimates: Basic Concepts 8-4 Interval Estimates and Confidence Intervals 8-5 Calculating Interval Estimates of the Mean from Large Samples 8-6 Calculating Interval Estimates of the Proportion from Large Samples 8-7 Interval Estimates Using the *t* Distribution 8-8 Determining the Sample Size in Estimation
New Terms New Equations Review Exercises Concepts Test Conceptual Case Computer Data Base Exercise Flow Chart

CHAPTER 9

TESTING HYPOTHESES 356

9-1 Introduction 9-2 Concepts Basic to the Hypothesis-Testing Procedure 9-3 Testing Hypotheses 9-4 Hypothesis Testing of Means—Samples with Population Standard Deviations Known 9-5 Measuring the Power of a Hypothesis Test 9-6 Hypothesis Testing of Proportions—Large Samples 9-7 Hypothesis Testing of Means Under Different Conditions 9-8 Hypothesis Testing for Differences Between Means and Proportions 9-9 Prob Values—Another Way to Look at Testing Hypotheses
New Terms New Equations Review Exercises Concepts Test Conceptual Case Computer Data Base Exercise Flow Chart

CHAPTER 10

CHI-SQUARE AND ANALYSIS OF VARIANCE 426

10-1 Introduction 10-2 Chi-Square as a Test of Independence 10-3 Chi-Square as a Test of Goodness of Fit: Testing the Appropriateness of a Distribution 10-4 Analysis of Variance 10-5 Inferences About a Population Variance 10-6 Inferences About Two Population Variances
New Terms New Equations Review Exercises Concepts Test Conceptual Case Computer Data Base Exercise Flow Chart

CHAPTER 11

SIMPLE REGRESSION AND CORRELATION 490

11-1 Introduction 11-2 Estimation Using the Regression Line 11-3 Correlation Analysis 11-4 Making Inferences About Population Parameters 11-5 Using Regression and Correlation Analysis: Limitations, Errors, and Caveats New Terms New Equations Review Exercises Concepts Test Conceptual Case Computer Data Base Exercise Flow Chart

CHAPTER 12

MULTIPLE REGRESSION AND MODELING TECHNIQUES 548

12-1 Multiple Regression and Correlation Analysis 12-2 Finding the Multiple Regression Equation 12-3 The Computer and Multiple Regression 12-4 Making Inferences About Population Parameters 12-5 Modeling Techniques New Terms New Equations Review Exercises Concepts Test Conceptual Case Computer Data Base Exercise Flow Chart

CHAPTER 13

NONPARAMETRIC METHODS 604

13-1 Introduction to Nonparametric Statistics 13-2 The Sign Test for Paired Data 13-3 A Rank Sum Test: The Mann-Whitney *U* Test 13-4 One-Sample Runs Test 13-5 Rank Correlation 13-6 The Kolmogorov-Smirnov Test New Terms New Equations Review Exercises Concepts Test Conceptual Case Computer Data Base Exercise Flow Chart

CHAPTER 14

TIME SERIES 660

14-1 Introduction 14-2 Variations in Time Series 14-3 Trend Analysis 14-4 Cyclical Variation 14-5 Seasonal Variation 14-6 Irregular Variation 14-7 A Problem Involving All Four Components of a Time Series 14-8 Time Series Analysis in Forecasting New Terms New Equations Review Exercises Concepts Test Conceptual Case Computer Data Base Exercise Flow Chart

CHAPTER 15

INDEX NUMBERS 706

15-1 Defining an Index Number 15-2 Unweighted Aggregates Index 15-3 Weighted Aggregates Index 15-4 Average of Relatives Methods 15-5 Quantity and Value Indices 15-6 Issues in Constructing an Index Number New Terms New Equations Review Exercises Concepts Test Conceptual Case Computer Data Base Exercise Flow Chart

CHAPTER 16

DECISION THEORY 746

16-1 The Decision Environment 16-2 Expected Profit Under Uncertainty: Assigning Probability Values 16-3 Using Continuous Distributions in Decision Theory: Marginal Analysis 16-4 Utility as a Decision Criterion 16-5 Helping Decision Makers Supply the Right Probabilities 16-6 Decision-Tree Analysis New Terms New Equations Review Exercises Concepts Test Conceptual Case

AFTERWORD 794

Falling Off the True Path

ANSWERS TO CHAPTER CONCEPTS TESTS 801

APPENDIX TABLES 804

ANSWERS TO SELECTED EVEN-NUMBERED EXERCISES 828

BIBLIOGRAPHY 861

INDEX 863

PREFACE

Subsequent editions of any successful book are a combination of approaches that have worked well in previous editions and new ideas designed to help people learn more effectively. A quick look at both.

10 Things That Are New in This Edition

Those who used the second edition of *Statistics for Management* will see ten significant additions in this edition; a word or two about each:

- We've included a section in Chapter 4 on exploratory data analysis: How do you get started with a bunch of "messy" data when you don't know anything about it?
- In Chapter 9, we discuss "prob values" as an alternative approach in hypothesis testing. The increased availability and use of computers in statistical analysis suggested to us that many instructors would find this useful.
- You'll find that we have expanded the use of the computer in statistical analysis, particularly in Chapters 4, 10, and 12. These new sections contain in-text computer output and analysis; they are designed so that they can be used or skipped at the instructor's option.
- The computer package we use in the text has been changed to SAS; the wide availability of this package suggests this will help those instructors who do make use of the computer in their approach to the course.
- Centered moving averages have been introduced as a part of our treatment of time series in Chapter 14.
- Chapter 13 on nonparametric tests now contains the Kolmogorov-Smirnov test.
- Each chapter now provides the student with a "conceptual case," a decision-making situation *without any data,* in which managers are being asked to reflect on (1) what data should be collected,

(2) what kinds of statistical analyses might be appropriate given the organization's needs, and (3) what we should do with the answer when we find it. Use of this approach will encourage students to worry more about what you do with the answer when you get it and somewhat less about how to "crank it out."

- The total number of exercises in the text has been increased to over 1,000.
- The end-of-chapter concepts quizzes have been lengthened.
- A flow chart has been provided in each chapter to help the student see the range of statistical procedures being discussed in that chapter, and to aid in making the right choice among those options and in using it properly.

3 Things That Haven't Changed

THE PHILOSOPHY OF THE BOOK. We are still deeply committed, as we were in the first and second editions of *Statistics for Management,* to helping students learn statistics without anxiety. To this end we have maintained our careful, step-by-step explanations of statistical approaches, using extensions of what the student already knows. Every step in the analysis of a problem is thoroughly covered, reinforced, and reviewed. The notation we use is necessary, simple, and consistent.

THE COMPREHENSIVE TOPIC COVERAGE. Our third edition covers the standard list of statistical topics with multiple-chapter expanded coverage of statistical inference, regression, use of the computer in statistical analysis, and use of statistics in decision making.

THE PEDAGOGICAL AIDS. Those who haven't used earlier editions of *Statistics for Management* will see a broad set of pedagogical aids built into the textbook and the accompanying manuals. A brief review of these may help:

- A comprehensive computer data base exercise continued throughout the book with problems and questions for each chapter.
- An annotated equation review at the end of each chapter.
- Consistent and complete numbering of every equation in the book each time it is used.
- A glossary of terms for each new idea introduced in the chapter.
- An extensive set of mixed chapter review exercises at the end of every chapter.
- Over 1,500 marginal notes to make studying easier.
- Over 1,000 text exercises, with answers provided for the even-numbered exercises.

- A chapter concepts test at the end of each chapter in which true-false, multiple-choice, and short-answer questions are used to reinforce what students have learned.
- Art and color have been used extensively to explain difficult concepts.
- A photographically described situation introducing each chapter, in which a decision maker is attempting to use statistical concepts in his or her work; this problem is later worked out in detail in the chapter.
- A comprehensive instructor's manual with completely worked-out answers to every exercise, a student workbook and study guide, and a test bank.

Other Folks' Help

No comprehensive venture such as this third edition of *Statistics for Management* is the work of one person. Many, many people are involved in this work, and I thank them all. In particular, I thank my friend, colleague, and collaborator, Dave Rubin of the University of North Carolina, who has left his mark on this edition. My gratitude also goes to the reviewers and users of the previous editions for their many excellent suggestions, and to the staff at Prentice-Hall for their help in making this edition possible.

I am also grateful to the literary executor of the late Sir Ronald Fisher, F.R.S., to Dr. Frank Yates, F.R.S., and to Longman Group Ltd., London, for permission to reprint Tables III and IV from their book, *Statistical Tables for Biological, Agricultural and Medical Research* (6th Edition, 1974).

I hope you like what we've done in the third edition, and I hope you find it useful in teaching and learning about statistics. Please write me with any suggestions you have about how we can improve it. Thanks!

DICK LEVIN
Chapel Hill, North Carolina

STATISTICS FOR MANAGEMENT

CHAPTER 1

INTRODUCTION

1. DEFINITIONS, 2
2. HISTORY, 3
3. SUBDIVISIONS WITHIN STATISTICS, 4
4. STRATEGY, ASSUMPTIONS, AND APPROACH, 4

This book was written for students taking statistics for the first time. A glance at this chapter should convince any concerned citizen and future manager that a working knowledge of basic statistics will be quite useful in coping with the complex problems of our society. Your first look will also convince you that this book is dedicated to helping you acquire that knowledge with virtually no previous formal mathematical training and with no pain at all.

1-1 DEFINITIONS

Different meanings of statistics depending on use

The word *statistics* means different things to different people. To a football fan, statistics are the information about rushing yardage, passing yardage, and first downs, given at halftime. To the manager of a power generating station, statistics may be information about the quantity of pollutants being released into the atmosphere. To a school principal, statistics are information on absenteeism, test scores, and teacher salaries. To a medical researcher investigating the effects of a new drug, statistics are evidence of the success of research efforts. And to a college student, statistics are the grades made on all the quizzes in a course this semester.

Each of these people is using the word *statistics* correctly, yet each uses it in a slightly different way and for a somewhat different purpose. *Statistics* is a word that can refer to quantitative data (such as wheat yield per acre) or to a field of study (you may, for example, major in statistics).

Today, statistics and statistical analysis are used in nearly every profession. For managers in particular, statistics have become a most valuable tool.

1-2 HISTORY

Origin of the word

The word *statistik* comes from the Italian word *statista* (meaning "statesman"). It was first used by Gottfried Achenwall (1719–1772), a professor at Marlborough and Göttingen. Dr. E.A.W. Zimmerman introduced the word *statistics* into England. Its use was popularized by Sir John Sinclair in his work, *Statistical Account of Scotland 1791–1799*. Long before the eighteenth century, however, people had been recording and using data.

Early government records

Official government statistics are as old as recorded history. The Old Testament contains several accounts of census taking. Governments of ancient Babylonia, Egypt, and Rome gathered detailed records of populations and resources. In the Middle Ages, governments began to register the ownership of land. In A.D. 762, Charlemagne asked for detailed descriptions of church-owned properties. Early in the ninth century, he completed a statistical enumeration of the serfs attached to the land. About 1086, William the Conqueror ordered the writing of the *Domesday Book*, a record of the ownership, extent, and value of the lands of England. This work was England's first statistical abstract.

An early prediction from statistics

Because of Henry VII's fear of the plague, England began to register its dead in 1532. About this same time, French law required the clergy to register baptisms, deaths, and marriages. During an outbreak of the plague in the late 1500s, the English government started publishing weekly death statistics. This practice continued, and by 1632 these *Bills of Mortality* listed births and deaths by sex. In 1662, Captain John Graunt used thirty years of these Bills to make predictions about the number of persons who would die from various diseases and the proportion of male and female births that could be expected. Summarized in his work, *Natural and Political Observations . . . Made upon the Bills of Mortality*, Graunt's study was a pioneer effort in statistical analysis. For his achievement in using past records to predict future events, Graunt was made a member of the original Royal Society.

The history of the development of statistical theory and practice is a lengthy one. We have only begun to list the people who have made significant contributions to this field. Later we will encounter others whose names are now attached to specific laws and methods. Many people have brought to the study of statistics refinements or innovations that, taken together, form the theoretical basis of what we will study in this book.

1-3 SUBDIVISIONS WITHIN STATISTICS

Managers apply some statistical technique to virtually every branch of public and private enterprise. These techniques are so diverse that statisticians commonly separate them into two broad categories: *descriptive statistics* and *inferential statistics.* Some examples will help us understand the difference between the two.

Descriptive statistics

Suppose a professor computes an average grade for one history class. Since statistics describe the performance of that one class but do not make a generalization about several classes, we can say that the professor is using *descriptive* statistics. Graphs, tables, and charts that display data so that they are easier to understand are all examples of descriptive statistics.

Inferential statistics

Now suppose that the history professor decides to use the average grade achieved by one history class to estimate the average grade achieved in all ten sections of the same history course. The process of estimating this average grade would be a problem in *inferential* statistics. Statisticians also refer to this category as *statistical inference.* Obviously, any conclusion the professor makes about the ten sections of the course will be based on a generalization that goes far beyond the data for the original history class; and the generalization may not be completely valid, so the professor must state how likely it is to be true. Similarly, statistical inference involves generalizations and statements about the *probability* of their validity.

Decision theory

The methods and techniques of statistical inference can also be used in a branch of statistics called *decision theory.* Knowledge of decision theory is very helpful for managers, because it is used to make decisions under conditions of uncertainty—when, for example, a manufacturer of stereo sets cannot specify precisely the demand for its products or when the chairperson of the English department at your school must schedule faculty teaching assignments without knowing precisely the student enrollment for next fall.

1-4 STRATEGY, ASSUMPTIONS, AND APPROACH

For students, not statisticians

This book is designed to help you get the feel of statistics—what it is, how and when to apply statistical techniques to decision-making situations, and how to interpret the results you get. Since we are not writing for professional statisticians, our writing is tailored to the backgrounds and needs of college students, who, as future citizens, probably accept the fact that statistics can be of considerable help to them in their future occupations but are very likely apprehensive about studying the subject.

We discard mathematical proofs in favor of intuitive ones. You will be guided through the learning process by reminders of what you already know, by examples with which you can identify, and by a step-by-step process instead of statements like, "it can be shown," or, "it therefore follows."

Symbols are simple and explained

As you thumb through this book and compare it with other basic business statistics textbooks, you will notice a minimum of mathematical notation. In the past, the complexity of the notation has intimidated many students, who got lost in the symbols even though they were motivated and intellectually capable of understanding the ideas. Each symbol and formula that is used is explained in detail, not only at the point at which it is introduced but also in a section at the end of the chapter.

No math beyond simple algebra required

If you felt reasonably comfortable when you finished your high school algebra course, you have enough background to understand *everything* in this book. Nothing beyond basic algebra is either assumed or used. Our goals are for you to be comfortable as you learn and for you to get a good intuitive grasp of statistical concepts and techniques. As a future manager, you will need to know when statistics can help your decision process and which tools to use. If you do need statistical help, you can find a statistical expert to handle the details.

Text problems cover a wide variety of situations

The problems used to introduce material in the chapters, the exercises at the end of each section within the chapter, and the chapter review exercises are drawn from a wide variety of situations you are already familiar with or are likely to confront quite soon. You will see problems involving all facets of the private sector of our economy: accounting, finance, individual and group behavior, marketing, and production. In addition, you will encounter managers in the public sphere coping with problems in public education, social services, the environment, consumer advocacy, and health systems.

Goals

In each problem situation, a manager is trying to use statistics creatively and productively. Helping you become comfortable doing exactly that is our goal.

CHAPTER 2

ARRANGING DATA TO CONVEY MEANING: TABLES AND GRAPHS

1. HOW CAN WE ARRANGE DATA? 8
2. EXAMPLES OF RAW DATA, 11
3. ARRANGING DATA USING THE DATA ARRAY AND THE FREQUENCY DISTRIBUTION, 12
4. CONSTRUCTING A FREQUENCY DISTRIBUTION, 20
5. GRAPHING FREQUENCY DISTRIBUTIONS, 28
6. TERMS, 37
7. EQUATIONS, 38
8. REVIEW EXERCISES, 39
9. CONCEPTS TEST, 45
10. CONCEPTUAL CASE, 47
11. COMPUTER DATA BASE EXERCISE, 50
12. FLOW CHART, 55

OBJECTIVES: Chapters 2, 3, and 4 will introduce the concepts and techniques of descriptive statistics. Chapter 2 examines two methods for describing a collection of items: tables and graphs. If you have ever heard a long-winded report droning about dues owed by all eighty club members, and you have wished for a quick graphic display to ease the pain, you already have an appreciation of what's to come in Chapter 2.

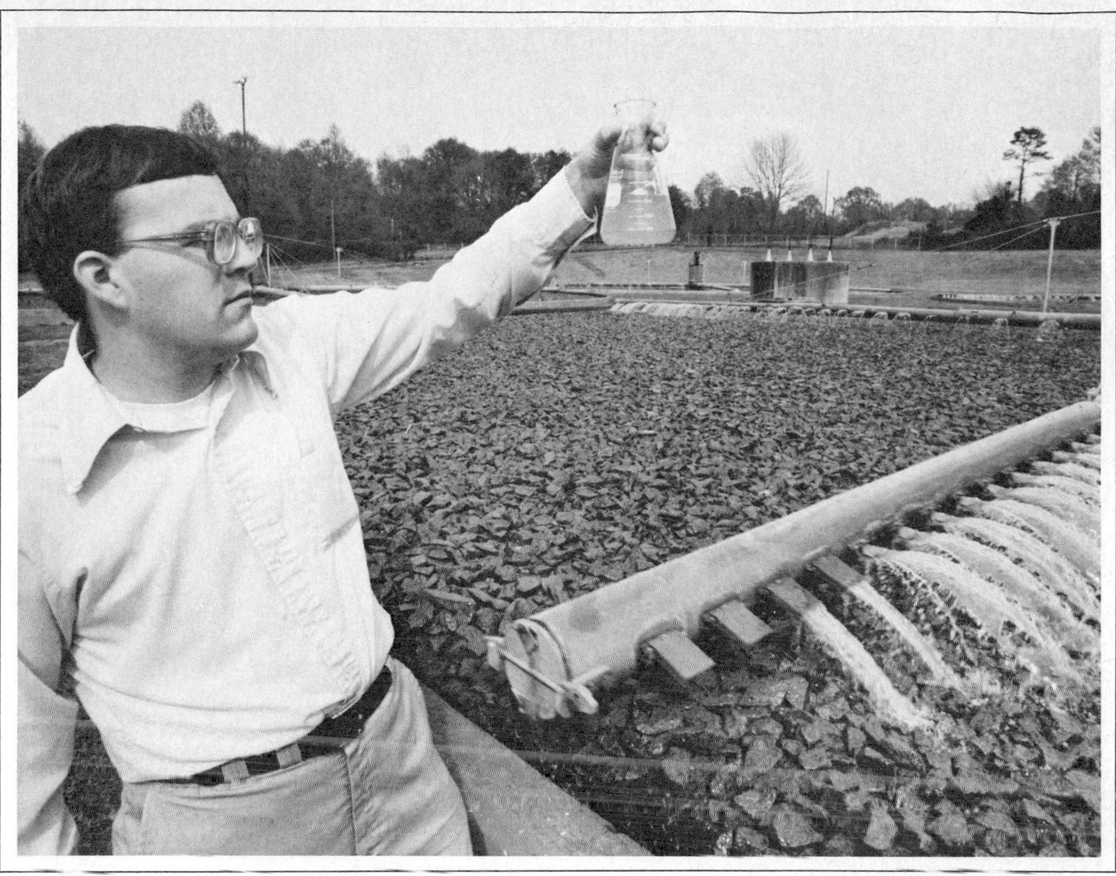

The water quality control engineer of Charlotte, North Carolina, is responsible for the chlorination level of the water. It must be close to the level required by the department of health. To watch the chlorine without checking every gallon of water leaving the plant, the engineer samples several gallons each day, measures chlorine content, and draws a conclusion about the average chlorination level of water treated that day. The table below shows the chlorine levels of the 30 gallons selected as one day's sample. These levels are the raw data from which the engineer can draw conclusions about the entire population of that day's treatment.

Chlorine levels in parts per million (ppm)
in 30 gallons of treated water

16.2	15.4	16.0	16.6	15.9	15.8	16.0	16.8	16.9	16.8
15.7	16.4	15.2	15.8	15.9	16.1	15.6	15.9	15.6	16.0
16.4	15.8	15.7	16.2	15.6	15.9	16.3	16.3	16.0	16.3

Using the methods introduced in this chapter, we can help the water quality control engineer draw the proper conclusions.

Some definitions

Data are collections of any number of related observations. We can collect the number of telephones that several workers install on a given day or that one worker installs per day over a period of several days, and we can call the results our data. A collection of data is called a *data set,* and a single observation a *data point.*

2-1 HOW CAN WE ARRANGE DATA?

For data to be useful, our observations need to be organized so that we can pick out trends and come to logical conclusions. This chapter introduces the techniques of arranging data in tabular and graphical forms. Chapter 3 will show how to use numbers to describe data.

Collecting Data

Represent all groups

Statisticians select their observations so that all relevant groups are represented in the data. To determine the potential market for a new product, for example, analysts might study 100 consumers in a certain geographical area. The analysts must be certain that this group contains a variety of people representing variables such as income level, race, education, and neighborhood.

Find data by observations or from records

Data can come from actual observations or from records that are kept for normal purposes. For billing purposes and doctors' reports, a hospital, for example, will record the number of patients using the X-ray facilities. But this information can also be organized to produce data that statisticians can describe and interpret.

Use data about the past to make decisions about the future

Data can assist decision makers in educated guesses about the *causes* and therefore the probable *effects* of certain characteristics in given situations. Also, knowledge of trends from past experience can enable concerned citizens to be aware of potential outcomes and to plan in advance. Our marketing survey may reveal that the product is preferred by black housewives of suburban communities, average incomes, and average education. The product's advertising copy should address this target audience. And if hospital records show that more patients used the X-ray facilities in June than in January, the hospital Personnel Division should determine if this was accidental to this year or an indication of a trend, and perhaps it should adjust its hiring and vacation practices accordingly.

When data are arranged in compact, usable form, decision makers can take reliable information from the environment and use it to make intelligent decisions. Today, computers allow statisticians to collect enormous volumes of observations and compress them instantly into tables, graphs, and numbers. These are all compact, usable forms—but are they reliable? Remember that the data that come out of a computer are only as accurate as the data that go in. As computer programmers say, "GIGO!" or "Garbage In, Garbage Out!" Managers must be very careful to be sure that the data they are using are based on correct assumptions and interpretations. Before relying on any interpreted data, from a computer or not, test the data by asking these questions:

Tests for data

1. Where did the data come from? Is the source biased; that is, is it likely to have an interest in supplying data points that will lead to one conclusion rather than another?
2. Do the data support or contradict other evidence we have?
3. Is evidence missing that might cause us to come to a different conclusion?
4. How many observations do we have? Do they represent all the groups we wish to study?
5. Is the conclusion logical? Have we made conclusions that the data do not support?

Study your answers to these questions. Are the data worth using? Or should we wait and collect more information before acting? If the hospital was caught short-handed because it hired too few nurses to staff the X-ray room, its administration relied on insufficient data. If the advertising agency targeted its copy only toward black suburban housewives when it could have tripled its sales by appealing to white suburban housewives too, it also relied on insufficient data. In both cases, testing available data would have helped managers make better decisions.

Difference Between Samples and Populations

Sample and population defined

Statisticians gather data from a sample. They use this information to make inferences about the population that the sample represents. Thus, *sample* and *population* are relative terms. A population is a whole, and a sample is a fraction or segment of that whole.

Function of samples

We will study samples in order to be able to describe populations. Our hospital may study a small, representative group of X ray records rather than examining each record for the last fifty years. The Gallup Poll may interview a sample of only 2,500 adult Americans in order to predict the opinion of all adults living in the United States. Studying samples is obviously easier than studying whole populations, and it is reliable if carefully and properly done.

Function of populations

A *population* is a collection of all the elements we are studying and about which we are trying to draw conclusions. We must define this population so that it is clear whether or not an element is a member of the population. The population for our marketing study may be all women within a 15-mile radius of center-city Cincinnati who have annual family incomes between $10,000 and $25,000 and have completed at least eleven years of school. A woman living in downtown Cincinnati with a family income of $15,000 and a college degree would be a part of this population. A woman living in San Francisco, or with a family income of $7,000, or with five years of schooling would not qualify as a member of this population.

Need for a representative sample

A *sample* is a collection of some, but not all, of the elements of the population. The population of our marketing survey is *all* women who meet the qualifications listed above. Any group of women who meet these qualifications can be a sample, as long as the group is only a fraction of the whole population. A large helping of cherry filling with only a few crumbs of crust is a sample of a pie, but it is not a representative sample because the proportions of the ingredients are not the same in the sample as they are in the whole.

A *representative sample* contains the relevant characteristics of the population *in the same proportion* as they are included in that population. If our population of women is one-third black, then a sample of the population that is representative in terms of race will also be one-third black. Specific methods for sampling will be covered in detail in Chapter 7.

Finding a Meaningful Pattern in the Data

Data come in a variety of forms

There are many ways to sort data. We can simply collect it and keep it in order. Or if the observations are measured in numbers, we can list the data points from the lowest to the highest in numerical value. But if the data are skilled workers (such as carpenters, masons, and ironworkers) required at construction sites, or the different types of automobiles manufactured by all automakers, or the various colors of sweaters manufactured by a given firm, we will need to organize them differently. We will need to present the data points in alphabetical order or by some other organizing principle. One useful way to organize data is to divide them into similar categories or classes and then count the number of observations that fall into each category. This method produces a *frequency distribution* and is discussed later in this chapter.

Why should we arrange data?

The purpose of organizing data is to enable us to see quickly all the possible characteristics in the data we have collected. We look for things such as the range (the largest and smallest values), apparent trends, what values the data may tend to group around, what values appear most often, and so on. The more information of this kind that we can learn from our sample, the better we can understand the population from which it came, and the better we can make decisions.

EXERCISES

2-1 Three out of four doctors recommend aspirin. Is this conclusion drawn from a sample or a population? Explain.

2-2 Sales have declined in the past 5 years at Donaldo's, a fast-food chain serving Italian food. A survey of 30 franchises from 5 states showed a mean decrease of 4.5 percent. Comment on this statement from the viewpoint of populations and samples.

2-3 An electronics firm recently introduced a new amplifier, and warranty cards indicate that 10,000 of these have been sold so far. The president of the firm, very upset after reading three letters of complaint about the new amplifiers, informed the production manager that costly control measures would be implemented immediately to ensure that the defects would not appear again. Comment on the president's reaction from the standpoint of the 5 tests for data given on page 9.

2-4 "Dewey Beats Truman," announced the newspaper headlines the morning following the 1948 election. For weeks, the pollsters had been predicting a Dewey landslide. Everyone was so confident Dewey would win that some newspapers had preset the headline type and printed the morning papers without waiting for full returns. Truman, however, was elected. Give some possible reasons for the pollsters' incorrect predictions.

2-5 Discuss the data given in the chapter-opening problem in terms of the 5 tests for data.

2-2 EXAMPLES OF RAW DATA

Information before it is arranged and analyzed is called *raw data*. It is "raw" because it is unprocessed by statistical methods.

Problem facing admissions staff

The chlorine data in the chapter-opening problem was one example of raw data. Consider a second: Suppose that the admissions staff of a university, concerned with the success of the students it selects for admission, wishes to compare the students' college performances with other achievements, such as high school grades, test scores, and extracurricular activities. Rather than study every student from every year, the staff can draw a sample of the population of all the students in a given time period and study only that group, to conclude what characteristics appear to predict success. The staff can, for example, compare high school grades with college grade point average (GPA) for students in the sample. The staff can assign each grade a numerical value. Then it can add the grades and divide by the total number of grades to get an average for each student. Table 2-1 shows a sample of this raw data in tabular form: 20 pairs of average grades in high school and college.

TABLE 2-1 High school and college grade point averages of 20 college seniors

H.S.	COLLEGE	H.S.	COLLEGE	H.S.	COLLEGE	H.S.	COLLEGE
3.6	2.5	3.5	3.6	3.4	3.6	2.2	2.8
2.6	2.7	3.5	3.8	2.9	3.0	3.4	3.4
2.7	2.2	2.2	3.5	3.9	4.0	3.6	3.0
3.7	3.2	3.9	3.7	3.2	3.5	2.6	1.9
4.0	3.8	4.0	3.9	2.1	2.5	2.4	3.2

Bridge-building problem

When designing a bridge, engineers are concerned with the stress that a given material, such as concrete, will withstand. Rather than test every cubic inch of concrete to determine its stress capacity, the engineers can take a sample of the concrete, test it, and conclude how much stress, on the average, that kind of concrete can withstand. Table 2-2 summarizes the raw data gathered from a sample of 40 batches of concrete that will be used in constructing a bridge.

TABLE 2-2 Pounds of pressure per square inch that concrete can withstand

2500.2	2497.8	2496.9	2500.8	2491.6	2503.7	2501.3	2500.0
2500.8	2502.5	2503.2	2496.9	2495.3	2497.1	2499.7	2505.0
2490.5	2504.1	2508.2	2500.8	2502.2	2508.1	2493.8	2497.8
2499.2	2498.3	2496.7	2490.4	2493.4	2500.7	2502.0	2502.5
2506.4	2499.9	2508.4	2502.3	2491.3	2509.5	2498.4	2498.1

EXERCISES

2-6 Look at the data in Table 2-1. Why do these data need further arranging? Can you form any conclusions from the data as they exist now?

2-7 The marketing manager of a large company receives a report each month on the sales activity of one of the company's products. The report is a listing of the sales of the product by state during the previous month. Is this an example of raw data?

2-8 The production manager in a large company receives a report each month from the quality control section. The report gives the reject rate for the production line (the number of rejects per 100 units produced), the machine causing the greatest number of rejects, and the average cost of repairing the rejected units. Is this an example of raw data?

2-3 ARRANGING DATA USING THE DATA ARRAY AND THE FREQUENCY DISTRIBUTION

Data array defined

The data array is one of the simplest ways to present data. It arranges values in ascending or descending order. Table 2-3 repeats the chlorine data from our chapter-opening problem, and Table 2-4 rearranges these numbers in a data array in ascending order.

TABLE 2-3 Chlorine levels in ppm of 30 gallons of treated water

16.2	15.8	15.8	15.8	16.3	15.6
15.7	16.0	16.2	16.1	16.8	16.0
16.4	15.2	15.9	15.9	15.9	16.8
15.4	15.7	15.9	16.0	16.3	16.0
16.4	16.6	15.6	15.6	16.9	16.3

TABLE 2-4 Data array of chlorine levels in ppm of 30 gallons of treated water

15.2	15.7	15.9	16.0	16.2	16.4
15.4	15.7	15.9	16.0	16.3	16.6
15.6	15.8	15.9	16.0	16.3	16.8
15.6	15.8	15.9	16.1	16.3	16.8
15.6	15.8	16.0	16.2	16.4	16.9

Advantages of data arrays

Data arrays offer several advantages over raw data:

1. We can quickly notice the lowest and highest values in the data. In our chlorination example, the range is from 15.2 ppm to 16.9 ppm.

2. We can easily divide the data into sections. In Table 2-4, the first 15 values (the lower half of the data) are between 15.2 and 16.0 ppm, and the last 15 values (the upper half) are between 16.0 and 16.9 ppm. Similarly, the lowest third of the values range from 15.2 to 15.8 ppm, the middle third from 15.9 to 16.2 ppm, and the upper third from 16.2 to 16.9 ppm.

3. We can see whether any values appear more than once in the array. Equal values appear together. Table 2-4 shows that 9 levels occurred more than once when the sample of 30 gallons of water was tested.

4. We can observe the distance between succeeding values in the data. In Table 2-4, 16.6 and 16.8 are succeeding values. The distance between them is .2 ppm (16.8 − 16.6).

Disadvantages of data arrays

In spite of these advantages, sometimes a data array isn't helpful. Since it lists every observation, it is a cumbersome form for displaying large quantities of data. We need to compress the information and still be able to use it for interpretation and decision making. How can we do this?

A Better Way to Arrange Data: The Frequency Distribution

Frequency distributions handle more data

One way we can compress data is to use a *frequency table* or a *frequency distribution*. To understand the difference between this and an array, take as an example the average inventory (in days) for 20 convenience stores:

TABLE 2-5 Data array of average inventory (in days) for 20 convenience stores

2.0	3.4	3.8	4.1	4.1	4.3	4.7	4.9	5.5	5.5
3.4	3.8	4.0	4.1	4.2	4.7	4.8	4.9	5.5	5.5

They lose some information

In Tables 2-5 and 2-6, we have taken identical data concerning the average inventory and displayed them first as an array in ascending order and then as a frequency distribution. To obtain Table 2-6, we had to divide the data into groups of similar values. Then we recorded the number of data

TABLE 2-6 Frequency distribution of average inventory (in days) for 20 convenience stores (6 classes)

CLASS (GROUP OF SIMILAR VALUES OF DATA POINTS)	FREQUENCY (NUMBER OF OBSERVATIONS IN EACH CLASS)
2.0 to 2.5	1
2.6 to 3.1	0
3.2 to 3.7	2
3.8 to 4.3	8
4.4 to 4.9	5
5.0 to 5.5	4

points that fell into each group. Notice that we lose some information in constructing the frequency distribution. We no longer know, for example, that the value 5.5 appears four times or that the value 5.1 does not appear at all. Yet we gain information concerning the *pattern* of average inventories. We can see from Table 2-6 that average inventory falls most often in the range from 3.8 to 4.3 days. It is unusual to find an average inventory in the range from 2.0 to 2.5 days or from 2.6 to 3.1 days. Inventories in the ranges of 4.4 to 4.9 days and 5.0 to 5.5 days are not prevalent but occur more frequently than some others. Thus, frequency distributions sacrifice some detail but offer us new insights into patterns of data.

But they gain other information

Function of classes in a frequency distribution

A frequency distribution is a table that organizes data into *classes;* that is, into groups of values describing one characteristic of the data. "The average inventory" is one characteristic of the 20 convenience stores. In Table 2-5, this characteristic has eleven different values. But these same data could be divided into any number of classes. Table 2-6, for example, uses six. We could compress the data even further and use only the two classes "less than 3.8" and "greater than, or equal to, 3.8." Or we could increase the number of classes by using smaller intervals, such as we have done in Table 2-7.

TABLE 2-7 Frequency distribution of average inventory (in days) for 20 convenience stores (12 classes)

CLASS	FREQUENCY	CLASS	FREQUENCY
2.0 to 2.2	1	3.8 to 4.0	3
2.3 to 2.5	0	4.1 to 4.3	5
2.6 to 2.8	0	4.4 to 4.6	0
2.9 to 3.1	0	4.7 to 4.9	5
3.2 to 3.4	2	5.0 to 5.2	0
3.5 to 3.7	0	5.3 to 5.5	4

Why it is called a "frequency" distribution

A frequency distribution shows **the number of observations from the data set that fall into each of the classes.** If you can determine the frequency with which values occur in each class of a data set, you can construct a frequency distribution.

Characteristics of Relative Frequency Distributions

Relative frequency distribution defined

So far, we have expressed the frequency with which values occur in each class as the total number of data points that fall within that class. We can also express the frequency of each value as a *fraction* or a *percentage* of the total number of observations. The frequency of an average inventory of 4.4 to 4.9 days, for example, is 5 in Table 2-6 but .25 in Table 2-8. To get this value of .25, we divided the frequency for that class (5) by the total number of observations in the data set (20). The answer can be expressed as a fraction (5/20), a decimal (.25), or a percentage (25%). A *relative frequency distribution* presents frequencies in terms of fractions or percentages.

TABLE 2-8 Relative frequency distribution of average inventory (in days) for 20 convenience stores

CLASS	FREQUENCY	RELATIVE FREQUENCY: FRACTION OF OBSERVATIONS IN EACH CLASS
2.0 to 2.5	1	.05
2.6 to 3.1	0	.00
3.2 to 3.7	2	.10
3.8 to 4.3	8	.40
4.4 to 4.9	5	.25
5.0 to 5.5	4	.20
	20	**1.00 sum of the relative frequencies of all classes**

Classes are all-inclusive

Notice in Table 2-8 that the sum of all the relative frequencies equals 1.00, or 100 percent. This is true because a relative frequency distribution pairs each class with its appropriate fraction or percentage of the total data. Therefore, the classes in any relative or simple frequency distribution are *all-inclusive*. All the data fit into one category or another. Also notice that the classes in Table 2-8 are *mutually exclusive;* that is, no data point falls into more than one category. Table 2-9 illustrates this concept by comparing mutually exclusive classes with ones that overlap. In frequency distributions, there are no overlapping classes.

They are mutually exclusive

TABLE 2-9 Mutually exclusive and overlapping classes

Mutually exclusive	1 to 4	5 to 8	9 to 12	13 to 16
Not mutually exclusive	1 to 4	3 to 6	5 to 8	7 to 10

Classes of qualitative data

Up to this point, our classes have consisted of numbers and have described some quantitative attribute of the items samples. We can also classify information according to qualitative characteristics, such as race, religion, and sex, which do not fall naturally into numerical categories. Like classes of quantitative attributes, these classes must be all-inclusive and mutually exclusive. Table 2-10 shows how to construct both simple and relative frequency distributions using the qualitative attribute of occupations.

TABLE 2-10 Occupations of sample of 100 graduates of Central College

OCCUPATIONAL CLASS	FREQUENCY DISTRIBUTION (1)	RELATIVE FREQUENCY DISTRIBUTION (1) ÷ 100
Actor	5	.05
Banker	8	.08
Businessperson	22	.22
Chemist	7	.07
Doctor	10	.10
Insurance representative	6	.06
Journalist	2	.02
Lawyer	14	.14
Teacher	9	.09
Other	17	.17
	100	**1.00**

Although Table 2-10 does not list every occupation held by the graduates of Central College, it is still all-inclusive. Why? The class "other" covers all the observations that fail to fit one of the enumerated categories. We will use a word like this whenever our list does not specifically list all the possibilities. If, for example, our characteristic can occur in any month of the year, a complete list would include twelve categories. But if we wish to list only the eight months from January to August, we can use the term "other" to account for our observations during the four months of September, October, November, and December. Although our list does not specifically list all the possibilities, it is all-inclusive. This "other" is called an

Open-ended classes for lists that are not exhaustive

TABLE 2-11 Ages of Bunder County residents

CLASS: AGE (1)	FREQUENCY (2)	RELATIVE FREQUENCY (2) ÷ 89,592
Birth to 7	8,873	.0990
8 to 15	9,246	.1032
16 to 23	12,060	.1346
24 to 31	11,949	.1334
32 to 39	9,853	.1100
40 to 47	8,439	.0942
48 to 55	8,267	.0923
56 to 63	7,430	.0829
64 to 71	7,283	.0813
72 and older	6,192	.0691
	89,592	**1.0000**

open-ended class when it allows either the upper or the lower end of a quantitative classification scheme to be limitless. The last class in Table 2-11 ("72 and older") is open-ended.

Discrete classes

Classification schemes can be either quantitative or qualitative *and* either discrete or continuous. *Discrete* classes are separate entities that do not progress from one class to the next without a break. Such classes as the number of children in each family, the number of trucks owned by moving companies, or the occupations of Central College graduates are discrete. Discrete data are data that can take on only a limited number of values. Central College graduates can be classified as either doctors or chemists but not something in between. The closing price of AT&T stock can be 66¾, or your basketball team can have a center who is 7 feet 1½ inches tall.

Continuous classes

Continuous data do progress from one class to the next without a break. They involve numerical measurement such as the weights of cans of tomatoes, the pounds of pressure on concrete, or the high school GPAs of college seniors. Continuous data can be expressed in either fractions or whole numbers.

EXERCISES

2-9 Arrange the data below in a data array from lowest to highest.

708	541	528	546	631	541	622	592	534	663
546	641	603	650	502	592	618	631	599	637
578	483	578	619	586	567	644	641	622	547
644	689	557	612	644	531	536	695	645	578

a) What are the highest and lowest data values?
b) Between what values do the lowest ¼ of the data fall? The highest ¼ of the data?
c) How many values appear more than once in the data set, and what are they?

2-10 For the data set in exercise 2-9, determine how many observations fall between 450.0 and 499.9, between 500.0 and 549.9, between 550.0 and 599.9, between 600.0 and 649.9, between 650.0 and 699.9, and between 700.0 and 749.9.

2-11 Construct a frequency distribution with intervals of .5 from the following set of measurements:

3.9	4.9	5.9	3.7	6.9	4.5	3.6	3.9	3.9
4.0	5.2	4.9	4.6	5.4	3.7	6.1	4.0	4.4
5.6	4.8	5.4	4.0	4.1	3.9	4.8	3.5	4.7
5.1	3.9	5.0	3.9	3.7	3.8	5.2	5.0	4.5
4.2	5.4	3.7	5.5	3.3	6.2	3.2	5.4	4.2

2-12 Given the following data set, construct a relative frequency distribution using (a) 7 equal intervals, and (b) 13 equal intervals:

80	52	67	59	60	79	62	55	52	90
64	87	65	64	50	71	72	64	71	67
40	56	74	69	97	67	81	77	77	57
35	86	71	99	88	43	54	48	68	77
93	70	84	78	68	63	47	56	66	57

2-13 Arrange the data in Table 2-2 on page 12 in an array from highest to lowest.

a) Suppose that state law requires bridge concrete to withstand at least 2,500 lbs./sq. in. How many samples would fail this test?

b) How many samples could withstand a pressure of at least 2,497 lbs./sq. in. but could not withstand a pressure greater than 2,504 lbs./sq. in.?

c) As you examine the array, you should notice that some samples can withstand identical amounts of pressure. List these pressures and the number of samples that can withstand each amount.

2-14 Using Table 2-1 on page 11 arrange the data in an array from highest to lowest high school GPA. Now, arrange the data into an array from highest to lowest college GPA.

2-15 The Environmental Protection Agency took water samples from 10 different rivers and streams that feed into Lake Erie. These samples were tested in the EPA laboratory and rated as to the amount of solid pollution suspended in each sample. The results of the testing are given in the following table:

Sample	1	2	3	4	5	6	7	8	9	10
Pollution rating (ppm)	27.2	38.7	64.3	52.8	47.6	23.4	33.9	45.0	56.7	41.1

a) Arrange the data into an array from highest to lowest.

b) Determine the number of samples having a pollution content between 20.0 and 29.9, 30.0 and 39.9, 40.0 and 49.9, 50.0 and 59.9, 60.0 and 69.9.

c) If 40.0 is the number used by the EPA to indicate excessive pollution, how many samples would be rated as having excessive pollution?

d) What is the largest distance between any two consecutive samples?

2-16 Suppose that the admissions staff mentioned in the discussion of Table 2-1 on page 11 wishes to examine the relationship between a student's differential on the college SAT examination (the difference between actual and expected score based on the student's high school GPA) and the spread between the student's high school and college GPA (the difference between the high school and college GPA). The admissions staff will use the following data:

H.S. GPA	COLLEGE GPA	SAT SCORE	H.S. GPA	COLLEGE GPA	SAT SCORE
3.6	2.5	1,090	3.4	3.6	1,170
2.6	2.7	955	2.9	3.0	1,025
2.7	2.2	940	3.9	4.0	1,315
3.7	3.2	1,170	3.2	3.5	1,160
4.0	3.8	1,330	2.1	2.5	925
3.5	3.6	1,190	2.2	2.8	975
3.5	3.8	1,240	3.4	3.4	1,160
2.2	3.5	1,050	3.6	3.0	1,110
3.9	3.7	1,300	2.6	1.9	850
4.0	3.9	1,345	2.4	3.2	1,080

In addition, the admissions staff has received the following information from the Educational Testing Service:

H.S. GPA	AVG. SAT SCORE	H.S. GPA	AVG. SAT SCORE
4.0	1,340	2.9	1,020
3.9	1,310	2.8	1,000
3.8	1,280	2.7	980
3.7	1,250	2.6	960
3.6	1,220	2.5	940
3.5	1,190	2.4	920
3.4	1,160	2.3	910
3.3	1,130	2.2	900
3.2	1,100	2.1	880
3.1	1,070	2.0	860
3.0	1,040		

a) Arrange these data into an array of spreads from highest to lowest. (Consider an increase in college GPA over high school GPA as positive and a decrease in college GPA below high school GPA as negative.) Include with each spread the appropriate SAT differential. (Consider an SAT score below expected as negative and above expected as positive.)
b) What is the most common spread?
c) For this spread in part b, what is the most common SAT differential?
d) From the analysis you have done, what do you conclude?

2-17 Construct a frequency distribution with intervals of 7 days from the following data obtained from shipping records of a mail order firm. Comment briefly on what your analysis shows.

TIME FROM RECEIPT OF ORDER TO DELIVERY (IN DAYS)									
3	11	7	13	10	5	5	12	14	10
12	22	6	23	9	14	22	8	25	5

2-18 Refer to Table 2-2 on page 12 and construct a relative frequency distribution using intervals of 4.0 lbs./sq. in. What do you conclude from this distribution?

2-19 The Bureau of Labor Statistics has sampled 30 communities nationwide and examined prices in each community at the beginning and end of August in order to find out approximately how the Consumer Price Index (CPI) has changed during August. The percentage change in prices for the 30 communities is given below:

1.1	0.5	0.2	0.4	−0.1	0.5	0.6	0.8	0.2	0.0
0.3	0.9	0.6	0.5	1.3	−0.4	0.2	0.3	0.6	0.4
−0.5	0.1	0.1	0.7	0.9	0.2	0.4	0.5	0.4	0.6

a) Arrange the data into an array from lowest to highest.
b) Using the following four equal-sized classes, create a frequency distribution and a relative frequency distribution: −0.5 to −0.1, 0.0 to 0.4, 0.5 to 0.9, 1.0 to 1.4.
c) How many communities had prices that either did not change or that increased less than 1.0%?
d) Are these data discrete or continuous?

2-20 Sarah Anne Rapp, the president of Baggit, Inc., has just obtained some raw data from a marketing survey that her company recently conducted. The survey was taken to determine the effectiveness of the new company slogan, "When you've given up on the rest, Baggit!" To determine the effect of the slogan on the sales of Luncheon Baggits, 20 people were asked how many boxes of Luncheon Baggits per month they bought before and after the slogan was used in an advertising campaign. The results were as follows:

BEFORE/AFTER		BEFORE/AFTER		BEFORE/AFTER		BEFORE/AFTER	
3	6	2	1	4	6	9	10
4	3	5	10	2	6	1	2
2	7	7	6	5	7	3	2
4	5	7	9	7	4	4	9
6	6	3	5	3	4	1	1

a) Create both frequency and relative frequency distributions for the "Before" responses, using as classes 1 to 2, 3 to 4, 5 to 6, 7 to 8, and 9 to 10.
b) Work part a for the "After" responses.
c) Give the most basic reason why it makes sense to use the same classes for both the "Before" and "After" responses.
d) For each pair of "Before/After" responses, subtract the "Before" response from the "After" response to get a number that we will call "Change" (example: $6 - 3 = +3$), and create frequency and relative frequency distributions for "Change" using classes -3 to -1, 0 to 2, and 3 to 5.
e) Based on your information collected above, state whether or not the new slogan has helped sales, and give one or two reasons to support your conclusion.

2-4 CONSTRUCTING A FREQUENCY DISTRIBUTION

Now that we have learned how to divide a sample into classes, we can take raw data and actually construct a frequency distribution. To solve the chlorination problem on the first page of the chapter, follow these three steps:

Classify the data

1. Decide on the type and number of classes for dividing the data. In this case, we have already chosen to classify the data by the quantitative measure of the number of ppm of chlorine in treated water rather than by a qualitative attribute like the color or odor of the water. Next, we need to decide how many different classes to use and the range (from where to

Divide the range by equal classes

where) each class should cover. The range must be divided by *equal* classes; that is, the width of the interval from the beginning of one class to the beginning of the next class needs to be the same for every class. If we choose

TABLE 2-12 Chlorine levels in samples of treated water with .5 ppm class intervals

CLASS IN PPM	FREQUENCY
15.1–15.5	2
15.6–16.0	16
16.1–16.5	8
16.6–17.0	4
	30

a width of .5 ppm for each class in our water example, the classes will be those shown in Table 2-12.

Problems with unequal classes

If the classes were unequal and the width of the intervals differed among the classes, then we would have a distribution that is much more difficult to interpret than one with equal intervals. Imagine how hard it would be to interpret the data presented in Table 2-13!

TABLE 2-13 Chlorine levels in samples of treated water using unequal class intervals

CLASS	WIDTH OF CLASS INTERVALS	FREQUENCY
15.1–15.5	15.6 − 15.1 = .5	2
15.6–15.8	15.9 − 15.6 = .3	8
15.9–16.1	16.2 − 15.9 = .3	9
16.2–16.5	16.6 − 16.2 = .4	7
16.6–16.9	17.0 − 16.6 = .4	4
		30

Use 6 to 15 classes

The number of classes depends on the number of data points and the range of the data collected. The more data points or the wider the range of the data, the more classes it takes to divide the data. Of course, if we have only ten data points, it is senseless to have as many as ten classes. As a rule, statisticians rarely use fewer than six or more than fifteen classes.

Determine the width of the class intervals

Because we need to make the class intervals of equal size, the number of classes determines the width of each class. To find the intervals, we can use this equation:

$$\text{Width of class intervals} = \frac{\text{Next unit value after largest value in data} - \text{Smallest value in data}}{\text{Total number of class intervals}} \quad [2\text{-}1]$$

We must use the *next value of the same units* because we are measuring the *interval* between the first value of one class and the first value of the next class. In our water study, the last value is 16.9, so 17.0 is the next value. Since we are using six classes in this example, the width of each class will be:

$$\frac{\text{Next unit value after largest value in data} - \text{Smallest value in data}}{\text{Total number of class intervals}} \quad [2\text{-}1]$$

$$= \frac{17.0 - 15.2}{6}$$

$$= \frac{1.8}{6}$$

$$= .3 \text{ ounces} \leftarrow \text{width of class intervals}$$

Examine the results

Step 1 is now complete. We have decided to classify the data by the quantitative measure of how many ppm of chlorine are in the treated water.

We have chosen six classes to cover the range of 15.2 to 16.9 and, as a result, will use .3 ppm as the width of our class intervals.

TABLE 2-14 Chlorine levels in samples of treated water with .3 ppm class intervals

CLASS	FREQUENCY
15.2–15.4	2
15.5–15.7	5
15.8–16.0	11
16.1–16.3	6
16.4–16.6	3
16.7–16.9	3
	30

Create the classes and count the frequencies

2. Sort the data points into classes and count the number of points in each class. This we have done in Table 2-14. Every data point fits into at least one class, and no data point fits into more than one class. Therefore, our classes are all-inclusive and mutually exclusive. Notice that the lower boundary of the first class corresponds with the smallest data point in our sample, and the upper boundary of the last class corresponds with the largest data point.

3. Illustrate the data in a chart. (See Fig. 2-1.)

These three steps enable us to arrange the data in both tabular and graphic form. In this case, our information is displayed in Table 2-14 and in Fig. 2-1. These two frequency distributions omit some of the detail contained in the raw data of Table 2-3, but they make it easier for us to notice trends in the data. One obvious characteristic, for example, is that the class 15.8–16.0 contains the most elements; class 15.2–15.4, the fewest.

Notice any trends

Notice in Fig. 2-1 that the frequencies in the classes of .3 ppm widths follow a regular progression: The number of data points begins with 2 for the

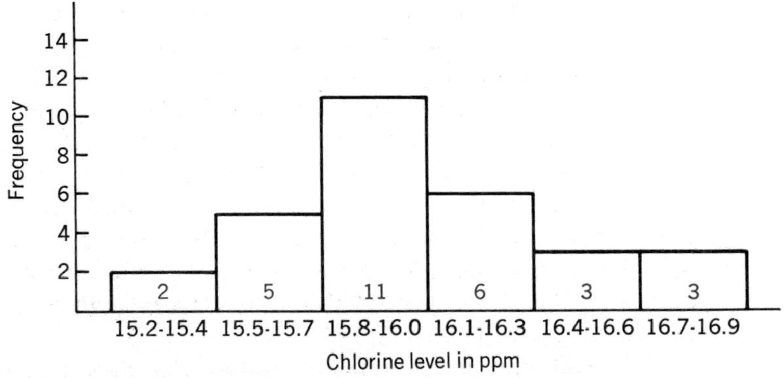

FIGURE 2-1 Frequency distribution of chlorine levels in samples of treated water, using .3 ppm class intervals

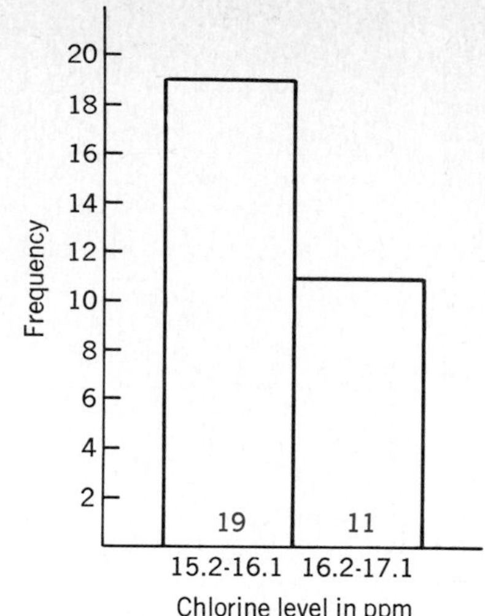

FIGURE 2-2 Frequency distribution of chlorine levels in samples of treated water, using 1 ppm class intervals

first class, builds to 5, reaches 11 in the third class, falls to 6, and tumbles to 3 in the fifth and sixth classes. We will find that the larger the width of the class intervals, the smoother this progression will be. However, if the classes are too wide, we lose so much information that the chart is almost meaningless. If, for example, we collapse Fig. 2-1 into only two categories, we obscure the trend. This is evident in Fig. 2-2.

Class Limits and Class Marks

Stated class limits vs. real class limits

Statisticians use the term *class limits* to refer to the smallest and largest values that go into any given class. But two different kinds of class limits exist. In Table 2-14, the lower and upper class limits for the first class are 15.2 and 15.4, respectively. These are the *stated* limits. The *real* limits, however, are 15.15 and 15.45. This is true because we round the values 15.15, 15.16, 15.17, 15.18, and 15.19 *up* to 15.2. As a result, *all* these values fall into the class with the lower limit equal to 15.2.

Distinction between real and stated class limits

The real limits of the next class are 15.45 and 15.75. Notice that the upper limit of one class is the lower limit of the succeeding class. Therefore, 15.45 is the upper limit of the class with stated limits of 15.2 and 15.4 *and* the lower limit of the class with stated limits of 15.5 and 15.7.

The distinction between real limits and stated limits is made only with continuous variables; we make this distinction because continuous variables are rounded. However, for discrete variables, which are usually counted (rather than measured), we do not make any distinction between the two kinds of limits. For instance, if we have a frequency distribution of weekly car sales by salespeople, and if one of the frequency classes is 0–5, then zero is *both* the real and the stated lower limit, and 5 is *both* the real and the stated upper limit.

Statisticians use another term, *class marks,* to describe the midpoints of the classes. To calculate the class mark, we simply average the lower and upper limits by applying Equation 2-2:

$$\text{Class mark} = \frac{\text{Stated lower limit} + \text{Stated upper limit}}{2} \quad \textbf{[2-2]}$$

Class marks or midpoints

Using this equation and Table 2-14, we can find the class mark for the class 15.2 – 15.4 like this:

$$\frac{\text{Stated lower limit} + \text{Stated upper limit}}{2} = \frac{15.2 + 15.4}{2} \quad \textbf{[2-2]}$$

$$= \frac{30.6}{2}$$

$$= 15.3 \text{ ppm} \leftarrow \text{class mark}$$

Now suppose that we are classifying a hi-fi store's accounts receivable, and our first two classes are \$0 – \$49.99 and \$50 – \$99.99. Then the class mark for the first class would be:

$$\frac{\text{Stated lower limit} + \text{Stated upper limit}}{2} = \frac{\$0 + \$49.99}{2} \quad \textbf{[2-2]}$$

$$= \$24.995 \leftarrow \text{class mark}$$

In this case, we would round up, so that \$25.00 would be the class mark. This rounding enables us to work with much more convenient values, and is usually done whenever we deal with discrete variables (cents, in this case) and with wide intervals (5,000 cents, in this case). In such situations, we use a modified version of Equation 2-2:

$$\text{Class mark} = \frac{\text{Stated lower limit} + \text{Stated lower limit of the next class}}{2} \quad \textbf{[2-3]}$$

So, in our accounts-receivable problem, we would find the class mark like this:

$$\frac{\text{Stated lower limit} + \text{Stated lower limit of the next class}}{2} = \frac{\$0 + \$50}{2} \quad \textbf{[2-3]}$$

$$= \$25 \leftarrow \text{class mark}$$

A Word of Advice

A hint when constructing class intervals

If possible, try to construct class intervals so that values *cluster* around the values of class marks. To do this, examine the raw data and look for values around which data points are concentrated. Look at Table 2-15, which illustrates the raw data from a sample of 20 weeks of penny production at the

Philadelphia mint. The director of the mint wants to know how many pennies are stamped each week.

TABLE 2-15 Philadelphia mint weekly penny production (in millions)

4	4	4	5	6	7	7	7	7	7	7	7	7	8	9	9	9	9	10	10

Notice that in Table 2-15 the values cluster around 4, 7, and 9. In constructing class intervals for the frequency distribution, then, we should attempt to have these three values as class marks. We have done this in Table 2-16. Of course, values do not always cluster so neatly. The important thing is to choose intervals so that as many values as possible are close to the values of the class marks.

TABLE 2-16 Frequency distribution of Philadelphia mint weekly penny production

CLASS IN MILLIONS	FREQUENCY	CLASS MARK
3 to 5	4	4
6 to 8	10	7
9 to 11	6	10

EXERCISES

2-21 For the following data, construct:
a) a 6-category closed classification
b) a 5-category open-ended classification
c) relative frequency distributions to go with the frequency distributions above

34.1	39.0	38.3	41.6	36.4	43.9	33.2	56.4	33.9	34.5
46.4	42.1	41.8	49.4	42.2	51.7	42.4	44.5	46.7	40.6
45.7	50.7	37.6	36.0	34.9	38.9	44.6	49.0	51.4	48.3

2-22 For the frequency distribution constructed above in exercise 21c, give the:
a) real class limits
b) stated class limits
c) class marks for the intervals used

2-23 Determine the class marks for the intervals of the following frequency distribution:

CLASS		
17.50–19.99	25.00–27.49	32.50–34.99
20.00–22.49	27.50–29.99	35.00–37.49
22.50–24.99	30.00–32.49	37.50–39.99

2-24 Given the following class marks for the intervals of a frequency distribution, determine the real and stated class limits of the intervals:

CLASS MARK			
8.50	14.50	20.50	26.50
11.50	17.50	23.50	29.50

2-25 Mr. Franks, a safety engineer for the Mars Point Nuclear Power Generating Station, has charted the peak reactor temperature each day for the past year and has prepared the following frequency distribution:

TEMPERATURES IN °C	FREQUENCY
Below 500	4
501–510	7
511–520	32
521–530	59
530–540	82
550–560	65
561–570	33
571–580	28
580–590	27
591–600	23
Total	**360**

List and explain any errors you can find in Mr. Franks's distribution.

2-26 Construct a discrete, closed classification for the possible responses to the "marital status" portion of an employment application. Also, construct a three-category, discrete, open-ended classification for the same responses.

2-27 Listings for a stock exchange usually contain the company name, high and low bids, closing price, and the change from the previous day's closing price. For example:

NAME	HIGH BID	LOW BID	CLOSING	CHANGE
Jefferson Pilot	28½	27¾	28¼	+1¼

Is a distribution of all

a) stocks on the New York Stock Exchange by industry
b) closing prices on a given day
c) changes in prices on a given day

1) quantitative or qualitative? 2) continuous or discrete? 3) open-ended or closed?
Would your answer to part c be different if the change were expressed simply as "higher," "lower," or "unchanged"?

2-28 The noise level in decibels of aircraft taking off from JFK Airport in New York City was rounded to the nearest tenth of a decibel and grouped in a table having the following class marks: 102.45, 107.45, 112.45, 117.45, 122.45, 127.45, 132.45, and 137.45. What are the stated and real class limits?

2-29 The production manager of Backtrail Jeeps collected data on the axles he was buying from Forged Products, Inc. His concern was their ability to meet required specifications. One of the variables of interest was the axles' circumference, recorded in inches and measured to the nearest one-thousandth of an inch. The data were compiled into a distribution with class marks for the intervals of 5.8695, 5.8895, 5.9095,

5.9295, 5.9495, 5.9695, and 5.9895. Determine the real limits and the stated limits for the intervals of the distribution.

2-30 The president of Ocean Airlines is trying to estimate when the Civil Aeronautics Board (CAB) is most likely to rule on the company's application for a new route between Charlotte and Nashville. Assistants to the president have assembled the following waiting times for applications filed during the past year. The data are given in days from the date of application until a CAB ruling.

32	38	26	29	32	41	28	31	45	36
45	35	40	30	31	40	27	33	28	30
30	41	39	38	33	35	31	36	37	32
23	45	39	37	38	36	33	35	42	38
34	22	37	43	52	32	35	30	46	36

a) Construct a frequency distribution using 10 closed intervals, equally spaced. Which interval occurs most often?

b) Construct a frequency distribution using 5 closed intervals, equally spaced. Which interval occurs most often?

2-31 For the purpose of performance evaluation and quota adjustment, Ralph Williams monitored the auto sales of his 40 salespeople. Over a one-month period, they sold the following numbers of cars:

7	8	5	10	9	10	5	12	8	6
10	11	6	5	10	11	10	5	9	13
8	12	8	8	10	15	7	6	8	8
5	6	9	7	14	8	7	5	5	14

a) Based on frequency, what would be the desired class marks?

b) Construct a frequency and relative frequency distribution having as many of these marks as possible. Make your intervals evenly spaced and at least 2 cars wide.

2-32 Warren Pad owns the Shake and Brake auto garage and is in the process of replenishing the shop's ice-cream freezer. Since his sales gimmick is to give each customer a free milkshake with every brake job, it is very important for Warren to have his customers' favorite flavors in stock. Warren has data indicating (to the nearest half gallon) the daily amount of each flavor of ice cream that is consumed, organized by the following categories: Rocky Road, Vanilla, Strawberry, Chocolate, and Other. The data have been collected for the past 30 days, and no more than 10 gallons of any one flavor was ever used on one day.

a) Is the flavor classification discrete or continuous? open or closed?

b) Is the "amount of ice cream" classification discrete or continuous? open or closed?

c) Are Warren's data qualitative or quantitative?

d) If Warren has exactly seven equal-spaced classes for the number of gallons of any one flavor sold on one day, what should they be?

2-33 Doug Atkinson is the owner and ticket collector for a ferry that transports people and cars from Long Island to Connecticut. Doug has data indicating the number of people, as well as the number of cars, that have ridden the ferry during the past two months. For example:

JULY 3   NUMBER OF PEOPLE, 173   NUMBER OF CARS, 32

might be a typical daily data entry for Doug. Doug has set up 6 equally spaced classes to record the daily number of people, and the class marks are 89.5, 109.5, 129.5, 149.5, 169.5, and 189.5. Doug's 6 equally spaced classes for the daily number of cars have class marks of 26.5, 34.5, 42.5, 50.5, 58.5, and 66.5.

a) Find the class limits for the daily number of people.

b) Find the class limits for the daily number of cars.

2-5 GRAPHING FREQUENCY DISTRIBUTIONS

Identifying the horizontal and vertical axes

Figures 2-1 and 2-2 (on pages 22 and 23) are previews of what we are going to discuss now: how to present frequency distributions graphically. Graphs give data in a two-dimensional picture. On the *horizontal* axis, we can show the values of the variable (the characteristic we are measuring), such as the chlorine level in ppm. On the *vertical* axis, we mark the frequencies of the classes shown on the horizontal axis. Thus, the height of the boxes in Fig. 2-1 measures the number of observations in each of the classes marked on the horizontal axis.

Function of graphs

Graphs of frequency distributions and relative frequency distributions are useful because they emphasize and clarify trends that are not so readily discernible in tables. They attract a reader's attention to trends in the data. Graphs can also help us do problems concerning frequency distributions. They will enable us to estimate some values at a glance and will provide us with a pictorial check on the accuracy of our solutions.

Histograms

Histograms described

Figures 2-1 and 2-2 (pp. 22, 23) are two examples of histograms. A *histogram* is a series of rectangles, each proportional in width to the range of values within a class and proportional in height to the number of items falling in the class. If the classes we use in the frequency distribution are of equal width, then the vertical bars in the histogram are also of equal width. The height of the bar for each class corresponds to the number of items in the class. As a result, the area contained in each rectangle (width times height) is the same percentage of the area of all the rectangles as the relative frequency of that class is to all the observations made.

Function of a relative frequency histogram

A histogram that uses the relative frequency of data points in each of the classes rather than the actual number of points is called a *relative frequency histogram*. The relative frequency histogram has the same shape as an absolute frequency histogram made from the same data set. This is true because in both, the relative size of each rectangle is the frequency of that class compared to the total number of observations.

Recall that the relative frequency of any class is the number of observations in that class divided by the total number of observations made. The sum of all the relative frequencies for any data set is equal to 1.0. With this in mind, we can convert the histogram of Fig. 2-1 into a relative frequency histogram such as we find in Fig. 2-3. Notice that the only difference between these two is the left-hand vertical scale. Whereas the scale in Fig. 2-1 is the *absolute* number of observations in each class, the scale in Fig. 2-3 is the number of observations in each class as a *fraction* of the total number of observations.

Advantage of the relative frequency

Being able to present data in terms of the relative rather than the absolute frequency of observations in each class is useful because, while the

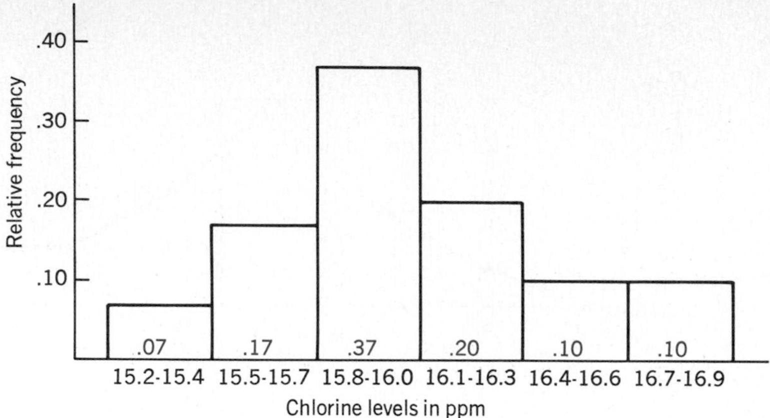

FIGURE 2-3 Relative frequency distribution of chlorine levels in samples of treated water, using .3 ppm class intervals

absolute numbers may change (as we test more gallons of water for example), the relationship among the classes may remain stable. Twenty percent of all the gallons of water may fall in the class "16.1 – 16.3 ppm" whether we test 30 gallons or 300 gallons. It is easy to compare the data from different sizes of samples when we use relative frequency histograms.

Frequency Polygons

Use class marks on the horizontal axis

Although less widely used, frequency polygons are another way to portray graphically both simple and relative frequency distributions. To construct a frequency polygon, we mark the frequencies on the vertical axis and the values of the variable we are measuring on the horizontal axis, as we did with histograms. Next, we plot each class frequency by drawing a dot above its class mark, or midpoint, and connect the successive dots with a straight line to form a polygon (a many sided figure).

Add two classes

Figure 2-4 is a frequency polygon constructed from the data in Table 2-14 on page 22. If you compare this figure with Fig. 2-1, you will notice that classes have been added at *each end* of the scale of observed values. These

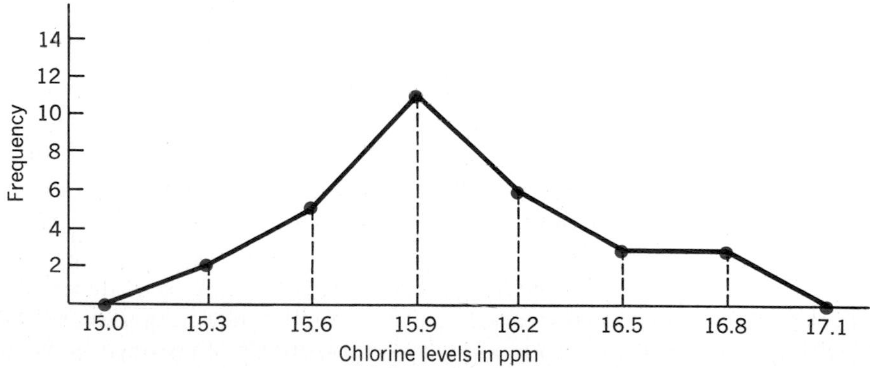

FIGURE 2-4 Frequency polygon of chlorine levels in samples of treated water, using .3 ppm class intervals

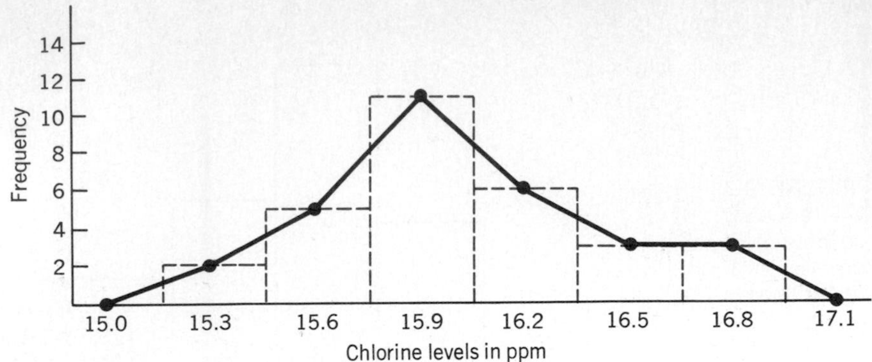

FIGURE 2-5 Histogram drawn from the points of the frequency polygon in Fig. 2-4

two new classes contain zero observations but allow the polygon to reach the horizontal axis at both ends of the distribution.

Converting a frequency polygon to a histogram

How can we turn a frequency polygon into a histogram? A frequency polygon is simply a line graph that connects the midpoints of all the bars in a histogram. Therefore, we can reproduce the histogram by drawing vertical lines from the bounds of the classes (as marked on the horizontal axis) and connecting them with horizontal lines at the heights of the polygon at each class mark. We have done this with dotted lines in Fig. 2-5.

Constructing a relative frequency polygon

A frequency polygon that uses the relative frequency of data points in each of the classes rather than the actual number of points is called a *relative frequency polygon*. The relative frequency polygon has the same shape as the frequency polygon made from the same data set but a different scale of values on the vertical axis. Rather than the absolute number of observations, the scale is the number of observations in each class as a fraction of the total number of observations.

Advantages of histograms

Histograms and frequency polygons are similar. Why do we need both? The advantages of histograms are:

1. The rectangle clearly shows each separate class in the distribution.
2. The area of each rectangle, relative to all the other rectangles, shows the proportion of the total number of observations that occur in that class.

Advantages of polygons

Frequency polygons, however, have certain advantages too.

1. The frequency polygon is simpler than its histogram counterpart.
2. It sketches an outline of the data pattern more clearly.
3. The polygon becomes increasingly smooth and curvelike as we increase the number of classes and the number of observations.

Creating a frequency curve

A polygon such as the one we have just described, smoothed by added classes and data points, is called a *frequency curve*. In Fig. 2-6, we have used our water example, but we have increased the number of observations to 300 and the number of classes to ten (the first and last dots do not

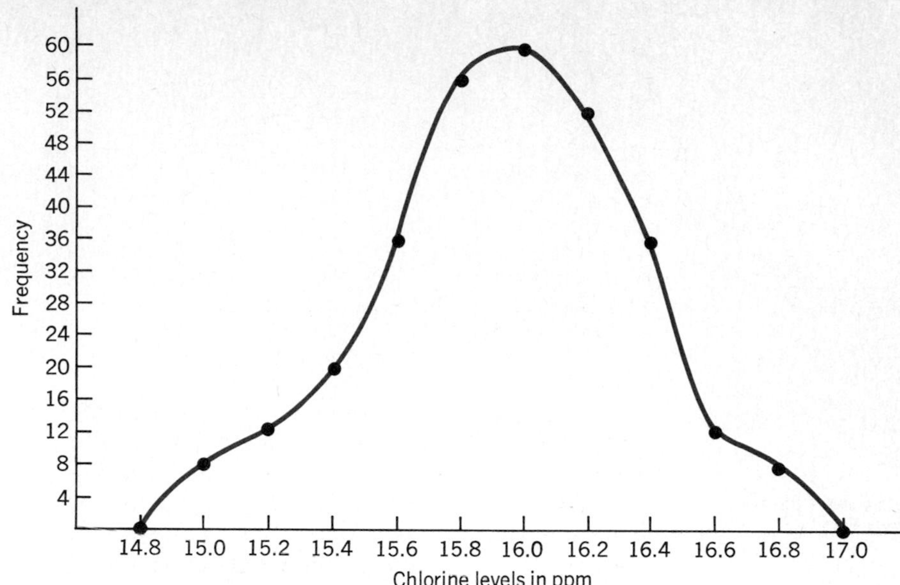

FIGURE 2-6 Frequency curve of the chlorine levels in 300 gallons of water, using .2 ppm intervals

represent class marks). Notice that we have connected the points with curved lines to approximate the way the polygon would look if we had an infinite number of data points and very small class intervals.

Ogives

Cumulative frequency distribution defined

A cumulative frequency distribution enables us to see how many observations lie above or below certain values, rather than merely recording the numbers of items within intervals. If, for example, we wish to know how many of our original 30 gallons of water contain more than 16.0 ppm of chlorine, we would refer to a table of cumulative "more-than" frequencies, such as Table 2-17. To know how many gallons contain less than 17.0 ppm, we can use a table recording the cumulative "less-than" frequencies in our sample, such as Table 2-18.

Tables of "more-than" and "less-than" frequencies

TABLE 2-17 Cumulative "more-than" frequency distribution of chlorine levels in ppm

CLASS	CUMULATIVE FREQUENCY
More than 15.1	30
More than 15.4	28
More than 15.7	23
More than 16.0	12
More than 16.3	6
More than 16.6	3
More than 16.9	0

TABLE 2-18 Cumulative "less-than" frequency distribution of chlorine levels in ppm

CLASS	CUMULATIVE FREQUENCY
Less than 15.2	0
Less than 15.5	2
Less than 15.8	7
Less than 16.1	18
Less than 16.4	24
Less than 16.7	27
Less than 17.0	30

A "more-than" ogive

A graph of a cumulative frequency distribution is called an *ogive* (pronounced "**oh**-jive"). The ogive for the cumulative distribution in Table 2-17 is shown in Fig. 2-7. The plotted points represent the number of gallons having more chlorine than the ppm shown on the horizontal axis. Notice that the upper bound of the classes in the table becomes the lower bound of the cumulative distribution of the ogive.

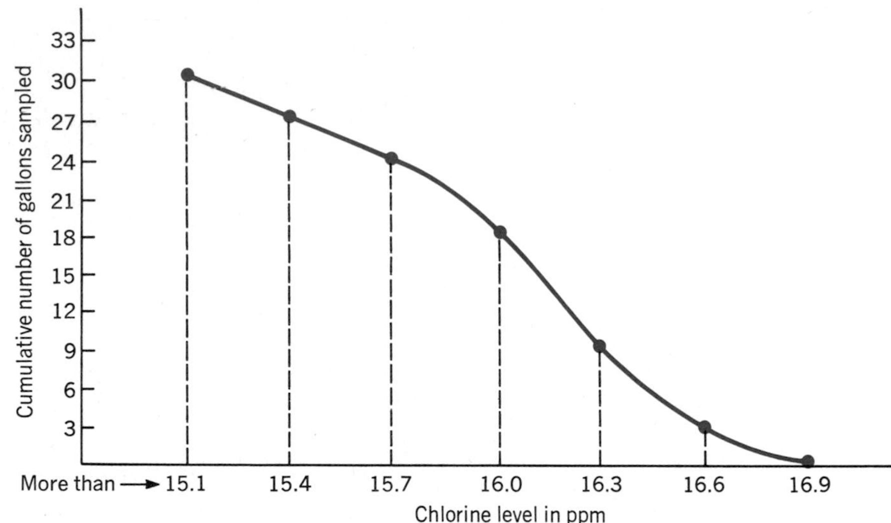

FIGURE 2-7 "More-than" ogive of the distribution of chlorine levels in ppm for 30 gallons of treated water

A "less-than" ogive

Likewise, we can use the ogive in Fig. 2-8, which plots the cumulative distribution of Table 2-18, to find the number of gallons having less chlorine than the ppm shown on the horizontal axis. In this case, the lower bound of the classes is the upper bound of the cumulative distribution in Fig. 2-8.

Shapes of ogives

The *S-shaped* curves shown in Figs. 2-7 and 2-8 are typical of ogives. Notice that the "more-than" curve slopes down and to the right. The "less-than" curve slopes up and to the right.

Ogives of relative frequencies

We can construct an ogive of a relative frequency distribution in the same manner in which we drew the ogives of absolute frequency distributions in Figs. 2-7 and 2-8. There will be one change—the vertical scale. As in

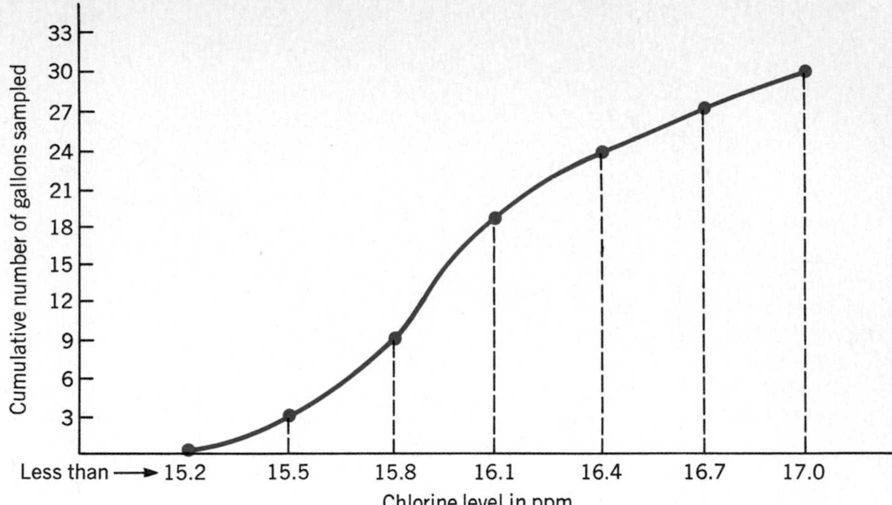

FIGURE 2-8 "Less-than" ogive of the distribution of chlorine levels in ppm for 30 gallons of treated water

Fig. 2-3, on page 29, this scale must mark the *fraction* of the total number of observations that fall into each class.

To construct a cumulative "less-than" ogive in terms of relative frequencies, we can refer to a relative frequency distribution (like Fig. 2-3) and set up a table using the data (like Table 2-19). Then we can convert the figures there to an ogive (as in Fig. 2-9). Notice that Figs. 2-8 and 2-9 are equivalent except for the left-hand vertical axis.

TABLE 2-19 Relative cumulative frequency distribution of chlorine levels in ppm

CLASS	CUMULATIVE FREQUENCY	CUMULATIVE RELATIVE FREQUENCY
Less than 15.2	0	.00
Less than 15.5	2	.07
Less than 15.8	7	.23
Less than 16.1	18	.60
Less than 16.4	24	.80
Less than 16.7	27	.90
Less than 17.0	30	1.00

Approximating the data array

Suppose we now draw a line perpendicular to the vertical axis at the .50 mark to intersect our ogive. (We have done this in Fig. 2-10.) In this way, we can read an approximate value for the chlorine level in the fifteenth gallon of an array of the 30 gallons. Thus, we are back to the first data arrangement discussed in this chapter. From the data array, we can construct frequency distributions. From frequency distributions, we can construct cumulative frequency distributions. From these, we can graph an ogive. And from this ogive, we can approximate the values we had in the data array. However, we cannot normally recover the *exact* original data from any of the graphic representations we have discussed.

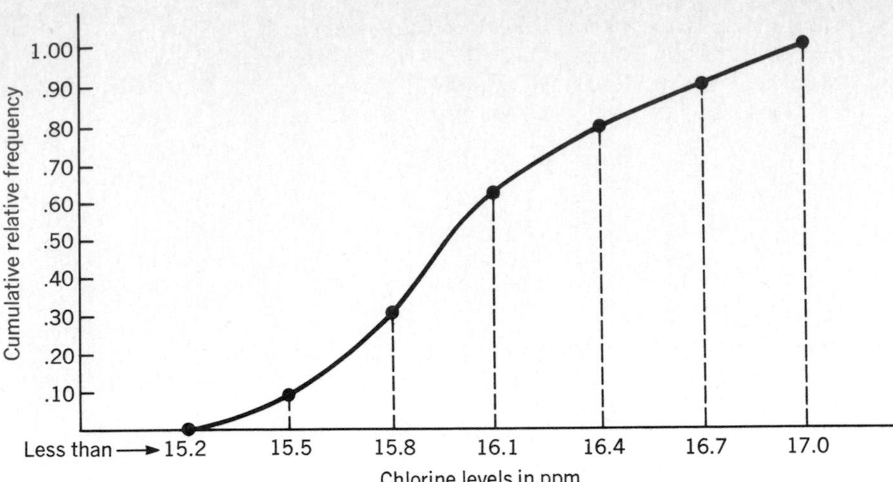

FIGURE 2-9
"Less-than" ogive of the distribution of chlorine levels in ppm for 30 gallons of treated water, using relative frequencies

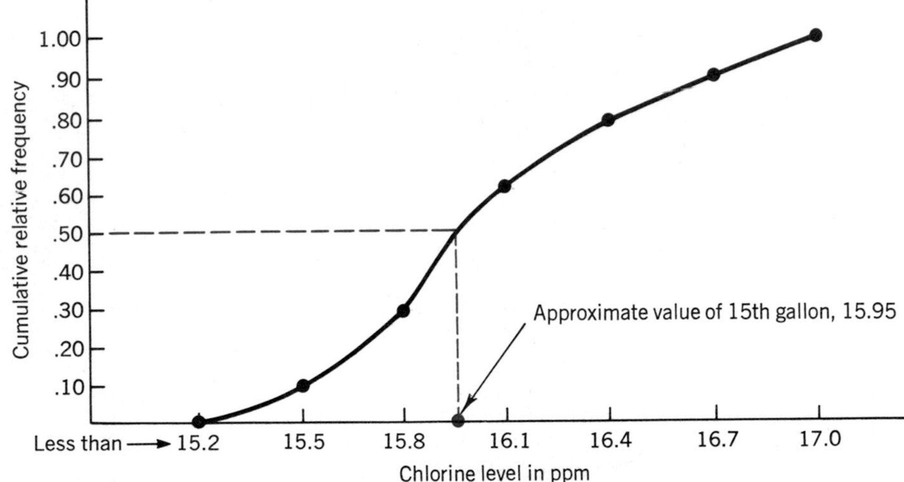

FIGURE 2-10
"Less-than" ogive of the distribution of chlorine levels in ppm for 30 gallons of treated water, indicating approximate middle value in original data array

EXERCISES

2-34 Construct a histogram for the data in the following frequency distribution:

CLASS	FREQUENCY	CLASS	FREQUENCY
75–89	9	150–164	24
90–104	12	165–179	10
105–119	24	180–194	8
120–134	25	195–209	6
135–149	30	210–224	2

2-35 Construct a frequency distribution for the data below.

a) Using intervals 50–59, 60–69,70–79, 80–89, and 90–99.
b) Using intervals 52–57, 58–63, 64–69, 70–75, 76–81, 82–87, 88–93, and 94–99.
c) Construct a frequency polygon for parts a and b.

67	63	95	79	70	82	83	84	71	93
92	67	97	72	60	57	58	86	54	68
98	80	85	84	74	66	60	56	78	79
59	81	78	69	74	90	71	82	73	65
80	72	76	88	83	70	71	91	69	83

2-36 For the following frequency distribution, construct:

a) A cumulative frequency distribution for frequencies of values "less than" the interval limits
b) An ogive based on part a
c) A cumulative frequency distribution for frequencies of values "more than" the interval limits
d) An ogive for part c

CLASS	FREQUENCY	CLASS	FREQUENCY
3.00–3.19	1	4.00–4.19	11
3.20–3.39	4	4.20–4.39	8
3.40–3.59	11	4.40–4.59	7
3.60–3.79	15	4.60–4.79	6
3.80–3.99	12		

2-37 For the following frequency distribution,

a) Construct a cumulative relative frequency ogive using frequencies of values "less than" the interval limits.
b) Estimate the value of the middle observation in the original data set.

CLASS	FREQUENCY	CLASS	FREQUENCY
0.5–0.9	13	2.5–2.9	30
1.0–1.4	20	3.0–3.4	35
1.5–1.9	22	3.5–3.9	41
2.0–2.4	24	4.0–4.4	15

2-38 Prior to constructing a dam on the Colorado River, the U.S. Army Corps of Engineers performed a series of tests to measure the water flow past the proposed location of the dam. The results of the testing were used to construct the following frequency distribution:

RIVER FLOW (THOUSANDS OF GALLONS PER MINUTE)	FREQUENCY
1,001–1,050	9
1,051–1,100	20
1,101–1,150	31
1,151–1,200	45
1,201–1,250	53
1,251–1,300	39
1,301–1,350	27
1,351–1,400	13
Total	**237**

a) Use the data given in the table to construct a "more-than" cumulative frequency distribution and ogive.
b) Use the data given in the table to construct a "less-than" cumulative frequency distribution and ogive.
c) Use your ogive to estimate what portion of the flow occurs at less than 1,300 thousands of gallons per minute.

2-39 Pamela Mason, a consultant for a small local brokerage firm, was attempting to design investment programs attractive to senior citizens. She knew that if potential customers could obtain a certain level of return, they would be willing to risk an investment; but below a certain level, they would be reluctant. From a group of 50 subjects, she obtained the following data regarding the various levels of return required for each respective subject to invest $1,000:

INDIFFERENCE POINT	FREQUENCY
$90– 94	2
95– 99	6
100–104	9
105–109	13
110–114	10
115–119	4
120–124	3
125–129	3
	50

a) Construct "more-than" and "less-than" cumulative relative frequency distributions.
b) Graph the two distributions in part a into relative frequency ogives.

2-40 At a newspaper office, the time required to set the entire front page in type was recorded for 50 days. The data, to the nearest tenth of a minute, are given below.

20.8	22.8	21.9	22.0	20.7	20.9	25.0	22.2	22.8	20.1
25.3	20.7	22.5	21.2	23.8	23.3	20.9	22.9	23.5	19.5
23.7	20.3	23.6	19.0	25.1	25.0	19.5	24.1	24.2	21.8
21.3	21.5	23.1	19.9	24.2	24.1	19.8	23.9	22.8	23.9
19.7	24.2	23.8	20.7	23.8	24.3	21.1	20.9	21.6	22.7

a) Arrange the data in an array from lowest to highest.
b) Construct a frequency distribution and a "less-than" cumulative frequency distribution from the data, using intervals of .8 minutes.
c) Construct a frequency polygon from the data.
d) Construct a "less-than" frequency ogive from the data.
e) From your ogive, estimate what percentage of the time the front page can be set in less than 24 minutes.

2-41 Jonathan Webb, insurance agent for the Safety Insurance Corporation, has data on the monthly dollar amount of insurance policies that he has sold over the past three years. He has arranged his data into the following frequency distribution.

MONTHLY SALES	FREQUENCY
$1,000–$1,149	1
1,150– 1,299	3
1,300– 1,449	6
1,450– 1,599	4
1,600– 1,749	8
1,750– 1,899	9
1,900– 2,049	3
2,050– 2,199	2

a) Construct a relative frequency distribution.
b) Construct, on the same graph, a relative frequency histogram and a relative frequency polygon.

2-42 Art Fulldodger, a skillful crooked accountant who has never paid a penny in federal taxes, has yearly data on the amount of money he has "saved" by cheating on his taxes over the last 25 years. With 10 years of free time coming to him in his cell at Fort Leavenworth, Art has plenty of time on his hands to analyze his data:

YEARLY TAXES EVADED	FREQUENCY
$ 1–$ 500	5
501– 1,000	1
1,001– 1,500	3
1,501– 2,000	4
2,001– 2,500	6
2,501– 3,000	6

a) Construct a relative frequency distribution and a "less-than" cumulative relative frequency distribution.
b) Construct an ogive based on part a.

2-43 Hans Orff, a tour guide at the Smithsonian Museum of Natural History in Washington, D.C., has been keeping track of how many minutes people spend in a certain dinosaur exhibit. His data, rounded to the nearest minute, for the most recent 400 people to visit the exhibit are summarized by the table below:

MINUTES SPENT IN EXHIBIT	FREQUENCY
Less than 2	30
2– 3	40
4 – 5	40
6– 7	90
8– 9	70
10–11	50
12–13	50
14–15	30
	400

a) Construct a "less-than" cumulative frequency distribution.
b) Construct an ogive based on part a.
c) Management has decided that an exhibit is a failure if 50% of the people spend less than 4 minutes in it. What is the percentage of the people observed spending less than 4 minutes? Also, management would like to know roughly how many minutes the 200th visitor spent in the exhibit, so give an approximate value for this.

2-6 TERMS INTRODUCED IN CHAPTER 2

CLASS LIMITS The smallest and largest values that go into any given class; there are stated limits and real limits.

CLASS MARK The midpoint of a class in a frequency distribution; the average of the lower and upper limits.

CONTINUOUS DATA Data that may progress from one class to the next without a break and may be expressed by either whole numbers or fractions.

CUMULATIVE FREQUENCY DISTRIBUTION A tabular display of data showing how many observations lie above, or below, certain values.

DATA A collection of any number of related observations on one or more variables.

DATA ARRAY The arrangement of raw data by observations in either ascending or descending order.

DATA POINT A single observation from a data set.

DATA SET A collection of data.

DISCRETE DATA Data that do not progress from one class to the next without a break; i.e., where classes represent distinct categories or counts and may be represented by whole numbers.

FREQUENCY CURVE A frequency polygon smoothed by adding classes and data points to a data set.

FREQUENCY DISTRIBUTION An organized display of data that shows the number of observations from the data set that fall into each of a set of mutually exclusive classes.

FREQUENCY POLYGON A line graph connecting the midpoints of each class in a data set, plotted at a height corresponding to the frequency of the class.

HISTOGRAM A graph of a data set, composed of a series of rectangles, each proportional in width to the range of values in a class and proportional in height to the number of items falling in the class, or the fraction of items in the class.

OGIVE A graph of a cumulative frequency distribution.

OPEN-ENDED CLASS A class that allows either the upper or lower end of a quantitative classification scheme to be limitless.

POPULATION A collection of all the elements we are studying and about which we are trying to draw conclusions.

RAW DATA Information before it is arranged or analyzed by statistical methods.

RELATIVE FREQUENCY DISTRIBUTION The display of a data set that shows the fraction or percentage of the total data set that falls into each of a set of mutually exclusive classes.

REPRESENTATIVE SAMPLE A sample that contains the relevant characteristics of the population in the same proportion as they are included in that population.

SAMPLE A collection of some, but not all, of the elements of the population under study, used to describe the population.

2-7 EQUATIONS INTRODUCED IN CHAPTER 2

[2-1]

$$\text{Width of class intervals} = \frac{\text{Next unit value after largest value in data} - \text{Smallest value in data}}{\text{Total number of class intervals}}$$

p. 21

To arrange raw data, decide the number of classes in which you will divide the data (normally, between 6 and 15), and then use Equation 2-1 to determine the *width of class intervals of equal size.* This formula uses the next value of the same units because it measures the interval between the first value of one class and the first value of the next class.

[2-2]

$$\text{Class mark} = \frac{\text{Stated lower limit} + \text{Stated upper limit}}{2}$$

p. 24

The midpoint of a class—that is, its *class mark*—is calculated by averaging the lower and upper limits of that class.

[2-3] $$\text{Class mark} = \frac{\text{Stated lower limit} + \text{Stated lower limit of the next class}}{2}$$ p. 24

When we are dealing with discrete variables and wide intervals, the midpoint of a class (its class mark) is calculated by using a slight modification of Equation 2-2. This enables us to work with more convenient values.

2-8 CHAPTER REVIEW EXERCISES

2-44 The following set of raw data gives income and education level for a sample of individuals. Would rearranging the data help us to draw some conclusions? Rearrange the data in a way that makes it more meaningful.

INCOME	EDUCATION	INCOME	EDUCATION	INCOME	EDUCATION
$17,000	High school	$ 21,200	B.S.	$17,200	2 yrs. college
20,800	B.S.	28,000	B.S.	19,600	B.A.
27,000	M.A.	30,200	High school	36,200	M.S.
70,000	M.D.	22,400	2 yrs. college	14,400	1 yr. college
29,000	Ph.D.	100,000	M.D.	18,400	2 yrs. college
14,400	10th grade	76,000	Law degree	34,400	B.A.
19,000	High school	44,000	Ph.D.	26,000	High school
23,200	M.A.	17,600	11th grade	52,000	Law degree
30,400	High school	25,800	High school	64,000	Ph.D.
25,600	B.A.	20,200	1 yr. college	32,800	B.S.

2-45 All 50 states send the following information to the Department of Labor: the average number of workers absent daily during each of the 13 weeks of a financial quarter, and the percentage of absentees for each state. Is this an example of raw data? Explain.

2-46 Knippon Cameras introduced a new 35-millimeter camera and invested heavily in a nationwide publicity campaign aimed at achieving substantial market penetration. Weekly sales increases for 40 districts were monitored and recorded in percentage figures (1.0 equals a 1 percent increase in sales); they are given below:

0.3	1.8	1.4	0.8	0.2	1.5	0.3	1.3	1.1	0.7
0.8	0.9	0.7	0.7	0.9	1.6	0.8	1.2	1.2	1.5
1.2	1.0	1.1	0.9	0.8	0.7	0.1	0.7	1.8	1.4
0.1	1.5	1.3	1.7	1.0	0.6	0.5	0.5	1.1	1.0

a) Arrange the data in an array from highest to lowest.

b) Construct a relative frequency distribution and a "more-than" cumulative relative frequency distribution using intervals of .25.

c) Construct a histogram from the data.
d) Construct a relative frequency "more-than" ogive.
e) Verify that the 20th data point in the array is close to the intersection of a horizontal line drawn from .50 on the vertical axis to the ogive curve.

2-47 The National Safety Council randomly sampled the tread depth of 60 right front tires on passenger vehicles stopped at a rest area on an interstate highway. From their data, they constructed the following frequency distribution:

TREAD DEPTH (INCHES)	FREQUENCY	TREAD DEPTH (INCHES)	FREQUENCY
16/32 (new tire)	5	4/32–6/32	7
13/32–15/32	10	1/32–3/32	4
10/32–12/32	20	0/32 bald	2
7/32–9/32	12		

Approximately what was the tread depth of the 30th tire in the data array?

2-48 The High Point Fastener Company produces 15 basic items. The company keeps records on the number of each item produced per month in order to examine the relative production levels. Records show the following numbers of each item were produced by the company for the last month of 20 operating days:

9,897	10,052	10,028	9,722	9,908
10,098	10,587	9,872	9,956	9,928
10,123	10,507	9,910	9,992	10,237

Construct both a frequency distribution and a relative frequency distribution of items produced per day, using intervals of 5 units per day.

2-49 The administrator of a hospital has ordered a study of the amount of time a patient must wait before being treated by emergency room personnel. The following data were collected during a typical day:

WAITING TIME (MIN.)									
15	13	19	23	22	5	15	12	28	20
28	2	8	17	24	7	20	26	13	9

a) Arrange the data in an array, lowest to highest.
b) Construct a frequency distribution, using 6 equal intervals.
c) Construct a frequency distribution, using 10 equal intervals.

2-50 The vice-president of finance for Home Plastics needed to invest a large amount of surplus cash generated from unexpectedly high sales. Various investment opportunities were classified according to potential risk and anticipated rate of return. The data regarding rate of return were recorded in a distribution with 14.65, 15.25, 15.85, 16.45, 17.05, 17.65, 18.25, and 18.85 as the real class limits (data recorded as a percentage and measured to the nearest tenth of a percentage point). Determine the stated class limits and class marks for each interval of the distribution.

2-51 Below are the measurements on an entire population of 100 elements.
a) Select two samples: one sample of the first 10 elements, and another sample of the largest 10 elements.
b) Are the two samples equally representative of the population? If not, which sample is more representative, and why?

226	198	210	233	222	175	215	191	201	175
264	204	193	244	180	185	190	216	178	190
174	183	201	238	232	257	236	222	213	207
233	205	180	267	236	186	192	245	218	193
189	180	175	184	234	234	180	252	201	187
155	175	196	172	248	198	226	185	180	175
217	190	212	198	212	228	184	219	196	212
220	213	191	170	258	192	194	180	243	230
180	135	243	180	209	202	242	259	238	227
207	218	230	224	228	188	210	205	197	169

2-52 In the population under study, there are 2,000 women and 8,000 men. If we are to select a sample of 250 individuals from this population, how many should be women, to make our sample considered strictly representative?

2-53 The U.S. Department of Labor publishes several classifications of the unemployment rate, as well as the rate itself. Recently, the unemployment rate was 7.3 percent. The department reported the following educational categories:

LEVEL OF EDUCATION	RELATIVE FREQUENCY (% OF THOSE UNEMPLOYED)
Did not complete high school	.38
Received high school diploma	.29
Attended college but did not receive a degree	.17
Received a college degree	.08
Attended graduate school but did not receive a degree	.05
Received a graduate degree	.03
Total	**1.00**

Using these data, construct a relative frequency histogram.

2-54 Using the relative frequency distribution given in problem 2-62, construct a relative frequency histogram and polygon. For the purposes of the present problem, assume that the upper limit of the last class is $51.00.

2-55 Using the frequency distribution given in problem 2-56 for miles per day of jogging, construct a frequency histogram and polygon. For the purpose of the present problem, assume that the upper limit of the last class is 5.39 miles.

2-56 A sports psychologist studying the effect of jogging on college students' grades collected data from a group of college joggers. Along with some other variables, he recorded the average number of miles run per day. He compiled his results into the following distribution:

MILES PER DAY	FREQUENCY
1.00–1.39	32
1.40–1.79	43
1.80–2.19	81
2.20–2.59	122
2.60–2.99	131
3.00–3.39	130
3.40–3.79	111
3.80–4.19	95
4.20–4.59	82
4.60–4.99	47
5.00 and up	53
	927

Determine the stated limits, real limits, and class marks for the intervals of the distribution.

2-57 City engineers made a study of the average time (in hours) cars remained parked at a new city parking lot. The data were rounded to the nearest tenth of an hour and grouped in a table whose classes have the following real limits: .05, .35, .65, .95, 1.25, 1.55, 1.85, 2.15, 2.45, 2.75, 3.05, and no limit for the last interval. Determine the stated limits and class marks for each interval.

2-58 If the following age groups are included in the proportions indicated, how many of each age group should be included in a sample of 3,000 people to make the sample representative?

AGE GROUP	RELATIVE PROPORTION IN POPULATION
12–17	.15
18–23	.33
24–29	.25
30–35	.17
36+	.10
	1.00

2-59 State University has 3 campuses, each with its own business school. Last year, State's business professors published numerous articles in prestigious professional journals, and the board of regents counted these articles as a measure of the productivity of each department.

JOURNAL NUMBER	NUMBER OF PUBLICATIONS	CAMPUS	JOURNAL NUMBER	NUMBER OF PUBLICATIONS	CAMPUS
9	3	North	14	20	South
12	6	North	10	18	South
3	12	South	3	12	West
15	8	West	5	6	North
2	9	West	7	5	North
5	15	South	7	15	West
1	2	North	6	2	North
15	5	West	2	3	West
12	3	North	9	1	North
11	4	North	11	8	North
7	9	North	14	10	West
6	10	West	8	17	South

a) Construct a frequency distribution and a relative frequency distribution by journal.
b) Construct a frequency distribution and a relative frequency distribution by university branch.
c) Construct a frequency distribution and a relative frequency distribution by number of publications (using intervals of 3).
d) Briefly interpret your results.

2-60 A questionnaire on attitudes about sex education in the schools is sent out to a random sample of 2,000 people; 880 are completed and returned to the researcher. Comment on the data available from these questionnaires in terms of the five tests for data.

2-61 With each appliance that Central Electric produces, the company includes a warranty card for the purchaser. In addition to validating the warranty and furnishing the company with the purchaser's name and address, the card also asks for certain other information that is used for marketing studies.

For each of the numbered blanks on the card, determine the most likely characteristics of the categories that would be used by the company to record the information. In particular, would they be (1) quantitative or qualitative? (2) continuous or discrete? (3) open-ended or closed? Briefly state the reasoning behind your answers.

Name______	Marital Status___ ③ ___
Address______	Where was appliance purchased?
City______ State______	___ ④ ___
Zip Code______	Why was appliance purchased?
Age_ ① _ Yearly Income___ ② ___	___ ⑤ ___

2-62 The following relative frequency distribution resulted from a study of the dollar amounts spent per visit by customers at a supermarket:

AMOUNT SPENT	RELATIVE FREQUENCY
$ 0–$ 5.99	1%
6.00–$10.99	3
11.00–$15.99	4
16.00–$20.99	6
21.00–$25.99	7
26.00–$30.99	9
31.00–$35.99	11
36.00–$40.99	19
41.00–$45.99	32
46.00 and above	8
Total	**100%**

Determine the class marks for each of the intervals.

2-63 The following responses were given by two groups of hospital patients, one receiving a new treatment, the other receiving a standard treatment for an illness. The question asked was, "What degree of discomfort are you experiencing?"

GROUP 1			GROUP 2		
Mild	Moderate	Severe	Moderate	Mild	Severe
None	Severe	Mild	Severe	None	Moderate
Moderate	Mild	Mild	Mild	Moderate	Moderate
Mild	Moderate	None	Moderate	Mild	Severe
Moderate	Mild	Mild	Severe	Moderate	Moderate
None	Moderate	Severe	Severe	Mild	Moderate

Suggest a better way to display these data. Explain why it is better.

2-64 The production manager of the Browner Typewriter Company posted final worker performance ratings based on total units produced, percentage of rejects, and total hours worked. Is this an example of raw data? Why, or why not? If not, what would the raw data be in this situation?

2-65 The head of a large business department wanted to classify the specialties of its 67 members. He asked Peter Wilson, a Ph.D. candidate, to get the information from the faculty members' publications. Peter compiled the following:

SPECIALTY	FACULTY MEMBERS PUBLISHING
Accounting only	1
Marketing only	5
Statistics only	4
Finance only	2
Accounting and marketing	7
Accounting and statistics	6
Accounting and finance	3
Marketing and finance	8
Statistics and finance	9
Statistics and marketing	21
No publications	1
	67

Construct a relative frequency distribution for the *types* of specialties. (*Hint:* the categories of your distribution will be mutually exclusive, but any individual may fall into several categories.)

2-66 The Ferebee Ergonomic Toy Company hired consultant Robin Clark to design a new management investment program. In order to estimate the various amounts managers would be willing to invest from their respective paychecks, Clark researched the second incomes of managers' families. His data reveal that no family has a second income over $20,000, and several families appear to have no second income. In a preliminary analysis, he decides to construct both frequency and relative frequency distributions for second income. He wants to use $2,000 intervals.

a) Develop a continuous, closed distribution that meets his requirements.
b) Develop a continuous distribution with 9 categories that meets his requirements and that is open at both ends. You may relax the requirement for $2,000 intervals for the open-ended category.

2-67 The Kawahondi Computer Company compiled data regarding the number of interviews required for each of its 20 salespeople to make a sale. Following are a frequency distribution and a relative frequency distribution of the number of interviews required per salesperson per sale. Fill in the missing data

NUMBER OF INTERVIEWS (CLASSES)	FREQUENCY	RELATIVE FREQUENCY
0–10	?	.05
11–20	0	?
21–30	1	?
31–40	?	?
41–50	?	.15
51–60	?	.20
61–70	2	?
71–80	?	.00
81–90	3	?
91–100	?	.00
Total	**?**	**?**

2-9 CHAPTER CONCEPTS TEST

Answers are in the back of the book.

T F 1. In comparison to a data array, the frequency distribution has the advantage of representing data in compressed form.

T F 2. The smallest and largest values that go into any given class of a frequency distribution are referred to as the class limits.

T F 3. A histogram is a series of rectangles, each proportional in width to the number of items falling within a specific class of data.

T F 4. A single observation is called a data point, whereas a collection of data is known as a tabular.

T F 5. The classes in any relative frequency distribution are all-inclusive and mutually exclusive.

T F 6. When a sample contains the relevant characteristics of a certain population in the same proportion as they are included in that population, the sample is said to be a representative sample.

T F 7. The distinction between real class limits and stated class limits is made only when we are dealing with continuous variables.

T F 8. If we were to connect the midpoints of the consecutive bars of a frequency histogram with a series of lines, we would be graphing a frequency polygon.

T F 9. Before information is arranged and analyzed, using statistical methods, it is known as preprocessed data.

T F 10. One disadvantage of the data array is that it does not allow us to easily find the highest and lowest values in the data set.

T F 11. Discrete data can be expressed only in whole numbers.

T F 12. As a general rule, statisticians regard a frequency distribution as incomplete if it has fewer than 20 classes.

T F 13. It is always possible to construct a histogram from a frequency polygon.

T F 14. The vertical scale of an ogive for a relative frequency distribution marks the fraction of the total number of observations that fall into each class.

T F 15. A data array is formed by arranging raw data in order of time of observation.

T F 16. A "less-than" ogive is S-shaped and slopes down and to the right.

T F 17. One advantage of a histogram in comparison with a frequency polygon is that it more clearly shows each separate class in the distribution.

18. Which of the following represents the most accurate scheme of classifying data?
    a) Quantitative methods
    b) Qualitative methods
    c) A combination of quantitative and qualitative methods
    d) A scheme can be determined only with specific information about the situation.

19. Which of the following is NOT an example of compressed data?
    a) Frequency distribution
    b) Data array
    c) Histogram
    d) Ogive

20. Which of the following statements about histogram rectangles is correct?
    a) The rectangles are proportional in height to the number of items falling in the classes.
    b) The rectangles are proportional in width to the size of the class marks.
    c) The area in a rectangle depends only upon the number of items in the class as compared to the number of items in all other classes.
    d) All of these.
    e) a and c but not b.

21. Why is it true that classes in frequency distributions are all-inclusive?
    a) No data point falls into more than one class.
    b) Every class has a class mark.
    c) All data fit into one class or another.
    d) All of these.
    e) a and c but not b.
22. When constructing a frequency distribution, the first step is:
    a) Calculate the class marks for the data.
    b) Sort the data points into classes and count the number of points in each class.
    c) Decide on the type and number of classes for dividing the data.
    d) None of these.
23. As the numbers of observations and classes increase, the shape of a frequency polygon:
    a) Tends to become increasingly smooth.
    b) Tends to become jagged.
    c) Stays the same.
    d) Varies only if data become more reliable.
24. Which of the following statements is true of cumulative frequency ogives for a particular set of data?
    a) Both "more-than" and "less-than" curves have the same slope.
    b) "More-than" curves slope up and to the right.
    c) "Less-than" curves slope down and to the right.
    d) "Less-than" curves slope up and to the right.
25. From an ogive constructed for a particular set of data:
    a) The original data can always be reconstructed exactly.
    b) The original data can always be approximated.
    c) The original data can never be approximated or reconstructed, but valid conclusions regarding the data can be drawn.
    d) None of these.
    e) a and b but not c.
26. When constructing a frequency distribution, the number of classes used depends upon:
    a) Number of data points.
    b) Range of the data collected.
    c) Size of the population.
    d) All of these.
    e) a and b but not c.
27. Which of the following statements is true?
    a) The size of a sample can never be as large as the size of the population from which it is taken.
    b) Classes describe only one characteristic of the data being organized.
    c) A class mark is calculated by averaging the lower and upper limits of a class.
    d) All of these.
    e) b and c but not a.
28. As a general rule, statisticians tend to use which of the following number of classes when arranging data?
    a) Fewer than 5.
    b) Between 1 and 5.
    c) More than 30.
    d) Between 20 and 25.
    e) None of these.
29. The distinction between real class limits and stated class limits is made only when you are using:
    a) Qualitative data.
    b) Discrete variables.
    c) Frequency polygons.
    d) Histograms.
    e) None of these.
30. A ______________ is a collection of all the elements in a group. A collection of some, but not all, of these elements is a ______________.
31. Dividing data points into similar classes and counting the number of observations in each class will give a ______________ distribution.

32. If data can take on only a limited number of values, the classes of these data are called ______. Otherwise, the classes are called ______.
33. The midpoint of a class is called the class ______.
34. A graph of cumulative frequency distributions is called a ______.
35. If a collection of data is called a data set, a single observation would be called a ______.

2-10 CONCEPTUAL CASE (Northern White Metals Company)

It was early in the autumn of 1980 that Dick Lennox began the job search that would ultimately lead him to the Northern White Metals Company. Dick had started his career in business as a sales representative with a large, diversified industrial firm. Late in 1974, after several successful years of sales work, he was lured away from life in a large corporation by one of his better customers, a medium-sized, highly profitable, family-owned metal manufacturing company. He accepted a job as marketing manager, bringing with him some fresh ideas and an eagerness to succeed. By the end of his first year, the company posted a record sales increase. Dick worked long hours, traveling extensively throughout the Northeast and industrial Midwest. Sales continued to grow, and Dick continued to develop his management expertise.

One midsummer's day in 1980, the president of the firm called Dick into his office and proudly announced that his two sons would be joining the company. One was to be shop foreman in the stamping department. The other, a recent graduate of a reputable eastern business school, was to be brought in as assistant marketing manager and would work closely with Dick. The long-run career implications of this development were strikingly clear, and that night, Dick began to consider the possibility of moving on.

After several months and many interviews, Dick began to get discouraged. He had received several offers, some quite attractive, but nothing that really matched what he wanted to do. Then, through a chance meeting with an old friend and fellow salesman, Dick heard of a small firm in New England. The Northern White Metals Company was seeking a qualified applicant to serve as general manager.

Northern White Metals began in the late 1940s as New England Metals Supply, a distributor of nonferrous metals, primarily aluminum, copper, and brass. These were sold in a variety of forms, such as sheet, rod, cable, and pipe, for a variety of industrial applications. Growth was never dramatic, but the company prospered in the postwar period, and sales and earnings increased steadily. Manufacturing capacity was added in 1952 with the purchase of an old, empty textile mill and a mid-sized, 1,850-ton aluminum extrusion press. Within three years, the copper and brass business was sold off. NWMC was by then fully involved in manufacturing and fabricating extruded aluminum products, primarily for the building and construction industry.

The aluminum extrusion manufacturing process begins with the raw material, aluminum billet. This is essentially aluminum ingot in cylindrical form, the shape necessary for use in the extrusion press. The billet is softened by being passed by a conveyor through high-heat ovens. It is then fed into the press and pushed with tremendous pressure through heavy steel dies. The result is long sections of aluminum with the desired cross-sectional shape. These are then stretched to remove twists and slight bends in the metal, cut into desired lengths, hardened in tempering ovens, packed, and shipped.

NWMC quickly developed a reputation for quality work and timely delivery. To better serve an expanding customer base, the company added an anodizing department, where a durable finish could be added to the metal; a fabricating department, with special cutting, bending, milling, and assembly capabilities; and a small machine shop, which offered tool and die and special repair capabilities.

Prosperity in the 1950s and the high growth potential of aluminum fostered a proliferation of small and medium-sized fabricating companies. Few developed primary manufacturing facilities, though, since the high capital investment made ventures into this area more difficult. With the rapid expansion of fabricating firms came an increasing intensity of competition. By the early 1960s, a recession and steep price declines pushed the industry into a profit squeeze from which many firms never recovered. NWMC operated its fabricating department unprofitably during this period, primarily to serve the overall needs of better customers. The extrusion department prospered, however, and served as a source of supply for many of the smaller fabricating firms that were forced to slash prices to preserve volume and utilize capacity.

The company performed well and, with the 1965 industry turnaround, had its most profitable year ever. Internal departments were expanded and NWMC flourished, securing a now smaller but very loyal group of customers. The 1970 downturn caused even this loyal group to shrink, though, as commercial construction slowed. Still, NWMC managed to remain profitable, and even grow a little, as new applications for extruded aluminum were sought in the rapidly emerging high-technology businesses.

The 1974 recession had a much more severe impact on the firm, however, as energy prices increased sharply. With its energy-intensive manufacturing process, NWMC's costs rose dramatically. The pressure on profits was severe. This, together with the sales decline that accompanied a depressed economy, left the company with its first unprofitable year ever.

Although general business conditions began to improve in 1975, NWMC never seemed to recover its previous position and exhibited a lackluster performance over the next few years. The president and principal owner of NWMC began to lose interest in the firm, and decided to contact a business broker about putting the company up for sale.

A prospect was found, and negotiations proceeded swiftly. NWMC was acquired with an exchange of common stock by Segue, Inc., a diversified architectural-products conglomerate that had long been interested in developing extrusion capability.

It was at this point that Dick Lennox first found out about NWMC. He arranged to meet with Segue management, and preliminary discussions ensued. A tour of the NWMC plant and offices followed and, although neither seemed particularly exciting, Dick thought there was potential in the operation. He was certainly enthusiastic about the prospect of stepping into a general manager's role.

That evening, Dick had dinner with the CEO of Segue. The man was an abrupt sort, but was relating the history and philosophy of his company with an almost reverential tone.

Suddenly he stopped. Looking directly at Dick with clear, penetrating eyes, he began to speak again.

"Lennox," he said with measured deliberation, "I want you to tell me why I should hire you."

Dick leaned forward and replied without hesitation.

"Two reasons, sir. I can increase sales, and I can increase profits."

Taken aback by the simplicity of the response, the CEO raised an eyebrow.

"Well, we shall see, young fellow," he chortled. He then snapped, "Report to Northern in three weeks, and be ready to go to work!"

The president of NWMC was to remain for an additional year and gradually turn over operating responsibility to Dick, his Segue-appointed successor. Running the company as it was did not seem to be exceptionally difficult, but sales gains and margin improvements would clearly be hard-won. It was to this task that Dick was to devote himself.

After three weeks of meeting the sales force, reviewing the production process, and getting to know the office staff, Dick was beginning to feel more comfortable in his new position. He also began to realize how formidable the challenge of this new position was. The company was in disarray, customer agreements were informal and subject to frequent changes, and the records systems were quite disorganized. Dick was in the process of addressing himself to these concerns when he received a late Friday afternoon call from corporate headquarters.

"Lennox," the CEO barked, "I want you in New York a week from Monday to make a presentation at the division presidents' meeting. We need a thorough analysis of sales and production cost trends at NWMC over the past three years and some kind of general suggestions about marketing and production plans for the coming year. Give us some thoughts on problem areas and potential problem areas—you know—the whole routine."

Dick swallowed hard as he hung up the phone. Back in his old job, he could have asked his M.B.A. assistant to punch up such information on the computer, draw up some projections, and there would be the report. Now he found himself staring at ten aging file cabinets packed with bills, orders, sales records, production records, and a plethora of other information.

Dick's task is to review a rather large body of data, select relevant information, and organize it into some meaningful and presentable form. How might he now proceed?

2-11 COMPUTER DATA BASE EXERCISE

Cold River Toy Company was founded in 1890 by the Mulford family to fill a demand for sleds in the burgeoning Rockies resort communities. The original Rough Rider sleds were handcrafted by the Mulford brothers and sold in hardware stores in resort towns in Colorado.

In the 1920s, sales of Rough Riders expanded throughout the Northwest as tourists spread their reputation for quality. Zelda and Scott Fitzgerald sledded on a Rough Rider in the French Alps, and the sled was instated as an adult toy.

The bottom dropped out in the Depression. Since purchases of toys and sports equipment are tied to disposable income, sales fell as the economy failed. Fortunately, Cold River was able to diversify into barrel staves from the seasoned oak that normally went into sleds and to integrate vertically with bootleg whiskey made of Rocky Mountain spring water. Not one employee was laid off, and Cold River prospered.

When prohibition was repealed, Cold River returned to sled production and increased distribution to the Midwest. Sales were beginning to climb when World War II began. The Mulfords of Cold River reproduced their turn-on-a-dime strategy and shifted to gun-stock and packing-crate production for the duration of the war.

Sales had been steadily building through the 1950s and 1960s as Rough Rider was rolled out to the East Coast. By 1978, Cold River had 50 distributors, and the main product line was a household word with phenomenal brand recognition.

The Mulfords began to diversify in the 1950s into small wooden toys and several additional sled sizes to catch the baby-boom market. Distribution on the toy line was primarily limited to Colorado, and volume frequently hovered at breakeven.

In 1977, Whizbang Conglomerate purchased a controlling share from the Mulford grandchildren and put Joe Walsh in power to clean up the operation, increase sales, and diversify the product line. Whizbang felt the toy and leisure-time industry had good growth prospects over the next ten years. With Cold River's name and debt-free balance sheet and Whizbang's dollars and administrative expertise, they hoped to expand sales and net income at a rapid rate.

U.S. census projections were anticipating an upswing in the birth rate in the 1980s. Projected births in 1985 were 4.2 million, up from a flat 3 million per year in the 1970s. Not only would more children be born, but more first-borns were expected after the 1970s tendency toward putting off childbearing. More disposable income per child was hypothesized, since typically both parents were working, and three adults (parents and a relative) were expected to be purchasing for each child. Appeals would be directed principally to those buying for preschoolers and to the good long-term possibilities of buyers for children under 15.

Despite the predicted growth in toy sales in the ensuing years, Whizbang knew the toy industry was a risky business. Two-thirds of all consumer purchases fell in the eight weeks before Christmas. Similarly, two-thirds of all retail purchases from the manufacturer are made from August to October. Fifty percent of all products every year are new products; 80 percent of those are unsuccessful. Most toy companies insulate profits against new-product failure by relying on stable sellers to supply cash flow. Since most annual sales take place in such a short period, manufacturers don't have time to produce large quantities of hot selling items after they determine which products will move. Initial production quantities of a new, untried line pose a difficult decision for the marketing staff, and inventory write-downs are a common phenomenon in the industry.

Joe Walsh took over Cold River in this industry environment. He planned to use Rough Rider and its two line extensions to subsidize the new product entries for the coming years. Whizbang had given him a 5-year contract to increase sales 50 percent and diversify the product line. After two years, Joe had streamlined production, cut costs, and introduced a best-selling aluminum sled. He was ready to expand to a new line of molded plastic toys when sales of Rough Riders began dropping. Joe is a competent administrator and a plodding thinker. He usually makes good decisions but likes convincing arguments from company personnel to sway his conservative bent. He had recently hired Laurel McRae and Frank Grove to fill a need at Cold River for data analysis and strategic planning. He felt a model toy company should rely on sophisticated marketing-analysis tools to keep on the edge of the industry, and Laurel and Frank had just graduated from a Midwestern business school with reputable skills in these disciplines.

Their first day at Cold River, Frank and Laurel shook hands briskly as they were ushered to a joint office. They had met during the interviewing process and felt they could work together. Although Laurel had doubts about Frank's statistical ability, she felt he would provide a valuable interface between marketing and statistical analysis. Frank thought Laurel a bit too brash and tactless, but he felt he could turn her computer background to a joint advantage.

Fred Walker, the VP of sales, broke into their extended coffee break as they were wondering when they'd get an assignment. He was the acting marketing chief at Cold River and had been with the Mulford family since he started selling sleds at 18. He had sold in every Cold River territory and had been regional manager of the Northwest and the Northeast before becoming VP of sales in 1970. Fred believed that experience was the best teacher and that education was only icing—to obscure the flavor of the cake. He'd opposed the Whizbang acquisition avidly from its inception. When James

Mulford finally acquiesced to the takeover, Fred forlornly agreed to continue to direct Cold River's marketing efforts.

Now, Fred greeted his new duo enthusiastically and introduced them around adjacent offices as the "marketeers." After telling them they'd better "hang up those diplomas so folks would know they were out of diapers," he mentioned a ten o'clock appointment scheduled for them with Joe Walsh.

As soon as Laurel and Frank sat down in the CEO's office, Joe began outlining the problem.

"This is an old company with old ideas. I've changed the way they think about production, but it's taken me two years to get a foothold with the old guard. Marketing was my next priority, but this sales decline has precipitated a crisis. I need you two to look at the distributor orders and find out what's happening out there.

"Fred seems to feel a sales meeting is in order, to tap the pulse of our market. He says salespeople know what's going on, and we don't need a computer to tell us.

"I know this is an abrupt introduction," Joe continued, "but can you look at these orders from the last three years and give me an opinion in a couple of days?"

With that, Joe hefted a sizable cardboard carton of orders across the table. Inside were hundreds of order requisitions, rubber-banded together by year.

"Oh no," whispered Frank as they snaked back down the hall lugging their hefty project between them. "I hope they have a keypunch operator."

"What's a keypunch?" asked Fred's secretary.

PROBLEMS AND QUESTIONS

1. Using the data for the number of units sold per order in each of the years 1977, 1978, and 1979, construct a histogram to plot the frequency distribution for each year. Use interval widths of 100, and let the first interval run from 0 to 100.
2. Calculate the relative frequency distributions, using the histograms developed in question 1.
3. What changing pattern do you see in the data from year to year? What are some possible explanations?

UNITS SOLD PER ORDER 1977

905	887	902	846	1119	1401	1299	858	702	441
874	896	923	1174	757	789	1234	927	999	1143
1004	1135	1005	1090	1270	999	812	1139	969	1348
802	656	658	482	709	426	825	362	799	731
652	345	321	396	662	365	651	321	846	580
475	543	418	390	607	562	831	598	828	655
517	343	528	722	632	655	547	848	452	333
283	285	326	176	235	198	196	190	244	208
246	258	317	270	392	242	294	336	251	214
203	200	236	238	293	294	187	256	260	246
238	339	317	293	276	250	283	293	295	202
291	303	331	257	219	285	270	338	219	367
301	274	327	201	214	208	190	329	249	230
273	340	335	214	241	257	215	262	245	320
219	274	296	297	375	247	310	228	227	248
282	226	251	204	289	284	236	232	362	312
291	314	280	230	213	256	226	251	305	333
275	219	231	174	200	264	224	261	330	185
266	191	224	225	273	276	300	229	333	196
234	288	234	214	240	190	297	202	260	307

UNITS SOLD PER ORDER 1978

1193	895	865	687	1337	588	1166	1136	1057	872
1326	727	1253	869	712	893	1382	1080	902	1156
990	998	919	818	770	1083	514	1047	1043	1096
1233	1129	628	1028	1159	992	935	319	659	559
484	763	557	593	633	465	329	319	871	371
380	560	411	500	454	319	649	338	525	454
524	555	507	743	524	504	876	531	403	881
839	626	421	522	721	498	330	658	192	209
290	156	271	217	203	253	202	231	303	221
178	181	219	162	235	258	228	197	228	155
201	173	249	183	309	203	252	241	272	162
184	165	220	257	142	215	256	286	188	235
212	203	192	198	212	267	181	147	269	149
313	228	290	236	228	223	258	178	273	187
245	235	206	209	171	166	205	191	198	256
262	258	249	162	300	185	146	197	158	165
268	292	239	272	198	219	191	203	196	146
218	180	228	201	156	160	229	242		

UNITS SOLD PER ORDER 1979

1041	983	822	549	963	1183	982	1108	856	1025
789	844	917	565	810	1013	1261	764	958	899
704	1112	1168	780	1002	923	999	920	776	869
694	755	979	826	939	855	1060	527	869	1037
1093	1003	687	701	873	428	427	867	816	478
522	553	627	838	314	841	372	416	439	690
651	761	717	626	326	460	404	810	828	424
547	617	829	365	488	768	492	332	770	613
653	247	177	210	171	145	286	200	213	234
228	181	198	179	82	203	142	255	133	280
161	181	220	161	205	295	201	227	188	291
240	177	280	225	214	185	189	88	218	191
179	198	261	245	177	163	216	156	174	190
244	181	171	218	228	126	155	160	175	126
224	185	223	260	113	194	135	202	151	213
223									

2-12 FLOW CHART

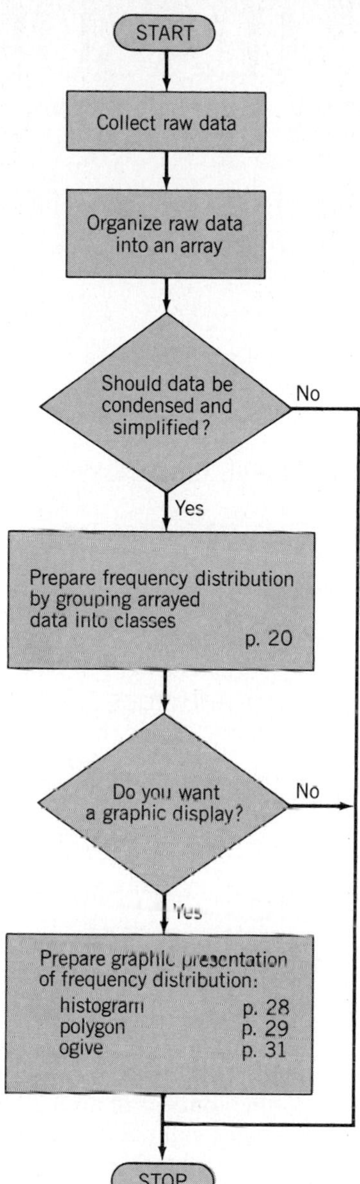

CHAPTER 3

SUMMARY MEASURES OF FREQUENCY DISTRIBUTIONS

1. BEYOND TABLES AND GRAPHS: Descriptive Measures of Frequency Distributions, 58
2. A MEASURE OF CENTRAL TENDENCY: The Arithmetic Mean, 62
3. A SECOND MEASURE OF CENTRAL TENDENCY: The Weighted Mean, 71
4. A THIRD MEASURE OF CENTRAL TENDENCY: The Geometric Mean, 74
5. A FOURTH MEASURE OF CENTRAL TENDENCY: The Median, 77
6. A FINAL MEASURE OF CENTRAL TENDENCY: The Mode, 84
7. COMPARING THE MEAN, MEDIAN, AND MODE, 90
8. TERMS, 91
9. EQUATIONS, 92
10. REVIEW EXERCISES, 94
11. CONCEPTS TEST, 97
12. CONCEPTUAL CASE, 99
13. COMPUTER DATA BASE EXERCISE, 100
14. FLOW CHART, 102

OBJECTIVES: Chapter 3 focuses on special ways to describe a collection of items, particularly the way observations tend to cluster or bunch up. Here, we shall encounter some familiar terms, such as the concept of an average. If the basketball coach at your university says the average height of the members of his team is 6′11″, he is really saying that there is a tendency for the heights of the players to bunch up around 6′11″. For a basketball team with this much height, you know intuitively that the chances of a winning season are quite good—even before you formally study statistics. In Chapter 3, we'll also study the mean, the median, and the mode—all ways of measuring and locating data.

The manager of a hydroelectric power plant has 10 generators in her system. She needs some measure of the time her 10 generators are out of service. With this information, she can plan manpower requirements, schedule maintenance, and arrange backup service. This table represents data from last year for each generator.

Generator	1	2	3	4	5	6	7	8	9	10
Days out of service	7	23	4	8	2	12	6	13	9	4

The manager would like some single measure of days out of service for all generators, to use in planning. This chapter introduces several measures useful to her and to others who must make similar plans.

3-1 BEYOND TABLES AND GRAPHS: Descriptive Measures of Frequency Distributions

Summary statistics describe the characteristics of a data set

In Chapter 2, we learned to construct tables and graphs using raw data. The resulting "pictures" of frequency distributions enabled us to discern trends and patterns in the data. But what if we need more exact measures of a data set? In that case, we can use single numbers, called *summary statistics,* to describe certain characteristics of a data set. From these, we can gain a more precise understanding of the data than we can from our tables and graphs. And these numbers will enable us to make quicker and better decisions because we will not need to consult our original observations.

Four of these characteristics are particularly important:

Middle of a data set

1. Measures of central tendency. Like averages, measures of central tendency tell us what we can expect a typical or middle data point to be. They are also called *measures of location.* In Fig. 3-1, the central location of curve B lies to the right of those of curve A and curve C. Notice that the central location of curve A is equal to that of curve C.

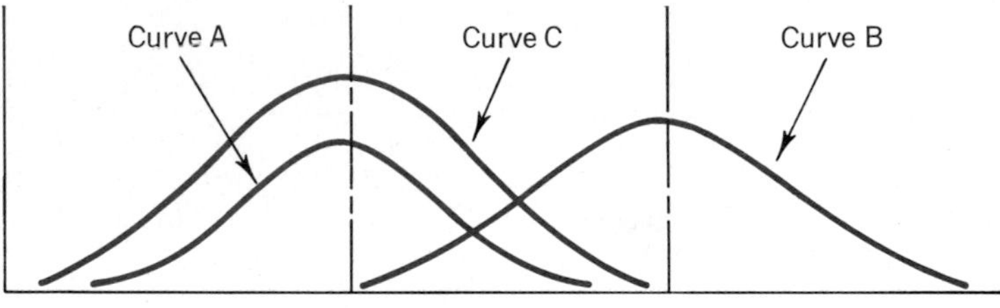

FIGURE 3-1 Comparison of central location of three curves

Range of a data set

2. Measures of dispersion. *Dispersion* refers to the spread of the data—that is, the extent to which the observations are scattered. In Chapter 2, we studied a measure of dispersion called the range. The range indicates how far it is from the lowest data point to the highest. Notice that curve A in Fig. 3-2 has a wider spread, or dispersion, than curve B.

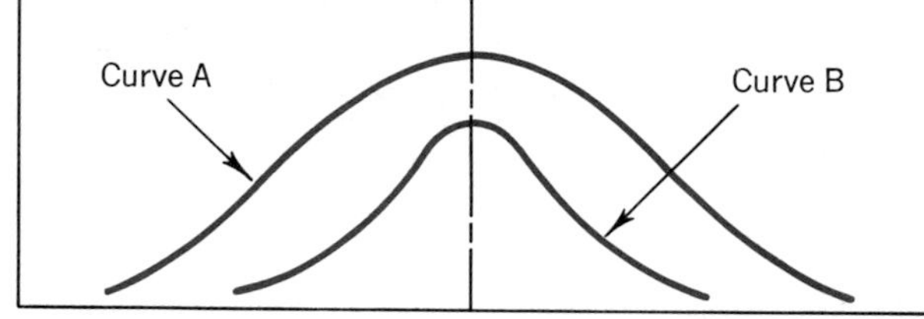

FIGURE 3-2 Comparison of dispersion of two curves

Symmetry of a data set

3. Measures of skewness. Curves representing the data points in the data set may be either symmetrical or skewed. *Symmetrical* curves, like the one in Fig. 3-3, are such that a vertical line drawn from the peak of the curve to the horizontal axis will divide the area of the curve into two equal parts. Each part is the mirror image of the other.

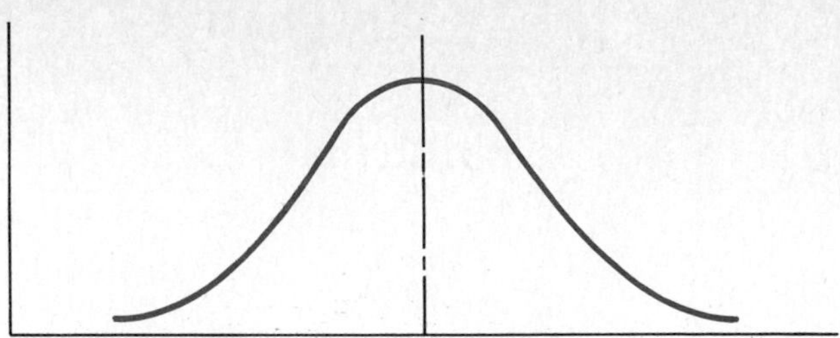

FIGURE 3-3
Symmetrical curve

Skewness of a data set

Curves A and B in Fig 3-4 are *skewed* curves. They are skewed because values in their frequency distributions are concentrated at either the low end or the high end of the measuring scale on the horizontal axis. The values are not equally distributed. Curve A is skewed to the right (or *positively* skewed), because it tails off toward the high end of the scale. Curve B is just the opposite. It is skewed to the left (*negatively* skewed), because it tails off toward the low end of the scale.

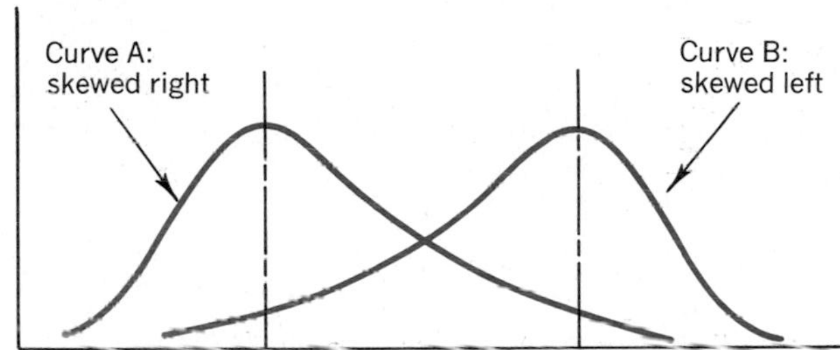

FIGURE 3-4
Comparison of two skewed curves

Curve A might represent the frequency distribution of the number of days' supply on hand in the wholesale fruit business. The curve would be skewed to the right, with many values at the low end and few at the high, because the inventory must turn over rapidly. Similarly, curve B could represent the frequency of the number of days a real-estate broker requires to sell a house. It would be skewed to the left, with many values at the high end and few at the low, because the inventory of houses turns over very slowly.

Peakedness of a data set

4. Measures of kurtosis. When we measure the *kurtosis* of a distribution, we are measuring its peakedness. In Fig. 3-5, for example, curves A and B differ only by the fact that one is more peaked than the other. They have the same central location and dispersion, and both are symmetrical. Statisticians say that the two curves have different degrees of kurtosis.

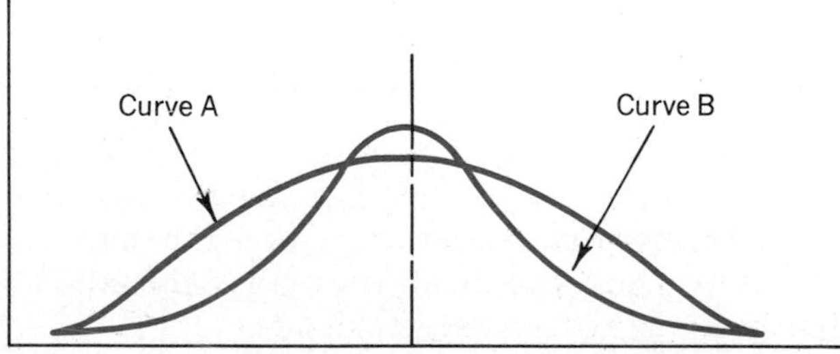

FIGURE 3-5
Two curves with the same central location but different kurtosis

Three degrees of peakedness

There are many different degrees of kurtosis, but statisticians commonly use three broad classes. A curve such as the one in Fig. 3-6 is called *mesokurtic;* a curve that is more peaked, like the one in Fig. 3-7, is called *leptokurtic;* and a curve that is less peaked, as in Fig. 3-8, is called *platykurtic.*

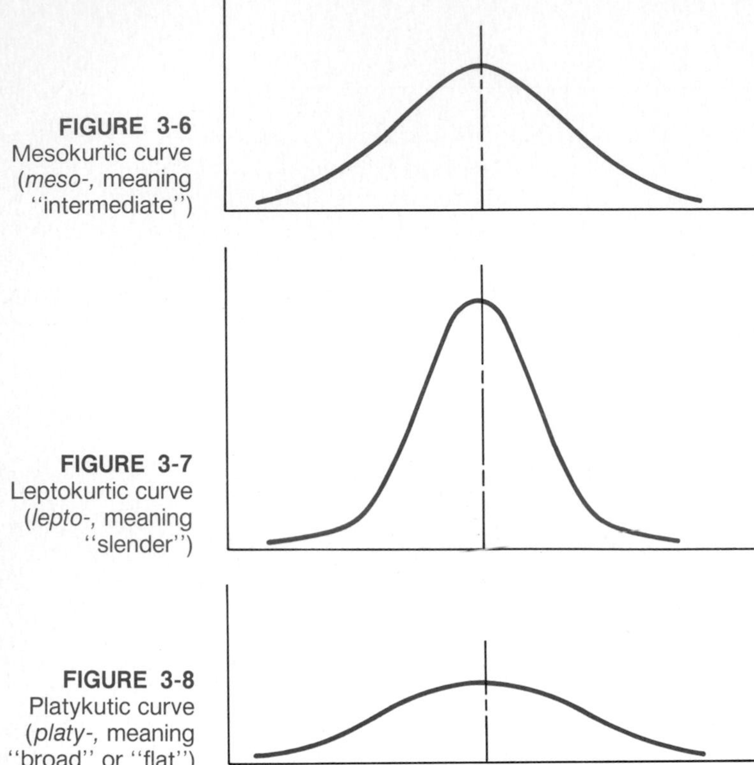

FIGURE 3-6 Mesokurtic curve (*meso-*, meaning "intermediate")

FIGURE 3-7 Leptokurtic curve (*lepto-*, meaning "slender")

FIGURE 3-8 Platykutic curve (*platy-*, meaning "broad" or "flat")

Now that we have briefly described these characteristics of frequency distributions, we can discuss in greater detail three common *measures of central tendency:* the *mean,* the *median,* and the *mode.*

EXERCISES

3-1 Draw examples of the following distributions, A and B:

a) A: Symmetrical, mesokurtic, range from −1.0 to +1.0, central tendency of 0.0.
   B: Symmetrical, platykurtic, range from −1.5 to +1.5, central tendency of 0.0.

b) A: Skewed left, mesokurtic, range from −1.0 to +1.0, peak at +0.5.
   B: Symmetrical, mesokurtic, range from −1.0 to +1.0, central tendency of 0.0.

c) A: Symmetrical, leptokurtic, range from −0.5 to +0.5, central tendency of 0.0.
   B: Skewed right, leptokurtic, range from −1.0 to +1.0, peak at −0.5.

3-2 Draw three curves, all symmetrical and with the same dispersion, but with the following central locations:

a) 0.0 b) 1.0 c) −1.0

3-3 Drawn below are four distribution curves. For each, indicate its peak, its degree of kurtosis, and whether it is symmetrical, positively skewed, or negatively skewed.

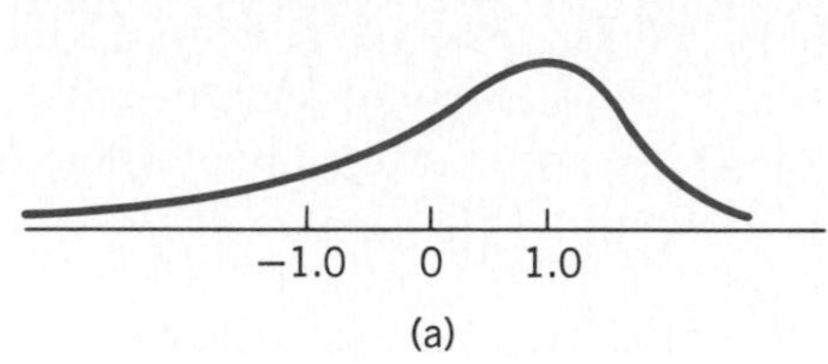

(a)

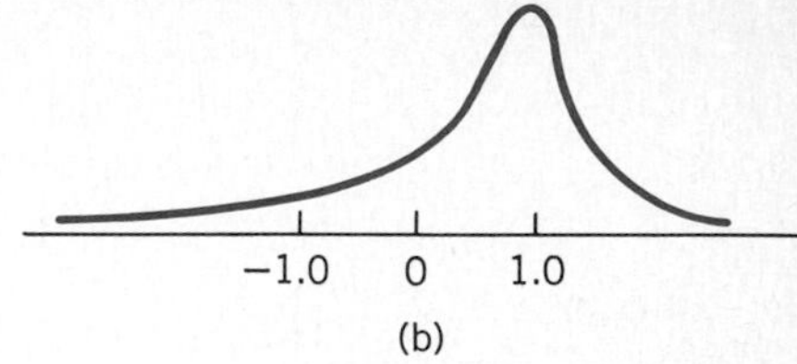

(b)

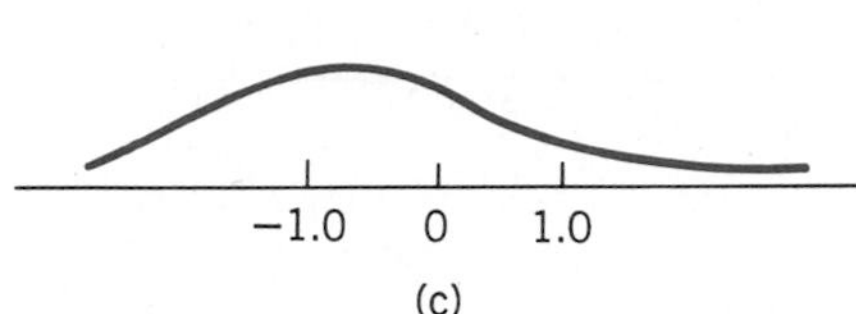

(c)

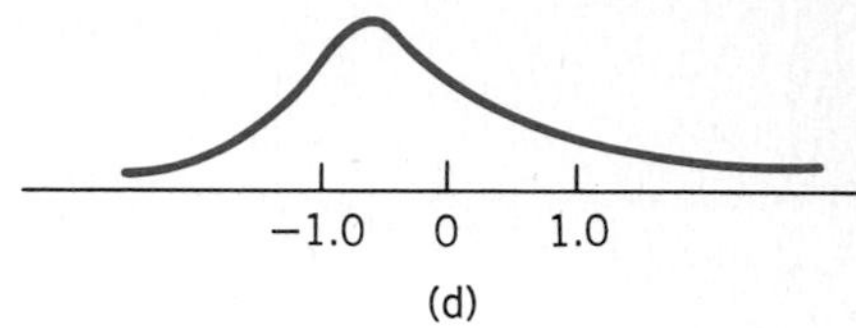

(d)

3-4 For the following distribution, indicate which distribution:

a) Has the larger average value.
b) Is more likely to produce a small value than a large value.

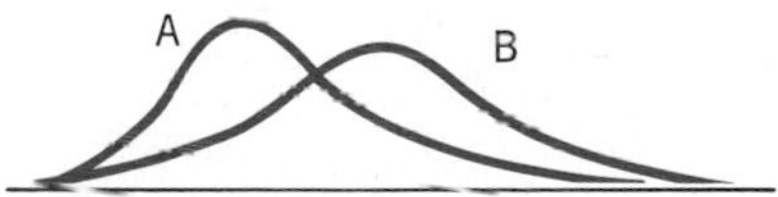

For the next two distributions, indicate which distribution, if any:

c) Has values most evenly distributed across the range of possible values.
d) Is more likely to produce a value near 0.
e) Has a greater likelihood of producing large values than small values.

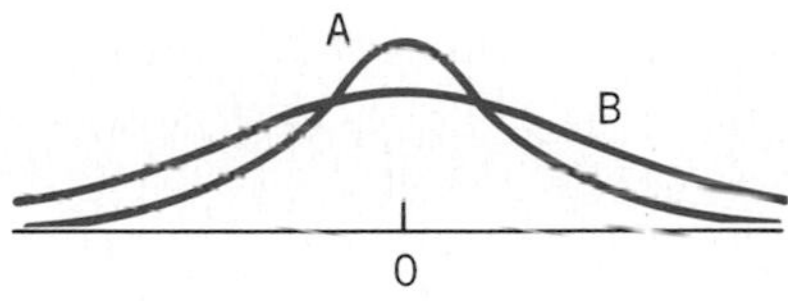

3-5 If the following two curves represent the distribution of scores for a group of students on two tests, which test appears to be more difficult for the students, A or B? Explain.

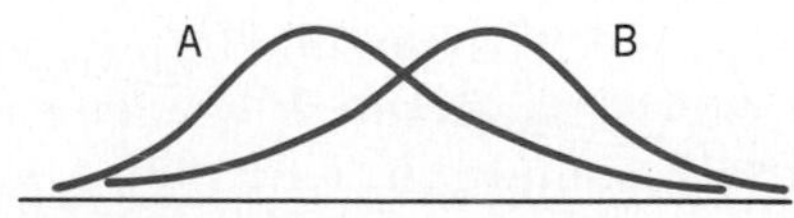

3-2 A MEASURE OF CENTRAL TENDENCY: The Arithmetic Mean

Most of the time when we refer to the "average" of something, we are talking about the arithmetic mean. This is true in cases such as the average winter temperature of New York City, the average life of a flashlight battery, and the average corn yield from an acre of land.

TABLE 3-1 Downtime of generators at Lake Ico station

GENERATOR	1	2	3	4	5	6	7	8	9	10
DAYS OUT OF SERVICE	7	23	4	8	2	12	6	13	9	4

The arithmetic mean is an average

Table 3-1 repeats the data from our chapter opening example. Data in the table represent the number of days the generators are out of service owing to regular maintenance or some malfunction. To find the arithmetic mean, we sum the values and divide by the number of observations:

$$\begin{aligned}\text{Arithmetic mean} &= \frac{7 + 23 + 4 + 8 + 2 + 12 + 6 + 13 + 9 + 4}{10}\\ &= \frac{88}{10}\\ &= 8.8 \text{ days}\end{aligned}$$

In this one-year period, the generators were out of service for an average of 8.8 days. With this figure, the power plant manager has a reasonable single measure of the behavior of *all* her generators.

Conventional Symbols

Characteristics of a sample are called statistics

Characteristics of a population are called parameters

To write equations for these measures of frequency distributions, we need to learn the mathematical notations used by statisticians. A *sample* of a population consists of n observations (a lower-case n) with a mean of $\bar{x}$ (read x-bar). Remember that the measures we compute for a sample are called *statistics.*

The notation is different when we are computing measures for the entire *population;* that is, for the group containing every element we are describing. The mean of a population is symbolized by μ, which is the Greek letter *mu*. The number of elements in a population is denoted by the capital italic letter N. Generally in statistics, we use Roman letters to symbolize sample information and Greek letters to symbolize population information.

Calculating the Mean from Ungrouped Data

Finding the population and sample means

In the example, the average of 8.8 days would be μ (the population mean) if the population of generators is exactly ten. It would be $\bar{x}$ (the sample mean) if the ten generators are a sample drawn from a larger population of generators. To write the formulas for these two means, we combine our mathematical symbols and the steps we used to determine the arithmetic mean. If we add the values of the observations and divide this sum by the number of observations, we will get:

Population mean — Sum of values of all observations

$$\mu = \frac{\Sigma x}{N} \qquad \textbf{[3-1]}$$

Number of elements in the population

and:

Sample mean — Sum of values of all observations

$$\bar{x} = \frac{\Sigma x}{n} \qquad \textbf{[3-2]}$$

Number of elements in the sample

Since μ is the *population arithmetic mean,* we use N to indicate that we divide by the number of observations or elements in the population. Similarly, $\bar{x}$ is the *sample arithmetic mean,* and n is the number of observations in the sample. The Greek letter sigma, Σ, indicates that all the values of x are summed together.

Another example: Table 3-2 lists the percentile increase in S.A.T. verbal scores shown by seven different students taking an S.A.T. preparatory course.

TABLE 3-2 Percentile increase in S.A.T. verbal scores

STUDENT	1	2	3	4	5	6	7
INCREASE	9	7	7	6	4	4	2

The data are arrayed in descending order. We assume that there are too many students in the course to survey each one. Therefore, we use our sample and compute the mean as follows:

$$\bar{x} = \frac{\Sigma x}{n} \qquad \textbf{[3-2]}$$

$$= \frac{9+7+7+6+4+4+2}{7}$$

$$= \frac{39}{7}$$

$= 5.6$ points per student ← sample mean

Dealing with ungrouped data

Notice that to calculate this mean, we added every observation separately, in no special order. Statisticians call this *ungrouped* data. The computations were not difficult, because our sample size was small. But suppose we are dealing with the weight of 5,000 head of cattle and prefer not to add each of our data points separately. Or suppose we have access to only the frequency distribution of the data, not to every individual observation. In these cases, we will need a different way to calculate the arithmetic mean.

Calculating the Mean from Grouped Data

Dealing with grouped data

A frequency distribution consists of data that are grouped by classes. Each value of an observation falls somewhere in one of the classes. Unlike the S.A.T. example, we do not know the separate values of every observation. Suppose we have a frequency distribution (illustrated in Table 3-3) of average monthly checking-account balances of 600 customers at a branch bank. From the information in this table, we can easily compute an *estimate* of the value of the mean of this grouped data. It is an estimate because we do not use all 600 data points in the sample. Had we used the original, ungrouped data, we could have calculated the actual value of the mean—but only after we had averaged the 600 separate values. For ease of calculation, we must give up accuracy.

Estimating the mean

TABLE 3-3 Average monthly balances of 600 customers

CLASS (DOLLARS)	FREQUENCY
0– 49.99	78
50.00– 99.99	123
100.00–149.99	187
150.00–199.99	82
200.00–249.99	51
250.00–299.99	47
300.00–349.99	13
350.00–399.99	9
400.00–449.99	6
450.00–499.99	4
	600

Calculating the mean

To find the arithmetic mean of grouped data, we first calculate the midpoint of each class (the class mark) using the modified form of Equation 2-2. Then we multiply each class mark by the frequency of observations in that class, sum all these results, and divide the sum by the total number of observations in the sample. The formula looks like this:

$$\bar{x} = \frac{\Sigma(f \times x)}{n} \qquad \textbf{[3-3]}$$

where:

- $\bar{x}$ is the sample mean
- Σ is the symbol meaning "the sum of"
- f is the frequency (number of observations) in each class
- x represents the class mark for each class in the sample
- n is the number of observations in the sample

Table 3-4 illustrates how to calculate the arithmetic mean from our grouped data, using Equation 3-3.

TABLE 3-4 Calculation of arithmetic sample mean from grouped data in Table 3-3

CLASS (DOLLARS) (1)	CLASS MARKS (x) (2)		FREQUENCY (f) (3)		$f \times x$ (3) × (2)
0- 49.99	25.00	×	78	=	1,950
50.00- 99.99	75.00	×	123	=	9,225
100.00-149.99	125.00	×	187	=	23,375
150.00-199.99	175.00	×	82	=	14,350
200.00-249.99	225.00	×	51	=	11,475
250.00-299.99	275.00	×	47	=	12,925
300.00-349.99	325.00	×	13	=	4,225
350.00-399.99	375.00	×	9	=	3,375
400.00-449.99	425.00	×	6	=	2,550
450.00-499.99	475.00	×	4	=	1,900
			$\Sigma f = n =$ **600**		**85,350** ← $\Sigma(f \times x)$

$$\bar{x} = \frac{\Sigma(f \times x)}{n} \quad [3\text{-}3]$$

$$= \frac{85,350}{600}$$

$$= 142.25 \leftarrow \text{sample mean (dollars)}$$

In our sample of 600 customers, the average monthly checking-account balance is $142.25. This is our approximation from the frequency distribution. Notice that since we did not know every data point in the sample, we assumed that every value in a class was equal to its class mark. Our results, then, can only approximate the actual average monthly balance.

Comparing the estimated mean with the actual mean

Let's compare an approximate mean calculated from grouped data with an actual mean compiled from ungrouped data. Consider the example presented in Tables 3-5 and 3-6 recording the annual snowfall (in inches) over 20 years in Harlan, Kentucky. If we use ungrouped data, the average annual snowfall is 21.65 inches. If we use grouped data, the estimated average is 21.5. The difference is small. And when the number of observations is large, you will appreciate the convenience offered by using grouped data.

TABLE 3-5 Annual snowfall in Harlan, Kentucky

YEAR	SNOWFALL (INCHES)	YEAR	SNOWFALL (INCHES)
1960	23	1970	12
1961	8	1971	28
1962	14	1972	8
1963	31	1973	36
1964	5	1974	16
1965	26	1975	9
1966	11	1976	42
1967	27	1977	30
1968	32	1978	7
1969	46	1979	22
			433 ← **total snowfall**

$$\bar{x} = \frac{\Sigma x}{n} \qquad \textbf{[3-2]}$$

$$= \frac{433}{20}$$

$$= 21.65 \leftarrow \text{average annual snowfall}$$

TABLE 3-6 Annual snowfall in Harlan, Kentucky

CLASS (GROUPED DATA) (1)	CLASS MARK (x) (2)		FREQUENCY (f) (3)		$f \times x$ (3) × (2)
0– 7	3.5	×	2	=	7.0
8–15	11.5	×	6	=	69.0
16–23	19.5	×	3	=	58.5
24–31	27.5	×	5	=	137.5
32–39	35.5	×	2	=	71.0
40–47	43.5	×	2	=	87.0
					430.0 ← $\Sigma(f \times x)$

$$\bar{x} = \frac{\Sigma(f \times x)}{n} \qquad \textbf{[3-3]}$$

$$= \frac{430}{20}$$

$$= 21.5 \leftarrow \text{average annual snowfall}$$

Coding

Giving codes to the class marks

We can further simplify our calculation of the mean from grouped data. Using a technique called *coding,* we eliminate the problem of large or inconvenient class marks. Instead of using the actual class marks to perform our calculations, we can assign small-value consecutive integers (whole numbers) called *codes* to each of the class marks. The integer zero can be assigned anywhere, but to keep the integers small, we will assign zero to the class mark in the *middle* (or the one nearest to the middle) of the frequency distribution. Then we can assign negative integers to values smaller than that class mark and positive integers to those larger, as follows:

Class	1–5	6–10	11–15	16–20	21–25	26–30	31–35	36–40	41–45
Code (u)	−4	−3	−2	−1	0 ↑ x_0	1	2	3	4

Calculating the mean from grouped data, using codes

Symbolically, statisticians use x_0 to represent the class mark that is assigned the code 0, and u for the coded class marks. The following formula is used to determine the sample mean using codes:

$$\bar{x} = x_0 + w\frac{\Sigma(u \times f)}{n} \quad \textbf{[3-4]}$$

where:

- $\bar{x}$ = mean of sample
- x_0 = value of the class mark assigned the code 0
- w = numerical width of the class interval
- u = code assigned to each class
- f = frequency or number of observations in each class
- n = total number of observations in the sample

Keep in mind that $\Sigma(u \times f)$ simply means that we (1) multiply u by f for every class in the frequency distribution, and (2) sum all of these products. Table 3-7 illustrates how to code the class marks and find the sample mean. The result is the same as it was when we calculated the mean from grouped data without coding (illustrated in Table 3-6).

TABLE 3-7 Annual snowfall in Harlan, Kentucky

CLASS (1)	CLASS MARK (x) (2)	CODE (u) (3)		FREQUENCY (f) (4)		$u \times f$ (3) × (4)
0–7	3.5	−2	×	2	=	−4
8–15	11.5	−1	×	6	=	−6
16–23	19.5 ← x_0	0	×	3	=	0
24–31	27.5	1	×	5	=	5
32–39	35.5	2	×	2	=	4
40–47	43.5	3	×	2	=	6
				$\Sigma f = n =$ **20**		**5** ← $\Sigma(u \times f)$

$$\bar{x} = x_0 + w\frac{\Sigma(u \times f)}{n} \quad \textbf{[3-4]}$$

$$= 19.5 + (8)\left(\frac{5}{20}\right)$$

$$= 19.5 + 2$$

$$= 21.5 \leftarrow \text{average annual snowfall}$$

Advantages and Disadvantages of the Arithmetic Mean

Advantages of the mean

The arithmetic mean, as a single number representing a whole data set, has important advantages. First, its concept is familiar to most people and intuitively clear. Second, every data set has a mean. It is a measure that can be calculated, and it is unique because every data set has one and only one mean. Finally, the mean is useful for performing statistical procedures such as comparing the means from several data sets (a procedure we will carry out in Chapter 9).

TABLE 3-8 Times for track-team members in a one-mile race

MEMBER	1	2	3	4	5	6	7
TIME IN MINUTES	4.2	4.3	4.7	4.8	5.0	5.1	9.0

Disadvantages of the mean

Yet, like any statistical measure, the arithmetic mean has disadvantages of which we must be aware. **First,** although the mean is reliable in that it reflects all the values in the data set, it may also be affected by extreme values that are not representative of the rest of the data. Notice that if the seven members of a track team have times in a mile race shown in Table 3-8, the mean time is:

$$\mu = \frac{\Sigma x}{N} \quad \textbf{[3-1]}$$

$$= \frac{4.2 + 4.3 + 4.7 + 4.8 + 5.0 + 5.1 + 9.0}{7}$$

$$= \frac{37.1}{7}$$

$$= 5.3 \text{ minutes} \leftarrow \text{population mean}$$

If we compute a mean time for the first six members, however, and exclude the 9.0 value, the answer is about 4.7 minutes. The one *extreme value* of 9.0 distorts the value we get for the mean. It would be more representative to calculate the mean *without* including such an extreme value.

A **second** problem with the mean is the same one we encountered with our 600 checking-account balances: it is tedious to compute the mean because we *do* use every data point in our calculation (unless, of course, we take the short-cut method of using grouped data to approximate the mean).

The **third** disadvantage is that we are unable to compute the mean for a data set that has open-ended classes at either the high or low end of the scale. Suppose the data in Table 3-8 had been arranged in the frequency distribution shown in Table 3-9. We could not compute a mean value for this data because of the open-ended class of "5.4 and above." We have no way of knowing whether the value is 5.4, near to 5.4, or far above 5.4.

TABLE 3-9 Times for track-team members in a one-mile race

CLASS IN MINUTES	4.2–4.5	4.6–4.9	5.0–5.3	5.4 and above
FREQUENCY	2	2	2	1

EXERCISES

3-6 Compute the sample mean for the following sets of data:

a) 10, 15, 16, 11, 18, 15, 13, 12
b) 1.472, 1.341, 1.403, 1.459, 1.299, 1.391, 1.430
c) 314, 237, 557, 425, 518, 473, 490, 316, 375, 341, 423, 479
d) 43.0, 48.7, 58.4, 40.9, 44.2, 43.6, 52.7, 48.6, 53.4, 46.5

3-7 Compute the sample mean for the following sets of grouped data, using the class mark method.

a)

Class	200–224	225–249	250–274	275–299	300–324	325–349
Frequency	6	21	32	26	10	5

b)

Class	.95–1.04	1.05–1.14	1.15–1.24	1.25–1.34	1.35–1.44	1.45–1.54	1.55–1.64
Frequency	2	6	7	10	9	5	1

3-8 Using the following set of data:

a) Construct a frequency distribution using intervals 35–44, etc.
b) Compute the sample mean from the raw data.
c) Compute the sample mean from the frequency distribution.
d) Compare b and c.

95	76	72	67	69	48	37	76	74	60
78	80	48	86	59	68	73	77	51	82
94	95	48	58	75	69	55	51	89	91
89	93	69	81	68	49	86	74	79	100

3-9 From the frequency distribution below:

a) Compute the sample mean, using the class mark method.
b) Compute the sample mean, using the coding method and assigning 0 to the fourth class.
c) Compute the sample mean, using the coding method and assigning 0 to the sixth class.
d) Verify that a, b, and c are equal.

CLASS	FREQUENCY	CLASS	FREQUENCY
10.0–10.9	2	15.0–15.9	10
11.0–11.9	3	16.0–16.9	9
12.0–12.9	5	17.0–17.9	6
13.0–13.9	7	18.0–18.9	8
14.0–14.9	12	19.0–19.9	2

3-10 Davis Furniture Company has a revolving credit agreement with the First National Bank. The loan showed the following ending monthly balances last year:

Jan.	$75,800	Apr.	$45,500	July	$36,700	Oct.	$33,000
Feb.	$70,100	May	$45,500	Aug.	$38,200	Nov.	$30,750
Mar.	$45,500	June	$35,800	Sept.	$31,500	Dec.	$28,800

The company is eligible for a reduced rate of interest if its average monthly balance is over $45,000; does it qualify?

3-11 A cosmetics manufacturer recently purchased a machine to fill 4-ounce cologne bottles. To test the accuracy of the machine's volume setting, 18 trial bottles were run. The resulting volumes (in ounces) for the trials were as follows:

4.01	3.90	3.91	3.85	3.89	3.98	3.94	3.95	3.92
4.00	3.98	3.94	3.91	3.93	3.97	3.98	4.00	3.96

The company does not normally recalibrate the filling machine for this cologne if the average volume is within .02 of 4.00 ounces; should it recalibrate?

3-12 The production manager of Hinton Press is determining the average time needed to photograph one printing plate. Using a stopwatch and observing the platemakers, he collects the following times (in seconds):

20.3	19.9	22.1	23.7	21.2	25.0	21.1	22.8	28.1	24.2
21.9	24.6	25.6	24.8	22.6	24.3	24.2	23.5	23.1	20.9

An average per-plate time of less than 23.5 seconds indicates satisfactory productivity. Should the production manager be concerned?

3-13 National Tire Company holds reserve funds in short-term marketable securities. The ending daily balance (in millions) of the marketable-securities account for two weeks is shown below:

Week 1	$1.973	$1.970	$1.972	$1.975	$1.976
Week 2	1.969	1.892	1.893	1.887	1.895

What was the average (mean) amount invested in marketable securities during (a) the first week? (b) the second week? (c) the two-week period? (d) An average balance over the two weeks of more than $1.970 qualifies National for special interest rates. Does it qualify?

3-14 M.T. Werds is the author of many best-selling books. He has kept track of the quarterly royalties he has received over the past three years, and these data are given in the table below. There are several ways to look at the data, and you can help out M.T. by answering the questions below.

	1ST QUARTER	2ND QUARTER	3RD QUARTER	4TH QUARTER
Year 1	$10,000	$ 5,000	$25,000	$15,000
Year 2	20,000	10,000	20,000	10,000
Year 3	30,000	15,000	45,000	50,000

a) Calculate separately M.T.'s average royalties in each of the four quarters.
b) Calculate separately M.T.'s average quarterly royalties in each of the three years.
c) Show that the mean of the four numbers you found in part a is equal to the mean of the three numbers you found in part b. Furthermore, show that both these numbers equal the mean of all twelve numbers in the data table. (This is M.T.'s average quarterly income over three years.)

3-15 Polly Tishon, mayor of Smallville, has been gathering data on the 15 most recent annual budgets for Smallville. She hopes to show that, while in office during the past 10 years, she has been saving the taxpayers money. The budget data are as follows:

YEAR	TOWN BUDGET	YEAR	TOWN BUDGET	YEAR	TOWN BUDGET
1984	$30,000	1979	$24,000	1974	$30,000
1983	28,000	1978	19,000	1973	20,000
1982	25,000	1977	21,000	1972	15,000
1981	27,000	1976	22,000	1971	10,000
1980	26,000	1975	24,000	1970	9,000

a) Calculate the average annual budget for the last five years (1980–1984).
b) Calculate the average annual budget for her first five years in office (1975–1979).

c) Calculate the average annual budget for the five years before she was elected (1970–1974).
d) Based on the answers you found for parts a, b, and c, do you think that there has been a decreasing or increasing trend in the annual budget? Has she been saving the taxpayers money?

3-3 A SECOND MEASURE OF CENTRAL TENDENCY: The Weighted Mean

A weighted mean

The weighted mean enables us to calculate an average that takes into account the importance of each value to the overall total. Consider, for example, the company in Table 3-10, which uses three grades of labor—unskilled, semiskilled, and skilled—to produce two end products. The company wants to know the average cost of labor per hour for each of the products.

TABLE 3-10 Labor input in manufacturing process

		Labor hours per unit of output	
GRADE OF LABOR	HOURLY WAGE (x)	PRODUCT 1	PRODUCT 2
Unskilled	$4.00	1	4
Semiskilled	6.00	2	3
Skilled	8.00	5	3

A simple arithmetic average of the labor wage rates would be:

$$\bar{x} = \frac{\Sigma x}{n} \qquad [3\text{-}2]$$

$$= \frac{\$4 + \$6 + \$8}{3}$$

$$= \frac{\$18}{3}$$

$$= \$6.00/\text{hour}$$

In this case, the arithmetic mean is incorrect

Using this average rate, we would compute the labor cost of one unit of product 1 to be $6(1 + 2 + 5) = $48, and of one unit of product 2 to be $6(4 + 3 + 3) = $60. But these answers are incorrect.

To be correct, the answers must take into account the fact that different amounts of each grade of labor are used. We can determine the correct answers in the following manner. For product 1, the total labor cost per unit is ($4 × 1) + ($6 × 2) + ($8 × 5) = $56, and, since there are eight hours of labor input, the average labor cost per hour is $56/8 = $7.00 per hour. For product 2, the total labor cost per unit is ($4 × 4) + ($6 × 3) + ($8 × 3) = $58, for an average labor cost per hour of $58/10, or $5.80 per hour.

The correct answer is the weighted mean

Another way to calculate the correct average cost per hour for the two products is to take a *weighted average* of the cost of the three grades of labor. To do this, we weight the hourly wage for each grade by its proportion of the total labor required to produce the product. One unit of product 1, for example, requires eight hours of labor. Unskilled labor uses 1/8 of this time, semiskilled labor uses 2/8 of this time, and skilled labor requires 5/8 of this time. If we use these fractions as our weights, then one hour of labor for product 1 costs an average of:

$$\left(\frac{1}{8} \times \$4\right) + \left(\frac{2}{8} \times \$6\right) + \left(\frac{5}{8} \times \$8\right) = \$7.00/\text{hour}$$

Similarly, a unit of product 2 requires ten labor hours, of which 4/10 is used for unskilled labor, 3/10 for semiskilled labor, and 3/10 for skilled labor. Using these fractions as weights, one hour of labor for product 2 costs:

$$\left(\frac{4}{10} \times \$4\right) + \left(\frac{3}{10} \times \$6\right) + \left(\frac{3}{10} \times \$8\right) = \$5.80/\text{hour}$$

Calculating the weighted mean

Thus, we see that the weighted averages give the correct values for the average hourly labor costs of the two products because **they take into account the fact that different amounts of each grade of labor are used in the products.**

Symbolically, the formula for calculating the weighted average is:

$$\bar{x}_w = \frac{\Sigma(w \times x)}{\Sigma w} \qquad \textbf{[3-5]}$$

where:

- $\bar{x}_w$ = the symbol for the weighted mean*
- w = weight assigned to each observation (1/8, 2/8, and 5/8 for product 1 in our example)
- $\Sigma(w \times x)$ = sum of the weight of each element times that element
- Σw = sum of all of the weights

If we apply Equation 3-5 to product 1 in our labor-cost example, we find:

* The symbol $\bar{x}_w$ is read *x-bar sub w*. The lower-case w is called a subscript and is a reminder that this is not an ordinary mean but one that is weighted according to the relative importance of the values of x.

$$\bar{x}_w = \frac{\Sigma(w \times x)}{\Sigma w} \quad [3\text{-}5]$$

$$= \frac{(1/8 \times \$4) + (2/8 \times \$6) + (5/8 \times \$8)}{1/8 + 2/8 + 5/8}$$

$$= \frac{\$7}{1}$$

$$= \$7.00/\text{hour}$$

The arithmetic mean of grouped data: the weighted mean

Notice that Equation 3-5 states more formally something we have done previously. When we calculated the arithmetic mean from grouped data (page 64), we actually found a weighted mean, using the class marks for the x values and the frequencies of each class as the weights. We divided this product by the sum of all the frequencies, which is the same as dividing by the sum of all the weights.

In like manner, *any* mean computed from all the values in a data set according to Equation 3-1 or 3-2 is really a weighted average of the components of the data set. What those components are, of course, determines what the mean measures. In a factory, for example, we could determine the weighted mean of all the wages (skilled, semiskilled, and unskilled), or of the wages of men workers, women workers, or union and nonunion members.

EXERCISES

3-16 A professor has decided to use a weighted average in figuring final grades for his seminar students. The homework average will count for 30 percent of a student's grade; the midterm, 20 percent; the final, 25 percent; the term paper, 15 percent; and quizzes, 10 percent. From the data below, compute the final average for the five students in the seminar.

STUDENT	HOMEWORK	QUIZZES	PAPER	MIDTERM	FINAL
1	85	89	94	87	90
2	78	84	88	91	92
3	94	88	93	86	89
4	82	79	88	84	93
5	95	90	92	82	88

3-17 Given the following prices and the number of each item sold, find the average price of the items sold.

Price	$1.29	$2.95	$3.49	$5.00	$7.50	$10.95
Number Sold	7	9	12	8	6	3

3-18 Keyes Home Furnishings ran six local newspaper advertisements during December. The following frequency distribution resulted:

Number of times subscriber saw ad during December	0	1	2	3	4	5	6
Frequency	998	983	1,417	727	294	236	210

What is the average number of times a subscriber saw a Keyes advertisement during December?

3-19 Bennett Distribution Company, a subsidiary of a major appliance manufacturer, is forecasting regional sales for next year. The Atlantic branch, with current yearly sales of $193.8 million, is expected to achieve a sales growth of 7.25 percent; the Midwest branch, with current sales of $79.3 million, is expected to grow by 8.20 percent; and the Pacific branch, with sales of $57.5 million, is expected to increase sales by 7.15 percent. What is the average rate of sales growth forecasted for next year?

3-20 The U.S. Postal Service handles 7 basic types of letters and cards: third class, second class, first class, air mail, special delivery, registered, and certified. The mail volume during 1977 is given in the following table:

TYPE OF MAILING	OUNCES DELIVERED (IN MILLIONS)	PRICE PER OUNCE
Third class	15,500	$.05
Second class	23,900	.08
First class	79,100	.13
Air mail	1,800	.17
Special delivery	1,200	.35
Registered	800	.40
Certified	700	.45

What was the average revenue per ounce for these services during the year?

3-21 The Fulcourt Press, printers extraordinaire of basketball books, has compiled data on the company's operations during the past year. Lane Zone, the company's statistical analyst, has divided all items sold by the company into the five categories below. For each category he has found a typical unit price and the number of units sold in the last year. What is Fulcourt's average revenue per unit?

CATEGORY	PRICE PER UNIT	UNITS SOLD
Instructional pamphlets	$ 6	3,212,000
Paperback books	12	1,475,000
Hardbound (B&W photos)	25	1,250,000
Hardbound (color photos)	35	1,600,000
Special editions	50	843,000

3-4 A THIRD MEASURE OF CENTRAL TENDENCY: The Geometric Mean

Finding the growth rate: the geometric mean

Sometimes when we are dealing with quantities that change over a period of time, we need to know an average rate of change, such as an average growth rate over a period of several years. In such cases, the simple arithmetic mean is inappropriate, because it gives the wrong answers. What we need to find is the *geometric mean,* called simply the G.M.

Consider, for example, the growth of a savings account. Suppose we deposit $100 initially and let it accrue interest at varying rates for five years. The growth is summarized in Table 3-11.

TABLE 3-11 Growth of $100 deposit in a savings account

YEAR	INTEREST RATE	GROWTH FACTOR	SAVINGS AT END OF YEAR
1	7%	1.07	$107.00
2	8	1.08	115.56
3	10	1.10	127.12
4	12	1.12	142.37
5	18	1.18	168.00

The entry labeled "growth factor" is equal to:

$$1 + \frac{\text{interest rate}}{100}$$

The growth factor is the amount by which we multiply the savings at the beginning of the year to get the savings at the end of the year. The simple arithmetic mean growth factor would be $(1.07 + 1.08 + 1.10 + 1.12 + 1.18)/5 = 1.11$, which corresponds to an average interest rate of 11 percent per year. If the bank gives interest at a constant rate of 11 percent per year, however, a $100 deposit would grow in five years to:

In this case, the arithmetic mean growth rate is incorrect

$$\$100 \times 1.11 \times 1.11 \times 1.11 \times 1.11 \times 1.11 = \$168.51$$

Table 3-11 shows that the actual figure is only $168.00. Thus, the correct average growth factor must be slightly less than 1.11.

Calculating the geometric mean

To find the correct average growth factor, we can multiply together the five years' growth factors and then take the fifth root of the product—the number that, when multiplied by itself four times, is equal to the product we started with. The result is the *geometric mean growth rate*, which is the appropriate average to use here. The formula for finding the geometric mean of a series of numbers is:

Number of x values →

$$\text{G.M.} = \sqrt[n]{\text{Product of all the } x \text{ values}} \quad \textbf{[3-6]}$$

If we apply this equation to our savings-account problem, we can determine that 1.1093 is the correct average growth factor.

$$\begin{aligned} \text{G.M.} &= \sqrt[n]{\text{Product of all the } x \text{ values}} \quad \textbf{[3-6]} \\ &= \sqrt[5]{1.07 \times 1.08 \times 1.10 \times 1.12 \times 1.18} \\ &= \sqrt[5]{1.679965} \\ &= 1.1093 \leftarrow \text{average growth factor} \end{aligned}$$

Warning: use the appropriate mean

Notice that the correct average interest rate of 10.93 percent per year obtained with the geometric mean is very close to the incorrect average rate of 11 percent obtained with the arithmetic mean. This happens because the interest rates are relatively small. Be careful, however, not to be tempted to use the arithmetic mean instead of the more complicated geometric mean. The following example demonstrates why.

In highly inflationary economies, banks must pay high interest rates to attract savings. Suppose that over five years in an unbelievably inflationary economy, banks pay interest at annual rates of 100, 200, 250, 300, and 400 percent, which corresponds to growth factors of 2, 3, 3.5, 4, and 5. (We've calculated these growth factors just as we did in Table 3-11.)

In five years, an initial deposit of \$100 would grow to $\$100 \times 2 \times 3 \times 3.5 \times 4 \times 5 = \$42{,}000$. The arithmetic mean growth factor is $(2 + 3 + 3.5 + 4 + 5)/5$, or 3.5. This corresponds to an average interest rate of 250 percent. Yet if the banks actually gave interest at a constant rate of 250 percent per year, then \$100 would grow to \$52,521.88 in five years:

$$\$100 \times 3.5 \times 3.5 \times 3.5 \times 3.5 \times 3.5 = \$52{,}521.88$$

This answer exceeds the actual \$42,000 by more than \$10,500, a sizable error.

Let's use the formula for finding the geometric mean of a series of numbers to determine the correct growth factor:

$$\begin{aligned} \text{G.M.} &= \sqrt[n]{\text{Product of all the } x \text{ values}} \qquad \textbf{[3-6]} \\ &= \sqrt[5]{2 \times 3 \times 3.5 \times 4 \times 5} \\ &= \sqrt[5]{420} \\ &= 3.347 \leftarrow \text{average growth factor} \end{aligned}$$

This growth factor corresponds to an average interest rate of 235 percent per year. In this case, the use of the appropriate mean *does* make a significant difference.

EXERCISES

3-22 Hayes Textiles has shown the following percentage increase in net worth over the last 5 years:

1978	1979	1980	1981	1982
5%	10.5%	9.0%	6.0%	7.5%

What is the average percentage increase in net worth over the 5-year period?

3-23 The growth in bad debt expense for Johnston Office Supply Company over the last few years is given below. Calculate the average percentage increase in bad-debt expense over this time period. If this rate continues, estimate bad debts for 1984.

1976	1977	1978	1979	1980	1981	1982
.11	.09	.075	.08	.095	.108	.120

3-24 The Birch Company, a manufacturer of electrical circuit boards, has manufactured the following number of units over the past 5 years:

1977	1978	1979	1980	1981
12,500	13,250	14,310	15,741	17,630

Calculate the average percentage increase in units produced over this time period, and use this to estimate production for 1984.

3-25 If the geometric mean of a set of 6 values is 1.24, and 5 of the values are 1.18, 1.32, 1.27, 1.15, and 1.22, find the last of the 6 values.

3-26 Over a 3-week period, a store owner purchased $60 worth of acrylic sheeting for new display cases in 3 equal purchases of $20 each. The first purchase was at $1.00 per square foot; the second, $1.10; and the third, $1.15. What was the average price per square foot paid for all the sheeting?

3-27 Mrs. Gibson has a standing policy of pricing the electronic equipment in her store at 10 percent above average cost. In preparation for the Christmas selling season, she placed three $1,000 orders for a particular turntable. However, because of the high inflation rate in the Japanese economy, the average unit prices for the shipments were $100.00, $111.11, and $125.00. What price should Mrs. Gibson charge?

3-28 Neilson Electronics calculates that the administrative cost of handling a credit account has increased from $43.00 to $46.50 to $49.80 to $53.65 per account during the last 4 years. What has been the average percent of increase in cost per account over the 4-year period? If the credit-department costs continue to rise at this rate, what will the handling cost per account be in 3 more years?

3-29 A sociologist has been studying the yearly changes in the number of convicts assigned to the largest correctional facility in the state. His data are expressed in terms of the percentage increase in the number of prisoners (a negative number indicates a percentage decrease). The sociologist's most recent data are given below.

1979	1980	1981	1982	1983	1984
−4%	5%	10%	3%	6%	−5%

a) Calculate the average percentage increase using only the 1980-through-1983 data.
b) Rework part a using the data from all 6 years.
c) A new penal code was passed in 1978. Previously, prison population grew at a rate of about 2% per year. What seems to be the effect of the new code?

3-5 A FOURTH MEASURE OF CENTRAL TENDENCY: The Median

Median defined

The median is a measure of central tendency different from any of the means we have discussed so far. The median is a single value from the data set that measures the central item in the data. This single item is the *middlemost* or *most central* item in the set of numbers. Half of the items lie above this point, and the other half lie below it.

Calculating the Median from Ungrouped Data

Finding the median of ungrouped data

To find the median of a data set, first array the data in ascending or descending order. If the data set contains an *odd* number of items, the middle item of the array is the median. If there is an *even* number of items, the median is the average of the two middle items. In formal language, the median is:

Number of items in the array

$$\text{Median} = \text{the} \left(\frac{n+1}{2}\right)\text{th item in a data array} \qquad \textbf{[3-7]}$$

An odd number of items

Suppose we wish to find the median of seven items in a data array. According to Equation 3-7, the median is the $(7 + 1)/2 = 4$th item in the array. If we apply this to our previous example of the times for seven members of a track team, we discover that the fourth element in the array is 4.8 minutes. This is the median time for the track team. Notice that unlike the arithmetic mean we calculated earlier, the median we calculated in Table 3-12 was *not* distorted by the presence of the last value (9.0). This value could have been 15.0 or even 45.0 minutes, and the median would have been the same!

Median not distorted by extreme values

TABLE 3-12 Times for track-team members

ITEM IN DATA ARRAY	1	2	3	4	5	6	7
TIME IN MINUTES	4.2	4.3	4.7	4.8	5.0	5.1	9.0
				↑ median			

An even number of items

Now let's calculate the median for an array with an even number of items. Consider the data shown in Table 3-13 concerning the number of patients treated daily in the emergency room of a hospital. The data are arrayed in descending order. The median of this data set would be:

$$\text{Median} = \text{the} \left(\frac{n+1}{2}\right)\text{th item in a data array} \qquad \textbf{[3-7]}$$

$$= \frac{8+1}{2}$$

$$= 4.5\text{th item}$$

TABLE 3-13 Patients treated in emergency room on 8 consecutive days

ITEM IN DATA ARRAY	1	2	3	4		5	6	7	8
NUMBER OF PATIENTS	86	52	49	43		35	31	30	11
					↑ median of 39				

Since the median is the 4.5th element in the array, we need to average the fourth and fifth elements. The fourth element in Table 3-13 is 43, and the fifth is 35. The average of these two elements is equal to $(43 + 35)/2$, or 39. Therefore, 39 is the median number of patients treated in the emergency room per day during the 8-day period.

Calculating the Median from Grouped Data

Finding the median of grouped data

Often, we have access to data only after it has been grouped in a frequency distribution. We do not, for example, know every observation that led to the construction of Table 3-14, the data on 600 bank customers originally introduced earlier. Instead, we have ten class intervals and a record of the frequency with which the observations appear in each of the intervals.

TABLE 3-14 Average monthly balances for 600 customers

CLASS IN DOLLARS	FREQUENCY
0– 49.99	78
50.00– 99.99	123
100.00–149.99	187 ← median class
150.00–199.99	82
200.00–249.99	51
250.00–299.99	47
300.00–349.99	13
350.00 399.99	9
400.00–449.99	6
450.00–499.99	4
	600

Locate the median class

Nevertheless, we can compute the median checking-account balance of these 600 customers by determining which of the ten class intervals *contains* the median. To do this, we must add the frequencies in the frequency column in Table 3-14 until we reach the $(n + 1)/2$th item. Since there are 600 accounts, the value for $(n + 1)/2$ is 300.5 (the average of the 300th and 301st items). The problem is to find the class intervals containing the 300th and 301st elements. The cumulative frequency for the first two classes is only $78 + 123 = 201$. But when we move to the third class interval, 187 elements are added to 201 for a total of 388. Therefore, the 300th and 301st observations must be located in this third class (the interval from $100.00 to $149.99).

Interpolate to find the median

The *median class* for this data set contains 187 items. If we assume that these 187 items begin at $100.00 and are *evenly spaced over the entire class interval* from $100.00 to $149.99, then we can interpolate and find values for the 300th and 301st items. First, we determine that the 300th item is the 99th element in the median class:

$$300 - 201 \text{ [items in the first two classes]} = 99$$

and that the 301st item is the 100th element in the median class:

$$301 - 201 = 100$$

Then we can calculate the *width* of the 187 equal steps from \$100.00 to \$149.99, as follows:

First item of next class

First item of median class

$$\frac{\$150.00 - \$100.00}{187} = \$.267 \text{ in width}$$

Now, if there are 187 steps of \$.267 each and if 98 steps will take us to the 99th item, then the 99th item is:

$$(\$.267 \times 98) + \$100 = \$126.17$$

and the 100th item is one additional step:

$$\$126.17 + \$.267 = \$126.44$$

Therefore, we can use \$126.17 and \$126.44 as the values of the 300th and 301st items, respectively.

The actual median for this data set is the value of the 300.5th item; that is, the average of the 300th and 301st items. This average is:

$$\frac{\$126.17 + \$126.44}{2} = \$126.30$$

This figure (\$126.30) is the median monthly checking account balance, as estimated from the grouped data in Table 3-14.

In summary, we can calculate the median of grouped data as follows:

Steps for finding the median of grouped data

1. Use Equation 3-7 to determine which element in the distribution is centermost (in this case, the average of the 300th and 301st items).
2. Add the frequencies in each class to find the class that contains that centermost element (the third class, or \$100.00–\$149.99).
3. Determine the number of elements in the class (187) and the location in the class of the median element (item 300 was the 99th element; item 301, the 100th element).
4. Learn the width of each step in the median class by dividing the class interval by the number of elements in the class (width = \$.267).
5. Determine the number of steps from the lower bound of the median class to the appropriate item for the median (98 steps for the 99th element; 99 steps for the 100th element).

6. Calculate the estimated value of the median element by multiplying the number of steps to the median element times the width of each step and by adding the result to the lower bound of the median class ($\$100 + 98 \times \$.267 = \$126.17$; $\$126.17 + \$.267 = \$126.44$).
7. If, as in our example, there is an even number of elements in the distribution, average the values of the median element calculated in step #6 ($126.30).

An easier method

To shorten this procedure, statisticians use an equation to determine the median of grouped data. For a sample, this equation would be:

Sample median

$$\tilde{m} = \left(\frac{(n+1)/2 - (F+1)}{f_m}\right) w + L_m \qquad \textbf{[3-8]}$$

where:

- $\tilde{m}$ = sample median
- n = total number of items in the distribution
- F = sum of all the class frequencies *up to,* but *not including,* the median class
- f_m = frequency of the median class
- w = class interval width
- L_m = lower limit of the median class interval

If we use Equation 3-8 to compute the median of our sample of checking-account balances, then $n = 600$, $F = 201$, $f_m = 187$, $w = \$50$, and $L_m = \$100$.

$$\begin{aligned}
\tilde{m} &= \left(\frac{(n+1)/2 - (F+1)}{f_m}\right) w + L_m \qquad \textbf{[3-8]}\\
&= \left(\frac{601/2 - 202}{187}\right) \$50 + \$100\\
&= \left(\frac{300.5 - 202}{187}\right) \$50 + \$100\\
&= \left(\frac{98.5}{187}\right) \$50 + \$100\\
&= (.527)(\$50) + \$100\\
&= \$126.35 \leftarrow \text{estimated sample median}
\end{aligned}$$

The slight difference between this answer and our answer calculated the long way is due to rounding.

Advantages and Disadvantages of the Median

Advantages of the median

The median has several advantages over the mean. The most important, demonstrated in our track-team example in Table 3-12, is that extreme values do not affect the median as strongly as they do the mean. The median is easy to understand and can be calculated from any kind of data—even for grouped data with open-ended classes such as the frequency distribution in Table 3-9—*unless* the median falls into an open-ended class.

We can find the median even when our data are qualitative descriptions like color or sharpness, rather than numbers. Suppose, for example, we have five runs of a printing press, the results from which must be rated according to sharpness of the image. We can array the results from best to worst: extremely sharp, very sharp, sharp, slightly blurred, and very blurred. The median of the five ratings is the $(5 + 1)/2$, or third rating (sharp).

Disadvantages of the median

The median has some disadvantages as well. Certain statistical procedures that use the median are more complex than those that use the mean. Also, because the median is an average of position, we must array the data before we can perform any calculations. This is time-consuming for any data set with a large number of elements. Therefore, if we want to use a sample statistic as an estimate of a population parameter, the mean is easier to use than the median. Chapter 8 will discuss estimation in detail.

EXERCISES

3-30 Calculate the median of the following data set:

810	444	748	593	762	729	528
1,190	843	824	858	802	579	485
622	734	432	500	524	733	676
733	604	555	484	740	831	673
485	605	803	881	720	657	609

3-31 Find the median of the following set of data:

1.08	.98	.97	1.10	1.03	1.13	1.07	1.24	.99	1.13
.99	1.43	1.18	1.02	1.12	1.17	.98	1.28	.98	1.09

3-32 For the frequency distribution below, determine:

a) Which is the median class.
b) Which number item represents the median item.
c) The width of the equal steps in the median class.
d) The estimated value of the median for this data.

CLASS	FREQUENCY	CLASS	FREQUENCY
100–149.5	12	300–349.5	72
150–199.5	14	350–399.5	63
200–249.5	27	400–449.5	36
250–299.5	58	450–499.5	18

3-33 For the following data, calculate an estimate of the median using Equation 3-8:

Class	0–24.9	25–49.9	50–74.9	75–99.9	100–124.9	125–149.9
Frequency	6	11	14	16	13	10

3-34 Calculate the median for the data given in the following table:

MINUTES FOR BUS RIDE FROM O'HARE AIRPORT TO JOHN HANCOCK CENTER

15	15	16	16	17	17	17	18	18	18
18	18	18	18	19	20	20	21	22	25
26	27	27	27	27	27	28	28	29	29
30	30	31	31	33	33	33	34	34	34
34	34	34	34	35	35	35	35	35	36
37	38	40	43	49	50	51	53	58	64

3-35 Mark Merritt, manager of Quality Upholstery Company, is researching the amount of material used in the firm's upholstery jobs. The amount varies between jobs, owing to different furniture styles and sizes. Merritt gathers the following data (in yards) from the jobs completed last week. Calculate the median yardage used on a job last week.

$5\frac{1}{4}$	$6\frac{1}{4}$	6	$7\frac{7}{8}$	$9\frac{1}{4}$	$9\frac{1}{2}$	$10\frac{1}{2}$
$5\frac{3}{8}$	6	$6\frac{1}{4}$	8	$9\frac{1}{2}$	$9\frac{7}{8}$	$10\frac{1}{4}$
$5\frac{1}{2}$	$5\frac{7}{8}$	$6\frac{1}{2}$	$8\frac{1}{4}$	$9\frac{3}{8}$	$10\frac{1}{4}$	$10\frac{1}{8}$
$5\frac{7}{8}$	$5\frac{3}{4}$	7	$8\frac{1}{2}$	$9\frac{1}{8}$	$10\frac{1}{2}$	$10\frac{1}{8}$
6	$5\frac{7}{8}$	$7\frac{1}{2}$	9	$9\frac{1}{4}$	$9\frac{7}{8}$	10

If there are 150 jobs scheduled in the next three weeks, use the median to predict how many yards of material will be required.

3-36 If insurance claims for automobile accidents follow the distribution given below, determine the median using the method outlined on page 80 in this chapter. Verify that you get the same answer using Equation 3-8.

AMOUNT OF CLAIM ($)	FREQUENCY	AMOUNT OF CLAIM ($)	FREQUENCY
less than 150	52	350–399.99	816
150–199.99	108	400–449.99	993
200–249.99	230	450–499.99	825
250–299.99	528	500 and above	650
300–349.99	663		

3-37 Ed Hughes, president of a local recording company, is busy evaluating the sales of all previous albums done by one of his weaker groups, the Band Aides. Ed understands very little about statistics, but even he recognizes the fact that the Band Aides' only million-seller would radically affect the mean of the sales of all six albums the group has made. The sales data are given on page 84:

NUMBER OF RECORDS SOLD		
1,430,000	251,700	100,526
483,900	401,000	657,000

a) Help Ed by finding the mean and median album sales for the Band Aides.
b) Several months later, Ed decides to reevaluate the Band Aides, using as additional information the fact that 359,000 records of the group's latest release have been sold. Adding this data value to those above, find the new mean and median album sales for the Band Aides.

3-6 A FINAL MEASURE OF CENTRAL TENDENCY: The Mode

Mode defined

The mode is a measure of central tendency that is different from the mean but somewhat like the median because it is not actually calculated by the ordinary processes of arithmetic. The mode is *that value that is repeated most often in the data set.*

Limited use of mode of ungrouped data

As in every other aspect of life, chance can play a role in the arrangement of data. Sometimes chance causes a single unrepresentative item to be repeated often enough to be the most frequent value in the data set. For this reason, we rarely use the mode of ungrouped data as a measure of central tendency. Table 3-15, for example, shows the number of delivery trips per day made by a Redi-mix concrete plant. The modal value is 15 because it occurs more often than any other value (three times). A mode of 15 implies that the plant activity is higher than 6.7 (6.7 is the answer we'd get if we calculated the mean). The mode tells us that 15 is the most frequent number of trips, but it fails to let us know that most of the values are under 10.

TABLE 3-15 Delivery trips per day in one 20-day period

TRIPS ARRAYED IN ASCENDING ORDER					
0	2	5	7	15	
0	2	5	7	15	← mode
1	4	6	8	15	
1	4	6	12	19	

Finding the modal class of grouped data

Now let's group this data into a frequency distribution, as we have done in Table 3-16. If we select the class with the most observations, which we can call the *modal class,* we would choose "4–7" trips. This class is more representative of the activity of the plant than is the mode of 15 trips per day. For this reason, whenever we use the mode as a measure of the central tendency of a data set, we should calculate the mode from grouped data.

TABLE 3-16 Frequency distribution of delivery trips

CLASS IN NUMBER OF TRIPS	0–3	4–7	8–11	12 and more
FREQUENCY	6	8 ↑ modal class	1	5

The Mode in Symmetrical and Skewed Distributions

Let's study Figs. 3-9 through 3-11, each of which shows a frequency distribution. Figure 3-9 is symmetrical, Fig. 3-10 is skewed to the right, and Fig. 3-11 is skewed to the left.

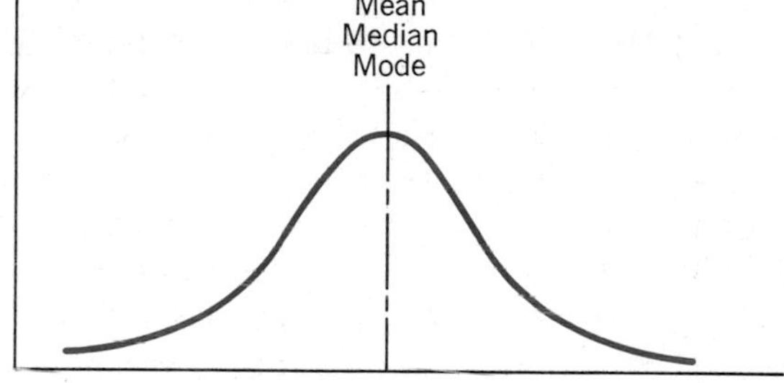

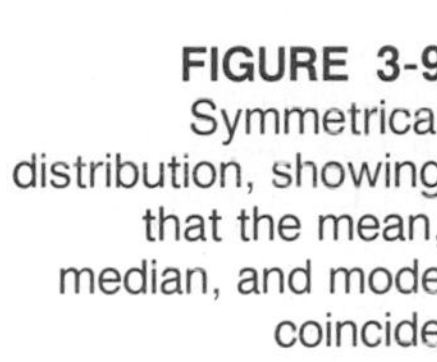

FIGURE 3-9 Symmetrical distribution, showing that the mean, median, and mode coincide

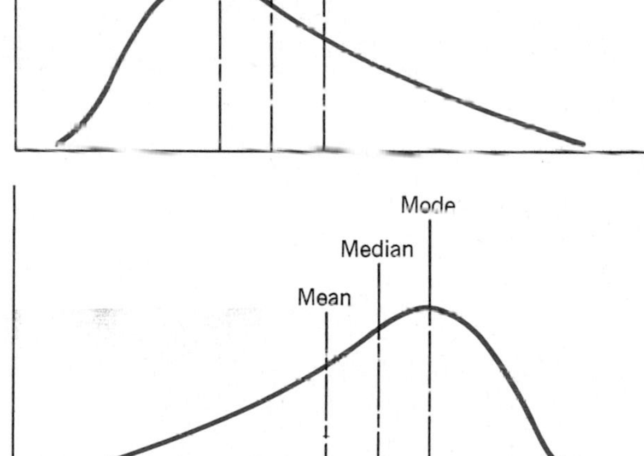

FIGURE 3-10 Distribution is skewed to the right

FIGURE 3-11 Distribution is skewed to the left

Location of the mode

In Fig. 3-9, where the distribution is symmetrical and there is only one mode, the three measures of central tendency—the mode, median, and mean—coincide with the highest point on the graph. In Fig. 3-10, the data set is skewed to the right. Here, the mode is still at the highest point on the graph, but the median lies to the right of this point and the mean falls to the right of the median. When the distribution is skewed to the left, as in Fig. 3-11, the mode is at the highest point on the graph, the median lies to the left of the mode, and the mean falls to the left of the median. **No matter what the shape of the curve, the mode is always located at the highest point.**

Calculating the Mode from Grouped Data

Finding the mode in the modal class

When our data are already grouped in a frequency distribution, we must assume that the mode is located in the class with the most items; that is, with the highest frequency. But how can we determine a single value for the mode from this modal class? Two methods are available to us. The first enables us to estimate the mode from a graph. The second method uses an equation.

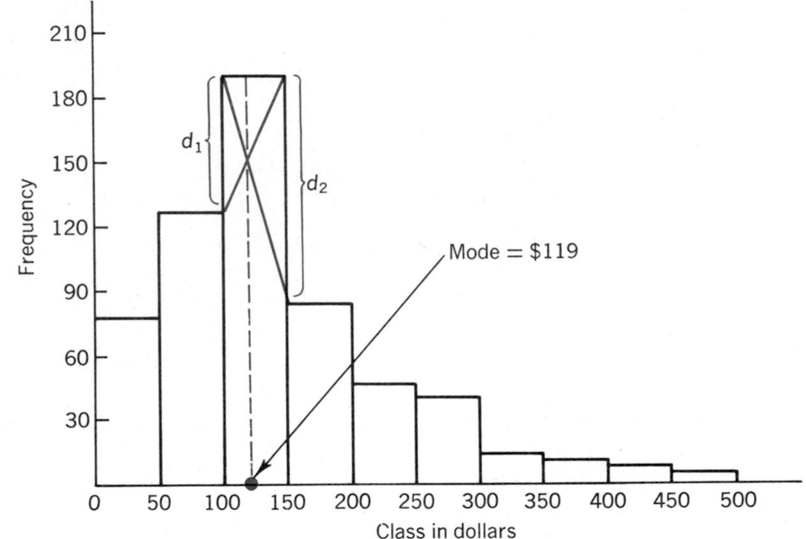

FIGURE 3-12 Calculation of the mode from grouped data using graph method

To demonstrate these two ways of finding the mode in grouped data, let's use the data in Table 3-14 on page 79 (our example of the checking account balances). First, we can construct a histogram of the data as shown in Fig. 3-12. Then, since the modal class is the tallest rectangle, we can locate the mode in it by:

A graphical solution

1. Drawing a line from the top right corner of the tallest rectangle to the top right corner of the rectangle to its immediate left.
2. Drawing a second line from the top left corner of the tallest rectangle to the top left corner of the rectangle to its immediate right.
3. Drawing a line perpendicular to the horizontal axis through the point where the lines drawn in steps 1 and 2 cross.

The value on the horizontal axis marked by the line drawn in step 3 will approximate the modal value. In this case, the mode is about 119.

A mathematical solution

A second way of finding the mode when we have grouped data is to use Equation 3-9:

Mode

$$Mo = L_{Mo} + \frac{d_1}{d_1 + d_2} w \qquad [3\text{-}9]$$

where:

- L_{Mo} = lower limit of the modal class
- d_1 = frequency of the modal class minus the frequency of the class *directly below it*
- d_2 = frequency of the modal class minus the frequency of the class *directly above it*
- w = width of the modal class interval

If we use Equation 3-9 to compute the mode of our checking-account balances, then L_{Mo} = \$100, $d_1 = 187 - 123 = 64$, $d_2 = 187 - 82 = 105$, and w = \$50.

$$\begin{aligned} Mo &= L_{Mo} + \frac{d_1}{d_1 + d_2} w \qquad [3\text{-}9] \\ &= \$100 + \frac{64}{64 + 105} \$50 \\ &= \$100 + (.38)(\$50) \\ &= \$100 + \$19 \\ &= \$119.00 \leftarrow \text{Mode} \end{aligned}$$

Our answer of \$119 is the estimate of the mode using either the graphic or the mathematical method of calculation.

Multimodal Distributions

Bimodal distributions

What happens when we have two different values that *each* appear the greatest number of times of any values in the data set? Table 3-17 shows the billing errors for a 20-day period in a hospital office. Notice that both 1 and 4 appear the greatest number of times in the data set. They each appear three times. This distribution, then, has two modes and is called a *bimodal distribution.*

TABLE 3-17 Billing errors per day in 20-day period

ERRORS ARRAYED IN ASCENDING ORDER					
0		2		6	9
0		4		6	9
1		4	←mode	7	10
1	←mode	4		8	12
1		5		8	12

In Fig. 3-13, we have graphed the data in Table 3-17. Notice that there are *two* highest points on the graph. They occur at the values 1 and 4 billing errors. The distribution in Fig. 3-14 is also called bimodal, even though the two highest points are not equal. Clearly, these points stand out above the neighboring values in the frequency with which they are observed.

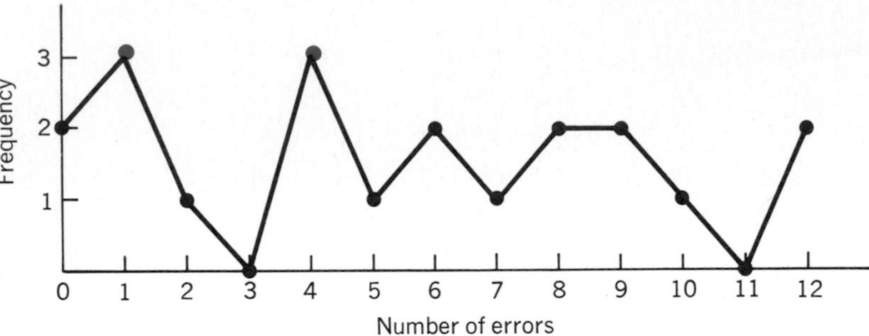

FIGURE 3-13 Data in Table 3-17, showing bimodal distribution

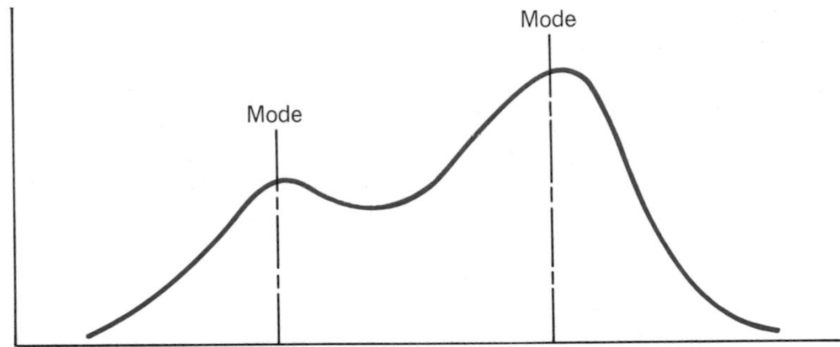

FIGURE 3-14 Bimodal distribution with two unequal modes

Advantages and Disadvantages of the Mode

Advantages of the mode

The mode, like the median, can be used as a central location for qualitative as well as quantitative data. If a printing press turns out five impressions, which we rate "very sharp," "sharp," "sharp," "sharp," and "blurred," then the modal value is "sharp." Similarly, we can talk about modal styles when, for example, furniture customers prefer Early American furniture to other styles.

Also like the median, **the mode is not unduly affected by extreme values.** Even if the high values are very high and the low values very low, we choose the most frequent value of the data set to be the modal value. We can use the mode no matter how large, how small, or how spread out the values in the data set happen to be.

A third advantage of the mode is that we can use it even when one or more of the classes are open-ended. Notice, for example, that Table 3-16 on page 85 contains the open-ended class "12 trips and more."

Disadvantages of the mode

Despite these advantages, the mode is not used as often to measure central tendency as are the mean and median. Too often, there is no modal value because the data set contains no values that occur more than once. Other times, every value is the mode, because every value occurs the same number of times. Clearly, the mode is a useless measure in these cases. Another disadvantage is that when data sets contain two, three, or many modes, they are difficult to interpret and compare.

EXERCISES

3-38 Find:

a) The modal class for the following data set:

Class	20–23	24–27	28–31	32–35	36–39	40–43	44–47
Frequency	3	4	7	15	12	6	2

b) The mode of the following sample: 5, 8, 11, 9, 8, 6, 8, 7, 12, 8, 7, 7, 11, 8, 6, 10, 13, 7, 8

3-39 Estimate the modal value of the following distribution by:

a) The graphical method b) Equation 3-9

Class	48–51.9	52–55.9	56–59.9	60–63.9	64–67.9	68–71.9	72–75.9
Frequency	2	8	20	32	56	28	4

3-40 What are the modal values for the following distributions?

a)

Hair color	Black	Brunette	Redhead	Blonde
Frequency	11	24	6	18

b)

Blood type	AB	O	A	B
Frequency	4	12	35	16

c)

Day of birth	Mon.	Tues.	Wed.	Thurs.	Fri.	Sat.	Sun.
Frequency	22	10	32	17	13	32	14

3-41 For the following data:

a) Find the mode of the data.
b) Construct a frequency distribution with intervals 10–14.9, 15–19.9, etc.
c) Estimate the modal value using Equation 3-9.
d) Compare a and c.

19	15	14	11	20	13	17	24	12	20
13	19	25	15	19	20	15	12	13	16
18	16	15	26	21	11	19	20	11	24
16	16	17	18	16	11	10	27	18	13

3-42 Estimate the mode for the distribution given in problem 3-36.

3-43 There are many different types of solar heating systems available to the public. Depending on the type of system, heat can be stored for varying lengths of time while the sun is not shining. The following frequency distribution gives the heat storage capacity in days for 20 systems that were tested:

Days	0–0.99	1–1.99	2–2.99	3–3.99	4–4.99	5–5.99	6 or more
Frequency	2	5	2	3	5	2	1

Estimate the modes for the distribution.

3-44 Ed Grant is the director of the Student Financial Aid Office at Wilderness College. He has used available data on the summer earnings of all students who have applied to his office for financial aid to develop the frequency distribution given below:

SUMMER EARNINGS	NUMBER OF STUDENTS
$ 0–$ 499	231
500– 999	304
1,000– 1,499	400
1,500– 1,999	296
2,000– 2,499	123
2,500– 2,999	68
3,000 or more	23

a) Find the modal class for Ed's data.
b) Use Equation 3-9 to find the mode for Ed's data.

3-7 COMPARING THE MEAN, MEDIAN, AND MODE

Mean, median, and mode are identical in symmetrical distribution

When we work statistical problems, we must decide whether to use the mean, the median, or the mode as the measure of central tendency. Symmetrical distributions that contain only one mode always have the same value for the mean, the median, and the mode, as illustrated in Fig. 3-9 on page 85. In these cases, we need not choose the measure of central tendency, because the choice has been made for us.

In a positively skewed distribution (one skewed to the right, such as the one in Fig. 3-10), the values are concentrated at the left end of the horizontal axis. Here, the mode is at the highest point of the distribution; the median is to the right of that; and the mean is to the right of both the mode and the median. In a negatively skewed distribution, such as in Fig. 3-11, the values are concentrated at the right end of the horizontal axis. The mode is at the highest point of the distribution, and the median is to the left of that. The mean is to the left of both the mode and the median.

The median may be best in skewed distributions

When the population is skewed negatively or positively, the median is often the best measure of location, because it is always between the mean and the mode. The median is not as highly influenced by the frequency of occurrence of a single value as the mode is, nor is it pulled by extreme values as the mean is.

Otherwise, there are no universal guidelines for applying the mean, median, or mode as the measure of central tendency for different populations. Each case must be judged independently, according to the guidelines we have discussed.

EXERCISES

3-45 When the distribution of data is symmetrical and bell-shaped, selection of a measure of location is considerably simplified. Why?

3-46 For which type of distribution (positively skewed, negatively skewed, or symmetric) is:
a) The mean less than the median?
b) The mode less than the mean?
c) The median less than the mode?

3-47 Sally Miller, the aggressive manager of the marketing division of Bindex Enterprises, has just stormed out of a rather frustrating meeting with her company's statistical analysts. They apparently bombarded her with various statistical information pertaining to the latest advertising campaign that she directed, including many measures of central tendency for several sections of the target population for the advertising blitz. She has ordered the head of the statistical analysis section to have an explanation of all measures of central tendency on her desk in exactly one hour! As the acting head of the analysis section, you must prepare a list containing exactly one strong point and one weakness of each of the measures of central tendency: mean, median, and mode.

3-8 TERMS INTRODUCED IN CHAPTER 3

BIMODAL DISTRIBUTION A distribution of data points in which two values occur more frequently than the rest of the values in the data set.

CODING A method of calculating the mean for grouped data by recoding values of class marks to more simple values.

GEOMETRIC MEAN A measure of central tendency used to measure the average rate of change or growth for some quantity, computed by taking the nth root of the product of n values representing change.

KURTOSIS The degree of peakedness of a distribution of points.

LEPTOKURTIC A strongly peaked distribution.

MEAN A central tendency measure representing the arithmetic average of a set of observations.

MEASURE OF CENTRAL TENDENCY A measure indicating the value to be expected of a typical or middle data point.

MEASURE OF DISPERSION A measure describing how scattered or spread out the observations in a data set are.

MEDIAN The middle point of a data set, a measure of location that divides the data set into halves.

MEDIAN CLASS The class in a frequency distribution that contains the median value for a data set.

MESOKURTIC A moderately peaked distribution.

MODE The value most often repeated in

the data set. It is represented by the highest point in the distribution curve of a data set.

PARAMETERS Numerical values that describe the characteristics of a whole population, commonly represented by Greek letters.

PLATYKURTIC A slightly peaked distribution.

SKEWNESS The extent to which a distribution of data points is concentrated at one end or the other; the lack of symmetry.

STATISTICS Numerical measures describing the characteristics of a sample.

SUMMARY STATISTICS Single numbers that describe certain characteristics of a data set.

SYMMETRICAL A characteristic of a distribution in which each half is the mirror image of the other half.

WEIGHTED MEAN An average calculated to take into account the importance of each value to the overall total; i.e., an average in which each observation value is weighted by some index of its importance.

3-9 EQUATIONS INTRODUCED IN CHAPTER 3

[3-1]

$$\mu = \frac{\Sigma x}{N}$$

p. 63

The *population arithmetic mean* is equal to the sum of the values of all the elements in the population (Σx) divided by the number of elements in the population (N).

[3-2]

$$\bar{x} = \frac{\Sigma x}{n}$$

p. 63

To derive the *sample arithmetic mean,* sum the values of all the elements in the sample (Σx) and divide by the number of elements in the sample (n).

[3-3]

$$\bar{x} = \frac{\Sigma(f \times x)}{n}$$

p. 64

To find the *sample arithmetic mean of grouped data,* calculate the class marks (x) for each class in the sample. Then multiply each class mark by the frequency (f) of observations in that class, sum (Σ) all these results, and divide by the total number of observations in the sample (n).

[3-4]

$$\bar{x} = x_0 + w\,\frac{\Sigma(u \times f)}{n}$$

p. 67

This formula enables us to calculate the *sample arithmetic mean of grouped data* using codes to eliminate dealing with large or inconvenient class marks. Assign these codes (u) as follows: Give the value of zero to the middle class mark (called x_0), positive consecutive integers to class marks larger than x_0, and negative consecutive integers to smaller class marks. Then, multiply the code assigned to each class (u) by the frequency (f) of observations in each class and sum (Σ) all of these products. Divide this result by the total number of observations in the sample (n), multiply by the numerical width of the class interval (w), and add the value of the class mark assigned the code zero (x_0).

[3-5]

$$\bar{x}_w = \frac{\Sigma(w \times x)}{\Sigma w}$$

p. 72

The *weighted mean*, $\bar{x}_w$, is an average that takes into account how important each value is to the overall total. We can calculate this average by multiplying the weight, or proportion, of each element (w) by that element (x), summing the results (Σ), and dividing this amount by the sum of all the weights (Σw).

[3-6]

$$\text{G.M.} = \sqrt[n]{\text{Product of all the } x \text{ values}}$$

p. 75

The *geometric mean*, or G.M., is appropriate to use whenever we need to measure the average rate of change (the growth rate) over a period of time. In this equation, n is equal to the number of x values dealt with in the problem.

[3-7]

$$\text{Median} = \text{the} \left(\frac{n+1}{2}\right)\text{th item in a data array}$$

p. 78

where: n = the number of items in the data array

The *median* is a single value that measures the central item in the data set. Half the items lie above the median, half below it. If the data set contains an odd number of items, the middle item of the array is the median. For an even number of items, the median is the average of the two middle items. Use this formula when the data are ungrouped.

[3-8]

$$\tilde{m} = \left(\frac{(n+1)/2 - (F+1)}{f_m}\right) w + L_m$$

p. 81

This formula enables us to find the *sample median of grouped data*. In it, n equals the total number of items in the distribution; F equals the sum of all the class frequencies up to, but not including, the median class; f_m is the frequency of observations in the median class; w is the class interval width; and L_m is the lower limit of the median class interval.

[3-9]

$$Mo = L_{Mo} + \frac{d_1}{d_1 + d_2} w$$

p. 87

The *mode* is that value most often repeated in the data set. To find the *mode of grouped data* (symbolized Mo), use this formula and let L_{Mo} = the lower limit of the modal class; d_1 = the frequency of the modal class minus the frequency of the class directly below it; d_2 = the frequency of the modal class minus the frequency of the class directly above it; and w = the width of the modal class interval.

3-10 CHAPTER REVIEW EXERCISES

3-48 The table below gives the relative distribution of sales calls made on Bancroft Pharmaceuticals' active accounts in the past month:

Number of sales calls	0	1	2	3	4	5 or more
Relative frequency	.21	.18	.38	.19	.03	.01

What is the mode of the distribution? Is the mode a good measure in this instance?

3-49 In a 4-week period, a utility company used the following kilotons of coal per day:

MONDAY	TUESDAY	WEDNESDAY	THURSDAY	FRIDAY	SATURDAY	SUNDAY
22.3	20.8	25.0	20.9	21.5	27.0	26.2
25.1	24.8	23.1	20.5	21.2	24.1	23.7
22.2	22.9	24.2	24.7	20.9	22.9	25.0
21.1	20.9	26.2	25.7	24.8	24.6	23.2

Using class intervals 20.00–20.99, 21.00–21.99, etc., find the modal class and the modal value.

3-50 Kerr Advertising Agency has developed a campaign for a new cereal. One of the television commercials was shown in a test market, and a sample of viewers were phoned to test recall of the message. Respondents who saw the ad were rated according to the percentage of the message recalled, and the following data resulted:

Recall (%)	0–9.9	10–19.9	20–29.9	30–39.9	40–49.9	50–59.9	60–69.9	70–79.9
Frequency	1	3	2	7	6	10	12	9

If the agency has established a minimum average recall of 50 percent for any advertisement, is this ad successful?

3-51 United Food Services operates four cafeterias within area manufacturing plants. The cafeterias are similar in terms of layout, equipment, and menu. During the past year, the average customer capacity per cafeteria was 420 people. This year, by adding employees and tables, two of the cafeterias increased their capacity by 10 percent, which made all four cafeterias equal in customer capacity. What capacities did the four cafeterias have before the increase?

3-52 For a skewed distribution, the best measure of central tendency to report is (choose one):

a) the mean
b) the median
c) the geometric mean
d) depends upon the direction of skewness
e) the mode

Why is this the case?

3-53 A firm that makes interviewing surveys for businesses and other organizations in New York City finds that the type of sampling its clients desire affects the cost of the interviews. If a client wants a sample by area, more work and time are involved, since more areas must be reached. The firm has divided the city into sectors and has arrived at the following schedule of charges for interviewing, depending on the number of people to be surveyed in a sector:

Dozens of Interviews/sector	First 10	next 5	next 5	next 10	next 10	next 10	all others
Cost (per dozen)	$12.00	$11.40	$10.80	$10.50	$10.20	$9.90	$9.60

If a particular organization using a sampling plan wants 660 (or 55 dozen) people interviewed in one of the sectors, what is the average cost per interview?

3-54 Using the frequency distribution given in problem 3-69:
a) Construct a frequency histogram. b) Graphically determine the mode.

3-55 Referring to problem 3-35:
a) What is the mode?
b) Construct a frequency distribution using 1-yard-wide classes. What is the modal class?
c) Estimate the mode from the distribution in part b using Equation 3-9. Compare your answer to that obtained by using a graphical calculation.

3-56 Suppose that the distributions illustrated in Fig. 3-1 represent the heat output distributions from 3 types of solar furnaces.
a) On average, which furnace produces the most heat?
b) Is it possible for all three types to have the same heat output?
c) Is it possible for type A to have a greater output than type B?
d) Is it possible for type C to have a smaller output than type A?
Briefly explain your answers.

3-57 Suppose that the two curves illustrated in Fig. 3-2 represent the distribution of possible winnings involved in 2 series of gambles in an experiment. Further suppose that both curves are symmetrical, with their centers (highest points) representing zero winnings. Positions to the left of center represent losses, and positions to the right of center represent winnings. Intuitively, which set of gambles, A or B, would you prefer?

3-58 Compare and contrast the central position, skewness, and kurtosis of the distributions of student/teacher ratios for all:
a) colleges in the United States
b) large state universities in the United States
c) private colleges in the United States

3-59 The gross displacement of each ship utilizing the Panama Canal during a one-week period was compiled into the frequency distribution below:

Gross displacement (Thousands of tons)	0–2.99	3–5.99	6–8.99	9–11.99	12–14.99	15–17.99	18–20.99
Frequency	30	47	69	32	18	3	1

a) Compute the sample mean of this data, using the class mark method.
b) Verify that you get the same result using the coding method.

3-60 From the data below, find the average age of the participants at a state sports meet:

Age	13	14	15	16	17	18	19	20	21	22	23	24	25
Frequency	25	48	62	81	105	75	54	40	63	32	24	22	19

3-61 The following table gives the distribution of miles per gallon (mpg) ratings for the engines produced by one Detroit automobile manufacturer:

MPG	10–12.99	13–15.99	16–18.99	19–21.99	22–24.99	25–27.99	28–30.99
Relative Frequency	.05	.10	.20	.30	.25	.05	.05

What is the mean value for the engines tested?

3-62 Joan Womble, supervisor of the telephone order department of Dover Paper Company, is working to reduce delays experienced by customers who phone in orders. She feels that minimum delays will reduce customers' dissatisfaction with the phone ordering system. To define the magnitude of the delays, she monitors a sample of phone calls and gathers the following data:

DELAY TIME (MINUTES)	FREQUENCY	DELAY TIME (MINUTES)	FREQUENCY
0.00–0.39	15	2.00–2.39	7
0.40–0.79	43	2.40–2.79	4
0.80–1.19	58	2.80–3.19	3
1.20–1.59	21	3.20–3.59	2
1.60–1.99	9	3.60–3.99	2

Using the coding method, show that you get the same value for the mean when you assign 0 to either the fifth or the sixth class.

3-63 For 5 years, Data Communications Corporation has increased its trade advertising by an average of 5.3 percent per year. The increases for the first 4 years were 6.2, 5.8, 5.0, and 4.2 percent. What was the increase in the fifth year?

3-64 A survey of 20 households concerning the quality of a particular TV program yielded the following distribution of ratings, with positive numbers indicating a favorable rating and negative numbers (denoted in parentheses) indicating an unfavorable one:

Quality rating	(30.0)–(20.1)	(20.0)–(10.1)	(10.0)–(0.1)	0.0–9.9	10.0–19.9	20.0–29.9
Frequency	3	7	5	2	2	1

Use the coding method to find the average rating given the TV program.

3-65 Over the past several years, the growth pattern in the population of a developing industrial town has followed the pattern given in the table below:

Year	1975	1976	1977	1978	1979	1980	1981	1982
Growth	.024	.062	.043	.201	.022	.005	.427	.201

Calculate the geometric mean of the increases.

3-66 Which measure of central tendency would you recommend to represent the following distributions?

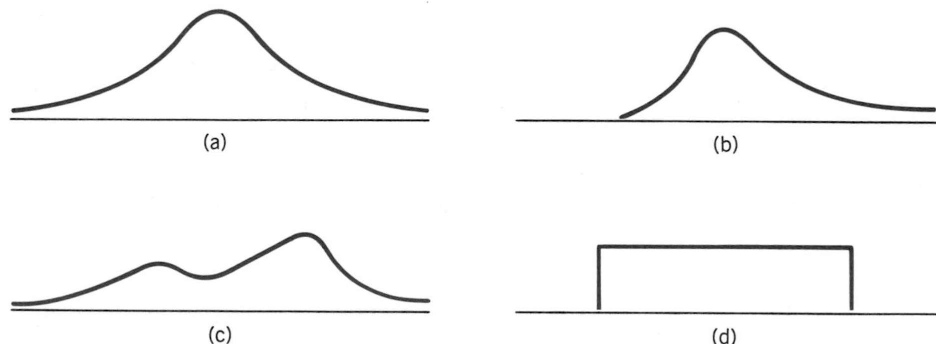

3-67 Business Products Company has shown the following unit sales of offset duplicators:

Year	1975	1976	1977	1978	1979
Unit sales	120,000	126,000	137,340	157,940	167,420

What is the average percentage increase in duplicator sales over the 5-year period?

3-68 Scientists categorize radiation according to wavelength. Typical categories are infrared, visible, ultraviolet, X-ray, and cosmic ray. What is the median category?

3-69 The weights of a sample of packages shipped by air freight are given in the following distribution:

Weight (lbs)	0–9.99	10.0–19.99	20.0–29.99	30.0–39.99	40.0–49.99	50.0 and above
Frequency	28	25	14	8	4	1

What is the median? Is it a good measure in this case?

3-70 On January 3rd, Don Ackerman had a better day than usual at the track. He placed the following bets in 5 races:

Race number	1	2	3	4	5
Number of tickets bought	10	20	10	25	10
Price per ticket	$15.40	$16.80	$5.00	$32.50	$3.20

a) What was the average price per ticket?
b) At the end of the races, Don received the following payoffs for each ticket:

Race number	1	2	3	4	5
Payoff per ticket	$1.00	$2.50	$.20	$.80	$.75

What was the average payoff on investment for these bets?

3-71 The operations manager of a digital watch manufacturer is considering switching from a batch production process to a continuous assembly line. To help him make a decision, he conducted a time study of the batch process. From the data he gathered, the following frequency distribution of total production time for one watch resulted:

PRODUCTION TIME (MINS.)	FREQUENCY	PRODUCTION TIME (MINS.)	FREQUENCY
5.00 and below	15	7.51– 8.00	58
5.01–5.50	21	8.01– 8.50	63
5.51–6.00	38	8.51– 9.00	27
6.01–6.50	39	9.01– 9.50	21
6.51–7.00	45	9.51– 10.00	19
7.01–7.50	51	Above 10.00	14

Determine the median. If the manager will switch processes any time the median is over 7.75 minutes, should he switch, based on this data?

3-11 CHAPTER CONCEPTS TEST

Answers are in the back of the book.

T F 1. The value of every observation in the data set is taken into account when we calculate its median.

T F 2. When the population is either negatively or positively skewed, it is often preferable to use the median as the best measure of location, because it always lies between the mean and the mode.

T F 3. Measures of central tendency in a data set refer to the extent to which the observations are scattered.

T F 4. A measure of the peakedness of a distribution curve is its skewness.

T F 5. With ungrouped data, the mode is most frequently used as the measure of central tendency.

T F 6. If we arrange the observations in a data set from highest to lowest, the data point lying in the middle is the median of the data set.

T F 7. When working with grouped data, we may compute an approximate mean by assuming that each value in a given class is equal to its class mark.

T F 8. The value most often repeated in a data set is called the arithmetic mean.

T F 9. If the curve of a certain distribution tails off toward the left end of the measuring scale on the horizontal axis, the distribution is said to be negatively skewed.

T F 10. After grouping a set of data into a number of classes, we may identify the median class as being the one that has the largest number of observations.

T F 11. A mean calculated from grouped data always gives a good estimate of the true value, although it is seldom exact.

T F 12. We can compute a mean for any data set, once we are given its frequency distribution.

T F 13. The mode is always found at the highest point of a graph of a data distribution.

T F 14. The number of elements in a population is denoted by n.

T F 15. For a data array with 50 observations, the median will be the value of the 25th observation in the array.

T F 16. Extreme values in a data set have a strong effect upon the median.

T F 17. The difference between the largest and smallest observations in a data set is called the geometric mean.

18. If a group of data has only one mode and its value is less than that of the mean, it can be concluded that the graph of the distribution is:
    a) Symmetrical
    b) Skewed to the left
    c) Skewed to the right
    d) Platykurtic

19. Which of the following curves would be expected to have the highest peak?
    a) Leptokurtic b) Platykurtic c) Mesokurtic

20. What is the major assumption we make when computing a mean from grouped data?
    a) All values are discrete.
    b) Every value in a class is equal to the class mark.
    c) No value occurs more than once.
    d) Each class contains exactly the same number of values.

21. Which of the following statements is NOT correct?
    a) Some data sets do not have means.
    b) Calculation of a mean is affected by extreme data values.
    c) A weighted mean should be used when it is necessary to take the importance of each value into account.
    d) All these statements are correct.

22. Which of the following is the first step in calculating the median of a data set?
    a) Average the middle two values of the data set.
    b) Array the data.
    c) Determine the relative weights of the data values in terms of importance.
    d) None of these.

23. Which of the following is NOT an advantage of using a median?
    a) Extreme values affect the median less strongly than they do the mean.
    b) A median can be calculated for qualitative descriptions.
    c) The median can be calculated for every set of data, even for all sets containing open-ended classes.
    d) The median is easy to understand.
    e) All these are advantages of using a median.

24. Why is it usually better to calculate a mode from grouped, rather than ungrouped, data?
   a) The ungrouped data tend to be bimodal.
   b) The mode for the grouped data will be the same, regardless of the skewness of the distribution.
   c) Extreme values have less effect on grouped data.
   d) The chance of an unrepresentative value being chosen as the mode is reduced.
25. In which of these cases would the mode be most useful as an indicator of central tendency?
   a) Every value in a data set occurs exactly once.
   b) All but three values in a data set occur once; three values occur 100 times each.
   c) All values in a data set occur 100 times each.
   d) Every observation in a data set has the same value.
26. Which of the following is an example of a parameter?
   a) $\bar{x}$ c) μ e) b and c, but not a
   b) n d) All of these
27. Which of the following is NOT a measure of central tendency?
   a) Geometric mean. c) Mode. e) All these are measures of central tendency.
   b) Median. d) Arithmetic mean.
28. When a distribution is symmetrical and has one mode, the highest point on the curve is referred to as the:
   a) Range c) Median e) All of these
   b) Mode d) Mean f) b, c, and d, but not a
29. When referring to a curve that tails off to the left end, you would call it:
   a) Symmetrical c) Positively skewed e) None of these
   b) Skewed right d) All of these
30. If a curve can be divided into two equal parts that are mirror images, it is __________. If it cannot be divided in this way, it is __________.
31. The symbol $\bar{x}$ denotes the mean of a __________. μ denotes the mean of a __________.
32. Assigning small-value consecutive integers to class marks during calculation of the mean is called __________.
33. When dealing with quantities that change over a period of time, it is better to calculate a __________ mean than a __________ mean.
34. If two values in a group of data occur more often than any others, the distribution of the data is said to be __________.
35. The extent to which values in a distribution are grouped together is a measure of __________.

3-12 CONCEPTUAL CASE (Northern White Metals Company)

Dick was truly impressed with the amount of information he, with the aid of two reluctant file clerks, had gleaned from the bulging file drawers. The purpose of these drawers had long been that of a repository for papers that seemed too important to discard, yet were of no immediate apparent use. Clearly, current invoices, orders, and other pertinent material had to be kept on hand, but Dick smiled as he tried to think of an occasion when an acknowledgement copy of a customer order dated May 12, 1954, might be needed.

A mandatory first step had been to clean out and update the record system, with all files more than three years old carted down to the basement for permanent storage. Unimportant material was discarded altogether. With much less clutter to deal with, Dick could organize the needed information into a form he felt was suitable for the presentation at Segue headquarters. Records were reviewed, and Dick developed a comprehensive analysis of sales volume, production volume, and raw-material price fluctuations and buying patterns.

Dick anxiously took the data he had accumulated and subsequently organized to the head draftsman, George Barbour, who had a strong artistic bent as well as considerable mechanical-drawing skill. An impressive series of tables and graphs was developed, and Dick felt the detail would make for a most effective presentation. George, on the other hand, was less convinced.

"Dick, from what I can tell, you've done quite a job in sizing up the company based on sales and production figures. As far as presentations go, though, I think you've got a real snoozer here," he offered cautiously.

"What makes you say that, George?" Dick asked, although he was beginning to see why as he perused the stack of information.

"Too complex, too much detail. Nothing really jumps out and says, 'Here's where we are,' in a nice concise way." George continued, "I don't know, it just seems by the time you make your point, everyone will be lost. This stuff is great supporting material, but it seems to me there should be some kind of summary measure in each of these areas that really lays out the situation."

Dick nodded, not unsurprised at George's concern or his perception. "I think you're right about this," he replied gratefully, "I'm going to review what we've got here and see what I can come up with."

Dick has identified three principal areas—sales volume, production volume, and raw-materials purchases—about which he will present some data and look at trends over the past three years. From this, a clearer picture should be gained about where the company is and how it got there. George has suggested that some summary measures of the rather large groupings of information Dick has developed might make his presentation more meaningful and more interesting. What might Dick do to more clearly depict sales, sales by customer class, sales by region, production volume, departmental breakdowns, and so forth, so that both he and corporate management might be better prepared to tackle the problem of charting NWMC's direction in the future?

3-13 COMPUTER DATA BASE EXERCISE

Faced with the fact of declining sales, Fred Walker compiled a comprehensive marketing strategy for wooden sleds after talking to his sales force. His subordinate, Dan Riffen, was feeling the side effects of the new marketing competition at Cold River.

"Those young computer jocks think they can tell me how to run a sales force!" Fred yelled. "What do they know about hustling sleds? They probably can't even wax a ski, don't even know which end of a Rough Rider to point downhill!

"Expand that section in the marketing plan on promotions for small toy stores. Put a free Cold River desk set in that complimentary retailer pack. We've got them now," he ranted.

Fred had designed a marketing strategy based on two assumptions:

1. The backbone of Cold River sales is the small store.
2. The sales force is the company's biggest asset.

He targeted his campaign to salespeople and to neighborhood stores, where sales were dropping. He laid out a two-pronged attack.

"First," he suggested, "we must motivate the sales force. We'll call them home for an overnight meeting at the opera house at Central City. We'll go heavy on the fancy food and have pretty girls demonstrating sleds. Then we'll sock it to them with our rabble-rousing sales pitch, and they'll get out there and sell sleds."

"The next step," Fred expanded, "is to charm the small-store owners. We'll start in heavy with a new Cold River winter sports calendar and a discount for orders over 30 units. If that doesn't pick up sales, maybe we'll advertise a weekend in Aspen for the store owner with the largest sales.

"Those kids don't have a chance against my hard knocks experience. We'll have them out of here by Christmas."

PROBLEMS AND QUESTIONS

1. Calculate the mean, median, and mode for the annual order size data presented in Chapter 2.
2. Total sales have been falling during the past three years. What has been happening to the mean order size? Are these trends consistent with each other? Explain.
3. If small stores place small orders and large stores place large orders, what is happening to the relative importance of the small stores? Is Fred correct in promoting sales to small stores exclusively?

3-14 FLOW CHART

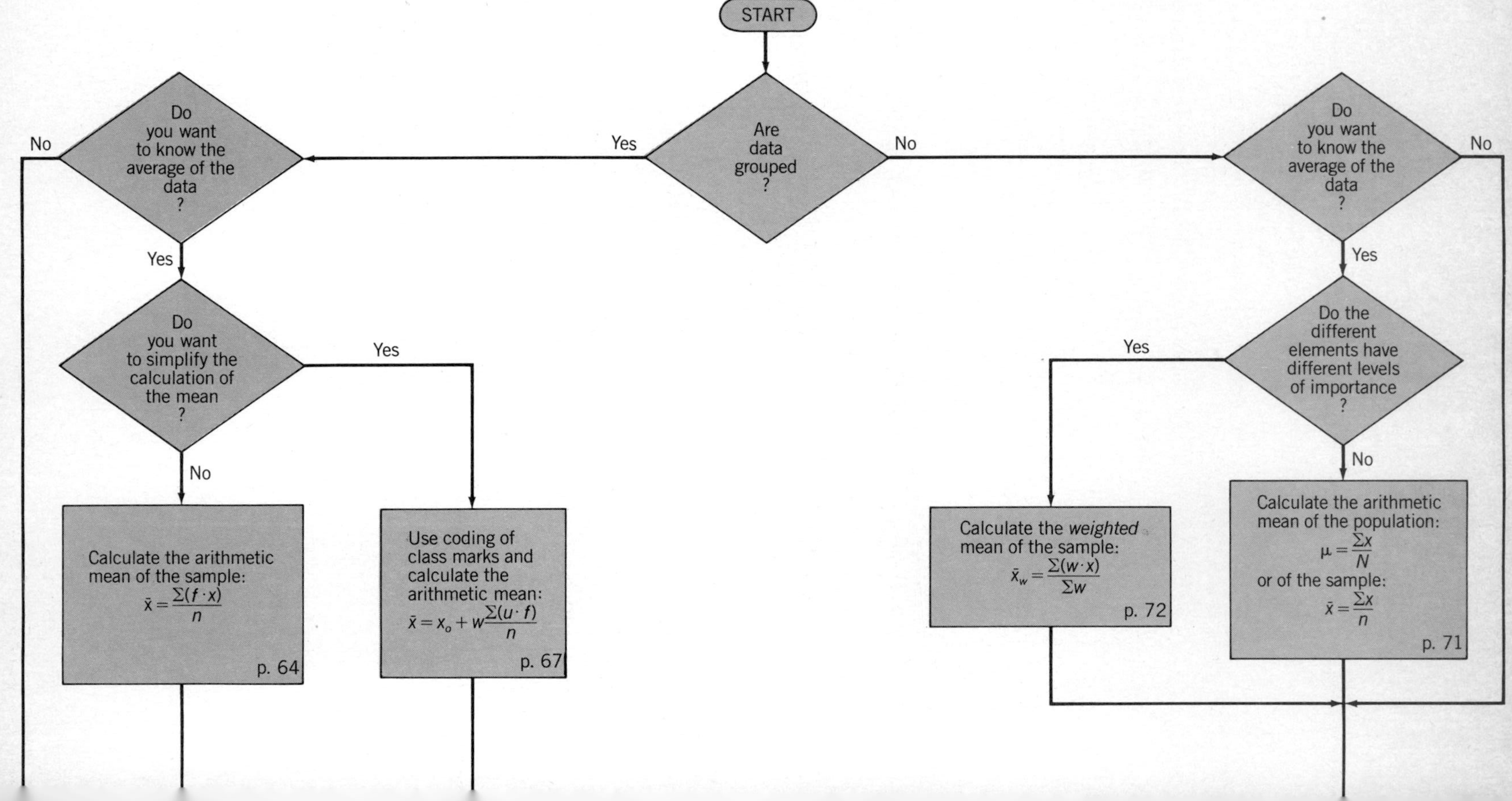
START
Are data grouped ?
Yes
No
Do you want to know the average of the data ?
No
Yes
Do you want to simplify the calculation of the mean ?
Yes
No
Calculate the arithmetic mean of the sample: $\bar{x} = \frac{\Sigma(f \cdot x)}{n}$ p. 64
Use coding of class marks and calculate the arithmetic mean: $\bar{x} = x_o + w\frac{\Sigma(u \cdot f)}{n}$ p. 67
Do you want to know the average of the data ?
No
Yes
Do the different elements have different levels of importance ?
Yes
No
Calculate the *weighted* mean of the sample: $\bar{x}_w = \frac{\Sigma(w \cdot x)}{\Sigma w}$ p. 72
Calculate the arithmetic mean of the population: $\mu = \frac{\Sigma x}{N}$ or of the sample: $\bar{x} = \frac{\Sigma x}{n}$ p. 71

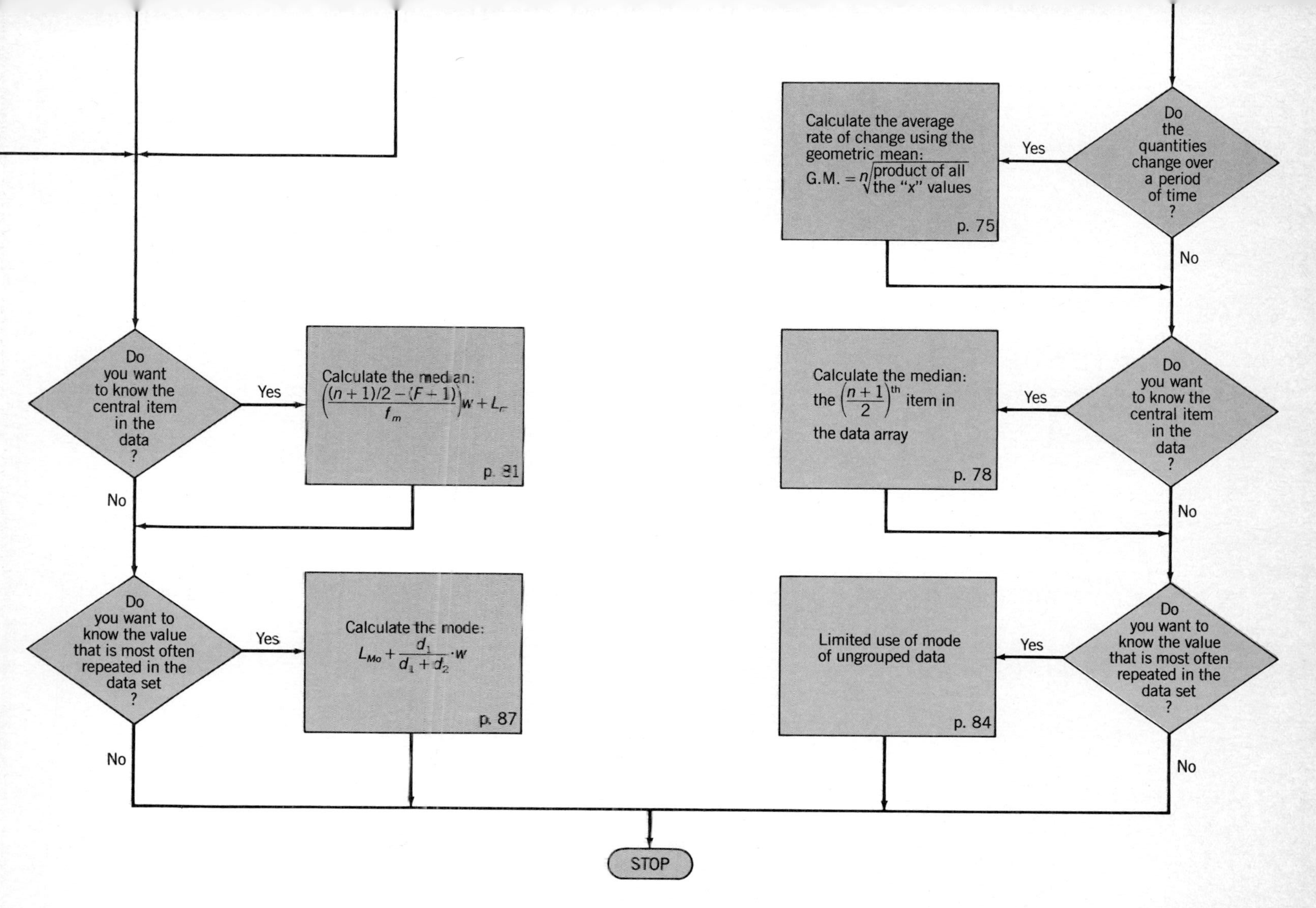
Do the quantities change over a period of time ?
Yes
No
Calculate the average rate of change using the geometric mean: G.M. = $\sqrt[n]{\text{product of all the "x" values}}$
p. 75
Do you want to know the central item in the data ?
Yes
No
Calculate the median: the $\left(\frac{n+1}{2}\right)^{th}$ item in the data array
p. 78
Do you want to know the value that is most often repeated in the data set ?
Yes
No
Limited use of mode of ungrouped data
p. 84
Do you want to know the central item in the data ?
Yes
No
Calculate the median: $\left(\frac{(n+1)/2-(F+1)}{f_m}\right)w+L_r$
p. 81
Do you want to know the value that is most often repeated in the data set ?
Yes
No
Calculate the mode: $L_{Mo}+\frac{d_1}{d_1+d_2}\cdot w$
p. 87
STOP

CHAPTER 4

MEASURING VARIABILITY

1. MEASURES OF DISPERSION, 106
2. DISPERSION: Distance Measures, 108
3. DISPERSION: Average Deviation Measures, 113
4. RELATIVE DISPERSION: The Coefficient of Variation, 126
5. EXPLORATORY DATA ANALYSIS, 128
6. TERMS, 130
7. EQUATIONS, 131
8. REVIEW EXERCISES, 133
9. CONCEPTS TEST, 136
10. CONCEPTUAL CASE, 138
11. COMPUTER DATA BASE EXERCISE, 139
12. FLOW CHART, 140

OBJECTIVES: Chapter 4 finishes our study of descriptive statistics by looking at methods that enable us to measure the tendency of a group of data to spread out, or disperse. Suppose an airline requires that its pilots be, on the average, 6′ tall, and you recruit a 4′ person and an 8′ person to apply for jobs. You would not get much praise for your efforts, even though these two unusual persons do average 6′. Instead, the airline is likely to reject both your candidates because their heights are too far from the desired average. In this situation, the 6′ average is an inadequate summary description of your two candidates. Chapter 4 provides better descriptions of variability.

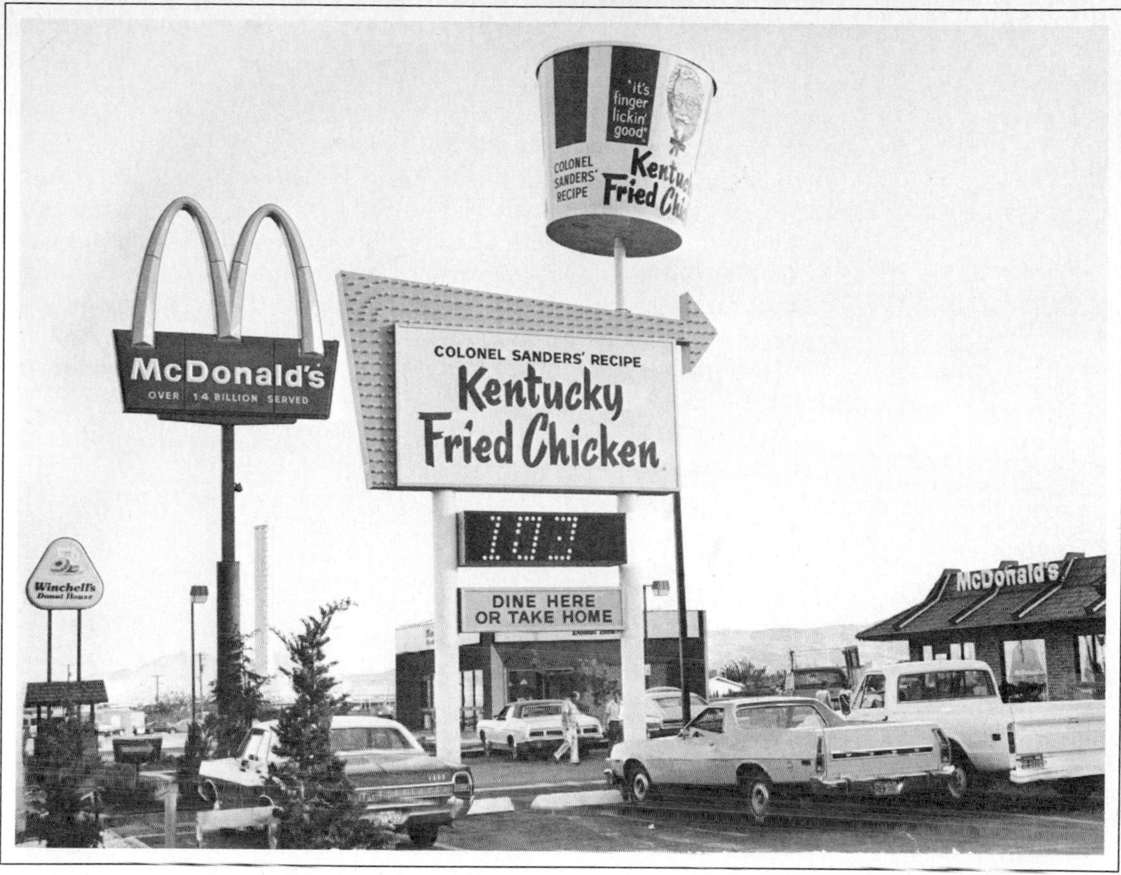

The vice-president of marketing of a fast-food chain is studying the sales performance of the 100 stores in his eastern district and has compiled this frequency distribution of annual sales:

SALES (000s)	FREQUENCY	SALES (000s)	FREQUENCY
700– 799	4	1,300–1,399	13
800– 899	7	1,400–1,499	10
900– 999	8	1,500–1,599	9
1,000–1,099	10	1,600–1,699	7
1,100–1,199	12	1,700–1,799	2
1,200–1,299	17	1,800–1,899	1

The vice-president would like to compare the eastern district with the other 3 districts in the country. To do so, he will summarize the distribution, but with an eye toward getting more information than just a measure of central tendency. This chapter discusses how he can measure the variability in a distribution and thus get a much better feel for the data.

4-1 MEASURES OF DISPERSION

Need to measure dispersion or variability

In Chapter 3, we learned that two sets of data can have the same central location and yet be very different if one is more spread out than the other. This is true of the three distributions in Fig. 4-1. The mean of all three curves is the same, but curve A has less spread (or *variability*) than curve B, and curve B has less variability than curve C. If we measure only the mean of these three distributions, we will miss an important difference among the three curves. Likewise for any data, the mean, the median, and the mode tell us only part of what we need to know about the characteristics of the data. To increase our understanding of the pattern of the data, we must also measure its *dispersion*—its spread, or variability.

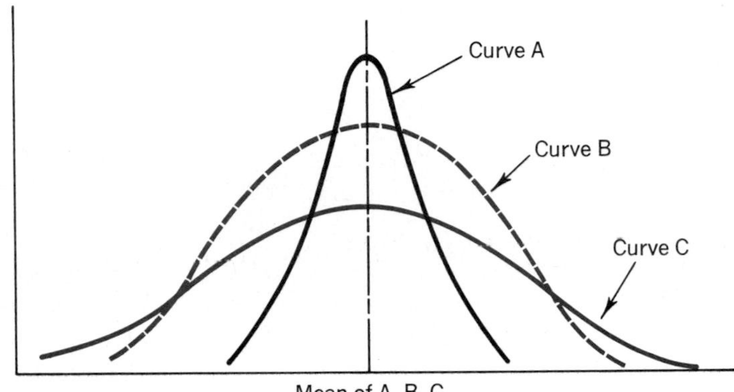

FIGURE 4-1 Three curves with the same mean but different variabilities

Uses of dispersion measures

Why is the dispersion of the distribution such an important characteristic to understand and measure? **First,** it gives us additional information that enables us to judge the reliability of our measure of the central tendency. If data are widely dispersed, such as those in curve C in Fig. 4-1, the central location is less representative of the data as a whole than it would be for data more closely centered around the mean, as in curve A. **Second,** because there are problems peculiar to widely dispersed data, we must be able to recognize that data are widely dispersed before we can tackle those problems. And, **third,** we may wish to compare dispersions of various samples. If a wide spread of values away from the center is undesirable or presents an unacceptable risk, we need to be able to recognize and avoid choosing those distributions with the greatest dispersion.

Financial use

Financial analysts are concerned about the dispersion of a firm's earnings. Widely dispersed earnings—those varying from extremely high to low or even negative levels—indicate a higher risk to stockholders and creditors than do earnings remaining relatively stable. Similarly, quality control experts analyze the dispersion of a product's quality levels. A drug that is average in purity but ranges from very pure to highly impure may endanger lives.

Quality control use

EXERCISES

4-1 A firm using two different methods to ship orders to its customers found the following distributions of delivery time for the two methods, based on past records. From available evidence, which shipment method would you recommend?

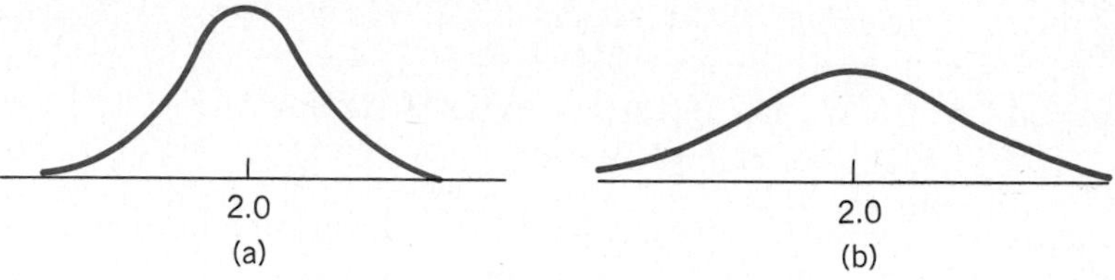

4-2 For which of the following distributions is the mean more representative of the data as a whole? Why?

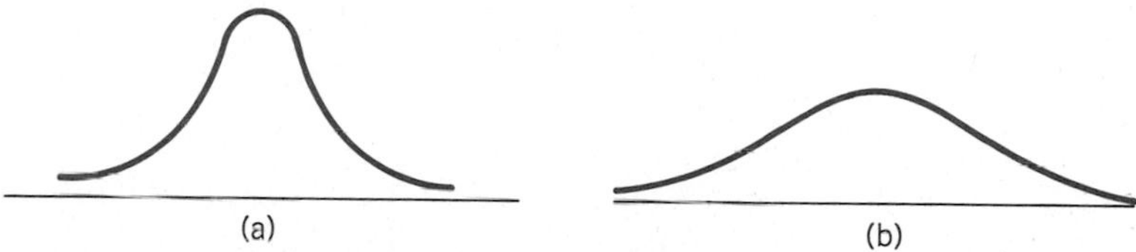

4-3 To measure scholastic achievement, educators need to test students' levels of knowledge and ability. Taking students' individual differences into account, teachers can plan their curricula better. The curves below represent distributions based on previous scores of two different tests. Which would you select as the better for the teachers' purpose?

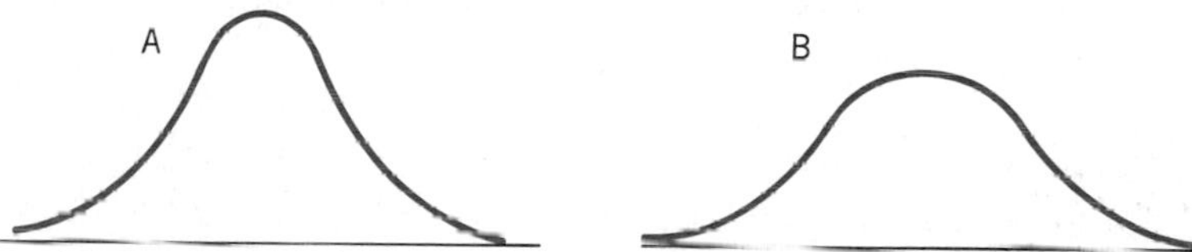

4-4 Which of the following is not one of the reasons for measuring the dispersion of a distribution?

a) It provides an indication of the reliability of the central tendency measure.
b) It enables us to compare several samples with similar averages.
c) It uses more data in describing a distribution.
d) It draws attention to problems associated with very small or very large variability in distributions.

4-5 Of the three curves shown in Fig. 4-1, choose one that would best describe the distribution of values for the ages of the following groups: members of Congress, newly elected members of the House of Representatives, the chairmen of major congressional committees. In making your choices, disregard the common mean of the curves in Fig. 4-1 and consider only the variability of the distributions. Briefly state your reasons for your choices.

4-6 How do you think the concept of variability might apply to an investigation by the Federal Trade Commission (FTC) into possible price fixing by a group of manufacturers?

4-7 Choose which of the three curves shown in Fig. 4-1 best describes the distribution of the following characteristics of various groups. Make your choices only on the basis of the variability of the distributions. Briefly state a reason for each choice.

a) The number of points scored by each player in a professional basketball league during an 80-game season

b) The salary of each of 100 people working roughly equivalent jobs in the federal government
c) The grade-point average of each of the 15,000 students at a major state university
d) The salary of each of 100 people working roughly equivalent jobs in a private corporation
e) The grade-point average of each student at a major state university who has been accepted for graduate school
f) The percentage of shots made by each player in a professional basketball league during an 80-game season

4-2 DISPERSION: Distance Measures

Three distance measures

Dispersion may be measured in terms of the difference between two values selected from the data set. In this section, we shall study three of these so-called *distance measures:* the range, the interfractile range, and the quartile deviation.

Range

Defining and computing the range

As we said in Chapter 2, *the range is the difference between the highest and lowest observed values.* In equation form, we can say:

$$\text{Range} = \begin{matrix}\text{Value of highest} \\ \text{observation}\end{matrix} - \begin{matrix}\text{Value of lowest} \\ \text{observation}\end{matrix} \qquad \textbf{[4-1]}$$

Using this equation, we compare the ranges of annual payments from Blue Cross–Blue Shield received by the two hospitals illustrated in Table 4-1.

The range of annual payments to Cumberland is \$1,883,000 − \$863,000 = \$1,020,000. For Valley Falls, the range is \$690,000 − \$490,000 = \$200,000.

TABLE 4-1 Annual payments from Blue Cross–Blue Shield (000s omitted)

Cumberland	863	903	957	1,041	1,138	1,204	1,354	1,624	1,698	1,745	1,802	1,883
Valley Falls	490	540	560	570	590	600	610	620	630	660	670	690

Characteristics of the range

The range is easy to understand and to find, but its usefulness as a measure of dispersion is limited. The range considers only the highest and lowest values of a distribution and fails to take account of any other observation in the data set. As a result, it ignores the nature of the variation among all the other observations, and it is heavily influenced by extreme values. Because it measures only two values, the range is likely to change drastically from one sample to the next in a given population, even though the values that fall between the highest and lowest values may be quite similar. Keep in mind, too, that open-ended distributions have no range, because no "highest" or "lowest" value exists in the open-ended class.

Interfractile Range

Fractiles

In a frequency distribution, a given fraction or proportion of the data lie at or below a *fractile*. The median, for example, is the .5 fractile, because half the data set are less than or equal to this value. You will notice that fractiles are similar to percentages. In any distribution, 25 percent of the data lie at or below the .25 fractile; likewise, 25 percent of the data lie at or below the 25th percentile. The *interfractile range* is a measure of the spread between two fractiles in a frequency distribution; that is, the difference between the values of two fractiles.

Meaning of the interfractile range

Calculating the interfractile range

Suppose we wish to find the interfractile range between the first and second *thirds* of Cumberland's receipts from Blue Cross–Blue Shield. We begin by dividing the observations into thirds, as we have done in Table 4-2. Each third contains four items (⅓ of the total of twelve items). Therefore, 33⅓ percent of the items lie at $1,041,000 or below it, and 66⅔ percent are equal to or less than $1,624,000. Now we can calculate the interfractile range between the ⅓ and ⅔ fractiles by subtracting the value $1,041,000 from the value $1,624,000. This difference of $583,000 is the spread between the top of the first third of the payments and the top of the second third.

TABLE 4-2 Blue Cross–Blue Shield annual payments to Cumberland Hospital (000s omitted)

FIRST THIRD	SECOND THIRD	LAST THIRD
863	1,138	1,698
903	1,204	1,745
957	1,354	1,802
1,041 ← ⅓ fractile	1,624 ← ⅔ fractile	1,883

Special fractiles: deciles, quartiles, and percentiles

Fractiles may have special names, depending on the number of equal parts into which they divide the data. Fractiles that divide the data into ten equal parts are called *deciles*. *Quartiles* divide the data into four equal parts. *Percentiles* divide the data into 100 equal parts. You've probably encountered percentiles in reported test scores. You know that if you scored in the 75th percentile, ¾ or 75 percent of all the people who took the test did no better than you did.

Interquartile Range and Quartile Deviation

Computing the interquartile range

The interquartile range measures approximately how far from the median we must go on either side before we can include one-half the values of the data set. To compute this range, we divide our data into four parts, each of which contains 25 percent of the items in the distribution. The *quartiles* are then the highest values in each of these four parts, and the *interquartile range* is the difference between the values of the first and third quartiles:

$$\text{Interquartile range} = Q_3 - Q_1 \qquad \textbf{[4-2]}$$

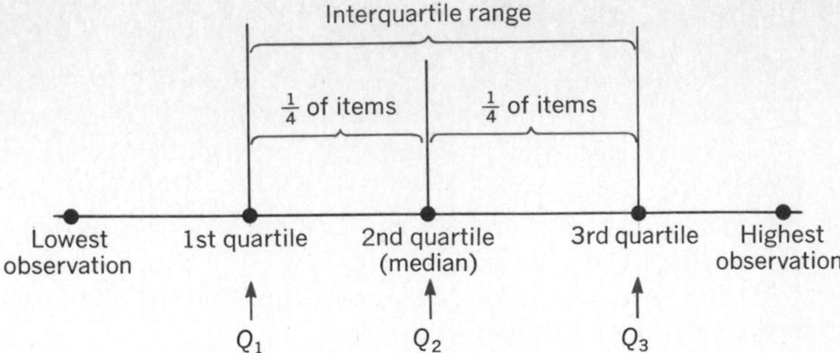

FIGURE 4-2
Interquartile range

Figure 4-2 shows the concept of the interquartile range graphically. Notice in that figure that the width of the four quartiles need *not* be the same.

In Fig. 4-3, another illustration of quartiles, the quartiles divide the area under the distribution into four equal parts, each containing 25 percent of the area.

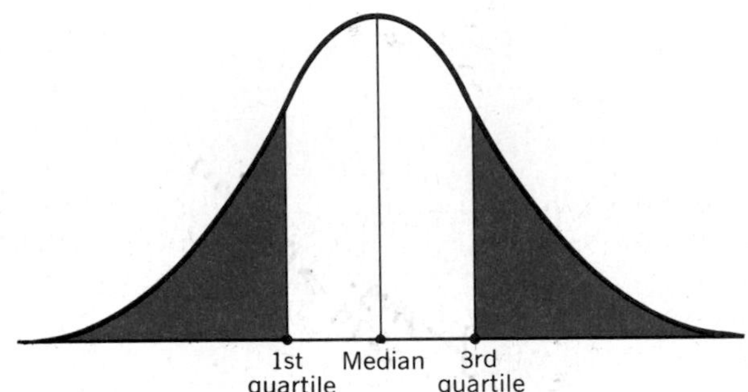

FIGURE 4-3
Quartiles

One-half of the interquartile range is a measure called the *quartile deviation:*

$$\text{Quartile deviation} = \frac{Q_3 - Q_1}{2} \qquad \textbf{[4-3]}$$

Quartile deviation

The quartile deviation, then, measures the *average* range of one-fourth of the data. It is representative of the spread of all the data, since it is found by taking an average of the middle half of the items rather than by choosing one of the fourths.

Illustrative problem for interquartile range and quartile deviation

Let's find the interquartile range and the quartile deviation of the Blue Cross–Blue Shield annual payments to Cumberland in Table 4-1. We begin by dividing the items into four equal parts, as we have done in Table 4-3. There, we see that the third quartile is \$1,698,000 and the first quartile is \$957,000. Using Equation 4-2, we find that the interquartile range is \$741,000:

$$\begin{aligned}\text{Interquartile range} &= Q_3 - Q_1 \qquad \textbf{[4-2]}\\ &= 1{,}698 - 957\\ &= 741 \text{ thousand dollars}\end{aligned}$$

and the *quartile deviation* is \$370,500:

$$\text{Quartile deviation} = \frac{Q_3 - Q_1}{2} \qquad [4\text{-}3]$$

$$= \frac{1{,}698 - 957}{2}$$

$$= \frac{741}{2}$$

$$= 370.5 \text{ thousand dollars}$$

TABLE 4-3 Blue Cross–Blue Shield annual payments to Cumberland Hospital (000s omitted)

FIRST FOURTH	SECOND FOURTH	THIRD FOURTH	LAST FOURTH
863	1,041	1,354	1,745
903	1,138	1,624	1,802
957 ←first quartile	1,204	1,698 ←third quartile	1,883

Advantages of interquartile range and quartile deviation

Like the range, the interquartile range and the quartile deviation are based on only two values from the data set. Although they are more complicated to calculate than the range, they avoid extreme values by using only the middle half of the data. Thus, they have a distinct advantage over the range, which is affected by the extreme values.

EXERCISES

4-8 For the data below, calculate the:

a) Range
b) Interfractile range between the third and seventh deciles
c) Interfractile range between the fourth and sixth deciles

98	69	58	87	73	89	83	65	82	63
88	91	77	68	94	86	96	89	98	85
55	59	87	84	59	82	73	95	68	81

4-9 Divide the following data set into 5 fractiles and list the elements of each. Calculate the:

a) Interfractile range between the second and fourth fractiles
b) Interfractile range between the second and third fractiles
c) Range

4.73	4.90	5.02	5.10	5.24	4.81	4.96	5.03	5.13	5.25
4.85	4.97	5.07	5.17	5.31	4.88	5.00	5.09	5.18	5.43

4-10 For the following data, compute the:
a) Interquartile range
b) Quartile deviation

97	72	87	57	39	81	70	84	93	79
84	81	65	97	75	72	84	46	94	77

4-11 For the sample below, compute the:
a) Range
b) Interfractile range between the 20th and 80th percentiles
c) Interquartile range
d) Quartile deviation
e) Interfractile range between the first and second quartiles
Compare parts d and e.

2,696	2,880	2,575	2,748	2,762	2,572	3,233	2,733	2,890	2,878
3,100	3,321	2,693	2,865	2,784	3,296	2,977	2,090	2,905	3,350

4-12 Redi-Mix Incorporated kept the following record of the time (to the nearest 100th of a minute) its trucks waited at the job to unload. Calculate the quartile deviation and interquartile range for their data.

.10	.20	.38	.45	.50	.61	.71	.83	.88	.98	1.02	1.18
.12	.28	.40	.46	.53	.68	.73	.84	.91	1.00	1.10	1.20
.15	.32	.42	.49	.59	.70	.75	.86	.96	1.01	1.15	1.24

4-13 Warlington Appliances has developed a new combination blender-crockpot. In a marketing demonstration, a price survey determined that most of those sampled would be willing to pay around $60, with a surprisingly small quartile deviation of $7.20. In an attempt to replicate the results, the demonstration and accompanying survey were repeated. The marketing department hoped to find an even smaller quartile deviation. The data are given below. Were their hopes confirmed?

PRICE (IN DOLLARS)											
52	35	48	46	43	40	61	49	57	58	65	46
72	69	38	37	55	52	50	31	41	60	45	41

4-14 The Casual Life Insurance Company is considering purchasing a new fleet of company cars. The financial department's director, Tom Dawkins, sampled 40 employees to determine the number of miles each drove over a 1-year period. The results of the study are given below. Calculate the quartile deviation and interquartile range.

3,600	4,200	4,700	4,900	5,300	5,700	6,700	7,300
7,700	8,100	8,300	8,400	8,700	8,700	8,900	9,300
9,500	9,500	9,700	10,000	10,300	10,500	10,700	10,800
11,000	11,300	11,300	11,800	12,100	12,700	12,900	13,100
13,500	13,800	14,600	14,900	16,300	17,200	18,500	20,300

4-15 The New Mexico State Highway Department is charged with maintaining all state roads in good condition. One measure of condition is the number of cracks present in each 100 feet of roadway. From the department's yearly survey, the following distribution was constructed:

CRACKS PER 100 FEET									
2	5	6	7	7	8	9	10	10	11
12	12	12	13	13	13	14	14	15	15
15	15	16	16	17	17	18	19	19	20

Calculate the interfractile range between the 20th, 40th, 60th, and 80th percentiles.

4-16 Ted Nichol is a statistical analyst who reports directly to the highest levels of management at Research Incorporated. He helped design the company slogan: "If you can't find the answer, then RESEARCH!" Ted has just received some disturbing data—the monthly dollar volume of research contracts that the company has won for the past year. Ideally, these monthly numbers should be fairly stable, since too much fluctuation in the amount of work to be done can result in an inordinate amount of hiring and firing of employees. Ted's data (in thousands of dollars) follow:

253	104	633	57	500	201
43	380	467	162	220	302

Calculate the following:

a) The interfractile range between the second and eighth deciles
b) The median, Q_1, and Q_3
c) The quartile deviation

4-3 DISPERSION: Average Deviation Measures

Two measures of average deviation

The most comprehensive descriptions of dispersion are those that deal with the average deviation from some measure of central tendency. Two of these measures are important to our study of statistics: the *variance* and the *standard deviation*. Both of these tell us an average distance of any observation in the data set from the mean of the distribution.

Average Absolute Deviation

Meaning of average absolute deviation

We will have a better understanding of the variance and the standard deviation if we focus first on what statisticians call the *average absolute deviation*. To compute this, we begin by finding the mean of our sample. Then we determine the absolute value of the difference between each item in the data set and the mean. In other words, we subtract the mean from every value in the data set and ignore the sign (positive or negative), thereby taking each to be positive. Finally, we add all these differences together and divide by the total number of items in our sample.

Symbolically, the formula for finding the average absolute deviation looks like this:

$$\text{Average absolute deviation} = \frac{\Sigma|x - \mu|}{N} \text{ for a population} \quad [4\text{-}4]$$

and like this:

$$\text{Average absolute deviation} = \frac{\Sigma|x - \bar{x}|}{n} \text{ for a sample} \qquad \textbf{[4-5]}$$

where:

- x = the item or observation
- μ = the population mean
- N = number of items in the population
- $\bar{x}$ = sample mean
- n = number of items in the sample

Remember that Σ means "the sum of all the values." In this case, they are $|x - \mu|$ or $|x - \bar{x}|$. Also notice the straight lines surrounding $|x - \mu|$ and $|x - \bar{x}|$, which indicate that we want the *absolute value* of that distance (expressed in positive, not negative, numbers). This means that if the distance $x - \bar{x}$ is -10, then the absolute value is 10. The absolute value of -25 is 25.

Calculating the average absolute deviation

Let's compute the average absolute deviation of the annual Blue Cross–Blue Shield payments to Cumberland in Table 4-1. First we find the mean:

$$\bar{x} = \frac{\Sigma x}{n} \qquad \textbf{[3-2]}$$

$$= \frac{863 + 903 + 957 + 1{,}041 + 1{,}138 + 1{,}204 + 1{,}354 + 1{,}624 + 1{,}698 + 1{,}745 + 1{,}802 + 1{,}883}{12}$$

$$= \frac{16{,}212}{12}$$

$$= 1{,}351 \text{ thousand dollars}$$

Using the step-by-step process outlined in Table 4-4, we find the absolute deviation of every observation from this mean of $1,351,000. Now we can divide the sum of these absolute deviations by the number of items in the sample to learn the value of the average absolute deviation:

$$\text{Average absolute deviation} = \frac{\Sigma|x - \bar{x}|}{n} \qquad \textbf{[4-5]}$$

$$= \frac{4{,}000}{12}$$

$$= 333.3 \text{ thousand dollars}$$

Characteristics of the average absolute deviation

This average absolute deviation is a better measure of dispersion than the ranges we have already calculated because it takes *every* observation into account. It weights each item equally and indicates how far, on average, each observation lies from the mean. In spite of this advantage,

TABLE 4-4 Determination of the average absolute deviation of annual Blue Cross–Blue Shield payments to Cumberland Hospital (000s omitted)

OBSERVATION (x) (1)		MEAN ($\bar{x}$) (2)		DEVIATION ($x - \bar{x}$) (1) − (2)	ABSOLUTE DEVIATION ($\lvert x - \bar{x}\rvert$) $\lvert(1) - (2)\rvert$
863	−	1,351	=	−488	488
903	−	1,351	=	−448	448
957	−	1,351	=	−394	394
1,041	−	1,351	=	−310	310
1,138	−	1,351	=	−213	213
1,204	−	1,351	=	−147	147
1,354	−	1,351	=	3	3
1,624	−	1,351	=	273	273
1,698	−	1,351	=	347	347
1,745	−	1,351	=	394	394
1,802	−	1,351	=	451	451
1,883	−	1,351	=	532	532
16,212 ← Σx					**4,000** ← $\Sigma\lvert x - \bar{x}\rvert$

however, for technical reasons beyond the scope of this text, this average deviation method is rarely used.

Population Variance

Variance

In the next two sections, we are going to focus on populations rather than samples. We shall begin with the fact that each population has a variance, which is symbolized by σ^2 (*sigma squared*).

Relationship of variance to average absolute deviation

The population variance is similar to an average absolute deviation computed for an entire population. But in this case, we are using the sum of the *squared* distances between the mean and each item divided by the total number of elements in the population. By squaring each distance, we automatically make every number positive and therefore have no need to take the absolute value of each deviation.

Formula for the variance

The formula for calculating the variance is similar to Equation 4-4. But this time, because we are finding the average squared distance between the mean and each item in the population, we will square each difference of $x - \mu$:

$$\sigma^2 = \frac{\Sigma(x - \mu)^2}{N} = \frac{\Sigma x^2}{N} - \mu^2 \qquad \textbf{[4-6]}$$

where:

- σ^2 = the population variance
- x = the item or observation
- μ = population mean
- N = total number of items in the population
- Σ = sum of all the values $(x - \mu)^2$, or all the values x^2

In Equation 4-6, the middle expression, $\frac{\Sigma(x-\mu)^2}{N}$, is the definition of σ^2. The last expression, $\frac{\Sigma x^2}{N}-\mu^2$, is *mathematically* equivalent to the definition but is often much more convenient to use if we must actually compute the value of σ^2, since it frees us from calculating the deviations from the mean. However, when the x values are large and the $x-\mu$ values are small, it may be more convenient to use the middle expression, $\frac{\Sigma(x-\mu)^2}{N}$, to compute σ^2. Before we can use this formula in an example, we need to discuss an important problem concerning the variance. In solving that problem, we will learn what the standard deviation is and how to calculate it. Then we can return to the variance itself.

Units in which the variance is expressed cause a problem

Earlier, when we calculated the range, the quartile deviation, and the average absolute deviation, the answers were expressed in the same units as the data. (In our examples, the units were "thousands of dollars of payments.") For the variance, however, the units are the *squares of the units* of the data—for example, "squared dollars" or "dollars squared." Squared dollars or dollars squared are not intuitively clear or easily interpreted. For this reason, we have to make a significant change in the variance to compute a useful measure of deviation, one that does not give us a problem with units of measure and thus is less confusing. **This measure is called the standard deviation, and it is the square root of the variance.** The square root of \$100 squared is \$10, because we take the square root of both the value and the units in which it is measured. The standard deviation, then, is in units that are the same as the original data.

Population Standard Deviation

Relationship of standard deviation to the variance

The population standard deviation, or σ, is simply the square root of the population variance. Since the variance is the average of the squared distances of the observations from the mean, **the standard deviation is the square root of the average of the squared distances of the observations from the mean.** While the variance is expressed in the square of the units used in the data, the standard deviation is in the same units as those used in the data. The formula for the standard deviation is:

$$\sigma=\sqrt{\sigma^2}=\sqrt{\frac{\Sigma(x-\mu)^2}{N}}=\sqrt{\frac{\Sigma x^2}{N}-\mu^2} \qquad \textbf{[4-7]}$$

where:

- x = the observation
- μ = the population mean
- N = the total number of elements in the population
- Σ = the sum of all the values $(x-\mu)^2$, or all the values x^2

- σ = the population standard deviation
- σ^2 = the population variance

Use the positive square root

The square root of a positive number may be either positive or negative, since $a^2 = (-a)^2$. When taking the square root of the variance to calculate the standard deviation, however, statisticians consider only the positive square root.

Computing the standard deviation

To calculate either the variance or the standard deviation, we construct a table, using every element of the population. If we have a population of fifteen vials of compound produced in one day and we test each vial to determine its purity, our data might look like Table 4-5. In Table 4-6, we show how to use these data to compute the mean (column 1 divided by N = 2.49/15), the deviation of each value from the mean (column 3), the square of the deviation of each value from the mean (column 4), and the sum of the squared deviations. From this, we can compute the variance, which is .0034 percent squared. (Table 4-6 also computes σ^2 using the second half of Equation 4-6, $\frac{\Sigma x^2}{N} - \mu^2$. Note that we get the same result but do a bit less work, since we do not have to compute the deviations from the mean.) Taking the square root of σ^2, we can compute the standard deviation, .058 percent.

TABLE 4-5 Results of purity test on compounds

OBSERVED PERCENT OF IMPURITY				
.04	.14	.17	.19	.22
.06	.14	.17	.21	.24
.12	.15	.18	.21	.25

Uses of the Standard Deviation

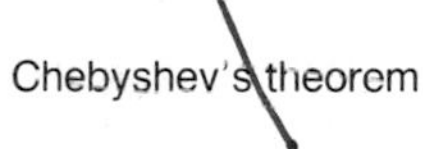

Chebyshev's theorem

The standard deviation enables us to determine, with a great deal of accuracy, where the values of a frequency distribution are located in relation to the mean. We can do this according to a theorem devised by the Russian mathematician, P. L. Chebyshev (1821–1894). Chebyshev's theorem says that no matter what the shape of the distribution, at least 75 percent of the values will fall within plus and minus 2 standard deviations from the mean of the distribution, and at least 89 percent of the values will lie within plus and minus 3 standard deviations from the mean.

We can measure with even more precision the percentage of items that fall within specific ranges under a symmetrical, bell-shaped curve like the one in Fig. 4-4. In these cases, we can say that:

1. About 68 percent of the values in the population will fall within plus and minus 1 standard deviation from the mean.

2. About 95 percent of the values will lie within plus and minus 2 standard deviations from the mean.
3. About 99 percent of the values will be in an interval ranging from 3 standard deviations below the mean to 3 standard deviations above the mean.

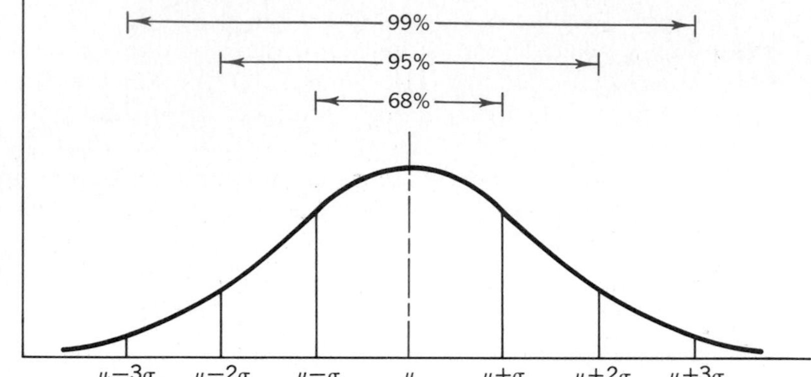

FIGURE 4-4 Location of observations around the mean of a bell-shaped frequency distribution

ignore

Using Chebyshev's theorem

In the light of Chebyshev's theorem, let's analyze the data in Table 4-6. There, the mean impurity of the fifteen vials of compound is .166 percent, and the standard deviation is .058 percent. Chebyshev's theorem tells us that at least 75 percent of the values (at least eleven of our fifteen items) are between $.166 - 2(.058) = .050$ and $.166 + 2(.058) = .282$. In fact, 93 percent of the values (fourteen of the fifteen values) are actually in that interval. Notice that the distribution is reasonably symmetrical and that 93 percent is close to the theoretical 95 percent for an interval of plus and minus 2 standard deviations from the mean of a bell-shaped curve.

Concept of the standard score

The standard deviation is also useful in describing how far individual items in a distribution depart from the mean of the distribution. A measure called the *standard score* gives us the number of standard deviations a particular observation lies below or above the mean. If we let x symbolize the observation, the standard score computed from population data is:

$$\text{Population standard score} = \frac{x - \mu}{\sigma} \qquad \textbf{[4-8]}$$

where:

- $x =$ the observation from the population
- $\mu =$ the population mean
- $\sigma =$ the population standard deviation

Suppose we observe a vial of compound that is .108 percent impure. Since our population has a mean of .166 and a standard deviation of .058, an observation of .108 would have a standard score of -1:

TABLE 4-6 Determination of the variance and standard deviation of percent impurity of compounds

OBSERVATION (x) (1)		MEAN (μ) = 2.49/15 (2)		DEVIATION ($x-\mu$) (3) = (1) − (2)	DEVIATION SQUARED $(x-\mu)^2$ (4) = [(1) − (2)]²	OBSERVATION SQUARED (x^2) (5) = (1)²
.04	−	.166	=	−.126	.016	.0016
.06	−	.166	=	−.106	.011	.0036
.12	−	.166	=	−.046	.002	.0144
.14	−	.166	=	−.026	.001	.0196
.14	−	.166	=	−.026	.001	.0196
.15	−	.166	=	−.016	.000	.0225
.17	−	.166	=	.004	.000	.0289
.17	−	.166	=	.004	.000	.0289
.18	−	.166	=	.014	.000	.0324
.19	−	.166	=	.024	.001	.0361
.21	−	.166	=	.044	.002	.0441
.21	−	.166	=	.044	.002	.0441
.22	−	.166	=	.054	.003	.0484
.24	−	.166	=	.074	.005	.0576
.25	−	.166	=	.084	.007	.0625
2.49 ← Σx					**.051** ← $\Sigma(x-\mu)^2$	**.4643** ← Σx^2

$$\sigma^2 = \frac{\Sigma(x-\mu)^2}{N} \quad \text{[4-6]}$$
$$= \frac{.051}{15}$$
$$= .0034 \text{ percent squared}$$

← OR →

$$\sigma^2 = \frac{\Sigma x^2}{N} - \mu^2 \quad \text{[4-6]}$$
$$= \frac{.4643}{15} - (.166)^2$$
$$= .0034 \text{ percent squared}$$

$$\sigma = \sqrt{\sigma^2} \quad \text{[4-7]}$$
$$= \sqrt{.0034}$$
$$= .058 \text{ percent}$$

Calculating the standard score

$$\text{Standard score} = \frac{x-\mu}{\sigma} \quad \text{[4-8]}$$
$$= \frac{.108 - .166}{.058}$$
$$= -\frac{.058}{.058}$$
$$= -1$$

An observed impurity of .282 percent would have a standard score of +2:

$$\text{Standard score} = \frac{x-\mu}{\sigma} \quad \text{[4-8]}$$
$$= \frac{.282 - .166}{.058}$$
$$= \frac{.116}{.058}$$
$$= 2$$

Interpreting the standard score

The standard score indicates that an impurity of .282 percent deviates from the mean by 2(.058) = .116 units, which is equal to +2 in terms of units of standard deviations away from the mean.

Calculation of Variance and Standard Deviation Using Grouped Data

Calculating the variance and standard deviation for grouped data

In our chapter-opening example, data on sales of 100 fast-food restaurants were already grouped in a frequency distribution. With such data we can use the following formulas to calculate the variance and the standard deviation:

$$\sigma^2 = \frac{\Sigma f(x - \mu)^2}{N} = \frac{\Sigma fx^2}{N} - \mu^2 \qquad \textbf{[4-9]}$$

and:

$$\sigma = \sqrt{\sigma^2} = \sqrt{\frac{\Sigma f(x - \mu)^2}{N}} = \sqrt{\frac{\Sigma fx^2}{N} - \mu^2} \qquad \textbf{[4-10]}$$

where:

- σ^2 = population variance
- σ = population standard deviation
- f = frequency of each of the classes
- x = class mark for each class
- μ = population mean
- N = size of the population

Table 4-7 shows how to apply these equations to find the variance and standard deviation of the sales of 100 fast-food restaurants.

We leave it as an exercise for the curious reader to verify that the second half of Equation 4-9, $\frac{\Sigma fx^2}{N} - \mu^2$, will yield the same value of σ^2.

Switching to sample variance and sample standard deviation

Now we are ready to compute the sample statistics that are analogous to the population variance σ^2 and the population standard deviation σ. These are the sample variance s^2 and the sample standard deviation s. In the next section, you'll notice we are changing from Greek letters (which denote population parameters) to the Latin letters of sample statistics.

Sample Standard Deviation

Computing the sample standard deviation

To compute the sample variance and the sample standard deviation, we use the same formulas as Equations 4-6 and 4-7, replacing μ with $\bar{x}$ and N with $n - 1$. The formulas look like this:

$$s^2 = \frac{\Sigma(x - \bar{x})^2}{n - 1} = \frac{\Sigma x^2}{n - 1} - \frac{n\bar{x}^2}{n - 1} \qquad \textbf{[4-11]}$$

TABLE 4-7 Determination of the variance and standard deviation of sales of 100 fast-food restaurants in the eastern district (000s omitted)

CLASS	CLASS MARK (x) (1)	FREQUENCY (f) (2)	$f \times x$ (3) = (2) × (1)	MEAN (μ) (4)	$x - \mu$ (1) − (4)	$(x - \mu)^2$ $[(1) - (4)]^2$	$f(x - \mu)^2$ $(2) \times [(1) - (4)]^2$
700– 799	750	4	3,000	1,250	−500	250,000	1,000,000
800– 899	850	7	5,950	1,250	−400	160,000	1,120,000
900– 999	950	8	7,600	1,250	−300	90,000	720,000
1,000–1,099	1,050	10	10,500	1,250	−200	40,000	400,000
1,100–1,199	1,150	12	13,800	1,250	−100	10,000	120,000
1,200–1,299	1,250	17	21,250	1,250	0	0	0
1,300–1,399	1,350	13	17,550	1,250	100	10,000	130,000
1,400–1,499	1,450	10	14,500	1,250	200	40,000	400,000
1,500–1,599	1,550	9	13,950	1,250	300	90,000	810,000
1,600–1,699	1,650	7	11,550	1,250	400	160,000	1,120,000
1,700–1,799	1,750	2	3,500	1,250	500	250,000	500,000
1,800–1,899	1,850	1	1,850	1,250	600	360,000	360,000
		100	**125,000**				**6,680,000**

$$\bar{x} = \frac{\Sigma(f \times x)}{n} \qquad [3\text{-}3]$$

$$= \frac{125,000}{100}$$

$$= 1,250 \text{ dollars} \leftarrow \text{mean}$$

$$\sigma^2 = \frac{\Sigma f(x - \mu)^2}{N} \qquad [4\text{-}9]$$

$$= \frac{6,680,000}{100}$$

$$= 66,800 \text{ (or 66,800 dollars squared)} \leftarrow \text{variance}$$

$$\sigma = \sqrt{\sigma^2} \qquad [4\text{-}10]$$

$$= \sqrt{66,800}$$

$$= 258.5 \leftarrow \text{standard deviation} = \$258,500$$

and:

$$s = \sqrt{s^2} = \sqrt{\frac{\Sigma(x - \bar{x})^2}{n - 1}} = \sqrt{\frac{\Sigma x^2}{n - 1} - \frac{n\bar{x}^2}{n - 1}} \qquad [4\text{-}12]$$

where:

- s^2 = sample variance
- s = sample standard deviation
- x = value of each of the n observations
- $\bar{x}$ = mean of the sample
- $n - 1$ = number of observations in the sample minus 1

Use of $n - 1$ as the denominator

Why do we use $n - 1$ as the denominator instead of n? Statisticians can prove that if we take many samples from a given population, find the sample variance (s^2) for each sample, and average each of these together, then this average tends not to equal the population variance, σ^2, unless we use $n - 1$ as the denominator. In Chapter 8, we shall learn the statistical explanation of why this is true.

Calculating sample variance and standard deviation for Cumberland Hospital data

Equations 4-11 and 4-12 enable us to find the sample variance and the sample standard deviation of the annual Blue Cross–Blue Shield payments to Cumberland Hospital discussed in Table 4-4 on page 115. We do this in Table 4-8, noting that both halves of Equation 4-11 yield the same result.

TABLE 4-8 Determination of the sample variance and standard deviation of annual Blue Cross–Blue Shield payments to Cumberland Hospital (000s omitted)

OBSERVATION (x) (1)	MEAN ($\bar{x}$) (2)	$x - \bar{x}$ (1) − (2)		$(x - \bar{x})^2$ $[(1) - (2)]^2$	x^2 $(1)^2$	
863	1,351	−488		238,144	744,769	
903	1,351	−448		200,704	815,409	
957	1,351	−394		155,236	915,849	
1,041	1,351	−310		96,100	1,083,681	
1,138	1,351	−213		45,369	1,295,044	
1,204	1,351	−147		21,609	1,449,616	
1,354	1,351	3		9	1,833,316	
1,624	1,351	273		74,529	2,637,376	
1,698	1,351	347		120,409	2,883,204	
1,745	1,351	394		155,236	3,045,025	
1,802	1,351	451		203,401	3,247,204	
1,883	1,351	532		283,024	3,545,689	
			$\Sigma(x - \bar{x})^2 \rightarrow$	**1,593,770**	**23,496,182**	$\leftarrow \Sigma x^2$

$$s^2 = \frac{\Sigma(x - \bar{x})^2}{n - 1} \qquad [4\text{-}11]$$

$$= \frac{1,593,770}{11}$$

$$= 144,888 \text{ (or \$144,888 million squared)} \leftarrow \text{sample variance}$$

$$s = \sqrt{s^2} \qquad [4\text{-}12]$$

$$= \sqrt{144,888}$$

$$= 380.64 \text{ (that is, \$380,640)} \leftarrow \text{sample standard deviation}$$

OR

$$s^2 = \frac{\Sigma x^2}{n - 1} - \frac{n\bar{x}^2}{n - 1} \qquad [4\text{-}11]$$

$$= \frac{23,496,182}{11} - \frac{12(1,351)^2}{11}$$

$$= \frac{1,593,770}{11}$$

$$= 144,888$$

Computing sample standard scores

Just as we used the population standard deviation to derive population standard scores, we may also use the sample standard deviation to compute sample standard scores. These sample standard scores tell us how many standard deviations a particular sample observation lies below or above the sample mean. The appropriate formula is:

$$\text{Sample standard score} = \frac{x - \bar{x}}{s} \qquad \textbf{[4-13]}$$

where:

- x = the observation from the sample
- $\bar{x}$ = the sample mean
- s = the sample standard deviation

In the example we just did, we see that the observation 863 corresponds to a standard score of -1.28:

$$\begin{aligned} \text{Sample standard score} &= \frac{x - \bar{x}}{s} \qquad \textbf{[4-13]} \\ &= \frac{863 - 1{,}351}{380.64} \\ &= \frac{-488}{380.64} \\ &= -1.28 \end{aligned}$$

Characteristics of the standard deviation

This section has demonstrated why the standard deviation is the measure of dispersion used most often. We can use it to compare distributions and to compute standard scores, an important element of statistical inference to be discussed later. Like the average absolute deviation, it takes into account every observation in the data set. But the standard deviation has some disadvantages too. It is not as easy to calculate as the range, and it cannot be computed from open-ended distributions. In addition, extreme values in the data set distort the value of the standard deviation, although to a lesser extent than they do the range.

EXERCISES

4-17 For the following measurements, compute the:

a) Average absolute deviation
b) Population variance
c) Population standard deviation

50	53	52	51	43	52	51	50	56	54
45	48	54	52	49	48	47	58	51	56

4-18 The following values represent a sample from a large population. Compute the:

a) Average absolute deviation for the sample
b) Sample variance
c) Sample standard deviation

26 17 24 29 26 21 33 31 29 27

4-19 In a set of 60 observations with a mean of 39.5, a variance of 17.64, and an unknown distribution shape:

a) Between what values should at least 75 percent of the observations fall, according to Chebyshev's theorem?
b) If the distribution is symmetrical and bell-shaped, approximately how many observations should be found in the interval 35.3 to 43.7?
c) Find the standard scores for the following observations from the distribution: 36.35, 44.54, 50.0, and 30.5.

4-20 Calculate the population variance for the following set of grouped data:

Class	0–199	200–399	400–599	600–799	800–999
Frequency	8	13	20	12	7

4-21 The Federal Reserve Board has given permission to all member banks to raise interest rates ½ percent for all depositors. Old rates for passbook savings were 5¼%; for certificates of deposit (CDs): 1-year CD, 7½%; 18-month CD, 8¾%; 2-year CD, 9%; 3-year CD, 10½%; 5-year CD, 11%. The president of the First State Bank wants to know what the characteristics of the new distribution of rates will be if the full ½ percent is added to all rates. How are the new characteristics related to the old ones?

4-22 The administrator of a Georgia hospital conducted a survey of the number of days patients stayed in the hospital following an operation. The data are given below:

Hospital stay (in days)	1–3	4–6	7–9	10–12	13–15	16–18	19–21	22–24
Frequency	32	108	67	28	14	7	3	1

a) Calculate the mean and standard deviation.
b) According to Chebyshev's theorem, how many stays should be between 0 and 15 days? How many are actually in that interval?
c) Since this distribution is roughly bell-shaped, how many of the stays can we expect to fall between 0 and 15 days?

4-23 In an attempt to estimate potential future demand, the National Motor Company did a study asking married couples how many cars the energy-minded family should own in 1990. For each couple, National averaged the husband's and wife's responses to get the overall couple response. The answers were then tabulated in a frequency distribution.

Number of cars	0–.49	.50–.99	1.00–1.49	1.50–1.99	2.00–2.49	2.50–2.99
Frequency	1	12	26	8	3	2

a) Calculate the variance and the standard deviation.
b) Since the distribution is bell-shaped, how many of the observations should theoretically fall between .8 and 1.8? between .3 and 2.3? How many actually do fall in those intervals?

4-24 Nell Berman, owner of the Earthbred Bakery, said that the average weekly production level of her company was 11,398 loaves, with a variance of 49,729. If the data used to compute the results were collected for 32 weeks, during how many weeks was the production level below 11,175? above 11,844?

4-25 The Creative Illusion Advertising Company has three offices in three different cities. Wage rates differ from state to state. In the Washington, D.C., office, the average wage increase for the past year was $1,250, with a standard deviation of $355. In the New York office, the average raise was $2,580, with a standard deviation of $578. In Durham, N.C., the average increase was $533, with a standard deviation of $42. Three employees were interviewed. The Washington employee received a raise of $1,000; the New York employee, a raise of $2,300; and the Durham employee, a raise of $500. Which of the three had the smallest raise in relation to the mean and standard deviation of his office?

4-26 American Foods heavily markets three different products nationally. One of the underlying objectives of each of the product's ads is to make the consumer recognize that American Foods makes that product. To measure how well each ad implants recognition, a group of consumers was asked to identify as quickly as possible the company responsible for each of a long list of products. The first American Foods product had an average response latency of 2 seconds, with a standard deviation of .005 seconds. The second had an average latency of 3 seconds, with a standard deviation of .007 seconds. The third had an average latency of 4 seconds, with a standard deviation of .10 seconds. One particular subject had the following latencies: 1.994 for the first, 3.007 for the second, and 3.990 for the third. For which product was this subject farthest from average performance, in standard deviation units?

4-27 Sid Levinson is a doctor who specializes in the knowledge and effective use of pain-killing drugs for the seriously ill. In order to know approximately how many nurses and office personnel to employ, he has begun to keep track of the number of patients that he sees each week. Each week he records the number of seriously ill patients and the number of routine patients. Sid has reason to believe that the number of routine patients per week would look like a bell-shaped curve if he had enough data. (This is not true of seriously ill patients.) However, he has data for only the past 5 weeks.

Seriously ill patients	30	41	23	26	45
Routine patients	30	29	33	32	26

a) Calculate the mean and variance for the number of seriously ill patients per week. Use Chebyshev's theorem to find boundaries within which the "middle 75%" of numbers of seriously ill patients per week should fall.

b) Calculate the mean, variance, and standard deviation for the number of routine patients per week. Within what boundaries should the "middle 68%" of these weekly numbers fall?

4-28 The superintendent of any local school district has two major problems: A tough job dealing with the elected school board is the first, and the second is the need to always be prepared to look for a new job because of the first problem. Tom Langley, superintendent of School District 18, is no exception. He has learned the value of understanding all numbers in any budget and being able to use them to his advantage. This year, the school board has proposed a budget of $350,000. From past experience, Tom knows that actual spending always exceeds the budget proposal, and the amount by which it exceeds the proposal has a mean of $40,000 and variance of 100,000,000 dollars squared. Tom learned about Chebyshev's theorem in college, and he thinks that this might be useful in finding a range of values within which the actual expenditure would fall 75% of the time in years when the budget proposal is the same as this year. Do Tom a favor and find this range.

4-29 Bea Reele, a well-known clinical psychologist, keeps very accurate data on all her patients. From these data, she has developed four categories within which to place all her patients: child, young adult, adult, and elderly. For each category, she has computed the mean IQ and the variance of IQs within that category. These numbers are given in the table below. If on a certain day Bea saw 4 patients (one from each category), and the IQs of those patients were as follows: child, 90; young adult, 92; adult, 100; elderly, 98; then which of the patients had the IQ farthest above the mean, in standard deviation units, for that particular category?

CATEGORY	MEAN IQ	IQ VARIANCE
Child	110	100
Young adult	90	64
Adult	95	49
Elderly	90	144

4-4 RELATIVE DISPERSION: The Coefficient of Variation

The standard deviation is an *absolute* measure of dispersion that expresses variation in the same units as the original data. The annual Blue Cross–Blue Shield payments to Cumberland Hospital (Table 4-8) have a standard deviation of \$380,640. The annual Blue Cross–Blue Shield payments to Valley Falls Hospital (Table 4-1) have a standard deviation (which you can compute) of \$57,390. Can we compare the values of these two standard deviations? Unfortunately, no.

Shortcomings of the standard deviation

The standard deviation cannot be the sole basis for comparing two distributions. If we have a standard deviation of 10 and a mean of 5, the values vary by an amount twice as large as the mean itself. If, on the other hand, we have a standard deviation of 10 and a mean of 5,000, the variation relative to the mean is insignificant. Therefore, we cannot know the dispersion of a set of data until we know the standard deviation, the mean, *and* how the standard deviation compares with the mean.

The coefficient of variation, a relative measure

What we need is a *relative* measure that will give us a feel for the magnitude of the deviation relative to the magnitude of the mean. The *coefficient of variation* is one such relative measure of dispersion. It relates the standard deviation and the mean by expressing the standard deviation as a percentage of the mean. The unit of measure, then, is "percent" rather than the same units as the original data. For a population, the formula for the coefficient of variation is:

Standard deviation of the population

$$\text{Population coefficient of variation} = \frac{\sigma}{\mu}(100) \quad \textbf{[4-14]}$$

Mean of the population

Using this formula in an example, we may suppose that each day, laboratory technician A completes 40 analyses with a standard deviation of 5. Technician B completes 160 analyses per day with a standard deviation of 15. Which employee shows less variability?

At first glance, it appears that technician B has three times more variation in the output rate than technician A. But B completes analyses at a rate four times faster than A. To take all this information into account, compute the coefficient of variation for both technicians:

Computing the coefficient of variation

$$\text{Coefficient of variation} = \frac{\sigma}{\mu}(100) \quad \textbf{[4-14]}$$

$$= \frac{5}{40}(100)$$

$$= 12.5\% \leftarrow \text{for technician A}$$

and:

$$\text{Coefficient of variation} = \frac{15}{160}(100)$$
$$= 9.4\% \leftarrow \text{for technician B}$$

So we find that technician B, who has more *absolute* variation in output than technician A, has less *relative* variation, because the mean output for B is much greater than for A.

EXERCISES

4-30 In two samples of size 50 each, the mean value for the first sample was 1.16 with a standard deviation of .21; the second sample had a mean of 1.75 and a standard deviation of .35. Which sample exhibits greater relative dispersion?

4-31 Bassart Electronics is considering employing one of two training programs. Two groups were trained for the same task. Group 1 was trained by program A; group 2, by program B. For the first group, it took an average of 28.74 hours to train each employee, with a variance of 79.39. For the second group, it took an average of 20.5 hours to train each employee, with a variance of 54.76. Which training program has less relative variability in its performance?

4-32 The following two samples are believed to represent the same population but were collected separately. Determine the relative dispersion of scores for the two samples and indicate which sample shows greater relative variability.

Sample 1	20	19	27	20	18	26	30	24	25	26
Sample 2	24	25	27	16	22	20	35	28	18	32

4-33 Dan Blaylock, owner of Blaylock's Television Outlet, must award a bonus to one of three salespeople. All three have achieved outstanding total sales, so Blaylock decided to grant the bonus to the most consistent. Over the last 5 years, they have sold the following numbers of televisions:

Archer	74	80	72	65	78
Quinn	82	76	69	70	84
Dutton	77	80	75	69	73

Which sales representative has the most consistent sales record?

4-34 The board of directors of Gothic Products is considering acquiring one of two companies and is closely examining the management of each company in regard to their inclinations toward risk. During the past 5 years, the first company had an average return on investment of 28 percent, with a standard deviation of 5.3 percent. The second company had an average return of 37.8 percent, with a standard deviation of 4.8 percent. If we consider risk to be associated with greater relative dispersion, which of these two companies has pursued a riskier strategy?

4-35 A drug company that supplies hospitals with premeasured doses of certain medications uses different machines for medications requiring different dosage amounts. One machine, designed to produce doses of 100 cc, has as its mean dose 100 cc, with a standard deviation of 2.6 cc. Another machine produces premeasured amounts of 180 cc of medication and has a standard deviation of 5.3 cc. Which machine has the least accuracy from the standpoint of relative dispersion?

4-36 Confederate Stereos, a wholesaler, was contemplating becoming the supplier to three retailers, but inventory shortages have forced Confederate to select only one. Confederate's credit manager is evaluating the credit record of these three retailers. Over the past 5 years, these retailers' accounts receivable have been outstanding for the following average number of days. The credit manager feels that consistency, in addition to lowest average, is important. Based on relative dispersion, which retailer would make the best customer?

Lee	62.1	61.8	63.2	62.9	61.7
Forrest	62.5	61.9	62.8	63.0	60.7
Davis	61.9	61.9	62.9	63.7	61.5

4-37 Frank N. Styne runs a rather unusual business named Rent-a-Monster. Frank offers two services to his customers: the basic Raid-a-Party (1 monster), and the deluxe Invade-a-Party (2 monsters minimum). Frank used to have no competition, but recently a similar business, Try-a-Troll, has gone into business under the direction of Ernest Gore. Try-a-Troll also offers two services: the basic (1 troll) service, and the deluxe (2 or more trolls) service. For the last 4 months, Frank and Ernest have waged a fierce battle for control of their rather limited market. The number of monthly rentals that each business has made are given below:

Rent-a-Monster, basic service	50	45	48	53
Rent-a-Monster, deluxe service	25	18	20	21
Try-a-Troll, basic service	30	35	40	35
Try-a-Troll, deluxe service	29	30	32	33

a) Compute the mean, variance, and coefficient of variation for each service of each business.
Using the coefficient of variation as a measure of consistency, answer the following questions:
b) Which basic service is more consistent?
c) Which deluxe service is more consistent?
d) Which of Frank's services is more consistent?

4-38 Sunray Appliance Company has just completed a study of three possible assembly-line configurations for producing its best selling two-slice toaster. Configuration I has yielded a mean time to construct a toaster of 31.5 minutes, with a standard deviation of 4 minutes. Configuration II has yielded a mean of 27 minutes, with a standard deviation of 9 minutes. Configuration III has yielded a mean of 33 minutes, with a standard deviation of 4.2 minutes. Which assembly-line configuration has the least relative variation in the time it takes to construct a toaster?

4-5 EXPLORATORY DATA ANALYSIS

Assumptions necessary in classical analysis

Chapters 2, 3, and 4 have been concerned with the *presentation* of data: how to organize and summarize raw data so we can recognize important characteristics of the data. The rest of the book is devoted almost entirely to classical methods of statistical analysis of data that can be used once the data have been collected and organized. As we shall see when we discuss these methods, many of these classical analyses depend on assumptions that must be made about the data being analyzed.

Robust analysis methods

Recent work, led principally by Prof. John W. Tukey of Princeton University and Bell Telephone Laboratories, has tried to develop methods for analyzing data that require very few prior assumptions. Statisticians call such methods *robust*. These techniques of *exploratory data analysis* (EDA) allow the statistician to examine the data and determine what further analyses may be appropriate.

Alternatives for doing exploratory analysis

There are several widely used computer packages for doing statistical analyses. Some of the more common are BMD, MINITAB, SAS, and SPSS. We will look at some outputs from SAS now, and also in Chapters 10 and 12. Table 4-9 gives the output when the SAS package is used to do an elementary exploratory analysis of the chlorine-level data from Chapter 2.

TABLE 4-9 An exploratory analysis of the chlorine-level data from Chapter 2, using the SAS computer package

```
        ILLUSTRATING THE USE OF SAS FOR EXPLORATORY DATA ANALYSIS

                     PPM = CHLORINE LEVELS IN PPM

                              UNIVARIATE

VARIABLE=PPM              CHLORINE LEVELS IN PPM

                               MOMENTS

             N                30          SUM WGTS          30
             MEAN        16.0367          SUM            481.1
             STD DEV    0.411459          VARIANCE    0.169299
             SKEWNESS   0.345475          KURTOSIS    -0.10233
             USS         7720.15          CSS          4.90967
             CV          2.56574          STD MEAN   0.0751219
             T:MEAN=0    213.475          PROB>|T|      0.0001
             SGN RANK      232.5          PROB>|S|      0.0001
             NUM ^= 0         30
             W:NORMAL   0.969853          PROB<W         0.571

                           QUANTILES(DEF=4)

              100% MAX      16.9            99%        16.9
               75% Q3       16.3            95%      16.845
               50% MED        16            90%       16.78
               25% Q1     15.775            10%        15.6
                0% MIN      15.2             5%       15.31
                                             1%        15.2
               RANGE         1.7
               Q3-Q1    0.524988
               MODE         15.9

                               EXTREMES

                        LOWEST            HIGHEST
                          15.2               16.4
                          15.4               16.6
                          15.6               16.8
                          15.6               16.8
                          15.6               16.9

             STEM LEAF                         #             BOXPLOT

              168 000                          3                |
              166 0                            1                |
              164 00                           2                |
              162 00000                        5             +-----+
              160 00000                        5             *--+--*
              158 0000000                      7             |     |
              156 00000                        5             +-----+
              154 0                            1                |
              152 0                            1                |
              150
                  ----+----+----+----+
                  MULTIPLY STEM.LEAF BY 10**-01
```

We will briefly glance at this output; if you wish to learn more about EDA, the bibliography at the end of the book gives several references.

The first section of the output (headed "moments") gives the mean, standard deviation, and numerical measures of the skewness and kurtosis of the data. As we have already seen in Chapters 2–4, these quantities tell us about the *shape* of the data.

Quartiles, ranges, and percentiles

The next section of output (headed "quantiles") gives the quartiles and various ranges, as well as several percentiles that delineate the upper (99%, 95%, 90%) and lower (10%, 5%, 1%) tails of the data. Thus EDA not only identifies the center of the data; it also calls our attention to the noncentral, atypical values in the data. Often, closer examination of these "outliers" will show that they really don't belong in the data set. (Perhaps they were incorrectly recorded.) We've already seen how such outliers distort sample means.

Graphical plots of the data

SAS then gives several different plots of the data. "Stem and leaf displays" are like histograms, but they simultaneously display all the data values while grouping them. Thus they have the histogram's advantage of summarizing the data without having its disadvantage of losing detail. "Boxplots" give a graphical representation of the median (the middle horizontal line in Table 4-9), the quartiles (the top and bottom horizontal lines of the box in Table 4-9), and the extremes (the "whiskers" extending from the box). You might want to think of a boxplot as a skeletal frequency distribution.

4-6 TERMS INTRODUCED IN CHAPTER 4

AVERAGE ABSOLUTE DEVIATION In a data set, the average distance of the observations from the mean.

CHEBYSHEV'S THEOREM No matter what the shape of a distribution, at least 75 percent of the values in the population will fall within 2 standard deviations of the mean, and at least 89 percent will fall within 3 standard deviations.

COEFFICIENT OF VARIATION A relative measure of dispersion, comparable across distributions, which expresses the standard deviation as a percentage of the mean.

DECILES Fractiles that divide the data into 10 equal parts.

DISPERSION The scatter or variability in a set of data.

DISTANCE MEASURE A measure of dispersion in terms of the difference between two values in the data set.

EXPLORATORY DATA ANALYSIS (EDA) Methods for analyzing data that require very few prior assumptions.

FRACTILE In a frequency distribution, the location of a value at, or above, a given fraction of the data.

INTERFRACTILE RANGE A measure of the spread between two fractiles in a distribution; i.e., the difference between the values of two fractiles.

INTERQUARTILE RANGE The difference between the values of the first and the third quartiles; this difference indicates the range of the middle half of the data set.

PERCENTILES Fractiles that divide the data into 100 equal parts.

QUARTILE DEVIATION Half of the interquartile range; a measure of the average range of one-fourth of the data.

QUARTILES Fractiles that divide the data into 4 equal parts.

RANGE The distance between the highest and lowest values in a data set.

STANDARD DEVIATION The positive square root of the variance; a measure of dispersion in the same units as the original data, rather than in the squared units of the variance.

STANDARD SCORE Expressing an observation in terms of standard deviation units above or below the mean; i.e., the transformation of an observation by subtracting the mean and dividing by the standard deviation.

VARIANCE A measure of the average squared distance between the mean and each item in the population.

4-7 EQUATIONS INTRODUCED IN CHAPTER 4

[4-1]

$$\text{Range} = \text{Value of highest observation} - \text{Value of lowest observation}$$

p. 108

The *range* is the difference between the highest and lowest observed values in a frequency distribution.

[4-2]

$$\text{Interquartile range} = Q_3 - Q_1$$

p. 109

The *interquartile range* measures approximately how far from the median we must go on either side before we can include one-half the values of the data set. To compute this range, divide the data into four equal parts. The *quartiles* (Q) are the highest values in each of these four parts. The *interquartile range* is the difference between the values of the first and third quartiles (Q_1 and Q_3).

[4-3]

$$\text{Quartile deviation} = \frac{Q_3 - Q_1}{2}$$

p. 110

The *quartile deviation* measures the spread of one-fourth of the data in a distribution. It is equal to one-half of the interquartile range.

[4-4]

$$\text{Average absolute deviation} = \frac{\Sigma|x - \mu|}{N}$$

p. 113

This formula enables us to calculate the *average absolute deviation for a population.* Because this measure of variability deals with the absolute value of the difference between each item in the data set and the mean, it is not as useful for further calculation as is the variance, which squares each distance.

Here, x represents the item or observation, μ the population mean, N the number of items in the population, and $\Sigma|x - \mu|$ the sum of all the values of $|x - \mu|$.

[4-5] $$\text{Average absolute deviation} = \frac{\Sigma|x - \bar{x}|}{n}$$ p. 114

For a *sample,* use this formula to determine the average absolute deviation. Unlike Equation 4-4, this formula uses the sample mean $\bar{x}$ and the numbers of items in the sample n.

[4-6] $$\sigma^2 = \frac{\Sigma(x - \mu)^2}{N} = \frac{\Sigma x^2}{N} - \mu^2$$ p. 115

This formula enables us to calculate the *population variance,* a measure of the average *squared* distance between the mean and each item in the population. The middle expression, $\frac{\Sigma(x - \mu)^2}{N}$, is the definition of σ^2. The last expression, $\frac{\Sigma x^2}{N} - \mu^2$, is mathematically equivalent to the definition but is often much more convenient to use, since it frees us from calculating the deviations from the mean.

[4-7] $$\sigma = \sqrt{\sigma^2} = \sqrt{\frac{\Sigma(x - \mu)^2}{N}} = \sqrt{\frac{\Sigma x^2}{N} - \mu^2}$$ p. 116

The population standard deviation, σ, is the square root of the population variance. It is a more useful parameter than the variance, because it is expressed in the same units as the data (whereas the units of the variance are the squares of the units of the data). Notice that the standard deviation is always the *positive* square root of the variance.

[4-8] $$\text{Population standard score} = \frac{x - \mu}{\sigma}$$ p. 119

The *standard score* of an observation is the number of standard deviations the observation lies below or above the mean of the distribution. The standard score enables us to make comparisons between distribution items that differ in order of magnitude or in the units employed. Use Equation 4-8 to find the standard score of an item in a *population.*

[4-9] $$\sigma^2 = \frac{\Sigma f(x - \mu)^2}{N} = \frac{\Sigma fx^2}{N} - \mu^2$$ p. 120

This formula in either form enables us to calculate the *variance* of data already *grouped* in a frequency distribution. Here, f represents the frequency of the class, and x represents the class mark.

[4-10] $$\sigma = \sqrt{\sigma^2} = \sqrt{\frac{\Sigma f(x - \mu)^2}{N}} = \sqrt{\frac{\Sigma fx^2}{N} - \mu^2}$$ p. 120

Take the square root of the variance, and you have the *standard deviation using grouped data.*

[4-11] $$s^2 = \frac{\Sigma(x - \bar{x})^2}{n - 1} = \frac{\Sigma x^2}{n - 1} - \frac{n\bar{x}^2}{n - 1}$$ p. 120

To compute the *sample variance,* use the same formula as Equation 4-6, replacing μ with $\bar{x}$ and N with $n - 1$. Chapter 8 contains an explanation of why we use $n - 1$ rather than n to calculate the sample variance.

[4-12]
$$s = \sqrt{s^2} = \sqrt{\frac{\Sigma(x - \bar{x})^2}{n - 1}} = \sqrt{\frac{\Sigma x^2}{n - 1} - \frac{n\bar{x}^2}{n - 1}}$$
p. 121

The *sample standard deviation* is the square root of the sample variance. It is similar to Equation 4-7, except that μ is replaced by the sample mean $\bar{x}$ and N is changed to $n - 1$.

[4-13]
$$\text{Sample standard score} = \frac{x - \bar{x}}{s}$$
p. 123

Use this equation to find the standard score of an item in a *sample.*

[4-14]
$$\text{Population coefficient of variation} = \frac{\sigma}{\mu}(100)$$
p. 126

The *coefficient of variation* is a relative measure of dispersion that enables us to compare two distributions. It relates the standard deviation and the mean by expressing the standard deviation as a percentage of the mean.

4-8 CHAPTER REVIEW EXERCISES

4-39 Hawker's Machined Parts supplies a part to Crowell Computers when Crowell is unable to meet its requirements from its regular supplier. The owner of Hawker's therefore has difficulty forecasting his production levels. For the past 9 years, he has supplied the following numbers of units to Crowell. Calculate the standard deviation for the following data. Does the value you have calculated for the standard deviation help explain Hawker's forecasting difficulty? Why?

36,500	31,850	18,885
29,750	29,900	25,510
47,000	16,275	30,000

4-40 The financial controller for the Bacchus Wine Company has the company's short-term cash in a variety of savings accounts and short-term notes with the following interest rates:

5.25%, 5.5%, 5.75%, 6%, 6.5%, 7%

Calculate the mean, variance, and standard deviation for these rates. Comment on your answers.

4-41 How would you reply to the following statement? "Variability is not an important factor, because even though the outcome is more uncertain, you still have an equal chance of falling either above or below the median. Therefore, on average, the outcome will be the same."

4-42 Following are three general sections of one year's defense budget, each of which was allocated the same amount of funding by Congress:

a) Officer salaries (total) b) Aircraft maintenance c) Food purchases (total)

Considering the distribution of possible outcomes for the funds actually spent in each of these areas, match each section to one of the curves in Fig. 4-1. Support your answers.

4-43 The Martin Rubber Company has a plant in Ohio and one in North Carolina. Both employ many high school students in the summer. In the North Carolina plant, the students average $98.20 a week, with a standard deviation of $15.40. In Ohio, students average $120.80, with a standard deviation of $21.40. Which plant has the greater relative dispersion?

4-44 The vice-president of sales for Vanguard Products has been studying records regarding the performances of his sales reps. He has noticed that in the last 2 years, the average level of sales per sales rep has remained the same, while the distribution of the sales levels has widened. Salespeople's sales levels from this period have significantly larger variations from the mean than in any of the previous 2-year periods for which he has records. What conclusions might be drawn from these observations?

4-45 Libby Bryan, president of Landscape Designs, utilizes large amounts of topsoil in her business, but ordering in advance is difficult because weekly needs fluctuate greatly. In an effort to accumulate information regarding potential topsoil needs, Bryan collected data on her past weekly utilization of topsoil. A sample of the data is given below:

TONS OF TOPSOIL USED (WEEKLY)				
2.65	2.89	3.02	3.51	3.78
3.98	4.02	4.15	4.39	4.59
4.88	5.01	5.90	6.01	6.95

Calculate the:

a) Range
b) Interfractile range between the one-third and two-thirds fractiles.
c) Interfractile range between the two-fifths and three-fifths fractiles.
d) Interfractile range between the three-fifths and four-fifths fractiles.

4-46 Two economists are studying fluctuations in the price of gold. One is examining the period of 1968–1972. The other is examining the period of 1975–1979. What differences would you expect to find in the variability of their data?

4-47 The Downhill Ski Boot Company runs two assembly lines in its plant. The production manager is interested in improving the consistency of the line with the greatest variation. Line number 1 produces a monthly average of 10,280 units, with a standard deviation of 1,051.5. Line number 2 produces a monthly average of 9,935, with a standard deviation of 1,020.8. Which line has the greater relative dispersion?

4-48 As part of a control program, samples are taken of welfare payments issued at each regional welfare office each week. The following data were collected during the final week in July at one such office:

INDIVIDUAL WELFARE PAYMENTS (IN DOLLARS)				
89.70	112.35	113.90	114.90	116.75
90.25	112.40	114.05	115.00	117.60
102.75	113.00	114.55	115.50	119.00

Calculate the range and the interfractile range between the ⅓ and ⅔ fractiles.

4-49 The owner of Records Anonymous, a large record retailer, employs two different formulas for predicting monthly sales. The first formula has an average miss of 700 records, with a standard deviation of 35 records. The second formula has an average miss of 300 records, with a standard deviation of 16. Which formula is relatively less accurate?

4-50 Using the following population data, calculate the average absolute deviation, variance, and standard deviation. What do your answers tell you about the cost behavior of heating fuel?

AVERAGE HEATING-FUEL COST PER GALLON FOR EIGHT STATES							
$1.03	$1.08	$1.04	$1.13	$1.12	$1.05	$1.09	$1.06

4-51 Below is the average number of New York City policemen and policewomen on duty each day between 8 and 12 P.M. in the borough of Manhattan:

Mon. 2,950 Tues. 2,900 Wed. 2,900 Thurs. 2,980 Fri. 3,285 Sat. 3,430 Sun 2,975

Calculate the variance and standard deviation of the distribution.

4-52 A psychologist wrote a computer program to simulate the way a person responds to a standard IQ test. To test the program, he gave the computer 15 different forms of a popular IQ test and computed its IQ from each form.

IQ VALUES				
121.85	123.50	124.75	125.15	125.15
130.05	131.00	131.75	132.50	132.95
133.10	133.50	133.75	135.50	141.40

a) Calculate the mean and standard deviation of the IQ scores.
b) According to Chebyshev's theorem, how many of the values should be between 120.11 and 140.67? How many are actually in that interval?

4-53 On a particular day, a city sanitation department measured the garbage weight in tons collected by the department's 40 trucks. The data were arranged in the following array:

GARBAGE WEIGHT (TONS)									
16.2	15.8	15.5	15.3	15.0	14.9	14.9	14.8	14.7	14.6
14.6	14.5	14.5	14.4	14.3	14.0	13.9	13.9	13.8	13.7
13.5	13.2	13.0	12.9	12.7	12.4	12.2	12.0	12.0	11.9
11.8	11.5	11.4	11.1	11.0	10.9	10.9	10.0	9.5	9.1

List the values in each decile. Ninety percent of the trucks brought in fewer than ______ tons.

4-54 Plummer Chevrolet has accumulated data for the average number of cars sold per day for each of the last ten months. Calculate the absolute deviation, variance, and standard deviation for the following daily averages, and comment on what your calculations tell you about its sales record.

AVERAGE CARS SOLD PER DAY FOR EACH MONTH									
3.21	3.10	2.33	2.05	2.68	3.05	2.91	2.87	2.55	2.85

4-55 On two successive days, a sample was taken of the lengths of missions flown by pilots at an overseas air-force base. The data are shown below:

LENGTH OF MISSION (HOURS)					
Day 1	1.1	1.3	1.4	1.5	3.0
Day 2	1.2	1.4	1.6	1.9	2.2

a) Calculate the range of the two distributions.
b) Comment on using the range as a measure of dispersion for these data.

4-9 CHAPTER CONCEPTS TEST

Answers are in the back of the book.

T F 1. The dispersion of a data set gives insight into the reliability of the measure of central tendency.

T F 2. The standard deviation is equal to the square root of the variance.

T F 3. The difference between the highest and lowest observations in a data set is called the quartile range.

T F 4. The quartile deviation is based upon only two values taken from the data set.

T F 5. The standard deviation is measured in the same units as the observations in the data set.

T F 6. A fractile is a location in a frequency distribution that a given proportion (or fraction) of the data lies at or above.

T F 7. The average absolute deviation, like the standard deviation, takes into account every observation in the data set.

T F 8. The coefficient of variation is an absolute measure of dispersion.

T F 9. The measure of dispersion most often used by statisticians is the standard deviation.

T F 10. One of the advantages of dispersion measures is that any statistic that measures absolute variation also measures relative variation.

T F 11. One disadvantage of using the range to measure dispersion is that it ignores the nature of the variations among most of the observations.

T F 12. The variance indicates the average distance of any observation in the data set from the mean.

T F 13. Every population has a variance, which is signified by s^2.

T F 14. According to Chebyshev's theorem, no more than 11 percent of the observations in a population can have population standard scores greater than 3 or less than -3.

T F 15. The interquartile range is a specific example of an interfractile range.

T F 16. It is possible to measure the range of an open-ended distribution.

T F 17. The quartile deviation measures the average range of the lower fourth of a distribution.

18. Which of the following is an example of a distance measure?
    a) Range
    b) Interfractile range
    c) Quartile deviation
    d) All of these
    e) a and b but not c

19. Which pair of phrases best completes this sentence? Fractiles that divide data into ________________ equal parts are called ________________ .
    a) 100 . . . . deciles
    b) 4 . . . . quartiles
    c) 10 . . . . percentiles
    d) 16 . . . . octiles

20. How does one calculate a quartile deviation?
    a) Divide the appropriate interquartile range by 4.
    b) Divide the appropriate interquartile range by 2.
    c) Multiply the appropriate interquartile range by 4.
    d) Multiply the appropriate interquartile range by 2.

21. Why is it necessary to square the differences from the mean when computing the population variance?
    a) So that extreme values will not affect the calculation.
    b) Because it is possible that N could be very small.
    c) Some of the differences will be positive and some will be negative.
    d) None of these.

22. Assume that a population has $\mu = 100$, $\sigma = 10$. If a particular observation has a standard score of 1, it can be concluded that:
   a) Its value is 110.
   b) It lies between 90 and 110, but its exact value cannot be determined.
   c) Its value is greater than 110.
   d) Nothing can be determined without knowing N.
23. Assume that a population has $\mu = 100$, $\sigma = 10$, and $N = 1{,}000$. According to Chebyshev's theorem, which of the following situations is NOT possible?
   a) 150 values are greater than 130.
   b) 930 values lie between 100 and 108.
   c) 22 values lie between 120 and 125.
   d) 90 values are less than 70.
   e) All these situations are possible.
24. Which of the following is an example of a relative measure of dispersion?
   a) Standard deviation
   b) Variance
   c) Coefficient of variation
   d) All of these
   e) a and b but not c
25. Which of the following is true?
   a) The variance can be calculated for grouped or ungrouped data.
   b) The standard deviation can be calculated for grouped or ungrouped data.
   c) The standard deviation can be calculated for grouped or ungrouped data, but the variance can be calculated only for ungrouped data.
   d) a and b but not c
26. If one were to divide the standard deviation of a population by the mean of the same population and multiply this value by 100, one would have calculated the:
   a) Population standard score
   b) Population variance
   c) Average absolute deviation
   d) Population coefficient of variation
   e) None of these
27. How does the computation of a sample variance differ from the computation of a population variance?
   a) μ is replaced by $\bar{x}$
   b) N Is replaced by $n - 1$
   c) N is replaced by n
   d) a and c but not b
   e) a and b but not c
28. The square of the variance of a distribution is the:
   a) Standard deviation
   b) Mean
   c) Range
   d) Absolute deviation
   c) a and d
   f) None of these
29. Chebyshev's theorem says that 99 percent of the values will lie within plus and minus 3 standard deviations from the mean for:
   a) Bell-shaped distributions
   b) Platykurtic distributions
   c) Left-tailed distributions
   d) All distributions
   e) No distributions
30. In a frequency distribution, the median is the .5 ______________ because half of the data set are less than or equal to this value.
31. The difference between the values of the first and third quartiles is the ______________ range.
32. The measure of the average squared distance between the mean and each item in the population is the ______________. The positive square root of this value is the ______________.
33. The expression of the standard deviation as a percentage of the mean is the ______________.

34. The number of standard deviation units that an observation lies above or below the mean is called the ____________________.
35. Fractiles that divide the data into 100 equal parts are called ____________________.

4-10 CONCEPTUAL CASE (Northern White Metals Company)

With a detailed, and now clearly summarized, three-year history of NWMC in hand, Dick was confident that his presentation would be a resounding success. As he reviewed his notes and figures, however, a feeling of concern crept over him. "This presentation is by no means complete," he thought. "Some of the departments have very high average sales growth rates, but the monthly sales figures themselves tend to fluctuate wildly. Other departments exhibit a lower growth rate, but on a higher sales volume that seems to fluctuate very little."

Similar situations were observable in sales grouped by customer class. Looking at certain account groupings, Dick had noticed the rapid appreciation in the importance of high-technology engineering firms to NWMC. Once again, though, this high-growth area seemed to be characterized by wide variations in observed data. Furthermore, accounts receivable collections among this group tended to jump around quite a bit as well. Slow collections were always troubling, but were even more so in view of the wide swings in primary aluminum ingot prices that had occurred over the past few years.

"Clearly," Dick thought, "the strategic policy NWMC pursues regarding departments and customer classes to develop must consider how reliable these descriptive measures we've come up with really are. Before I put the wrap on this presentation, I need to develop some feel for the consistency and reliability of all these accumulated data." As he pondered what he hoped would be the final phase of his presentation plight, the telephone rang.

"Lennox!" barked the by now familiar voice of the CEO, "we're looking forward to your pitch on Monday. Much of what you come up with is going to be used in the budget allocation for 1982. How's it coming?"

"In the process of wrapping it up, sir," Dick replied. "I'm looking at sales volume and I've analyzed the figures so we can get an idea of trends in a variety of areas of the firm's operations. I'm also reviewing production volume and purchasing, too. I've also done some calculations to make the rather large body of supportive data easier to interpret." He added, "I've noticed some interesting behavior in sales and cash-flow patterns. . . ."

"Good, good," the CEO responded, cutting Dick off. "Sounds like you're right on track."

Dick hung up the phone, reassured. "Now back to the business at hand," he thought.

It has occurred to Dick that his presentation, although currently broad in scope, will be incomplete without some further analysis. He has noticed that certain figures tend to fluctuate considerably more than others. Not wanting to make a hasty or erroneous recommendation, Dick has decided it would be useful to assess the variability of the data he is presenting. How should he go about doing this? What measures would be useful? How might they be interpreted and used in a planning function?

4-11 COMPUTER DATA BASE EXERCISE

Wednesday morning, after another late night session of punching cards, Frank and Laurel received a phone call from Joe.

"We've got a strategy meeting scheduled for 10 A.M. tomorrow to thrash out this sales decline. Fred will present his proposal, and I want a recommendation from you two. See what you can put together; if it's any good, we'll flesh in details later."

"Oh, no," said Frank as they hung up, "we still don't have a clear picture. And this may be our only opportunity to get a foothold in the Rockies."

"Calm down," answered Laurel. "We've got the data punched; let's start testing the variability."

PROBLEMS AND QUESTIONS

1. What is the average absolute deviation from the mean order size each year? (Use data from Chapter 2.)
2. What are the variance and standard deviation for each year? (Use the raw data.) Using the grouped data from the histogram you developed in Chapter 2, compute the variance and standard deviation for 1979.
3. Use Chebyshev's theorem to calculate the range in order size that will include at least 89 percent of all orders.
4. Examine the histograms plotted for Chapter 2 and compare them to the Chebyshev ranges calculated above. How precise is Chebyshev's theorem in establishing the range in each case?
5. In which year was an individual order size most likely to be 700 or greater?
6. How would you present your analysis to Fred? Is Fred correct in promoting sales to small stores exclusively? How do you reconcile the fact that sales are falling with your position?
7. Cold River has been staging equivalent promotion efforts at both small and large stores. Suppose, at the strategy meeting, it is decided that Fred's strategy ought to be followed. What pattern will the data for 1980 show? And how will it be different from the present pattern? Will the data support Fred's strategy? How will the 1980 data differ from the previous years' in accurately reflecting the market environment?

4-12 FLOW CHART

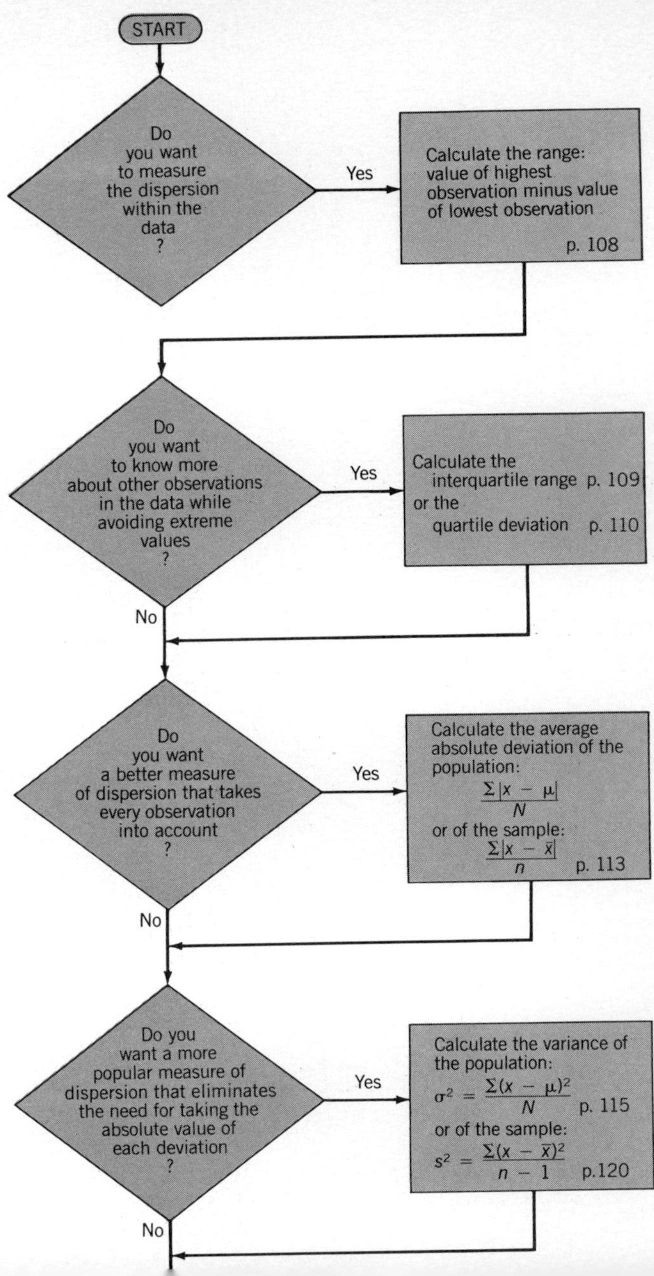

START
Do you want to measure the dispersion within the data ?
Yes
Calculate the range: value of highest observation minus value of lowest observation p. 108
Do you want to know more about other observations in the data while avoiding extreme values ?
Yes
Calculate the interquartile range p. 109 or the quartile deviation p. 110
No
Do you want a better measure of dispersion that takes every observation into account ?
Yes
Calculate the average absolute deviation of the population: $\frac{\Sigma|x - \mu|}{N}$ or of the sample: $\frac{\Sigma|x - \bar{x}|}{n}$ p. 113
No
Do you want a more popular measure of dispersion that eliminates the need for taking the absolute value of each deviation ?
Yes
Calculate the variance of the population: $\sigma^2 = \frac{\Sigma(x - \mu)^2}{N}$ p. 115 or of the sample: $s^2 = \frac{\Sigma(x - \bar{x})^2}{n - 1}$ p.120
No

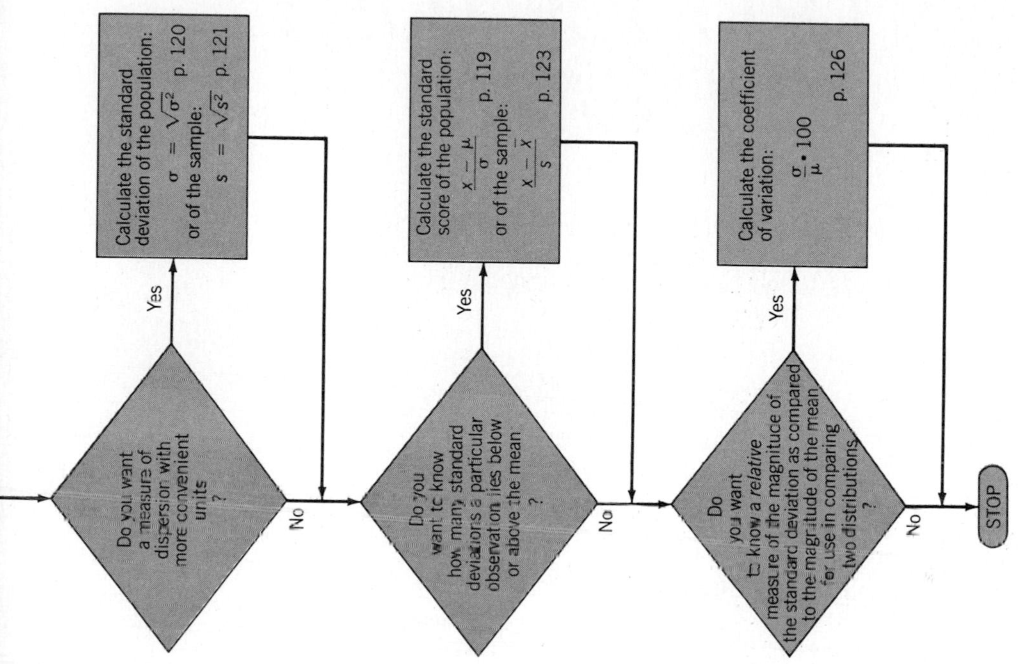

Do you want a measure of dispersion with more convenient units ?
Yes
No
Calculate the standard deviation of the population:
$\sigma = \sqrt{\sigma^2}$ p. 120
or of the sample:
$s = \sqrt{s^2}$ p. 121
Do you want to know how many standard deviations a particular observation lies below or above the mean ?
Yes
No
Calculate the standard score of the population:
$\frac{X - \mu}{\sigma}$ p. 119
or of the sample:
$\frac{X - \bar{X}}{s}$ p. 123
Do you want to know a *relative* measure of the magnitude of the standard deviation as compared to the magnitude of the mean for use in comparing two distributions ?
Yes
No
Calculate the coefficient of variation:
$\frac{\sigma}{\mu} \cdot 100$ p. 126
STOP

CHAPTER 5

PROBABILITY I: INTRODUCTORY IDEAS

1. HISTORY AND RELEVANCE OF PROBABILITY THEORY, 144
2. SOME BASIC CONCEPTS IN PROBABILITY, 145
3. THREE TYPES OF PROBABILITY, 147
4. PROBABILITY RULES, 152
5. PROBABILITIES UNDER CONDITIONS OF STATISTICAL INDEPENDENCE, 158
6. PROBABILITIES UNDER CONDITIONS OF STATISTICAL DEPENDENCE, 167
7. REVISING PRIOR ESTIMATES OF PROBABILITIES: Bayes' Theorem, 175
8. TERMS, 182
9. EQUATIONS, 183
10. REVIEW EXERCISES, 184
11. CONCEPTS TEST, 188
12. CONCEPTUAL CASE, 190
13. COMPUTER DATA BASE EXERCISE, 192
14. FLOW CHART, 197

OBJECTIVES: Chapter 5 introduces the basic concepts of probability (or chance). With Chapter 6, it is a foundation for our study of statistical inference in later chapters. Here, we examine methods of calculating and using probabilities under various conditions. If you are one of 200 students in a class and it seems that the professor calls on you each time the class meets, you might accuse that professor of not calling on students at random. If, on the other hand, you are one student in a class of eight and you never prepare for class, assuming that the professor will not get around to you, then you may be the one who needs to examine probability ideas a bit more.

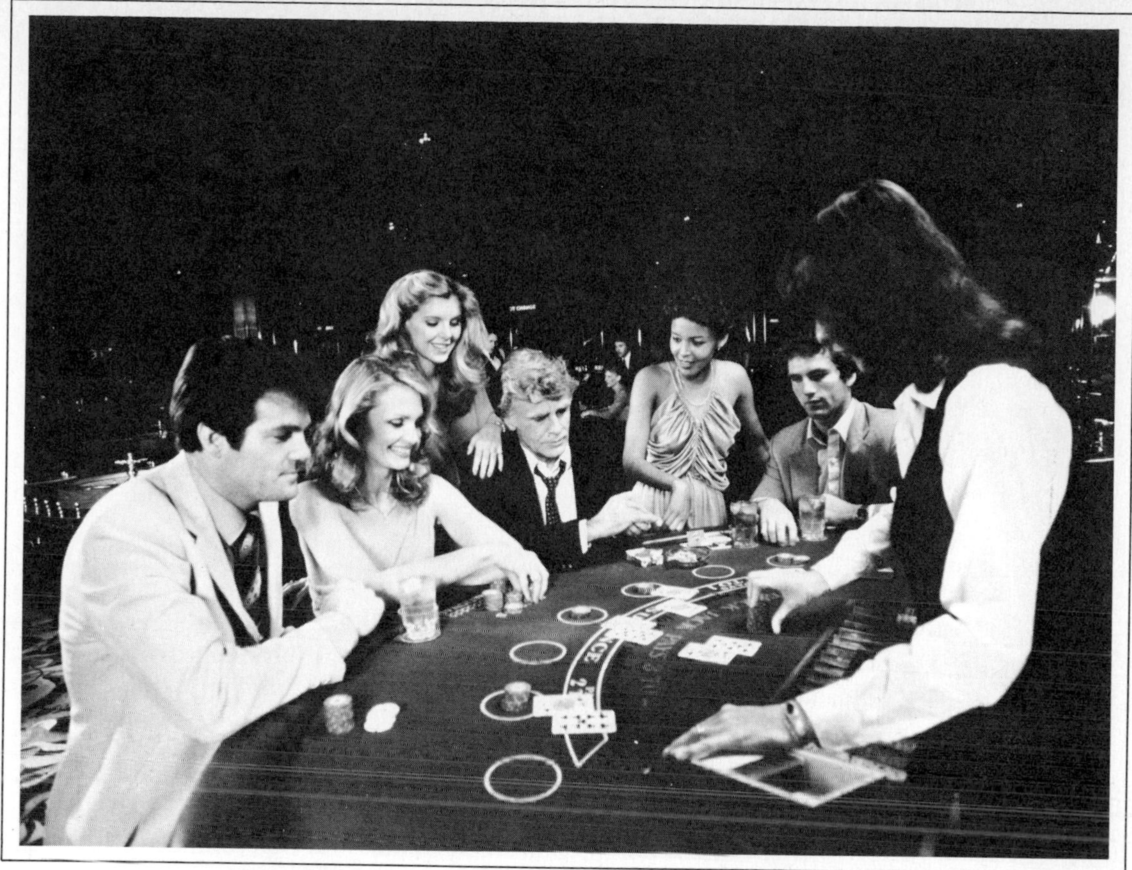

Gamblers have used odds to make bets during most of recorded history. But it wasn't until the seventeenth century that a French nobleman named Antoine Gombauld (1607–1684) questioned the mathematical basis for success and failure at the dice tables. He asked the French mathematician Blaise Pascal (1623–1662), "What are the odds of rolling two sixes at least once in twenty-four rolls of a pair of dice?" Pascal solved the problem, having become as interested in the idea of probabilities as was Gombauld. They shared their ideas with the famous mathematician Pierre de Fermat (1601–1665), and the letters written by these three constitute the first academic journals in probability theory. We have no record of the degree of success enjoyed by these gentlemen at the dice tables, but we do know that their curiosity and research introduced many of the concepts we shall study in this chapter and the next.

5-1 HISTORY AND RELEVANCE OF PROBABILITY THEORY

Jacob Bernoulli (1654–1705), Abraham de Moivre (1667–1754), the Reverend Thomas Bayes (1702–1761), and Joseph Lagrange (1736–1813) developed probability formulas and techniques. In the nineteenth century, Pierre Simon, Marquis de Laplace (1749–1827), unified all these early ideas and compiled the first general theory of probability.

Need for probability theory

Probability theory was successfully applied at the gambling tables and, more relevant to our study, eventually to other social and economic problems. The insurance industry, which emerged in the nineteenth century, required precise knowledge about the risk of loss in order to calculate premiums. Within fifty years, many learning centers were studying probability as a tool for understanding social phenomena. Today, the mathematical theory of probability is the basis for statistical applications in both social and decision-making research.

Examples of the use of probability theory

Probability is a part of our everyday lives. In personal and managerial decisions, we face uncertainty and use probability theory whether or not we admit the use of something so sophisticated. When we hear a weather forecast of a 70 percent chance of rain, we change our plans from a picnic to a pool game. Playing bridge, we make some probability estimate before attempting a finesse. Managers who deal with inventories of highly styled women's clothing must wonder about the chances that sales will reach or exceed a certain level, and the buyer who stocks up on skateboards considers the probability of the life of this particular fad. Before Muhammad Ali's highly publicized fight with Leon Spinks, Ali was reputed to have said, "I'll give you **odds** I'm still the greatest when it's over." And when you begin to study for the inevitable quiz attached to the use of this book, you may ask yourself, "What are the chances the professor will ask us to recall something about the history of probability theory?"

We live in a world in which we are unable to forecast the future with complete certainty. Our need to cope with uncertainty leads us to the study and use of probability theory. In many instances we, as concerned citizens, will have some knowledge about the possible outcomes of a decision. By organizing this information and considering it systematically, we will be able to recognize our assumptions, communicate our reasoning to others, and make a sounder decision than we could by using a shot-in-the-dark approach.

EXERCISES

5-1 The insurance industry uses probability theory to calculate premium rates; but life insurers know for certain that every policyholder is going to die. Does this mean that probability theory does not apply to the life insurance business? Explain.

5-2 "Warning: the Surgeon General has determined that cigarette smoking is hazardous to your health." How might probability theory have played a part in that statement?

5-3 Is there really any such thing as an "uncalculated risk"? Explain.

5-4 A well-known manufacturer of children's clothing decides to expand its product line by adding preteen clothing. In what ways do you think the decision involves probability theory?

5-2 SOME BASIC CONCEPTS IN PROBABILITY

In general, probability is the chance something will happen. Probabilities are expressed as fractions (1/6, 1/2, 8/9) or as decimals (.167, .500, .889) between zero and 1. Assigning a probability of zero means that something can never happen; a probability of 1 indicates that something will always happen.

In probability theory, an *event* is one or more of the possible outcomes of doing something. If we toss a coin, getting a tail would be an *event*, and getting a head would be another event. Similarly, if we are drawing from a deck of cards, selecting the ace of spades would be an event. An example of an event closer to your life, perhaps, is being picked from a class of 100 students to answer a question. When we hear the frightening predictions of highway traffic deaths, we hope not to be one of those events.

The activity that produces such an event is referred to in probability theory as an *experiment*. Using this formal language, we could ask the question, "In a coin toss *experiment*, what is the probability of the event *head?*" And, of course, if it is a fair coin with an equal chance of coming down on either side (and no chance of landing on its edge), we would answer, "1/2" or ".5." The set of all possible outcomes of an experiment is called the *sample space* for the experiment. In the coin-toss experiment, the sample space is:

Sample space

$$S = \{\text{head, tail}\}$$

In the card-drawing experiment, the sample space has 52 members: ace of hearts, deuce of hearts, and so on.

Most of us are less excited about coins or cards than we are interested in questions like, "What are the chances of making that plane connection?" or, "What are my chances of getting a second job interview?" In short, we are concerned with the chances that certain events will happen.

Mutually exclusive events

Events are said to be *mutually exclusive* if one and only one of them can take place at a time. Consider again our example of the coin. We have two possible outcomes, heads and tails. On any toss, either heads or tails may turn up, but not both. As a result, the events heads and tails on a single toss are said to be mutually exclusive. Similarly, you will either pass or fail this course or, before the course is over, you may drop it without a grade. Only one of those three outcomes can happen; they are said to be mutually exclusive events. The crucial question to ask in deciding whether events are really mutually exclusive is, "Can two or more of these events occur at one time?" If the answer is yes, the events are *not* mutually exclusive.

A collectively exhaustive list

When a list of the possible events that can result from an experiment includes every possible outcome, the list is said to be *collectively exhaustive*. In our coin example, the list "head and tail" is collectively exhaustive (unless, of course, the coin stands on its edge when we toss it). In a presidential campaign, the list of outcomes "Democratic candidate and Republican candidate" is *not* a collectively exhaustive list of outcomes, since an independent candidate or the candidate of another party could conceivably win.

EXERCISES

5-5 Give a collectively exhaustive list of the possible outcomes of tossing two dice.

5-6 Which of the following are pairs of mutually exclusive events in the drawing of a single card from a standard deck of 52?

a) A heart and a queen
b) A club and a red card
c) An even number and a spade
d) An ace and an even number

Which of the following are mutually exclusive outcomes in the rolling of two dice?

a) A total of 5 and a 5 on one die
b) A total of 7 and an even number of points on both dice
c) A total of 8 and an odd number of points on both dice
d) A total of 9 points and a 2 on one die
e) A total of 10 points and a 4 on one die

5-7 Give the sample space of outcomes for the following "experiments" in terms of their sex makeup: the birth of (a) twins, (b) triplets.

5-8 Give the probability for each of the following totals in the rolling of two dice: 1, 2, 5, 6, 7, 10, 11.

5-9 In a recent meeting of union members supporting Joe Royal for union president, Royal's leading supporter said "chances are good" that Royal will defeat the single opponent facing him in the election.

a) What are the "events" that could take place with regard to the election?
b) Is your list collectively exhaustive? Are the events in your list mutually exclusive?
c) Disregarding the supporter's comments and knowing no additional information, what probabilities would you assign to each of your events?

5-10 New Jersey Telephone is considering the distribution of funds for a campaign to increase long distance calls in the state. The following table lists the markets in the state that the company considers worthy of focused promotions.

MARKET SEGMENT	COST OF SPECIAL CAMPAIGN AIMED AT GROUP
Minorities	$500,000
Businesspeople	750,000
Women	250,000
Professionals and middle class	250,000
Working class	500,000

There is up to $1 million available for these special campaigns.

a) Are the market segments listed in the table collectively exhaustive? Are they mutually exclusive?
b) Make a collectively exhaustive and mutually exclusive list of the possible events of the spending decision.
c) Suppose the company has decided to spend the entire $1 million on special campaigns. Does this change your answer to part b? If so, what is your new answer?

5-3 THREE TYPES OF PROBABILITY

There are three basic ways of classifying probability. These three represent rather different conceptual approaches to the study of probability theory; in fact, experts disagree about which approach is the proper one to use. Let us begin by defining the:

1. Classical approach
2. Relative frequency approach
3. Subjective approach

Classical Probability

Classical probability defined

Classical probability defines the probability that an event will occur as:

$$\text{Probability of an event} = \frac{\text{Number of outcomes where the event occurs}}{\text{Total number of possible outcomes}} \quad [5\text{-}1]$$

It must be emphasized that in order for Equation 5-1 to be valid, each of the possible outcomes must be equally likely. This is a rather complex way of defining something that may seem intuitively obvious to us, but we can use it to write our coin-toss and dice-rolling examples in symbolic form. First, we would state the question, "What is the probability of getting a head on one toss?" as:

$$P(\text{Head})$$

Then, using formal terms, we get:

$$P(\text{Head}) = \frac{1}{1+1} = .5, \text{ or } \frac{1}{2}$$

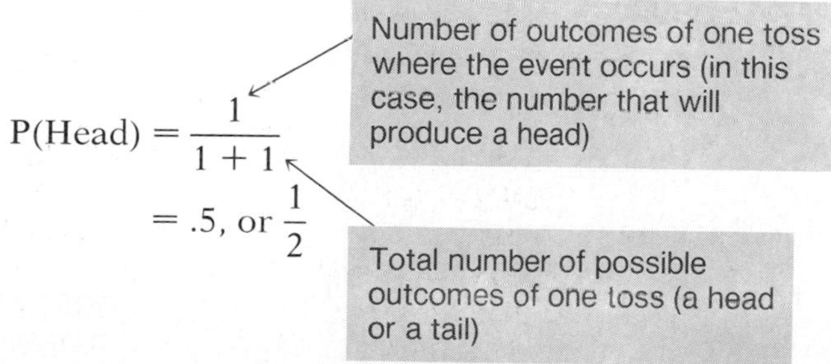

Number of outcomes of one toss where the event occurs (in this case, the number that will produce a head)
Total number of possible outcomes of one toss (a head or a tail)

And for the dice-rolling example:

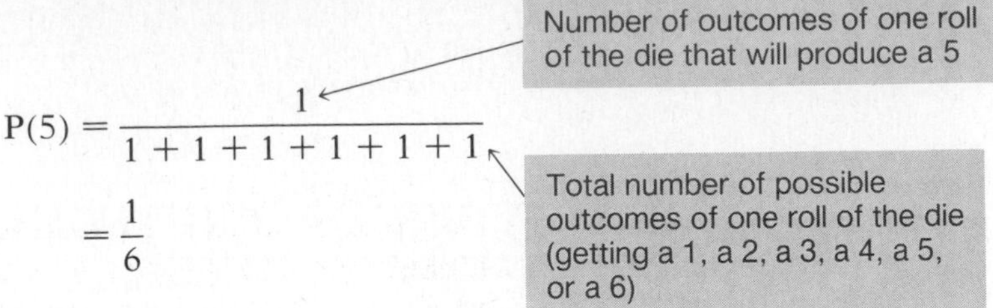

$$P(5) = \frac{1}{1+1+1+1+1+1}$$

$$= \frac{1}{6}$$

A priori probability

Classical probability is often called *a priori* probability, because if we keep using orderly examples like fair coins, unbiased dice, and standard decks of cards, we can state the answer in advance (a priori) *without* tossing a coin, rolling a die, or drawing a card. We do not have to perform experiments to make our probability statements about fair coins, standard card decks, and unbiased dice. Instead, we can make statements based on logical reasoning before any experiments take place.

Shortcomings of the classical approach

This approach to probability is useful when we deal with card games, dice games, coin tosses, and the like but has serious problems when we try to apply it to the less orderly decision problems we encounter in management. The classical approach to probability assumes a world that does not exist. It assumes away situations that are very unlikely but that could conceivably happen. Such occurrences as a coin landing on its edge, your classroom burning down during a discussion of probabilities, or your eating pizza while on a business trip at the North Pole are all extremely unlikely but not impossible. Nevertheless, the classical approach assumes them all away. Classical probability also assumes a kind of symmetry about the world, and that assumption can get us into trouble. Real-life situations, disorderly and unlikely as they often are, make it useful to define probabilities in other ways.

Relative Frequency of Occurrence

Suppose we begin asking ourselves complex questions such as, "What is the probability that I will live to be 85?" or, "What are the chances that I will blow one of my stereo speakers if I turn my 200-watt amplifier up to wide open?" or, "What is the probability that the location of a new paper plant on the river near our town will cause a substantial fish kill?" We quickly see that we may not be able to state in advance, without experimentation, what these probabilities are. Other approaches may be more useful.

Probability redefined

In the 1800s, British statisticians, interested in a theoretical foundation for calculating risk of losses in life insurance and commercial insurance, began defining probabilities from statistical data collected on births and deaths. Today this approach is called *relative frequency of occurrence*. It defines probability as either:

1. The observed relative frequency of an event in a very large number of trials, or
2. The proportion of times that an event occurs in the long run when conditions are stable.

Using the relative frequency of occurrence approach

This method uses the relative frequencies of past occurrences as probabilities. We determine how often something has happened in the past and use that figure to predict the probability that it will happen again in the future. Let us look at an example. Suppose an insurance company knows from past actuarial data that of all males 40 years old, about 60 out of every 100,000 will die within a one-year period. Using this method, the company estimates the probability of death for that age group as:

$$\frac{60}{100{,}000}, \text{ or } .0006$$

More trials, greater accuracy

A second characteristic of probabilities established by the relative frequency of occurrence method can be shown by tossing one of our fair coins 300 times. Figure 5-1 illustrates the outcomes of these 300 tosses. Here we can see that although the proportion of heads was far from .5 in the first 100 tosses, it seemed to stabilize and approach .5 as the number of tosses increased. In statistical language, we would say that the relative frequency becomes stable as the number of tosses becomes large (if we are tossing the coin under uniform conditions). Thus, when we use the relative frequency approach to establish probabilities, our probability figure will gain accuracy as we increase the number of observations. Of course, this improved accuracy is not free; although more tosses of our coin will produce a more accurate probability of heads occurring, we must bear both the time and the cost of additional observations.

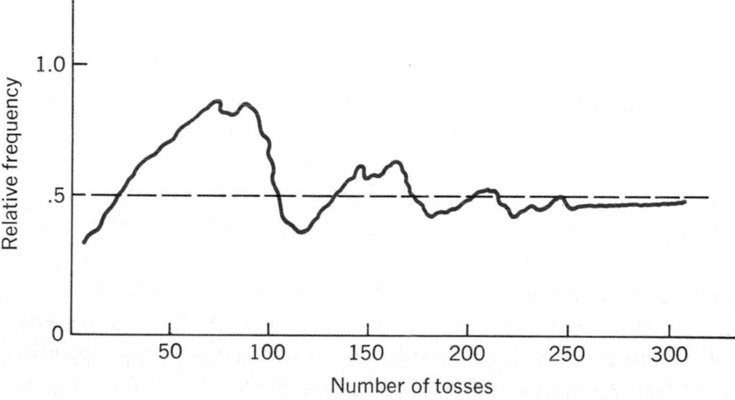

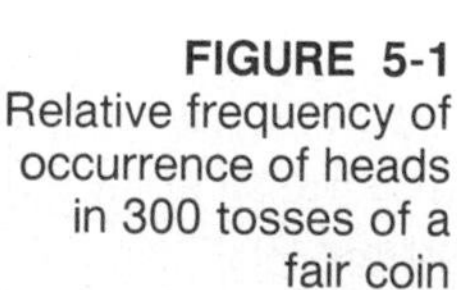
FIGURE 5-1 Relative frequency of occurrence of heads in 300 tosses of a fair coin

One difficulty with the relative frequency approach is that people often use it without evaluating a sufficient number of outcomes. If you heard someone say, "My aunt and uncle got the flu this year, and they are both over 65, so everyone in that age bracket will probably get the flu," you would know that your friend did not base his assumptions on enough evidence. He had insufficient data for establishing a relative frequency of occurrence probability.

But what about a different kind of estimate, one that seems not to be based on statistics at all? Suppose your school's basketball team lost the first ten games of the year. You were a loyal fan, however, and bet $100 that your team would beat Indiana's in the eleventh game. To everyone's surprise, you won your bet. We would have difficulty convincing you that you were statistically incorrect. And you would be right to be skeptical about our argument. Perhaps without knowing that you did so, you may have based your bet on the statistical foundation described in the next approach to establishing probabilities.

Subjective Probabilities

Subjective probability defined

Subjective probabilities are based on the beliefs of the person making the probability assessment. In fact, subjective probability can be defined as the probability assigned to an event by an individual, based on whatever evidence is available. This evidence may be in the form of relative frequency of past occurrences, or it may be just an educated guess. Probably the earliest subjective probability estimate of the likelihood of rain occurred when someone's Aunt Bess said, "My corns hurt; I think we're in for a downpour." Subjective assessments of probability permit the widest flexibility of the three concepts we have discussed. The decision maker can use whatever evidence is available and temper this with personal feelings about the situation.

Subjective probability assignments are frequently found when events occur only once or at most a very few times. Say that it is your job to interview and select a new social services caseworker. You have narrowed your choice to three people. Each has an attractive appearance, a high level of energy, abounding self-confidence, a record of past accomplishments, and a state of mind that seems to welcome challenges. What are the chances each will relate to clients successfully? Answering this question and choosing among the three will require you to assign a subjective probability to each person's potential.

Using the subjective approach

Here is one more illustration of this kind of probability assignment. A judge is deciding whether to allow the construction of a nuclear power plant on a site where there is some evidence of a geological fault. He must ask himself the question, "What is the probability of a major nuclear accident at this location?" The fact that there is no relative frequency of occurrence evidence of previous accidents at this location does not excuse him from making a decision. He must use his best judgment in trying to determine the subjective probabilities of a nuclear accident.

Since most higher level social and managerial decisions are concerned with specific, unique situations, rather than with a long series of identical situations, decision makers at this level make considerable use of subjective probabilities.

The subjective approach to assigning probabilities was introduced in 1926 by Frank Ramsey, in his book, *The Foundation of Mathematics and Other Logical Essays*. The concept was further developed by Bernard Koopman, Richard Good, and Leonard Savage, names that appear regularly in advanced work in this field. Professor Savage pointed out that two reasonable people faced with the same evidence could easily come up with quite different subjective probabilities for the same event. The two people who made opposing bets on the outcome of the Indiana basketball game would understand quite well what he meant.

EXERCISES

5-11 A purchasing agent for a trucking firm is considering changing the brand of tires he buys. To test two other brands, he purchases 25 of each, places them on randomly selected trucks, and measures miles to first recap. Below are the frequency distributions for the two tires:

MILES TO RECAP (THOUSANDS)	BRAND A	BRAND B
48–51	2	4
52–55	4	5
56–59	3	7
60–63	8	6
64–67	7	3
68–71	1	0
	25	**25**

a) What is the probability that a tire selected at random from the group of Brand B tires lasts between 52,000 and 56,000 miles?
b) What is the probability that a tire selected from the group of Brand A tires lasts between 60,000 and 64,000 miles?
c) Suppose we were to combine both brands into one group and form a new frequency distribution. What would be the probability of selecting a tire that lasts between 52,000 and 56,000 miles, based on this new distribution?
d) What type of probability estimates are these?

5-12 Determine the probabilities of the following events in drawing a card from a standard deck of 52:
a) A queen
b) A club
c) An ace in a red suit
d) A red card
e) A face card (king, queen, or jack)
f) What type of probability estimates are these?

5-13 Below is a frequency distribution of annual sales commission from a survey of 225 media salespeople. Based on this information, what is the probability that a media salesperson makes a commission:

a) between $8,000 and $12,000
b) less than $8,000
c) more than $24,000
d) between $12,000 and $16,000

ANNUAL COMMISSIONS	FREQUENCY
$ 0– 3,999	5
4,000– 7,999	15
8,000–11,999	40
12,000–15,999	90
16,000–19,999	30
20,000–23,999	25
24,000+	20

5-14 A marketing manager for a calculator manufacturer is trying to predict the demand for the new programmable calculator the company has introduced. He has limited his possible predictions to 200,000 or 250,000 or 300,000 or 350,000 or 400,000 units demanded. He feels unable to decide whether 300,000 or 350,000 units are more likely. But he feels that 350,000 units are twice as likely as 400,000 and that 300,000 units are four times as likely as 200,000 units. Finally, he thinks that 250,000 units are only half as likely as 350,000 units.

a) What are the probabilities of the five quantities being demanded, according to the marketing manager?
b) What has the marketing manager implicitly said concerning the probability of demand being greater than 400,000 or fewer than 200,000 units?

5-15 The office manager of an insurance company has the following data on the functioning of the copiers in the office:

COPIER NUMBER	DAYS FUNCTIONING	DAYS OUT OF SERVICE
1	244	16
2	252	8
3	237	23
4	208	52
5	254	6

What is the probability of a copier's being out of service on a given day?

5-16 Classify the following probability estimates as to their type (classical, relative frequency, or subjective):

a) The probability that you will make a B in this course is .75.
b) The probability that a randomly selected family from a particular community has two children is .25.
c) The probability that my candidate will win the election is .60.
d) The probability that a student from this high school will go on to college is .90.
e) The probability of my ticket's winning a raffle drawing for which 1,000 tickets were sold is .001.

5-4 PROBABILITY RULES

Most managers who use probabilities are concerned with two conditions:

1. The case where one event *or* another will occur
2. The situation where two or more events will *both* occur

We are interested in the first case when we ask, "What is the probability that today's demand will exceed our inventory?" To illustrate the second situation, we could ask, "What is the probability that today's demand will exceed our inventory *and* that more than 10 percent of our sales force will not report for work?" In the sections to follow, we shall illustrate methods of determining answers to questions like these under a variety of conditions.

Some Commonly Used Symbols, Definitions, and Rules

SYMBOL FOR A MARGINAL PROBABILITY. In probability theory, we use symbols to simplify the presentation of ideas. As we discussed earlier in this chapter, the probability of the event *A* would be expressed as:

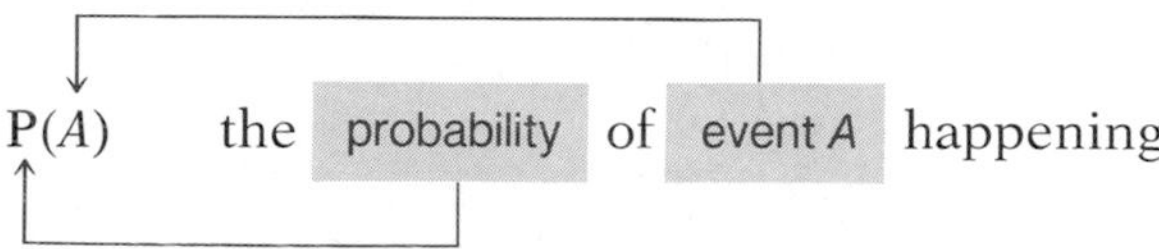

Marginal or unconditional probability

A *single* probability means that only one event can take place. It is called a *marginal* or *unconditional probability*. To illustrate, let us suppose that 50 members of a school class drew tickets to see which student would get a free trip to the National Rock Festival. Any one of the students could calculate his or her chances of winning by the formulation:

$$
\begin{aligned}
\text{P(Winning)} &= \frac{1}{50} \\
&= .02
\end{aligned}
$$

In this case, a student's chance is one in 50, because we are certain that the possible events are mutually exclusive; that is, only one student can win at a time.

There is a nice diagrammatic way to illustrate this example and other probability concepts. We use a pictorial representation called a *Venn diagram,* after the nineteenth-century English mathematician, John Venn. In these diagrams, the entire sample space is represented by a rectangle, and events are represented by parts of the rectangle. If two events *are* mutually exclusive, their parts of the rectangle will not overlap each other, as shown in Fig. 5-2(a). If two events are *not* mutually exclusive, their parts of the rectangle *will* overlap, as in Fig. 5-2(b).

Venn diagrams

Since probabilities behave a lot like areas, we shall let the rectangle have an area of 1 (because the probability of *something* happening is 1). Then the probability of an event is the area of *its* part of the rectangle. Figure 5-2(c) illustrates this for the National Rock Festival example. There the rectangle is divided into 50 equal, nonoverlapping parts.

FIGURE 5-2 Some Venn diagrams

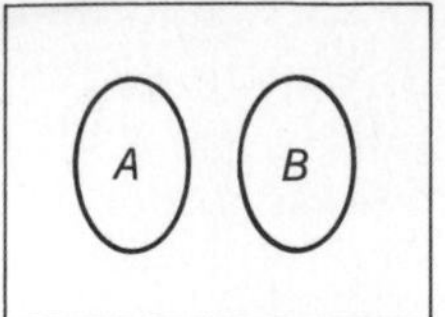

Two mutually exclusive events

(a)

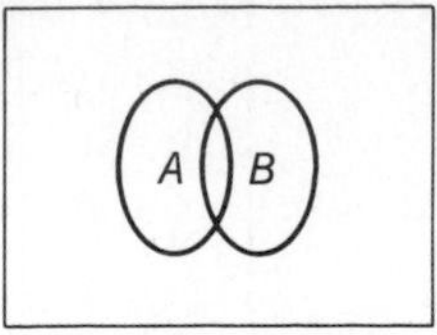

Two nonmutually exclusive events

(b)

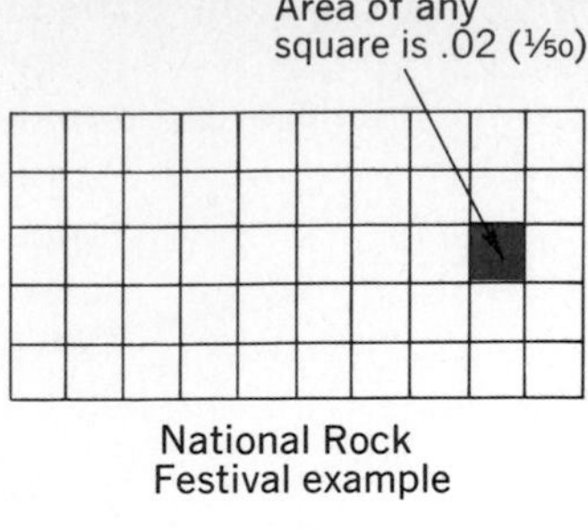

National Rock Festival example

(c)

Probability of one or more mutually exclusive events

ADDITION RULE FOR MUTUALLY EXCLUSIVE EVENTS. Often, however, we are interested in the probability that one thing *or* another will occur. If these two events are mutually exclusive, we can express this probability using the addition rule for mutually exclusive events. This rule is expressed symbolically as:

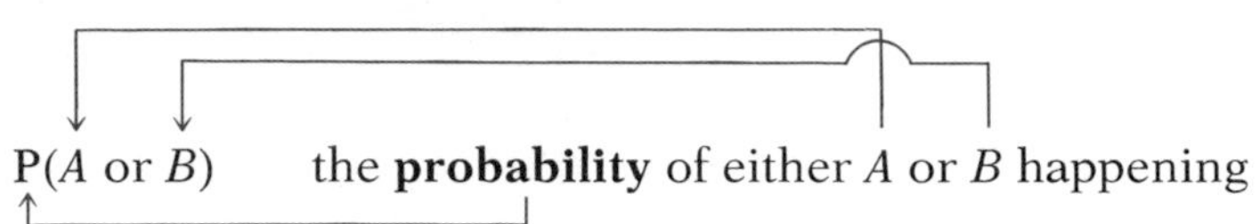

and is calculated as follows:

$$P(A \text{ or } B) = P(A) + P(B) \qquad \textbf{[5-2]}$$

This addition rule is illustrated by the Venn diagram in Fig. 5-3, where we note that the area in the two circles together (denoting the event *A or B*) is the sum of the areas of the two circles.

FIGURE 5-3 Venn diagram for the addition rule for mutually exclusive events

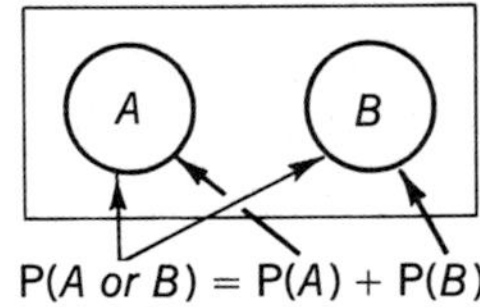

Now to use this formula in an example. Five equally capable students are waiting for a summer job interview with a company that has announced that it will hire only one of five by random drawing. The group consists of Bill, Helen, John, Sally, and Walter. If our question is, "What is the probability that John will be the candidate?" we can use Equation 5-1 and give the answer:

$$P(\text{John}) = \frac{1}{5}$$
$$= .2$$

If, however, we ask, "What is the probability that either John *or* Sally will be the candidate?" we would use Equation 5-2:

$$\begin{aligned} P(\text{John or Sally}) &= P(\text{John}) + P(\text{Sally}) \\ &= \frac{1}{5} + \frac{1}{5} \\ &= \frac{2}{5} \\ &= .4 \end{aligned}$$

Let's calculate the probability of two or more events happening once more. Table 5-1 contains data on the size of families in a certain town. We are interested in the question, "What is the probability that a family chosen at random from this town will have four or more children (that is, four, five, six or more children)?" Using Equation 5-2, we can calculate the answer as:

$$\begin{aligned} P(4, 5, 6 \text{ or more}) &= P(4) + P(5) + P(6 \text{ or more}) \\ &= .15 + .10 + .05 \\ &= .30 \end{aligned}$$

TABLE 5-1 Family-size data

Number of children	0	1	2	3	4	5	6 or more
Proportion of families having this many children	.05	.10	.30	.25	.15	.10	.05

A special case of Equation 5-2

There is an important special case of Equation 5-2. For any event A, either A happens or it doesn't. So the events A and *not* A are exclusive and exhaustive. Applying Equation 5-2 yields the result:

$$P(A) + P(not\ A) = 1$$

or equivalently:

$$P(A) = 1 - P(not\ A)$$

For example, referring back to Table 5-1, the probability of a family's having five or fewer children is most easily obtained by subtracting from 1 the probability of the family's having six or more children, and thus is seen to be .95.

Probability of one or more events *not* mutually exclusive

ADDITION RULE FOR EVENTS THAT ARE NOT MUTUALLY EXCLUSIVE. If two events are not mutually exclusive, it is possible for both events to occur. In these cases, our addition rule must be modified. For example, what is the probability of drawing either an ace *or* a heart from a deck of cards? Obviously, the events ace and heart can occur together because we could draw the ace of hearts. Thus, ace and heart are not mutually exclusive events. We must adjust our Equation 5-2 to avoid double counting; that is, we have to *reduce* the probability of drawing either an ace or a heart *by the chance* that we could draw both of them together. As a result, the correct equation for the probability of one or more of two events that are not mutually exclusive is:

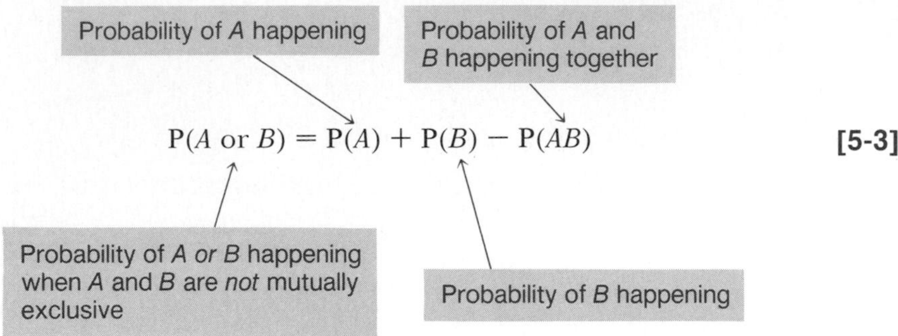

$$P(A \text{ or } B) = P(A) + P(B) - P(AB) \qquad [5\text{-}3]$$

A Venn diagram illustrating Equation 5-3 is given in Fig. 5-4. There, the event *A or B* is outlined with a heavy line. The event *A and B* is the cross-hatched wedge in the middle. If we add the areas of circles *A* and *B*, we *double count* the area of the wedge, and so we must subtract it, to make sure it is counted only once.

A B

A or B A and B

FIGURE 5-4
Venn diagram for the addition rule for two events not mutually exclusive

Using Equation 5-3 to determine the probability of drawing either an ace *or* a heart, we can calculate:

$$\begin{aligned} P(\text{Ace or Heart}) &= P(\text{Ace}) + P(\text{Heart}) - P(\text{Ace and Heart}) \\ &= \frac{4}{52} + \frac{13}{52} - \frac{1}{52} \\ &= \frac{16}{52} \text{ or } \frac{4}{13} \end{aligned}$$

Let's do a second example. The employees of a certain company have elected five of their number to represent them on the employee–management productivity council. Profiles of the five are as follows:

1. male	age 30
2. male	32
3. female	45
4. female	20
5. male	40

This group decides to elect a spokesperson by drawing a name from a hat. Our question is, "What is the probability the spokesperson will be *either* female *or* over 35?" Using Equation 5-3, we can set up the solution to our question like this:

$$\begin{aligned} P(\text{Female or Over 35}) &= P(\text{Female}) + P(\text{Over 35}) - P(\text{Female and Over 35}) \\ &= \frac{2}{5} + \frac{2}{5} - \frac{1}{5} \\ &= \frac{3}{5} \end{aligned}$$

We can check our work by inspection and see that, of the five people in the group, three would fit the requirements of being either female or over 35.

EXERCISES

From the Venn diagrams below, which indicate the number of outcomes of an experiment corresponding to each event and the number of outcomes that do not correspond to either event, give the probabilities indicated:

5-17 Total outcomes = 60

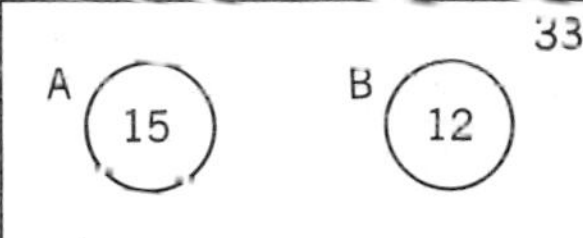

$P(A) =$
$P(B) =$
$P(A \text{ or } B) =$

5-18 Total outcomes = 50

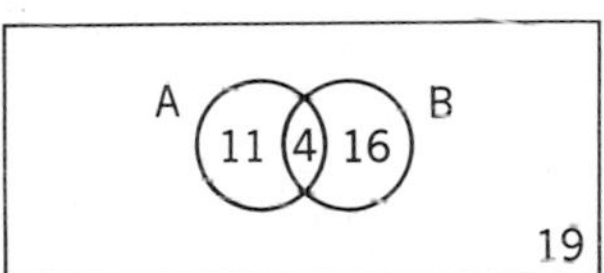

$P(A) =$
$P(B) =$
$P(A \text{ or } B) =$

5-19 An urn contains 60 marbles: 40 are blue, and 15 of these blue marbles are swirled. The rest of the marbles are red, and 10 of the red ones are swirled. The marbles that are not swirled are clear. What is the probability of drawing:

a) A red marble from the urn?
b) A clear marble from the urn?
c) A red, swirled marble?
d) A blue, clear marble?
e) A swirled marble?

5-20 As the safety officer of an airline, Debbie Best has been asked to give a talk to the press concerning engine safety. As part of her talk, she has decided to include the probability of a two-engine jet having engine failure on a flight. After consulting her records, she finds the following information about last year's operating record for two-engine aircraft:

> Twenty-nine reported failure of the right engine alone.
> Thirty-three reported failure of the left engine alone.
> There was one crash attributed to double engine failure.
> There were 345,000 flights during the year.

What probability should she report to the press?

5-21 Mary Harper, member of a women's activist group, feels that the Equal Rights Amendment will pass within the next three years in six states if one of two things happens: (1) enough pro-ERA candidates are elected to office (and none of its current supporters voted out of office), or (2) the lobby in each state can change the minds of a certain number of current congressmen who are nonsupporters. The following estimates are available to her:

State	1	2	3	4	5	6
Probability of electing enough pro-ERA congressmen	.025	.10	.15	.15	.05	.025
Probability of changing minds of current nonsupporters	.005	.02	.075	.10	.15	.15

Ms. Harper also believes that there is no chance that both these events will happen within three years in any of the states. In which state is the ERA most likely to be passed in the next three years, given these probability estimates?

5-22 The manager of a chemical plant located on the Mississippi River knows that in an upcoming court case the company may be found guilty of polluting the river. Further, he knows that if found guilty, the company will be required to install a water purification system, pay a fine, or both. Thus far, only 10 percent of the companies involved in similar cases have been both fined and required to install the purification system. In addition, when the court's ruling has not involved both penalties, a company has been 3 times more likely to be fined than to be required to install the purification system. If 28 percent of the companies have been found guilty thus far, what is the probability that this company will be required to install a purification system?

5-23 In this section, two expressions were developed for the probability of either of two events, *A* or *B*, occurring. Referring to Equations 5-2 and 5-3:

a) What can you say about the probability of *A* and *B* occurring simultaneously when *A* and *B* are *mutually exclusive?*
b) Develop an expression for the probability that at least one of three events, *A, B,* or *C*, could occur; i.e., P(*A* or *B* or *C*). Do *not* assume that *A, B,* and *C* are mutually exclusive of each other.
c) Rewrite your expression for the case in which *A* and *B* are mutually exclusive, but *A* and *C* and *B* and *C* are not mutually exclusive.
d) Rewrite your expression for the case in which *A* and *B* and *A* and *C* are mutually exclusive, but not *B* and *C*.
e) Rewrite your expression for the case in which *A, B,* and *C* are mutually exclusive of the others.

5-5 PROBABILITIES UNDER CONDITIONS OF STATISTICAL INDEPENDENCE

Independence defined

When two events happen, the outcome of the first event may or may not have an effect on the outcome of the second event. That is, the events may be either dependent or independent. In this section, we examine events that are *statistically independent:* The occurrence of one event *has no effect* on the probability of the occurrence of any other event. There are three types of probabilities under statistical independence:

1. Marginal
2. Joint
3. Conditional

Marginal Probabilities Under Statistical Independence

Marginal probability of independent events

As we explained previously, a marginal or unconditional probability is the simple probability of the occurrence of an event. In a fair coin toss, $P(H) = .5$, and $P(T) = .5$; that is, the probability of heads equals .5, and the probability of tails equals .5. This is true for every toss, no matter how many tosses have been made or what their outcomes have been. Every toss stands alone and is in no way connected with any other toss. Thus the outcome of *each* toss of a fair coin is a statistically independent event.

Imagine that we have a biased or unfair coin that has been altered in such a way that heads occurs .90 of the time and tails .10 of the time. On each individual toss, $P(H) = .90$, and $P(T) = .10$. The outcome of any particular toss is completely unrelated to the outcomes of the tosses that may precede or follow it. The outcome of each toss of *this* coin is a statistically independent event, too, even though the coin is biased.

Joint Probabilities Under Statistical Independence

Multiplication rule for joint, independent events

The probability of two or more independent events occurring together or in succession is the product of their marginal probabilities. Mathematically, this is stated:

$$P(AB) = P(A) \times P(B) \qquad \textbf{[5-4]}$$

where:

- $P(AB)$ = probability of events A and B occurring together or in succession; this is known as a *joint probability*
- $P(A)$ = marginal probability of event A occurring
- $P(B)$ = marginal probability of event B occurring

In terms of the fair coin example, the probability of heads on two successive tosses is the probability of heads on the first toss (which we shall call H_1) times the probability of heads on the second toss (H_2). That is, $P(H_1H_2) = P(H_1) \times P(H_2)$. We have shown that the events are statistically independent, because the probability of any outcome is not affected by any preceding outcome. Therefore, the probability of heads on any toss is .5, and $P(H_1H_2) = .5 \times .5 = .25$. Thus, the probability of heads on two successive tosses is .25.

Likewise, the probability of getting three heads on three successive tosses is $P(H_1H_2H_3) = .5 \times .5 \times .5 = .125$.

Assume next that we are going to toss an unfair coin that has $P(H) = .8$ and $P(T) = .2$. The events (outcomes) are independent, because the probabilities of all tosses are exactly the same—the individual tosses are completely separate and in no way affected by any other toss or outcome. Suppose our question is, "What is the probability of getting three heads on three successive tosses?" We use Equation 5-4 and discover that:

$$P(H_1H_2H_3) = P(H_1) \times P(H_2) \times P(H_3) = .8 \times .8 \times .8 = .512$$

Now let us ask the probability of getting three tails on three successive tosses:

$$P(T_1T_2T_3) = P(T_1) \times P(T_2) \times P(T_3) = .2 \times .2 \times .2 = .008$$

Note that these two probabilities do not add up to 1 because the events $H_1H_2H_3$ and $T_1T_2T_3$ do not constitute a collectively exhaustive list. They *are* mutually exclusive, because if one occurs, the other cannot.

Using a probability tree

We can make the probabilities of events even more explicit using a *probability tree*. Figure 5-5 is a probability tree showing the possible outcomes and their respective probabilities for one toss of a fair coin.

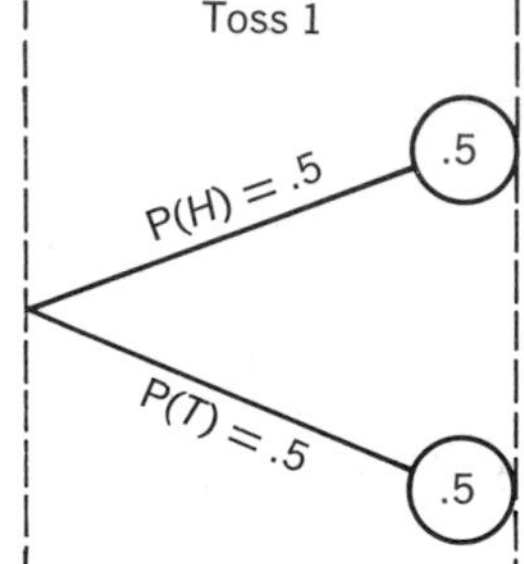

FIGURE 5-5 Probability tree of one toss

One toss, two possible outcomes

For toss 1 we have two possible outcomes, heads and tails, each with a probability of .5. Assume that the outcome of toss 1 is heads. We toss again. The second toss has two possible outcomes, heads and tails, each with a probability of .5. In Fig. 5-6 we add these two branches of the tree.

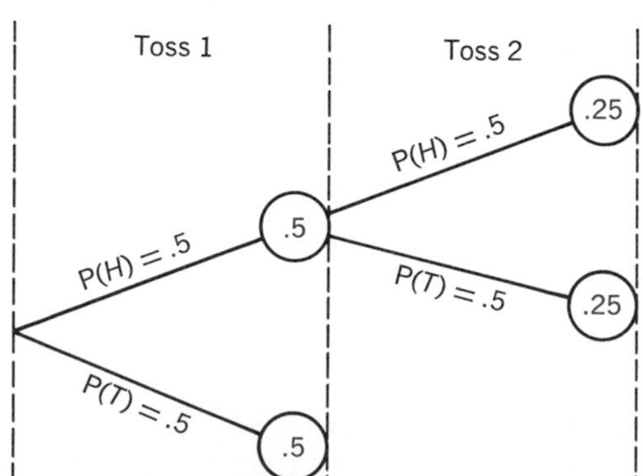

FIGURE 5-6 Probability tree of partial second toss

Two tosses, four possible outcomes

Next we consider the possibility that the outcome of toss 1 is tails. Then the second toss must stem from the second branch representing toss 1. Thus in Fig. 5-7, we add two more branches to the tree. Notice that on two tosses, we have four possible outcomes: H_1H_2, H_1T_2, T_1H_2, and T_1T_2 (remember that the subscripts indicate the toss number and that T_2, for example, means tails on toss 2). Thus, after two tosses, we may arrive at any one of four possible points. Since we are going to toss three times, we must add more branches to the tree.

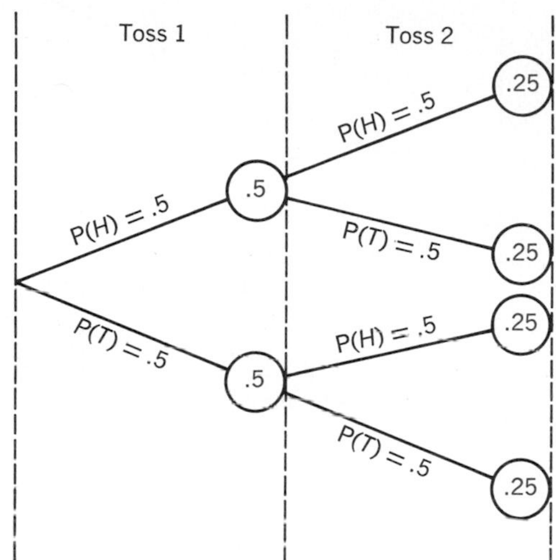

FIGURE 5-7 Probability tree of two tosses

Three tosses, eight possible outcomes

Assuming that we have had heads on the first two tosses, we are now ready to begin adding branches for the third toss. As before, the two possible outcomes are heads and tails, each with a probability of .5. The first step is shown in Fig. 5-8. The additional branches are added in exactly the same

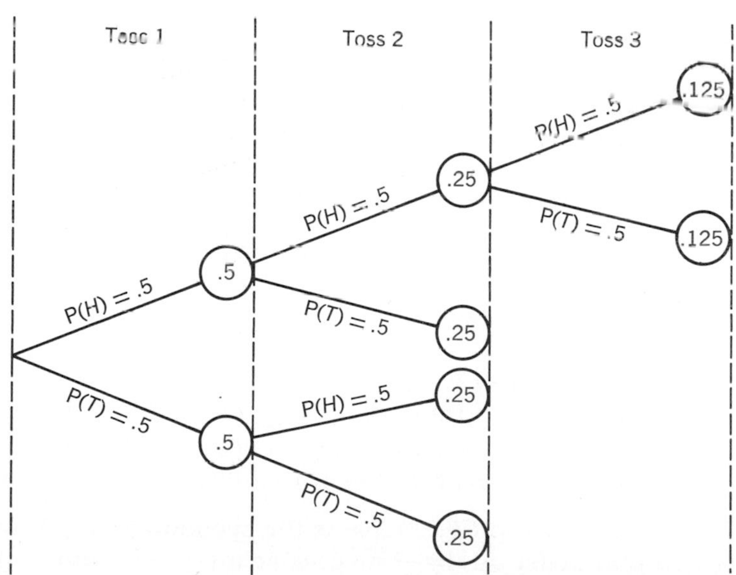

FIGURE 5-8 Probability tree of partial third toss

All tosses are independent

manner. The completed probability tree is shown in Fig. 5-9. Notice that both heads and tails have a probability of .5 of occurring no matter how far from the origin (first toss) any particular toss may be. **This follows from our definition of independence: No event is affected by the events preceding or following it.**

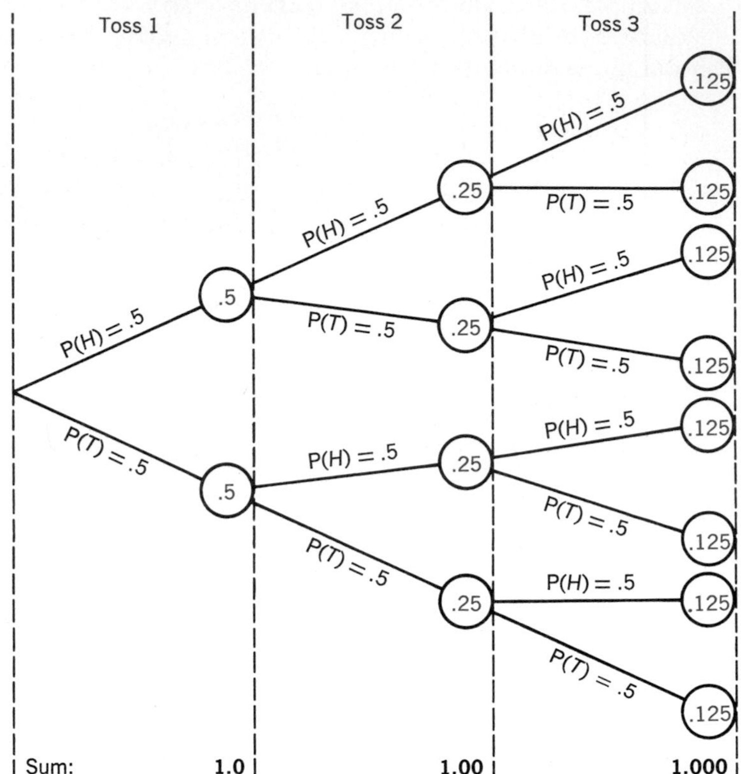

FIGURE 5-9 Completed probability tree

Suppose we are going to toss a fair coin and want to know the probability that all three tosses will result in heads. Expressing the problem symbolically, we want to know $P(H_1H_2H_3)$. From the mathematical definition of the joint probability of independent events, we know that:

$$P(H_1H_2H_3) = P(H_1) \times P(H_2) \times P(H_3) = .5 \times .5 \times .5 = .125$$

We could have read this answer from the probability tree in Fig. 5-9 by following the branches giving $H_1H_2H_3$.

Try solving these problems using the probability tree in Fig. 5-9:

◆ **EXAMPLE 1: What is the probability of getting tails, heads, tails *in that order* on three successive tosses of a fair coin?**

◆ **SOLUTION: $P(T_1H_2T_3) = P(T_1) \times P(H_2) \times P(T_3) = .125$. Following the prescribed path on the probability tree will give us the same answer.**

◆ **EXAMPLE 2: What is the probability of getting tails, tails, heads *in that order* on three successive tosses of a fair coin?**

◆ **SOLUTION:** If we follow the branches giving tails on the first toss, tails on the second toss, and heads on the third toss, we arrive at the probability of .125. Thus, $P(T_1T_2H_3) = .125$.

It is important to notice that the probability of arriving at a given point by a given route is *not* the same as the probability of, say, heads on the third toss. $P(H_1T_2H_3) = .125$, but $P(H_3) = .5$. The first is a case of *joint probability;* that is, the probability of getting heads on the first toss, tails on the second, and heads on the third. The latter, by contrast, is simply the *marginal probability* of getting heads on a particular toss, in this instance toss 3.

Notice that the sum of the probabilities of all the possible outcomes for each toss is 1. This results from the fact that we have mutually exclusive and collectively exhaustive lists of outcomes. These are given in Table 5-2.

TABLE 5-2 Lists of outcomes

1 TOSS		2 TOSSES		3 TOSSES	
Possible outcomes	Probability	Possible outcomes	Probability	Possible outcomes	Probability
H_1	.5	H_1H_2	.25	$H_1H_2H_3$	.125
T_1	.5	H_1T_2	.25	$H_1H_2T_3$	.125
	1.0	T_1H_2	.25	$H_1T_2H_3$	.125
		T_1T_2	.25	$H_1T_2T_3$	.125
			1.00	$T_1H_2H_3$	.125
				$T_1H_2T_3$	.125
				$T_1T_2H_3$	.125
				$T_1T_2T_3$	.125
					1.000

◆ **EXAMPLE 3:** What is the probability of *at least* two heads on three tosses?

◆ **SOLUTION:** Recalling that the probabilities of mutually exclusive events are additive, we can note the possible ways that at least two heads on three tosses can occur, and we can sum their individual probabilities. The outcomes satisfying the requirement are $H_1H_2H_3$, $H_1H_2T_3$, $H_1T_2H_3$, and $T_1H_2H_3$. Since each of these has an individual probability of .125, the sum is .5. Thus the probability of at least two heads on three tosses is .5.

◆ **EXAMPLE 4:** What is the probability of *at least* one tail on three tosses?

◆ **SOLUTION:** There is only one case in which no tails occur, namely, $H_1H_2H_3$. Therefore we can simply subtract for the answer:

$$1 - P(H_1H_2H_3) = 1 - .125 = .875$$

The probability of at least one tail occurring in three successive tosses is .875.

◆ **EXAMPLE 5: What is the probability of *at least* one head on two tosses?**

◆ **SOLUTION: The possible ways a head may occur are H_1H_2, H_1T_2, T_1H_2. Each of these has a probability of .25. Therefore, the probability of at least one head on two tosses is .75. Alternatively, we could consider the case in which no head occurs—namely, T_1T_2—and subtract its probability from 1; that is:**

$$1 - P(T_1T_2) = 1 - .25 = .75$$

Conditional Probabilities Under Statistical Independence

Conditional probability

Thus far we have considered two types of probabilities, marginal (or unconditional) probability and joint probability. Symbolically, marginal probability is P(A) and joint probability is P(AB). Besides these two, there is one other type of probability, known as *conditional* probability. Symbolically, conditional probability is written:

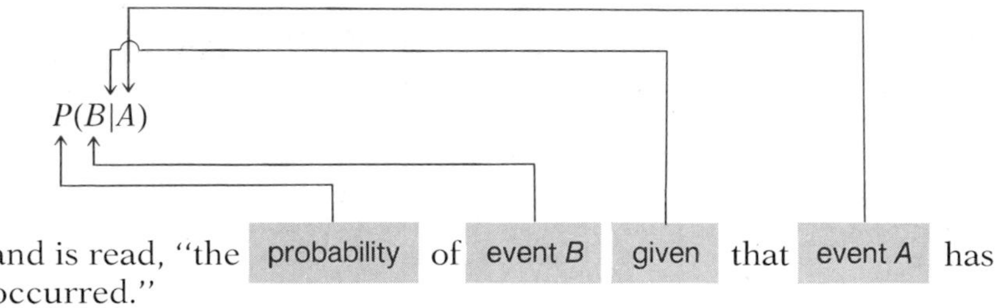

and is read, "the probability of event B given that event A has occurred."

Conditional probability is the probability that a second event (B) will occur *if* a first event (A) has already happened.

Conditional probability of independent events

For statistically independent events, the conditional probability of event B given that event A has occurred is simply the probability of event B:

$$P(B|A) = P(B) \qquad \textbf{[5-5]}$$

At first glance, this may seem contradictory. Remember, however, that by definition, independent events are those whose probabilities are in no way affected by the occurrence of each other. In fact, statistical independence is defined symbolically as the condition in which $P(B|A) = P(B)$.

We can understand conditional probability better by solving an illustrative problem. Our question is, "What is the probability that the second toss of a fair coin will result in heads, given that heads resulted on the first toss? Symbolically, this is written as $P(H_2|H_1)$. Remember that for two independent events, the results of the first toss have absolutely no effect on the results of the second toss. Since the probabilities of heads and tails are identical for every toss, the probability of heads on the second toss is .5. Thus, we must say that $P(H_2|H_1) = .5$.

Table 5-3 summarizes the three types of probabilities and their mathematical formulas under conditions of statistical independence.

TABLE 5-3 Probabilities under statistical independence

TYPE OF PROBABILITY	SYMBOL	FORMULA
Marginal	$P(A)$	$P(A)$
Joint	$P(AB)$	$P(A) \times P(B)$
Conditional	$P(B\|A)$	$P(B)$

EXERCISES

5-24 What is the probability that a couple's second child will be:

a) A boy, given that their first child was a girl?

b) A girl, given that their first child was a girl?

5-25 In rolling two dice, what is the probability of rolling:

a) A total of 7 on the first roll, followed by a total of 5 on the second roll and another total of 5 on the third roll?

b) Three sets of doubles in three rolls?

c) Two sets of doubles in two rolls?

5-26 What is the probability that, in selecting two cards, one at a time, from a deck with replacement, the second card is:

a) A spade, given that the first card was a heart?

b) Black, given that the first card was red?

c) A queen, given that the first card was a queen?

5-27 Use a probability tree to answer the following questions. Assuming A, B, and C are independent events with marginal probabilities $P(A) = .2$, $P(B) = .5$, $P(C) = .3$, and that the subscripts represent trial numbers, find:

a) $P(A_1B_2C_3)$ b) $P(C_1C_2C_3)$ c) $P(A_1C_2B_3C_4)$ d) $P(A_1B_2)$ e) $P(B_1B_2)$

5-28 Sue Martin, quality control manager of Gibson Electric, questions the reliability of the two quality control checks in the food-processor manufacturing process. One check is performed by a worker who manually checks the processors, and a second check is performed by a computer monitor. Sue knows that 5 percent of the time the worker is apt to miss a defective processor and that 2 percent of the time the computer will malfunction and fail to detect defective processors.

a) If Martin finds that the computer was malfunctioning, what is the probability that the worker will have missed a defective processor?

b) If she knows that the worker missed a defective processor, what is the probability that she will find the computer had malfunctioned?

c) What is the probability that the worker will miss a defective processor and the computer will malfunction at the same time, allowing a defective processor to leave manufacturing?

5-29 A social psychologist plans to use two current topics of interest—abortion and support for nuclear power plants—in a proposed study of attitude changes. He knows from a questionnaire completed at the beginning of the experiment that 35 percent of the subjects favor the construction of nuclear power plants and 50 percent are in favor of federally subsidized abortions. He also knows that individual support for one issue is independent of support for the other issue.

a) What is the probability that a subject supports both federally funded abortions and the construction of nuclear power plants?
b) What is the probability that a person supports federally funded abortions or nuclear power plants, but not both?

5-30 Al Wright, a pollster for the Republican party in Colorado, has just issued some opinions based on the results of his latest statewide poll. According to Al, the probability of either the Republicans increasing their control of the state legislature in the next election or the economy improving significantly by November is .75. The probability of the economy improving significantly by November is .55. The probability that the Republicans will increase their control of the state legislature in the next election *and* that the economy will improve significantly by November is .4. Assuming that Al's estimates are correct, what is the probability that the Republicans will increase their control of the state legislature in the next election?

5-31 Sol O'Tarry, a prison guard, has been reviewing prison records on attempted escapes by inmates. He has data covering the last 40 years that the prison has been open, arranged by seasons. The data are summarized in the table below.

ATTEMPTED ESCAPES	WINTER	SPRING	SUMMER	FALL
1– 5	18	12	7	6
6–10	10	15	8	19
11–15	6	10	5	10
16–20	4	1	13	5
21–25	2	1	4	0
26–30	0	1	3	0
	40	**40**	**40**	**40**

a) What is the probability that in a year selected at random, the number of attempted escapes was between 11 and 15 during the winter?
b) What is the probability that more than 15 escapes were attempted during a randomly chosen summer season?
c) What is the probability that more than 5 but fewer than 21 escapes will be attempted during a randomly chosen fall season?
d) If all the data are grouped together, what is the probability that between 1 and 5 escapes would be attempted during a randomly chosen season?

5-32 Bill Borde, top advertising executive for the ad agency Grapevine Concepts, has just launched a publicity campaign for a new restaurant in town, The Black Angus. Bill has just installed three billboards on a highway outside of town, and he knows from experience the probabilities that each will be noticed by a randomly chosen motorist. The probability of the first billboard's being noticed by a motorist is .8. The probability of the second's being noticed is .7, and the third has a .9 probability of being noticed. Assuming that the event that a motorist notices any particular billboard is independent of whether or not he notices the others, answer the following questions for Bill:

a) What is the probability that all three billboards will be noticed by a randomly chosen motorist?
b) What is the probability that the first and third billboards are noticed, but not the second billboard?
c) What is the probability that none of the billboards are noticed?
d) What is the probability that at least one billboard is noticed?
e) What is the probability that the first two billboards are noticed?

5-6 PROBABILITIES UNDER CONDITIONS OF STATISTICAL DEPENDENCE

Dependence defined

Statistical dependence exists when the probability of some event is dependent upon or affected by the occurrence of some other event. Just as with independent events, the types of probabilities under statistical dependence are:

1. Conditional
2. Joint
3. Marginal

Conditional Probabilities Under Statistical Dependence

Conditional and joint probabilities under statistical dependence are more involved than marginal probabilities are. We shall discuss conditional probabilities first, because the concept of joint probabilities is best illustrated by using conditional probabilities as a basis.

Examples of conditional probability of dependent events

Assume that we have one box containing ten balls distributed as follows:

- 3 are colored and dotted
- 1 is colored and striped
- 2 are gray and dotted
- 4 are gray and striped

The probability of drawing any one ball from this box is .1, since there are ten balls, each with equal probability of being drawn. The discussion of the following examples will be facilitated by reference to Table 5-4 and to Fig. 5-10, which shows the contents of the box in diagram form.

TABLE 5-4 Color and configuration of 10 balls

Event	Probability of event	
1	.1	colored and dotted
2	.1	
3	.1	
4	.1	colored and striped
5	.1	gray and dotted
6	.1	
7	.1	gray and striped
8	.1	
9	.1	
10	.1	

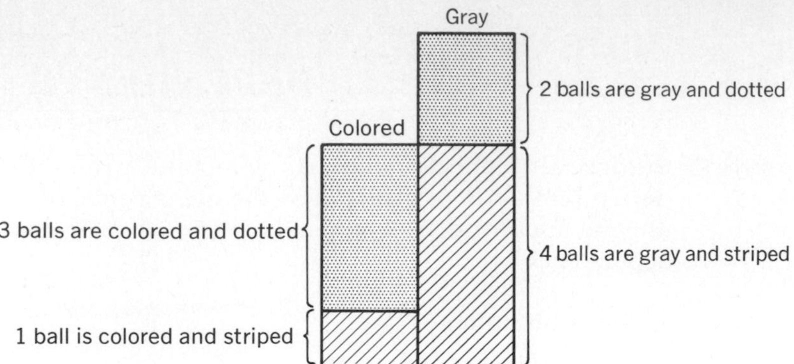
Gray
2 balls are gray and dotted
Colored
3 balls are colored and dotted
4 balls are gray and striped
1 ball is colored and striped

FIGURE 5-10
Contents of the box

◆ **EXAMPLE 1: Suppose someone draws a colored ball from the box. What is the probability that it is dotted? What is the probability it is striped?**

◆ **SOLUTION: This question can be expressed symbolically as $P(D|C)$, or, "What is the conditional probability that this ball is dotted, *given* that it is colored?"**

We have been told that the ball that was drawn is colored. Therefore, to calculate the probability that the ball is dotted, we will ignore *all* the gray balls and concern ourselves with colored only. In diagram form, we consider only what is shown in Fig. 5-11.

From the statement of the problem, we know that there are four colored balls, three of which are dotted and one of which is striped. Our problem is now to find the simple probabilities of dotted and striped. To do so, we divide the number of balls in each category by the total number of colored balls:

$$P(D|C) = \frac{3}{4} = .75$$

$$P(S|C) = \frac{1}{4} = \underline{.25}$$

$$1.00$$

In other words, three-fourths of the colored balls are dotted, and one-fourth of the colored balls are striped. Thus, the probability of dotted, given that the ball is colored, is .75. Likewise, the probability of striped, given that the ball is colored, is .25.

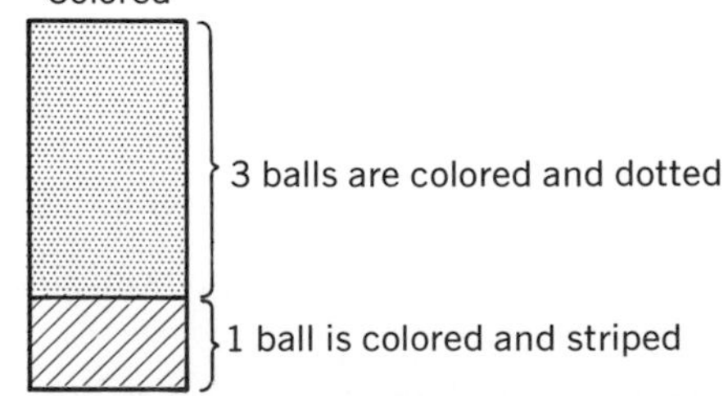
Colored
3 balls are colored and dotted
1 ball is colored and striped

FIGURE 5-11
Probability of dotted and striped, given colored

Now we can see how our reasoning will enable us to develop the formula for conditional probability under statistical dependence. We can first assure ourselves that these events *are* statistically dependent by observing that the color of the balls determines the probabilities that they are either striped or dotted. For example, a gray ball is more likely to be striped than a colored ball is. Since color affects the probability of striped or dotted, these two events are dependent.

Formula for conditional probability of dependent events

To calculate the probability of dotted given colored, $P(D|C)$, we divided the probability of colored and dotted balls (3 out of 10, or .3) by the probability of colored balls (4 out of 10, or .4):

$$P(D|C) = \frac{P(DC)}{P(C)}$$

Expressed as a general formula using the letters A and B to represent the two events, the equation is:

$$P(B|A) = \frac{P(BA)}{P(A)} \qquad [5\text{-}6]$$

This is the formula for *conditional probability under statistical dependence.*

◆ EXAMPLE 2: Continuing with our example of the colored and gray balls, let's answer the question, "What is $P(D|G)$?" and, "What is $P(S|G)$?"

◆ SOLUTION:

$$P(D|G) = \frac{P(DG)}{P(G)} = \frac{.2}{.6} = \frac{1}{3}$$

$$P(S|G) = \frac{P(SG)}{P(G)} = \frac{.4}{.6} = \frac{2}{3}$$

$$\overline{1.0}$$

The problem is shown diagrammatically in Fig. 5-12.

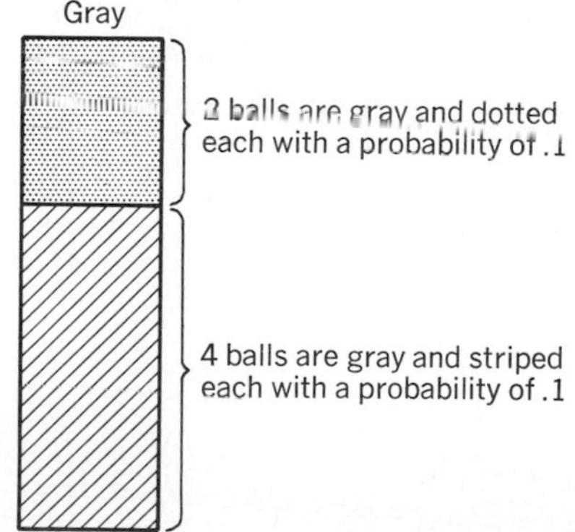
Gray
2 balls are gray and dotted each with a probability of .1
4 balls are gray and striped each with a probability of .1

FIGURE 5-12 Probability of dotted and striped, given gray

The total probability of gray is .6, (6 out of 10 balls). To determine the probability that the ball (which we know is gray) will be dotted, we divide the probability of gray and dotted (.2) by the probability of gray (.6), or .2/.6 = 1/3. Similarly, to determine the probability that the ball will be striped, we divide the probability of gray and striped (.4) by the probability of gray (.6), or .4/.6 = 2/3.

◆ **EXAMPLE 3:** Calculate $P(G|D)$ and $P(C|D)$.

◆ **SOLUTION:** Figure 5-13 shows the contents of the box arranged according to the striped or dotted markings on the balls. Since we have been told that the ball that was drawn is dotted, we can disregard striped and consider only dotted.

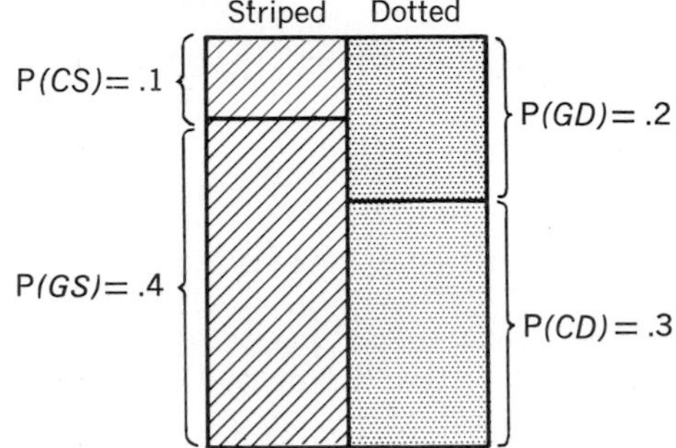

FIGURE 5-13 Contents of the box arranged by configuration, striped and dotted

Now see Figure 5-14, showing the probabilities of colored and gray, given dotted. Notice that the relative proportions of the two are as

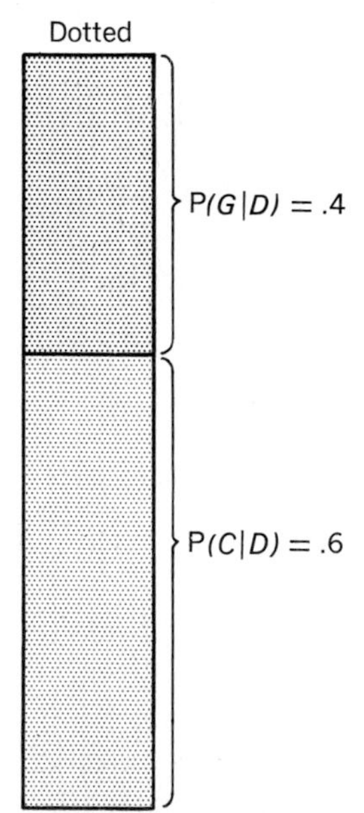

FIGURE 5-14 Probability of colored and gray, given dotted

.4 is to .6. The calculations used to arrive at these proportions were:

$$\mathbf{P}(G|D) = \frac{\mathbf{P}(GD)}{\mathbf{P}(D)} = \frac{.2}{.5} = .4$$

$$\mathbf{P}(C|D) = \frac{\mathbf{P}(CD)}{\mathbf{P}(D)} = \frac{.3}{.5} = \underline{.6}$$

$$1.0$$

- **EXAMPLE 4: Calculate P($C|S$) and P($G|S$).**
- **SOLUTION:**

$$\mathbf{P}(C|S) = \frac{\mathbf{P}(CS)}{\mathbf{P}(S)} = \frac{.1}{.5} = .2$$

$$\mathbf{P}(G|S) = \frac{\mathbf{P}(GS)}{\mathbf{P}(S)} = \frac{.4}{.5} = \underline{.8}$$

$$1.0$$

Joint Probabilities Under Statistical Dependence

We have shown that the formula for conditional probability under conditions of statistical dependence is:

$$\mathrm{P}(B|A) = \frac{\mathrm{P}(BA)}{\mathrm{P}(A)} \qquad \textbf{[5-6]}$$

If we solve this for P(BA) by cross multiplication, we have the formula for *joint probability under conditions of statistical dependence:*

Joint probability of events *B* and *A* happening together or in succession

Probability of event *B* given that event *A* has happened

$$\mathrm{P}(BA) = \mathrm{P}(B|A) \times \mathrm{P}(A)^{*} \qquad \textbf{[5-7]}$$

Probability that event *A* will happen

Notice that this formula is *not* P(BA) = P(B) × P(A), as it would be under conditions of statistical independence.

Converting the general formula P(BA) = P($B|A$) × P(A) to our example and to the terms of colored, gray, dotted, and striped, we have P(CD) =

* To find the joint probability of events A and B, you could also use the formula P(BA) = P(AB) = P($A|B$) × P(B). This is because $BA = AB$.

$P(C|D) \times P(D)$, or $P(CD) = .6 \times .5 = .3$. Here, .6 is the probability of colored, given dotted (computed in example 3 above), and .5 is the probability of dotted (also computed in example 3).

$P(CD) = .3$ can be verified in Table 5-4, where we originally arrived at the probability by inspection: Three balls out of ten are colored and dotted.

Several examples

The following joint probabilities are computed in the same manner and can also be substantiated by reference to Table 5-4.

$$P(CS) = P(C|S) \times P(S) = .2 \times .5 = .1$$
$$P(GD) = P(G|D) \times P(D) = .4 \times .5 = .2$$
$$P(GS) = P(G|S) \times P(S) = .8 \times .5 = .4$$

Marginal Probabilities Under Statistical Dependence

Marginal probabilities under statistical dependence are computed by summing up the probabilities of all the joint events in which the simple event occurs. In the example above, we can compute the marginal probability of the event colored by summing the probabilities of the two joint events in which colored occurred:

$$P(C) = P(CD) + P(CS) = .3 + .1 = .4$$

Similarly, the marginal probability of the event gray can be computed by summing the probabilities of the two joint events in which gray occurred:

$$P(G) = P(GD) + P(GS) = .2 + .4 = .6$$

In like manner, we can compute the marginal probability of the event dotted by summing the probabilities of the two joint events in which dotted occurred:

$$P(D) = P(CD) + P(GD) = .3 + .2 = .5$$

And finally, the marginal probability of the event striped can be computed by summing the probabilities of the two joint events in which gray occurred:

$$P(S) = P(CS) + P(GS) = .1 + .4 = .5$$

These four marginal probabilities, $P(C) = .4$, $P(G) = .6$, $P(D) = .5$, and $P(S) = .5$, can be verified by inspection of Table 5-4.

We have now considered the three types of probability (conditional, joint, and marginal) under conditions of statistical dependence. Table 5-5 provides a résumé of our development of probabilities under both statistical independence and statistical dependence.

TABLE 5-5 Probabilities under statistical independence and dependence

TYPE OF PROBABILITY	SYMBOL	FORMULA UNDER STATISTICAL INDEPENDENCE	FORMULA UNDER STATISTICAL DEPENDENCE
Marginal	P(*A*)	P(*A*)	Sum of the probabilities of the joint events in which *A* occurs
Joint	P(*AB*) or P(*BA*)	P(*A*) × P(*B*) P(*B*) × P(*A*)	P(*A*|*B*) × P(*B*) P(*B*|*A*) × P(*A*)
Conditional	P(*B*|*A*)	P(*B*)	$\frac{P(BA)}{P(A)}$
	or P(*A*|*B*)	P(*A*)	$\frac{P(AB)}{P(B)}$

EXERCISES

5-33 In a study of the number of men and women employed at a plant, data show that 65 percent of the employees are males, 40 percent of the employees are production workers, and the probability that an employee is a male production worker is .30. If a randomly selected employee turns out to be a production worker, what is the probability that the employee is a male?

5-34 According to a survey, the probability that a family owns 2 cars if their annual income is greater than $15,000 is .70. Of the households surveyed, 50 percent had incomes over $15,000 and 40 percent had 2 cars. What is the probability that a family has 2 cars and an income over $15,000 a year?

5-35 Two events, *A* and *B*, are statistically dependent. P(*A*) = .25, P(*B*) = .33, and P(*A* or *B*) = .43. Find the probability that:

a) Neither *A* nor *B* will occur.
b) Both *A* and *B* will occur.
c) *B* will occur, given that *A* has occurred.
d) *A* will occur, given that *B* has occurred.

5-36 Given that P(*A*) = 1/6, P(*B*) = 1/3, P(*C*) = 4/9, P(*A* and *C*) = 1/12, and P(*B*|*C*) = 1/4, find the following probabilities:

P(*A*|*C*); P(*C*|*A*); P(*B* and *C*); P(*C*|*B*)

5-37 The Virginia National Bank estimates that 10 percent of adults in Charlottesville have checking accounts with Virginia National, and 5 percent of adults there have passbook savings accounts at that bank. In addition, 3 percent of adults in Charlottesville have both checking and passbook savings accounts with the Virginia National Bank.

a) What is the probability that an adult in Charlottesville will have a checking account with the bank, if that depositor has a savings account with it?
b) What is the probability that an adult in Charlottesville will have a savings account with the bank, if he or she has a Virginia National Bank checking account?

5-38 Myers Clothiers knows that 1 out of 10 families in its trading area qualifies for their charge accounts and that 1 out of 15 families in this area has applied for an account. From past records, 90 percent of credit applications are accepted. What is the probability that an area family will apply for a Myers charge card and be accepted?

5-39 A product manager is trying to determine how likely it is that a new competitor will damage sales of his product. He knows from past experience with new competitors that he will have 2 chances out of 10 of seeing sales decline, provided the competitor's price is not lower than his product's price and provided the competitor's advertising budget is less than $2 million a year. If the competitor's price is lower, there is a 5 out of 10 chance of a sales decline. If the competitor's ad budget is over $2 million, he knows that there is a 7 out of 10 chance of a sales decline. If the competitor's price is lower and the ad budget greater than $2 million, the chance of a sales decline is 8 out of 10. After reviewing the new product's performance in test markets, the manager predicts a 60 percent chance of his competitor's ad budget being over $2 million and a 30 percent chance of the competitor's product being priced below his product. (Advertising budget and price may be assumed to be independent of each other.) What is the probability of:

a) The competitor's product being priced under his product and the competitor's ad budget being over $2 million?
b) Lower price or greater than a $2 million ad budget, but not both; lower price but not greater ad budget; greater ad budget but not lower price?
c) Neither lower price nor greater advertising budget?
d) Sales damage?

5-40 Referring to problem 39, suppose that the product manager's brand did, in fact, suffer a sales decline during the year. What is the probability that:

a) The competitive price was below his brand, but the competitive advertising budget was below $2 million?
b) There was a competitive ad budget over $2 million, but the competitor's price was not lower than his brand?
c) The competitor both priced lower and used an ad budget over $2 million?
d) The competitor neither priced lower nor used an ad budget over $2 million?

5-41 Friendly's department store has been the target of many shoplifters during the past month, but owing to increased security precautions, 200 shoplifters have been caught. In order to better understand the security problem, the store has compiled data on each shoplifter caught. Each shoplifter's sex is noted and also whether the culprit was a first-time or a repeat offender. The data are summarized in the table below:

	FIRST-TIME OFFENDER	REPEAT OFFENDER
Male	70	26
Female	90	14
	160	**40**

Assuming that a shoplifter is chosen at random, find:

a) The probability that the shoplifter is male
b) The probability that the shoplifter is a first-time offender, given that the shoplifter is female
c) The probability that the shoplifter is male, given that the shoplifter is a repeat offender
d) The probability that the shoplifter is female, given that the shoplifter is a repeat offender
e) The probability that the shoplifter is both male and a first-time offender

5-42 Alan Adazewerk is in charge of the produce section at Food N' Crude, the local supermarket and gas station combination. Alan has noticed that for any given customer, the purchase of lettuce seems to be dependent upon the purchase of tomatoes, and vice versa. Through his vast experience, he has produced the following probabilities: The probability of a customer's buying lettuce is .72. The probability of a customer's buying tomatoes is .5. The probability of a customer's buying tomatoes, given that the customer is buying lettuce, is .625. Help Alan by answering the following questions:

a) What is the probability of a customer's buying both lettuce and tomatoes?
b) What is the probability of a customer's buying lettuce, given that the customer is buying tomatoes?

5-7 REVISING PRIOR ESTIMATES OF PROBABILITIES: Bayes' Theorem

At the beginning of the baseball season, the fans of last year's pennant winner thought their team had a good chance of winning again. As the season progressed, however, injuries sidelined their shortstop and their chief rivals drafted a terrific home run hitter. The team began to lose. Late in the season, the fans realized that they must alter their prior probabilities of winning.

A similar situation often occurs in business. If a manager of a boutique finds that most of the purple and chartreuse ski jackets that she thought would sell so well are hanging on the rack, she must revise her prior probabilities and order a different color combination or have a sale.

Posterior probabilities defined

In both these cases, certain probabilities were altered after the people involved got additional information. The new probabilities are known as revised, or *posterior* probabilities. Because probabilities can be revised as more information is gained, probability theory is of great value in managerial decision making.

Bayes' theorem

The origin of the concept of obtaining posterior probabilities with limited information is attributable to the Reverend Thomas Bayes (1702–1761), and the basic formula for conditional probability under dependence:

$$P(B|A) = \frac{P(BA)}{P(A)} \qquad \textbf{[5-6]}$$

is called *Bayes' theorem*.

Bayes, an Englishman, was a Presbyterian minister and a competent mathematician. He pondered how he might prove the existence of God by examining whatever evidence the world about him provided. Attempting to show "that the Principal End of the Divine Providence . . . is the Happiness of His Creatures," the Reverend Bayes used mathematics to study God. Unfortunately, the theological implications of his findings so alarmed the good Reverend Bayes that he refused to permit publication of his work during his lifetime. Nevertheless, his work outlived him, and modern decision theory is often called Bayesian decision theory in his honor.

Value of Bayes' theorem

Bayes' theorem offers a powerful statistical method of evaluating new information and revising our prior estimates (based upon limited information only) of the probability that things are in one state or another. **If correctly used, it makes it unnecessary to gather masses of data over long periods of time in order to make decisions based upon probabilities.**

Calculating Posterior Probabilities

Finding a new posterior estimate

Assume, as a first example of revising prior probabilities, that we have equal numbers of two types of deformed (biased or weighted) dice in a bowl. On half of them, ace (or one dot) comes up 40 percent of the time; therefore, P(ace) = .4. On the other half, ace comes up 70 percent of the time, and P(ace) = .7. Let us call the former type 1 and the latter type 2. One die is drawn, rolled once, and comes up ace. What is the probability that it is a type 1 die? Knowing the bowl contains the same number of both types of dice, we might incorrectly answer that the probability is one-half; but we can do better than this. To answer the question correctly, we set up Table 5-6.

TABLE 5-6 Finding the marginal probability of getting an ace

ELEMENTARY EVENT	PROBABILITY OF ELEMENTARY EVENT	P(ACE|ELEMENTARY EVENT)	P(ACE, ELEMENTARY EVENT)*
Type 1	.5	.4	$.4 \times .5 = .20$
Type 2	.5	.7	$.7 \times .5 = .35$
	1.0		**P(ace) = .55**

* A comma is used to separate joint events. We can join individual letters to indicate joint events without confusion (*AB*, for example), but joining whole words in this way could produce strange looking events (aceelementaryevent) in this table, and they could be confusing.

The sum of the probabilities of the elementary events (drawing either a type 1 or a type 2 die) is 1.0, because there are only two types of dice. The probability of each type is .5. The two types constitute a mutually exclusive and collectively exhaustive list.

The sum of P(ace|elementary event) does *not* equal 1.0. The figures .4 and .7 simply represent the conditional probabilities of getting an ace, given type 1 and type 2, respectively.

The fourth column shows the joint probability of ace and type 1 occurring together ($.4 \times .5 = .20$), and the joint probability of ace and type 2 occurring together ($.7 \times .5 = .35$). The sum of these joint probabilities (.55) is the marginal probability of getting an ace. Notice that in each case, the joint probability was obtained by using the formula:

$$P(AB) = P(A|B) \times P(B) \quad \textbf{[5-7]}$$

To find the probability that the die we have drawn is type 1, we use the formula for conditional probability under statistical dependence:

$$P(B|A) = \frac{P(BA)}{P(A)} \quad \textbf{[5-6]}$$

Converting to our problem, we have:

$$P(\text{type 1}|\text{ace}) = \frac{P(\text{type 1, ace})}{P(\text{ace})}$$

or:

$$P(\text{type 1}|\text{ace}) = \frac{.20}{.55} = .364$$

Thus, the probability that we have drawn a type 1 die is .364.

Let us compute the probability that the die is type 2:

$$P(\text{type 2}|\text{ace}) = \frac{P(\text{type 2, ace})}{P(\text{ace})} = \frac{.35}{.55} = .636$$

Revision after one roll

What have we accomplished with one additional piece of information made available to us? What inferences have we been able to draw from one roll of the die? Before we rolled this die, the best we could say was that there is a .5 chance it is a type 1 die and a .5 chance it is a type 2 die. However, after rolling the die, we have been able to *alter*, or revise, *our prior probability estimate*. Our new posterior estimate is that there is a higher probability (.636) that the die we have in our hand is a type 2 than that it is a type 1 (only .364).

Posterior Probabilities With More Information

Finding a new posterior estimate with more information

We may feel that one roll of the die is not sufficient to indicate its characteristics (whether it is type 1 or type 2). In this case, we can obtain additional information by rolling the die again. (Obtaining more information in most decision-making situations, of course, is more complicated and time-consuming.) Assume that the same die is rolled a second time and again comes up ace. What is the further revised probability that the die is type 1? To determine this answer, see Table 5-7.

We have one new column in this table, P(2 aces|elementary event). This column gives the *joint* probability of two aces on two successive rolls if the die is type 1 and if it is type 2: P(2 aces|type 1) = .4 × .4 = .16, and P(2 aces|type 2) = .7 × .7 = .49. In the last column, we see the joint probabilities of two aces on two successive rolls and the elementary events (type 1 and type 2). That is, P(2 aces, type 1) equals P(2 aces|type 1) times the

TABLE 5-7 Finding the marginal probability of two aces on two successive rolls

ELEMENTARY EVENT	PROBABILITY OF ELEMENTARY EVENT	P(ACE| ELEMENTARY EVENT)	P(2 ACES| ELEMENTARY EVENT)	P(2 ACES, ELEMENTARY EVENT)
Type 1	.5	.4	.16	.16 × .5 = .080
Type 2	.5	.7	.49	.49 × .5 = .245
	1.0			**P(2 aces) = .325**

probability of type 1, or $.16 \times .5 = .080$. And P(2 aces, type 2) equals P(2 aces|type 2) times the probability of type 2, or $.49 \times .5 = .245$. The sum of these (.325) is the marginal probability of two aces on two successive rolls.

We are now ready to compute the probability that the die we have drawn is type 1, given an ace on each of two successive rolls. Using the same general formula as before, we convert to:

$$P(\text{type } 1|2 \text{ aces}) = \frac{P(\text{type } 1, 2 \text{ aces})}{P(2 \text{ aces})} = \frac{.080}{.325} = .246$$

Similarly,

$$P(\text{type } 2|2 \text{ aces}) = \frac{P(\text{type } 2, 2 \text{ aces})}{P(2 \text{ aces})} = \frac{.245}{.325} = .754$$

What have we accomplished with two rolls? When we first drew the die, all we knew was that there was a probability of .5 that it was type 1 and a probability of .5 that it was type 2. In other words, there was a 50-50 chance that it was either type 1 or type 2. After rolling the die once and getting an ace, we revised these original probabilities to the following:

Probability that it is type 1 = .364
Probability that it is type 2 = .636

After the second roll (another ace), we revised the probabilities again:

Probability that it is type 1 = .246
Probability that it is type 2 = .754

Revision after two rolls

We have thus changed the original probabilities from .5 for each type to .246 for type 1 and .754 for type 2. This means that we can now assign a probability of .754 that if a die turns up ace on two successive rolls, it is type 2.

In both these experiments, we gained new information free of charge. We were able to roll the die twice, observe its behavior, and draw inferences from that behavior without any monetary cost. Obviously, there are few situations in which this is true, and managers must not only understand how to utilize new information to revise prior probabilities, but also be able to determine *how much that information is worth* to them before the fact. In many cases, the value of the information obtained may be considerably less than its cost.

A Problem with Three Revisions

Example of posterior probability based on three trials

Consider the problem of a Little League baseball team that has been using an automatic pitching machine. If the machine is correctly set up—that is, properly adjusted—it will pitch strikes 85 percent of the time. If it is incorrectly setup, it will pitch strikes only 35 percent of the time. Past experience indicates that 75 percent of the setups of the machine are correctly done. After the machine has been set up at batting practice one day, it throws three strikes on the first three pitches. What is the revised probability that the setup has been done correctly? Table 5-8 illustrates how we can answer this question.

We can interpret the numbered table headings in Table 5-8 as follows:

(1) P(*event*) describes the individual probabilities of correct and incorrect. P(correct) = .75 is given in the problem. Thus we can compute:

$$\text{P(incorrect)} = 1.00 - \text{P(correct)} = 1.00 - .75 = .25$$

(2) P(*1* strike|*event*) represents the probability of a strike given that the setup is correct or incorrect. These probabilities are given in the problem.

(3) P(*3* strikes|*event*) is the probability of getting three strikes on three successive pitches, given the event; that is, given correct or incorrect. The probabilities are computed as follows:

$$\text{P(3 strikes|correct)} = .85 \times .85 \times .85 = .6141$$

$$\text{P(3 strikes|incorrect)} = .35 \times .35 \times .35 = .0429$$

(4) P(*event, 3* strikes) is the probability of the joint occurrence of the event (correct or incorrect) and three strikes. We can compute the probabilities in this problem as follows:

$$\text{P(correct, 3 strikes)} = .6141 \times .75 = .4606$$

$$\text{P(incorrect, 3 strikes)} = .0429 \times .25 = .0107$$

Notice that if A = event and B = strikes, these last two probabilities conform to the general mathematical formula for joint probabilities under conditions of dependence: $P(AB) = P(BA) = P(B|A) \times P(A)$, Equation 5-7.

TABLE 5-8 Posterior probabilities with joint events

EVENT	P(EVENT) (1)	P(1 STRIKE| EVENT) (2)	P(3 STRIKES| EVENT) (3)	P(EVENT, 3 STRIKES) (4)
Correct	.75	.85	.6141	.6141 × .75 = .4606
Incorrect	.25	.35	.0429	.0429 × .25 = .0107
	1.00			**P(3 strikes) = .4713**

After finishing the computations in Table 5-8, we are ready to determine the revised probability that the machine is correctly set up. We use the general formula

$$P(A|B) = \frac{P(AB)}{P(B)} \quad \textbf{[5-6]}$$

and convert it to the terms and numbers in this problem:

$$P(\text{correct}|3\text{ strikes}) = \frac{P(\text{correct, 3 strikes})}{P(3\text{ strikes})}$$

$$= \frac{.4606}{.4713} = .9773$$

The *posterior probability* that the machine is correctly set up is .9773, or 97.73 percent. We have thus revised our original probability of a correct setup from 75 to 97.73 percent, based on three strikes being thrown in three pitches.

Posterior Probabilities with Inconsistent Outcomes

An example with inconsistent outcomes

In each of our problems so far, the behavior of the experiment was consistent—the die came up ace on two successive rolls, and the automatic machine threw strikes on each of the first three pitches. In most situations, we would expect a less consistent distribution of outcomes. In the case of the pitching machine for example, we might find the five pitches to be: strike, ball, strike, strike, strike. Calculating our posterior probability that the machine is correctly set up in this case is really no more difficult than it was with a set of perfectly consistent outcomes. Using the notation S = strike and B = ball, we have solved this example in Table 5-9.

TABLE 5-9 Posterior probabilities with inconsistent outcomes

EVENT	P(EVENT)	P(*S*|EVENT)	P(*SBSSS*|EVENT)	P(EVENT, *SBSSS*)
Correct	.75	.85	.85 × .15 × .85 × .85 × .85 = .07830	.07830 × .75 = .05873
Incorrect	.25	.35	.35 × .65 × .35 × .35 × .35 = .00975	.00975 × .25 = .00244
	1.00			**P(SBSSS) = .06117**

$$P(\text{correct setup}|\text{SBSSS}) = \frac{P(\text{correct setup, SBSSS})}{P(\text{SBSSS})}$$

$$= \frac{.05873}{.06117}$$

$$= .9601$$

EXERCISES

5-43 Given: The probabilities of three events, A, B, and C, occurring are: $P(A) = .5$, $P(B) = .3$, and $P(C) = .2$. Assuming that, A, B, or C has occurred, the probabilities of another event, X, occurring are: $P(X|A) = .6$, $P(X|B) = .8$, and $P(X|C) = .4$. Find $P(A|X)$; $P(B|X)$; $P(C|X)$.

5-44 Martin Coleman, credit manager for Beck's, knows that the company uses 3 methods to encourage collection of delinquent accounts. From past collection records, he knows that 60 percent of the accounts are called on personally to collect, 25 percent are phoned, and 15 percent are sent a letter. The probability of collecting an overdue amount from an account with the 3 methods is .80, .50, and .40 respectively. Mr. Coleman has just received payment from a past-due account.

a) Given this information, what is the probability that the account was called on personally?
b) What is the probability that the account remitted payment after receiving a phone call?
c) What is the probability that the account received a letter and sent payment?

5-45 A public-interest group was planning to make a court challenge to auto insurance rates in one of three cities: Atlanta, Denver, or Indianapolis. The probability that it would choose Atlanta was .40; Denver, .30; Indianapolis, .30. The group also knew that it had a 50 percent chance of a favorable court ruling if it chose Atlanta, 60 percent if it chose Denver, and 75 percent if it chose Indianapolis. If the group did receive a favorable ruling, which city did it most likely choose?

5-46 In a particular town, there are two Sunday newspapers, the *Times* and the *Herald,* each of which has a classified ad section. Twenty percent of the employers in the city place want ads only in the *Times,* 10 percent place ads only in the *Herald,* and 70 percent place ads in both newspapers. In the past, 75 percent of the ads appearing only in the *Times* have received more than one reply, 65 percent of the ads appearing only in the *Herald* have received more than one reply, and 90 percent of the ads appearing in both newspapers have received more than one reply. If an employer places an ad and receives only one reply, what is the probability that the ad appeared in both papers?

5-47 An independent research group has been making a study of the chances that an accident at a nuclear power plant will result in radiation leakage. The group considers that the only possible types of accidents at a reactor are fire, material failure, and human error, and that two or more accidents never occur together. It has performed studies that indicate that if there were a fire, a radiation leak would occur 10 percent of the time; if there were a mechanical failure, a radiation leak would occur 40 percent of the time; and if there were human error, a radiation leak would occur 5 percent of the time. Its studies have also shown that the probability of:

- a fire and a radiation leak occurring together is .0005.
- a mechanical failure and a radiation leak occurring together is .0010.
- human error and a radiation leak occurring together is .0007.

a) What are the respective probabilities of having a fire, mechanical failure, and human error upon which the probabilities given above are based?
b) What are the respective probabilities that a radiation leak would be caused by fire, mechanical failure, or human error?
c) What is the probability of a radiation leak?

5-48 Data on readership of a certain magazine indicate that the proportion of male readers over 30 years old is .20. The proportion of male readers under 30 is .40. If the proportion of readers under 30 is .70, what is

a) The proportion of subscribers that are male?
b) The probability that a randomly selected male subscriber is under 30?

5-49 Last year, Village Communications Company hired 12 engineers, 25 salespersons, 18 announcers, and 5 technicians. Three of the engineers, 5 of the salespersons, 6 of the announcers, and 2 of the technicians received promotions during the year. If an employee is selected randomly from the group hired in the past year and is found to have received a promotion, what is the probability that the employee is (a) an announcer, (b) a technician, (c) a salesperson, (d) an engineer?

5-50 The federal government has just released its economic forecasts for the next year. If there is no oil embargo, the gross national product (GNP) will increase 1 percent with probability .1, 2 percent with probability .1, 3 percent with probability .2, 4 percent with probability .4, and 5 or more percent with probability .2. If there is an oil embargo, but no war in the Middle East, the GNP will increase 1 percent with probability .2, 2 percent with probability .2, 3 percent with probability .3, 4 percent with probability .2, and 5 or more percent with probability .1. If war breaks out in the Middle East, there will definitely be an embargo, and then the probabilities are .4, .3, .1, .1, and .1 of 1, 2, 3, 4, and 5 or more percent increases in the GNP.

The prior probability for no embargo is .6, for an embargo without war is .1, and for a war is .3. Given that a 5 or more percent increase in GNP is observed, find the posterior probability that:

a) There was no embargo.
b) There was an embargo, but no war.
c) There was a war.

If instead, a 2 percent increase in GNP is observed, find the posterior probability that:

d) There was no embargo.
e) There was an embargo, but no war.
f) There was a war.

5-51 The executives at Sole Source Shoes estimate that the prior probability of their latest advertising campaign being successful is .5, being only marginally successful is .3, and being unsuccessful is .2. After the advertising campaign, the company expects sales of its shoes to increase 10 percent, remain unchanged, or decrease 10 percent, with probabilities determined by the success of the advertising campaign (see table below). The executives are trying to anticipate all possible outcomes that could affect the company and need to answer the questions below, so they have hired you as a consultant.

GIVEN THAT ADVERTISING IS:	SALES UP 10%	SALES UNCHANGED	SALES DOWN 10%
Successful	.4	.4	.2
Marginally successful	.2	.5	.3
Unsuccessful	.0	.6	.4

a) If the company finds that sales have increased 10 percent, find each of the posterior probabilities that the advertising campaign was successful, marginally successful, and unsuccessful.
b) If sales remain unchanged, find the posterior probabilities that the advertising campaign was successful, marginally successful, and unsuccessful.

5-8 TERMS INTRODUCED IN CHAPTER 5

A PRIORI PROBABILITY Probability estimate made prior to receiving new information.

BAYES' THEOREM The formula for conditional probability under statistical dependence.

CLASSICAL PROBABILITY The number of outcomes favorable to the occurrence of an event divided by the total number of possible outcomes.

COLLECTIVELY EXHAUSTIVE EVENTS The list of events that represents all the possible outcomes of an experiment.

CONDITIONAL PROBABILITY The probability of one event occurring, given that another event has occurred.

EVENT One or more of the possible outcomes of doing something, or one of the possible outcomes of an experiment.

EXPERIMENT The activity that results in, or produces, an event.

JOINT PROBABILITY The probability of two events occurring together or in succession.

MARGINAL PROBABILITY The unconditional probability of one event occurring; the probability of a single event.

MUTUALLY EXCLUSIVE EVENTS Events that cannot happen together.

POSTERIOR PROBABILITY A probability that has been revised after additional information was obtained.

PROBABILITY The chance that something will happen.

PROBABILITY TREE A graphical representation showing the possible outcomes of a series of experiments and their respective probabilities.

RELATIVE FREQUENCY OF OCCURRENCE The proportion of times that an event occurs in the long run when conditions are stable, or the observed relative frequency of an event in a very large number of trials.

SAMPLE SPACE The set of all possible outcomes of an experiment.

STATISTICAL DEPENDENCE The condition when the probability of some event is dependent upon, or affected by, the occurrence of some other event.

STATISTICAL INDEPENDENCE The condition when the occurrence of one event has no effect upon the probability of occurrence of any other event.

SUBJECTIVE PROBABILITY Probabilities based on the personal beliefs of the person making the probability estimate.

VENN DIAGRAM A pictorial representation of probability concepts, in which the sample space is represented as a rectangle and the events in the sample space as portions of that rectangle.

5-9 EQUATIONS INTRODUCED IN CHAPTER 5

[5-1] $$\text{Probability of an event} = \frac{\text{The number of outcomes where the event occurs}}{\text{The total number of possible outcomes}}$$ *p. 147*

This is the definition of the *classical* probability that an event will occur.

$$\mathrm{P}(A) = \text{The probability of an event } A \text{ happening}$$ *p. 153*

A single probability refers to the probability of one particular event occurring, and it is called *marginal* probability.

$$\mathrm{P}(A \text{ or } B) = \text{The probability of } either\ A \text{ or } B \text{ happening}$$ *p. 154*

This notation represents the probability that one event *or* the other will occur.

[5-2] $$\mathrm{P}(A \text{ or } B) = \mathrm{P}(A) + \mathrm{P}(B)$$ *p. 154*

The probability of either A or B happening when A and B are mutually exclusive equals the sum of the probability of event A happening and the probability of event B happening. This is the *addition rule for mutually exclusive events.*

[5-3] $$\mathrm{P}(A \text{ or } B) = \mathrm{P}(A) + \mathrm{P}(B) - \mathrm{P}(AB)$$ *p. 156*

The addition rule for events that are not mutually exclusive shows that the probability of A or B happening when A and B are not mutually exclusive is equal to the probability of event A happening plus the probability of event B happening minus the probability of A and B happening together, symbolized $\mathrm{P}(AB)$.

[5-4] $$P(AB) = P(A) \times P(B)$$ *p. 159*

where:

$P(AB)$ = the joint probability of events A and B occurring together or in succession
$P(A)$ = the marginal probability of event A happening
$P(B)$ = the marginal probability of event B happening

The *joint* probability of two or more *independent* events occurring together or in succession is the product of their marginal probabilities.

$P(B|A)$ = The probability of event B, *given* that event A has happened *p. 164*

This notation shows *conditional* probability, the probability that a second event (B) will occur if a first event (A) has already happened.

[5-5] $$P(B|A) = P(B)$$ *p. 164*

For *statistically independent* events, the *conditional* probability of event B, given that event A has occurred, is simply the probability of event B. Independent events are those whose probabilities are in no way affected by the occurrence of each other.

[5-6] $$P(B|A) = \frac{P(BA)}{P(A)}$$ *p. 169*

and $$P(A|B) = \frac{P(AB)}{P(B)}$$

For statistically *dependent* events, the *conditional* probability of event B, given that event A has occurred, is equal to the joint probability of events A and B divided by the marginal probability of event A.

[5-7] $$P(AB) = P(A|B) \times P(B)$$ *p. 171*

and $$P(BA) = P(B|A) \times P(A)$$

Under conditions of statistical *dependence*, the *joint* probability of events A and B happening together or in succession is equal to the probability of event A, given that event B has already happened, multiplied by the probability that event B will happen.

5-10 CHAPTER REVIEW EXERCISES

5-52 Life insurance premiums are higher for older people, but auto insurance premiums are generally higher for younger people. What does this suggest about the risks and probabilities associated with these two areas of the insurance business?

5-53 "The chance of rain today is 80 percent." Which of the following best explains this statement?

a) It will rain 80 percent of the day today.
b) It will rain in 80 percent of the area for which this forecast applies today.
c) In the past, weather conditions of this sort have produced rain in this area 80 percent of the time.

5-54 "There is a .25 probability that a restaurant in the United States will go out of business this year." When researchers make such statements, how have they arrived at their conclusions?

5-55 Using probability theory, explain the success of gambling and poker establishments.

5-56 If we assume that a person is equally likely to be born on any day of the week, what are the probabilities of a certain baby being born:

a) On a Tuesday?
b) On a day beginning with the letter S?
c) Between Wednesday and Friday, inclusive?
d) What type of probability estimates are these?

5-57 A real estate agent estimates that your house will go up in market value by 15 percent or more in the next 6 months, with probability .60. He estimates that the probability that my house will increase in market value by 15 percent or more in the next 6 months is .8. He also estimates that the probability of a certain client taking his advice and buying your house is .7. If at the end of 6 months, the client's new home has indeed increased in value by 15 percent or more, what is the probability that the client bought (a) my house, (b) your house?

5-58 Betty Barnes has worked with the U.S. Postal Service for 12 years. During this time, she has inspected many letters and has made a list of the most common mistakes that people make when addressing letters. Here is her list:

No zip code	Too much postage
No return address	Not enough postage
No street address	

a) In probability theory, would each item on the list be classified as an "event"?
b) Are all the items on the list mutually exclusive? Are any of them mutually exclusive?
c) Is Betty's list collectively exhaustive? (Remember, if you answer no, then you should be able to add at least one more item to the list. Can you?)

5-59 Which of the following sets of two events are mutually exclusive?

a) You choose a target market of women only, all between the ages of 18 and 49.
b) You find in a study that verbally rewarding employees for good performance increases their motivation and that the amount of verbal reward influences their job satisfaction.
c) You decide to give an across-the-board raise to all employees, and you decide to give performance bonuses rather than an across-the-board raise.
d) You give an across-the-board raise to employees, and you give them performance bonuses as well.
e) You intend to expand your plant size this year but not to make any capital expenditures this year.

5-60 The scheduling officer for a local police department is trying to decide whether to schedule additional patrol units in each of two neighborhoods. She knows that on any given day during the past year, the probabilities of major crimes and minor crimes being committed in the northern neighborhood were .589 and .342, respectively, and that the corresponding probabilities in the southern neighborhood were .507 and .863.

a) What is the probability that a crime of either type will be committed in the northern neighborhood on a given day?
b) What is the probability that a crime of either type will be committed in the southern neighborhood on a given day?
c) What is the probability that *no* crime will be committed in either neighborhood on a given day?

5-61 The Environmental Protection Agency is trying to assess the pollution effect of a paper mill that is to be built near Spokane, Washington. In studies of six similar plants built during the last year, the EPA determined the following pollution factors:

Plant	1	2	3	4	5	6
Sulfur dioxide emission in parts per million (ppm)	15	12	18	16	11	19

EPA defines excessive pollution as a sulfur dioxide emission of 18 ppm or greater.

a) Calculate the probability that the new plant will be an excessive sulfur dioxide polluter.
b) Classify this probability according to the three types discussed in the chapter: classical, relative frequency, and subjective.
c) How would you judge the accuracy of your result?

5-62 The American Cancer Society is planning to mail out questionnaires concerning breast cancer. From past experience with questionnaires, the society knows that only 12 percent of the persons receiving questionnaires will respond. It also knows that 1 percent of the questionnaires mailed out will have a mistake in the address and will never be delivered, that 3 percent will be lost or destroyed by the post office, that 22 percent will be mailed to people who have moved, and that only 52 percent of those who move leave forwarding addresses.

a) Do the percentages given in the problem represent classical, relative frequency, or subjective probability estimates?
b) What is the probability that the society will receive a reply from a given questionnaire?

5-63 A contractor knows that in the past year, his revenue declined by 10 percent, revenues from government contracts declined by 12 percent, and revenues from private contracts increased by 2 percent. Is the probability of an increase in next year's sales revenue for the contractor greater with private or government contracts?

5-64 As the administrator of a hospital, Cindy Turner wants to know what the probability is that a person checking into the hospital will require X-ray treatment and will also have hospital insurance that will cover the X-ray treatment. She knows that during the past 5 years, 12 percent of the people entering the hospital required X rays and that during the same period, 58 percent of the people checking into the hospital had insurance that covered X-ray treatments. What is the correct probability?

5-65 The air traffic controller at O'Hare Airport has specific regulations that require him to divert one of two airplanes if the probability of the aircraft meeting at the same point exceeds .225. The controller has two inbound aircraft scheduled to arrive 10 minutes apart. He knows that Flight 100, scheduled to arrive first, has a history of being 5 minutes late 20 percent of the time. He also knows that Flight 200, scheduled to arrive second, has a history of being 5 minutes early 25 percent of the time.

a) If the controller finds out that Flight 200 will definitely arrive 5 minutes early, should he divert Flight 100?
b) If the controller finds out that Flight 100 will definitely arrive 5 minutes late, should he divert Flight 200?

5-66 A production process is designed to produce 3-mm ball bearings. Because of the rigid standards required by the customers, samples of bearings are frequently tested. The results of the most recent test are shown below.

Total bearings tested	1,000
Number with diameter less than 2.9 mm	4
Number with diameter more than 3.1 mm	10
Number with diameter of 2.9 mm–3.1 mm	986

If only bearings with diameters between 2.9 mm and 3.1 mm are acceptable, what is the probability that a bearing selected at random will be too large or too small?

5-67 Which of the following pairs of events are statistically independent?

a) The number of union members in a unionized aluminum can factory and the number of men working in the plant.

b) The number of women in the United States who have annual incomes over $20,000 and the number of women who have college degrees.
c) The number of seconds it takes worker A to assemble a switch and the number of seconds it takes worker B to assemble the switch.
d) The number of people who have checking accounts with a certain bank and the number of people who have other types of accounts, such as savings and charge cards, with that bank.
e) The number of applicants for brand-manager positions at one cosmetic company and the number of applicants for brand manager at another cosmetic company in the same city.

5-68 Susan Dugan, an administrator in research and development for a packaged-foods producer, is preparing a presentation for top management on 3 new product developments (a dessert, a dessert topping, and a seasoning mix). She estimates that there is an 80 percent chance that the dessert will be accepted by management and a 50 percent chance that if they do accept it, the product will be a success in the test market. She estimates that there is a 60 percent chance that they will adopt the dessert topping and a 70 percent chance that if they do adopt it, the product will succeed in the test market. Finally, she estimates that there is a 40 percent chance of the managers accepting the new seasoning mix and a 90 percent chance that if they do, the product will be successful in the test market. Suppose that at the end of next year, we find that none of these three products made it to national distribution.
a) For each product, what is the probability that the managers did not accept it?
b) For each product, what is the probability that the managers accepted the product, but it was not successful in the test market?

5-69 An electronics manufacturer is considering expansion of its plant in the next few years. The decision will be influenced by increased production that will occur if either government or consumer sales increase. Specifically, the plant will be expanded if one of two events occur: (1) consumer sales increase 50 percent over the present sales level, or (2) a major government contract is obtained. The company also feels that both these events will not happen in the same year. Therefore, the planning director has obtained the following estimates:
1. The probability of consumer sales increasing by 50 percent within one year is .10, and the probability of obtaining a major government contract within one year is .05.
2. The probability of consumer sales increasing by 50 percent during the next two years is .25, and the probability of obtaining a major government contract during the next two years is .20.
3. The probability of consumer sales increasing by 50 percent during the next three years is .40, and the probability of obtaining a major government contract during the next three years is .45.

a) What are the probabilities that the electronics manufacturer will increase its plant size in years 1, 2, or 3, respectively?
b) What is the probability it will increase the plant size at all during the three-year period?

5-70 Draw Venn diagrams to represent the following situations involving three events, *A*, *B*, and *C*, which are part of a sample space of events but do not include the whole sample space
a) Each pair of events (*A* and *B*, *A* and *C*, and *B* and *C*) may occur together, but all three may not occur together.
b) *A* and *B* are mutually exclusive, but not *A* and *C* nor *B* and *C*.
c) *A*, *B*, and *C* are all mutually exclusive of one another.
d) *A* and *B* are mutually exclusive, *B* and *C* are mutually exclusive, but *A* and *C* are not mutually exclusive.

5-71 As an aid in diagnosing the cause of automobile malfunctions, small computers are currently being used in dealerships of a German car. The company that supplies the dealerships with the computers claims that they make errors in pinpointing the cause of malfunctions only .1 percent of the time.
a) Suppose that in a nationwide screening of 10,000 cars, 6,000 are diagnosed by Model #101 computers and 4,000 are diagnosed by Model #102 computers. If the cause of one car's malfunctioning is found to be misdiagnosed, what is the probability that the diagnosis was made by Model #101?
b) Suppose that after three years, records indicate that .2 percent of the diagnoses made by Model #101 were incorrect and .3 percent of the diagnoses made by Model #102 were incorrect. In another screening of 10,000 cars, 6,000 are diagnosed on Model #101 and 4,000 on Model #102. If an

automobile is found to be misdiagnosed in this group, what is the probability that the diagnosis was done by Model #102?

5-72 Determine the probability that:

a) A person is a heroin addict and smokes marijuana, given that 62 percent of all heroin addicts smoke marijuana and that the probability of a person being a heroin addict is .005.

b) A child in a certain school district comes from an intact family with an income over $20,000, given that 50 percent of the intact families in the district have incomes over $20,000 and 95 percent of the families in the district are intact.

c) A man on campus is a business major and lives in James Dorm, given that 30 percent of the men are business majors and 10 percent of them live in James Dorm.

5-73 A company faced with a problem of distribution of its new product at the retail level studied the relationship between personal sales calls to outlets and the number of outlets that carry the product. It found that 72 percent of the stores called upon by a company salesperson now carried the brand. If 20 percent of total retail outlets have had a visit from a sales representative, what is the probability that a retail outlet has both received a sales call and carries the product? What information would you need in order to determine the probability of a given store carrying the brand?

5-11 CHAPTER CONCEPTS TEST

Answers are in the back of the book.

T F 1. In probability theory, the outcome from some experiment is known as an activity.

T F 2. The probability of two or more statistically independent events occurring together or in succession is equal to the sum of their marginal probabilities.

T F 3. Using Bayes' theorem, we may develop revised probabilities based upon new information; these revised probabilities are also known as posterior probabilities.

T F 4. In classical probability, we can determine a priori probabilities based upon logical reasoning before any experiments take place.

T F 5. The set of all possible outcomes of an experiment is called the sample space for the experiment.

T F 6. Under statistical dependence, a marginal probability may be computed for some simple event by taking the product of the probabilities of all joint events in which the simple event occurs.

T F 7. When a list of events resulting from some experiment includes all possible outcomes, the list is said to be collectively exclusive.

T F 8. An unconditional probability is also known as a marginal probability.

T F 9. A subjective probability may be nothing more than an educated guess.

T F 10. When the occurrence of some event has no effect upon the probability of occurrence of some other event, the two events are said to be statistically independent.

T F 11. When using the relative frequency approach, probability figures become less accurate for large numbers of observations.

T F 12. Symbolically, a marginal probability is denoted $P(AB)$.

T F 13. If A and B are statistically dependent events, the probability of *A and B* occurring is $P(A) \times P(B)$.

T F 14. Classical probability assumes that each of the possible outcomes of an experiment is equally likely.

T F 15. One reason that decision makers at high levels often use subjective probabilities is that they are concerned with unique situations.

T F 16. In assessing the probability of some event, the relative frequency of occurrence approach gives the greatest flexibility.

T F 17. Bayes' theorem is the formula for conditional probability under statistical dependence.

18. Why are the events of a coin toss mutually exclusive?
   a) The outcome of any toss is not affected by the outcomes of those preceding it.
   b) Both a head and a tail cannot turn up on any one toss.
   c) The probability of getting a head and the probability of getting a tail are the same.
   d) All of these.
   e) a and b but not c.

19. If a Venn diagram were drawn for events *A* and *B*, which are mutually exclusive, which of the following would always be true of *A* and *B*?
   a) Their parts of the rectangle will overlap.
   b) Their parts of the rectangle will be equal in area.
   c) Their parts of the rectangle will not overlap.
   d) None of these.
   e) b and c but not a.

20. What is the probability that a value chosen at random from a particular population is larger than the median of the population?
   a) .25 b) .5 c) 1.0 d) .67

21. Assume that a single fair die is rolled once. Which of the following is true?
   a) The probability of rolling a number higher than one is 1 − P(one is rolled).
   b) The probability of rolling a three is 1 − P(1, 2, 4, 5, or 6 is rolled).
   c) The probability of rolling a 5 or 6 is higher than the probability of rolling a 3 or 4.
   d) All of these.
   e) a and b but not c.

22. If *A* and *B* are mutually exclusive events, then P(*A* or *B*) = P(*A*) + P(*B*). How does the calculation of P(*A* or *B*) change if *A* and *B* are *not* mutually exclusive?
   a) P(*AB*) must be subtracted from P(*A*) + P(*B*).
   b) P(*AB*) must be added to P(*A*) + P(*B*).
   c) [P(*A*) + P(*B*)] must be multiplied by P(*AB*).
   d) [P(*A*) + P(*B*)] must be divided by P(*AB*).
   e) None of these.

23. Leo C. Swartz, a taxi driver in Chicago, has found that the weather affects his customers' tipping. If it is raining, his customers usually tip poorly. When it is not raining, however, they usually tip well. Which of the following is true?
   a) Tips and weather are statistically independent.
   b) The weather conditions Leo cited are not mutually exclusive.
   c) P(good tip|rain) is larger than P(bad tip|rain).
   d) None of these.
   e) a and c but not b.

24. Assume that a die is rolled twice in succession and that you are asked to draw the probability tree showing all possible outcomes of the two rolls. How many branches will your tree have?
   a) 6 b) 12 c) 36 d) 42 e) 48

Questions 25–28 refer to the following situation: Ten numbered balls are placed in an urn. Numbers 1–4 are red and numbers 5–10 are blue.

25. What is the probability that a ball drawn at random from the urn is blue?
   a) .1 b) .4 c) .6 d) 1.0
   e) Cannot be determined from the information given.

26. The probability of drawing the ball numbered 3, of course, is .1. A ball is drawn, and it is red. Which of the following is true?
   a) P(ball drawn is #3|ball drawn is red) = .1
   b) P(ball drawn is #3|ball drawn is red) < .1
   c) P(ball drawn is #3|ball drawn is red) > .1
   d) P(ball drawn is red|ball drawn is #3) = .25
   e) c and d only
27. In question 26, the probability of drawing the #3 ball was reconsidered after it was found that the ball drawn was red. The new probabilities we considered are called:
   a) Exhaustive b) A priori c) Marginal d) Subjective e) None of these
28. Symbolically, a marginal probability is:
   a) P(*AB*) b) P(*BA*) c) P(*B*|*A*) d) P(*ABC*) e) None of these
29. If we sum all the probabilities of the conditional events in which the event *A* occurs while under statistical dependence, the result is:
   a) The marginal probability of *A*
   b) The joint probability of *A*
   c) The conditional probability of *A*
   d) None of these
30. One of the possible outcomes of doing something is a ________________. The activity that produced this outcome is a ________________.
31. The set of all possible outcomes of an activity is the ________________.
32. A pictorial representation of probability concepts, using symbols to represent outcomes, is a ________________.
33. Events that cannot happen together are called ________________.
34. The probability of one event occurring, given that another event has occurred, is called ________________ probability.
35. In terms of its assumptions, the least restrictive approach to the study of probability is the ________________.

5-12 CONCEPTUAL CASE (Northern White Metals Company)

The 7:00 A.M. shuttle out of New York was crowded and noisier than usual, but Dick Lennox sat back in his seat, undisturbed and deep in thought. His presentation and status report on NWMC had been well received. Segue management had decided to increase substantially the capital resources available to Northern in the coming year. Sales and earnings gains were expected, and Dick had been granted considerable latitude in ensuring that they were realized. Sufficient funding and operating flexibility were all that was needed, he had asserted, to make NWMC a significant contributor to the Segue system.

Three principal objectives were established. First, sales dollars were to be increased through greater utilization of fabricating and anodizing departments by present customers. Sales growth would also come from increasing marketing efforts with the engineering and high-technology industries, although it was suspected that stiff competition would leave this area less profitable than traditional lines of business for some time yet. A second major objective was profit improvement through the introduction of production efficiencies. NWMC had an unusually high amount of waste material compared to finished products, and it was felt that some investment in better quality assurance procedures was sorely needed. Additionally, it was felt that inefficient scheduling led to shorter and more frequent production runs, resulting in higher costs and more unproductive time than was necessary.

The third objective Dick had defined was a review and possible restructuring of the company's credit policy. Current procedures had left Northern with an average collection period of more than 60 days. The company's terms were 1½ 10 net 20, and having receivables outstanding more than three times Northern's net limit was intolerable. Just thinking about the cash flow implications made Dick wince.

Back at the office and ready to formulate his "action plan," as he liked to call it, Dick was considering various ways of expanding sales. He felt he could either add additional sales representatives or simply require the current sales force to make more calls. Management had in the past frequently adjusted the size of the sales force both up and down, and had occasionally raised call quotas to burdensome levels. Dick felt the sales force had been poorly managed, but he still had no real feeling as to which choice would be the better one. Dick was also considering implementing a program suggested by one of his bright young salesmen, Bill Hamilton. Bill had proposed that the company engage in a direct mail campaign to some of the newer high-tech firms with the hope of generating productive new leads for the sales reps. The program was a costly one, but Bill felt sure it would be well worth it. His excitement was infectious, but Dick knew better than to get caught up in the enthusiasm of impetuous youth. The firm had no data available on this kind of program, but Dick felt he could get his hands on some industry figures that might help him make a decision.

Production efficiency improvements, although complex, were less uncertain. Dick had assigned NWMC's chief foreman and expediter, Neill Jansen, a man with considerable operations experience, the task of coordinating production runs and improving scheduling procedures. He had made rapid progress in this area, but quality problems remained. Although many of the extruded aluminum shapes were quite simple, customer specifications were often very precise and there was generally little room for tolerance error. Tolerance tests were being conducted as the extruded metal came out of the press as well as just after the stretching procedure. Dick believed some further examination of past Q/A test data could provide some insight into where the problem might lie.

Some additional insight into the outstanding credit problem was necessary too. The major primary aluminum producers, NWMC's principal raw-material suppliers, were not nearly as flexible with their credit terms as Northern was. Pay early and collect late hardly seemed like an effective financial strategy to Dick. He was quite adamant, then, when he suggested to

Northern's financial officer that an analysis of outstanding past-due accounts was warranted, and quickly too.

In deciding what actions to take to reach his established objectives, Dick once again recognizes the need for more information and analysis. In resolving the sales-force question, data regarding past actions may help Dick in his current situation. What kind of information might he gather, and how should it be used in helping him select the alternative most likely to lead to success? Company data are not available to assess the viability of a direct-mail marketing program. How might external information be applied in determining whether the benefits of the program justify the costs? Quality problems occur in two steps of the manufacturing process. How might Dick determine which is more likely the problem area in most situations? Finally, in resolving Northern's payables-receivables timing disparity and its detrimental effects on cash flow, how might the financial officer determine how likely past-due collections are at all? How likely within some acceptable time frame? How might Dick and the financial officer utilize this information in credit policy formulation?

5-13 COMPUTER DATA BASE EXERCISE

During 1980, Cold River launched a new Rider toy, Polaris. Joe Walsh hoped the toy, named after a popular science fiction movie, would capture market share in the sunbelt, an area impervious to the charms of the Rough Rider because of climate. Polaris is manufactured of a fiber-reinforced, brightly colored plastic, designed for children aged 6 to 12. The toy was an immediate success in the 1980 Christmas retail market.

Polaris is propelled by pedaling; but unlike other pedal toys, it has a mainspring and a flywheel. The toy can be wound up by foot power or as it moves down hill. The toy is self-propelled and emits a whirring noise like a jet turbine as it travels along its range of 100 yards.

Now, in preparing for the 1981 season, Cold River encountered a production problem. The flywheel was mounted on a shaft that turned inside a sleeve. If the space between the shaft and the sleeve were too tight—say .003″ or less—it would be hard to pedal the toy. However, if the space were larger than .006″, the toy would wear out quickly. Another factor influencing the durability of the toy was the average weight of the child riding it.

Although the toy was selling well, Fred had started receiving complaints about it from his sales force. "Aha," he thought, "here's something to keep the dynamic duo off my back for a while."

"Hey, you," he yelled, as he noticed Laurel casually ransacking his order file. "I've got an important job for you. Straighten out Nick Pappas in Production on this. Find out why Polaris is breaking, or we'll have to close out the line."

Laurel groaned as she recalled her 3 painful hours of college credit in production and went to track down Nick Pappas for data.

PROBLEMS AND QUESTIONS

1. Using market survey data for a sample of 500 toys, find the relative frequency of each clearance in the first 50 pedal toys. (Use classes of less than 0.003 inches, between 0.003 and 0.006 inches, and more than 0.006 inches.) Then do the same for the first 100, 150, 200, 250, 300, 400, 500. Assuming that the sample relative frequencies are the same as the population frequencies, what is the probability that a toy leaving the factory will be easy to pedal?
2. What is the probability that a .006 or greater clearance toy will be used by a 140-lb. child? (Assume clearance and user weight are independent.)
3. An estimated .6 percent of all toys sold broke within 2 years of the warranty period. The following data apply to broken toys that were returned. What is the relative frequency of a .006″ or greater clearance given a broken toy?
4. If we have a broken toy, what was its relative frequency of use by a 140-lb. or heavier child?
5. What is the probability that a pedal toy will be given to a 140-lb. child and will break during the warranty period?
6. What is the probability that a pedal toy will break before the end of the warranty period if it is given to a 140-lb. child?
7. What is the probability that a toy will break before the end of the warranty if the clearance is more than .006″?

MARKET SURVEY DATA

BEARING CLEARANCE (IN.)	USER WEIGHT (LBS.)	BEARING CLEARANCE (IN.)	USER WEIGHT (LBS.)	BEARING CLEARANCE (IN.)	USER WEIGHT (LBS.)	BEARING CLEARANCE (IN.)	USER WEIGHT (LBS.)
0.0024	96	0.0041	88	0.0044	77	0.0033	75
0.0046	75	0.0040	100	0.0047	98	0.0035	79
0.0030	109	0.0046	77	0.0021	115	0.0040	94
0.0042	83	0.0041	81	0.0052	107	0.0038	88
0.0040	71	0.0045	78	0.0044	89	0.0044	85
0.0048	104	0.0038	90	0.0039	106	0.0038	82
0.0032	86	0.0044	84	0.0029	91	0.0039	87
0.0028	90	0.0038	92	0.0026	104	0.0029	95
0.0046	65	0.0055	114	0.0044	104	0.0046	53
0.0032	125	0.0039	71	0.0048	122	0.0028	76
0.0031	67	0.0032	97	0.0036	109	0.0053	121
0.0036	98	0.0046	99	0.0037	112	0.0038	102
0.0042	96	0.0037	93	0.0044	100	0.0026	87
0.0048	106	0.0047	107	0.0028	144	0.0034	97
0.0044	127	0.0047	119	0.0033	60	0.0035	76
0.0038	112	0.0037	69	0.0039	104	0.0044	86

MARKET SURVEY DATA *(Continued)*

BEARING CLEARANCE (IN.)	USER WEIGHT (LBS.)	BEARING CLEARANCE (IN.)	USER WEIGHT (LBS.)	BEARING CLEARANCE (IN.)	USER WEIGHT (LBS.)	BEARING CLEARANCE (IN.)	USER WEIGHT (LBS.)
0.0032	73	0.0045	108	0.0044	93	0.0034	93
0.0051	77	0.0041	117	0.0041	95	0.0033	111
0.0027	91	0.0044	101	0.0051	64	0.0044	111
0.0045	84	0.0050	111	0.0040	96	0.0040	94
0.0042	120	0.0040	119	0.0060	95	0.0042	97
0.0034	117	0.0041	59	0.0038	92	0.0037	91
0.0041	73	0.0032	83	0.0051	90	0.0033	83
0.0040	103	0.0046	105	0.0038	82	0.0040	82
0.0051	114	0.0050	105	0.0037	62	0.0048	142
0.0021	88	0.0032	109	0.0041	102	0.0031	94
0.0027	115	0.0043	143	0.0029	117	0.0034	109
0.0040	95	0.0031	91	0.0037	102	0.0035	94
0.0036	114	0.0043	100	0.0039	87	0.0040	111
0.0039	91	0.0031	109	0.0032	77	0.0033	78
0.0037	74	0.0041	90	0.0051	88	0.0029	91
0.0035	104	0.0034	99	0.0037	92	0.0041	54
0.0033	125	0.0036	101	0.0034	65	0.0051	75
0.0046	110	0.0035	109	0.0049	75	0.0031	88
0.0020	102	0.0038	88	0.0046	57	0.0047	108
0.0031	117	0.0041	69	0.0032	71	0.0027	92
0.0044	65	0.0036	110	0.0039	95	0.0027	86
0.0032	79	0.0045	82	0.0040	113	0.0034	97
0.0039	102	0.0039	78	0.0026	105	0.0034	92
0.0027	93	0.0031	105	0.0048	69	0.0039	124
0.0045	93	0.0039	86	0.0038	98	0.0037	86
0.0044	90	0.0046	58	0.0046	110	0.0050	121
0.0041	93	0.0046	128	0.0049	117	0.0031	98
0.0036	112	0.0035	74	0.0025	110	0.0042	60
0.0039	85	0.0032	91	0.0046	83	0.0044	94
0.0042	70	0.0038	107	0.0039	83	0.0047	76
0.0042	81	0.0033	103	0.0027	123	0.0039	92
0.0036	68	0.0039	82	0.0030	101	0.0045	55
0.0039	107	0.0045	83	0.0042	46	0.0044	60
0.0031	84	0.0044	86	0.0031	102	0.0022	93
0.0045	90	0.0032	118	0.0037	67	0.0042	100
0.0037	92	0.0031	64	0.0036	84	0.0054	76
0.0042	113	0.0041	118	0.0041	73	0.0051	118
0.0052	80	0.0052	91	0.0031	100	0.0043	93
0.0039	100	0.0029	118	0.0018	91	0.0039	89
0.0035	42	0.0044	85	0.0039	88	0.0033	113
0.0061	88	0.0027	101	0.0031	88	0.0038	109
0.0046	92	0.0048	108	0.0035	69	0.0027	124
0.0041	52	0.0038	73	0.0050	78	0.0039	100
0.0038	101	0.0045	103	0.0063	85	0.0042	100
0.0039	113	0.0046	90	0.0042	77	0.0043	83
0.0036	112	0.0037	115	0.0038	74	0.0045	86
0.0027	97	0.0035	102	0.0035	103	0.0025	88
0.0024	119	0.0050	72	0.0042	109	0.0037	67
0.0033	116	0.0036	93	0.0030	106	0.0033	71
0.0029	85	0.0027	73	0.0047	65	0.0030	89
0.0042	96	0.0035	112	0.0049	91	0.0040	92

MARKET SURVEY DATA *(Continued)*

BEARING CLEARANCE (IN.)	USER WEIGHT (LBS.)	BEARING CLEARANCE (IN.)	USER WEIGHT (LBS.)	BEARING CLEARANCE (IN.)	USER WEIGHT (LBS.)	BEARING CLEARANCE (IN.)	USER WEIGHT (LBS.)
0.0033	98	0.0034	93	0.0044	61	0.0040	68
0.0050	68	0.0044	67	0.0039	49	0.0042	60
0.0040	113	0.0039	82	0.0042	84	0.0042	115
0.0040	112	0.0037	82	0.0042	108	0.0037	73
0.0034	69	0.0033	110	0.0042	102	0.0043	110
0.0031	119	0.0039	73	0.0034	84	0.0044	79
0.0036	98	0.0032	106	0.0041	52	0.0041	48
0.0037	82	0.0042	83	0.0037	96	0.0038	103
0.0036	111	0.0037	72	0.0042	106	0.0044	80
0.0044	103	0.0042	90	0.0040	87	0.0031	89
0.0042	106	0.0043	72	0.0032	80	0.0039	116
0.0034	96	0.0043	112	0.0036	103	0.0033	80
0.0037	74	0.0037	91	0.0028	73	0.0024	127
0.0042	96	0.0034	81	0.0037	114	0.0034	62
0.0046	115	0.0029	81	0.0038	85	0.0032	91
0.0036	48	0.0042	59	0.0043	115	0.0041	53
0.0043	89	0.0046	108	0.0033	64	0.0032	99
0.0052	108	0.0032	95	0.0037	83	0.0042	80
0.0032	92	0.0037	91	0.0047	80	0.0033	103
0.0038	67	0.0041	68	0.0040	78	0.0030	122
0.0037	77	0.0049	99	0.0037	92	0.0041	95
0.0050	104	0.0031	80	0.0048	113	0.0033	95
0.0047	81	0.0049	99	0.0050	116	0.0045	89
0.0022	95	0.0036	78	0.0050	157	0.0031	99
0.0041	111	0.0035	62	0.0035	92	0.0053	103
0.0036	106	0.0045	45	0.0046	100	0.0032	115
0.0026	88	0.0040	62	0.0041	114	0.0044	87
0.0047	83	0.0043	68	0.0041	60	0.0054	90
0.0047	63	0.0033	117	0.0042	140	0.0032	49
0.0042	88	0.0044	84	0.0036	70	0.0038	108
0.0066	107	0.0030	80	0.0033	114	0.0036	112
0.0046	127	0.0035	81	0.0034	123	0.0040	133
0.0042	86	0.0032	80	0.0039	71	0.0031	91
0.0036	112	0.0038	78	0.0040	80	0.0039	65
0.0033	115	0.0026	76	0.0039	85	0.0048	106
0.0029	58	0.0029	95	0.0036	60	0.0046	87
0.0042	112	0.0039	102	0.0034	96	0.0050	80
0.0033	69	0.0038	73	0.0039	35	0.0027	62
0.0036	113	0.0036	125	0.0050	103	0.0032	104
0.0048	95	0.0039	109	0.0025	100	0.0048	107
0.0035	54	0.0047	84	0.0047	104	0.0032	100
0.0046	108	0.0043	72	0.0040	61	0.0040	106
0.0040	78	0.0043	58	0.0022	86	0.0047	116
0.0051	88	0.0036	85	0.0034	81	0.0039	70
0.0031	85	0.0036	68	0.0033	95	0.0048	102
0.0043	93	0.0039	93	0.0043	102	0.0043	102
0.0035	79	0.0038	97	0.0037	70	0.0038	75
0.0037	108	0.0035	93	0.0037	71	0.0052	87
0.0051	99	0.0038	75	0.0038	84	0.0029	64
0.0037	74	0.0035	98	0.0055	71	0.0028	107
0.0044	93	0.0042	117	0.0033	94	0.0041	95

MARKET SURVEY DATA *(Continued)*

BEARING CLEARANCE (IN.)	USER WEIGHT (LBS.)	BEARING CLEARANCE (IN.)	USER WEIGHT (LBS.)	BEARING CLEARANCE (IN.)	USER WEIGHT (LBS.)	BEARING CLEARANCE (IN.)	USER WEIGHT (LBS.)
0.0033	54	0.0043	100	0.0035	37	0.0038	101
0.0032	58	0.0042	118	0.0036	77	0.0041	72
0.0039	74	0.0043	71	0.0041	105	0.0050	96
0.0037	105	0.0045	73	0.0031	81	0.0037	119
0.0055	92	0.0050	67	0.0031	79	0.0036	106
0.0038	127	0.0028	120	0.0048	81	0.0053	88
0.0032	46	0.0047	68	0.0049	90	0.0027	95

DATA REPRESENTING TOYS THAT BROKE DURING WARRANTY PERIOD

BEARING CLEARANCE (IN.)	USER WEIGHT (LBS.)	BEARING CLEARANCE (IN.)	USER WEIGHT (LBS.)	BEARING CLEARANCE (IN.)	USER WEIGHT (LBS.)	BEARING CLEARANCE (IN.)	USER WEIGHT (LBS.)
0.0050	146	0.0067	138	0.0066	129	0.0059	131
0.0062	125	0.0066	150	0.0063	148	0.0061	129
0.0056	145	0.0062	127	0.0047	135	0.0066	144
0.0066	133	0.0067	131	0.0064	143	0.0064	138
0.0066	131	0.0065	128	0.0064	139	0.0066	135
0.0064	146	0.0064	140	0.0065	140	0.0064	132
0.0058	136	0.0070	134	0.0055	141	0.0065	137
0.0054	140	0.0064	142	0.0052	150	0.0055	145
0.0068	139	0.0061	132	0.0070	152	0.0060	153
0.0058	125	0.0065	129	0.0060	130	0.0054	126
0.0057	135	0.0058	147	0.0062	143	0.0059	135
0.0062	148	0.0066	149	0.0063	144	0.0064	152
0.0064	146	0.0063	143	0.0064	150	0.0052	137
0.0068	140	0.0065	147	0.0054	144	0.0060	147
0.0068	127	0.0065	131	0.0059	136	0.0061	126
0.0064	140	0.0063	137	0.0065	148	0.0070	136
0.0058	129	0.0067	140	0.0070	143	0.0060	143
0.0061	129	0.0065	129	0.0067	145	0.0059	141
0.0053	141	0.0062	147	0.0059	142	0.0062	143
0.0063	134	0.0054	139	0.0066	146	0.0066	144
0.0064	134	0.0066	137	0.0048	145	0.0064	147
0.0060	133	0.0067	143	0.0064	142	0.0063	141
0.0067	127	0.0058	133	0.0057	140	0.0059	133
0.0066	147	0.0064	149	0.0064	132	0.0066	132
0.0059	136	0.0058	145	0.0063	134	0.0058	142

5-14 FLOW CHART

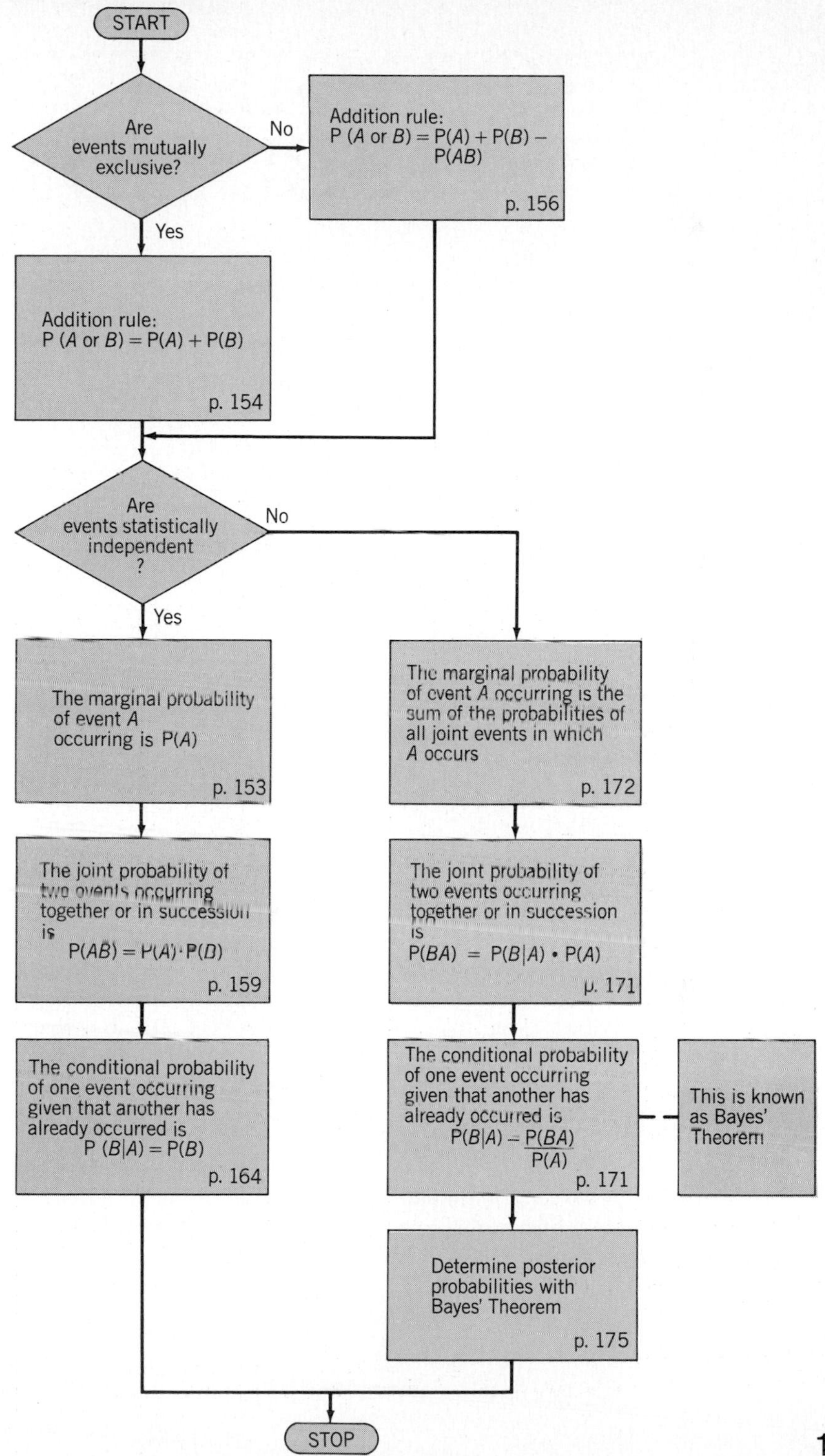

START
Are events mutually exclusive?
No
Addition rule:
P (A or B) = P(A) + P(B) − P(AB)
p. 156
Yes
Addition rule:
P (A or B) = P(A) + P(B)
p. 154
Are events statistically independent ?
No
Yes
The marginal probability of event A occurring is P(A)
p. 153
The marginal probability of event A occurring is the sum of the probabilities of all joint events in which A occurs
p. 172
The joint probability of two events occurring together or in succession is
P(AB) = P(A)·P(B)
p. 159
The joint probability of two events occurring together or in succession is
P(BA) = P(B|A) • P(A)
p. 171
The conditional probability of one event occurring given that another has already occurred is
P (B|A) = P(B)
p. 164
The conditional probability of one event occurring given that another has already occurred is
P(B|A) = P(BA) / P(A)
p. 171
This is known as Bayes' Theorem
Determine posterior probabilities with Bayes' Theorem
p. 175
STOP

CHAPTER 6

PROBABILITY II: DISTRIBUTIONS

1. INTRODUCTION TO PROBABILITY DISTRIBUTIONS, 200
2. RANDOM VARIABLES, 204
3. USE OF EXPECTED VALUE IN DECISION MAKING, 210
4. THE BINOMIAL DISTRIBUTION, 214
5. THE POISSON DISTRIBUTION, 224
6. THE NORMAL DISTRIBUTION: A Distribution of a Continuous Random Variable, 230
7. CHOOSING THE CORRECT PROBABILITY DISTRIBUTION, 246
8. TERMS, 247
9. EQUATIONS, 247
10. REVIEW EXERCISES, 249
11. CONCEPTS TEST, 253
12. CONCEPTUAL CASE, 255
13. COMPUTER DATA BASE EXERCISE, 257
14. FLOW CHART, 264

OBJECTIVES: In Chapter 6, we are concerned with probability distributions; that is, the various ways data array themselves when we graph them. Here again we are laying the foundation for later work in statistical inference. You may have a notion about probability distributions if you have dealt with the bell-shaped curve in psychology or mathematics. Or if you are a male who wears a 16EE shoe or a female who wears size 3AAAA, you may have an intuitive idea about probability distributions. When you cannot be fitted, you probably wish the shoe-store manager would order a larger distribution of sizes; but a manager who thinks in terms of correct probability distributions will probably not order such unusual sizes and won't be able to accommodate people with very large or very small feet.

Most consequential managerial decisions are made under conditions of uncertainty, because decision makers seldom have complete information about what the future will bring. Also introduced in Chapter 6 is statistical decision theory, those methods that are useful when we must decide among alternatives despite uncertain conditions.

Modern filling machines are designed to work efficiently and with high reliability. Machines like the one pictured can fill soft-drink bottles to within .1 ounce of the desired level 80 percent of the time. A visitor to the bottling plant, watching filled bottles being placed into six-pack cartons, asked, "What's the chance that exactly half the bottles in a six pack selected at random will be filled to within .1 ounce of the desired level?" Although we cannot make an exact forecast, the ideas about probability distributions discussed in this chapter enable us to give a pretty good answer to the question.

6-1 INTRODUCTION TO PROBABILITY DISTRIBUTIONS

In Chapters 2, 3, and 4, we described frequency distributions as a useful way of summarizing variations in observed data. We prepared frequency distributions by listing all the possible outcomes of an experiment and then indicating the observed frequency of each possible outcome. *Probability distributions* are related to frequency distributions. **In fact, we can think of a probability distribution as a theoretical frequency distribution.** Now, what does that mean? A theoretical frequency distribution is a probability distribution that describes how outcomes are *expected* to vary. Since these distributions deal with expectations, they are useful models in making inferences and decisions under conditions of uncertainty. In later chapters, we will discuss the methods we use under these conditions.

Probability distributions and frequency distributions

Examples of Probability Distributions

Experiment using a fair coin

To begin our study of probability distributions, let's go back to the idea of a fair coin, which we introduced in Chapter 5. Suppose we toss a fair coin twice. Table 6-1 illustrates the possible outcomes from this two-toss experiment.

TABLE 6-1 Possible outcomes from two tosses of a fair coin

FIRST TOSS	SECOND TOSS	NUMBER OF TAILS ON TWO TOSSES	PROBABILITY OF THE FOUR POSSIBLE OUTCOMES
T	*T*	2	.5 × .5 = .25
T	*H*	1	.5 × .5 = .25
H	*H*	0	.5 × .5 = .25
H	*T*	1	.5 × .5 = .25
			1.00

Now suppose that we are interested in formulating a probability distribution of the number of tails that could possibly result when we toss the coin twice. We would begin by noting any outcome that did *not* contain a tail. With a fair coin, that is only the third outcome in Table 6-1: *H, H*. Then we would note those outcomes containing only one tail (the second and fourth outcomes in Table 6-1), and finally we would note that the first outcome contains two tails. In Table 6-2 we rearrange the outcomes of Table 6-1 to emphasize the number of tails contained in each outcome. We must be careful to note at this point that Table 6-2 is *not* the actual outcome of tossing a fair coin twice. Rather, it is a *theoretical* outcome; that is, it represents the way in which we would *expect* our two-toss experiment to behave over time.

We can illustrate in graphic form the probability distribution in Table 6-2. To do this, we graph the number of tails we might see on two tosses against the probability that this number would happen. We have shown this graph in Fig. 6-1.

TABLE 6-2 Probability distribution of possible number of tails from two tosses of a fair coin

NUMBER OF TAILS *T*	TOSSES	PROBABILITY OF THIS OUTCOME P(*T*)
0	(*H*, *H*)	.25
1	(*T*, *H*) + (*H*, *T*)	.50
2	(*T*, *T*)	.25

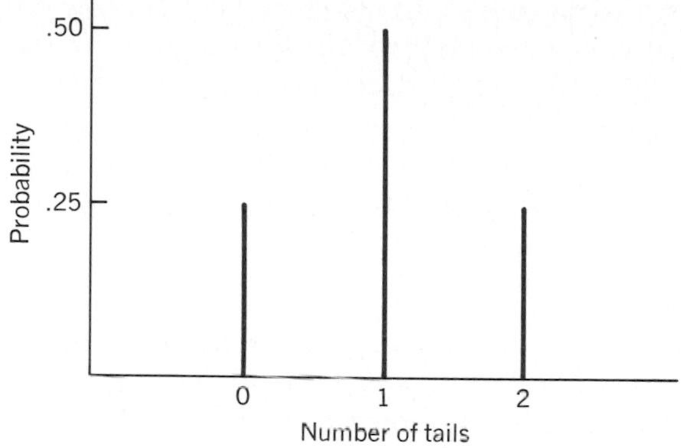

FIGURE 6-1 Probability distribution of the number of tails in two tosses of a fair coin

Voting example

Consider another example. A political candidate for local office is considering the votes she can get in a coming election. Assume that votes can take on only four possible values. If the candidate's assessment is like this:

Number of votes	1,000	2,000	3,000	4,000	
Probability this will happen	.1	.3	.4	.2	**Total 1.0**

then the graph of the probability distribution representing her expectations will be like the one shown in Fig. 6-2.

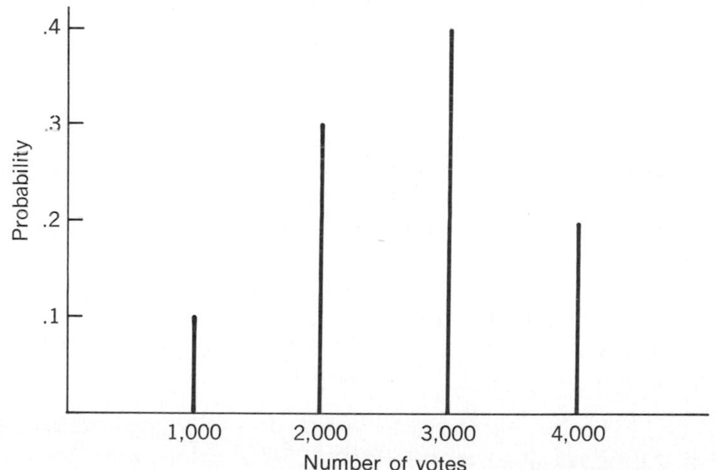

FIGURE 6-2 Probability distribution of number of votes

Difference between frequency distributions and probability distributions

Before we move on to other aspects of probability distributions, we should point out that a **frequency distribution is a listing of the observed frequencies of all the outcomes of an experiment that actually occurred when the experiment was done, whereas a probability distribution is a listing of the probabilities of all the possible outcomes that *could* result if the experiment were done.** Also, as we can see in the two examples we presented in Figs. 6-1 and 6-2, probability distributions can be based on theoretical considerations (the tosses of a coin) or on a subjective assessment of the likelihood of certain outcomes (the candidate's estimate). Probability distributions can also be based on experience. Insurance company actuaries determine insurance premiums, for example, by using long years of experience with death rates to establish probabilities of dying among various age groups.

Types of Probability Distributions

Discrete probability distributions

Probability distributions are classified as either *discrete* or *continuous*. A discrete probability is allowed to take on only a limited number of values. An example of a discrete probability distribution is shown in Fig. 6-2, where we expressed the candidate's ideas about the coming election. There, votes were allowed to take on only four possible values (1,000, 2,000, 3,000, or 4,000). Similarly, the probability that you were born in a given month is also discrete, since there are only twelve possible values (the twelve months of the year).

Continuous probability distributions

In a continuous probability distribution, on the other hand, the variable under consideration is allowed to take on any value within a given range. Suppose we were examining the level of effluent in a variety of streams, and we measured the level of effluent by parts of effluent per million parts of water. We would expect quite a continuous range of ppm (parts per million), all the way from very low levels in clear mountain streams to extremely high levels in polluted streams. In fact, it would be quite normal for the variable "parts per million" to take on an enormous number of values. We would call the distribution of this variable (ppm) a continuous distribution. Continuous distributions are convenient ways to represent discrete distributions that have many possible outcomes, all very close to each other.

EXERCISES

6-1 The manager of Nickels Department Store is attempting to estimate how many people he will have to hire over the next year. Historical information regarding the turnover rate resulted in the following data concerning the probabilities of hiring various numbers of employees. Draw a graph illustrating this probability distribution.

Number of employees hired	0	5	10	15	25
Probability	.08	.18	.30	.24	.20

6-2 Based on the following graph of a probability distribution, construct the table that corresponds to the graph.

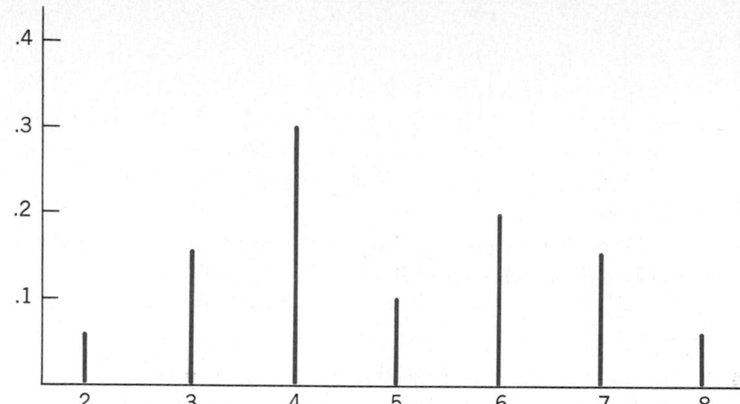

6-3 In the last chapter, we looked at the possible outcomes of tossing two dice, and we calculated some probabilities associated with various outcomes. Construct a table and a graph of the probability distribution representing the outcomes (in terms of total number of dots showing on both dice) for this experiment.

6-4 Which of the following statements regarding probability distributions are correct?

a) A probability distribution provides information about the long-run or expected frequency of each outcome of an experiment.
b) The graph of a probability distribution has the possible outcomes of an experiment marked on the horizontal axis.
c) A probability distribution lists the probabilities that each outcome is random.
d) A probability distribution is always constructed from a set of observed frequencies like a frequency distribution.
e) A probability distribution may be based on subjective estimates of the likelihood of certain outcomes.

6-5 Southport Autos offers a variety of luxury options on its cars. Because of the 6- to 8-week waiting period for custom orders, Larry Toppman, the dealer, stocks his cars with a variety of options. Currently, Mr. Toppman, who prides himself on being able to meet his customers' needs immediately, is worried because of an industrywide shortage of cars with sun roofs. Toppman offers the following luxury combinations:

1. Power windows	Vinyl roof	Electric sun roof
2. Electric sun roof	FM stereo	Power windows
3. Vinyl roof	FM stereo	Leather interior
4. FM stereo	Electric sun roof	Vinyl roof

Toppman assigns an equal chance that any of the combinations will be ordered.

a) What is the probability that any one customer ordering a luxury car will order one including a sun roof?
b) Assume that two customers order luxury cars. Construct a table showing the probability distribution of the number of sun roofs ordered.

6-6 Erika Rosenberg, the product manager for a new support hose recently designed by Knees, is on the verge of releasing her product in a test market. Before releasing the product, Rosenberg must clearly tell her superiors how she expects the product to perform. In this test market, she feels that she can sell 16,000 pairs, with a 60 percent probability. Her marketing assistants feel, however, that 4,000 of these sales are tenuous. They feel that there is half as much chance of getting 12,000 sales as there is of getting all 16,000. The assistants and Rosenberg also agree that with a slight change in the product's positioning, the product could, with some probability, pick up an additional 2,000 sales; but they feel this is the maximum the product could obtain. Looking at the blocks of sales as Rosenberg and her assistants see it, construct a table and draw a graph of the probability distribution of sales.

6-2 RANDOM VARIABLES

Random variable defined

A random variable is a variable that takes on different values as a result of the outcomes of a random experiment. A random variable can be either discrete or continuous. If a random variable is allowed to take on only a limited number of values, it is a *discrete random variable*. On the other hand, if it is allowed to assume any value within a given range, it is a *continuous random variable*.

Example of discrete random variables

You can think of a random variable as a value or magnitude that changes from occurrence to occurrence in no predictable sequence. A breast-cancer screening clinic, for example, has no way of knowing exactly how many women will be screened on any one day. So tomorrow's number of patients is a random variable. The values of a random variable are the numerical values corresponding to each possible outcome of the random experiment. If past daily records of the clinic indicate that the values of the random variable range from 100 to 115 patients daily, the random variable is a discrete random variable.

Table 6-3 illustrates the number of times each level has been reached during the last 100 days. Note that Table 6-3 gives a frequency distribution. To the extent that we believe that the experience of the past 100 days has been typical, we can use this historical record to assign a probability to each

Finding a probability distribution

possible number of patients and find a probability distribution. We have accomplished this in Table 6-4, by normalizing the observed frequency

TABLE 6-3 Number of women screened daily during 100 days

NUMBER SCREENED	NUMBER OF DAYS THIS LEVEL WAS OBSERVED
100	1
101	2
102	3
103	5
104	6
105	7
106	9
107	10
108	12
109	11
110	9
111	8
112	6
113	5
114	4
115	2
	100

TABLE 6-4 Probability distribution for number of women screened

NUMBER SCREENED (VALUE OF THE RANDOM VARIABLE)	PROBABILITY THAT THE RANDOM VARIABLE WILL TAKE ON THIS VALUE
100	.01
101	.02
102	.03
103	.05
104	.06
105	.07
106	.09
107	.10
108	.12
109	.11
110	.09
111	.08
112	.06
113	.05
114	.04
115	.02
	1.00

distribution (in this case, dividing each value in the right-hand column of Table 6-3 by 100, the total number of days for which the record has been kept). The probability distribution for the random variable "daily number screened" is illustrated graphically in Fig. 6-3. Notice that the probability distribution for a random variable provides a probability for each possible value and that these probabilities must sum to 1. Table 6-4 shows that both these requirements have been met. Furthermore, both Table 6-4 and Fig. 6-3 give us information about the long-run frequency of occurrence of daily patient screenings we would expect to observe if this random "experiment" is repeated.

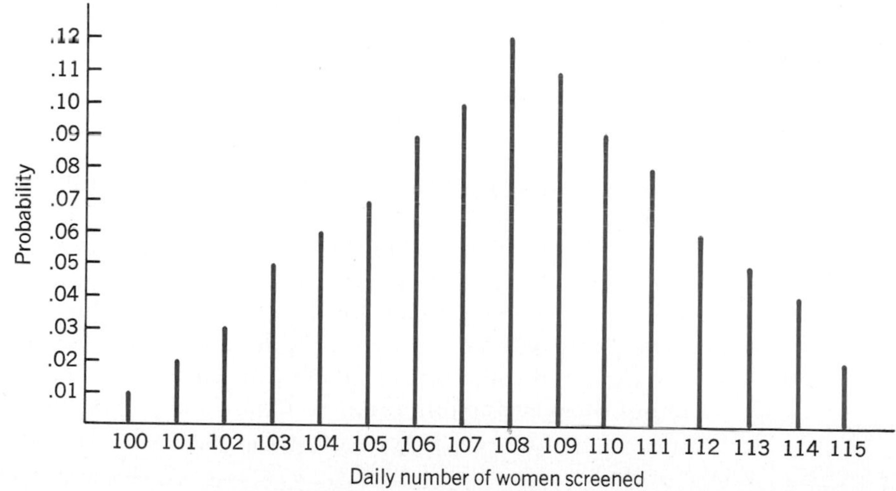

FIGURE 6-3 Probability distribution for the discrete random variable "daily number screened"

The Expected Value of a Random Variable

Suppose you toss a coin ten times and get seven heads, like this:

HEADS	TAILS	TOTAL
7	3	10

Hmm, strange, you say. You then ask a friend to try tossing the coin 20 times; she gets fifteen heads and five tails. So now you have, in all, 22 heads and eight tails out of 30 tosses.

What did you expect? Was it something closer to fifteen heads and fifteen tails (half and half)? Now suppose you turn the tossing over to a machine and get 792 heads and 208 tails out of 1,000 tosses of the same coin. You might now be suspicious of the coin because it didn't live up to what you expected.

Expected value is a fundamental idea in the study of probability distributions. For many years, the concept has been put to considerable practical use in the insurance industry, and in the last twenty years, it has been widely used by many others who must make decisions under conditions of uncertainty.

Expected value defined

To obtain the **expected value of a discrete random variable,** we multiply each value that the random variable can assume by the probability of occurrence of that value and then sum these products. Table 6-5 illustrates this procedure for our clinic problem. The total in Table 6-5 tells us that the expected value of the discrete random variable "number screened" is 108.02 women. What does this mean? It means that over a long period of time, the number of daily screenings should average about 108.02. Remember that an expected value of 108.02 does *not* mean that tomorrow exactly 108.02 women will visit the clinic.

The clinic director would base her decisions on the expected value of daily screenings because the expected value is a *weighted average of the outcomes she expects in the future*. Expected value weights each possible outcome by the frequency with which it is expected to occur. Thus, more common occurrences are given more weight than are less common ones. As conditions change over time, the director would recompute the expected value of daily screenings and use this new figure as a basis for decision making.

Deriving expected value

In our clinic example, the director used past patients' records as the basis for calculating the expected value of daily screenings. The expected value can also be derived from the director's subjective assessments of the probability that the random variable will take on certain values. In that case, the expected value represents nothing more than her personal convictions about the possible outcome.

In this section, we have worked with the probability distribution of a

TABLE 6-5 Calculating the expected value of the discrete random variable "daily number screened"

POSSIBLE VALUES OF THE RANDOM VARIABLE (1)	PROBABILITY THAT THE RANDOM VARIABLE WILL TAKE ON THESE VALUES (2)	(1) × (2)
100	.01	1.00
101	.02	2.02
102	.03	3.06
103	.05	5.15
104	.06	6.24
105	.07	7.35
106	.09	9.54
107	.10	10.70
108	.12	12.96
109	.11	11.99
110	.09	9.90
111	.08	8.88
112	.06	6.72
113	.05	5.65
114	.04	4.56
115	.02	2.30
	Expected value of the random variable "daily number screened" →	**108.02**

random variable in tabular form (Table 6-5) and in graphic form (Fig. 6-3). In many situations, however, we will find it more convenient, in terms of the computations that must be done, to represent the probability distribution of a random variable in *algebraic* form. By doing this, we can make probability calculations by substituting numerical values directly into an algebraic equation. In the following sections, we shall illustrate situations in which this is appropriate and methods for accomplishing it.

EXERCISES

6-7 Construct a table for a possible probability distribution based on the frequency distribution given below.

Outcome	10	12	14	16	18	20
Frequency	15	20	45	42	18	10

a) Draw a graph of the hypothetical probability distribution.
b) Compute the expected value of the outcome.

6-8 From the following graph of a probability distribution:
a) Construct a table of the probability distribution.
b) Find the expected value of the random variable.

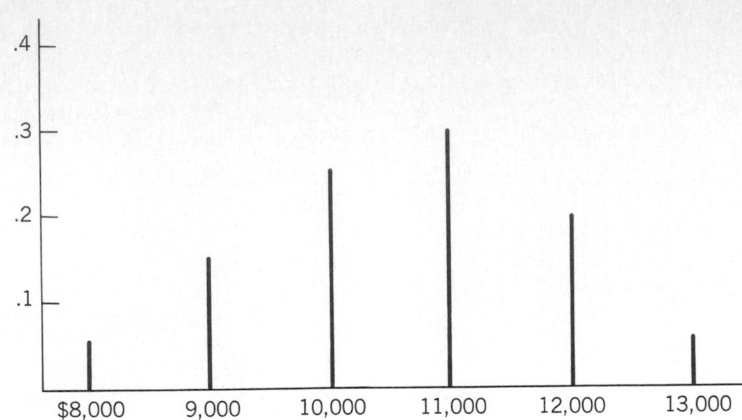

6-9 Bob Walters, who frequently invests in the stock market, carefully studies any potential investment. He is currently examining the possibility of investing in the Trinity Power Company. Through studying past performance, Walters has broken the potential results of an investment into 5 possible outcomes with accompanying probabilities. The outcomes are annual rates of return on a single share of stock that currently costs $100. Find the expected value of the return on investing in a single share of Trinity Power.

Return on investment ($)	0.00	5.00	10.00	25.00	50.00
Probability	.25	.40	.20	.10	.05

If Walters purchases stock only if the expected rate of return exceeds 10 percent, will he purchase this stock, according to these data?

6-10 The only information available to you regarding the probability distribution of a set of outcomes is the following list of frequencies:

X	0	1	2	3	4	5
Frequency	18	48	180	252	72	30

a) Construct a possible probability distribution for the set of outcomes.
b) Find the expected value of an outcome.

6-11 A Las Vegas gambling-casino owner has hired a behavior-modification expert to help him figure out ways to make larger profits from the slot machines. One specific machine, located in the lobby of the convention hall, is chosen for study. The owner of the casino wants the psychologist to focus on the months of August and September, pivotal months in the gambling-casino business. The psychologist hopes to alter the design of the slot machine to take advantage of his knowledge of the clientele and gambling behavior in general. The owner and psychologist agree that a preliminary analysis should be done of past activity on this machine. The psychologist decides to prepare a probability distribution and compute the expected value of gross profits for August and September. The following data are available:

	Dollars taken from slot machine											
YEAR	J	F	M	A	M	J	J	A	S	O	N	D
1980	9,500	7,000	7,000	7,500	7,000	8,000	6,500	8,000	10,000	7,500	6,000	8,000
1981	6,500	7,500	6,000	9,000	9,500	7,000	7,500	6,500	6,000	9,000	5,500	6,500
1982	9,000	7,000	7,500	10,000	7,000	8,000						

6-12 Dr. James Sperling, chief psychiatrist at a mental institution, recently became concerned about the institution's treatment of patients having acute anxiety neuroses. Specifically, he felt these patients were being kept in the institution too long. Dr. Sperling specialized in therapy but did not feel that he handled figures very well, so he assigned his assistant, Dr. Alice Thorndike, to compile a summary report to help him investigate his belief. When Dr. Thorndike presented a probability distribution to Dr. Sperling, he was less than appreciative. He commented that she had been assigned to compile figures, not to attempt creativity by drawing pictures. She returned to her office with the realization that all Dr. Sperling desired was one figure—the expected length of time one of these patients stayed in the institution. What answer should she give him?

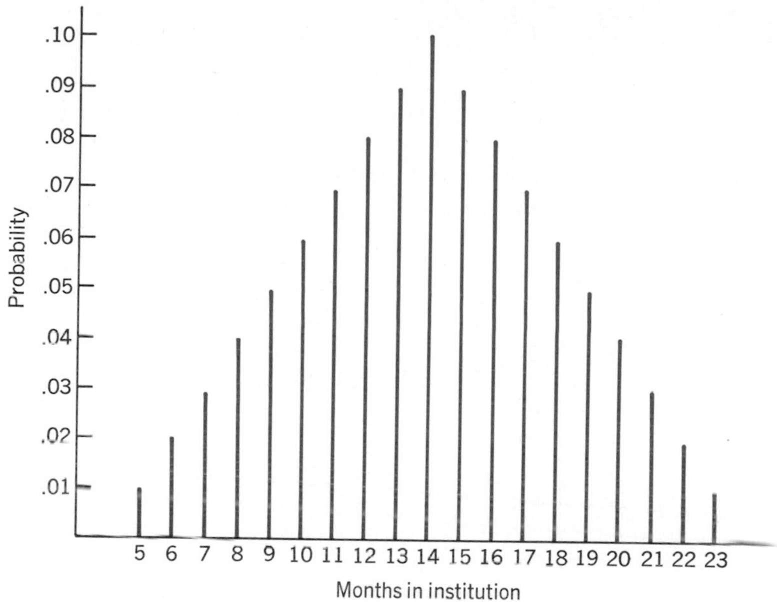

6-13 Production levels for Giles Fashion vary greatly according to consumer acceptance of the latest styles. Therefore, the company's weekly orders of wool cloth are difficult to predict in advance. On the basis of 5 years of data, the following probability distribution for the company's weekly demand for wool has been computed:

Amount of wool (lbs.)	3,000	4,000	4,500	5,000
Probability	.2	.4	.2	.2

From these data, the raw-materials purchaser computed the expected number of pounds required. Recently he noticed that the company's sales were lower in the last year than in years before. Extrapolating, he observed that the company will be lucky if its weekly demand averages 2,500 this year.

a) What was the expected weekly demand for wool based on the distribution from past data?
b) If each pound of wool generates $5 in revenue and costs $4 to purchase, ship, and handle, how much would Giles Fashion stand to gain or lose each week if it orders wool based on past data and the company's demand is only 2,500?

6-14 Betty Jackson owns Jackson's Bakeshop, which is well known for the delicious cakes that are baked daily. Betty's problem is that to keep up her good reputation, she never sells a cake that is not fresh. Each morning, Betty bakes five cakes, which cost her approximately $6.50 each, and any cakes that are not sold by the end of the day are thrown away. Betty sells each cake for $11, and the number of cakes that she sells in a day has a probability distribution given below. Calculate Betty's expected daily profits from cake sales.

Number of cakes sold	0	1	2	3	4	5
Probability	.05	.10	.20	.30	.25	.10

Is it profitable for Betty to bake 5 cakes each day?

6-3 USE OF EXPECTED VALUE IN DECISION MAKING

In the preceding section, we calculated the expected value of a random variable and noted that it can have significant value to decision makers. Now we need to take a moment to illustrate how decision makers combine the probabilities that a random variable will take on certain values with the monetary gain or loss that results when it does take on those values. Doing just this enables them to make intelligent decisions under uncertain conditions.

Combining Probabilities and Monetary Values

Wholesaler problem

Let us look at the case of a fruit and vegetable wholesaler who sells strawberries. This product has a very limited useful life. If not sold on the day of delivery, it is worthless. One case of strawberries costs \$20, and the wholesaler receives \$50 for it. The wholesaler cannot specify the number of cases customers will call for on any one day, but her analysis of past records has produced the information in Table 6-6.

TABLE 6-6 Sales during 100 days

DAILY SALES	NUMBER OF DAYS SOLD	PROBABILITY OF EACH NUMBER BEING SOLD
10	15	.15
11	20	.20
12	40	.40
13	25	.25
	100	**1.00**

Types of Losses Defined

Two types of losses are incurred by the wholesaler: (1) *obsolescence losses,* caused by stocking too much fruit on any one day and having to throw it away the next day; and (2) *opportunity losses,* caused by being out of strawberries any time that customers call for them. (Customers will not wait beyond the day a case is requested.)

Table of conditional losses

Table 6-7 is a table of conditional losses. Each value in the table is conditional on a specific number of cases being stocked and a specific number being requested. The values in Table 6-7 include not only losses from decaying berries but also those losses resulting from lost revenue when the wholesaler is unable to supply the requests she receives for the berries.

Neither of these two types of losses is incurred when the number of cases stocked on any one day is the same as the number of cases requested. When that happens, the wholesaler sells all she has stocked and incurs no losses. This situation is indicated by a colored zero in the appropriate column. Figures **above** any zero represent losses arising from spoiled berries. In each case here, the number of cases stocked is greater than the number requested. For example, if the wholesaler stocks twelve cases but receives requests for only ten cases, she loses $40 (or $20 per case for spoiled strawberries).

TABLE 6-7 Conditional loss table

POSSIBLE REQUESTS FOR STRAWBERRIES	Possible stock actions			
	10	11	12	13
10	$ 0	$20	$40	$60
11	30	0	20	40
12	60	30	0	20
13	90	60	30	0

Opportunity losses

Values **below** the colored zeros represent opportunity losses resulting from requests that cannot be filled. If only ten cases are stocked on a day that eleven requests are received, the wholesaler suffers an opportunity loss of $30 for the case she cannot sell ($50 income per case that would have been received minus $20 cost equals $30).

Calculating Expected Losses

Examining each possible stock action, we can compute the expected loss. We do this by weighting each of the four possible loss figures in each column of Table 6-7 by the probabilities from Table 6-6. For a stock action of ten cases, the expected loss is computed as in Table 6-8.

TABLE 6-8 Expected loss from stocking 10 cases

POSSIBLE REQUESTS	CONDITIONAL LOSS		PROBABILITY OF THIS MANY REQUESTS		EXPECTED LOSS
10	$ 0	×	.15	=	$ .00
11	30	×	.20	=	6.00
12	60	×	.40	=	24.00
13	90	×	.25	=	22.50
			1.00		**$52.50**

Meaning of expected loss

The conditional losses in Table 6-8 are taken from the first column of Table 6-7 for a stock action of ten cases. The fourth column total in Table 6-8 shows us that if ten cases are stocked each day, over a long period of time the average or expected loss will be \$52.50 a day. There is no guarantee that *tomorrow's* loss will be exactly \$52.50.

Optimum solution

Tables 6-9 through 6-11 show the computations of the expected loss resulting from decisions to stock eleven, twelve, and thirteen cases, respectively. **The optimum stock action is the one that will minimize expected losses.** This action calls for the stocking of twelve cases each day, at which point the expected loss is minimized at \$17.50. We could just as easily have solved this problem by taking an alternative approach; that is, *maximizing expected gain* (\$50 received per case less \$20 cost per case) instead of minimizing expected loss. The answer, twelve cases, would have been the same.

TABLE 6-9 Expected loss from stocking 11 cases

POSSIBLE REQUESTS	CONDITIONAL LOSS		PROBABILITY OF THIS MANY REQUESTS		EXPECTED LOSS
10	\$20	×	.15	=	\$ 3.00
11	0	×	.20	=	.00
12	30	×	.40	=	12.00
13	60	×	.25	=	15.00
			1.00		**\$30.00**

TABLE 6-10 Expected loss from stocking 12 cases

POSSIBLE REQUESTS	CONDITIONAL LOSS		PROBABILITY OF THIS MANY REQUESTS		EXPECTED LOSS
10	\$40	×	.15	=	\$ 6.00
11	20	×	.20	=	4.00
12	0	×	.40	=	.00
13	30	×	.25	=	7.50
			1.00	**minimum expected loss →**	**\$17.50**

TABLE 6-11 Expected loss from stocking 13 cases

POSSIBLE REQUESTS	CONDITIONAL LOSS		PROBABILITY OF THIS MANY REQUESTS		EXPECTED LOSS
10	\$60	×	.15	=	\$ 9.00
11	40	×	.20	=	8.00
12	20	×	.40	=	8.00
13	0	×	.25	=	.00
			1.00		**\$25.00**

In our brief treatment of expected value, we have made quite a few assumptions. To name only two, we've assumed that demand for the product can take on only four values, and that the berries are worth nothing one day later. Both these assumptions reduce the value of the answer we got. In Chapter 16, you will again encounter expected-value decision making, but there we will develop the ideas as a part of statistical decision theory (a broader use of statistical methods to make decisions), and we shall devote an entire chapter to expanding the basic ideas we have developed at this point.

EXERCISES

6-15 The luggage department of Madison Rhodes Department Store featured a special Day-After-Christmas Sale on unsold Christmas merchandise. The luggage brand on sale was Imagemaker. The manager of the luggage department was planning his order. Because the store did not carry Imagemaker during the year, the manager wanted to avoid overstocking; yet because of a special price the manufacturer offered on the line, he also wanted to minimize stockouts. He was currently attempting to decide the number of women's tote bags to purchase. His estimate of the probable sales, based in part on past performance, is shown below.

Bags	27	28	29	30	31	32	33
Probability	.11	.13	.17	.20	.15	.14	.10

The store is planning to sell the tote bag for $37.30. His cost is $22.00. How many bags should he order for the sale? Use the method of minimizing expected loss to compute your answer.

6-16 Airport Rent-a-Car is a locally operated business in competition with several major firms. ARC is planning a new deal for prospective customers who want to rent a car for only one day and will return it to the airport. For $17, the company will rent a small economy car to a customer, whose only other expense is to fill the car with gas at day's end. ARC is planning to buy a number of small cars from the manufacturer at a reduced price of $1,600. The big question is how many to buy. Company executives have decided on the following probable average demands per day for the service.

Number of cars rented	8	9	10	11	12	13
Probability	.17	.18	.20	.16	.15	.14

The company intends to offer the plan 6 days a week (312 days per year) and anticipates that its variable cost per car per day will be $1.50. After the end of one year, the company expects to sell the cars and recapture 50 percent of the original cost. Disregarding the time value of money and any noncash expenses, use the expected-loss method to determine the optimal number of cars for ARC to buy.

6-17 Mario, owner of Mario's Pizza Emporium, has a difficult decision on his hands. He has found that he always sells between 1 and 4 of his famous "everything but the kitchen sink" pizzas per night. These pizzas take so long to prepare, however, that Mario prepares all of them in advance and stores them in the refrigerator. Because the ingredients go bad within one day, Mario always throws out any unsold pizzas at the end of each evening. The cost of preparing each pizza is $7, and Mario sells each one for $12. In addition to the usual costs, Mario also calculates that each "everything but" pizza that is ordered but he cannot deliver due to insufficient stock costs him $5 in future business. What number of "everything but" pizzas should Mario stock each night in order to minimize expected loss if the number of such pizzas ordered has the probability distribution given below?

Number of pizzas demanded	1	2	3	4
Probability	.40	.30	.20	.10

6-4 THE BINOMIAL DISTRIBUTION

The binomial distribution, a Bernoulli process

One widely used probability distribution of a discrete random variable is the binomial distribution. It describes a variety of processes of interest to managers. The binomial distribution describes discrete, not continuous, data, resulting from an experiment known as a *Bernoulli process* after the seventeenth-century Swiss mathematician Jacob Bernoulli. The tossing of a fair coin a fixed number of times is a Bernoulli process, and the outcomes of such tosses can be represented by the binomial probability distribution. The success or failure of interviewees on an aptitude test may also be described by a Bernoulli process. On the other hand, the frequency distribution of the lives of fluorescent lights in a factory would be measured on a continuous scale of hours and would not qualify as a binomial distribution.

Use of the Bernoulli Process

Bernoulli process defined

We can use the outcomes of a fixed number of tosses of a fair coin as an example of a Bernoulli process. We can describe this process as follows:

1. Each trial (each toss, in this case) has only *two* possible outcomes: heads or tails, yes or no, success or failure.
2. The probability of the outcome of any trial (toss) remains *fixed* over time. With a fair coin, the probability of heads remains .5 for each toss regardless of the number of times the coin is tossed.
3. The trials are *statistically independent;* that is to say, the outcome of one toss does not affect the outcome of any other toss.

Characteristic probability defined

Each Bernoulli process has its own characteristic probability. Take the situation in which historically seven-tenths of all persons who applied for a certain type of job passed the job test. We would say that the characteristic probability here is .7, but we could describe our testing results as Bernoulli only if we felt certain that the proportion of those passing the test (.7) remained constant over time. The other characteristics of the Bernoulli process would also have to be met, of course. Each test would have to have only two outcomes (success or failure), and the results of each test would have to be statistically independent.

In more formal language, the symbol p represents the probability of a success (in our example .7), and the symbol q, ($q = 1 - p$), the probability of a failure (.3). To represent a certain number of successes, we will use the symbol r, and to symbolize the total number of trials, we use the symbol n. In the situations we will be discussing, the number of trials is fixed before the experiment is begun.

Using this language in a simple problem, we can calculate the chances of getting exactly two heads (in any order) on three tosses of a fair coin. Symbolically, we express the values as follows:

- p = Characteristic probability or probability of success = .5
- $q = 1 - p$ = Probability of failure = .5
- r = Number of successes desired = 2
- n = Number of trials undertaken = 3

Binomial formula

We can solve the problem by using the *binomial formula:*

$$\text{Probability of } r \text{ successes in } n \text{ trials} = \frac{n!}{r!(n-r)!} p^r q^{n-r} \qquad \textbf{[6-1]}$$

Although this formula may look somewhat complicated, it can be used quite easily. The symbol ! means *factorial,* which is computed as follows: 3! means $3 \times 2 \times 1$, or 6. To calculate 5!, we multiply $5 \times 4 \times 3 \times 2 \times 1 = 120$. Mathematicians define 0! as equal to 1. Using the binomial formula to solve our problem, we discover:

$$\begin{aligned}\text{Probability of 2 successes in 3 trials} &= \frac{3!}{2!(3-2)!}(.5^2)(.5^1) \\ &= \frac{3 \times 2 \times 1}{(2 \times 1)(1 \times 1)}(.5^2)(.5^1) \\ &= \frac{6}{2}(.25)(.5) \\ &= .375\end{aligned}$$

Thus, there is a .375 probability of getting two heads on three tosses of a fair coin.

By now you've probably recognized that we can use the binomial distribution to determine the probabilities for the soft-drink bottling problem we introduced at the beginning of this chapter. Recall that historically, eight-tenths of the bottles were correctly filled (successes). If we want to compute the probability of getting exactly three of six bottles (half a six pack) correctly filled, we can define our symbols this way:

$$\begin{aligned} p &= .8 \\ q &= .2 \\ r &= 3 \\ n &= 6 \end{aligned}$$

and then use the binomial formula as follows:

$$\text{Probability of } r \text{ successes in } n \text{ trials} = \frac{n!}{r!(n-r)!} p^r q^{n-r} \quad \textbf{[6-1]}$$

$$\begin{aligned} \text{Probability of 3 out of 6 bottles correctly filled} &= \frac{6 \times 5 \times 4 \times 3 \times 2 \times 1}{(3 \times 2 \times 1)(3 \times 2 \times 1)} (.8^3)(.2^3) \\ &= \frac{720}{(6 \times 6)} (.512)(.008) \\ &= (20)(.512)(.008) \\ &= .08192 \end{aligned}$$

Of course, we *could* have solved these two problems using the probability trees we developed in Chapter 5; but for larger problems, trees become quite cumbersome. In fact, using the binomial formula (Equation 6-1) is no easy task when we have to compute the value of something like 46 factorial. For this reason, binomial probability tables have been developed, and we shall use them shortly.

Some Graphic Illustrations of the Binomial Distribution

To this point, we have dealt with the binomial distribution only in terms of the binomial formula, but the binomial, like any other distribution, can be expressed graphically as well.

To illustrate several of these distributions, consider a situation at Kerr Elementary School, where students are often late. Five students are in kindergarten. The principal has studied the situation over a period of time and has determined that there is a .4 chance of any one student being late and that students arrive independently of one another. How would we draw a binomial probability distribution illustrating the probabilities of 0, 1, 2, 3, 4, or 5 students being late simultaneously? To do this, we would need to use the binomial formula where:

$$\begin{aligned} p &= .4 \\ q &= .6 \\ n &= 5^* \end{aligned}$$

and to make a separate computation for each r, from 0 through 5. Remember that mathematically, any number to the zero power is defined as being equal to one. Beginning with our binomial formula:

$$\text{Probability of } r \text{ late arrivals out of } n \text{ students} = \frac{n!}{r!(n-r)!} p^r q^{n-r} \quad \textbf{[6-1]}$$

* When we define n, we look at the number of students. The fact that there is a possibility that none will be late does not alter our choice of $n = 5$.

Using the formula to derive the binomial probability distribution

For $r = 0$, we get:

$$
\begin{aligned}
P(0) &= \frac{5!}{0!(5-0)!}(.4^0)(.6^5) \\
&= \frac{5 \times 4 \times 3 \times 2 \times 1}{(1)(5 \times 4 \times 3 \times 2 \times 1)}(1)(.6^5) \\
&= \frac{120}{120}(1)(.07776) \\
&= (1)(1)(.07776) \\
&= .07776
\end{aligned}
$$

For $r = 1$, we get:

$$
\begin{aligned}
P(1) &= \frac{5!}{1!(5-1)!}(.4^1)(.6^4) \\
&= \frac{5 \times 4 \times 3 \times 2 \times 1}{(1)(4 \times 3 \times 2 \times 1)}(.4)(.6^4) \\
&= \frac{120}{24}(.4)(.1296) \\
&= (5)(.4)(.1296) \\
&= .2592
\end{aligned}
$$

For $r = 2$, we get:

$$
\begin{aligned}
P(2) &= \frac{5!}{2!(5-2)!}(.4^2)(.6^3) \\
&= \frac{5 \times 4 \times 3 \times 2 \times 1}{(2 \times 1)(3 \times 2 \times 1)}(.4^2)(.6^3) \\
&= \frac{120}{12}(.16)(.216) \\
&= (10)(.03456) \\
&= .3456
\end{aligned}
$$

For $r = 3$, we get:

$$
\begin{aligned}
P(3) &= \frac{5!}{3!(5-3)!}(.4^3)(.6^2) \\
&= \frac{5 \times 4 \times 3 \times 2 \times 1}{(3 \times 2 \times 1)(2 \times 1)}(.4^3)(.6^2) \\
&= (10)(.064)(.36) \\
&= .2304
\end{aligned}
$$

For $r = 4$, we get:

$$\begin{aligned} P(4) &= \frac{5!}{4!(5-4)!}(.4^4)(.6^1) \\ &= \frac{5 \times 4 \times 3 \times 2 \times 1}{(4 \times 3 \times 2 \times 1)(1)}(.4^4)(.6) \\ &= (5)(.0256)(.6) \\ &= .0768 \end{aligned}$$

Finally, for $r = 5$, we get:

$$\begin{aligned} P(5) &= \frac{5!}{5!(5-5)!}(.4^5)(.6^0) \\ &= \frac{5 \times 4 \times 3 \times 2 \times 1}{(5 \times 4 \times 3 \times 2 \times 1)(1)}(.4^5)(1) \\ &= (1)(.01024)(1) \\ &= .01024 \end{aligned}$$

The binomial distribution for this example is shown graphically in Fig. 6-4.

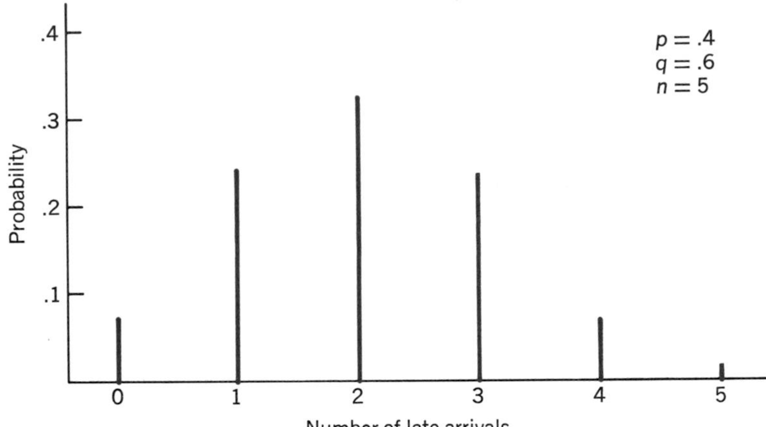

FIGURE 6-4 Binomial probability distribution of late arrivals

General appearance of binomial distributions

Without doing all the calculations involved, we can illustrate the general appearance of a family of binomial probability distributions. In Fig. 6-5, for example, each distribution represents $n = 5$. In each case, the p and q have been changed and are noted beside each distribution. From Fig. 6-5, we can make the following generalizations:

1. When p is small (.1), the binomial distribution is skewed to the right.
2. As p increases (to .3, for example), the skewness is less noticeable.
3. When $p = .5$, the binomial distribution is symmetrical.
4. When p is larger than .5, the distribution is skewed to the left.

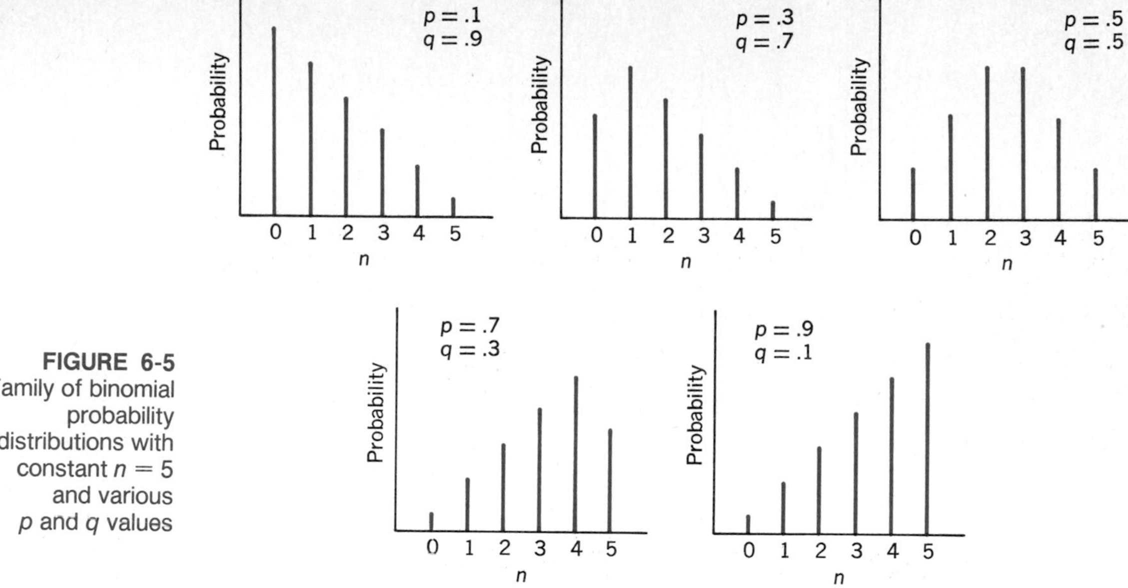

FIGURE 6-5 Family of binomial probability distributions with constant $n = 5$ and various p and q values

5. The probabilities for .3, for example, are the same as those for .7 except that the values of p and q are *reversed*. This is true for any pair of complementary p and q values (.3 and .7, .4 and .6, and .2 and .8).

Let us examine graphically what happens to the binomial distribution when p stays constant but n is increased. Figure 6-6 illustrates the general shape of a family of binomial distributions with a constant p of .4 and n's from 5 to 30. As n increases, the vertical lines not only become more numerous but also tend to bunch up together to form a *bell shape*. We shall have more to say about this bell shape shortly.

Using the Binomial Tables

Solving problems using the binomial tables

Earlier we recognized that it is tedious to calculate probabilities using the binomial formula when n is a large number. Fortunately, we can use Appendix Table 3 to determine binomial probabilities quickly.

To illustrate the use of the binomial tables, consider this problem. What is the probability that eight or more of the fifteen registered Democrats on Prince Street will fail to vote in the coming primary if the probability of any individual's not voting is .30, and if people decide independently of each other whether or not to vote? First we represent the elements in this problem in binomial distribution notation:

$n = 15$ number of registered Democrats

$p = .30$ probability that any one individual won't vote

$r = 8$ number of individuals who will fail to vote

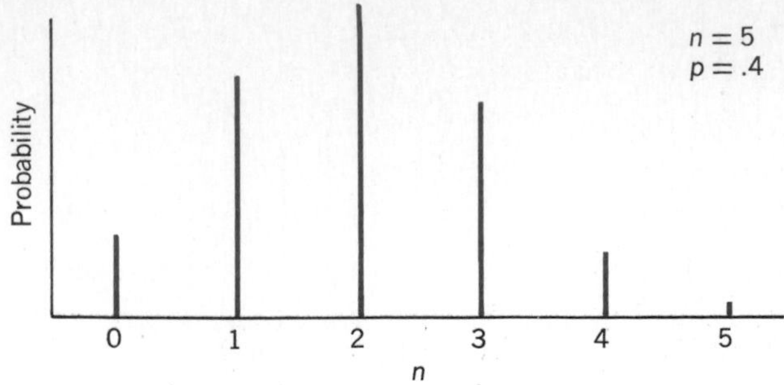

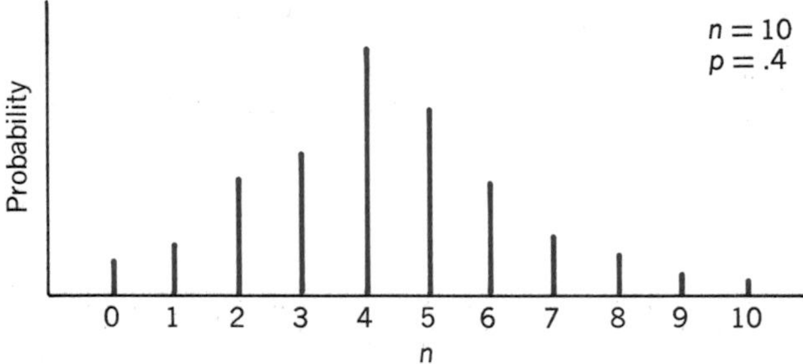

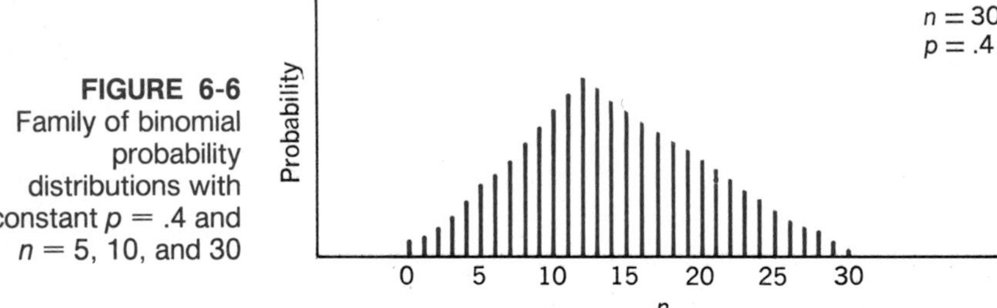

FIGURE 6-6 Family of binomial probability distributions with constant $p = .4$ and $n = 5$, 10, and 30

Then, since the problem involves fifteen trials, we must find the table corresponding to $n = 15$. Since the probability of an individual's not voting is .30, we must look through the $n = 15$ table until we find the column where $p = .30$. (This is denoted as 30.) We then move down that column until we are opposite the $r = 8$ row. The answer there is 0500, which can be interpreted as being a probability value of .0500. This represents the probability of eight or more nonvoters, since the tables are so constructed.

Our problem asked for the probability of eight or more nonvoters. If it had asked for the probability of more than eight nonvoters, we would have looked up the probability of nine or more nonvoters. Had the problem asked for the probability of exactly eight nonvoters we would have subtracted .0152 (the probability of nine or more nonvoters) from .0500 (the probability of eight or more nonvoters). The answer would be .0348 = the probability of exactly eight nonvoters. Finally, if the problem had asked for the probability of fewer than eight nonvoters, we would have subtracted .0500 (the probability of eight or more nonvoters) from 1.0, for an answer of .9500. (Note that

Appendix Table 3 only goes up to $p = .50$. Instructions for using the table when p is larger than .50 are found on the first page of Appendix Table 3.)

Measures of Central Tendency and Dispersion for the Binomial Distribution

Computing the mean and the standard deviation

Earlier in this chapter, we encountered the concept of the expected value or mean of a probability distribution. The binomial distribution has an expected value or mean (μ) and a standard deviation (σ), and we should be able to compute both these statistical measures. Intuitively, we can reason that if a certain machine produces good parts with a $p = .5$, then, over time, the mean of the distribution of the good parts in the output would be .5 times the total output. If there is a .5 chance of tossing a head with a fair coin, over a large number of tosses the mean of the binomial distribution of the number of heads would be .5 times the total number of tosses.

Symbolically, we can represent the mean of a binomial distribution as:

$$\mu = np \tag{6-2}$$

where:

- n = number of trials
- p = probability of success

And we can calculate the standard deviation of a binomial distribution by using the formula:

$$\sigma = \sqrt{npq} \tag{6-3}$$

where:

- n = number of trials
- p = probability of success
- q = probability of failure $= 1 - p$

To see how to use Equations 6-2 and 6-3, take the case of a packaging machine that produces 20 percent defective packages. If we take a random sample of ten packages, we can compute the mean and the standard deviation of the binomial distribution of that process like this:

$$\begin{aligned}\mu &= np \\ &= (10)(.2) \\ &= 2 \leftarrow \text{mean}\end{aligned} \tag{6-2}$$

$$\begin{aligned}\sigma &= \sqrt{npq} \\ &= \sqrt{(10)(.2)(.8)} \\ &= \sqrt{1.6} \\ &= 1.265 \leftarrow \text{standard deviation}\end{aligned} \tag{6-3}$$

Meeting the Conditions for Using the Bernoulli Process

Applying the binomial distribution to real-life situations

We need to be careful in the use of the binomial probability distribution to make certain that the three conditions necessary for a Bernoulli process introduced earlier are met, particularly conditions 2 and 3. Condition 2 requires the probability of the outcome of any trial to remain fixed over time. In many industrial processes, however, it is extremely difficult to guarantee that this is indeed the case. Each time an industrial machine produces a part, for instance, there is some infinitesimal wear on the machine. If this wear accumulates beyond a reasonable point, the proportion of acceptable parts produced by the machine will be altered, and condition 2 for the use of the binomial distribution may be violated. This problem is not present in a coin-toss experiment, but it is an integral consideration of all real applications of the binomial probability distribution.

Condition 3 requires that the trials of a Bernoulli process be statistically independent; that is, the outcome of one trial cannot affect in any way the outcome of any other trial. Here, too, we can encounter some problems in real applications. Consider an interviewing process in which high-potential candidates are being screened for top political positions. If the interviewer has talked with five unacceptable candidates in a row, he may not view the sixth with complete impartiality. The trials, therefore, would not be statistically independent.

EXERCISES

6-18 For a binomial distribution with $n = 6$ and $p = 3$, find:
a) $P(r = 5)$ b) $P(r > 4)$ c) $P(r < 2)$ d) $P(r \geqslant 3)$

6-19 For a binomial distribution with $n = 15$ and $p = .2$, use Appendix Table 3 to find:
$P(r = 6)$ $P(r > 9)$ $P(r \leqslant 12)$

6-20 Find the mean and standard deviation of the following binomial distributions:
a) $n = 12$, $p = .25$
b) $n = 25$, $q = .4$
c) $n = 500$, $p = .10$
d) $n = 40$, $p = .05$
e) $n = 2{,}250$, $p = .95$

6-21 For $n = 10$ trials, compute the probability that $r \geqslant 1$ for each of the following values of p:
a) $p = .2$ b) $p = .4$ c) $p = .5$ d) $p = .7$

6-22 The financial manager for the Aycock Sheetrock Company will randomly sample 4 customers' accounts. Aycock offers a 2 percent trade discount for payments received within 10 days of the order. The manager knows from previous research that 60 percent of Aycock's customers capitalize on this discount.
a) What is the probability that the manager's sample will contain exactly 2 accounts that utilize the discount? Do not use the tables.
b) What is the probability that there will be 4 accounts in the sample that utilize the discount? Solve this without using the tables. Use the binomial formula.

6-23 The Hart Ketchup Company offers a semiannual national consumer discount through the use of coupons. Historical data supplied by Hart's marketing department shows that 80 percent of the consumers buying ketchup during the discount period do not take advantage of the coupon. Find the following probabilities (to 4 decimal places) without the use of Appendix Table 3.

a) One day during the discount period, 8 customers at Ken's Quik-Mart bought Hart's ketchup. What is the probability that exactly 6 did not use the coupons?
b) Exactly 7?

6-24 Kandid Film Company distributes its product through drugstores and allows them to buy large quantities on credit. Kandid carefully screens the financial condition of the stores. The president of Kandid instituted a policy that 80 percent of the new distributors granted credit must have a ratio of current assets to liabilities greater than 2. The company's chief accountant has argued that raising this criterion to 90 percent would reduce the chance of getting exactly 2 distributors without the minimum ratio requirement in a sample of 5. The president disagreed, saying that the probability would have to be the same, since all probabilities have to add to 1.00. The accountant presented the president with a graph and chart that reflected the company's current acceptance criterion. His attempt to explain how the increased acceptance level would change the probabilities, however, was unsuccessful.

Probability distribution

NUMBER NOT SATISFYING REQUIREMENTS	PROBABILITY
0	.3277
1	.4096
2	.2048
3	.0512
4	.0064
5	.0003
	1.0000

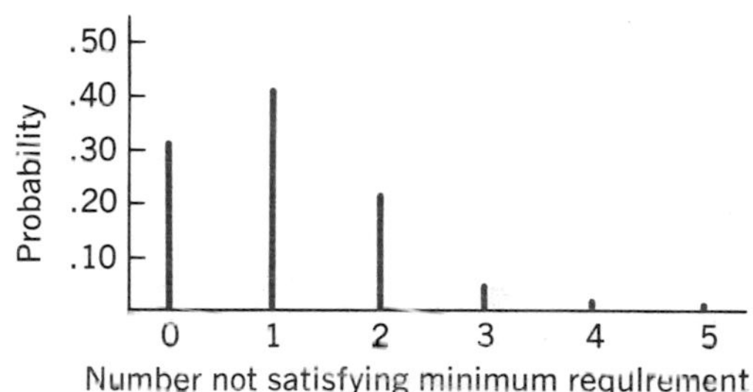

a) Draw a similar graph for a credit-extension policy that requires 90 percent of accepted stores to have the minimum ratio requirement. Construct a similar chart of the probabilities.
b) What will be the difference, if any, in the probability of obtaining exactly 2 stores with a ratio above 2 from a sample of 5, once the credit policy is changed?

6-25 The latest nationwide political poll indicates that if an American is randomly selected, the probability that he is conservative is .5, the probability that he is liberal is .3, and the probability that he is middle-of-the-road is .2. Assuming that these probabilities are accurate, answer the following questions pertaining to a randomly chosen group of 10 Americans. (Do not use Appendix Table 3.)

a) What is the probability that 5 are conservative?
b) What is the probability that none are liberal?
c) What is the probability that 4 are middle-of-the-road?
d) What is the probability that at least 9 are conservative?

6-26 Harry Ohme is in charge of the electronics section of a large department store. He has noticed that the probability that a customer who is just browsing will buy something is .3. Suppose that 15 customers browse in the electronics section each hour. Use Appendix Table 3 in the back of the book to answer the following questions:

a) What is the probability that at least 1 browsing customer will buy something during a specified hour?
b) What is the probability that at least 4 browsing customers will buy something during a specified hour?
c) What is the probability that no browsing customers will buy anything during a specified hour?
d) What is the probability that no more than 4 browsing customers will buy something during a specified hour?

6-5 THE POISSON DISTRIBUTION

There are many discrete probability distributions, but our discussion will focus on only two: the *binomial*, which we have just concluded, and the *Poisson*, which is the subject of this section. The Poisson distribution is named for Siméon Denis Poisson (1781–1840), a Frenchman who developed the distribution from studies during the latter part of his lifetime.

Examples of Poisson distributions

The Poisson distribution is used to describe a number of processes, including the distribution of telephone calls going through a switchboard system, the demand (needs) of patients for service at a health institution, the arrivals of trucks and cars at a tollbooth, and the number of accidents at an intersection. These examples all have a common element: They can be described by a discrete random variable that takes on integer (whole) values (0, 1, 2, 3, 4, 5, and so on). The number of patients who arrive at a physician's office in a given interval of time will be 0, 1, 2, 3, 4, 5, or some other whole number. Similarly, if you count the number of cars arriving at a tollbooth on the New Jersey Turnpike during some ten-minute period, the number will be 0, 1, 2, 3, 4, 5, and so on.

Characteristics of Processes that Produce a Poisson Probability Distribution

Conditions leading to a Poisson probability distribution

The number of vehicles passing through a single turnpike tollbooth at rush hour serves as an illustration of Poisson probability distribution characteristics:

1. The average (mean) arrivals of vehicles per rush hour can be estimated from past traffic data.
2. If we divide the rush hour into periods (intervals) of one second each, we will find these statements to be true:
   a) The probability that exactly one vehicle will arrive at the single booth per second is a very small number and is constant for every one-second interval.
   b) The probability that two or more vehicles will arrive within a one-second interval is so small that we can assign it a zero value.
   c) The number of vehicles that arrive in a given one-second interval is independent of the time at which that one-second interval occurs during the rush hour.
   d) The number of arrivals in any one-second interval is not dependent on the number of arrivals in any other one-second interval.

Now, we can generalize from these four conditions described for our tollbooth example and apply them to other processes. If these new processes meet the same four conditions, then we can use a Poisson probability distribution to describe them.

Calculating Probabilities Using the Poisson Distribution

The Poisson probability distribution, as we have shown, is concerned with certain processes that can be described by a discrete random variable. The letter X usually represents that discrete random variable, and X can take on integer values (0, 1, 2, 3, 4, 5, and so on). We use capital X to represent the random variable and lowercase x to represent a specific value that capital X can take. The probability of exactly x occurrences in a Poisson distribution is calculated with the formula:

Poisson distribution formula

$$P(x) = \frac{\lambda^x \times e^{-\lambda}}{x!} \quad \textbf{[6-4]}$$

Look more closely at each part of this formula:

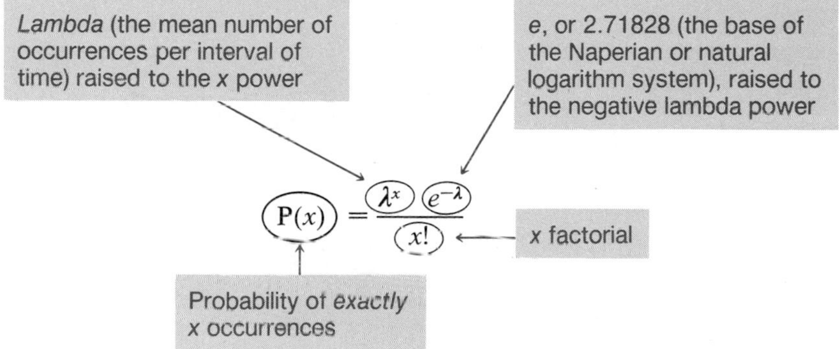

Suppose that we are investigating the safety of a dangerous intersection. Past police records indicate a mean of five accidents per month at this intersection. The number of accidents is distributed according to a Poisson distribution, and the Highway Safety Division wants us to calculate the probability in any month of exactly 0, 1, 2, 3, and 4 accidents. We can use Appendix Table 4 to avoid having to calculate e's to negative powers. Applying the formula:

An example using the Poisson formula

$$P(x) = \frac{\lambda^x \times e^{-\lambda}}{x!} \quad \textbf{[6-4]}$$

we can calculate the probability of exactly 0 accidents:

$$\begin{aligned} P(0) &= \frac{(5^0)(e^{-5})}{0!} \\ &= \frac{(1)(.00674)}{1} \\ &= .00674 \end{aligned}$$

For exactly one accident:

$$\begin{aligned} P(1) &= \frac{(5^1)(e^{-5})}{1!} \\ &= \frac{(5)(.00674)}{1} \\ &= .03370 \end{aligned}$$

For exactly two accidents:

$$\begin{aligned} P(2) &= \frac{(5^2)(e^{-5})}{2!} \\ &= \frac{(25)(.00674)}{2 \times 1} \\ &= .08425 \end{aligned}$$

For exactly three accidents:

$$\begin{aligned} P(3) &= \frac{(5^3)(e^{-5})}{3!} \\ &= \frac{(125)(.00674)}{3 \times 2 \times 1} \\ &= \frac{.8425}{6} \\ &= .14042 \end{aligned}$$

Finally, for exactly four accidents:

$$\begin{aligned} P(4) &= \frac{(5^4)(e^{-5})}{4!} \\ &= \frac{(625)(.00674)}{4 \times 3 \times 2 \times 1} \\ &= \frac{4.2125}{24} \\ &= .17552 \end{aligned}$$

What the answers to the formula mean

Our calculations will answer several questions. Perhaps we want to know the probability of there being 0, 1, or 2 accidents in any month. We find this by adding together the probabilities of exactly 0, 1, and 2 accidents like this:

$$\begin{aligned} P(0) &= .00674 \\ P(1) &= .03370 \\ P(2) &= \underline{.08425} \\ P(0, 1, 2) &= \mathbf{.12469} \end{aligned}$$

We will take action to improve the intersection if the probability of more than three accidents per month exceeds .65. Should we act? To solve this problem, we need to calculate the probability of having 0, 1, 2, or 3 accidents and then subtract the sum from 1.0 to get the probability for more than three accidents. We begin like this:

$$\begin{aligned} P(0) &= .00674 \\ P(1) &= .03370 \\ P(2) &= .08425 \\ P(3) &= \underline{.14042} \\ P(3 \text{ or fewer}) &= \mathbf{.26511} \end{aligned}$$

Because the Poisson probability of three or fewer accidents is .26511, the probability of more than three must be .73489, (1.00000 − .26511). Since .73489 exceeds .65, steps should be taken to improve the intersection.

Constructing a Poisson probability distribution

We could continue calculating the probabilities for more than four accidents and eventually produce a Poisson probability distribution of the number of accidents per month at this intersection. Table 6-12 illustrates such a distribution. To produce this table, we have used Formula 6-4. Try doing the calculations yourself for the probabilities beyond exactly four accidents. Figure 6-7 illustrates graphically the Poisson probability distribution of the number of accidents.

TABLE 6-12 Poisson probability distribution of accidents per month

x = NUMBER OF ACCIDENTS	P(x) = PROBABILITY OF EXACTLY THAT NUMBER	
0	.00674	
1	.03370	
2	.08425	
3	.14042	
4	.17552	
5	.17552	
6	.14627	
7	.10448	
8	.06530	
9	.03628	
10	.01814	
11	.00824	
	.99486	← Probability for 0 through 11 accidents
12 or more	.00514	← Probability for 12 or more (1.0 − .99486)
	1.00000	

Poisson Distribution as an Approximation of the Binomial Distribution

Using a modification of the Poisson formula to approximate binomial probabilities

Sometimes, if we wish to avoid the tedious job of calculating binomial probability distributions, we can use the Poisson instead. The Poisson distribution can be a reasonable approximation of the binomial, but only under

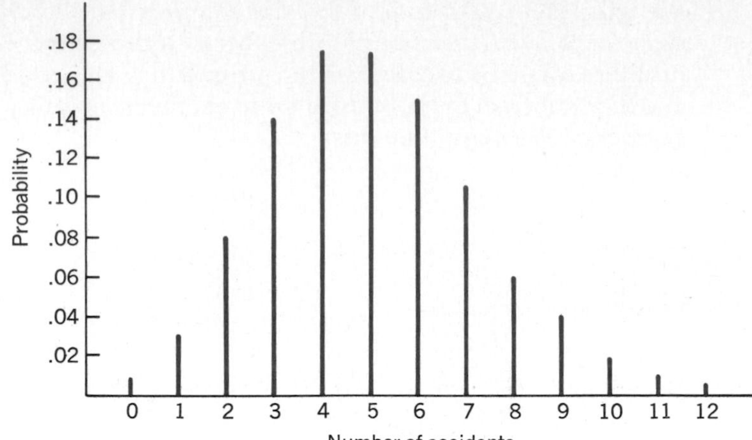

FIGURE 6-7
Poisson probability distribution of the number of accidents

certain conditions. These conditions are when n is large and p is small; that is, when the number of trials is large and the binomial probability of success is small. **The rule most often used by statisticians is that the Poisson is a good approximation of the binomial when n is equal to or greater than 20, and p is equal to or less than .05.** In cases that meet these conditions, we can substitute the mean of the binomial distribution (np) in place of the mean of the Poisson distribution (λ), so that the formula becomes:

$$P(x) = \frac{(np)^x \times e^{-np}}{x!} \qquad \textbf{[6-5]}$$

Comparing the Poisson and binomial formulas

Let us use both the binomial probability formula (6-1) and the Poisson approximation formula (6-5) on the same problem to determine the extent to which the Poisson is a good approximation of the binomial. Say that we have a hospital with 20 kidney dialysis machines and that the chance of

TABLE 6-13 Comparison of Poisson and binomial probability approaches to the kidney dialysis situation

POISSON APPROACH	BINOMIAL APPROACH
$P(x) = \frac{(np)^x \times e^{-np}}{x!}$ **[6-5]**	$P(r) = \frac{n!}{r!(n-r)!} p^r q^{n-r}$ **[6-1]**
$P(3) = \frac{(20 \times .02)^3 e^{-(20 \times .02)}}{3!}$	$P(3) = \frac{20!}{3!(20-3)!} (.02^3)(.98^{17})$
$= \frac{(.4^3)(e)^{-.4*}}{(3 \times 2 \times 1)}$	$= .0065$
$= \frac{(.064)(.67032)^*}{6}$	
$= .00715$	

* Use Appendix Table 4 to find the value of $(e)^{-.4}$.

any one of them malfunctioning during any day is .02. What is the probability that exactly three machines will be out of service on the same day? Table 6-13 shows the answers to this question. As we can see, the difference between the two probability distributions is slight (only about a 10 percent error, in this example).

EXERCISES

6-27 If OPEC is successful in raising the price of oil an average of 4 times every 3 years, find the probability of:
a) No price hikes in a randomly selected period of 3 years
b) 2 price hikes
c) 4 price hikes
d) 5 or more

6-28 Given $\lambda = 3.5$, for a Poisson distribution, find:
a) $P(X \leq 2)$ b) $P(X \geq 4)$ c) $P(X = 6)$

6-29 Given a binomial distribution with $n = 25$ trials and $p = .02$, use the Poisson approximation to the binomial to find:
a) $P(r = 20)$ b) $P(r = 5)$ c) $P(r = 2)$

6-30 Given a binomial distribution with $n = 20$ trials and $p = .04$, use the Poisson approximation to the binomial to find:
a) $P(r \geq 2)$ b) $P(r < 5)$ c) $P(r = 0)$

6-31 In addition to doing the interviewing and hiring for the PAKE Company's production facility, Kern Buckner, personnel manager, also has to handle all worker–supervisor problems. Buckner complained to his superior that he was currently overworked in his advisory capacity. Buckner had kept a record showing that the mean number of employees daily visiting his office was 10. His superior agreed (without knowing of his record) that if there were 7 or more visits from employees on a particular day on which he kept track, he would appoint an assistant to aid Buckner. If the probability that there will be more than 7 visits is .7798, what is the probability that Buckner will get an assistant?

6-32 Guy Ford, production supervisor for the Winstead Company's Charlottesville plant, is worried about an elderly employee's ability to keep up the minimum work pace. In addition to the normal daily breaks, this employee stops for short rest periods an average of 4.1 times per hour. The rest period is a fairly consistent 3 minutes each time. Ford has decided that if the probability of the employee's resting for 12 minutes (not including normal breaks) or more per hour is greater than .5, he will move the employee to a different job. Should he do so?

6-33 Owing to both a sugar shortage and an increasing tendency for consumers to hoard commodities, the demand for sugar has skyrocketed. During this current rush, Peggy Sackett, inventory manager for an Atlanta Squiggly Piggly food store, has determined that the shelves empty an average of 5.4 times a day.
a) What is the probability that the shelves will be emptied exactly 5 times?
b) If the probability that the shelves will be emptied 4 or fewer times is .3733, what is the probability that the shelves will be emptied more than 5 times?

6-34 Southwestern Electronics has developed a new calculator that performs a series of functions not yet performed by any calculator. The marketing department is planning to demonstrate this calculator to a group of potential customers but is worried about some initial production problems, which have resulted in 4 percent of the new calculators developing mathematical inconsistencies. The marketing VP is planning on randomly selecting a group of calculators for this demonstration and is worried about the chances of selecting a calculator that could start malfunctioning. He believes that whether or not a calculator malfunctions is a Bernoulli process, and he is convinced that the probability of malfunction is really about .04.

a) Assuming that the VP selects exactly 50 calculators to use in the demonstration, and using the Poisson distribution as an approximation to the binomial, what chance will he have of getting at least 1 calculator that malfunctions?

b) No calculators malfunctioning?

6-35 Southcentral Telephone Company employs the Boynton Delivery Service to deliver its telephone books. Southcentral has been pleased with the service, because over the years, Boynton has delivered telephone books to 97 percent of the names that were supplied to it by the phone company. Nevertheless, Southcentral continues to make spot checks, randomly calling numbers that should be supplied with new telephone books.

a) What is the probability that out of 100 calls made, exactly 3 people will not have received telephone books?

b) Exactly one person?

6-36 The Home Appliance Store has just recently opened in Plainville, and the owner, Max Voltz, is determined to obtain some estimates for the probabilities that specific numbers of refrigerators will be ordered each week. Max thinks that he will sell 0.7 refrigerators per week on the average. In Plainville, such an expensive purchase certainly qualifies as a rare event. It seems reasonable to assume that the number of refrigerators sold each week has a Poisson distribution. For a given week, find:

a) The probability that no refrigerators will be sold.

b) The probability that exactly 2 refrigerators will be sold.

c) The probability that exactly 3 refrigerators will be sold.

d) The probability that exactly 1 refrigerator will be sold.

e) The probability that 3 or more refrigerators will be sold.

6-6 THE NORMAL DISTRIBUTION: A Distribution of a Continuous Random Variable

Continuous distribution defined

So far in this chapter, we have been concerned with discrete probability distributions. In this section, we shall turn to cases in which the variable can take on *any* value within a given range and in which the probability distribution is continuous.

A very important continuous probability distribution is the *normal* distribution. Several mathematicians were instrumental in its development, among them the eighteenth-century mathematician-astronomer Karl Gauss. In honor of his work, the normal probability distribution is often called the Gaussian distribution.

Importance of the normal distribution

There are two basic reasons why the normal distribution occupies such a prominent place in statistics. First, it has some properties that make it applicable to a great many situations in which it is necessary to make inferences by taking samples. In Chapter 7, we will find that the normal distribution is a useful sampling distribution. Second, the normal distribution comes close to fitting the actual observed frequency distributions of many phenomena, including human characteristics (weights, heights, and

IQs), outputs from physical processes (dimensions and yields), and other measures of interest to managers in both the public and private sectors.

Characteristics of the Normal Probability Distribution

The normal curve described

Look for a moment at Fig. 6-8. This diagram suggests several important features of a normal probability distribution:

1. The curve has a single peak; thus, it is unimodal. It has the bell shape that we described earlier.
2. The mean of a normally distributed population lies at the center of its normal curve.
3. Because of the symmetry of the normal probability distribution, the median and the mode of the distribution are also at the center; thus, for a normal curve, the mean, median, and mode are the same value.
4. The two tails of the normal probability distribution extend indefinitely and never touch the horizontal axis. (Graphically, of course, this is impossible to show.)

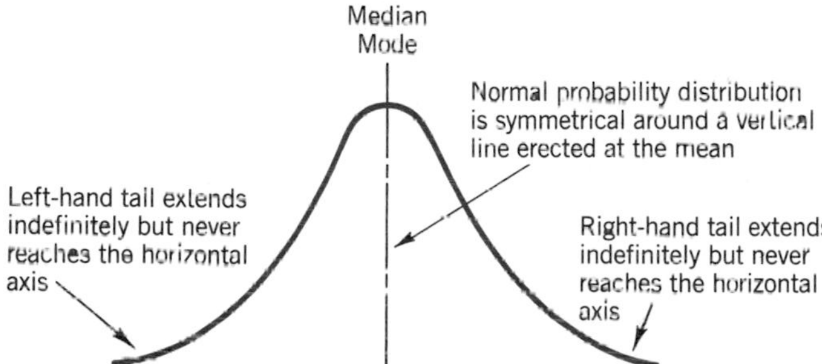

FIGURE 6-8 Frequency curve for the normal probability distribution

Significance of the two parameters

Most real-life populations do not extend forever in both directions; but for such populations, the normal distribution is a convenient approximation. There is no single normal curve, but rather a family of normal curves. To define a particular normal probability distribution, we need only two parameters: the mean (μ) and the standard deviation (σ). In Table 6-14, each of the populations is described only by the mean and the standard deviation, and each has a particular normal curve.

Figure 6-9 shows three normal probability distributions, each of which has the same mean but a different standard deviation. Although these curves differ in appearance, all three are "normal curves."

Figure 6-10 illustrates a "family" of normal curves, all with the same standard deviation but each with a different mean.

TABLE 6-14 Different normal probability distributions

NATURE OF THE POPULATION	ITS MEAN	ITS STANDARD DEVIATION
Annual earnings of employees at one plant	\$10,000/year	\$1,000
Length of standard 8′ building lumber	8′	.5″
Air pollution in one community	2,500 particles per million	750 particles per million
Per capita income in a single developing country	\$1,400	\$300
Violent crimes per year in a given city	8,000	900

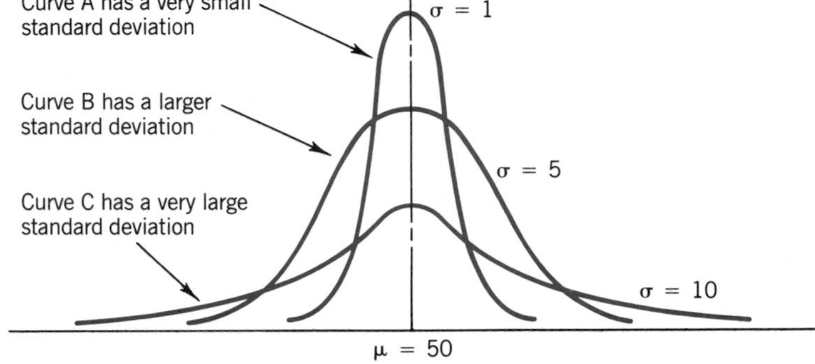

Curve A has a very small standard deviation
Curve B has a larger standard deviation
Curve C has a very large standard deviation
σ = 1
σ = 5
σ = 10
μ = 50

FIGURE 6-9 Normal probability distributions with identical means but different standard deviations

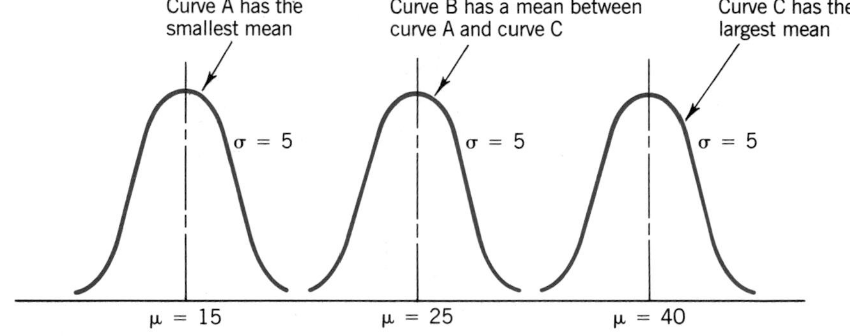

Curve A has the smallest mean
Curve B has a mean between curve A and curve C
Curve C has the largest mean
σ = 5
σ = 5
σ = 5
μ = 15
μ = 25
μ = 40

FIGURE 6-10 Normal probability distributions with different means but the same standard deviation

Finally, Fig. 6-11 shows three different normal probability distributions, each with a different mean *and* a different standard deviation. The normal probability distributions illustrated in Figs. 6-9, 6-10, and 6-11 demonstrate that the normal curve can describe a large number of populations, differentiated only by the mean and/or the standard deviation.

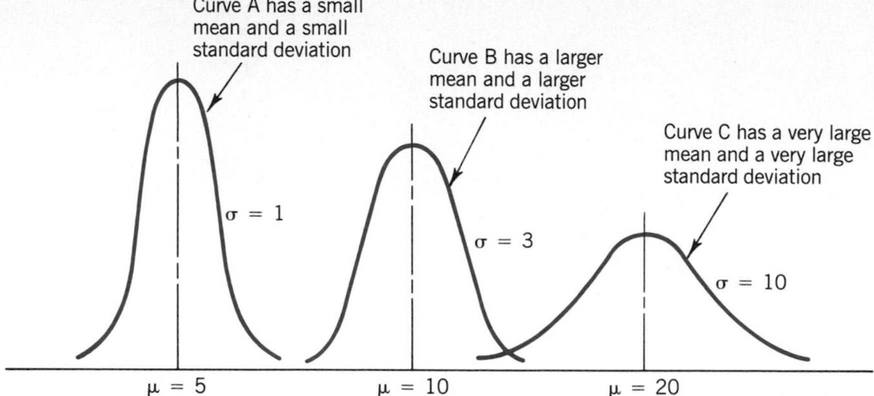
Curve A has a small mean and a small standard deviation
Curve B has a larger mean and a larger standard deviation
Curve C has a very large mean and a very large standard deviation
σ = 1
σ = 3
σ = 10
μ = 5
μ = 10
μ = 20

FIGURE 6-11 Three normal probability distributions, each with a different mean and a different standard deviation

Areas Under the Normal Curve

Measuring the area under a normal curve

No matter what the values of μ and σ are for a normal probability distribution, the total area under the normal curve is 1.00, so that we may think of areas under the curve as probabilities. Mathematically, it is true that:

1. Approximately 68 percent of all the values in a normally distributed population lie within 1 standard deviation (plus and minus) from the mean.
2. Approximately 95.5 percent of all the values in a normally distributed population lie within 2 standard deviations (plus and minus) from the mean.
3. Approximately 99.7 percent of all the values in a normally distributed population lie within 3 standard deviations (plus and minus) from the mean.

These three statements are shown graphically in Fig. 6-12.

Figure 6-12 shows three different ways of measuring the area under the normal curve. However, very few of the applications we shall make of the normal probability distribution involve intervals of *exactly* 1, 2, or 3 standard deviations (plus and minus) from the mean. What should we do about all these other cases? Fortunately, we can refer to statistical tables constructed for precisely these situations. They indicate portions of the area under the normal curve that are contained within any number of standard deviations (plus and minus) from the mean.

Standard normal probability distribution

It is not possible or necessary to have a different table for every possible normal curve. Instead, we can use a **standard normal probability distribution** to find areas under any normal curve. With this table, we can determine the area, or probability, that the normally distributed random variable will lie within certain distances from the mean. These distances are defined in terms of standard deviations.

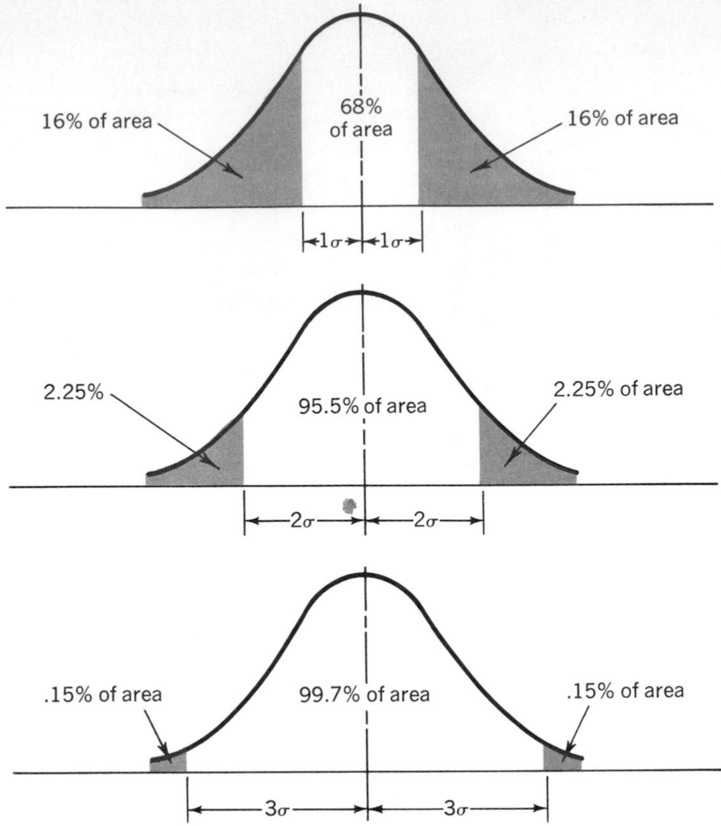

FIGURE 6-12 Relationship between the area under the curve for a normal probability distribution and the distance from the mean measured in standard deviations

We can better understand the concept of the standard normal probability distribution by examining the special relationship of the standard deviation to the normal curve. Look at Fig. 6-13. Here we have illustrated two normal probability distributions, each with a different mean and a different standard deviation. Both area *a* and area *b*, the shaded areas under the curves, contain the *same* proportion of the total area under the normal curve. Why? Because both these areas are defined as being the area between

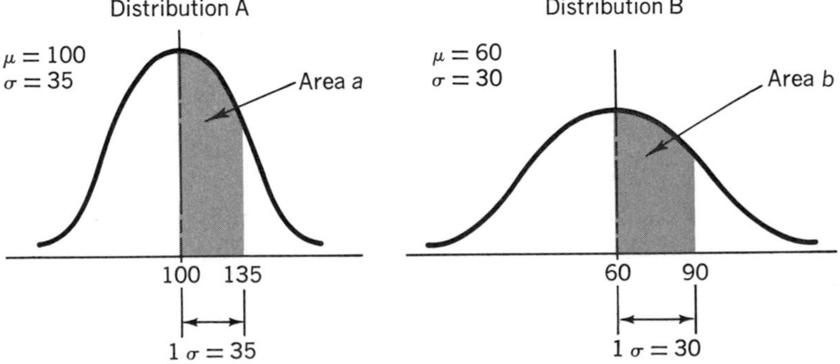

FIGURE 6-13 Two intervals, each one standard deviation to the right of the mean

the mean and one standard deviation to the right of the mean. *All* intervals containing the same number of standard deviations from the mean will contain the same proportion of the total area under the curve for *any* normal probability distribution. This makes possible the use of only one standard normal probability distribution table.

Deriving the percentage of the total area under the curve

Let's find out what proportion of the total area under the curve is represented by colored areas in Fig. 6-13. In Fig. 6-12, we saw that an interval of one standard deviation (plus *and* minus) from the mean contained about 68 percent of the total area under the curve. In Fig. 6-13, however, we are interested only in the area between the mean and one standard deviation to the *right* of the mean (plus, *not* plus and minus). This area must be half of 68 percent, or 34 percent, for both distributions.

One more example will reinforce our point. Look at the two normal probability distributions in Fig. 6-14. Each of these has a different mean and a different standard deviation. The colored area under *both* curves, however, contains the same proportion of the total area under the curve. Why? Because the problem states that both colored areas fall within 2 standard deviations plus and minus from the mean. Two standard deviations plus and minus from the mean include the same proportion of the total area under any normal probability distribution. In this case, we can refer to Fig. 6-12 again and see that the colored area in both distributions in Fig. 6-14 contains about 95.5 percent of the total area under the curve.

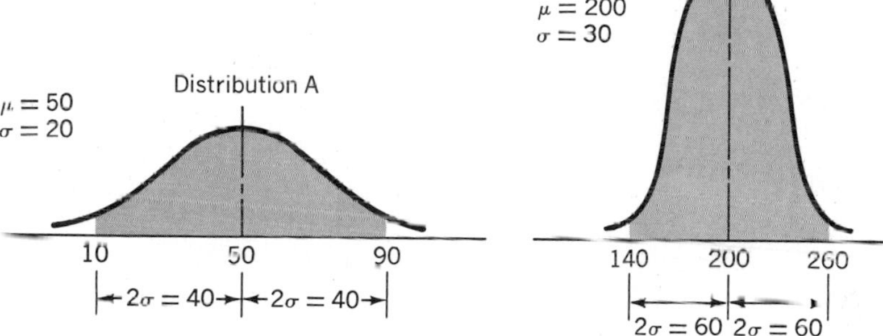

FIGURE 6-14 Two intervals, each two standard deviations plus and minus from the mean

Using the Standard Normal Probability Distribution Table

Formula for measuring distances under the normal curve

Appendix Table 1 shows the area under the normal curve between the mean and any value of the normally distributed random variable. Notice in this table the location of the column labeled z. The value for z is derived from the formula:

$$z = \frac{x - \mu}{\sigma} \qquad [6\text{-}6]$$

where:

- x = value of the random variable with which we are concerned
- μ = mean of the distribution of this random variable
- σ = standard deviation of this distribution
- z = number of standard deviations from x to the mean of this distribution

Why do we use z rather than "the number of standard deviations"? Normally distributed random variables take on many *different units* of measure: dollars, inches, parts per million, pounds, time. Since we shall use one table, Table 1 in the Appendix, we talk in terms of *standard units* (which really means standard deviations), and we give them a symbol of z.

Using z values

We can illustrate this graphically. In Fig. 6-15, we see that the use of z is just a change of the scale of measurement on the horizontal axis.

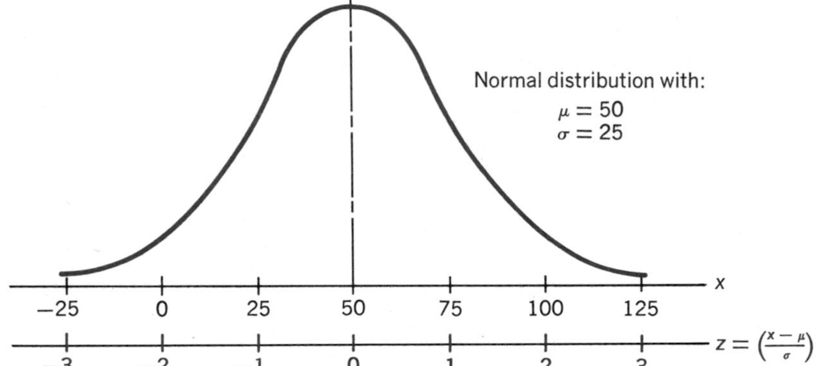

FIGURE 6-15 Normal distribution illustrating comparability of z values and standard deviations

Standard Normal Probability Distribution Table

The Standard Normal Probability Distribution Table, Appendix Table 1, is organized in terms of standard units, or z values. It gives the values for only *half* the area under the normal curve, beginning with 0.0 at the mean. Since the normal probability distribution is symmetrical (return to Fig. 6-8 to review this point), the values true for one half of the curve are true for the other. We can use this one table for problems involving both sides of the normal curve. Working a few examples will help us to feel comfortable with the table.

Using the table to find probabilities (an example)

We have a training program designed to upgrade the supervisory skills of production-line supervisors. Because the program is self-administered, supervisors require different numbers of hours to complete the program. A study of past participants indicates that the mean length of time spent on the program is 500 hours and that this normally distributed random variable has a standard deviation of 100 hours.

- **EXAMPLE 1: What is the probability that a participant selected at random will require more than 500 hours to complete the program?**

◆ **SOLUTION: In Fig. 6-16, we see that half of the area under the curve is located on either side of the mean of 500 hours. Thus, we can deduce that the probability that the random variable will take on a value higher than 500 is the colored half, or .5.**

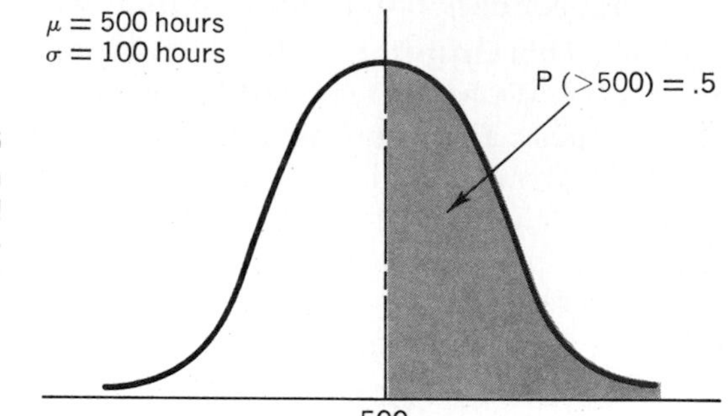

FIGURE 6-16 Distribution of time required to complete the training program, with interval more than 500 hours in color

◆ **EXAMPLE 2: What is the probability that a candidate selected at random will take between 500 and 650 hours to complete the training program?**

◆ **SOLUTION: We have shown this situation graphically in Fig. 6-17. The probability that will answer this question is represented by the colored area between the mean (500 hours) and the *x* value in which we are interested (650 hours). Using Equation 6-6, we get a *z* value of:**

$$z = \frac{x - \mu}{\sigma} \tag{6-6}$$

$$= \frac{650 - 500}{100}$$

$$= \frac{150}{100}$$

$$= 1.5 \text{ standard deviations}$$

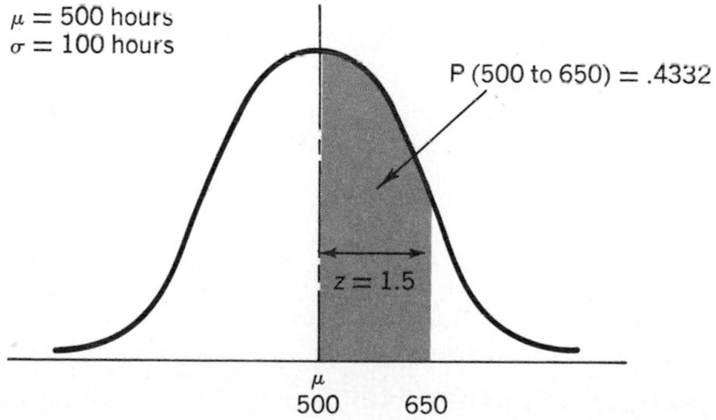

μ = 500 hours
σ = 100 hours
P (500 to 650) = .4332
z = 1.5
μ
500 650

FIGURE 6-17 Distribution of time required to complete the training program, with interval 500 to 650 hours in color

If we look up $z = 1.5$ in Appendix Table 1, we find a probability of .4332. Thus, the chance that a candidate selected at random would require between 500 and 650 hours to complete the training program is slightly higher than .4.

◆ EXAMPLE 3: What is the probability that a candidate selected at random will take more than 700 hours to complete the program?

◆ SOLUTION: This situation is different from our previous examples. Look at Fig. 6-18. We are interested in the colored area to the right of the value "700 hours." How can we solve this problem? We can begin by using Equation 6-6:

$$z = \frac{x - \mu}{\sigma} \tag{6-6}$$

$$= \frac{700 - 500}{100}$$

$$= \frac{200}{100}$$

$$= 2 \text{ standard deviations}$$

Looking in Appendix Table 1 for a z value of 2.0, we find a probability of .4772. That represents the probability the program will require *between* 500 and 700 hours. However, we want the probability it will take *more* than 700 hours (the colored area in Fig. 6-18). Since the right half of the curve (between the mean and the right-hand tail) represents a probability of .5, we can get our answer (the area to the right of the 700-hour point) if we subtract .4772 from .5; $.5000 - .4772 = .0228$. Therefore, there are just over two chances in 100 that a participant chosen at random would take more than 700 hours to complete the course.

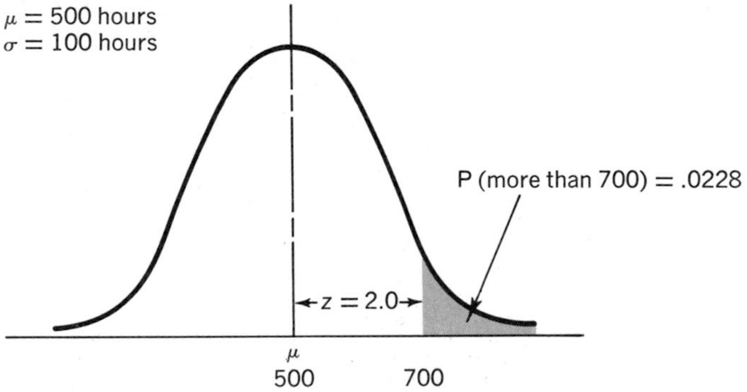

FIGURE 6-18 Distribution of time required to complete the training program, with interval above 700 hours in color

◆ EXAMPLE 4: Suppose the training-program director wants to know the probability that a participant chosen at random would require between 550 and 650 hours to complete the required work.

◆ SOLUTION: This probability is represented by the colored area in Fig. 6-19. This time, our answer will require two steps. First, we calculate a z value for the 650-hour point, as follows:

$$\begin{aligned} z &= \frac{x-\mu}{\sigma} \qquad [6\text{-}6] \\ &= \frac{650-500}{100} \\ &= \frac{150}{100} \\ &= 1.5 \text{ standard deviations} \end{aligned}$$

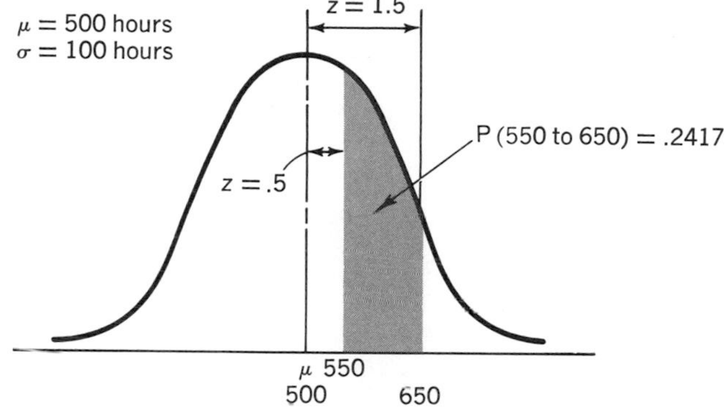

FIGURE 6-19 Distribution of time required to complete the training program, with interval between 550 and 650 hours in color

When we look up a z of 1.5 in Appendix Table 1, we see a probability value of .4332 (the probability that the random variable will fall between the mean and 650 hours). Now for step 2. We calculate a z value for our 550-hour point like this:

$$\begin{aligned} z &= \frac{x-\mu}{\sigma} \qquad [6\text{-}6] \\ &= \frac{550-500}{100} \\ &= \frac{50}{100} \\ &= .5 \text{ standard deviations} \end{aligned}$$

In Appendix Table 1, the z value of .5 has a probability of .1915 (the chance that the random variable will fall between the mean and 550 hours). To answer our question, we must subtract as follows:

.4332	Probability that the random variable will lie between the mean and 650 hours
−.1915	Probability that the random variable will lie between the mean and 550 hours
.2417 ←	Probability that the random variable will lie between 550 and 650 hours

Thus, the chance of a candidate selected at random taking between 550 and 650 hours to complete the program is a bit less than one in four.

◆ **EXAMPLE 5:** What is the probability that a candidate selected at random will require less than 580 hours to complete the program?

◆ **SOLUTION:** This situation is illustrated in Fig. 6-20. Using Equation 6-6 to get the appropriate z value for 580 hours, we have:

$$z = \frac{x - \mu}{\sigma} \qquad [6\text{-}6]$$

$$= \frac{580 - 500}{100}$$

$$= \frac{80}{100}$$

$$= .8 \text{ standard deviations}$$

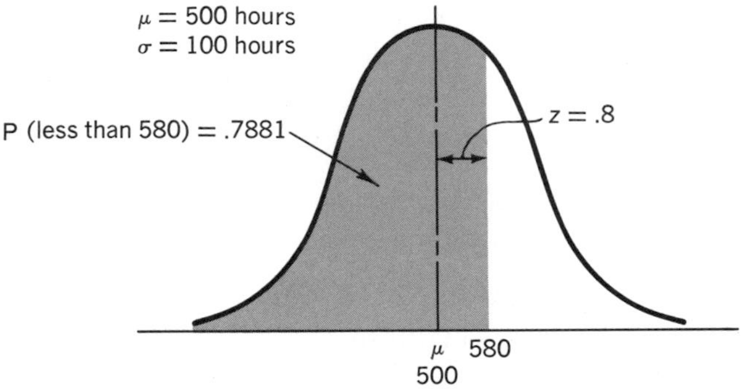

μ = 500 hours
σ = 100 hours
P (less than 580) = .7881
z = .8
μ 500
580

FIGURE 6-20 Distribution of time required to complete the training program, with interval less than 580 hours in color

Looking in Appendix Table 1 for a z value of .8, we find a probability of .2881—the probability that the random variable will lie between the mean and 580 hours. We must add to this the probability that the random variable will be between the left-hand tail and the mean. Since the distribution is symmetrical with half the area on each side of the mean, we know this value must be .5. As a final step, then, we add the two probabilities:

.2881	Probability that the random variable will lie between the mean and 580 hours
+.5000	Probability that the random variable will lie between the left-hand tail and the mean
.7881 ←	Probability that the random variable will lie between the left-hand tail and 580 hours

Thus, the chances of a candidate requiring less than 580 hours to complete the program are slightly higher than 75 percent.

◆ **EXAMPLE 6:** What is the probability that a candidate chosen at random will take between 420 and 570 hours to complete the program?

◆ **SOLUTION:** Figure 6-21 illustrates the interval in question, from 420 to 570 hours. Again the solution requires two steps. First, we calculate a z value for the 570-hour point:

$$z = \frac{x - \mu}{\sigma} \qquad [6\text{-}6]$$

$$= \frac{570 - 500}{100}$$

$$= \frac{70}{100}$$

$$= .7 \text{ standard deviations}$$

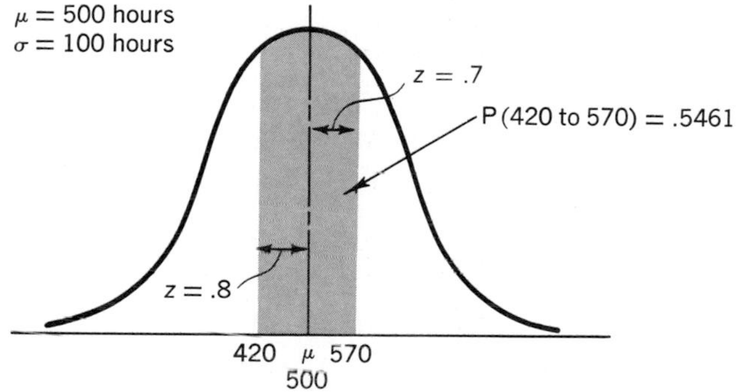

FIGURE 6-21 Distribution of time required to complete the training program, with interval between 420 and 570 hours in color

We look up the z value of .7 in Appendix Table 1 and find a probability value of .2580. Second, we calculate the z value for the 420-hour point:

$$z = \frac{x - \mu}{\sigma} \qquad [6\text{-}6]$$

$$= \frac{420 - 500}{100}$$

$$= \frac{-80}{100}$$

$$= -.8 \text{ standard deviations}$$

Since the distribution is symmetrical, we can disregard the sign and look for a z value of .8. The probability associated with this z value is .2881. We find our answer by adding these two values as follows:

.2580	Probability that the random variable will lie between the mean and 570 hours
+.2881	Probability that the random variable will lie between the mean and 420 hours
.5461 ←	Probability that the random variable will lie between 420 and 570 hours

Thus, there is slightly better than a 50 percent chance that a participant chosen at random will take between 420 and 570 hours to complete the training program.

Shortcomings of the Normal Probability Distribution

Theory and practice

Earlier in this section, we noted that the tails of the normal distribution approach but never touch the horizontal axis. This implies that there is *some* probability (although it may be very small) that the random variable can take on enormous values. It is possible for the right-hand tail of a normal curve to assign a minute probability of a person's weighing 2,000 pounds. Of course, no one would believe that such a person exists. (A weight of one ton or more would lie about 50 standard deviations to the right of the mean and would have a probability that began with 250 zeroes to the right of the decimal point!) **We do not lose much accuracy by ignoring values far out in the tails. But in exchange for the convenience of using this theoretical model, we must accept the fact that it can assign impossible empirical values.**

The Normal Distribution as an Approximation of the Binomial Distribution

Sometimes the normal is used to approximate the binomial

Although the normal distribution is continuous, it is interesting to note that it can sometimes be used to approximate discrete distributions. To see how we can use it to approximate the binomial distribution, suppose we would like to know the probability of getting five, six, seven, or eight heads in ten tosses of a fair coin. We could use Appendix Table 3 to find this probability, as follows:

$$\begin{aligned}\text{Probability of 5, 6, 7, or 8 heads} &= \text{Probability of 5 or more heads} - \text{Probability of 9 or more heads}\\ &= .6230 - .0107\\ &= .6123\end{aligned}$$

Two distributions with the same means and standard deviations

Figure 6-22 shows the binomial distribution for $n = 10$ and $p = \frac{1}{2}$ with a normal distribution superimposed on it with the *same* mean ($\mu = np = 10(\frac{1}{2}) = 5$) and the *same* standard deviation ($\sigma = \sqrt{npq} = \sqrt{10(\frac{1}{2})(\frac{1}{2})} = \sqrt{2.5} = 1.581$).

Look at the area under the normal curve between $5 + \frac{1}{2}$ and $5 - \frac{1}{2}$. We see that this area is *approximately* the same size as the area of the colored bar representing the binomial probability of getting five heads. The two ½s that we add to and subtract from 5 are called *continuity correction factors* and are used to improve the accuracy of the approximation.

Continuity correction factors

Using the continuity correction factors, we see that the binomial probability of 5, 6, 7, or 8 heads can be approximated by the area under the

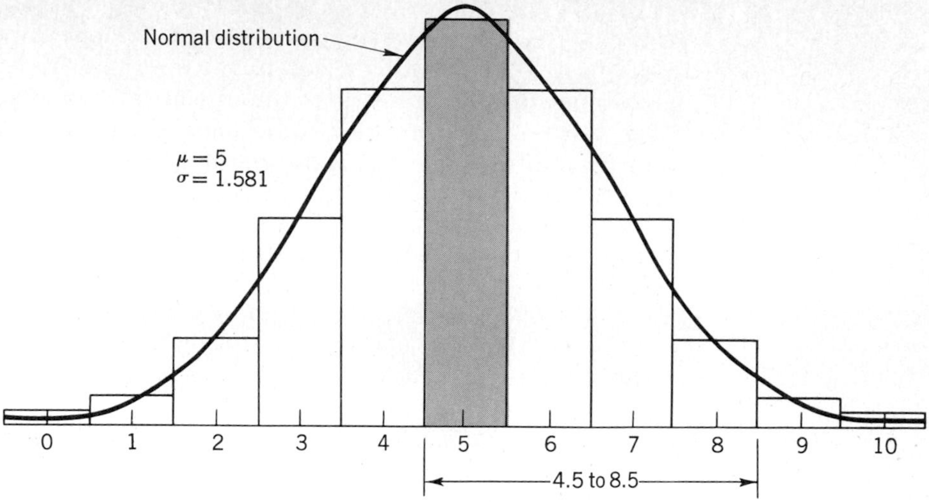

FIGURE 6-22 Binomial distribution with $n = 10$ and $p = \frac{1}{2}$, with superimposed normal distribution with $\mu = 5$ and $\sigma = 1.581$

normal curve between 4.5 and 8.5. Compute that probability by finding the z values corresponding to 4.5 and 8.5.

$$\text{At } x = 4.5,\ z = \frac{x - \mu}{\sigma} \qquad \textbf{[6-6]}$$

$$= \frac{4.5 - 5}{1.581}$$

$$= -0.32 \text{ standard deviations}$$

$$\text{At } x = 8.5,\ z = \frac{x - \mu}{\sigma} \qquad \textbf{[6-6]}$$

$$= \frac{8.5 - 5}{1.581}$$

$$= 2.21 \text{ standard deviations}$$

Now, from Appendix Table 1, we find:

.1255	The probability that z will be between -0.32 and 0 (and correspondingly, that x will be between 4.5 and 5)
+.4864	The probability that z will be between 0 and 2.21 (and correspondingly, that x will be between 5 and 8.5)
.6119	The probability that x will be between 4.5 and 8.5

The error in estimating is slight

Comparing the binomial probability of .6123 (which we got from Appendix Table 3) with this normal approximation of .6119, we can see that the error in the approximation is less than 1/10 of 1 percent.

The normal approximation to the binomial distribution is very convenient, since it enables us to solve the problem without extensive tables of the binomial distribution. (You might note that Appendix Table 3, which gives binomial probabilities for values of n up to 15, is already thirteen pages long. **We should note that some care needs to be taken in using this approximation, but it is quite good whenever both *np* and *nq* are at least 5.**

Care must be taken

EXERCISES

6-37 Given that a random variable, X, has a normal distribution with mean 5.6 and standard deviation 1.4, find:
a) $P(5.0 < x < 6.0)$ b) $P(x > 7.0)$ c) $P(x < 4.4)$ d) $P((x < 3.4) \text{ or } (x > 6.4))$

6-38 Given that a random variable has a binomial distribution with $n = 80$ trials and $p = .40$, use the normal approximation to the binomial to find:
a) $P(x > 25)$ b) $P(x > 40)$ c) $P(x < 35)$ d) $P(30 < x < 36)$

6-39 In a normal distribution with a standard deviation of 4.0, the probability that an observation selected at random exceeds 30 is .06.
a) Find the mean of the distribution.
b) Find the value below which 10 percent of the values in the distribution lie.

6-40 The financial controller for Rocky Mountain Airlines is having some problems with cash flow. Daily revenues fluctuate greatly and are difficult to predict, whereas daily expenses remain fairly constant regardless of the daily number of passengers. If daily revenue has a normal distribution with a mean of 72 (× \$1,000), and 85 percent of the values lie below 82, what is the standard deviation of the distribution? What is the value above which 5 percent of the values in the distribution lie?

6-41 Use the normal approximation to compute the following binomial probabilities:
a) $n = 50$ $p = .36$, between 10 and 20 successes
b) $n = 64$ $p = .81$, 48 or more successes
c) $n = 19$ $p = .44$, at most 7 successes
d) $n = 26$ $p = .52$, between 9 and 12 successes

6-42 The Gilbert Machinery Company has received a big order to produce electric motors for a manufacturing company. The drive shaft of the motor must fit in a groove with a diameter of $4.2 \pm .05$ (inches). The company's inventory manager realized that there was a large stock of steel rods in inventory with a mean diameter of 4.18″ with a standard deviation of .06″. What is the probability of a steel rod from inventory fitting the groove?

6-43 A new restaurant manager for Speedies, a national chain, wanted to compare his restaurant's performance with that of the rest of the chain. He took his revenue figures to an accountant and explained, "I know the mean monthly gross revenue of a Speedies restaurant is \$200,000, but I don't know the standard deviation. I do know that my predecessor's final month resulted in a gross of \$68,000, and his supervisors told him the probability of a gross that low or lower was .1210." The accountant quickly computed the standard deviation. What was it?

6-44 Ellen Bonder, owner of the Fancy Foods Store, is assembling a special gourmet food package for the holiday season. In addition to other items, a package contains two types of cheese: cheddar and gouda. Each package contains exactly 2.6 pounds of precut cheddar. However, Fancy Foods cuts its own gouda. Because of the difference in cost, Bonder does not want any of the packages to contain more than one-sixth gouda by weight. On the average, there are .4 lbs of gouda in each package. One of Bonder's assistants tells her that in 68 percent of the packages, the total weight of the gouda added to the cheddar is within plus or minus .05 of .4 pounds. What is the probability that Bonder will have to recut the gouda cheese in a package because of weight composition?

6-45 The Thirst Killer Corporation has developed a new instant drink and is currently considering various prices for the product. The marketing department developed an initial daily sales estimate of 2,400 packages, with a standard deviation of 450. Prices for the product were then determined, based on that forecast. A revised estimate from marketing predicted an average daily sales level of 2,350 packages.

a) According to the revised estimate, what is the probability that a day's sale will still be over 2,400, given that the standard deviation remains the same?
b) According to the revised estimate, what is the probability that a day's sales will be at least 98 percent of 2,400?

6-46 Glenn Howell, vice-president of personnel for the Standard Insurance Company, has developed a new training program that is entirely self-paced. New employees work through various stages at their own pace; completion occurs when the material is learned. Howell's program has been especially effective in speeding up the training process, as an employee's salary during training is only 67 percent of that earned upon completion of the program. In the last several years, average completion of the program has been 56 days, with a standard deviation of 14 days.

a) What is the probability an employee will finish the program between 40 and 51 days?
b) What is the probability of finishing the program in fewer than 35 days?
c) Fewer than 34 or more than 84 days?

6-47 On the basis of past experience, automobile inspectors in New Jersey have noticed that 7 percent of all cars coming in for their annual inspection fail to pass. Using the normal approximation to the binomial distribution, find the probability that between 10 and 20 of the next 200 cars to enter the Eatontown, N.J., inspection station will fail the inspection.

6-48 Ron Ledwith is the service manager for Johnson Car Refinishing, Inc., a firm that paints cars. His records indicate an average incoming level of 24 cars daily, with a standard deviation of 4.6, and he believes the distribution to be normal. On any day when more than 30 cars arrive to be painted, Ron must call in 2 extra shop helpers. What proportion of the time should he plan on employing these helpers?

6-49 Maurine Lewis, an editor for a large publishing company, calculates that it requires 11 months on average to complete the publication process from manuscript to finished book, with a standard deviation of 2.4 months. She believes that the normal distribution well describes the distribution of publication times. Out of 19 books she will handle this year, approximately how many will complete the process in less than a year?

6-50 The Quickie Sales Corporation has just been given two conflicting estimates of sales for the upcoming quarter. Estimate I says that sales (in millions of dollars) will be normally distributed with mean 250 and standard deviation of 50. Estimate II says that sales will be normally distributed with mean 270 and standard deviation of 30. The board of directors finds that each estimate appears to be equally believable a priori. In order to determine which estimate should be used for future predictions, the board of directors has decided to meet again at the end of the quarter to use updated sales information to make a statement about the believability of each estimate.

a) Assuming that estimate I is accurate, what is the probability that Quickie will have quarterly sales in excess of $330 million?
b) Rework part *a* assuming that estimate II is accurate.

At the end of the quarter, the board of directors finds that Quickie Sales Corp. has had sales in excess of $330 million.

c) Given this updated information, what is the probability that estimate I was originally the accurate one? (*Hint:* Remember Bayes' theorem.)
d) Rework part *c* for estimate II.

6-51 The Nobb Door Company manufactures both frames of doors and the doors themselves. They have two conflicting objectives: They want to build doors as small as possible to save on material costs, but to preserve their good reputation with the public, they feel obliged to manufacture doors that are tall enough for 99 percent of the adult population in the United States to pass through. In order to determine the height at which to manufacture doors, Nobb is willing to assume that the height of adults in the United States is normally distributed with mean 70 inches and standard deviation of 6 inches. How tall should Nobb's doors be?

6-7 CHOOSING THE CORRECT PROBABILITY DISTRIBUTION

If we plan to use a probability distribution to describe a situation, we must be careful to choose the right one. We need to be certain that we are not using the *Poisson* probability distribution when it is the *binomial* that more nearly describes the situation we are studying. Remember that the binomial distribution is applied when the number of trials is fixed before the experiment begins, and each trial is independent and can result in only two mutually exclusive outcomes (success/failure, either/or, yes/no). Like the binomial, the Poisson distribution applies when each trial is independent. But although the probabilities in a Poisson distribution approach zero after the first few values, the possible values are infinite. The results are not limited to two mutually exclusive outcomes. Under some conditions, the Poisson distribution can be used as an approximation of the binomial, but not always. All the assumptions that form the basis of a distribution must be met if our use of that distribution is to produce usable results.

Even though the normal probability distribution is the only continuous distribution we have discussed in this chapter, we should realize that there are other useful continuous distributions. In the chapters to come, we shall study three additional continuous distributions, each of interest to decision makers who solve problems using statistics.

EXERCISES

6-52 Which probability distribution is most likely the appropriate one to use for the following variables: binomial, Poisson, or normal?

a) Number of customers arriving at a complaint office
b) Scores on an intelligence test
c) Number of sales made in 10 house calls by a sales representative
d) Amount of daily rainfall

6-53 What characteristics of a situation help to determine which is the appropriate distribution to use?

6-54 Explain in your own words the difference between discrete and continuous random variables. What difference does such classification make in determining the probabilities of future events?

6-55 In practice, managers see many different types of distributions. Often, the nature of these distributions is not as apparent as are some of the examples provided in this book. What alternatives are open to students, teachers, and researchers who want to use probability distributions in their work but who are not sure exactly which distributions are appropriate for given situations?

6-8 TERMS INTRODUCED IN CHAPTER 6

BERNOULLI PROCESS A process in which each trial has only two possible outcomes, the probability of the outcome of any trial remains fixed over time, and the trials are statistically independent.

BINOMIAL DISTRIBUTION A discrete distribution describing the results of an experiment known as a Bernoulli process.

CONTINUITY CORRECTION FACTOR Corrections used to improve the accuracy of the approximation of a binomial distribution by a normal distribution.

CONTINUOUS PROBABILITY DISTRIBUTION A probability distribution in which the variable is allowed to take on any value within a given range.

CONTINUOUS RANDOM VARIABLE A random variable allowed to take on any value within a given range.

DISCRETE PROBABILITY DISTRIBUTION A probability distribution in which the variable is allowed to take on only a limited number of values.

DISCRETE RANDOM VARIABLE A random variable that is allowed to take on only a limited number of values.

EXPECTED VALUE A weighted average of the outcomes of an experiment.

EXPECTED VALUE OF A RANDOM VARIABLE The sum of the products of each value of the random variable with that value's probability of occurrence.

NORMAL DISTRIBUTION A distribution of a continuous random variable with a single-peaked, bell-shaped curve. The mean lies at the center of the distribution, and the curve is symmetrical around a vertical line erected at the mean. The two tails extend indefinitely, never touching the horizontal axis.

POISSON DISTRIBUTION A discrete distribution in which the probability of the occurrence of an event within a very small time period is a very small number, the probability that two or more such events will occur within the same small time interval is effectively 0, and the probability of the occurrence of the event within one time period is independent of where that time period is.

PROBABILITY DISTRIBUTION A list of the outcomes of an experiment with the probabilities we would expect to see associated with these outcomes.

RANDOM VARIABLE A variable that takes on different values as a result of the outcomes of a random experiment.

STANDARD NORMAL PROBABILITY DISTRIBUTION A normal probability distribution, with mean $\mu = 0$ and standard deviation $\sigma = 1$.

6-9 EQUATIONS INTRODUCED IN CHAPTER 6

[6-1]

$$\text{Probability of } r \text{ successes in } n \text{ Bernoulli or binomial trials} = \frac{n!}{r!(n-r)!} p^r q^{n-r}$$

p. 215

where:

r = number of success desired
n = number of trials undertaken
p = probability of success (characteristic probability)
q = probability of failure ($q = 1 - p$)

This *binomial formula* enables us to calculate algebraically the probability of success. We can apply it to any Bernoulli process, where (1) each trial has only two possible outcomes—a success or a failure; (2) the probability of success remains the same trial after trial; and (3) the trials are statistically independent.

[6-2] $$\mu = np$$ *p. 221*

The *mean* of a *binomial distribution* is equal to the number of trials multiplied by the probability of success.

[6-3] $$\sigma = \sqrt{npq}$$ *p. 221*

The *standard deviation* of a *binomial distribution* is equal to the square root of the product of (1) the number of trials, (2) the probability of a success, and (3) the probability of a failure (found by taking $q = 1 - p$).

[6-4] $$P(x) = \frac{\lambda^x \times e^{-\lambda}}{x!}$$ *p. 225*

This formula enables us to calculate the probability of a discrete random variable occurring in a *Poisson distribution*. The formula states that the probability of *exactly* x occurrences is equal to λ, or lambda (the mean number of occurrences per interval of time in a Poisson distribution), raised to the x power and multiplied by e, or 2.71828 (the base of the natural logarithm system), raised to the negative lambda power, and the product divided by x factorial. The table of values for $e^{-\lambda}$ is Appendix Table 4.

[6-5] $$P(x) = \frac{(np)^x \times e^{-np}}{x!}$$ *p. 228*

If we substitute in Equation 6-4 the mean of the binomial distribution (np) in place of the mean of the Poisson distribution (λ), we can use the Poisson probability distribution as a reasonable approximation of the binomial. The approximation is good when n is equal to or greater than 20 and p is equal to or less than .05.

[6-6] $$z = \frac{x - \mu}{\sigma}$$ *p. 235*

where:

x = value of the random variable with which we are concerned
μ = mean of the distribution of this random variable
σ = standard deviation of this distribution
z = number of standard deviations from x to the mean of this distribution

Once we have derived z using this formula, we can use the Standard Normal Probability Distribution Table (which gives the values for half the area under the normal curve, beginning with 0.0 at the mean) and determine the probability that the random variable with which we are concerned is within that distance from the mean of this distribution.

6-10 CHAPTER REVIEW EXERCISES

6-56 Capital City Coach maintains a fleet of buses and operates as a commercial carrier with scheduled buses and charters. Over the last several years, Capital City Coach has maintained an excellent safety record and has averaged only 1 accident for every 250,000 bus miles (including fender-benders and bus station mishaps). For the week of June 17, Capital City Coach has buses scheduled (including charters) for 50,000 bus miles.

a) What is the probability that in the seven-day period, Capital City Coach will experience only 1 accident?
b) No accidents?

6-57 The Sureflight Golf Company recently purchased a patent on a small portable device designed to measure the loft of a golf club. The president of Sureflight believes that the device is as accurate as the large mounted machines used for this. He had 100 of these produced for testing. On each one produced, a reading was taken on a club that had also been measured by a large mounted machine. As long as the reading on the portable was within .0004 inches of the reading on the larger machine, he considered it acceptable. Otherwise, the portable was rejected. He had heard of the Bernoulli process and thought it might be applicable if he could establish the probability of a defect. As described, do you think the production of the portable machines is a Bernoulli process?

6-58 The regional office of the Environmental Protection Agency annually hires second-year law students as summer interns to help the agency prepare court cases. The agency is under a budget and wishes to keep its costs at a minimum. However, hiring student interns is less costly than hiring full-time employees. Accordingly, the agency wishes to hire the maximum number of students without overstaffing. On the average, it takes two interns all summer to research a case. The interns turn their work over to staff attorneys, who prosecute the case in the fall when the circuit court convenes. The legal staff coordinator has to place his budget request in June of the preceding summer for the number of positions he wishes to maintain. It is therefore impossible for him to know with certainty how many cases will be researched in the following summer. The data from preceding summers are as follows:

YEAR	1974	1975	1976	1977	1978	1979	1980	1981	1982	1983
Number of cases	6	4	8	7	5	6	4	5	4	5

Using these data as his probability distribution for the number of cases, the legal staff coordinator wishes to hire enough interns to research the expected number of cases that will arise. How many intern positions should be requested in the budget?

6-59 Label the following probability distributions as discrete or continuous:

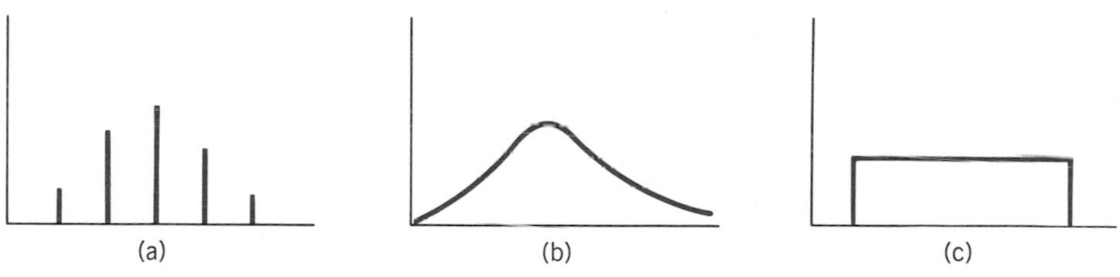

6-60 Which probability distribution would you use in the following situations: binomial, Poisson, or normal?

a) 10 trials, probability of success .5
b) 200 trials, probability of success .01
c) 500 trials, probability of success .04
d) 30 trials, probability of success .10

6-61 Lauch Faircloth, a produce broker at the Pompano Beach, Florida, market, buys and resells vegetables. It is squash season now, and Lauch is currently buying squash at $9 a crate (400 crates per truckload). If he resells it by the next day, he gets $15 a crate. If it takes longer than a day, his receipts drop to $8 a crate. Tomorrow's demand for squash is a random variable with demand for either 2, 3, 4, or 5 truckloads with probability .1, .3, .4, and .2, respectively. How much can Lauch expect to clear a day if he buys very sensibly?

6-62 The billing process for Oxxen Petroleum's credit-card sales involves mailing a different communication to those accounts past due over 60 days. A computer identifies these accounts by processing all accounts. Over the past years, an average of 4.6 accounts out of every 30 were over 60 days outstanding.

a) What is the probability that exactly 6 of the next 30 accounts processed will be over 60 days outstanding?
b) Exactly 9?

6-63 British Recording Laboratories produces long-playing records from master tapes supplied to it by recording studios. British Recording Laboratories takes the magnetic tape, cuts a master copy of the record, and makes a mold to press other records. Blanks are purchased from a plastics manufacturer. Periodically, blanks are inserted improperly into the press, causing imperfections in the record grooves and distortion when the record is played. Ian Cambridge, production manager for British Recording Laboratories, reports that on the average, 3 records are mispressed per day.

a) What is the probability that exactly 4 records will be mispressed in one day?
b) After the records are pressed, appropriate labels are glued to each side. Cambridge noted that on the average, 4.2 records are mislabeled every day. What is the probability that exactly 3 records will be mislabeled?

6-64 The City Bank of Durham has recently begun a new credit program. Customers meeting certain credit requirements can obtain a credit card that is accepted by participating area merchants and which carries a discount. Past numbers show that 30 percent of all applicants for this card are rejected. Given that credit acceptance or rejection is a Bernoulli process, out of 15 applicants, what is the probability that:

a) Exactly 3 will be rejected?
b) Exactly 10?
c) Fewer than 4?
d) More than 6?

6-65 U.S. Customs agents check the documents of incoming foreigners to see if each person entering the country has been vaccinated for smallpox. Departmental records show that 50 percent of all foreigners entering the United States have been vaccinated.

a) From a sample of 15, what is the probability that 6 or more will not have been vaccinated?
b) 8 or more?
c) Fewer than 5?

6-66 A farmer on the Delmarva Peninsula recently planted 15 hills of Half-Runner green beans. Both the seed producer and the local seed store guarantee an 80 percent fertility rate, based on years of past experience with that particular brand of seed.

a) What is the probability that more than 12 hills will come up?
b) 12 or more fertile hills?
c) Fewer than 12 fertile hills?
d) 8 or fewer fertile hills?

6-67 The Virginia Department of Health and Welfare publishes a pamphlet, *A Guide to Selecting Your Doctor.* Free copies are available to individuals, institutions, and organizations that are willing to pay the postage. Most of the copies have gone to a small number of groups who, in turn, have disseminated the literature. Mailings for 5 years have been as follows:

	Year				
	1979	1980	1981	1982	1983
Virginia Medical Association	6,000	4,000	1,000	—	3,000
Octogenarian clubs	2,000	1,000	1,000	2,000	1,000
Virginia Federation of Women's Clubs	3,000	2,000	1,000	5,000	2,000
Medical College of Virginia	500	300	600	800	1,000
U.S. Department of Health, Education, and Welfare	1,000	—	—	—	1,000

Additionally, an average of 1,500 copies per year were mailed or given to walk-in customers. Assistant Secretary Susan Fleming has to estimate the number of pamphlets to print for 1984. She knows that the pamphlet will be revised in 1984 and a new edition published. She feels that the demand in 1984 will most likely resemble that of 1982; however, she has constructed this assessment of the probabilities.

	Year				
	1979	1980	1981	1982	1983
Probability that 1984 will resemble this year	.05	.20	.10	.40	.25

a) Construct a table of a probability distribution of demand for the pamphlet, and draw a graph representing that distribution.
b) Assuming Fleming's assessment of the probabilities was correct, how many pamphlets should she order to be certain there will be enough for 1984?

6-68 The Silent Running Boat Company distributes a sailboat made by Tall Ships. On August 1, Carter Fletcher, the company's owner, learned that Tall Ships was halting production for a few weeks. Fletcher found that he had 2 dozen boats left. Fletcher knows how many boats he has sold in the last 2 years, and he consults his records for these figures:

	J	F	M	A	M	J	J	A	S	O	N	D
1982	31	30	28	29	30	29	30	32	30	27	33	32
1983	31	26	31	28	27	29	30	34	28	33	30	32

a) From Fletcher's data, compute the probability of each value indicated for the number of boats sold in a given month.
b) Compute the expected number of boats sold per month.
c) What is Fletcher's expected sales loss for August in total boats?

6-69 The financial VP of The Eversharp Knife Company must use short-term borrowing every month to ensure adequate cash flow. The VP has the figures over many months for the amount Eversharp has borrowed.

Dollars borrowed (× $1,000)	22	23	24	25	26	27	28	29	30	31	32	33	34	35
Frequency	1	2	3	4	4	5	7	6	5	4	3	3	2	1

a) Using these past data, compute the probability distribution for the random variable "monthly amount borrowed."
b) How much should the VP plan on borrowing next month if he uses expected value to do his forecasting?

6-70 The Executive Camera Company provides full expenses for its sales force. When attempting to budget automobile expenses for its employees, the financial department uses mileage figures to estimate gas, tire, and repair expenses. Salespeople average 6,250 miles a month, with a standard deviation of 178. In the interest of conservatism, the financial department wants its expense estimate and subsequent budget to be adequately high and therefore does not want to use the data from drivers who drove less than 6,000 miles. What percentage of drivers drove 6,000 miles or more?

6-71 Carolina Airlines flies a small number of routes in North and South Carolina. A flight carries an average of 30 passengers. In the summer, however, travel is heavier, and Carolina Airlines expects to average 45 passengers per flight in June.

a) Does the airline's expectation provide any insight into expected value computation?
b) Assume that the number of passengers is normally distributed with a given mean (30) and some standard deviation. The probability of having 45 passengers on a flight is very low. Does that fact cause Carolina Airlines not to expect them? Is this situation similar to the one previously described?

6-72 The purchasing agent in charge of procuring automobiles for the state of Minnesota's interagency motor pool was considering two different models. Both were 4-door, 4-cylinder cars with comparable service warranties. The decision was to choose the automobile that achieved the best mileage per gallon. The state had done some tests of its own, which produced the following results for the two automobiles in question:

	AVERAGE MPG	STANDARD DEVIATION
Automobile A	23	7
Automobile B	25	1

The purchasing agent was uncomfortable with the standard deviations, so she set her own decision criterion for the car that would be most likely to get more than 26 miles per gallon.

a) Using the data provided in combination with the purchasing agent's decision criterion, which car should she choose?
b) If the purchasing agent's decision criterion was to reject the automobile that most often obtained fewer than 24 mpg, which car should she buy?

6-73 Last year, Herb Williams invested his life savings in an antique store. Williams figured that during the first year, he took in an average of $400 dollars a week, with a standard deviation of $100.

a) According to these data, what is the probability that in any given week he took in between $350 and $420?
b) What is the probability that in any given week he took in between $380 and $500?

6-74 For a local cancer fund, the Rothman Candy Company plans to sell boxes of candy door-to-door, with the profits going to the fund. The president is convinced that the media exposure and door-to-door public contact will prove beneficial to public relations. He plans to solicit 25,000 homes. The marketing department has predicted the following probability distribution regarding number of sales:

Number of sales	14,000	15,000	16,000	17,000	18,000	19,000	20,000
Probability	.10	.15	.20	.30	.15	.05	.05

Since a unique package is being used for this project, Rothman must order the boxes in advance. The president feels that enough boxes should be ordered so that all 25,000 homes have the opportunity to purchase. The marketing VP feels that a 95 percent assurance level (5 percent chance of more demand than available boxes) is sufficient.

a) How many boxes does the president want to order (based on the validity of the probability distribution above)?
b) How many does the assistant want to order?
c) If the company decided on a 90 percent assurance level, how many boxes should be ordered?
d) If they decided on an 80 percent assurance level, how many should be ordered?

6-75 Surveys by the Federal Deposit Insurance Corporation have shown that the life of a regular savings account maintained in one of its member banks averages 18 months, with a standard deviation of 6.45 months.

a) If a depositor opens an account at a bank that is a member of the FDIC, what is the probability that there will still be money in that account in 22 months?

b) What is the probability that the account will have been closed before 2 years?

6-76 Sensurex Productions, Incorporated, has recently patented and developed an ultrasensitive smoke detector for use in both residential and commercial buildings. Whenever a detectable amount of smoke is in the air, a wailing siren is set off. In recent tests conducted in a 20′ × 15′ × 8′ room, the smoke levels that activated the smoke detector averaged 372 parts per million (ppm) of smoke in the room, with a standard deviation of 13 ppm.

a) If a cigarette introduces 75 ppm into the atmosphere of a 20′ × 15′ × 8′ room, what is the probability that 5 people simultaneously smoking cigarettes will set off the alarm?

b) Three people?

6-77 Rework problem 6-65, using the normal approximation. Compare the approximate and the exact answers.

6-78 Try to use the normal approximation for problem 6-66. Notice that nq is only 3. Comment on the accuracy of the approximation.

6-11 CHAPTER CONCEPTS TEST

Answers are in the back of the book.

T F 1. The expected value of an experiment is obtained by computing the arithmetic average value over all possible outcomes of the experiment.

T F 2. The value of z for some point x lying in a normal distribution is the area between x and the mean of the distribution.

T F 3. The right and left tails of the normal distribution extend indefinitely, never touching the horizontal axis.

T F 4. For a normal distribution, the mean always lies between the mode and the median.

T F 5. All but about three-tenths of 1 percent of the area in a normal distribution lies within plus and minus 3 standard deviations from the mean.

T F 6. Developing a conditional loss table is cumbersome when there are many possible actions and outcomes, because the loss resulting from every action/outcome pair must be included in the table.

T F 7. The area under the curve of a normal distribution between the mean and a point 1.8 standard deviations above the mean is greater for a distribution having a mean of 100 than it is for a distribution having a mean of 0.

T F 8. The normal distribution may be used to approximate the binomial distribution when the number of trials, n, is equal to or greater than 60.

T F 9. The two types of losses we consider in solving an inventory-stocking problem are (a) opportunity losses and (b) activity losses.

T F 10. When the probability of success in a Bernoulli process is 50 percent ($p = .5$), its binomial distribution is symmetrical.

T F 11. A frequency distribution lists observed frequencies for an experiment that has already been performed; a probability distribution lists those outcomes that could result *if* the experiment were performed.

T F 12. The value of a random variable can usually be predicted in advance of a particular occurrence.

T F 13. Once the value of p has been decided for a Bernoulli process, the value of q is calculated as $(1 - p)$.

T F 14. If the expected number of arrivals in an office is calculated as 5 per hour, one can be reasonably confident that 5 people will arrive within the next hour.

T F 15. The binomial distribution is not really necessary, since its values can always be approximated by another distribution.

T F 16. The height of adult humans can be described by a Poisson distribution.

T F 17. Any action that minimizes expected loss will also minimize expected gain.

T F 18. Which of the following is a characteristic of a probability distribution for a random variable?
a) A probability is provided for every possible value.
b) The sum of all probabilities is 1.
c) No given probability occurs more than once.
d) All of these.
e) a and b but not c.

19. Which of the following could never be described by a binomial distribution?
a) The number of defective widgets produced by an assembly process.
b) The amount of water used daily by a single household.
c) The number of people in your class who can answer this question correctly.
d) All of these could always be described by a binomial distribution.

20. If $p = .4$ for a particular Bernoulli process, the calculation $\frac{7!}{3! \times 4!}(.4)^3(.6)^4$ gives the probability of getting:
a) Exactly 3 successes in 7 trials
b) Exactly 4 successes in 7 trials
c) 3 or more successes in 7 trials
d) 4 or more successes in 7 trials
e) None of these.

21. For binomial distributions with $p = .2$:
a) A distribution for $n = 2{,}000$ would more closely approximate the normal distribution than one for $n = 50$.
b) No matter what the value of n, the distribution is skewed to the right.
c) The graph of this distribution with $p = .2$ and $n = 100$ would be the exact reverse of the graph for the binomial distribution with $n = 100$ and $p = .8$.
d) All of these.
e) a and b but not c.

22. Which of the following is a necessary condition for use of a Poisson distribution?
a) Probability of 1 arrival per second is constant.
b) The number of arrivals in any 1-second interval is independent of arrivals in other intervals.
c) The probability of 2 or more arrivals in the same second is zero.
d) All of these.
e) b and c but not a.

23. In which of these cases would the Poisson distribution be a good approximation of the binomial?
a) $n = 40, p = .32$
b) $n = 40, q = .79$
c) $n = 200, q = .98$
d) $n = 10, p = .03$
e) All of these.

24. For a normal curve with $\mu = 55$ and $\sigma = 10$, how much area will be found under the curve to the right of the value 55?
a) 1.0 d) .32
b) .68 e) Cannot be determined from the information given.
c) .5

25. Suppose you are using a normal distribution to approximate a binomial distribution with $\mu = 5$, $\sigma = 2$ and wish to determine the probability of getting more than 7 successes. From the normal table, you would determine the probability that z is greater than:
a) 0 b) .5 c) .75 d) 1.0 e) 1.25

26. For a normal curve with a mean of 120 and a standard deviation of 35, what proportion of the area under the curve will lie between the values of 40 and 82?

27. Which of the following normal curves looks most like the curve for $\mu = 10$, $\sigma = 5$?
a) Curve for $\mu = 10$, $\sigma = 10$. c) Curve for $\mu = 20$, $\sigma = 5$.
b) Curve for $\mu = 20$, $\sigma = 10$. d) Curve for $\mu = 12$, $\sigma = 3$.

28. A binomial distribution may be approximated by a Poisson distribution if:
a) n is large and p is large d) None of these
b) n is small and p is large c) n is small and p is small

29. The standard deviation of a binomial distribution depends on:
a) Probability of success d) a and b but not c
b) Probability of failure e) b and c but not a
c) Number of trials f) a, b, and c

30. The weighted average of the outcomes of an experiment is called the ______________.

31. The distribution that deals only in successes and failures is the ______________ distribution. It is usually used to describe a ______________ process.

32. When approximating a binomial distribution by a normal distribution, a ______________ correction factor should be used.

33. The mean of a binomial distribution, μ, can be calculated as ______________, once n and p are known. The standard deviation, σ, is calculated as ______________.

34. For a Poisson distribution, the symbol that represents the mean number of occurrences per interval of time is ______________.

35. A list of the probabilities of outcomes that could result if an experiment were performed is called a ______________.

6-12 CONCEPTUAL CASE (Northern White Metals Company)

Late in January 1981, Dick Lennox made the decision to expand NWMC's sales force. The economy had rebounded from the brief 1980 recession, the prospects for a spring boom in commercial construction were strong, and continual gains were being posted in the high-tech applications area. NWMC aluminum was being increasingly accepted as both a structural material and exterior trim, largely through the efforts of Bill Hamilton, who had made microprocessor, computer, and instrumentation businesses his specialty.

Four experienced sales reps were hired to service the upsurge in building, and three new reps, all midyear graduates from a local engineering school, were taken on to service the burgeoning technology field. It was planned that growth in this industry would lead to growth for Northern, too.

And so it went, with all three new reps bringing in at first small, but soon larger and larger orders. Of the new salespeople, one, Lynn Martin, seemed to progress faster than the rest and was soon rivaling Bill as top producer in the special-applications area. By mid-May, the total order backlog had increased 20 percent, and Dick was quite pleased. An additional, somewhat unexpected benefit of increased sales in this area was a greater demand for services of the fabricating and anodizing departments. Capacity utilization in each of these had risen nearly 50 percent, since the newer applications frequently required cut, milled, finished material and not just raw extruded aluminum.

This growth spurt, though, carried with it some problems. Particularly troubled was the anodizing department. Anodizing involves putting a protective, often decorative, oxide film on the aluminum by an electrolytic process in which the metal serves as an anode. The metal is placed on special racks and dipped sequentially in large tanks containing concentrated solutions of acid, caustic soda, and a neutral rinse. There are six tanks in all, and the aluminum sections must spend a certain amount of time in each tank before being transferred to the next. When the metal is brought out of the sixth tank and dried, the process is complete. The process is a fairly delicate one, and it is important to maintain the proper pH levels, or acid and alkaline concentrations, in the different solutions.

Improper pH levels, either too acid or too alkaline, could result in a finish that is either too light or too heavy. If too light a finish is imparted, the entire cycle has to be repeated. If the finish is too heavy, or textured, the metal is suitable only for scrap.

In the past, the anodizing foreman could use a judgment born of years of experience and compensate for concentration deviations by using longer or shorter dipping periods. The significantly increased volume had begun to strain the process, though, and this system was no longer practicable. Mike Schutzer, the foreman, was growing increasingly frustrated, and he stopped in to talk with Dick one afternoon at quitting time.

"We've reached the limit!" he erupted with dismay.

"The limit of what?" Dick replied curiously. The growing bottleneck problem in anodizing had not yet been brought to his attention.

"The limit of reason," the foreman responded. "I can't go on juggling orders through the line anymore. Each pass-through changes the solution concentrations from the ideal levels. Either we have to monitor levels continuously to keep them at the ideal mark or risk turning out batch after batch of bad product."

Dick thought for a moment, then replied, "Mike, I think there's a compromise solution here. It's true that there is actually some acceptable range of concentrations around the ideal, isn't there?"

"Well, yes, I suppose there is," the foreman answered cautiously.

Dick was relieved to know that was true. The cost of maintaining a constant, unchanging pH would easily exceed the price addition of an anodized finish, of that he was sure.

"We both know how costly it is to maintain a fixed concentration," he continued, "so it seems to me we have to determine a tradeoff point. We'll select a waste/reject level that will allow us to operate the process continuously while only requiring periodic concentration adjustments."

Clearly, increased demand has introduced an unforeseen problem into the anodizing department. Dick seems to have an idea about how to get operations under control, and fortunately, he has the support of his foreman. What information is now needed? Once acquired, how should the information be used to better manage the anodizing department?

6-13 COMPUTER DATA BASE EXERCISE

Since its founding in 1890, Cold River had always built its Rough Rider sleds the same time-proven way. Each of the fifteen craftsmen would build a complete sled by hand. First he would cut, bend, weld, grind, and paint the channel iron to make sled runners. After shaping the wooden frame pieces, he would assemble them together with the runners and the steering mechanism. Once he was through, he added the final touch by stenciling a stallion and the name, Rough Rider, on the steering bar.

Joe periodically assessed the feasibility of installing an assembly line for Rough Rider, similar to production of his other lines. He thought the old way of building sleds was less efficient than a production line. Industrial engineering consultants had estimated that a production line could reduce the number of craftsmen to twelve and maintain the same output.

Nick Pappas, the production manager, approached Joe one day with a request. "Those kids did such a good job on the Polaris problem, how about if we turn them loose on our annual efficiency study and see if they can settle the argument. I'd love to see a good assembly line in here for next year's Rough Riders."

"Great idea, Nick," Joe agreed. "I had that scheduled to worry about next week, and they've been looking a little bored recently."

Frank and Laurel began gathering information that afternoon. The comptroller estimated that the firm's cost of capital required that an investment in a new production line achieve at least an 18 percent reduction in per-unit labor costs after downtime was taken into account, in order to break even.

A discussion with Nick gave them several additional insights. He told them that under the present system, if a craftsman were absent, production would continue. With a production line, if two or more workers were absent from the production stations, it would stop the whole line for the entire day. The workers reporting to work would have to be paid, but no sleds would be built. Although the line would be equally productive every day it operated, regardless of how many workers were present, it could not be understaffed permanently with only eleven workers.

Personnel gave Laurel and Frank the file on worker absenteeism (Exhibit 1) and said the data were stable and representative, and would not change if the production line were installed.

PROBLEMS AND QUESTIONS

1. What is the probability that a given worker will be absent on any given day?
2. With 250 work days per year and 12 employees on the line, how many days per year will there be exactly 1 worker absent? 2, 3, 4, 5 absent?
3. If employees are paid in full for the days when they are not absent, but the production line has stopped, how much will Cold River spend in nonproductive wages? How much will the company save with a production line (amount and percentage)? (Assume a $50 per diem wage rate.)

The head of Personnel, Irene MacDonald (who doubled as office manager and purchaser for raw materials), thought that if people came to work and had nothing to do, serious morale problems would result. "Idle hands are the devil's workshop" was a favorite saying of hers. She insisted that the production line could not be down more than twice per year on the average.

Nick Pappas argued with her for a while and then conceded that this could be done with overstaffing, and still the production line would be cheaper.

PROBLEMS AND QUESTIONS

4. How many extra production workers are needed to overstaff the production line so that downtime will not be greater than twice per year on the average?
5. How much more will be produced with overstaffing? What will be the change in per-unit labor costs? Should the line be installed?

The comptroller, Eric Thomasson, was so pleased with the thorough job Frank and Laurel had done with the production problem that he asked them to help him out with a minor cash flow problem.

Exhibit I

WORKERS																									
Present	15	15	15	15	15	15	15	15	15	15	15	15	15	15	15	15	13	15	12	15	15	15	14	15	15
Absent	0	0	0	0	0	0	0	0	0	0	0	0	0	0	0	0	2	0	3	0	0	0	1	0	0
Present	15	14	15	15	14	13	15	15	15	15	15	14	14	15	15	15	14	13	15	15	15	15	15	15	15
Absent	0	1	0	0	1	2	0	0	0	0	0	1	1	0	0	0	1	2	0	0	0	0	0	0	0
Present	15	15	15	15	15	13	14	15	15	13	14	15	15	15	15	15	15	15	14	15	14	15	15	14	15
Absent	0	0	0	0	0	2	1	0	0	2	1	0	0	0	0	0	0	0	1	0	1	0	0	1	0
Present	15	15	15	15	14	15	15	14	15	13	14	15	15	15	14	15	14	15	15	14	15	15	15	15	15
Absent	0	0	0	0	1	0	0	1	0	2	1	0	0	0	1	0	1	0	0	1	0	0	0	0	0
Present	15	15	14	14	14	15	14	14	15	15	15	12	14	14	14	15	15	15	15	14	15	15	14	15	15
Absent	0	0	1	1	1	0	1	1	0	0	0	3	1	1	1	0	0	0	0	1	0	0	1	0	0
Present	15	15	15	15	15	15	15	15	15	15	14	14	15	14	15	15	15	15	15	15	13	14	14	14	15
Absent	0	0	0	0	0	0	0	0	0	0	1	1	0	1	0	0	0	0	0	0	2	1	1	1	0
Present	14	15	14	15	15	15	14	14	15	15	15	14	15	15	15	15	15	15	15	15	15	15	14	13	15
Absent	1	0	1	0	0	0	1	1	0	0	0	1	0	0	0	0	0	0	0	0	0	0	1	2	0
Present	15	15	15	14	15	13	15	14	13	15	15	15	15	14	15	14	15	15	14	15	14	14	14	15	14
Absent	0	0	0	1	0	2	0	1	2	0	0	0	0	1	0	1	0	0	1	0	1	1	1	0	1
Present	15	14	15	14	15	15	15	15	15	15	15	15	14	15	13	15	15	14	15	15	15	15	15	14	15
Absent	0	1	0	1	0	0	0	0	0	0	0	0	1	0	2	0	0	1	0	0	0	0	0	1	0
Present	14	14	14	14	15	15	15	15	15	14	15	16	14	15	13	15	14	13	14	15	14	15	15	15	15
Absent	1	1	1	1	0	0	0	0	0	1	0	0	1	0	2	0	1	2	1	0	1	0	0	0	0

"When Joe and I joined Cold River, we noticed dollar sales were dropping drastically whenever we instituted a promotion to our distributors. Retail sales were constant, but we lost money. To overcome this, we initiated a policy of continuous promotion. Each Rough Rider came with a refund coupon that entitled the purchaser to a $10 rebate. After the purchaser sent us his coupon, we'd mail him a check the following Monday."

"Sounds great," said Frank. "What's the problem?"

"We're running tight here at Cold River. With the expected product line expansions, we're holding on to every penny we can and reinvesting it till we need it. Except for receivables and inventories, all our current assets are in cash deposits and marketable securities, and we keep the cash as low as possible. We need 3 weeks lead time to convert securities into cash, and I'd like a good idea of how much I'll need every Monday in cash to pay the rebates."

"That's a hard one to get with any accuracy. If we could get a figure for the average number of coupon redemptions per week, we could use the

Poisson distribution to get a handle on the figure; but the only way to be 100 percent sure that the Monday balance is high enough is to have a very large balance equal to all the outstanding coupons," responded Laurel.

Eric felt that this amount defeated the purpose of cash management; and besides, that level of certainty was not necessary, since they could delay mailing the checks for a week if the balance was too low. Only a minor disruption would result.

PROBLEMS AND QUESTIONS

6. If a delay in mailing the checks once every 5 weeks were acceptable, how large should the balance for coupons be?

7. How much should the balance be to cut the number of delays to once every 10 weeks?

8. How much larger should the balance be to cut the average number of delays to once every 20 years?

NUMBER OF COUPONS EACH WEEK
(Data are to be read row by row)

173	182	182	168	172	163	144	143	135	143	124	104	92
80	85	75	56	57	50	23	28	15	24	16	19	15
10	9	14	16	35	41	40	52	49	71	89	83	90
102	118	132	150	140	147	176	163	170	185	184	179	187

The day after the cash flow study was completed, Frank and Laurel were packing their knapsacks for an afternoon of crosscountry skiing when Joe caught them in the employees' lounge.

"If you folks have a second, I have a minor project for you. We're considering launching a new line of wooden toys and want to know who buys the old line. Here are the warranty cards for the last couple of years. See what you can find out, then take the afternoon off."

The two market statisticians exchanged woebegone glances and headed back to the office.

The preschool line of wooden puzzle toys on wheels was sold in 20 stores in Denver and in 20 more in resort towns like Aspen and Telluride.

"A consumer profile won't be difficult to capture," said Frank. "Wonder what questions are on the warranty cards?"

"Let's start with income bracket for the last year. You keypunch this stack," said Laurel.

Four hours later they had finished coding in the income bracket and were ready to run the data and look at the distribution.

"I'm sure glad this toy isn't more widely distributed," said Laurel. "We'd have been here for days."

PROBLEMS AND QUESTIONS

9. What distribution appears to describe the purchasers' incomes?

10. What were the mean, median, and standard deviation?

"There's something else on my mind," said Joe. "It's crucial that we establish income group proportions accurately if we are going to use our budget efficiently. I want to be sure we are advertising to the right income brackets."

QUESTION

11. Suppose that purchasers' incomes are normally distributed with μ and σ calculated in 10. What proportion of the toy purchasers would you expect to earn more than \$20,000 per year? Less than \$15,000? What proportions actually do fall in these ranges?

PURCHASER INCOME

SEQUENCE ⟶

17378	15098	14582	18511	16421	14178	21752	15690	15515	14183
12850	20375	16506	13431	18797	16519	15002	16694	19112	14864
16700	17725	15829	16863	18052	13947	18612	17377	16561	16155
16900	13831	16604	17522	19862	16933	18016	17066	15090	16190
15817	12185	17568	15876	15228	15269	14526	14898	17489	14555
17393	16968	16793	16929	15284	15589	12326	13790	20080	16963
16964	16466	15387	15265	18375	13640	13443	16576	18290	17662
13978	13008	12901	15457	17227	17982	11641	14954	14886	13600
18599	15528	17426	14861	15414	13388	14325	16979	14487	17602
13376	14239	14632	15185	16362	17041	14974	17205	16228	14964
16442	12987	10783	18949	15918	17949	13698	14146	17892	16110
12171	18151	16092	13155	16049	15022	15805	18141	12421	12371
14757	17783	13778	17394	15734	16651	18990	19087	17822	18685
17536	13700	17919	13943	12031	14303	14006	17221	17509	15819
13077	14853	16925	14929	15935	12786	13288	14379	16290	12057
17439	15930	15608	14334	18745	21036	14621	14043	12527	16624
16827	12946	17451	15834	15856	16156	13773	15736	17010	16352
20101	13626	14435	16647	14793	14453	17717	17166	16782	17134
12123	17607	16551	18207	14727	17063	14706	15794	15383	15526
17307	15815	15512	14637	15462	17516	18667	13330	18308	12671
15038	15951	17557	14621	20592	14486	17294	13656	15202	15739
13211	15824	16539	16174	17120	12816	12264	15594	15003	17325
14233	13808	16997	16820	16902	13525	17035	18006	18205	15920
19891	14189	14664	17684	16505	14296	16391	18387	19572	18451
14331	13761	14600	18072	15282	15381	12930	17810	12596	20745
17125	12606	17839	15996	17824	18311	18442	14744	14530	19346
14526	16942	17601	12456	16688	18244	15991	17451	16534	17259
12573	13917	19495	19412	11697	15138	18562	13378	16071	15194
13812	14359	18414	17472	14584	15806	14411	14648	14187	14995
15457	17406	18754	13264	17695	19458	16921	12721	14044	14117
17326	17143	13237	15223	18318	17298	18098	16206	15636	15911
14848	16776	14450	17697	16137	11160	14467	17869	18005	16519
11022	17011	18875	15192	17285	14757	15521	15336	16741	17387
18259	14819	14488	13573	19217	13734	19785	14251	15881	19300
13567	16167	13964	15575	15929	15772	13627	13858	20741	13541
16235	14064	14292	16560	18382	17725	16427	15924	16737	13421
16698	13679	16916	19044	17537	14557	13190	15628	18540	14811

PURCHASER INCOME (*continued*)

SEQUENCE ⟶

16530	12713	15808	15938	17919	14688	18327	15199	18015	17098
14866	14872	15272	15927	15442	11884	15760	15168	13721	14898
19651	12712	14462	16036	14602	17453	16217	11855	15982	16664
19978	16693	19092	17663	17234	18808	17794	18656	16242	14761
15666	17568	17593	16482	15981	17035	20698	14085	17646	15650
12095	18646	16573	16486	15130	15589	13386	19688	15930	18540
16284	13995	16189	11254	16322	13579	15934	16525	14812	16184
14088	13832	15920	13400	16626	16311	17983	14632	15773	13146
15558	15417	15127	15345	11965	15601	16083	15198	16849	14852
15748	16865	15857	17023	14878	19186	17833	15672	17988	16518
13750	16941	20248	16109	15055	18084	15827	14440	13751	14541
18262	15256	16941	17175	19531	12337	16692	13736	10977	13967
16673	16713	15861	14783	15500	15261	16971	16245	17567	14822
19377	16107	15610	16302	11794	14824	16235	19412	15410	17147
11428	14757	14000	17699	15967	13552	17497	12503	15593	17582
14176	13313	18026	15567	17032	16093	14862	18484	16279	17298
17323	14916	16892	18173	16846	20591	14687	18287	13434	18798
12566	15309	11842	16959	17668	13431	17878	15877	14045	14118
15390	16447	13304	15445	16765	17105	15536	18371	16491	20888
16625	18418	16195	14813	19321	14703	13543	13951	18185	15621
14786	15472	16500	17157	15574	17650	12008	13939	19409	16955
13419	17107	16735	15535	16050	14491	13816	14216	15927	16426
16298	12905	18213	16726	15852	17469	15352	17868	17341	18350
17119	13506	17406	15312	15209	17365	16567	15346	16071	17225
17383	15912	14563	17297	15544	19664	13838	17259	15148	17871
11415	16666	16743	15772	16466	14798	14314	17831	13762	17537
18689	16713	15168	14731	16090	14765	18144	16074	13869	15055
14805	14626	18189	16816	14287	13038	16559	14330	17985	17903
15349	16310	14321	17869	17372	17414	14760	11838	16212	16269
13891	14531	13633	15458	14934	14873	17988	16102	15496	17550
19082	15349	15501	17138	15423	14976	13986	17742	15906	16310
15987	15966	16674	13734	16868	13550	15560	15246	19605	14155
13608	15714	16634	14598	14934	17892	15969	16785	13650	18607
14379	15484	16701	18155	18686	17745	17627	11728	14814	14983
16051	20523	15752	13281	16700	14384	16135	13863	16211	15252
13831	14922	15089	16971	16397	13768	13677	14877	15907	14713
15749	19650	13371	20286	18051	16475	10188	17946	14627	18111
15440	15020	12680	18002	14296	14667	13480	12989	13608	16146
16545	13913	15526	15887	16281	16056	13193	18778	14277	11524
18088	13696	18608	12157	12205	18152	14784	16607	15642	18632
12759	16809	18109	15574	13310	15589	15745	14169	13385	15749
15702	16103	17276	17421	13332	12480	16399	11428	16541	16257
13428	14836	16893	15251	15883	15927	17725	14594	16346	14915
14429	18154	15146	15149	16062	15865	16767	17720	14495	14803
14777	12531	14251	17194	15526	17413	17012	16963	16165	16730
16108	16080	20321	13993	16520	18199	18042	12832	14926	18700
14837	16550	16024	15303	17451	17269	16219	14422	15251	14589
13328	13365	13345	15618	17894	14719	16544	14465	13671	16035
18343	15393	13682	17785	19695	14129	17951	16929	13871	15679
19881	16693	18775	15326	12469	16926	15254	15211	17011	14895
16658	13300	14958	15781	11046	16499	17373	17670	15168	16128
15168	15731	15959	15997	12520	15493	16110	13415	14441	14713
16524	15755	16691	16340	17901	18352	14918	15580	16659	12912

PURCHASER INCOME (*continued*)

SEQUENCE ⟶

18844	17191	17252	15934	15436	18078	21296	16818	19435	12735
17329	15215	18030	18653	19524	17667	14299	16332	17479	19707
21393	21629	17630	17534	15227	15440	17388	14971	13072	13216
12968	15684	13496	13226	14042	14018	14390	18191	17624	16463
18331	13528	13881	14308	17421	14291	18930	15567	18352	14996
18780	16054	14679	13781	14745	15658	17795	16760	15231	14401
17886	17110	17245	14612	18655	15123	13960	15000	17572	14907
14292	16101	17825	12437	18047	17387	19313	15260	12375	14289
19590	15085	15110	14782	17153	16917	17184	13672	16274	16351
15396	11730	15651	14736	12765	14514	17175	16874	17765	15866

6-14 FLOW CHART

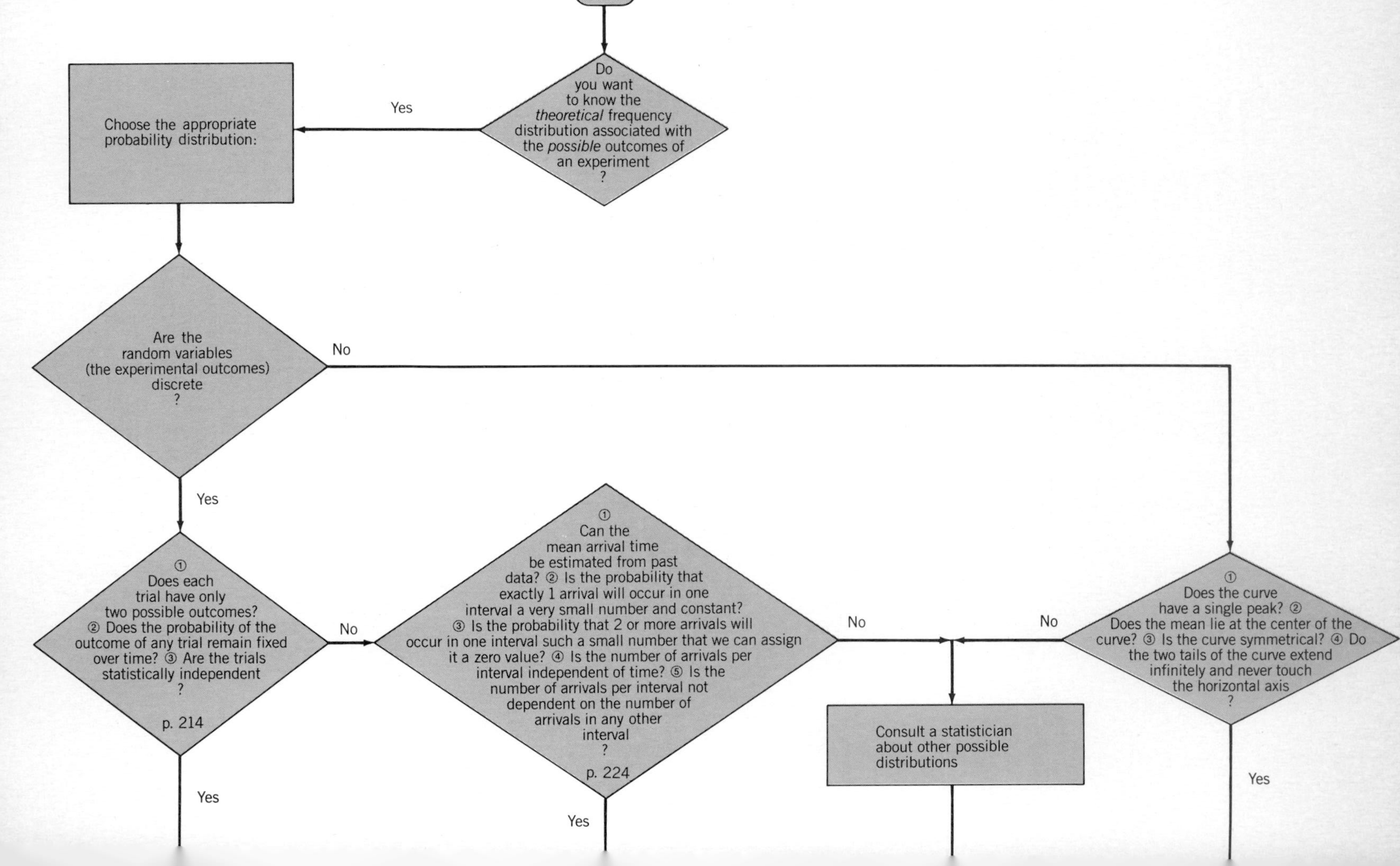

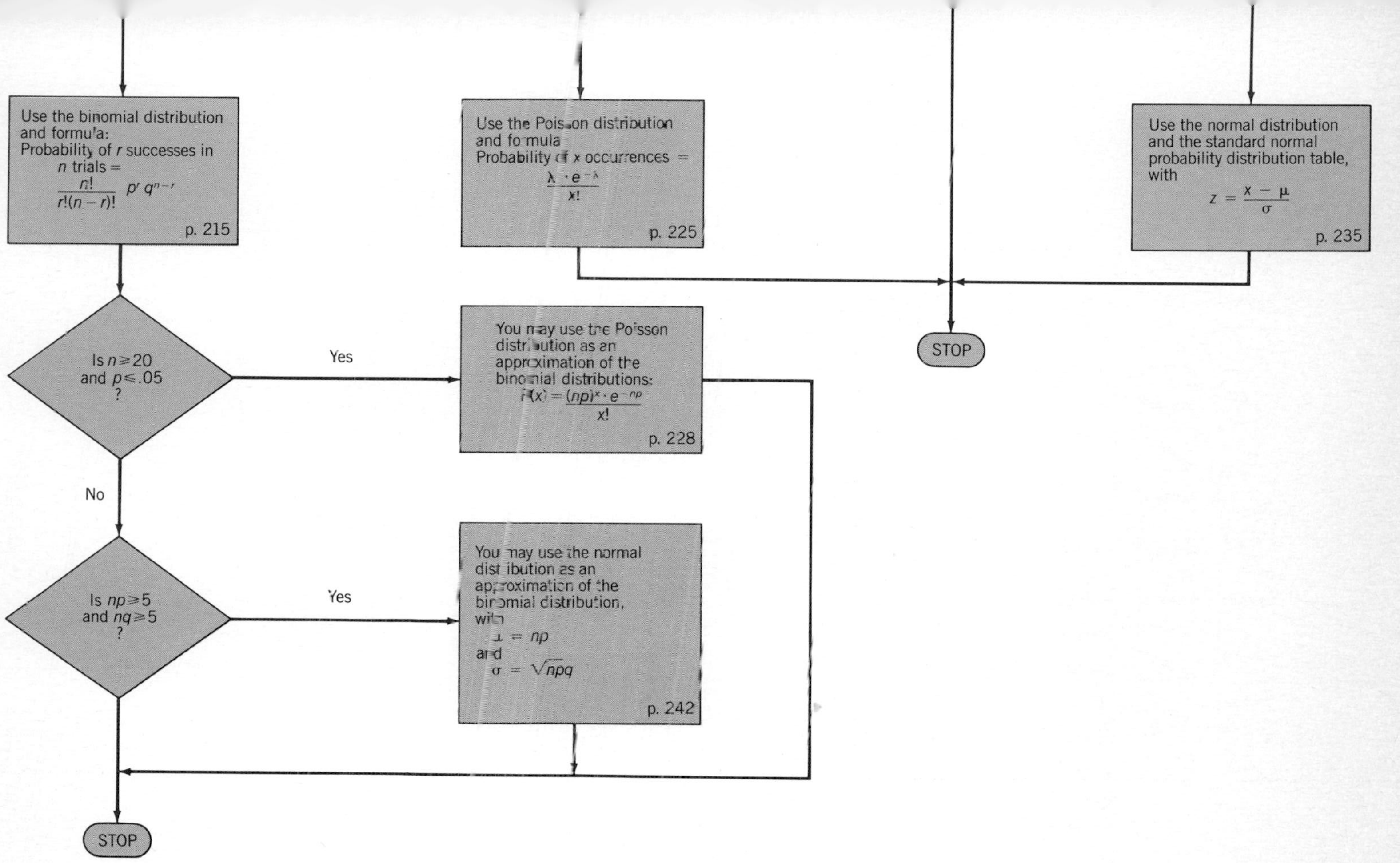
Use the binomial distribution and formula:
Probability of r successes in n trials = $\frac{n!}{r!(n-r)!} p^r q^{n-r}$
p. 215
Use the Poisson distribution and formula
Probability of x occurrences = $\frac{\lambda^x \cdot e^{-\lambda}}{x!}$
p. 225
Use the normal distribution and the standard normal probability distribution table, with
$z = \frac{x - \mu}{\sigma}$
p. 235
STOP
Is $n \geq 20$ and $p \leq .05$?
Yes
You may use the Poisson distribution as an approximation of the binomial distributions:
$f(x) = \frac{(np)^x \cdot e^{-np}}{x!}$
p. 228
No
Is $np \geq 5$ and $nq \geq 5$?
Yes
You may use the normal distribution as an approximation of the binomial distribution, with
$\mu = np$
and
$\sigma = \sqrt{npq}$
p. 242
STOP

CHAPTER 7

SAMPLING AND SAMPLING DISTRIBUTIONS

1. INTRODUCTION TO SAMPLING, 268
2. RANDOM SAMPLING, 270
3. INTRODUCTION TO SAMPLING DISTRIBUTIONS, 277
4. SAMPLING DISTRIBUTIONS IN MORE DETAIL, 280
5. AN OPERATIONAL CONSIDERATION IN SAMPLING: The Relationship Between Sample Size and Standard Error, 291
6. DESIGN OF EXPERIMENTS, 295
7. TERMS, 299
8. EQUATIONS, 301
9. REVIEW EXERCISES, 301
10. CONCEPTS TEST, 303
11. CONCEPTUAL CASE, 306
12. COMPUTER DATA BASE EXERCISE, 307
13. FLOW CHART, 308

OBJECTIVES: Statistical sampling, the subject of Chapter 7, is a systematic approach to selecting a few elements (a *sample*) from an entire collection of data (a *population*) in order to make some inferences about the total collection. We shall learn methods that help to ensure that samples represent the entire collection. If you have ever examined a peach on the top of a basket, bought the whole basket on the basis of that peach, and then found the bottom of the basket filled with overripe fruit, you have a good (if somewhat expensive) understanding of statistical sampling and the need for better sampling methods.

Although there are over 150 million TV viewers in the United States and somewhat over half that many TV sets, only about 1,000 of those sets are sampled to determine what programs Americans watch. Why select only about 1,000 sets out of 75 million? Because time and the average cost of an interview prohibit the rating companies from trying to reach millions of people. And since polls are reasonably accurate, interviewing everybody is unnecessary. In this chapter, we examine questions such as these: How many people should be interviewed? How should they be selected? How do we know when our sample accurately reflects the entire population?

7-1 INTRODUCTION TO SAMPLING

Reasons for sampling

Shoppers often sample a small piece of cheese before purchasing any. They decide from one piece what the larger chunk will taste like. A chemist does the same thing when he takes a sample of whiskey from a vat, determines that it is 90 proof, and infers that all whiskey in the vat is 90 proof. If the chemist tests all the whiskey or the shoppers taste all the cheese, there will be none to sell. Testing all of the product often destroys it and is unnecessary. To determine the characteristics of the whole, we have to sample only a portion.

Suppose that, as the personnel director of a large bank, you need to write a report describing all the employees who have voluntarily left the company in the last ten years. You would have a difficult task locating all these thousands of people. They are not easily accessible as a group — many have died, moved from the community, left the country, or acquired a new name by marriage. How do you write the report? The best idea is to locate a representative sample and interview them, in order to generalize about the entire group.

Time is also a factor when managers need information quickly in order to adjust an operation or change a policy. Take an automatic machine that sorts thousands of pieces of mail daily. Why wait for an entire day's output to check whether the machine is working accurately (whether the *population characteristics* are those required by the postal service)? Instead, samples can be taken at specific intervals, and if necessary, the machine can be adjusted right away.

Census or sample

Sometimes it is possible and practical to examine every person or item in the population we wish to describe. We call this a *complete enumeration,* or *census*. We use sampling when it is not possible to count or measure every item in the population.

Examples of populations and samples

Statisticians use the word *population* to refer not only to people but to all items that have been chosen for study. In the cases we have just mentioned, the populations are all the cheese in the chunk, all the whiskey in the vat, all the employees of the large bank who voluntarily left in the last ten years, and all mail sorted by the automatic machine since the previous sample check. **Statisticians use the word *sample* to describe a portion chosen from the population.**

Statistics and Parameters

Function of statistics and parameters

Mathematically, we can describe samples and populations by using measures such as the mean, median, mode, and standard deviation, which we introduced in Chapters 3 and 4. When these terms describe the characteristics of a sample, they are called *statistics*. When they describe the characteristics of a population, they are called *parameters*. **A statistic is a characteristic of a sample, and a parameter is a characteristic of a population.**

Suppose that the mean height in inches of all tenth graders in the United States is 60 inches. In this case, 60 inches is a characteristic of the population "all tenth graders" and can be called a *population parameter*. On the other hand, if we say that the mean height in Ms. Jones's tenth-grade class in Bennetsville is 60 inches, we are using 60 inches to describe a characteristic of the sample "Ms. Jones's tenth graders." In that case, 60 inches would be a *sample statistic*. If we are convinced that the mean height of Ms. Jones's tenth graders is an accurate estimate of the mean height of all tenth graders in the United States, we could use the sample statistic "mean height of Ms. Jones's tenth graders" to estimate the population parameter "mean height of all U.S. tenth-graders" without having to count all the millions of tenth graders in the United States.

Using statistics to estimate parameters

N, μ, σ, and n, $\bar{x}$, s: standard symbols

To be consistent, statisticians use lowercase Roman letters to denote sample statistics and Greek or capital letters for population parameters. Table 7-1 lists these symbols and summarizes the definitions we have studied so far in this chapter.

TABLE 7-1 Differences between populations and samples

	POPULATION	SAMPLE
Definition	Collection of items being considered	Part or portion of the population chosen for study
Characteristics	"Parameters"	"Statistics"
Symbols	Population size = N Population mean = μ Population standard deviation = σ	Sample size = n Sample mean = $\bar{x}$ Sample standard deviation = s

Types of Sampling

Judgment and probability sampling

There are two methods of selecting samples from populations: *nonrandom* or *judgment* sampling, and *random* or *probability* sampling. In probability sampling, all the items in the population have a chance of being chosen in the sample. In judgment sampling, personal knowledge and opinion are used to identify those items from the population that are to be included in the sample. A sample selected by judgment sampling is based on someone's expertise about the population. A forest ranger, for example, would have a judgment sample if he decided ahead of time which parts of a large forested area he would walk through to estimate the total board feet of lumber that could be cut. Sometimes a judgment sample is used as a pilot or trial sample to decide how to take a random sample later. Judgment samples avoid the statistical analysis that is necessary to make probability samples. They are more convenient and can be used successfully even though we are unable to measure their validity. But if a study uses judgment sampling and loses a significant degree of "representativeness," it will have purchased convenience at too high a price.

EXERCISES

7-1 What is the major drawback of judgment sampling?

7-2 Depending on the extent of conclusions drawn from a statistical analysis, a given set of observations may be thought of as a sample or as a population. Explain.

7-3 List the advantages of sampling over complete enumeration, or census.

7-4 What are some of the disadvantages of probability sampling versus judgment sampling?

7-5 Dick Barron, quality control manager for Set-Rite Typewriter Company, was in a heated discussion with his Trenton plant assistant concerning the company's quality control tests. The company has built its reputation on high-quality merchandise; therefore, in the Trenton plant as in all the company plants, typewriters are tested as they come off the assembly line. The Trenton plant tests 100 percent of its typewriters. For this reason, the Trenton assistant argued that he was dealing with a population, as far as statistics were concerned, and that the plant's average defect rate and standard deviation were parameters. Barron argued that since the plant was only one of several in which the typewriters were produced and tested, the information from the Trenton plant was simply a sample of a larger set of tests. Accordingly, any statistics generated were sample statistics, not parameters. Who was right?

7-6 Jean Mason, who was hired by Former Industries to determine employee attitudes toward the upcoming union vote, met with some difficulty after reporting her findings to management. Mason's study was based on statistical sampling, and from the beginning data it was clear (or so Jean thought) that the employees were favoring a unionized shop. Jean's report was shrugged off with the comment, "This is no good. Nobody can make statements about employee sentiments when she talks to only a little over 15 percent of our employees. Everyone knows you have to check 50 percent to have any idea of what the outcome of the union vote will be. We didn't hire you to make guesses." Is there any defense for Jean's position?

7-7 A corporation wants to conduct an investigation of possible increases in employee stress and job dissatisfaction due to the increased production rate necessary in one of its manufacturing plants. The corporation has hired a research firm to conduct employee interviews. The corporation has a choice of getting interview data on a sample of the total employee population or getting data on all employees. The corporation knows that the sample will be less costly but has heard from a fairly reliable source that a census is always better than a sample, since the census provides more accurate information. The corporation thought that by omitting other research projects, it could use the extra funds for purchasing the information on all employees. Evaluate the information from the reliable source and advise the corporation what type of data it should obtain from the research firm.

7-2 RANDOM SAMPLING

In a random or probability sample, we know what the chances are that an element of the population will or will not be included in the sample. As a result, we can assess objectively the estimates of the population characteristics that result from our sample; that is, we can describe mathematically how objective our estimates are. Let us begin our explanation of this process by introducing four methods of random sampling:

1. Simple random sampling
2. Systematic sampling

3. Stratified sampling
4. Cluster sampling

Simple Random Sampling

An example of simple random sampling

Simple random sampling selects samples by methods that allow *each possible sample to have an equal probability of being picked* and *each item in the entire population to have an equal chance of being included in the sample.* We can illustrate these requirements with an example. Suppose we have a population of four students in a seminar and we want samples of two students at a time for interviewing purposes. Table 7-2 illustrates the possible combinations of samples of two students in a population size of four, the probability of each sample being picked, and the probability that each student will be in the sample.

TABLE 7-2 Chances of selecting samples of 2 students from a population of 4 students

STUDENTS A, B, C, AND D		
Possible samples of two persons: *AB, AC, AD, BC, CD, BD*		
Probability of drawing this sample of two persons must be:		
	$AB = 1/6$	
	$AC = 1/6$	
	$AD = 1/6$	(There are only six possible samples of two
	$BC = 1/6$	persons)
	$CD = 1/6$	
	$BD = 1/6$	
Probability of this student being in the sample must be:		
	$A = 1/2$	[In Chapter 5, we saw that the marginal proba-
	$B = 1/2$	bility is equal to the *sum* of the joint probabili-
	$C = 1/2$	ties of the events within which the event is
	$D = 1/2$	contained: $P(A) = P(AB + AC + AD) = 1/2$]

Defining *finite* and *replacement*

Our example illustrated in Table 7-2 uses a *finite* population of four students. By *finite,* we mean that the population has a stated or limited size; that is to say, there is a whole number (N) that tells us how many items there are in the population. Certainly, if we sample without "replacing" the student, we shall soon exhaust our small population group. Notice, too, that if we sample *with replacement* (that is, if we replace the sampled student immediately after he or she is picked and before the second student is chosen), the same person could appear twice in the sample.

An infinite population

We have used this example only to help us think about sampling from an infinite population. An *infinite* population is a population in which it is theoretically impossible to observe all the elements. Although many populations appear to be exceedingly large, no truly infinite population of physical objects actually exists. After all, given unlimited resources and time, we could enumerate any finite population, even the grains of sand on the beaches of North America. As a practical matter, then, we will use the term *infinite population* when we are talking about a population that could not be enumerated in a reasonable period of time. In this way, we will use the theoretical concept of infinite population as an approximation of a large finite population, just as we earlier used the theoretical concept of continuous random variable as an approximation of a discrete random variable that could take on many closely spaced values.

How to Do Random Sampling

The easiest way to select a sample randomly is to use random numbers. These numbers can be generated either by a computer programmed to scramble numbers or by a table of random numbers, which should properly be called a *table of random digits.*

Table 7-3 illustrates a portion of such a table. Here we have 1,250 random digits in sets of ten digits. These numbers have been generated by a completely random process. The probability that any one digit from 0 through 9 will appear is the same as that for any other digit, and the probability of one sequence of digits occurring is the same as that for any other sequence of the same length.

Using a table of random digits

To see how to use this table, suppose that we have 100 employees in a company and wish to interview a randomly chosen sample of ten. We could get such a random sample by assigning every employee a number from 00 to 99, consulting Table 7-3, and picking a systematic method of selecting two-digit numbers. In this case, let's do the following:

1. Go from the top to the bottom of the columns beginning with the left-hand column, and read only the first two digits in each row. Notice that our first number using this method would be 15, the second 09, the third 41, and so on.

2. If we reach the bottom of the last column on the right and are still short of our desired 10 two-digit numbers of 99 and under, we can go back to the beginning (the top of the left-hand column) and start reading the third and fourth digits of each number. These would begin 81, 28, and 12.

Using slips of paper

Another way to select our employees would be to write the name of each one on a slip of paper and deposit the slips in a box. After mixing them thoroughly, we could draw ten slips at random. This method works well with a small group of people but presents problems if the people in the population number in the thousands. There is the added problem, too, of not being certain that the slips of paper are mixed well. In the draft lottery of 1970, for example, when capsules were drawn from a bowl to determine by birthdays the order of selecting draftees for the armed services, December birthdays appeared more often than the probabilities would have suggested. As it turned out, the December capsules had been placed in the bowl last, and the capsules had not been mixed properly. Thus, December capsules had the highest probability of being drawn.

TABLE 7-3 1,250 random digits*

1581922396	2068577984	8262130892	8374856049	4637567488
0928105582	7295088579	9586111652	7055508767	6472382934
4112077556	3440672486	1882412963	0684012006	0933147914
7457477468	5435810788	9670852913	1291265730	4890031305
0099520858	3090908872	2039593181	5973470495	9776135501
7245174840	2275698645	8416549348	4676463101	2229367983
6749420382	4832630032	5670984959	5432114610	2966095680
5503161011	7413686599	1198757695	0414294470	0140121598
7164238934	7666127259	5263097712	5133648980	4011966963
3593969525	0272759769	0385998136	9999089966	7544056852
4192054466	0700014629	5169439659	8408705169	1074373131
9697426117	6488888550	4031652526	8123543276	0927534537
2007950579	9564268448	3457416988	1531027886	7016633739
4584768758	2389278610	3859431781	3643768456	4141314518
3840145867	9120831830	7228567652	1267173884	4020651657
0190453442	4800088084	1165628559	5407921254	3768932478
6766554338	5585265145	5089052204	9780623691	2195448096
6315116284	9172824179	5544814339	0016943666	3828538786
3908771938	4035554324	0840126299	4942059208	1475623997
5570024586	9324732596	1186563397	4425143189	3216653251
2999997185	0135968938	7678931194	1351031403	6002561840
7864375912	8383232768	1892857070	2323673751	3188881718
7065492027	6349104233	3382569662	4579426926	1513082455
0654683246	4765104877	8149224168	5468631609	6474393896
7830555058	5255147182	3519287786	2481675649	8907598697

* Source: Dudley J. Cowden and Mercedes S. Cowden, *Practical Problems in Business Statistics*, 2d ed. (Englewood Cliffs, N.J.: Prentice-Hall, 1960).

Systematic Sampling

In systematic sampling, elements are selected from the population at a uniform interval that is measured in time, order, or space. If we wanted to interview every twentieth student on a college campus, we would choose a random starting point in the first twenty names in the student directory and then pick every twentieth name thereafter.

Characteristics of systematic sampling

Systematic sampling differs from simple random sampling in that each *element* has an equal chance of being selected but each *sample* does *not* have an equal chance of being selected. This would have been the case if, in our earlier example, we had assigned numbers between 00 and 99 to our employees and then had begun to choose a sample of ten by picking every tenth number beginning 1, 11, 21, 31, and so forth. Employees numbered 2, 3, 4, and 5 would have had no chance of being selected.

Shortcomings of the systematic approach

In systematic sampling, there is the problem of introducing an error into the sampling process. Suppose we were sampling paper waste produced by households, and we decided to sample 100 households every Monday. Chances are high that our sample would not be representative, because Monday's trash would very likely include the Sunday newspaper. Thus, the amount of waste would be biased upward by our choice of this sampling procedure.

Systematic sampling has advantages too, however. Even though systematic sampling may be inappropriate when the elements lie in a sequential pattern, this method may require less time and sometimes results in lower costs than the simple random sampling method.

Stratified Sampling

Two ways to take stratified samples

To use stratified sampling, we divide the population into relatively homogeneous groups, called *strata*. Then we use one of two approaches. Either we select at random from each stratum a specified number of elements corresponding to the proportion of that stratum in the population as a whole, or we draw an equal number of elements from each stratum and give weight to the results according to the stratum's proportion of total population. With either approach, stratified sampling guarantees that every element in the population has a chance of being selected.

Stratified sampling is appropriate when the population is already divided into groups of different sizes and we wish to acknowledge this fact. Suppose that the patients of a physician are divided into four groups according to age, as shown in Table 7-4. The physician wants to find out how many hours his patients sleep. To obtain an estimate of this characteristic of the population, he could take a random sample from each of the four age groups and give weight to the samples according to the percentage of patients in that group. This would be an example of a stratified sample.

The advantage of stratified samples is that when they are properly designed, they more accurately reflect characteristics of the population from which they were chosen than do other kinds of sampling.

TABLE 7-4 Composition of patients by age

AGE GROUP	PERCENTAGE OF TOTAL
Birth–19 years	30%
20–39 years	40
40–59 years	20
60 years and older	10

Cluster Sampling

In cluster sampling, we divide the population into groups, or *clusters*, and then select a random sample of these clusters. We assume that these individual clusters are representative of the population as a whole. If a market research team is attempting to determine by sampling the average number of television sets per household in a large city, they could use a city map to divide the territory into blocks and then choose a certain number of blocks (clusters) for interviewing. Every household in each of these blocks would be interviewed. A well-designed cluster sampling procedure can produce a more precise sample at considerably less cost than that of simple random sampling.

Comparison of stratified and cluster sampling

With both stratified and cluster sampling, the population is divided into well-defined groups. We use *stratified* sampling when each group has small variation within itself but there is wide variation between the groups. We use *cluster* sampling in the opposite case—when there is considerable variation within each group but the groups are essentially similar to each other.

Basis of Statistical Inference: Simple Random Sampling

Systematic sampling, stratified sampling, and cluster sampling attempt to approximate simple random sampling. All are methods that have been developed for their precision, economy, or physical ease. Even so, assume for the rest of the examples and problems in this book that we obtain our data using simple random sampling. This is necessary because the principles of simple random sampling are the foundation for *statistical inference,* the process of making inferences about populations from information contained in samples. Once these principles have been developed for simple random sampling, their extension to the other sampling methods is conceptually quite simple but somewhat involved mathematically. If you understand the basic ideas involved in simple random sampling, you will have a good grasp of what is going on in the other cases, even if you must leave the technical details to the professional statistician.

EXERCISES

7-8 In the example below, probability distributions for 3 natural subgroups of a larger population are shown. For which situation would you recommend stratified sampling?

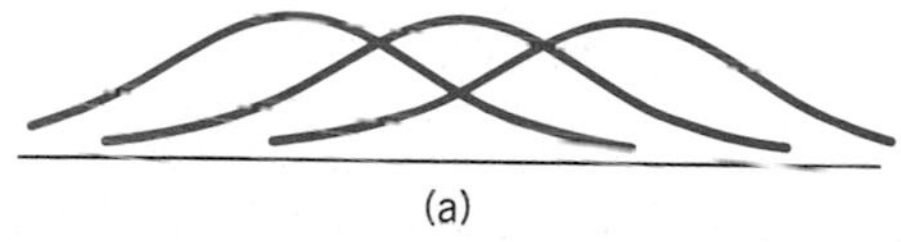

(a)

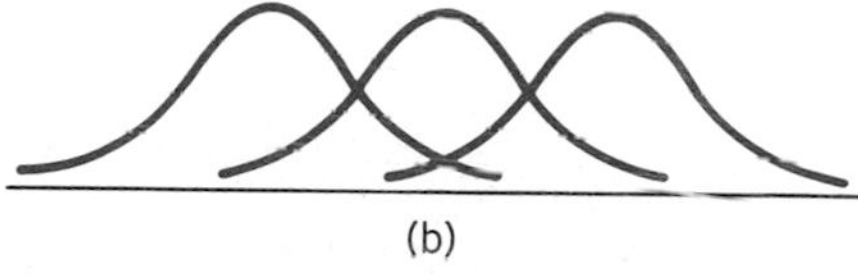

(b)

7-9 If we have a population of 1,000 individuals and we wish to sample 25 randomly, use the random digits table (Table 7-3) to select 25 individuals from the 1,000. List the numbers of those elements selected, based on the random digits table.

7-10 Using a calendar, systematically sample every 14th day of one year, beginning with January 3rd.

7-11 A population is made up of groups that have wide variation within each group but little variation from group to group. The appropriate type of sampling for this population is:
a) Stratified b) Systematic c) Cluster d) Judgment

7-12 Morrisville Tobacco Company has recently implemented a wage incentive program to help increase productivity and worker motivation. Management wishes to find out overall employee response to the program. The study will include all of Morrisville's plants, which are under the wage incentive plan, and will sample a large number of employees throughout the company. The management is drawing the sample from a list of all employees who have worked at the company at least 1 year. Is it a random sample?

7-13 Bob Peterson, public relations manager for Piedmont Power and Light, has implemented an institutional advertising campaign to promote energy consciousness among its customers. Peterson, anxious to know if the campaign has been effective, plans to conduct a telephone survey of area residents. He plans to look in the telephone book and select random numbers with addresses that correspond to the company's service area. Will Peterson's sample be a random one?

7-14 Consult Table 7-3. What is the probability that a 3 will appear as the rightmost digit in each set of 10 digits? That a six will appear? 8? How many times would you expect to see each of those digits in the rightmost position? How many times is each found in that position? Can you explain any differences in the number found and the number expected?

7-15 In a study of changing consumer attitudes, an assistant for a marketing research firm is required to listen to taped consumer interviews and to keypunch the responses on computer cards. He usually does approximately 10 tape programmings per day before changing to another type of work, since there are certain fatigue effects involved in listening and coding the data. His supervisor wishes to do a reliability check on his work with this study and is considering a statistical method of sampling to check his accuracy. Would systematic sampling be appropriate?

7-16 The state occupational safety board has decided to do a study of work-related accidents within the state, to examine some of the variables involved in the accidents; e.g., the type of job, the cause of the accident, the extent of the injury, the time of day, and whether the employer was negligent. It has been decided that 250 of the 2,500 work-related accidents reported last year in the state will be sampled. The accident reports are filed by date in a filing cabinet. Marsha Gulley, a department employee, has proposed that the study use a systematic sampling technique and select every tenth report in the file for the sample. Would her plan of systematic sampling be appropriate here? Explain.

7-17 Bob Bennett, product manager for Clipper Mowers Company, is interested in looking at the kinds of lawn mowers used throughout the country. Assistant product manager Mary Wilson has recommended a stratified random sampling process in which the cities and communities studied are separated into substrata, depending on the size and nature of the community. Mary Wilson proposes the following classification:

CATEGORY	TYPE OF COMMUNITY
Urban	Inner city (population 100,000+)
Suburban	Outlying areas of cities or smaller communities (pop. 20,000 to 100,000)
Rural	Small communities (fewer than 20,000 residents)

Is stratified random sampling appropriate here?

7-18 A Senate study on the issue of self-rule for the District of Columbia involved surveying 2,000 people from the population of the city regarding their opinions on a number of issues related to self-rule. Washington, D.C., is a city in which many neighborhoods are poor and many neighborhoods are rich, with very few neighborhoods falling between the extremes. The researchers who were administering the survey had reason to believe that the opinions expressed on the various questions would be highly dependent upon income. Which method was more appropriate, stratified sampling or cluster sampling? Explain briefly.

7-3 INTRODUCTION TO SAMPLING DISTRIBUTIONS

Statistics differ among samples from the same population

In Chapters 3 and 4, we introduced methods by which we can use sample data to calculate statistics such as the mean and the standard deviation. So far in this chapter, we have examined how samples can be taken from populations. If we apply what we have learned and take several samples from a population, the statistics we would compute for each sample need not be the same and most probably would vary from sample to sample.

Sampling distribution defined

Suppose our samples each consist of ten 25-year-old women from a city with a population of 100,000 (an infinite population, according to our usage). By computing the mean height and standard deviation of that height for each of these samples, we would quickly see that the mean of each sample and the standard deviation of each sample would be different. **A probability distribution of all the possible means of the samples is a distribution of the sample means. Statisticians call this a *sampling distribution of the mean.***

We could also have a sampling distribution of a proportion. Assume that we have determined the proportion of beetle-infested pine trees in samples of 100 trees taken from a very large forest. We have taken a large number of those 100-item samples. If we plot a probability distribution of the possible proportions of infested trees in all these samples, we would see a distribution of the sample proportions. In statistics, this is called a *sampling distribution of the proportion*. (Notice that the term *proportion* refers to the proportion that is infested.)

Describing Sampling Distributions

Any probability distribution (and, therefore, any sampling distribution) can be partially described by its mean and standard deviation. Table 7-5 illustrates several populations. Beside each, we have indicated the sample taken

TABLE 7-5 Examples of populations, samples, sample statistics, and sampling distributions

POPULATION	SAMPLE	SAMPLE STATISTIC	SAMPLING DISTRIBUTION
Water in a river	10-gallon containers of water	Mean number of parts of mercury per million parts of water	Sampling distribution of the mean
All professional basketball teams	Groups of 5 players	Median height	Sampling distribution of the median
All parts produced by a manufacturing process	50 parts	Proportion defective	Sampling distribution of the proportion

from that population, the sample statistic we have measured, and the sampling distribution that would be associated with that statistic.

Now, how would we describe each of the sampling distributions in Table 7-5? In the first example, the sampling distribution of the mean can be partially described by its mean and standard deviation. The sampling distribution of the median in the second example can be partially described by the mean and standard deviation of the distribution of the medians. And in the third, the sampling distribution of the proportion can be partially described by the mean and standard deviation of the distribution of the proportions.

Concept of Standard Error

Derivation of the term *standard error*

Rather than say "standard deviation of the distribution of sample means" to describe a distribution of sample means, statisticians refer to the *standard error of the mean*. Similarly, the "standard deviation of the distribution of sample proportions" is shortened to the *standard error of the proportion*. The term *standard error* is used because it conveys a specific meaning. An example will help explain the reason for the name. Suppose we wish to learn something about the height of freshmen at a large state university. We could take a series of samples and calculate the mean height for each sample. It is highly unlikely that all of these sample means would be the same; we expect to see some variability in our observed means. This variability in the sample statistic results from *sampling error* due to chance; that is, there are differences between each sample and the population, and among the several samples, owing solely to the elements we happened to choose for the samples.

The standard deviation of the distribution of sample means measures the extent to which we expect the means from the different samples to vary because of this chance error in the sampling process. Thus, **the standard deviation of the distribution of a sample statistic is known as the *standard error of the statistic.***

Size of the standard error

The standard error indicates not only the size of the chance error that has been made but also the accuracy we are likely to get if we use a sample statistic to estimate a population parameter. A distribution of sample means that is less spread out (that has a small standard error) is a better

TABLE 7-6 Conventional terminology used to refer to sample statistics

WHEN WE WISH TO REFER TO THE:	WE USE THE CONVENTIONAL TERM:
Standard deviation of the distribution of sample means	Standard error of the mean
Standard deviation of the distribution of sample proportions	Standard error of the proportion
Standard deviation of the distribution of sample medians	Standard error of the median
Standard deviation of the distribution of sample ranges	Standard error of the range

estimator of the population mean than a distribution of sample means that is widely dispersed and has a larger standard error.

Table 7-6 indicates the proper use of the term *standard error.* In Chapter 8, we shall discuss how to *estimate* population parameters using sample statistics.

EXERCISES

7-19 A restaurant with a limited number of seats serving businesspeople in a downtown office building is known to have a mean of 120 persons served per day and a standard deviation of 12. Two potential buyers of the restaurant were discussing the probability that in the next 30 days, the average number of persons served per day would be 120. One buyer, who had been in the restaurant business for years, said that it was entirely chance that the average number of persons served in the 30-day period would equal the mean of the population. The younger buyer thought there was a great probability that the sample would average 120, since that was the expected number of daily customers. Which of the buyers is right? Explain.

7-20 The term *error,* in standard error of the mean, refers to what type of error?

7-21 A machine that fills bottles is known to have a mean filling amount of 100 grams and a standard deviation of 15 grams. A quality control manager took a random sample of filled bottles and found the sample mean to be 105. The quality control manager assumed the sample must not have been representative. Is his conclusion correct?

7-22 An electric company has determined that the mean cost per 100 sq. ft. for the residential population electrical service is $0.242 with a standard error of $0.05. Two different samples are selected at random, and the means are $0.20 and $0.27, respectively. The assistant in charge of data collection concludes that the second sample is the better one because it is better to overestimate than underestimate the true mean. Comment. Is one of the sample means "better" in some way, given the true population mean?

7-23 A survey researcher has mailed out questionnaires to a large sample of people in cities across the nation. Different numbers of questionnaires are sent to different geographic regions, based on the population density of the area. Not all the questionnaires sent out are returned. Upon receiving the ones that were completed, he sorts them according to region and computes the mean response for each region. He then plots the frequency distribution of these means. Does this represent a sampling distribution of the mean for the population? Why, or why not?

7-24 Marilyn Swinford, a financial officer for Northwestern Bank, is studying the time needed to make a loan decision since the implementation of stricter loan guidelines. From a sample of loans, she recorded the length of time before a decision was announced. The loan policy has been studied by others in the bank, and Marilyn is attempting to present the results of these studies to the president. She has with her two graphs that, she explained, represent frequency distributions of the length of time it took to make a loan decision. The president, however, does not get the point. Can you explain to the president the significance of the two graphs shown on page 280?

7-25 In times of declining SAT scores and problems of functional illiteracy, the admissions committee of a prestigious university is concerned with keeping high standards of admission. Each year, after decisions on acceptance are made, the committee publishes and distributes statistics on students admitted, giving, for example, the average SAT score. On the report containing the statistics are the words, "Standard Error of the Mean." The secretary who types the report knows that for several years, the average SAT score was about 1,200 and has assumed that the standard error of the mean was how much the committee allowed an admitted student's score to deviate from the mean. Is the assumption correct? Explain.

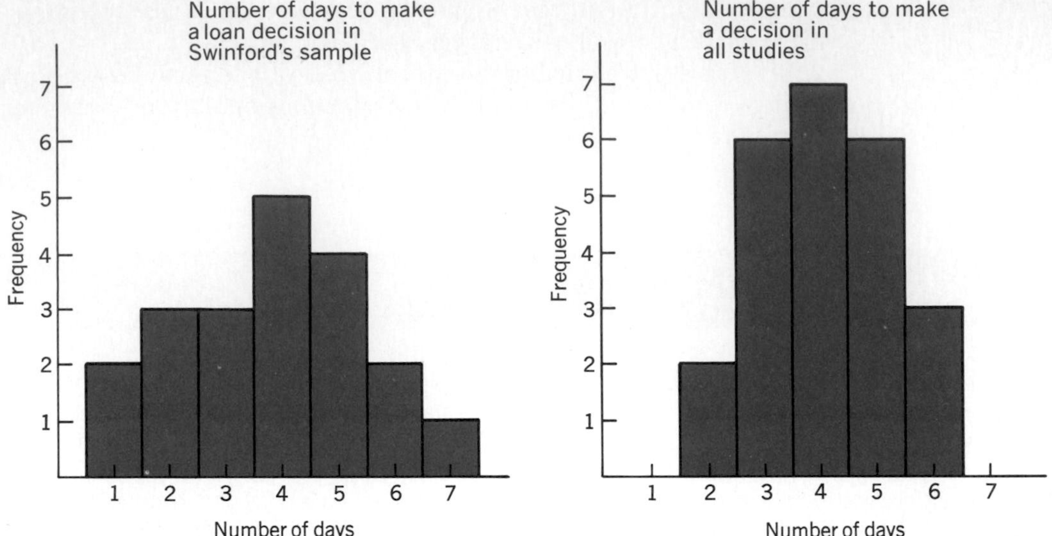

7-26 A fast-food chain, Super Chicken, has been randomly sampling specific franchises in order to determine the time it takes an employee to construct the Super Jr. chicken sandwich. At each selected franchise, 10 employees are timed, and the mean time for that franchise is recorded. When the study was concluded, 50 franchises had been sampled in the manner just described. The 50 numbers associated with the franchises, plus the mean and standard deviation of these numbers, were turned over to the board of directors of Super Chicken. Did the board receive information about the distribution of time for a single employee to construct a sandwich, or about the distribution of a sample mean of times for groups of employees?

7-4 SAMPLING DISTRIBUTIONS IN MORE DETAIL

In the last section of this chapter, we introduced the idea of a sampling distribution. We examined the reasons why sampling from a population and developing a distribution of these sample statistics would produce a sampling distribution, and we introduced the concept of standard error. Now we will study these concepts further, so that we will not only be able to understand them conceptually but also be able to handle them computationally.

Conceptual Basis for Sampling Distributions

Deriving the sampling distribution of the mean

Figure 7-1 will help us examine sampling distributions without delving too deeply into statistical theory. We have divided this illustration into three parts. Part *a* of Fig. 7-1 illustrates a *population distribution*. Assume that this population is all the filter screens in a large industrial pollution-control

(a)

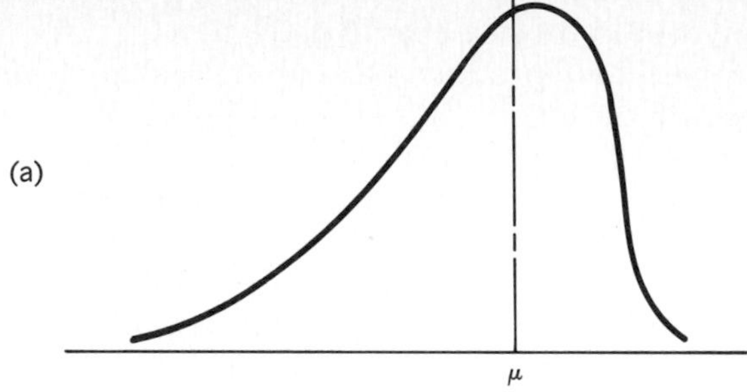

The population distribution:
This distribution is the distribution of the operating hours of *all* the filter screens. It has:

μ = the mean of this distribution

σ = the standard deviation of this distribution

If somehow we were able to take *all* the possible samples of a given size from this *population distribution,* they would be represented graphically by these four samples below. Although we have shown only four such samples, there would actually be an enormous number of them.

(b)

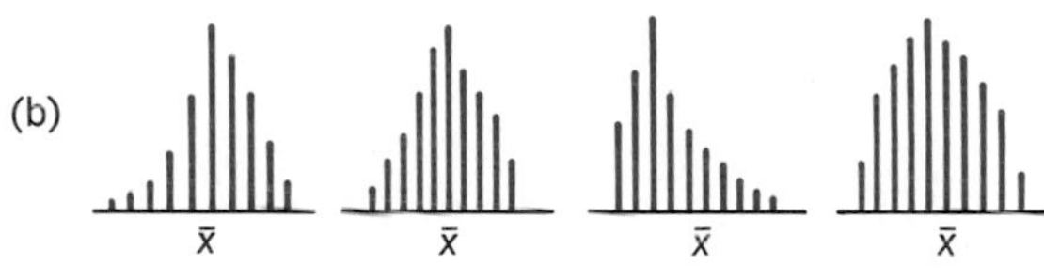

The sample frequency distributions:
These only *represent* the enormous number of sample distributions possible. *Each* sample distribution is a discrete distribution and has:

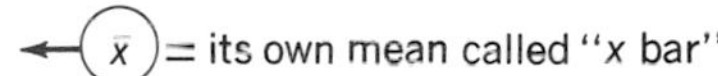 = its own mean called "x bar"

s = its own standard deviation

Now, if we were able to take the means from all the *sample distributions* and produce a distribution of these sample means, it would look like this:

(c)

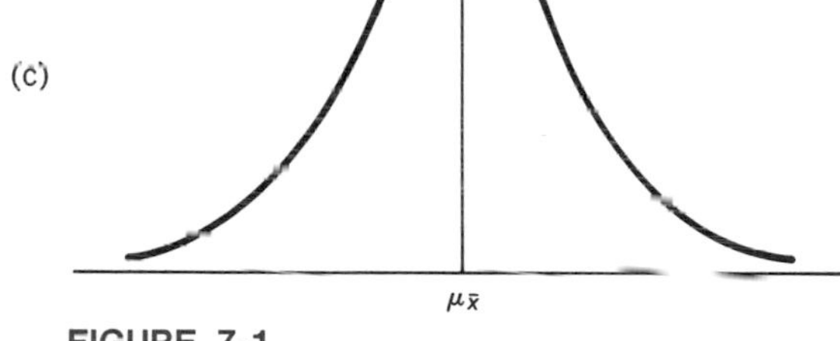

The sampling distribution of the mean:
This distribution is the distribution of all the sample means and has:

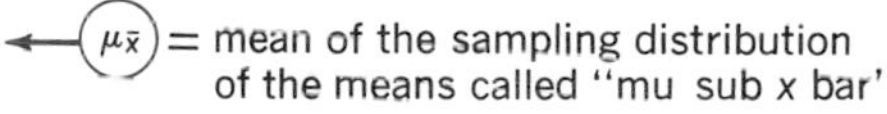 = mean of the sampling distribution of the means called "mu sub x bar"

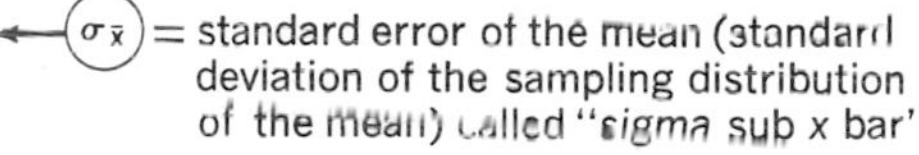 = standard error of the mean (standard deviation of the sampling distribution of the mean) called "sigma sub x bar"

FIGURE 7-1
Conceptual population distribution, sample distributions, and sampling distribution

system and that this distribution is the operating hours before a screen becomes clogged. The distribution of operating hours has a mean μ (*mu*) and a standard deviation σ (*sigma*).

Suppose that somehow we are able to take all the possible samples of ten screens from the population distribution (actually, there would be far too many for us to consider). Next we would calculate the mean and the standard deviation for each one of these *samples* as represented in part *b* of Fig. 7-1. As a result, *each* sample would have its own mean, $\bar{x}$ (*x bar*), and its own standard deviation, *s*. All the individual sample means would *not* be the same as the population mean. They would tend to be near the population mean, but only rarely would they be exactly that value.

As a last step, we would produce a distribution of all the means from every sample that could be taken. This distribution, called the *sampling distribution of the mean,* is illustrated in part *c* of Fig. 7-1. This distribution of the sample means (the sampling distribution) would have its own mean $\mu_{\bar{x}}$ (*mu sub x bar*) and its own standard deviation, or standard error, $\sigma_{\bar{x}}$ (*sigma sub x bar*).

Function of theoretical sampling distributions

In statistical terminology, the sampling distribution we would obtain by taking all the samples of a given size is a *theoretical sampling distribution*. Part *c* of Fig. 7-1 describes such an example. In practice, the size and character of most populations prohibit decision makers from taking all the possible samples from a population distribution. Fortunately, statisticians have developed formulas for estimating the characteristics of these theoretical sampling distributions, making it unnecessary for us to collect large numbers of samples. In most cases, decision makers take only one sample from the population, calculate statistics for that sample, and from those statistics infer something about the parameters of the entire population. We shall illustrate this shortly.

Why we use the sampling distribution of the mean

In each example of sampling distributions in the remainder of this chapter, we shall use the sampling distribution of the mean. We could study the sampling distribution of the median, range, or proportion, but we will stay with the mean for the continuity it will add to the explanation. Once you develop an understanding of how to deal computationally with the sampling distribution of the mean, you will be able to apply it to the distribution of any other sample statistic.

Sampling from Normal Populations

Sampling distribution of the mean from normally distributed populations

Suppose we draw samples from a normally distributed population with a mean of 100 and a standard deviation of 25, and that we start by drawing samples of five items each and by calculating their means. The first mean might be 95, the second 106, the third 101, and so on. Obviously, there is just as much chance for the sample mean to be above the population mean of 100 as there is for it to be below 100. Since we are *averaging* five items to get each sample mean, very large values in the sample would be averaged down and very small values up. We would reason that we would get less spread among the sample means than we would among the individual items in the original population. That is the same as saying that the standard error of the mean, or standard deviation of the sampling distribution of the mean, would be less than the standard deviation of the *individual* items in the population. Figure 7-2 illustrates this point graphically.

Now suppose we increase our sample size from five to 20. This would not change the standard deviation of the items in the original population. But with samples of 20, we have increased the effect of averaging in each sample and would expect even *less* dispersion among the sample means. Figure 7-3 illustrates this point.

FIGURE 7-2 Relationship between the population distribution and the sampling distribution of the mean for a normal population

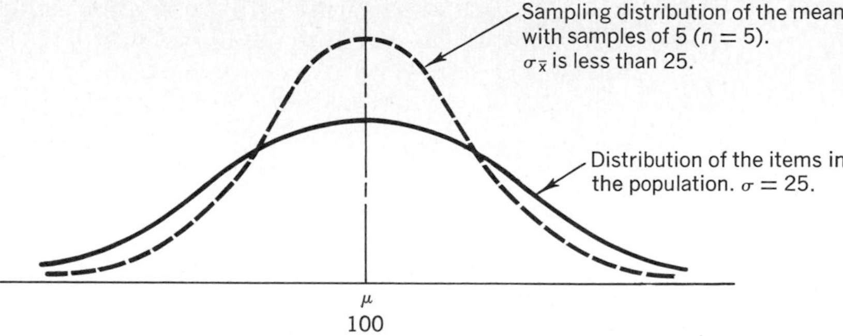

FIGURE 7-3 Relationship between the population distribution and sampling distribution of the mean with increasing n's

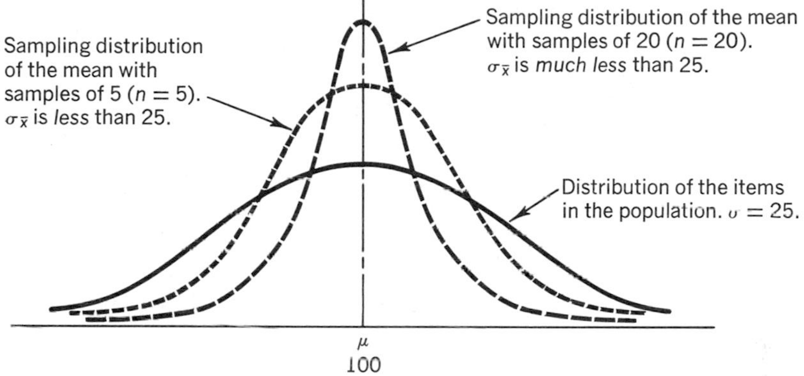

Properties of the sampling distribution of the mean

The sampling distribution of a mean of a normally distributed population demonstrates the important properties summarized in Table 7-7. An example will further illustrate these properties. A bank calculates that its individual savings accounts are normally distributed with a mean of \$2,000 and a standard deviation of \$600. If the bank takes a random sample of 100 accounts, what is the probability that the sample mean will lie between \$1,900 and \$2,050? This is a question about the sampling distribution of the mean; therefore, we must first calculate the standard error of the mean. In this case, we shall use the equation for the standard error of the mean

TABLE 7-7 Properties of the sampling distribution of the mean when the population is normally distributed

PROPERTY	ILLUSTRATED SYMBOLICALLY
The sampling distribution has a mean equal to the population mean	$\mu_{\bar{x}} = \mu$
The sampling distribution has a standard deviation (a standard error) equal to the population standard deviation divided by the square root of the sample size	$\sigma_{\bar{x}} = \frac{\sigma}{\sqrt{n}}$
The sampling distribution is normally distributed	

designed for situations in which the population is infinite (later, we shall introduce an equation for finite populations):

Standard error of the mean → $$\sigma_{\bar{x}} = \frac{\sigma}{\sqrt{n}} \qquad \textbf{[7-1]}$$

where:

Finding the standard error of the mean for infinite populations

- σ = population standard deviation
- n = sample size

Applying this to our example, we get:

$$\begin{aligned}\sigma_{\bar{x}} &= \frac{\$600}{\sqrt{100}} \\ &= \frac{\$600}{10} \\ &= \$60 \leftarrow \text{standard error of the mean}\end{aligned}$$

Next, we need to use the table of z values (Appendix Table 1) and Equation 6-6, which enables us to use the Standard Normal Probability Distribution Table. With these we can determine the probability that the sample mean will lie between \$1,900 and \$2,050.

$$z = \frac{x - \mu}{\sigma} \qquad \textbf{[6-6]}$$

Equation 6-6 tells us that to convert any normal random variable to a standard normal random variable, we must subtract the mean of the variable being standardized and divide by the standard error (the standard deviation of that variable). Thus, in this particular case, Equation 6-6 becomes:

Converting the sample mean to a z value

Sample mean → $\bar{x}$; Population mean → μ; Standard error of the mean $= \frac{\sigma}{\sqrt{n}}$ → $\sigma_{\bar{x}}$

$$z = \frac{\bar{x} - \mu}{\sigma_{\bar{x}}} \qquad \textbf{[7-2]}$$

Now we are ready to compute the two z values as follows:

For $\bar{x}$ = \$1,900

$$\begin{aligned}z &= \frac{\bar{x} - \mu}{\sigma_{\bar{x}}} \qquad \textbf{[7-2]} \\ &= \frac{\$1{,}900 - \$2{,}000}{\$60} \\ &= -\frac{100}{60} \\ &= -1.67 \leftarrow \text{standard deviations from the mean of a standard normal probability distribution}\end{aligned}$$

For $\bar{x} = \$2{,}050$

$$z = \frac{\bar{x} - \mu}{\sigma_{\bar{x}}} \qquad [7\text{-}2]$$

$$= \frac{\$2{,}050 - \$2{,}000}{\$60}$$

$$= \frac{50}{60}$$

$= .83 \leftarrow$ standard deviations from the mean of a standard normal probability distribution

Appendix Table 1 gives us an area of .4525 corresponding to a z value of -1.67, and it gives an area of .2967 for a z value of .83. If we add these two together, we get .7492 as the total probability that the sample mean will lie between \$1,900 and \$2,050. We have shown this problem graphically in Fig. 7-4.

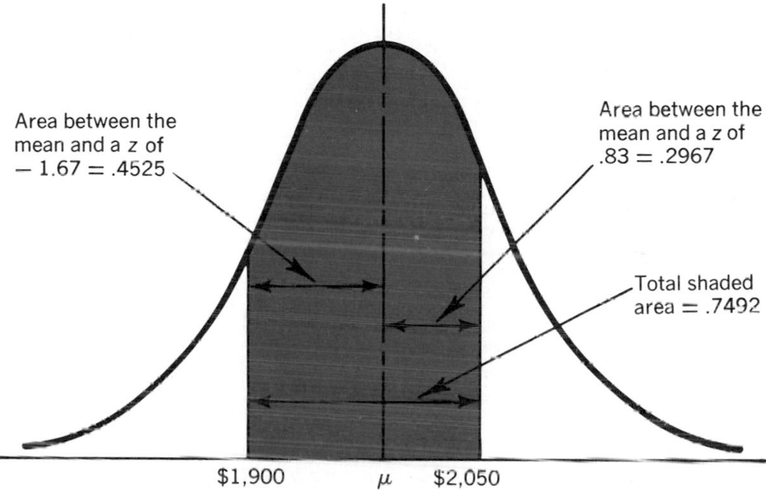

FIGURE 7-4 Probability of sample mean lying between \$1,900 and \$2,050

Sampling from Non-normal Populations

In the preceding section, we concluded that when the population is normally distributed, the sampling distribution of the mean is also normal. Yet decision makers must deal with many populations that are not normally distributed. How does the sampling distribution of the mean react when the population from which the samples are drawn is *not* normal? An illustration will help us answer this question.

The mean of the sampling distribution of the mean equals population mean

Consider the data in Table 7-8, concerning five motorcycle owners and the lives of their tires. Since only five people are involved, the population is too small to be approximated by a normal distribution. We'll take all of the possible samples of the owners in groups of three, compute the sample means ($\bar{x}$), list them, and compute the mean of the sampling distribution ($\mu_{\bar{x}}$).

TABLE 7-8 Experience of five motorcycle owners with life of tires

Owner	Carl	Debbie	Elizabeth	Frank	George	
Tire life (months)	3	3	7	9	14	**Total: 36 months**
			Mean $= \frac{36}{5} = 7.2$ months			

We have done this in Table 7-9. These calculations show that even in a case in which the population is not normally distributed, $\mu_{\bar{x}}$, the mean of the sampling distribution, is *still* equal to the population mean, μ.

TABLE 7-9 Calculation of sample mean tire life with $n = 3$

SAMPLES OF THREE	SAMPLE DATA (TIRE LIVES)	SAMPLE MEAN
EFG*	7 + 9 + 14	10
DFG	3 + 9 + 14	8⅔
DEG	3 + 7 + 14	8
DEF	3 + 7 + 9	6⅓
CFG	3 + 9 + 14	8⅔
CEG	3 + 7 + 14	8
CEF	3 + 7 + 9	6⅓
CDF	3 + 3 + 9	5
CDE	3 + 3 + 7	4⅓
CDG	3 + 3 + 14	6⅔
		72 months
		$\mu_{\bar{x}} = \frac{72}{10}$
		$= 7.2$ months

* Names abbreviated by first initial.

Now look at Fig. 7-5. Part *a* is the population distribution of tire lives for the five motorcycle owners, a distribution that is anything but normal in shape. In part *b* of Fig. 7-5, we have shown the sampling distribution of the mean for a sample size of three, taking the information from Table 7-9.

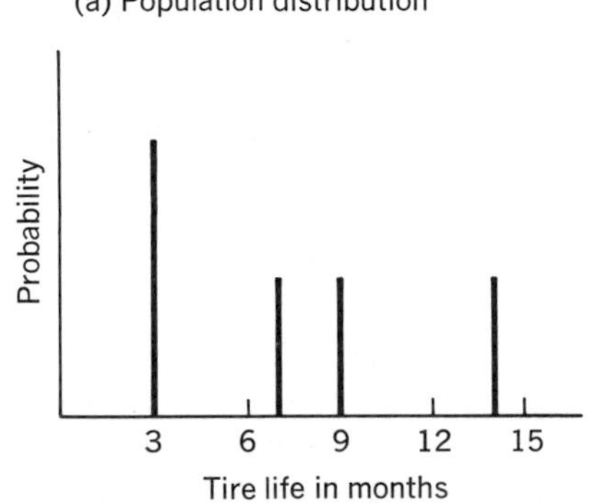

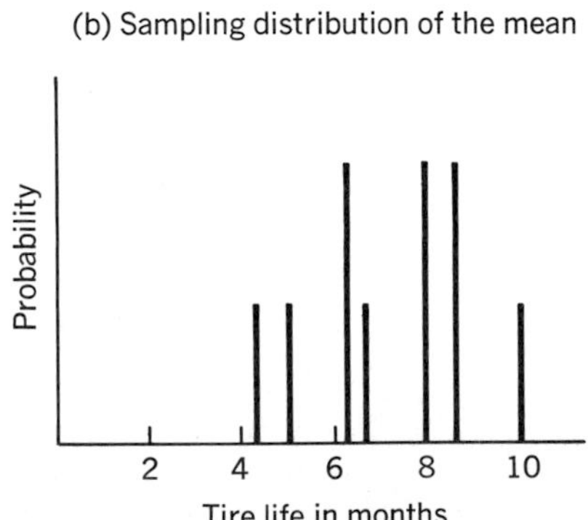

FIGURE 7-5 Population distribution and sampling distribution of the mean tire life

Notice the difference between the probability distributions in *a* and *b*. In part *b*, the distribution looks a little more like the bell shape of the normal distribution.

Increase in size of samples leads to a more normal sampling distribution

If we had a long time and much space, we could repeat this example and enlarge the population size to 20. Then we could take samples of *every* size. Next we would plot the sampling distribution of the mean that would occur in *each* case. Doing this would show quite dramatically how quickly the sampling distribution of the mean approaches normality, regardless of the shape of the population distribution. Figure 7-6 simulates this process graphically without all the calculations.

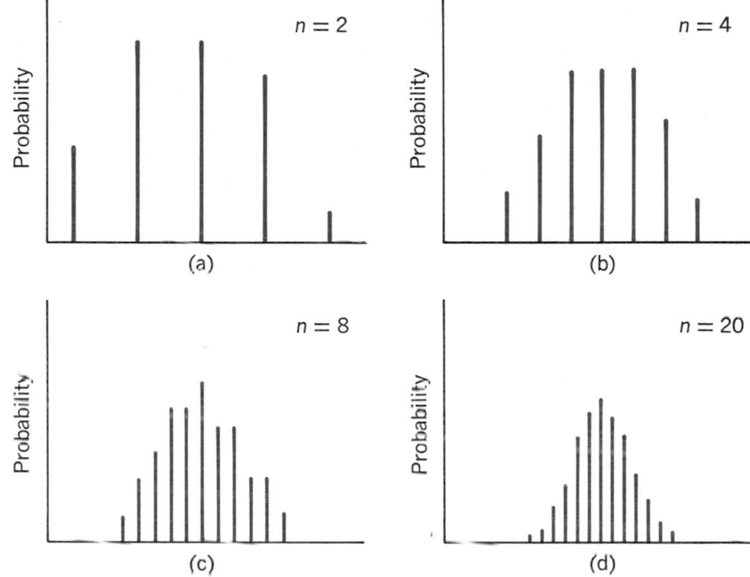

FIGURE 7-6 Simulated effect of increases in the sample size on appearance of sampling distribution

The Central Limit Theorem

Results of increasing sample size

The example in Table 7-9 and the two probability distributions in Fig. 7-5 should suggest several things to you. First, **the mean of the sampling distribution of the mean will equal the population mean** regardless of the sample size, even if the population is not normal. Second, as the sample size increases, **the sampling distribution of the mean will approach normality,** regardless of the shape of the population distribution.

Significance of the central limit theorem

This relationship between the shape of the population distribution and the shape of the sampling distribution of the mean is called the *central limit theorem*. The central limit theorem is perhaps the most important theorem in all of statistical inference. **It assures us that the sampling distribution of the mean approaches normal as the sample size increases.** There are theoretical situations in which the central limit theorem fails to hold, but they are almost never encountered in practical decision making. Actually, a sample does not have to be very large for the sampling distribution of the mean to approach normal. Statisticians use the normal distribution as an approximation to the sampling distribution whenever the sample size is at least 30, but the sampling distribution of the mean can be nearly normal with samples of even half that size. **The significance of the central limit theorem is that it permits us to use sample statistics to make inferences about population parameters without knowing anything about the shape of the frequency distribution of that population other than what we can get from the sample.** Putting this ability to work is the subject of much of the material in the subsequent chapters of this book.

Using the central limit theorem

Let's illustrate the use of the central limit theorem. The distribution of annual earnings of all bank tellers with five years' experience is skewed negatively, as shown in part *a* of Fig. 7-7. This distribution has a mean of \$15,000 and a standard deviation of \$2,000. If we draw a random sample of 30 tellers, what is the probability that their earnings will average more than \$15,750 annually? In part *b* of Fig. 7-7, we show the sampling distribution of the mean that would result, and we have colored the area representing "earnings over \$15,750."

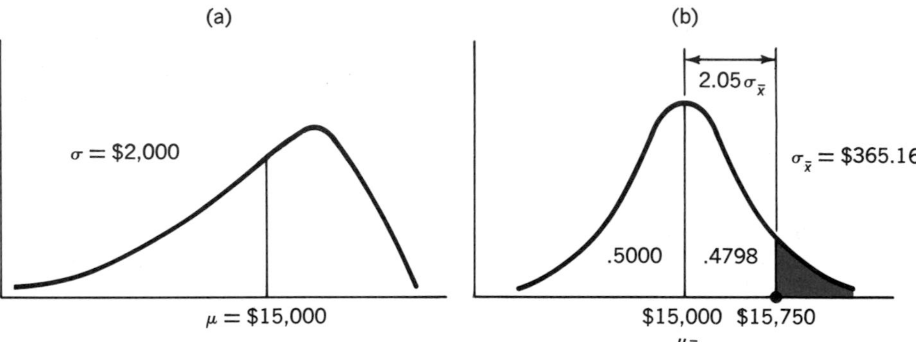

FIGURE 7-7 Population distribution and sampling distribution for bank tellers' earnings

Our first task is to calculate the standard error of the mean from the population standard deviation, as follows:

$$\sigma_{\bar{x}} = \frac{\sigma}{\sqrt{n}} \qquad \textbf{[7-1]}$$

$$= \frac{\$2,000}{\sqrt{30}}$$

$$= \frac{\$2,000}{5.477}$$

$$= \$365.16 \leftarrow \text{standard error of the mean}$$

Since we are dealing with a sampling distribution, we must now use Equation 7-2 and the table of z values (Appendix Table 1):

For $\bar{x} = \$15,750$

$$z = \frac{\bar{x} - \mu}{\sigma_{\bar{x}}} \quad [7\text{-}2]$$

$$= \frac{\$15,750 - \$15,000}{\$365.16}$$

$$= \frac{\$750.00}{\$365.16}$$

$$= 2.05 \leftarrow \text{standard deviations from the mean of a standard normal probability distribution}$$

This gives us an area of .4798 for a z value of 2.05. We show this area in Fig. 7-7 as the area between the mean and \$15,750. Since half, or .5000, of the area under the curve lies between the mean and the right-hand tail, the colored area must be:

.5000	Area between the mean and the right-hand tail
−.4798	Area between the mean and \$15,750
.0202 ←	Area between the right-hand tail and \$15,750

Thus, we have determined that there is slightly more than a 2 percent chance of average earnings being more than \$15,750 annually in a group of 30 tellers.

EXERCISES

7-27 In a sample of 36 observations from a normal distribution with a mean of 125 and a variance of 225, what is:
a) $P(\bar{x} < 127)$ b) $P(\bar{x} > 130)$
If, instead of 36 observations, 81 observations are taken, find:
c) $P(\bar{x} < 127)$ d) $P(\bar{x} > 130)$

7-28 In a sample of 9 observations from a normal distribution with mean 76.8 and standard deviation 4.8, what is:
a) $P(75 < \bar{x} < 80)$
b) The corresponding probability given a sample of 25.

7-29 In a normal distribution with mean 72 and standard deviation of 10, how large a sample must be taken so that there will be a 90 percent chance that its mean is greater than 70?

7-30 In a normal distribution with mean of 250 and standard deviation of 20, how large a sample must be taken so that the probability will be .95 that the sample mean falls between 240 and 260?

7-31 Kelly's Home Entertainment Center averages 15 television service calls per week, with a variance of 16 calls squared. What is the probability that:
a) In a sample of one week, between 14 and 16 service calls will be made?
b) In a sample of two weeks, the average number of service calls made will be between 14 and 16?
c) In a sample of three weeks, the average number of service calls made will be between 14 and 16?
d) Explain the difference in your answers.

7-32 The average cost of a studio condominium in the Cedar Lakes development is $25,000 with a standard deviation of $1,700.

a) What is the probability that a condominium in this development will cost at least $26,000?

b) Is the probability that the average cost of a sample of two condominiums will be at least $26,000 greater or less than the probability of one condominium's costing that much?

7-33 Robertson Employment Service customarily gives standard intelligence and aptitude tests to all persons who seek employment through the firm. The firm has collected data for several years and has found that the distribution of scores is not normal, but is skewed to the left with a mean of 83 and a standard deviation of 18. What is the probability that in a sample of 75 applicants taking the test, the mean score will be less than 82.5 or greater than 84?

7-34 An oil refinery has backup monitors to keep track of the refinery flows continuously and to prevent machine malfunctions from disrupting the process. One particular monitor has an average life of 4,300 hours with a standard deviation of 730 hours. In addition to the primary monitor, the refinery has set up 2 standby units, which are duplicates of the primary one. In the case of malfunction of one of the monitors, another will automatically take over in its place. The operating life of each monitor is independent of the others.

a) What is the probability that a given set of monitors will last at least 13,000 hours?

b) At most 12,630 hours?

7-35 Modern Buick sells an average of 10 cars a day, with a variance of 35.5 cars squared. If a sample of 7 days is studied, what is the probability that the sample mean will be:

a) More than 16 or fewer than 12 cars sold?

b) Fewer than 16 and more than 5 cars sold?

7-36 Matthews Toy Company, manufacturer of metal toy trucks, estimates that the average direct labor cost per unit is 50.2 cents with a standard deviation of 1.2 cents. If a sample of 20 trucks is taken and the direct labor cost for each determined, can you say with a 98 percent probability that the average direct labor cost per unit of output will be between 49.5 and 50.7 cents?

7-37 Clara Voyant, whose job is to statistically predict the future for her venture capital company, has just received the statistics describing her company's performance on 1,600 investments last year. Clara knows that each investment generates a profit that has a normal distribution with mean $5,000 and standard deviation $2,500. Even before she looked at the specific results from each of the 1,600 investments from last year, Clara was able to accurately make some predictions by using her knowledge of the sampling distribution. Follow her analysis by finding the probability:

a) That the sample mean of last year's 1,600 investments will exceed $5,050.

b) That the sample mean of last year's investments will be less than $4,975.

c) That the sample mean of last year's investments will be greater than $4,950, but less than $5,025.

7-38 Farmer Braun, who sells grain to West Germany, owns 50 acres of wheatfields. Based on past experience, Farmer Braun knows that weather affects the crop drastically, so that the yield from each individual acre is normally distributed with mean 100 bushels and standard deviation 8 bushels. Help Farmer Braun plan for his next year's crop by finding:

a) The expected mean of the yields from Farmer Braun's 50 acres of wheat.

b) The standard deviation of the sample mean of the yields from Farmer Braun's 50 acres.

c) The probability that the mean yield per acre will exceed 102.5 bushels.

d) The probability that the mean yield per acre will fall between 98 and 102.5 bushels.

7-39 A ferry carries 25 passengers. The weight of each passenger has a normal distribution with mean 150 pounds and variance 400 pounds squared. Safety regulations state that for this particular ferry, the total weight of passengers on the ferry should not exceed 4,000 pounds more than 1% of the time. As a service to the ferry owners, find:

a) The probability that the total weight of passengers on the ferry will exceed 4,000 pounds.

b) The 99th percentile of the distribution of the total weight of passengers on the ferry.

Is the ferry complying with safety regulations?

7-5 AN OPERATIONAL CONSIDERATION IN SAMPLING: The Relationship Between Sample Size and Standard Error

Precision of the sample mean

We saw earlier in this chapter that the standard error, $\sigma_{\bar{x}}$, is a measure of dispersion of the sample means around the population mean. If the dispersion decreases (if $\sigma_{\bar{x}}$ becomes smaller), then the values taken by the sample mean tend to cluster *more* closely around μ. Conversely, if the dispersion increases (if $\sigma_{\bar{x}}$ becomes larger), the values taken by the sample mean tend to cluster *less* closely around μ. We can think of this relationship this way: **As the standard error decreases, the value of any sample mean will probably be closer to the value of the population mean.** Statisticians describe this phenomenon in another way: As the standard error decreases, the *precision* with which the sample mean can be used to estimate the population mean increases.

If we refer to Equation 7-1, we can see that as n increases, $\sigma_{\bar{x}}$ decreases. This happens because in Equation 7-1, a larger denominator on the right side would produce a smaller $\sigma_{\bar{x}}$ on the left side. Two examples will show this relationship; both assume the same population standard deviation σ of 100.

$$\sigma_{\bar{x}} = \frac{\sigma}{\sqrt{n}} \qquad \textbf{[7-1]}$$

When $n = 10$:

$$\begin{aligned}\sigma_{\bar{x}} &= \frac{100}{\sqrt{10}}\\ &= \frac{100}{3.162}\\ &= 31.63 \leftarrow \text{standard error of the mean}\end{aligned}$$

And when $n = 100$:

$$\begin{aligned}\sigma_{\bar{x}} &= \frac{100}{\sqrt{100}}\\ &= \frac{100}{10}\\ &= 10 \leftarrow \text{standard error of the mean}\end{aligned}$$

Increasing the sample size: diminishing returns

What have we shown? As we increased our sample size from 10 to 100 (a tenfold increase), the standard error dropped from 31.63 to 10, which is only about one-third of its former value. **Our examples suggest that, owing to the fact that $\sigma_{\bar{x}}$ varies inversely with the square root of n, there is a diminishing return in sampling.**

It is true that sampling more items will decrease the standard error, but this benefit may not be worth the cost. A statistician would say, "The increased precision is not worth the additional sampling cost." In a statistical sense, it seldom pays to take excessively large samples. Managers should always assess *both* the worth and the cost of the additional precision they will obtain from a larger sample before they commit resources to take it.

The Finite Population Multiplier

Modifying Equation 7-1

To this point in our discussions of sampling distributions, we have used Equation 7-1 to calculate the standard error of the mean:

$$\sigma_{\bar{x}} = \frac{\sigma}{\sqrt{n}} \quad \textbf{[7-1]}$$

This equation is designed for situations in which the population is infinite, or in which we sample from a finite population with replacement (that is to say, after each item is sampled it is put back into the population before the next item is chosen, so that the same item can possibly be chosen more than once). If you will refer back to page 284 where we introduced Equation 7-1, you will recall our parenthesized note, which said, "Later we shall introduce an equation for finite populations." Introducing this new equation is the purpose of this section.

Many of the populations that decision makers examine are finite; that is, of stated or limited size. Examples of these include the employees in a given company, the clients of a city social-services agency, the students in a specific class, and a day's production in a given manufacturing plant. Not one of these populations is infinite, so we need to modify Equation 7-1 to deal with them. The formula designed to find the standard error of the mean when the population is *finite* is:

Finding the standard error of the mean for finite populations

$$\sigma_{\bar{x}} = \frac{\sigma}{\sqrt{n}} \times \sqrt{\frac{N-n}{N-1}} \quad \textbf{[7-3]}$$

where:

- N = size of the population
- n = size of the sample

This new term on the right-hand side, which we multiply by our original standard error, is called the *finite population multiplier:*

$$\text{Finite population multiplier} = \sqrt{\frac{N-n}{N-1}} \quad \textbf{[7-4]}$$

A few examples will help us become familiar with interpreting and using Equation 7-3. Suppose we are interested in a population of 20 textile companies of the same size, all of which are experiencing excessive labor turnover. Our study indicates that the standard deviation of the distribution of annual turnover is 75 employees. If we sample five of these textile companies and wish to compute the standard error of the mean, we would use Equation 7-3 as follows:

$$\sigma_{\bar{x}} = \frac{\sigma}{\sqrt{n}} \times \sqrt{\frac{N-n}{N-1}} \quad \textbf{[7-3]}$$

$$= \frac{75}{\sqrt{5}} \times \sqrt{\frac{20-5}{20-1}}$$

$$= \frac{75}{2.236} \times \sqrt{\frac{15}{19}}$$

$$= 33.54 \times \sqrt{.798}$$

$$= (33.54)(.888)$$

$$= 29.8 \leftarrow \text{standard error of the mean of a finite population}$$

In this example, a finite population multiplier of .888 reduced the standard error from 33.54 to 29.8.

Sometimes the finite population multiplier is close to 1

In cases in which the population is very large in relation to the size of the sample, this finite population multiplier is close to 1 and has little effect on the calculation of the standard error. Say that we have a population of 1,000 items and that we have taken a sample of 20 items. If we use Equation 7-4 to calculate the finite population multiplier, the result would be:

$$\text{Finite population multiplier} = \sqrt{\frac{N-n}{N-1}} \quad \textbf{[7-4]}$$

$$= \sqrt{\frac{1{,}000-20}{1{,}000-1}}$$

$$= \sqrt{\frac{980}{999}}$$

$$= \sqrt{.981}$$

$$= .99$$

Using this multiplier of .99 would produce little effect on the calculation of the standard error of the mean.

Sampling fraction defined

This last example shows that when we sample a small fraction of the entire population (that is, when the population size N is very large relative to the sample size n), the finite population multiplier takes on a value close to 1.0. Statisticians refer to the fraction n/N as the *sampling fraction,* because it is the fraction of the population N that is contained in the sample.

When the sampling fraction is small, the standard error of the mean for finite populations is so close to the standard error of the mean for infinite populations that we might as well use the same formula for both, namely Equation 7-1: $\sigma_{\bar{x}} = \frac{\sigma}{\sqrt{n}}$. The generally accepted rule is: **When the sampling fraction is less than .05, the finite population multiplier need not be used.**

Sample size determines sampling precision

When we use Equation 7-1, σ is constant, and so the measure of sampling precision, $\sigma_{\bar{x}}$, depends only on the sample size n and not on the proportion of the population sampled. That is, to make $\sigma_{\bar{x}}$ smaller, it is necessary to make only n larger. **Thus it turns out that it is the absolute size of the sample that determines sampling precision, not the fraction of the population sampled.**

EXERCISES

7-40 Every unit in the sample for a certain study costs \$2. The information value of various sample sizes may be figured according to the formula $\$6{,}400/\sigma_{\bar{x}}$. If a researcher wants to increase the sample until cost equals information value, how many individuals should she sample if the population standard deviation is 200?

7-41 Given a population of size $N = 65$ with a mean of 12 and a standard deviation of 2.1, what is the probability that a sample of size 16 will have a mean between 11.5 and 12.5?

7-42 From a population of 145 items with a mean of 120 and a standard deviation of 15, 64 items were chosen.
a) What is the standard error of the mean?
b) What is the $P(122 < \bar{x} < 124)$?

7-43 For a population of size $N = 120$ with a mean of 7.5 and a standard deviation of 1.5, find the standard error of the mean for the following sample sizes:
a) $n = 9$ b) $n = 25$ c) $n = 49$

7-44 George Bransford is the owner of a chain of 25 clothing stores. He has been considering retiring, because his health is bad and also because he feels the business is not as profitable as it once was. Over the past several years, the mean net income for each of the 25 stores has been \$21,000 with a standard deviation of \$3,400. George has said that if the first 5 stores audited at year end do not show profits of at least \$100,000, he will sell the business. What is the probability that George will sell out?

7-45 Jonida Martinez, researcher for the Colombian Coffee Corporation, is interested in determining the rate of coffee usage per household in the United States. She believes that yearly consumption per household is normally distributed with an unknown mean μ and a standard deviation of about 2 pounds.
a) If Martinez takes a sample of 16 households and records their consumption of coffee for 1 year, what is the probability that the sample mean is within 1 pound of the population mean?
b) How large a sample must she take in order to be 98 percent certain that the sample mean is within 1 pound of the population mean?

7-46 Sara Gordon is heading a fund-raising drive for Milford College. She wishes to concentrate on the current tenth-reunion class, and hopes to get contributions from 40 percent of the 160 members of that class. Past data indicate that those who contribute to the tenth-year reunion gift will donate 3 percent of their annual salaries. Sara believes that the reunion class members have an average annual salary of \$18,000 with a standard deviation of \$8,000. If her expectations are met (40 percent of the class donate 3 percent of their salaries), what is the probability that the tenth-reunion gift will be between \$32,000 and \$38,400?

7-47 A stockbroker has named 100 stocks that he predicts will rise in market value an average of 12 percent during the next quarter, with a standard deviation of 4 percent. He is challenging his colleagues to choose 10 stocks at random from the list, to see if his prediction comes true. If his expectations are correct, what is the probability that a colleague following his instructions will see an average market-value increase of 10 to 15 percent for the quarter?

7-48 Food Place, a chain of 101 supermarkets, has been bought out by a larger nationwide supermarket chain. Before the deal is finalized, the larger chain wants to have some assurance that Food Place will be a consistent money-maker. The larger chain has decided to look at the financial records for 36 of the Food Place stores. Food Place management claims that each store's profits have a normal distribution with the same mean and a standard deviation of $1,000. If the Food Place management is correct, what is the probability that the sample mean for the 36 stores will fall within $150 of the actual mean?

7-49 Miss Joanne Happ, chief executive officer of Southeastern Life & Surety Corp., wants to undertake a survey of the huge number of insurance policies that her company has underwritten. Miss Happ's firm makes on each policy a yearly profit that is distributed with mean $150 and standard deviation $90. Her personal accuracy requirements dictate that the survey must be large enough to reduce the standard error to no more than .1 percent of the population mean. How large should her sample be?

7-6 DESIGN OF EXPERIMENTS

Events and experiments revisited

We have encountered the term *experiment* in Chapter 5, "Probability I." There we defined an *event* as one or more of the possible outcomes of doing something, and an *experiment* as an activity that would produce such events. In a coin-toss experiment, the possible events would be heads and tails.

Planning Experiments

Sampling is only one part

If we are to conduct experiments that produce meaningful results in the form of usable conclusions, the way in which these experiments are designed is of the utmost importance. A good part of this chapter was taken up with ways of ensuring that random sampling was indeed being done. The way in which sampling is conducted is only a *part* of the total design of an experiment. In fact, the design of experiments is itself the subject of quite a number of books, some of them rather formidable in both scope and volume.

Phases of Experimental Design

A claim is made

To get a better feel for the complexity of experimental design without actually getting involved with the complex details, take an example from the many that confront us every day, and follow that example through from beginning to end.

The statement is made that a Crankmaster Battery will start your car's engine better than Battery X. Crankmaster might design its experiment this way:

Objectives are set

OBJECTIVE. This is our beginning point. Crankmaster wants to test its battery against the leading competitor. Although it is possible to design an experiment that would test the two batteries on several characteristics (life, size, cranking power, weight, and cost, to name but a few), Crankmaster has decided to limit this experiment to cranking power.

The response variable is selected

WHAT IS TO BE MEASURED. This is often referred to as the response variable. If Crankmaster is to design an experiment that measures cranking power of its battery against that of another, it must define how cranking power is to be measured. Again, there are quite a few ways in which this can be done. For example, Crankmaster could measure (1) the time it took for the batteries to run down completely while cranking engines, (2) the total number of engine starts it took to run down the batteries, or (3) the number of months in use that the two batteries could be expected to last. Crankmaster decides that the response variable in its experiment will be (1) the time it takes for batteries to run down completely while cranking engines.

How many to test

HOW LARGE A SAMPLE SIZE. Crankmaster wants to be sure that it chooses a sample size large enough to support claims it makes for its battery, without fear of being challenged; however, it knows that the more batteries it tests, the higher the cost of conducting the experiment. As we pointed out in section 5 of this chapter, there is a diminishing return in sampling; and although sampling more items does, in fact, decrease the standard error, the benefit may not be worth the cost. Not wishing to choose a sample size that is too expensive to contend with, Crankmaster decides that comparing ten batteries from each of the two companies (itself and its competitor) will suffice.

Experimental conditions

CONDUCTING THE EXPERIMENT. Crankmaster must be careful to conduct its experiment under controlled conditions; that is, it has to be sure that it is measuring *cranking power*, and that the other variables (such as temperature, age of engine, and condition of battery cables, to name only a few) are held as nearly constant as practicable. In an effort to accomplish just this, Crankmaster's statistical group uses new cars of the same make and model, conducts the tests at the same outside air temperature, and is careful to be quite precise in measuring the time variable. Crankmaster gathers experimental data on the performance of the 20 batteries in this manner.

Data are analyzed

ANALYZING THE DATA. Data on the 20 individual battery tests are subjected to hypothesis testing in the same way that we shall see in Chapter 9, "Testing Hypotheses." Crankmaster is interested in whether there is a significant difference between the cranking power of its battery and that of its competitor. It turns out that the difference between the mean cranking life of Crankmaster's battery and that of its competitor *is* significant. Crankmaster incorporates the result of this experiment into its advertising.

Reacting to Experimental Claims

How should the consumer react?

How should we, as consumers, react to Crankmaster's new battery-life claims in its latest advertising? Should we conclude from the tests it has run that the Crankmaster battery *is* superior to the competitive battery? If we stop for a moment to consider the nature of the experiment, we may not be too quick to come to such a conclusion.

Are we sure?

How do we know that the ages and conditions of the cars' engines in the experiment *were* identical? And are we absolutely sure that the battery cables were identical in size and resistance to current? And what about the air temperature during the tests: Was it the same? These are the normal kinds of questions that we should ask.

How should we react to the statement, if it is made, that "we subjected the experimental results to extensive statistical testing"? The answer to that will have to wait until Chapter 9, "Testing Hypotheses," where we can determine if such a difference in battery lives is too large to be attributed to chance. At this point we, as consumers, need to be appropriately skeptical.

Other Options Open

Another route for Crankmaster

Of course, Crankmaster would have had the same concerns we did, and in all likelihood would *not* have made significant advertising claims solely on the basis of the experimental design we have just described. One possible course of action to avoid criticism is to *ensure* that all variables except the one being measured have indeed been controlled. Despite the care taken to produce such controlled conditions, it turns out that these overcontrolled experiments do not really solve our problem. Normally, instead of investing resources in attempts to *eliminate* experimental variations, we choose a *completely different route*. The next few paragraphs show how we can accomplish this.

Factorial Experiments

Handling all the test conditions at the same time

In the Crankmaster situation, we had two batteries (let's refer to them now as A and B) and three test conditions that were of some concern to us: (1) temperature, (2) age of the engine, and (3) condition of the battery cable. Let's introduce the notion of factorial experiments by using this notation:

H = Hot temperature	N = New engine	G = Good cable
C = Cold temperature	O = Old engine	W = Worn cable

Of course, in most experiments, we could find more than two temperature conditions and, for that matter, more than two categories for engine condition and battery-cable condition. But it's better to introduce the idea of factorial experiments using a somewhat simplified example.

How many combinations?

Now, since there are two batteries, two temperature possibilities, two engine condition possibilities, and two battery-cable possibilities, there are $2 \times 2 \times 2 \times 2 = 16$ possible combinations of factors. If we wanted to write these sixteen possibilities down, they would look like Table 7-10.

Levels and factors to be handled

Having set up all the possible combinations of factors involved in this experiment, we could now conduct the sixteen tests in the table. If we did this, we would have conducted a complete factorial experiment, because each of the two *levels* of each of the four *factors* would have been used once

TABLE 7-10 Sixteen possible combinations of factors for battery test

TEST	BATTERY	TEMPERATURE	ENGINE CONDITION	CABLE CONDITION
1	A	H	N	G
2	A	H	N	W
3	A	H	O	G
4	A	H	O	W
5	A	C	N	G
6	A	C	N	W
7	A	C	O	G
8	A	C	O	W
9	B	H	N	G
10	B	H	N	W
11	B	H	O	G
12	B	H	O	W
13	B	C	N	G
14	B	C	N	W
15	B	C	O	G
16	B	C	O	W

with each possible combination of other levels of other factors. Designing the experiment this way would permit us to use techniques we shall introduce in Chapter 10, "Chi-Square and Analysis of Variance," to test the effect of each of the factors.

Randomizing

We need to point out, before we leave this section, that in an actual experiment we would hardly conduct the tests in the order in which they appear in the table. They were arranged in that order to facilitate your counting the combinations and determining that all possible combinations were indeed represented. In actual practice, we would randomize the order of the tests, perhaps by putting sixteen numbers in a hat and drawing out the order of the experiment in that simple manner.

Being More Efficient in Experimental Design

A bit of efficiency

As you saw from our four-factor experiment, sixteen tests were required to compare all levels with all factors. If we were to compare the same two batteries, but this time with five levels of temperature, four measures of engine condition, and three measures of battery-cable condition, it would take $2 \times 5 \times 4 \times 3 = 120$ tests for a complete factorial experiment.

Fortunately, statisticians have been able to help us reduce the number of tests in cases like this. To illustrate how this works, look at the consumer-products company that wants to test market a new toothpaste in four different cities with four different kinds of packages and with four different advertising programs. In such a case, a complete factorial experiment would take $4 \times 4 \times 4 = 64$ tests. However, if we do some clever planning, we can actually do it with far fewer tests—sixteen, to be precise.

Let's use the notation:

A = City 1	I = Package 1	1 = Ad program 1
B = City 2	II = Package 2	2 = Ad program 2
C = City 3	III = Package 3	3 = Ad program 3
D = City 4	IV = Package 4	4 = Ad program 4

Now we arrange the cities, packages, and advertising programs in a design called a Latin square (Fig. 7-8).

Advertising program

Packages	1	2	3	4
I	C	B	D	A
II	B	C	A	D ← Cities
III	D	A	B	C
IV	A	D	C	B

FIGURE 7-8
A Latin square

The statistical analysis

In the experimental design represented by the Latin square, we would need only sixteen tests instead of 64 as originally calculated. Each combination of city, package, and advertising program would be represented in the sixteen tests. The actual statistical analysis of the data obtained from such a Latin square experimental design would require a form of analysis of variance a bit beyond the scope of this book.

7-7 TERMS INTRODUCED IN CHAPTER 7

CENSUS The measurement or examination of every element in the population.

CENTRAL LIMIT THEOREM A rule assuring that the sampling distribution of the mean approaches normal as the sample size increases, regardless of the shape of the population distribution from which the sample is selected.

CLUSTERS Within a population, groups that are essentially similar to each other, although the groups themselves have wide internal variation.

CLUSTER SAMPLING A method of random sampling in which the population is divided into groups, or clusters of elements, and then a random sample of these clusters is selected.

FACTORIAL EXPERIMENT Experiment in which each factor involved is used once with each other factor. In a complete factorial experiment, every level of each factor is used once with each level of every other factor.

FINITE POPULATION A population having a stated or limited size.

FINITE POPULATION MULTIPLIER A factor used to correct the standard error of the mean for studying a population of finite size that is small in relation to the size of the sample.

INFINITE POPULATION A population in which it is theoretically impossible to observe all the elements.

JUDGMENT SAMPLING A method of selecting a sample from a population in which personal knowledge or expertise is used to identify those items from the population that are to be included in the sample.

LATIN SQUARE An efficient experimental design that makes it unnecessary to use a complete factorial experiment.

PARAMETERS Values that describe the characteristics of a population.

PRECISION The degree of accuracy with which the sample mean can estimate the population mean, as revealed by the standard error of the mean.

RANDOM OR PROBABILITY SAMPLING A method of selecting a sample from a population in which all the items in the population have an equal chance of being chosen in the sample.

SAMPLE A portion of the elements in a population chosen for direct examination or measurement.

SAMPLING DISTRIBUTION OF A STATISTIC For a given population, a probability distribution of all the possible values a statistic may take on for a given sample size.

SAMPLING DISTRIBUTION OF THE MEAN A probability distribution of all the possible means of samples of a given size, n, from a population.

SAMPLING ERROR Error or variation among sample statistics due to chance; i.e., differences between each sample and the population, and among several samples, which are due solely to the elements we happened to choose for the sample.

SAMPLING FRACTION The fraction or proportion of the population contained in a sample.

SIMPLE RANDOM SAMPLING Methods of selecting samples that allow each possible sample an equal probability of being picked *and* each item in the entire population an equal chance of being included in the sample.

STANDARD ERROR The standard deviation of the sampling distribution of a statistic.

STANDARD ERROR OF THE MEAN The standard deviation of the sampling distribution of the mean; a measure of the extent to which we expect the means from different samples to vary from the population mean, owing to the chance error in the sampling process.

STATISTICAL INFERENCE The process of making inferences about populations from information contained in samples.

STATISTICS Measures describing the characteristics of a sample.

STRATA Groups within a population formed in such a way that each group is relatively homogeneous, but wider variability exists among the separate groups.

STRATIFIED SAMPLING A method of random sampling in which the population is divided into homogeneous groups, or strata, and elements within each stratum are selected at random according to one of two rules: (1) A specified number of elements is drawn from each stratum corresponding to the proportion of that stratum in the population, or (2) an equal number of elements is drawn from each stratum, and the results are weighted according to the stratum's proportion of the total population.

SYSTEMATIC SAMPLING A method of random sampling used in statistics in which elements to be sampled are selected from the population at a uniform interval that is measured in time, order, or space.

7-8 EQUATIONS INTRODUCED IN CHAPTER 7

[7-1]
$$\sigma_{\bar{x}} = \frac{\sigma}{\sqrt{n}}$$
p. 284

Use this formula to derive the *standard error of the mean* when the population is *infinite;* that is, when the elements of the population cannot be enumerated in a reasonable period of time or when we sample with replacement. This equation explains that the sampling distribution has a standard deviation, which we also call a standard error, equal to the population standard deviation divided by the square root of the sample size.

[7-2]
$$z = \frac{\bar{x} - \mu}{\sigma_{\bar{x}}}$$
p. 284

A modified version of Equation 6-6, this formula allows us to determine the distance of the *sample mean* $\bar{x}$ from the population mean μ when we divide the difference by the standard error of the mean $\sigma_{\bar{x}}$. Once we have derived a z value, we can use the Standard Normal Probability Distribution Table and compute the probability that the sample mean will be that distance from the population mean. Because of the central limit theorem, we can use this formula for non-normal distributions if the sample size is at least 30.

[7-3]
$$\sigma_{\bar{x}} = \frac{\sigma}{\sqrt{n}} \times \sqrt{\frac{N-n}{N-1}}$$
p. 292

where:

N = size of the population

n = size of the sample

This is the formula for finding the *standard error of the mean* when the population is *finite;* that is, of stated or limited size.

[7-4]
$$\text{Finite population multiplier} = \sqrt{\frac{N-n}{N-1}}$$
p. 292

In Equation 7-3, the term $\sqrt{(N-n)/(N-1)}$, which we multiply by the standard error from Equation (7-1), is called the *finite population multiplier.* When the population is small in relation to the size of the sample, the finite population multiplier reduces the size of the standard error. Any decrease in the standard error increases the precision with which the sample mean can be used to estimate the population mean.

7-9 CHAPTER REVIEW EXERCISES

7-50 Donna Ayscue is in charge of training consumer interviewers for a market-research firm. Since she has other responsibilities, she is not able to observe all the practice interviews. She arbitrarily observes the trainees interviewing consumers and sometimes watches from an adjoining room, without forewarning the trainees that they will be observed. She feels that this makes her testing and evaluations objective. Is she using random sampling or judgment sampling?

7-51 Jim Ford, advertising manager for a retail department store chain, is responsible for choosing the final advertisements from sample layouts designed by his staff. He has been in the retail advertising business for years and has been responsible for the chain's advertising for quite some time. His assistant, however, having learned the latest advertising effectiveness measurement techniques while at a New York agency, wants to do effectiveness tests for each advertisement considered on random samples of consumers in the store's retail trading district. These tests will be quite costly. Jim is sure that his experience enables him to decide on appropriate ads, so there has been some disagreement between the two. Can you defend either position?

7-52 Burt Perdue, manager of the Sea Island Development Company, wants to find out residents' feeling toward the development's recreation facilities and the improvements they would like to see implemented. The development includes residents of various ages and income levels, but a large proportion are middle-class residents between the ages of 30 and 50. As yet, Burt is unsure of whether there are differences among age groups or income levels in their desire for recreation facilities. Would stratified random sampling be appropriate here?

7-53 A camera manufacturer is attempting to find out what employees feel are the major problems with the company and what improvements are needed. To assess the opinions of the 37 departments, the management is considering a sampling plan. It has been recommended to the personnel director that the management adopt a cluster sampling plan. The management would choose 6 departments and interview all the employees. Upon collecting and assessing the data gathered from these employees, the company could then make changes and plan for areas of job improvement. Is a cluster sampling plan appropriate in this situation?

7-54 By reviewing sales since the business opened 6 months ago, a restaurant owner found that the average bill for a couple was \$16, with a standard deviation of \$4. How large would a sample of customers have to be for the probability to be 95.44 percent that the mean cost per meal for the sample would fall between \$15.20 and \$16.80?

7-55 Hartford Products has recently sent a direct-mail advertising piece to area contractors. The literature sent out explains the advantages of using Hartford's insulated windows for both residential and commercial construction. The company now wants to see how many contractors read the information, and it is considering telephoning the contractors who should have received the information. The company has all their phone numbers, and management feels that the task could be accomplished by the receptionists in the office during their spare time. Since the company apparently has both the time and manpower, are there any reasons for it to poll a sample of the contractors rather than the entire population?

7-56 A drug manufacturer knows that for a certain antibiotic, the average number of doses ordered for a patient is 20. Steve Simmons, a salesman for the company, after looking at 1 day's prescription order for the drug in his territory, announced that the sample mean for this drug should be lower. He said, "For any sample, the mean should be lower, since the sampling mean always understates the population mean because of sample variation." Is there any truth to what Simmons said?

7-57 Several weeks later at a sales meeting, Steve Simmons again demonstrated his expertise in statistics. He had drawn a graph and presented it to the group, saying, "This is a sampling distribution of means. It is a normal curve and represents a distribution of all observations in each possible sample combination." Is Simmons right? Explain.

7-58 Low-Cal Foods Company uses estimates of the level of activity for various market segments to determine the nutritional composition of its diet food products. Low-Cal is considering the introduction of a liquid diet food for older women, since this segment has special weight problems not met by the competitor's diet foods. To determine the desired calorie content of this new product, Dr. Nell Watson, researcher for the company, conducted tests on a sample of women, to determine calorie consumption per day. Her results showed that the average number of calories expended per day for older women is 1,424 with a standard deviation of 240. Dr. Watson estimates that the benefits she obtains with a sample size of 25 are worth

$1,440. She expects that reducing the standard error by half its current value will double the benefit. If it costs $20 for every woman in the sample, should Watson reduce her standard error?

7-59 The U.S. Customs Agency routinely checks all passengers arriving from foreign countries as they enter the United States. The department reports that on the average, 35 people per day, with a standard deviation of 6, are found to be carrying contraband material as they enter the United States through the John F. Kennedy Airport in New York. What is the probability that in 4 days at that airport, the average number of passengers found carrying contraband will exceed 40?

7-60 HAL Corporation manufactures large computer systems and has always prided itself on the reliability of its System 666 central processing units. In fact, past experience has shown that the monthly downtime of System 666 CPUs averages 40 minutes, with a standard deviation of 8 minutes. The computer center at a large state university maintains an installation built around five System 666 CPUs. James Batter, the director of the computer center, feels that a satisfactory level of service is provided to the university community if the average downtime of the five CPUs is less than three-quarters of an hour per month. In any given month, what is the probability that Batter will be satisfied with the level of service?

7-61 Members of the Organization for Consumer Action send more than 100 volunteers a day all over the state to increase support for a consumer protection bill that is currently before the state legislature. Usually, each volunteer will visit a household and talk briefly with the resident, in the hope that the resident will sign a petition to be given to the state legislature. On the average, a volunteer will obtain 4.2 signatures for the petition each day, with a standard deviation of .6. What is the probability that a sample of 70 volunteers will result in an average between 4.05 and 4.1 signatures per day?

7-62 Jill Johnson, product manager for Southern Electric's smoke alarm, is concerned over recent complaints from a consumer group about the short life of the device. She has decided to gather evidence to counteract the complaints by testing a sample of the alarms. For the test, it costs $3 per unit in the sample. Since precision is desirable for presenting persuasive statistical evidence to the consumer group, Johnson figures the benefits she will receive for various sample sizes are determined by the formula: Benefits = $\$4.608/\sigma_{\bar{x}}$. If Johnson wants to increase her sample until the cost equals the benefit, how many units should she sample? The population standard deviation is 240.

7-63 A sales manager is concerned about what he considers a high rate of turnover in the sales force. Since the company sells highly technical industrial products, a considerable investment is involved in training a salesperson, and selling effectiveness tends to increase with experience. The manager reviews the records of the 29 salespeople and finds that the average number of years a salesperson has been with the company is 4 with a standard deviation of 2. What is the probability that, in a sample of 3 salespeople, the mean will be more than 6 years with the company?

7-10 CHAPTER CONCEPTS TEST

Answers are in the back of the book.

T F 1. When the items included in a sample are based upon the judgment of the individual conducting the sample, the sample is said to be nonrandom.

T F 2. A statistic is a characteristic of a population.

T F 3. A sampling plan that selects members from a population at uniform intervals in time, order, or space is called stratified sampling.

T F 4. As a general rule, it is not necessary to include a finite population multiplier in a computation for standard error of the mean when the size of the sample is greater than 50.

T F 5. The probability distribution of all the possible means of samples is known as the sample distribution of the mean.

T F 6. The principles of simple random sampling are the theoretical foundation for statistical inference.

T F 7. The standard error of the mean is the standard deviation of the distribution of sample means.

T F 8. A sampling plan that divides the population into well-defined groups from which random samples are drawn is known as cluster sampling.

T F 9. With increasing sample size, the sampling distribution of the mean approaches normality, regardless of the distribution of the population.

T F 10. The standard error of the mean decreases in direct proportion to sample size.

T F 11. To perform a complete enumeration, one would examine every item in a population.

T F 12. In everyday life, we see many examples of infinite populations of physical objects.

T F 13. To obtain a theoretical sampling distribution, we consider all the samples of a given size.

T F 14. Large samples are always a good idea, since they decrease the standard error.

T F 15. If the mean for a certain population were 15, it is likely that most of the samples we could take from that population would have means of 15.

T F 16. The precision of a sample is determined by the number of items in the sample and not the proportion of the total population that is sampled.

T F 17. The standard error of a sample statistic is the standard deviation of its sampling distribution.

18. Which of the following is a method of selecting samples from a population?
    a) Judgment sampling c) Probability sampling e) a and b but not c
    b) Random sampling d) All of these

19. Choose the pair of symbols that best completes this sentence:
    ____________________ is a parameter, whereas ____________________ is a statistic.
    a) $N \ldots \mu$ c) $N \ldots n$ e) b and c but not a
    b) $\sigma \ldots s$ d) All of these

20. In random sampling, we can describe mathematically how objective our estimates are. Why is this?
    a) We always know the chance that a population element will be included in the sample.
    b) Every sample always has an equal chance of being selected.
    c) All the samples are of exactly the same size and can be counted.
    d) None of these. e) a and b but not c.

21. Suppose you are performing stratified sampling on a particular population and have divided the population into strata of different sizes. How can you now make your sample selection?
    a) Select at random an equal number of elements from each stratum.
    b) Draw an equal number of elements from each stratum and give weights to the results.
    c) Draw a number of elements from each stratum proportional to its weight in the population.
    d) a and b only. e) b and c only.

22. In which of the following situations would $\sigma_{\bar{x}} = \frac{\sigma}{\sqrt{n}}$ be the correct formula to use for computing $\sigma_{\bar{x}}$?
    a) Sampling is from an infinite population.
    b) Sampling is from a finite population with replacement.
    c) Sampling is from a finite population without replacement.
    d) a and b only. e) b and c only.

23. The dispersion among sample means is less than the dispersion among the sampled items themselves because:
    a) Each sample is smaller than the population from which it is drawn.
    b) Very large values are averaged down, and very small values are averaged up.
    c) The sampled items are all drawn from the same population.
    d) None of these. e) b and c but not a.

24. Suppose that a normally distributed population with $N = 144$ has $\mu = 24$. What is the mean of the sampling distribution of the mean for samples of size 25?
a) 24 b) 2 c) 4.8 d) Cannot be determined from the information given.

25. The central limit theorem assures us that the sampling distribution of the mean:
a) Is always normal. b) Is always normal for large sample sizes.
c) Approaches normality as sample size increases.
d) Appears normal only when N is greater than 1,000.

26. Suppose that, for a certain population, $\sigma_{\bar{x}}$ is calculated as 20 when samples of size 25 are taken and as 10 when samples of size 100 are taken. A quadrupling of sample size, then, only halved $\sigma_{\bar{x}}$. We can conclude that increasing sample size is:
a) Always cost-effective b) Sometimes cost-effective c) Never cost-effective

27. Refer again to the data of question 26. What must be the value of σ for this infinite population?
a) 1,000 b) 500 c) 377.5 d) 100
e) Cannot be determined from the information given

28. The finite population multiplier does not have to be used when the sampling fraction is:
a) Greater than .05 c) Less than .50 e) None of these
b) Greater than .50 d) Greater than .90

29. The standard error of the mean for a sample size of 2 or more is:
a) Always greater than the standard deviation of the population
b) Generally greater than the standard deviation of the population
c) Usually less than the standard deviation of the population
d) None of these

30. A portion of the elements in a population chosen for direct examination or measurement is a __________________.

31. The proportion of the population contained in a sample is the __________________.

32. A method of random sampling in which elements are selected from the population at uniform intervals is called __________________ sampling.

33. __________________ is the degree of accuracy with which the sample mean can estimate the population mean.

34. Within a population, groups that are similar to each other (although the groups themselves have wide internal variation) are called __________________.

35. A sampling distribution of the proportion is a probability distribution of __________________.

7-11 CONCEPTUAL CASE (Northern White Metals Company)

Dick looked down at the memo in his hand and frowned. One of Northern's best customers, NES Electronics, had refused to accept an entire shipment of aluminum mounting brackets because of late delivery. A month earlier, a shipment of a similar product had been returned for quality reasons. Lynn Martin had worked for months in developing the NES account and was quite upset at the poor service this valued customer had been getting.

"Something has got to be done, Dick," she said with obvious irritation. "Not only is our company being hurt, but my credibility is being questioned as well. I think we have a real problem here."

"Yes, I agree, Lynn," Dick replied, laying her memo aside. "We do have a problem, and we've got to fix it soon. Can you patch things up with Morty at NES while we work on their next order?" he asked anxiously.

"Probably, but the next foul-up will be the last foul-up as far as they're concerned, I can tell you that much," Lynn grumbled as she turned to leave Dick's office.

Dick sat back in his chair, pondering the problem of disgruntled sales reps and dissatisfied customers. Problems such as those with NES had been occurring more and more frequently. First, the anodizing department had had some difficulty in adjusting to the increasing volume of orders. Now it appeared the fabricating department was having problems as well. Increased demand on this area saw the established, formal quality control procedures becoming increasingly ineffective. Consequently, more and more orders were being shipped that did not meet customer standards.

The first NES quality problem had originated in this way: The mounting brackets NES had ordered were formed in the fabricating area by cutting long lengths of extruded aluminum into small, one-inch sections. An automatic high-speed saw was used in the process, and the lengths of aluminum were fed into the cutting area by continuous conveyor.

For small orders, the saw, once set, did not need to be adjusted. With larger orders, however, the extended use of the machinery would occasionally cause the process to require readjustment. The saw and the conveyor would then have to be shut down and the measuring control recalibrated.

This particular difficulty had first become evident when NES returned the earlier shipment, two-thirds of which was outside of size tolerance limits. To prevent such an egregious error from recurring, Dick had suggested to the fabricating department supervisor that large orders coming through the automatic saw be monitored. The next large order had indeed been monitored, with each individual piece tested for conformance to size specifications. This resulted in continual delays, as the saw was periodically shut down so the testing could catch up with the process.

Similar problems were being observed on other pieces of equipment, and Dick realized that some formal, more sophisticated quality control procedures were needed. He called the New York office.

"Sir," he said as the CEO answered, "we've got a QC situation here that calls for some corporate assistance. Can you spare some technical people for awhile?"

"Sure thing, Lennox," the CEO replied, surprisingly agreeable. "I've got two top people, Jody Wallis and Sarah Porter, just finishing up a big project. I'll send them up on the morning plane." He added, "These two are all business, so be ready to put them to work!"

Increased sales volume has again created some difficulties, this time in the fabricating department. Dick has recognized the need for better quality control procedures and will be receiving some much needed technical assistance in this area. What kind of information will Dick and the fabricating area supervisor need to provide to the technical support staff to aid them in their task? How will Jody and Sarah use this information to help Dick solve the quality control problem?

7-12 COMPUTER DATA BASE EXERCISE

Fred notified Laurel and Frank of a strategy meeting to discuss the new wooden toy product line hot off the drawing board of Dunlap Sandell.

Dunlap had spent most of his career drawing for a West Coast animation studio and was personally responsible for several nationally famous hamsters. At age 45, he had tired of the excitement and pressure of L.A., and with his wife and three children, he abandoned his backyard swimming pool to get closer to nature in Colorado. He often said he adored Cold River because he could do his job with a blindfold and mittens on.

Dunlap had created the Polaris Rider 2 years before, and Joe Walsh had recently directed his efforts toward the preschool market because of predicted growth potential. Today, Dunlap is surrounded by a gaggle of wooden animals.

Joe opened the meeting with some ideas about the new line. He felt the toy industry had increasing sales possibilities in sturdy natural toys of good quality. The new toys would be a spinoff of the current preschool products sold only in Colorado. The present distribution system might be used to introduce the experimental animals in Colorado for a test market before Cold River began national distribution.

The menagerie of new animals received applause from the corporate staff as Dunlap held them high for introduction. Made like the old line, each animal was a chunky wooden puzzle toy on wheels, so a child could pull it behind him or reassemble the pieces. Dunlap had added a new twist: The five pieces of each animal fit with the five pieces of every other animal, so a child could create a penguin with an anteater snout or a cow with a lion's head. He felt the diversity would lead the purchaser to add to the child's zoo and bankroll Dunlap for years.

"They look great," Joe affirmed. "What did you kids find out about the purchasers of the old line?"

"Just the income levels of known purchasers over the last year," said Frank. "For last year's sales, the mean was about \$16,000, and the standard deviation was about \$1,600."

"Hmm," pondered Joe. "You had to use lots of data to get those figures. What would happen if you used smaller samples?"

Laurel smiled and said, "Joe, we're going to give you a demonstration of the central limit theorem in action."

PROBLEM

1. Using the purchasers' income data in Chapter 6, compute the sample mean and standard deviation for the incomes of the first 25 purchasers. Then do the same for the first 50, 100, 200, and 400.

7-13 FLOW CHART

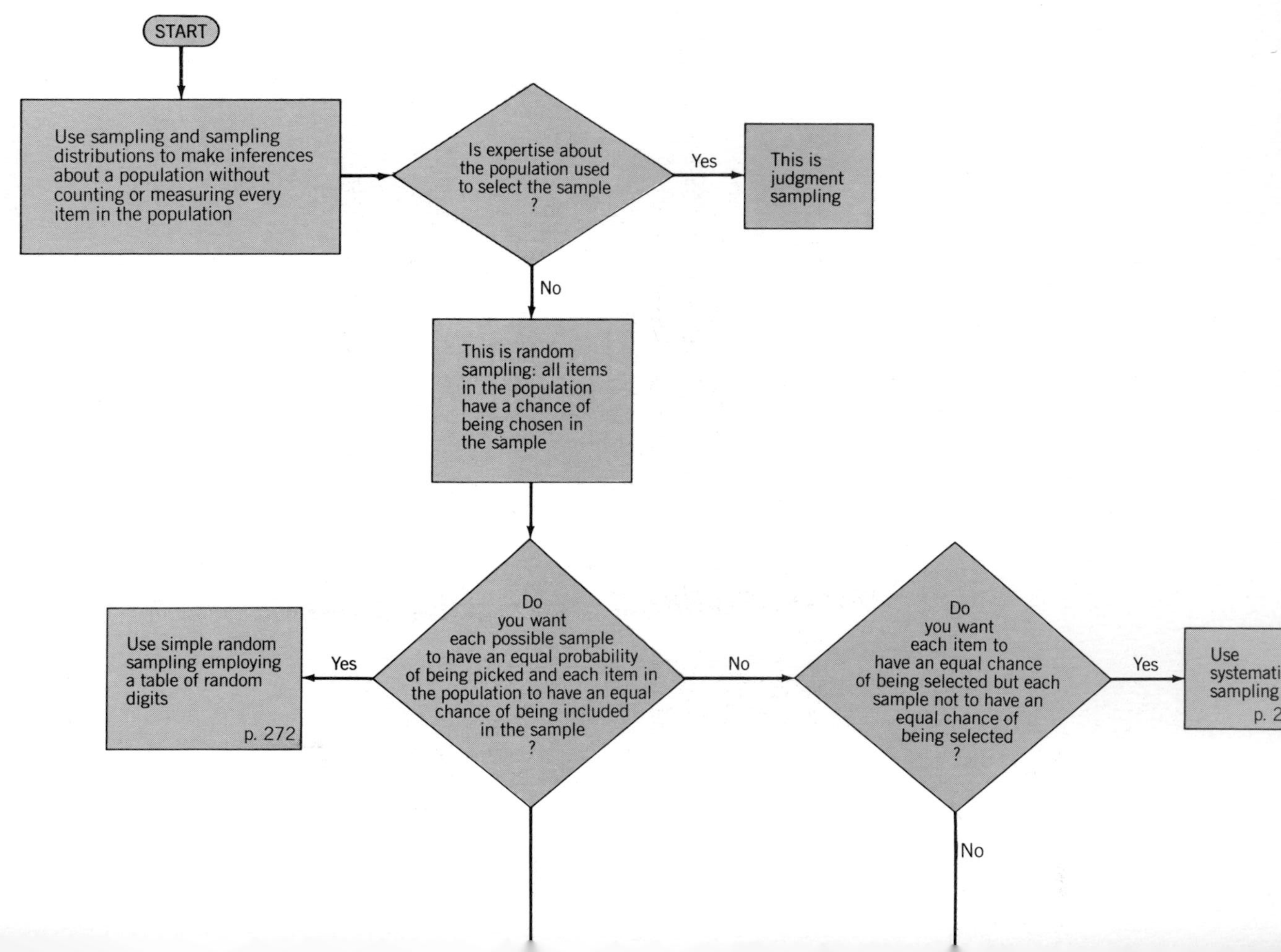

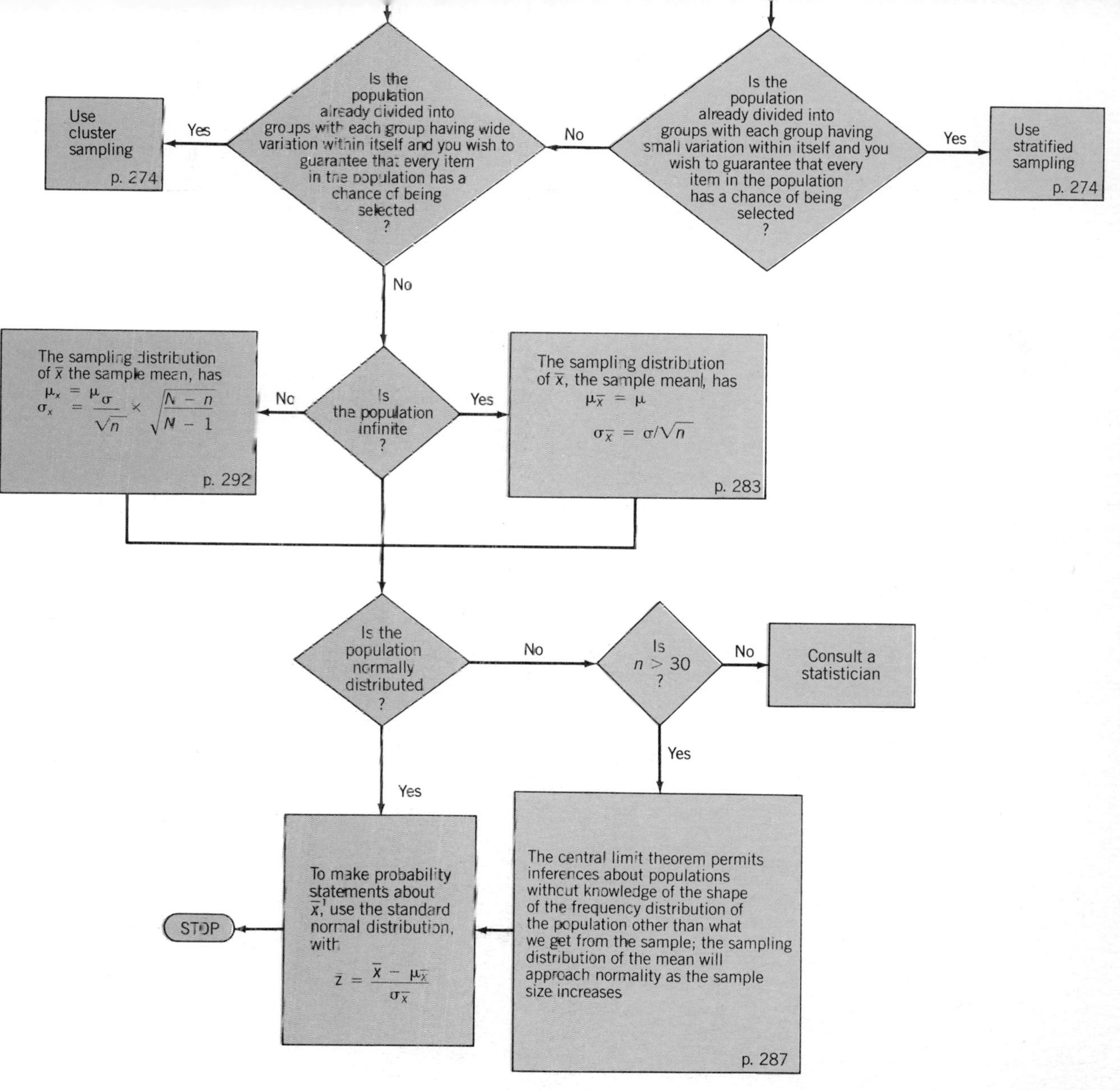

Is the population already divided into groups with each group having small variation within itself and you wish to guarantee that every item in the population has a chance of being selected ?
Yes
Use stratified sampling p. 274
No
Is the population already divided into groups with each group having wide variation within itself and you wish to guarantee that every item in the population has a chance of being selected ?
Yes
Use cluster sampling p. 274
No
Is the population infinite ?
Yes
The sampling distribution of $\overline{x}$, the sample mean, has $\mu_{\overline{x}} = \mu$ $\sigma_{\overline{x}} = \sigma/\sqrt{n}$ p. 283
No
The sampling distribution of $\overline{x}$ the sample mean, has $\mu_x = \mu$ $\sigma_x = \frac{\sigma}{\sqrt{n}} \times \sqrt{\frac{N-n}{N-1}}$ p. 292
Is the population normally distributed ?
Yes
To make probability statements about $\overline{x}$, use the standard normal distribution, with $z = \frac{\overline{x} - \mu_{\overline{x}}}{\sigma_{\overline{x}}}$
No
Is $n > 30$?
No
Consult a statistician
Yes
The central limit theorem permits inferences about populations without knowledge of the shape of the frequency distribution of the population other than what we get from the sample; the sampling distribution of the mean will approach normality as the sample size increases p. 287
STOP

CHAPTER 8

ESTIMATION

1. INTRODUCTION, 312
2. POINT ESTIMATES, 315
3. INTERVAL ESTIMATES: Basic Concepts, 319
4. INTERVAL ESTIMATES AND CONFIDENCE INTERVALS, 323
5. CALCULATING INTERVAL ESTIMATES OF THE MEAN FROM LARGE SAMPLES, 326
6. CALCULATING INTERVAL ESTIMATES OF THE PROPORTION FROM LARGE SAMPLES, 330
7. INTERVAL ESTIMATES USING THE *t* DISTRIBUTION, 334
8. DETERMINING THE SAMPLE SIZE IN ESTIMATION, 340
9. TERMS, 345
10. EQUATIONS, 346
11. REVIEW EXERCISES, 347
12. CONCEPTS TEST, 349
13. CONCEPTUAL CASE, 351
14. COMPUTER DATA BASE EXERCISE, 352
15. FLOW CHART, 354

OBJECTIVES: Chapters 8 and 9 deal with statistical inference. In Chapter 8, we shall learn to estimate the characteristics of a population by observing the characteristics of a sample. Two characteristics of special interest will be how a population tends to "bunch up" and how it spreads out.

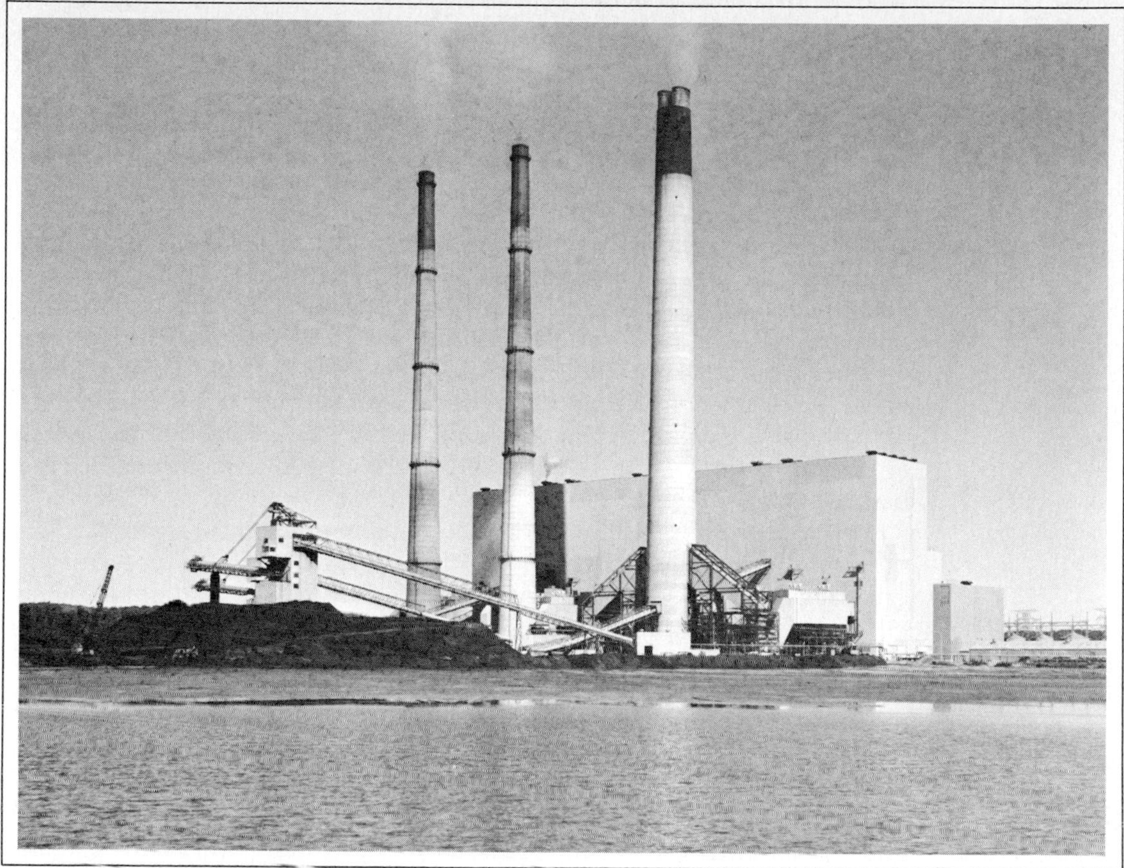

As part of the budgeting process for next year, the manager of the Far Point electric generating plant must estimate the coal he will require for this year. Last year, the plant almost ran out, so he is reluctant to budget for that same amount again. The plant manager, however, does feel that past usage data will help him *estimate* the number of tons of coal to order. A random sample of ten plant operating weeks chosen over the last five years yielded a mean usage of 11,400 tons a week, with a sample standard deviation of 700 tons a week. With the data he has and the methods we shall discuss in this chapter, the plant manager can make a sensible estimate of the amount to order this year, including some idea of the accuracy of the estimate he has made.

8-1 INTRODUCTION

Everyone makes estimates. When you get ready to cross a street, you estimate the speed of any car that is approaching, the distance between you and that car, and your own speed. Having made these quick estimates, you decide whether to wait, walk, or run.

Reasons for estimates

All managers must make quick estimates, too. The outcome of these estimates can affect their organizations as seriously as the outcome of your decision as to whether to cross the street. University department heads make estimates of next fall's enrollment in statistics. Credit managers estimate whether a purchaser will eventually pay his bills. Prospective home buyers make estimates concerning the behavior of interest rates in the mortgage market. All these people make estimates without worry about whether they are scientific but with the hope that the estimates bear a reasonable resemblance to the outcome.

Managers use estimates because in all but the most trivial decisions, they must make rational decisions without complete information and with a great deal of uncertainty about what the future will bring. As educated citizens and professionals, you will be able to make more useful estimates by applying the techniques described in this and subsequent chapters.

Making statistical inferences

The material on probability theory covered in Chapters 5, 6, and 7 forms the foundation for *statistical inference,* the branch of statistics concerned with using probability concepts to deal with uncertainty in decision making. Statistical inference is based on *estimation,* which we shall introduce in this chapter, and *hypothesis testing,* which is the subject of Chapters 9 and 10. In both estimation and hypothesis testing, we shall be making inferences about characteristics of populations from information contained in samples.

How do managers use sample statistics to estimate population parameters? The department head attempts to estimate enrollments next fall from current enrollments in the same courses. The credit manager attempts to estimate the creditworthiness of prospective customers from a sample of their past payment habits. The home buyer attempts to estimate the future course of interest rates by observing the current behavior of those rates. In each case, somebody is trying to infer something about a population from information taken from a sample.

Estimating population parameters

This chapter introduces methods that enable us to estimate with reasonable accuracy the *population proportion* (the proportion of the population that possesses a given characteristic) and the *population mean.* To calculate the exact proportion or the exact mean would be an impossible goal. Even so, we will be able to make an estimate, make a statement about the error that will probably accompany this estimate, and implement some controls to avoid as much of the error as possible. As decision makers, we will be forced at times to rely on blind hunches. Yet in other situations, in which information is available and we apply statistical concepts, we can do better than that.

Types of Estimates

Point estimate defined

We can make two types of estimates about a population: a *point* estimate and an *interval* estimate. **A point estimate is a single number that is used to estimate an unknown population parameter.** If, while watching the first members of a football team come onto the field, you say, "Why, I bet their line must weigh 250 pounds," you have made a point estimate. A department chairwoman would make a point estimate if she said, "Our current data indicate that this course will have 350 students in the fall."

Shortcomings of point estimates

A point estimate is often insufficient, because it is either right or wrong. If you are told only that the chairwoman's point estimate of enrollment is wrong, you do not know *how* wrong it is, and you cannot be certain of the estimate's reliability. If you learn that it is off by only ten students, you would accept 350 students as a good estimate of future enrollment. But if the estimate is off by 90 students, you would reject it as an estimate of future enrollment. Therefore, a point estimate is much more useful if it is accompanied by an estimate of the error that might be involved.

Interval estimate defined

An interval estimate is a range of values used to estimate a population parameter. It indicates the error in two ways: by the extent of its range and by the probability of the true population parameter lying within that range. In this case, the department chairwoman would say something like, "I estimate that the true enrollment in this course in the fall will be between 330 and 380 and that it is very likely that the exact enrollment will fall within this interval." The chairwoman has a better idea of the reliability of her estimate. If the course is taught in sections of about 100 students each, and if the chairwoman had tentatively scheduled five sections, then on the basis of her estimate, she can now cancel one of those sections and offer an elective instead.

Estimator and Estimates

Estimator defined

Any sample statistic that is used to estimate a population parameter is called an estimator; that is, **an estimator is a sample statistic used to estimate a population parameter.** The sample mean $\bar{x}$ can be an estimator of the population mean μ, and the sample proportion can be used as an estimator of the population proportion. We can also use the sample range as an estimator of the population range.

Estimate defined

When we observe a specific numerical value of our estimator, we call that value an estimate. In other words, **an estimate is a specific observed value of a statistic.** We form an estimate by taking a sample and computing the value taken by our estimator in that sample. Suppose that we calculate the mean odometer reading (mileage) from a sample of used taxis and find it to be 98,000 miles. If we use this specific value to estimate the mileage for a whole fleet of used taxis, the value 98,000 miles would be an estimate. Table 8-1 illustrates several populations, population parameters, estimators, and estimates.

TABLE 8-1 Populations, population parameters, estimators, and estimates

POPULATION IN WHICH WE ARE INTERESTED	POPULATION PARAMETER WE WISH TO ESTIMATE	SAMPLE STATISTIC WE WILL USE AS AN ESTIMATOR	ESTIMATE WE MAKE
Employees in a furniture factory	Mean turnover per year	Mean turnover for a period of 1 month	8.9% turnover per year
Applicants for town manager of Chapel Hill	Mean formal education (years)	Mean formal education of every 5th applicant	17.9 years of formal education
Teenagers in a given community	Proportion who have criminal records	Proportion of a sample of 50 teenagers who have criminal records	.02, or 2%, have criminal records

Criteria of a Good Estimator

Qualities of a good estimator

Some statistics are better estimators than are others. Fortunately, we can evaluate the quality of a statistic as an estimator by using four criteria:

1. **Unbiasedness.** This is a desirable property for a good estimator to have. The term *unbiasedness* refers to the fact that a sample mean is an unbiased estimator of a population mean because **the mean of the sampling distribution of sample means taken from the same population is equal to the population mean itself.** We can say that a statistic is an unbiased estimator if, on the average, it tends to assume values that are above the population parameter being estimated as frequently and to the same extent as it tends to assume values that are below the population parameter being estimated.

2. **Efficiency.** Another desirable property of a good estimator is that it be efficient. *Efficiency* refers to the size of the standard error of the statistic. If we compare two statistics from a sample of the same size and try to decide which one is the more efficient estimator, we would pick the statistic that has the smaller standard error, or standard deviation of the sampling distribution. Suppose we choose a sample of a given size and must decide whether to use the sample mean or the sample median to estimate the population mean. If we calculate the standard error of the sample mean and find it to be 1.05 and then calculate the standard error of the sample median and find it to be 1.6, we would say that the sample mean is a *more efficient estimator* of the population mean *because its standard error is smaller.* It makes sense that an estimator with a smaller standard error (with less variation) will have more chance of producing an estimate nearer to the population parameter under consideration.

3. **Consistency.** A statistic is a consistent estimator of a population parameter if *as the sample size increases, it becomes almost certain that the value of the statistic comes very close to the value of the population parameter.* If an estimator is consistent, it becomes more reliable with large samples. Thus, if you are wondering whether to increase the sample size to get more information about a population parameter, find out first whether your

statistic is a consistent estimator. If it is not, you will waste time and money by taking larger samples.

4. Sufficiency. An estimator is sufficient if it makes so much use of the information in the sample that no other estimator could extract from the sample additional information about the population parameter being estimated. We present these criteria here to make you aware of the care that statisticians must use in picking an estimator.

Finding the best estimator

A given sample statistic is not always the best estimator of its analogous population parameter. Consider a symmetrically distributed population in which the values of the median and the mean coincide. In this instance, the sample mean would be an *unbiased* estimator of the population median because it would assume values that on the average would equal the population median. Also, the sample mean would be a *consistent* estimator of the population median because, as the sample size increases, the value of the sample mean would tend to come very close to the population median. And the sample mean would be a more *efficient* estimator of the population median than the sample median itself because in large samples, the sample mean has a smaller standard error than the sample median. At the same time, the sample median in a symmetrically distributed population would be an unbiased and consistent estimator of the population mean but *not the most efficient* estimator because in large samples, its standard error is larger than that of the sample mean.

EXERCISES

8-1 What two basic tools are used in making statistical inferences?

8-2 Why do decision makers often measure samples rather than entire populations? What is the disadvantage?

8-3 Explain a shortcoming that occurs in a point estimate but not in an interval estimate. What measure is included with a point estimate to compensate for this problem?

8-4 What is an estimator? How does an estimate differ from an estimator?

8-5 List and describe briefly the criteria of a good estimator.

8-6 What role does consistency play in determining sample size?

8-2 POINT ESTIMATES

Using the sample mean to estimate the population mean

The sample mean $\bar{x}$ is the best estimator of the population mean μ. It is unbiased, consistent, the most efficient estimator, and, as long as the sample is sufficiently large, its sampling distribution can be approximated by the normal distribution.

If we know the sampling distribution of $\bar{x}$, we can make statements about any estimate we may make from sampling information. Let's look at a medical supplies company that produces disposable hypodermic syringes. Each syringe is wrapped in a sterile package and then jumble-packed in a large corrugated carton. Jumble packing causes the cartons to contain differing numbers of syringes. Since the syringes are sold on a per unit basis, the company needs an estimate of the number of syringes per carton for billing purposes. We have taken a sample of 35 cartons at random and recorded the number of syringes in each carton. Table 8-2 illustrates our results. Using the results of Chapter 3, we can obtain the sample mean $\bar{x}$ by finding the sum of all our results, Σx, and dividing this total by n, the number of cartons we have sampled:

Finding the sample mean

$$\bar{x} = \frac{\Sigma x}{n} \qquad [3\text{-}2]$$

TABLE 8-2 Results of sample of 35 cartons of hypodermic syringes (syringes per carton)

101	103	112	102	98	97	93
105	100	97	107	93	94	97
97	100	110	106	110	103	99
93	98	106	100	112	105	100
114	97	110	102	98	112	99

Using this equation to solve our problem, we get:

$$\bar{x} = \frac{3570}{35}$$
$$= 102 \text{ syringes}$$

Thus, using the sample mean $\bar{x}$ as our estimator, the point estimate of the population mean μ is 102 syringes per carton. Since the manufactured price of a disposable hypodermic syringe is quite small (about 25¢), both the buyer and seller would accept the use of this point estimate as the basis for billing, and the manufacturer can save the time and expense of counting each syringe that goes into a carton.

Point Estimate of the Population Variance and Standard Deviation

Using the sample standard deviation to estimate the population standard deviation

Suppose the management of the medical-supplies company wants to estimate the variance and/or standard deviation of the distribution of the number of packaged syringes per carton. The most frequently used estimator of the population standard deviation σ is the sample standard deviation s. We can calculate the sample standard deviation as in Table 8-3 and discover that the sample standard deviation is 6.01 syringes.

TABLE 8-3 Calculation of sample variance and standard deviation for syringes per carton

VALUES OF x (NEEDLES PER CARTON) (1)	x^2 (2)	SAMPLE MEAN $\bar{x}$ (3)	$(x - \bar{x})$ (4) = (1) − (3)	$(x - \bar{x})^2$ (5) = $(4)^2$
101	10,201	102	−1	1
105	11,025	102	3	9
97	9,409	102	−5	25
93	8,649	102	−9	81
114	12,996	102	12	144
103	10,609	102	1	1
100	10,000	102	−2	4
100	10,000	102	−2	4
98	9,604	102	−4	16
97	9,409	102	−5	25
112	12,544	102	10	100
97	9,409	102	−5	25
110	12,100	102	8	64
106	11,236	102	4	16
110	12,100	102	8	64
102	10,404	102	0	0
107	11,449	102	5	25
106	11,236	102	4	16
100	10,000	102	−2	4
102	10,404	102	0	0
98	9,604	102	−4	16
93	8,649	102	−9	81
110	12,100	102	8	64
112	12,544	102	10	100
98	9,604	102	−4	16
97	9,409	102	−5	25
94	8,836	102	−8	64
103	10,609	102	1	1
105	11,025	102	3	9
112	12,544	102	10	100
93	8,649	102	−9	81
97	9,409	102	−5	25
99	9,801	102	−3	9
100	10,000	102	2	4
99	9,801	102	−3	9
3,570	**365,368**	Sum of all the squared differences $\Sigma(x - \bar{x})^2$ →		**1,228**

[4-11] $s^2 = \dfrac{\Sigma x^2}{n-1} - \dfrac{n\bar{x}^2}{n-1}$

$= \dfrac{365{,}368}{34} - \dfrac{35(102)^2}{34}$

$= \dfrac{1228}{34}$ ← or →

$= 36.12$

Sum of the squared differences divided by 34, the number of items in the sample − 1 (sample variance) $\dfrac{\Sigma(x - \bar{x})^2}{n-1}$ → 36.12

[4-12] $s = \sqrt{s^2}$

$= \sqrt{36.12}$

$= 6.01$ syringes

Sample standard deviation s $\sqrt{\dfrac{\Sigma(x - \bar{x})^2}{n-1}}$ → 6.01 syringes

If, instead of considering:

$$s^2 = \frac{\Sigma(x - \bar{x})^2}{n - 1} \qquad \text{[4-11]}$$

Why is $n - 1$ the divisor?

as our sample variance, we had considered:

$$s^2 = \frac{\Sigma(x - \bar{x})^2}{n}$$

the result would have some *bias* as an estimator of the population variance; specifically, it would tend to be too low. Using a divisor of $n - 1$ gives us an unbiased estimator of σ^2. Thus, we will use s^2 (as defined in Equation 4-11) and s (as defined in Equation 4-12) to estimate σ^2 and σ.

Point Estimate of the Population Proportion

Using the sample proportion to estimate the population proportion

The proportion of units that have a particular characteristic in a given population is symbolized p. If we know the proportion of units in a sample that has that same characteristic (symbolized $\bar{p}$), we can use this $\bar{p}$ as an estimator of p. It can be shown that $\bar{p}$ has all the desirable properties we discussed earlier; it is unbiased, consistent, efficient, and sufficient.

Continuing our example of the manufacturer of medical supplies, we shall try to estimate the population proportion from the sample proportion. Suppose the management wishes to estimate the number of cartons that will arrive damaged, owing to poor handling in shipment after the cartons leave the factory. We can check a sample of 50 cartons from their shipping point to the arrival at their destination and then record the presence or absence of damage. If, in this case, we find that the proportion of damaged cartons in the sample is .08, we would say that:

$$\bar{p} = .08 \leftarrow \text{sample proportion damaged}$$

And since the sample proportion $\bar{p}$ is a convenient estimator of the population proportion p, we can estimate that the proportion of damaged cartons in the population will also be .08.

EXERCISES

8-7 Golden Cigarettes has developed a new blended tobacco product. Golden's marketing department has yet to determine the factory price. A sample of 20 wholesalers received information about the product and were asked to set a reasonable price. Determine the sample mean for the following prices supplied by the wholesalers:

$.61	.70	.63	.76	.72	.64	.82	.88	.82	.67
.78	.84	.83	.74	.85	.73	.85	.87	.75	.82

8-8 Sensing a potential downturn in the demand for cyclamates, Sweetners' principal product, the financial VP was considering shifting his company's resources to a new product area. He selected a sample of 10 firms in the pharmaceutical industry and discovered that they were earning the following percentage returns on investment. Find point estimates of the mean and the variance of the population from which the following sample came:

17.0	25.0	13.0	8.5	27.5	20.0	18.5	17.0	16.0	12.0

8-9 Electric Pizza was considering national distribution of its regionally successful product and was compiling *pro forma* sales data. Below are listed the average monthly sales figures (in thousands of dollars) from its 35 current distributors. Treating them as (a) a sample and (b) a population, compute the standard deviation.

4.7	5.0	8.0	3.5	5.0	4.3	7.0
5.6	8.1	8.0	4.0	7.8	6.0	10.0
6.8	2.0	5.9	7.3	5.8	4.7	6.1
3.9	8.0	5.0	8.0	6.4	7.0	8.0
6.8	4.4	7.0	5.5	6.4	5.0	4.2

8-10 In a sample of 500 textile workers, 284 expressed extreme dissatisfaction regarding a prospective plan to modify working conditions. This dissatisfaction was vehement enough to allow management to interpret plan reaction as being highly undesirable, and they were curious about the proportion of total workers harboring this sentiment. Give a point estimate of this proportion.

8-11 Fred B. Klogg, owner of Fred's Plumbing Service, prides himself on the reputation that his company has earned for speedy service. Open day and night, Fred's Plumbing Service advertises that it responds to customers' service requests within 30 minutes on the average. At the end of each month, Fred samples 20 of the hundreds of service completion forms that his company fills out each month, and he calculates a sample mean response time to determine if his company is living up to its claim of having a mean response of less than 30 minutes. Each plumber fills out a service completion form after each customer's service request is completed, and the response time is one of several numbers that is entered on the form. The service completion forms are then filed by the date and month, and whenever a customer complaint is received, the appropriate service completion form is photocopied, and the copy is filed under "Consumer Complaints." This particular month, Fred hasn't been able to locate the service completion form files, so he has randomly chosen 20 copies from the Consumer Complaint file. The times (in minutes) for Fred's plumbers to respond to customers' requests are given below:

17	27	35	29	26	30	32	33	39	30
31	28	29	38	45	25	22	41	33	34

a) Find the mean for the sample above.
b) From what population was this sample drawn?
c) What is the sample mean an appropriate point estimate for?
d) Can Fred claim that his company lived up to its claim last month? Explain briefly.

8-3 INTERVAL ESTIMATES: Basic Concepts

The purpose of gathering samples is to learn more about a population. We can compute this information from the samples as either *point* estimates, which we have just discussed, or as *interval* estimates, the subject of the rest

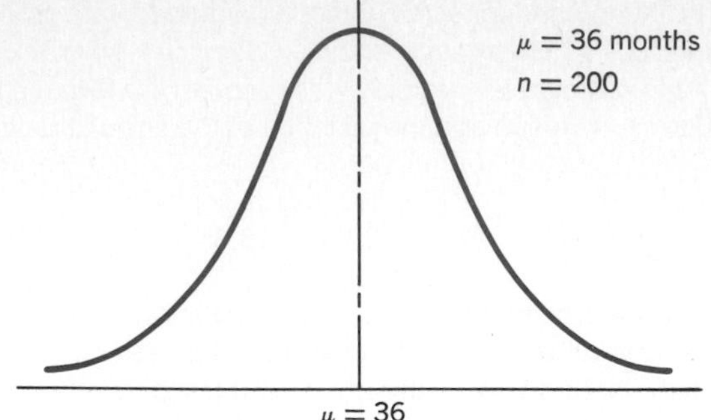

FIGURE 8-1 Sampling distribution of the mean for samples of 200 batteries

of this chapter. *An interval estimate describes a range of values within which a population parameter is likely to lie.*

Finding the point estimate

Suppose the marketing research director needs an estimate in months of the average life of car batteries his company manufactures. We select a random sample of 200 batteries, record the car owners' names and addresses as listed in store records, and interview these owners about the battery life they have experienced. Our sample of 200 users has a mean battery life of 36 months. If we use the point estimate of the sample mean $\bar{x}$ as the best estimator of the population mean μ, we would report that the mean life of the company's batteries is 36 months.

Finding the likely error of this estimate

But the director also asks for a statement about the uncertainty that will be likely to accompany this estimate; that is, a statement about the range within which the unknown population mean is likely to lie. To provide such a statement, we need to find *the standard error of the mean.*

We learned from Chapter 7 that if we select and plot a large number of sample means from a population, the distribution of these means will approximate a normal curve. Furthermore, the mean of the sample means will be the same as the population mean. Our sample size of 200 is large enough so that we can apply the central limit theorem, as we have done graphically in Fig. 8-1. To measure the spread, or dispersion, in our distribution of sample means, we can use the following formula* and calculate the standard error of the mean:

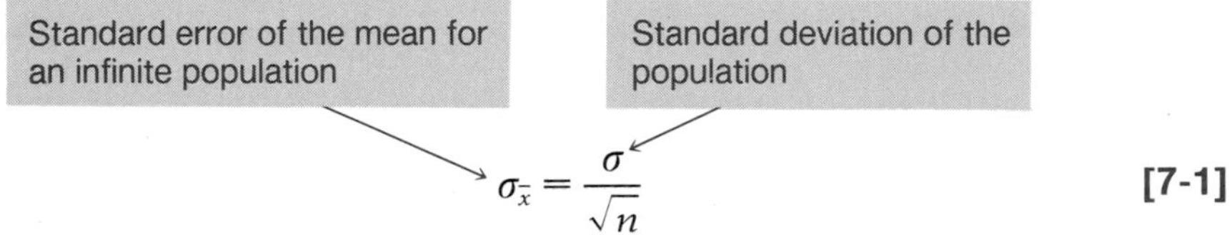

$$\sigma_{\bar{x}} = \frac{\sigma}{\sqrt{n}} \qquad [7\text{-}1]$$

In this case, we have already estimated the standard deviation of the population of the batteries and reported that it is ten months. Using this standard

* We have not used the finite population multiplier to calculate the standard error of the mean because the population of batteries is large enough to be considered infinite.

deviation and the first equation from Chapter 7, we can calculate the standard error of the mean:

$$\sigma_{\bar{x}} = \frac{\sigma}{\sqrt{n}} \quad \textbf{[7-1]}$$

$$= \frac{10}{\sqrt{200}}$$

$$= \frac{10}{14.14}$$

$$= .707 \text{ months} \leftarrow \text{one standard error of the mean}$$

We could now report to the director that our estimate of the life of the company's batteries is 36 months, and the standard error that accompanies this estimate is .707. In other words, the actual mean life for all the batteries *may* lie somewhere in the interval estimate of from 35.293 to 36.707 months. This is helpful but insufficient information for the director. Next, we need to calculate the chance that the actual life will lie in this interval *or* in other intervals of different widths that we might choose, $\pm 2\sigma$ $(2 \times .707)$, $\pm 3\sigma$ $(3 \times .707)$, and so on.

Probability of the True Population Parameter Falling Within the Interval Estimate

To begin to solve this problem, we should review relevant parts of Chapter 6. There we worked with the normal probability distribution and learned that specific portions of the area under the normal curve are located between plus and minus any given number of standard deviations from the mean. In Fig. 6-12, we saw how to relate these portions to specific probabilities.

Finding the chance the mean will fall in this interval estimate

Fortunately, we can apply these properties to the standard error of the mean and make the following statement about the range of values in an interval estimate for our battery problem.

The probability is .955 that the mean of a sample size of 200 will be within plus and minus 2 standard errors of the population mean. Stated differently, 95.5 percent of all the sample means are within plus and minus 2 standard errors from μ, and hence **μ is within plus and minus 2 standard errors of 95.5 percent of all the sample means.** Theoretically, if we select 1,000 samples at random from a given population and then construct an interval of plus and minus 2 standard errors around the mean of each of these samples, about 955 of these intervals will include the population mean. Similarly, the probability is .683 that the mean of the sample will be within plus and minus 1 standard error of the population mean, and so forth. This theoretical concept is basic to our study of interval construction and of statistical inference. In Fig. 8-2, we have illustrated the concept graphically, showing five such intervals. Only the interval constructed around the sample mean $\bar{x}_4$ does not contain the population mean. In words, statisticians would describe the interval estimate represented in Fig. 8-2 by saying, "The

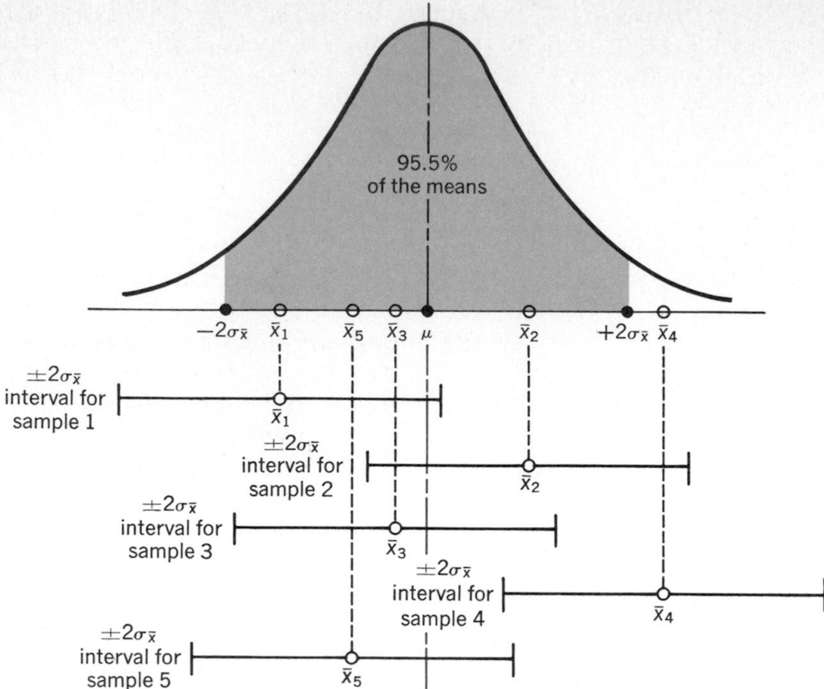

FIGURE 8-2
A number of intervals constructed around sample means; all except one include the population mean

population mean μ will be located within plus and minus 2 standard errors from the sample mean 95.5 percent of the time."

As far as any particular interval in Fig. 8-2 is concerned, it either contains the population mean or it does not, because the population mean is a fixed parameter and does not vary. Since we know that in 95.5 percent of all samples, the interval will contain the population mean, we say that we are 95.5 percent confident that the interval contains the population mean.

Applying this to the battery example, we can now report to the director. Our best estimate of the life of the company's batteries is 36 months, *and* we are 68.3 percent confident that the life lies in the interval from 35.293 to 36.707 months ($36 \pm 1\sigma_{\bar{x}}$). Similarly, we are 95.5 percent confident that the life falls within the interval of 34.586 to 37.414 months ($36 \pm 2\sigma_{\bar{x}}$), and we are 99.7 percent confident that battery life falls within the interval of 33.879 to 38.121 months ($36 \pm 3\sigma_{\bar{x}}$).

EXERCISES

8-12 From a population known to have a standard deviation of .9, a sample of 36 individuals is taken. The mean for this sample is found to be 9.6.

a) Find the standard error of the mean.
b) Establish an interval estimate around the mean, using one standard error of the mean.

8-13 The personnel manager for the California Citrus Company had been assigned the long-term objective of hiring younger workers. To monitor his progress, he needed to determine the mean age of the company's workers. He selected a sample of 81 employees from a population whose standard deviation is known to be 3.6. The mean for this sample turned out to be 24.5.

a) Find the standard error of the mean.
b) What is the interval around the sample mean that will include the population mean 95.5 percent of the time?

8-14 For a population with a known variance of 196, a sample of 49 leads to 210 as an estimate of the mean.

a) Find the standard error of the mean.
b) Establish an interval estimate that should include the population mean 68.3 percent of the time.

8-15 The owner of The Bard's Nook, a recently opened restaurant, has had difficulty estimating the quantity of food to be prepared for each evening. He decided to determine the mean number of customers served each night. He selected a sample of 25 nights, which resulted in a mean of 68. The population standard deviation has been established as 4.25.

a) Give an interval estimate that has a 68.3 percent probability of including the population mean.
b) Give an interval estimate that has a 99.7 percent chance of including the population mean.

8-16 The manager of the Neuse River Bridge is concerned about the number of cars "running" the toll gates and is considering altering the toll-collection procedure if such alteration would be cost-effective. She randomly sampled 100 hours to determine the rate of violation. The resulting average violations per hour was 6. If the population standard deviation is known to be .8, estimate an interval that has a 95.5 percent chance of containing the true mean.

8-17 Doug Thompson, an entrepreneur seeking new investment opportunities, studied the dating habits of young metropolitan adults in 36 randomly sampled cities and determined that an average of 36,000 per location frequented discotheques. He knows the standard deviation of this type of data to be 12,000.

a) Establish an interval estimate for the average number of disco goers, so that we are 68.3 percent certain that the population mean lies within this interval.
b) Establish an interval estimate for the average number of disco goers, so that we are 95.5 percent certain that the population mean lies within this interval.

8-18 The school board of Forsight County considers its most important task to be keeping the average class size in Forsight County schools less than the average class size in neighboring Hindsight County. Miss Dee Marks, the school superintendent for Forsight County, has just received reliable information indicating that the average class size in Hindsight County this year is 26.9 students. She does not yet have the figures for all 532 classes in her own school system, so Dee is forced to rely upon the 81 classes that have reported class sizes, yielding an average class size of 25.1 students. Dee knows that the class size of any Forsight County class has a distribution with unknown mean and standard deviation equal to 7.2 students. Assuming that the sample of size 81 that Miss Marks possesses is randomly chosen from the population of all Forsight County class sizes:

a) Find an interval that Dee can be 95.5 percent certain will contain the true mean.
b) Do you think that Dee has met her goal?

8-4 INTERVAL ESTIMATES AND CONFIDENCE INTERVALS

In using interval estimates, we are not confined to plus and minus 1, 2, and 3 standard errors. According to Appendix Table 1, for example, plus and minus 1.64 standard errors includes about 90 percent of the area under the curve; it includes .4495 of the area on either side of the mean in a normal distribution. Similarly, plus and minus 2.58 standard errors includes about 99 percent of the area, or 49.51 percent on each side of the mean.

Confidence level defined

In statistics, the probability that we associate with an interval estimate is called the confidence level. This probability, then, indicates how confident we are that the interval estimate will include the population parameter. A higher probability means more confidence. In estimation, the most commonly used confidence levels are 90 percent, 95 percent, and 99 percent, but we are free to apply *any* confidence level. In Fig. 8-2, for example, we used a 95.5 percent confidence level.

Confidence intervals and confidence limits

The confidence interval is the range of the estimate we are making. If we report that we are 90 percent confident that the mean of the population of incomes of persons in a certain community will lie between \$8,000 and \$24,000, then the range \$8,000–\$24,000 is our confidence interval. Often, however, we will express the confidence interval in standard errors rather than in numerical values. Thus, we will frequently express confidence intervals like this: $\bar{x} \pm 1.64\sigma_{\bar{x}}$, where:

$$\bar{x} + 1.64\sigma_{\bar{x}} = \text{upper limit of the confidence interval}$$

$$\bar{x} - 1.64\sigma_{\bar{x}} = \text{lower limit of the confidence interval}$$

Thus, confidence limits are the upper and lower limits of the confidence interval. In this case, $\bar{x} + 1.64\sigma_{\bar{x}}$ is called the *upper confidence limit,* and $\bar{x} - 1.64\sigma_{\bar{x}}$ is the *lower confidence limit.*

Relationship Between Confidence Level and Confidence Interval

The shortcoming of high confidence levels

You may think that we should use a high confidence level, such as 99 percent, in all estimation problems. After all, a high confidence level seems to signify a high degree of accuracy in the estimate. In practice, however, high confidence levels will produce large confidence intervals, and such large intervals are not precise; they give very fuzzy estimates.

Consider an appliance store customer who inquires about the delivery of a new washing machine. In Table 8-4 are several of the questions the customer might ask and the likely responses. This table indicates the direct relationship that exists between the confidence level and the confidence interval for any estimate. As the customer sets a tighter and tighter confidence interval, the store manager agrees to a lower and lower confidence level. Notice, too, that when the confidence interval is too wide, as is the case with a one-year delivery, the estimate may have little real value, even though the store manager attaches a 99 percent confidence level to that estimate. Similarly, if the confidence interval is too narrow ("Will my washing machine get home before I do?"), the estimate is associated with such a low confidence level (1 percent) that we question its value.

TABLE 8-4 Illustration of the relationship between confidence level and confidence interval

CUSTOMER'S QUESTION	STORE MANAGER'S RESPONSE	IMPLIED CONFIDENCE LEVEL	IMPLIED CONFIDENCE INTERVAL
Will I get my washing machine within 1 year?	I am absolutely certain of that.	Better than 99%	1 year
Will you deliver the washing machine within 1 month?	I am almost positive it will be delivered this month.	At least 95%	1 month
Will you deliver the washing machine within a week?	I am pretty certain it will go out within this week.	About 80%	1 week
Will I get my washing machine tomorrow?	I am not certain we can get it to you then.	About 40%	1 day
Will my washing machine get home before I do?	There is little chance it will beat you home.	Near 1%	1 hour

Using Sampling and Confidence Interval Estimation

Estimating from only one sample

In our discussion of the basic concepts of interval estimation, particularly in Fig. 8-2, we described samples being drawn repeatedly from a given population in order to estimate a population parameter. We also mentioned selecting a large number of sample means from a population. In practice, however, it is often difficult to take more than one sample from a population. Based on just one sample, we estimate the population parameter. We must be careful, then, about interpreting the results of such a process.

If we calculate from one sample in our battery example the following confidence interval and confidence level: "We are 95 percent confident that the mean battery life of the population lies within 30 and 42 months," **this statement does not mean that the chance is .95 that the mean life of all our batteries falls within the interval established from this one sample. Instead, it means that if we select many random samples of this sample size and if we calculate a confidence interval for each of these samples, then in about 95 percent of these cases, the population mean will lie within that interval.**

EXERCISES

8-19 Define the confidence level for an interval estimate.

8-20 Define the confidence interval.

8-21 Suppose you wish to use a confidence level of 80 percent. Give the upper limit of the confidence interval in terms of sample mean, $\bar{x}$, and the standard error, $\sigma_{\bar{x}}$.

8-22 In what way may an estimate be less meaningful because of:
a) A high confidence level? b) A narrow confidence interval?

8-23 Suppose that, using one random sample of 50 elements of a population, you have established a confidence interval of 70–90 around the sample mean, with a confidence level of 95 percent that the population mean falls within this interval. What statement can you make concerning the population mean if 99 other 50-element random samples are also taken from this population?

8-24 Is the confidence level for an estimate based on the interval constructed from 1 sample?

8-25 Given the following confidence levels, express the lower and upper limits of the confidence interval for these levels in terms of $\bar{x}$ and $\sigma_{\bar{x}}$.
a) 50% b) 75% c) 85% c) 98%

8-26 Steve Klippers, the owner of Steve's Barbershop, has built quite a reputation among the residents of Cullowhee. As each customer enters his barbershop, Steve yells out the number of minutes that the customer can expect to wait before getting his haircut. The only statistician in town, after being frustrated by Steve's inaccurate point estimates, has determined that the actual waiting time for any customer is normally distributed with mean equal to Steve's estimate in minutes and standard deviation equal to 6 minutes divided by the customer's position in the waiting line. Help Steve's customers develop 95 percent probability intervals for the following situations:
a) The customer is third in line, and Steve's estimate is 30 minutes.
b) The customer is first in line, and Steve's estimate is 12 minutes.
c) The customer is fourth in line, and Steve's estimate is 35 minutes.
d) The customer is second in line, and Steve's estimate is 18 minutes.
How are these intervals different from confidence intervals?

8-5 CALCULATING INTERVAL ESTIMATES OF THE MEAN FROM LARGE SAMPLES

Finding a 95 percent confidence interval

A large automotive-parts wholesaler needs an estimate of the mean life it can expect from windshield wiper blades under typical driving conditions. Already, management has determined that the standard deviation of the population life is six months. When we select a simple random sample of 100 wiper blades and collect data on their useful lives, we obtain these results:

$n = 100 \leftarrow$ sample size

$\bar{x} = 21$ months $\leftarrow$ sample mean

$\sigma = 6$ months $\leftarrow$ population standard deviation

Since the wholesaler uses tens of thousands of these wiper blades annually, it requests that we find an interval estimate with a confidence level of 95 percent. Since the sample size is greater than 30, we can use the normal distribution as our sampling distribution and calculate the standard error of the mean by using Equation 7-1:

$$\sigma_{\bar{x}} = \frac{\sigma}{\sqrt{n}} \qquad [7\text{-}1]$$

$$= \frac{6 \text{ months}}{\sqrt{100}}$$

$$= \frac{6}{10}$$

$$= .6 \text{ months} \leftarrow \text{standard error of the mean for an infinite population}$$

Next, we consider the confidence level with which we are working. Since a 95 percent confidence level will include 47.5 percent of the area on either side of the mean of the sampling distribution, we can search in the body of Appendix Table 1 for the .475 value. We discover that .475 of the area under the normal curve is contained between the mean and a point 1.96 standard errors to the right of the mean. Therefore, we know that (2)(.475) = .95 of the area is located between plus and minus 1.96 standard errors from the mean and that our confidence limits are:

$$\bar{x} + 1.96\sigma_{\bar{x}} \leftarrow \text{upper confidence limit}$$

$$\bar{x} - 1.96\sigma_{\bar{x}} \leftarrow \text{lower confidence limit}$$

Then we substitute numerical values into these two expressions:

$$\begin{aligned} \bar{x} + 1.96\sigma_{\bar{x}} &= 21 \text{ months} + 1.96(.6 \text{ months}) \\ &= 21 + 1.18 \text{ months} \\ &= 22.18 \text{ months} \leftarrow \text{upper confidence limit} \end{aligned}$$

$$\begin{aligned} \bar{x} - 1.96\sigma_{\bar{x}} &= 21 \text{ months} - 1.96(.6 \text{ months}) \\ &= 21 - 1.18 \text{ months} \\ &= 19.82 \text{ months} \leftarrow \text{lower confidence limit} \end{aligned}$$

We can now report that we estimate the mean life of the population of wiper blades to be between 19.82 and 22.18 months with 95 percent confidence.

When the Population Standard Deviation Is Unknown

Finding a 90 percent confidence interval

A more complex interval estimate problem comes from a social-service agency in a local government. It is interested in estimating the mean annual income of 700 families living in a four-square-block section of a community. We take a simple random sample and find these results:

$n = 50 \leftarrow$ sample size

$\bar{x} = \$4{,}800 \leftarrow$ sample mean

$s = \$950 \leftarrow$ sample standard deviation

The agency asks us to calculate an interval estimate of the mean annual income of all 700 families so that it can be 90 percent confident that the population means falls within that interval. Since the sample size is over 30, we can use the normal distribution as the sampling distribution.

Estimating the population standard deviation

Notice that one part of this problem differs from our previous examples: we do *not* know the population standard deviation, and so we will use the sample standard deviation to estimate the *population standard deviation:*

Estimate of the population standard deviation $\rightarrow$

$$\hat{\sigma} = s = \sqrt{\frac{\Sigma(x - \bar{x})^2}{n - 1}} \qquad \textbf{[8-1]}$$

The value \$950.00 is our estimate of the standard deviation of the population. We can also symbolize this *estimated* value by $\hat{\sigma}$, which is called *sigma hat.*

Now we can estimate the standard error of the mean. Since we have a finite population size of 700, we will use the formula for deriving the standard error of the mean of finite populations:

$$\sigma_{\bar{x}} = \frac{\sigma}{\sqrt{n}} \times \sqrt{\frac{N - n}{N - 1}} \qquad \textbf{[7-3]}$$

Estimating the standard error of the mean

But since we are calculating the standard error of the mean using an *estimate* of the standard deviation of the population, we rewrite this equation so that it is correct symbolically:

Symbol that indicates an estimated value

Estimate of the population standard deviation

$$\hat{\sigma}_{\bar{x}} = \frac{\hat{\sigma}}{\sqrt{n}} \times \sqrt{\frac{N - n}{N - 1}} \qquad \textbf{[8-2]}$$

$$= \frac{\$950.00}{\sqrt{50}} \times \sqrt{\frac{700 - 50}{700 - 1}}$$

$$= \frac{\$950.00}{7.07} \sqrt{\frac{650}{699}}$$

$$= \$134.37\ \sqrt{.9299}$$

$= (\$134.37)(.9643)$

$= \$129.57 \leftarrow$ estimate of the standard error of the mean of a finite population (derived from an *estimate* of the population standard deviation)

Next we consider the 90 percent confidence level, which would include 45 percent of the area on either side of the mean of the sampling distribution. Looking in the body of Appendix Table 1 for the .45 value, we find that about .45 of the area under the normal curve is located between the mean and a point 1.64 standard errors from the mean. Therefore, 90 percent of the area is located between plus *and* minus 1.64 standard errors from the mean, and our confidence limits are:

$$\begin{aligned} \bar{x} + 1.64\sigma_{\bar{x}} &= \$4{,}800 + 1.64(\$129.57) \\ &= \$4{,}800 + \$212.50 \\ &= \$5{,}012.50 \leftarrow \text{upper confidence limit} \end{aligned}$$

$$\begin{aligned} \bar{x} - 1.64\sigma_{\bar{x}} &= \$4{,}800 - 1.64(\$129.57) \\ &= \$4{,}800 - \$212.50 \\ &= \$4{,}587.50 \leftarrow \text{lower confidence limit} \end{aligned}$$

Our report to the social-service agency would be: With 90 percent confidence, we estimate that the average annual income of all 700 families living in this four-square-block section falls between \$4,587.50 and \$5,012.50.

EXERCISES

8-27 The VP of sales for The National Food Company must project total sales expenses for the upcoming year. This entails determining the mean number of miles salespeople travel per day. A sample of 64 salespeople yielded a mean of 120 miles. The population's standard deviation is 12.

a) Compute the standard error of the mean.

b) Construct a 90 percent confidence interval for the true population mean.

8-28 Upon collecting a sample of size 100 from a population with known standard deviation of 4.96, the mean is found to be 68.4.

a) Find a 95 percent confidence interval for the mean.

b) Find a 99 percent confidence interval for the mean.

8-29 Dave Lonquest, owner of Sureflite Golf, has utilized a new club-casting process to produce a special limited production run of 1,800 five-irons. Before he can set a price for the club, Lonquest must determine its percentage increase in performance. A sample of 145 clubs drove balls 25 percent farther on the average than his other clubs did, and the standard deviation was 7.2 percent.

a) Calculate the estimated standard error of the mean.

b) Construct a 90 percent confidence interval for the mean.

8-30 From a population of size 240, a sample of 49 individuals is taken. From this sample, the mean is found to be 15.8 and the standard deviation 4.2.

a) Find the estimated standard error of the mean.

b) Construct a 98 percent confidence interval for the mean.

8-31 In an automotive safety test conducted by the North Carolina Highway Safety Research Center, the average tire pressure in a sample of 81 tires was found to be 26 pounds per square inch, and the standard deviation was 1.8 pounds per square inch.

a) Calculate the estimated population standard deviation for this population. (There are about a million cars registered in North Carolina.)
b) Calculate the estimated standard error of the mean.
c) Construct a 90 percent confidence interval for the population mean.

8-32 The financial controller for Home Electronics is concerned about rising personnel costs. Recruiting expenses appear to be too high, and the controller suspects that an undue number of applicants are being examined for each new position. From the recently filled positions, he sampled 36 and learned that the mean number of applicants interviewed for each position was 38, with a standard deviation of 4.5. Construct a 95 percent confidence interval for the mean number of applicants screened for each new job at Home Electronics.

8-33 Christopher Chambers, the chief accountant for the Airtight Insulation Company, believes that the company's 1,500 small accounts are not providing enough revenue to justify their administrative costs. Chambers sampled 36 small accounts. Their mean revenue was $1,800 with a sample standard deviation of $150.

a) Estimate the population standard deviation from the sample standard deviation.
b) Estimate the standard error of the mean for this finite population.
c) Construct a 98 percent confidence interval for the mean revenue of small accounts.

8-34 Chief of Police Kathy Ackert has recently instituted a crackdown on drug dealers in her city. Since the crackdown began, 625 of the 10,001 drug dealers in the city have been caught. The mean dollar value of drugs found on these 625 dealers is $200,000. The standard deviation of the dollar value of drugs for these 625 dealers is $40,000. Construct for Chief Ackert a 95 percent confidence interval for the mean dollar value of drugs possessed by the city's drug dealers.

8-6 CALCULATING INTERVAL ESTIMATES OF THE PROPORTION FROM LARGE SAMPLES

Statisticians often use a sample to estimate a *proportion* of occurrences in a population. For example, the government estimates by a sampling procedure the unemployment rate, or the proportion of unemployed persons, in the U.S. work force.

Review of the binomial distribution

In Chapter 6, we introduced the binomial distribution, a distribution of discrete, not continuous, data. Also, we presented the two formulas for deriving the mean and the standard deviation of the binomial distribution:

$$\mu = np \qquad \textbf{[6-2]}$$

$$\sigma = \sqrt{npq} \qquad \textbf{[6-3]}$$

where:

- n = number of trials
- p = probability of a success
- q = probability of a failure found by taking $1 - p$

Theoretically, the binomial distribution is the correct distribution to use in constructing confidence intervals to estimate a population proportion.

Shortcomings of the binomial distribution

Because the computation of binomial probabilities is so tedious (recall that the probability of r successes in n trials is $[n!/r!(n-r)!][p^r q^{n-r}]$), using the binomial distribution to form interval estimates of a population proportion is a complex proposition. Fortunately, as the sample size increases, the binomial can be approximated by an appropriate normal distribution, which we can use to approximate the sampling distribution. Statisticians recommend that in estimation, n be large enough for both np and nq to be at least 5 when you use the normal distribution as a substitute for the binomial.

Finding the mean and variance of the sample proportion

Symbolically, let's express the proportion of successes in a sample by $\bar{p}$ (pronounced *p-bar*). Then modify Equation 6-2, so that we can use it to derive the *mean of the sampling distribution of the proportion of successes.* In words, $\mu = np$ shows that the mean of the binomial distribution is equal to the product of the number of trials, n, and the probability of success, p; that is, np equals the mean number of successes. To change this *number* of successes to the *proportion* of successes, we divide np by n and get p alone. The mean in the left-hand side of the equation becomes $\mu_{\bar{p}}$, or the mean of the sampling distribution of the proportion of successes:

$$\mu_{\bar{p}} = p \qquad \textbf{[8-3]}$$

Similarly, we can modify the formula for the standard deviation of the binomial distribution, $\sqrt{npq}$, which measures the standard deviation in the number of successes. To change number of successes to proportion of successes, we divide $\sqrt{npq}$ by n and get $\sqrt{pq/n}$. In statistical terms, the standard deviation for the proportion of successes in a sample is symbolized:

Standard error of the proportion →

$$\sigma_{\bar{p}} = \sqrt{\frac{pq}{n}} \qquad \textbf{[8-4]}$$

and is called the *standard error of the proportion*

When the Population Proportion Is Unknown

We can illustrate how to use these formulas if we estimate for a very large organization what proportion of the employees prefer to provide their own retirement benefits in lieu of a company sponsored plan. First, we conduct a simple random sample of 75 employees and find that .4 of them are interested in providing their own retirement plan. Our results are:

$n = 75$ ← sample size

$\bar{p} = .4$ ← sample proportion in favor

$\bar{q} = .6$ ← sample proportion not in favor

Next, management requests that we use this sample to find an interval about which they can be 99 percent confident that it contains the true population proportion.

Estimating a population proportion

But what are p and q for the *population?* We can estimate the population parameters by substituting the corresponding sample statistics $\bar{p}$ and $\bar{q}$ (*p-bar* and *q-bar*) in the formula for the standard error of the proportion.* Doing this, we get:

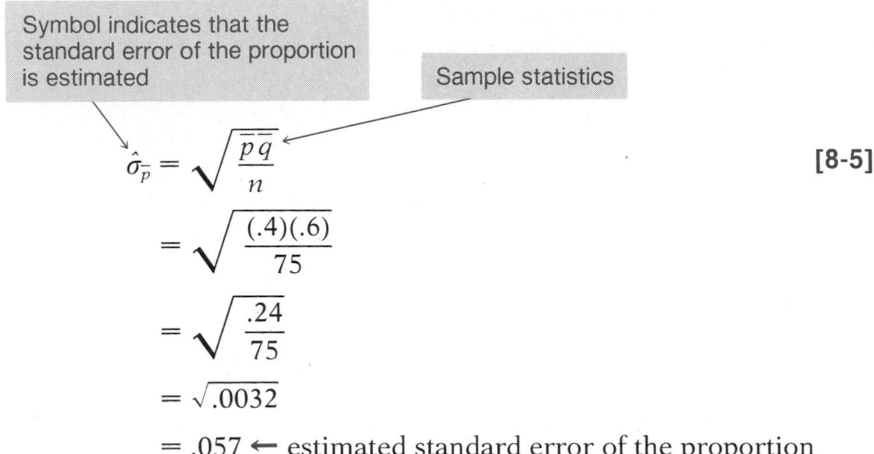

$$\hat{\sigma}_{\bar{p}} = \sqrt{\frac{\bar{p}\bar{q}}{n}} \qquad [8\text{-}5]$$

$$= \sqrt{\frac{(.4)(.6)}{75}}$$

$$= \sqrt{\frac{.24}{75}}$$

$$= \sqrt{.0032}$$

$$= .057 \leftarrow \text{estimated standard error of the proportion}$$

Computing the confidence limits

Now we can provide the estimate management needs by using the same procedure we have used previously. A 99 percent confidence level would include 49.5 percent of the area on either side of the mean in the sampling distribution. The body of Appendix Table 1 tells us that .495 of the area under the normal curve is located between the mean and a point 2.58 standard errors from the mean. Thus, 99 percent of the area is contained between plus *and* minus 2.58 standard errors from the mean. Our confidence limits then become:

$$\begin{aligned} \bar{p} + 2.58\hat{\sigma}_{\bar{p}} &= .4 + 2.58(.057) \\ &= .4 + .147 \\ &= .547 \leftarrow \text{upper confidence limit} \end{aligned}$$

$$\begin{aligned} \bar{p} - 2.58\hat{\sigma}_{\bar{p}} &= .4 - 2.58(.057) \\ &= .4 - .147 \\ &= .253 \leftarrow \text{lower confidence limit} \end{aligned}$$

Thus, we estimate from our sample of 75 employees that with 99 percent confidence we believe that the proportion of the total population of employees who wish to establish their own retirement plans lies between .253 and .547.

* Notice that we do not use the finite population multiplier, because our population is so large compared with the sample size.

EXERCISES

8-35 Jack B. Craven, chief executive officer for the brokerage firm Craven, Craven, and Craven, surveyed 100 of his clients and learned that 60 percent were extremely satisfied with the firm's service.

a) Estimate the standard error of the proportion of clients extremely satisfied.

b) Construct a 98 percent confidence interval for the proportion of clients extremely satisfied with Craven's service.

8-36 When a sample of 64 retail executives were surveyed regarding the poor November performance of the retail industry, 72 percent believed that decreased sales were due to unseasonably warm temperatures, resulting in consumers delaying purchase of cold-weather items.

a) Estimate the standard error of the proportion of retail executives who blame warm weather for low sales.

b) Find the upper and lower confidence limits for this proportion, given a confidence level equal to .90.

8-37 The product manager for the new lemon-lime Clear 'n Light dessert topping was worried about both the product's poor performance and her future with Clear 'n Light. Concerned that her marketing strategy had not properly identified the attributes of the product, she sampled 1,200 consumers and learned that 780 thought that the product was a floor wax.

a) Estimate the standard error of the proportion of people holding this severe misconception.

b) Construct a 95 percent confidence interval for the true population proportion.

8-38 The vice-president of production for McCormick Tires determined that the production costs for the company's new radials were running over budget. In an effort to target the reasons, he sampled 500 workers and learned that 36 percent were lower on the learning curve than he had expected.

a) Estimate the standard error of the proportion.

b) Construct a 90 percent confidence interval for the true proportion.

8-39 In the examination of 400 salespeople at a national sales convention, 64 were found to exhibit the classic symptoms of ego distortion.

a) Estimate the standard error of the proportion.

b) Construct a 99 percent confidence interval for the true proportion.

8-40 The owner of the Home Loan Company randomly surveyed 120 of the company's 2,500 accounts and determined that 72 percent were in excellent standing.

a) Find a 95 percent confidence interval for the proportion in excellent standing.

b) Based on part a, what kind of interval estimate might you give for the absolute number of accounts that meet the requirement of excellence, keeping the same 95 percent confidence level?

8-41 For a year and a half now, sales have been falling consistently in all 1,200 franchises of a fast-food chain. A consulting firm has determined that 45 percent of a sample of 64 indicate clear signs of mismanagement. Construct a 95 percent confidence interval for this proportion.

8-42 By randomly surveying 49 of *Fortune* magazine's list of the 500 largest companies, consultant Milton S. Hulme discovered that 80 percent displayed basic management policies roughly equivalent to those taught in most reputable M.B.A. programs. Give the upper and lower limits for a 96 percent confidence interval for the proportion of *Fortune*'s 500 companies employing M.B.A. management techniques.

8-43 Barry Turnbull, the noted Wall Street analyst, is interested in knowing the proportion of individual stockholders who are planning on selling at least one-quarter of all their stock in the next month. Barry has conducted a random survey of 900 individuals who hold stock and has learned that 20 percent of his sample plan to sell at least one-quarter of all their stock in the next month. Barry is about to issue his much-anticipated monthly report, "The Wall Street Pulse—the Tape's Ticker," and would like to be able to report a confidence interval to his subscribers. He is more worried about being correct than he is about the width of the interval. Construct a 99 percent confidence interval for the true proportion of individual stockholders who plan to sell at least one-quarter of their stock during the next month.

8-7 INTERVAL ESTIMATES USING THE *t* DISTRIBUTION

In our three examples so far, the sample sizes were all larger than 30. We sampled 100 windshield wiper blades, 50 families living in a four-square-block section of a community, and 75 employees of a very large organization. Each time, the normal distribution was the appropriate sampling distribution to use to determine confidence intervals.

However, this is not always the case. How can we handle estimates where the normal distribution is *not* the appropriate sampling distribution; that is, when we are estimating the population standard deviation and the sample size is 30 or less? For example, in our chapter-opening problem of coal usage, we had data from only ten weeks. Fortunately, another distribution exists that is appropriate in these cases. It is called the *t distribution*.

Background of the *t* distribution

Early theoretical work on *t* distributions was done by a man named W.S. Gossett in the early 1900s. Gossett was employed by the Guinness Brewery in Dublin, Ireland, which did not permit employees to publish research findings under their own names. So Gossett adopted the pen name "Student" and published under that name. Consequently, the *t* distribution is commonly called *Student's t distribution*, or simply *Student's distribution*.

Conditions for using the *t* distribution

Since it is used when the sample size is 30 or less, statisticians often associate the *t* distribution with small sample statistics. This is misleading, because the size of the sample is only *one* of the conditions that lead us to use the *t* distribution. The second condition is that the population standard deviation must be unknown. **Use of the *t* distribution for estimating is required whenever the sample size is 30 or less and the population standard deviation is not known. Furthermore, in using the *t* distribution, we assume that the population is normal or approximately normal.**

Characteristics of the *t* Distribution

t distribution compared to normal distribution

Without deriving the *t* distribution mathematically, we can gain an intuitive understanding of the relationship between the *t* distribution and the *normal* distribution. Both are symmetrical. In general, the *t* distribution is flatter than the normal distribution, and there is a different *t* distribution for every possible sample size. Even so, as the sample size gets larger, the shape of the *t* distribution loses its flatness and becomes approximately equal to the normal distribution. In fact, for sample sizes of more than 30, the *t* distribution is so close to the normal distribution that we will use the normal to approximate the *t*.

Figure 8-3 compares one normal distribution with two *t* distributions of different sample sizes. This figure shows two characteristics of *t* distributions: **a *t* distribution is lower at the mean and higher at the tails than a normal distribution.** The figure also demonstrates how the *t* distribution has proportionally more of its area in its tails than the normal does. This is the reason why it will be necessary to go farther out from the mean of

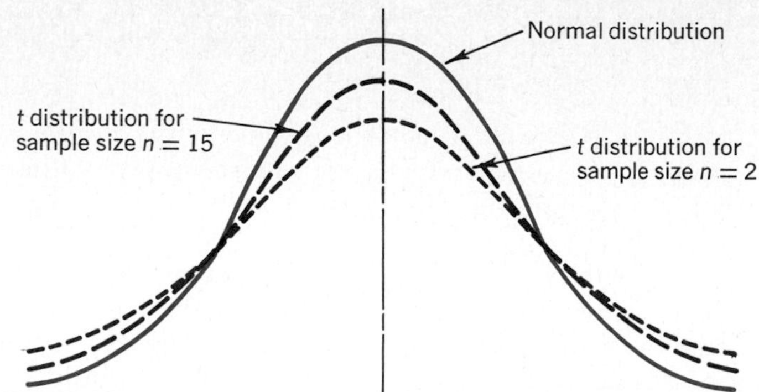

FIGURE 8-3 Normal distribution, t distribution for sample size $n = 15$, and t distribution for sample size $n = 2$

a t distribution to include the same area under the curve. Interval widths from t distributions are, therefore, wider than those based on the normal distribution.

Degrees of Freedom

Degrees of freedom defined

We said earlier that there is a separate t distribution for each sample size. In proper statistical language, we would say, "There is a different t distribution for each of the possible *degrees of freedom*." **What are degrees of freedom? We can define them as the number of values we can choose freely.**

Assume that we are dealing with two sample values, a and b, and we know that they have a mean of 18. Symbolically, the situation is:

$$\frac{a+b}{2} = 18$$

How can we find what values a and b can take on in this situation? The answer is that a and b can be any two values whose sum is 36, because $36 \div 2 = 18$.

Suppose we learn that a has a value of 10. Now b is no longer free to take on any value but *must* have the value of 26, because:

$$\begin{array}{rr} \text{if} & a = 10 \\ & \dfrac{10+b}{2} = 18 \\ \text{so} & 10 + b = 36 \\ \text{therefore} & b = 26 \end{array}$$

This example shows that when there are two elements in a sample and we know the sample mean of these two elements, we are free to specify only one of the elements, because the other element will be determined by the fact that the two elements sum to twice the sample mean. Statisticians say, "We have one degree of freedom."

Another example

Look at another example. There are seven elements in our sample, and we learn that the mean of these elements is 16. Symbolically, we have this situation:

$$\frac{a+b+c+d+e+f+g}{7} = 16$$

In this case, the degrees of freedom, or the number of variables we can specify freely, are $7 - 1 = 6$. We are free to give values to six variables, and then we are no longer free to specify the seventh variable. It is determined automatically.

With two sample values, we had one degree of freedom ($2 - 1 = 1$), and with seven sample values, we had six degrees of freedom. In each of these two examples, then, we had $n - 1$ degrees of freedom, assuming n is the sample size. Similarly, a sample of 23 would give us 22 degrees of freedom.

Function of degrees of freedom

We will use degrees of freedom when we select a t distribution to estimate a population mean, and we will use $n - 1$ degrees of freedom, letting n equal the sample size. If, for example, we use a sample of 20 to estimate a population mean, we will use nineteen degrees of freedom in order to select the appropriate t distribution.

Using the *t* Distribution Table

t table compared to *z* table: 3 differences

The table of t distribution values (Appendix Table 2) differs in construction from the z table we have used previously. **The *t* table is more compact and shows areas and *t* values for only a few percentages (10, 5, 2, and 1 percent).** Since there is a different t distribution for each number of degrees of freedom, a more complete table would be quite lengthy. Although we can conceive of the need for a more complete table, in fact Appendix Table 2 contains all the commonly used values of the t distribution.

A second difference in the *t* table is that it does *not* focus on the chance that the population parameter being estimated will fall *within* our confidence interval. Instead, it measures the chance that the population parameter we are estimating will *not* be within our confidence interval (that is, that it will lie *outside* it). If we are making an estimate at the 90 percent confidence level, we would look in the t table under the .10 column (100 percent − 90 percent = 10 percent). This .10 chance of error is symbolized by α, which is the Greek letter *alpha*. We would find the appropriate t values for confidence intervals of 95 percent, 98 percent, and 99 percent under the α columns headed .05, .02, and .01, respectively.

A third difference in using the *t* table is that we must specify the degrees of freedom with which we are dealing. Suppose we make an estimate at the 90 percent confidence level with a sample size of 14, which is thirteen degrees of freedom. Look in Appendix Table 2 under the .10 column until you encounter the row labeled 13 *df* (degrees of freedom). Like a z value, the t value there of 1.771 shows that if we mark off plus and minus 1.771 $\hat{\sigma}_{\bar{x}}$'s (estimated standard errors of $\bar{x}$) on either side of the mean, the area under the curve between these two limits will be 90 percent, and the area outside these limits (the chance of error) will be 10 percent (see Fig. 8-4).

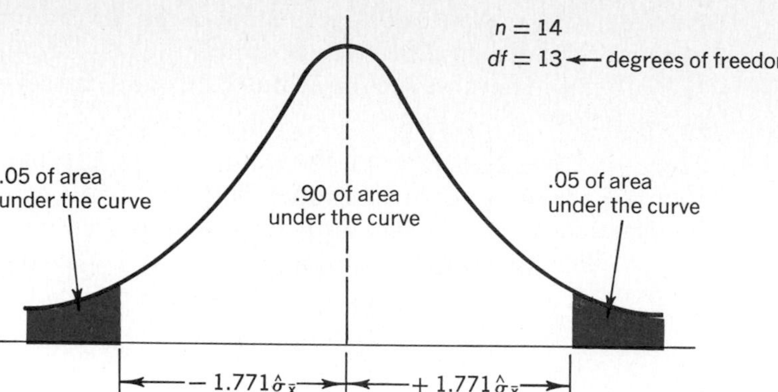

FIGURE 8-4 A t distribution for 13 degrees of freedom, showing a 90 percent confidence interval

Recall that in our chapter-opening problem, the generating plant manager wanted to estimate the coal needed for this year, and he took a sample by measuring coal usage for ten weeks. The sample data are summarized below:

$n = 10$ weeks ← sample size
$df = 9$ ← degrees of freedom
$\bar{x} = 11{,}400$ tons ← sample mean
$s = 700$ tons ← sample standard deviation

Using the t table to compute confidence limits

The plant manager wants an interval estimate of the mean coal consumption, and he wants to be 95 percent confident that the mean consumption falls within that interval. **This problem requires the use of a t distribution, because the sample size is less than 30 and the population standard deviation is unknown.**

As a first step in solving this problem, recall that we *estimate* the population standard deviation with the sample standard deviation; thus:

$$\hat{\sigma} = s \qquad \textbf{[8-1]}$$
$$= 700 \text{ tons}$$

Using this estimate of the population standard deviation, we can estimate the standard error of the mean by modifying Equation 8-2 to omit the finite population multiplier (because the population of days is infinite):

$$\hat{\sigma}_{\bar{x}} = \frac{\hat{\sigma}}{\sqrt{n}} \qquad \textbf{[8-6]}$$
$$= \frac{700}{\sqrt{10}}$$
$$= \frac{700}{3.162}$$
$$= 221.38 \text{ tons} \leftarrow \text{estimated standard error of the mean of an infinite population}$$

Now we look in Appendix Table 2 down the .05 column (100 percent − 95 percent = 5 percent) until we encounter the row of nine degrees of freedom (10 − 1 = 9). There we see the t value 2.262 and can set our confidence limits accordingly:

$$\begin{aligned} \bar{x} + 2.262\hat{\sigma}_{\bar{x}} &= 11{,}400 \text{ tons} + 2.262(221.38 \text{ tons}) \\ &= 11{,}400 + 500.76 \\ &= 11{,}901 \text{ tons} \leftarrow \text{upper confidence limit} \end{aligned}$$

$$\begin{aligned} \bar{x} - 2.262\hat{\sigma}_{\bar{x}} &= 11{,}400 \text{ tons} - 2.262(221.38 \text{ tons}) \\ &= 11{,}400 - 500.76 \\ &= 10{,}899 \text{ tons} \leftarrow \text{lower confidence limit} \end{aligned}$$

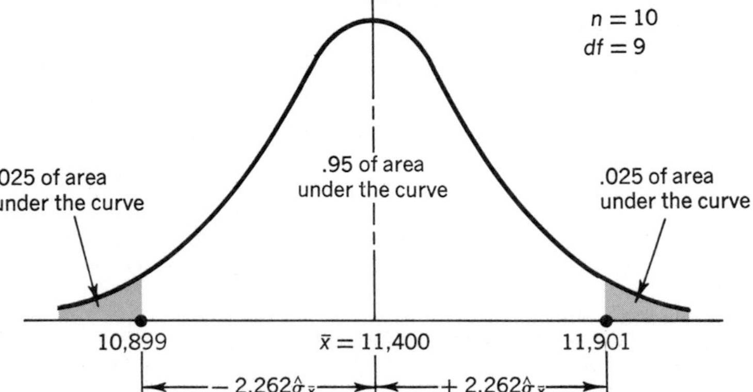

FIGURE 8-5 Coal problem: a t distribution with 9 degrees of freedom and a confidence interval of 95 percent

We can report to the plant manager with 95 percent confidence that the mean weekly usage of coal lies between 10,899 and 11,901 tons, and we can use the 11,901-ton figure to estimate how much coal to order.

The only difference between the process we used to make this coal-usage estimate and the previous estimating problems is the use of the t distribution as the appropriate distribution. **Remember that in any estimation problem in which the sample size is 30 or less *and* the standard deviation of the population is unknown, we use the t distribution.**

Summary of Confidence Limits Under Various Conditions

Table 8-5 summarizes the various approaches to estimation introduced in this chapter and the confidence limits appropriate for each.

EXERCISES

8-44 For the following sample sizes and confidence levels, find the appropriate t values for constructing confidence intervals:

a) $n = 5$; 99%
b) $n = 18$; 99%
c) $n = 27$; 95%
d) $n = 16$; 95%
e) $n = 18$; 95%
f) $n = 14$; 90%

TABLE 8-5 Summary of formulas for confidence limits estimating mean and proportion

	WHEN THE POPULATION IS FINITE	WHEN THE POPULATION IS INFINITE
Estimating μ (the population mean): When σ (the population standard deviation) is known	upper limit: $\bar{x} + z\frac{\sigma}{\sqrt{n}} \times \sqrt{\frac{N-n}{N-1}}$	$\bar{x} + z\frac{\sigma}{\sqrt{n}}$
	lower limit: $\bar{x} - z\frac{\sigma}{\sqrt{n}} \times \sqrt{\frac{N-n}{N-1}}$	$\bar{x} - z\frac{\sigma}{\sqrt{n}}$
When σ (the population standard deviation) is not known [$\hat{\sigma} = s$] **When n (the sample size) is larger than 30**	upper limit: $\bar{x} + z\frac{\hat{\sigma}}{\sqrt{n}} \times \sqrt{\frac{N-n}{N-1}}$	$\bar{x} + z\frac{\hat{\sigma}}{\sqrt{n}}$
	lower limit: $\bar{x} - z\frac{\hat{\sigma}}{\sqrt{n}} \times \sqrt{\frac{N-n}{N-1}}$	$\bar{x} - z\frac{\hat{\sigma}}{\sqrt{n}}$
When n (the sample size) is 30 or less*	upper limit: $\bar{x} + t\frac{\hat{\sigma}}{\sqrt{n}} \times \sqrt{\frac{N-n}{N-1}}$	$\bar{x} + t\frac{\hat{\sigma}}{\sqrt{n}}$
	lower limit: $\bar{x} - t\frac{\hat{\sigma}}{\sqrt{n}} \times \sqrt{\frac{N-n}{N-1}}$	$\bar{x} - t\frac{\hat{\sigma}}{\sqrt{n}}$
Estimating p (the population proportion): When n (the sample size) is larger than 30	upper limit: $\bar{p} + z\hat{\sigma}_{\bar{p}} \times \sqrt{\frac{N-n}{N-1}}$	$\bar{p} + z\hat{\sigma}_{\bar{p}}$
$\left[\hat{\sigma}_{\bar{p}} = \sqrt{\frac{\bar{p}\bar{q}}{n}}\right]$	lower limit: $\bar{p} - z\hat{\sigma}_{\bar{p}} \times \sqrt{\frac{N-n}{N-1}}$	$\bar{p} - z\hat{\sigma}_{\bar{p}}$

* Remember that the appropriate t distribution to use is the one with $n - 1$ degrees of freedom.

8-45 Given the following sample sizes and t values used to construct confidence intervals, find the corresponding confidence levels:
a) $n = 20$; $t = \pm 1.729$ b) $n = 12$; $t = \pm 2.201$ c) $n = 7$; $t = \pm 3.707$

8-46 Sandra Cummings, the financial manager of the Fike Lumber Company, wanted to evaluate the receivables collection policy she had recently implemented. She sampled 24 accounts, and the average collection period was 27.3 days, with a standard deviation of 1.9. Construct a 98 percent confidence interval for the mean of the population.

8-47 A sample of size 15 had a mean of 56 and a standard deviation of 12. Construct a 95 percent confidence interval for the population mean.

8-48 The following sample of 8 observations is from an infinite population:

12.1 11.9 12.4 12.3 11.9 12.1 12.4 12.1

a) Find the mean.
b) Estimate the population standard deviation.
c) Construct a 90 percent confidence interval for the mean.

8-49 Six housewives were randomly sampled, and it was determined that they walked an average of 34.6 miles per week in their housework, with a sample deviation of 2.8 miles per week. Construct a 95 percent confidence interval for the population mean.

8-50 State senator Hanna Rowe has ordered an investigation of the large number of boating accidents that have occurred in the state in recent summers. Acting upon her instructions, her aide, Geoff Spencer, has randomly selected 8 summer months within the last few years and has compiled data on the number of boating accidents that occurred during each of these months. The mean number of boating accidents to occur in these 8 months was 35, and the standard deviation in this sample was 10 boating accidents per month. Geoff was told to construct a 90 percent confidence interval for the true mean number of boating accidents per month, but he was in such an accident himself recently, so you will have to do this for him.

8-8 DETERMINING THE SAMPLE SIZE IN ESTIMATION

In all our discussions so far, we have used for sample size the symbol n instead of a specific number. Now we need to know how to determine what number to use. How large should the sample be? If it is too small, we may fail to achieve the objectives of our analysis. But if it is too large, we waste resources when we gather the sample.

What sample size is adequate?

Some sampling error will arise because we have not studied the whole population. Whenever we sample, we always miss *some* helpful information about the population. If we want a high level of precision (that is, if we want to be quite sure of our estimate), we have to sample enough of the population to provide the required information. Sampling error is controlled by selecting a sample that is adequate in size. In general, the more precision you want, the larger the sample you will need to take. Let us examine some methods that are useful in determining what sample size is necessary for any specified level of precision.

Sample Size for Estimating a Mean

Suppose a university is performing a survey of the annual earnings of last year's graduates from its business school. It knows from past experience that the standard deviation of the annual earnings of the entire population (1,000) of these graduates is about $1,500. How large a sample size should the university take in order to estimate the mean annual earnings of last year's class within plus and minus $500 and at a 95 percent confidence level?

Two ways to express a confidence limit

Exactly what is this problem asking? The university is going to take a sample of *some* size, determine the mean of the sample, $\bar{x}$, and use it as a point estimate of the population mean. It wants to be 95 percent certain that the true mean annual earnings of last year's class are not more than $500 above or below the point estimate. Row *a* in Table 8-6 summarizes in symbolic terms how the university is defining its confidence limits for us. Row *b* shows symbolically how we normally express confidence limits for an infinite population. When we compare these two sets of confidence limits, we can see that:

$$z\sigma_{\bar{x}} = \$500$$

TABLE 8-6 Comparison of two ways of expressing the same confidence limits

LOWER CONFIDENCE LIMIT	UPPER CONFIDENCE LIMIT
a. $\bar{x} - \$500$	a. $\bar{x} + \$500$
b. $\bar{x} - z\sigma_{\bar{x}}$	b. $\bar{x} + z\sigma_{\bar{x}}$

Thus, the university is actually saying that it wants $z\sigma_{\bar{x}}$ to be equal to \$500. If we look in Appendix Table 1, we find that the necessary z value for a 95 percent confidence level is 1.96. Step by step:

$$\text{If } z\sigma_{\bar{x}} = \$500$$

$$\text{and } z = 1.96$$

$$\text{then } 1.96\,\sigma_{\bar{x}} = \$500$$

$$\text{and } \sigma_{\bar{x}} = \frac{\$500}{1.96}$$

$$= \$255 \leftarrow \text{standard error of the mean}$$

Remember that the formula for the standard error is Equation 7-1:

$$\sigma_{\bar{x}} = \frac{\sigma \leftarrow \text{Population standard deviation}}{\sqrt{n}} \quad [7\text{-}1]$$

Finding an adequate sample size

Using Equation 7-1, we can substitute our known population standard deviation value of \$1,500 and our calculated standard error value of \$255 and solve for n:

$$\sigma_{\bar{x}} = \frac{\sigma}{\sqrt{n}} \quad [7\text{-}1]$$

$$\$255 = \frac{\$1{,}500}{\sqrt{n}}$$

$$(\sqrt{n})(\$255) = \$1{,}500$$

$$\sqrt{n} = \frac{\$1{,}500}{\$255}$$

$$\sqrt{n} = 5.882 \text{ now square both sides}$$

$$n = 34.6 \leftarrow \text{sample size for precision specified}$$

Therefore, since n must be greater than or equal to 34.6, the university should take a sample of 35 business-school graduates to get the precision it wants in estimating the class's mean annual earnings.

Estimating the standard deviation from the range

In this example, we knew the standard deviation of the population, but in many cases, the standard deviation of the population is not available. Remember, too, that we have not yet taken the sample, and we are trying to

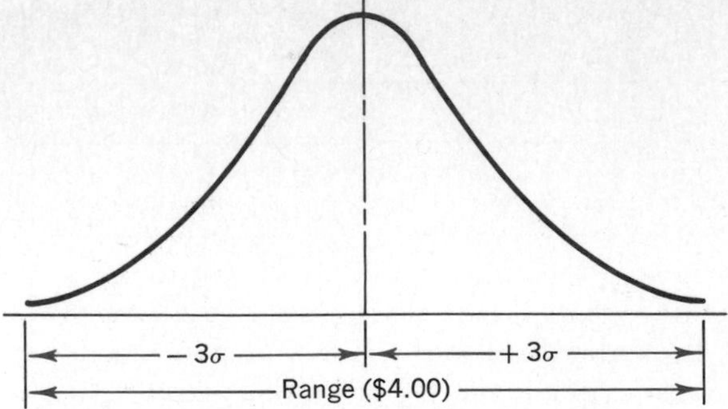

FIGURE 8-6 Approximate relationship between the range and population standard deviation

decide how large to make it. We cannot estimate the population standard deviation using methods from the first part of this chapter. If we have a notion about the range of the population, we can use that to get a crude but workable estimate.

Suppose we are estimating hourly manufacturing wage rates in a city and are fairly confident that there is a $4.00 difference between the highest and lowest wage rates. We know that plus and minus 3 standard deviations include 99.7 percent of all the area under the normal curve; that is, plus 3 standard deviations and minus 3 standard deviations include almost all of the distribution. To symbolize this relationship, we have constructed Fig. 8-6, in which $4.00 (the range) equals 6 standard deviations (plus 3 and minus 3). Thus, a rough estimate of the population standard deviation would be:

$$6\hat{\sigma} = \$4.00$$

$$\hat{\sigma} = \frac{\$4.00}{6}$$

Estimate of the population standard deviation ⟶

$$\hat{\sigma} = \$0.667$$

Our estimate of the population standard deviation using this rough method is not precise, but it may mean the difference between getting a working idea of the required sample size and knowing nothing about that sample size.

Sample Size for Estimating a Proportion

The procedures for determining sample sizes for estimating a population proportion are similar to those for estimating a population mean. Suppose we wish to poll students at a large state university. We want to determine what proportion of them are in favor of a new grading system. We would like a sample size that will enable us to be 90 percent certain of estimating the true proportion that are in favor of the new system within plus and minus .02.

We begin to solve this problem by looking in Appendix Table 1 to find the z value for a 90 percent confidence level. That value is plus and minus 1.64 standard errors from the mean. Since we want our estimate to be within .02, we can symbolize the step-by-step process like this:

$$\text{If } z\sigma_{\bar{p}} = .02$$

$$\text{and } z = 1.64$$

$$\text{then } 1.64\,\sigma_{\bar{p}} = .02$$

If we now substitute the right side of Equation 8-4 for $\sigma_{\bar{p}}$, we get:

$$1.64\left(\sqrt{\frac{pq}{n}}\right) = .02$$

$$\sqrt{\frac{pq}{n}} = .0122 \quad \text{now square both sides}$$

$$\frac{pq}{n} = .0001488 \quad \text{multiply both sides by } n$$

$$pq = .0001488n$$

$$n = \frac{pq}{.0001488}$$

Finding an adequate sample size

To find n, we still need an estimate of the population parameters p and q. If we have strong feelings about the actual proportion in favor of the new system, we can use that as our best guess to calculate n. But if we have no idea what p is, then our best strategy is to guess at p in such a way that we choose n in a conservative manner (that is, so that the sample size *is* large enough to supply at least the precision we require no matter what p actually is). At this point in our problem, n is equal to the product of p and q divided by .0001488. The way to get the largest n is to generate the largest possible numerator of that expression, which happens if we pick $p = .5$ and $q = .5$. Then n becomes:

$$\begin{aligned} n &= \frac{pq}{.0001488} \\ &= \frac{(.5)(.5)}{.0001488} \\ &= \frac{.25}{.0001488} \\ &= 1680 \leftarrow \text{sample size for precision specified} \end{aligned}$$

As a result, to be 90 percent certain of estimating the true proportion within .02, we should pick a simple random sample of 1,680 students to interview.

Picking the most conservative proportion

In the problem we have just solved, we picked a value for p that represented the most conservative strategy. The value .5 generated the largest possible sample. We would have used another value of p if we had been able to estimate one *or* if we had a strong feeling about one. Whenever all these solutions are absent, assume the most conservative possible value for p, or .5.

To illustrate that .5 yields the largest possible sample, Table 8-7 solves the grading-system problem using several different values of p. You

TABLE 8-7 Sample size n associated with different values of p and q

CHOOSE THIS VALUE FOR p	VALUE OF q, OR $1-p$	$\left(\frac{pq}{.0001488}\right)$		INDICATED SAMPLE SIZE n
.2	.8	$\frac{(.2)(.8)}{.0001488}$	=	1,075
.3	.7	$\frac{(.3)(.7)}{.0001488}$	=	1,411
.4	.6	$\frac{(.4)(.6)}{.0001488}$	=	1,612
.5	.5	$\frac{(.5)(.5)}{.0001488}$	=	1,680 ← most conservative
.6	.4	$\frac{(.6)(.4)}{.0001488}$	=	1,612
.7	.3	$\frac{(.7)(.3)}{.0001488}$	=	1,411
.8	.2	$\frac{(.8)(.2)}{.0001488}$	=	1,075

can see from the sample sizes associated with these different values that for the range of p's from .3 to .7, the change in the appropriate sample size is relatively small. Therefore, even if you knew that the true population proportion was .3 and you used a value of .5 for p anyway, you would have sampled only 269 more people $(1{,}680 - 1{,}411)$ than was actually necessary for the desired degree of precision. Obviously, guessing values of p in cases like this is not as critical as it seems at first glance.

EXERCISES

8-51 If the population standard deviation is 200, find the sample size necessary to estimate the true mean within 100 points for a confidence level of 90 percent.

8-52 For a test market, find the sample size needed to estimate the true proportion of consumers satisfied with a certain new product within $\pm.03$ at the 95 percent confidence interval. Assume you have no strong feeling about what the proportion is.

8-53 Given a population with a standard deviation of .8, what size sample is needed to estimate the mean of the population within $\pm.25$ with 98 percent confidence?

8-54 We have strong indications that the proportion is around .75. Find the sample size needed to estimate the proportion within $\pm.04$ with confidence level 90 percent.

8-55 The management of Southern Textiles has recently come under extreme fire regarding the supposedly detrimental effects on health caused by their manufacturing process. A social scientist has advanced a theory that the employees who die from natural causes exhibit remarkable consistency in their life span; the upper and lower limits of their life spans differ by no more than 600 weeks (about 11½ years). For a confidence level of 90 percent, how large a sample should be examined to find the average life span of these employees within ±30 weeks?

8-56 The manager of an industrial chemical plant needs to determine the average life span of the vats extensively employed in the manufacturing process. From prior studies, he knows that the population standard deviation is 9 years. How large a sample should be chosen to be 95 percent confident that the sample average is within 2 years of the true average?

8-57 A speed-reading course guarantees a certain reading rate increase within 2 days. The teacher knows a few people will not be able to achieve this increase; so before stating the guaranteed reading rate increase, he wants to be 95 percent confident that the percentage has been estimated to within ± 3 percent of the true value. What is the most conservative sample size needed for this problem?

8-58 A local store that specializes in candles and clocks, Wicks and Ticks, is interested in obtaining an interval estimate for the mean number of customers that enter the store daily. The owners are reasonably sure that the actual standard deviation of the daily number of customers is 19 customers. Help Wicks and Ticks out of a fix by determining the sample size they should use in order to develop a 90 percent confidence interval for the true mean that will have a width of only 4 customers.

8-9 TERMS INTRODUCED IN CHAPTER 8

CONFIDENCE INTERVAL A range of values that has some designated probability of including the true population parameter value.

CONFIDENCE LEVEL The probability that we associate with an interval estimate of a population parameter indicating how confident we are that the interval estimate will include the population parameter.

CONFIDENCE LIMITS The upper and lower boundaries of a confidence interval.

CONSISTENT ESTIMATOR An estimator that yields values more closely approaching the population parameter as the sample size increases.

DEGREES OF FREEDOM The number of values in a sample we can specify freely, once we know something about that sample.

EFFICIENT ESTIMATOR An estimator with a smaller standard error than some other estimator of the population parameter; i.e., the smaller the standard error of an estimator, the more efficient that estimator is.

ESTIMATE A specific observed value of an estimator.

ESTIMATOR A sample statistic used to estimate a population parameter.

INTERVAL ESTIMATE A range of values used to estimate an unknown population parameter.

POINT ESTIMATE A single number that is used to estimate an unknown population parameter.

STUDENT'S *t* DISTRIBUTION A family of probability distributions distinguished by their individual degrees of freedom, similar in form to the normal distribution, and used when the population standard deviation is unknown and the sample size is relatively small ($n \leq 30$).

SUFFICIENT ESTIMATOR An estimator that uses all the information available in the data concerning a parameter.

UNBIASED ESTIMATOR An estimator of a population parameter that, on the average, assumes values above the population parameter as often, and to the same extent, as it tends to assume values below the population parameter.

8-10 EQUATIONS INTRODUCED IN CHAPTER 8

[8-1] Estimator of the population standard deviation $\hat{\sigma} = s = \sqrt{\frac{\Sigma(x - \bar{x})^2}{n - 1}}$ *p. 328*

This formula indicates that the sample standard deviation can be used as an estimator of the population standard deviation.

[8-2] $$\hat{\sigma}_{\bar{x}} = \frac{\hat{\sigma}}{\sqrt{n}} \times \sqrt{\frac{N - n}{N - 1}}$$ *p. 328*

This formula enables us to derive an *estimated* standard error of the mean of a *finite* population from an *estimate* of the population standard deviation. The symbol ˆ, called a hat, indicates that the value is estimated. Equation 8-6 is the same formula for an infinite population.

[8-3] $$\mu_{\bar{p}} = p$$ *p. 331*

Use this formula to derive the *mean* of the sampling distribution *of the proportion* of successes. The right-hand side, p, is equal to $(n \times p)/n$, where the numerator is the product of the number of trials and the probability of successes, and the denominator is the number of trials. Symbolically, the proportion of successes *in a sample* is written $\bar{p}$ and is pronounced *p-bar.*

[8-4] $$\sigma_{\bar{p}} = \sqrt{\frac{pq}{n}}$$ *p. 331*

To get the *standard error of the proportion,* take the square root of the product of the probabilities of success and failure divided by the number of trials.

[8-5] $$\hat{\sigma}_{\bar{p}} = \sqrt{\frac{\bar{p}\bar{q}}{n}}$$ *p. 332*

This is the formula to use to derive an *estimated* standard error of the proportion when the population proportion is unknown and you are forced to use $\bar{p}$ and $\bar{q}$, the sample proportions of successes and failures.

[8-6] $$\hat{\sigma}_{\bar{x}} = \frac{\hat{\sigma}}{\sqrt{n}}$$ *p. 337*

This formula enables us to derive an *estimated* standard error of the mean of an *infinite* population from an *estimate* of the population standard deviation. It is exactly like Equation 8-2 except that it lacks the finite population multiplier.

8-11 CHAPTER REVIEW EXERCISES

8-59 The average daily fluctuation of a sample of 49 stocks is \$2.45. Previous studies have determined that the population standard deviation is \$.70. If intervals were constructed by a brokerage firm around sample means that would include the true mean daily fluctuation 99.7 percent of the time, what interval would the firm construct for this particular sample?

8-60 What are the advantages of using an interval estimate over a point estimate?

8-61 Why is the size of a statistic's standard error important in its use as an estimator? To which characteristic of estimators does this relate?

8-62 Scott Eames, president of a local bank in Lexington, North Carolina, has determined that the average level of deposit in savings accounts must be \$85 in order to cover minimum costs. He wants to determine with a 95% confidence level what proportion of accounts (within $\pm .04$) have savings levels below that figure. Conservatively, how many accounts should be sampled to determine this proportion?

8-63 A 95 percent confidence interval for the population mean is given by (84,116), and a 75 percent confidence interval is given by (90.96, 109.04). What are the advantages and disadvantages of each of these interval estimates?

8-64 In a random selection of 81 of the 2,200 employees of the Cambridge Carpet Company, the mean number of absences per month was determined to be 3.2 and the sample standard deviation .9.

a) Estimate the standard deviation of the population from the sample standard deviation.
b) Estimate the standard error of the mean for this finite population.
c) If the desired confidence level is .95, what will be the upper and lower limits of the confidence interval for the mean number of absences per employee per month?

8-65 Given a sample mean of 96, a population standard deviation of 4.8, and a sample size of 36, find the confidence level associated with each of the following intervals:

a) (94.4; 97.6) b) (94; 98) c) (95.328; 96.672)

8-66 Based on knowledge about the desirable qualities of estimators, for what reasons might $\bar{x}$ be considered the "best" estimator of the true population mean?

8-67 The president of Offshore Oil has been concerned about the number of fights on his rigs and has been considering various courses of action. In an effort to understand the catalysts of offshore fighting, he randomly sampled 35 days on which a crew had returned from mainland leave. For this sample, the average proportion of workers involved in fisticuffs each day is .045, and the associated standard deviation is .0120.

a) Give a point estimate for the average proportion of workers involved in fights on any given day that a crew has returned from the mainland.
b) Estimate the population standard deviation associated with this fighting rate.

8-68 Given the following expressions for the limits of a confidence interval, find the confidence level associated with the interval:

a) $\bar{x} - 1.5\sigma_{\bar{x}}$ to $\bar{x} + 1.5\sigma_{\bar{x}}$ b $\bar{x} - 1.7\sigma_{x}$ to $\bar{x} + 1.7\sigma_{\bar{x}}$ c) $\bar{x} - 2.3\sigma_{\bar{x}}$ to $\bar{x} + 2.3\sigma_{\bar{x}}$

8-69 From previous studies, the population standard deviation for the performance ratings of the sales for the Dutch Food Company has been determined to be 12.4; the ratings fall within a scale of 0-100. Ann Clark, vice-president of sales, wants to be 98 percent certain that the average performance rating of a sample falls within ± 3 points of the population's rating. How large a sample should she select?

8-70 The Taylor Glass Company's production manager, Bill Bohannon, has been concerned about the high percentage of defectives coming off the line. He recently obtained the trial use of a machine reportedly capable of removing the flaws in most defectives. The advertised "cure" rate of this machine is 75 percent. How large a sample should Bohannon run in order to be 98 percent certain that the sample proportion of repaired defectives is within $\pm .04$ of the proportion of all defectives the machine would repair if purchased?

8-71 A ski resort manager in Vermont wants to know the resort's average daily registration. The following table presents the number of guests registered each of 30 randomly selected days. Calculate the sample mean.

60	58	52	61	63	56	55	57	62	63
58	51	57	61	56	59	63	62	61	58
62	53	53	55	60	52	54	61	58	59

8-72 Using the information in problem 8-71 as a:

a) Sample, find the sample standard deviation.

b) Population, find the population standard deviation.

8-73 In evaluating the effectiveness of a federal rehabilitation program, a survey of 49 of a prison's 800 inmates found that 47 percent were repeat offenders.

a) Estimate the standard error of the proportion of repeat offenders.

b) Construct a 99 percent confidence interval for the proportion of repeat offenders among the inmates of this prison.

8-74 In a Utah sample of 64 automotive repair jobs covered by warranty, the average cost was found to be \$43. Previous studies in that state had determined a population standard deviation of \$24.

a) Calculate the standard error of the mean.

b) Establish an interval estimate around the mean using one standard error of the mean.

8-75 From a random sample of 64 buses, Montreal's mass transit office has calculated the mean number of passengers per kilometer to be 3.5. From previous studies, the population standard deviation is known to be 1.6 passengers per kilometer.

a) Find the standard error of the mean. (Assume the bus fleet is very large.)

b) Construct a 95 percent confidence interval for the mean number of passengers per kilometer for the population.

8-76 Richard D. Austin, owner of the Julius Employment Agency, believes that his average cost of placing a candidate may have increased considerably. He randomly sampled 40 placements over the past year and calculated the average cost of placement at \$360, with a corresponding standard deviation of \$30. Using that information, estimate the average cost and standard deviation for all placements during the past year.

8-77 The executive vice-president of Zayes, a large national retail chain, is contemplating adjusting his store managers' salary mix of base pay and commission. He sampled 100 store managers and found their mean base pay to be \$28,640. The population standard deviation was known to be \$850. For the mean base salary of Zayes' store managers, construct a confidence interval with confidence level (a) 95 percent; (b) 98 percent.

8-78 Bill Wenslaff, an engineer on the staff of a water purification plant, measures the chlorine content in 100 different samples daily. Over a period of years, he has established the population standard deviation to be 1.2 milligrams of chlorine per liter. The latest samples averaged 4.8 milligrams of chlorine per liter.

a) Find the standard error of the mean.

b) Establish the interval around 5.0, the population mean, which will include the sample mean, with a probability of 68.7 percent.

8-79 Ellen Harris, a time-methods engineer, was accumulating normal times for various tasks on a labor-intensive assembly process. This process included 200 separate job stations, each performing the same assembly task. She sampled 5 stations and obtained the following assembly times for each station: 1.8; 2.4; 2.2; 2.6; and 1.6 minutes.

a) Calculate the mean assembly time and the corresponding standard deviation for the sample.

b) Estimate the population standard deviation.

c) Construct a 98 percent confidence interval for the mean assembly time.

8-80 Larry Culler, the federal grain inspector at a seaport, found spoilage in 35 of 100 randomly selected lots of wheat shipped from the port. Construct a 95 percent confidence interval for him for the actual proportion of lots with spoilage in shipments from that port.

8-81 The credit manager for Prangles, a clothing retailer, sampled 300 accounts and found 120 to be a minimum of 30 days delinquent. Given a confidence level equal to .98, construct a confidence interval for the proportion of accounts at least 30 days delinquent.

8-82 Mason Exports negotiated a shipping contract that was based on a flat rate per container shipped. The agreement specified that most of the containers had to weigh the same, since the flat rate per container would be based on a standard weight. The shipping company sampled 144 containers and found the mean weight to be 128.4 ounces, with a standard deviation of .6.

a) Find the standard error of the mean.
b) What is the interval around the sample mean that would contain the population mean 95.5 percent of the time?

8-83 Mark Semmes, owner of the Aurora Restaurant, is considering purchasing new furniture. To assist him in deciding on the amount he can afford to invest in tables and chairs, he wishes to determine the average revenue per customer. He randomly sampled 8 customers, whose average check turned out to be \$10.50, with a standard deviation of \$2.50. Construct a 95 percent confidence interval for the size of the average check per customer.

8-12 CHAPTER CONCEPTS TEST

Answers are in the back of the book.

T F 1. A statistic is said to be an efficient estimator of a population parameter if, with increasing sample size, it becomes almost certain that the value of the statistic comes very close to that of the population parameter.

T F 2. An interval estimate is a range of values used to estimate the shape of a population's distribution.

T F 3. If a statistic tends to assume values higher than the population parameter as frequently as it tends to assume values that are lower, we say that the statistic is an unbiased estimate of the parameter.

T F 4. The probability that a population parameter will lie within a given interval estimate is known as the confidence level.

T F 5. With increasing sample size, the *t* distribution tends to become flatter in shape.

T F 6. We must always use the *t* distribution, rather than the normal, whenever the standard deviation of the population is not known.

T F 7. We may obtain a crude estimate of the standard deviation of some population if we have some information about its range.

T F 8. When using the *t* distribution in estimation, we must assume that the population is approximately normal.

T F 9. Using high confidence levels is not always desirable, because high confidence levels produce large confidence intervals.

T F 10. There is a different *t* distribution for each possible sample size.

T F 11. A point estimate is often insufficient, because it is either right or wrong.

T F 12. A sample mean is said to be an unbiased estimator of a population mean because no other estimator could extract from the sample additional information about the population mean.

T F 13. The most frequently used estimator of σ is s.

T F 14. The standard error of the proportion is calculated as $\sqrt{\frac{p(1-p)}{n}}$.

T F 15. The degrees of freedom used in a *t*-distribution estimation are equal to the sample size.

T F 16. The t distribution is less able to approximate a normal distribution as the sample size increases.

T F 17. The t distribution need not be used in estimating if you know the standard deviation of the population.

18. When choosing an estimator of a population parameter, one should consider:
a) Sufficiency c) Efficiency e) a and c but not b
b) Clarity d) All of these

19. Suppose that 200 members of a group were asked whether or not they liked a particular product. Fifty said yes; 150 said no. Assuming "yes" means a success, which of the following is correct?
a) $\bar{p} = .33$ b) $\bar{p} = .25$ c) $p = .33$ d) $p = .25$ e) b and d only

20. Assume that you take a sample and calculate $\bar{x}$ as 100. You then calculate the upper limit of a 90 percent confidence interval for μ; its value is 112. What is the lower limit of this confidence interval?
a) 88 c) 100
b) 92 d) Cannot be determined from the information given

21. After taking a sample and computing $\bar{x}$, a statistician says, "I am 88 percent confident that the population mean is between 106 and 122." What does she really mean?
a) The probability is .88 that μ is between 106 and 122.
b) The probability is .88 that $\mu = 114$, the midpoint of the interval.
c) 88 percent of the intervals calculated from samples of this size will contain the population mean.
d) All of these.
e) a and c but not b.

22. Which of the following is a necessary condition for using a t-distribution table?
a) n is small. d) All of these.
b) s is known but a is not. e) a and b but not c.
c) The population is infinite.

23. Which of the following t distributions would be expected to have the most area in its tails?
a) $\bar{x} = .83$, degrees of freedom $= 12$ c) $\bar{x} = 15$, $n = 19$
b) $\bar{x} = 15$, degrees of freedom $= 19$ d) $\bar{x} = 8.3$, $n = 12$

24. Which of the following is a difference between z tables and t tables?
a) The t table has values for only a few percentages.
b) The t table measures the chance that the population parameter we are estimating will be in our confidence interval.
c) We must specify the degrees of freedom with which we are dealing when using a z table.
d) All of these.
e) a and b but not c.

25. Suppose we are attempting to estimate a population variance by using s^2. It is incorrect to calculate s^2 as $\frac{\Sigma(x - \bar{x})^2}{n}$ because the value would be:
a) Biased b) Inefficient c) Inconsistent d) Insufficient

26. When considering samples with size greater than 30, we use the normal table, even if the population standard deviation is unknown. Why is this?
a) Calculation of degrees of freedom becomes difficult for large sample sizes.
b) The number of percentages we need for calculation of confidence intervals exceeds the number contained in the t tables.
c) It is difficult to calculate $\bar{x}$ (and hence s^2) for large samples.
d) None of these.
e) a and c but not b.

27. Assume that, from a population with $N = 50$, a sample of size 15 is drawn; σ^2 is known to be 36, and s^2 for the sample is 49; $\bar{x}$ for the sample is calculated as 104. Which of the following should be used for calculating a 95 percent confidence interval for μ?
a) Student's *t* distribution
b) Normal distribution
c) Finite population multiplier
d) a and c but not b
e) b and c but not a

28. We can use the normal distribution to represent the sampling distribution of the population when:
a) The sample size is more than 10
b) The sample size is less than 50
c) The sample size is more than 5
d) None of these

29. If a statistic underestimates a population parameter as much as it overestimates it, we would call it:
a) Consistent
b) Sufficient
c) Efficient
d) All of these
e) None of these

30. A single number used to estimate an unknown population parameter is a ______________ estimate.

31. A range of values used to estimate an unknown population parameter is a ______________ estimate.

32. Once we know something about a sample, the number of values in the sample we can specify freely is called ______________.

33. The family of probability distributions used when population standard deviation is unknown, sample size is small, and values approximate the normal is the ______________.

34. When we give an interval estimate of a population parameter, we show how sure we are that the interval contains the actual population parameter by setting a ______________ level.

35. The upper confidence limit and lower confidence limit are the same ______________ from the ______________.

8-13 CONCEPTUAL CASE (Northern White Metals Company)

Jody Wallis had begun her career in the statistical services department of a large health care insurance company, but soon decided to switch to the more glamorous atmosphere of a diversified manufacturing enterprise. Sarah, although less experienced, was highly respected for her technical competence and well liked for her friendly, open manner.

Both had set right to work, as the CEO has said they would, and Dick was very pleased with their progress. A thorough analysis of automated operations in the fabricating department had ultimately resulted in more efficient quality control procedures. Improvements were suggested and effected in the anodizing department as well. Impressed with their dedication and teamwork and the easy way they got along with the employees at Northern, Dick thought what a valuable addition they would be to his staff. His thoughts were interrupted as NWMC's two top sales reps, Bill Hamilton and Lynn Martin, rapped on his half-open office door.

Dick beckoned them in and inquired as to the nature of the unexpected visit.

"We didn't think this should wait until next week's sales meeting,"

Bill began. "As you know, there have been problems with a few of my accounts, similar to those with NES Electronics."

"I am painfully aware of them," Dick replied, "but I believe our corporate technical staff people have the quality control situation in hand. They've really done a good job," he said enthusiastically.

"That's exactly why we're here," Lynn noted. "Bill and I were hoping that Jody and Sarah could help us gain back some of the ground we've lost with some important customers." She went on to explain that some of these accounts were displaying a lack of confidence in the quality of NWMC's products, and were now reluctant to commit to large volume orders.

At that moment, Jody appeared in the doorway, a stack of paper in hand.

"Sorry to intrude," she started.

"No, not at all," Dick interrupted, "come in."

"Sarah and I have just about finished and I wanted to go over this with you," she said.

"Good," Dick responded. "While you are here, perhaps you can help Lynn and Bill with a sales problem."

Jody answered that she would be happy to try, and Lynn continued where she had left off.

"A few important customers have recently had problems with some of our products. We need something specific, something more than fast talk, to convince them that the situation has improved," Lynn said earnestly. "What kind of assurances can be given about our product quality now?" she asked.

"Well," Jody answered with a smile, "what kind of assurances do you need?"

Lynn and Bill need some technical support for their sales presentations to some customers who have become a bit unsure of NWMC's ability to deliver a product that will conform to specifications. What kind of evidence might be provided that new, more effective quality control procedures are in place? What kind of information will Jody require to provide such evidence?

8-14 COMPUTER DATA BASE EXERCISE

A month later, Laurel and Frank were tabulating daily sales made in the four stores chosen for the test market of the Menagerie. Laurel wanted to use these data for estimating the first season's sales of the new toy. Nick told her that Cold River needed to sell at least 100,000 of the Menagerie toys to break even.

For questions 1 through 4, assume daily sales are independent from store to store and from day to day.

PROBLEMS AND QUESTIONS

1. Estimate the population mean and standard deviation of daily sales.
2. Estimate the standard error of the mean for this sample.
3. Construct a 90 percent confidence interval for the mean daily sales of the new toy in a single store.
4. Should Cold River produce the toy if it wants to be 99 percent certain first-year sales will be above 100,000 units? Toys will be sold in 100 stores, with 60 shopping days anticipated.

DAILY TEST MARKET SALES			
Store A	Store B	Store C	Store D
29	15	34	25
29	16	22	19
13	32	31	25
22	31	28	35
23	32	23	25
20	15	20	20
29	16	26	34
17	46	39	29
22	27	24	24
26	20	35	33
19	28	37	36
21	2	20	39
47	28	27	38
11	29	30	12
32	36	34	33
42	33	25	26
32	18	21	35
13	33	26	30
19	28	16	28
23	27	31	34
20	34	23	20
20	16	25	29
17	30	12	20
31	32	22	36

Of the purchasers, the following numbers expressed a desire to buy another animal.

STORE	NUMBER OF REPEAT PURCHASERS																						
A	23	18	3	20	16	19	22	13	17	20	12	17	41	5	22	39	19	7	10	11	19	8	14	27
B	12	12	27	27	17	7	11	34	23	18	20	2	26	24	30	28	7	20	19	24	30	14	22	29
C	28	19	27	24	20	13	15	32	20	18	34	18	18	21	28	23	17	13	11	22	13	20	9	18
D	22	17	17	17	19	13	28	22	22	28	26	34	32	10	23	18	28	23	24	30	17	18	12	29

5. Estimate the proportion and the standard error of the proportion for repeat purchasers.
6. Construct a 90 percent confidence interval for the proportion of repeat purchasers among the Menagerie buyers.

8-15 FLOW CHART

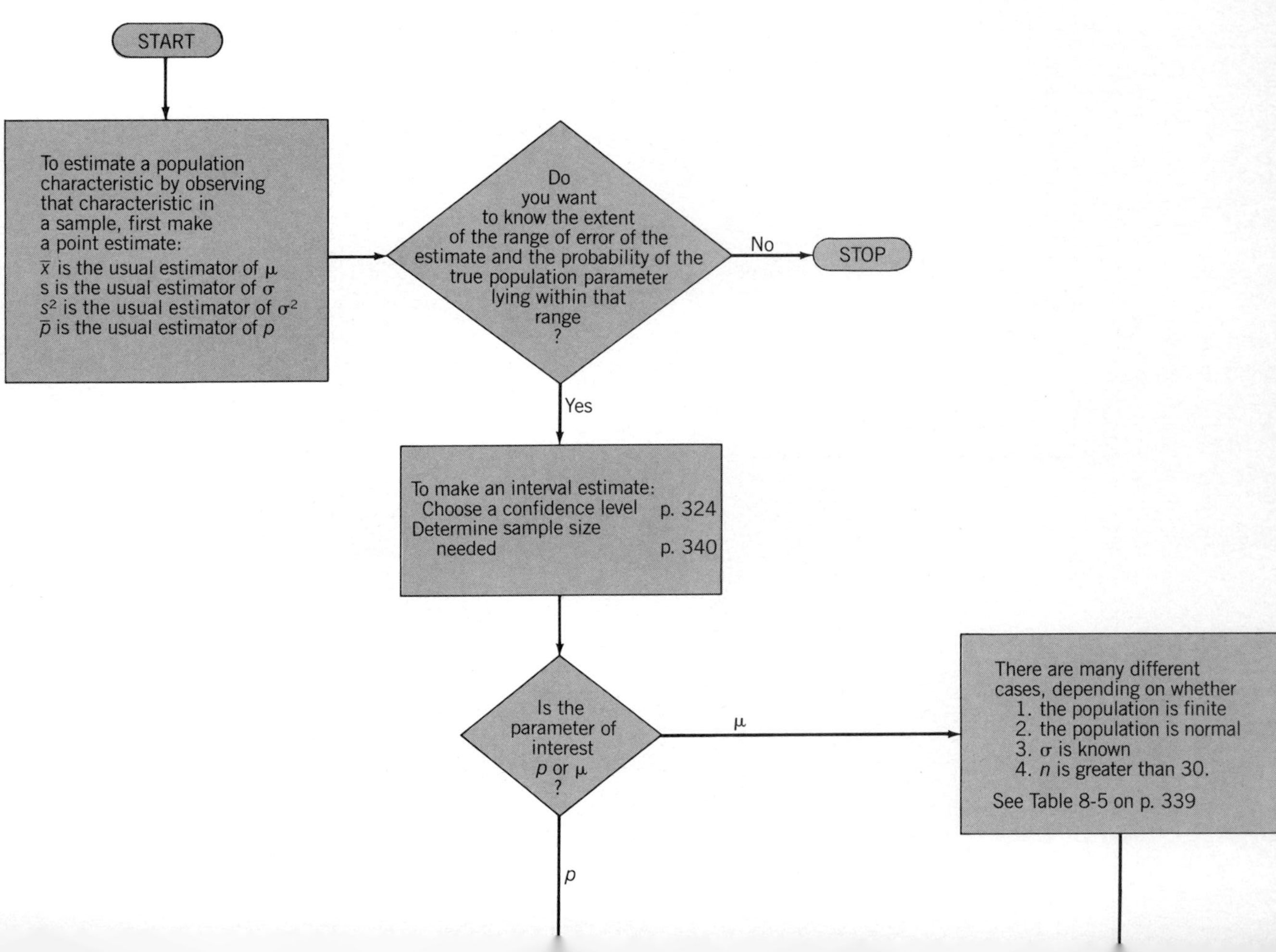

START
To estimate a population characteristic by observing that characteristic in a sample, first make a point estimate:
$\bar{x}$ is the usual estimator of μ
s is the usual estimator of σ
s^2 is the usual estimator of σ^2
$\bar{p}$ is the usual estimator of p
Do you want to know the extent of the range of error of the estimate and the probability of the true population parameter lying within that range ?
No
STOP
Yes
To make an interval estimate:
Choose a confidence level p. 324
Determine sample size needed p. 340
Is the parameter of interest p or μ ?
μ
There are many different cases, depending on whether
1. the population is finite
2. the population is normal
3. σ is known
4. n is greater than 30.
See Table 8-5 on p. 339
p

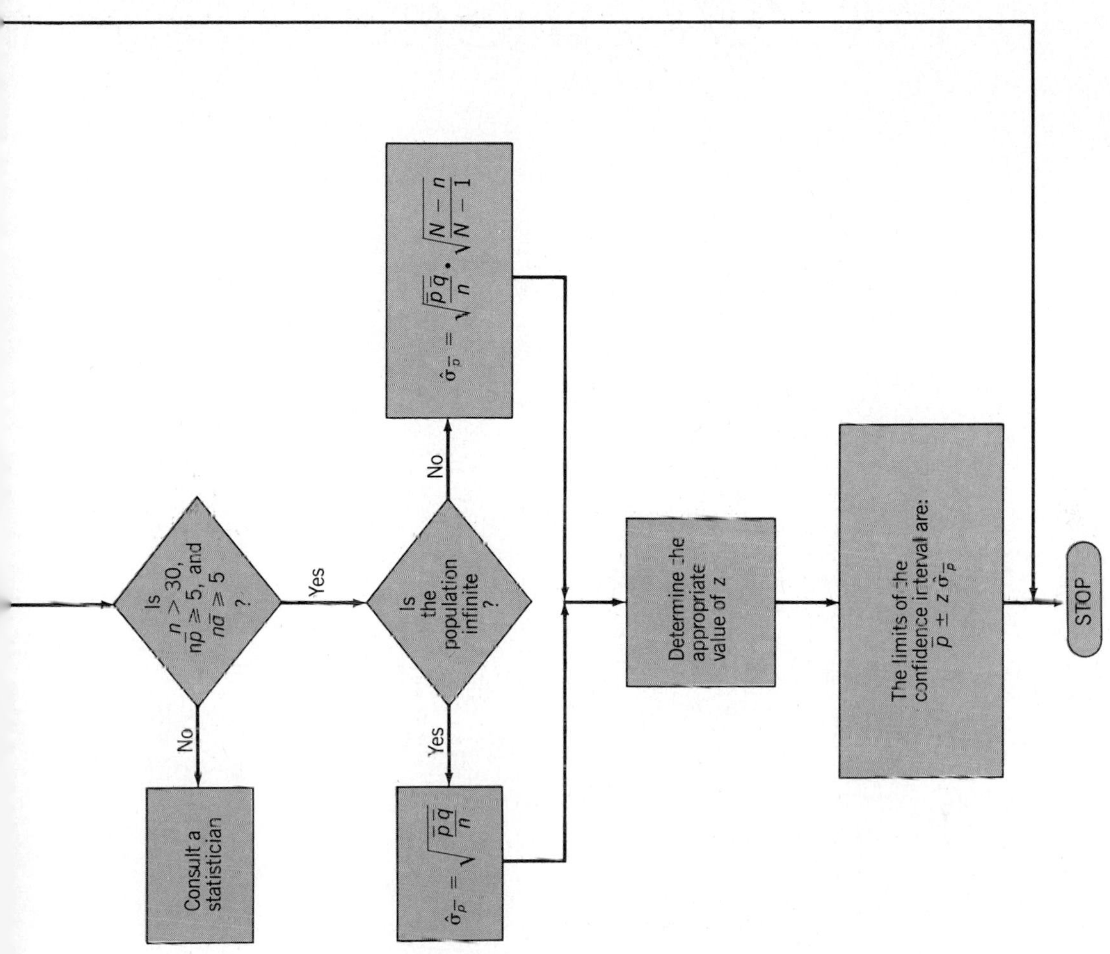

Is $n > 30$, $n\bar{p} \geq 5$, and $n\bar{q} \geq 5$?
No
Consult a statistician
Yes
Is the population infinite ?
Yes
$\hat{\sigma}_{\bar{p}} = \sqrt{\frac{\bar{p}\bar{q}}{n}}$
No
$\hat{\sigma}_{\bar{p}} = \sqrt{\frac{\bar{p}\bar{q}}{n}} \cdot \sqrt{\frac{N-n}{N-1}}$
Determine the appropriate value of z
The limits of the confidence interval are: $\bar{p} \pm z\,\hat{\sigma}_{\bar{p}}$
STOP

CHAPTER 9

TESTING HYPOTHESES

1. INTRODUCTION, 358
2. CONCEPTS BASIC TO THE HYPOTHESIS-TESTING PROCEDURE, 359
3. TESTING HYPOTHESES, 361
4. HYPOTHESIS TESTING OF MEANS—SAMPLES WITH POPULATION STANDARD DEVIATIONS KNOWN, 369
5. MEASURING THE POWER OF A HYPOTHESIS TEST, 375
6. HYPOTHESIS TESTING OF PROPORTIONS—LARGE SAMPLES, 377
7. HYPOTHESIS TESTING OF MEANS UNDER DIFFERENT CONDITIONS, 382
8. HYPOTHESIS TESTING FOR DIFFERENCES BETWEEN MEANS AND PROPORTIONS, 386
9. PROB VALUES—ANOTHER WAY TO LOOK AT TESTING HYPOTHESES, 408
10. TERMS, 412
11. EQUATIONS, 413
12. REVIEW EXERCISES, 415
13. CONCEPTS TEST, 419
14. CONCEPTUAL CASE, 421
15. COMPUTER DATA BASE EXERCISE, 422
16. FLOW CHART, 425

OBJECTIVES: The subject of Chapter 9 is *hypothesis testing*. Here we are trying to determine when it is reasonable to conclude, from analysis of a sample, that the entire population possesses a certain property, and when it is not reasonable to reach such a conclusion. Suppose a student purchases a $500 second-hand car from a dealer who advertises, "Our cars are the finest, most dependable in town." If the car's repair bills during the first month are $600, that one-car sample may cause the student to conclude that the dealer's population of used cars is probably not as advertised. Chapter 9 will allow us to test and evaluate larger samples than those available to the buyer of the used car.

The roofing contract for a new sports complex in San Francisco has been awarded to Parkhill Associates, a large architectural firm. Building specifications call for a movable roof covered by approximately 10,000 sheets of .04-inch-thick aluminum. The aluminum sheets cannot be appreciably thicker than .04 inches because the structure could not support the additional weight. Nor can the sheets be appreciably thinner than .04 inches because the strength of the roof would be inadequate. Because of this restriction on thickness, Parkhill carefully checks the aluminum sheets from its supplier. Of course, Parkhill does not want to measure each sheet, so it randomly samples 100. The sheets in the sample have a mean thickness of .0408 inches. From past experience with this supplier, Parkhill believes that these sheets come from a thickness population with a standard deviation of .004 inches. On the basis of this data, Parkhill must decide whether the 10,000 sheets meet specifications. In Chapter 8, we used sample statistics to estimate population parameters. Now, to solve problems like Parkhill's, we shall learn how to use characteristics of samples to test an assumption we have about the population from which that sample came. Our test for Parkhill, later in the chapter, may lead Parkhill to accept the shipment, or it may indicate that Parkhill should reject the aluminum sheets sent by the supplier because they do not meet the architectural specifications.

9-1 INTRODUCTION

Function of hypothesis testing

Hypothesis testing begins with an assumption, called a *hypothesis,* that we make about a population parameter. Then we collect sample data, produce sample statistics, and use this information to decide how likely it is that our hypothesized population parameter is correct. Say that we assume a certain value for a population mean. To test the validity of our assumption, we gather sample data and determine the difference between the hypothesized value and the actual value of the sample mean. Then we judge whether the difference is significant. The smaller the difference, the greater the likelihood that our hypothesized value for the mean is correct. The larger the difference, the smaller the likelihood.

Unfortunately, the difference between the hypothesized population parameter and the actual sample statistic is more often neither so large that we automatically reject our hypothesis nor so small that we just as quickly accept it. So in hypothesis testing as in most significant real-life decisions, clear-cut solutions are the exception, not the rule.

When to accept or reject the hypothesis

Suppose a manager of a large shopping mall tells us that the average work efficiency of her employees is 90 percent. How can we test the validity of her hypothesis? Using the sampling methods we learned in Chapter 7, we could calculate the efficiency of a *sample* of her employees. If we did this and the sample statistic came out to be 93 percent, we would readily accept the manager's statement. However, if the sample statistic were 46 percent, we would reject her assumption as untrue. We can interpret both these outcomes, 93 percent and 46 percent, using our common sense.

The basic problem will be dealing with uncertainty

Now suppose that our sample statistic reveals an efficiency of 81 percent. This value is relatively close to 90 percent. But is it close enough for us to accept the manager's hypothesis? Whether we accept or reject the manager's hypothesis, we cannot be absolutely certain that our decision is correct; therefore we will have to learn to deal with uncertainty in our decision making. **We cannot accept or reject a hypothesis about a population parameter simply by intuition. Instead, we need to learn how to decide objectively, on the basis of sample information, whether to accept or reject a hunch.**

EXERCISES

9-1 Why must we be required to deal with uncertainty in our decisions, even when using statistical techniques?

9-2 Theoretically speaking, how might one go about testing the hypothesis that a coin is fair? that a die is fair?

9-3 Is it possible that a false hypothesis will be accepted? How would you explain this?

9-4 Describe the hypothesis-testing process.

9-5 How would you explain a large difference between a hypothesized population parameter and a sample statistic, if, in fact, the hypothesis is true?

9-2 CONCEPTS BASIC TO THE HYPOTHESIS-TESTING PROCEDURE

Sports-complex problem

Before we introduce the formal statistical terms and procedures, we'll work our chapter-opening sports-complex problem all the way through. Recall that the aluminum roofing sheets have a claimed average thickness of .04 inches and that they will be unsatisfactory if they are too thick *or* too thin. The contractor takes a sample of 100 sheets and determines that the sample mean thickness is .0408 inches. On the basis of past experience, he knows that the population standard deviation is .004 inches. Does this sample evidence indicate that the batch of 10,000 sheets of aluminum is suitable for constructing the roof of the new sports complex?

Formulating the hypothesis

If we assume that the true mean thickness is .04 inches, and we know that the population standard deviation is .004 inches, how likely is it that we would get a sample mean of .0408 or more from that population? In other words, **if the true mean is .04 inches, and the standard deviation is .004 inches, what are the chances of getting a sample mean that differs from .04 inches by .0008 inches or more?**

These questions show that **to determine whether the population mean is actually .04 inches, we must calculate the probability that a random sample with a mean of .0408 inches will be selected from a population with a μ of .04 inches and a σ of .004 inches. This probability will indicate whether it is *reasonable* to observe a sample like this if the population mean is actually .04 inches.** If this probability is far too low, we must conclude that the aluminum company's statement is false and that the mean thickness of the aluminum sheets is not .04 inches.

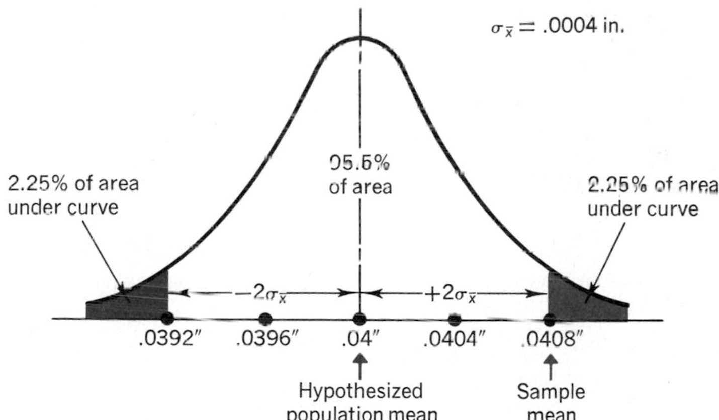

FIGURE 9-1 Probability that $\bar{x}$ will differ from hypothesized μ by 2 standard errors or more

To answer the question illustrated in Fig. 9-1: If the hypothesized population mean is .04 inches and the population standard deviation is .004 inches, what are the chances of getting a sample mean (.0408 inches) that differs from .04 inches by .0008 inches? First we calculate the standard error of the mean from the population standard deviation:

Calculating the standard error of the mean

$$\sigma_{\bar{x}} = \frac{\sigma}{\sqrt{n}} \qquad [7\text{-}1]$$

$$= \frac{.004 \text{ in.}}{\sqrt{100}}$$

$$= \frac{.004 \text{ in.}}{10}$$

$$= .0004 \text{ in.}$$

Next we use Equation 7-2 to discover that the mean of our sample (.0408 inches) lies 2 standard errors to the right of the hypothesized population mean:

$$z = \frac{\bar{x} - \mu}{\sigma_{\bar{x}}} \qquad [7\text{-}2]$$

$$= \frac{.0408 - .04}{.0004}$$

$$= 2 \leftarrow \text{standard errors of the mean}$$

Interpreting the probability associated with this difference

Using Appendix Table 1, we learn that 4.5 percent is the *total chance* of our sample mean differing from the population mean by 2 or more standard errors; that is, the chances that the sample mean would be .0408 inches or larger or .0392 inches or smaller are only 4.5 percent ($P(z \geq 2 \text{ or } z \leq -2) = 2(.5 - .4722) = .0456$, or about 4.5 percent). **With this low a chance, Parkhill could conclude that a population with a true mean of .04 inches would not be likely to produce a sample like this.** The project supervisor would reject the aluminum company's statement about the mean thickness of the sheets.

The decision maker's role in formulating hypotheses

In this case, the difference between the sample mean and the hypothesized population mean is too large, and the chance that the population would produce such a random sample is far too low. Why this probability of 4.5 percent is too low, or wrong, is a judgment for decision makers to make. Certain situations demand that decision makers be very sure about the characteristics of the items being tested, and then 4.5 percent is too high to be attributable to chance. Other processes allow for a wider latitude or variation, and a decision maker might accept a hypothesis with a 20 percent probability of chance variation. In each situation, we must try to determine the costs resulting from an incorrect decision and the precise level of risk we are willing to assume.

Risk of rejection

In our example, we rejected the aluminum company's contention that the population mean is .04 inches. But suppose for a moment that the population mean is *actually* .04 inches. If we then stuck to our rejection rule of 2 standard errors or more (the 4.5 percent probability or less in the tails of Fig. 9-1), we would reject a perfectly good lot of aluminum sheets 4.5 percent of the time. Therefore, **our minimum standard for an acceptable probability, 4.5 percent, is *also* the *risk* we take of *rejecting a hypothesis that is true.* In this or any decision making, there can be no risk-free tradeoff.**

EXERCISES

9-6 What do we mean when we reject a hypothesis on the basis of a sample?

9-7 Explain why there is no single level of probability used to reject or accept in hypothesis testing.

9-8 If we reject a hypothesized value because it differs from a sample statistic by more than one standard error, what is the probability that we have rejected a hypothesis that is in fact true?

9-9 How many standard deviations around the hypothesized value should we use to be 95.5 percent certain that we accept the hypothesis when it is correct?

9-10 A tire manufacturer claims that its 4-ply economy tire lasts an average of 18,300 miles, with a standard deviation of 2,400 miles. *Consumer* magazine takes a sample of 25 tires and finds they last an average of 17,000 miles. Using 2 standard errors as the criterion, can the magazine accept the manufacturer's claim and the hypothesis that the population mean is 18,300 miles?

9-11 For a certain population with a standard deviation of 12, the mean is hypothesized to be 84. If a sample of 64 observations is taken and yields a mean of 87.2, determine whether such a sample estimate is reasonable (within 2 standard errors) if, in fact, the hypothesis is true.

9-12 An automobile manufacturer claims that a particular model gets 24 miles to the gallon. The Environmental Protection Agency, using a sample of 36 automobiles of this model, finds the sample mean to be 23.1 miles per gallon. From previous studies, the population standard deviation is known to be 3 miles per gallon. Could we reasonably expect (within 2 standard deviations) that we could select such a sample if indeed the population mean is actually 24 miles per gallon?

9-3 TESTING HYPOTHESES

Making a formal statement of the null hypothesis

In hypothesis testing, we must state the assumed or hypothesized value of the population parameter *before* we begin sampling. The assumption we wish to test is called the *null hypothesis* and is symbolized H_0, or "H sub-zero."

Suppose we want to test the hypothesis that the population mean is equal to 500. We would symbolize it as follows and read it, "The null hypothesis is that the population mean is equal to 500":

$$H_0: \mu = 500$$

The term *null hypothesis* arises from earlier agricultural and medical applications of statistics. In order to test the effectiveness of a new fertilizer or drug, the tested hypothesis (the null hypothesis) was that it had *no effect;* that is, there was no difference between treated and untreated samples.

If we use a hypothesized value of a population mean in a problem, we would represent it symbolically as:

$$\mu_{H_0}$$

This is read, "The hypothesized value of the population mean."

If our sample results fail to support the null hypothesis, we must conclude that something else is true. **Whenever we reject the null hypothesis, the conclusion we do accept is called the *alternative hypothesis* and**

is symbolized H_1 ("H sub-one"). For the null hypothesis:

$H_0: \mu = 200$ (Read: "The null hypothesis is that the population mean is equal to 200.")

Making a formal statement of the alternative hypothesis

we will consider three possible alternative hypotheses:

- $H_1: \mu \neq 200 \leftarrow$ "The alternative hypothesis is that the population mean is *not equal* to 200."
- $H_1: \mu > 200 \leftarrow$ "The alternative hypothesis is that the population mean is *greater than* 200."
- $H_1: \mu < 200 \leftarrow$ "The alternative hypothesis is that the population mean is *less than* 200."

Interpreting the Significance Level

The purpose of hypothesis testing is not to question the computed value of the sample statistic but to make a judgment about the *difference* between that sample statistic and a hypothesized population parameter. The next step after stating the null and alternative hypotheses, then, is to decide what criterion to use for deciding whether to accept or reject the null hypothesis.

In our sports-complex example, we decided that a difference observed between the sample mean $\bar{x}$ and the hypothesized population mean μ_{H_0} had only a 4.5 percent, or .045, chance of occurring. Therefore, we rejected the null hypothesis that the population mean was .04 inches (H_0: $\mu = .04$ inches). In statistical terms, the value .045 is called the *significance level.*

Function of the significance level

What if we test a hypothesis at the 5 percent level of significance? This means that we will reject the null hypothesis if the difference between the sample statistic and the hypothesized population parameter is so large that it or a larger difference would occur, on the average, only five or fewer times in every 100 samples when the hypothesized population parameter is correct. **Assuming the hypothesis is correct, then, the significance level indicates the percentage of sample means that is outside certain limits.** (In estimation, you remember, the confidence level indicated the percentage of sample means that fell *within* the defined confidence limits.)

Area where no significant difference exists

Figure 9-2 illustrates how to interpret a 5 percent level of significance. Notice that 2.5 percent of the area under the curve is located in each tail. From Appendix Table 1, we can determine that 95 percent of all the area under the curve is included in an interval extending $1.96\sigma_{\bar{x}}$ on either side of the hypothesized mean. In 95 percent of the area, then, there is no significant difference between the sample statistic and the hypothesized population parameter. In the remaining 5 percent (the colored regions in Fig. 9-2), a significant difference does exist.

Also called the area where we accept the null hypothesis

Figure 9-3 examines this same example in a different way. Here, the .95 of the area under the curve is where we would accept the null hypothesis.

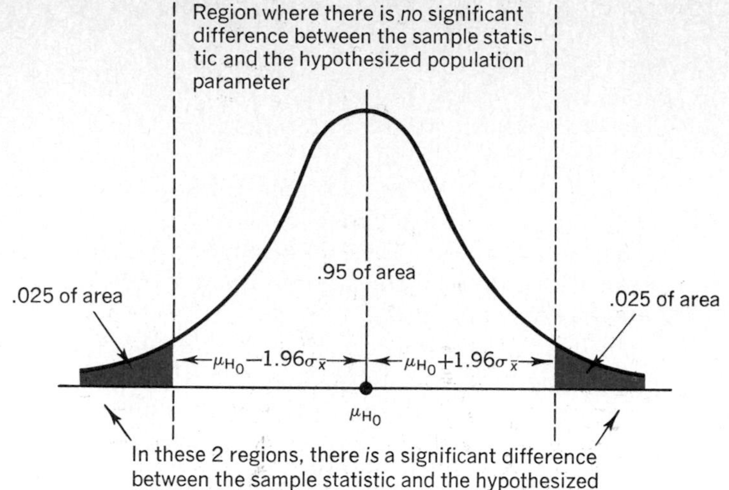
Region where there is no significant difference between the sample statistic and the hypothesized population parameter
.95 of area
.025 of area
.025 of area
$\mu_{H_0} - 1.96\sigma_{\bar{x}}$
$\mu_{H_0} + 1.96\sigma_{\bar{x}}$
μ_{H_0}
In these 2 regions, there is a significant difference between the sample statistic and the hypothesized population parameter

FIGURE 9-2 Regions of significant difference and of no significant difference at a 5 percent level of significance

The two colored parts under the curve, representing a total of 5 percent of the area, are where we would reject the null hypothesis.

A word of caution is appropriate here. Even if our sample statistic in Fig. 9-3 does fall in the nonshaded region (that region comprising 95 percent of the area under the curve), **this *does not prove* that our null hypothesis (H_0) is true; it simply does not provide statistical evidence to reject it.** Why? Because the only way in which the hypothesis can be accepted with certainty is for us to know the population parameter, and unfortunately, this is not possible. Therefore, whenever we say that we accept the null hypothesis, we actually mean that there is not sufficient statistical evidence to reject it. **Use of the term *accept,* instead of *do not reject,* has become standard. It means simply that when sample data do not cause us to reject a null hypothesis, we behave as though that hypothesis is true.**

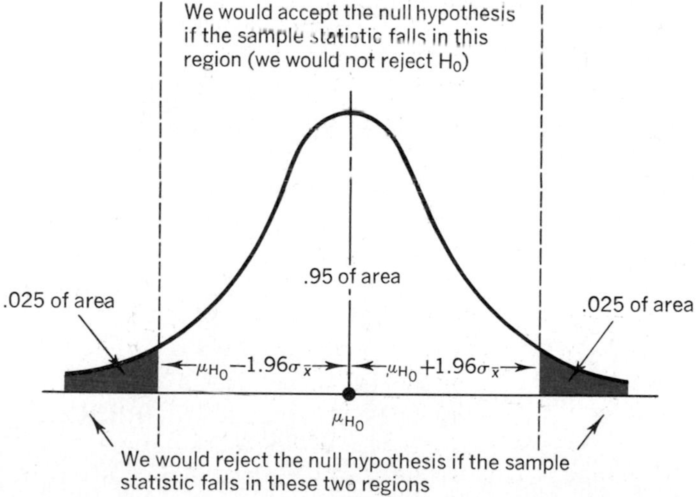
We would accept the null hypothesis if the sample statistic falls in this region (we would not reject H_0)
.95 of area
.025 of area
.025 of area
$\mu_{H_0} - 1.96\sigma_{\bar{x}}$
$\mu_{H_0} + 1.96\sigma_{\bar{x}}$
μ_{H_0}
We would reject the null hypothesis if the sample statistic falls in these two regions

FIGURE 9-3 A 5 percent level of significance, with acceptance and rejection regions designated

Selecting a Significance Level

Tradeoffs when choosing a significance level

There is no single standard or universal level of significance for testing hypotheses. In some instances, a 5 percent level of significance is used. Published research results often test hypotheses at the 1 percent level of significance. It is possible to test a hypothesis at *any* level of significance. But remember that our choice of the minimum standard for an acceptable probability, or the significance level, is also the risk we assume of rejecting a null hypothesis when it is true. **The higher the significance level we use for testing a hypothesis, the higher the probability of rejecting a null hypothesis when it is true.**

Examining this concept, we refer to Fig. 9-4. Here we have illustrated a hypothesis test at three different significance levels: .01, .10, and .50. Also, we have indicated the location of the same sample mean $\bar{x}$ on each distribution. In parts *a* and *b*, we would accept the null hypothesis that the population mean is equal to the hypothesized value. But notice that in part *c*, we would reject this same null hypothesis. Why? Our significance level there of .50 is so high that we would rarely accept a null hypothesis when it is *not* true but, at the same time, frequently reject one when it *is* true.

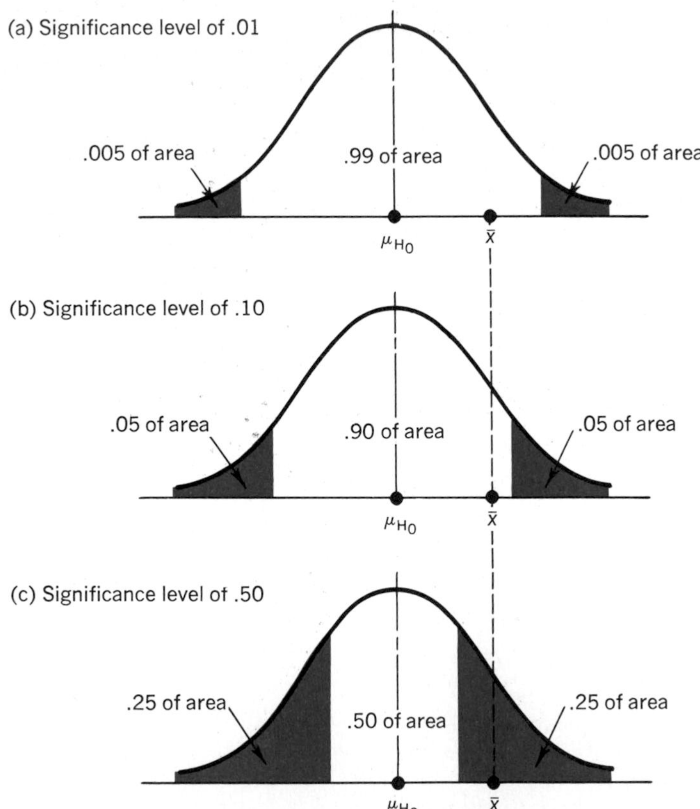

FIGURE 9-4 Three different levels of significance

Type I and Type II Errors

Type I and Type II errors defined

Statisticians give specific definitions and symbols to the concept illustrated in Fig. 9-4. **Rejecting a null hypothesis when it is true is called a Type I error**, and its probability (which, as we have seen, is also the significance level of the test) is symbolized α (alpha). Alternately, **accepting a null hypothesis when it is false is called a Type II error**, and its probability is symbolized β (beta). There is a tradeoff between these two types of errors: the probability of making one type of error can be reduced only if we are willing to increase the probability of making the other type of error. Notice in part *c*, Fig. 9-4, that our acceptance region is quite small (.50 of the area under the curve). With an acceptance region this small, we will rarely accept a null hypothesis when it is not true, but as a cost of being this sure, we will frequently reject a null hypothesis when it is true. Put another way, in order to get a low β, we will have to put up with a high α. To deal with this tradeoff in personal and professional situations, decision makers decide the appropriate level of significance by examining the costs or penalties attached to both types of errors.

Preference for a Type I error

Suppose that making a Type I error (rejecting a null hypothesis when it is true) involves the time and trouble of reworking a batch of chemicals that should have been accepted. At the same time, making a Type II error (accepting a null hypothesis when it is false) means taking a chance that an entire group of users of this chemical compound will be poisoned. Obviously, the management of this company will prefer a Type I error to a Type II error and, as a result, will set very high levels of significance in its testing to get low βs.

Preference for a Type II error

Suppose, on the other hand, that making a Type I error involves disassembling an entire engine at the factory, but making a Type II error involves relatively inexpensive warranty repairs by the dealers. Then the manufacturer is more likely to prefer a Type II error and will set low significance levels in its testing.

Deciding Which Distribution to Use in Hypothesis Testing

Selecting the correct distribution prior to the test

After deciding what level of significance to use, our next task in hypothesis testing is to determine the appropriate probability distribution. We have a choice between the normal distribution, Appendix Table 1, and the *t* distribution, Appendix Table 2. The rules for choosing the appropriate distribution are similar to those we encountered in Chapter 8 on estimation. Table 9-1 summarizes when to use the normal and *t* distributions in making tests of means. Later in this chapter, we shall examine the distributions appropriate for testing hypotheses about proportions.

Remember one more rule when testing the hypothesized value of a mean. As in estimation, use the *finite population multiplier* whenever the population is finite in size, sampling is done without replacement, and the sample is more than 5 percent of the population.

TABLE 9-1 Conditions for using the normal and *t* distributions in testing hypotheses about means

	WHEN THE POPULATION STANDARD DEVIATION IS KNOWN	WHEN THE POPULATION STANDARD DEVIATION IS *NOT* KNOWN
Sample size *n* is larger than 30	Normal distribution, *z* table	Normal distribution, *z* table
Sample size *n* is 30 or less and we assume the population is normal or approximately so	Normal distribution, *z* table	*t* distribution, *t* table

Two-Tailed and One-Tailed Tests of Hypotheses

Description of a two-tailed hypothesis test

In the tests of hypothesized population means that follow, we shall illustrate two-tailed tests and one-tailed tests. These new terms need a word of explanation. A *two-tailed test* of a hypothesis will reject the null hypothesis if the sample mean is significantly higher than *or* lower than the hypothesized population mean. Thus, in a two-tailed test, there are *two* rejection regions. This is illustrated in Fig. 9-5.

A two-tailed test is appropriate when the null hypothesis is $\mu = \mu_{H_0}$ (μ_{H_0} being some specified value) and the alternative hypothesis is $\mu \neq \mu_{H_0}$. Assume that a manufacturer of light bulbs wants to produce bulbs with a mean life of $\mu = \mu_{H_0} = 1{,}000$ hours. If the lifetime is shorter, he will lose customers to his competition; if the lifetime is longer, he will have a very high production cost because the filaments will be excessively thick. In order to see if his production process is working properly, he takes a sample of the output to test the hypothesis $H_0 : \mu = 1{,}000$. Since he does not want to deviate significantly from 1,000 hours *in either direction,* the appropriate

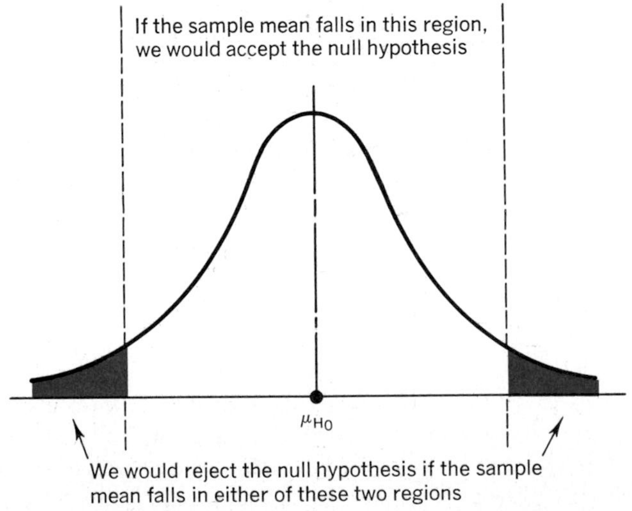
If the sample mean falls in this region, we would accept the null hypothesis
μ_{H_0}
We would reject the null hypothesis if the sample mean falls in either of these two regions

FIGURE 9-5 Two-tailed test of a hypothesis, showing the two rejection regions

alternative hypothesis is $H_1: \mu \neq 1{,}000$, and he uses a two-tailed test. That is, he rejects the null hypothesis if the mean life of bulbs in the sample is *either too far above* 1,000 hours *or too far below* 1,000 hours.

Conditions when a two-tailed test may not be appropriate and we must use a one-tailed test

However, there are situations in which a two-tailed test is not appropriate, and we must use a one-tailed test. Consider the case of a wholesaler that buys light bulbs from the manufacturer discussed above. The wholesaler buys bulbs in large lots and does not want to accept a lot of bulbs unless their mean life is 1,000 hours. As each shipment arrives, the wholesaler tests a sample to decide whether it should accept the shipment. The company will reject the shipment only if it feels that the mean life is below 1,000 hours. If it feels that the bulbs are better than expected (with a mean life above 1,000 hours), it certainly will not reject the shipment, because the longer life comes at no extra cost. So the wholesaler's hypotheses are: $H_0: \mu = 1{,}000$ hours and $H_1: \mu < 1{,}000$ hours. It rejects H_0 only if the mean life of the sampled bulbs is significantly *below* 1,000 hours. This situation is illustrated in Fig. 9-6. From this figure we can see why this test is called a *left-tailed test* (or a *lower-tailed test*).

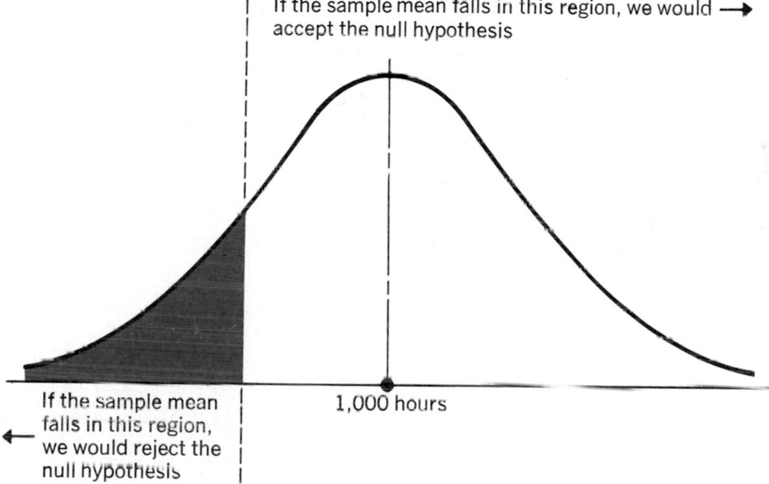
If the sample mean falls in this region, we would accept the null hypothesis →
If the sample mean falls in this region, we would reject the null hypothesis
1,000 hours

FIGURE 9-6 Left-tailed test (a lower-tailed test) with the rejection region on the left side (lower side)

In general, a left-tailed (lower-tailed) test is used if the hypotheses are $H_0: \mu = \mu_{H_0}$ and $H_1: \mu < \mu_{H_0}$. In such a situation, it is sample evidence with the sample mean significantly below the hypothesized population mean that leads us to reject the null hypothesis in favor of the alternative hypothesis. Stated differently, the rejection region is in the lower tail (left tail) of the distribution of the sample mean, and that is why we call this a lower-tailed test.

Left-tailed tests and right-tailed tests

A left-tailed test is one of the two kinds of one-tailed tests. As you have probably guessed by now, the other kind of one-tailed test is a *right-tailed test* (or an *upper-tailed test*). An upper-tailed test is used when the hypotheses are H_0: $\mu = \mu_{H_0}$ and H_1: $\mu > \mu_{H_0}$. Only values of the sample mean that are *significantly* above the hypothesized population mean will cause us to reject the null hypothesis in favor of the alternative hypothesis. This is called an upper-tailed test because the rejection region is in the upper tail of the distribution of the sample mean.

The following situation is illustrated in Fig. 9-7; it calls for the use of an upper-tailed test. A sales manager has asked her salespersons to observe a limit on traveling expenses. The manager hopes to keep expenses to an average of $100 per salesperson per day. One month after the limit is imposed, a sample of submitted daily expenses is taken to see if the limit is being observed. The null hypothesis is $H_0: \mu = \$100.00$, but the manager is concerned only with excessively high expenses. Thus, the appropriate alternative hypothesis is $H_1: \mu > \$100.00$, and an upper-tailed test is used. The null hypothesis is rejected (and corrective measures taken) only if the sample mean is significantly higher than $100.00.

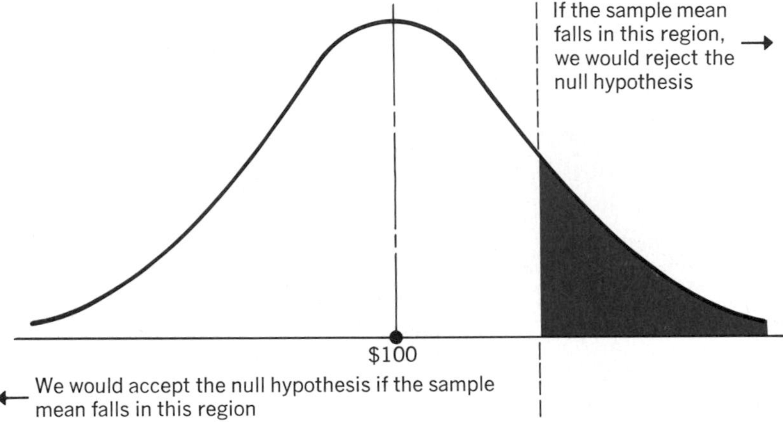

If the sample mean falls in this region, we would reject the null hypothesis
$100
We would accept the null hypothesis if the sample mean falls in this region

FIGURE 9-7 Right-tailed (upper-tailed) test

Finally, we should remind you again that in each example of hypothesis testing, when we accept a null hypothesis on the basis of sample information, we are really saying that there is no statistical evidence to reject it. We are not saying that the null hypothesis is true. The only way to prove a null hypothesis is to know what the population parameter is, and that is not possible with sampling. Thus, we accept the null hypothesis and behave as though it is true simply because we can find no evidence to reject it.

EXERCISES

9-13 Formulate the null and alternative hypotheses to test whether the mean lifetime for men is 68 years.

9-14 Describe what the null and alternative hypotheses typically represent in the hypothesis-testing process.

9-15 Define the term *significance level.*

9-16 Define Type I and Type II errors.

9-17 In a trial, the null hypothesis is that an individual is innocent of a certain crime. Would the legal system prefer to commit a Type I or a Type II error with this hypothesis?

9-18 What is the relationship between the significance level of a test and Type I error?

9-19 If our goal is to accept a null hypothesis with 99 percent certainty when it's true, and our sample size is more than 30, diagram the acceptance and rejection regions for the following alternative hypotheses:
a) $\mu \neq 0$ b) $\mu < 0$ c) $\mu > 0$
Specify the percentage of the area under each region of the curves.

9-20 For the following cases, specify which probability distribution to use in a hypothesis test:
a) $H_0: \mu = 25$ $H_1: \mu > 25, \bar{x} = 28.2, \sigma = 4, n = 12$
b) $H_0: \mu = 1{,}024$ $H_1: \mu \neq 1024, \bar{x} = 976, \sigma = 60, n = 30$
c) $H_0: \mu = 100$ $H_1: \mu > 100, \bar{x} = 107, s = 3.2, n = 16$
d) $H_0: \mu = 500$ $H_1: \mu > 500, \bar{x} = 508, s = 4, n = 40$
e) $H_0: \mu = 6$ $H_1: \mu \neq 6, \bar{x} = 5.4, s = .5, n = 25$

9-21 Our hypothesis is that a bridge will safely withstand 50 tons of traffic.
a) Would we rather commit a Type I or a Type II error?
b) Based on your answer to part a, should we use a high or a low significance level?

9-22 Under what conditions is it appropriate to use a one-tailed test? a two-tailed test?

9-23 If you have decided that a one-tailed test is the appropriate test to use, how do you decide whether it should be a lower-tailed test or an upper-tailed test?

9-24 Martha Inman, a highway safety engineer, decides to test the load-bearing capacity of a bridge that is 20 years old. Considerable data are available from similar tests on the same type of bridge. Which is appropriate, a one-tailed or a two-tailed test? If the minimum load-bearing capacity of this bridge must be 10 tons, what are the null and alternative hypotheses?

9-25 Reggie Lowe, manager of the Blues and Reggae Music Store, is interested in knowing whether or not he sells fewer records than his local competition, Colt's 45s and Albums. Reggie is also interested in knowing whether or not his estimate of his monthly overhead expenses is accurate.
a) Suppose Reggie knows that Colt's sells an average of 100 records per week. State the null and alternative hypotheses that he is interested in testing.
b) Suppose Reggie thinks that his average monthly overhead is $1,000. State the null and alternative hypotheses that he is interested in testing.

9-4 HYPOTHESIS TESTING OF MEANS—SAMPLES WITH POPULATION STANDARD DEVIATIONS KNOWN

Two-Tailed Tests of Means

A manufacturer supplies the rear axles for U.S. Postal Service mail trucks. These axles must be able to withstand 80,000 pounds per square inch in stress tests, but an excessively strong axle raises production costs significantly. Long experience indicates that the standard deviation of the strength of its axles is 4,000 pounds per square inch. The manufacturer selects a sample of 100 axles from the latest production run, tests them, and finds that the mean stress capacity of the sample is 79,600 pounds per square inch. Written symbolically, the data in this case are:

Setting up the problem symbolically

$$\mu_{H_0} = 80{,}000 \leftarrow \text{hypothesized value of the population mean}$$
$$\sigma = 4{,}000 \leftarrow \text{population standard deviation}$$
$$n = 100 \leftarrow \text{sample size}$$
$$\bar{x} = 79{,}600 \leftarrow \text{sample mean}$$

If the axle manufacturer uses a significance level (α) of .05 in testing, will the axles meet his stress requirements? Symbolically, we can state the problem:

$H_0: \mu = 80{,}000 \leftarrow$ null hypothesis: the true mean is 80,000 pounds per square inch

$H_1: \mu \neq 80{,}000 \leftarrow$ alternative hypothesis: the true mean is not 80,000 pounds per square inch

$\alpha = .05 \leftarrow$ level of significance for testing this hypothesis

Calculating the standard error of the mean

Since we know the population standard deviation, and since the size of the population is large enough to be treated as infinite, we can use the normal distribution in our testing. First, we calculate the standard error of the mean using Equation 7-1:

$$\sigma_{\bar{x}} = \frac{\sigma}{\sqrt{n}} \quad [7\text{-}1]$$
$$= \frac{4{,}000}{\sqrt{100}}$$
$$= \frac{4{,}000}{10}$$
$$= 400 \text{ pounds per square inch} \leftarrow \text{standard error of the mean}$$

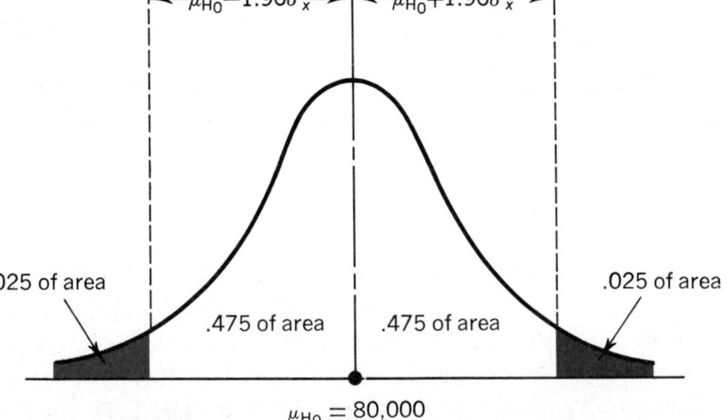

FIGURE 9-8 Two-tailed hypothesis test at the .05 significance level

Illustrating the problem

Figure 9-8 illustrates this problem, showing the significance level of .05 as the two shaded regions that each contain .025 of the area. The .95 acceptance region contains two equal areas of .475 each. From the normal distribution table (Appendix Table 1), we can see that the appropriate z value for .475 of the area under the curve is 1.96. Now we can determine the limits of the acceptance region:

Determining the limits of the acceptance region

$$\begin{aligned} \mu_{H_0} + 1.96\sigma_{\bar{x}} &= 80{,}000 + 1.96(400) \\ &= 80{,}000 + 784 \\ &= 80{,}784 \text{ pounds per square inch} \leftarrow \text{upper limit} \end{aligned}$$

and:

$$\begin{aligned} \mu_{H_0} - 1.96\sigma_{\bar{x}} &= 80{,}000 - 1.96(400) \\ &= 80{,}000 - 784 \\ &= 79{,}216 \text{ pounds per square inch} \leftarrow \text{lower limit} \end{aligned}$$

Interpreting the results

These two limits of the acceptance region (80,784 and 79,216) are shown in Fig. 9-9. Also, we have indicated the sample mean (79,600 pounds per square inch). Obviously, the sample mean lies within the acceptance region; the manufacturer should accept the null hypothesis, because there is no significant difference between the hypothesized mean of 80,000 and the observed mean of the sample axles. On the basis of this sample, the manufacturer should accept the production run as meeting the stress requirements.

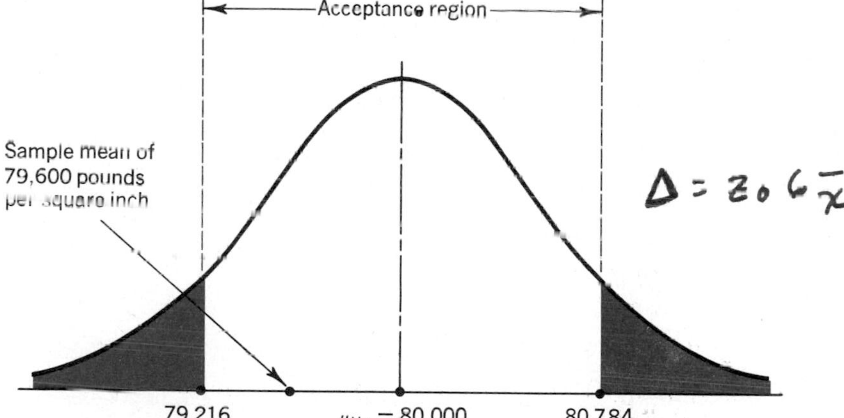

FIGURE 9-9 Two-tailed hypothesis test at the .05 significance level, showing acceptance region and sample mean

One-Tailed Tests of Means

For a one-tailed test of a mean, suppose a hospital uses large quantities of packaged doses of a particular drug. The individual dose of this drug is 100 cubic centimeters (100 cc). The action of the drug is such that the body will harmlessly pass off excessive doses. On the other hand, insufficient doses do not produce the desired medical effect, and they interfere with patient treatment. The hospital has purchased its requirements of this drug from the same manufacturer for a number of years and knows that the population standard deviation is 2 cc. The hospital inspects 50 doses of this drug at random from a very large shipment and finds the mean of these doses to be 99.75 cc.

$$\mu_{H_0} = 100 \leftarrow \text{hypothesized value of the population mean}$$
$$\sigma = 2 \leftarrow \text{population standard deviation}$$
$$n = 50 \leftarrow \text{sample size}$$
$$\bar{x} = 99.75 \leftarrow \text{sample mean}$$

Setting up the problem symbolically

If the hospital sets a .10 significance level and asks us whether the dosages in this shipment are too small, how can we find the answer?

To begin, we can state the problem symbolically:

$$H_0: \mu = 100 \leftarrow \text{null hypothesis: the mean of the shipments' dosages is 100 cc}$$
$$H_1: \mu < 100 \leftarrow \text{alternative hypothesis: the mean is less than 100 cc}$$
$$\alpha = .10 \leftarrow \text{level of significance for testing this hypothesis}$$

Calculating the standard error of the mean

Then we can calculate the standard error of the mean, using the known population standard deviation and Equation 7-1 (because the population size is large enough to be considered infinite):

$$\sigma_{\bar{x}} = \frac{\sigma}{\sqrt{n}} \qquad [7\text{-}1]$$
$$= \frac{2}{\sqrt{50}}$$
$$= \frac{2}{7.07}$$
$$= .2829 \text{ cc} \leftarrow \text{standard error of the mean}$$

Illustrating the problem

The hospital wishes to know whether the actual dosages are 100 cc or whether, in fact, the dosages are too small. The hospital must determine that the dosages are *more* than a certain amount, or it must reject the shipment. This is a *left-tailed* test, which we have shown graphically in Fig. 9-10. Notice that the colored region corresponds to the .10 significance level. Also notice that the acceptance region consists of 40 percent on the left side of the distribution *plus* the entire right side (50 percent), for a total

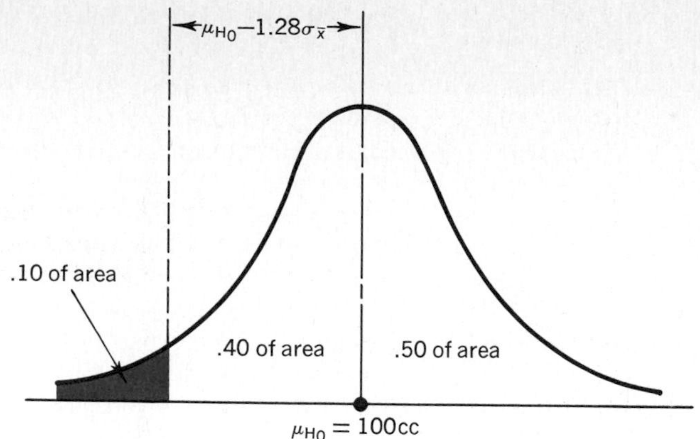

FIGURE 9-10 Left-tailed hypothesis test at the .10 significance level

area of 90 percent. Since we know the population standard deviation, and n is larger than 30, we can use the normal distribution. From Appendix Table 1, we can determine that the appropriate z value for 40 percent of the area under the curve is 1.28. Using this information, we can calculate the acceptance region's *lower* limit:

Determining the limit of the acceptance region

$$\begin{aligned}\mu_{H_0} - 1.28\sigma_{\bar{x}} &= 100 - 1.28(.2829) \\ &= 100 - .36 \\ &= 99.64 \text{ cc} \leftarrow \text{lower limit}\end{aligned}$$

Interpreting the results

This lower limit of the acceptance region, 99.64 cc, and the sample mean, 99.75, are both shown in Fig. 9-11. In this figure, we can see that the sample mean lies within the acceptance region. Therefore, the hospital should accept the null hypothesis, because there is no significant difference between our hypothesized mean of 100 cc and the observed mean of the sample. On the basis of this sample of 50 doses, the hospital should accept the doses in the shipment as being sufficient.

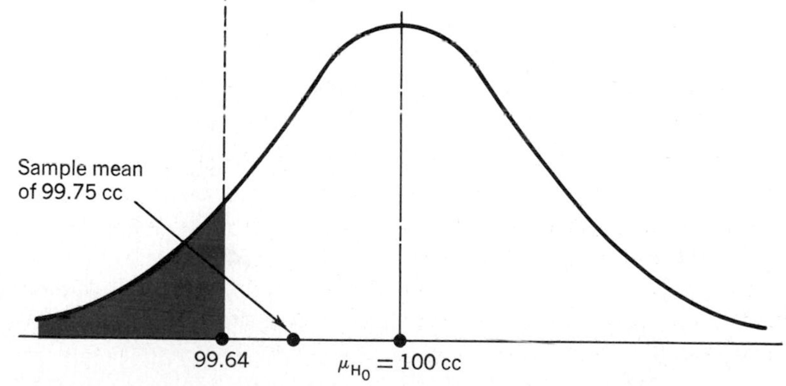

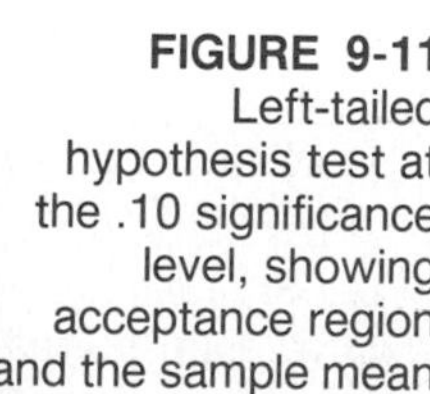
FIGURE 9-11 Left-tailed hypothesis test at the .10 significance level, showing acceptance region and the sample mean

EXERCISES

9-26 Atlas Sporting Goods has implemented a special trade promotion for its propane stove, and it suspects that the promotion may have resulted in a price change for the consumer. Atlas knows that before the promotion began, the average retail price of the stove was \$34, with a standard deviation of \$4.20. Atlas sampled 25 of its retail distributors after the promotion began and found the mean price for the stoves was \$32.40. At a .05 significance level, using a two-tailed test, does Atlas have reason to believe that the average retail price to the consumer has changed?

9-27 A moped manufacturer hypothesizes that the mean miles per gallon for its moped is 115.2. It takes a sample of 49 mopeds and finds the sample mean to be 117.6 miles per gallon. If the population standard deviation is known to be 8.4, test the hypothesis that the true mean miles per gallon is 115.2 against the alternative that it is greater than 115.2, using the .04 significance level.

9-28 Hinton Press hypothesizes that the life of its largest web press is 13,000 hours, with a known standard deviation of 2,000 hours. From a sample of 16 presses, the company finds the sample mean to be 12,000 hours. At a .01 level of significance, should the company conclude that the average life of the presses is less than the hypothesized 13,000 hours?

9-29 American Theaters knows that a certain hit movie ran an average of 76 days in each city, and the corresponding standard deviation was 8 days. The manager of the northwestern district was interested in comparing the movie's popularity in his region with that in all of American's other theaters. He randomly chooses 100 theaters in his region and finds that they ran the movie an average of 72 days.

a) The manager wishes to know if there is a significant difference between the mean number of days for the theaters in the Northwest and all of American's other theaters. What are the null and alternative hypotheses?

b) At a significance level of .05, test your hypothesis in part a.

9-30 A computer leasing firm has stated that the average monthly cost for a certain model is \$4,800, with a population standard deviation of \$900. The firm has sampled 40 of its customers who lease this model and found that the average monthly cost is \$4,500. At a 5 percent significance level, is the firm overestimating the cost for this model?

9-31 Marshall Bank and Trust Company offers a telephone-bill-paying service for its customers. Originally, the bank charged \$.05 per bill, and found that customers using the service paid an average of 9.5 bills per month through the bank, with a standard deviation of 4 bills. Last month the bank withdrew the service charge and offered the service free. This month, the bank sampled 36 accounts and found that the average number of bills paid through the service was 10.5. Using a significance level of .02, should the bank conclude that the change to free service has led to an increase in the number of bills per account paid through the service?

9-32 A chair manufacturing company knows that the average number of chairs a worker can assemble in one hour is 15, with a standard deviation of 5. It is proposed that a new glue may speed up assembly and increase hourly output, so a test is made using the new glue and 100 hours of labor time. The average number of chairs assembled per hour during the test is 16. At the .10 level of significance, does management have reason to believe that the new glue speeds up assembly output?

9-33 The Bay City Bigleaguers, a semiprofessional baseball team, have the player who led the league in batting average for many years. For the past several years, Joe Carver has compiled a mean batting average of .325 with a standard deviation of .020. This year, however, Joe's batting average was only .290. Joe's contract with the team has just ended, and the salary that he will be able to obtain for his next contract is highly dependent upon his ability to convince the team owner that his batting average was not significantly worse than in previous years. At the .05 level of significance, is Joe's average worse than it was previously?

9-5 MEASURING THE POWER OF A HYPOTHESIS TEST

What should a good hypothesis test do?

Now that we have considered two examples of hypothesis testing, a step back is appropriate, to discuss what a good hypothesis test *should* do. Ideally, α and β (the probabilities of Type I and Type II errors) should both be small. Recall that a Type I error occurs when we reject a null hypothesis that is true, and that α (the significance level of the test) *is* the probability of making a Type I error. In other words, once we decide upon the significance level, there is nothing else we can do about α. A Type II error occurs when we accept a null hypothesis that is false; the probability of a Type II error is β. What can we say about β?

Meaning of β and $1 - \beta$

Suppose the null hypothesis *is* false. Then managers would like the hypothesis test to reject it all the time. Unfortunately, hypothesis tests cannot be foolproof; sometimes when the null hypothesis is false, a test does not reject it, and thus a Type II error is made. When the null hypothesis is false, μ (the *true* population mean) does not equal μ_{H_0} (the hypothesized population mean); instead, μ equals some other value. For each possible value of μ for which the alternative hypothesis is true, there is a different probability (β) of incorrectly accepting the null hypothesis. Of course, we would like this β (the probability of accepting a null hypothesis when it is false) to be as small as possible, or equivalently, we would like $1 - \beta$ (the probability of rejecting a null hypothesis when it is false) to be as large as possible.

Interpreting the values of $1 - \beta$

Since rejecting a null hypothesis when it is false is exactly what a good test ought to do, a high value of $1 - \beta$ (something near 1.0) means the test is working quite well (it is rejecting the null hypothesis when it is false); a low value of $1 - \beta$ (something near 0.0) means that the test is working very poorly (it's not rejecting the null hypothesis when it is false). Since the value of $1 - \beta$ is the measure of how well the test is working, it is known as the *power of the test.* If we plot the values of $1 - \beta$ for each value of μ for which the alternative hypothesis is true, the resulting curve is known as a *power curve*.

Computing the values of $1 - \beta$

In part *a* of Fig. 9-12, we have reproduced the left-tailed test first introduced in Fig. 9-10. In part *b* of Fig. 9-12, we show the power curve that is associated with this test. Computing the values of $1 - \beta$ to plot the power curve is not difficult; three such points are shown in *b*, Fig. 9-12. Recall that with this test we were deciding whether or not to accept a drug shipment. Our test dictated that we should reject the null hypothesis if the sample mean dosage is less than 99.64 cc.

Consider point *C* on the power curve in *b*, Fig. 9-12. The population mean dosage is 99.42 cc. Given that the population mean is 99.42 cc, we must compute the probability that the mean of a random sample of 50 doses from this population will be less than 99.64 cc (the point below which we decided to reject the null hypothesis). Now look at *c*, Fig. 9-12. Earlier we computed the standard error of the mean to be .2829 cc, so 99.64 cc is

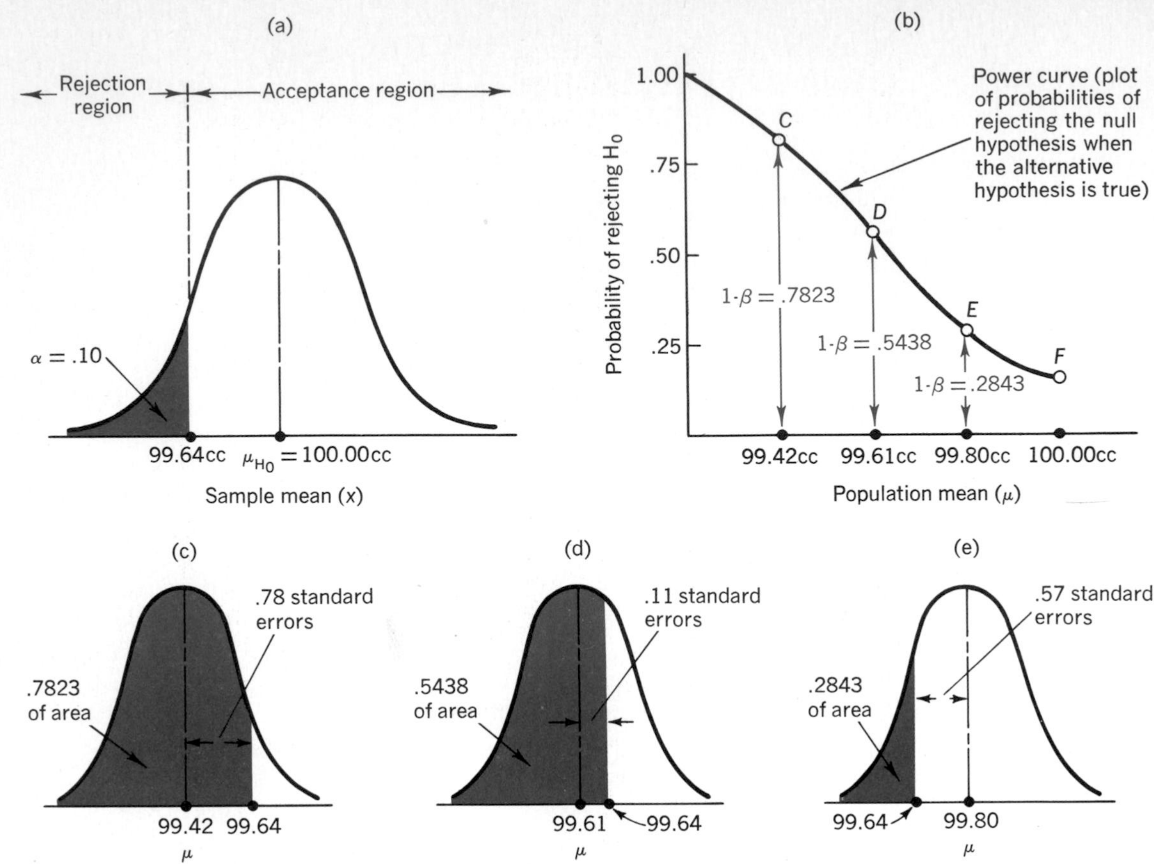

FIGURE 9-12
Left-tailed hypothesis test, associated power curve, and three values of μ

(99.64 − 99.42)/.2829, or .78 standard errors above 99.42 cc. Using Appendix Table 1, we can see that the probability of observing a sample mean less than 99.64 cc and thus rejecting the null hypothesis is .7823, the colored area in *c*, Fig. 9-12. Thus, the power of the test $(1-\beta)$ at $\mu = 99.42$ is .7823. This simply means that at $\mu = 99.42$, the probability that this test will reject the null hypothesis when it is false is .7823.

Interpreting a point on the power curve

Now look at point *D* in *b*, Fig. 9-12. For this population mean dosage of 99.61 cc, what is the probability that the mean of a random sample of 50 doses from this population will be less than 99.64 cc and thus cause the test to reject the null hypothesis? Look at *d*, Fig. 9-12. Here we see that 99.64 is (99.64 − 99.61)/.2829, or .11 standard errors above 99.61 cc. Using Appendix Table 1 again, we can see that the probability of observing a sample mean less than 99.64 cc and thus rejecting the null hypothesis is .5438, the colored area in *d*, Fig. 9-12. Thus, the power of the test $(1-\beta)$ at $\mu = 99.61$ cc is .5438.

Termination point of the power curve

Using the same procedure at point *E*, we find the power of the test at $\mu = 99.80$ cc is .2843; this is illustrated as the colored area in *e*, Fig. 9-12. The values of $1 - \beta$ continue to decrease to the right of point E. How low do they get? As the population mean gets closer and closer to 100.00 cc, the power of the test $(1 - \beta)$ must get closer and closer to the probability of rejecting the null hypothesis when the population mean is exactly 100.00 cc. And we know *that* probability is nothing but the significance level of the test—in this case, .10. Thus, the curve terminates at point F, which lies at a height of .10 directly over the population mean.

Interpreting the power curve

What does our power curve in b, Fig. 9-12, tell us? Just that as the shipment becomes less satisfactory (as the doses in the shipment become smaller), our test is more powerful (it has a greater probability of recognizing that the shipment is unsatisfactory). It also shows us, however, that because of sampling error, when the dosage is only slightly less than 100.00 cc, the power of the test to recognize this situation is quite low. Thus, if having *any* dosage below 100.00 cc is completely unsatisfactory, the test we have been discussing is not appropriate.

EXERCISES

9-34 See problem 9-31. Compute the power of the test for $\mu = 9.5$, 10.0, and 10.5 bills.

9-35 See problem 9-32. Compute the power of the test for $\mu = 15.4$, 15.7, and 16.0 chairs.

9-36 In problem 9-31, what happens to the power of the test for $\mu = 9.5$, 10.0, and 10.5 bills if the significance level is changed to .01?

9-37 In problem 9-32, what is the effect on the power of the test for $\mu = 15.4$, 15.7, and 16.0 chairs of raising the significance level to 20 percent?

9-6 HYPOTHESIS TESTING OF PROPORTIONS—LARGE SAMPLES

Two-Tailed Tests of Proportions

Dealing with proportions

In this section, we'll apply what we have learned about tests concerning means to tests for *proportions* (that is, the proportion of occurrences in a population). But before we apply it, we'll review the important conclusions we made about proportions in Chapter 8. First, remember that the binomial is the theoretically correct distribution to use in dealing with proportions, since the data are discrete, not continuous. As the sample size increases, the binomial distribution approaches the normal in its characteristics, and we can use the normal distribution to approximate the sampling distribution. Specifically, *np and nq each need to be at least 5* before we can use the normal distribution as a substitute for the binomial.

Setting up the problem symbolically

Consider, as an example, a company that is evaluating the promotability of its employees; that is, determining the proportion of them whose ability, training, and supervisory experience qualify them for promotion to the next higher level of management. The human resources director tells the president that 80 percent, or .8, of the employees in the company are "promotable." The president assembles a special committee to assess the promotability of all the employees. This committee conducts in-depth interviews with 150 employees and finds that in their judgment, only 70 percent of the sample are qualified for promotion.

$p_{H_0} = .8 \leftarrow$ hypothesized value of the population proportion of successes (judged promotable, in this case)

$q_{H_0} = .2 \leftarrow$ hypothesized value of the population proportion of failures (judged not promotable)

$n = 150 \leftarrow$ sample size

$\bar{p} = .7 \leftarrow$ sample proportion of promotables

$\bar{q} = .3 \leftarrow$ sample proportion judged not promotable

---

The president wants to test at the .05 significance level the hypothesis that .8 of the employees are promotable:

$H_0: p = .8 \leftarrow$ null hypothesis: 80 percent of the employees are promotable

$H_1: p \neq .8 \leftarrow$ alternative hypothesis: the proportion of promotable employees is not 80 percent

$\alpha = .05 \leftarrow$ level of significance for testing the hypothesis

---

Calculating the standard error of the proportion

To begin, we can calculate the standard error of the proportion, using the hypothesized values of p_{H_0} and q_{H_0} in Equation 8-4:

$$\sigma_{\bar{p}} = \sqrt{\frac{p_{H_0}q_{H_0}}{n}} \qquad \textbf{[8-4]}$$

$$= \sqrt{\frac{(.8)(.2)}{150}}$$

$$= \sqrt{.0010666}$$

$$= .0327 \leftarrow \text{standard error of the proportion}$$

Illustrating the problem

In this instance, the company wants to know whether the true proportion is larger or smaller than the hypothesized proportion. Thus, a two-tailed test of a proportion is appropriate, and we have shown it graphically in Fig. 9-13. The significance level corresponds to the two colored regions, each containing .025 of the area. The acceptance region of .95 is illustrated as two areas of .475 each. Since np and nq are each larger than 5,

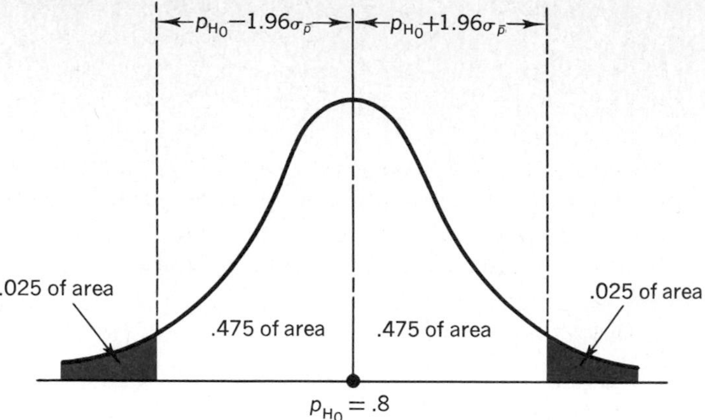

FIGURE 9-13 Two-tailed hypothesis test of a proportion at the .05 level of significance

Determining the limits of the acceptance region

we can use the normal approximation of the binomial distribution. From Appendix Table 1, we can determine that the appropriate z value for .475 of the area under the curve is 1.96. Thus, the limits of the acceptance region are:

$$
\begin{aligned}
p_{H_0} + 1.96\sigma_{\bar{p}} &= .8 + 1.96(.0327) \\
&= .8 + .0641 \\
&= .8641 \leftarrow \text{upper limit} \\
p_{H_0} - 1.96\sigma_{\bar{p}} &= .8 - 1.96(.0327) \\
&= .8 - .0641 \\
&= .7359 \leftarrow \text{lower limit}
\end{aligned}
$$

Interpreting the results

Figure 9-14 illustrates these two limits of the acceptance region, .8641 and .7359, as well as our sample proportion, .7. We can see that our sample proportion does *not* lie within the acceptance region. Therefore, in this case, the president should reject the null hypothesis and conclude that there *is* a significant difference between the director of human resources' hypothesized proportion of promotable employees (.8) and the observed proportion of promotable employees in the sample. From this, he should infer that the

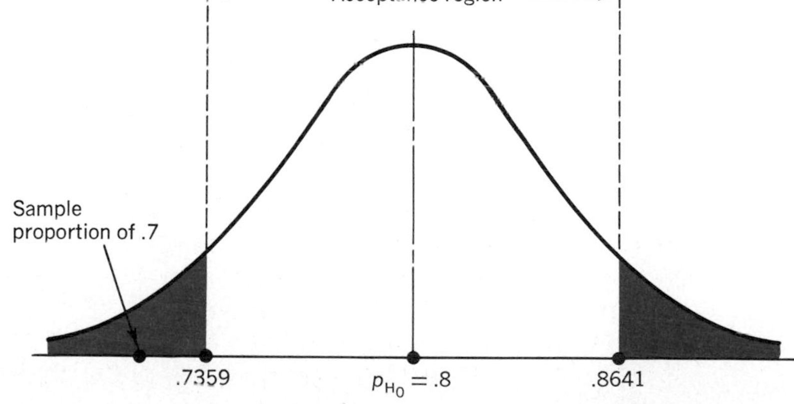

FIGURE 9-14 Two-tailed hypothesis test of a proportion at the .05 significance level, showing acceptance region and sample proportion

true proportion of promotable employees in the entire company is not 80 percent.

One-Tailed Tests of Proportions

A one-tailed test of a proportion is conceptually equivalent to a one-tailed test of a mean, as can be illustrated with this example. A member of a public interest group concerned with environmental pollution asserts at a public hearing that "fewer than 60 percent of the industrial plants in this area are complying with air pollution standards." Attending this meeting is an official of the Environmental Protection Agency who believes that 60 percent of the plants *are* complying with the standards; she decides to test that hypothesis at the .02 significance level.

$H_0: p = .6 \leftarrow$ null hypothesis: the proportion of plants complying with air pollution standards is .6

$H_1: p < .6 \leftarrow$ alternative hypothesis: the proportion complying with the standards is less than .6

$\alpha = .02 \leftarrow$ level of significance for testing the hypothesis

---

The official makes a thorough search of the records in her office. She samples 60 plants from a population of over 10,000 plants and finds that 33 are complying with air pollution standards. Is the assertion by the member of the public interest group a valid one?

We begin by summarizing the case symbolically:

Setting up the problem symbolically

$p_{H_0} = .6 \leftarrow$ hypothesized value of the population proportion that are complying with air pollution standards

$q_{H_0} = .4 \leftarrow$ hypothesized value of the population proportion that are not complying and thus polluting

$n = 60 \leftarrow$ sample size

$\bar{p} = 33/60$ or $.55 \leftarrow$ sample proportion complying

$\bar{q} = 27/60$ or $.45 \leftarrow$ sample proportion polluting

---

Calculating the standard error of the proportion

Next, we can calculate the standard error of the proportion using the hypothesized population proportion as follows:

$$\sigma_{\bar{p}} = \sqrt{\frac{p_{H_0}q_{H_0}}{n}} \qquad \textbf{[8-4]}$$

$$= \sqrt{\frac{(.6)(.4)}{60}}$$

$$= \sqrt{.004}$$

$$= .0632 \leftarrow \text{standard error of the proportion}$$

Illustrating the problem

This is a one-tailed test: The EPA official wonders only whether the actual proportion is less than .6. Specifically, this is a left-tailed test. In order to reject the null hypothesis that the true proportion of plants in compliance is 60 percent, the EPA representative must accept the alternative hypothesis that fewer than .6 have complied. In Fig. 9-15, we have shown this hypothesis test graphically.

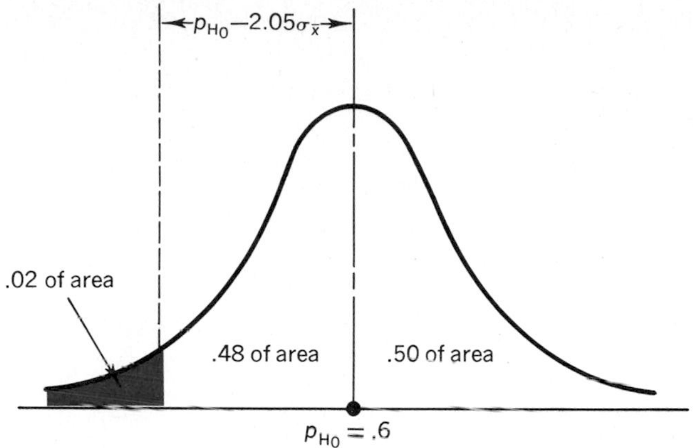

FIGURE 9-15 One-tailed hypothesis test at the .02 level of significance

Determining the limit of the acceptance region

Since np and nq are each over 5, we can use the normal approximation of the binomial distribution. The appropriate z value from Appendix Table 1 for .48 of the area under the curve is 2.05. Thus, we can calculate the limit of the acceptance region as follows:

$$\begin{aligned} p_{H_0} - 2.05\sigma_{\bar{p}} &= .6 - 2.05(.0632) \\ &= .6 - .13 \\ &= .47 \leftarrow \text{lower limit} \end{aligned}$$

Interpreting the results

Figure 9-16 illustrates the limit of the acceptance region, .47, and the sample proportion, .55, (33/60). Looking at this figure, we can see that the sample proportion lies within the acceptance region. Therefore, the EPA official

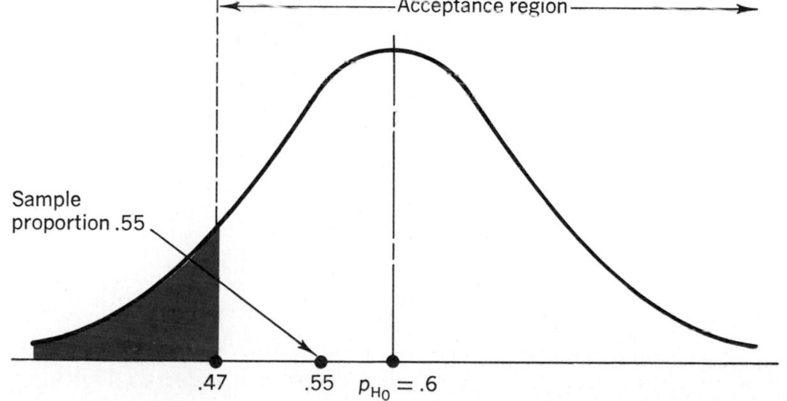

FIGURE 9-16 One-tailed (left-tailed) hypothesis test at .02 significance level, showing acceptance region and sample proportion

should accept the null hypothesis that the true proportion of complying plants is .6. **Although the observed sample proportion is below .6, *it is not significantly below* .6; that is, it is not far enough below .6 to make us accept the assertion by the member of the public interest group.**

EXERCISES

9-38 Grant, Inc., a manufacturer of men's dress shirts, knows that its brand is carried in 15 percent of the men's clothing stores in the United States. Grant recently sampled 75 men's clothing stores on the West Coast and found that 18.7 percent of the stores sampled carried the brand. At the .05 level of significance, is there evidence that Grant has better distribution on the West Coast than nationally?

9-39 From a total of 8,000 loans made by a state's employees' credit union in the most recent 5-year period, 300 were sampled to determine what proportion was made to women. This sample showed 37 percent of the loans made by the credit union were made to women employees. A similar study made 5 years ago showed that 32 percent of the borrowers were women. At a significance level of .10, has there been a significant change in the proportion of women receiving loans?

9-40 Marvin Hendrix, brand manager of a fluoride toothpaste, knows that his brand has consistently been favored by 58 percent of the population. However, a competitor has increased its advertising budget in the past year; and from a recent sample of 500 consumers, the proportion preferring Hendrix's brand was 54 percent.

a) At the .10 level of significance, should Hendrix conclude that his brand's share has declined?
b) Reconsider the question in part a at the .05 level of significance.

9-41 A furniture store with a loose credit policy expects that 8 percent of its credit accounts will default on payments. Looking at the 500 accounts sold to last year, however, we see that 49 have defaulted. Using a 5 percent level of significance, do you think the store has reason to believe that the estimate of 8 percent is too low?

9-42 A ketchup manufacturer is in the process of deciding whether to produce a new extra-spicy brand. The marketing research department of the company used a national telephone survey of 5,000 housewives and found that 235 said that they would purchase an extra-spicy brand. A similar study made 2 years ago showed the percentage of housewives who said they would purchase the brand was 4 percent. At a 2 percent significance level, should the company conclude that there is an increased interest in the extra-spicy flavor?

9-43 Steve Cutter sells Big Blade lawn mowers in his hardware store, and he is interested in comparing the reliability of the Big Blade mowers he sells to the reliability of Big Blade mowers nationwide. Steve knows that only 20 percent of all Big Blade mowers sold nationwide require repairs during the first year of ownership. A sample of 100 of Steve's customers revealed that exactly 27 of them required mower repairs in the first year of ownership. At the .05 level of significance, is there evidence that Steve's Big Blade mowers are less reliable than all Big Blade mowers sold nationwide?

9-7 HYPOTHESIS TESTING OF MEANS UNDER DIFFERENT CONDITIONS

When to use the *t* distribution

When we estimated confidence intervals in Chapter 8, we learned that the difference in size between large and small samples is important when the population standard deviation σ is unknown and must be estimated from the sample standard deviation. If the sample size n is 30 or less and σ is not known, we should use the t distribution. The appropriate t distribution has $n - 1$ degrees of freedom. These rules apply to hypothesis testing, too.

Two-Tailed Tests of Means Using the *t* Distribution

Setting up the problem symbolically

A personnel specialist of a major corporation is recruiting a large number of employees for an overseas assignment. During the testing process, management asks how things are going, and she replies, "Fine. I think the average score on the aptitude test will be 90." When management reviews 20 of the test results compiled, it finds that the mean score is 84, and the standard deviation of this score is 11.

$$\mu_{H_0} = 90 \leftarrow \text{hypothesized value of the population mean}$$
$$n = 20 \leftarrow \text{sample size}$$
$$\bar{x} = 84 \leftarrow \text{sample mean}$$
$$s = 11 \leftarrow \text{sample standard deviation}$$

If management wants to test her hypothesis at the .10 level of significance, what is the procedure?

$$H_0: \mu = 90 \leftarrow \text{null hypothesis: the true population mean score is 90}$$
$$H_1: \mu \neq 90 \leftarrow \text{alternative hypothesis: the mean score is not 90}$$
$$\alpha = .10 \leftarrow \text{level of significance for testing this hypothesis}$$

Calculating the standard error of the mean

Since the population standard deviation is not known, we must estimate it using the sample standard deviation and Equation 8-1:

$$\hat{\sigma} = s \qquad [8\text{-}1]$$
$$= 11$$

Now we can compute the standard error of the mean. Since we are using $\hat{\sigma}$, an estimate of the population standard deviation, the standard error of the mean will also be an estimate. We can use Equation 8-6, as follows:

$$\hat{\sigma}_{\bar{x}} = \frac{\hat{\sigma}}{\sqrt{n}} \qquad [8\text{-}6]$$
$$= \frac{11}{\sqrt{20}}$$
$$= \frac{11}{4.47}$$
$$= 2.46 \leftarrow \text{estimated standard error of the mean}$$

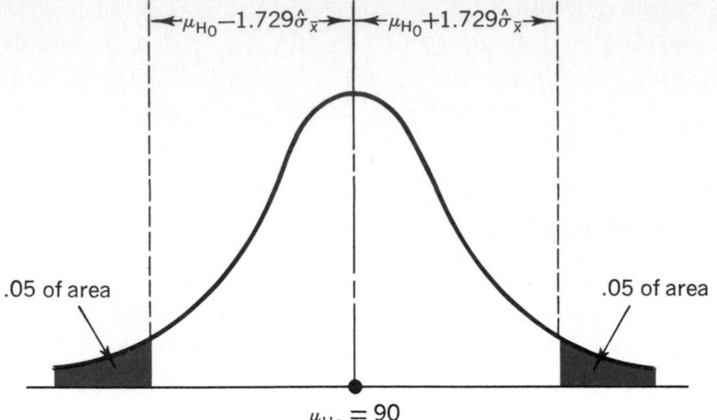

FIGURE 9-17 Two-tailed test of hypothesis at the .10 level of significance using the *t* distribution

Illustrating the problem

Figure 9-17 illustrates this problem graphically. Since management is interested in knowing whether the true mean score is *larger* or *smaller* than the hypothesized score, a *two-tailed test* is the appropriate one to use. The significance level of .10 is shown in Fig. 9-17 as the two colored areas, each containing .05 of the area under the *t* distribution. Since the sample size is 20, the appropriate number of degrees of freedom is 19; that is, 20 − 1. Therefore, we look in the *t* distribution table, Appendix Table 2, under the .10 column until we reach the 19 degrees of freedom row. There we find the *t* value of 1.729.

This value is the appropriate one to use in calculating the limits of the acceptance region:

Determining the limits of the acceptance region

$$\begin{aligned}\mu_{H_0} + 1.729\hat{\sigma}_{\bar{x}} &= 90 + 1.729(2.46)\\ &= 90 + 4.25\\ &= 94.25 \leftarrow \text{upper limit}\end{aligned}$$

$$\begin{aligned}\mu_{H_0} - 1.729\hat{\sigma}_{\bar{x}} &= 90 - 1.729(2.46)\\ &= 90 - 4.25\\ &= 85.75 \leftarrow \text{lower limit}\end{aligned}$$

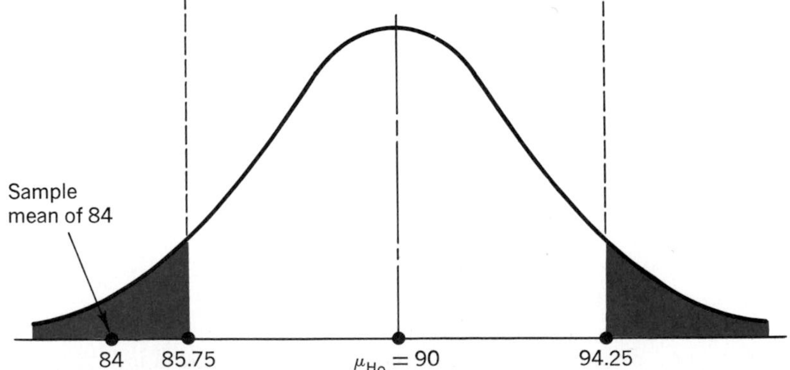

FIGURE 9-18 Two-tailed hypothesis test at the .10 level of significance, showing acceptance region and the sample mean

Interpreting the results

Figure 9-18 illustrates these two limits of the acceptance region, 94.25 and 85.75, and sample mean, 84. From this figure, we can see that the sample mean lies outside the acceptance region. Therefore, management should reject the null hypothesis (the personnel specialist's assertion that the true mean score of the employees being tested is 90).

One-Tailed Tests of Means Using the *t* Distribution

One difference from the z tables

The procedure for a one-tailed hypothesis test using the t distribution is the same conceptually as for a one-tailed test using the normal distribution and the z table. Performing such one-tailed tests may cause some difficulty, however. Notice that the column headings in Appendix Table 2 represent the *area in both tails combined*. Thus, they are appropriate to use in a two-tailed test with *two* rejection regions.

Using the t tables for one-tailed tests

If we use the t distribution for a one-tailed test, we need to determine the area located in only one tail. So to find the appropriate t value for a one-tailed test at a significance level of .05 with 12 degrees of freedom, we would look in Appendix Table 2 under the .10 column opposite the 12 degrees of freedom row. The answer in this case is 1.782. **This is true because the .10 column represents .10 of the area under the curve contained in *both tails combined,* and so it also represents .05 of the area under the curve contained in each of the tails separately.**

EXERCISES

9-44 Given a sample mean of 19.1, a sample standard deviation of 4, and a sample of size 25, test the hypothesis that the value of the population mean is 17, against the alternative that it is greater than 17. Use the .01 significance level.

9-45 If a sample of 10 observations reveals a sample mean of 12 and a sample variance of 1.96, test the hypothesis that the population mean is 13, against the alternative that it is some other value. Use the .05 level of significance.

9-46 Ferrell Realty Company took a random sample of 16 homes in a prestigious area of Chicago and found the average appraised market value to be $210,500, with a standard deviation of $30,000. Test the hypothesis that in the entire population of 120 homes in the area, the mean appraised value is $200,000, against the alternative that it is greater than $200,000. Use the .01 level of significance.

9-47 For a sample of 50 taken from a population of 2,000, the sample mean is 105.1 and the sample standard deviation is 21.5. Using the .05 level of significance, test the hypothesis that the true population mean is 102, against the alternative that it is some other value.

9-48 A data-processing department of an insurance company has installed new video display terminals to replace the old machines. The 160 operators trained to run the new machines averaged 14.1 trials before a perfect performance, with a standard deviation of 4 trials. Long experience with operators on the old machines showed that they average 12.6 trials before a perfect performance. At the .05 significance level, should the supervisor of the department conclude that the new terminals are harder to learn to operate?

9-49 The present best-selling remedy for headaches is reported to bring relief in 15 minutes. In a pilot study of 9 individuals, scientists at a pharmaceutical company found that their new formula brought relief in an average of 13.5 minutes, with a standard deviation of 1.2 minutes. At the .025 level of significance, is there reason to believe that the average relief time for the new medication is shorter than that for the old?

9-50 A television documentary on overeating claimed that Americans are 16 pounds overweight on average. To test this claim, 9 randomly selected individuals were examined, and the average excess weight was found to be 18 pounds with a standard deviation of 4 pounds. At the .05 level of significance, is there reason to believe the claim of 16 pounds to be in error?

9-51 A scientist researching giraffes in Africa has been gathering data from one very large herd. Due to some rather obvious problems in measuring the length of a giraffe's neck, he has only been able to measure the neck lengths of 36 randomly chosen giraffes from the herd. The mean neck length of the sample was 9.7 feet, with sample variance of 4 feet squared. At the .05 level of significance, is it reasonable to conclude that the mean neck length of all giraffes in the herd is exactly 9 feet?

9-8 HYPOTHESIS TESTING FOR DIFFERENCES BETWEEN MEANS AND PROPORTIONS

Comparing two populations

In many decision-making situations, people need to determine whether the parameters of two populations are alike or different. A company may want to test, for example, whether its female employees receive lower salaries than its male employees for the same work. A training director may wish to determine whether the proportion of promotable employees at one government installation is different from that at another. A drug manufacturer may need to know whether a new drug causes one reaction in one group of experimental animals but a different reaction in another group.

In each of these examples, decision makers are concerned with the parameters of two populations. In these situations, they are not as interested in the actual value of the parameters as they are in the *relation between* the values of the two parameters—that is, how these parameters differ. *Do* female employees earn less than male employees for the same work? *Is* the proportion of promotable employees at one installation different from that at another? *Did* one group of experimental animals react differently from the other? In this section, we shall introduce methods by which these questions can be answered, using hypothesis-testing procedures.

Sampling Distribution for the Difference Between Two Population Parameters—Basic Concepts

A new way to generate a sampling distribution

In Chapter 7, we introduced the concept of the sampling distribution of the mean as the foundation for the work we would do in estimation and hypothesis testing. For a quick review of the sampling distribution of the mean, you may refer to Fig. 7-1.

Since we now wish to study two populations, not just one, the sampling distribution of interest is the *sampling distribution of the difference*

Deriving the sampling distribution of the difference between sample means

between sample means. Figure 9-19 may help us conceptualize this particular sampling distribution. At the top of this figure, we have drawn two populations, identified as Population 1 and Population 2. These two have means of μ_1 and μ_2 and standard deviations of σ_1 and σ_2, respectively. Beneath each population, we show the sampling distribution of the mean for that population. At the bottom of the figure is the sampling distribution of the difference between the sample means.

The two theoretical sampling distributions of the mean in Fig. 9-19 are each made up of all the possible samples of a given size that can be drawn

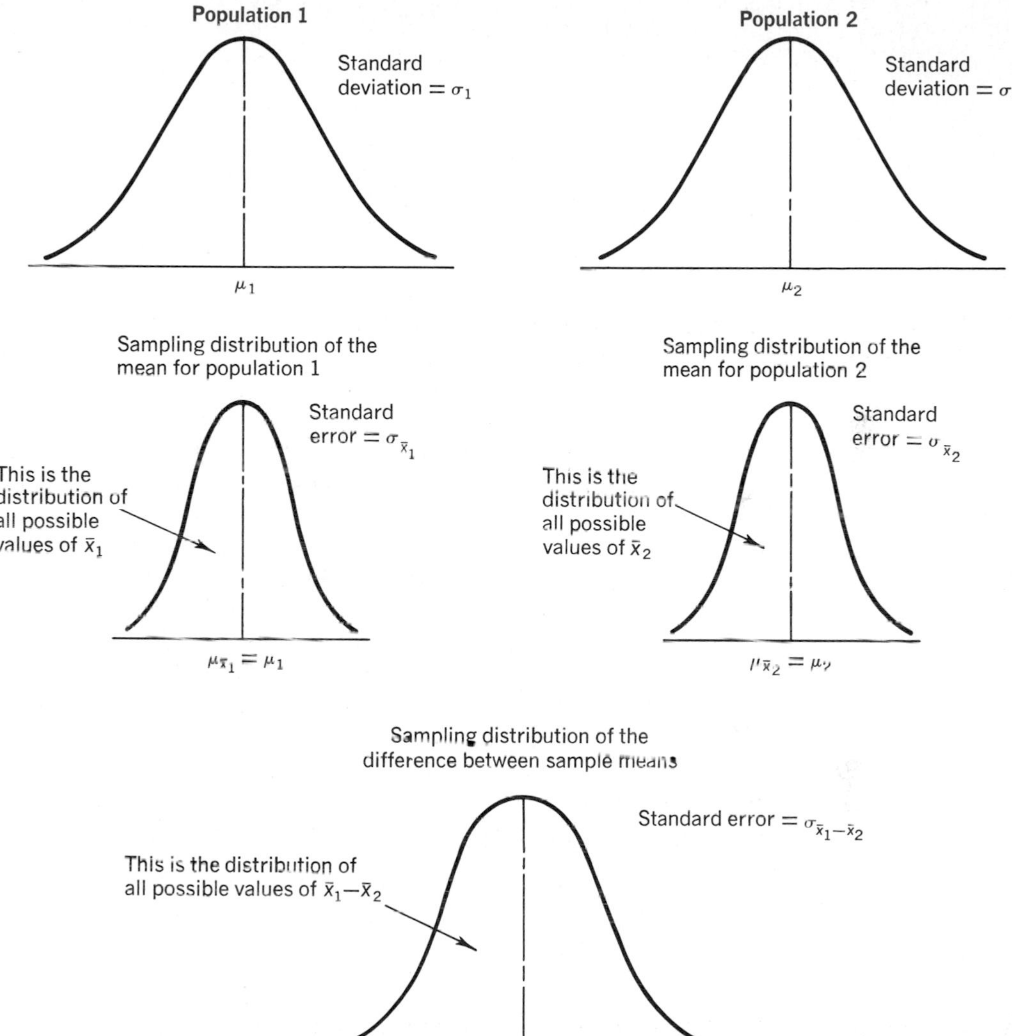

FIGURE 9-19
Basic concepts of population distributions, sampling distributions of the mean, and the sampling distribution of the difference between sample means

from the corresponding population distribution. Now, suppose we take a random sample from the distribution of Population 1 and another random sample from the distribution of Population 2. If we then subtract the two sample means, we get:

$$\bar{x}_1 - \bar{x}_2 \leftarrow \text{difference between sample means}$$

This difference will be positive if $\bar{x}_1$ is larger than $\bar{x}_2$, and negative if $\bar{x}_2$ is greater than $\bar{x}_1$. By constructing a distribution of *all* the possible sample differences of $\bar{x}_1 - \bar{x}_2$, we end up with the sampling distribution of the difference between sample means, which is shown at the bottom of Fig. 9-19.

Parameters of this sampling distribution

The *mean of the sampling distribution of the difference between sample means* is symbolized $\mu_{\bar{x}_1 - \bar{x}_2}$ and is equal to $\mu_{\bar{x}_1} - \mu_{\bar{x}_2}$, which, as we saw in Chapter 7, is the same as $\mu_1 - \mu_2$. If $\mu_1 = \mu_2$, then $\mu_{\bar{x}_1} - \mu_{\bar{x}_2} = 0$.

The standard deviation of the distribution of the difference between the sample means is called the *standard error of the difference between two means* and is calculated using this formula:

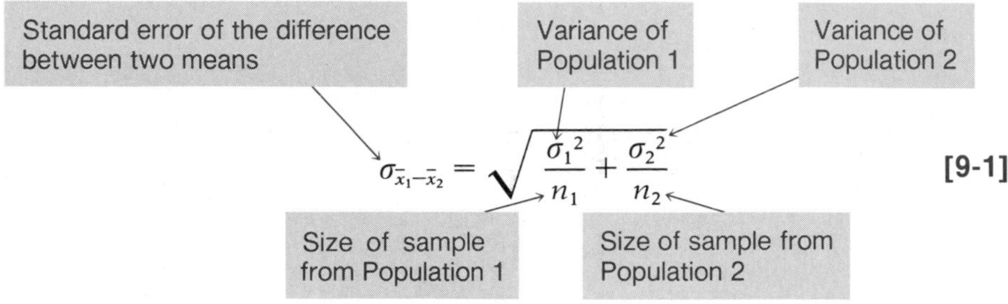

[9-1]

How to estimate the standard error of this sampling distribution

If the two population standard deviations are *not* known, we can *estimate* the standard error of the difference between two means. We can use the same method of estimating the standard error that we have used before by letting sample standard deviations estimate the population standard deviations as follows:

$$\hat{\sigma} = s \longleftarrow \text{Sample standard deviation} \qquad \textbf{[8-1]}$$

Therefore, the formula for the estimated standard error of the difference between two means becomes:

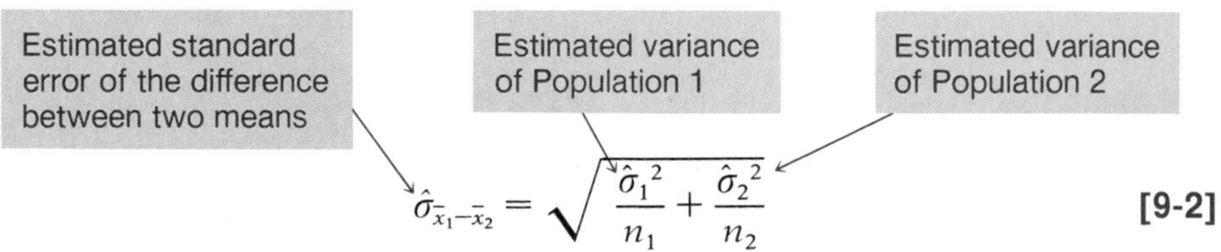

[9-2]

As the following examples show, depending on the sample sizes, we shall use different estimates for $\hat{\sigma}_1$ and $\hat{\sigma}_2$ in Equation 9-2.

Two-Tailed Tests for Difference Between Means (Large Sample Sizes)

Setting up the problem symbolically

When both sample sizes are greater than 30, this example illustrates how to do a two-tailed test of a hypothesis about the difference between two means. A manpower-development statistician is asked to determine whether the hourly wages of semiskilled workers are the same in two cities. The statistician takes simple random samples of hourly earnings in both cities. The results of this survey are presented in Table 9-2. Suppose the company wants to test the hypothesis at the .05 level that there is no difference between hourly wages for semiskilled workers in the two cities:

$H_0: \mu_1 = \mu_2$ ← null hypothesis: there is no difference

$H_1: \mu_1 \neq \mu_2$ ← alternative hypothesis: a difference exists

$\alpha = .05$ ← level of significance for testing this hypothesis

TABLE 9-2 Data from sample survey of hourly wages

CITY	MEAN HOURLY EARNINGS FROM SAMPLE	STANDARD DEVIATION OF SAMPLE	SIZE OF SAMPLE
Apex	$6.95	$.40	200
Eden	7.10	.60	175

Calculating the standard error of the difference between two means

Since the company is interested only in whether the means are *or* are not equal, this is a two-tailed test.

The standard deviations of the two populations are not known. Therefore, our first step is to estimate them, as follows:

$$\hat{\sigma}_1 = s_1 \qquad \hat{\sigma}_2 = s_2 \qquad \textbf{[8-1]}$$
$$= \$.40 \qquad = \$.60$$

Now the estimated standard error of the difference between the two means can be determined by:

$$\hat{\sigma}_{\bar{x}_1 - \bar{x}_2} = \sqrt{\frac{\hat{\sigma}_1^2}{n_1} + \frac{\hat{\sigma}_2^2}{n_2}} \qquad \textbf{[9-2]}$$
$$= \sqrt{\frac{(.40)^2}{200} + \frac{(.60)^2}{175}}$$
$$= \sqrt{\frac{.16}{200} + \frac{.36}{175}}$$
$$= \sqrt{.0028}$$
$$= \$.053 \leftarrow \text{estimated standard error}$$

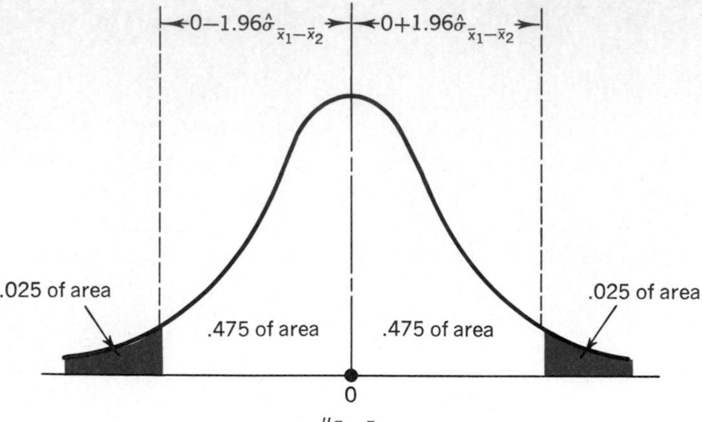

FIGURE 9-20 Two-tailed hypothesis test of the difference between two means at the .05 level of significance

Illustrating the problem

We can illustrate this hypothesis test graphically. In Fig. 9-20, the significance level of .05 corresponds to the two colored areas, each of which contains .025 of the area. The acceptance region contains two equal areas of .475 each. Since both samples are large, we can use the normal distribution. From Appendix Table 1, we can determine the appropriate z value for .475 of the area under the curve to be 1.96. Now we can calculate the limits of the acceptance region:

Determining the limits of the acceptance region

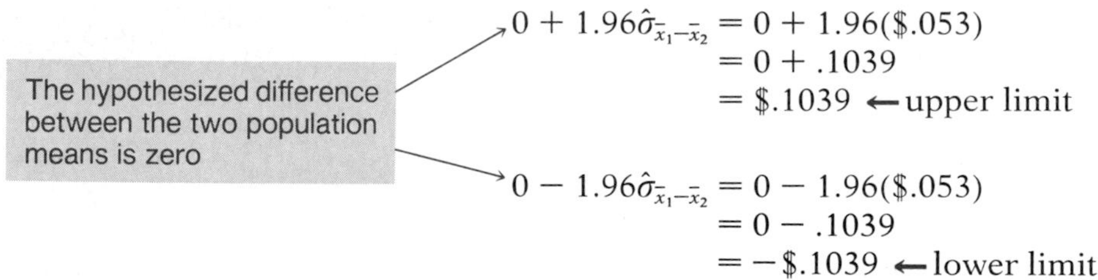

$$\begin{aligned} 0 + 1.96\hat{\sigma}_{\bar{x}_1-\bar{x}_2} &= 0 + 1.96(\$.053) \\ &= 0 + .1039 \\ &= \$.1039 \leftarrow \text{upper limit} \end{aligned}$$

$$\begin{aligned} 0 - 1.96\hat{\sigma}_{\bar{x}_1-\bar{x}_2} &= 0 - 1.96(\$.053) \\ &= 0 - .1039 \\ &= -\$.1039 \leftarrow \text{lower limit} \end{aligned}$$

Interpreting the results

Figure 9-21 illustrates these two limits of the acceptance region (\$.1039 and −\$.1039) and indicates the difference between the sample means. It is calculated:

$$\begin{aligned} \text{Difference} &= \bar{x}_1 - \bar{x}_2 \text{ (from Table 9-2)} \\ &= \$6.95 - \$7.10 \\ &= -\$0.15 \end{aligned}$$

Figure 9-21 demonstrates that the difference between the two sample means lies outside the acceptance region. Thus, we reject the null hypothesis of no difference and conclude that the population means (the average semiskilled wages in these two cities) differ.

One-Tailed Tests for Difference Between Means (Small Sample Sizes)

Setting up the problem symbolically

The procedure for a one-tailed test of the difference between means is conceptually like that for the one-tailed tests of means we have already discussed. The only major difference will be in how we compute the esti-

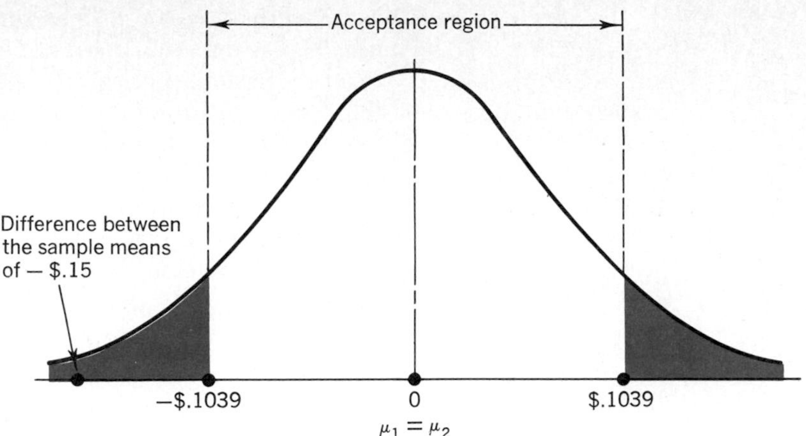

FIGURE 9-21 Two-tailed hypothesis test of the difference between two means at the .05 level of significance, showing acceptance region and difference between sample means

mated standard error of the difference between the two means. Suppose that a company has been investigating two education programs for increasing the sensitivity of its managers to the needs of its Spanish-speaking employees. The original program consisted of several informal question-and-answer sessions with leaders of the Spanish-speaking community. Over the past few years, a program involving formal classroom contact with professional psychologists and sociologists has been developed. The new program is considerably more expensive, and the president wants to know at the .05 level of significance whether this expenditure has resulted in greater sensitivity. Let's test the following:

$H_0: \mu_1 = \mu_2$ ← null hypothesis: there is no difference in sensitivity levels achieved by the two programs

$H_1: \mu_1 > \mu_2$ ← alternative hypothesis: the new program results in higher sensitivity levels

$\alpha = .05$ ← level of significance for testing this hypothesis

---

Table 9-3 contains the data resulting from a sample of the managers trained in both programs. Because only limited data are available for the two programs, the population standard deviations are estimated from the data. The sensitivity level is measured as a percentage on a standard psychometric scale.

TABLE 9-3 Data from sample of two sensitivity programs

PROGRAM SAMPLED	MEAN SENSITIVITY AFTER THIS PROGRAM	NUMBER OF MANAGERS OBSERVED	ESTIMATED STANDARD DEVIATION OF SENSITIVITY AFTER THIS PROGRAM
Formal	92%	12	15%
Informal	84%	15	19%

The company wishes to test whether the sensitivity achieved by the new program is *significantly higher* than that achieved under the older, more informal program. To reject the null hypothesis (a result that the company desires), the observed difference of sample means would need to fall sufficiently high in the *right* tail of the distribution. Then we would accept the alternative hypothesis that the new program leads to higher sensitivity levels and that the extra expenditures on this program are justified.

Our first task in performing the test is to calculate the standard error of the difference between the two means. Since the population standard deviations are not known, we must use Equation 9-2:

$$\hat{\sigma}_{\bar{x}_1-\bar{x}_2} = \sqrt{\frac{\hat{\sigma}_1^2}{n_1} + \frac{\hat{\sigma}_2^2}{n_2}} \qquad \textbf{[9-2]}$$

In the previous example, where the sample sizes were large (both greater than 30), we used Equation 8-1 and estimated $\hat{\sigma}_1^2$ by s_1^2, and $\hat{\sigma}_2^2$ by s_2^2. Now, with small sample sizes, that procedure is not appropriate. If we can assume that the unknown population variances are equal (and this assumption can be tested using a method discussed in Section 6 of the next chapter), we can continue. If we cannot assume that $\sigma_1^2 = \sigma_2^2$, then the problem is beyond the scope of this text.

Estimating σ^2 with small sample sizes

Assuming for the moment that $\sigma_1^2 = \sigma_2^2$, how can we estimate the common variance σ^2? If we use either s_1^2 or s_2^2, we get an unbiased estimator of σ^2, but we don't use all the information available to us, since we ignore one of the samples. Instead we use a weighted average of s_1^2 and s_2^2, and the weights are the numbers of degrees of freedom in each sample. This weighted average is called a "pooled estimate" of σ^2. It is given by:

Pooled estimate of σ^2 ⟶

$$s_p^2 = \frac{(n_1 - 1)s_1^2 + (n_2 - 1)s_2^2}{n_1 + n_2 - 2} \qquad \textbf{[9-3]}$$

Plugging this into Equation 9-2 and simplifying gives us:

$$\hat{\sigma}_{\bar{x}_1-\bar{x}_2} = s_p \sqrt{\frac{1}{n_1} + \frac{1}{n_2}} \qquad \textbf{[9-4]}$$

When we want to test hypotheses about differences of population means, and we have small samples but equal population variances, we use Equation 9-4 to estimate the standard error of the difference between the two means. Then, as you might have guessed, the test is based on the t distribution. The appropriate number of degrees of freedom is $(n_1 - 1) + (n_2 - 1)$, or $n_1 + n_2 - 2$, which is the denominator in Equation 9-3.

Applying these results to our sensitivity example:

$$s_p^2 = \frac{(n_1 - 1)s_1^2 + (n_2 - 1)s_2^2}{n_1 + n_2 - 2} \qquad \textbf{[9-3]}$$

$$= \frac{(12 - 1)(15)^2 + (15 - 1)(19)^2}{12 + 15 - 2}$$

$$= \frac{11(225) + 14(361)}{25}$$

$$= 301.160$$

Taking square roots on both sides, we get $s_p = \sqrt{301.160}$, or 17.354, and so:

$$\hat{\sigma}_{\bar{x}_1 - \bar{x}_2} = s_p \sqrt{\frac{1}{n_1} + \frac{1}{n_2}} \quad \textbf{[9-4]}$$

$$= 17.354 \sqrt{\frac{1}{12} + \frac{1}{15}}$$

$$= 17.354(.387)$$

$$= 6.721$$

Illustrating the problem

In Fig. 9-22, a graphic illustration of this hypothesis test, the significance level of .05 is represented by the colored region at the right of the distribution. Since both sample sizes are less than 30, the t distribution with $12 + 15 - 2 = 25$ degrees of freedom is the appropriate sampling distribution. The t value for .05 of the area under the curve is 1.708, according to Appendix Table 2. The value of $\mu_{\bar{x}_1 - \bar{x}_2}$, the mean of the sampling distribution of the hypothesized difference between the two sensitivity means, is equal to zero. Thus, the calculation for determining the limit of the acceptance region is:

Determining the limit of the acceptance region

$$0 + 1.708\hat{\sigma}_{\bar{x}_1 - \bar{x}_2} = 0 + 1.708(6.721)$$
$$= 0 + 11.48$$
$$= 11.48\% \leftarrow \text{upper limit}$$

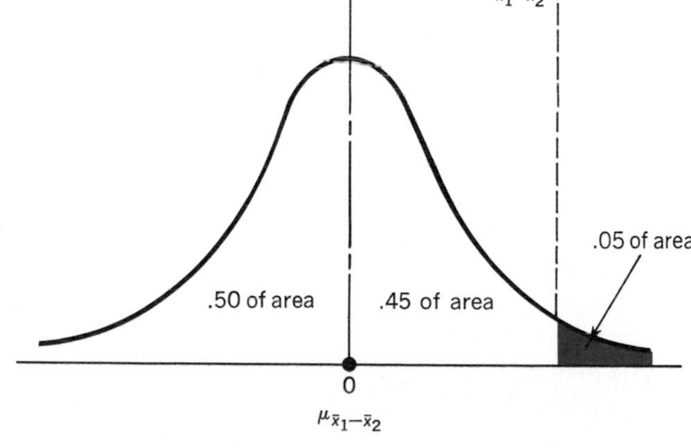

FIGURE 9-22 Right-tailed hypothesis test of the difference between two means at the .05 level of significance

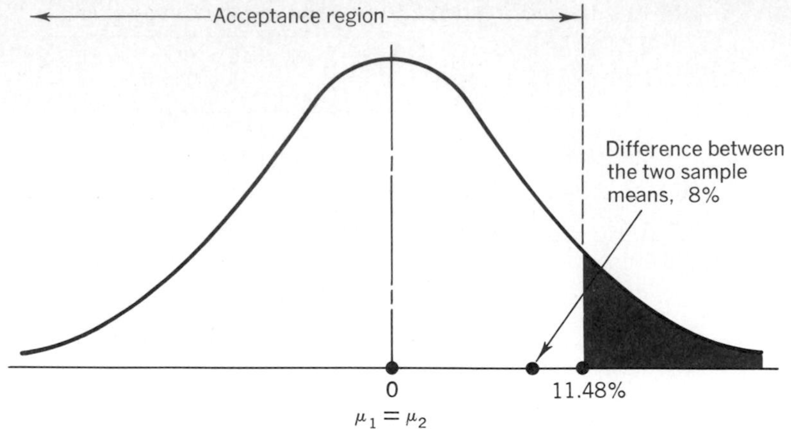

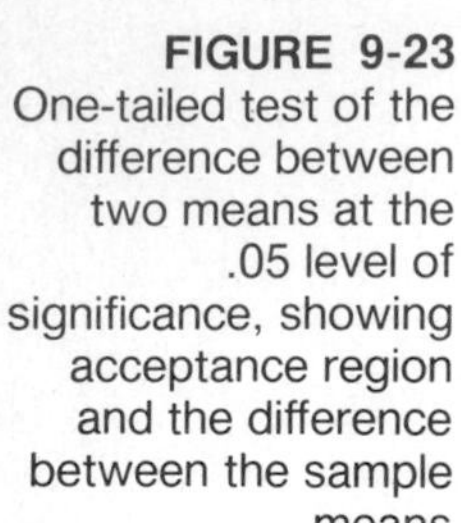
FIGURE 9-23 One-tailed test of the difference between two means at the .05 level of significance, showing acceptance region and the difference between the sample means

Interpreting the results

In Fig. 9-23, we have illustrated this limit of the acceptance region and the difference between the two sample sensitivities (92% − 84% = 8%). We can see in Fig. 9-23 that the difference between the two sample means lies within the acceptance region. Thus, we accept the null hypothesis that there is no difference between the sensitivities achieved by the two programs. The company's expenditures on the formal instructional program have not produced significantly higher sensitivities among its managers.

Testing Differences Between Means with Dependent Samples

Conditions under which paired samples aid analysis

In the last two examples, our samples were chosen *independently* of each other. In the wage example, the samples were taken in two different cities. In the sensitivity example, samples were taken of managers who had gone through two different training programs. Sometimes, however, it will make sense to take samples that are not independent of each other. Often the use of such *dependent* (or *paired*) samples will enable us to perform a more precise analysis, because they will allow us to control for extraneous factors. With dependent samples, we still follow the same basic procedure we have followed in all our hypothesis testing. The only differences are that we will use a different formula for the estimated standard error of the sample differences and that we will require that both samples be of the same size.

A health spa has advertised a weight-reducing program and has claimed that the average participant in the program loses at least seventeen pounds. A somewhat overweight executive is interested in the program but is skeptical about the claims and asks for some hard evidence. The spa allows him to select randomly the records of ten participants and record their weights before and after the program. These data are recorded in Table 9-4. Here we have two samples (a *before* sample and an *after* sample) that are clearly dependent on each other, since the same ten people have been observed twice.

TABLE 9-4 Weights before and after a reducing program

Before	189	202	220	207	194	177	193	202	208	233
After	170	179	203	192	172	161	174	187	186	204

The overweight executive wants to test at the 5 percent significance level the claimed average weight loss of at least seventeen pounds. Formally, we may state this problem:

$H_0: \mu_1 - \mu_2 = 17$ ← null hypothesis: average weight loss is only 17 pounds

$H_1: \mu_1 - \mu_2 > 17$ ← alternative hypothesis: average weight loss exceeds 17 pounds

$\alpha = .05$ ← level of significance

Conceptual understanding of differences

What we are really interested in is not the weights before and after but only their *differences*. **Conceptually, what we have is *not two* samples of before and after weights, but rather *one sample* of weight losses.** If the population of weight losses has a mean μ_ℓ, we can restate our hypotheses as:

$$H_0: \mu_\ell = 17$$
$$H_1: \mu_\ell > 17$$

Now we compute the individual losses, their mean and standard deviation, and proceed exactly as we did when testing hypotheses about a single mean. The computations are done in Table 9-5.

TABLE 9-5 Finding the mean weight loss and its standard deviation

BEFORE	AFTER	LOSS x	LOSS SQUARED x^2
189	170	19	361
202	179	23	529
220	203	17	289
207	192	15	225
194	172	22	484
177	161	16	256
193	174	19	361
202	187	15	225
208	186	22	484
233	204	29	841
		$\Sigma x =$ **197**	$\Sigma x^2 =$ **4,055**

$$\bar{x} = \frac{\Sigma x}{n} \quad [3\text{-}2]$$
$$= \frac{197}{10}$$
$$= 19.7$$

$$s = \sqrt{\frac{\Sigma x^2}{n-1} - \frac{n\bar{x}^2}{n-1}} \quad [4\text{-}12]$$
$$= \sqrt{\frac{4{,}055}{9} - \frac{10(19.7)^2}{9}}$$
$$= \sqrt{19.34}$$
$$= 4.40$$

We use Equation 8-1 to estimate the unknown population standard deviation:

$$\hat{\sigma} = s \qquad [8\text{-}1]$$
$$= 4.40$$

and now we can estimate the standard error of the mean:

$$\hat{\sigma}_{\bar{x}} = \frac{\hat{\sigma}}{\sqrt{n}} \qquad [8\text{-}6]$$
$$= \frac{4.40}{\sqrt{10}}$$
$$= \frac{4.40}{3.16}$$
$$= 1.39 \leftarrow \text{estimated standard error of the mean}$$

Figure 9-24 illustrates this problem graphically. Since we want to know if the mean weight loss *exceeds* seventeen pounds, an upper-tailed test is appropriate. The .05 significance level is shown in Fig. 9-24 as the colored area under the t distribution. We use the t distribution because the sample size is only ten; the appropriate number of degrees of freedom is 9, (10 − 1). Appendix Table 2 gives the t value of 1.833.

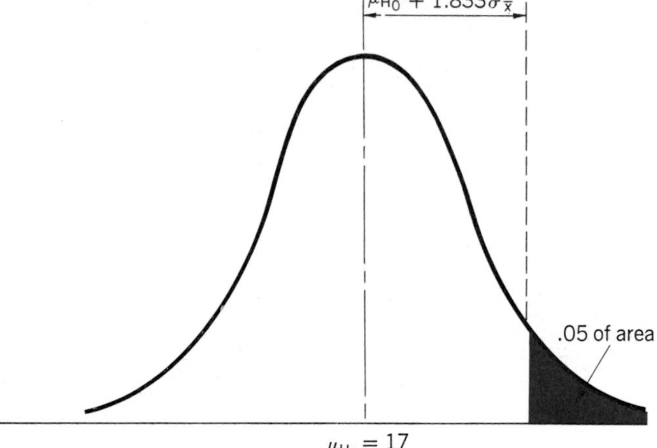

FIGURE 9-24 One-tailed hypothesis test at the .05 level of significance

We use this t value to calculate the upper limit of the acceptance region:

$$\mu_{H_0} + 1.833\hat{\sigma}_{\bar{x}} = 17 + 1.833(1.39)$$
$$= 17 + 2.55$$
$$= 19.55 \text{ pounds} \leftarrow \text{upper limit}$$

Interpreting the results

Figure 9-25 illustrates the acceptance region and the sample mean, 19.7. We see that the sample mean lies outside the acceptance region, so the executive can reject the null hypothesis and conclude that the claimed weight loss in the program is legitimate.

How does the paired difference test differ?

Let's see how this *paired difference* test differs from a test of the

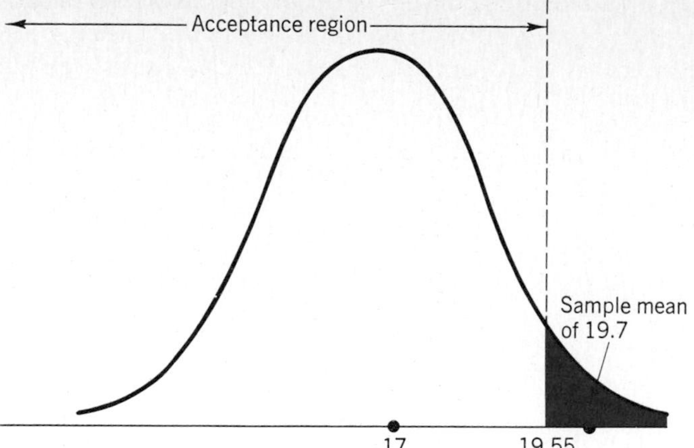

FIGURE 9-25 One-tailed hypothesis test at the .05 level of significance, showing acceptance region and sample mean

difference of means of *two independent* samples. Suppose that the data in Table 9-4 represent two independent samples of ten individuals *entering* the program and *another* ten randomly selected individuals *leaving* the program. The means and variances of the two samples are given in Table 9-6.

TABLE 9-6 Before and after means and variances

SAMPLE	SIZE	MEAN	VARIANCE
Before	10	202.5	253.61
After	10	182.8	201.96

Since the sample sizes are small, we use Equation 9-3 to get a pooled estimate of σ^2 and Equation 9-4 to estimate $\hat{\sigma}_{\bar{x}_1-\bar{x}_2}$:

$$s_p^2 = \frac{(n_1 - 1)s_1^2 + (n_2 - 1)s_2^2}{n_1 + n_2 - 2} \quad [9\text{-}3]$$

$$= \frac{(10 - 1)(253.61) + (10 - 1)(201.96)}{10 + 10 - 2}$$

$$= \frac{2282.49 + 1817.64}{18}$$

$$= 227.79 \leftarrow \text{estimate of common population variance}$$

$$\hat{\sigma}_{\bar{x}_1-\bar{x}_2} = s_p \sqrt{\frac{1}{n_1} + \frac{1}{n_2}} \quad [9\text{-}4]$$

$$= \sqrt{227.79} \sqrt{\frac{1}{10} + \frac{1}{10}}$$

$$= 15.09 \sqrt{0.2}$$

$$= 15.09(0.45)$$

$$= 6.79 \leftarrow \text{estimate of } \hat{\sigma}_{\bar{x}_1-\bar{x}_2}$$

The appropriate test is now based on the t distribution with 18 degrees of freedom $(10 + 10 - 2)$. With a significance level of .05, the appropriate t value from Appendix Table 2 is 1.734, so the upper limit of the acceptance region is:

$$\begin{aligned} 17 + 1.734\hat{\sigma}_{\bar{x}_1-\bar{x}_2} &= 17 + 1.734(6.79) \\ &= 17 + 11.77 \\ &= 28.77 \text{ pounds} \end{aligned}$$

The observed difference of the sample means is:

$$\begin{aligned} \bar{x}_1 - \bar{x}_2 &= 202.5 - 182.8 \\ &= 19.7 \text{ pounds} \end{aligned}$$

so this test will *not* reject H_0.

Explaining differing results

Why did these two tests give such different results? In the paired sample test, the sample standard deviation of the individual differences was relatively small, so 19.7 pounds was significantly larger than the hypothesized weight loss of 17 pounds. With independent samples, however, the estimated standard deviation of the difference between the means depended on the standard deviations of the before weights and the after weights. Since both of these were relatively large, $\hat{\sigma}_{\bar{x}_1-\bar{x}_2}$ was also large, and thus 19.7 was not significantly larger than 17. The paired sample test controlled this initial and final variability in weights by looking only at the individual changes in weights. Because of this, it was better able to detect the significance of the weight loss.

We conclude this section with two examples showing when to treat two samples of equal size as dependent or independent:

Should we treat samples as dependent or independent?

1. An agricultural extension service wishes to determine whether a new hybrid seed corn has a greater yield than an old standard variety. If the service asks ten farmers to record the yield of an acre planted with the new variety and asks another ten farmers to record the yield of an acre planted with the old variety, the two samples are independent. If, however, it asks ten farmers to plant one acre with each variety and record the results, then the samples are dependent, and the paired difference test is appropriate. In the latter case, differences due to fertilizer, insecticide, rainfall, and so on are controlled, because each farmer treats his two acres identically. Thus, any differences in yield can be attributed solely to the variety planted.

2. The director of the secretarial pool at a large legal office wants to determine whether typing speed depends upon the kind of typewriter used by a secretary. If she tests seven secretaries using electric typewriters and seven using manual typewriters, she should treat her samples as independent. If she tests the same seven secretaries twice (once on each type of machine), then the two samples are dependent. In the paired difference test, differences among the secretaries are eliminated as a contributing factor, and the differences in typing speeds can be attributed to the different types of machines.

Two-Tailed Tests for Difference Between Proportions

Consider the case of a pharmaceutical manufacturing company testing two new compounds intended to reduce blood-pressure levels. The compounds are administered to two different sets of laboratory animals. In group one, 71 of 100 animals tested respond to drug 1 with lower blood-pressure levels. In group two, 58 of 90 animals tested respond to drug 2 with lower blood-pressure levels. The company wants to test at the .05 level whether there is a difference between the efficacies of these two drugs. How should we proceed with this problem?

As in our previous examples, we can begin by calculating the standard deviation of the sampling distribution we are using in our hypothesis test. In this example, the binomial distribution is the correct sampling distribution.

$\bar{p}_1 = .71$ ← sample proportion of successes with drug 1

$\bar{q}_1 = .29$ ← sample proportion of failures with drug 1

$n_1 = 100$ ← sample size for testing drug 1

$\bar{p}_2 = .644$ ← sample proportion of successes with drug 2

$\bar{q}_2 = .356$ ← sample proportion of failures with drug 2

$n_2 = 90$ ← sample size for testing drug 2

$H_0: p_1 = p_2$ ← null hypothesis: there is no difference between these two drugs

$H_1: p_1 \neq p_2$ ← alternative hypothesis: there is a difference between them

$\alpha = .05$ ← level of significance for testing this hypothesis

Calculating the standard error of the difference between two proportions

We want to find the *standard error of the difference between two proportions;* therefore, we should recall the formula for the *standard error of the proportion:*

$$\sigma_{\bar{p}} = \sqrt{\frac{pq}{n}} \qquad \textbf{[8-4]}$$

Using this formula and the same form we previously used in Equation 9-1 for the standard error of the difference between two *means,* we get:

$$\sigma_{\bar{p}_1-\bar{p}_2} = \sqrt{\frac{p_1q_1}{n_1} + \frac{p_2q_2}{n_2}} \qquad \textbf{[9-5]}$$

How to estimate this standard error

To test the two compounds, we do not know the population parameters p_1, p_2, q_1, and q_2, and thus we need to estimate them from the sample statistics $\bar{p}_1$, $\bar{p}_2$, $\bar{q}_1$, and $\bar{q}_2$. In this case, we might suppose that the practical formula to use would be:

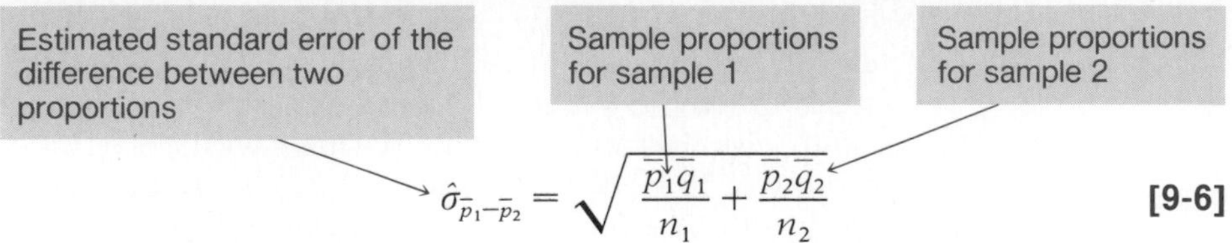

$$\hat{\sigma}_{\bar{p}_1-\bar{p}_2} = \sqrt{\frac{\bar{p}_1\bar{q}_1}{n_1} + \frac{\bar{p}_2\bar{q}_2}{n_2}} \qquad \textbf{[9-6]}$$

But think about this a bit more. After all, if we hypothesize that there is *no difference* between the two population proportions, then our best estimate of the overall population proportion of successes is probably the *combined* proportion of successes in both samples; that is:

Best estimate of the overall proportion of successes in the population if the 2 proportions are hypothesized to be equal = (Number of successes in sample 1 + Number of successes in sample 2) / Total size of both samples

And in the case of the two compounds, we use this equation with symbols rather than words:

$$\hat{p} = \frac{(n_1)(\bar{p}_1) + (n_2)(\bar{p}_2)}{n_1 + n_2} \qquad \textbf{[9-7]}$$

$$= \frac{(100)(.71) + (90)(.644)}{100 + 90}$$

$$= \frac{71 + 58}{190}$$

$= .6789 \leftarrow$ estimate of the overall proportion of successes in the combined populations using combined proportions from both samples ($\hat{q}$ would be $1 - .6789 = .3211$)

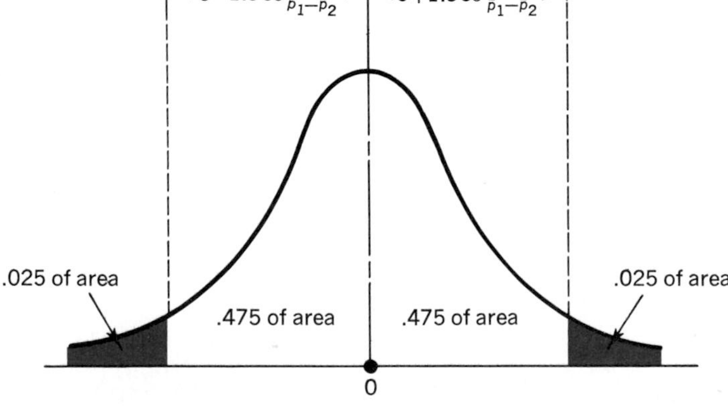

FIGURE 9-26 Two-tailed hypothesis test of the difference between two proportions at the .05 level of significance

Now we can appropriately modify Equation 9-6 using the values $\hat{p}$ and $\hat{q}$ from Equation 9-7:

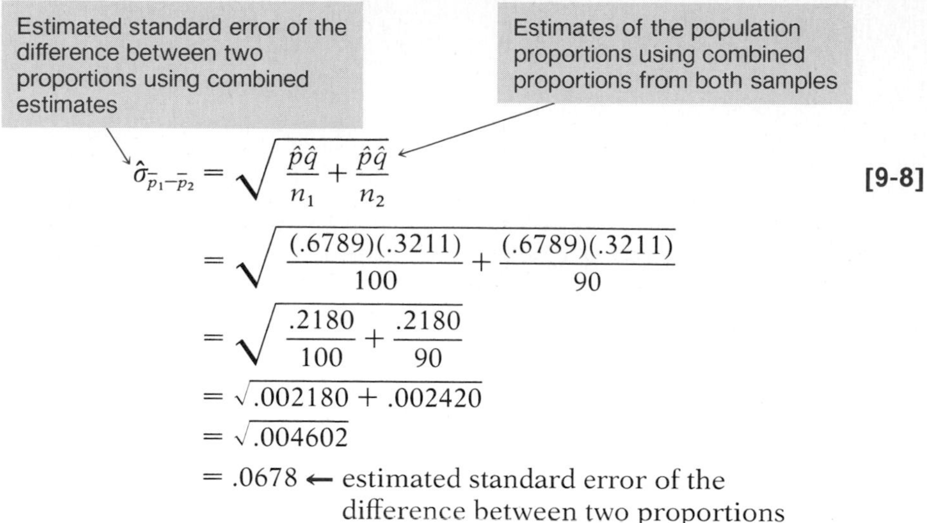

$$\hat{\sigma}_{\bar{p}_1-\bar{p}_2} = \sqrt{\frac{\hat{p}\hat{q}}{n_1} + \frac{\hat{p}\hat{q}}{n_2}} \qquad [9\text{-}8]$$

$$= \sqrt{\frac{(.6789)(.3211)}{100} + \frac{(.6789)(.3211)}{90}}$$

$$= \sqrt{\frac{.2180}{100} + \frac{.2180}{90}}$$

$$= \sqrt{.002180 + .002420}$$

$$= \sqrt{.004602}$$

$$= .0678 \leftarrow \text{estimated standard error of the difference between two proportions}$$

What did we save by using Equation 9-8 instead of Equation 9-6? In Equation 9-8, we needed only *one* value for $\hat{p}$ and *one* value for $\hat{q}$; thus we avoided some of the calculations involved in the use of Equation 9-6.

Illustrating the problem

Figure 9-26 illustrates this hypothesis test graphically. Since the management of the pharmaceutical company wants to know whether there is a difference between the two compounds, this is a two-tailed test. The significance level of .05 corresponds to the colored regions in the figure. Both samples are large enough to justify using the normal distribution to approximate the binomial. From Appendix Table 1, we can determine that the appropriate z value for .475 of the area under the curve is 1.96. We can calculate the two limits of the acceptance region as follows:

Determining the limits of the acceptance region

The hypothesized difference between the 2 proportions is zero

$$0 + 1.96\hat{\sigma}_{\bar{p}_1-\bar{p}_2} = 0 + 1.96(.0678)$$
$$= 0 + .1329$$
$$= .1329 \leftarrow \text{upper limit}$$

$$0 - 1.96\hat{\sigma}_{\bar{p}_1-\bar{p}_2} = 0 - 1.96(.0678)$$
$$= 0 - .1329$$
$$= -.1329 \leftarrow \text{lower limit}$$

Figure 9-27 illustrates these two limits of the acceptance region, .1329 and −.1329. It also indicates the difference between the sample proportions, calculated as:

$$\text{Difference} = \bar{p}_1 - \bar{p}_2$$
$$= .71 - .644$$
$$= .066$$

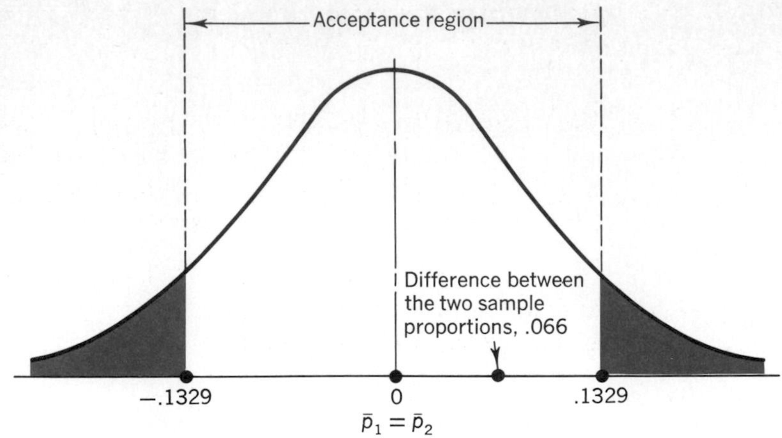

FIGURE 9-27 Two-tailed hypothesis test of the difference between two proportions at the .05 level of significance, showing acceptance region and the difference between sample proportions

Interpreting the results

We can see in Fig. 9-27 that the difference between the two sample proportions lies within the acceptance region. Thus, we accept the null hypothesis and conclude that these two compounds produce effects on blood pressure that are *not* different.

One-Tailed Tests for Difference Between Proportions

Setting up the problem symbolically

Conceptually, the one-tailed test for the difference between two population proportions is similar to a one-tailed test for the difference between two means. Suppose that for tax purposes, a city government has been using two methods of listing property. The first requires the property owner to appear in person before a tax lister, but the second permits the property owner to mail in a tax form. The city manager thinks the personal-appearance method produces far fewer mistakes than the mail-in method. She authorizes an examination of 50 personal-appearance listings and 75 mail-in listings. Ten percent of the personal-appearance forms contain errors; 13.3 percent of the mail-in forms contain them. The result of her sample can be summarized:

$\bar{p}_1 = .10 \leftarrow$ proportion of personal-appearance forms with errors

$\bar{q}_1 = .90 \leftarrow$ proportion of personal-appearance forms without errors

$n_1 = 50 \leftarrow$ sample size of personal-appearance forms

$\bar{p}_2 = .133 \leftarrow$ proportion of mail-in forms with errors

$\bar{q}_2 = .867 \leftarrow$ proportion of mail-in forms without errors

$n_2 = 75 \leftarrow$ sample size of mail-in forms

The city manager wants to test at the .15 level of significance the hypothesis that the personal-appearance method produces a lower proportion of errors. What should she do?

$H_0: p_1 = p_2 \leftarrow$ null hypothesis: there is no difference between the two methods

$H_1: p_1 < p_2 \leftarrow$ alternative hypothesis: the personal-appearance method has a lower proportion of errors than the mail-in method

$\alpha = .15 \leftarrow$ level of significance for testing the hypothesis

Calculating the standard error of the difference between two proportions

To estimate the *standard error of the difference between two proportions,* we first use the combined proportions from both samples to estimate the overall proportion of successes:

$$\hat{p} = \frac{(n_1)(\bar{p}_1) + (n_2)(\bar{p}_2)}{n_1 + n_2} \quad [9\text{-}7]$$

$$= \frac{(50)(.10) + (75)(.133)}{50 + 75}$$

$$= \frac{5 + 10}{125}$$

$$= .12 \leftarrow \text{estimate of the overall proportion of successes in the population using combined proportions from both samples}$$

Now this answer can be used to calculate the standard error of the difference between the two proportions, using Equation 9-8:

$$\hat{\sigma}_{\bar{p}_1 - \bar{p}_2} = \sqrt{\frac{\hat{p}\hat{q}}{n_1} + \frac{\hat{p}\hat{q}}{n_2}} \quad [9\text{-}8]$$

$$= \sqrt{\frac{(.12)(.88)}{50} + \frac{(.12)(.88)}{75}}$$

$$= \sqrt{\frac{.10560}{50} + \frac{.10560}{75}}$$

$$= \sqrt{.002112 + .001408}$$

$$= \sqrt{.00352}$$

$$= .0593 \leftarrow \text{estimated standard error of the difference between two proportions using combined estimates}$$

Illustrating the problem

Figure 9-28 illustrates this hypothesis test. Since the city manager wishes to test whether the personal-appearance listing is better than the mailed-in listing, the appropriate test is a one-tailed test. Specifically, it is a *left-tailed* test, because to reject the null hypothesis, the test result must fall in the colored portion of the left tail, indicating that *significantly fewer errors* exist in the personal-appearance forms. This colored region in Fig. 9-28 corresponds to the .15 significance level.

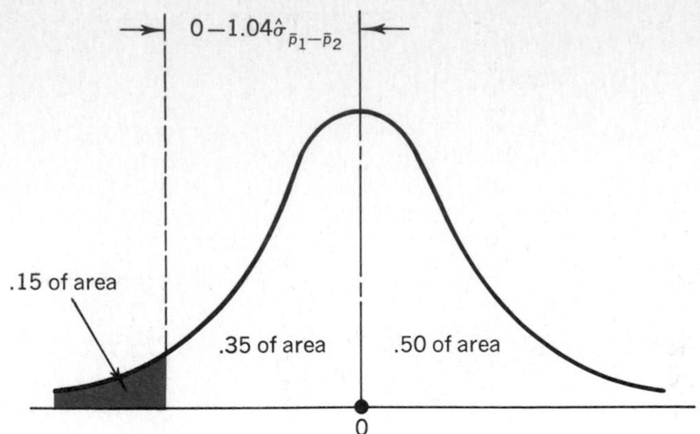

FIGURE 9-28 One-tailed hypothesis test of the difference between two proportions at the .15 level of significance

With samples of this size, we can use the standard normal distribution and Appendix Table 1 to determine the appropriate z value for .35 of the area under the curve. We can use this value, 1.04, to calculate the lower limit of the acceptance region:

Determining the limit of the acceptance region

The hypothesized difference between the 2 population proportions is zero

$$
\begin{aligned}
0 - 1.04\hat{\sigma}_{\bar{p}_1-\bar{p}_2} &= 0 - 1.04(.0593) \\
&= 0 - .0617 \\
&= -.0617 \leftarrow \text{lower limit}
\end{aligned}
$$

Interpreting the results

We have illustrated this limit to the acceptance region and the difference between the two sample proportions $(.10 - .133 = -.033)$ in Fig. 9-29. This figure shows us that the difference between the two sample proportions lies well within the acceptance region, and the city manager should accept the null hypothesis that there is no difference between the two methods of tax listing. Therefore, if mailed-in listing is considerably less expensive to the city, the city manager should consider increasing the use of this method.

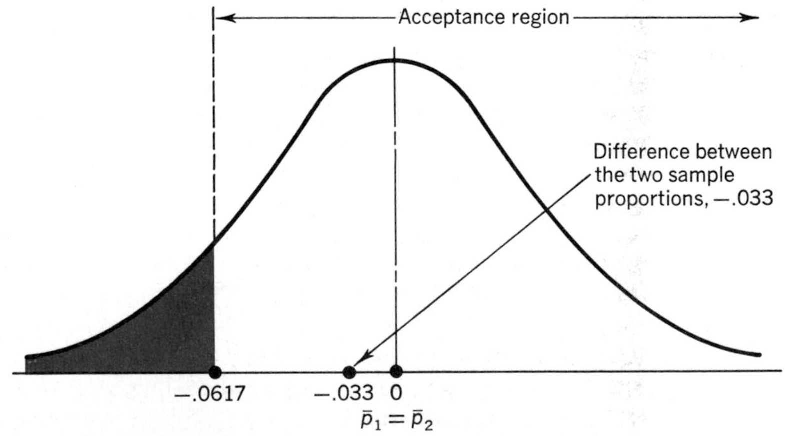

FIGURE 9-29 One-tailed hypothesis test of the difference between two proportions at the .15 level of significance, showing acceptance region and the difference between the sample proportions

EXERCISES

9-52 Two independent samples of observations were collected. For the first sample of 36 elements, the mean was 240 and the standard deviation 14. The second sample of 49 elements had a mean of 230 and a standard deviation of 10.

a) Compute the standard error of the difference between the two means.
b) Test the hypothesis that the two samples are from populations with the same mean. Use the .05 level of significance.

9-53 In order to compare the performance of two training methods, samples of individuals from each of the methods were checked. For the six individuals from training method 1, the mean efficiency score was 35, with a variance of 40. For the eight individuals in training method 2, the mean efficiency score was 27, with a variance of 45.

a) Compute the standard error of the difference between the two means.
b) Test whether the efficiency scores by individuals from the two training methods may be concluded to be equal. Use the .01 level of significance.

9-54 The following two samples are units sold by distributors in the month before and after the addition of a cents-off promotion.

a) Find the mean change in units sold after the promotion.
b) Find the standard deviation of the change and the standard error of the mean.
c) Test for a significant difference between the units sold before and after the promotion. Use the .05 level of significance.

Distributor	1	2	3	4	5	6	7	8
Before	97	106	106	95	102	111	115	104
After	113	113	101	119	111	122	121	106

9-55 Whitman Manufacturing surveyed employees to see whether they preferred a large increase in retirement benefits or a smaller increase in salary. From a group of 1,000 male employees polled, 850 supported increased retirement benefits. Of 500 female employees surveyed, 400 supported the increase in retirement benefits.

a) Calculate $\hat{p}$.
b) Compute the standard error of the difference between the two proportions.
c) Test the hypothesis that the proportions of men and women supporting increased retirement benefits are equal. Use the .01 level of significance.

9-56 Elizabeth Kerr, supervisor of a typing pool, is interested in knowing whether typists required to correct their own errors have the same error rate as typists not required to correct their own errors. Of the 40 typists required to correct their own errors, the average number of errors per day is 20.2 with a standard deviation of 2.5. Of the 56 typists not required to correct their own errors, the average number of errors per day is 21.0 with a standard deviation of 3.1. At a significance level of 10 percent, is there a significant difference in the number of errors made by the two kinds of typists?

9-57 Two research laboratories have independently produced drugs that provide relief to arthritis sufferers. The first drug was tested on a group of 100 arthritis victims and produced an average of 8.5 hours of relief with a standard deviation of 2 hours. The second drug was tested on 75 arthritis victims, producing an average of 7.8 hours of relief with a standard deviation of 1.5 hours. At the .02 level of significance, does the first drug provide a significantly longer period of relief?

9-58 Two different areas of a city are being considered as sites for day-care centers. Of 150 households surveyed in one section, the proportion in which the mother worked full-time was .44. In the other section, 38 percent of the 100 households surveyed had mothers working at full-time jobs. At the .05 level of significance, is there a significant difference in the proportion of working mothers in the two areas of the city?

9-59 Morgan Glass Works recently instituted a job enrichment program to help increase employee motivation. To test the effectiveness of this program, an organizational psychologist administered job motivation tests to two types of employees: those with "enriched" jobs and those without changes in their jobs. Of the 40 employees tested after job enrichment, the average score on the motivation test was 28.8 with a standard deviation of 1.35. Among the 45 employees tested who had not been affected by the job enrichment program, the mean score on the motivation test was 27.7 with a standard deviation of 1.49. At the .05 significance level, is a significant difference in motivation achieved by the job enrichment program?

9-60 A coal-fired power plant is comparing two different systems for pollution abatement. The first system has reduced the emission of pollutants to acceptable levels 63 percent of the time, as determined from 200 air samples. The second (and more expensive) system has reduced the emission of pollutants to acceptable levels 79 percent of the time, as determined from 300 air samples. At the .10 level of significance, can management conclude that the more expensive system is not significantly more effective than the inexpensive system?

9-61 An advertising research firm is studying differences in coupon redemption rates depending on the location of the coupon in a magazine. The firm looked at one coupon and corresponding advertisement that was placed in a variety of magazines. In some of the magazines, the coupon was placed on the inside back cover; in others, the coupon was placed on the inside front cover. The data below give the redemption rate for the coupon placement in 18 different magazines.

PLACEMENT	PERCENT OF COUPONS REDEEMED									
Inside front cover	6.2	5.8	7.1	6.5	6.7	7.0	6.6	6.3	6.9	6.0
Inside back cover	4.9	5.2	5.4	5.8	5.9	6.1	6.3	6.5		

Does it appear that coupons placed in two different parts of the magazine have different redemption rates? (Use the .05 level of significance to do the test.)

9-62 A consumer research organization routinely selects several car models a year and tests their claims regarding safety, mileage, and comfort. In one study of two similar subcompact models manufactured by two different automakers, the average gas mileage for 7 cars of make A was 21 miles per gallon with a standard deviation of 5.8. For 9 cars of make B, the average gas mileage was 26 miles per gallon with a standard deviation of 5.3 miles per gallon. Test the hypothesis that the average gas mileage for cars of make B is greater than the average gas mileage for cars of make A. Use the .05 level of significance.

9-63 Is the amount of responsibility for an action ascribed in relation to the severity of the consequences of that action? That question was the basis of a study of responsibility in which subjects read a description of an accident on an interstate highway. The consequences, in terms of cost and injury, were described as either very minor or serious. A questionnaire tested the subjects' comprehension of the facts in the story and asked them to rate the degree of responsibility that should be placed on the main figure in the story. Below are these ratings for the mild-consequences group and the severe-consequences group. High ratings indicate more responsibility attributed to the primary actor. Test the hypothesis that severe consequences lead to greater attribution of responsibility. Use the .01 level of significance.

CONSEQUENCES	DEGREE OF RESPONSIBILITY							
Mild	4	5	3	3	4	1	2	6
Severe	4	5	4	6	7	8	6	5

9-64 The quality control manager of Taylor Sportswear suggested that the piece-rate wage system should be changed so that employees are not paid for defective goods they produce. The company made this change on 10 workers and recorded their daily number of defectives before and after the change. The data are shown below. Test the hypothesis that the change in the wage system reduces defective merchandise. Use the .05 level of significance.

Worker	1	2	3	4	5	6	7	8	9	10
Before	12	14	12	13	15	13	14	13.5	12	12.5
After	9	13	14	10	12	11	13	10	11	13

9-65 A mouthwash brand implemented two different trade promotions last year in the United States. The company divided the country into 9 sales regions, and during the month of each promotion, sales to distributors were recorded (in thousands of cases). The data are given below. Test the hypothesis that the average sales per region (in thousands of cases) during the two promotions were different. Use the .10 level of significance.

Region	1	2	3	4	5	6	7	8	9
Promotion #1	46	54	49	39	42	48	51	55	44
Promotion #2	53	52	49	42	51	50	49	60	43

9-66 Many companies subscribe to music systems that play softly and are thought to produce a relaxing, comfortable work setting, leading to greater productivity. Mr. Kingpin, however, is not convinced of these benefits, especially for certain departments that he feels involve jobs requiring greater concentration. He assigns his personnel manager to run the music system for one week, to measure the productivity of the 6 employees in one of these departments, and to measure the same 6 employees' productivity in a week when the music is not piped in. The data given below are the productivity measures for the 2 week-long periods.

Employee	1	2	3	4	5	6
Week with music	142	136	158	145	150	148
Week without music	139	138	150	145	145	142

Test the hypothesis that when the music is piped in, the mean productivity for these employees is different from the mean productivity when the music is not piped in. Use the .05 level of significance.

9-67 Block Enterprises, a manufacturer of silicon computer chips, is in the process of attempting to decide whether to replace its current semiautomated assembly-line process with a fully automated assembly-line process. Block has gathered some preliminary test data, summarized in the table below, and would like to know whether it should upgrade its assembly-line process. At the .05 level of significance, state and test the hypothesis that will allow Block Enterprises to make its decision.

	TYPE OF ASSEMBLY LINE	
	Semiautomatic	Automatic
Mean number of chips/hour	195	205
Sample standard deviation	30	20
Number of hours tested	200	100

9-68 Smoothy Peanut Butter has interviewed 8 randomly chosen customers to gauge the success of its latest advertising campaign. The customers were asked how many ounces of Smoothy they purchased per week, both before and after the advertising campaign began. The answers are given in the table below. At the .05 level of significance, do these data indicate that the advertising campaign has been successful in increasing customers' demand for Smoothy?

Before	64	32	16	32	24	48	64	64
After	72	32	48	16	16	64	64	56

9-69 A group of clinical doctors is performing tests on patients to determine the effect of a new antihypertensive drug in combating high blood pressure. Patients with high blood pressure were randomly chosen, and then randomly put into either the control group or the treatment group. The control group did not receive the drug; the treatment group did receive the antihypertensive drug. The doctors noted the percentage of people whose high blood pressure was reduced to a normal level within 1 year. At the .05 level, test an appropriate hypothesis to help the doctors determine if the drug is significantly effective in reducing high blood pressure.

GROUP	PROPORTION THAT IMPROVED	NUMBER OF PATIENTS
1. Treatment	.4	50
2. Control	.3	100

9-9 PROB VALUES—ANOTHER WAY TO LOOK AT TESTING HYPOTHESES

In all the work we've done so far on hypothesis testing, one of the first things we had to do was choose a level of significance, α, for the test. It has been traditional to choose a significance level of $\alpha = 10$ percent, 5 percent, 2 percent, or 1 percent, and almost all our examples have been done at these levels. But why use only these few values?

How do we choose a significance level?

When we discussed Type I and Type II errors on page 365, we saw that the choice of the significance level depended on a tradeoff between the costs of each of these two kinds of errors. If the cost of a Type I error (incorrectly rejecting H_0) is relatively high, we want to avoid making this kind of error, so we choose a small value of α. On the other hand, if a Type II error (incorrectly accepting H_0) is relatively more expensive, we are more willing to make a Type I error, and we choose a high value of α. **However, understanding the nature of the tradeoff still doesn't tell us how to choose a significance level.**

Deciding before we take a sample

When we test the hypotheses:

$$H_0: \mu = \mu_{H_0}$$
$$H_1: \mu \neq \mu_{H_0}$$
$$\alpha = .05$$

we take a sample, compute $\bar{x}$, and reject H_0 if $\bar{x}$ is so far from μ_{H_0} that the probability of seeing a value of $\bar{x}$ this far (or farther) from μ_{H_0} is less than

.05. In other words, **before we take the sample**, we specify how unlikely the observed results will have to be in order for us to reject H_0. There is another way to approach this decision about rejecting or accepting H_0 that doesn't require that we specify the significance level before taking the sample. Let's see how it works.

Prob values

Suppose we take our sample, compute $\bar{x}$, and then ask the question, "Supposing H_0 were true, what's the probability of getting a value of $\bar{x}$ this far or farther from μ_{H_0}?" This probability is called a *prob value* or a *p-value*. **Whereas before we asked, "Is the probability of what we've observed less than α?" now we are merely asking, "How unlikely is the result we have observed?" Once the prob value for the test is reported, *then* the decision maker can weigh all the relevant factors and decide whether to accept or reject H_0, without being bound by a prespecified significance level.**

Another advantage

Another benefit of using prob values is that they provide more information. If you know that I rejected H_0 at $\alpha = .05$, you only know that $\bar{x}$ was *at least* 1.96 standard errors away from μ_{H_0}. However, a prob value of .05 tells you that $\bar{x}$ was *exactly* 1.96 standard errors away from μ_{H_0}. Let's look at an example.

Two-Tailed Prob Values When σ Is Known

A machine is used to cut wheels of Swiss cheese into blocks of specified weight. On the basis of long experience, it has been observed that the weight of the blocks is normally distributed with a standard deviation of .3 ounce. The machine is currently set to cut blocks that weigh 12 ounces. A sample of nine blocks is found to have an average weight of 12.25 ounces. Should we conclude that the cutting machine needs to be recalibrated?

Written symbolically, the data in our problem are:

Setting up the problem symbolically

$\mu_{H_0} = 12 \leftarrow$ hypothesized value of the population mean

$\sigma = .3 \leftarrow$ population standard deviation

$n = 9 \leftarrow$ sample size

$\bar{x} = 12.25 \leftarrow$ sample mean

The hypotheses we wish to test are:

$H_0: \mu = 12 \leftarrow$ null hypothesis: the true population mean weight is 12 ounces

$H_1: \mu \neq 12 \leftarrow$ alternative hypothesis: the true population mean weight is not 12 ounces

Since this is a two-tailed test, our prob value is the probability of observing a value of $\bar{x}$ at least as far away (on either side) from 12 as 12.25, if H_0 is true. In other words, the prob value is the probability of getting

$\bar{x} \geq 12.25$ or $\bar{x} \leq 11.75$ if H_0 is true. To find this probability, we first use Equation 7-1 to calculate the standard error of the mean:

Calculating the standard error of the mean

$$\sigma_{\bar{x}} = \frac{\sigma}{\sqrt{n}} \qquad [7\text{-}1]$$

$$= \frac{.3}{\sqrt{9}}$$

$$= \frac{.3}{3}$$

$$= .1 \text{ ounce} \leftarrow \text{standard error of the mean}$$

Then we use this to convert $\bar{x}$ to a standard z score:

Finding the z score and the prob value

$$z = \frac{\bar{x} - \mu}{\sigma_{\bar{x}}} \qquad [7\text{-}2]$$

$$= \frac{12.25 - 12}{.1}$$

$$= \frac{.25}{.1}$$

$$= 2.5$$

From Appendix Table 1, we see that the probability that z is greater than 2.5 is $.5000 - .4938 = .0062$. Hence, since this is a two-tailed hypothesis test, the prob value is $2(.0062) = .0124$. Our results are illustrated in Fig. 9-30. Given this information, our cheese packer can now decide whether to recalibrate the machine (reject H_0) or not (accept H_0).

Relationship between prob values and significance levels

How is this related to what we did before, when we specified a significance level? If a significance level of $\alpha = .05$ were adopted, we would

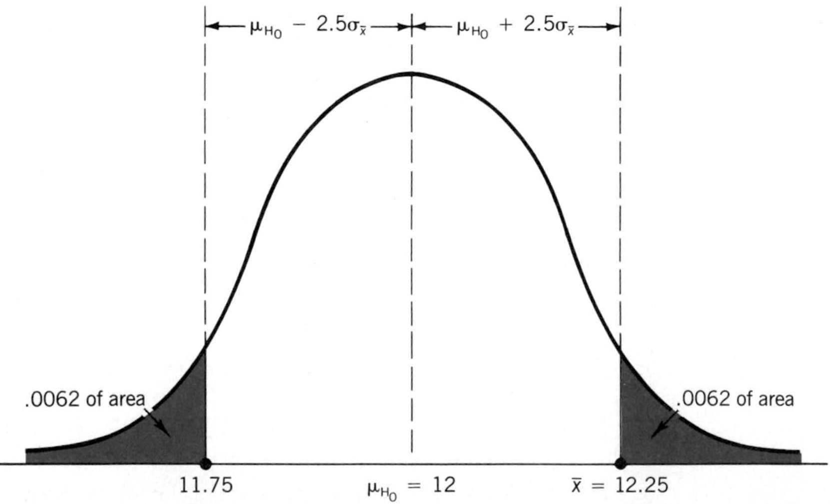

FIGURE 9-30 Two-tailed hypothesis test, showing prob value of .0124

reject H_0. You can easily see this by looking at Fig. 9-30. At a significance level of $\alpha = .05$, we reject H_0 if $\bar{x}$ is so far from μ_{H_0} that less than .05 of the area under the curve is left in the two tails. Since our observed value of $\bar{x} = 12.25$ leaves only .0124 of the total area in the tails, we would reject H_0 at a significance level of $\alpha = .05$. (You can also verify this result by noting that the upper limit of the acceptance region is $\mu_{H_0} + 1.96\sigma_{\bar{x}} = 12 + 1.96(.1) = 12.20$, so our observed value of $\bar{x} = 12.25$ is *outside* the acceptance region.)

Similarly, we can see that at a significance level of $\alpha = .01$, we would accept H_0, because $\bar{x} = 12.25$ leaves more than .01 of the total area in the tails. (In this case, the upper limit of the acceptance region would be $\mu_{H_0} + 2.57\sigma_{\bar{x}} = 12 + 2.57(.1) = 12.26$, so our observed value of $\bar{x} = 12.25$ is *inside* the acceptance region.) In fact, at any level of α above .0124, we would reject H_0. **Thus we see that the prob value is precisely the largest significance level at which we would accept H_0.**

Prob Values Under Other Conditions

In our example, we did a two-tailed hypothesis test using the normal distribution. How would we proceed in other circumstances?

One-tailed prob values

1. If σ was known, and we were doing a one-tailed test, we would compute the prob value in exactly the same way except that we would not multiply the probability that we got from Appendix Table 1 by 2, since that table gives one-tailed probabilities directly.

Using the *t* distribution

2. If σ was not known, we would use the t distribution with $n - 1$ degrees of freedom and Appendix Table 2. This table gives two-tailed probabilities, but only a few of them, so we can't get exact prob values from it. For example, for a two-tailed test, if $\mu_{H_0} = 50$, $\bar{x} = 49.2$, $s = 1.4$, and $n = 16$, we find that:

$$\hat{\sigma}_{\bar{x}} = \frac{\hat{\sigma}}{\sqrt{n}} \qquad [8\text{-}6]$$

$$= \frac{1.4}{\sqrt{16}}$$

$$= .35$$

and that $\bar{x}$ is 2.286 estimated standard errors below μ_{H_0} $[(49.2 - 50)/.35 = -2.286]$. Looking at the 15 degrees of freedom row in Appendix Table 2, we see that 2.286 is between 2.131 ($\alpha = .05$) and 2.602 ($\alpha = .02$). Our prob value is therefore something between .02 and .05, but we can't be more specific.

Prob values in other contexts

Most computer statistics packages report exact prob values, not only for tests about means based on the normal distribution, but for other tests such as chi-square and analysis of variance (which we will discuss in Chapter 10) and tests in the context of linear regression (which we will discuss in Chapters 11 and 12). The discussion we have provided in this section will enable you to understand prob values in those contexts too. Although different statistics and distributions will be involved, the ideas are the same.

EXERCISES

9-70 A car tire retailer thinks that a 35,000 mile claim for tire life by the manufacturer is too high. She carefully records the mileage obtained from a sample of 50 such tires; this mean turns out to be 33,750 miles. The standard deviation of the life of all tires of this type has previously been calculated by the manufacturer to be 5,000 miles. Assuming that the mileage is normally distributed, determine the largest significance level at which we would accept the manufacturer's mileage claim.

9-71 Avionics, Inc., manufactures distance measuring equipment for aircraft. It advertises a mean life of 1,200 hours between repairs for model 100-AS, with a standard deviation of 125 hours. Ben Oliver, a local Avionics repair manager, has sold a number of these distance measuring devices and has tracked their repair records. For 30 such devices, the mean time between repair has been 1,250 hours. Assuming the time between repairs is normally distributed, determine the largest significance level at which Ben would conclude that the mean time between repairs is significantly greater than 1,200 hours.

9-72 Kelly's machine shop uses a machine controlled metal saw to cut sections of tubing used in pressure measuring devices. The length of the sections is normally distributed with a standard deviation of .05 inches. At a setting of 2.0″, after the machine has cut 50 pieces, their mean length is measured and found to be 2.02″. Use prob values to determine whether the machine should be recalibrated because the mean length is significantly different from 2.0″.

9-73 A new car distributor advertises that the cars sold in her district will get an average of 28 mpg. An EPA inspector conducts a mileage test on 20 of those cars with a result of only 26.9 mpg. The sample standard deviation was 2.6 mpg. Using prob values, decide whether the distributor's claim is overly optimistic.

9-10 TERMS INTRODUCED IN CHAPTER 9

ALPHA (α) The probability of a Type I error.

ALTERNATIVE HYPOTHESIS The conclusion we accept when the data fail to support the null hypothesis.

BETA (β) The probability of a Type II error.

DEPENDENT SAMPLES Samples drawn from two populations in such a way that the elements were not chosen independently of one another, in order to allow a more precise analysis or to control for some extraneous factors.

HYPOTHESIS An assumption or speculation we make about a population parameter.

LOWER-TAILED TEST A one-tailed hypothesis test in which a sample value significantly below the hypothesized population value will lead us to reject the null hypothesis.

NULL HYPOTHESIS The hypothesis, or assumption, about a population parameter we wish to test, usually an assumption of the status quo.

ONE-TAILED TEST A hypothesis test in which there is only one rejection region; i.e., we are concerned only with whether the observed value deviates from the hypothesized value in one direction.

PAIRED DIFFERENCE TEST A hypothesis test of the difference between the sample means of two dependent samples.

POWER CURVE A graph of the values of the power of a test for each value of μ, or other population parameter, for which the alternative hypothesis is true.

POWER OF THE HYPOTHESIS TEST The probability of rejecting the null hypothesis when it is false; i.e., a measure of how well the hypothesis test is working.

PROB VALUE The largest significance level at which we would accept the null hypothesis. It enables us to test hypotheses without first specifying a value for α.

SIGNIFICANCE LEVEL A value indicating the percentage of sample values that is outside certain limits, assuming the null hypothesis is correct; i.e., the probability of rejecting the null hypothesis when it is true.

TWO-TAILED TEST A hypothesis test in which the null hypothesis is rejected if the sample value is significantly higher or lower than the hypothesized value of the population parameter; a test involving two rejection regions.

TYPE I ERROR Rejecting a null hypothesis when it is true.

TYPE II ERROR Accepting a null hypothesis when it is false.

UPPER-TAILED TEST A one-tailed hypothesis test in which a sample value significantly above the hypothesized population value will lead us to reject the null hypothesis.

9-11 EQUATIONS INTRODUCED IN CHAPTER 9

[9-1]

$$\sigma_{\bar{x}_1-\bar{x}_2} = \sqrt{\frac{\sigma_1^2}{n_1} + \frac{\sigma_2^2}{n_2}}$$

p. 388

This formula enables us to derive the standard deviation of the distribution of the difference between the sample means; that is, *the standard error of the difference between two means*. To do this, we take the square root of the value equal to the sum of Population 1's variance divided by its sample size and of Population 2's variance divided by its sample size.

[9-2]

$$\hat{\sigma}_{\bar{x}_1-\bar{x}_2} = \sqrt{\frac{\hat{\sigma}_1^2}{n_1} + \frac{\hat{\sigma}_2^2}{n_2}}$$

p. 388

If the two population standard deviations are unknown, we can use this formula to derive the *estimated* standard error of the difference between two means. We can use this equation after we have used the two sample standard deviations and Equation 8-1 to determine the estimated standard deviations of Population 1 and Population 2 ($\hat{\sigma} = s$).

[9-3]

$$s_p^2 = \frac{(n_1 - 1)s_1^2 + (n_2 - 1)s_2^2}{n_1 + n_2 - 2}$$

p. 392

With this formula we can get a "pooled estimate" of σ^2. It uses a weighted average of s_1^2 and s_2^2, where the weights are the numbers of degrees of freedom in each sample. Use of this formula assumes that $\sigma_1^2 = \sigma_2^2$ (that the unknown population variances are equal). We use this formula when testing for the differences between means in situations with small sample sizes (less than 30).

[9-4] $$\hat{\sigma}_{\bar{x}_1-\bar{x}_2} = s_p \sqrt{\frac{1}{n_1} + \frac{1}{n_2}}$$ p. 392

With the "pooled estimate" of σ^2 we obtained from Equation 9-3, we put this value into Equation 9-2 and simplify the expression. This gives us a formula to estimate the standard error of the difference between sample means when we have small samples (less than 30) but equal population variances.

[9-5] $$\sigma_{\bar{p}_1-\bar{p}_2} = \sqrt{\frac{p_1q_1}{n_1} + \frac{p_2q_2}{n_2}}$$ p. 399

This is the formula to use to derive the standard error of the difference between two *proportions*. The symbols p_1 and p_2 represent the proportion of successes in Population 1 and Population 2, respectively, and q_1 and q_2 are the proportion of failures in Populations 1 and 2, respectively.

[9-6] $$\hat{\sigma}_{\bar{p}_1-\bar{p}_2} = \sqrt{\frac{\bar{p}_1\bar{q}_1}{n_1} + \frac{\bar{p}_2\bar{q}_2}{n_2}}$$ p. 400

If the population parameters p and q are unknown, we can use the sample statistics $\bar{p}$ and $\bar{q}$ and this formula to *estimate* the standard error of the difference between two proportions.

[9-7] $$\hat{p} = \frac{(n_1)(\bar{p}_1) + (n_2)(\bar{p}_2)}{n_1 + n_2}$$ p. 400

Because the null hypothesis assumes that there is *no difference* between the two population proportions, it would be more appropriate to modify Equation 9-6 and to use the combined proportions from both samples to estimate the overall proportion of successes in the combined populations. Equation 9-7 combines the proportions from both samples. Notice that the value of $\hat{q}$ is equal to $1 - \hat{p}$.

[9-8] $$\hat{\sigma}_{\bar{p}_1-\bar{p}_2} = \sqrt{\frac{\hat{p}\hat{q}}{n_1} + \frac{\hat{p}\hat{q}}{n_2}}$$ p. 401

Now we can substitute the results of Equation 9-7, both $\hat{p}$ and $\hat{q}$, into Equation 9-6 and get a more correct version of Equation 9-6. This new equation, 9-8, gives us the *estimated* standard error of the difference between the two proportions using combined estimates from both samples.

9-12 CHAPTER REVIEW EXERCISES

9-74 For the following situations, state the null and alternative hypotheses:

a) A researcher wishes to test whether a certain enrichment class leads to test scores greater than the population average of 85 points.

b) An airlines employee wishes to determine if the average height of stewardesses is at least 66 inches.

c) A university official wishes to determine if average enrollment for the past 10 years is significantly different from a hypothesized value of 12,500.

9-75 Health Electronics, Inc., a manufacturer of pacemaker batteries, specifies that the life of each battery is equal to or greater than 28 months. If scheduling for replacement surgery for the batteries is to be based upon this claim, explain to the management of this company the consequences of Type I and Type II errors.

9-76 A manufacturer of petite women's sportswear has hypothesized that the average weight of the women buying their clothing is 110 pounds. The company takes two samples of its customers and finds one sample's estimate of the population mean is 98 pounds, and another sample produces a mean weight of 122 pounds. In the test of the company's hypothesis that the population mean is 110 pounds versus the hypothesis that the mean does not equal 110 pounds, is one of these sample values more likely to lead us to accept the null hypothesis? Why, or why not?

9-77 A firm has tested two types of point-of-purchase displays for its new erasable pen. A shelf display was placed in a random sample of 36 stores in the test market, and a floor display was placed in 36 other stores in the area. The mean number of pens sold per store in one month with the shelf display was 40 with a standard deviation of 3. With the floor display, the mean number of pens sold per store in the same month was 42 with a standard deviation of 5. At the .05 significance level, was there a significant difference between sales with the two types of displays?

9-78 A university librarian suspects that the average number of books checked out to each student per visit has changed recently. In the past, an average of 3.5 books were checked out. However, a sample of 20 students averaged 4.2 books per visit, with a standard deviation of 1.8 books. At the .05 level of significance, has the average checkout changed?

9-79 A puppy-food manufacturer is interested in knowing whether there is a significant difference between the calorie content of its brand and the competitor's brand. Analysis of 80 ounces of the manufacturer's product showed the mean calories per ounce to be 64.3, with a standard deviation of .5. The competitor's brand, after analysis of 60 ounces, showed a mean caloric content per ounce of 64.1 with a standard deviation of .25. At the significance level of .05, can we conclude that there is a significant difference between the calorie content of the two puppy foods?

9-80 The production manager of a cigarette manufacturer charges that at least 20 percent of employees' time on the job is idle because of poor job design and excessive machine breakdowns. The standards department, upon hearing this charge, undertakes an extensive study in which 800 employees in all job areas are studied to determine the percentage of idle time on the job. The study finds that only 15 percent of their time is idle. At a 5 percent level of significance, should the standards department's statement be accepted or rejected?

9-81 In response to criticism concerning lost mail, the U.S. Postal Service maintains that its historic loss rate of .3 percent or less has not changed. Concerned with this controversy, a government committee sponsors an investigation in which a total of 5,000 pieces of mail are mailed from various parts of the country. This mailing results in a total of 19 pieces not reaching their destination. At the .05 level of significance, is the U.S. Postal Service losing significantly more mail than its historic rate?

9-82 What is the probability that we are rejecting a true hypothesis when we reject the hypothesized value because of the following:

a) The sample statistic differs from it by more than 1.5 standard errors in either direction.

b) The value of the sample statistic is more than 2 standard errors above it.

c) The value of the sample statistic is more than 1 standard error below it.

9-83 If we wish to accept the null hypothesis 80 percent of the time when it is correct, how many standard errors around the hypothesized value should be used in determining whether to reject it, based on sample information? How many for 90 percent certainty of accepting the null hypothesis when it is true?

9-84 Federal environmental statutes applying to a particular nuclear power plant specify that recycled water must, on the average, be no warmer than 82° F (28° C) before it can be released back into the river. From 100 samples, the average temperature of the recycled water was found to be 84° F (29° C). If the population standard deviation is 7.2° F (4° C), should the plant be cited for exceeding the limitations of the statute? Use a significance level of .04.

9-85 State inspectors, investigating charges that a Louisiana soft-drink bottling company underfills its product, have sampled 100 bottles and found the average contents to be 31.8 fluid ounces. The bottles are advertised to contain 32 fluid ounces. If the population standard deviation is 2 fluid ounces, should we reject at the 5 percent significance level the claim that the average is at least 32 fluid ounces?

9-86 A department store has instituted a sales training program for its sales staff. Ms. Lacock, head of the sales staff, wants to see if the employees who have been through the program sell more than employees who have not. Sales data (in thousands) for both groups of employees for the year are given below. Test the hypothesis that the average yearly sales for trained employees are greater than for employees who have not completed the training program. Use the .025 level of significance.

NO TRAINING

64	65	92	81	91	69	89	70	86	72	85	74	75	79	82

TRAINING

68	75	95	89	78	94	79	91	84	88	82	85

9-87 An upholstery center has just received a shipment of 200 bolts of fabric. Each bolt is supposed to have 64 yards, with a standard deviation of 4 yards. A sample of 36 of the bolts is checked and shows an average of 64.8 yards. The upholstery center wants to know if, at the .02 level of significance level, it can assume that the bolts contain 64 yards.

9-88 A company is trying to improve distribution of its brand of frozen desserts. To accomplish this goal, it has hired a sales force to push the product into new outlets. Prior to hiring the sales force, the company sampled 300 grocery outlets and found that 43 percent carried at least one of its products. After hiring the salespeople, the company sampled 400 grocery outlets and found that 51 percent carried the brand. At the .05 level of significance, can the company conclude that distribution has improved?

9-89 A stereo manufacturer, deciding on the appropriate market for a lower-priced stereo system, has estimated that no more than 14 percent of college students purchase stereo systems costing over $800. To test this claim, the company surveyed 150 of a college's 1,200 students. The study showed that 17 of the 150 students had purchased stereos that cost over $800. If the company is willing to run a 10 percent risk of rejecting the original estimate when it is true, what should the company conclude?

9-90 Allen Distribution Company hypothesizes that a phone call is more effective than a letter in speeding up collection of a slow account. Two groups of slow accounts were contacted by these 2 methods, and the length of time between receipt of the call or the letter and the time the payment was received was recorded. Below are the collection times (in days) for the two groups:

METHOD USED	DAYS TO COLLECTION					
Letter	6	8	9	10	12	9
Phone call	4	5	4	8	6	9

At the .05 level of significance, is there a difference between the average collection time for the two collection methods?

9-91 Vista Garden Center has received a contract to plant grass for 300 patio gardens in the Golden Ages retirement development. The garden center has estimated that on the average, it takes 11 pounds of seed for each garden. After seeding 14 of the gardens, the center finds that the average number of pounds used per garden is 9, with a sample standard deviation of 5. At the .05 level of significance, is the estimate of 11 pounds per garden reasonable?

9-92 A buffered aspirin recently lost some of its market share to a new competitor. The competitor advertised that its brand enters the bloodstream faster than buffered aspirin does; therefore, it relieves pain sooner. The buffered-aspirin company would like to prove that there is no significant difference between the two products and therefore the competitor's claim is false. As a preliminary test, 7 subjects were given buffered aspirin once a day for 3 weeks, and the length of time it took the medication to reach the bloodstream was measured. For another 3 weeks, the subjects were given the competitive product. The length of time to the bloodstream was again measured. The data below are the average number of minutes it took the medication to reach the bloodstream during the two 3-week periods.

Subject	1	2	3	4	5	6	7
Buffered aspirin	15.00	25.50	22.25	14.50	28.00	10.00	20.50
Competitor	12.00	20.00	25.75	18.25	24.00	12.50	17.00

At the .05 level of significance, test the hypothesis that the average amount of time it takes buffered aspirin to reach the bloodstream is different from the average time it takes the competitor's product to do so.

9-93 Eastgate Hardware hypothesizes that an average of 3 percent of its sales per day this year will be on bank credit cards. A sample mean of 2.7 percent per day is found from the first 25 operating days this year. For the entire year of 200 operating days, the standard deviation is known to be 0.4 percent. Using the .10 level of significance, test whether we can accept that the mean credit-card sales per day over the year is 3 percent.

9-94 A chemist developing insect repellents wishes to know whether a new formula leads to greater protection from insect bites than that given by the most popular product on the market. Sixteen volunteers were used in the experiment, and each had one arm sprayed with the old product and one arm sprayed with the new formula. Then each subject placed his arms in 2 insect chambers filled with equal numbers of mosquitoes, gnats, and other biting insects. The number of bites received on each arm was recorded and is given below. Test the hypothesis that there is a difference in the amount of protection provided by the 2 insect repellents. Use the .05 level of significance.

Subject Formulas:	1	2	3	4	5	6	7	8	9	10	11	12	13	14	15	16
Old	5	2	5	4	3	6	2	4	2	6	5	7	1	3	4	1
New	3	1	5	1	1	3	4	2	5	2	1	2	1	2	1	4

9-95 A company was recently criticized for not paying women as much as men working in the same positions. It claims that its average salary paid to all employees is $12,500. From a random sample of 36 women in the company, the average salary was calculated to be $11,900. If the population standard deviation is known to be $900 for these jobs, determine whether or not we could reasonably (within 2 standard deviations) expect to find $11,900 as the sample mean if, in fact, the company's claim is true.

9-96 A regional grocery chain has installed new computerized checkout centers to reduce customer waiting and labor costs, as well as to aid in inventory control. The 49 employees trained on the new machines averaged 12 trials before making an error-free transaction. Long experience with training cashiers to run the old registers showed that they made 11 trials before a perfect transaction, on the average, with a standard deviation of 3.5 trials. At a significance level of .10, should the chain conclude that the new computerized registers are harder to learn to operate?

9-97 A landscaping firm has contracted to landscape 120 homes in a new development. In order not to exceed its budget, a landscaping team can spend no more than 8 days, on average, per house. After the completion of 15 houses, the average number of days spent per house is found to be 10, with a sample standard deviation of 3 days. At the .05 level of significance, is there significant reason to believe that the number of days spent per house will exceed an average of 8 for the contract?

9-98 An electronics manufacturer has changed some of its welders from a straight salary to piece rate. To see if this change improved worker output, the foreman was asked to keep a record of one day's output for each employee. Below are the number of units produced in one day, according to the employee's method of compensation.

PIECE-RATE WORKERS		STRAIGHT SALARY WORKERS	
110	118	108	119
115	122	106	103
99	106	114	128
125	102	95	117
109	100	110	130
92	103	101	121
113	129		

At the .05 level of significance, test the hypothesis that there are output differences between the two forms of compensation.

9-99 Refer to Exercise 9-27. Compute the power of the test for $\mu = 116$, 117, and 117.6

9-100 A personnel manager hypothesized that 15 percent of the company employees work overtime every week. If the observed proportion is .17 for a sample of 200 of the 2,000 employees, test whether we can accept his hypothesis as correct at the .10 level of significance or if we must conclude that some other value is more appropriate.

9-101 In Exercise 9-28, what would be the power of the test for $\mu = 12{,}500$, 12,000, and 11,500 if the significance level were changed to .05.

9-102 A stockbroker claims that she can predict with 80 percent accuracy whether a stock's market value will rise or fall during the coming month. As a test, she predicts the outcome of 40 stocks and is correct in 28 of the predictions. Does this evidence support the stockbroker's claim, or may we conclude that her percentage accuracy is less than 80 percent? Use the .05 level of significance.

9-103 In Exercise 9-27, what would be the power of the test for $\mu = 116$, 117, and 117.6 if the significance level were changed to .01?

9-104 Given that 55 of 1,000 failed a test in which the proportion that was hypothesized to fail was .04, test the hypothesis that the true proportion is .04 versus the alternative that it is greater than .04. Use the .01 level of significance.

9-105 An innovator in the motor-drive industry hypothesized that its new electric motor drive would capture 48 percent of the regional market within 1 year because of the product's low price and superior performance. There are 5,000 users of motor drives in the region. After sampling 10 percent of these users a year later, the company found that 45 percent of the drives purchased by the sample were the new brand. At the .05 level of significance, should we conclude that the company did not reach its market-share goal?

9-106 Refer to Exercise 9-28. Compute the power of the test for $\mu = 12{,}500$, 12,000, and 11,500.

9-13 CHAPTER CONCEPTS TEST

Answers are in the back of the book.

T F 1. In hypothesis testing, we assume that some population parameter takes on a particular value before we sample. This assumption to be tested is called an alternative hypothesis.

T F 2. Assuming that a given hypothesis about a population mean is correct, then the percentage of sample means that could fall outside certain limits from this hypothesized mean is called the significance level.

T F 3. In hypothesis testing, the appropriate probability distribution to use is always the normal distribution.

T F 4. If we were to make a Type I error, we would be rejecting a null hypothesis when it is really true.

T F 5. A paired difference test is appropriate when the two samples being tested are dependent samples.

T F 6. A one-tailed test for the difference between means may be undertaken when the sample sizes are either large or small and the procedures are similar. The only difference is that when sample sizes are large, we employ a normal distribution, whereas the *t* distribution is used when sample sizes are small.

T F 7. If our null and alternative hypotheses are $H_0: \mu = 80$ and $H_1: \mu < 80$, it is appropriate to use a left-tailed test.

T F 8. Suppose a hypothesis test is to be made regarding the difference in means between two populations, and our sample sizes are large. If we do not know the actual standard deviations of the two populations, we can use the sample standard deviations as estimates.

T F 9. The value $1 - \beta$ is known as the power of the test.

T F 10. If we took two independent samples and performed a hypothesis test to evaluate significant differences in their means, we would find the results very similar to a paired difference test performed on the same two samples.

T F 11. It is often, but not always, possible to set the value of α so that we obtain a risk-free tradeoff in hypothesis testing.

T F 12. You are performing a two-tailed hypothesis test on a population mean and have set $\alpha = .05$. If the sample statistic falls within the .95 of area around μ_{H_0}, you have proved that the null hypothesis is true.

T F 13. If hypothesis tests were done with a significance level of .60, the null hypothesis would usually be accepted when it was not true.

T F 14. If $\mu_{H_0} = 50$ and $\alpha = .05$, then $1 - \beta$ must be equal to .95 when $\mu = 50$.

T F 15. When performing a two-tailed test for the difference between means, with a null hypothesis of $\mu_1 = \mu_2$, the hypothesized difference between the two population means is zero.

T F 16. Selecting the appropriate significance level is easier than selecting the proper test to use.

T F 17. Mathematical methods exist that guarantee that the significance level chosen will be appropriate.

18. If we say that $\alpha = .10$ for a particular hypothesis test, then we are saying that:
    a) 10 percent is our minimum standard for acceptable probability.
    b) 10 percent is the risk we take of rejecting a hypothesis that is true.
    c) 10 percent is the risk we take of accepting a hypothesis that is false.
    d) a and b only.
    e) a and c only.

19. Suppose we wish to test whether a population mean is significantly larger or smaller than 10. We take a sample and find $\bar{x}$ to be 8. What should our alternative hypothesis be?
    a) $\mu < 10$ b) $\mu \neq 10$ c) $\mu > 10$ d) Cannot be determined from information given

20. Suppose that a hypothesis test is being performed for a process in which a Type I error will be very costly, but a Type II error will be relatively inexpensive and unimportant. Which of the following would be the best choice for α in this test?
a) .01 b) .10 c) .25 d) .50

21. You are performing a right-tailed test of a population mean and σ is not known. A sample of size 26 is taken, and $\bar{x}$ and s are computed. At a significance level of .01, where would you look for a value from a distribution?
a) z table where .99 of the area is to the left of the z value.
b) z table where .98 of the area is to the left of the z value.
c) t table where, with 25 degrees of freedom, the column heading is .02.
d) t table where, with 25 degrees of freedom, the column heading is .01.

22. Suppose you are going to test the difference between two sample means, which you have calculated as $\bar{x}_1 = 22$ and $\bar{x}_2 = 27$. You wish to test whether the difference is significant. What is the value of $\mu_{\bar{x}_1 - \bar{x}_2}$ which you will use?
a) 5 b) -5 c) 0 d) Cannot be determined from information given

23. Why do we sometimes use paired, as opposed to independent, samples?
a) The cost of taking paired samples is always less than the cost of independent sampling.
b) Paired samples allow us to control for extraneous factors.
c) The sample sizes must be the same for paired samples.
d) All of these.
e) b and c but not a.

24. A set of two dependent samples of size 15 was taken and a hypothesis test was performed. A t value with 14 degrees of freedom was used. If the two sets of samples had been treated as independent, how many degrees of freedom would have been used?
a) 14 b) 28 c) 29 d) 30

25. A farmer has 12 fields of corn in different parts of a certain county. Testing for significantly different yields from year to year, he checks his records for the past 2 years and is able to gather information about production in 11 of the fields for the first year and second years. Should he treat these samples as:
a) Dependent? c) Cannot be determined from information given.
b) Independent?

26. In a test of difference between proportions, two samples are under consideration. In the first, a sample of size 100 shows 20 successes; in the second, a sample of size 50 shows 13 successes. What is the value of $\hat{p}$ for this situation?
a) $\frac{20 + 13}{150}$ b) $\frac{20}{100} + \frac{13}{50}$ c) $\frac{33}{150} \times \frac{117}{150}$ d) None of these

27. What is the major assumption we made when performing one-tailed tests for differences between means with small samples?
a) Unknown population variances were equal.
b) Sampling fractions were quite small.
c) The samples were chosen using judgmental sampling techniques.
d) None of these.

28. With a lower significance level, the probability of rejecting a null hypothesis that is actually true:
a) Decreases. c) Increases.
b) Remains the same. d) All of these.

29. Decision makers make decisions on the appropriate significance level by examining the cost of:
a) Performing the test c) A type II error e) a and c
b) A type I error d) a and b f) b and c

30. An assumption or speculation made about a population parameter is a ____________________ .

31. Accepting a null hypothesis when it is false is a Type ________ error. Its probability is denoted by ________.
32. The assumption about a population parameter that we wish to test is the ________ hypothesis. The conclusion we accept when the data fail to support this assumption is the ________ hypothesis.
33. A hypothesis test of the difference between the sample means of two dependent samples is a ________ difference test.
34. A hypothesis test involving two rejection regions is called a two-________ test.
35. If the null hypothesis is $\mu = 10$ and the alternative hypothesis is $\mu > 10$, the appropriate test to use is a ________ test.

9-14 CONCEPTUAL CASE (Northern White Metals Company)

Dick was so pleased with the work that Sarah and Jody had done, that he called the CEO to ask if they could be reassigned from corporate headquarters to Northern for the next few months.

"No way, Lennox!" the CEO growled. "We've got plenty of problems right here that require their attention." Then he softened and added, "Maybe they'll be able to help out from time to time on an ad hoc basis. We'll have to play it by ear."

"Thanks, sir," Dick replied. "I'll check back with them when problems arise."

Although Dick was disappointed that the CEO had turned down his request to have Sarah and Jody transferred from corporate headquarters to Northern, he was pleased that the product quality situation was now under control. Customer problems had been smoothed over, and the sales force's outlook was once again refreshingly optimistic.

The original president of Northern had by now retired, and Dick formally assumed the role of president and general manager. With production running smoothly and sales still growing, Dick decided to turn his attention to improving other phases of Northern's operations. The shipping department first came to mind, as Dick noticed activity in this area becoming increasingly hectic and a bit disorganized. Making the department more efficient, thought Dick, would surely enable the company to serve its customers better.

The shipping department comprised two separate operations, packing and loading. In the packing process, long sections of aluminum extrusions were stacked, forming a sort of bundle. This was then wrapped with heavy-duty cardboard and secured with a series of steel bands. The cardboard served mainly to protect the metal, and the banding actually held the stacked bundle together. The entire process was performed manually, with two employees working at each of the packing stations. The number of stations could be increased or decreased, depending on demand. Wrapped and banded bundles were taken from the packing stations by an overhead hoist, weighed, and then stacked in a holding area to await loading unto trucks. The shipping department was always a flurry of activity; occasionally it became chaotic.

Dick had noted, by observation and by frequent discussions with the chief shipping coordinator, that problems tended to arise most frequently in the packing area. The number of stations was near capacity. Even so, the packers, although good workers, frequently had difficulty in keeping up with the volume of material coming off the production line. Dick was particularly interested in this problem, as he had recently been approached by Rich Gochnauer, a sales representative from a packing-materials company, about a new, automatic banding machine the firm had developed.

The new equipment would offer little in the way of packing-material cost savings, but the sales rep claimed it would greatly reduce the time it took to wrap and band a bundle. It would not only make packing operations more efficient, he stated, but would substantially reduce labor costs as well.

Dick was skeptical, although he was anxious to improve the packing area. Mr. Gochnauer agreed that, to convince Dick of the equipment's benefits, a sample unit could be installed at NWMC for a 30-day trial period. Dick felt this would be more than enough time to evaluate the machine, and arrangements were made to set up the trial.

Dick decided that if the new automatic bander provided a significant improvement over current methods, he would have several installed in the packing area. What troubled him now was how to decide if the new equipment was truly superior to manual banding—that is, would it really do the same job in less time? He decided to confer with his new-found "consultants" at corporate technical services.

"Would you be free to come up here and help us out with this?" Dick asked Jody after explaining the situation.

"There is really no need for us to come up there, Dick," Jody replied calmly. "The problem seems to be rather clear-cut. Just send me the data at the end of the trial period and we'll try to give you an answer straightaway."

What kind of data and general information will Dick need to provide to technical services? How will technical services make use of these data, and what sort of "answer" might Jody give Dick about the new equipment?

9-15 COMPUTER DATA BASE EXERCISE

Since the test market on the Menagerie toys was going so well, Fred suggested to Laurel and Frank that they might want to proceed with some production calculations before distribution expanded and things got hot.

"For example," he said, "we've already had a few complaints about some of the toys sticking; and if 3-year-olds can't pull a puzzle toy apart, nobody can."

"I suppose we'd better check with Nick about the gap size between pieces and see what other problems he anticipates with production while we're at it," answered Frank. "We've got a potential star toy on our hands, and we'd better check out the difficulties now."

Laurel and Frank wandered off to corner Nick. "This is so exciting," bubbled Laurel. "I've never been in on a new product before, and I feel like I'm helping with the discovery of the hula hoop."

"Nick, we've been looking for you to chat about the Menagerie," continued Laurel, as they entered the Rough Rider factory and spotted their prey.

"We need to know the planned average gap size and the standard deviation on the puzzle pieces. Fred's been getting some complaints on the tightness, so we'd like to see if samples from production are significantly different from what they're supposed to be," said Frank.

"Good idea, kids. You can check this last batch of 100 and compare it to the planned average of .16 centimeters with a standard deviation of .03."

QUESTION

1. At a significance level of .05, should Laurel and Frank conclude that the pieces are too tight?

"You know what, Nick," Laurel said as they finished the testing. "It's almost as bad for the product if the gap is too big and the pieces fall apart."

GAP SIZE (IN CENTIMETERS)				
0.18	0.17	0.22	0.22	0.17
0.20	0.20	0.24	0.17	0.20
0.21	0.14	0.17	0.15	0.34
0.13	0.18	0.19	0.20	0.17
0.20	0.20	0.21	0.21	0.22
0.20	0.21	0.18	0.25	0.14
0.22	0.20	0.25	0.11	0.21
0.15	0.23	0.28	0.15	0.22
0.14	0.24	0.17	0.22	0.27
0.20	0.12	0.16	0.21	0.19
0.29	0.20	0.15	0.20	0.21
0.18	0.20	0.16	0.22	0.19
0.24	0.16	0.16	0.22	0.27
0.17	0.15	0.19	0.19	0.15
0.15	0.16	0.17	0.26	0.22
0.16	0.18	0.16	0.19	0.20
0.21	0.20	0.17	0.18	0.13
0.17	0.17	0.23	0.23	0.20
0.18	0.20	0.11	0.20	0.24
0.15	0.15	0.13	0.12	0.23

PROBLEM

2. Formulate a new set of hypotheses to take Laurel's observation into account. Use the sample from the previous question. Test at the .10 level.

"That's valuable information," Nick responded when they presented the results. "You've saved me a fair amount of time later on when we go into full production. While you're at it, I've got one more problem that applies to this toy as well as to the Rough Rider."

"Be glad to help," offered Laurel.

"It seems that the wood we buy has been getting worse. We used to figure 12 percent of the load of wood was unsuitable for use because of knot-holes and splits. Our costs seem to be rising; and since the price of wood has been constant over the last couple of months, I think the problem is in the quality. If I get someone to check the last load we got, will you two see if the proportion of bad wood has changed?"

"Certainly," said Frank. "I can handle that myself."

QUESTION

3. A six-foot board is considered unusable if its percentage of waste is 16 percent or more. Each of the 125 six-foot boards in the load was checked for the percentage of waste, with the following results:

PERCENTAGE OF WASTE PER BOARD				
0.17	0.12	0.11	0.15	0.17
0.18	0.15	0.15	0.16	0.16
0.16	0.16	0.14	0.17	0.11
0.14	0.15	0.13	0.12	0.13
0.14	0.17	0.10	0.16	0.14
0.16	0.15	0.11	0.15	0.16
0.11	0.14	0.14	0.12	0.16
0.16	0.12	0.11	0.12	0.16
0.11	0.09	0.13	0.13	0.11
0.13	0.12	0.14	0.14	0.13
0.16	0.17	0.16	0.12	0.14
0.17	0.14	0.13	0.15	0.14
0.12	0.10	0.17	0.14	0.12
0.15	0.19	0.16	0.14	0.15
0.20	0.15	0.15	0.15	0.12
0.14	0.16	0.12	0.11	0.14
0.16	0.16	0.16	0.15	0.10
0.18	0.14	0.14	0.18	0.12
0.17	0.16	0.16	0.17	0.12
0.19	0.18	0.08	0.16	0.16
0.14	0.14	0.15	0.15	0.16
0.11	0.14	0.13	0.13	0.16
0.14	0.13	0.16	0.11	0.15
0.14	0.12	0.16	0.14	0.20
0.14	0.12	0.12	0.16	0.16

Was there a significant change (at the .05 significance level) in the proportion of suitable boards?

9-16 Flow Chart

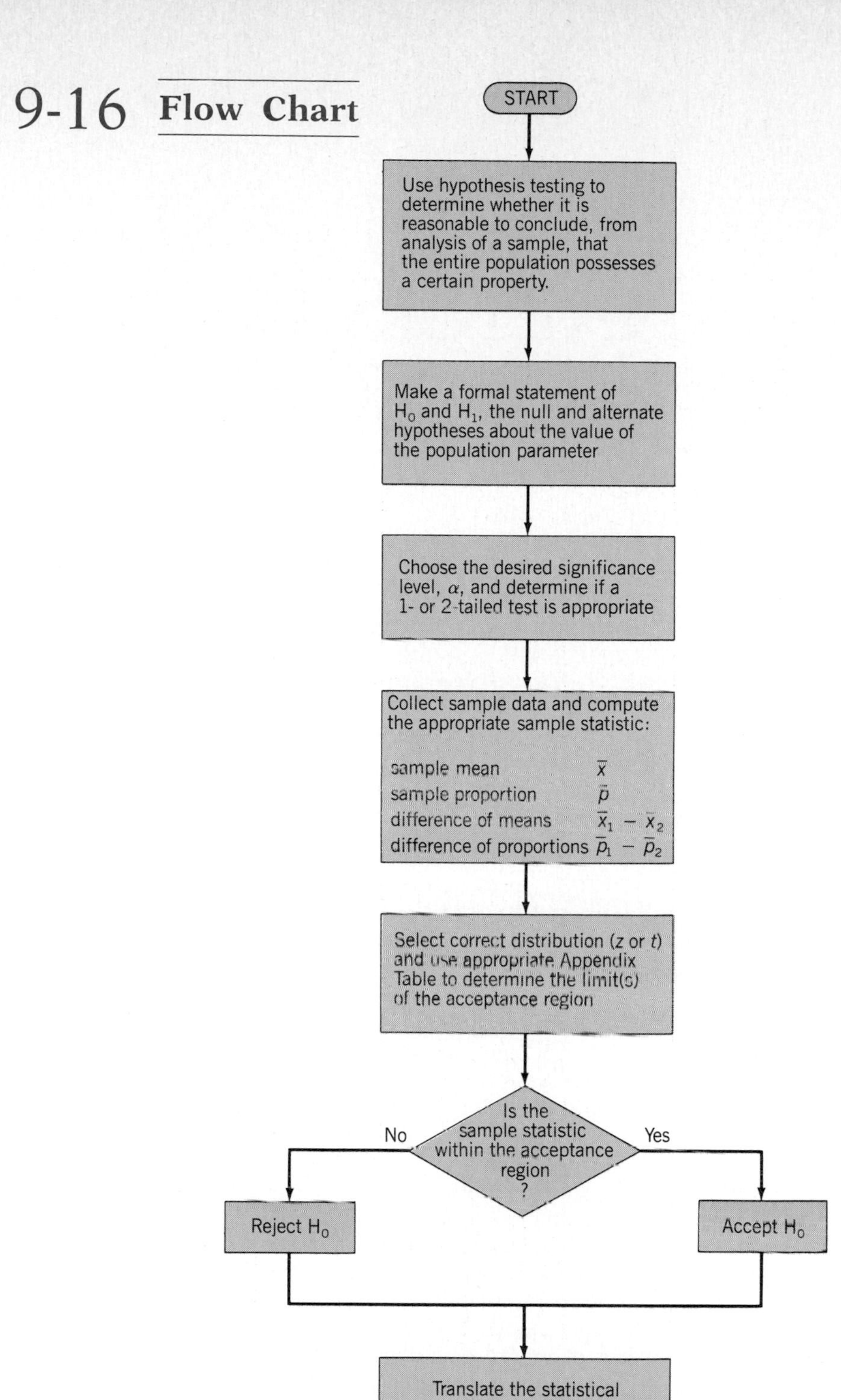

START
Use hypothesis testing to determine whether it is reasonable to conclude, from analysis of a sample, that the entire population possesses a certain property.
Make a formal statement of H_0 and H_1, the null and alternate hypotheses about the value of the population parameter
Choose the desired significance level, α, and determine if a 1- or 2-tailed test is appropriate
Collect sample data and compute the appropriate sample statistic:
sample mean $\bar{x}$
sample proportion $\bar{p}$
difference of means $\bar{x}_1 - \bar{x}_2$
difference of proportions $\bar{p}_1 - \bar{p}_2$
Select correct distribution (z or t) and use appropriate Appendix Table to determine the limit(s) of the acceptance region
Is the sample statistic within the acceptance region ?
No
Yes
Reject H_0
Accept H_0
Translate the statistical results into appropriate managerial action
STOP

CHAPTER 10

CHI-SQUARE AND ANALYSIS OF VARIANCE

1. INTRODUCTION, 428
2. CHI-SQUARE AS A TEST OF INDEPENDENCE, 429
3. CHI-SQUARE AS A TEST OF GOODNESS OF FIT: Testing the Appropriateness of a Distribution, 443
4. ANALYSIS OF VARIANCE, 449
5. INFERENCES ABOUT A POPULATION VARIANCE, 463
6. INFERENCES ABOUT TWO POPULATION VARIANCES, 469
7. TERMS, 475
8. EQUATIONS, 476
9. REVIEW EXERCISES, 478
10. CONCEPTS TEST, 482
11. CONCEPTUAL CASE, 485
12. COMPUTER DATA BASE EXERCISE, 485
13. FLOW CHART, 488

OBJECTIVES: Chapter 10 discusses three statistical techniques: chi-square tests, analysis of variance, and making inferences about population variances. *Chi-square tests* are useful in analyzing more than two populations. They can be helpful in marketing data—for example, to test whether preference for a certain product differs from state to state or region to region. Chi-square tests also enable us to determine whether a group of data that we think could be described by the normal distribution actually does conform to that pattern. *Analysis of variance,* the second subject of Chapter 10, is used to test the difference between several sample means. It is a method an automobile manufacturer might use to evaluate five series of tests on the same model. This method can help in answering the question, "Are the miles-per-gallon results really the same, or do they only appear to be?" The last sections of the chapter show us how to make inferences about the variability present in one or two populations.

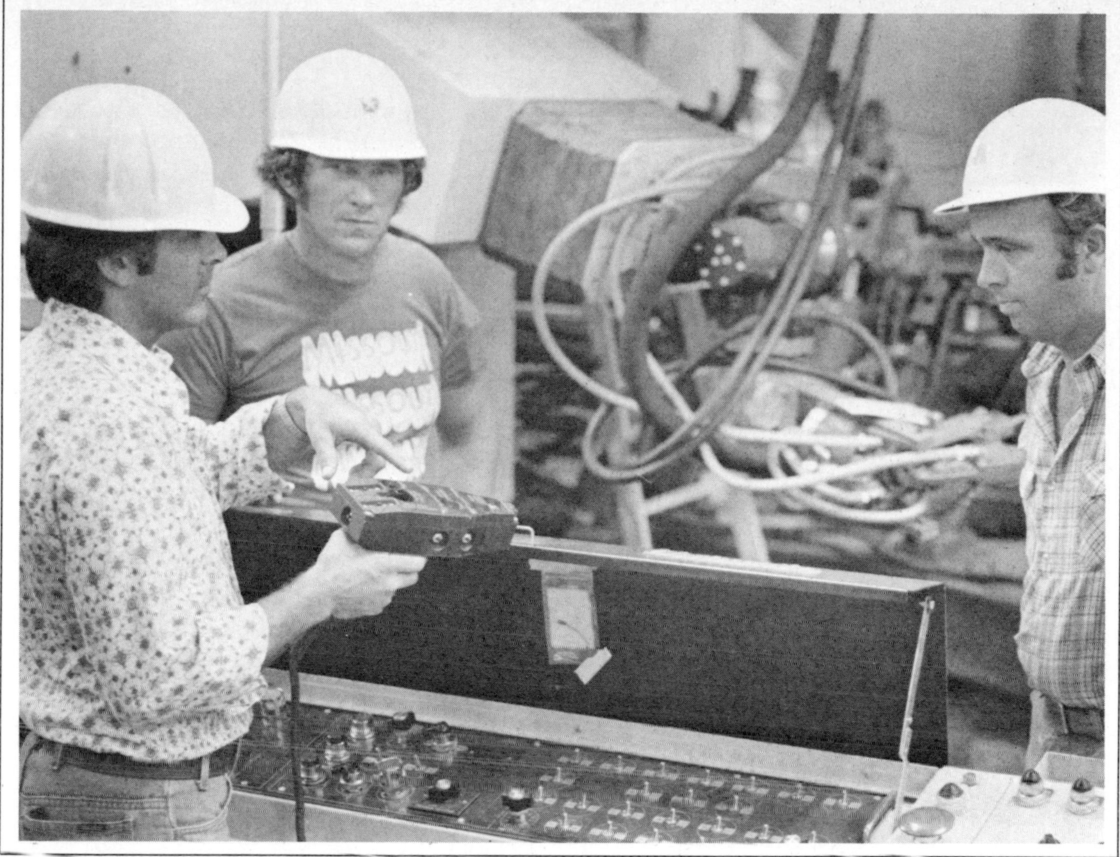

The training director of a company is trying to evaluate three different methods of training new employees. The first method assigns each to an experienced employee for individual help in the factory. The second method puts all new employees in a training room separate from the factory, and the third method uses training films and programmed learning materials. The training director chooses 16 new employees assigned at random to the 3 training methods and records their daily production after they complete the programs:

Method 1	15	18	19	22	11	
Method 2	22	27	18	21	17	
Method 3	18	24	19	16	22	15

The director wonders if there are differences in effectiveness among the methods. Using techniques learned in this chapter, we can help answer that question.

10-1 INTRODUCTION

In the last chapter, we learned how to test hypotheses using data from either one or two samples. We used one-sample tests to determine whether a mean or a proportion was significantly different from a hypothesized value. In the two-sample tests, we examined the difference between either two means or two proportions, and we tried to learn whether this difference was significant.

Uses of the chi-square test

Suppose we have proportions from five populations instead of only two. In this case, the methods for comparing proportions described in Chapter 9 do *not* apply; we must use the *chi-square test,* the subject of the first portion of this chapter. Chi-square tests enable us to test whether more than two population proportions can be considered equal.

Actually, chi-square tests allow us to do a lot more than just test for the equality of several proportions. If we classify a population into several categories with respect to two attributes (for example, age and job performance), we can then use a chi-square test to determine if the two attributes are independent of each other.

Function of analysis of variance

Managers also encounter situations in which it is useful to test for the equality of more than two population means. Again, we cannot apply the methods introduced in Chapter 9, because they are limited to testing for the equality of only two means. The *analysis of variance,* discussed in the fourth section of this chapter, will enable us to test whether more than two population means can be considered equal.

Inferences about population variances

It is clear that we will not always be interested in means and proportions. There are many managerial situations where we will be concerned about the variability in a population. Section 5 of this chapter shows how to use the chi-square distribution to form confidence intervals and test hypotheses about a population variance. In Section 6, we show that hypotheses comparing the variances of two populations can be tested using the F distribution.

EXERCISES

10-1 Why do we use a chi-square test?

10-2 Why do we use analysis of variance?

10-3 What type of statistical test could be used in the following situations?

a) We wish to know whether the average sales per outlet of a product is significantly affected by 3 different in-store promotions.

b) A research group is interested in determining whether there is a significant difference between the purchasing habits of men and women.

c) We need to compare the differences in the proportions of consumers favoring each of 4 brands.

10-4 To make comparisons in the following groups, what type of statistical test is appropriate or what probability distribution is used?

a) Percentage of the labor force from each age group: 16–23, 24–31, 32–39, 40–47, 48–55, and 56 and over

b) Average income of these age groups: 16–23, 24–31, 32–39, 40–47, 48–55, 56 and over

c) Average income of men and women, aged 16–56

d) Amount of dispersion in the earnings of men and women, aged 16–56

10-5 To help remember which distribution or technique is used, complete the following table with either the name of a distribution or the technique involved. The row classification refers to the number of parameters involved in a test, and the column classification refers to the type of parameter involved. Some cells may not have an entry; others may have more than one possible entry.

NUMBER OF PARAMETERS INVOLVED	TYPE OF PARAMETER		
	μ	σ	p
1			
2			
3 or more			

10-2 CHI-SQUARE AS A TEST OF INDEPENDENCE

Sample differences among proportions: significant or not?

Many times, managers need to know whether the differences they observe among several sample proportions are significant or only due to chance. Suppose the campaign manager for a presidential candidate studies three geographically different regions and finds that 35 percent, 42 percent, and 51 percent of those voters surveyed in the three regions, respectively, recognize the candidate's name. If this difference is significant, the manager may conclude that location will affect the way the candidate should act. But if the difference is not significant (that is, if the manager concludes that the difference is solely due to chance), then he may decide that the place chosen to make a particular policy-making speech will have no effect on its reception. To run the campaign successfully, then, the manager needs to determine whether location and acceptance are dependent or independent.

Contingency Tables

Describing a contingency table

Suppose that in four regions, the National Health Care Company samples its hospital employees' attitudes toward job performance reviews. Respondents are given a choice between the present method (two reviews a year) and a proposed new method (quarterly reviews). Table 10-1, which illustrates the response to this question from the sample polled, is called a *contingency table*. A table such as this is made up of rows and columns; rows run horizontally, columns vertically.

TABLE 10-1 Sample response concerning review schedules for National Health Care hospital employees

	NORTHEAST	SOUTHEAST	CENTRAL	WEST COAST	**TOTAL**
Number who prefer present method	68	75	57	79	**279**
Number who prefer new method	32	45	33	31	**141**
Total employees sampled in each region	**100**	**120**	**90**	**110**	**420**

Notice that the four columns in Table 10-1 provide one basis of classification—geographical regions—and that the two rows classify the information another way: preference for review methods. Table 10-1 is called a "2 × 4 contingency table," because it consists of two rows and four columns. We describe the dimensions of a contingency table by first stating the number of rows and then the number of columns. The "total" column and the "total" row are not counted as part of the dimensions.

Observed and Expected Frequencies

Stating the hypotheses

Suppose we now symbolize the true proportions of the total population of employees who prefer the present plan as:

- $p_N \leftarrow$ proportion in Northeast who prefer present plan
- $p_S \leftarrow$ proportion in Southeast who prefer present plan
- $p_C \leftarrow$ proportion in Central region who prefer present plan
- $p_W \leftarrow$ proportion in West Coast region who prefer present plan

Using these symbols, we can state the null and alternative hypotheses as follows:

H_0: $p_N = p_S = p_C = p_W \leftarrow$ null hypothesis

H_1: p_N, p_S, p_C, and p_W are not all equal $\leftarrow$ alternative hypothesis

If the null hypothesis is true, we can combine the data from the four samples and then estimate the proportion of the total work force (the total population) that prefers the present review method:

Combined proportion who prefer present method assuming the null hypothesis of no difference is true

$$= \frac{68 + 75 + 57 + 79}{100 + 120 + 90 + 110}$$

$$= \frac{279}{420}$$

$$= .664$$

Determining expected frequencies

Obviously, if the value .664 estimates the population proportion expected to prefer the present compensation method, then .336, (= 1 − .664) is the estimate of the population proportion expected to prefer the proposed new method. Using .664 as the *estimate* of the population proportion who prefer the present review method, and .336 as the *estimate* of the population proportion who prefer the new method, we can estimate the number of sampled employees in each region whom we would expect to prefer each of the review methods. These calculations are done in Table 10-2.

TABLE 10-2 Proportion of sampled employees in each region expected to prefer the two review methods

	NORTHEAST	SOUTHEAST	CENTRAL	WEST COAST
Total number sampled	100	120	90	110
Estimated proportion who prefer present method	×.664	×.664	×.664	×.664
Number *expected* to prefer present method	**66**	**80**	**60**	**73**
Total number sampled	100	120	90	110
Estimated proportion who prefer new method	×.336	×.336	×.336	×.336
Number *expected* to prefer new method	**34**	**40**	**30**	**37**

Comparing expected and observed frequencies

Table 10-3 combines all the information from Tables 10-1 and 10-2. It illustrates both the actual, or observed, frequency of the employees sampled who prefer each type of job-review method and the theoretical, or expected, frequency of sampled employees preferring each type of method.

TABLE 10-3 Comparison of observed and expected frequencies of sampled employees

	NORTHEAST	SOUTHEAST	CENTRAL	WEST COAST
FREQUENCY PREFERRING PRESENT METHOD:				
Observed (actual) frequency	68	75	57	79
Expected (theoretical) frequency	**66**	**80**	**60**	**73**
FREQUENCY PREFERRING NEW METHOD:				
Observed (actual) frequency	32	45	33	31
Expected (theoretical) frequency	**34**	**40**	**30**	**37**

Remember that the expected frequencies, those in color, were estimated from our combined proportion estimate.

Reasoning intuitively about chi-square tests

To test the null hypothesis, $p_N = p_S = p_C = p_W$, we must compare the frequencies that were observed (the black ones in Table 10-3) with the frequencies we would expect if the null hypothesis is true (those in color). If the sets of observed and expected frequencies are nearly alike, we can reason intuitively that we will accept the null hypothesis. If there is a large difference between these frequencies, we may intuitively reject the null hypothesis, and conclude that there are significant differences in the proportions of employees in the four regions preferring the new method.

The Chi-Square Statistic

To go beyond our intuitive feelings about the observed and expected frequencies, we can use the chi-square statistic, which is calculated this way:

Calculating the chi-square statistic

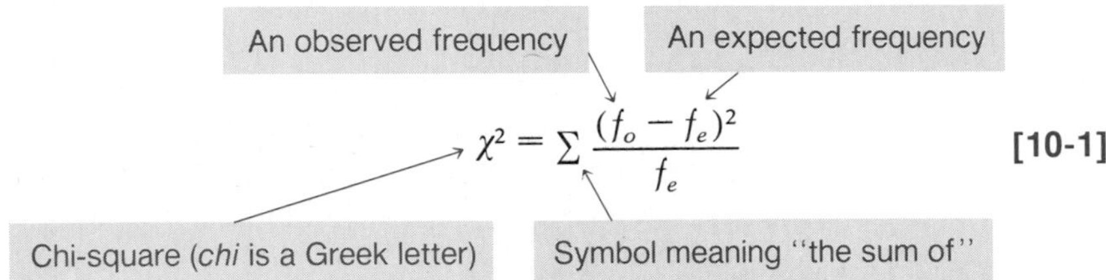

$$\chi^2 = \sum \frac{(f_o - f_e)^2}{f_e} \qquad [10\text{-}1]$$

This formula says that chi-square, or χ^2, is the sum we will get if we:

1. Subtract f_e from f_o for each of the eight boxes, or cells, of Table 10-3
2. Square each of the differences
3. Divide each squared difference by f_e
4. Sum all eight of the answers

TABLE 10-4 Calculation of χ^2 (chi-square) statistic from data in Table 10-3

		Step 1	Step 2	Step 3
f_o	f_e	$f_o - f_e$	$(f_o - f_e)^2$	$\frac{(f_o - f_e)^2}{f_e}$
68	66	2	4	.0606
75	80	−5	25	.3125
57	60	−3	9	.1500
79	73	6	36	.4932
32	34	−2	4	.1176
45	40	5	25	.6250
33	30	3	9	.3000
31	37	−6	36	.9730
				3.0319

Step 4 $\sum \frac{(f_o - f_e)^2}{f_e} = 3.032 \leftarrow \chi^2$ (chi-square)

Numerically, the calculations are easy to do using a table such as Table 10-4, which shows the steps.

Interpreting the chi-square statistic

The answer of 3.032 is the value for chi-square in our problem comparing preferences for review methods. If this value were as large as, say, 20, it would indicate a substantial difference between our observed values and our expected values. A chi-square of zero, on the other hand, indicates that the observed frequencies exactly match the expected frequencies. The value of chi-square can never be negative, since the differences between the observed and expected frequencies are always *squared*.

The Chi-Square Distribution

Describing a chi-square distribution

If the null hypothesis is true, then the sampling distribution of the chi-square statistic, χ^2, can be closely approximated by a continuous curve known as a *chi-square distribution*. As in the case of the t distribution, there is a different chi-square distribution for each different number of degrees of freedom. Figure 10-1 indicates the three different chi-square distributions that would correspond to 1, 5, and 10 degrees of freedom. For very small numbers of degrees of freedom, the chi-square distribution is severely skewed to the right. As the number of degrees of freedom increases, the curve rapidly becomes more symmetrical until the number reaches large values, at which point the distribution can be approximated by the normal.

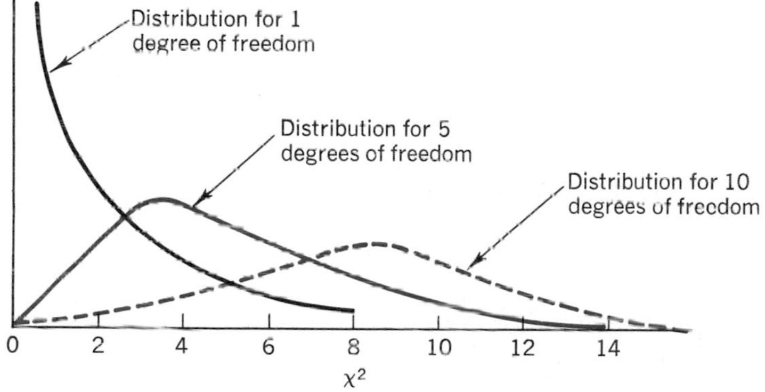

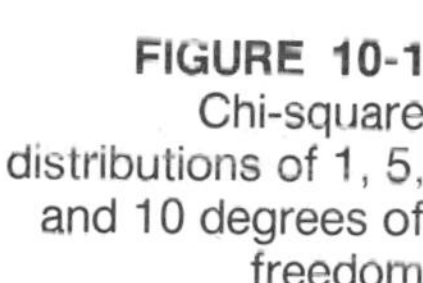
FIGURE 10-1 Chi-square distributions of 1, 5, and 10 degrees of freedom

Finding probabilities when using a chi-square distribution

The chi-square distribution is a probability distribution. Therefore, the total area under the curve in each chi-square distribution is 1.0. Like the t distribution, so many different chi-square distributions are possible that it is not practical to construct a table that illustrates the areas under the curve for all possible values of the area. Appendix Table 5 illustrates only the areas in the tail most commonly used in significance tests using the chi-square distribution.

Determining Degrees of Freedom

Calculating degrees of freedom

To use the chi-square test, we must calculate the number of degrees of freedom in the contingency table by applying Equation 10-2:

$$\text{Number of degrees of freedom} = (\text{Number of rows} - 1)(\text{Number of columns} - 1) \quad \textbf{[10-2]}$$

Let's examine the appropriateness of this equation. Suppose we have a 3 × 4 contingency table like the one in Fig. 10-2. We know the row and column totals that are designated RT_1, RT_2, RT_3, and CT_1, CT_2, CT_3, CT_4. As we discussed in Chapter 8, the number of degrees of freedom is equal to the number of values that we can freely specify.

Look now at the first row of the contingency table in Fig. 10-2. Once we specify the first three values in that row (denoted by checks in the figure), the fourth value in that row (denoted by a circle) is already determined; we are not free to specify it, because we know the row total.

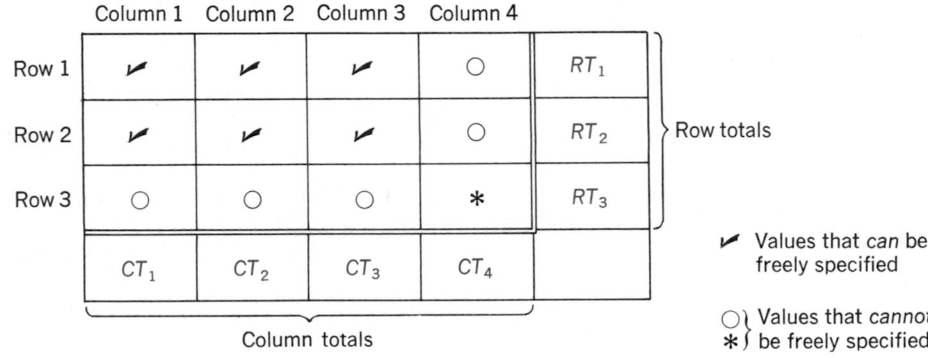

FIGURE 10-2 A 3 × 4 contingency table illustrating determination of the number of degrees of freedom

Likewise, in the second row of the contingency table in Fig. 10-2, once we specify the first three values (denoted again by checks), the fourth value is determined and cannot be freely specified. We have denoted this fourth value by a circle.

Turning now to the third row, we see that its first entry is determined, *because we already know the first two entries in the first column and the column total;* again we have denoted this entry with a circle. We can apply this same reasoning to the second and third entries in the third row, both of which have been denoted by a circle too.

Turning finally to the last entry in the third row (denoted by a star), we see that we cannot freely specify its value, because we have already determined the first two entries in the fourth column. By counting the number of checks in the contingency table in Fig. 10-2, you can see that the number of values we are free to specify is six (the number of checks). This is equal to 2 × 3, or (the number of rows − 1) times (the number of columns − 1).

This is exactly what we have in Equation 10-2. Table 10-5 illustrates the row-and-column dimensions of three more contingency tables and indicates the appropriate degrees of freedom in each case.

TABLE 10-5 Determination of degrees of freedom in three contingency tables

CONTINGENCY TABLE	NUMBER OF ROWS (r)	NUMBER OF COLUMNS (c)	$(r-1)$	$(c-1)$	DEGREES OF FREEDOM $(r-1)(c-1)$
A	3	4	$3-1=2$	$4-1=3$	$(2)(3)=6$
B	5	7	$5-1=4$	$7-1=6$	$(4)(6)=24$
C	6	9	$6-1=5$	$9-1=8$	$(5)(8)=40$

Using the Chi-Square Test

Stating the problem symbolically

Returning to our example of job-review preferences of National Health Care hospital employees, we use the chi-square test to determine whether attitude about reviews is independent of geographical region. If the company wants to test the null hypothesis at the .10 level of significance, our problem can be summarized:

H_0: $p_N = p_S = p_C = p_W$ ← null hypothesis

H_1: p_N, p_S, p_C, and p_W are *not* all equal ← alternative hypothesis

$\alpha = .10$ ← level of significance for testing these hypotheses

Calculating degrees of freedom

Since our contingency table for this problem (Table 10-1) has two rows and four columns, the appropriate number of degrees of freedom is:

Number of rows — Number of columns

$$\text{Number of degrees of freedom} = (r-1)(c-1) \quad \textbf{[10-2]}$$
$$= (2-1)(4-1)$$
$$= (1)(3)$$
$$= 3 \leftarrow \text{degrees of freedom}$$

Illustrating the hypothesis test

Figure 10-3 illustrates a chi-square distribution for 3 degrees of freedom, showing the significance level in color. In Appendix Table 5, we can look under the .10 column and move down to the 3 degrees of freedom row.

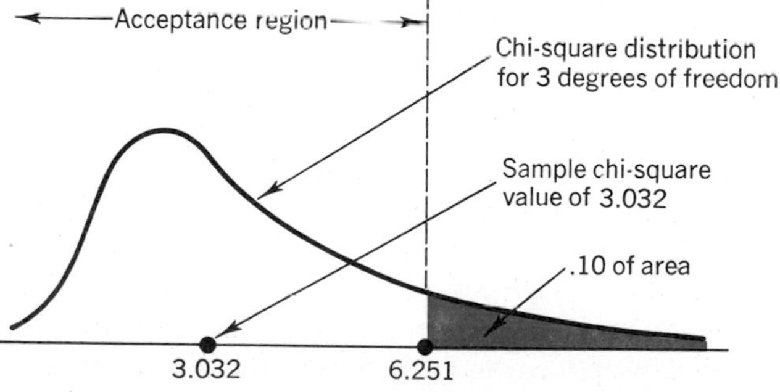

FIGURE 10-3 Chi-square hypothesis test at the .10 level of significance, showing acceptance region and sample chi-square value of 3.032

There we find the value of the chi-square statistic, 6.251. We can interpret this to mean that with 3 degrees of freedom, the region to the right of a chi-square value of 6.251 contains .10 of the area under the curve. Thus, the acceptance region for the null hypothesis in Fig. 10-3 goes from the left tail of the curve to the chi-square value of 6.251.

Interpreting the results

As we can see from Fig. 10-3, the sample chi-square value of 3.032, which we calculated in Table 10-4, falls within the acceptance region. Therefore, we accept the null hypothesis that there is no difference between the attitudes about job interviews in the four geographical regions. In other words, we conclude that attitude about performance reviews is independent of geography.

Contingency Tables with More Than Two Rows

Are hospital stay and insurance coverage independent?

Mr. George McMahon, president of National General Health Insurance Company, is opposed to national health insurance. He argues that it would be too costly to implement, particularly since the existence of such a system would, among other effects, tend to encourage people to spend more time in hospitals. George believes that lengths of stays in hospitals are dependent on the types of health insurance that people have. He asked Donna McClish, his staff statistician, to check the matter out. Donna collected data on a random sample of 660 hospital stays and summarized it in Table 10-6.

TABLE 10-6 Hospital-stay data classified by the type of insurance coverage and length of stay

		Days in hospital <5	5–10	>10	TOTAL
Fraction of costs covered by insurance	<25%	40	75	65	**180**
	25–50%	30	45	75	**150**
	>50%	40	100	190	**330**
	TOTAL	**110**	**220**	**330**	**660**

Table 10-6 gives observed frequencies in the nine different lengths of stay and the types of insurance categories (or "cells") into which we have divided the sample. Donna wishes to test the hypotheses:

H_0: length of stay and type of insurance are independent

H_1: length of stay depends on type of insurance

$\alpha = .01 \leftarrow$ level of significance for testing these hypotheses

Finding expected frequencies

We will use a chi-square test, so we first have to find the expected frequencies for each of the nine cells. Let's demonstrate how to find them by looking at the cell that corresponds to stays of less than five days and insurance covering less than 25 percent of costs.

Estimating the proportions in the cells

A total of 180 of the 660 stays in the sample had insurance covering less than 25 percent of costs. So we can use the figure 180/660 to *estimate* the proportion in the population having insurance covering less than 25 percent of the costs. Similarly, 110/660 *estimates* the proportion of all hospital stays that last fewer than five days. If length of stay and type of insurance really are independent, we can use Equation 5-4 to *estimate* the proportion in the first cell (less than five days and less than 25 percent coverage).

We let:

A = the event "a stay corresponds to someone whose insurance covers less than 25 percent of the costs," and

B = the event "a stay lasts less than 5 days."

Then,

$$\begin{aligned} \text{P(first cell)} &= \text{P}(A \text{ and } B) \\ &= \text{P}(A) \times \text{P}(B) \\ &= \left(\frac{180}{660}\right)\left(\frac{110}{660}\right) \\ &= 1/22 \end{aligned} \qquad \textbf{[5-4]}$$

Since 1/22 is the expected *proportion* in the first cell, the expected *frequency* in that cell is:

$$(1/22)(660) = 30 \text{ observations}$$

Calculating the expected frequencies for the cells

In general, we can calculate the expected frequency for any cell with Equation 10-3:

$$f_e = \frac{RT \times CT}{n} \qquad \textbf{[10-3]}$$

where:

- f_e = the expected frequency in a given cell
- RT = the row total for the row containing that cell
- CT = the column total for the column containing that cell
- n = the total number of observations

Now we can use Equations 10-3 and 10-1 to compute all of the expected frequencies and the value of the chi-square statistic. The computations are done in Table 10-7.

TABLE 10-7 Calculation of expected frequencies and chi-square from data in Table 10-6

ROW	COLUMN	f_o	f_e	$= \frac{RT \times CT}{n}$	$f_o - f_e$	$(f_o - f_e)^2$	$\frac{(f_o - f_e)^2}{f_e}$
1	1	40	30	$\frac{180 \times 110}{660}$	10	100	3.333
1	2	75	60	$\frac{180 \times 220}{660}$	15	225	3.750
1	3	65	90	$\frac{180 \times 330}{660}$	−25	625	6.944
2	1	30	25	$\frac{150 \times 110}{660}$	5	25	1.000
2	2	45	50	$\frac{150 \times 220}{660}$	−5	25	0.500
2	3	75	75	$\frac{150 \times 330}{660}$	0	0	0.000
3	1	40	55	$\frac{330 \times 110}{660}$	−15	225	4.091
3	2	100	110	$\frac{330 \times 220}{660}$	−10	100	0.909
3	3	190	165	$\frac{330 \times 330}{660}$	25	625	3.788

$$[10\text{-}1] \quad \sum \frac{(f_o - f_e)^2}{f_e} = 24.315 \leftarrow \chi^2 \text{ chi-square}$$

Figure 10-4 illustrates a chi-square distribution with 4 degrees of freedom (number of rows − 1 = 2) × (number of columns − 1 = 2), showing the .01 significance level in color. Appendix Table 5 (in the .01 column and the 4 degrees of freedom row) tells Donna that for her problem, the region to the right of a chi-square value of 13.277 contains .01 of the area under the curve. Thus, the acceptance region for the null hypothesis in Fig. 10-4 goes from the left tail of the curve to the chi-square value of 13.277.

Interpreting the results of the test

As Fig. 10-4 shows Donna, the sample chi-square value of 24.315 she calculated in Table 10-7 is not within the acceptance region. Thus Donna must reject the null hypothesis and inform Mr. McMahon that the evidence supports his belief that length of hospital stay and insurance coverage are dependent on each other.

Precautions About Using the Chi-Square Test

Use large sample sizes

To use a chi-square hypothesis test, we must have a sample size large enough to guarantee the similarity between the theoretically correct distribution

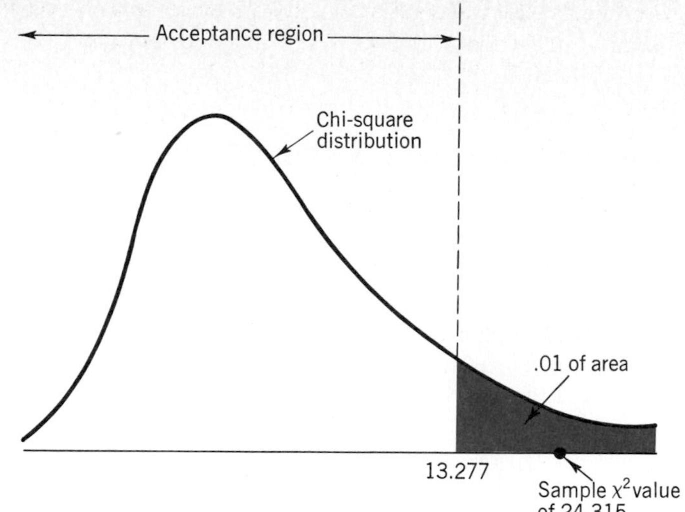

FIGURE 10-4 Chi-square hypothesis test at the .01 level of significance, showing acceptance region and sample chi-square value of 24.315

and our sampling distribution of χ^2, the chi-square statistic. When the expected frequencies are too small, the value of χ^2 will be overestimated and will result in too many rejections of the null hypothesis. **To avoid making incorrect inferences from χ^2 hypothesis tests, follow the general rule that an expected frequency of less than 5 in one cell of a contingency table is too small to use.*** When the table contains more than one cell with an expected frequency of less than 5, we can combine these in order to get an expected frequency of 5 or more. But in doing this, we reduce the number of categories of data and will gain less information from the contingency table.

Use carefully collected data

This rule will enable us to use the chi-square hypothesis test properly, but unfortunately, each test can only reflect (and not improve) the quality of the data we feed into it. So far, we have rejected the null hypothesis if the difference between the observed and expected frequencies—that is, the computed chi-square value—is too large. In the case of the job-review preferences, we would reject the null hypothesis at a .10 level of significance if our chi-square value was 6.251 or more. **But if the chi-square value was zero, we should be careful to question whether *absolutely no difference* exists between observed and expected frequencies.** If we have strong feelings that some difference *ought* to exist, we should examine either the way the data were collected or the manner in which measurements were taken, or both, to be certain that existing differences had not been obscured or missed in collecting sample data.

Mendel's pea data

Experiments with the characteristics of peas led the monk Gregor Mendel to propose the existence of genes. Mendel's experimental results were astoundingly close to those predicted by his theory. Some time later, statisticians looked at Mendel's "pea data," performed a chi-square test, and

* Statisticians have developed correction factors that, in some cases, allow us to use cells with expected frequencies of less than 5. The derivation and use of these correction factors are beyond the scope of this book.

concluded that chi-square was too small; that is, Mendel's reported experimental data were so close to what was expected that they could only conclude that he had fudged the data.

Using the Computer To Do Chi-Square Tests

Using SAS for a chi-square test

Even though the computations necessary to do a chi-square test of independence are relatively simple, for large sets of data they can become rather tedious. Most commonly used computer statistics packages contain routines for doing these tests. In Table 10-8, we see the output that results when we use the SAS package to analyze the hospital-stay data in Table 10-6. Let's compare the computer output with the analysis we did by hand on pages 436–438.

Comparing computer and hand-computed outputs

In each cell of Table 10-8, SAS prints out the observed frequency (f_o), the expected frequency (f_e), and the contribution of that cell to the χ^2 statistic $[(f_o - f_e)^2/f_e]$. Then, at the bottom of the table, SAS prints out the sample chi-square value, the number of degrees of freedom, and a prob value. The last of these (the prob value) is the probability of getting an observed chi-square value as large (or larger) than the sample chi-square value if the hypothesis of independence is valid.

Interpreting the results

Recalling our discussion of prob values in Chapter 9, we know that we will reject H_0 if the prob value is less than α, the significance level of the

TABLE 10-8 Output from SAS for the hospital-stay problem

```
       ILLUSTRATING THE USE OF SAS FOR A TEST OF INDEPENDENCE

                      DAYS = LENGTH OF STAY
              COVERAGE = % OF COSTS COVERED BY INSURANCE

                     TABLE OF DAYS BY COVERAGE

   DAYS           COVERAGE

   FREQUENCY     |
   EXPECTED      |
   CELL CHI2     | UNDER  |        | OVER   |
                 |  25%   |25%-50% | 50%    |  TOTAL
   --------------+--------+--------+--------+
   LESS THAN 5   |     40 |     30 |     40 |    110
                 |   30.0 |   25.0 |   55.0 |
                 |    3.3 |    1.0 |    4.1 |
   --------------+--------+--------+--------+
   5 TO 10       |     75 |     45 |    100 |    220
                 |   60.0 |   50.0 |  110.0 |
                 |    3.8 |    0.5 |    0.9 |
   --------------+--------+--------+--------+
   MORE THAN 10  |     65 |     75 |    190 |    330
                 |   90.0 |   75.0 |  165.0 |
                 |    6.9 |    0.0 |    3.8 |
   --------------+--------+--------+--------+
   TOTAL              180      150      330      660

                   STATISTICS FOR 2-WAY TABLES

 CHI-SQUARE                     24.316    DF=     4   PROB=0.0001
```

test. In our example, $\alpha = .01$ and the prob value reported by SAS is .0001, so again we reject H_0, and conclude that length of stay and insurance coverage are not independent.

EXERCISES

10-6 Given the following dimensions for contingency tables, how many degrees of freedom will the chi-square statistic for each have?

a) 2 rows, 5 columns
b) 3 rows, 4 columns
c) 4 rows, 6 columns
d) 5 rows, 5 columns
e) 3 rows, 6 columns

10-7 A brand manager is concerned that her brand's share may be unevenly distributed throughout the country. In a survey in which the country was divided into 4 geographic regions, a random sampling of 100 consumers in each region was surveyed, with the following results:

	REGION				
	A	B	C	D	TOTAL
Purchase the brand	47	52	43	49	**191**
Do not purchase	53	48	57	51	**209**
Total	**100**	**100**	**100**	**100**	**400**

Develop a table of observed and expected frequencies (similar to Table 10-3) for this problem.

10-8 For problem 10-7:

a) Calculate χ^2, using a frequency table similar to Table 10-4.
b) State the null and alternative hypotheses.
c) Using a .05 level of significance, should the null hypothesis be rejected?

10-9 To determine whether different income groups have different purchasing habits concerning a certain brand, a marketing researcher asked 4 income groups, "Do you always purchase the brand, never purchase the brand, or sometimes purchase the brand?" The results of this survey were:

	INCOME GROUP (HOUSEHOLD)				
	<$7,000	$7,000–12,999	$13,000–19,999	$20,000+	TOTAL
Always	25	40	47	46	**158**
Never	69	51	74	57	**251**
Sometimes	36	29	19	37	**121**
Total	**130**	**120**	**140**	**140**	**530**

Calculate a table of observed and expected frequencies for this problem.

10-10 For problem 10-9:

a) State the null and the alternative hypotheses.
b) Calculate χ^2.
c) At the .10 significance level, should the null hypothesis be rejected?

10-11 A financial consultant is interested in the differences in capital structure within different firm sizes in a certain industry. The consultant surveys a group of firms with assets of different amounts and divides the firms into three groups. Each firm is classified according to whether its total debt is greater than stockholders' equity or whether its total debt is less than stockholders' equity. The results of the survey are:

	FIRM ASSET SIZE (IN THOUSANDS) <\$500	\$500–2,000	\$2,000+	**TOTAL**
Debt less than equity	7	10	8	**25**
Debt greater than equity	10	18	9	**37**
Total	**17**	**28**	**17**	**62**

Do the three firm sizes have the same capital structure? Use the .10 significance level.

10-12 A newspaper publisher, trying to pinpoint his market's characteristics, wondered whether newspaper readership in the community is related to readers' educational achievement. A survey questioned adults in the area on their level of education and their frequency of readership. The results are shown in the following table.

	LEVEL OF EDUCATIONAL ACHIEVEMENT				
FREQUENCY OF READERSHIP	PROFESSIONAL OR POSTGRADUATE	COLLEGE GRADUATE	HIGH SCHOOL GRADUATE	DID NOT COMPLETE HIGH SCHOOL	**TOTAL**
Never	6	13	14	17	**50**
Sometimes	12	16	8	8	**44**
Morning or evening	38	40	11	6	**95**
Both editions	21	22	9	13	**65**
Total	**77**	**91**	**42**	**44**	**254**

At the .05 significance level, does the frequency of newspaper readership in the community differ according to the readers' level of education?

10-13 A school educator has the opinion that the grades high school students make are dependent on the amount of time they spend listening to music. To test this theory, he has randomly given 400 students a questionnaire. Within the questionnaire are the two questions, "How many hours per week do you listen to music?" and, "What is the average grade for all your classes?" The data from the survey are in the table below. Using a 10 percent significance level, test whether these factors are independent or dependent.

HOURS SPENT LISTENING TO MUSIC	AVERAGE GRADE A	B	C	D	F	**TOTAL**
<5 hrs.	12	9	10	15	4	**50**
5–10 hrs.	21	28	28	20	3	**100**
11–20 hrs.	8	26	70	15	31	**150**
>20 hrs.	9	12	42	25	12	**100**
Total	**50**	**75**	**150**	**75**	**50**	**400**

10-3 CHI-SQUARE AS A TEST OF GOODNESS OF FIT: Testing the Appropriateness of a Distribution

In the preceding section of this chapter, we used the chi-square test to decide whether to accept a null hypothesis that was a hypothesis of independence between two variables. In our example, these two variables were (1) attitude toward job performance reviews and (2) geographical region.

Function of a goodness-of-fit test

The chi-square test can also be used to decide whether a particular probability distribution, such as the binomial, Poisson, or normal, is the *appropriate* distribution. This is an important ability, because as decision makers using statistics, we will need to choose a certain probability distribution to approximate the distribution of the data we happen to be considering. We will need the ability to question how far we can go from the assumptions that underlie a particular distribution before we must conclude that this distribution is no longer applicable. **The chi-square test enables us to ask this question and to test whether there is a significant difference between an observed frequency distribution and a theoretical frequency distribution.** In this manner, we can determine the *goodness of fit* of a theoretical distribution (that is, how well it fits the distribution of data that we have actually observed). Thus we can determine whether we should believe that the observed data constitute a sample drawn from the hypothesized theoretical distribution.

Calculating Observed and Expected Frequencies

Suppose that the Gordon Company requires that college seniors who are seeking positions with it be interviewed by three different executives. This enables the company to obtain a consensus evaluation of each candidate. Each executive gives the candidate either a positive or a negative rating. Table 10-9 contains the interview results of the last 100 candidates.

TABLE 10-9 Interview results of 100 candidates

POSSIBLE POSITIVE RATINGS FROM 3 INTERVIEWS	NUMBER OF CANDIDATES RECEIVING EACH OF THESE RATINGS
0	18
1	47
2	24
3	11
	100

For manpower planning purposes, the director of recruitment for this company thinks that the interview process can be approximated by a binomial distribution with $p = .40$; that is, with a 40 percent chance of any candidate receiving a positive rating on any one interview. If the director wants to test this hypothesis at the .20 level of significance, how should he proceed?

Stating the problem symbolically

H_0: A binomial distribution with
$p = .40$ is a good description ← null hypothesis
of the interview process
H_1: A binomial distribution with
$p = .40$ is *not* a good description ← alternative hypothesis
of the interview process
$\alpha = .20$ ← level of significance for testing these hypotheses

---

Calculating the binomial probabilities

To solve this problem, we must determine whether the discrepancies between the observed frequencies and those we would expect (if the binomial distribution is the proper model to use) are actually due to chance. We can begin by determining what the binomial probabilities would be for this interview situation. For three interviews, we would find the probability of success in the Cumulative Binomial Distribution Table (Appendix Table 3) by looking for the column labeled $n = 3$ and $p = .40$. The results are summarized in Table 10-10.

TABLE 10-10 Binomial probabilities for interview problem

POSSIBLE POSITIVE RATINGS FROM 3 INTERVIEWS	BINOMIAL PROBABILITIES OF THESE OUTCOMES
0	1.0 − .7840 = .2160
1	.7840 − .3520 = .4320
2	3520 − .0640 = .2880
3	.0640
	1.0000

Now we can use the theoretical binomial probabilities of the outcomes to compute the expected frequencies. By comparing these expected frequencies with our observed frequencies using the χ^2 test, we can examine the extent of the difference between them. Table 10-11 lists the observed

TABLE 10-11 Observed frequencies, appropriate binomial probabilities, and expected frequencies for interview problem

POSSIBLE POSITIVE RATINGS FROM 3 INTERVIEWS	OBSERVED FREQUENCY OF CANDIDATES RECEIVING THESE RATINGS	BINOMIAL PROBABILITY OF POSSIBLE OUTCOMES		NUMBER OF CANDIDATES INTERVIEWED		EXPECTED FREQUENCY OF CANDIDATES RECEIVING THESE RATINGS
0	18	.2160	×	100	=	22
1	47	.4320	×	100	=	43
2	24	.2880	×	100	=	29
3	11	.0640	×	100	=	6
	100	**1.0000**				**100**

frequencies, the appropriate binomial probabilities from Table 10-10, and the expected frequencies for the sample of 100 interviews.

Calculating the Chi-Square Statistic

To compute the chi-square statistic for this problem, we can use Equation 10-1:

$$\chi^2 = \sum \frac{(f_o - f_e)^2}{f_e} \qquad \textbf{[10-1]}$$

and the format we introduced in Table 10-4. This process is illustrated in Table 10-12.

TABLE 10-12 Calculation of χ^2 statistic from interview data listed in Table 10-11

OBSERVED FREQUENCY f_o	EXPECTED FREQUENCY f_e	$f_o - f_e$	$(f_o - f_e)^2$	$\frac{(f_o - f_e)^2}{f_e}$
18	22	−4	16	.7273
47	43	4	16	.3721
24	29	−5	25	.8621
11	6	5	25	4.1667
				6.1282
	$\sum \frac{(f_o - f_e)^2}{f_e} = 6.1282 \leftarrow \chi^2$			

Determining Degrees of Freedom in a Goodness-of-Fit Test

First count the number of classes

Before we can calculate the appropriate number of degrees of freedom for a chi-square goodness-of-fit test, we must count the number of classes (symbolized k) for which we have compared the observed and expected frequencies. Our interview problem contains four such classes: 0, 1, 2, and 3 positive ratings. Thus we begin with 4 degrees of freedom. Yet since the four observed frequencies must sum to 100, the total number of observed frequencies we can freely specify is only $k - 1$, or 3. The fourth is determined, because the total of the four has to be 100.

Then subtract degrees of freedom lost from estimating population parameters

To solve a goodness-of-fit problem, we may be forced to impose additional restrictions on the calculations of the degrees of freedom. Suppose we are using the chi-square test as a goodness-of-fit test to determine whether a normal distribution fits a set of observed frequencies. If we have six classes of observed frequencies ($k = 6$), then we would conclude that we have only $k - 1$, or 5 degrees of freedom. If, however, we also have to use the sample mean as an estimate of the population mean, we will have to subtract an additional degree of freedom, which leaves us with only 4. And third, if we have to use the sample standard deviation to estimate the population standard deviation, we will have to subtract *one more* degree of freedom, leaving us with 3. Our general rule in these cases is, **first employ the ($k - 1$) rule and then subtract an additional degree of freedom for each population parameter that has to be estimated from the sample data.**

In the interview example, we have four classes of observed frequencies. As a result, $k = 4$, and the appropriate number of degrees of freedom is $k - 1$, or 3. We are not required to estimate any population parameter, so we need not reduce this number further.

Using the Chi-Square Goodness-of-Fit Test

Calculating the limit of the acceptance region

In the interview problem, the company desires to test the hypothesis of goodness of fit at the .20 level of significance. In Appendix Table 5, then, we must look under the .20 column and move down to the row labeled 3 degrees of freedom. There we find that the value of the chi-square statistic is 4.642. We can interpret this value as follows: With 3 degrees of freedom, the region to the right of a chi-square value of 4.642 contains .20 of the area under the curve.

Illustrating the problem

Figure 10-5 illustrates a chi-square distribution for 3 degrees of freedom, showing in color a .20 level of significance. Notice that the acceptance region for the null hypothesis (the hypothesis that the sample data came from a binomial distribution with $p = .4$) extends from the left tail to the chi-square value of 4.642. Obviously, the sample chi-square value of 6.1282 falls outside this acceptance region. Therefore, we reject the null hypothesis and conclude that the binomial distribution with $p = .4$ fails to provide a good description of our observed frequencies.

Interpreting the results

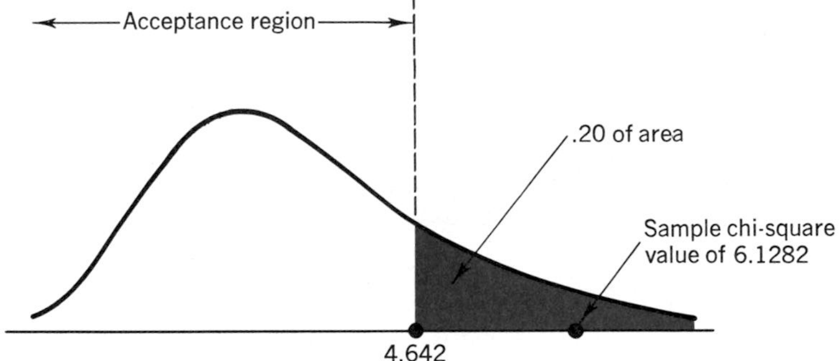

FIGURE 10-5 Goodness-of-fit test at the .20 level of significance, showing acceptance region and sample chi-square value of 6.1282

EXERCISES

10-14 Louis Armstrong, salesman for Dillard Paper Company, has 5 accounts to visit per day. It is suggested that the variable, sales by Mr. Armstrong, may be described by the binomial distribution, with the probability of selling each account being .3. Given the following observed frequency distribution of Armstrong's number of sales per day, can we conclude that the distribution does in fact follow the suggested distribution? Use the .05 significance level.

Number of sales per day	0	1	2	3	4	5
Frequency of the number of sales	20	65	42	14	6	3

10-15 At the .10 level of significance, can we conclude that the following distribution follows a Poisson distribution with $\lambda = 2$?

Number of arrivals per hour	0	1	2	3	4	5 or more
Number of hours	10	19	31	26	11	3

10-16 Below is a table of observed frequencies, along with the frequencies to be expected under a normal distribution.

a) Calculate the chi-square statistic.
b) Can we conclude that this distribution does in fact follow a normal distribution? Use the .05 level of significance.

	SCORE				
	51-60	61-70	71-80	81-90	91-100
Observed frequency	3	10	44	50	13
Expected frequency	2	17	50	41	10

10-17 Below is an observed frequency distribution. Using a normal distribution with $\mu = 2.44$ and $\sigma = .4$:

a) Find the probability of falling in each class.
b) From part *a*, compute the expected frequency of each category.
c) Calculate the chi-square statistic.
d) At the .10 level of significance, does this distribution seem to be well described by the suggested normal distribution?

Observed value of the variable	less than 1.8	1.8-2.19	2.2-2.59	2.6-2.99	3.0 and above
Observed frequency	3	17	33	22	5

10-18 An account executive of an advertising agency is reviewing the results of a telephone survey measuring the audience exposure to a commercial that was aired 3 times last week. According to ratings of the time slots chosen, she believes that any person in the area owning a television had a 40 percent chance of seeing each ad. She also believes that exposure to each ad was independent, since the commercials were run during different time slots on different stations. A sample of the results from 200 people surveyed showed that the number of people seeing 0, 1, 2, or 3 ads were 46, 73, 58, and 23, respectively. At the .10 level of significance, is the number of ads seen per person well described by a binomial distribution with $p = .4$?

10-19 A chemical extraction plant processes sea water to collect sodium chloride and magnesium. From scientific analysis, sea water is known to contain sodium chloride, magnesium, and other elements in the ratio 62 : 4 : 34. A sample of 200 tons of extracted minerals has resulted in 130 tons of sodium chloride and 6 tons of magnesium. Are these data consistent with the scientific model? Use the .05 level of significance.

10-20 Dennis Barry, a hospital administrator, has examined past records from 300 randomly selected 8-hour shifts to determine the frequency with which the hospital treats fractures. The number of days in which 0, 1, 2, 3, 4, 5, or 6 or more patients with broken bones were treated was 25, 45, 63, 71, 48, 26, and 22, respectively. At the .05 level of significance, can we reasonably believe that the incidence of broken bone cases follows a Poisson distribution with $\lambda = 3$?

10-21 A large city fire department calculates that for any given precinct, during any given 8-hour shift, there is a 30 percent chance of receiving at least 1 fire alarm. Here is a random sampling of 60 days:

Number of shifts during which alarms were received	1	2	3
Number of days	27	11	6

At the .05 level of significance, do these fire alarms follow a binomial distribution? (*Hint:* Combine the last two groups so that all expected frequencies will be greater than 5.)

10-22 A marketing researcher studying sales per distributor has compiled the following table classifying 150 distributors by the number of units they sell per month:

UNIT SALES/MONTH	50 OR LESS	51–100	101–150	151 OR MORE
Number of distributors in each group	13	53	62	22

Before the individual distributors were combined into these groups, the sample mean and standard deviation were calculated to be 106.3 and 36.5 units per month, respectively.

a) What is the probability (using a normal distribution with $\mu = 106.3$ and $\sigma = 36.5$) that a distributor's monthly unit sales will be less than 50.5 units; between 50.5 and 100.5 units; between 100.5 and 150.5 units; greater than 150.5 units?
b) Using the probabilities in part *a*, find the expected frequencies for the 150 distributors' monthly unit sales.
c) At the .05 level of significance, does the observed distribution follow the normal distribution found in part *b*?

10-23 A supermarket manager is keeping track of the arrival of customers at checkout counters, to see how many cashiers are needed to handle the flow. In a sample of 800 5-minute time periods, there were 36, 117, 194, 167, 138, 94, and 54 periods in which 0, 1, 2, 3, 4, 5, or 6 or more customers arrived at a checkout counter, respectively. Are these data consistent at the .05 level of significance with a Poisson distribution with $\lambda = 3$?

10-24 After years of working at a weighing station for trucks, Jeff Simpson feels that the weight per truck follows a normal distribution with $\mu = 70$ and $\sigma = 10$. In order to test this assumption, Jeff collected the data below one Monday, recording the weight of each truck that entered his station (in 000's of pounds).

75	82	84	68	78	15	40	60	62	73
45	72	83	71	92	89	35	105	69	75
75	60	74	80	66	82	80	87	76	74
81	69	65	95	76	55	49	80	84	73
77	78	64	65	71	69	64	73	62	66

If Jeff used a chi-square goodness-of-fit test on these data, what would he conclude about the trucks' weight distribution? (Use a .10 significance level and be sure to state the hypothesis of interest.) *Hint:* Use 5 equally probable intervals.

10-25 A company that manufactures kitchen appliances has stated that the probability of a blender's being defective is 15 percent. A certain retail store receives these blenders in boxes of 5. In unpacking 200 of these boxes, the clerk was asked to keep a record of the number in each box that were defective. If the shipment the store gets is similar to that claimed by the manufacturing company, the store will keep the blenders. However, they must be 95 percent confident of this fit. Based on the following tabulation, use a chi-square goodness-of-fit test. What is the null hypothesis? (*Hint:* Classes can be combined if the expected value is less than 5.)

NUMBER DEFECTIVE IN BOX	NUMBER OF BOXES
0	100
1	70
2	20
3	5
4	3
5	2

10-4 ANALYSIS OF VARIANCE

Function of analysis of variance

Earlier in this chapter, we used the chi-square test to examine the difference between more than two sample proportions and to make inferences about whether such samples are drawn from populations each having the same proportion. In this section, we will learn a technique known as **analysis of variance (often abbreviated ANOVA), which will enable us to test for the significance of the difference between more than two sample means.** Using analysis of variance, we will be able to make inferences about whether our samples are drawn from populations having the same mean.

Analysis of variance will be useful in such situations as comparing the mileage achieved by five different brands of gasoline, testing which of four different training methods produces the fastest learning record, or comparing the first-year earnings of the graduates of half a dozen different schools of business. In each of these cases, we would compare the means of *more* than two samples.

Statement of the Problem

In the training director's problem that opened this chapter, she wanted to evaluate three different training methods, to determine whether there was any difference in their effectiveness.

TABLE 10-13 Daily production of 16 new employees

METHOD 1	METHOD 2	METHOD 3
		18
15	22	24
18	27	19
19	18	16
22	21	22
11	17	15
85	**105**	**114**
÷5	÷5	÷6
$17 = \bar{x}_1$	$21 = \bar{x}_2$	$19 = \bar{x}_3$ ← sample means
$n_1 = 5$	$n_2 = 5$	$n_3 = 6$ ← sample sizes

Calculating the grand mean

After completion of the training period, the company's statistical staff chose sixteen new employees assigned at random to the three training methods.* Counting the production output by these sixteen trainees, the staff has summarized the data and calculated the mean production of the trainees (see Table 10-13). Now if we wish to determine the *grand mean,* or $\bar{\bar{x}}$ (the mean for the entire group of sixteen trainees), we can use one of two methods:

1. $\bar{\bar{x}} = \frac{15+18+19+22+11+22+27+18+21+17+18+24+19+16+22+15}{16}$

$= \frac{304}{16}$

$= 19 \leftarrow$ grand mean using all the data

2. $\bar{\bar{x}} = (5/16)(17) + (5/16)(21) + (6/16)(19)$

$= \frac{304}{16}$

$= 19 \leftarrow$ grand mean as a weighted average of the sample means, using the relative sample sizes as the weights

Statement of the Hypotheses

In this case, our reason for using analysis of variance is to decide whether these three samples (a *sample* is the small group of employees trained by any one method) were drawn from populations (a *population* is the total number of employees who could be trained by that method) having the same means. Because we are testing the effectiveness of the three training methods, we must determine whether the three samples, represented by the sample means $\bar{x}_1 = 17$, $\bar{x}_2 = 21$, and $\bar{x}_3 = 19$, could have been drawn from populations having the same mean, μ. A formal statement of the null and alternative hypotheses we wish to test would be:

Stating the problem symbolically

$H_0: \mu_1 = \mu_2 = \mu_3 \leftarrow$ null hypothesis

$H_1: \mu_1, \mu_2$, and μ_3 are *not* all equal $\leftarrow$ alternative hypothesis

Interpreting the results

If we can conclude from our test that the sample means do not differ significantly, we can infer that the choice of training method does not influence the productivity of the employee. On the other hand, if we find a difference among the sample means that is too large to attribute to chance sampling error, we can infer that the method used in training *does* influence the productivity of the employee. In that case, we would adjust our training program accordingly.

* Although in real practice, sixteen trainees would not constitute an adequate statistical sample, we have limited the number here, to be able to demonstrate the basic techniques of analysis of variance and to avoid tedious calculations.

Analysis of Variance: Basic Concepts

Assumptions made in analysis of variance

In order to use analysis of variance, we must assume that each of the samples is drawn from a normal population and that each of these populations has the same variance, σ^2. If, however, the sample sizes are large enough, we do not need the assumption of normality.

In our training-methods problem, our null hypothesis states that the three populations have the same mean. If this hypothesis is true, classifying the data into three columns in Table 10-13 is unnecessary, and the entire set of sixteen measurements of productivity can be thought of as a sample from one population. This overall population also has a variance of σ^2.

Analysis of variance is based on a comparison of two different estimates of the variance, σ^2, of our overall population. In this case, we can calculate one of these estimates by examining **the variance among the three sample means,** which are 17, 21, and 19. The other estimate of the population variance is determined by **the variation within the three samples** themselves; that is, (15, 18, 19, 22, 11), (22, 27, 18, 21, 17), and (18, 24, 19, 16, 22, 15). Then we compare these two estimates of the population variance. Since both are estimates of σ^2, they should be approximately equal in value *when the null hypothesis is true*. If the null hypothesis is *not* true, these two estimates will differ considerably. The three steps in analysis of variance, then, are:

Steps in analysis of variance

1. Determine one estimate of the population variance from the variance *among the sample means.*
2. Determine a second estimate of the population variance from the variance *within the samples.*
3. Compare these two estimates. If they are approximately equal in value, *accept* the null hypothesis.

In the remainder of this section, we shall learn how to calculate these two estimates of the population variance, how to compare these two estimates, and how to make a hypothesis test and interpret the results. As we learn how to do these computations, however, keep in mind that all are based on the concepts we have presented in this section.

Calculating the Variance Among the Sample Means

Finding the first estimate of the population variance

Step 1 in analysis of variance indicates that we must obtain one estimate of the population variance from the variance among the three sample means. In statistical language, this estimate is called the *between-column variance.*

In Chapter 4, we used Equation 4-11 to calculate the sample variance:

Sample variance

$$s^2 = \frac{\Sigma(x - \bar{x})^2}{n - 1} \qquad [4\text{-}11]$$

First find the variance among sample means

Now, because we are working with three sample means and a grand mean, let's substitute $\bar{x}$ for x, $\bar{\bar{x}}$ for $\bar{x}$, and k (the number of samples) for n to get a formula for the variance among the sample means:

Variance among sample means →

$$s_{\bar{x}}^2 = \frac{\Sigma(\bar{x} - \bar{\bar{x}})^2}{k - 1} \qquad [10\text{-}4]$$

Then find the population variance using this variance among sample means

Next, we can return for a moment to Chapter 7, where we defined the standard error of the mean as the standard deviation of all possible samples of a given size. The formula to derive the standard error of the mean is Equation 7-1:

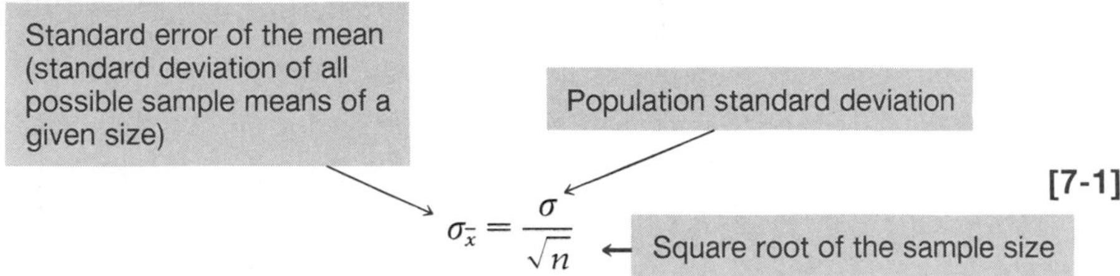

$$\sigma_{\bar{x}} = \frac{\sigma}{\sqrt{n}}$$

We can simplify this equation by cross-multiplying the terms and then squaring both sides in order to change the population standard deviation, σ, into the population variance, σ^2:

Population variance →

$$\sigma^2 = \sigma_{\bar{x}}^2 \times n \qquad [10\text{-}5]$$

Standard error squared (this is the variance among the sample means)

An acceptable substitution

For our training-method problem, we do not have all the information we need to use this equation to find σ^2. Specifically, we do not know $\sigma_{\bar{x}}^2$. We could, however, calculate the variance among the three sample means, $s_{\bar{x}}^2$, using Equation 10-4. So why not substitute $s_{\bar{x}}^2$ for $\sigma_{\bar{x}}^2$ in Equation 10-5 and calculate an estimate of the population variance? This will give us:

$$\hat{\sigma}^2 = s_{\bar{x}}^2 \times n = \frac{\Sigma n(\bar{x} - \bar{\bar{x}})^2}{k - 1}$$

Which sample size to use

There is a slight difficulty in using this equation as it stands. In Equation 7-1, n represents the sample size, but *which* sample size should we use when the different samples have different sizes? We solve this problem with Equation 10-6, where each $(\bar{x}_j - \bar{\bar{x}})^2$ is multiplied by its own appropriate n_j.

First estimate of the population variance →

$$\hat{\sigma}^2 = \frac{\Sigma n_j(\bar{x}_j - \bar{\bar{x}})^2}{k - 1} \qquad [10\text{-}6]$$

where:

- $\hat{\sigma}^2$ = our first estimate of the population variance based on the variance among the sample means (the *between-column variance*)
- n_j = the size of the jth sample
- $\bar{x}_j$ = the sample mean of the jth sample
- $\bar{\bar{x}}$ = the grand mean
- k = the number of samples

Now we can use Equation 10-6 and the data from Table 10-13 to calculate the between-column variance. Table 10-14 shows how to make these calculations.

TABLE 10-14 Calculation of the between-column variance

n	$\bar{x}$	$\bar{\bar{x}}$	$\bar{x} - \bar{\bar{x}}$	$(\bar{x} - \bar{\bar{x}})^2$	$n(\bar{x} - \bar{\bar{x}})^2$
5	17	19	$17 - 19 = -2$	$(-2)^2 = 4$	$5 \times 4 = 20$
5	21	19	$21 - 19 = 2$	$(2)^2 = 4$	$5 \times 4 = 20$
6	19	19	$19 - 19 = 0$	$(0)^2 = 0$	$6 \times 0 = 0$
					$\Sigma n_j(\bar{x}_j - \bar{\bar{x}})^2 \rightarrow$ **40**

$$\hat{\sigma}^2 = \frac{\Sigma n_j(\bar{x}_j - \bar{\bar{x}})^2}{k-1} = \frac{40}{3-1} \quad [10\text{-}6]$$

$$= \frac{40}{2}$$

$$= 20 \leftarrow \text{the between-column variance}$$

Calculating the Variance Within the Samples

Finding the second estimate of the population variance

Step 2 in ANOVA requires a second estimate of the population variance based on the variance within the samples. In statistical terms, this can be called the *within-column variance*. Our employee training problem has three samples of five or six items each. We can calculate the variance within each of these three samples using Equation 4-11:

Sample variance

$$s^2 = \frac{\Sigma(x - \bar{x})^2}{n - 1} \quad [4\text{-}11]$$

Since we have assumed that the variances of our three populations are the same, we could use any one of the three sample variances (s_1^2 or s_2^2 or s_3^2) as the second estimate of the population variance. Statistically, we can get a better estimate of the population variance by using a weighted average of all three sample variances. The general formula for this second estimate of σ^2 is:

Second estimate of the population variance

$$\hat{\sigma}^2 = \sum\left(\frac{n_j - 1}{n_T - k}\right) s_j^2 \qquad [10\text{-}7]$$

where:

- $\hat{\sigma}^2$ = our second estimate of the population variance based on the variances within the samples (the *within-column variance*)
- n_j = the size of the jth sample
- s_j^2 = the sample variance of the jth sample
- k = the number of samples
- $n_T = \Sigma n_j$ = the total sample size

Using all the information at our disposal

This formula uses all the information that we have at our disposal, not just a portion of it. Had there been seven samples instead of three, we would have taken a weighted average of all seven. The weights used in Equation 10-7 will be explained shortly. Table 10-15 illustrates how to calculate this second estimate of the population variance using the variances within all three of our samples.

TABLE 10-15 Calculation of variances within the samples and the within-column variance

Training method 1 Sample mean: $\bar{x} = 17$		Training method 2 Sample mean: $\bar{x} = 21$		Training method 3 Sample mean: $\bar{x} = 19$	
$x - \bar{x}$	$(x - \bar{x})^2$	$x - \bar{x}$	$(x - \bar{x})^2$	$x - \bar{x}$	$(x - \bar{x})^2$
$15 - 17 = -2$	$(-2)^2 = 4$	$22 - 21 = 1$	$(1)^2 = 1$	$18 - 19 = -1$	$(-1)^2 = 1$
$18 - 17 = 1$	$(1)^2 = 1$	$27 - 21 = 6$	$(6)^2 = 36$	$24 - 19 = 5$	$(5)^2 = 25$
$19 - 17 = 2$	$(2)^2 = 4$	$18 - 21 = -3$	$(-3)^2 = 9$	$19 - 19 = 0$	$(0)^2 = 0$
$22 - 17 = 5$	$(5)^2 = 25$	$21 - 21 = 0$	$(0)^2 = 0$	$16 - 19 = -3$	$(3)^2 = 9$
$11 - 17 = -6$	$(-6)^2 = 36$	$17 - 21 = -4$	$(-4)^2 = 16$	$22 - 19 = 3$	$(3)^2 = 9$
	$\Sigma(x - \bar{x})^2 = \mathbf{70}$		$\Sigma(x - \bar{x})^2 = \mathbf{62}$	$15 - 19 = -4$	$(-4)^2 = 16$
					$\Sigma(x - \bar{x})^2 = \mathbf{60}$
	$\frac{\Sigma(x - \bar{x})^2}{n - 1} = \frac{70}{5 - 1} = \frac{70}{4}$		$\frac{\Sigma(x - \bar{x})^2}{n - 1} = \frac{62}{5 - 1} = \frac{62}{4}$		$\frac{\Sigma(x - \bar{x})^2}{n - 1} = \frac{60}{6 - 1} = \frac{60}{5}$
sample variance → $s_1^2 = 17.5$		sample variance → $s_2^2 = 15.5$		sample variance → $s_3^2 = 12.0$	

And:

$$\hat{\sigma}^2 = \sum\left(\frac{n_j - 1}{n_T - k}\right)s_j^2 = (4/13)(17.5) + (4/13)(15.5) + (5/13)(12.0) \qquad [10\text{-}7]$$

$$= \frac{192}{13}$$

$= 14.769$ ← Second estimate of the population variance based on the variances within the samples (the within-column variance)

The *F* Hypothesis Test: Computing and Interpreting the *F* Statistic

Finding the *F* ratio

Step 3 in ANOVA compares these two estimates of the population variance by computing their ratio, called *F*, as follows:

$$F = \frac{\begin{array}{c}\text{First estimate of the population variance}\\ \text{based on the variance among the sample means}\end{array}}{\begin{array}{c}\text{Second estimate of the population variance}\\ \text{based on the variances within the samples}\end{array}} \quad [10\text{-}8]$$

If we substitute the statistical shorthand for the numerator and denominator of this ratio, Equation 10-8 becomes:

$$F = \frac{\text{Between-column variance}}{\text{Within-column variance}} \quad [10\text{-}9]$$

Now we can find the *F* ratio for the training-method problem with which we have been working:

$$F = \frac{\text{Between-column variance}}{\text{Within-column variance}} \quad [10\text{-}9]$$

$$= \frac{20}{14.769}$$

$$= 1.354 \leftarrow F \text{ ratio}$$

Interpreting the *F* ratio

Having found this *F ratio* of 1.354, how can we interpret it? First, examine the denominator, which is based on the variance within the samples. The denominator is a good estimator of σ^2 (the population variance) whether the null hypothesis is true or not. What about the numerator? If the null hypothesis that the three methods of training have equal effects is true, then the numerator, or the variation among the sample means of the three methods, is also a good estimate of σ^2 (the population variance). As a result, **the denominator and numerator should be about equal if the null hypothesis is true.** The nearer the *F* ratio comes to 1, then, the more we are inclined to accept the null hypothesis. Conversely, as the *F* ratio becomes larger, we will be more inclined to reject the null hypothesis and accept the alternative (that a difference does exist in the effects of the three training methods).

Shortly, we shall learn a more formal way of deciding when to accept or reject the null hypothesis. But even now, you should understand the basic logic behind the *F statistic*. **When populations are not the same, the between-column variance (which was derived from the variance among the sample means) will tend to be larger than the within-column variance (which was derived from the variances within the samples), and the value of *F* will tend to increase. This will lead us to reject the null hypothesis.**

The *F* Distribution

Describing an *F* distribution

Like other statistics we have studied, if the null hypothesis is true, then the *F* statistic has a particular sampling distribution. Like the *t* and chi-square distributions, this *F* distribution is actually a whole family of distributions, three of which are shown in Fig. 10-6. Notice that each is identified by a *pair* of degrees of freedom, unlike the *t* and chi-square distributions, which have only one value for the number of degrees of freedom. **The first number refers to the number of degrees of freedom in the numerator of the *F* ratio; the second, to the degrees of freedom in the denominator.**

As we can see in Fig. 10-6, the *F* distribution has a single mode. The specific shape of an *F* distribution depends upon the number of degrees of freedom in both the numerator and the denominator of the *F* ratio. But in general, the *F* distribution is skewed to the right and tends to get more symmetrical as the number of degrees of freedom in the numerator and denominator increase.

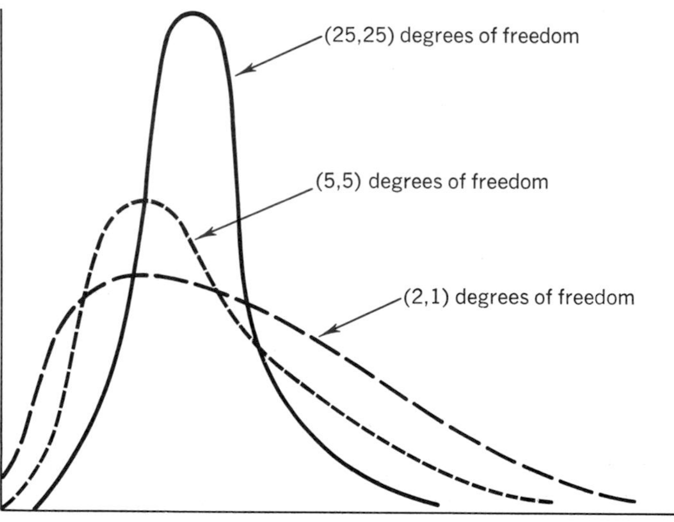

FIGURE 10-6 Three *F* distributions (first value in parentheses equals number of degrees of freedom in the numerator of the *F* ratio; second equals number of degrees of freedom in the denominator)

Using the *F* Distribution: Degrees of Freedom

Calculating degrees of freedom

As we have mentioned, each *F* distribution has a pair of degrees of freedom, one for the numerator of the *F* ratio and the other for the denominator. How can we calculate both of these?

Finding the numerator degrees of freedom

First, think about the numerator, the between-column variance. In Table 10-14, we used three values of $(\bar{x} - \bar{\bar{x}})^2$, one for each sample, to calculate $\Sigma(\bar{x} - \bar{\bar{x}})^2$. Once we knew two of these $(\bar{x} - \bar{\bar{x}})^2$ values, the third was *automatically determined* and could not be freely specified. Thus, one degree of freedom is lost when we calculate the between-column variance, and the number of degrees of freedom for the numerator of the *F* ratio is always one fewer than the number of samples. The rule, then, is:

Number of degrees of freedom in *numerator* of the F ratio $= (\text{Number of samples} - 1)$ **[10-10]**

Finding the denominator degrees of freedom

Now, what of the denominator? Look at Table 10-15 for a moment. There we calculated the variances within the samples, and we used all three samples. For the jth sample, we used n_j values of $(x - \bar{x})$ to calculate the $\Sigma(x - \bar{x})^2$ for that sample. Once we knew all but one of these $(x - \bar{x})$ values, the last was *automatically determined* and could not be freely specified. Thus, we lost 1 degree of freedom in the calculations for *each* sample, leaving us with 4, 4, and 5 degrees of freedom in the samples. Since we had three samples, we were left with $4 + 4 + 5 = 13$ degrees of freedom (which could also be calculated as $5 + 5 + 6 - 3 = 13$). We can state the rule like this:

Number of degrees of freedom in *denominator* of the F ratio $= \Sigma(n_j - 1) = n_T - k$ **[10-11]**

where:

- n_j = the size of the jth sample
- k = the number of samples
- $n_T = \Sigma n_j$ = the total sample size

Now we can see that the weight assigned to s_j^2 in Equation 10-7 was just its fraction of the total number of degrees of freedom in the denominator of the F ratio.

Using the *F* Table

To do F hypothesis tests, we shall use an F table in which the columns represent the number of degrees of freedom for the numerator and the rows represent the degrees of freedom for the denominator. Separate tables exist for each level of significance.

Suppose we are testing a hypothesis at the .01 level of significance, using the F distribution. Our degrees of freedom are 8 for the numerator and 11 for the denominator. In this instance, we would turn to Appendix Table 6. In the body of that table, the appropriate value for 8 and 11 degrees of freedom is 4.74. If our calculated value of F exceeds this table value of 4.74, we would reject the null hypothesis. If not, we would accept it.

Testing the Hypothesis

Finding the F statistic and the degrees of freedom

We can now test our hypothesis that the three different training methods produce identical results, using the material we have developed to this point. Let's begin by reviewing how we calculated the F ratio:

$$F = \frac{\text{First estimate of the population variance based on the variance among the sample means}}{\text{Second estimate of the population variance based on the variances within the samples}} \quad \textbf{[10-8]}$$

$$= \frac{20}{14.769}$$

$$= 1.354 \leftarrow F \text{ statistic}$$

Next, calculate the number of degrees of freedom in the numerator of the F ratio, using Equation 10-10 as follows:

$$\text{Number of degrees of freedom in } \textit{numerator} \text{ of the } F \text{ ratio} = (\text{Number of samples} - 1) \quad \textbf{[10-10]}$$

$$= 3 - 1$$

$$= 2 \leftarrow \text{degrees of freedom in the numerator}$$

And we can calculate the number of degrees of freedom in the denominator of the F ratio by use of Equation 10-11:

$$\text{Number of degrees of freedom in } \textit{denominator} \text{ of the } F \text{ ratio} = \Sigma(n_j - 1) = n_T - k \quad \textbf{[10-11]}$$

$$= (5 - 1) + (5 - 1) + (6 - 1)$$

$$= 16 - 3$$

$$= 13 \leftarrow \text{degrees of freedom in the denominator}$$

Calculating the limit of the acceptance region

Suppose the director of training wants to test at the .05 level the hypothesis that there is no difference among the three training methods. We can look in Appendix Table 6 for 2 degrees of freedom in the numerator and 13 in the denominator. The value we find there is 3.81. Figure 10-7 shows this hypothesis test graphically. The colored region represents the level of signif-

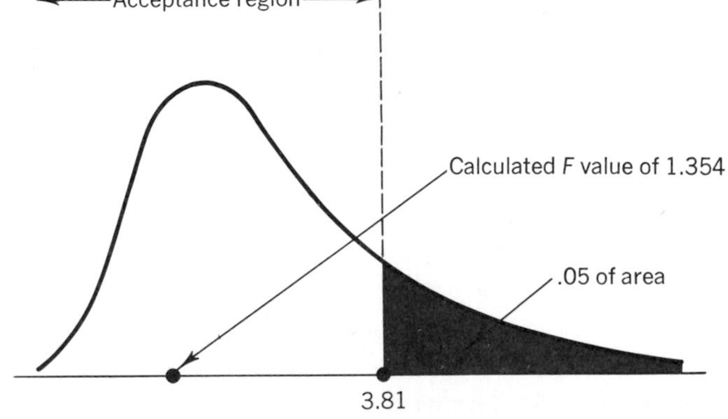

FIGURE 10-7 Hypothesis test at the .05 level of significance, using the F distribution and showing the acceptance region and the calculated F value

Interpreting the results

icance. The table value of 3.81 sets the upper limit of the acceptance region. Since the calculated value for *F* of 1.354 lies within the acceptance region, we would accept the null hypothesis and conclude that, according to the sample information we have, there is no difference in the effects of the three training methods on employee productivity.

Precautions About Using the *F* Test

Use large sample sizes

As we stated earlier, our sample sizes in this problem are too small for us to be able to draw valid inferences about the effectiveness of the various training methods. We chose small samples so that we could explain the logic of analysis of variance without tedious calculations. In actual practice, our methodology would be the same, but our samples would be larger.

Control all factors but the one being tested

In our example, we have assumed the absence of many factors that might have affected our conclusions. We accepted as given, for example, the fact that all the new employees we sampled had the same demonstrated aptitude for learning—which may or may not be true. We assumed that all the instructors of the three training methods had the same ability to teach and to manage, which may not be true. And we assumed that the company's statistical staff collected the data on productivity during work periods that were similar in terms of time of day, day of the week, time of the year, and so on. To be able to make significant decisions based on analysis of variance, we need to be certain that all these factors are effectively controlled.

A test for one factor only

Finally, notice that we have discussed only *one-way*, or one-factor, analysis of variance. Our problem examined the effect of the type of training method on employee productivity, nothing else. Had we wished to measure the effect of two factors, such as the training program and the age of the employee, we would need the ability to use two-way analysis of variance, a statistical method best saved for more advanced textbooks.

Using the Computer for Analysis of Variance

Once again, let us repeat that we used small sample sizes in our ANOVA example so we could explain the logic of the method without getting bogged down in tedious calculations. For a realistic problem, it would be very convenient to use the ANOVA routines that can be found in all the commonly used statistical packages. So that you can compare one of these with the analysis that we did by hand, Table 10-16 gives the output when SAS is used to analyze the data in our training-method problem.

Using the SAS package for ANOVA

Let's look at the column of SAS's "ANOVA table" headed "MEAN SQUARE." In the row labeled "MODEL," this column contains the value 20.000, which we recognize as the between-column variance we calculated in Table 10-14. In the row labeled "ERROR," we find the value 14.769, which is the within-column variance we calculated in Table 10-15. Notice also the column headed "DF" (meaning degrees of freedom). It tells us that the MODEL MEAN SQUARE (the between-column variance) has 2 degrees of freedom and the ERROR MEAN SQUARE (the within-column variance) has 13 degrees of freedom.

TABLE 10-16 Output from SAS for the employee training problem

```
ILLUSTRATING THE USE OF SAS FOR ANOVA

UNITS = UNITS PRODUCED BY TRAINEE
METHOD = TRAINING METHOD USED

ANALYSIS OF VARIANCE PROCEDURE

DEPENDENT VARIABLE: UNITS        UNITS PRODUCED BY TRAINEE

SOURCE                 DF      SUM OF SQUARES         MEAN SQUARE

MODEL                   2         40.00000000         20.00000000

ERROR                  13        192.00000000         14.76923077

CORRECTED TOTAL        15        232.00000000

MODEL F =            1.35                          PR > F = 0.2923
```

Interpreting the results

The last line of the output gives the value of the F statistic, $F = 1.35$, and the prob value .2923, which is the probability of getting an F statistic as large or larger than 1.35 if H_0 is true. Since the prob value is larger than our significance level of $\alpha = .05$, we again conclude that we cannot reject H_0. On the basis of the sample evidence, these three training methods do not appear to have different effects on employee productivity.

EXERCISES

10-26 A study compared the effects of 4 one-month point-of-purchase promotions on sales. Below are the unit sales for 5 stores using all 4 promotions in different months.

Free sample	77	86	80	88	84
On-pack gift	95	92	88	91	89
Cents-off	72	77	68	82	75
Refund by mail	80	84	79	70	82

a) Compute the mean unit sales for each promotion and then determine the grand mean.
b) Estimate the population variance using the between-column variance (Equation 10-6).
c) Estimate the population variance using the within-column variance computed from the variances within the samples.
d) Calculate the F ratio. At the .05 level of significance, do the promotions produce different effects on sales?

10-27 Three training methods were compared to see if they led to greater productivity after training. Below are productivity measures for individuals trained by each method.

Method 1	36	26	31	20	34	25
Method 2	40	29	38	32	39	34
Method 3	32	18	23	21	33	27

At the .05 level of significance, do the three training methods lead to different levels of productivity?

10-28 The following data show the number of claims processed per day for a group of 5 insurance-company employees observed for a number of days. Test the hypothesis that the employees' mean claims per day are all the same. Use the .01 level of significance.

Employee 1	15	17	14	11		
Employee 2	12	10	13	17	14	
Employee 3	10	14	13	15	12	
Employee 4	14	9	7	10	8	7
Employee 5	13	12	9	14	10	9

10-29 Given the measurements on the 4 samples below, can we conclude that they come from populations having the same mean value? Use the .05 level of significance.

Sample 1	17	22	25	29	30	
Sample 2	29	18	20	19	30	21
Sample 3	13	14	20	18	27	16
Sample 4	21	28	20	22	18	

10-30 The manager of an assembly line in a clock-manufacturing plant decided to study how different speeds of the conveyor belt affect the rate of defective units produced in an 8-hour shift. To examine this, he ran the belt at 4 different speeds for five 8-hour shifts each and measured the number of defective units found at the end of each shift. The results of the study follow:

DEFECTIVE UNITS PER SHIFT			
SPEED 1	SPEED 2	SPEED 3	SPEED 4
36	29	31	36
34	34	35	28
37	34	32	34
35	36	33	32
33	32	39	30

a) Calculate the mean number of defective units, $\bar{x}$, for each speed; then determine the grand mean, $\bar{\bar{x}}$.
b) Using Equation 10-6, estimate the population variance (the between-column variance).
c) Calculate the variances *within* the samples and estimate the population variance based upon these variances (the within-column variance).
d) Calculate the F ratio. At the .05 level of significance, do the four different conveyor-belt speeds produce the same rate of defective clocks per shift?

10-31 A camera shop is studying the effects of special film-processing promotions on the number of rolls of film processed per week. The first promotion, which ran in early summer for 6 weeks, offered a free roll of film with each roll processed. The second promotion, which ran in late summer, offered $1.00 off the price of processing 1 roll. The data for each 6-week promotion were recorded, along with the number of rolls processed per week for the 5-week period before the promotion began.

	NUMBER OF ROLLS PROCESSED PER WEEK					
Free roll	65	79	73	55	68	74
$1.00 off	60	64	57	75	62	56
No promotion	61	54	74	59	46	

a) Calculate the average number, $\bar{x}$, of rolls processed per week during the 3 periods, and then determine the grand mean, $\bar{\bar{x}}$.

b) Estimate the population variance by the between-column variance.

c) Calculate the variances within the samples and estimate the population variance based upon these variances (the within-column variance).

d) Calculate the F ratio. At the .05 level of significance, do the 3 time periods show the same number of rolls processed per week? In other words, were the promotions ineffective?

10-32 The supervisor of security at a large department store would like to know if the store apprehends relatively more shoplifters during the Christmas holiday season than in the weeks before or after the holiday. He gathered data on the number of shoplifters apprehended in the store during the months of November, December, and January over the past 6 years. The information is shown in the table below:

	NUMBER OF SHOPLIFTERS					
November	42	36	58	54	37	47
December	51	38	45	32	47	46
January	37	29	35	42	31	33

At the .05 level of significance, is the number of apprehended shoplifters the same during these 3 months?

10-33 A research company has designed 4 different systems to clean up oil spills. The following table contains the results, measured by how much surface area (in meters^2) is cleared in one hour. The data were found by testing each method in five trials. Are the four systems equally effective? Use .05 level of significance.

System A	55	60	58	61	54
System B	47	53	54	49	52
System C	63	59	58	64	63
System D	51	56	54	59	54

10-34 In an effort to set a standard time for a certain batch assembly process, 5 workers were monitored for their unit output per hour for 9 randomly selected hours. The data gathered are shown below in units of output per hour. At the .01 level of significance, is the output per hour of the 5 workers the same?

Worker 1	24	11	19	27	15	16	22	32	17
Worker 2	29	35	37	26	45	26	29	35	38
Worker 3	30	28	29	32	22	17	23	29	11
Worker 4	16	14	5	19	21	17	11	26	9
Worker 5	21	16	19	15	16	28	23	29	17

10-35 A lumber company is concerned about how rising interest rates are affecting the new housing starts in the area. To explore this question, the company has gathered data on new housing starts during the past 3 quarters for 5 surrounding counties. This information is presented in the following table. At the .05 level of significance, is there any difference in the number of new housing starts during the three quarters?

Quarter 1	41	53	54	55	43
Quarter 2	45	51	48	43	39
Quarter 3	34	44	46	45	51

10-36 Morristown Shoe Company sets sales quotas every December for each of its 15 salespeople. Unexpected competition, production problems, and an increase in prices prevented Morristown's salespeople from meeting their quotas. The company has divided its sales force into 3 regions and compiled the table on page 463 to show the percentage of goal that each salesperson reached. At the .05 level of significance, did the 3 regions meet an equal percentage of their sales goals?

PERCENT OF SALES GOALS MET BY EACH SALESPERSON						
West Coast	85	84	79	84	88	
East Coast	83	94	96	85	87	90
Midwest	74	76	73	81		

10-37 The owner of Bressler Incorporated, a company that manufactures soft drinks, has asked one of its employees to measure exactly how much of the soft drink is being put into its 12-ounce bottles. The employee decides to take a sample of the bottles coming off the production line at three separate times during the week and measure their contents. As his measurement, he records how the contents of each bottle differ from the nominal 12 ounces. After he collects these data, one of his fellow employees mentions that some of the machinery was adjusted during the week, and that this adjustment might affect how much of the soft drink was put into each bottle. Now it is of interest to the employee to know if the difference from 12 ounces is the same for the three time periods. Give the employee an answer. Use a .05 significance level.

Sample 1	+.02	−.04	−.03	−.005	−.01	0
Sample 2	+.01	+.005	+.01	−.01	−.02	−.01
Sample 3	+.02	0	−.005	+.01	+.005	+.03

10-38 In Bigville, a fast-food chain feels it is gaining a bad reputation because it takes too long to serve the customers. Since the chain has 4 restaurants in this town, it is concerned with whether all 4 restaurants have the same average service time. One of the owners of the fast-food chain has decided to visit each of the stores and monitor the service time for 5 randomly selected customers. At his 4 noon-time visits, he records the following service times in minutes:

Restaurant 1	4	5	6.5	4.5	5
Restaurant 2	3	3.5	4.5	4	5.5
Restaurant 3	2	3.5	5	6.5	7
Restaurant 4	3	4	5.5	2.5	2.5

a) Using a 1 percent significance level, do all the restaurants have the same mean service time?
b) Based on his results, should the owner make any policy recommendations to any of the restaurant managers?

10-5 INFERENCES ABOUT A POPULATION VARIANCE

Need to make decisions about variability in a population

In Chapters 8 and 9, we learned how to form confidence intervals and test hypotheses about one or two population means or proportions. Earlier in this chapter, we used chi-square and *F* tests to make inferences about more than two means or proportions. But we are not always interested in means and proportions. In many situations, responsible decision makers have to make inferences about the variability in a population. In order to schedule the labor force at harvest time, a peach grower needs to know not only the mean time to maturity of the peaches, but also their variance around that mean. A sociologist investigating the effect of education on earning power wants to know if the incomes of college graduates are more variable than those of high school graduates. Precision instruments used in laboratory work must be quite accurate on the average; but in addition, repeated measurements should show very little variation. In this section, we shall see how to make inferences about a single population variance. The next section looks at problems involving the variances of two populations.

The Distribution of the Sample Variance

In response to a number of complaints about slow mail delivery, the Postmaster General initiates a preliminary investigation. An investigator follows nine letters from New York to Chicago, to estimate the standard deviation in time of delivery. Table 10-17 gives the data and computes $\bar{x}$, s^2, and s. As we saw in Chapter 8, we use s to estimate σ.

Determining the uncertainty attached to estimates of the population standard deviation

We can tell the Postmaster General that the *population* standard deviation, as estimated by the *sample* standard deviation, is approximately 23 hours. But he also wants to know how accurate that estimate is and what uncertainty is associated with it. In other words, he wants a confidence interval, not just a point estimate of σ. In order to find such an interval, we must know the sampling distribution of s. It is traditional to talk about s^2 rather than s, but this will cause us no trouble, since we can always go from s^2 and σ^2 to s and σ by taking square roots; and we can go in the other direction by squaring.

If the population variance is σ^2, then the statistic:

$$\chi^2 = \frac{(n-1)s^2}{\sigma^2} \qquad \textbf{[10-12]}$$

TABLE 10-17 Delivery time (in hours) for letters going between New York and Chicago

TIME x	$\bar{x}$	$x - \bar{x}$	$(x - \bar{x})^2$
50	59	−9	81
45	59	−14	196
27	59	−32	1,024
66	59	7	49
43	59	−16	256
96	59	37	1,369
45	59	−14	196
90	59	31	961
69	59	10	100
$\Sigma x = \mathbf{531}$			$\Sigma(x - \bar{x})^2 = \mathbf{4{,}232}$

$$\bar{x} = \frac{\Sigma x}{n} = \frac{531}{9} \qquad \textbf{[3-2]}$$

$$= 59 \text{ hours}$$

$$s^2 = \frac{\Sigma(x - \bar{x})^2}{n-1} = \frac{4{,}232}{8} \qquad \textbf{[4-11]}$$

$$= 529 \text{ hours squared}$$

$$s = \sqrt{s^2} = \sqrt{529} \qquad \textbf{[4-12]}$$

$$= 23 \text{ hours}$$

has a chi-square distribution with $n - 1$ degrees of freedom. This result is exact if the population is normal; but even for samples from non-normal populations, it is frequently a good approximation. We can now use the chi-square distribution to form confidence intervals and test hypotheses about σ^2.

Confidence Intervals for the Population Variance

Constructing a confidence interval for a variance

Suppose we want a 95 percent confidence interval for the variance in our mail-delivery problem. Figure 10-8 shows how to begin constructing this interval.

We locate two points on the χ^2 distribution: $\chi_U{}^2$ cuts off .025 of the area in the upper tail of the distribution, and $\chi_L{}^2$ cuts off .025 of the area in the lower tail. (For a 99 percent confidence interval, we would put .005 of the area in each tail, and similarly for other confidence levels.) The values of $\chi_L{}^2$ and $\chi_U{}^2$ can be found in Appendix Table 5. In our mail problem, with $9 - 1 = 8$ degrees of freedom, $\chi_L{}^2 = 2.180$, and $\chi_U{}^2 = 17.535$.

Now Equation 10-12 gives χ^2 in terms of s^2, n, and σ^2. To get a confidence interval for σ^2, we solve Equation 10-12 for σ^2:

$$\sigma^2 = \frac{(n-1)s^2}{\chi^2} \qquad \textbf{[10-13]}$$

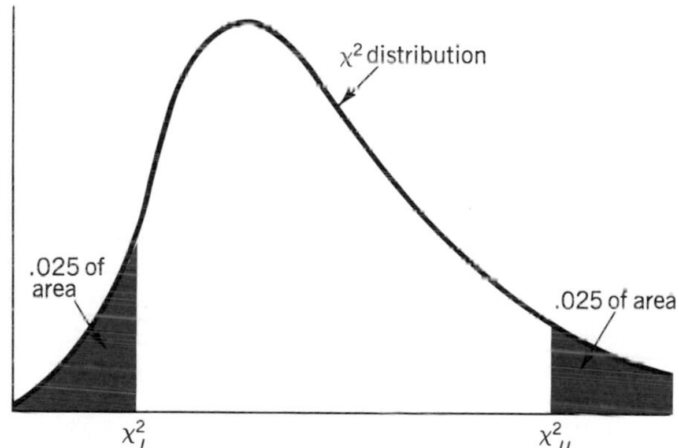

FIGURE 10-8 Constructing a confidence interval for σ^2

and then our confidence interval is given by:

Upper and lower limits for the confidence interval

$$\sigma_L{}^2 = \frac{(n-1)s^2}{\chi_U{}^2} \leftarrow \text{lower confidence limit}$$

$$\sigma_U{}^2 = \frac{(n-1)s^2}{\chi_L{}^2} \leftarrow \text{upper confidence limit} \qquad \textbf{[10-14]}$$

Notice that since χ^2 appears in the denominator in Equation 10-13, we can use $\chi_U{}^2$ to find $\sigma_L{}^2$ and $\chi_L{}^2$ to find $\sigma_U{}^2$. Continuing with the Postmaster General's problem, we see he can be 95 percent confident that the population variance lies between 241.35 and 1,941.28 hours squared:

$$\sigma_L^2 = \frac{(n-1)s^2}{\chi_U^2} = \frac{8(529)}{17.535} = 241.35$$

$$\sigma_U^2 = \frac{(n-1)s^2}{\chi_L^2} = \frac{8(529)}{2.180} = 1{,}941.28 \qquad \textbf{[10-14]}$$

So a 95 percent confidence interval for σ would be from $\sqrt{241.35}$ to $\sqrt{1{,}941.28}$ hours; that is, from 15.54 to 44.06 hours.

A Two-Tailed Test of a Variance

Testing hypotheses about a variance: two-tailed tests

A management professor has given careful thought to the design of examinations. In order for him to be reasonably certain that an exam does a good job of distinguishing the differences in achievement shown by the students, the standard deviation in scores on the examination cannot be too small. On the other hand, if the standard deviation is too large, there will tend to be a lot of very low scores, which is bad for student morale. Past experience has led the professor to believe that a standard deviation of about thirteen points on a 100-point exam indicates that the exam does a good job of balancing these two objectives.

The professor just gave an examination to his class of 31 freshmen and sophomores. The mean score was 72.7, and the sample standard deviation was 15.9. Does this exam meet his goodness criterion? We can summarize the data:

$\sigma_{H_0} = 13$ ← hypothesized value of the population standard deviation

$s = 15.9$ ← sample standard deviation

$n = 31$ ← sample size

If the professor uses a significance level of .10 in testing his hypothesis, we can symbolically state the problem:

Statement of the problem

$H_0: \sigma = 13$ ← null hypotheses: the true standard deviation is 13 points

$H_1: \sigma \neq 13$ ← alternative hypothesis: the true standard deviation is not 13 points

$\alpha = .10$ ← level of significance for testing these hypotheses

The first thing we do is to use Equation 10-12 to calculate the χ^2 statistic:

Calculating the χ^2 statistic

$$\chi^2 = \frac{(n-1)s^2}{\sigma^2} \qquad \textbf{[10-12]}$$

$$= \frac{30(15.9)^2}{(13)^2}$$

$$= 44.88$$

This statistic has a χ^2 distribution with $n - 1$ (= 30 in this case) degrees of freedom. We will accept the null hypothesis if χ^2 is neither too big nor too small. From the χ^2 distribution table (Appendix Table 5), we can see that the appropriate χ^2 values for .05 of the area to lie in each tail of the curve are 18.493 and 43.773. These two limits of the acceptance region and the observed sample statistic ($\chi^2 = 44.88$) are shown in Fig. 10-9. We see that the sample value of χ^2 is not in the acceptance region, so the professor should reject the null hypothesis; this exam does not meet his goodness criterion.

Interpreting the results

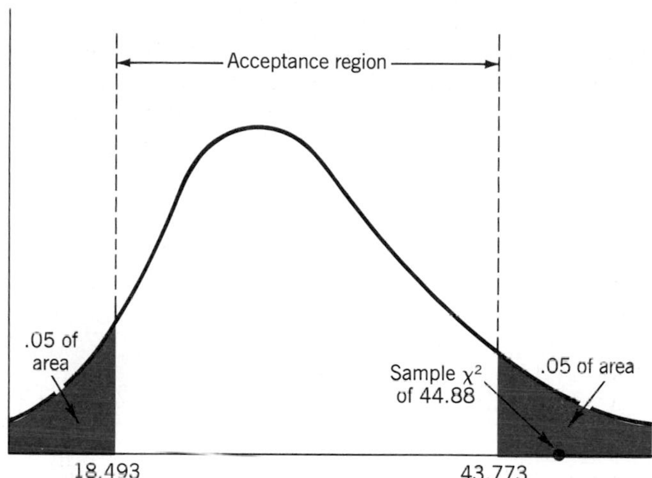

FIGURE 10-9 Two-tailed hypothesis test at the .05 level of significance, showing acceptance region and sample χ^2

A One-Tailed Test of a Variance

Testing hypotheses about a variance: one-tailed tests

Precision Analytics manufactures a wide line of precision instruments and has a fine reputation in the field for the quality of its instruments. In order to preserve that reputation, it maintains strict quality control on all of its output. It will not release an analytic balance for sale, for example, unless that balance shows a variability significantly below one microgram (at $\alpha = .01$) when weighing quantities of about 500 grams. A new balance has just been delivered to the quality control division from the production line.

The new balance is tested by using it to weigh the same 500-gram standard weight thirty different times. The sample standard deviation turns out to be 0.73 micrograms. Should this balance be sold? We summarize the data:

Statement of the problem

$\sigma_{H_0} = 1$ ← hypothesized value of the population standard deviation

$s = 0.73$ ← sample standard deviation

$n = 30$ ← sample size

and state the problem:

$H_0: \sigma = 1$ ← null hypothesis: the true standard deviation is 1 microgram

$H_1: \sigma < 1$ ← alternative hypothesis: the true standard deviation is less than 1 microgram

$\alpha = .01$ ← level of significance for testing these hypotheses

Calculating the χ^2 statistic

We begin by using Equation 10-12 to calculate the χ^2 statistic:

$$\chi^2 = \frac{(n-1)s^2}{\sigma^2} \quad [10\text{-}12]$$

$$= \frac{29(.73)^2}{(1)^2}$$

$$= 15.45$$

We will reject the null hypothesis and release the balance for sale, if this statistic is sufficiently small. From Appendix Table 5, we see that with 29 degrees of freedom (30 − 1), the value of χ^2 that leaves an area of .01 in the lower tail of the curve is 14.256. The acceptance region and the observed value of χ^2 are shown in Fig. 10-10. We see that we cannot reject the null hypothesis. The balance should be returned to the production line for adjusting.

Interpreting the results

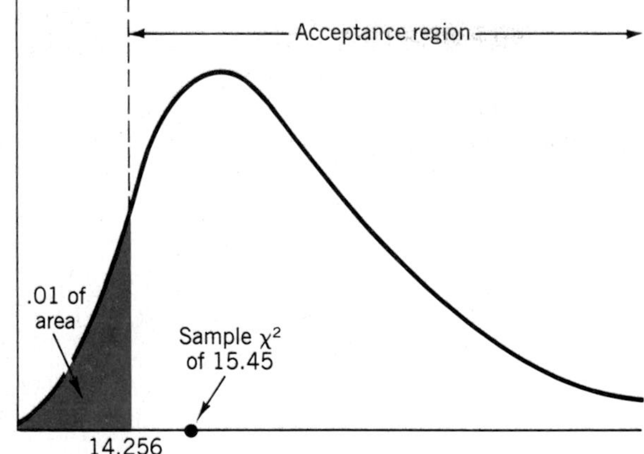

FIGURE 10-10 One-tailed hypothesis test at the .01 significance level, showing acceptance region and sample χ^2

EXERCISES

10-39 A sample of 16 observations from a normal distribution has a mean of 32.5 and a variance of 16.9. Construct a 95 percent confidence interval for the true population variance.

10-40 The standard deviation of a distribution is hypothesized to be 310. If an observed sample of 10 yields a sample standard deviation of 220, should we reject the null hypothesis that the true standard deviation is 310? Use the .05 level of significance.

10-41 Based on past data, the variance of a population is hypothesized to be 48. If a sample of 15 observations yields a variance of 55, should we reject the hypothesized value and conclude that the variance has increased? Use the .10 significance level.

10-42 Given a sample variance of 224 from a set of 12 observations, construct a 90 percent confidence interval for the population variance.

10-43 A production manager feels that the output rate of experienced employees is surely greater than that of new employees, but he does not expect the variability in output rates to differ for the two groups. In previous output studies, it has been shown that the average unit output per hour for new employees at this particular type of work is 20 units per hour with a variance of 56 units squared. For a group of 20 employees with 5 years' experience, the average output for this same type of work is 30 units per hour, with a sample variance of 28 units squared. Does the variability in output appear to differ at the two experience levels? Test the hypotheses at the .05 significance level.

10-44 An organizational psychologist, giving a popular job-motivation questionnaire to company employees, has been informed by the questionnaire developer that the population variance for scores on the questionnaire, from a large standardized group employed in the development of the test, is 45 points squared. The sample variance for the 24 company employees tested is 25 points squared. At the .05 level of significance, is there evidence to indicate that the company employees questioned are less variable than the population in their scores?

10-45 In checking its cars for adherence to emissions standards set by the government, an automaker measured emissions of 25 cars. The average number of particles of pollutants emitted was found to be within the required levels, but the sample variance was 54. Find the 95 percent confidence interval for the variance in emission particles for these cars.

10-46 A bank is considering ways to reduce the costs associated with passbook savings accounts. The bank has found that the variance in the number of days between account transactions for passbook accounts is 84 days squared. The bank wants to reduce the variance by discouraging the present use of accounts as short-term storage of cash. Therefore, after implementing a new policy that penalizes the customer with a service charge for withdrawals more than once a month, the bank decides to test for a change in the variance of days between account transactions. From a sample of 15 savings accounts, the bank finds the variability between transactions to be 28 days squared. Is the bank justified in claiming that the new policy reduces the variance of days between transactions? Test the hypotheses at the .05 level of significance.

10-47 Sam Bogart, the owner of the Play-It-Again Stereo Company, offers 1-year warranties on all the stereos his company sells. For those 30 stereos that were serviced under the warranty last year, the average cost to fix a stereo was $75 and sample standard deviation was $15. Calculate a 95 percent confidence interval for the true standard deviation of the cost of repair. Sam has decided that unless the true standard deviation is less than $20, he will buy his stereos from a different retailer. Help Sam test the appropriate hypotheses, using a significance level of .01. Should he switch retailers?

10-6 INFERENCES ABOUT TWO POPULATION VARIANCES

Comparing the variances of two populations

In Chapter 9, we saw several situations in which we wanted to compare the means of two different populations. Recall that we did this by looking at the *difference* of the means of two samples drawn from those populations. Here, we want to compare the variances of two populations. However, rather than looking at the *difference* of the two sample variances, it turns out to be more convenient if we look at their *ratio*. The next two examples show how this is done.

A One-Tailed Test of Two Variances

A prominent sociologist at a large midwestern university believes that incomes earned by college graduates show much greater variability than the earnings of those who did not attend college. In order to test out this theory, she dispatches two research assistants to Chicago to look at the earnings of these two populations. The first assistant takes a random sample of 21 college graduates and finds that their earnings have a sample standard deviation of $s_1 = \$17,000$. The second assistant samples 25 nongraduates and obtains a standard deviation in earnings of $s_2 = \$7,500$. The data of our problem can be summarized as follows:

Statement of the problem

$s_1 = 17,000 \leftarrow$ standard deviation of first sample

$n_1 = 21 \leftarrow$ size of first sample

$s_2 = 7,500 \leftarrow$ standard deviation of second sample

$n_2 = 25 \leftarrow$ size of second sample

Why a one-tailed test is appropriate

Since the sociologist theorizes that the earnings of college graduates are *more* variable than those of people not attending college, a one-tailed test is appropriate. She wishes to verify her theory at the .01 level of significance. We can formally state her problem:

H_0: $\sigma_1^2 = \sigma_2^2$ (or $\sigma_1^2/\sigma_2^2 = 1$) $\leftarrow$ null hypothesis: the two variances are the same

H_1: $\sigma_1^2 > \sigma_2^2$ (or $\sigma_1^2/\sigma_2^2 > 1$) $\leftarrow$ alternative hypothesis: earnings of college graduates have more variance

$\alpha = .01 \leftarrow$ level of significance for testing these hypotheses

We know that s_1^2 can be used to estimate σ_1^2, and s_2^2 can be used to estimate σ_2^2. If the alternative hypothesis is true, we would expect that s_1^2 will be greater than s_2^2 (or, equivalently, that s_1^2/s_2^2 will be greater than 1). But how much greater must s_1^2 be in order for us to be able to reject the null hypothesis? To answer this question, we must know the distribution of s_1^2/s_2^2. If we assume that the two populations are reasonably well described by normal distributions, then the ratio:

Description of the *F* statistic

$$F = s_1^2/s_2^2 \qquad [10\text{-}15]$$

has an F distribution with $n_1 - 1$ degrees of freedom in the numerator and $n_2 - 1$ degrees of freedom in the denominator.

In the earnings problem, we calculate the sample F statistic:

$$F = s_1^2/s_2^2 \quad [10\text{-}15]$$
$$= \frac{(17{,}000)^2}{(7{,}500)^2}$$
$$= \frac{289{,}000{,}000}{56{,}250{,}000}$$
$$= 5.14$$

Interpreting the results

For 20 degrees of freedom (21 − 1) in the numerator and 24 degrees of freedom (25 − 1) in the denominator, Appendix Table 6 tells us that the critical value that separates the acceptance and rejection regions is 2.74. Figure 10-11 shows the acceptance region and the observed F statistic of 5.14. Our sociologist rejects the null hypothesis, and the sample data support her theory.

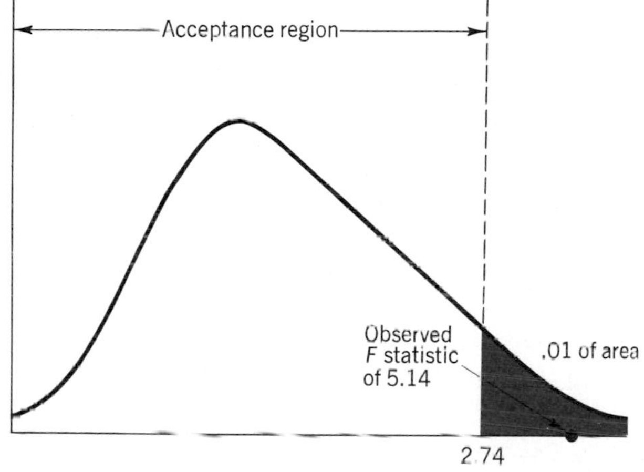

FIGURE 10-11 One-tailed hypothesis test at the .01 level of significance, showing the acceptance region and the sample F statistic

Handling lower-tailed tests in Table 6

A word of caution about the use of Appendix Table 6 is necessary at this point. You will notice that the table gives values of the F statistic that are appropriate for only *upper-tailed* tests. Contrast this with Appendix Table 5, which gives values appropriate for both upper- and lower-tailed tests. How can we handle alternative hypotheses of the form $\sigma_1^2 < \sigma_2^2$ (or $\sigma_1^2/\sigma_2^2 < 1$)? This is easily done if we notice that $\sigma_1^2/\sigma_2^2 < 1$ is equivalent to $\sigma_2^2/\sigma_1^2 > 1$. Thus, all we need to do is calculate the ratio s_2^2/s_1^2, which also has an F distribution (but with $n_2 - 1$ numerator degrees of freedom and $n_1 - 1$ denominator degrees of freedom), and then we can use Appendix Table 6. There is another way to say the same thing: **whenever you are doing a one-tailed test of two variances, number the populations so that the alternative hypothesis has the form:**

$$H_1: \sigma_1^2 > \sigma_2^2 \text{ (or } \sigma_1^2/\sigma_2^2 > 1)$$

and then proceed as we did in the earnings example.

A Two-Tailed Test of Two Variances

Finding the critical value in a two-tailed test

The procedure for a two-tailed test of two variances is similar to that for a one-tailed test. The only problem arises in finding the critical value in the lower tail. This is related to the problem about lower-tailed tests discussed in the last paragraph, and we will resolve it in a similar way.

One criterion in evaluating oral anesthetics for use in general dentistry is the variability in the length of time between injection and complete loss of sensation in the patient. (This is called the effect delay time.) A large pharmaceutical firm has just developed two new oral anesthetics, which it will market under the names Oralcaine and Novasthetic. From similarities in the chemical structure of the two compounds, it has been predicted that they should show the same variance in effect delay time. Sample data from tests of the two compounds (which controlled other variables such as age and weight) are given in Table 10-18.

TABLE 10-18 Effect delay times for two anesthetics

ANESTHETIC	SAMPLE SIZE n	SAMPLE VARIANCE (SECONDS SQUARED) s^2
Oralcaine	31	1,296
Novasthetic	41	784

The company wants to test at a 2 percent significance level whether the two compounds have the same variance in effect delay time. Symbolically, the hypotheses are:

Statement of the problem

H_0: $\sigma_1^2 = \sigma_2^2$ (or $\sigma_1^2/\sigma_2^2 = 1$) ← null hypothesis: the two variances are the same

H_1: $\sigma_1^2 \neq \sigma_2^2$ (or $\sigma_1^2/\sigma_2^2 \neq 1$) ← alternative hypothesis: the two variances are different

$\alpha = .02$ ← significance level of the test

Calculating the F statistic

To test these hypotheses, we again use Equation 10-15:

$$F = s_1^2/s_2^2 \qquad \textbf{[10-15]}$$
$$= 1{,}296/784$$
$$= 1.65$$

This statistic comes from an F distribution with $n_1 - 1$ degrees of freedom in the numerator (30, in this case) and $n_2 - 1$ degrees of freedom in the denominator (40, in this case). Let us use the notation:

Some useful notation for the test

$$F(n, d, \alpha)$$

to denote that value of F with n numerator degrees of freedom, d denominator degrees of freedom, and an area of α in the upper tail. In our problem, the

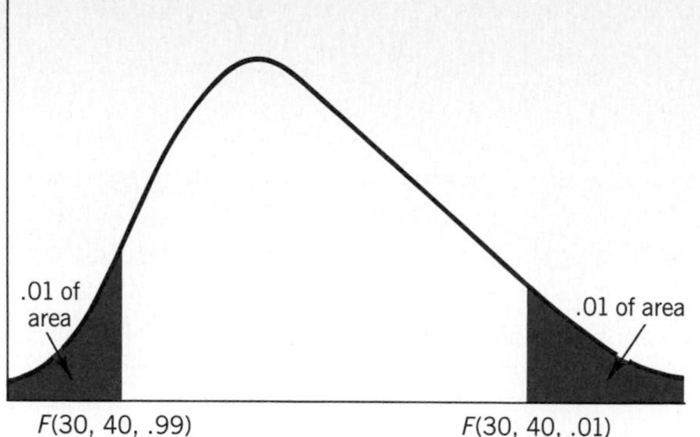

FIGURE 10-12 Two-tailed test of hypotheses at the .02 significance level

acceptance region extends from $F(30, 40, .99)$ to $F(30, 40, .01)$, as illustrated in Fig. 10-12.

We can get the value of $F(30, 40, .01)$ directly from Appendix Table 6; it is 2.20. However, the value of $F(30, 40, .99)$ is not in the table. Now $F(30, 40, .99)$ will correspond to a *small* value of s_1^2/s_2^2, but to a *large* value of s_2^2/s_1^2, which is just the reciprocal of s_1^2/s_2^2. Given the discussion on page 471 about lower-tailed tests, we might suspect that:

$$F(n, d, \alpha) = \frac{1}{F(d, n, 1-\alpha)} \qquad \textbf{[10-16]}$$

and this turns out to be true. We can use this equation to find $F(30, 40, .99)$:

$$F(30, 40, .99) = \frac{1}{F(40, 30, .01)} \qquad \textbf{[10-16]}$$
$$= \frac{1}{2.30}$$
$$= 0.43$$

Interpreting the results

In Fig. 10-13, we have illustrated the acceptance region for this hypothesis test and the observed value of F. We see there that the null hypothesis is

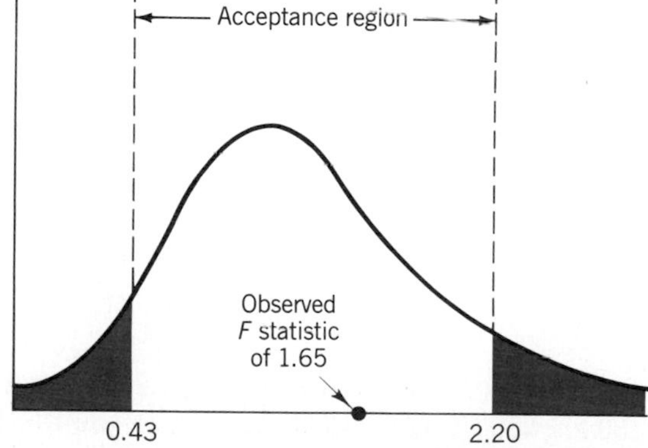

FIGURE 10-13 Two-tailed hypothesis test at the .02 level of significance, showing acceptance region and the sample F statistic

accepted, so we conclude that the observed difference in the sample variances of effect delay times for the two anesthetics is not statistically significant.

EXERCISES

10-48 The table below shows the ratings for ABC and CBS programming during one Sunday night this year. Test the hypothesis that their variances in ratings are equal. Use the .05 significance level.

CBS	38	27	34	25	28	
ABC	34	37	35	40	30	34

Can we conclude that their variances are equal, or must we accept the alternative that CBS has a larger variance?

10-49 From a sample of 16 observations, the estimate of the standard deviation of a population was found to be 8.2. From another sample of 12 observations, the estimate was found to be 4.8. Can we accept the hypothesis that the two samples come from populations with equal variances, or must we conclude that the variance of the second sample is smaller? Use the .05 level of significance.

10-50 Graphico Corporation knows that the unit manufacturing costs for two lithographic film processors are normally distributed. A sample of 15 Model 1000 units has a variance in manufacturing costs of 146 dollars squared, while a sample of 18 Model 2000 units has a variance of 124 dollars squared. Can we accept the hypothesis that the population variances of the two models are equal, or does the evidence appear to indicate that the Model 1000's variance is larger? Use the .05 level of significance.

10-51 For two populations thought to have the same variance, the following information was found. A sample of 12 from population 1 exhibited a sample variance of 1.96, while a sample of 10 from population 2 had a variance of 3.64.

a) Calculate the F ratio for the test of equality of variances.
b) Find the critical F value for the upper tail, using the .05 significance level.
c) Find the corresponding F value for the lower tail.
d) State the conclusion of your test.

10-52 In our study of comparisons between the means of 2 groups, it was noted that the most common form of the two-group t test for the difference between 2 means assumes that the population variances for the 2 groups are the same. One experimenter, using a control condition and an experimental condition in his study of drug reactions, wished to verify that this assumption held; i.e., that the treatment administered affected only the mean, not the variance of the variable under study. From his data, he calculated the variance of the experimental group to be 27.8 and that of the control group to be 18.6. The experimental group had 35 subjects, and the control group had 32. Can he proceed to use the t test, which assumes equal variances for the two groups?

10-53 Ben Morris, a dedicated football fan, is taking a statistics course this semester and has become enthralled by using his knowledge to compare his team with its opponents. This week, he wants to see whether there is a difference between the variance in weight of the home team and that of the visiting team. Weights of the 11 members of the starting offensive lineup for both teams are shown in the table. Calculate the sample variances and test the hypothesis that the variance in weight is the same for the two teams. Use the .10 level of significance.

Home team	191	189	183	201	193	198	244	218	208	225	238
Visitors	172	196	180	185	188	223	215	244	245	252	212

10-54 A manager of quality control suspects that the variability of breaking points for two different grades of glass may be different. Using a standard instrument for measuring glass strength, he tests 25 pieces each of high-grade and low-grade glass. He finds that the sample variance of breaking points for low-grade glass is 12.4; for high-grade, 5.2. Does there seem to be a difference in the variability of breaking points for the two grades of glass? Use the .10 level of significance to test the hypothesis.

10-55 Two brand managers were in disagreement over the issue of whether urban housewives had greater variability in grocery shopping patterns than did rural housewives. To test their conflicting ideas, they took random samples of 65 women from urban areas and 65 women from rural areas. They found that the variance in days squared between shopping visits for urban women was 9.6, while the sample variance for the rural women was 4.2. Is the difference between the variances in days between shopping visits significant at the .05 level?

10-56 A writer for a consumer magazine is doing a comparison study between sports cars and economy cars. He has found 21 owners of each type of car who are willing to participate in his study. After asking each driver to give the average mileage per tank over a month's time, the writer has discovered the sample standard deviation for the sports-car drivers is 9.8 miles and the sample standard deviation for the economy-car drivers is 7.5. At a .05 significance level, do the two groups have the same variability, or does the sports-car group have more variation?

10-7 TERMS INTRODUCED IN CHAPTER 10

ANALYSIS OF VARIANCE (ANOVA) A statistical technique used to test the equality of 3 or more sample means and thus make inferences as to whether the samples come from populations having the same mean.

BETWEEN-COLUMN VARIANCE An estimate of the population variance derived from the variance among the sample means.

CHI-SQUARE DISTRIBUTION A family of probability distributions, differentiated by their degrees of freedom, used to test a number of different hypotheses about variances, proportions, and distributional goodness of fit.

CONTINGENCY TABLE A table having *R* rows and *C* columns. Each row corresponds to a level of one variable; each column, to a level of another variable. Entries in the body of the tables are the frequencies with which each variable combination occurred.

EXPECTED FREQUENCIES The frequencies we would expect to see in a contingency table or frequency distribution if the null hypothesis is true.

***F* DISTRIBUTION** A family of distributions differentiated by two parameters (df-numerator, df-denominator), used primarily to test hypotheses regarding variances.

***F* RATIO** A ratio used in the analysis of variance, among other tests, to compare the magnitude of two estimates of the population variance to determine if the two estimates are approximately equal; in ANOVA, the ratio of between-column variance to within-column variance is used.

GOODNESS-OF-FIT TEST A statistical test for determining whether there is a significant difference between an observed frequency distribution and a theoretical probability distribution hypothesized to describe the observed distribution.

GRAND MEAN The mean for the entire group of subjects from all the samples in the experiment.

TEST OF INDEPENDENCE A statistical test of proportions or frequencies, to determine if membership in categories of one variable is different as a function of membership in the categories of a second variable.

WITHIN-COLUMN VARIANCE An estimate of the population variance based on the variances within the k samples, using a weighted average of the k sample variances.

10-8 EQUATIONS INTRODUCED IN CHAPTER 10

[10-1]
$$\chi^2 = \sum \frac{(f_o - f_e)^2}{f_e}$$
p. 432

This formula says that the *chi-square statistic* (χ^2) is equal to the sum (Σ) we will get if we:

1. Subtract the expected frequencies, f_e, from the observed frequencies, f_o, for each category of our contingency table.
2. Square each of the differences.
3. Divide each squared difference by f_e.
4. Sum all the results of step 3.

[10-2]
$$\text{Number of degrees of freedom} = (\text{Number of rows} - 1)(\text{Number of columns} - 1)$$
p. 434

To calculate number of *degrees of freedom in a chi-square test of independence,* multiply the number of rows (less 1) times the number of columns (less 1).

[10-3]
$$f_e = \frac{RT \times CT}{n}$$
p. 437

With this formula, we can calculate the expected frequency for any cell within a contingency table. RT is the row total for the row containing the cell, CT is the column total for the column containing the cell, and n is the total number of observations.

[10-4]
$$s_{\bar{x}}^2 = \frac{\Sigma(\bar{x} - \bar{\bar{x}})^2}{k - 1}$$
p. 452

To calculate the *variance among the sample means,* use this formula.

[10-5]
$$\sigma^2 = \sigma_{\bar{x}}^2 \times n$$
p. 452

The *population variance* is equal to the product of the square of the standard error of the mean and the sample size.

[10-6]
$$\hat{\sigma}^2 = \frac{\Sigma n_j(\bar{x}_j - \bar{\bar{x}})^2}{k - 1}$$ *p. 452*

One estimate of the population variance (the between-column variance) can be obtained by using this equation. We obtain this equation by first substituting $s_{\bar{x}}^2$ for $\sigma_{\bar{x}}^2$ in Equation 10-5, and then by weighting each $(\bar{x}_j - \bar{\bar{x}})^2$ by its own appropriate sample size (n_j).

[10-7]
$$\hat{\sigma}^2 = \Sigma\left(\frac{n_j - 1}{n_T - k}\right)s_j^2$$ *p. 454*

A second estimate of the population variance (the within-column variance) can be obtained from this equation. This equation uses a weighted average of all the sample variances. In this formulation, $n_T = \Sigma n_j$, the total sample size.

[10-8]
$$F = \frac{\text{First estimate of the population variance based on the variance among the sample means}}{\text{Second estimate of the population variance based on the variances within the samples}}$$ *p. 455*

This ratio is the way we can compare the two estimates of the population variance, which we calculated in Equations 10-6 and 10 7. In a hypothesis test based on an F distribution, we are more likely to accept the null hypothesis if this *F ratio* or *F statistic* is near to the value of one. As the F ratio increases, the more likely it is that we will reject the null hypothesis.

[10-9]
$$F = \frac{\text{Between-column variance}}{\text{Within-column variance}}$$ *p. 455*

This restates Equation 10-8, using statistical shorthand for the numerator and the denominator of the F ratio.

[10-10]
$$\frac{\text{Number of degrees of freedom}}{\text{in numerator of the } F \text{ ratio}} = (\text{Number of samples} - 1)$$ *p. 457*

To do an analysis of variance, we calculate the number of *degrees of freedom in the between-column variance* (the numerator of the F ratio) by subtracting one from the number of samples collected.

[10-11]
$$\text{Number of degrees of freedom in denominator of the } F \text{ ratio} = \Sigma(n_j - 1) = n_T - k$$ *p. 457*

We use this equation to calculate the number of degrees of freedom in the denominator of the F ratio. This turns out to be the total sample size, n_T, minus the number of samples, k.

[10-12] $$\chi^2 = \frac{(n-1)s^2}{\sigma^2}$$ *p. 464*

With a population variance of σ^2, the χ^2 statistic given by this equation has a chi-square distribution with $n - 1$ degrees of freedom. This result is exact if the population is normal, but even in samples from non-normal populations, frequently it is still a good approximation.

[10-13] $$\sigma^2 = \frac{(n-1)s^2}{\chi^2}$$ *p. 465*

To get a confidence interval for σ^2, we solve Equation 10-12 for σ^2.

[10-14] $$\sigma_L^2 = \frac{(n-1)s^2}{\chi_U^2} \leftarrow \text{lower confidence limit}$$
$$\sigma_U^2 = \frac{(n-1)s^2}{\chi_L^2} \leftarrow \text{upper confidence limit}$$ *p. 465*

These formulas give the lower and upper confidence limit for a confidence interval for σ^2. (Notice that since χ^2 appears in the denominator, we use χ_U^2 to find σ_L^2 and χ_L^2 to find σ_U^2.)

[10-15] $$F = \frac{s_1^2}{s_2^2}$$ *p. 470*

This ratio has an F distribution with $n_1 - 1$ degrees of freedom in the numerator and $n_2 - 1$ degrees of freedom in the denominator. (This assumes that the two populations are reasonably well described by normal distributions.) It is used to test hypotheses about two population variances.

[10-16] $$F(n, d, \alpha) = \frac{1}{F(d, n, 1-\alpha)}$$ *p. 473*

Appendix Table 6 gives values of F for upper-tailed tests only, but this equation enables us to find appropriate values of F for lower-tailed and two-tailed tests.

10-9 CHAPTER REVIEW EXERCISES

10-57 A television manufacturer is investigating the amount of variation in retail prices of its 19-inch portable black-and-white set. In a sample of 20 retailers, the average price was \$95 with a standard deviation of \$8. Find a 90 percent confidence interval for the variance in price for this set.

10-58 For the contingency table below, calculate the observed and expected frequencies and the chi-square statistic. Test the appropriate hypotheses at the .10 significance level.

	ATTITUDE TOWARD SOCIAL LEGISLATION		
Occupation	Favor	Neutral	Oppose
Blue-collar	18	12	36
White-collar	11	15	42
Professional	24	8	32

10-59 A Lexington bank is considering the acquisition of a fully automated, tellerless branch-banking system. To test whether the public's acceptance of this innovation would be affected by income level, the bank has installed experimental units in 3 shopping centers, each catering to one of 3 general economic groups—lower, middle, or upper class. The results of this survey were the following:

	FREQUENCY OF RESPONSES			
	Low	Middle	Upper	Total
Approve: Observed	30	45	23	98
Expected	31	41	26	
Disapprove: Observed	30	35	27	92
Expected	29	39	24	

a) What are the null and alternative hypotheses for this problem?
b) Calculate the value of χ^2.
c) Using a .05 level of significance, should the null hypothesis be rejected?

10-60 What probability distribution is used in each of these types of statistical tests?
a) Comparing 2 population proportions
b) Value of a single population variance
c) Comparing 3 or more population means
d) Comparing 2 population means from small, dependent samples

10-61 What probability distribution is used in each of these types of statistical tests?
a) Comparing the means of 2 small samples from populations with unknown variances
b) Comparing 2 population variances
c) Value of a single population mean based on large samples
d) Comparing 3 or more population proportions

10-62 A production manager experiments with 3 different processes making the same product, to see if different processes produce different unit manufacturing costs. The table below shows 6 samples of unit manufacturing costs for each process.

	MANUFACTURING COST PER UNIT (IN DOLLARS)					
Process 1	6.50	7.20	6.80	6.90	6.40	7.30
Process 2	4.90	5.30	4.80	4.60	5.90	5.00
Process 3	6.10	5.90	5.80	6.10	6.00	5.70

At the .01 level of significance, do the 3 production processes have the same unit manufacturing cost?

10-63 An outdoor advertising company must know whether significantly different traffic volumes pass 3 billboard locations in Newark, since the company charges different rates for different traffic volumes. The company measures the volume of traffic at the 3 locations during randomly selected 5-minute intervals. The table below shows the data gathered. At the .05 level of significance, is the volume of traffic passing the 3 billboards the same?

	VOLUME OF TRAFFIC								
Billboard 1	30	45	26	44	18	38	42	29	
Billboard 2	24	33	31	16	31	13	12	25	27
Billboard 3	35	47	43	46	27	31	21		

10-64 Janet Peterson, media buyer for the Johnston Advertising Agency, is deciding which of 3 television spots to use. She randomly selects 6 weeks out of the year and looks at the percentage of each program's audience that falls within her defined target market. From the data shown below, can she conclude that the 3 spots are equal in the percentage of their audiences falling within the target market? Use an F test at the .05 level of significance.

	PERCENT					
Program 1	85	71	78	89	74	95
Program 2	65	77	84	75	71	96
Program 3	72	86	77	76	84	85

10-65 For the following contingency table:

a) Construct a table of observed and expected frequencies.
b) Calculate the chi-square statistic.
c) State the null and alternative hypotheses.
d) Using a .05 level of significance, should the null hypothesis be rejected?

	INCOME LEVEL		
CHURCH ATTENDANCE	Low	Middle	High
Never	28	52	16
Occasional	25	66	14
Regular	18	73	8

10-66 For the following contingency table:

a) Construct a table of observed and expected frequencies.
b) Calculate the chi-square statistic.
c) State the null and alternative hypotheses.
d) Using a .01 level of significance, should the null hypothesis be rejected?

	AGE GROUP			
TYPE OF CAR DRIVEN	16–21	22–30	31–45	46+
Sports car	10	15	12	8
Compact	5	7	6	8
Midsize	12	14	20	25
Full size	8	12	21	25

10-67 As part of a federal air-traffic study at a local airport, a record was made of the number of transient aircraft arrivals during 250 half-hour time intervals. The table below presents the observed number of periods in which there were 0, 1, 2, 3, or 4 or more arrivals, as well as the expected number of such periods if arrivals per half hour have a Poisson distribution with $\lambda = 2$. At the .05 level of significance, does this Poisson distribution describe the observed arrivals?

Number of observed arrivals (per half hour)	0	1	2	3	4 or more
Number of periods observed	47	56	71	44	32
Number of periods expected (Poisson, $\lambda = 2$)	34	68	68	45	36

10-68 There has been some sociological evidence that women as a group are more variable than men in their attitudes and beliefs. A large private research organization has conducted a survey of men's attitudes on a certain issue and found the standard deviation on this attitude scale to be 15 points. A sociologist gave the same scale to a group of 30 women and found that the sample variance was 360 points. At the .05 significance level, is there reason to believe that women do indeed show greater variability on this attitude scale?

10-69 A social psychologist has tested 150 subjects to construct an attitude scale measuring feelings toward the women's movement. She presents a number of statements varying in their favorability toward the movement, and the subjects respond either "agree" or "disagree." The final attitude score or measure for each subject is the number of statements agreed with. She thinks that attitudes reflected by her scale should follow a normal distribution. Using the sample mean and sample standard deviation as parameters for the normal distribution, the psychologist constructed the following table. Do the data in this table confirm the conclusion, at the .025 level of significance, that attitudes as measured by this scale follow a normal distribution?

Number of items agreed with	10 or fewer	11–12	13–14	15–16	17–18	19+
Number of subjects in each group	8	27	53	48	26	4
Number of subjects in normal distribution	14	26	41	36	22	11

10-70 Psychologists have often wondered about the effects of stress and anxiety on test performance. An aptitude test was given to two randomly chosen groups of 18 college students, one group in a nonstressful situation and the other in a stressful situation. The experimenter expects the stress treatment to increase the variance of scores on the test, because he feels some students perform better under stress while others experience adverse reactions to stress. The variances computed for the two groups are $s_1^2 = 22.8$ for the nonstress group and $s_2^2 = 78.5$ for the stress group. Was his hypothesis confirmed? Use the .05 level of significance to test the hypothesis.

10-71 A sales manager made a study of the possible relationship between the salespersons' experience before working for the company and their success with the company. Sales representatives were classified by number of years' experience in sales before joining the company and their performance during the first year with the company. The results of the study were:

	PRIOR EXPERIENCE (YEARS)				
PERFORMANCE	Over 5	2–5	Under 2	None	Total
Poor	24	42	38	29	**133**
Satisfactory	70	41	45	47	**203**
Exceptional	36	27	27	29	**119**
Total	**130**	**110**	**110**	**105**	**455**

At the .025 level of significance, is sales experience a significant factor in the performance of salespersons during the first year?

10-72 In the development of new drugs for the treatment of anxiety, it is important to check the drugs' effects on various motor functions, one of which is driving. The Confab Pharmaceutical Company is testing 4 different tranquilizing drugs for their effects on driving skill. Subjects take a simulated driving test, and their scores reflect their errors. The more severe errors lead to higher scores. The results of these tests produced the following table:

Drug 1	230	258	239	241	
Drug 2	285	276	263	274	
Drug 3	215	232	204	247	226
Drug 4	241	253	237	246	210

At a .05 level of significance, do the 4 drugs affect driving skill differently?

10-73 In test theory, which is concerned with the construction of reliable and valid measuring instruments for a variety of uses, there is a concept known as parallel tests. Parallel tests measure the same attribute or ability, so that individuals should score about the same on both of two parallel tests. One of the characteristics of parallel tests is that they have the same variance in their scores. A professor of accounting teaches 2 sections of the course, which meet on consecutive days. He has constructed 2 tests that he believes are parallel, to be sure that nobody on the second day will know any of the questions on the test, even though the 2 tests cover the same material. After giving the tests, he computes the basic statistics, including the two variances. For the first test, given to a class of 32, $s^2 = 396$; and for the second test, given to 30 students, $s^2 = 344$. Can he feel secure in the assumption that the variances are equal, based on these groups representing random samples from the same population? Use the .10 level of significance to test the hypothesis.

10-74 Andrea Johnson, a social psychologist studying attitude change, is searching for the most effective type of persuasion in modifying attitudes toward a company policy. She measures subjects' attitudes before and after a persuasive manipulation involving either a film, a lecture, or role-playing activity. The data used are composite measures of change in attitude toward the target group.

Film	46	48	52	43	47	51
Lecture	38	43	39	45	36	43
Role-playing	45	44	47	46	46	39

At the .05 level of significance, can the researcher conclude that the 3 methods of inducing attitude change are equally effective?

10-10 CHAPTER CONCEPTS TEST

Answers are in the back of the book.

T F 1. Analysis of variance may be used to test whether the means of more than two populations can be considered equal.

T F 2. Analysis of variance is based upon a comparison of two estimates of the variance of the overall population that contains all samples.

T F 3. When comparing the variances of two populations, it is convenient to look at the difference in the sample variances, just as we looked at the difference in sample means to make inferences about population means.

T F 4. When the chi-square distribution is used as a test of independence, the number of degrees of freedom is related to both the number of rows and the number of columns in the contingency table.

T F 5. Chi-square may be used as a test to decide whether a particular distribution closely approximates a sample from some population. We refer to such tests as goodness-of-fit tests.

T F 6. If samples are taken from two populations that are both nearly normal, then the ratio of all possible sets of the two sample variances is also normally distributed.

T F 7. When using a chi-square test, we must ensure an adequate sample size, so that we can avoid any tendency for the value of the chi-square statistic to be overestimated.

T F 8. When testing hypotheses about a population's variance, we may form confidence intervals by using the chi-square distribution.

T F 9. The specific shape of an F distribution depends on the number of degrees of freedom in both the numerator and denominator of the F ratio.

T F 10. One convenient aspect of hypothesis testing using the *F* statistic is that all such tests are upper-tailed tests.

T F 11. Chi-square tests enable us to test whether more than two population proportions can be considered equal.

T F 12. A "3 × 5 contingency table" has three columns and five rows.

T F 13. The total area under the curve of a chi-square distribution, like that of other distributions, is 1.

T F 14. The expected frequency for any cell in a contingency table can be immediately calculated, once we know only the row and column totals for that cell.

T F 15. If the chi-square value for an observation is zero, we know that there will never be any difference between observed and expected frequencies.

T F 16. Sample sizes in analysis of variance need not be equal.

T F 17. The smaller the value of the *F* statistic, the more we tend to believe there is a difference among the various samples.

18. Suppose you have observed proportions for three different geographic regions. You wish to test whether the regions have significantly different proportions. Assuming p_1, p_2, p_3 are the true proportions, which of the following would be your null hypothesis?
    a) $p_1 \neq p_2 \neq p_3$ c) p_1, p_2, p_3 are not all equal
    b) $p_1 = p_2 = p_3$ d) None of these

19. A chi-square value can never be negative because:
    a) Differences between expected and observed frequencies are squared.
    b) A negative value would mean that the observed frequencies were negative.
    c) The absolute value of the differences is computed.
    d) None of these.
    e) a and b but not c.

20. Suppose that there are 8 possible classes under consideration for a goodness-of-fit test. How many degrees of freedom should be used?
    a) 8 c) 6
    b) 7 d) Cannot be determined from the information given

21. Which of the followng is a step in performing analysis of variance?
    a) Determine an estimate of population variance from within the samples.
    b) Determine an estimate of population variance among the sample means.
    c) Determine the difference between expected and observed frequency for each class.
    d) All of these.
    e) a and b but not c.

22. Suppose you calculated the following variances for several different groups of samples, and all the groups had the same degrees of freedom. For which ratio would you be most likely to accept the null hypothesis of equal means, at a given significance level?
    a) Between-column variance = 8, within-column variance = 3
    b) Between-column variance = 6, within-column variance = 3
    c) Between-column variance = 4, within-column variance = 3
    d) Between-column variance = 30, within-column variance = 20

23. Suppose σ^2 for a certain population is hypothesized to be 25. You take a sample of size 16 and find s^2 to be 15. To perform a two-tailed test of variance, you would:
    a) Compare $\chi^2 = 9$ with values from a chi-square distribution with 16 degrees of freedom.
    b) Compare $\chi^2 = 9$ with values from a chi-square distribution with 15 degrees of freedom.
    c) Compare $\chi^2 = 25$ with values from a chi-square distribution with 15 degrees of freedom.
    d) Compare $\chi^2 = 25$ with values from a chi-square distribution with 16 degrees of freedom.

24. A two-tailed test of two variances is to be performed for samples 1 and 2 with $n_1 = 15$ and $n_2 = 12$. If $\alpha = .10$, which of the following represents the upper value to which s_1^2/s_2^2 should be compared?

a) $\dfrac{1}{F(14, 11, .05)}$ c) $F(11, 14, .05)$ e) None of these

b) $\dfrac{1}{F(14, 11, .95)}$ d) $F(14, 11, .05)$

25. Assume that a chi-square test is to be performed on a contingency table with 4 rows and 4 columns. How many degrees of freedom should be used?
a) 16   b) 8   c) 9   d) 6

26. When performing a chi-square hypothesis test, what happens when expected frequencies in several cells are too small?
a) The value of χ^2 will be overestimated.
b) The null hypothesis will be more likely to be rejected than it should be.
c) The degrees of freedom are greatly reduced.
d) None of these.
e) a and b but not c.

27. Suppose you are comparing 5 groups exposed to different methods of treatment and have taken a sample of size 10 from each group. You have calculated $\bar{x}$ for each sample. How could you now calculate the grand mean?
a) Multiply each sample mean by ⅕ and add these values. Then divide this sum by 50.
b) Add the 5 sample means and divide by 50.
c) Add the 5 sample means and multiply by ⅕.
d) Add the 5 sample means.
e) None of these.

28. If we want to test whether the proportions of more than 2 populations are equal, we use:
a) Analysis of variance   c) The variance   e) None of these
b) Estimation   d) Interval estimates

29. Which of these distributions has a pair of degrees of freedom:
a) Poisson   c) Chi-square   e) All of these
b) Normal   d) Binomial   f) None of these

30. The mean for the entire group of subjects from all the samples in an experiment is called the ____________ mean.

31. A statistical technique used to test the equality of three or more population means is called ____________.

32. A test of ____________ is used to determine if membership in categories of one variable is different as a function of membership in the categories of a second variable.

33. A family of distributions differentiated by two parameters and used primarily to test hypotheses regarding variances is called the ____________ distribution.

34. The ____________ test determines whether there is a significant difference between the observed and hypothesized distributions for a sample.

35. Analysis of variance compares the ____________ with the ____________ to get the ____________ statistic.

10-11 CONCEPTUAL CASE (Northern White Metals Company)

Very soon after the agreement was reached to test the new automatic banding machine, Dick was visited by Chip Yamaguchi, another packing-equipment sales representative. His company, too, was introducing a new automatic banding machine. This machine, however, was mounted on heavy steel casters, so that, despite its rather large size, it was actually portable. This feature intrigued Dick, for movable equipment could give the shipping department greater flexibility. Still, he thought as Mr. Yamaguchi continued extolling the wonders of this new machine, what was really needed was equipment that would speed up routine packing operations. Dick explained this to the sales rep, and mentioned the upcoming trial that had been arranged with the Bondurant Band and Strap Company's new banding machine.

Mr. Yamaguchi eagerly assured Dick that his banding machine was every bit as efficient as his competitor's, and that he would welcome any comparison.

"Would a three-way test be possible?" he asked.

"I don't see why not," Dick replied after considering the matter for a moment. "Talk to Jan Hazel, my shipping supervisor, about the details."

They shook hands and the sales rep was barely out of the office before Dick was calling technical services at corporate headquarters.

Sarah Porter answered and, after exchanging pleasantries, replied that yes, she was familiar with the pending banding-machine trial in NWMC's shipping department. Dick told her of the addition of another machine to the trial and anxiously asked if this would pose any analytical difficulties.

"Not at all, Dick," Sarah responded, cheerfully amused at his concern. "You deliver the information, as Jody suggested, and we'll handle the rest."

There are now three alternative processes that might be used in the packing area of the shipping department, the manual banding method and two new automatic banding machines. Since Dick is still interested in determining if different methods will speed up packing operations, should the new test situation have data requirements different from the two-method test? How might Sarah and Jody proceed to analyze the data to determine which method offers the fastest banding time?

10-12 COMPUTER DATA BASE EXERCISE

Eric, the comptroller, advanced threateningly on Laurel and Frank as they sat sipping coffee in the sun, chattering about their proposed ski trip to Vail.

"Boy, did you guys mess me up with those funny cash-flow estimates. [See Chapter 6.] Poisson distribution, my eye. During the last two months, we've had to delay checks twice instead of less than once."

"I thought normal things were normally distributed with a bell-shaped curve," interposed Frank. "Besides, what good is the Poisson distribution if it doesn't give us the right answer?"

"I'm sure that's just a chance occurrence," responded Laurel. "Let's check with a chi-square."

"Well, be sure you get back to me when you straighten out the problem," said Eric.

PROBLEMS AND QUESTIONS

1. Check the coupon-arrival data in Chapter 6 to see if it is Poisson distributed. Be sure to choose intervals wide enough so the expected frequencies are all at least 5. Test at the 1 percent significance level.
2. Check the assumption that the data follow a normal distribution.
3. Plot the time-series data for week number versus number of coupons. Can you hypothesize a reason for the discrepancy Eric has noted?

Cold River's production manager, Nick Pappas, was so pleased with the excellent job that Frank and Laurel did in Chapter 6 that he sought Joe's approval to get them to do another production study.

"It is plain as day that some of the pedal-toy assembly workers get more work done than others. It is only fair that they get paid more," he said. "I believe in an honest day's pay for an honest day's work. If some people get less done than others, they should be paid less."

"Hold your horses!" Irene interjected. "There is no point in getting excited. Although there are differences from day to day, on average all the assembly workers produce the same number of toys each week."

"Joe, let's get Frank and Laurel to test that assumption," Nick quickly responded.

"Why not?" Joe agreed.

"One question before we start," Frank added. "Does each worker do the same job, assembling a pedal toy from start to finish?"

"Of course they do!" Laurel said. "Haven't you been in the shop?"

QUESTION

4. Do the sampled data come from populations with the same mean? Test Irene's assumption at the 1 percent significance level for the weekly production output of the sixteen workers sampled.

	WORKER															
WEEK	1	2	3	4	5	6	7	8	9	10	11	12	13	14	15	16
1	103	117	101	129	97	90	99	109	107	88	90	99	112	87	118	105
2	113	100	101	119	81	125	97	103	99	103	122	79	76	98	120	101
3	113	119	108	115	101	112	105	100	89	100	96	108	92	111	114	96
4	85	109	93	108	101	100	103	118	105	114	87	73	67	102	102	97
5	96	107	103	97	110	116	100	80	93	94	84	92	123	118	98	112
6	101	119	85	84	88	96	105	109	83	102	73	84	97	120	99	78
7	119	100	141	97	81	108	68	115	91	91	94	91	73	117	81	106
8	98	87	108	102	79	111	96	122	111	102	116	96	93	102	81	106
9	125	124	137	99	82	72	102	89	105	87	94	91	89	109	99	102
10	99	102	97	87	84	77	112	124	94	87	130	117	84	83	94	87
11	87	97	110	111	99	89	98	113	84	93	118	84	80	114	84	85
12	128	101	96	92	106	103	105	91	81	93	116	80	90	87	100	110
13	91	119	115	103	94	92	102	99	74	79	95	106	105	93	119	91
14	94	105	107	86	88	120	86	71	98	95	113	109	101	94	102	92
15	113	103	82	121	110	96	94	100	96	112	86	84	101	91	124	102

10-13 FLOW CHART

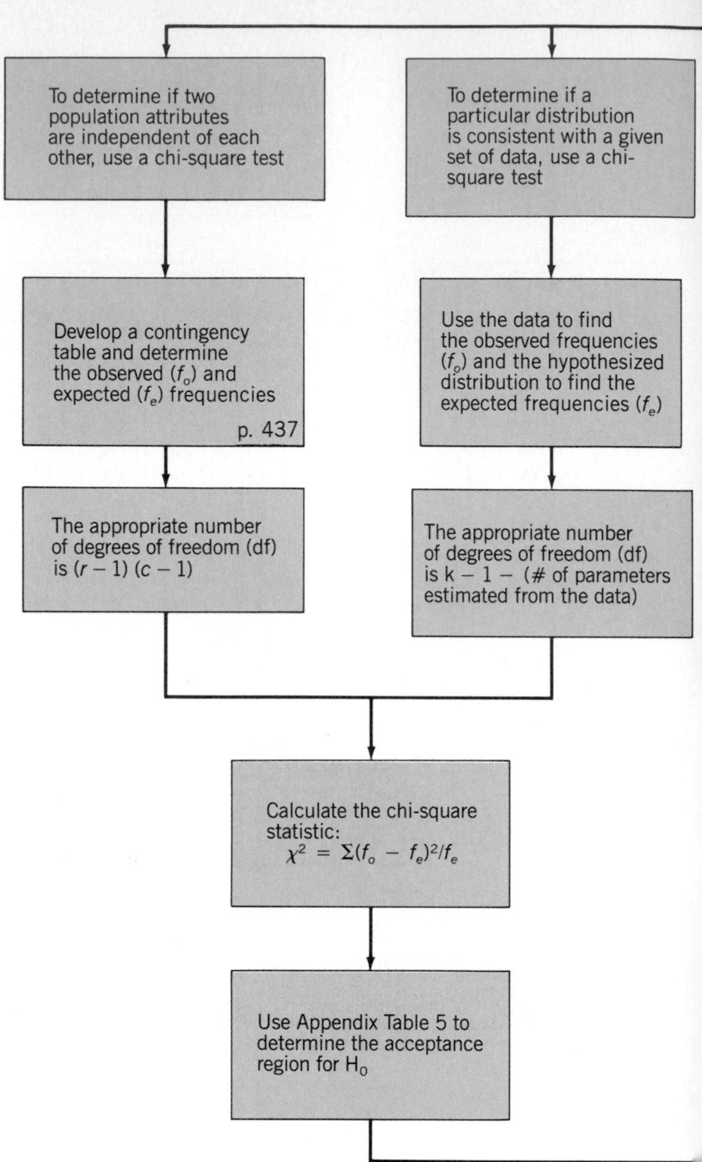

To determine if two population attributes are independent of each other, use a chi-square test
To determine if a particular distribution is consistent with a given set of data, use a chi-square test
Develop a contingency table and determine the observed (f_o) and expected (f_e) frequencies
p. 437
Use the data to find the observed frequencies (f_o) and the hypothesized distribution to find the expected frequencies (f_e)
The appropriate number of degrees of freedom (df) is $(r - 1)(c - 1)$
The appropriate number of degrees of freedom (df) is k − 1 − (# of parameters estimated from the data)
Calculate the chi-square statistic:
$\chi^2 = \Sigma(f_o - f_e)^2/f_e$
Use Appendix Table 5 to determine the acceptance region for H_0

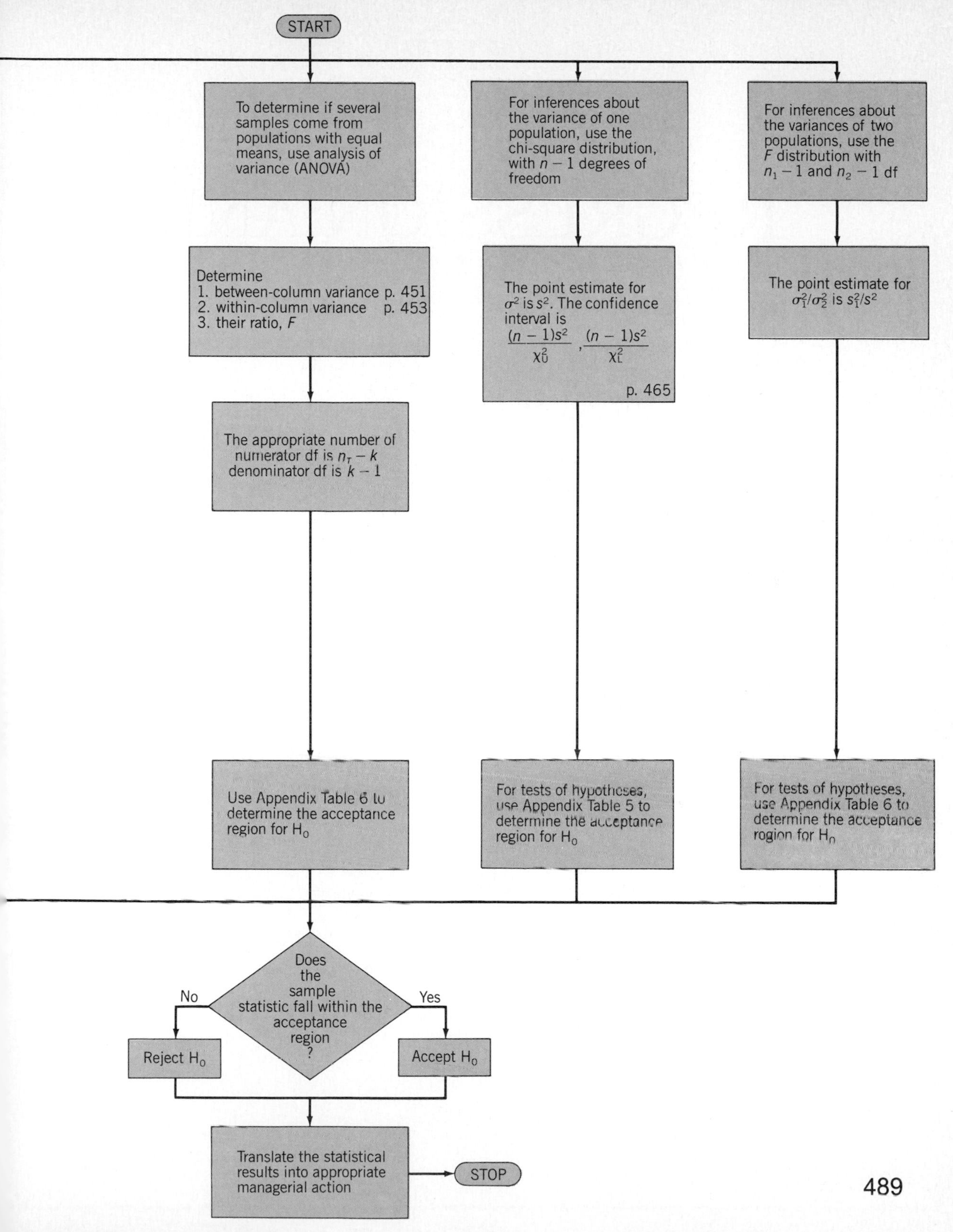
START
To determine if several samples come from populations with equal means, use analysis of variance (ANOVA)
For inferences about the variance of one population, use the chi-square distribution, with $n - 1$ degrees of freedom
For inferences about the variances of two populations, use the F distribution with $n_1 - 1$ and $n_2 - 1$ df
Determine
1. between-column variance p. 451
2. within-column variance p. 453
3. their ratio, F
The point estimate for σ^2 is s^2. The confidence interval is
$\frac{(n-1)s^2}{\chi_U^2}, \frac{(n-1)s^2}{\chi_L^2}$
p. 465
The point estimate for σ_1^2/σ_2^2 is s_1^2/s^2
The appropriate number of numerator df is $n_T - k$ denominator df is $k - 1$
Use Appendix Table 6 to determine the acceptance region for H_0
For tests of hypotheses, use Appendix Table 5 to determine the acceptance region for H_0
For tests of hypotheses, use Appendix Table 6 to determine the acceptance region for H_0
Does the sample statistic fall within the acceptance region ?
No
Yes
Reject H_0
Accept H_0
Translate the statistical results into appropriate managerial action
STOP

CHAPTER 11

SIMPLE REGRESSION AND CORRELATION

1. INTRODUCTION, 492
2. ESTIMATION USING THE REGRESSION LINE, 497
3. CORRELATION ANALYSIS, 518
4. MAKING INFERENCES ABOUT POPULATION PARAMETERS, 527
5. USING REGRESSION AND CORRELATION ANALYSES: Limitations, Errors, and Caveats, 533
6. TERMS, 535
7. EQUATIONS, 536
8. REVIEW EXERCISES, 538
9. CONCEPTS TEST, 541
10. CONCEPTUAL CASE, 543
11. COMPUTER DATA BASE EXERCISE, 544
12. FLOW CHART, 546

OBJECTIVES: If your university used your high school grade-point average to predict your college grade-point average, it may have used the technique of *regression analysis,* one of the subjects of Chapter 11. And if you have heard the statement that there is a high correlation between smoking and lung cancer, then the word *correlation* (another topic in Chapter 11) is not strange to you. *Correlation analysis* is used to measure the degree of association between two variables.

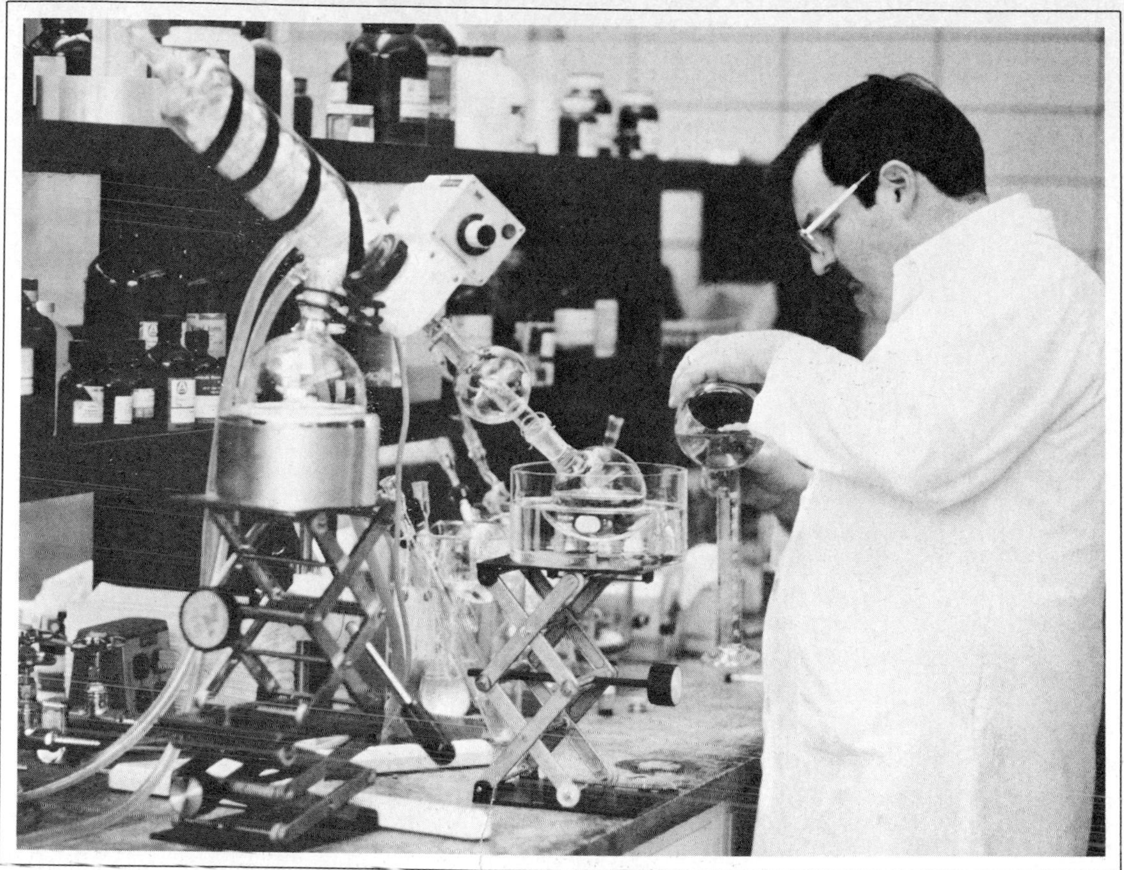

The vice-president for research and development of a large chemical and fiber manufacturing company believes that the firm's annual profits depend on the amount spent on R&D. The new chief executive officer does not agree and has asked for evidence. Here are data for 6 years:

YEAR	MILLIONS SPENT ON RESEARCH AND DEVELOPMENT	ANNUAL PROFIT (MILLIONS)
1978	2	20
1979	3	25
1980	5	34
1981	4	30
1982	11	40
1983	5	31

The vice-president for R&D wants an equation for predicting annual profits from the amount budgeted for R&D. With methods in this chapter, we can supply such a decision-making tool and tell him something about the accuracy he can expect in using it to make decisions.

11-1 INTRODUCTION

Relationship between variables

Every day, managers make personal and professional decisions that are based upon predictions of future events. To make these forecasts, they rely upon the relationship (intuitive and calculated) between what is already known and what is to be estimated. If decision makers can determine how the known is related to the future event, they can aid the decision-making process considerably. That is the subject of this chapter: how to determine the *relationship between variables.*

Difference between chi-square and topics in this chapter

In Chapter 10, we used chi-square tests of independence to determine whether a statistical relationship existed between two variables. The chi-square test tells us *if* there is such a relationship, but it does not tell us *what* that relationship is. **Regression and correlation analyses will show us how to determine both the nature and the strength of a relationship between two variables.** We will learn to predict, with some accuracy, the value of an unknown variable based on past observations of that variable and others.

Origin of terms *regression* and *multiple regression*

The term *regression* was first used as a statistical concept in 1877 by Sir Francis Galton. Galton made a study that showed that the height of children born to tall parents will tend to move back, or "regress," toward the mean height of the population. He designated the word *regression* as the name of the general process of predicting one variable (the height of the children) from another (the height of the parent). Later, statisticians coined the term *multiple regression* to describe the process by which several variables are used to predict another.

Development of an estimating equation

In *regression analysis,* we shall develop an *estimating equation*—that is, a mathematical formula that relates the known variables to the unknown variable. Then, after we have learned the pattern of this relationship, we can apply *correlation analysis* to determine the degree to which the variables are related. Correlation analysis, then, tells us how well the estimating equation actually describes the relationship.

Types of Relationships

Independent and dependent variables

Regression and correlation analyses are based on the relationship, or association, between two (or more) variables. The known variable (or variables) is called the *independent* variable(s). The variable we are trying to predict is the *dependent* variable.

Scientists know, for example, that there is a relationship between the annual sales of aerosol spray cans and the quantity of fluorocarbons released into the atmosphere each year. If we studied this relationship, "the number of aerosol cans sold each year" would be the independent variable, and "the quantity of fluorocarbons released annually" would be the dependent variable.

Let's take another example. Economists might base their predictions of the annual gross national product, or GNP, on the final consumption spending within the economy. Thus, "the final consumption spending" is the independent variable, and "the GNP" would be the dependent variable.

In regression, we can have only one dependent variable in our estimating equation. However, we can use more than one independent variable. Often when we add independent variables, we improve the accuracy of our prediction. Economists, for example, frequently add a second independent variable, "the level of investment spending," to improve their estimate of the nation's GNP.

Direct relationship between X and Y

Our two examples of fluorocarbons and GNP are illustrations of direct associations between independent and dependent variables. As the independent variable increases, the dependent variable also increases. In like manner, we expect the sales of a company to increase as the advertising budget increases. We can graph such a *direct relationship,* plotting the independent variable of the X-axis and the dependent variable on the Y-axis. We have done this in *a*, Fig. 11-1. Notice how the line slopes up as X takes on larger and larger values. The slope of this line is said to be *positive,* because Y increases as X increases.

Inverse relationship between X and Y

Relationships can also be *inverse* rather than direct. In these cases, the dependent variable decreases as the independent variable increases. The government assumes that such an inverse association exists between a company's increased annual expenditures for pollution-abatement devices and decreased pollution emissions. This type of relationship is illustrated in *b*, Fig. 11-1, and is characterized by a *negative* slope (the dependent variable Y decreases as the independent variable X increases).

Frequently, we find a *causal* relationship between variables; that is, the independent variable "causes" the dependent variable to change. This is true in the antipollution example above. But in many cases, some other factor causes the change in both the dependent and the independent variables. We might be able to predict the sales of diamond earrings from the sale of new Cadillacs, but we could not say that one is caused by the other. Instead, we realize that the sales levels of both Cadillacs and diamond earrings are caused by another factor, such as the level of disposable income.

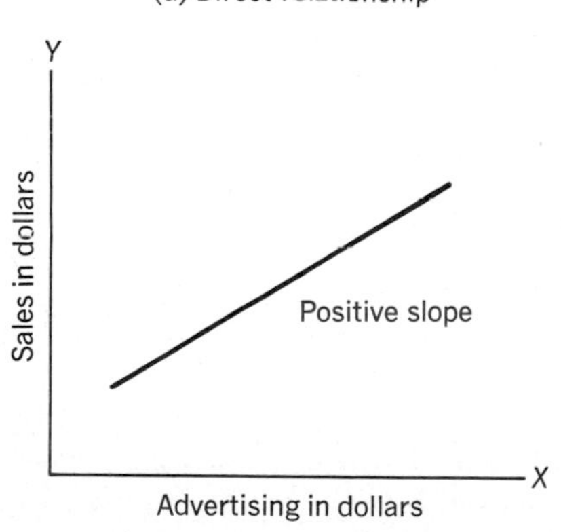

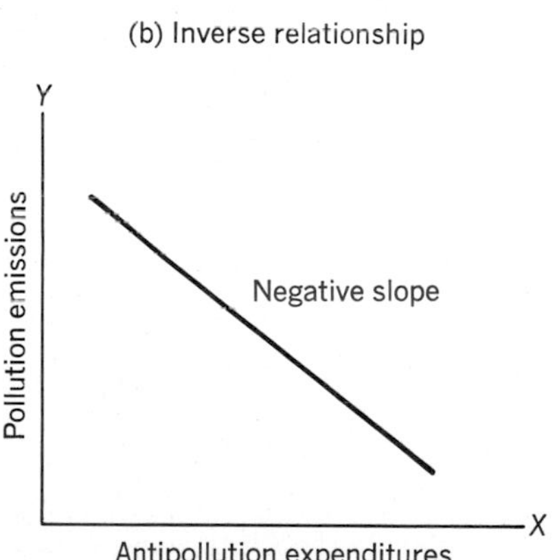

FIGURE 11-1 Direct and inverse relationships between independent variable X and dependent variable Y

Relationships of association, *not* cause and effect

For this reason, it is important that you consider the relationships found by regression to be relationships of association but *not* necessarily of cause and effect. Unless you have specific reasons for believing that the values of the dependent variable are caused by the values of the independent variable(s), do not infer causality from the relationships you find by regression.

Scatter Diagrams

Scatter diagram

The first step in determining whether there is a relationship between two variables is to examine the graph of the observed (or known) data. This graph, or chart, is called a *scatter diagram.*

A scatter diagram can give us two types of information. Visually, we can look for patterns that indicate that the variables are related. Then, if the variables are related, we can see what kind of line, or estimating equation, describes this relationship.

We are going to develop and use a specific scatter diagram. Suppose a university admissions director asks us to determine whether any relationship exists between a student's scores on an entrance examination and that student's cumulative grade-point average (GPA) upon graduation. The administrator has accumulated a random sample of data from the records of the university. This information is recorded in Table 11-1.

TABLE 11-1 Student scores on entrance examinations and cumulative grade-point averages at graduation

Student	A	B	C	D	E	F	G	H
Entrance examination scores (100 = maximum possible score)	74	69	85	63	82	60	79	91
Cumulative GPA (4.0 = A)	2.6	2.2	3.4	2.3	3.1	2.1	3.2	3.8

Transfer tabular information to a graph

To begin, we should transfer the information in Table 11-1 to a graph. Since the director wishes to use examination scores to predict success in college, we have placed the cumulative GPA (the dependent variable) on the vertical or Y-axis and the entrance examination score (the independent variable) on the horizontal or X-axis. Figure 11-2 shows the completed scatter diagram.

At first glance we can see why we call this a scatter diagram. The pattern of points results from the fact that each pair of data from Table 11-1 has been recorded as a single point. When we view all these points together, we can visualize the relationship that exists between the two variables. As a result, we can draw, or "fit," a straight line through our scatter diagram to represent the relationship. We have done this in Fig. 11-3. It is common to try to draw these lines so that an equal number of points lie on either side of the line.

Drawing, or "fitting," a straight line through a scatter diagram

Interpreting our straight line

In this case, the line drawn through our data points represents a direct relationship, because Y increases as X increases. Because the data points are relatively close to this line, we can say that there is a high degree of

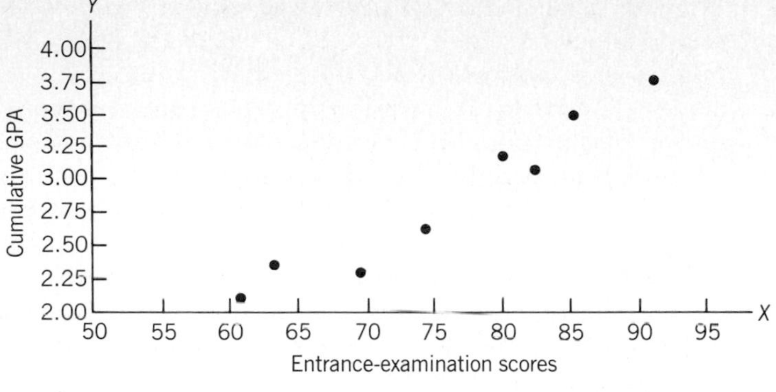

FIGURE 11-2 Scatter diagram of student scores on entrance examinations plotted against cumulative grade-point averages

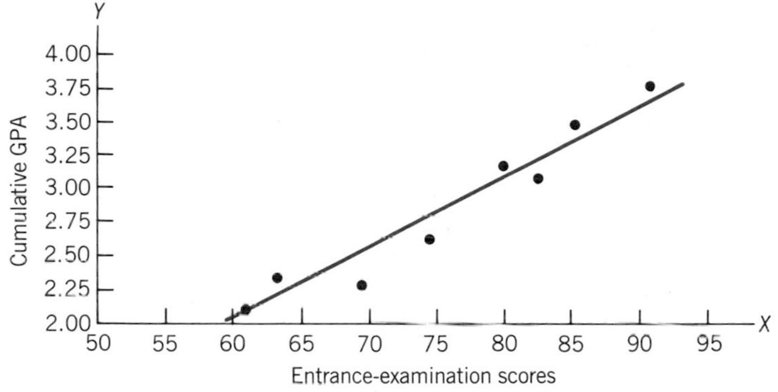

FIGURE 11-3 Scatter diagram with straight line representing the relationship between *X* and *Y* "fitted" through it

association between the examination scores and the cumulative GPAs. In Fig. 11-3, we can see that the relationship described by the data points is well described by a straight line. Thus, we can say that it is a *linear* relationship.

Curvilinear relationships

The relationship between *X* and *Y* variables can also take the form of a curve. Statisticians call such a relationship *curvilinear*. The employees of many industries, for example, experience what is called a "learning curve"; that is, as they produce a new product, the time required to produce one unit is reduced by some fixed proportion as the total number of units doubles. One such industry is aviation. Manufacturing time per unit for a new aircraft tends to decrease by 20 percent each time the total number of completed new planes doubles. Figure 11-4 illustrates the curvilinear relationship of this "learning-curve" phenomenon.

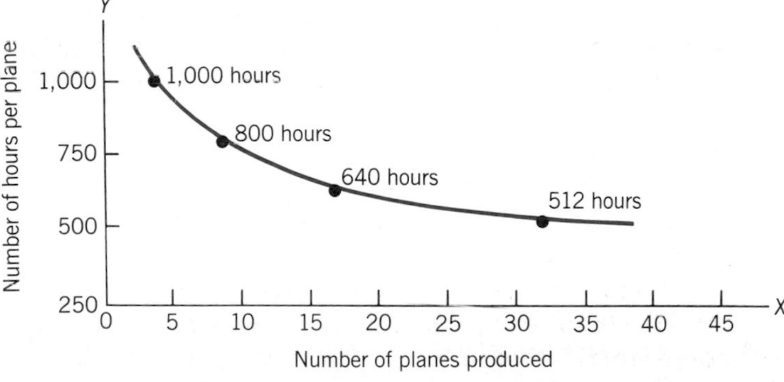

FIGURE 11-4 Curvilinear relationship between new-aircraft construction time and number of units produced

The direction of the curve can indicate whether the curvilinear relationship is direct or inverse. The curve in Fig. 11-4 describes an inverse relationship, because Y decreases as X increases.

Review of possible relationships

To review the relationships possible in a scatter diagram, examine the graphs in Fig. 11-5. Graphs a and b show direct and inverse linear relationships. Graphs c and d are examples of curvilinear relationships that demonstrate direct and inverse associations between variables, respectively. Graph e illustrates an inverse linear relationship with a widely scattered pattern of points. This wider scattering indicates that there is a lower degree of association between the independent and dependent variables than there is in graph b. The pattern of points in graph f seems to indicate that there is no relationship between the two variables; therefore, knowledge of the past concerning one variable will not allow us to predict future occurrences of the other.

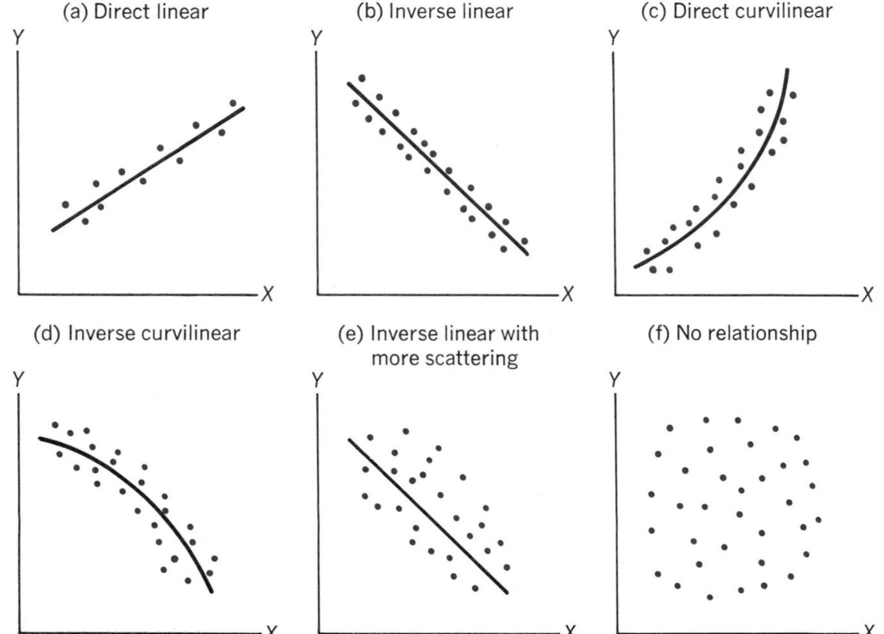

FIGURE 11-5 Possible relationships between X and Y in scatter diagrams

EXERCISES

11-1 What is regression analysis?

11-2 In regression analysis, what is an estimating equation?

11-3 What is the purpose of correlation analysis?

11-4 Define direct and inverse relationships.

11-5 To what does the term *causal relationship* refer?

11-6 Explain the difference between linear and curvilinear relationships.

11-7 Explain why and how we construct a scatter diagram.

11-8 What is multiple regression analysis?

11-9 The president of Decade Real Estate, a large southwestern real estate company, is conducting a study on sales techniques. One relationship of interest is the average length of time an agent spends with each customer and the success of that agent. A group of agents were sampled and the following data were collected. Row *X* is the average length of time (minutes) a particular agent spends with a prospect, and row *Y* is the number of houses that agent has sold in the last year. Construct a scatter diagram for this data. Is there a relationship between the variables? If so, is it linear or curvilinear, direct or inverse?

X	40	58	33	65	80	80	56	30	33	90	72
Y	15	14	12	20	26	26	14	12	12	30	22

11-10 For each of the following scatter diagrams, indicate whether a relationship exists and, if so, whether it is direct or inverse and linear or curvilinear.

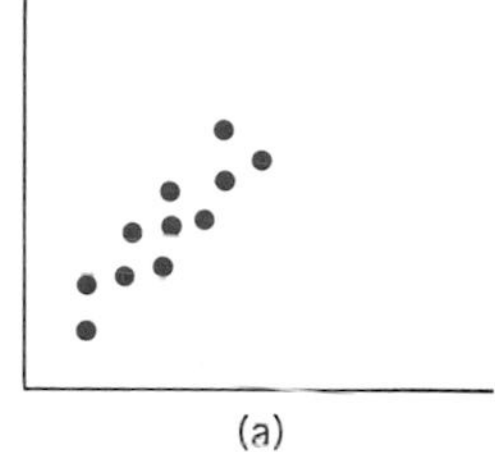
(a)

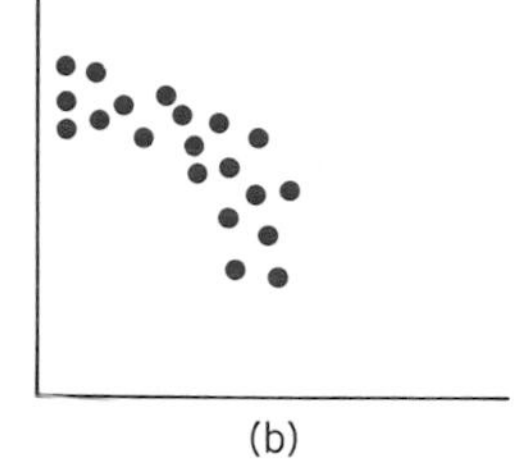
(b)

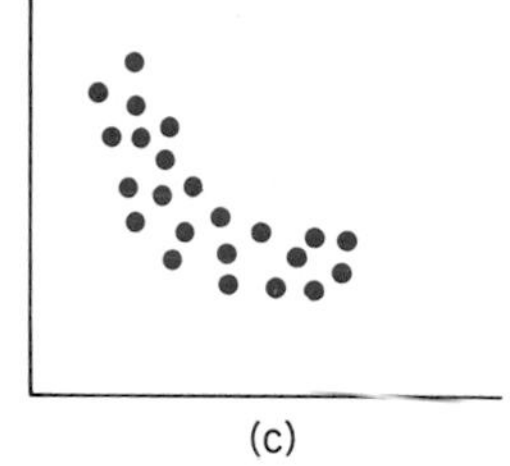
(c)

11-11 William Hawkins, vice-president of personnel for International Motors, is working on the relationship between a worker's salary and absentee rate. Hawkins divided the salary range of International into 25 grades or levels (1 being the lowest grade, 25 the highest) and then randomly sampled a group of workers. He determined the salary grade for each worker and the number of days that employee had missed over the last 3 years.

Salary ranking	22	20	16	10	18	18	15	6	21	16	13	3	17	15	11	5
Absences	7	15	27	34	9	24	26	33	12	20	30	37	14	24	29	38

Construct a scatter diagram for the data above and indicate the type of relationship.

11-12 The National Institute of Environmental Health Sciences (NIEHS) has been studying the statistical relationships between many different variables and the common cold. One of the variables being examined is the use of facial tissues. The data given below indicate the number of facial tissues (*X*) and the number of days that cold symptoms were exhibited (*Y*) by 7 people over a 12-month period. What relationship, if any, seems to hold between the two variables? Does this indicate any causal effect?

X	2,000	1,500	500	750	600	900	1,000
Y	40	30	10	15	5	20	25

11-2 ESTIMATION USING THE REGRESSION LINE

Calculating the regression line using an equation

In the scatter diagrams we have used to this point, the *regression lines* were put in place by fitting the lines visually among the data points. In this section, we shall learn how to calculate the regression line somewhat more precisely, using an equation that relates the two variables mathematically. Here, we examine only linear relationships involving two variables. We shall deal with relationships among more than two variables in the next chapter.

Equation for a straight line

The equation for a straight line where the dependent variable Y is determined by the independent variable X is:

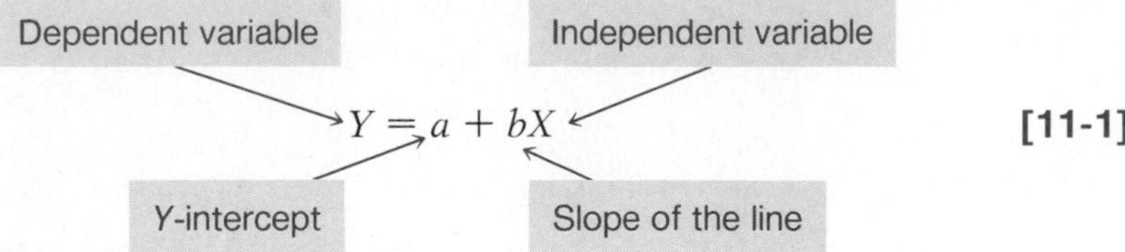

$$Y = a + bX \qquad [11\text{-}1]$$

Interpreting the equation

Using this equation, we can take a given value of X and compute the value of Y. The a is called the "Y-intercept" because its value is the point at which the regression line crosses the Y-axis—that is, the vertical axis. The b in Equation 11-1 is the "slope" of the line. It represents how much each unit change of the independent variable X changes the dependent variable Y. Both a and b are numerical *constants,* since, for any given straight line, their value does not change.

Calculating Y from X using the equation for a straight line

Suppose we know that a is 3 and b is 2. Let us determine what Y would be for an X equal to 5. When we substitute the values for a, b, and X in Equation 11-1, we find the corresponding value of Y to be:

$$\begin{aligned} Y &= a + bX \qquad [11\text{-}1] \\ &= 3 + 2(5) \\ &= 3 + 10 \\ &= 13 \leftarrow \text{value for } Y \text{ given } X = 5 \end{aligned}$$

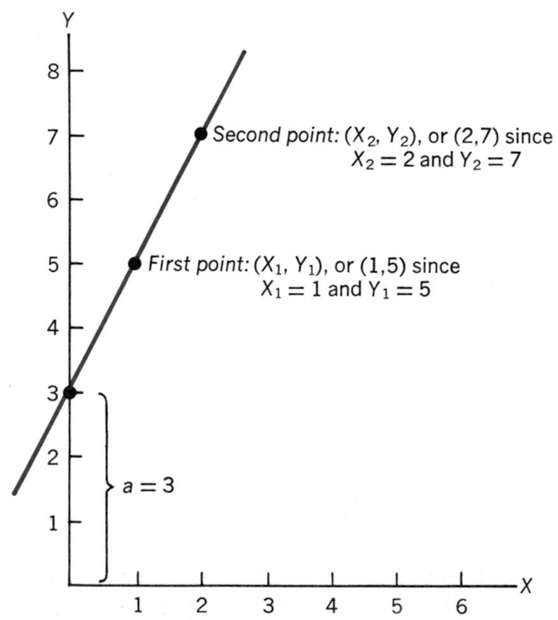

FIGURE 11-6 Straight line with a positive slope, with Y-intercept and two points on the line designated

Using the Estimating Equation for a Straight Line

Finding the values for *a* and *b*

How can we find the values of the numerical constants, a and b? To illustrate this process, let's use the straight line in Fig. 11-6.

Visually, we can find a (the Y-intercept) by locating the point where the line crosses the Y-axis. In Fig. 11-6, this happens where $a = 3$.

To find the slope of the line, b, we must determine how the dependent variable, Y, changes as the independent variable, X, changes. We can begin by picking two points on the line in Fig. 11-6. Now, we must find the values of X and Y (the *coordinates*) of both points. We can call the coordinates of our first point (X_1, Y_1) and those of the second point (X_2, Y_2). By examining Fig. 11-6, we can see that $(X_1, Y_1) = (1,5)$ and $(X_2, Y_2) = (2,7)$. At this point, then, we can calculate the value of b, using this equation:

$$b = \frac{Y_2 - Y_1}{X_2 - X_1} \quad \textbf{[11-2]}$$

$$= \frac{7 - 5}{2 - 1}$$

$$= \frac{2}{1}$$

$$= 2 \leftarrow \text{slope of the line}$$

Writing and using the equation for a straight line

In this manner, we can learn the values of the numerical constants, a and b, and write the equation for a straight line. The line in Fig. 11-6 can be described by Equation 11-1, where $a = 3$ and $b = 2$. Thus:

$$Y = a + bX \quad \textbf{[11-1]}$$

and: $Y = 3 + 2X$ in Fig. 11-6

Using this equation, we can determine the corresponding value of the dependent variable for any value of X. Suppose we wish to find the value of Y when $X = 7$. The answer would be:

$$Y = a + bX \quad \textbf{[11-1]}$$

$$= 3 + 2(7)$$

$$= 3 + 14$$

$$= 17$$

Direct relationship; positive slope

If you substitute more values for X into the equation, you will notice that Y increases as X increases. Thus, the relationship between the variables is *direct*, and the slope is *positive*.

Now consider the line in Fig. 11-7. We see that it crosses the Y-axis at 6. Therefore, we know that $a = 6$. If we select the two points where

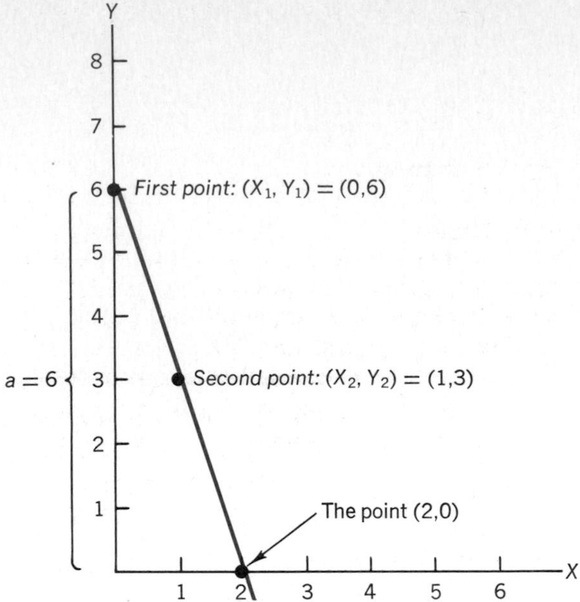

FIGURE 11-7
Straight line with negative slope

$(X_1, Y_1) = (0,6)$ and $(X_2, Y_2) = (1,3)$, we will find that the slope of the line is -3:

$$\begin{aligned} b &= \frac{Y_2 - Y_1}{X_2 - X_1} \\ &= \frac{3 - 6}{1 - 0} \\ &= -\frac{3}{1} \\ &= -3 \end{aligned} \qquad \textbf{[11-2]}$$

Determining the equation for the line

Notice that when b is negative, the line represents an *inverse* relationship, and the slope is *negative* (Y decreases as X increases). Now, with the numerical values of a and b determined, we can substitute them into the general equation for a straight line:

$$\begin{aligned} Y &= a + bX \\ Y &= 6 + (-3)X \\ Y &= 6 - 3X \end{aligned} \qquad \textbf{[11-1]}$$

Finding Y from X

Assume that we wish to find the value of the dependent variable that corresponds to $X = 2$. Substituting into the equation above, we get:

$$\begin{aligned} Y &= 6 - (3)(2) \\ &= 6 - 6 \\ &= 0 \end{aligned}$$

Thus, when $X = 2$, Y must equal 0. If we refer to the line in Fig. 11-7, we can see that the point (2,0) does lie on the line.

The Method of Least Squares

Fitting a regression line mathematically

Now that we have seen how to determine the equation for a straight line, let's think about how we can calculate an equation for a line that is drawn through the middle of a set of points in a scatter diagram. How can we "fit" a line mathematically if none of the points lie on the line? To a statistician, the line will have a "good fit" if it *minimizes the error* between the estimated points on the line and the actual observed points that were used to draw it.

Introduction of $\hat{Y}$

Before we proceed, we need to introduce a new symbol. So far, we have used Y to represent the individual values of the observed points measured along the Y-axis. Now we should begin to use $\hat{Y}$ (*Y-hat*) to symbolize the individual values of the *estimated* points—that is, those points that lie on the estimating line. Accordingly, we shall write the equation for the estimating line as:

$$\hat{Y} = a + bX \qquad \textbf{[11-3]}$$

Which line fits best?

In Fig. 11-8, we have two estimating lines that have been fitted to the same set of three data points. These three given, or observed, data points are shown in black. Two very different lines have been drawn to describe the relationship between the two variables. Obviously, we need a way to decide which of these lines gives us a better fit.

Using total error to determine best fit

One way we can "measure the error" of our estimating line is to *sum* all the individual differences, or errors, between the estimated points shown in color and the observed points shown in black. In Table 11-2, we have calculated the individual differences between the corresponding Y and $\hat{Y}$, and then we have found the sum of them.

FIGURE 11-8
Two different estimating lines fitted to the same three observed data points, showing errors in both cases

(a)

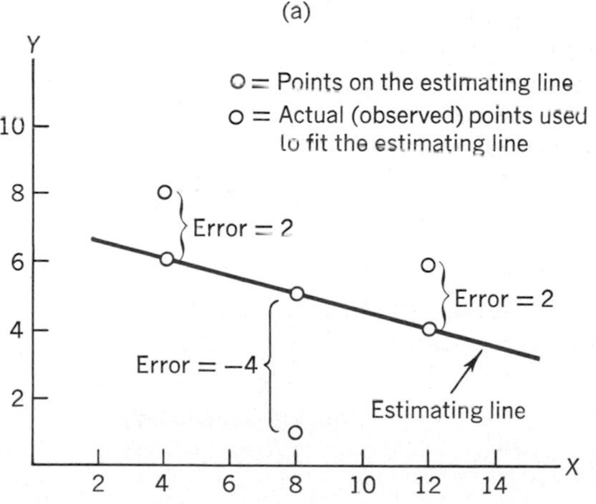

(b)

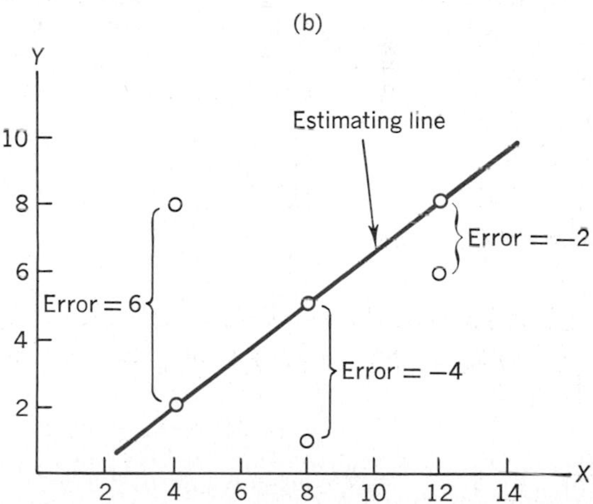

TABLE 11-2 Summing the errors of the two estimating lines in Fig. 11-8

GRAPH *a* $Y - \hat{Y}$	GRAPH *b* $Y - \hat{Y}$
$8 - 6 = 2$	$8 - 2 = 6$
$1 - 5 = -4$	$1 - 5 = -4$
$6 - 4 = 2$	$6 - 8 = -2$
0 ← **total error**	**0** ← **total error**

A quick visual examination of the two estimating lines in Fig. 11-8 reveals that the line in graph *a* fits the three data points better than the line in graph *b*.* However, our process of summing the individual differences in Table 11-2 indicates that both lines describe the data equally well (the total error in both cases is zero). Thus, we must conclude that the process of summing individual differences for calculating the error is not a reliable way to judge the goodness of fit of an estimating line.

Using absolute value of error to measure best fit

The problem with adding the individual errors is the canceling effect of the positive and negative values. From this, we might deduce that the proper criterion for judging the goodness of fit would be to add the *absolute values* (the values without their algebraic signs) of each error. We have done this in Table 11-3. (The symbol for absolute value is two parallel vertical lines, | |.) Since the total absolute error in graph *a* is smaller than the total absolute error in graph *b*, and since we are looking for the "minimum absolute error," we have confirmed our intuitive impression that the estimating line in graph *a* is the better fit.

TABLE 11-3 Summing the absolute values of the errors of the two estimating lines in Fig. 11-8

GRAPH *a* $\lvert Y - \hat{Y} \rvert$	GRAPH *b* $\lvert Y - \hat{Y} \rvert$
$\lvert 8 - 6 \rvert = 2$	$\lvert 8 - 2 \rvert = 6$
$\lvert 1 - 5 \rvert = 4$	$\lvert 1 - 5 \rvert = 4$
$\lvert 6 - 4 \rvert = 2$	$\lvert 6 - 8 \rvert = 2$
8 ← **total absolute error**	**12** ← **total absolute error**

On the basis of this success, we might conclude that minimizing the sum of the absolute values of the error is the best criterion for finding a good fit. But before we feel too comfortable with it, we should examine a different situation.

In Fig. 11-9, we again have two identical scatter diagrams with two different estimating lines fitted to the three data points. In Table 11-4, we have added the absolute values of the errors and found that the estimating

* We can reason that this is so by noticing that whereas both estimating lines miss the second and third points (reading from left to right) by an equal distance, the line in graph *a* misses the first point by considerably less than the line in graph *b*.

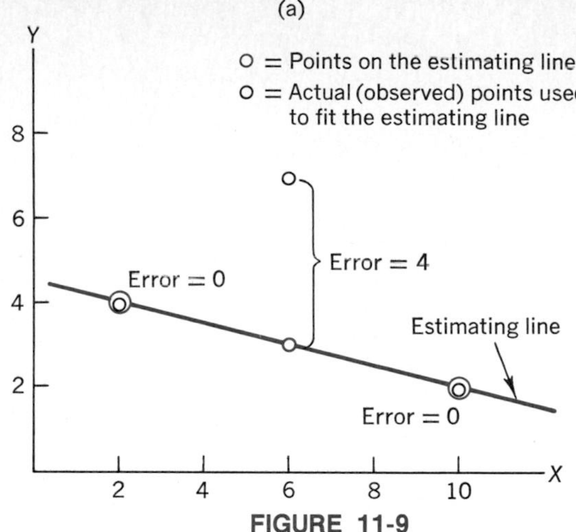

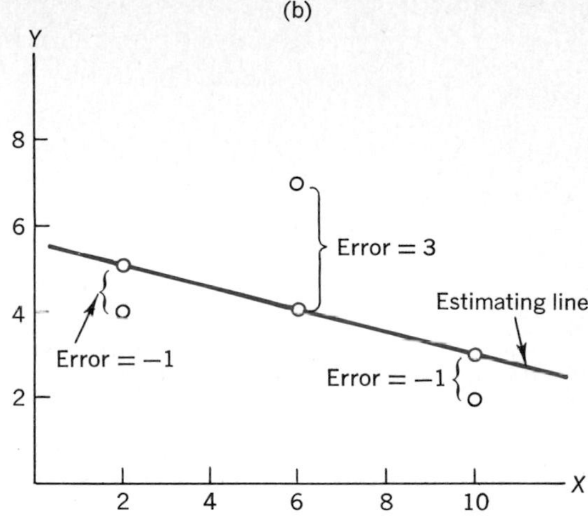

FIGURE 11-9
Two different estimating lines fitted to the same three observed data points, showing errors in both cases

line in graph *a* is a better fit than the line in graph *b*. Intuitively, however, it appears that the line in graph *b* is the better fit line, because it has been moved vertically to take the middle point into consideration. Graph *a*, on the other hand, seems to ignore the middle point completely. So we would probably discard this second criterion for finding the best fit. Why? **The sum of the absolute values does not stress the *magnitude* of the error.**

Giving more weight to farther points; squaring the error

It seems reasonable that the farther away a point is from the estimating line, the more serious is the error. We would rather have several small absolute errors than one large one, as we saw in the last example. **In effect, we want to find a way to "penalize" large absolute errors, so that we can avoid them. We can accomplish this if we *square* the individual errors before we add them.** Squaring each term accomplishes two purposes:

1. It magnifies, or penalizes, the larger errors.
2. It cancels the effect of the positive and negative values (a negative error squared is still positive).

Using least squares as a measure of best fit

Since we are looking for the estimating line that minimizes the sum of the squares of the errors, we call this the *least squares method*.

TABLE 11-4 Summing the absolute values of the errors of the two estimating lines in Fig. 11-9

GRAPH *a* $\lvert Y - \hat{Y} \rvert$	GRAPH *b* $\lvert Y - \hat{Y} \rvert$
$\lvert 4 - 4 \rvert = 0$	$\lvert 4 - 5 \rvert = 1$
$\lvert 7 - 3 \rvert = 4$	$\lvert 7 - 4 \rvert = 3$
$\lvert 2 - 2 \rvert = \underline{0}$	$\lvert 2 - 3 \rvert = \underline{1}$
4 ← total absolute error	**5 ← total absolute error**

Let's apply the least squares criterion to the problem in Fig. 11-9. After we have organized the data and summed the squares in Table 11-5, we can see that, as we thought, the estimating line in graph b is the better fit.

TABLE 11-5 Applying the least squares criterion to the estimating lines

GRAPH *a* $(Y - \hat{Y})^2$	GRAPH *b* $(Y - \hat{Y})^2$
$(4 - 4)^2 = (0)^2 = 0$	$(4 - 5)^2 = (-1)^2 = 1$
$(7 - 3)^2 = (4)^2 = 16$	$(7 - 4)^2 = (3)^2 = 9$
$(2 - 2)^2 = (0)^2 = 0$	$(2 - 3)^2 = (-1)^2 = 1$
16 ← sum of the squares	**11 ← sum of the squares**

Finding best-fitting least squares line mathematically

Using the criterion of least squares, we can now determine whether one estimating line is a better fit than another. But for a set of data points through which we could draw an infinite number of estimating lines, how can we tell when we have found *the best-fitting line?*

Statisticians have derived two equations we can use to find the slope and the Y-intercept of the best-fitting regression line. The first formula calculates the slope:

Slope of the least squares regression line

Slope of best-fitting estimating line

$$b = \frac{\Sigma XY - n\bar{X}\bar{Y}}{\Sigma X^2 - n\bar{X}^2} \quad \textbf{[11-4]}$$

where:

- b = slope of the best-fitting estimating line
- X = values of the independent variable
- Y = values of the dependent variable
- $\bar{X}$ = mean of the values of the independent variable
- $\bar{Y}$ = mean of the values of the dependent variable
- n = number of data points (that is, the number of the pairs of values for the independent and dependent variables)

The second formula calculates the Y-intercept of the line whose slope we calculated using Equation 11-4:

Intercept of the least squares regression line

Y-intercept

$$a = \bar{Y} - b\bar{X} \quad \textbf{[11-5]}$$

where:

- a = Y-intercept
- b = slope from Equation 11-4

- $\overline{Y}$ = mean of the values of the dependent variable
- $\overline{X}$ = mean of the values of the independent variable

With these two equations, we can find the best-fitting regression line for any two-variable set of data points.

Using the Least Squares Method in Two Problems

Suppose the director of the Chapel Hill Sanitation Department is interested in the relationship between the age of a garbage truck and the annual repair expense he should expect to incur. In order to determine this relationship, the director has accumulated information concerning four of the trucks the city currently owns (Table 11-6).

TABLE 11-6 Annual truck-repair expenses

TRUCK NUMBER	AGE OF TRUCK IN YEARS (X)	REPAIR EXPENSE DURING LAST YEAR IN HUNDREDS OF $ (Y)
101	5	7
102	3	7
103	3	6
104	1	4

Example of the least squares method

The first step in calculating the regression line for this problem is to organize the data as outlined in Table 11-7. This allows us to substitute

TABLE 11-7 Calculation of inputs for Equations 11-4 and 11-5

TRUCKS ($n = 4$) (1)	AGE (X) (2)	REPAIR EXPENSE (Y) (3)	XY (2) × (3)	X^2 $(2)^2$
101	5	7	35	25
102	3	7	21	9
103	3	6	18	9
104	1	4	4	1
	$\Sigma X =$ **12**	$\Sigma Y =$ **24**	$\Sigma XY =$ **78**	$\Sigma X^2 =$ **44**

$$\overline{X} = \frac{\Sigma X}{n} \qquad \textbf{[3-2]}$$

$$= \frac{12}{4}$$

$$= 3 \leftarrow \text{mean of the values of the independent variable}$$

$$\overline{Y} = \frac{\Sigma Y}{n} \qquad \textbf{[3-2]}$$

$$= \frac{24}{4}$$

$$= 6 \leftarrow \text{mean of the values of the dependent variable}$$

directly into Equations 11-4 and 11-5 in order to find the slope and the Y-intercept of the best-fitting regression line.

With the information in Table 11-7, we can now use the equations for the slope (Equation 11-4) and the Y-intercept (Equation 11-5) to find the numerical constants for our regression line. The slope is:

Finding the value of *b*

$$b = \frac{\Sigma XY - n\bar{X}\bar{Y}}{\Sigma X^2 - n\bar{X}^2} \qquad [11\text{-}4]$$

$$= \frac{78 - (4)(3)(6)}{44 - (4)(3)^2}$$

$$= \frac{78 - 72}{44 - 36}$$

$$= \frac{6}{8}$$

$$= .75 \leftarrow \text{the slope of the line}$$

And the Y-intercept is:

Finding the value of *a*

$$\begin{aligned} a &= \bar{Y} - b\bar{X} \qquad [11\text{-}5] \\ &= 6 - (.75)(3) \\ &= 6 - 2.25 \\ &= 3.75 \leftarrow \text{the } Y\text{-intercept} \end{aligned}$$

Determining the estimating equation

Now, to get the estimating equation that describes the relationship between the age of a truck and its annual repair expense, we can substitute the values of a and b in the general equation for a straight line:

$$\hat{Y} = a + bX \qquad [11\text{-}3]$$

$$\hat{Y} = 3.75 + .75X$$

Using the estimating equation

Using this estimating equation (which we could plot as a regression line if we wished), the Sanitation Department director can estimate the annual repair expense, given the age of his equipment. If, for example, the city has a truck that is four years old, the director could use the equation to predict the annual repair expense for this truck as follows:

$$\begin{aligned} \hat{Y} &= 3.75 + .75(4) \\ &= 3.75 + 3 \\ &= 6.75 \leftarrow \text{expected annual repair expense of \$675.00} \end{aligned}$$

Thus, the city might expect to spend about $675 annually in repairs on a 4-year-old truck.

Another example

Now we can solve the chapter-opening problem concerning the relationship between money spent on research and development and the chemical firm's annual profits. Table 11-8 presents the information for the preceding six years. With this, we can determine the regression equation describing the relationship.

TABLE 11-8 Annual relationship between research and development and profits

YEAR	MILLIONS SPENT ON RESEARCH AND DEVELOPMENT (X)	ANNUAL PROFIT ($ MILLION) (Y)
1983	$ 5	$31
1982	11	40
1981	4	30
1980	5	34
1979	3	25
1978	2	20

Again, we can facilitate the collection of the necessary information if we perform the calculations in a table such as Table 11-9.

With this information, we are ready to find the numerical constants a and b for the estimating equation. The value of b is:

Finding b

$$b = \frac{\Sigma XY - n\overline{X}\overline{Y}}{\Sigma X^2 - n\overline{X}^2} \quad [11\text{-}4]$$

$$= \frac{1{,}000 - (6)(5)(30)}{200 - (6)(5)^2}$$

$$= \frac{1{,}000 - 900}{200 - 150}$$

$$= \frac{100}{50}$$

$$= 2 \leftarrow \text{the slope of the line}$$

Finding a

And the value for a is:

$$a = \overline{Y} - b\overline{X} \quad [11\text{-}5]$$
$$= 30 - (2)(5)$$
$$= 30 - 10$$
$$= 20 \leftarrow \text{the } Y\text{-intercept}$$

Determining the estimating equation

So we can substitute these values a and b into Equation 11-3 and get:

$$\hat{Y} = a + bX \quad [11\text{-}3]$$
$$\hat{Y} = 20 + 2X$$

Using the estimating equation to predict

Using this estimating equation, the vice-president for research and development can predict what the annual profits will be from the amount budgeted for R&D. If the firm spends $8 million for R&D in 1984, it can expect to earn approximately $36 million in profits during that year:

$$\hat{Y} = 20 + 2(8)$$
$$= 20 + 16$$
$$= 36 \leftarrow \text{expected annual profit (millions)}$$

TABLE 11-9 Calculation of inputs for Equations 11-4 and 11-5

YEAR ($n = 6$)	EXPENDITURES FOR R&D (X)	ANNUAL PROFITS (Y)	XY	X^2
1983	5	31	155	25
1982	11	40	440	121
1981	4	30	120	16
1980	5	34	170	25
1979	3	25	75	9
1978	2	20	40	4
	$\Sigma X =$ **30**	$\Sigma Y =$ **180**	$\Sigma XY =$ **1,000**	$\Sigma X^2 =$ **200**

$$\bar{X} = \frac{\Sigma X}{n} \qquad \textbf{[3-2]}$$

$$= \frac{30}{6}$$

$$= 5 \leftarrow \text{mean of the values of the independent variable}$$

$$\bar{Y} = \frac{\Sigma Y}{n} \qquad \textbf{[3-2]}$$

$$= \frac{180}{6}$$

$$= 30 \leftarrow \text{mean of the values of the dependent variable}$$

Shortcoming of the estimating equation

Estimating equations are not perfect predictors. In Fig. 11-10, which plots the points found in Table 11-8, the \$36 million estimate of profit for 1984 is only that—an estimate. Even so, the regression does give us an idea of what to expect for the coming year.

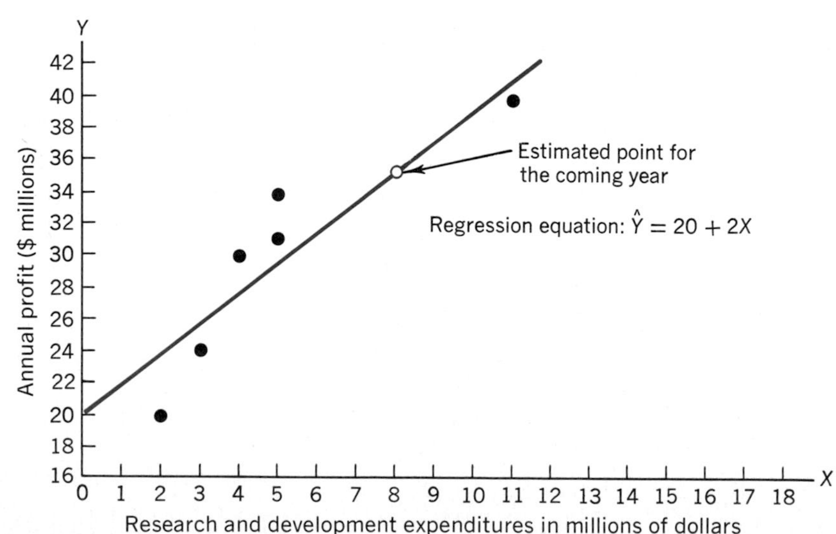

FIGURE 11-10 Scattering of points around regression line

Checking the Estimating Equation

Checking the estimating equation: one way

Now that we know how to calculate the regression line, we can learn how to check our work. A crude way to verify the accuracy of the estimating equation is to examine the graph of the sample points. As we can see from the previous problem, the regression line in Fig. 11-10 does appear to follow the path described by the sample points.

Another way to check the estimating equation

A more sophisticated method comes from one of the mathematical properties of a line fitted by the method of least squares; that is, the individual positive and negative errors must sum to zero. Using the information from Table 11-9, check to see whether the sum of the errors in the last problem is equal to zero. This is done in Table 11-10.

Since the sum of the errors in Table 11-10 does equal zero, and since the regression line appears to "fit" the points in Fig. 11-10, we can be reasonably certain that we have not committed any serious mathematical mistakes in determining the estimating equation for this problem.

TABLE 11-10 Calculating the sum of the individual errors in Table 11-9

Y		$\hat{Y}$ (THAT IS, $20 + 2X$)		INDIVIDUAL ERROR
31	−	[20 + (2)(5)]	=	1
40	−	[20 + (2)(11)]	=	−2
30	−	[20 + (2)(4)]	=	2
34	−	[20 + (2)(5)]	=	4
25	−	[20 + (2)(3)]	=	−1
20	−	[20 + (2)(2)]	=	−4
				0 ← total error

The Standard Error of Estimate

Measuring the reliability of the estimating equation

The next process we need to learn in our study of regression analysis is how to measure the reliability of the estimating equation that we have developed. We alluded to this topic when we introduced scatter diagrams. There, we realized intuitively that a line must be more accurate as an estimator when the data points lie close to the line (as in graph *a* of Fig. 11-11) than when the points are farther away from the line (as graph *b* of Fig. 11-11).

Definition and use of standard error of estimate

To measure the reliability of the estimating equation, statisticians have developed the *standard error of estimate*. This standard error is symbolized s_e and is similar to the standard deviation (which we first examined in Chapter 4), in that both are measures of dispersion. You will recall that the standard deviation is used to measure the dispersion of a set of observations about the mean. **The standard error of estimate, on the other hand, measures the variability, or scatter, of the observed values around the regression line.** Even so, you will see the similarity between the standard error of estimate and the standard deviation if you compare Equation 11-6,

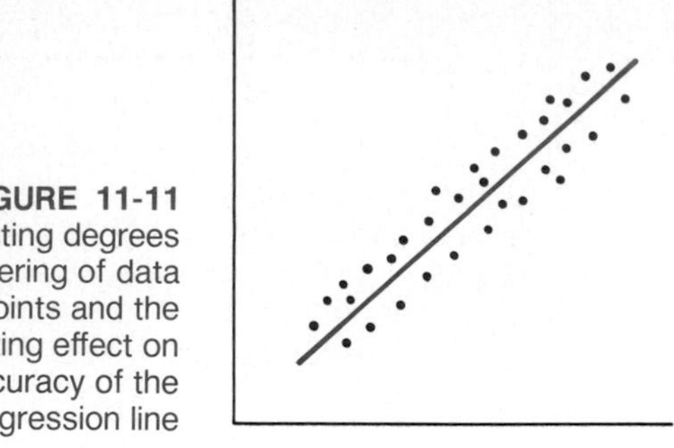

(a) This regression line is a more accurate estimator of the relationship between X and Y
Y
X

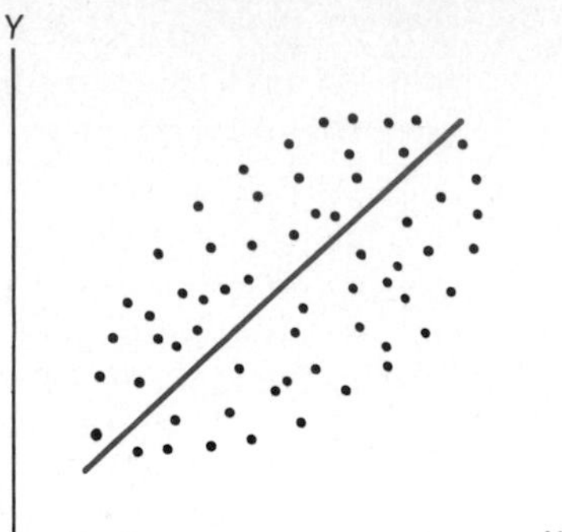

(b) This regression line is a less accurate estimator of the relationship between X and Y
Y
X

FIGURE 11-11 Contrasting degrees of scattering of data points and the resulting effect on accuracy of the regression line

which defines the standard error of estimate, with Equation 4-12, which defines the standard deviation:

Equation for calculation of standard error of estimate

Standard error of estimate

$$s_e = \sqrt{\frac{\Sigma(Y - \hat{Y})^2}{n - 2}} \qquad \textbf{[11-6]}$$

where:

- Y = values of the dependent variable
- $\hat{Y}$ = estimated values from the estimating equation that correspond to each Y value
- n = number of data points used to fit the regression line

$n - 2$ is the divisor in Equation 11-6

Notice that in Equation 11-6, the sum of the squared deviations is divided by $n - 2$ and not by n. This happens because we have lost 2 degrees of freedom in estimating the regression line. We can reason that since the values of a and b were obtained from a sample of data points, we lose 2 degrees of freedom when we use these points to estimate the regression line.

Now let's refer again to our earlier example of the Sanitation Department director who related the age of his trucks to the amount of annual repairs. We found the estimating equation in that situation to be:

$$\hat{Y} = 3.75 + .75X$$

where X is the age of the truck and $\hat{Y}$ is the estimated amount of annual repairs (in hundreds of dollars).

Calculating the standard error of estimate

To calculate s_e for this problem, we must first determine the value of $\Sigma(Y - \hat{Y})^2$; that is, the numerator of Equation 11-6. We have done this in Table 11-11, using $(3.75 + .75X)$ for $\hat{Y}$ wherever it was necessary. Since

TABLE 11-11 Calculating the numerator of the fraction in Equation 11-6

X (1)	Y (2)	$\hat{Y}$ (THAT IS, $3.75 + .75X$) (3)	INDIVIDUAL ERROR $(Y - \hat{Y})$ (2) − (3)	$(Y - \hat{Y})^2$ $[(2) - (3)]^2$
5	7	3.75 + (.75)(5)	7 − 7.5 = −.5	.25
3	7	3.75 + (.75)(3)	7 − 6.0 = 1.0	1.00
3	6	3.75 + (.75)(3)	6 − 6.0 = 0.0	.00
1	4	3.75 + (.75)(1)	4 − 4.5 = −.5	.25
				$\Sigma(Y - \hat{Y})^2 = 1.50$ ← **sum of squared errors**

$\Sigma(Y - \hat{Y})^2$ is equal to 1.50, we can now use Equation 11-6 to find the standard error of estimate:

$$s_e = \sqrt{\frac{\Sigma(Y - \hat{Y})^2}{n - 2}} \qquad \textbf{[11-6]}$$

$$= \sqrt{\frac{1.50}{4 - 2}}$$

$$= \sqrt{\frac{1.50}{2}}$$

$$= \sqrt{.75}$$

$$= .866 \leftarrow \text{standard error of estimate of \$86.60}$$

Using a Short-Cut Method to Calculate the Standard Error of Estimate

To use Equation 11-6, we must do the tedious series of calculations outlined in Table 11-11. For every value of Y, we must compute the corresponding value of $\hat{Y}$. Then we must substitute these values into the expression $\Sigma(Y - \hat{Y})^2$.

Fortunately, we can eliminate some of the steps in this task by using the short cut provided by Equation 11-7; that is:

A quicker way to calculate s_e

$$s_e = \sqrt{\frac{\Sigma Y^2 - a\Sigma Y - b\Sigma XY}{n - 2}} \qquad \textbf{[11-7]}$$

where:

- X = values of the independent variable
- Y = values of the dependent variable
- a = Y-intercept from Equation 11-5
- b = slope of the estimating equation from Equation 11-4
- n = number of data points

This equation is a short cut because, when we first organized the data in this problem so that we could calculate the slope and the Y-intercept (Table

TABLE 11-12 Calculation of inputs for Equation 11-7

TRUCKS $n = 4$ (1)	AGE X (2)	REPAIR EXPENSE Y (3)	XY (2) × (3)	X^2 $(2)^2$	Y^2 $(3)^2$
101	5	7	35	25	49
102	3	7	21	9	49
103	3	6	18	9	36
104	1	4	4	1	16
	$\Sigma X =$ **12**	$\Sigma Y =$ **24**	$\Sigma XY =$ **78**	$\Sigma X^2 =$ **44**	$\Sigma Y^2 =$ **150**

11-7), we determined every value we will need for Equation 11-7 except one—the value of ΣY^2. Table 11-12 is a repeat of Table 11-7 with the Y^2 column added.

Now we can refer to Table 11-12 and our previous calculations of a and b in order to calculate s_e using the short-cut method:

$$s_e = \sqrt{\frac{\Sigma Y^2 - a\Sigma Y - b\Sigma XY}{n-2}} \quad \textbf{[11-7]}$$

$$= \sqrt{\frac{150 - (3.75)(24) - (.75)(78)}{4-2}}$$

$$= \sqrt{\frac{150 - 90 - 58.5}{2}}$$

$$= \sqrt{\frac{1.5}{2}}$$

$$= \sqrt{.75}$$

$$= .866 \leftarrow \text{standard error of \$86.60}$$

This is the same result as the one we obtained using Equation 11-6, but think of how many steps we saved!

Interpreting the Standard Error of Estimate

Interpreting and using the standard error of estimate

As was true of the standard deviation, the larger the standard error of estimate, the greater the scattering (or dispersion) of points around the regression line. Conversely, if $s_e = 0$, we expect the estimating equation to be a "perfect" estimator of the dependent variable. In that case, all the data points should lie directly on the regression line, and no points would be scattered around it.

Using s_e to form bounds around the regression line

We shall use the standard error of estimate as a tool in the same way that we can use the standard deviation. That is to say, assuming that the observed points are normally distributed around the regression line, we can expect to find 68 percent of the points within $\pm 1s_e$ (or plus and minus 1 standard error of estimate), 95.5 percent of the points within $\pm 2s_e$, and 99.7 percent of the points within $\pm 3s_e$. Figure 11-12 illustrates these "bounds" around the regression line. Another thing to notice in Fig. 11-12 is

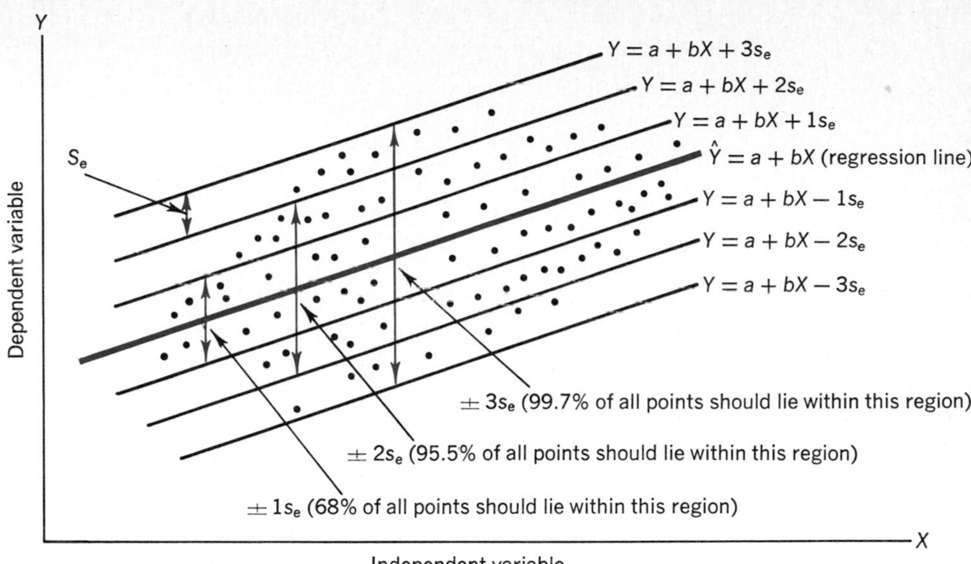

FIGURE 11-12 $\pm 1s_e$, $\pm 2s_e$, and $\pm 3s_e$ bounds around the regression line

that the standard error of estimate is measured along the Y-axis, rather than perpendicularly from the regression line.

Assumptions we make in use of s_e

At this point, we should state the assumptions we are making, because shortly, we shall make some probability statements based on these assumptions. Specifically, we have assumed that:

1. The observed values for Y are normally distributed around each estimated value of $\hat{Y}$.
2. The variance of the distributions around each possible value of $\hat{Y}$ is the same.

If this second assumption were not true, then the standard error at one point on the regression line could differ from the standard error at another point on the line.

Approximate Prediction Intervals

Using s_e to generate prediction intervals

One way to view the standard error of estimate is to think of it as the statistical tool we can use to make a probability statement about the interval around an estimated value of $\hat{Y}$, within which the actual value of Y lies. We can see, for instance, in Fig. 11-12 that we can be 95.5 percent certain that the actual value of Y will lie within 2 standard errors of the estimated value of $\hat{Y}$. We call these intervals around the estimated $\hat{Y}$ *approximate prediction intervals.* They serve the same function as the confidence intervals did in Chapter 8.

Now, applying the concept of approximate prediction intervals to the Sanitation Department director's repair expenses, we know that the estimating equation used to predict the annual repair expense is:

$$\hat{Y} = 3.75 + .75X$$

Applying prediction intervals

And we know that if the department has a 4-year-old truck, we predict it will have an annual repair expense of \$675:

$$\begin{aligned}\hat{Y} &= 3.75 + .75(4)\\ &= 3.75 + 3.00\\ &= 6.75 \leftarrow \text{expected annual repair expense of \$675}\end{aligned}$$

One standard error prediction interval

Finally, you will recall that we calculated the standard error of estimate to be $s_e = .866$, (\$86.60). We can now combine these two pieces of information and say that we are roughly 68 percent confident that the actual repair expense will be within ± 1 standard error of estimate from $\hat{Y}$. We can calculate the upper and lower limits of this prediction interval as follows:

$$\begin{aligned}\hat{Y} + 1s_e &= \$675 + (1)(\$86.60)\\ &= \$761.60 \leftarrow \text{upper limit of prediction interval}\end{aligned}$$

and:

$$\begin{aligned}\hat{Y} - 1s_e &= \$675 - (1)(\$86.60)\\ &= \$588.40 \leftarrow \text{lower limit of prediction interval}\end{aligned}$$

Two standard error prediction intervals

If, instead, we say that we are roughly 95.5 percent confident that the actual repair expense will be within ± 2 standard errors of estimate from $\hat{Y}$, we would calculate the limits of this new prediction interval like this:

$$\begin{aligned}\hat{Y} + 2s_e &= \$675 + (2)(\$86.60)\\ &= \$848.20 \leftarrow \text{upper limit}\end{aligned}$$

and:

$$\begin{aligned}\hat{Y} - 2s_e &= \$675 - (2)(\$86.60)\\ &= \$501.80 \leftarrow \text{lower limit}\end{aligned}$$

n is too small to use the normal distribution

Keep in mind that statisticians apply prediction intervals based on the normal distribution (68 percent for $1s_e$, 95.5 percent for $2s_e$, and 99.7 percent for $3s_e$) *only* to large samples; that is, where $n > 30$. In this problem, our sample size is too small ($n = 4$). Thus, *our conclusions are inaccurate*. But the method we have used nevertheless demonstrates the principle involved in prediction intervals.

Using the *t* distribution for prediction intervals

If we wish to avoid the inaccuracies caused by the size of the sample, we need to use the *t* distribution. Recall that the *t* distribution is appropriate when *n* is less than 30 and the population standard deviation is unknown. We meet both these conditions, since $n = 4$, and s_e is an estimate rather than the known population standard deviation.

An example using the *t* distribution to calculate prediction intervals

Now suppose the Sanitation Department director wants to be roughly 90 percent certain that the annual truck-repair expense will lie within the prediction interval. How should we calculate this interval? Since the *t* distribution table focuses on the probability that the parameter we are estimating will lie *outside* the prediction interval, we need to look in Appendix Table 2 under the 100% − 90% = 10% value column. Once we locate that column, we look for the row representing 2 degrees of freedom; since $n = 4$ and since we know we lose 2 degrees of freedom (in estimating the values of a and b), then $n - 2 = 2$. Here we find the appropriate t value to be 2.920.

Now we can make a more accurate calculation of our prediction interval limits, as follows:

$$\begin{aligned} \hat{Y} + t(s_e) &= \$675 + (2.920)(\$86.60) \\ &= \$675 + \$252.87 \\ &= \$927.87 \leftarrow \text{upper limit} \end{aligned}$$

and:

$$\begin{aligned} \hat{Y} - t(s_e) &= \$675 - (2.920)(\$86.60) \\ &= \$675 - \$252.87 \\ &= \$422.13 \leftarrow \text{lower limit} \end{aligned}$$

So the director can be 90 percent certain that the annual repair expense on a 4-year-old truck will lie between \$422.13 and \$927.87.

We stress again that the prediction intervals above are only *approximate*. In fact, statisticians can calculate the exact standard error for the prediction, s_p, using this formula:

$$s_p = s_e \sqrt{1 + \frac{1}{n} + \frac{(\bar{X} - X_0)^2}{\Sigma X^2 - n\bar{X}^2}}$$

where X_0 = the specific value of X at which we want to predict the value of Y.

Notice that if we use this formula, s_p will be different for each value of X_0. In particular, if X_0 is *far* from $\bar{X}$, then s_p will be large, because $(\bar{X} - X_0)^2$ will be large. If, on the other hand, X_0 is close to X, and n is moderately large (greater than 10), then s_p will be close to s_e. This happens because $1/n$ will be small and $(\bar{X} - X_0)^2$ will be small. Therefore, the value under the square-root sign will be close to 1, the square root will be even closer to 1, and s_e will be very close to s_p. This justifies our use of s_e to compute approximate prediction intervals.

EXERCISES

11-13 For the following set of data:

a) Plot the scatter diagram.
b) Develop the estimating equation that best describes the data.
c) Predict Y for $X = 4$, 9, and 12.

X	7	10	8	5	11	3	7	11	12	6
Y	2.0	3.0	2.4	1.8	3.2	1.5	2.1	3.8	4.0	2.2

11-14 Using the data in the table below:

a) Plot the scatter diagram.
b) Develop the estimating equation that best describes the data.
c) Predict Y for $X = 12$, 14, and 18.

X	20	11	15	10	17	19
Y	5	15	14	17	8	9

11-15 Given the following set of data:

a) Find the best-fitting line.
b) Compute the standard error of estimate.
c) Find a prediction interval (with a 95 percent confidence level) for the dependent variable given that X is 44.

X	56	48	42	58	40	39	50
Y	9.5	7.5	7.0	9.5	6.2	6.6	8.7

11-16 Richard Specker, the sales manager for a large appliance retailer, is measuring his radio advertising campaign featuring major appliances (washers, dryers, and dishwashers). Over the last 7 weeks he has purchased varying amounts of radio time (line X, in minutes). Line Y displays the number of major appliances sold that week.

X (minutes)	25	18	32	21	35	28	30
Y	16	11	20	15	26	32	20

a) Find the best-fitting line.
b) Calculate the standard error of estimate.
c) Find a prediction level (with 90 percent confidence level) for Y when X is 27.

11-17 The production manager for the Continental Television Company is conducting a study examining the relationship between the absentee rate and number of defects produced. She sampled production data for 12 weeks and found the following average daily absentee rate (line X) and corresponding number of defects produced during that week (line Y).

X	7.3	6.4	6.2	5.5	6.4	4.7	5.8	7.9	6.7	9.6	10.3	7.2
Y	22	17	9	8	12	5	7	19	13	29	33	18

a) Develop the estimating equation that best describes these data.
b) Calculate the standard error of estimate for this relationship.
c) Find a prediction interval (with 95 percent confidence level) for the number of defects produced in a week with an average daily absentee rate of 6.0.

11-18 A study by the Atlanta, Georgia, Department of Transportation on the effect of bus-ticket prices upon the number of passengers produced the following results:

Ticket price (cents)	15	20	25	30	40	50
Passengers per 100 miles	440	430	450	370	340	370

a) Plot these data.
b) Develop the estimating equation that best describes these data.
c) Predict the number of passengers per mile if the ticket price were 35 cents.

11-19 William C. Andrews, an organizational-behavior consultant for Victory Motorcycles, has designed a test to show the company's foremen the dangers of oversupervising their workers. A worker from the assembly line is given a series of complicated tasks to perform. During the worker's performance, a foreman constantly interrupts the worker to assist him in completing the tasks. The worker, upon completion of the tasks, is then given a psychological test designed to measure the worker's hostility toward authority (a high score equals low hostility). Eight different workers were assigned the tasks and then interrupted for the purpose of instructional assistance varying numbers of times (line *X*). Their corresponding scores on the hostility test are revealed in line *Y*.

X (number of times worker interrupted)	5	10	10	15	15	20	20	25
Y (worker's score on hostility test)	58	41	45	27	26	12	16	3

a) Plot these data.
b) Develop the equation that best describes the relationship between number of times interrupted and test score.
c) Predict the expected test score if the worker is interrupted 18 times.

11-20 The editor-in-chief of a major metropolitan newspaper has been trying to convince the paper's owner to improve the working conditions in the pressroom. He is convinced that the noise level when the presses are running creates unhealthy levels of tension and anxiety. He recently had a psychologist conduct a test during which pressmen were placed in rooms with varying levels of noise and then given a test to measure mood and anxiety levels. The following table shows the index of their degree of arousal or nervousness and the level of noise to which they were exposed. (5.0 is low and 10.0 is high.)

Noise level	7.0	6.5	5.5	6.0	8.0	8.5	6.0	6.5
Degree of arousal	23	38	45	36	16	18	39	41

a) Plot these data.
b) Develop an estimating equation that describes these data.
c) Predict the degree of arousal that we might expect when the noise level is 7.25.

11-21 The production supervisor of the Packerd Container Company is convinced of the need to assign strenuous jobs according to age. He randomly selected 10 workers and measured the amount of time they were able to maintain a strenuous loading activity.

Age	42	27	36	25	22	39	57	19	33	30
Strenuous minutes	2	7	5	9	10	4	4	8	6	5

a) Plot these data.
b) Develop the equation that best describes the relationship between age and physical stamina.
c) How long might a 30-year-old man be expected to maintain strenuous physical activity of the sort in this task?

11-22 The city council of Bowie, Maryland, has gathered data on the number of minor traffic accidents and the number of youth soccer games that occur in town over a weekend.

X (soccer games)	25	45	10	15	20	30	40
Y (minor accidents)	6	9	4	3	8	7	10

a) Plot these data.
b) Develop the estimating equation that best describes these data.
c) Predict the number of minor traffic accidents that will occur on a weekend during which 35 soccer games take place in Bowie.
d) Calculate the standard error of estimate.

11-23 The sales manager at a men's clothing store is looking into the effect of the number of salesmen in the store each hour on the hourly dollar value of clothing sold. He has gathered the following data during 8 randomly chosen hours of observation.

X (salesmen)	1	2	3	1	4	2	3	1
Y (sales in \$)	50	40	75	150	275	120	150	70

a) Find the best-fitting line.
b) Calculate the standard error of estimate.
c) Develop an 80 percent approximate prediction interval for sales when 3 salesmen are on the floor.

11-24 Mel, the owner of Cheap Mel's Used Cars, is interested in the relationship between the prime interest rate at the beginning of a month and the number of used cars that he sells that month. He has collected 7 months' worth of data:

X (prime rate)	17	16	16	14	15	13	14
Y (cars sold)	250	150	200	100	130	110	160

a) Plot these data.
b) Develop the estimating equation that best fits the data.
c) Predict the number of used cars that Mel will sell if the prime interest rate is 14 at the beginning of a month.

11-3 CORRELATION ANALYSIS

What correlation analysis does

Correlation analysis is the statistical tool that we can use to describe *the degree to which one variable is linearly related to another.* Frequently, correlation analysis is used in conjunction with regression analysis to measure how well the regression line explains the variation of the dependent variable, Y. Correlation can also be used by itself, however, to measure the degree of association between two variables.

Two measures that describe correlation

Statisticians have developed two measures for describing the correlation between two variables: the *coefficient of determination* and the *coefficient of correlation*. Introducing these two measures of association is the purpose of this section.

The Coefficient of Determination

Developing the sample coefficient of determination

The coefficient of determination is the primary way we can measure the extent, or strength, of the association that exists between two variables, X and Y. Since we have used a sample of points to develop regression lines, we refer to this measure as the *sample coefficient of determination.*

The sample coefficient of determination is developed from the relationship between two kinds of variation: the variation of the Y values in a data set around:

1. The fitted regression line
2. Their own mean

The term *variation* in both these cases is used in its usual statistical sense to mean "the sum of a group of squared deviations." Using this definition, then, it is reasonable to express the variation of the Y values around the regression line with this equation:

$$\text{Variation of the } Y \text{ values around the regression line} = \Sigma(Y - \hat{Y})^2 \quad \textbf{[11-8]}$$

And the second variation, that of the Y values around their own mean, is determined by:

$$\text{Variation of the } Y \text{ values around their own mean} = \Sigma(Y - \overline{Y})^2 \quad \textbf{[11-9]}$$

One minus the ratio between these two variations is the sample coefficient of determination, which is symbolized r^2:

Sample coefficient of determination

$$r^2 = 1 - \frac{\Sigma(Y - \hat{Y})^2}{\Sigma(Y - \overline{Y})^2} \quad \textbf{[11-10]}$$

The next two sections will show you that r^2, as defined by Equation 11-10, is a measure of the degree of linear association between X and Y.

An Intuitive Interpretation of r^2

Consider the two extreme ways in which the variables X and Y can be related. In Table 11-13, every observed value of Y lies on the estimating line, as can be proven visually by Fig. 11-13. This is *perfect correlation.*

TABLE 11-13 Illustration of perfect correlation between two variables, X and Y

DATA POINT	VALUE OF X	VALUE OF Y
1st	1	4
2nd	2	8
3rd	3	12
4th	4	16
5th	5	20
6th	6	24
7th	7	28
8th	8	32
		$\Sigma Y =$ **144**
		$\overline{Y} = \frac{144}{8}$
		$= 18$ ← mean of the values of Y

Estimating equation appropriate for perfect correlation example

The estimating equation appropriate for these data is easy to determine. Since the regression line passes through the origin, we know that the Y-intercept is zero; and since Y increases by 4 every time X increases by 1, the slope must equal 4. Thus, the regression line is:

$$\hat{Y} = 4X$$

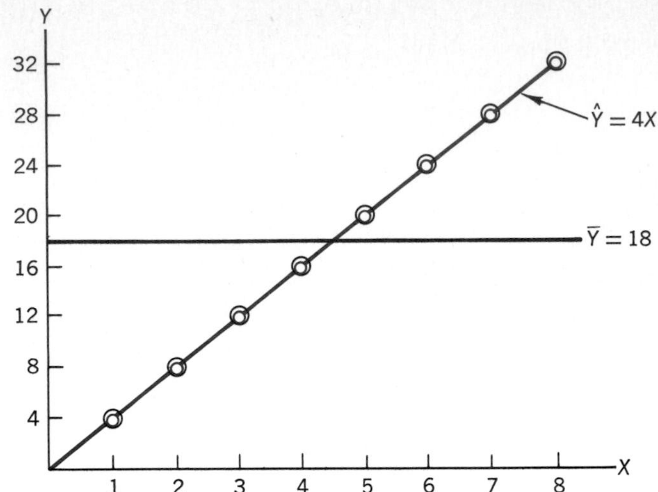

FIGURE 11-13 Perfect correlation between X and Y: Every data point lies on the regression line

Now, to determine the sample coefficient of determination for the regression line in Fig. 11-13, we first calculate the numerator of the fraction in Equation 11-10:

$$\begin{aligned}\text{Variation of the } Y \text{ values around the regression line} &= \Sigma(Y-\hat{Y})^2 \quad \textbf{[11-8]}\\ &= \Sigma(0)^2\\ &= 0\end{aligned}$$

Since every Y value is on the regression line, the difference between Y and $\hat{Y}$ is zero in each case.

Then we can find the denominator of the fraction:

Determining sample coefficient of determination for perfect correlation example

$$\begin{aligned}\text{Variation of the } Y \text{ values around their own mean} &= \Sigma(Y-\overline{Y})^2 \quad \textbf{[11-9]}\\ &= (4-18)^2 = (-14)^2 = 196\\ &+ (8-18)^2 = (-10)^2 = 100\\ &+ (12-18)^2 = (-6)^2 = 36\\ &+ (16-18)^2 = (-2)^2 = 4\\ &+ (20-18)^2 = (2)^2 = 4\\ &+ (24-18)^2 = (6)^2 = 36\\ &+ (28-18)^2 = (10)^2 = 100\\ &+ (32-18)^2 = (14)^2 = \underline{196}\\ &\qquad\qquad \mathbf{672} \leftarrow \Sigma(Y-\overline{Y})^2\end{aligned}$$

With these values to substitute into Equation 11-10, we can find that the sample coefficient is equal to +1:

$$r^2 = 1 - \frac{\Sigma(Y - \hat{Y})^2}{\Sigma(Y - \bar{Y})^2} \quad [11\text{-}10]$$

$$= 1 - \frac{0}{672}$$

$$= 1 - 0$$

$$= 1 \leftarrow \text{sample coefficient of determination when there is perfect correlation}$$

The value of r^2 is equal to +1, then, whenever the regression line is a perfect estimator.

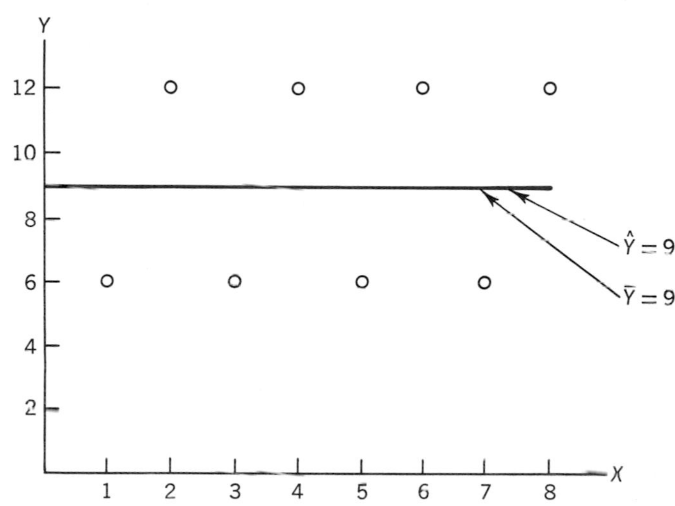

FIGURE 11-14 Zero correlation between X and Y: Same values of Y appear for different values of X

A second extreme way in which the variables X and Y can be related is that the points could lie at equal distances on both sides of a horizontal regression line, as is pictured in Fig. 11-14. The data set here consists of eight points, all of which have been recorded in Table 11-14.

TABLE 11-14 Illustration of zero correlation between two variables, X and Y

DATA POINT	VALUE OF X	VALUE OF Y
1st	1	6
2nd	2	12
3rd	3	6
4th	4	12
5th	5	6
6th	6	12
7th	7	6
8th	8	12
		$\Sigma Y = \mathbf{72}$
		$\bar{Y} = \frac{72}{8}$
		$= 9 \leftarrow$ mean of the values of Y

Determining sample coefficient of determination for zero correlation

From Fig. 11-14, we can see that the least-squares regression line appropriate for these data is of the form $\hat{Y} = 9$. The slope of the line is *zero*, because the same values of Y appear for all the different values of X. Both the Y-intercept and the mean of the Y values are equal to 9.

Now we'll compute the two variations using Equations 11-8 and 11-9, so that we can determine the sample coefficient of determination for this regression line. First, the variation of the Y values around the estimating line $\hat{Y} = 9$:

$$\begin{aligned}
\text{Variation of the } Y \text{ values around the regression line} &= \Sigma(Y - \hat{Y})^2 \qquad \textbf{[11-8]} \\
&= (6-9)^2 = (-3)^2 = 9 \\
&+ (12-9)^2 = (3)^2 = 9 \\
&+ (6-9)^2 = (-3)^2 = 9 \\
&+ (12-9)^2 = (3)^2 = 9 \\
&+ (6-9)^2 = (-3)^2 = 9 \\
&+ (12-9)^2 = (3)^2 = 9 \\
&+ (6-9)^2 = (-3)^2 = 9 \\
&+ (12-9)^2 = (3)^2 = \underline{9} \\
&\qquad\qquad\qquad\quad \mathbf{72} \leftarrow \Sigma(Y - \hat{Y})^2
\end{aligned}$$

Then, the variation of the Y values around the mean of 9:

$$\begin{aligned}
\text{Variation of the } Y \text{ values around their own mean} &= \Sigma(Y - \overline{Y})^2 \qquad \textbf{[11-9]} \\
&= (6-9)^2 = (-3)^2 = 9 \\
&+ (12-9)^2 = (3)^2 = 9 \\
&+ (6-9)^2 = (-3)^2 = 9 \\
&+ (12-9)^2 = (3)^2 = 9 \\
&+ (6-9)^2 = (-3)^2 = 9 \\
&+ (12-9)^2 = (3)^2 = 9 \\
&+ (6-9)^2 = (-3)^2 = 9 \\
&+ (12-9)^2 = (3)^2 = \underline{9} \\
&\qquad\qquad\qquad\quad \mathbf{72} \leftarrow \Sigma(Y - \overline{Y})^2
\end{aligned}$$

Substituting these two values into Equation 11-10, we see that the sample coefficient of determination is 0:

$$\begin{aligned}
r^2 &= 1 - \frac{\Sigma(Y - \hat{Y})^2}{\Sigma(Y - \overline{Y})^2} \qquad \textbf{[11-10]} \\
&= 1 - \frac{72}{72} \\
&= 1 - 1 \\
&= 0 \leftarrow \text{sample coefficient of determination when there is no correlation}
\end{aligned}$$

Thus, the value of r^2 is zero when there is no correlation.

Interpreting r^2 values

In the problems most decision makers encounter, r^2 will lie somewhere between these two extremes of 1 and 0. Keep in mind, however, that an r^2 close to 1 indicates a strong correlation between X and Y, while an r^2 near 0 means there is little correlation between these two variables.

One point that we must emphasize strongly is that r^2 measures only the strength of a linear relationship between two variables. For example, if we had a lot of X,Y points that all fell on the circumference of a circle but at randomly scattered places, clearly there would be a relationship among these points (they all lie on the same circle). But in this instance, if we computed r^2, it would turn out in fact to be close to zero, because the points do not have a *linear* relationship with each other.

Interpreting r^2 Another Way

Another way to interpret the sample coefficient of determination

Explained and unexplained deviation

Statisticians also interpret the sample coefficient of determination by looking at the *amount of the variation in Y that is explained by the regression line.* To understand this meaning of r^2, consider the regression line (shown in color) in Fig. 11-15. Here, we have singled out one observed value of Y, shown as the upper black circle. If we use the mean of the Y values, $\bar{Y}$, to estimate this black-circled value of Y, then the *total deviation* of this Y from its mean would be $(Y - \bar{Y})$. Notice that if we used the regression line to estimate this black-circled value of Y, we would get a better estimate. However, even though the regression line accounts for, or explains, $(\hat{Y} - \bar{Y})$ of the total deviation, the remaining portion of the total deviation, $(Y - \hat{Y})$, is still *unexplained.*

But consider a whole set of observed Y values instead of only one value. The total variation—that is, the sum of the squared total deviations —of these points from their mean would be:

$$\Sigma(Y - \bar{Y})^2 \qquad \textbf{[11-9]}$$

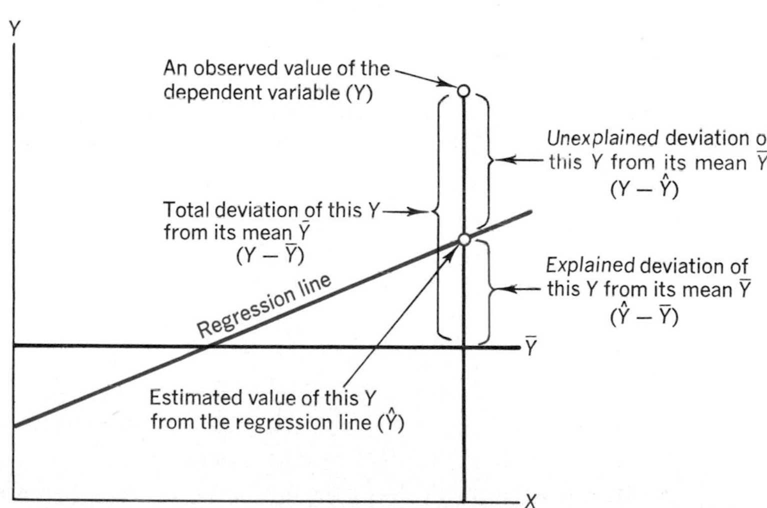

FIGURE 11-15 Total deviation, explained deviation, and unexplained deviation for *one* observed value of Y

Explained and unexplained variation

and the *explained* portion of the total variation, or the sum of the squared explained deviations of these points from their mean, would be:

$$\Sigma(\hat{Y} - \bar{Y})^2$$

The *unexplained* portion of the total variation (the sum of the squared unexplained deviations) of these points from the regression line would be:

$$\Sigma(Y - \hat{Y})^2 \quad \textbf{[11-8]}$$

If we want to express the fraction of the total variation that remains *unexplained,* we would divide the unexplained variation, $\Sigma(Y - \hat{Y})^2$, by the total variation, $\Sigma(Y - \bar{Y})^2$, as follows:

$$\frac{\Sigma(Y - \hat{Y})^2}{\Sigma(Y - \bar{Y})^2} \leftarrow \text{fraction of the total variation that is unexplained}$$

and finally, if we subtract the fraction of the total variation that remains unexplained from 1, we will have the formula for finding that fraction of the total variation of Y that *is* explained by the regression line. That formula is:

$$r^2 = 1 - \frac{\Sigma(Y - \hat{Y})^2}{\Sigma(Y - \bar{Y})^2} \quad \textbf{[11-10]}$$

the same equation that we have previously used to calculate r^2. It is in this sense, then, that r^2 measures how well X explains Y; that is, the degree of association between X and Y.

Short-cut method to calculate r^2

One final word about calculating r^2. To obtain r^2 using Equations 11-8, 11-9, and 11-10 requires a series of tedious calculations. To bypass these calculations, statisticians have developed a short-cut version, using values we would have determined already in the regression analysis. The formula is:

r^2 calculated by short-cut method →

$$r^2 = \frac{a\Sigma Y + b\Sigma XY - n\bar{Y}^2}{\Sigma Y^2 - n\bar{Y}^2} \quad \textbf{[11-11]}$$

where:

- r^2 = sample coefficient of determination
- a = Y-intercept
- b = slope of the best-fitting estimating line
- n = number of data points
- X = values of the independent variable
- Y = values of the dependent variable
- $\bar{Y}$ = mean of the observed values of the dependent variable

TABLE 11-15 Calculations of inputs for Equation 11-11

YEAR $n = 6$ (1)	RESEARCH AND DEVELOPMENT EXPENSE X (2)	ANNUAL PROFIT Y (3)	XY (2) × (3)	X^2 $(2)^2$	Y^2 $(3)^2$
1983	5	31	155	25	961
1982	11	40	440	121	1,600
1981	4	30	120	16	900
1980	5	34	170	25	1,156
1979	3	25	75	9	625
1978	2	20	40	4	400
	$\Sigma X = \mathbf{30}$	$\Sigma Y = \mathbf{180}$	$\Sigma XY = \mathbf{1{,}000}$	$\Sigma X^2 = \mathbf{200}$	$\Sigma Y^2 = \mathbf{5{,}642}$
		$\bar{Y} = \frac{180}{6}$			
		$= 30$ ← mean of the values of the dependent variable			

Applying the short-cut method

To see why this formula is a short cut, apply it to our earlier regression relating research and development expenditures to profits. In Table 11-15, we have repeated the columns from Table 11-9, adding a Y^2 column. Recall that when we found the values for a and b, the regression line for this problem was described by:

$$\hat{Y} = 20 + 2X$$

Using this line and the information in Table 11-15, we can solve for r^2 as follows:

$$r^2 = \frac{a\Sigma Y + b\Sigma XY - n\bar{Y}^2}{\Sigma Y^2 - n\bar{Y}^2} \quad \textbf{[11-11]}$$

$$= \frac{(20)(180) + (2)(1{,}000) - (6)(30)^2}{5{,}642 - (6)(30)^2}$$

$$= \frac{3{,}600 + 2{,}000 - 5{,}400}{5{,}642 - 5{,}400}$$

$$= \frac{200}{242}$$

$$= .826 \leftarrow \text{sample coefficient of determination}$$

Interpreting r^2

Thus, we can conclude that the variation in the research and development expenditures (the independent variable X) explains 82.6 percent of the variation in the annual profits (the dependent variable Y).

The Coefficient of Correlation

Sample coefficient of correlation

The coefficient of correlation is the second measure that we can use to describe how well one variable is explained by another. When we are dealing with samples, the *sample coefficient of correlation* is denoted by r and is the square root of the sample coefficient of determination:

$$r = \sqrt{r^2} \tag{11-12}$$

When the slope of the estimating equation is positive, r is the positive square root, but if b is negative, r is the negative square root. Thus, **the sign of r indicates the direction of the relationship between the two variables X and Y.** If an inverse relationship exists—that is, if Y decreases as X increases—then r will fall between 0 and -1. Likewise, if there is a direct relationship (if Y increases as X increases), then r will be a value within the range of 0 to 1. Figure 11-16 illustrates these various characteristics of r.

Interpreting r

The coefficient of correlation is more difficult to interpret than r^2. What does $r = .9$ mean? To answer that question, we must remember that $r = .9$ is the same as $r^2 = .81$. The latter tells us that 81 percent of the variation in Y is explained by the regression line. So we see that r is nothing more than the square root of r^2, and we cannot interpret its meaning directly.

Calculating r for the research and development problem

Now let's find the coefficient of correlation for our problem relating research and development expenditures and annual profits. Since, in the previous section, we found that the sample coefficient of determination is $r^2 = .826$, we can substitute this value into Equation 11-12 and find that:

$$\begin{aligned} r &= \sqrt{r^2} \qquad \textbf{[11-12]} \\ &= \sqrt{.826} \\ &= .909 \leftarrow \text{sample coefficient of correlation} \end{aligned}$$

The relation between the two variables is direct and the slope is positive; therefore, the sign for r is positive.

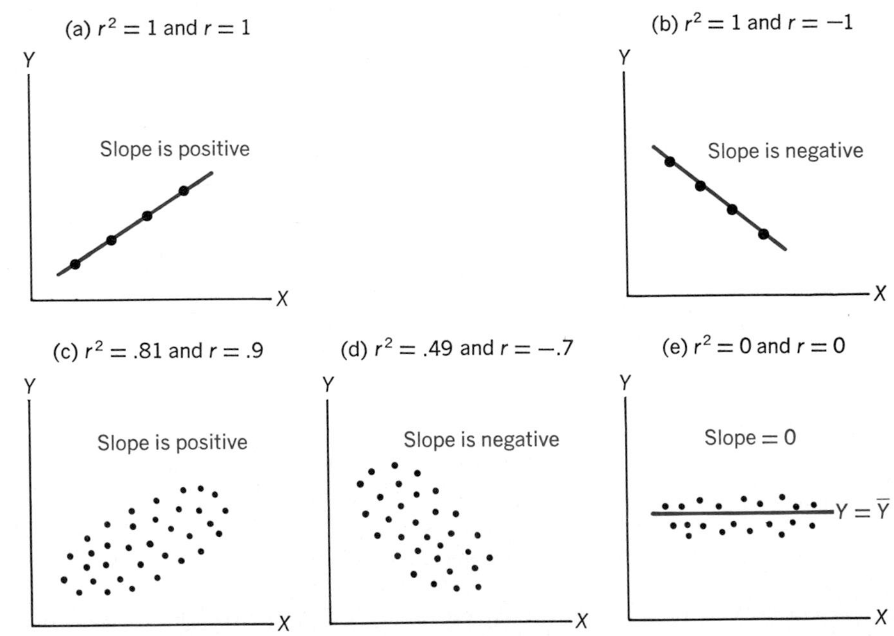

FIGURE 11-16 Various characteristics of r, the sample coefficient of correlation

EXERCISES

In the following exercises, calculate the sample coefficient of determination and the sample coefficient of correlation for the problems specified.

11-25 Problem 11-17

11-26 Problem 11-18

11-27 Problem 11-19

11-28 Problem 11-20

11-29 Problem 11-21

11-30 What type of correlation (positive, negative, or zero) should we expect from these variables?

a) Ability of supervisors and output of their subordinates
b) Age at first full-time job and number of years of education
c) Weight and blood pressure
d) College grade-point average and student's height

11-31 The Environmental Protection Agency (EPA) is conducting a study of the relationship between age and systolic blood pressure. A small subset of the huge data base is given below:

X (age in years)	30	55	60	45	40	65	50	75
Y (blood pressure in mm/Hg)	120	160	170	180	130	140	150	180

a) Develop the estimating equation that best fits the data.
b) Calculate the sample coefficient of determination and the sample coefficient of correlation.

11-32 Zippy Cola is studying the effect of its latest advertising campaign. People chosen at random were called and asked how many cans of Zippy Cola they had bought in the past week and how many Zippy Cola advertisements they had either read or seen in the past week.

X (number of ads)	5	10	4	0	2	7	3	6
Y (cans purchased)	10	12	5	4	1	3	4	8

a) Develop the estimating equation that best fits the data.
b) Calculate the sample coefficient of determination and the sample coefficient of correlation.

11-4 MAKING INFERENCES ABOUT POPULATION PARAMETERS

Relationship of sample regression line and population regression line

So far, we have used regression and correlation analyses to relate two variables on the basis of sample information. But data from a sample represent only part of the total population. Because of this, we may think of our estimated sample regression line as an estimate of a true, but unknown population regression line of the form:

$$Y = A + BX \quad [11\text{-}13]$$

Recall our discussion of the Sanitation Department director who tried to use the age of a truck to explain the annual repair expense on it. That expense will probably consist of two parts:

1. Regular maintenance that does not depend on the age of the truck: tune-ups, oil changes, and lubrication. This expense is captured in the intercept term A in Equation 11-13 on page 527.
2. Expenses for repairs due to aging: relining brakes, engine and transmission overhauls, and painting. Such expenses will tend to increase with the age of the truck, and they are captured in the BX term of the population regression line $Y = A + BX$ in Equation 11-13 on page 527.

Why data points do not lie exactly on the regression line

Of course, all the brakes of all the trucks will not wear out at the same time, and some of the trucks will run years without engine overhauls. Because of this, the individual data points will probably not lie exactly on the population regression line. Some will be above it; some will fall below it. So, instead of satisfying:

$$Y = A + BX \tag{11-13}$$

the individual data points will satisfy the formula:

$$Y = A + BX + e \tag{11-13a}$$

Random disturbance e and its behavior

where e is a random disturbance from the population regression line. On the average, e equals zero, because disturbances above the population regression line are canceled out by disturbances below the line. We can denote the standard deviation of these individual disturbances by σ_e. The standard error of estimate s_e, then, is an estimate of σ_e, the standard deviation of the disturbances.

Let us look more carefully at Equations 11-13 and 11-13a. Equation 11-13a expresses the individual values of Y (in this case, annual repair expense) in terms of (1) the individual values of X (the age of the truck), and (2) the random disturbance (e). Since disturbances above the population regression line are canceled out by those below the line, we know that the expected value of e is zero, and we see that if we had several trucks of the same age, X, we would expect the average annual repair expense on these trucks to be $Y = A + BX$. This shows us that the population regression line (Equation 11-13) gives the mean value of Y associated with each value of X.

Making inferences about B from b

Since our *sample* regression line, $\hat{Y} = a + bX$ (Equation 11-3), estimates the *population* regression line, $Y = A + BX$ (Equation 11-13), we should be able to use it to make inferences about the population regression line. In this section then, we shall make inferences about the slope B of the "true" regression equation (the one for the entire population) that are based upon the slope b of the regression equation estimated from a sample of values.

Slope of the Population Regression Line

Difference between true regression equation and one estimated from sample observations

The regression line is derived from a sample and not from the entire population. As a result, we cannot expect the true regression equation, $Y = A + BX$ (the one for the entire population), to be exactly the same as the quation estimated from the sample observations, or $\hat{Y} = a + bX$. Even so, we can use the value of b, the slope we calculate from a sample, to test hypotheses about the value of the B, the slope of the regression line for the entire population.

Testing a hypothesis about B

The procedure for testing a hypothesis about B is similar to procedures discussed in Chapter 9, on hypothesis testing. To understand this process, return to the problem that related annual expenditures for research and development to profits. On page 507, we pointed out that $b = 2$. The first step is to find some value for B to compare with $b = 2$.

Suppose that over an extended past period of time, the slope of the relationship between X and Y was 2.1. To test if this were still the case, we could define the hypotheses as:

H_0: $B = 2.1$ ← null hypothesis
H_1: B is not equal to 2.1 ← alternative hypothesis

In effect, then, we are testing to learn whether current data indicate that B has changed from its historical value of 2.1.

Standard error of the regression coefficient

To find the test statistic for B, it is necessary first to find the *standard error of the regression coefficient*. Here, the regression coefficient we are working with is b, so the standard error of this coefficient is denoted s_b. Equation 11-14 presents the mathematical formula for s_b.

Standard error of the regression coefficient

$$s_b = \frac{s_e}{\sqrt{\Sigma X^2 - n\bar{X}^2}} \quad \textbf{[11-14]}$$

where:

- s_b = standard error of the regression coefficient
- s_e = standard error of estimate
- X = values of the independent variable
- $\bar{X}$ = mean of the values of the independent variable
- n = number of data points

Finding upper and lower limits of the acceptance region for our hypothesis test

Once we have calculated s_b, we can use the t distribution with $n - 2$ degrees of freedom and the following equation to calculate the upper and lower limits of the acceptance region:

$$\left.\begin{aligned}\text{Upper limit of acceptance region} &= B + t(s_b)\\ \text{Lower limit of acceptance region} &= B - t(s_b)\end{aligned}\right\} \quad \textbf{[11-15]}$$

where:

- t = appropriate t value (with $n - 2$ degrees of freedom) for the significance level of the test
- B = actual slope hypothesized for the population
- s_b = standard error of the regression coefficient

Of course, for a one-tailed test, you would calculate only an upper or lower limit as appropriate.

A glance at Table 11-15 on page 525 enables us to calculate the values of ΣX^2 and $n\bar{X}^2$. To obtain s_e, we can take the short-cut method, as follows:

Calculating s_e

$$s_e = \sqrt{\frac{\Sigma Y^2 - a\Sigma Y - b\Sigma XY}{n-2}} \quad \textbf{[11-7]}$$

$$= \sqrt{\frac{5{,}642 - (20)(180) - (2)(1{,}000)}{6-2}}$$

$$= \sqrt{\frac{5{,}642 - 3{,}600 - 2{,}000}{4}}$$

$$= \sqrt{\frac{42}{4}}$$

$$= \sqrt{10.5}$$

$$= 3.24 \leftarrow \text{standard error of estimate}$$

Now we can determine the standard error of the regression coefficient:

Calculating s_b

$$s_b = \frac{s_e}{\sqrt{\Sigma X^2 - n\bar{X}^2}} \quad \textbf{[11-14]}$$

$$= \frac{3.24}{\sqrt{200 - (6)(5)^2}}$$

$$= \frac{3.24}{\sqrt{50}}$$

$$= \frac{3.24}{7.07}$$

$$= .46 \leftarrow \text{standard error of the regression coefficient}$$

Conducting the hypothesis test

Suppose we have reason to test our hypothesis at the 10 percent level of significance. Since we have six observations in our sample data, we know that we have $n - 2$ or $6 - 2 = 4$ degrees of freedom. We look in Appendix Table 2 under the 10 percent column and come down until we find the 4-degrees-of-freedom row. There, we see that the appropriate t value is 2.132. Since we are concerned whether b (the slope of the sample regression line) is significantly *different* from B (the hypothesized slope of the population regression line), this is a two-tailed test, and the limits of the acceptance region are found using Equation 11-15:

$$B + t(s_b) = 2.1 + 2.132(0.46)$$
$$= 3.081 \leftarrow \text{upper limit of acceptance region}$$

$$B - t(s_b) = 2.1 - 2.132(0.46)$$
$$= 1.119 \leftarrow \text{lower limit of acceptance region}$$

The slope of our regression line (b) is 2.0, which is inside the acceptance region. Therefore, we accept the null hypothesis that B still equals 2.1. In other words, there is not enough difference between b and 2.1 for us to conclude that B has changed from its historical value. Because of this, we feel that each additional million dollars spent on research and development still increases annual profits by about $2.1 million, as it has in the past.

In addition to hypothesis testing, we can also construct a *confidence interval* for the value of B. In the same way that b is a point estimate of B, such confidence intervals are interval estimates of B. The problem we just completed, and for which we did a hypothesis test, will illustrate the process of constructing a confidence interval. There, we found that:

$$b = 2.0$$
$$s_b = 0.46$$
$$t = 2.132 \leftarrow \text{10\% level of significance and 4 degrees of freedom}$$

Confidence interval for B

With this information, we can calculate confidence intervals like this:

$$b + t(s_b) = 2 + (2.132)(.46)$$
$$= 2 + .981$$
$$= 2.981 \leftarrow \text{upper limit}$$

$$b - t(s_b) = 2 - (2.132)(.46)$$
$$= 2 - .981$$
$$= 1.019 \leftarrow \text{lower limit}$$

Interpreting the confidence interval

In this situation, then, we are 90 percent confident that the true value of B lies between 1.019 and 2.981; that is, each additional million dollars spent on research and development increases annual profits by some amount between $1.02 million and $2.98 million.

EXERCISES

11-33 The vice-president of marketing for the Smooth Peanut Butter Company is conducting a study on the success of his company's trade promotions. Over the last 3 years, the company's twice-a-year 10 percent discount promotion has been run for varying numbers of days. He is currently examining the relationship between the amount of peanut butter sold during each promotion and the number of days the promotion ran. From the data below, test the hypothesis that the population slope is 1.2 against the alternative that it is not equal to that value.

X	9	17	20	19	20	23	(number of days promotion ran)
Y	23	35	29	33	43	32	(number of carloads of peanut butter sold during promotion)

11-34 In a regression problem with a sample of size 6, the slope was found to be .75 and the standard error of estimate 30.412. The quantity $(\Sigma X^2 - n\bar{X}^2) = 240{,}083.3$.
a) Find the standard error of the regression coefficient.
b) Construct a 90 percent confidence interval for the population slope.

11-35 A broker for a local investment firm has been studying the relationship between significant increases in the price of gold and his customers' requests to liquidate stocks. From a data set based on 12 observations, the sample slope was found to be 2.4. If the standard error of the regression coefficient is .15, is there reason to believe (at the .05 significance level) that the slope has changed from its past value of 2.8?

11-36 For a sample of size 10, the slope was found to be .265 and the standard error of the regression coefficient was .02. Is there reason to believe that the slope has changed from its past value of .30? Use the .01 significance level.

11-37 The research and development department for a major breakfast-cereal company has developed a new package design for one of its products. The researchers wonder if the colors of new and old lettering respond differently to light intensity. A consumer was tested for the distance at which he could read the product's name under different light intensities. From the following data, should the researchers conclude (at the .10 level of significance) that the slope of the relationship is significantly different from that of the old package, for which it is 2.8?

Light intensity	7.3	6.6	6.4	6.8	5.9
Reading distance (feet)	20	18	19	20	18

11-38 In 1969, a government health agency found that in a number of countries, the relationship between smokers and heart disease fatalities per 100,000 population had a slope of .08. A recent study of 12 countries produced a slope of .14 and a standard error of the regression coefficient of .02.
a) Construct a 95 percent confidence interval estimate of the slope of the true regression line. Does the result from this recent study indicate that the true slope has changed?
b) Construct a 99 percent confidence interval estimate of the slope of the true regression line. Does the result from this recent study indicate that the true slope has changed?

11-39 The Energy Research Administration specifies that the relationship between the number of cars in a train and a diesel engine's consumption of fuel oil has a slope of .046. A particular railroad company has compiled the operation records for 10 different train lengths. From this information, the slope of this relationship (train length versus fuel-oil consumption) was calculated to be .061, and the standard error of the regression coefficient was determined to be .005.
a) Construct a 95 percent confidence interval estimate of the slope of the true regression line. Does the information from this study indicate that the ERA claim is invalid?
b) Repeat the analysis from part *a* at the 99 percent level of confidence.

11-40 The College Board constantly monitors the reliability of SAT scores as a predictor of college grade-point average. Past data have indicated that a slope of 200 was appropriate. A recent small study of 15 students found that the slope was 190 and the standard error of the estimate was 20. The quantity $(\Sigma X^2 - n\bar{X}^2)$ was equal to 25. At the .05 level of significance, should the College Board conclude that the slope has changed?

11-5 USING REGRESSION AND CORRELATION ANALYSES: Limitations, Errors, and Caveats

Misuse of regression and correlation

Regression and correlation analyses are statistical tools that, when properly used, can significantly help people make decisions. Unfortunately, they are frequently misused. As a result, decision makers often make inaccurate forecasts and less-than-desirable decisions. We'll mention the most common errors made in the use of regression and correlation in the hope that you will avoid them.

Extrapolation Beyond the Range of the Observed Data

Specific limited range over which regression equation holds

A common mistake is to assume that the estimating line can be applied over any range of values. Hospital administrators can properly use regression analysis to predict the relationship between costs per bed and occupancy levels at various occupancy levels. Some administrators, however, incorrectly use the same regression equation to predict the costs per bed for occupancy levels that are significantly higher than those that were used to estimate the regression line. Although one relationship holds over the range of sample points, an entirely different relationship may exist for a different range. As a result, these people make decisions on one set of costs and find that the costs change drastically as occupancy increases (owing to things such as overtime costs and capacity constraints). Remember that **an estimating equation is valid only over the same range as the one from which the sample was taken initially.**

Cause and Effect

Regression and correlation analyses do not determine cause and effect

Another mistake we can make when we use regression analysis is to assume that a change in one variable is "caused" by a change in the other variable. As we discussed earlier, **regression and correlation analyses can in no way determine cause and effect.** If we say that there is a correlation between students' grades in college and their annual earnings five years after graduation, we are *not* saying that one causes the other. Rather, both may be caused by other factors, such as sociological background, parental attitudes, quality of teachers, effectiveness of the job-interviewing process, and economic status of parents—to name only a few potential factors.

We have extensively used the example about research and development expenses and annual profits to illustrate various aspects of regression analysis. But it is really highly unlikely that profits in a given year are *caused* by R&D expenditures in that year. Certainly it would be foolhardy for the VP for R&D to suggest to the chief executive that profits could immediately be increased merely by increasing R&D expenditures. Particularly in high-technology industries, the R&D activity can be used to explain profits, but a better way to do so would be to predict current profits in terms of past research and development expenditures as well as in terms of economic conditions, dollars spent on advertising, and other variables. This can be done by using the multiple regression techniques to be discussed in the next chapter.

Using Past Trends to Estimate Future Trends

Conditions change and invalidate the regression equation

We must take care to reappraise the historical data we use to estimate the regression equation. Conditions can change and violate one or more of the assumptions on which our regression analysis depends. Earlier in this chapter, we made the point that we assume that the variance of the disturbance e around the mean is constant. In many situations, however, this variance changes from year to year.

Values of variables change over time

Another error that can arise from the use of historical data concerns the dependence of some variables on time. Suppose a firm uses regression analysis to determine the relationship between the number of employees and the production volume. If the observations used in the analysis extend back for several years, the resulting regression line may be too steep, because it may fail to recognize the effect of changing technology.

Misinterpreting the Coefficients of Correlation and Determination

Misinterpreting r and r^2

The coefficient of correlation is occasionally misinterpreted as a percentage. If $r = .6$, it is incorrect to state that the regression equation "explains" 60 percent of the total variation in Y. Instead, if $r = .6$, then r^2 must be $.6 \times .6 = .36$. Only 36 percent of the total variation is explained by the regression line.

The coefficient of determination is misinterpreted if we use r^2 to describe the percentage of the change in the dependent variable that is *caused* by a change in the independent variable. This is wrong because r^2 is a measure only of how well one variable describes another, *not* of how much of the change in one variable is caused by the other variable.

Finding Relationships When They Do Not Exist

Relationships that have no common bond

When applying regression analysis, people sometimes find a relationship between two variables that, in fact, have no common bond. Even though one variable does not "cause" a change in the other, they think that there must be some factor common to both variables. It might be possible, for example, to find a statistical relationship between a random sample of the number of miles per gallon consumed by eight different cars and the distance from earth to each of the other eight planets. But since there is absolutely no common bond between gas mileage and the distance to other planets, this "relationship" would be meaningless.

EXERCISES

11-41 Explain why an estimating equation is valid over only the range of values used for its development.

11-42 Explain the difference between the coefficient of determination and the coefficient of correlation.

11-43 Why should we be cautious in using past data to predict future trends?

11-44 Why must we not attribute causality in a relationship even when there is strong correlation between the variables or events?

11-6 TERMS INTRODUCED IN CHAPTER 11

COEFFICIENT OF CORRELATION The square root of the coefficient of determination. Its sign indicates the direction of the relationship between two variables, direct or inverse.

COEFFICIENT OF DETERMINATION A measure of the proportion of variation in Y, the dependent variable, that is explained by the regression line; i.e., by Y's relationship with the independent variable.

CORRELATION ANALYSIS A technique to determine the degree to which variables are linearly related.

CURVILINEAR RELATIONSHIP An association between two variables that is described by a curved line.

DEPENDENT VARIABLE The variable we are trying to predict in regression analysis.

DIRECT RELATIONSHIP A relationship between two variables such that, as the independent variable's value increases, so does the value of the dependent variable.

ESTIMATING EQUATION A mathematical formula that relates the unknown variable to the known variables in regression analysis.

INDEPENDENT VARIABLES The known variable, or variables, in regression analysis.

INVERSE RELATIONSHIP A relationship between two variables such that, as the independent variable increases, the dependent variable decreases.

LEAST SQUARES METHOD A technique for fitting a straight line through a set of points in such a way that the sum of the squared vertical distances from the n points to the line is minimized.

LINEAR RELATIONSHIP A particular type of association between two variables that can be described mathematically by a straight line.

MULTIPLE REGRESSION The statistical process by which several variables are used to predict another variable.

REGRESSION The general process of predicting one variable from another by statistical means, using previous data.

REGRESSION LINE A line fitted to a set of data points to estimate the relationship between two variables.

SCATTER DIAGRAM A graph of points on a rectangular grid; the X and Y coordinates of each point correspond to the two measurements made on some particular sample element, and the pattern of points illustrates the relationship between the two variables.

SLOPE A constant for any given straight line, whose value represents how much each unit change of the independent variable changes the dependent variable.

STANDARD ERROR OF ESTIMATE A measure of the reliability of the estimating equation, indicating the variability of the observed points around the regression line; i.e., the extent to which observed values differ from their predicted values on the regression line.

STANDARD ERROR OF THE REGRESSION COEFFICIENT A measure of the variability of sample regression coefficients around the true population regression coefficient.

***Y*-INTERCEPT** A constant for any given straight line, whose value represents the predicted value of the Y variable when the X variable has a value of 0.

11-7 EQUATIONS INTRODUCED IN CHAPTER 11

[11-1]

$$Y = a + bX$$

p. 498

This is the equation for a *straight line* where the dependent variable Y is "determined" by the independent variable X. The a is called the *Y-intercept* because its value is the point at which the line crosses the Y-axis (the vertical axis). The b is the slope of the line; that is, it tells how much each unit change of the independent variable X changes the dependent variable Y. Both a and b are numerical constants, since for any given straight line, their values do not change.

[11-2]

$$b = \frac{Y_2 - Y_1}{X_2 - X_1}$$

p. 499

To calculate the numerical constant b for any given line, find the value of the coordinates, X and Y, for two points that lie on the line. The coordinates of the first point are (X_1, Y_1) and the second point (X_2, Y_2). Remember that b is the slope of the line.

[11-3]

$$\hat{Y} = a + bX$$

p. 501

In regression analysis, $\hat{Y}$(*Y-hat*) symbolizes the individual Y values of the *estimated* points; that is, those points that lie on the estimating line. Accordingly, Equation 11-3 is the equation for the estimating line.

[11-4]

$$b = \frac{\Sigma XY - n\bar{X}\bar{Y}}{\Sigma X^2 - n\bar{X}^2}$$

p. 504

The equation enables us to calculate the *slope of the best-fitting regression line* for any two-variable set of data points. We introduce two new symbols in this equation, $\bar{X}$ and $\bar{Y}$, which represent the means of the values of the independent variable and the dependent variable, respectively. In addition, this equation contains n, which, in this case, represents the number of data points with which we are fitting the regression line.

[11-5]

$$a = \bar{Y} - b\bar{X}$$

p. 504

Using this formula, we can compute the *Y-intercept of the best-fitting regression line* for any two-variable set of data points.

[11-6] $$s_e = \sqrt{\frac{\Sigma(Y - \hat{Y})^2}{n - 2}}$$ p. 510

The *standard error of estimate, s_e,* measures the variability or scatter of the observed values around the regression line. In effect, it indicates the reliability of the estimating equation. The denominator is $n - 2$ because we lose 2 degrees of freedom (for the values a and b) in estimating the regression line.

[11-7] $$s_e = \sqrt{\frac{\Sigma Y^2 - a\Sigma Y - b\Sigma XY}{n - 2}}$$ p. 511

Since Equation 11-6 requires tedious calculations, statisticians have devised this *short-cut method for finding the standard error of estimate.* In calculating the values for b and a, we have already calculated every quantity in Equation 11-7 except ΣY^2, which we can do easily.

[11-8] Variation of the Y values around the regression line $= \Sigma(Y - \hat{Y})^2$ p. 519

The variation of the Y values in a data set around the fitted regression line is one of two quantities from which the sample coefficient of determination is developed. Equation 11-8 shows how to measure this particular dispersion, which is the *unexplained* portion of the total variation.

[11-9] Variation of the Y values around their own mean $= \Sigma(Y - \bar{Y})^2$ p. 519

This formula measures the *total variation* of a whole set of Y values; that is, the dispersion of these Y values around their own mean.

[11-10] $$r^2 = 1 - \frac{\Sigma(Y - \hat{Y})^2}{\Sigma(Y - \bar{Y})^2}$$ p. 519

The *sample coefficient of determination, r^2,* gives the fraction of the total variation of Y that is explained by the regression line. It is an important measure of the degree of association between X and Y. If the value of r^2 is $+1$, then the regression line is a perfect estimator. If $r^2 = 0$, there is no correlation between X and Y.

[11-11] $$r^2 = \frac{a\Sigma Y + b\Sigma XY - n\bar{Y}^2}{\Sigma Y^2 - n\bar{Y}^2}$$ p. 524

This is a short-cut equation for calculating r^2.

[11-12] $$r = \sqrt{r^2}$$ p. 526

The *sample coefficient of correlation* is denoted by r and is found by taking the square root of the sample coefficient of determination. It is a second measure (in addition to r^2) we can use to describe how well one variable is explained by another. The sign of r indicates the direction of the relationship between the two variables X and Y.

[11-13] $$Y = A + BX$$ p. 527

Each *population regression line* is of the form in Equation 11-13, where A is the Y-intercept for the population, and B is the slope.

[11-13a] $$Y = A + BX + e$$ p. 528

Because all the individual points in a population do not lie on the population regression line, the *individual* data points will satisfy Formula 11-13a, where e is a random disturbance from the population regression line. On the average, e equals zero, because disturbances above the population regression line are canceled out by disturbances below it.

[11-14] $$s_b = \frac{s_e}{\sqrt{\Sigma X^2 - n\overline{X}^2}}$$ p. 529

When we are dealing with a sample, we can use this formula to find the *standard error of the regression coefficient, b.*

[11-15] $$\text{Upper limit of acceptance region} = B + t(s_b)$$ $$\text{Lower limit of acceptance region} = B - t(s_b)$$ p. 529

Once we have calculated s_b using Equation 11-14, we can determine the upper and lower limits of the acceptance region for a hypothesis test using this pair of equations.

11-8 CHAPTER REVIEW EXERCISES

11-45 Melinda Wilde, an HEW economist, speculates about the relationship between a family's income and its expenditures for food. The following table presents the results of a survey of 8 randomly selected families:

Income (×$1,000)	8	12	9	24	13	37	19	16
Percent spent for food	36	25	33	15	28	19	20	22

a) Develop an estimating equation that best describes these data.
b) Calculate the standard error of estimate, s_e, for this relationship.
c) Find an approximate 90 percent confidence interval for the percentage of income spent on food by a family earning $25,000 annually.

11-46 The financial controller for the Pleasurecraft Boat Company is examining his forecasts for the past 10 months in relation to the actual figures. Of particular interest are the data below, regarding monthly sales levels (×$1,000). For the following table of observed and predicted values of Y, compute the sample coefficient of determination and sample correlation coefficient.

Y	55	64	54	63	68	70	76	66	75	74
$\hat{Y}$	55.5	59.5	60.5	63.5	67.5	65.5	73.5	70.5	72.5	76.5

11-47 (Fill in the blanks.) Regression and correlation analyses deal with the ________________ between variables. Regression analysis, through ________________ equations, enables us to ________________ an unknown variable from a set of known variables. The unknown variable is called the ________________ variable; known variables are referred to as ________________ variables. The correlation between two variables indicates the ________________ of the linear relationship between them and thus gives an idea of how well the ________________ ________________ in regression describes the relationship between the variables.

11-48 Calculate the sample coefficient of determination and sample correlation coefficient for problem 11-14.

11-49 The president of Wonx Computers is interested in studying the relationship between the size of the annual raise and the performance of a sales representative over the subsequent year. He sampled 12 sales representatives and determined the sizes of their respective raises (given as a percentage of their individual salaries) and the number of sales made by each one during the 12 months following raises.

Size of raise	7.3	6.4	6.2	5.5	6.4	4.7	5.8	7.9	6.7	9.6	10.3	7.2
Number of sales	64	53	42	29	71	26	32	68	53	64	85	73

a) Develop the best-fitting estimating equation that describes these data.
b) Calculate the standard error of estimate for this relationship.
c) Develop a 90 percent interval for the number of sales made by a salesperson after receiving an 8.6 percent raise.

11-50 For each of the following pairs of plots, state which has a higher value of r, the correlation coefficient, and what the sign of r is:

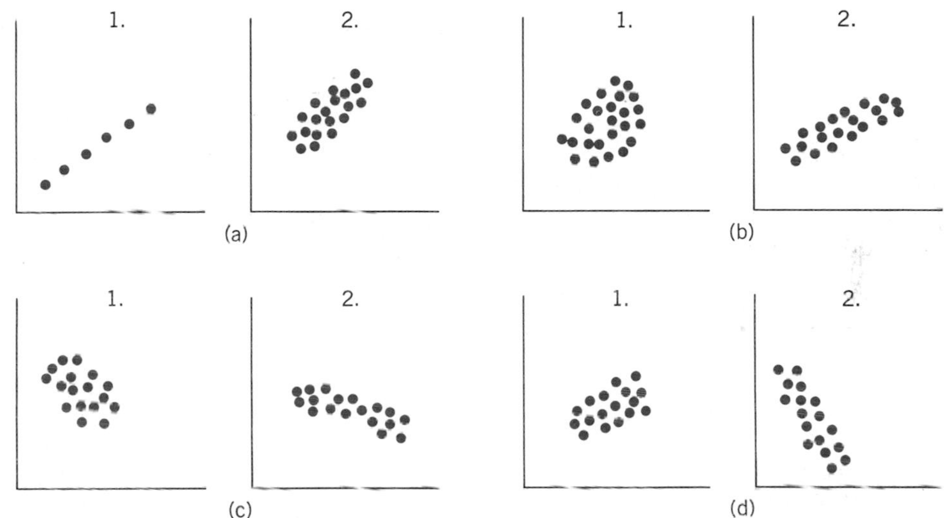

11-51 The manager of the Durham, N.C., water purification plant has compiled the data shown below to determine whether or not water usage has changed. These pairs of data are the volumes of water consumed and the corresponding number of households serviced for six recent months. Previous studies indicated that the relationship describing these two variables has a slope of 13. At the .10 level of significance, has the slope of this relationship increased?

Number of households (1,000s)	8.1	7.8	8.4	7.6	8.0	8.1
Water consumed (10 million gallons)	94	83	97	85	89	92

11-52 Calculate the sample coefficient of determination and the sample correlation coefficient for problem 11-13.

11-53 We should not extrapolate to predict values outside the range of the data used in constructing the regression line. The reason (choose one):
a) The relationship between the variables may not be the same for different values of the variables.
b) The independent variable may not have the causal effect on the dependent variable for these values.
c) The variables' values may change over time.
d) There may be no common bond to explain the relationship.

11-54 A survey of 10 sales regions of the Westchester Motorcycle Company indicated that the amount budgeted for advertising and the number of cycles sold has a slope of 1.5 and a standard error of the regression coefficient of .35. Does this information contradict, at the .10 level of significance, the marketing department's claim that 60,000 more cycles would be sold through an additional advertising expenditure of $25 million? (Sales are measured in 1,000s, advertising expenditures in $100,000s.)

11-55 Unlike the coefficient of determination, the coefficient of correlation (choose one):

a) Indicates whether the slope of the regression line is positive or negative.
b) Measures the strength of association between the two variables more exactly.
c) Can never have an absolute value greater than 1.
d) Measures the percentage of variance explained by the regression line.

11-56 Worth Ketcham, president of Streamlined, a southeastern bathing-suit company, knows that sales in April are historically unstable. He has investigated the relationship between temperature and sales during this period. Measurements over a period of years produced the following results:

Average temperature (°C)	19°	23°	25°	24°	26°	21°
Sales (×$1,000)	$66	$74	$72	$76	$78	$72

a) Plot these data.
b) Develop the estimating equation that best describes these data.

11-57 Marc Applestein, president of a consulting firm, is interested in the relationship between environmental work factors and the employee turnover rate. He defines environmental factors as those aspects of a job other than salary and benefits. He visited 10 similar plants and gave each plant a rating from 1 to 25 on its environmental factors. He then obtained each plant's turnover rate and examined the relationship.

Environmental rating	11	19	7	12	13	10	16	22	14	12
Turnover rate (annual %)	6	4	8	3	7	8	3	2	5	6

a) Plot these data.
b) Develop the estimating equation that best describes these data.
c) Predict the turnover rate that might be expected if a plant received a rating of 15.

11-58 The Dipit Donut chain has experienced large fluctuations in revenue over the last several years. Numerous specials, new products, and advertising techniques have been employed during this time, so it is difficult to determine which devices have had the strongest influence on sales. The marketing department has studied a variety of relationships and believes that the monthly expenditures on billboards may be significant. It sampled 7 months and determined the following:

Monthly expenditure on billboards (×$1,000)	27	18	44	36	12	23	22
Monthly sales revenue (×$100,000)	32	12	46	30	24	27	18

a) Develop an estimating equation that best describes these data.
b) Calculate the standard error of estimate for this relationship.
c) If a month had a billboard expenditure of $30,000, predict (with 95 percent confidence) the expected monthly sales for that month.

11-59 In a CAB study of airline operations, a survey of 12 companies disclosed that the relationship between the number of pilots employed and the number of planes in service has a slope of 3.5. Previous studies indicated that the slope of this relationship was 4.0. If the standard error of the regression coefficient has been calculated to be .20, is there reason to believe that, at the .01 level of significance, the true slope has changed?

11-9 CHAPTER CONCEPTS TEST

Answers are in the back of the book.

T F 1. Regression analysis is used to described how well an estimating equation describes the relationship being studied.

T F 2. Given that the equation for a line is $Y = 26 - 24X$, we may say that the relationship of Y to X is direct linear.

T F 3. An r^2 value close to 0 indicates a strong correlation between X and Y.

T F 4. Regression and correlation analyses are used to determine cause-and-effect relationships.

T F 5. The sample coefficient of correlation, r, is nothing more than $\sqrt{r^2}$, and we cannot interpret its meaning directly as a percentage of some kind.

T F 6. The standard error of estimate measures the variability of the observed values around the regression equation.

T F 7. The regression line is derived from a sample and not the entire population.

T F 8. We may interpret the sample coefficient of determination as the amount of the variation in Y that is explained by the regression line.

T F 9. Lines drawn on either side of the regression line at ±1, ±2 and ±3 times the value of the standard error of estimate are called confidence lines.

T F 10. The estimating equation is valid over only the same range as that given by the original sample data upon which it was developed.

T F 11. In the equation $Y = a + bX$ for dependent variable Y and independent variable X, the Y-intercept is b.

T F 12. If a line is fitted to a set of points by the method of least squares, the individual positive and negative errors from the line sum to zero.

T F 13. If $s_e = 0$ for an estimating equation, it must perfectly estimate the dependent variable at the observed points.

T F 14. Suppose the slope of an estimating equation is positive. Then the value of r must be the positive square root of r^2.

T F 15. If $r = .8$, then the regression equation explains 80 percent of the total variation in the dependent variable.

T F 16. The coefficient of correlation explains the percentage of the total variation of the dependent variable.

T F 17. The standard error of estimate is measured perpendicularly from the regression line rather than on the Y-axis.

18. Suppose that we know the height of a student but do not know her weight. We use an estimating equation to determine an estimate of her weight based upon her height. We can therefore surmise that:
    a) Weight is the independent variable. b) Height is the dependent variable.
    c) The relationship between weight and height is an inverse one.
    d) None of these. e) b and c but not a.

19. Suppose you are told that there is a direct relationship between the price of artichokes and the amount of rain that fell during the growing season. It can be concluded that:
    a) Prices tend to be high when rainfall is high.
    b) Prices tend to be low when rainfall is high.
    c) A large amount of rain causes prices to rise.
    d) A lack of rain causes prices to rise.

20. Suppose it is calculated that *a* is 4 and *b* is 2 for a particular estimating line with one independent variable. If the independent variable has a value of 2, what value should be expected for the dependent variable?
a) 8 b) 10 c) −1 d) 0

21. Suppose the estimating equation $\hat{Y} = 5 - 2X$ has been calculated for a set of data. Which of the following is true for this situation?
a) The *Y*-intercept of the line is 2.
b) The slope of the line is negative.
c) The line represents an inverse relationship.
d) All of these. e) b and c but not a.

22. We know that the standard error is the same at all points on a regression line because we assumed that:
a) Observed values for *Y* are normally distributed around each estimated value of $\hat{Y}$.
b) The variance of the distributions around each possible value of $\hat{Y}$ is the same.
c) All available data were taken into account when the regression line was calculated.
d) None of these.

23. The variation of the *Y* values around the regression line is best expressed as:
a) $\Sigma(Y + \bar{Y})^2$ b) $\Sigma(Y - \bar{Y})^2$ c) $\Sigma(Y - \hat{Y})^2$ d) $\Sigma(Y + \hat{Y})^2$

24. The value of r^2 for a particular situation is .49. What is the coefficient of correlation in this situation?
a) .49 c) .07
b) .7 d) Cannot be determined from information given

25. The fraction $\dfrac{\Sigma(Y - \hat{Y})^2}{\Sigma(Y - \bar{Y})^2}$ represents:
a) Fraction of total variation in *Y* that is unexplained
b) Fraction of total variation in *Y* that is explained
c) Fraction of total variation in *Y* that was caused by changes in *X*
d) None of these

26. In the equation $Y = A + BX + e$, the *e* represents:
a) The *X*-intercept of the observed data
b) The value of *Y* to which others are compared to determine the "best fit"
c) Random disturbances from the population regression line
d) None of these

27. Suppose you wish to compare the hypothesized value of *B* to a sample value of *b* that has been calculated. Which of the following *must* be calculated before the others?
a) s_b c) s_p
b) s_e d) Calculations can be made in any order.

28. For the estimating equation to be a perfect estimator of the dependent variable, which of these would have to be true?
a) The standard error of the estimate is zero.
b) All the data points are on the regression line.
c) The coefficient of determination is −1.
d) a and b but not c.
e) All of these.

29. If the dependent variable increases as the independent variable increases in an estimating equation, the coefficient of correlation will be in the range:
a) 0 to −1 b) 0 to −.5 c) 0 to −2 d) None of these

30. If the dependent variable in a relationship decreases as the independent variable increases, the relationship is ________________ .

31. An association between two variables that is described by a curved line is a ______________ one.
32. Every straight line has a ______________, which represents how much each change of the independent variable changes the dependent variable.
33. The extent to which observed values differ from their predicted values on the regression line is measured by the ______________.
34. ______________ is a measure of the proportion of variation in the dependent variable that is explained by the regression line.
35. If 75 percent of the variation in the dependent variable is explained by the regression line, then the value of r will be about ______________.

11-10 CONCEPTUAL CASE (Northern White Metals Company)

By December 1982, Dick felt that most of Northern's immediate difficulties had been taken care of. Except for an occasional problem, production and shipping operations were running quite smoothly. Sales had continued to climb steadily, and costs seemed to be under control. The end of Dick's first full year at Northern saw the company achieve record profits.

The company began 1983 with employee morale high. The past year's success and the bonus reward that went along with it generated an enthusiasm the firm had not seen in years. It was with this spirit that the January production meeting started. Goals and manufacturing improvements were discussed and an overall production plan established.

A small, but potentially very profitable, component of this plan was the introduction of an idea suggested by Northern's production supervisor, M. J. Sabeau. M. J. had been approached a week earlier by Tar Reid, the stooped and wizened proprietor of Reid's Recycling, Inc. Reid, a scrap hauler of some renown, had suggested that his company purchase all of Northern's scrap aluminum.

Although much had been done to improve the quality of manufacturing operations at Northern, large amounts of scrap metal still resulted as a natural by-product of the production process. This waste material was at present discarded, and Northern incurred significant disposal costs, since the metal had to be trucked more than 70 miles to a dumping facility.

Dick was anxious to take advantage of this opportunity to sell Northern's scrap aluminum. Not only would transport costs and dumping fees be eliminated, but a handsome compensation would be received as well. A favorable price per pound was negotiated, and Reid agreed to pick up the scrap metal every Friday afternoon. His only requirement was one week's advance notice of the total scrap poundage to be hauled. This was necessary so that the recycler could schedule his trucks and compacting equipment.

From experience, Dick knew that waste was directly related to production volume. The greater the poundage of aluminum coming out of the extrusion press, the more scrap would result. The following week's production was always scheduled—based on customer orders—each Friday morning at the weekly production meeting. Production volume was known a week in advance, therefore, and Dick felt it would be a small matter to forecast the amount of scrap that could be expected as well.

He was uncertain as to how an accurate forecast should be made, however, and he pondered the problem as he picked up the phone.

"Hi, Dick," Sarah said happily. "What can we do for you today?"

Dick explained his situation and requested Sarah's help in developing a means to predict weekly scrap volume.

"Sure thing, Dick," Sarah replied. She was eager to try out a new statistical software package she had recently ordered. "I can run that through on my minicomputer with no problem at all. One thing, though. Do you have much in the way of past data on finished output and scrap poundage?" she asked.

"Yes," Dick responded. "We have readily available weekly records going back at least three years."

"Excellent," Sarah responded. "Now, here's the information that I'm going to need . . . "

Sarah will assist Dick in developing the ability to predict the amount of scrap aluminum that will result from a week's expected production. What data will Sarah require to conduct her analysis? What kind of analytical procedures will she have her computer perform on these data? What cautions should Sarah offer to Dick in using whatever conclusions might be drawn from the analysis?

11-11 COMPUTER DATA BASE EXERCISE

In the early spring, Joe cornered Laurel in the hall with a request.

"It's about time to start scheduling production requirements for the fall sled shipments. We need to estimate materials requirements and assembly time as closely as possible. In the past, we just added 10 percent to last year's final sales figure, but I'd like a more reliable estimate from you two. Fred will be glad to help you."

"Oh no," moaned Laurel as she headed back to the production area to find Frank, "More hassling with that old coot.

"Frank," she said, "looks as if we need to work up some estimating equations for the Rough Rider. Do you want to bell the cat and ask Fred's help, or shall I?"

"Why don't we just send Fred a memo?" Frank suggested. "Let's be assertive and direct. We'll say, 'Please, sir, what factors influence sled sales?' "

"And," Laurel chimed in, "he'll say—'SALESMEN, good salesmen are the only thing that matters!' "

"At any rate, we'd better brainstorm some independent variables, so we'll have half a leg to stand on," Frank answered. "It seems like toy sales would be affected most severely by economic factors—disposable income, GNP—all the things that affect general retail sales."

"That makes sense," Laurel said. "Let's do a simple regression with retail toy sales over the past ten years, to predict Rough Rider sales and see what they look like."

QUESTION

1. What are the coefficient of determination and coefficient of correlation for sled sales vs. retail sales?

   "Rotten-fitting regression," Frank announced. "Even I know that."

YEAR	RETAIL TOY SALES (000)	SLED SALES (UNITS)
1949	671	10,767
1950	683	16,633
1951	747	15,646
1952	902	15,614
1953	1,572	15,893
1954	2,092	21,211
1955	2,602	16,552
1956	3,393	18,853
1957	4,422	18,373
1958	5,474	18,331
1959	6,222	19,135
1960	7,626	17,225
1961	8,877	22,928
1962	10,332	20,688
1963	11,643	21,789
1964	13,340	19,436
1965	14,931	21,876
1966	16,925	18,355
1967	18,688	25,599
1968	20,597	21,044
1969	22,868	24,409
1970	24,731	25,706
1971	27,317	24,476
1972	29,403	19,706
1973	32,118	21,725
1974	34,566	26,806
1975	37,524	22,471
1976	40,276	25,112
1977	42,985	23,944
1978	46,520	26,819

11-12 FLOW CHART

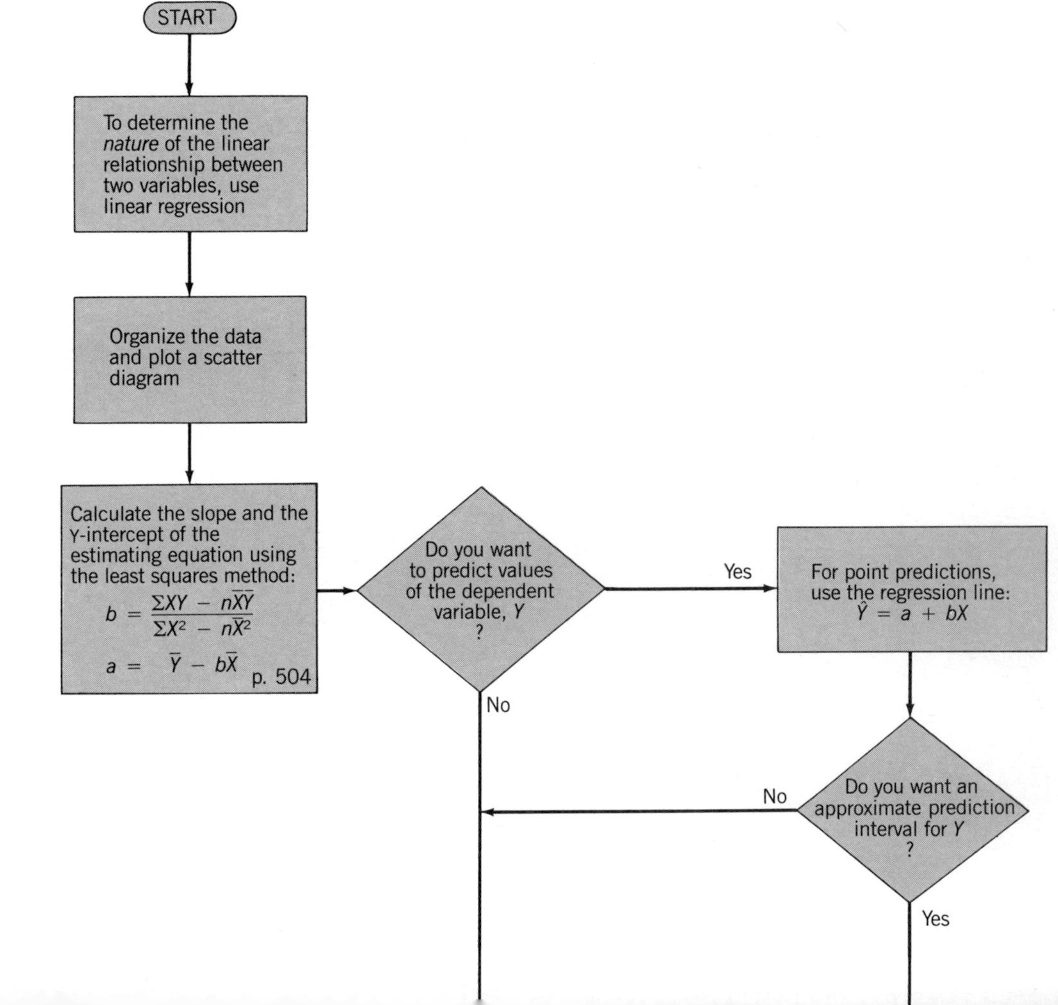

START
To determine the *nature* of the linear relationship between two variables, use linear regression
Organize the data and plot a scatter diagram
Calculate the slope and the Y-intercept of the estimating equation using the least squares method:
$b = \frac{\Sigma XY - n\bar{X}\bar{Y}}{\Sigma X^2 - n\bar{X}^2}$
$a = \bar{Y} - b\bar{X}$
p. 504
Do you want to predict values of the dependent variable, Y ?
Yes
No
For point predictions, use the regression line: $\hat{Y} = a + bX$
Do you want an approximate prediction interval for Y ?
No
Yes

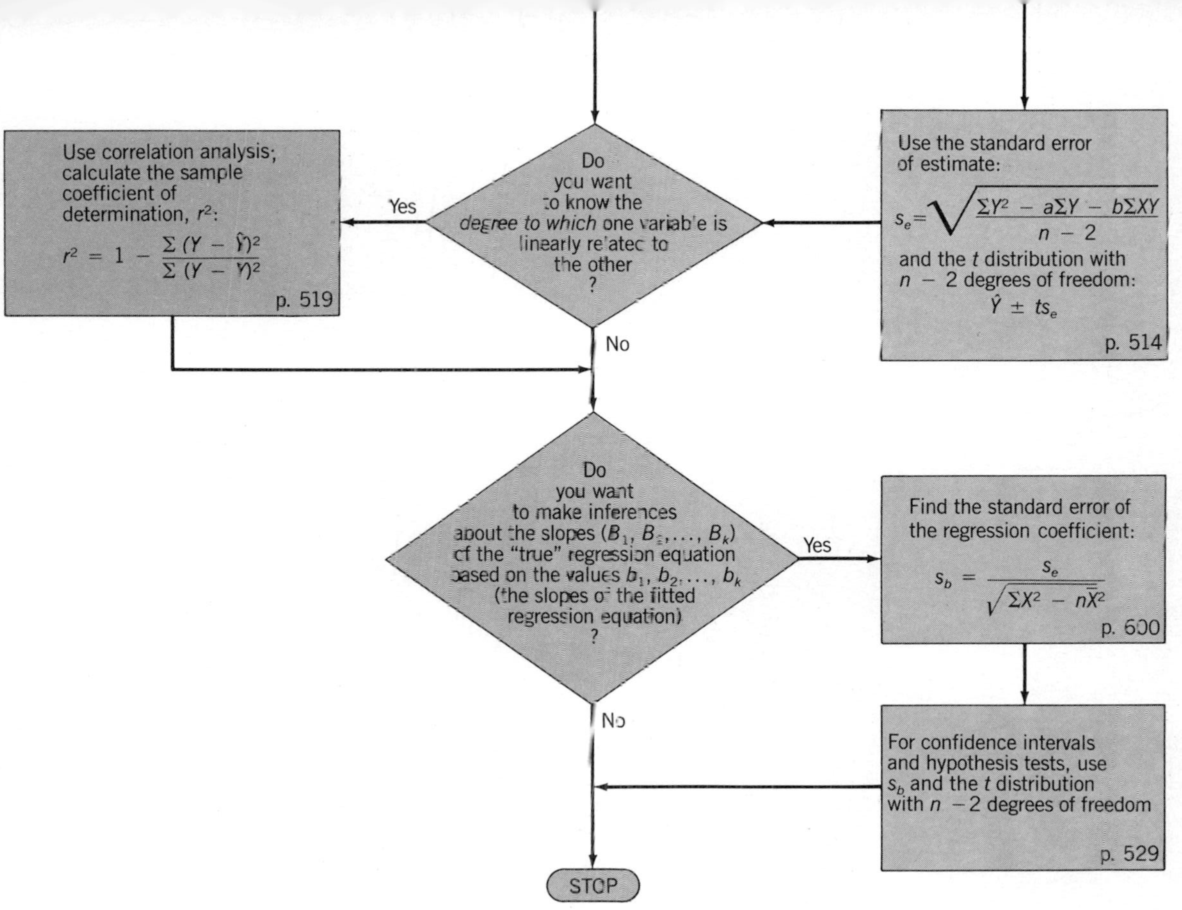

Use the standard error of estimate:
$s_e = \sqrt{\dfrac{\Sigma Y^2 - a\Sigma Y - b\Sigma XY}{n - 2}}$
and the t distribution with $n - 2$ degrees of freedom:
$\hat{Y} \pm ts_e$
p. 514
Do you want to know the *degree to which* one variable is linearly related to the other?
Yes
Use correlation analysis; calculate the sample coefficient of determination, r^2:
$r^2 = 1 - \dfrac{\Sigma (Y - \hat{Y})^2}{\Sigma (Y - \bar{Y})^2}$
p. 519
No
Do you want to make inferences about the slopes ($B_1, B_2, \ldots, B_k$) of the "true" regression equation based on the values $b_1, b_2, \ldots, b_k$ (the slopes of the fitted regression equation)?
Yes
Find the standard error of the regression coefficient:
$s_b = \dfrac{s_e}{\sqrt{\Sigma X^2 - n\bar{X}^2}}$
p. 500
For confidence intervals and hypothesis tests, use s_b and the t distribution with $n - 2$ degrees of freedom
p. 529
No
STOP

CHAPTER 12

MULTIPLE REGRESSION AND MODELING TECHNIQUES

1. MULTIPLE REGRESSION AND CORRELATION ANALYSIS, 550
2. FINDING THE MULTIPLE REGRESSION EQUATION, 551
3. THE COMPUTER AND MULTIPLE REGRESSION, 559
4. MAKING INFERENCES ABOUT POPULATION PARAMETERS, 566
5. MODELING TECHNIQUES, 579
6. TERMS, 591
7. EQUATIONS, 592
8. REVIEW EXERCISES, 593
9. CONCEPTS TEST, 597
10. CONCEPTUAL CASE, 599
11. COMPUTER DATA BASE EXERCISE, 600
12. FLOW CHART, 602

OBJECTIVES: Chapter 12 is a continuation of some of the regression ideas introduced in Chapter 11. Here we shall examine how to use regression when we feel that more than one factor is involved in something we are trying to predict. For example, if your university used your high school grade-point average as well as your college board scores to predict your college grade-point average, chances are they were using multiple regression. Also in Chapter 12, we'll try a bit of modeling with regression; that is, we'll get a bit deeper into how we can predict some things by looking at others, and what those others ought to be.

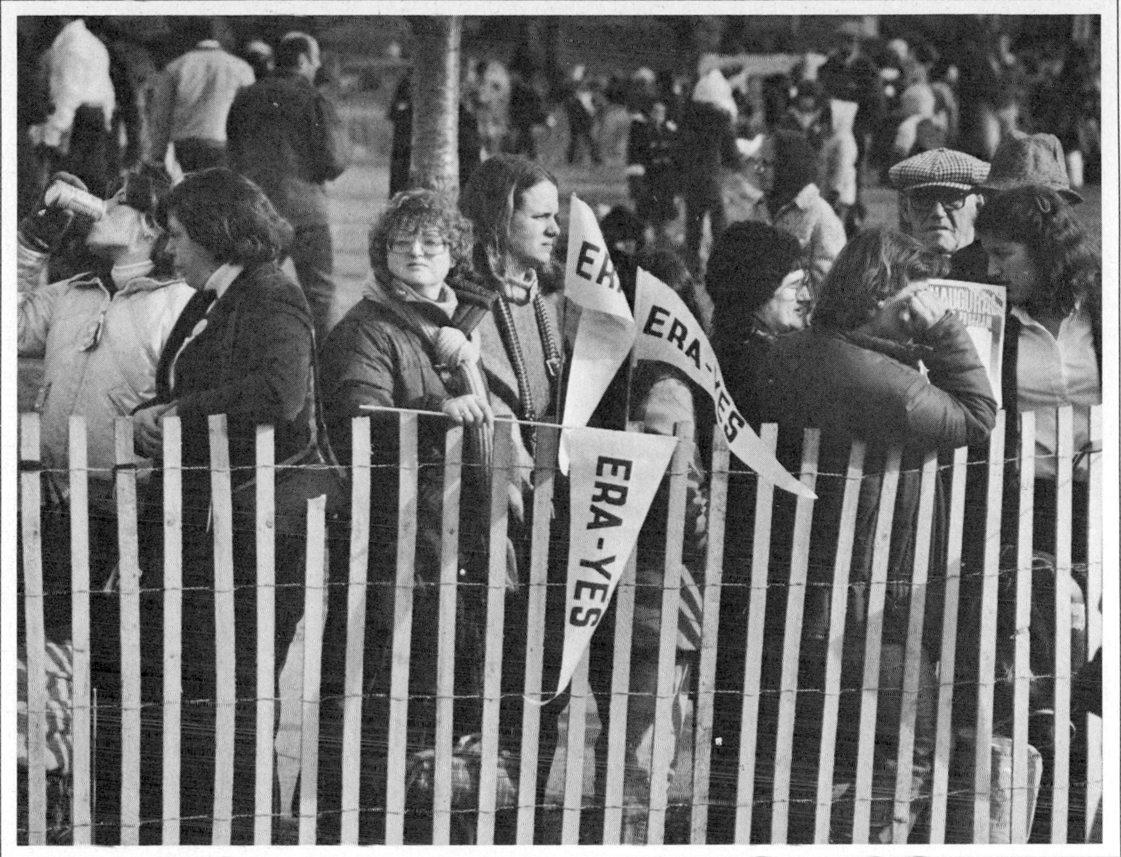

A manufacturer of small office copiers and word-processing machinery pays its salespersons a base salary plus a commission equal to a fixed percent of the person's sales. One of the salespersons charges that this salary structure discriminates against women. Current base salaries for the firm's 9 salespersons are as follows:

Salesmen		Saleswomen	
MONTHS EMPLOYED	BASE SALARY ($1,000s)	MONTHS EMPLOYED	BASE SALARY ($1,000s)
6	7.5	5	6.2
10	8.6	13	8.7
12	9.1	15	9.4
18	10.3	21	9.8
30	13.0		

The director of personnel sees that base salary depends on length of service, but she does not know how to use the data to learn if it also depends on sex and if there is discrimination against women. Methods in this chapter will enable her to find out.

12-1 MULTIPLE REGRESSION AND CORRELATION ANALYSIS

Using more than one independent variable to estimate the dependent variable

As we mentioned in Chapter 11, we may use more than one independent variable to estimate the dependent variable and, in this way, attempt to increase the accuracy of the estimate. This process is called multiple regression and correlation analysis. It is based on the same assumptions and procedures we have encountered using simple regression.

Consider the real estate agent who wishes to relate the number of houses the firm sells in a month to the amount of her monthly advertising. Certainly we can find a simple estimating equation that relates these two variables. Could we also improve the accuracy of our equation by including in the estimating process the number of salespersons she employs each month? The answer is probably yes. And now, since we want to use both the number of sales agents and the advertising expenditures to predict monthly house sales, we must use *multiple,* not simple, regression to determine the relationship.

Advantage of multiple regression

The principal advantage of multiple regression is that it allows us to utilize more of the information available to us to estimate the dependent variable. Sometimes the correlation between two variables may be insufficient to determine a reliable estimating equation. Yet, if we add the data from more independent variables, we may be able to determine an estimating equation that describes the relationship with greater accuracy.

Steps in multiple regression and correlation

Multiple regression and correlation analysis is a three-step process such as the one we used in simple regression. In this process, we must:

1. Describe the multiple regression equation.
2. Examine the multiple regression standard error of estimate.
3. Use multiple correlation analysis to determine how well the regression equation describes the observed data.

In addition, in multiple regression, we can look at each of the individual independent variables and test whether it contributes significantly to the way the regression describes the data.

Computer regression packages

In this chapter, we shall see how to find the best-fitting regression equation for a given set of data and how to analyze the equation that we get. Although we shall show how to do multiple regression by hand or on a hand-held calculator, it will quickly become obvious to you that you would not want to do even a modest-size real-life problem by hand. Fortunately, there are available many computer "packages" for doing multiple regressions and other statistical analyses. We shall also discuss the regression output from a typical package.

Multiple regression will also enable us to fit curves as well as lines. Using the techniques of "dummy variables," we can even include qualitative factors such as sex in our multiple regression. This technique will enable us to analyze the discrimination problem opening this chapter. Dummy variables and fitting curves are only two of the many *modeling techniques* that can be used in multiple regression.

EXERCISES

12-1 Why would we use multiple regression instead of simple regression in estimating a dependent variable?

12-2 How will dummy variables be used in our study of multiple regression?

12-3 To what does the word *multiple* refer in the phrase *multiple regression?*

12-4 Suppose that a manager was trying to measure the effects of several variables on sales levels. She found that the income of the customers explained a large portion of sales variation. If she had also considered the effects of customer age, do you think the model would have explained more or less of the sales variation? Why?

12-5 Describe the 3 steps in the process of multiple regression and correlation analysis.

12-6 Will the procedures used in multiple regression differ greatly from those we used in simple regression? Why, or why not?

12-2 FINDING THE MULTIPLE REGRESSION EQUATION

A problem to demonstrate multiple regression

Let's see how we can compute the multiple regression equation. For convenience, we shall use only two independent variables in the problem we work in this section. Keep in mind, however, that the same sort of technique is in principle applicable to any number of independent variables.

The Internal Revenue Service is trying to estimate the monthly amount of unpaid taxes discovered by its auditing division. In the past, the IRS estimated this figure on the basis of the expected number of field-audit labor hours. In recent years, however, field-audit labor hours have become an erratic predictor of the actual unpaid taxes. As a result, the IRS is looking for another factor with which it can improve the estimating equation.

The auditing division does keep a record of the number of hours its computers are used to detect unpaid taxes. Could we combine this information with the data on field-audit labor hours and come up with a more accurate estimating equation for the unpaid taxes discovered each month? Table 12-1 presents these data for the last ten months.

Appropriate symbols

In simple regression, X is the symbol used for the values of the independent variable. In multiple regression, we have more than one independent variable. So we shall continue to use X, but we shall add a subscript (for example, X_1, X_2) to distinguish between the independent variables we are using.

TABLE 12-1 Data from IRS auditing records during last 10 months

MONTH	X_1 FIELD-AUDIT LABOR HOURS (00s OMITTED)	X_2 COMPUTER HOURS (00s OMITTED)	Y ACTUAL UNPAID TAXES DISCOVERED (MILLIONS OF DOLLARS)
January	45	16	$29
February	42	14	24
March	44	15	27
April	45	13	25
May	43	13	26
June	46	14	28
July	44	16	30
August	45	16	28
September	44	15	28
October	43	15	27

Defining the variables

In this problem, X_1, will represent the number of field-audit labor hours and X_2 the number of computer hours. The dependent variable, Y, will be the actual unpaid taxes discovered.

Estimating equation for multiple regression

Recall that in simple regression, the estimating equation $\hat{Y} = a + bX$ describes the relationship between the two variables X and Y. In multiple regression, we must extend that equation, adding one term for each new variable. In symbolic form, Equation 12-1 is the formula we can use when we have two independent variables:

$$\hat{Y} = a + b_1X_1 + b_2X_2 \qquad \textbf{[12-1]}$$

where:

- $\hat{Y}$ = estimated value corresponding to the dependent variable
- a = Y-intercept
- X_1 and X_2 = values of the two independent variables
- b_1 and b_2 = slopes associated with X_1 and X_2, respectively

Visualizing multiple regression

We can visualize the simple estimating equation as a line on a graph; similarly, we can picture a two-variable multiple regression equation as a plane, such as the one shown in Fig. 12-1. Here we have a three-dimensional shape that possesses depth, length, and width. To get an intuitive feel for this three-dimensional shape, visualize the intersection of the axes, Y, X_1, and X_2 as one corner of a room.

Figure 12-1 is a graph of the ten sample points from Table 12-1 and the plane about which these points seem to cluster. Some points lie above

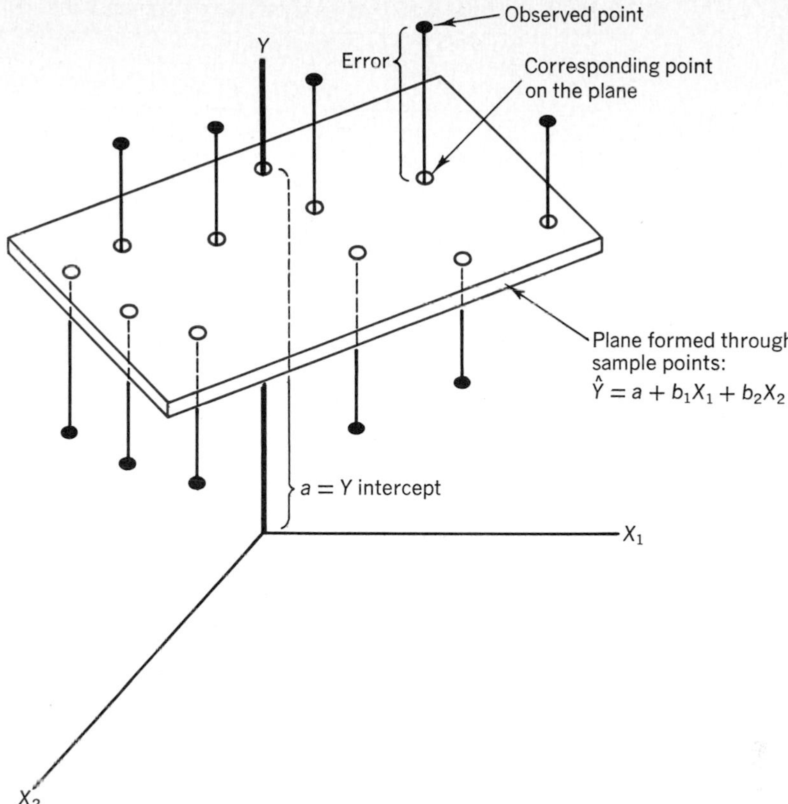

FIGURE 12-1 Multiple regression plane for 10 data points

the plane, and some fall below it—just as points lay above and below the simple regression line.

Using the least squares criterion to fit a regression plane

Our problem is to decide which of the possible planes that we could draw will be the best fit. To do this, we shall again use the least squares criterion and locate the plane that minimizes the sum of the squares of the errors, that is, the distances from the points around the plane to the corresponding points *on* the plane. We use our data and the following three equations to determine the values of the numerical constants a, b_1, and b_2.

$$\Sigma Y = na + b_1\Sigma X_1 + b_2\Sigma X_2 \qquad [12\text{-}2]$$

$$\Sigma X_1Y = a\Sigma X_1 + b_1\Sigma X_1^2 + b_2\Sigma X_1X_2 \qquad [12\text{-}3]$$

$$\Sigma X_2Y = a\Sigma X_2 + b_1\Sigma X_1X_2 + b_2\Sigma X_2^2 \qquad [12\text{-}4]$$

Solving Equations 12-2, 12-3, and 12-4 for a, b_1, and b_2 will give us the coefficients for the regression plane. Obviously, the best way to compute all the sums in these three equations is to use a table to collect and organize the necessary information, just as we did in simple regression. This we have done for the IRS problem in Table 12-2.

TABLE 12-2 Values for fitting least squares plane, where $n = 10$

Y (1)	X_1 (2)	X_2 (3)	X_1Y (2) × (1)	X_2Y (3) × (1)	X_1X_2 (2) × (3)	X_1^2 $(2)^2$	X_2^2 $(3)^2$	Y^2 $(1)^2$
29	45	16	1,305	464	720	2,025	256	841
24	42	14	1,008	336	588	1,764	196	576
27	44	15	1,188	405	660	1,936	225	729
25	45	13	1,125	325	585	2,025	169	625
26	43	13	1,118	338	559	1,849	169	676
28	46	14	1,288	392	644	2,116	196	784
30	44	16	1,320	480	704	1,936	256	900
28	45	16	1,260	448	720	2,025	256	784
28	44	15	1,232	420	660	1,936	225	784
27	43	15	1,161	405	645	1,849	225	729
272	**441**	**147**	**12,005**	**4,013**	**6,485**	**19,461**	**2,173**	**7,428**
↑ ΣY	↑ ΣX_1	↑ ΣX_2	↑ ΣX_1Y	↑ ΣX_2Y	↑ ΣX_1X_2	↑ ΣX_1^2	↑ ΣX_2^2	↑ ΣY^2

$\bar{Y} = 27.2$
$\bar{X}_1 = 44.1$
$\bar{X}_2 = 14.7$

Equations 12-2, 12-3, and 12-4 used to solve for a, b_1, and b_2

Now, using the information from Table 12-2 in Equations 12-2, 12-3, and 12-4, we get three equations in the three unknown constants (a, b_1, and b_2), which we denote below as ①, ②, and ③.

$$272 = 10a + 441b_1 + 147b_2 \quad ①$$

$$12{,}005 = 441a + 19{,}461b_1 + 6{,}485b_2 \quad ②$$

$$4{,}013 = 147a + 6{,}485b_1 + 2{,}173b_2 \quad ③$$

Solving Equations 12-2, 12-3, and 12-4 simultaneously

We can find the values for the three numerical constants by solving these three equations simultaneously, as follows:

STEP 1. Multiply equation ① by −441. Multiply Equation ② by 10. Add ① to ②. This eliminates a and produces Equation ④.

$$① \times (-441): -119{,}952 = -4410a - 194{,}481b_1 - 64{,}827b_2$$
$$② \times (10): \quad 120{,}050 = 4410a + 194{,}610b_1 + 64{,}850b_2$$
$$④: \quad 98 = 129b_1 + 23b_2$$

STEP 2. Multiply Equation ① by −147 and Equation ③ by 10. Add ① to ③. This eliminates a and produces Equation ⑤.

$$① \times (-147): -39{,}984 = -1470a - 64{,}827b_1 - 21{,}609b_2$$
$$③ \times 10: \quad 40{,}130 = 1470a + 64{,}850b_1 + 21{,}730b_2$$
$$⑤: \quad 146 = 23b_1 + 121b_2$$

STEP 3. Multiply Equation ④ by -23 and Equation ⑤ by 129. Add ④ to ⑤ to eliminate b_1. This produces Equation ⑥, which can be solved for b_2:

$$\begin{aligned} ④ \times (-23)&: -2{,}254 = -2{,}967b_1 - 529b_2 \\ ⑤ \times (129)&: \underline{18{,}834 = 2{,}967b_1 + 15{,}609b_2} \\ ⑥&: 16{,}580 = 15{,}080b_2 \end{aligned}$$

$$b_2 = 1.099$$

STEP 4. Find the value of b_1 by substituting the value for b_2 into Equation ④:

$$\begin{aligned} ④: 98 &= 129b_1 + 23b_2 \\ 98 &= 129b_1 + (23)(1.099) \\ 98 &= 129b_1 + 25.277 \\ 72.723 &= 129b_1 \end{aligned}$$

$$b_1 = .564$$

STEP 5. Substitute the values of b_1 and b_2 into Equation ① to determine the value of a:

$$\begin{aligned} ①: 272 &= 10a + 441b_1 + 147b_2 \\ 272 &= 10a + (441)(.564) + (147)(1.099) \\ 272 &= 10a + 248.724 + 161.553 \\ -138.277 &= 10a \end{aligned}$$

$$a = -13.828$$

STEP 6 Substitute the values of a, b_1, and b_2 into the general two-variable regression equation (Equation 12-1). The resulting Equation ⑦ describes the relationship among the number of field-audit labor hours, the number of computer hours, and the unpaid taxes discovered by the auditing division.

$$\hat{Y} = a + b_1X_1 + b_2X_2 \qquad \textbf{[12-1]}$$

$$⑦: \hat{Y} = -13.828 + .564X_1 + 1.099X_2$$

The auditing division can use this equation monthly to estimate the amount of unpaid taxes it will discover.

Using the multiple regression equation to estimate

Suppose the IRS wants to increase its discoveries in the coming month. Since trained auditors are scarce, the IRS does not intend to hire additional personnel. The number of field-audit labor hours, then, will remain at October's level of about 4,300 hours. But in order to increase its discoveries of unpaid taxes, the IRS expects to increase the number of computer hours to about 1,600. As a result:

$$X_1 = 43 \leftarrow \text{4,300 hours of field-audit labor}$$
$$X_2 = 16 \leftarrow \text{1,600 hours of computer time}$$

Substituting these values into Equation ⑦, we get:

$$\begin{aligned}\hat{Y} &= -13.828 + .564X_1 + 1.099X_2 \qquad ⑦\\ &= -13.828 + (.564)(43) + (1.099)(16)\\ &= -13.828 + 24.252 + 17.584\\ &= 28.008 \leftarrow \text{estimated discoveries of \$28,008,000}\end{aligned}$$

Interpreting our estimate

Therefore, in the November forecast, the audit division can indicate that it expects about $28 million of discoveries for this combination of factors.

a, b_1, and b_2 are the estimated regression coefficients

So far, we have referred to a as the Y-intercept and to b_1 and b_2 as the slopes of the multiple regression line. But to be more precise, we should say that these numerical constants are the *estimated regression coefficients*. The constant a is the value of $\hat{Y}$ (in this case, the estimated unpaid taxes) *if* both X_1 and X_2 happen to be zero. The coefficients b_1 and b_2 describe how changes in X_1 and X_2 affect the value of $\hat{Y}$. In Equation ⑦, for example, we can hold the number of field-audit labor hours, X_1, constant and change the number of computer hours, X_2. When we do, the value of $\hat{Y}$ will increase $1,099,000 for every additional 100 hours of computer time. Likewise, we can hold X_2 constant and find that, for every 100-hour increase in the number of field-audit labor hours, $\hat{Y}$ increases by $564,000.

EXERCISES

12-7 Given the following set of data:

a) Calculate the multiple regression plane.
b) Predict Y when $X_1 = 4.8$ and $X_2 = 4.0$.

Y	X_1	X_2
34	5.0	5.0
29	4.2	4.5
43	8.5	10.0
12	1.4	2.5
35	3.6	5.0
27	1.3	3.0

12-8 For the following set of data:

a) Calculate the multiple regression plane.
b) Predict Y for $X_1 = 36$ and $X_2 = 16$.

Y	X_1	X_2
8	10	8
36	37	21
23	18	14
27	29	11
14	14	9
12	21	4

12-9 Jean Barker, a reading specialist, wants to develop an estimating equation to predict reading achievement for first graders. She believes that achievement is related to both the perceptual motor development of a child and the degree to which he or she is above average in mental age. She has compiled the following information from 5 students:

STUDENT	X_1 PERCEPTUAL MOTOR TASK SCORE	X_2 YEARS DIFFERENCE BETWEEN MENTAL AND CHRONOLOGICAL AGES	Y READING ACHIEVEMENT SCORE
1	100	1.05	71
2	103	1.21	82
3	112	1.26	91
4	104	1.35	98
5	116	1.47	104

a) Calculate the least squares equation that best relates these 3 variables.
b) If a child's perceptual motor score is 120 and her mental age is 1.56 years above her chronological age, what score would you expect her to obtain on the reading achievement test at the end of the year?

12-10 A developer of food for pigs would like to determine what relationship exists among the age of a pig when it starts receiving a newly developed food supplement, the initial weight of the pig at the same time, and the amount it gains in a 1-week period with the food supplement. The following information is the result of a study of 8 piglets:

PIGLET NUMBER	X_1 INITIAL WEIGHT (LBS)	X_2 INITIAL AGE (WEEKS)	Y WEIGHT GAIN
1	39	8	7
2	52	6	6
3	48	7	7
4	46	12	10
5	61	9	9
6	34	6	4
7	25	10	3
8	55	4	4

a) Calculate the least squares equation that best describes these 3 variables.
b) How much might we expect a pig to gain in a week with the food supplement if it was 9 weeks old and weighed 48 pounds?

12-11 Given the following set of data:

a) Calculate the multiple regression plane.

b) Predict Y when $X_1 = 5$ and $X_2 = 7$.

Y	X_1	X_2
2	1	0
8	3	4
5	2	1
6	3	3
12	5	3
19	8	8

12-12 Radio station WILD is contemplating a new contest that will require listeners to call the station and guess the identity of a "secret spy." WILD hopes that the contest will capture a larger share of the listening market. Prizes and the number of times per day that calls will be accepted have yet to be determined. The past 5 contests that WILD has run have yielded the following data:

X_1 NUMBER OF CALLS PER DAY	X_2 PRIZES	Y TOTAL % OF LISTENING MARKET DURING CONTEST
15	$15.00	39%
8	3.50	23
19	5.00	28
24	10.00	35
10	1.50	23

a) Calculate the least squares equation that best relates these 3 variables.

b) If WILD takes 13 calls per day and each prize is worth $7.50, what market share should be expected during the contest?

12-13 The Federal Reserve is performing a preliminary study to determine the relationship between certain economic indicators and annual percentage change in the gross national product (GNP). Two such indicators being examined are the amount of the federal government's deficit (in billions of dollars) and the Dow Jones Industrial Average (the mean value over the year). Data for 6 years are given below:

Y CHANGE IN GNP	X_1 FEDERAL DEFICIT	X_2 DOW JONES
2.5	50	950
−1.0	200	700
4.0	60	1,100
1.0	100	800
1.5	90	850
3.0	40	900

a) Calculate the least squares equation that best describes the data.

b) What percentage change in GNP would be expected in a year in which the federal deficit was $120 billion and the mean Dow Jones value was 1,000?

12-3 THE COMPUTER AND MULTIPLE REGRESSION

Impracticality of computing regressions by hand

In Chapter 11, and so far in this chapter, we have presented simplified problems and samples of small sizes. After the example in the last section, you have probably concluded that you are not interested in regression if you have to do the computations by hand. In fact, as sample size gets larger and the number of independent variables in the regression increases, it quickly becomes impractical to do the computations even on a hand-held calculator.

As managers, however, we will have to deal with complex problems requiring larger samples and additional independent variables. To assist us in solving these more detailed problems, we will make use of a computer, which allows us to perform a large number of computations in a very small period of time.

Suppose that we have not one or two independent variables but rather that we have k of them: $X_1, X_2, \ldots, X_k$. As before, we will let n denote the number of data points that we have. The regression equation we are trying to estimate is:

$$\hat{Y} = a + b_1X_1 + b_2X_2 + \cdots + b_kX_k \qquad \textbf{[12-5]}$$

Now we'll see how we can use a computer to estimate the regression coefficients.

Demonstration of multiple regression using the computer

To demonstrate how a computer handles multiple regression analysis, take our IRS problem from the preceding section. Suppose the auditing division adds to its model the information concerning rewards to informants. The IRS wishes to include his third independent variable, X_3, because it feels certain that there is some relationship between these payments and the unpaid taxes discovered. Information for the last ten months is recorded in Table 12-3.

TABLE 12-3 Factors related to the discovery of unpaid taxes

MONTH	FIELD-AUDIT LABOR HOURS (00s OMITTED) X_1	COMPUTER HOURS (00s OMITTED) X_2	REWARDS TO INFORMANTS (000s OMITTED) X_3	ACTUAL UNPAID TAXES DISCOVERED (000,000s OMITTED) Y
January	45	16	71	29
February	42	14	70	24
March	44	15	72	27
April	45	13	71	25
May	43	13	75	26
June	46	14	74	28
July	44	16	76	30
August	45	16	69	28
September	44	15	74	28
October	43	15	73	27

Using SAS to solve multiple regression problems

To solve this problem, the auditing division has used the multiple regression procedure in the SAS package that we saw previously in Chapters 4 and 10. Of course, we don't yet know how to interpret the solution provided by SAS, but as we shall see, most of the numbers given in the solution correspond fairly closely to things we have already discussed in the context of simple regression.

SAS Output

Output from the SAS program

Once all the data have been entered and the independent and dependent variables chosen, SAS computes the regression coefficients and several statistics associated with the regression equation. Let's look at the output for the IRS problem and see what all the numbers mean. The first part of the output is given in Table 12-4 below.

TABLE 12-4 SAS output

```
      ROOT MSE          0.286128          R-SQUARE            0.9834

                        PARAMETER         STANDARD     T FOR H0:
VARIABLE    DF          ESTIMATE             ERROR   PARAMETER=0      PROB > |T|

INTERCEP     1        -45.796348          4.877651        -9.389          0.0001
AUDIT        1          0.596972          0.081124         7.359          0.0003
COMPUTER     1          1.176838          0.084074        13.998          0.0001
REWARDS      1          0.405109          0.042234         9.592          0.0001
```

1. *The regression equation.* From the numbers in the "parameter estimate" column, we can read the estimating equation:

$$\hat{Y} = a + b_1X_1 + b_2X_2 + b_3X_3 \quad [12\text{-}5]$$

$$\hat{Y} = -45.796 + .597X_1 + 1.177X_2 + .405X_3$$

Finding and interpreting the regression equation

We can interpret this equation in much the same way that we interpreted the two-variable regression equation on page 556. If we hold the number of field-audit labor hours, X_1, and the number of computer hours, X_2, constant and change the rewards to informants, X_3, then the value of $\hat{Y}$ will increase \$405,000 for each additional \$1,000 paid to informants. Similarly, holding X_1 and X_3 constant, we see that each additional 100 hours of computer time used will increase $\hat{Y}$ by \$1,177,000. Finally, if X_2 and X_3 are held constant, we estimate that an additional 100 hours spent in the field audits will uncover an additional \$597,000 in unpaid taxes.

Suppose that in November, the IRS intends to leave the field-audit labor hours and computer hours at their October levels (4,300 and 1,500) but to increase the rewards paid to informants to \$75,000. How much unpaid taxes do they expect to discover in November? Substituting these values into the estimated regression equation, we get:

$$\begin{aligned}\hat{Y} &= -45.796 + .597X_1 + 1.177X_2 + .405X_3\\ &= -45.796 + .597(43) + 1.177(15) + .405(75)\\ &= -45.796 + 25.671 + 17.655 + 30.375\\ &= 27.905 \leftarrow \text{estimated discoveries of \$27,905,000}\end{aligned}$$

So the audit division expects to discover about \$28 million in unpaid taxes in November.

Measuring dispersion around the multiple regression plane; using the standard error of estimate

2. *A measure of dispersion, the standard error of estimate for multiple regression.* Now that we have determined the equation that relates our three variables, we need some measure of the dispersion around this multiple regression plane. In simple regression, the estimation becomes more accurate as the degree of dispersion around the regression line gets smaller. The same is true of the sample points around the multiple regression plane. To measure this variation, we shall again use the measure called the standard error of estimate:

$$s_e = \sqrt{\frac{\Sigma(Y - \hat{Y})^2}{n - k - 1}} \quad \textbf{[12-6]}$$

where:

- Y = sample values of the dependent variable
- $\hat{Y}$ = corresponding estimated values from the regression equation
- n = number of data points in the sample
- k = number of independent variables (=3 in our example)

The denominator of this equation indicates that in multiple regression with k independent variables, the standard error has $n - k - 1$ degrees of freedom. This occurs because the degrees of freedom are reduced by the $k + 1$ numerical constants, a, b_1, b_2, . . . b_k that have all been estimated from the same sample.

To compute s_e, we look at the individual *errors* $(Y - \hat{Y})$ in the fitted regression plane, *square* them, compute their *mean* (dividing by $n - 1 - k$ instead of n), and take the square *root* of the result. Because of the way it is computed, s_e is sometimes called the *root mean square error* (or *root mse* for short). From the SAS output, we see that the root mse in our IRS problem is .286; that is to say, \$286,000.

Confidence intervals for $\hat{Y}$

As was the case in simple regression, we can use the standard error of the estimate and the t distribution to form an *approximate confidence interval* around our estimated value $\hat{Y}$. In the unpaid tax problem, for 4,300 field-audit labor hours, 1,500 computer hours, and \$75,000 paid to informants, our $\hat{Y}$ is \$27,905,000 estimated unpaid taxes discovered, and our s_e is \$286,000. If we want to construct a 95 percent confidence interval around this estimate of \$27,905,000, we look in Appendix Table 2 under the 5 percent column until we locate the $n - k - 1 = 10 - 3 - 1 = 6$ degrees of freedom row. The appropriate t value for our interval estimate is 2.447. Therefore, we can calculate the limits of our confidence interval like this:

$$\begin{aligned}\hat{Y} + t(s_e) &= 27{,}905{,}000 + (2.447)(286{,}000)\\ &= 27{,}905{,}000 + 699{,}800\\ &= 28{,}604{,}800 \leftarrow \text{upper limit}\end{aligned}$$

$$\begin{aligned}\hat{Y} - t(s_e) &= 27{,}905{,}000 - (2.447)(286{,}000)\\ &= 27{,}905{,}000 - 699{,}800\\ &= 27{,}205{,}200 \leftarrow \text{lower limit}\end{aligned}$$

Interpreting the confidence interval

With a confidence level as high as 95 percent, the auditing division can feel certain that the actual discoveries will lie in this large interval from \$27,205,200 to \$28,604,800. If the IRS wishes to use a lower confidence level, such as 90 percent, it can narrow the range of values in estimating the unpaid taxes discovered. As was true with simple regression, we can use the standard normal distribution, Appendix Table 1, to approximate the t distribution whenever our degrees of freedom (n minus the number of estimated regression coefficients) are greater than 30.

Value of additional variables

Did adding the third independent variable (rewards to informants) make our regression better? Since s_e measures the dispersion of the data points around the regression plane, smaller values of s_e should indicate better regressions. For the two-variable regression done earlier in this chapter, s_e turns out to be 1.076. Since the addition of the third variable reduced s_e to .286, we see that adding the third variable *did* improve the fit of the regression in this example. **It is not true in general, however, that adding variables always reduces s_e.**

Meaning of the coefficient of determination

3. *The coefficient of multiple determination.* In our discussion of simple correlation analysis, we measured the strength of the relation between two variables using the sample coefficient of determination, r^2. This coefficient of determination is the fraction of the total variation of the dependent variable Y that is explained by the estimating equation.

Using the coefficient of multiple determination

Similarly, in multiple correlation, we shall measure the strength of the relationship among three variables using the *coefficient of multiple determination,* R^2, or its square root, R (the coefficient of multiple correlation). **This coefficient of multiple determination is also the fraction that represents the proportion of the total variation of Y that is "explained" by the regression plane.**

Notice that the SAS output gives the value of R^2 as .9834. This tells us that 98.34 percent of the total variation in unpaid taxes discovered is explained by the three independent variables. For the two-variable regression done earlier, R^2 is only .7289, so 72.89 percent of the variation is explained by field-audit labor hours and computer hours. Adding in rewards to informants explains another 25.45 percent of the variation.

We still have not explained the numbers in the columns headed "standard error," "t for H_0: parameter $= 0$," or "prob $> |t|$." These numbers will be used to make inferences about the population regression plane, the topic of the next section.

EXERCISES

12-14 Given the following set of data, use whatever computer package is available to find the best-fitting regression equation and answer the following:

a) What is the regression equation?
b) What is the standard error of the estimate?

c) What is R^2 for this regression?
d) What is the predicted value of Y when $X_1 = 5.8$, $X_2 = 4.2$, and $X_3 = 6.1$?

Y	X_1	X_2	X_3
74.6	5.3	4.0	6.8
90.8	6.1	4.7	7.2
64.2	5.0	3.6	6.4
103.4	7.7	5.4	9.1
77.7	5.5	4.1	7.0
60.2	3.8	2.9	6.0
96.6	7.2	5.2	8.6
34.3	2.1	2.2	4.1

12-15 Given the following set of data, use whatever computer package is available to find the best-fitting regression equation and answer the following:
a) What is the regression equation?
b) What is the standard error of the estimate?
e) What is R^2 for this regression?
d) Give an approximate 95 percent confidence interval for the value of Y when the values of X_1, X_2, X_3, and X_4 are 15.6, 71.8, 93.4, and 1.7, respectively.

X_1	X_2	X_3	X_4	Y
12.4	92.6	91.2	.8	108.22
15.7	70.4	92.4	1.5	127.39
14.8	81.8	89.6	1.2	119.46
11.8	101.4	90.9	.6	102.91
17.6	62.2	92.1	1.8	138.55
19.9	51.6	90.3	2.0	170.32

12-16 Pam Schneider owns and operates an accounting firm in Ithaca, New York. Pam feels that it would be useful to be able to predict in advance the number of rush income tax returns during the busy March 1–April 15 season, so that she can better plan her personnel needs during this time. She has hypothesized that several factors may be useful in her prediction. Data for these factors and numbers of rush returns for past years are:

X_1 ECONOMIC INDEX	X_2 POPULATION WITHIN 1 MILE OF OFFICE	X_3 AVERAGE INCOME IN ITHACA	Y NUMBER OF RUSH RETURNS, MARCH 1–APRIL 15
199	9,188	$11,465	1,906
206	7,566	12,228	1,566
200	9,557	17,665	1,422
229	9,219	15,200	1,721
279	8,662	16,300	2,344

a) Using whatever computer package is available, determine the best-fitting regression equation for these data.
b) What percentage of the total variation in the number of rush returns is explained by this equation?
c) For 1984, the economic index is 269, the population within 1 mile of the office is 9,212, and the average income in Ithaca is $16,925. How many rush returns should Pam expect to process during March 1–April 15?

12-17 David Mathews is a loan officer for a bank in Richmond, Virginia. He is trying to use past knowledge to determine the value of loans defaulting in given months. David feels that this value will be related to the average size of outstanding loans, the total number of loans outstanding, and the rate of inflation during the previous month. David has compiled these data from past months:

Y TOTAL VALUE OF LOANS DEFAULTING	X_1 AVERAGE SIZE OF OUTSTANDING LOANS	X_2 NUMBER OF LOANS OUTSTANDING	X_3 RATE OF INFLATION IN PRECEDING MONTH
$2,033	$1,722	697	1.2%
1,908	2,100	528	0.7
1,541	2,694	466	0.9
3,406	1,229	806	1.1
926	3,661	512	0.8
802	2,944	405	1.0

a) Using whatever computer package is available, determine the best-fitting regression equation for these data.
b) What is R^2 for this equation?
c) What is the standard error of the estimate?
d) For October, David estimates that the average dollar amount of outstanding loans is $1,995. There are 516 loans outstanding, and the inflation rate in September was 1.2 percent. Give an approximate 95 percent confidence interval for the total value of loans defaulting in October.

12-18 Bill Buxton, a statistics professor in a leading business school, has a keen interest in factors affecting students' performance on exams. The mid-term exam for the past semester had a wide distribution of grades, but Bill feels certain that several factors explain the distribution: He allowed his students to study from as many different books as they liked, their IQs vary, they are of different ages, and they study varying amounts of time for exams. To develop a predicting formula for exam grades, Bill asked each student to answer, at the end of the exam, questions regarding study time and number of books used. Bill's teaching records already contained the IQs and ages for the students, so he compiled the data for the class and ran a multiple regression with SAS. The output from Bill's computer run was as follows:

```
        ROOT MSE      11.657308        R-SQUARE         0.7672

                      PARAMETER        STANDARD    T FOR H0:
       VARIABLE   DF   ESTIMATE           ERROR  PARAMETER=0     PROB > |T|

       INTERCEP    1  -49.947647      41.549391       -1.202         0.2684
       HOURS       1    1.069316       0.981632        1.089         0.3121
       IQ          1    1.364595       0.376270        3.627         0.0084
       BOOKS       1    2.039817       1.507990        1.353         0.2182
       AGE         1   -1.798903       0.673319       -2.672         0.0319
```

a) What is the best-fitting regression equation for these data?
b) What percentage of the variation in grades is explained by this equation?
c) What grade would you expect for a 21-year-old student with an IQ of 113, who studied 5 hours and used 3 different books?

12-19 Mary L. Webb owns an investment firm in Boston. Her firm specializes in the sale of bonds, and most of her salespeople are hired after graduation from business school. A little over a year ago, Mary became concerned about the apparent lack of knowledge many of her salespeople displayed regarding the intricacies of bonds. She contracted with a local college to have a series of 15 courses made available to her sales force. Only one of the courses was required of all sales personnel; it covered basic principles, such as the difference between premiums and discounts. The remaining 14 courses were staggered so that any salesperson who wished could take all courses, but few took advantage of more than 10. Mary is now interested in the effects of the courses on sales levels, so she is asking us to prepare an analysis of the data. Because she admits that factors other than training may also influence sales ability, she has added additional information about years of experience and number of clients visited this month for each member of her sales force. The result of a multiple regression run using these data to explain this month's sales (in $1,000s) is:

```
      ROOT MSE        5.302171       R-SQUARE          0.9450

                      PARAMETER     STANDARD    T FOR H0:
VARIABLE    DF        ESTIMATE         ERROR  PARAMETER=0     PROB > |T|

INTERCEP     1        8.497472      8.803709        0.965         0.3717
COURSES      1        5.076890      1.016650        4.994         0.0025
YEARS        1       -0.304431      0.664944       -0.458         0.6632
CLIENTS      1       -0.103262      0.238443       -0.433         0.6801
```

a) What is the best-fitting regression equation, as given by SAS?
b) What is the standard error of the estimate for this equation?
c) What fraction in the variation in sales is explained by this regression?
d) What sales level should Mary expect from a salesperson who took 2 courses, has 3 years of selling experience, and visited 61 clients during the month?

12-20 Norm Elsey manages a department store in Charlotte, North Carolina. Norm has noticed that the number of umbrellas that his store sells on any given day seems to be related to the percent chance of precipitation that day, the predicted high temperature for the day, and the percentage of people unemployed locally. Norm has collected data on 10 different days:

Y NO. OF UMBRELLAS	X_1 PERCENT CHANCE OF PRECIPITATION	X_2 HIGH TEMPERATURE	X_3 PERCENTAGE UNEMPLOYED
35	60	71	6.1
15	20	51	7.3
20	90	82	10.1
10	30	45	11.2
29	40	67	7.2
6	50	30	10.5
21	70	40	6.7
19	55	90	7.5
31	80	63	5.3
30	65	42	8.9

a) Using whatever computer package is available, determine the best-fitting regression equation for these data.
b) What is R^2 for this equation?
c) How many umbrellas should Norm expect to sell on a day when the predicted high temperature is 60, the percent chance of precipitation is 40, and the local unemployment rate is 8.1?

12-21 Allegheny Steel Corporation has been looking into the factors that influence how many millions of tons of steel they are able to sell each year. The management suspects that the following are major factors: the annual national inflation rate, the average price per ton by which imported steel undercuts Allegheny's prices (in dollars), and the number of cars (in millions) that U.S. automakers are planning to produce in that year. Data for the past 7 years have been collected:

YEAR	Y MILLIONS OF TONS SOLD	X_1 INFLATION RATE	X_2 IMPORTED UNDERCUT	X_3 NO. OF CARS
1983	3.2	4.7	3.10	6.1
1982	2.1	5.1	5.00	5.0
1981	3.0	8.5	2.20	5.7
1980	3.7	11.7	4.50	7.2
1979	3.3	16.5	4.35	6.8
1978	2.7	14.0	2.60	6.3
1977	2.5	12.0	3.05	6.0

a) Using whatever computer package is available, determine the best-fitting regression equation for these data.
b) What percentage of the total variation in the number of millions of tons of steel sold by Allegheny each year is explained by this equation?
c) How many tons of steel should Allegheny expect to sell in a year in which the inflation rate is 7.1, American automakers are planning to produce 5.9 million cars, and the average imported price undercut per ton is $3.50?

12-4 MAKING INFERENCES ABOUT POPULATION PARAMETERS

In the preceding chapter, we noted that the *sample* regression line, $\hat{Y} = a + bX$ (Equation 11-3), estimates the *population* regression line, $Y = A + BX$ (Equation 11-13). The reason we could only estimate the population regression line rather than find it exactly was that the data points didn't fall exactly on the population regression line. Because of random disturbances, the data points satisfied $Y = A + BX + e$ (Equation 11-13a) rather than $Y = A + BX$.

Exactly the same sort of thing happens in multiple regression. Our estimated regression plane:

$$\hat{Y} = a + b_1X_1 + b_2X_2 + \cdots + b_kX_k \qquad [12\text{-}5]$$

Population regression plane

is an estimate of a true but unknown population regression plane of the form:

$$Y = A + B_1X_1 + B_2X_2 + \cdots + B_kX_k \qquad [12\text{-}7]$$

Once again, the individual data points usually won't lie exactly on the population regression plane. Consider our IRS problem to see why this is so. Not all payments to informants will be equally effective. Some of the computer hours may be used for collecting and organizing data; others may be used for analyzing those data to seek errors and fraud. The success of the computer in discovering unpaid taxes may depend on how much time is devoted to each of these activities. For these and other reasons, some of the data points will be above the regression plane and some will be below it. Instead of satisfying:

$$Y = A + B_1X_1 + B_2X_2 + \cdots + B_kX_k \qquad \textbf{[12-7]}$$

Random disturbances move points off the regression plane

the individual data points will satisfy:

$$Y = A + B_1X_1 + B_2X_2 + \cdots + B_kX_k + e \qquad \textbf{[12-7a]}$$

The quantity e in Equation 12-7a is a random disturbance, which equals zero on the average. The standard deviation of the individual disturbances is σ_e, and the standard error of estimate, s_e, which we looked at in the last section, is an estimate of σ_e.

Since our *sample* regression plane, $\hat{Y} = a + b_1X_1 + b_2X_2 + \cdots + b_kX_k$ (Equation 12-5) estimates the unknown population regression plane $Y = A + B_1X_1 + B_2X_2 + \cdots + B_kX_k$ (Equation 12-7), we should be able to use it to make inferences about the population regression plane. In this section, we shall make inferences about the slopes ($B_1, B_2, \ldots, B_k$) of the "true" regression equation (the one for the entire population) that are based on the slopes ($b_1, b_2, \ldots, b_k$) of the regression equation estimated from the sample of data points.

Inferences About an Individual Slope B_i

Difference between true regression equation and one estimated from sample observations

The regression plane is derived from a sample and not from the entire population. As a result, we cannot expect the true regression equation, $Y = A + B_1X_1 + B_2X_2 + \cdots + B_kX_k$ (the one for the entire population), to be exactly the same as the equation estimated from the sample observations, $\hat{Y} = a + b_1X_1 + b_2X_2 + \cdots + b_kX_k$. Even so, we can use the value of b_i, one of the slopes we calculate from a sample, to test hypotheses about the value of the B_i, one of the slopes of the regression plane for the entire population.

Testing a hypothesis about B_i

The procedure for testing a hypothesis about B_i is similar to procedures discussed in Chapter 9, on hypothesis testing. To understand this process, return to the problem that related unpaid taxes discovered to field-audit labor hours, computer hours, and rewards to informants. On page 560, we pointed out that $b_1 = .597$. The first step is to find some value for B_1 to compare with $b_1 = .597$.

Suppose that over an extended past period of time, the slope of the relationship between X and Y_1 was .400. To test if this were still the case, we could define the hypotheses as:

H_0: $B_1 = .400 \leftarrow$ null hypothesis

H_1: B_1 is not equal to $.400 \leftarrow$ alternative hypothesis

In effect, then, we are testing to learn whether current data indicate that B_1 has changed from its historical value of .400.

Standard error of the regression coefficient

To find the test statistic for B_1, it is necessary first to find the *standard error of the regression coefficient.* Here, the regression coefficient we are working with is b_1, so the standard error of this coefficient is denoted s_{b_1}.

It is too difficult to compute s_{b_1} by hand, but fortunately, SAS computes the standard errors of all the regression coefficients for us. For convenience, Table 12-4 is repeated.

TABLE 12-4 SAS output

ROOT MSE		0.286128	R-SQUARE	0.9834	
VARIABLE	DF	PARAMETER ESTIMATE	STANDARD ERROR	T FOR H0: PARAMETER=0	PROB > |T|
INTERCEP	1	-45.796348	4.877651	-9.389	0.0001
AUDIT	1	0.596972	0.081124	7.359	0.0003
COMPUTER	1	1.176838	0.084074	13.998	0.0001
REWARDS	1	0.405109	0.042234	9.592	0.0001

Finding upper and lower limits of the acceptance region for our hypothesis test

From the output, we see that s_{b_1} is 0.0811. (Similarly, if we want to test a hypothesis about B_2, we see that the appropriate standard error to use is $s_{b_2} = 0.0841$.) Once we have found s_{b_1} we can use the t distribution with $n - k - 1$ degrees of freedom and the following equation to calculate the upper and lower limits of the acceptance region.

$$\left.\begin{array}{l}\text{Upper limit of acceptance region} = B_i + t(s_{b_i}) \\ \text{Lower limit of acceptance region} = B_i - t(s_{b_i})\end{array}\right\} \quad \textbf{[12-8]}$$

where:

- t = appropriate t value (with $n - k - 1$ degrees of freedom) for the significance level of the test
- B_i = actual slope hypothesized for the population
- s_{b_i} = standard error of the regression coefficient

Conducting the hypothesis test

Suppose we are interested in testing our hypothesis at the 10 percent level of significance. Since we have ten observations in our sample data, and three independent variables, we know that we have $n - k - 1$ or $10 - 3 - 1 = 6$ degrees of freedom. We look in Appendix Table 2 under the 10 percent column and come down until we find the 6 degrees of freedom row. There, we see that the appropriate t value is 1.943. Since we are concerned whether b_1 (the slope of the sample regression plane) is significantly different from B_1 (the hypothesized slope of the population regression plane), this is a two-tailed test, and the limits of the acceptance region are found using Equation 12-8, with $i = 1$, since we are testing hypotheses about B_1.

$$B_1 + t(s_{b_1}) = .400 + 1.943(0.0811)$$
$$= .558 \leftarrow \text{upper limit of acceptance region}$$

$$B_1 - t(s_{b_1}) = .400 - 1.943(0.0811)$$
$$= .242 \leftarrow \text{lower limit of acceptance region}$$

The slope of our regression plane (b_1) is .597, which is *not* inside the acceptance region. Therefore, we reject the null hypothesis that B_1 still equals .400. In other words, there *is* enough difference between b_1 and .400 for us to conclude that B_1 has changed from its historical value. Because of this, we feel that each additional 100 hours of field-audit labor no longer increases unpaid taxes discovered by $400,000 as it did in the past.

Confidence interval for B_i

In addition to hypothesis testing, we can also construct a *confidence interval* for any one of the values of B_i. In the same way that b_i is a point estimate of B_i, such confidence intervals are interval estimates of B_i. To illustrate the process of constructing a confidence interval, let's find a 95 percent confidence interval for B_3 in our IRS problem. The relevant data are:

$$\left.\begin{array}{l} b_3 = 0.405 \\ s_{b_3} = 0.0422 \end{array}\right\} \text{from Table 12.4}$$

$$t = 2.447 \leftarrow \text{5 percent level of significance and 6 degrees of freedom}$$

With this information, we can calculate confidence intervals like this:

$$b_3 + t(s_{b_3}) = 0.405 + 2.447(0.0422)$$
$$= .508 \leftarrow \text{upper limit}$$

$$b_3 - t(s_{b_3}) = 0.405 - 2.447(0.0422)$$
$$= .302 \leftarrow \text{lower limit}$$

We see that we can be 95 percent confident that each additional $1,000 paid to informants increases the unpaid taxes discovered by some amount between $302,000 and $508,000.

Is an explanatory variable significant?

We will often be interested in questions of the form: Does Y really depend on X_i? For example, we could ask whether unpaid taxes discovered really depend on computer hours. Frequently this question is phrased as, "Is X_i a significant explanatory variable for Y?" A bit of thought should convince you that Y depends on X_i (that is, Y varies when X_i varies) if $B_i \neq 0$, and it doesn't depend on X_i if $B_i = 0$.

We see that our question leads to hypotheses of the form:

H_0: $B_i = 0 \leftarrow$ null hypothesis: X_i is not a significant explanatory variable.

H_1: $B_i \neq 0 \leftarrow$ alternative hypothesis: X_i is a significant explanatory variable.

We can test these hypotheses using Equation 12-8 just as we did when we tested our hypotheses about whether B_1 still equaled .400. However, there is an easier way to do this, using the column on the output in Table 12-4 headed "t for H_0: parameter = 0." Look at Equation 12-8 again:

$$\text{Upper limit of acceptance region} = B_i + t(s_{b_i})$$
$$\text{Lower limit of acceptance region} = B_i - t(s_{b_i}) \qquad \textbf{[12-8]}$$

If we let U denote the upper limit and L the lower limit, and note that $B_i = 0$ in the hypothesis test, Equation 12-8 becomes:

$$U = B_i + t(s_{b_i}) = 0 + t(s_{b_i}) = t(s_{b_i})$$
$$L = B_i - t(s_{b_i}) = 0 - t(s_{b_i}) = -t(s_{b_i})$$

and we accept H_0 if:

$$-t(s_{b_i}) \leqslant b_i \leqslant t(s_{b_i})$$

which is the same as saying, accept H_0 if:

$$-t \leqslant \frac{b_i}{s_{b_i}} \leqslant t$$

Using "computed t values" from SAS output

Now the t value in this last expression is the "critical" t value that we look up in Appendix Table 2. Let's call this t_c. The ratio b_i/s_{b_i} is called the "observed" or "computed" t value, denoted t_o. This is the number that appears in the column headed "t for H_0: parameter = 0" in Table 12-4. So, to test hypotheses about whether X_i is a significant explanatory variable, we need only check whether:

$$-t_c \leqslant t_o \leqslant t_c \qquad \textbf{[12-9]}$$

where:

- t_c = appropriate t value (with $n - k - 1$ degrees of freedom) for the significance level of the test
- $t_o = b_i/s_{b_i}$ = observed (or computed) t value obtained from the computer output

If t_o falls between $-t_c$ and t_c, we accept H_0 and conclude X_i is not a significant explanatory variable. Otherwise, we reject H_0 and conclude that X_i is a significant explanatory variable.

Testing the significance of computer hours in the IRS problem

Let's test, at the .01 significance level, whether computer hours are a significant explanatory variable for unpaid taxes discovered. From Appendix Table 2, with $n - k - 1 = 10 - 3 - 1 = 6$ degrees of freedom and $\alpha = .01$, we see that $t_c = 3.707$. From Table 12-4, we see that $t_o = 13.997$. Since $t_o > t_c$, we conclude that computer hours *are* a significant explanatory variable. In fact, looking at the computed t values for the other two independent variables (field-audit labor hours $t_o = 7.359$ and rewards to informants, $t_o = 9.592$), we see that each of them is also a significant explanatory variable.

We can also use the column headed "prob $> |t|$" to test if X_i is a significant explanatory variable. In fact, using that information, we don't even need to use Appendix Table 2. The entries in this column are *prob values* for the hypotheses:

$$H_0: B_i = 0$$
$$H_1: B_i \neq 0$$

Recall from the discussion of section 9 in Chapter 9 that these prob values are the probabilities that each b_i would be as far (or farther) away from zero than the observed value obtained from our regression, *if H_0 is true*. As Fig. 12-2 illustrates, we need only compare these prob values with α, the significance level of the test, to determine whether or not X_i is a significant explanatory variable for Y.

The absolute-value sign is included in "prob $> |t|$" because testing the significance of an explanatory variable is a two-tailed test. The independent variable X_i is a significant explanatory variable if b_i is significantly *different* from zero; that is, if t_o is a large positive or a large negative number.

In the IRS example, let's repeat our tests at $\alpha = .01$. For each of the three independent variables, prob $> |t|$ is less than .01, so we again conclude that each one is a significant explanatory variable.

FIGURE 12-2
Using "prob $> |t|$" to see if X_i is a significant explanatory variable

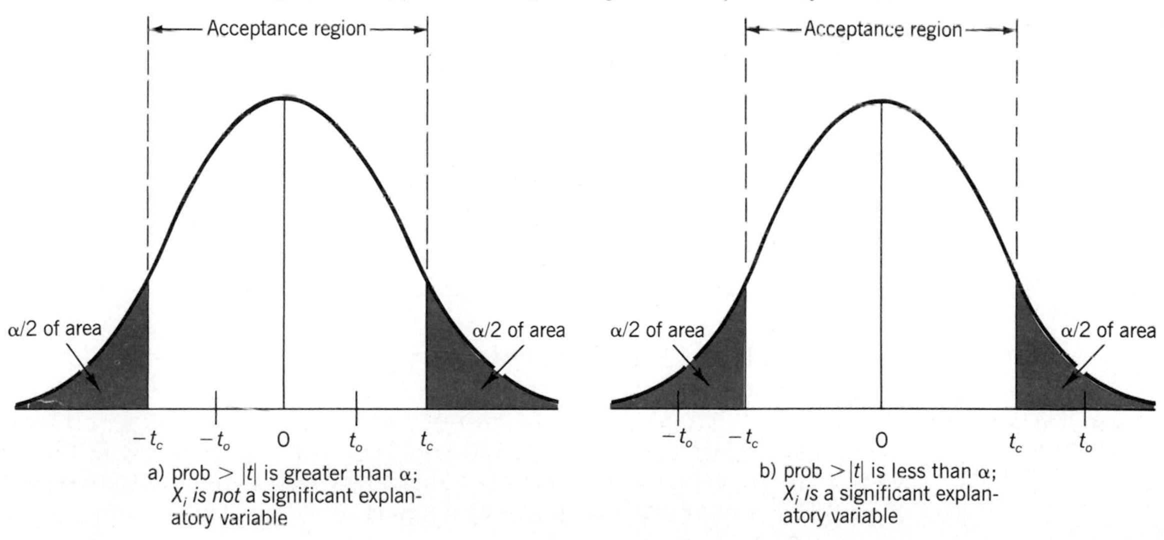

Inferences About the Regression as a Whole

Suppose you put a piece of graph paper over a dartboard and randomly tossed a bunch of darts at it. After you took the darts out, you would have something that looked very much like a scatter diagram. Suppose you then fit a simple regression line to this set of "observed data points" and calculated r^2. Because the darts were randomly tossed, you would expect to get a low value of r^2, since in this case, X really doesn't explain Y. However, if you did this many times, occasionally you would observe a high value of r^2, just by pure chance.

Significance of the regression as a whole

Well, then, given any simple (or multiple) regression, **it's natural to ask whether the value of r^2 (or R^2) really indicates that the independent variables explain Y, or might this have happened just by chance?** This question is often phrased, Is the regression as a whole significant? In the last section, we looked at how to tell whether an individual X_i was a significant explanatory variable; now we see how to tell whether all the X_i's taken together significantly explain the variability observed in Y. Our hypotheses are:

H_0: $B_1 = B_2 \ . \ . \ . = B_k = 0$ ← null hypothesis: Y doesn't depend on the X_i's

H_1: at least one $B_i \neq 0$ ← alternative hypothesis: Y depends on at least one of the X_i's

---

Analyzing the variation in the Y values

When we discussed r^2 in Chapter 11, we looked at the total variation in Y, $\Sigma(Y - \overline{Y})^2$, the part of that variation which is explained by the regression, $\Sigma(\hat{Y} - \overline{Y})^2$, and the unexplained part of that variation, $\Sigma(Y - \hat{Y})^2$. Figure 12-3 is a duplicate of Fig. 11-15. It reviews the relationship between total deviation, explained deviation, and unexplained deviation for a single data point in a simple regression. Although we can't draw a similar picture for a multiple regression, we are doing the same thing conceptually.

Sums of squares and their degrees of freedom

In discussing the variation in Y, then, we look at three different terms, each of which is a sum of squares. We denote these by:

$$\left.\begin{aligned} \text{SST} &= \text{the total sum of squares} = \Sigma(Y - \overline{Y})^2 \\ \text{SSR} &= \text{the regression sum of squares} = \Sigma(\hat{Y} - \overline{Y})^2 \\ &\quad \text{(i.e., the explained part)} \\ \text{SSE} &= \text{the error sum of squares} = \Sigma(Y - \hat{Y})^2 \\ &\quad \text{(i.e., the unexplained part)} \end{aligned}\right\} \quad \textbf{[12-10]}$$

These are related by the equation

$$\text{SST} = \text{SSR} + \text{SSE} \quad \textbf{[12-11]}$$

which says that the total variation in Y can be broken down into two parts, the explained part and the unexplained part.

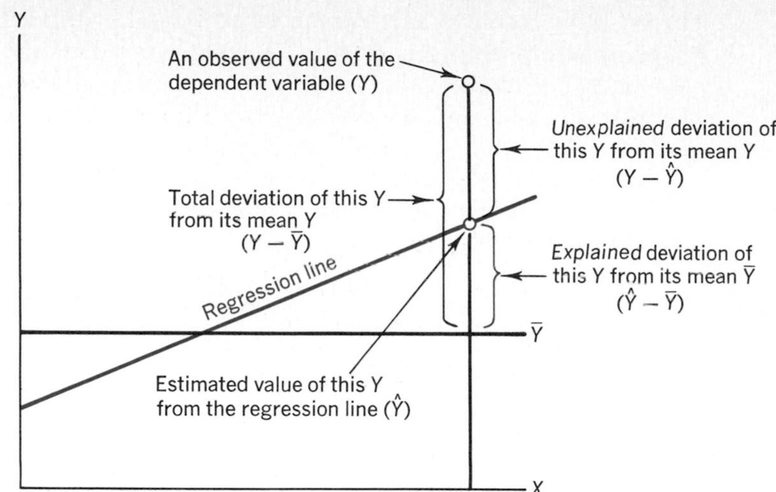

FIGURE 12-3 Total deviation, explained deviation, and unexplained deviation for *one* observed value of Y

Each of these sums of squares has an associated number of degrees of freedom. SST has $n - 1$ degrees of freedom (n observations, but we lose a degree of freedom because the sample mean is fixed). SSR has k degrees of freedom, because there are k independent variables being used to explain Y. Finally, SSE has $n - k - 1$ degrees of freedom, because we used our n observations to estimate $k + 1$ constants, $a, b_1, b_2, \ldots, b_k$. If the null hypothesis is true, the ratio:

$$F = \frac{\text{SSR}/k}{\text{SSE}/(n - k - 1)} \quad \textbf{[12-12]}$$

F test on the regression as a whole

has an F distribution with k numerator degrees of freedom and $n - k - 1$ denominator degrees of freedom. If the null hypothesis is false, then the F ratio tends to be larger than it is when the null hypothesis is true. So if the F ratio is too high (as determined by the significance level of the test and the appropriate value from Appendix Table 6), we reject H_0 and conclude that the regression as a whole *is* significant.

Analysis of variance for the regression

Table 12-5 gives more of the SAS output for the IRS problem. This part of the output includes the computed F ratio for the regression, and is sometimes called "the analysis of variance for the regression." You are probably wondering whether this has anything to do with the analysis of variance we discussed in Chapter 10. Yes, it does. Although we did not do so, it is possible to show that the analysis of variance in Chapter 10 also looks at the total variation of all of the observations about the grand mean, and

TABLE 12-5 More SAS output: the analysis of variance

DEP VARIABLE: DISCOVER UNPAID TAXES DISCOVERED ($MILLIONS)

SOURCE	DF	SUM OF SQUARES	MEAN SQUARE	F VALUE	PROB>F
MODEL	3	29.108784	9.702928	118.517	0.0001
ERROR	6	0.491216	0.081869		
C TOTAL	9	29.600000			

breaks it up into two parts: one part explained by the differences among the several groups (corresponding to what we called the "between-column variance") and the other part unexplained by those differences (corresponding to what we called the "within-column variance"). This is precisely analogous to what we just did in Equation 12-11.

For the IRS problem, we see that SSR = 29.109 (with $k = 3$ degrees of freedom), SSE = 0.491 (with $n - k - 1 = 10 - 3 - 1 = 6$ degrees of freedom) and that:

Testing the significance of the IRS regression

$$F = \frac{29.109/3}{0.491/6} = \frac{9.703}{0.082} = 118.517$$

The entries in the "mean square" column are just the sums of squares divided by their degrees of freedom. For 3 numerator degrees of freedom and 6 denominator degrees of freedom, Appendix Table 6 tells us that 9.78 is the upper limit of the acceptance region for a significance level of $\alpha = .01$. Our calculated F value of 118.517 is far above 9.78, so we see that the regression as a whole is highly significant. We can also reach the same conclusion by noting that the output tells us that "prob > F" is .0001. Since this prob value is less than our significance level of $\alpha = .01$, we conclude that the regression as a whole is significant. Using "prob > F" analogously to the way we used "prob > $|t|$" in testing the significance of the individual explanatory variables, we see that we can do the test without having to use Appendix Table 6.

Multicollinearity in Multiple Regression

Definition and effect of multicollinearity

In multiple regression analysis, the regression coefficients often become less reliable as the degree of correlation between the independent variables increases. If there is a high level of correlation between them, we have a problem that statisticians call *multicollinearity*.

Multicollinearity might occur if we wished to estimate a firm's sales revenue, and we used both the number of salespersons employed and their total salaries. Since the values associated with these two independent variables are highly correlated, we need to use only one set of them to make our estimate. In fact, adding a second variable that is correlated with the first distorts the values of the regression coefficients. Nevertheless, we can often predict Y well, even when multicollinearity is present.

An example of multicollinearity

Let's look at an example in which multicollinearity is present, to see how it affects the regression. For the past twelve months, the manager of Pizza Shack has been running a series of advertisements in the local newspaper. The ads are scheduled and paid for in the month before they appear. Each of the ads contains a two-for-one coupon, which entitles the bearer to receive two Pizza Shack pizzas while paying for only the more expensive of the two. The manager has collected the data in Table 12-6 and would like to use it to predict pizza sales.

Two simple regressions

In Tables 12-7 and 12-8, we have given the SAS outputs for the regression of total sales on number of ads and cost of ads respectively.

TABLE 12-6 Pizza Shack sales and advertising data

MONTH	X_1 NUMBER OF ADS APPEARING	X_2 COST OF ADS APPEARING (00s OF DOLLARS)	Y TOTAL PIZZA SALES (000s OF DOLLARS)
May	12	$13.9	$43.6
June	11	12.0	38.0
July	9	9.3	30.1
Aug.	7	9.7	35.3
Sept.	12	12.3	46.4
Oct.	8	11.4	34.2
Nov.	6	9.3	30.2
Dec.	13	14.3	40.7
Jan.	8	10.2	38.5
Feb.	6	8.4	22.6
March	8	11.2	37.6
April	10	11.1	35.2

For the regression on number of ads, we see that the observed t value is 3.952. With 10 degrees of freedom and a significance level of $\alpha = .01$, the critical t value (from Appendix Table 2) is found to be 3.169. Since $t_o > t_c$ (or equivalently, since prob $> |t|$ is less than .01), we conclude that the number of ads is a highly significant explanatory variable for total sales. Note also

TABLE 12-7 Regression of sales on number of ads

```
MODEL: ADS
DEP VARIABLE: SALES     TOTAL PIZZA SALES (THOUSANDS OF $)
                         SUM OF           MEAN
SOURCE      DF          SQUARES          SQUARE        F VALUE         PROB>F
MODEL        1          276.308         276.308         15.621         0.0027
ERROR       10          176.879       17.687880
C TOTAL     11          453.187
    ROOT MSE           4.205696        R-SQUARE         0.6097

                      PARAMETER        STANDARD     T FOR H0:
VARIABLE    DF         ESTIMATE           ERROR   PARAMETER=0     PROB > |T|

INTERCEP     1        16.936911        4.981827         3.400         0.0068
ADS          1         2.083246        0.527086         3.952         0.0027
```

TABLE 12-8 Regression of sales on cost of ads

```
MODEL: COST
DEP VARIABLE: SALES     TOTAL PIZZA SALES (THOUSANDS OF $)
                         SUM OF           MEAN
SOURCE      DF          SQUARES          SQUARE        F VALUE         PROB>F
MODEL        1          305.039         305.039         20.590         0.0011
ERROR       10          148.148       14.814803
C TOTAL     11          453.187
    ROOT MSE           3.849000        R-SQUARE         0.6731


                      PARAMETER        STANDARD     T FOR H0:
VARIABLE    DF         ESTIMATE           ERROR   PARAMETER=0     PROB > |T|

INTERCEP     1         4.172700        7.108790         0.587         0.5702
COST         1         2.872484        0.633036         4.538         0.0011
```

that $r^2 = .6097$, so that the number of ads explains about 61 percent of the variation in pizza sales.

For the regression on cost of ads, the observed t value is 4.538, so that cost of ads is even more significant as an explanatory variable for total sales than was number of ads (for which the observed t value was only 3.952). In this regression, $r^2 = .6731$, so about 67 percent of the variation in pizza sales is explained by the cost of ads.

Using both explanatory variables in a multiple regression

Since both explanatory variables are highly significant by themselves, we try to use both of them in a multiple regression. The output is in Table 12-9.

TABLE 12-9 Regression of sales on number and cost of ads

```
MODEL: BOTH
DEP VARIABLE: SALES     TOTAL PIZZA SALES (THOUSANDS OF $)
                        SUM OF          MEAN
SOURCE        DF       SQUARES        SQUARE       F VALUE       PROB>F
MODEL          2       309.986       154.993         9.741       0.0056
ERROR          9       143.201     15.911202
C TOTAL       11       453.187
    ROOT MSE          3.988885      R-SQUARE        0.6840

                     PARAMETER      STANDARD     T FOR H0:
VARIABLE      DF      ESTIMATE         ERROR   PARAMETER=0   PROB > |T|

INTERCEP       1      6.583578      8.542155         0.771       0.4606
ADS            1      0.624675      1.120277         0.558       0.5907
COST           1      2.138864      1.470150         1.455       0.1797
```

The multiple regression is highly significant as a whole, since prob $> F$ is 0.0056.

The multiple coefficient of determination is $R^2 = .6840$, so the two variables together explain about 68 percent of the variation in total sales.

Loss of individual significance

However, if we look at the prob $> |t|$ values for the variables in the multiple regression, we see that even at $\alpha = .1$, neither variable is a significant explanatory variable.

What has happened here? In the simple regression, each variable is highly significant, and in the multiple regression, they are collectively very significant, but individually not significant.

Correlation between the two explanatory variables

This apparent contradiction is explained once we notice that the number of ads is highly correlated with the cost of ads. In fact, the correlation between these two variables is $r = .8949$, so we have a problem with multicollinearity in our data. You might wonder why these two variables are not perfectly correlated. This is because the cost of an ad varies slightly, depending on where it appears in the newspaper. For instance, in the Sunday paper, ads in the TV section cost more than ads in the news section, and the manager of Pizza Shack has placed Sunday ads in each of these sections on different occasions.

Both variables explain the same thing

Since X_1 and X_2 are closely related to each other, in effect they each explain the same part of the variability in Y. That's why we get $r^2 = .6097$ in the first simple regression, $r^2 = .6731$ in the second simple regression, but an r^2 of only .6840 in the multiple regression: Adding number of ads as a second explanatory variable to cost of ads explains only about 1 percent more of the variation in total sales.

Individual contributions can't be separated out

At this point, it is fair to ask, "Which variable is really explaining the variation in total sales in the multiple regression?" The answer is that both are, but **we cannot separate out their individual contributions, because they are so highly correlated with each other. As a result of this, their coefficients in the multiple regression have high standard errors and relatively small computed *t* values, and relatively large prob > |*t*| values.**

How does this multicollinearity affect us? We are still able to make relatively precise predictions when it is present: Note that for the multiple regression (output in Table 12-9) the standard error of estimate, which determines the width of confidence intervals for predictions, is 3.99, while for the simple regression with cost of ads as the explanatory variable (output in Table 12-8), we have $s_e = 3.85$. What we can't do is tell with much precision how sales will change if we increase the number of ads by 1. The multiple regression says $b_1 = .625$ (that is, each ad increases total pizza sales by about \$625), but the standard error of this coefficient is 1.12 (that is, about \$1,120).

EXERCISES

12-22 Suppose that regressions have been run each month for several years on variables 1, 2, and 3. Variable 3 has always been labeled the "dependent variable" and variables 1 and 2 have always been labeled the "independent variables." Historically, the value of B_1 in these regressions has been .150. The regression for this month is based on 8 data points and has just been run on SAS. Here are the results:

VARIABLE	DF	PARAMETER ESTIMATE	STANDARD ERROR	T FOR HØ: PARAMETER=Ø	PROB > |T|
INTERCEP	1	18.012141	1.180060	15.264	0.0043
VARIABL1	1	0.232491	0.083367	2.789	0.1081
VARIABL2	1	1.150570	0.099667	11.544	0.0074

a) At a significance level of .05, is there significant evidence that the value of B_1 has changed from the historical value?

b) Give a 90 percent confidence interval for the value of B_2 in this regression.

12-23 Refer to problem 12-18. At a significance level of .05, is IQ a significant explanatory variable for exam scores? (There were 12 students in the sample.)

12-24 Refer to problem 12-18. The following additional output was provided by SAS when Bill ran the multiple regression:

DEP VARIABLE: SCORE EXAM SCORE

SOURCE	DF	SUM OF SQUARES	MEAN SQUARE	F VALUE
MODEL	4	3134.417	783.604	
ERROR	7	951.250	135.893	
C TOTAL	11	4085.667		

a) What is the observed value of F?
b) At a significance level of .01, what is the appropriate critical value of F to use in determining if the regression is as a whole significant?
c) Based upon your answers to *a* and *b*, *is* the regression significant as a whole?

12-25 Refer to problem 12-19. At a significance level of .05, is the number of courses taken this year a significant explanatory variable for monthly sales? (There were 10 salespeople in Mary's sample.)

12-26 Refer to problem 12-19. The following additional output was provided by SAS when the multiple regression was run:

```
DEP VARIABLE: SALES     SALES THIS MONTH (THOUSANDS OF $)
                          SUM OF             MEAN
SOURCE       DF          SQUARES           SQUARE          F VALUE          PROB>F
MODEL         3         2900.065          966.688           34.386          0.0004
ERROR         6          168.678        28.113020
C TOTAL       9         3068.744
```

At a .05 level of significance, is the regression significant as a whole?

12-27 Henry Lander is director of production for the Alecos Corporation of Caracas, Venezuela. Henry has asked you to help him determine a predicting formula for absenteeism in a meat-packing facility. He hypothesizes that percentage absenteeism can be explained by average daily temperature. Data are gathered for several months, you run the simple regression, and you find that temperature explains 66 percent of the variation in absenteeism. But Henry is not convinced that this is a satisfactory predictor. He suggests that daily rainfall may also have something to do with absenteeism. So you gather data, run a regression of absenteeism during rainfall, and get an R^2 of .59. "Eureka!" you cry, "I've got it! With one predictor that explains 66 percent and another that explains 59 percent, all I have to do is run a multiple regression using both predictors, and I'll surely have an almost perfect predictor!" To your dismay, however, the multiple regression has an R^2 of only 68 percent, which is just slightly better than the temperature variable alone. How can you account for this apparent discrepancy?

12-28 Juan Armenlegg, manager of Rocky's Diamond and Jewelry Store, is interested in developing a model to estimate consumer demand for his rather expensive merchandise. Since most customers buy diamonds and jewelry on credit, Juan is sure that 2 factors that must influence consumer demand are the current annual inflation rate and the current prime lending rate at the leading banks in the country. Explain some of the problems that Juan might encounter if he were to set up a regression model based on his two predictor variables.

12-29 Edith Pratt is a busy executive in a nationwide trucking company. Edith is late for a meeting because she has been unable to locate the multiple regression computer output that a subordinate produced for her. If the total regression was significant at the .05 level, then she wanted to use the computer output as evidence to support some of her ideas for the company at the meeting. The subordinate, however, called in sick today and she has been unable to locate his work. As a matter of fact, all the information she possesses concerning the multiple regression is a piece of scrap paper with the following on it:

REGRESSION FOR E. PRATT

SSR		, with 6 *df*
SSE	743.5	, with *df*
SST	2015.7	, with 17 *df*

Since the scrap paper doesn't even have a complete set of numbers on it, Edith has concluded that it must be useless. You, however, should know better. Should Edith go directly to the meeting, or continue looking for the computer output?

12-30 Mike Murphy, the owner of Murphy Airlines, is attempting to determine what factors influence the number of passengers that fly Murphy each year. He is currently looking at various measures of his company's performance; service level (measured between 0 and 100, with 100 being perfect) to customers on board, the percentage of passengers whose luggage is lost, and the percentage of Murphy flights that are on time. Each of these measures has been calculated for the past 6 years.

YEAR	Y PASSENGERS	X_1 SERVICE	X_2 % LUGGAGE LOST	X_3 % ON TIME
1983	2,600	72	7.2	91
1982	3,125	81	6.5	97
1981	2,710	78	6.2	94
1980	2,900	75	8.5	93
1979	3,251	76	7.0	96
1978	3,475	85	5.1	98

a) Using whatever computer package is available, determine the best-fitting regression equation for these data.
b) Historically, Murphy Airlines has found B_3 to be 50. At the .05 significance level, has this changed?
c) Give an 80 percent confidence interval for B_1.

12-5 MODELING TECHNIQUES

Looking at different models

Given a variable we want to explain and a bunch of potential explanatory variables, there may be several different regression equations we can look at, depending on which explanatory variables we include and how we include them. Each such regression equation is called a *model. Modeling techniques* are the various ways in which we can include the explanatory variables and check the appropriateness of our regression models. There are many different modeling techniques, but we shall look at only two of the most commonly used devices.

Qualitative Data and Dummy Variables

In all the regression examples we have looked at so far, the data have been numerical, or *quantitative*. But occasionally we will be faced with a variable that is categorical, or *qualitative*. In our chapter opening problem, the director of personnel wanted to see if the base salary of a salesperson depended on the person's sex. Table 12-10 repeats the data of that problem.

TABLE 12-10 Data for sex-discrimination problem

Salesmen		Saleswomen	
MONTHS EMPLOYED	BASE SALARY ($1,000s)	MONTHS EMPLOYED	BASE SALARY ($1,000s)
6	7.5	5	6.2
10	8.6	13	8.7
12	9.1	15	9.4
18	10.3	21	9.8
30	13.0		

Reviewing a previous way to approach the problem

For the moment, ignore the length of employment and use the technique developed in Chapter 9 for testing the difference between means of two populations, to see if men earn more than women. Test this at $\alpha = .01$. If we let the men be population 1 and the women be population 2, we are testing:

$H_0: \mu_1 = \mu_2$ ← null hypothesis: There is no sex discrimination in base salaries.

$H_1: \mu_1 > \mu_2$ ← alternative hypothesis: Women are discriminated against in base salary.

$\alpha = .01$ ← level of significance

We sketch the analysis below. If you have any trouble following it, you should review briefly pages 386–394.

$$n_1 = 5 \qquad n_2 = 4$$
$$\bar{x}_1 = 9.7 \qquad \bar{x}_2 = 8.525$$
$$s_1^2 = 4.415 \qquad s_2^2 = 2.609$$

$$s_p^2 = \frac{(n_1 - 1)s_1^2 + (n_2 - 1)s_2^2}{n_1 + n_2 - 2} \qquad \textbf{[9-3]}$$
$$= \frac{4(4.415) + 3(2.609)}{5 + 4 - 2}$$
$$= 3.641$$

$$s = s_p\sqrt{\frac{1}{n_1} + \frac{1}{n_2}} \qquad \textbf{[9-4]}$$
$$= 1.28$$

With 7 degrees of freedom, the upper limit of the acceptance region is $0 + 1.28(2.998) = 3.84$. The observed value of $\bar{x}_1 - \bar{x}_2 = 1.175$, which we see is less than 3.84, so we cannot reject H_0.

The old approach doesn't detect any discrimination

Our analysis therefore concludes that there does not appear to be any sex discrimination in base salaries. But recall that we have ignored the length-of-employment data thus far in the analysis.

"Eyeballing" the data

Before we go any farther, look at a scatter diagram of the data. In Fig. 12-4, the black points correspond to men and the colored circles correspond to women. The scatter diagram clearly shows that base salary increases with length of service; but if you try to "eyeball" the regression line, you'll note that the black points tend to be above it, and the colored circles tend to be below it.

Table 12-11 gives the output from a regression of base salary on months employed. From that output we see that months employed is a very highly significant explanatory variable.

Also, $r^2 = .9260$, indicating that months employed explains about 93 percent of the variation in base salary. Table 12-11 contains part of the

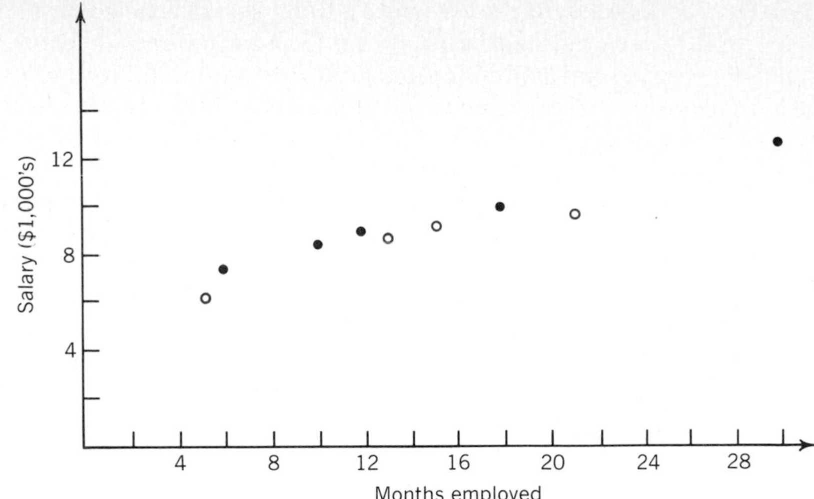

FIGURE 12-4 Scatter diagram of base salaries plotted against months employed

output that we haven't seen before, a table of *residuals*. For each data point, the residual is just $Y - \hat{Y}$, which we recognize as the error in the fit of the regression line at that point.

"Squeezing the residuals"

Perhaps the most important part of analyzing a regression output is looking at the residuals. If the regression includes all the relevant explanatory factors, these residuals ought to be random. Looking at this in another way, if the residuals show any nonrandom patterns, this

TABLE 12-11 Regression of base salary on months employed

MODEL: MONTHS
DEP VARIABLE: SALARY BASE SALARY (THOUSANDS OF $)

SOURCE	DF	SUM OF SQUARES	MEAN SQUARE	F VALUE	PROB>F
MODEL	1	26.442724	26.442724	87.607	0.0001
ERROR	7	2.112831	0.301833		
C TOTAL	8	28.555556			
ROOT MSE		0.549393	R-SQUARE	0.9260	

VARIABLE	DF	PARAMETER ESTIMATE	STANDARD ERROR	T FOR H0: PARAMETER=0	PROB > |T|
INTERCEP	1	5.809278	0.403802	14.386	0.0001
MONTHS	1	0.233204	0.024915	9.360	0.0001

OBS	ACTUAL	PREDICT VALUE	RESIDUAL
1	7.500	7.209	0.291499
2	8.600	8.141	0.458684
3	9.100	8.608	0.492276
4	10.300	10.007	0.293053
5	13.000	12.805	0.194607
6	6.200	6.975	-.775297
7	8.700	8.841	-.140928
8	9.400	9.307	0.092665
9	9.800	10.707	-.906559

indicates that there is something systematic going on that we have failed to take into account. So we look for patterns in the residuals; or to put it somewhat more picturesquely, we "squeeze the residuals until they talk."

Noticing a pattern in the residuals

As we look at the residuals in Table 12-11, we note that the first five residuals are positive. So for the salesmen, we have $Y - \hat{Y} > 0$, or $Y > \hat{Y}$; that is to say, the regression line falls below these five data points. Three of the last four residuals are negative. And thus for the saleswomen, we have $Y - \hat{Y} < 0$, or $Y < \hat{Y}$, so the regression line lies above three of the four data points. This confirms the observation we made when we looked at the scatter diagram in Fig. 12-4. This nonrandom pattern in the residuals suggests that sex *is* a factor in determining base salary.

Using dummy variables

How can we incorporate the salesperson's sex *into* the regression model? We do this by using a device called a *dummy variable* (or an *indicator variable*). For the points representing salesmen, this variable is given the value 0, and for the points representing saleswomen, it is given the value 1. The input data for our regression using dummy variables are given in Table 12-12.

TABLE 12-12 Input data for sex-discrimination regression

	X_1 MONTHS EMPLOYED	X_2 SEX	Y BASE SALARY ($1,000s)
Men	6	0	7.5
	10	0	8.6
	12	0	9.1
	18	0	10.3
	30	0	13.0
Women	5	1	6.2
	13	1	8.7
	15	1	9.4
	21	1	9.8

To the data in Table 12-12, we fit a regression of the form:

$$\hat{Y} = a + b_1X_1 + b_2X_2 \quad \textbf{[12-5]}$$

Let's see what happens if we use this regression to predict the base salary of an individual with X_1 months of service:

$$\text{Salesman:} \quad \hat{Y} = a + b_1X_1 + b_2(0) = a + b_1X_1$$

$$\text{Saleswoman:} \quad \hat{Y} = a + b_1X_1 + b_2(1) = a + b_1X_1 + b_2$$

Interpreting the coefficient of the dummy variable

For salesmen and saleswomen with the same length of employment, we predict a base salary difference of b_2 thousands of dollars. Now, b_2 is just our estimate of B_2 in the population regression:

$$Y = A + B_1X_1 + B_2X_2 \quad \textbf{[12-7]}$$

Testing for discrimination

If there really is discrimination against women, they should earn less than men with the same length of service. In other words, B_2 should be negative. We can test this at the .01 level of significance.

$H_0: B_2 = 0$ ← null hypothesis: There is no sex discrimination in base salaries.

$H_1: B_2 < 0$ ← alternative hypothesis: Women are discriminated against.

$\alpha = .01$ ← level of significance

In order to test these hypotheses, we run a regression on the data in Table 12-12. The results of that regression are given in Table 12-13.

TABLE 12-13 Output from sex-discrimination regression

MODEL: BOTH
DEP VARIABLE: SALARY BASE SALARY (THOUSANDS OF $)

SOURCE	DF	SUM OF SQUARES	MEAN SQUARE	F VALUE	PROB>F
MODEL	2	27.807744	13.903872	111.556	0.0001
ERROR	6	0.747812	0.124635		
C TOTAL	8	28.555556			
ROOT MSE		0.353037	R-SQUARE	0.9738	

VARIABLE	DF	PARAMETER ESTIMATE	STANDARD ERROR	T FOR H0: PARAMETER=0	PROB > |T|
INTERCEP	1	6.248479	0.291450	21.439	0.0001
MONTHS	1	0.227074	0.016117	14.089	0.0001
SEX	1	-0.788975	0.238404	-3.309	0.0162

OBS	ACTUAL	PREDICT VALUE	RESIDUAL
1	7.500	7.611	-.110921
2	8.600	8.519	0.080704
3	9.100	8.973	0.126636
4	10.300	10.336	-.035807
5	13.000	13.061	-.060692
6	6.200	6.595	-.394873
7	8.700	8.411	0.288537
8	9.400	8.866	0.534389
9	9.800	10.228	-.428053

Our hypothesis test is based on the t distribution with $n - k - 1 = 9 - 2 - 1 = 6$ degrees of freedom. The appropriate t value from Appendix Table 2 is 3.143. The lower limit of the acceptance region is:

$$\begin{aligned} \text{Lower limit of acceptance region} &= B_2 - t(s_{b_2}) \\ &= 0 - 3.143(.238) \\ &= -0.748 \end{aligned} \quad \textbf{[12-8]}$$

Concluding that discrimination is present

Figure 12-5 illustrates this limit of the acceptance region and the observed value of $b_2 = -0.789$. **We see that the observed b_2 lies outside the acceptance region, so we reject the null hypothesis and conclude that the firm**

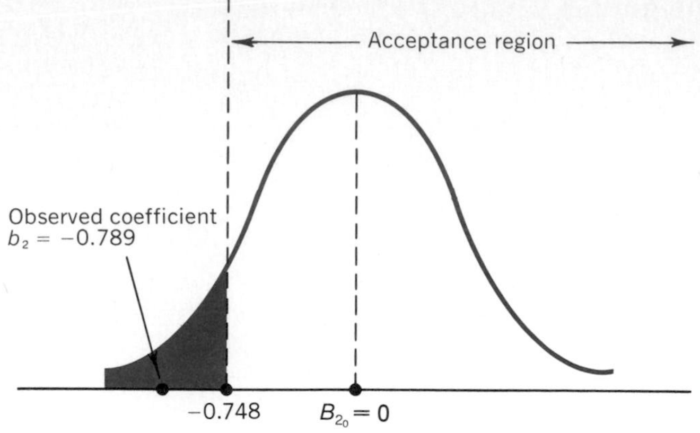

FIGURE 12-5 Left-tailed hypothesis test at the .01 significance level, showing acceptance region and the observed regression coefficient

does discriminate against its saleswomen. We also note, in passing, that the computed t value for b_1 in this regression is 14.089, so including sex as an explanatory variable makes months employed even more significant an explanatory variable than it was before. Finally, we note that the residuals for this regression don't seem to show any nonrandom pattern.

Interpreting the coefficient of the dummy variable

Now to review how we handled the qualitative variable in this problem. We set up a dummy variable, which we gave the value 0 for the men and the value 1 for the women. Then the coefficient of the dummy variable can be interpreted as the difference between a woman's base salary and the base salary for a man. Suppose we had set the dummy variable to 0 for women and 1 for men. Then is coefficient would be the difference between a man's base salary and the base salary for a woman. Can you guess what the regression would have been in this case? It shouldn't surprise you to learn that it would have been:

$$\hat{Y} = 5.459504 + 0.227074X_1 + .788975X_2$$

The choice of which category is given the value 0 and which the value 1 is totally arbitrary and affects only the sign, not the numerical value of the coefficient of the dummy variable.

Extensions of dummy variable techniques

Our example had only one qualitative variable (sex), and that variable had only two possible categories (male and female). Although we won't pursue the details here, dummy variable techniques can also be used in problems with several qualitative variables, and those variables can have more than two possible categories.

Transforming Variables and Fitting Curves

A manufacturer of small electric motors uses an automatic milling machine to produce the slots in the shafts of the motors. A batch of shafts is run and then checked. All shafts in the batch that do not meet required dimensional tolerances are discarded. At the beginning of each new batch, the milling machine is readjusted, since its cutter head wears slightly during the production of the batch. The manufacturer is trying to pick an optimal batch size;

TABLE 12-14 Number of defective shafts per batch

BATCH SIZE	NUMBER DEFECTIVE	BATCH SIZE	NUMBER DEFECTIVE
100	5	250	37
125	10	250	41
125	6	250	34
125	7	275	49
150	6	300	53
150	7	300	54
175	17	325	69
175	15	350	82
200	24	350	81
200	21	350	84
200	22	375	92
225	26	375	96
225	29	375	97
225	25	400	109
250	34	400	112

but in order to do this, he must know how the size of a batch affects the number of defective shafts in the batch. Table 12-14 gives data for a sample of 30 batches, arranged by ascending size of batch.

Noticing a pattern in the residuals

Figure 12-6 is a scatter diagram for these data. Since there are two batches of size 250 with 34 defective shafts, two of the points in the scatter diagram coincide (this is indicated by a colored data point in Fig. 12-6).

We are going to run a regression of number of defective shafts on the batch size. The output from the regression is in Table 12-15. What does this output tell us? First of all, we note that batch size does a fantastic job of

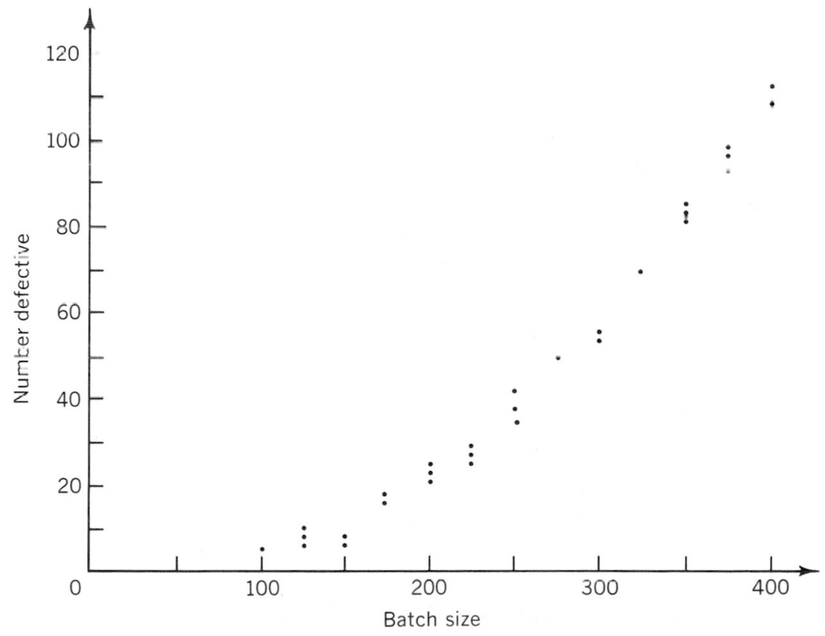

FIGURE 12-6 Scatter diagram of defective shafts plotted against size of batch

TABLE 12-15 Regression of number of defects on batch size

MODEL: LINE
DEP VARIABLE: DEFECTS DEFECTIVE PIECES IN BATCH

SOURCE	DF	SUM OF SQUARES	MEAN SQUARE	F VALUE	PROB>F
MODEL	1	32744.455	32744.455	572.905	0.0001
ERROR	28	1600.345	57.155169		
C TOTAL	29	34344.800			
ROOT MSE		7.560104	R-SQUARE	0.9534	

VARIABLE	DF	PARAMETER ESTIMATE	STANDARD ERROR	T FOR H0: PARAMETER=0	PROB > |T|
INTERCEP	1	-47.900695	4.111558	-11.650	0.0001
BATCHSIZ	1	0.367131	0.015338	23.935	0.0001

OBS	ACTUAL	PREDICT VALUE	RESIDUAL
1	5.000	-11.188	16.188
2	10.000	-2.009	12.009
3	6.000	-2.009	8.009
4	7.000	-2.009	9.009
5	6.000	7.169	-1.169
6	7.000	7.169	-.169025
7	17.000	16.347	0.652688
8	15.000	16.347	-1.347
9	24.000	25.526	-1.526
10	21.000	25.526	-4.526
11	22.000	25.526	-3.526
12	26.000	34.704	-8.704
13	29.000	34.704	-5.704
14	25.000	34.704	-9.704
15	34.000	43.882	-9.882
16	37.000	43.882	-6.882
17	41.000	43.882	-2.882
18	34.000	43.882	-9.882
19	49.000	53.060	-4.060
20	53.000	62.239	-9.239
21	54.000	62.239	-8.239
22	69.000	71.417	-2.417
23	82.000	80.595	1.405
24	81.000	80.595	0.404682
25	84.000	80.595	3.405
26	92.000	89.774	2.226
27	96.000	89.774	6.226
28	97.000	89.774	7.226
29	109.000	98.952	10.048
30	112.000	98.952	13.048

explaining the number of defective shafts: the computed t value is 23.935 and $r^2 = .9534$. However, despite the incredibly high t value, and despite the fact that batch size explains 95 percent of the variation in number of defectives, the residuals in this regression are far from random. Notice how they start out as large positive values, become smaller, then go negative, then become more negative, and then turn around again, finishing up with large positive values.

What the pattern suggests

What does this indicate? Look at Fig. 12-7, where we have fit a black regression line ($\hat{Y} = -7 + 7X$) to the eight points $(X,Y) = (0,0), (1,1), (2,4), (3,9), \ldots, (7,49)$, all of which lie on the colored curve ($Y = X^2$). The figure also shows the residuals and their signs.

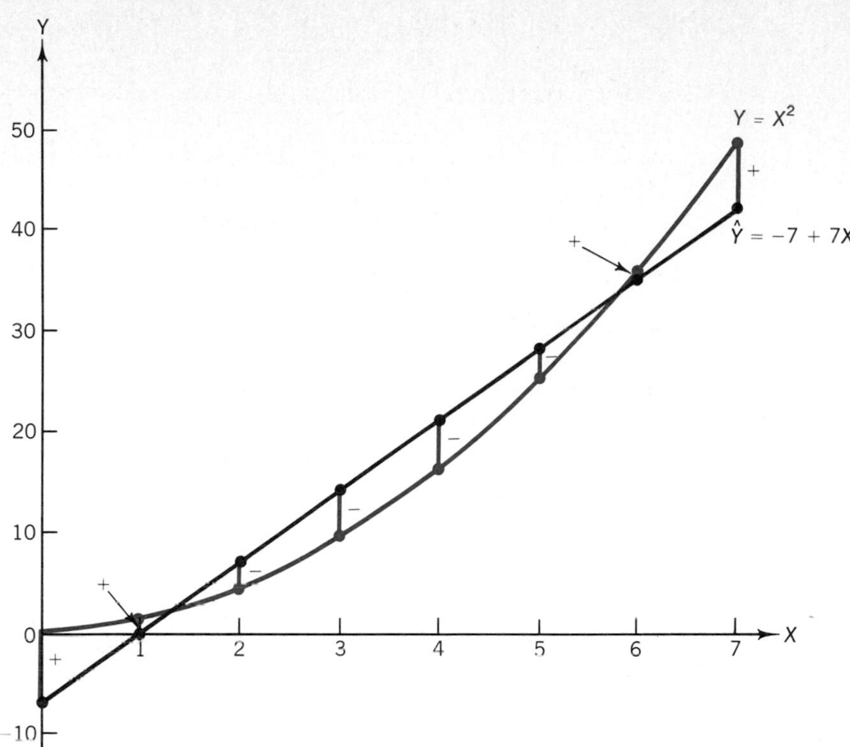

FIGURE 12-7
Fitting a straight line to points on a curve

TABLE 12-16 Input for fitting a curve to the motor-shaft data

X_1 BATCH SIZE	X_2 (BATCH SIZE)^2	Y NUMBER DEFECTIVE	X_1 BATCH SIZE	X_2 (BATCH SIZE)^2	Y NUMBER DEFECTIVE
100	10,000	5	250	62,500	37
125	15,625	10	250	62,500	41
125	15,625	6	250	62,500	34
125	15,625	7	275	75,625	49
150	22,500	6	300	90,000	53
150	22,500	7	300	90,000	54
175	30,625	17	325	105,625	69
175	30,625	15	350	122,500	82
200	40,000	24	350	122,500	81
200	40,000	21	350	122,500	84
200	40,000	22	375	140,625	92
225	50,625	26	375	140,625	96
225	50,625	29	375	140,625	97
225	50,625	25	400	160,000	109
250	62,500	34	400	160,000	112

The pattern of residuals that we got in our motor-shaft problem is quite similar to the pattern seen in Fig. 12-7. Maybe the shaft data are better approximated by a curve than a straight line. Look back at Fig. 12-6; what do you think?

Fitting a curve to the data

But we've fitted only straight lines before. How do we go about fitting a curve? It's simple; all we do is introduce another variable, $X_2 =$ (batch size)^2, and then run a multiple regression. The input data are in Table 12-16 on the previous page, and the results are in Table 12-17 below.

TABLE 12-17 Regression on batch size and (batch size)^2

```
MODEL: CURVE
DEP VARIABLE: DEFECTS  DEFECTIVE PIECES IN BATCH
                     SUM OF           MEAN
SOURCE      DF      SQUARES         SQUARE       F VALUE         PROB>F
MODEL        2    34186.277      17093.139      2911.349         0.0001
ERROR       27      158.523       5.871209
C TOTAL     29    34344.800
    ROOT MSE       2.423058       R-SQUARE        0.9954


                  PARAMETER       STANDARD     T FOR H0:
VARIABLE    DF     ESTIMATE          ERROR   PARAMETER=0     PROB > |T|

INTERCEP     1     6.897585       3.736894         1.846         0.0759
BATCHSIZ     1    -0.120103       0.031478        -3.815         0.0007
SIZESQU      1 0.0009495387 .00006059274        15.671         0.0001

                  PREDICT
  OBS    ACTUAL     VALUE RESIDUAL

    1     5.000     4.383 0.617284
    2    10.000     6.721    3.279
    3     6.000     6.721 -.721307
    4     7.000     6.721 0.278693
    5     6.000    10.247   -4.247
    6     7.000    10.247   -3.247
    7    17.000    14.959    2.041
    8    15.000    14.959 0.040740
    9    24.000    20.859    3.141
   10    21.000    20.859 0.141379
   11    22.000    20.859    1.141
   12    26.000    27.945   -1.945
   13    29.000    27.945    1.055
   14    25.000    27.945   -2.945
   15    34.000    36.218   -2.218
   16    37.000    36.218 0.781887
   17    41.000    36.218    4.782
   18    34.000    36.218   -2.218
   19    49.000    45.678    3.322
   20    53.000    56.325   -3.325
   21    54.000    56.325   -2.325
   22    69.000    68.159 0.840723
   23    82.000    81.180 0.819821
   24    81.000    81.180 -.180179
   25    84.000    81.180    2.820
   26    92.000    95.388   -3.388
   27    96.000    95.388 0.611997
   28    97.000    95.388    1.612
   29   109.000   110.783   -1.783
   30   112.000   110.783    1.217
```

The curve is much better than the line

Looking at Table 12-17, we see that batch size and (batch size)^2 are *both* significant explanatory variables, since their t values are -3.815 and 15.671 respectively. The multiple coefficient of determination is $R^2 = .9954$; so together, our two variables explain 99.5 percent of the variation in the number of defective motor shafts. As a final comparison of our two regressions, notice that the standard error of estimate, which measures the dispersion of the sample points around the fitted model, is 7.560 for the straight-line model but only 2.423 for the curved model. **The curved model is far superior to the straight-line model, even though the latter explained 95 percent of the variation! And remember, it was the pattern that we observed in the residuals for the straight-line model that suggested to us that a curved model would be more appropriate.**

Transforming variables

In our curved model, we got our second variable, (batch size)^2, by doing a *mathematical transformation* of our first variable, batch size. Because we squared a variable, the resulting curved model is known as a *second-degree* (or *quadratic*) regression model. There are many other ways in which we can transform variables to get new variables, and most computer regression packages have these transformations built into them. You do not have to compute the transformed variables by hand as we did in Table 12-16. SAS has the capability to compute all sorts of transformations of one or more variables: sums, differences, products, quotients, roots, powers, logarithms, exponentials, trigonometric functions, and many more.

EXERCISES

12-31 Describe three situations in everyday life in which dummy variables could be used in regression models.

12-32 Russ Andrews owns a company that manufactures Whizzos. The failure rate for Whizzos seems to vary from batch to batch, and Russ wants an equation that will help him predict failure rates. Russ feels that one possible explanation for failure rates may be the number of gears in the Whizzo. Although the company's models are essentially similar, some contain more gears than others. Also, the material from which the Whizzo is made may affect the failure rate (a Whizzo can be made from either aluminum or wood). Russ has collected data for several days and presented you with a table containing the number of gears, type of material, and failure rate for each of 35 batches of Whizzos. He has asked you to help with his predictions.

a) Describe a model using a dummy variable that the company could use to estimate batch failure rates from number of gears and type of material.

b) Russ also wants to know if the type of material really has any effect on failure rates. Based upon your answer to part *a*, give the hypotheses you would use for this test.

12-33 Pam Buckthal is a time-study engineer in Bethel, North Carolina. Recently, her firm instituted a new technique for use on a production line. Since it is hoped that employees will be more productive each day that they use the new technique, Pam has collected data for the total units produced each day for the first 17 days. Numbering the first day as 0, then numbering each day sequentially, she has performed a regression of units of production on number of days since the new technique was introduced. The results are:

```
DEP VARIABLE: UNITS     UNITS PRODUCED
                           SUM OF           MEAN
SOURCE        DF          SQUARES          SQUARE         F VALUE          PROB>F
MODEL          1         80812001        80812001         109.881          0.0001
ERROR         15         11031775          735452
C TOTAL       16         91843776
    ROOT MSE              857.585        R-SQUARE          0.8799


                        PARAMETER        STANDARD      T FOR H0:
VARIABLE      DF         ESTIMATE           ERROR    PARAMETER=0     PROB > |T|

INTERCEP       1         7158.431         398.280         17.973         0.0001
DAYS           1          445.049       42.456774         10.482         0.0001

                        PREDICT
   OBS     ACTUAL         VALUE  RESIDUAL

     1       8210          7158      1052
     2       8400          7603   796.520
     3       8490          8049   441.471
     4       8680          8494   186.422
     5       8870          8939   -68.627
     6       9150          9384  -233.676
     7       9340          9829  -488.725
     8       9630         10274  -643.775
     9       9820         10719  -898.824
    10      10190         11164  -973.873
    11      10950         11609  -658.922
    12      11510         12054  -543.971
    13      11700         12499  -799.020
    14      12170         12944  -774.069
    15      14160         13389   770.882
    16      15190         13834      1356
    17      15760         14279      1481
```

Are you satisfied with these results as a predictor for future days' production? If so, why? If not, tell why not and suggest a better model.

12-34 Dr. Linda Frazer runs a medical clinic in Philadelphia. She collected data on age, reaction to penicillin, and systolic blood pressure for 13 patients. She established systolic blood pressure as the dependent variable, age as X_1 (independent variable), and reaction to penicillin as X_2 (independent variable). Letting 0 stand for a positive reaction to penicillin, and 1 stand for a negative reaction, she performed a SAS multiple regression. The predicting equation was: $\hat{Y} = 13.7 + 3.5X_1 + .206X_2$.

a) After the regression had already been run, Linda discovered that she had meant to code a positive reaction as 1 and a negative reaction as 0. Does she have to rerun the regression? If so, why? If not, give her the equation she would have gotten if the variable had been coded as she had originally intended.

b) If s_{b_2} has a value of .09, is there evidence at a significance level of .01 that reaction to penicillin is a significant explanatory variable for systolic blood pressure?

12-35 A statistician collected a set of 17 pairs of data points. He called the independent variable X_1 and the dependent variable Y. He ran a linear regression of Y on X_1, and he was unsatisfied with the results. Because of some nonrandom patterns he observed in the residuals, he decided to square the values of X_1; he called these squared values X_2. The statistician then ran a multiple regression of Y on X_1 and X_2. The resulting equation was: $\hat{Y} = 200.4 + 7.99X_1 - 2.08X_2$. The value of s_{b_1} was 3.734 and the value of s_{b_2} was 1.01. At a .05 level of significance, determine if:

a) The set of unsquared values of X_1 is a significant explanatory variable for Y.

b) The set of squared values of X_1 is a significant explanatory variable for Y.

12-36 Suppose you have a set of data points to which you have fitted a linear regression equation. Even though the R^2 for the line is very high, you wonder whether it would be a good idea to fit a second-degree equation to the data. Describe how you would make your decision based on:

a) A scattergram of the data

b) A table of residuals from the linear regression

12-37 NASA is interested in determining the factors that seem to have the greatest effect on the mission performance level (MPL) of any launched space mission. The MPL is an aggregate measure (0 to 100) of the performance of all systems in the rocket, shuttle, or other spacecraft over the course of its mission. NASA has determined that three possible predictors of MPL for any mission are actual length of the mission (in days), whether or not the mission returned to earth from space, and the number of new subsystems being tried out on this mission.

a) Develop a model for NASA that could be used to estimate the MPL of any mission from the three predictor variables. Indicate exactly what each independent variable in the model represents.

b) To account for any serious mishaps early in the mission, NASA has decided to include a fourth predictor variable in the model to indicate whether or not the mission succeeded in leaving the earth's atmosphere. How would you add this to your model?

c) Suppose NASA thought that the square of actual length of the mission was also an important predictor of MPL. How would you add this to the model? State the hypotheses you would test to determine if this actually had any effect on MPL.

12-6 TERMS INTRODUCED IN CHAPTER 12

ANALYSIS OF VARIANCE FOR REGRESSION The procedure for computing the F ratio used to test the significance of the regression as a whole. It is related to the analysis of variance discussed in Chapter 10.

COEFFICIENT OF MULTIPLE CORRELATION, R The positive square root of R^2.

COEFFICIENT OF MULTIPLE DETERMINATION, R^2 The fraction of the variation of the dependent variable that is explained by the regression. R^2 measures how well the multiple regression fits the data.

COMPUTED F-RATIO A statistic used to test the significance of the regression as a whole.

COMPUTED t A statistic used for testing the significance of an individual explanatory variable.

DUMMY VARIABLE A variable taking the value 0 or 1, enabling us to include in a regression model qualitative factors such as sex, marital status, and education level.

MODELING TECHNIQUES Methods for deciding which variables to include in a regression model and the different ways in which they can be included.

MULTICOLLINEARITY A statistical problem sometimes present in multiple regression analysis in which the reliability of the regression coefficients is reduced, owing to a high level of correlation between the independent variables.

MULTIPLE REGRESSION The statistical process by which several variables are used to predict another variable.

SAS A computer program for doing regression and other statistical analyses. Other commonly available packages include MINITAB and SPSS.

STANDARD ERROR OF A REGRESSION COEFFICIENT A measure of our uncertainty about the exact value of a regression coefficient.

TRANSFORMATIONS Mathematical manipulations for converting one variable into a different form, so we can fit curves as well as lines by regression.

12-7 EQUATIONS INTRODUCED IN CHAPTER 12

[12-1] $$\hat{Y} = a + b_1X_1 + b_2X_2$$ p. 552

In multiple regression, this is the formula for the estimating equation that describes the relationship between three variables: Y, X_1, and X_2. Picture a two-variable multiple regression equation as a plane, rather than a line.

[12-2] $$\Sigma Y = na + b_1\Sigma X_1 + b_2\Sigma X_2$$

[12-3] $$\Sigma X_1Y = a\Sigma X_1 + b_1\Sigma X_1^2 + b_2\Sigma X_1X_2$$ p. 553

[12-4] $$\Sigma X_2Y = a\Sigma X_2 + b_1\Sigma X_1X_2 + b_2\Sigma X_2^2$$

Solving these three equations determines the values of the numerical constants a, b_1, and b_2 and thus the best-fitting multiple regression plane in a two-variable multiple regression.

[12-5] $$\hat{Y} = a + b_1X_1 + b_2X_2 + \cdots + b_kX_k$$ p. 559

This is the formula for the estimating equation describing the relationship between Y and the k independent variables $X_1, X_2, \ldots, X_k$. Equation 12-1 is the special case of this equation for $k = 2$.

[12-6] $$s_e = \sqrt{\frac{\Sigma(Y - \hat{Y})^2}{n - k - 1}}$$ p. 561

To measure the variation around a multiple regression equation when there are k independent variables, use this equation to find the *standard error of estimate*. The standard error, in this case, has $n - k - 1$ degrees of freedom, owing to the $k + 1$ numerical constants that must be calculated from the data ($a, b_1, \ldots, b_k$).

[12-7] $$Y = A + B_1X_1 + B_2X_2 + \cdots + B_kX_k$$ p. 566

This is the *population regression equation* for the multiple regression. Its Y intercept is A, and it has k slope coefficients, one for each of the independent variables.

[12-7a] $$Y = A + B_1X_1 + B_2X_2 + \cdots + B_kX_k + e$$ p. 567

Because all the individual points in a population do not lie on a population regression equation, the *individual* data points will satisfy this equation, where e is a random disturbance from the population regression equation. On the average, e equals zero, because disturbances above the population regression equation are canceled out by disturbances below it.

[12-8] $$\text{Upper limit of acceptance region} = B_i + t(s_{b_i})$$ $$\text{Lower limit of acceptance region} = B_i - t(s_{b_i})$$ p. 568

To test hypotheses about the slopes of multiple regression equations, we use this pair of equations to find the limits of the acceptance region. The standard error of the coefficient (s_{b_i}) is obtained from the computer package we are using, and the t value is taken from the t distribution with $n - k - 1$ degrees of freedom.

[12-9] $$-t_c \leq t_o \leq t_c$$ *p. 570*

To test whether a given independent variable is significant, we use this formula to see if the observed t value (taken from the computer output) lies between plus and minus the critical t value (taken from the t distribution with $n - k - 1$ degrees of freedom). The variable *is* significant when t_o is *not* in the indicated range. If your computer package gives you "prob $> |t|$" values, the variable *is* significant when this value is *less than* α, the significance level of the test.

[12-10]

$$\left.\begin{array}{lll} \text{SST} & = \text{Total sum of squares} & = \Sigma(Y - \overline{Y})^2 \\ \text{SSR} & = \text{Regression sum of squares (the explained part of SST)} & = \Sigma(\hat{Y} - \overline{Y})^2 \\ \text{SSE} & = \text{Error sum of squares (the unexplained part of SST)} & = \Sigma(Y - \hat{Y})^2 \end{array}\right\}$$ *p. 572*

[12-11] $$\text{SST} = \text{SSR} + \text{SSE}$$ *p. 572*

These two equations enable us to break down the variability of the dependent variable into two parts (one explained by the regression and the other unexplained) so we can test for the significance of the regression as a whole.

[12-12] $$F = \frac{\text{SSR}/k}{\text{SSE}/(n - k - 1)}$$ *p. 573*

This F-ratio, which has k numerator degrees of freedom and $n - k - 1$ denominator degrees of freedom, is used to test the significance of the regression as a whole. If F is *bigger* than the critical value, then we conclude that the regression as a whole *is* significant. The same conclusion holds if the "prob F" value (from the computer output) is *less than* α, the significance level of the test.

12-8 CHAPTER REVIEW EXERCISES

12-38 Homero Martinez is a judge in Barcelona, Spain. He has recently called you in as a statistical consultant to investigate what purports to be a significant finding. He claims that the number of days a case is in court can be used to estimate the amount of damages that should be awarded. He has gathered data from his court and from the courts of several of his fellow judges. For each of the numbers 1 to 10, he has located a case that took that many days in court, and he has determined the amount (in millions of pesetas) of damages awarded in that case. The following SAS results were generated when damages awarded were regressed on days in court.

```
DEP VARIABLE: DAMAGES  DAMAGES AWARDED (MILLIONS OF PESETAS)
                    SUM OF           MEAN
SOURCE     DF      SQUARES          SQUARE         F VALUE         PROB>F
MODEL       1    16.094260       16.094260         102.765         0.0001
ERROR       7     1.096290        0.156613
C TOTAL     8    17.190550
   ROOT MSE       0.395743        R-SQUARE          0.9362


                 PARAMETER        STANDARD    T FOR H0:
VARIABLE   DF     ESTIMATE           ERROR  PARAMETER=0     PROB > |T|

INTERCEP    1    -0.406250        0.287501        -1.413         0.2005
DAYS        1     0.517917        0.051090        10.137         0.0001

                PREDICT
 OBS    ACTUAL    VALUE RESIDUAL

   1 0.645000 0.111667 0.533333
   2 0.750000 0.629583 0.120417
   3    1.000    1.147 -.147500
   4    1.300    1.665 -.365417
   5    1.750    2.183 -.433333
   6    2.205    2.701 -.496250
   7    3.500    3.219 0.280833
   8    4.000    3.737 0.262917
   9    4.500    4.255 0.245000
```

Of course, you are quite pleased with these results, since the value of R^2 is very high. But the judge is not convinced that you are right. He says, "This is the worst job I've ever seen! I don't care if this line *does* fit the data I gave you. I can tell by looking at the output that it won't work for other data! If you can't do any better, just let me know, and I'll hire a *smart* statistician!"

a) Why is the judge upset?
b) Suggest a better model that will calm the judge.

12-39 Jon Grant, supervisor of the Carven Manufacturing Facility, is examining the relationship between an employee's score on an aptitude test, prior work experience, and success on the job. An employee's prior work experience is studied and weighted, yielding a rating between 2 and 12. The measure of on-the-job success is based on a point system involving total output and efficiency with a maximum possible value of 50. Grant sampled 6 first-year employees and obtained the following:

X_1 APTITUDE TEST SCORE	X_2 PRIOR EXPERIENCE	Y PERFORMANCE EVALUATION
84	7	36
74	5	28
89	8	39
78	7	30
92	10	45
70	3	22

a) Develop the estimating equation best describing these data.
b) If an employee scored 83 on the aptitude test and had prior work rating of 7, what performance evaluation would be expected?

12-40 Just one year ago, Bobby Spalding was making a fortune as a soccer player in England. Today, Bobby has been forced into retirement by advancing age and declining ability to score. Using the savings he accumulated during his active years, he purchased a trout farm in southern France. Convinced that he can make a killing by controlling the environmental factors, he has gathered data from the former owner regarding production in the past 9 years. When Bobby used SAS to regress annual trout production (in thousands of kilograms) on thousands of fish stocked in the farm's pools, average water temperature (°C), and food added to the pools (thousands of kilograms), he got these results:

```
DEP VARIABLE: WEIGHT    TROUT PRODUCED (THOUSANDS OF KG)
                          SUM OF          MEAN
SOURCE      DF          SQUARES         SQUARE       F VALUE          PROB>F
MODEL        3          756.664        252.221        28.592          0.0014
ERROR        5        44.106871       8.821374
C TOTAL      8          800.771
     ROOT MSE          2.970080       R-SQUARE        0.9449


                     PARAMETER        STANDARD    T FOR H0:
VARIABLE    DF        ESTIMATE           ERROR  PARAMETER=0      PROB > |T|

INTERCEP     1      -14.316828       10.226069       -1.400          0.2204
TROUT        1        1.196342        0.223357        5.356          0.0030
DEGREES      1        0.195845        0.387032        0.506          0.6344
FOOD         1        1.467678        0.800879        1.833          0.1263
```

a) Give an equation that Bobby can use to predict how many kilograms of trout can be expected.
b) How much of the variation in trout production is explained by the environmental factors?
c) At a significance level of 5 percent, which of the environmental factors are significant explanatory variables for trout production?
d) This year, Bobby plans to add 20,000 trout to the pools and keep the average water temperature at 10° Celsius. If he estimates the total amount of trout that can be sold as 24,000 kilograms, what is your best estimate of the amount of food he should add to the pools?

12-41 David Howell, VP of sales for Landon Clothes, is studying the relationship between a product's wholesale margin, retail margin, and sales level. He sampled 5 items from Landon's product line with the following respective margins (percentage) and annual sales levels (number of units).

RETAIL MARGIN (%)	WHOLESALE MARGIN (%)	NUMBER OF UNITS SOLD (×10,000)
20	11	7
40	16	26
35	19	13
30	12	5
50	26	33

a) Develop an estimating equation best describing these data.
b) If an item had a retail margin of 30 percent and a wholesale margin of 15 percent, what unit sales would be expected?

12-42 Dr. Harden Ricci is a veterinarian in Sacramento, California. Recently, he has been trying to develop a predicting equation for the amount of anesthesia (measured in milliliters) to be used in operations. He feels that the amount used will be affected by the weight of the animal (in pounds), length of the operation (in hours), and whether the animal is a cat (coded 0) or a dog (coded 1). He used SAS to run a regression on his data from 13 recent operations, and got these results:

```
DEP VARIABLE: ANESTHES MILLILITERS OF ANESTHETIC USED
                         SUM OF           MEAN
SOURCE      DF          SQUARES         SQUARE       F VALUE      PROB>F
MODEL        3           590880         196960        60.474      0.0001
ERROR        9        29312.398       3256.933
C TOTAL     12           620192
    ROOT MSE          57.069547       R-SQUARE        0.9527


                      PARAMETER       STANDARD    T FOR H0:
VARIABLE    DF         ESTIMATE          ERROR  PARAMETER=0    PROB > |T|

INTERCEP     1        90.032476      56.842294        1.584        0.1477
TYPE         1        99.485929      42.373539        2.348        0.0435
WEIGHT       1        21.536329       2.668117        8.072        0.0001
HOURS        1       -34.460982      28.606709       -1.205        0.2591
```

a) What is the predicting equation for amounts of anesthesia, as given by SAS?
b) Give an approximate 90 percent confidence interval for the amount of anesthesia to be used in a 2-hour operation on a 20-pound dog.
c) At a significance level of 5 percent, is the amount of anesthesia needed significantly different for dogs and cats?
d) At a significance level of 1 percent, is this regression significant as a whole?

12-43 Gerald Chrisco owns and operates Gerald's Cleaning Service in Winston-Salem, N.C. Gerald stocks his own brand of cleaning solvent, and he feels that this gives his service a distinctive edge over the competition. One of the problems with his method, though, is that he has to be careful to give each of his workers the proper amount of solvent before they begin cleaning an establishment. If they are given too little, they cannot properly clean the total area. If they are given too much, they tend to "lose" the excess, and this costs Gerald quite a bit in unnecessary expenses. Gerald has compiled the following data regarding solvent use for 6 recent cleaning projects:

OUNCES OF SOLVENT USED	TOTAL SQUARE FEET	DAYS SINCE LAST CLEANING
8.0	1,206	2
10.0	1,771	5
11.0	1,502	4
12.6	1,603	3
13.0	864	9
16.0	1,355	10

a) Use a computer package to calculate the best-fitting regression equation for these data.
b) How much additional solvent should Gerald allow for each additional 100 square feet of area?
c) Suppose that Gerald has a *very* important cleaning job of 1,150 square feet that hasn't been cleaned for 7 days. Because of the importance of the job, he is much more concerned with whether his crew will have sufficient solvent than whether they "lose" any excess. Find the upper limit of a 99 percent confidence interval for the amount of solvent that Gerald should give his crew for this job.

12-9 CHAPTER CONCEPTS TEST

Answers are in the back of the book.

T F 1. The principal advantage of multiple regression over simple regression is that it allows us to use more of the information available to us to estimate the dependent variable.

T F 2. Suppose, in the multiple regression equation $\hat{Y} = 24.4 + 5.6X_1 + 6.8X_2$, $\hat{Y}$ stands for weight (in pounds) and X_2 stands for age (in years). For each additional year of age, then, it can be expected that weight will increase by 24.4 pounds.

T F 3. Although it is theoretically possible to do multiple regression calculations by hand, we seldom do so.

T F 4. Suppose you are attempting to form a confidence interval for a value of Y from a multiple regression equation. If there are 20 elements in the sample and 4 independent variables are used in the regression, you should use 16 degrees of freedom when you get a value from the t table.

T F 5. The standard error of the coefficient b_2 in a multiple regression is denoted s_2.

T F 6. Suppose we wish to test whether the values of Y in a multiple regression really depend upon the values of X_1. The null hypothesis for our test would be: $B_1 = 0$.

T F 7. To determine whether a regression is significant as a whole, an observed value of F is calculated and compared to a value from a table.

T F 8. If one knows the total sum of squares and regression sum of squares for a multiple regression, the error sum of squares can always be quickly calculated.

T F 9. If a multiple regression includes all the relevant explanatory factors for the dependent variable, the residuals are usually nonrandom.

T F 10. Simple regressions of Y on X_1 and Y on X_2 show that X_1 and X_2 are both significant explanatory variables for Y. But a multiple regression of Y on X_1 and X_2 says that neither X_1 nor X_2 is a significant explanatory variable for Y. Clearly, this is a case of multicollinearity.

T F 11. Dummy variables are often used to incorporate qualitative data into multiple regressions.

T F 12. When using a dummy variable with values of 0 and 1, it is very important to make sure that the 0's and 1's are used according to standard practice. Reversing the coding will completely destroy the results of the multiple regression.

T F 13. We can form a second-degree regression model by multiplying observed values of an independent variable by 2.

T F 14. Adding additional variables to a multiple regression will always reduce the standard error of the estimate.

T F 15. Suppose a multiple regression yielded this equation: $Y = 5.6 + 2.8X_1 - 3.9X_2 + 5.6X_3$. If X_1, X_2, and X_3 all had values of zero, then Y could be expected to have a value of 5.6.

T F 16. The analysis of the residuals in a straight-line regression model is done to determine the correct value for s_e.

T F 17. Although it is possible to make inferences about the regression as a whole, it is not possible to make inferences about the estimated regression coefficients.

18. Suppose that a multiple regression yielded this equation: $\hat{Y} = 51.21 + 6.88X_1 + 7.06X_2 - 3.71X_3$. The value of b_2 for this equation is:
    a) 51.21
    b) 6.88
    c) 7.06
    d) −3.71
    e) Cannot be determined from information given

19. We have said that the standard error of estimate has $n - k - 1$ degrees of freedom. What does the k stand for in this expression?
    a) Number of elements in the sample

b) Number of independent variables in the multiple regression
c) Mean of the sample values of the dependent variable
d) None of these

20. Suppose that you have run a multiple regression and have found that the value of b_1 is 1.66. Historical data, however, indicate that the value of B_1 should be 1.34. You wish to test, at a .05 level of significance, the null hypothesis that B_1 is still 1.34. Assuming that you have access to any tables you may need, what other information is required for you to perform your test?
a) Degrees of freedom
b) s_{b_1}
c) s_e
d) a and b but not c
e) a and c but not b

21. Suppose that a toy manufacturer wishes to determine if his red toys sell better than his blue toys. He gathered data regarding sales levels, color, price, and average age levels for which the toys are intended. He entered these into a computer run. The resulting multiple regression equation was: $\hat{Y} = 70663 - 713X_1 - 59.6X_2 + 66.4X_3$, where $\hat{Y}$ refers to sales levels in units, X_1 refers to color (0 = blue, 1 = red), X_2 refers to retail price (in dollars), and X_3 refers to average age level (in years). Which of the following is true if factors of price and age level are held constant?
a) Red toys should sell 713 more units than blue toys.
b) Red toys should sell 713 fewer units than blue toys.
c) Children will always choose a blue toy over a red one.
d) b and c but not a.

Questions 22 through 27 deal with a director of personnel who is trying to determine a predicting equation for longevity in his plant. He has used SAS to regress months employed for several employees on their education level (years of schooling), age when hired, score on the company's psychological maturity test, and number of dependents (including the employee). Here are his results:

```
DEP VARIABLE: LONGEV    LENGTH OF EMPLOYMENT (MONTHS)
                          SUM OF           MEAN
SOURCE        DF         SQUARES          SQUARE        F VALUE        PROB>F
MODEL          4        7325.325        1831.331         10.194        0.0127
ERROR          5         898.275         179.655
C TOTAL        9        8223.600
     ROOT MSE          13.403541        R-SQUARE         0.8908


                       PARAMETER        STANDARD     T FOR H0:
VARIABLE      DF        ESTIMATE           ERROR   PARAMETER=0    PROB > |T|

INTERCEP       1       82.237454       81.737817         1.006        0.3605
SCHOOL         1       -1.552644        4.362058        -0.356        0.7364
AGE            1       -1.685367        1.252534        -1.346        0.2362
SCORE          1        0.110216        0.290813         0.379        0.7203
DEPENDEN       1        6.875539        7.657836         0.898        0.4104
```

22. The regression equation for these data is:
a) $\hat{Y} = 82.24 - 1.55X_1 - 1.69X_2 + 0.11X_3 + 6.88X_4$
b) $\hat{Y} = 13.40 - 1.55X_1 - 1.69X_2 + 0.11X_3 + 6.88X_4$
c) $\hat{Y} = 82.24 + 4.36X_1 + 1.25X_2 + 0.29X_3 + 7.66X_4$
d) $\hat{Y} = 82.24 - 0.36X_1 - 1.35X_2 + 0.38X_3 + 0.90X_4$

23. How much of the variation in length of employment is explained by the regression?
a) 94% b) 82% c) 89% d) 13%

24. Suppose you wish to test whether years of school are a significant explanatory variable for longevity. The degrees of freedom you would use would be:
a) 4 b) 10 c) 6 d) 5

25. What is the value of s_{b_3}?
a) 13.4 b) .29 c) .38 d) .11
26. How many denominator degrees of freedom would there be for an F test to determine if this regression was significant as a whole?
a) 5 b) 4 c) 9 d) 10
27. How many data points did the director enter?
a) 9 b) 10 c) 18 d) 19
28. In the equation $Y = A + B_1X_1 + B_2X_2$, Y is independent of X_1 if:
a) $B_2 = 0$ c) $B_1 = 1$
b) $B_2 = -1$ d) None of these
29. A normal distribution can be used to approximate the t distribution for multiple regression whenever the degrees of freedom (n minus the number of estimated regression coefficients) are:
a) Less than 40 c) Equal to 5 e) None of these
b) More than 10 d) More than 50
30. ______________ are methods for deciding which variables to include in a regression model and the different ways in which they can be included.
31. Mathematical manipulations for converting a variable into a different form so that we can fit regression curves are called ______________.
32. The ______________ is a statistic used to test the significance of a regression as a whole.
33. A ______________ variable takes on the values 0 and 1 to describe qualitative data.
34. A measure of our uncertainty about the exact value of a multiple regression coefficient is the ______________ of the coefficient.
35. The coefficient of multiple determination in multiple regression measures the ______________.

12-10 CONCEPTUAL CASE (Northern White Metals Company)

Dick's predecessor at NWMC had often remarked that the company was "adrift in a sea of unpredictable circumstance. Sales go up, sales go down," he would say, "and that's all there is to it." This cavalier, somewhat fatalistic attitude had struck Dick as strange, and he was determined to provide a little more insight and direction into the planning process at Northern than had existed previously.

On his next trip to corporate headquarters in New York, he made it a point to arrange a short meeting with Sarah and Jody. Looking out their office window at the cold, cloudy October afternoon, Dick thought how well the weather matched his mood.

Despite some indications from an earlier analysis that Northern's advertising program was perhaps not a very significant factor in explaining sales, Dick had proceeded to accelerate advertising efforts throughout the third quarter. A subsequent analysis revealed little difference from the first one. Expenses were up considerably, and Dick finally decided to scrap the project.

"Probably a wise choice," offered Sarah as Dick related his plight.

"Dick, you're interested in getting a better understanding of the behavior of sales so you can improve your planning capabilities," Jody said. "Why don't we look at some other factors that might explain sales volume? We should be able to draw some useful conclusions for you," she stated confidently.

"That would be great," Dick said as his eyes brightened a bit. "You know, one of my top sales reps thought the number of people out making calls was more important than advertising; and sales did grow rather briskly as I expanded the sales force last year."

"There you go," said Jody. "Sales force size might be a factor."

"We would probably want to segregate building-products and high-tech-applications products sales," Dick said, "since these are probably affected differently by general economic conditions."

"We could check it out," Sarah offered. "Why don't you talk with your sales reps, decide what you think are the major determinants of sales, and we'll take it from there."

Dick left, grateful for their counsel and convinced that the planning process at Northern was soon to be improved considerably.

After Dick and the sales force decide upon some principal determinants of sales volume, what information will they need to provide to Jody and Sarah? What analyses can they be expected to perform? What results might they obtain that would be useful to Dick in a decision-making or planning capacity?

12-11 COMPUTER DATA BASE EXERCISE

"Fred, oh, Fred," Laurel trilled, as a three-piece-suited hulk passed the door. "Joe asked us to formulate some sales predictions for next season, and we need your valuable assistance. What do you think affects sales the most?"

"SALESPEOPLE, good salespeople are all that matters," pronounced Fred. "Forget all those fancy promotion and pricing strategies. A good salesman can turn those sleds over better than anything."

"And how many of our salespeople are good?" queried Frank.

"They're all good," yelped Fred, "or I'd fire them!" He stomped to the door.

"OK, Frank, do an equation of sales against number of salespeople, and we'll see," said Laurel.

QUESTION

1. What were the coefficients of correlation and determination for a simple regression of sales vs. the number of salespeople? (Use sales data from Chapter 11).

"Better," said Frank, "but not much. What now?"
"Throw in the retail toy sales, too," answered Laurel.

QUESTION

2. What equation did they get? Was it better than the previous two?

"Not perfect yet," Frank commented after another hour. "You know, I just saw Nick, and he said that he always felt the number of inches of snow before Christmas was the most important influence on sales. Neat idea."

"Try all three," said Laurel.

QUESTION

3. What was their new predicting equation? Was it better or worse than the previous tries? Why?

YEAR	SALESPEOPLE	SNOWFALL (INCHES)
1949	6	1
1950	10	17
1951	9	14
1952	12	4
1953	12	1
1954	12	18
1955	14	10
1956	16	1
1957	16	12
1958	15	18
1959	16	12
1960	18	1
1961	19	8
1962	18	7
1963	19	12
1964	19	4
1965	19	0
1966	20	6
1967	20	15
1968	22	14
1969	22	10
1970	22	11
1971	22	17
1972	24	7
1973	25	6
1974	23	18
1975	24	2
1976	24	12
1977	26	0
1978	25	14

12-12 FLOW CHART

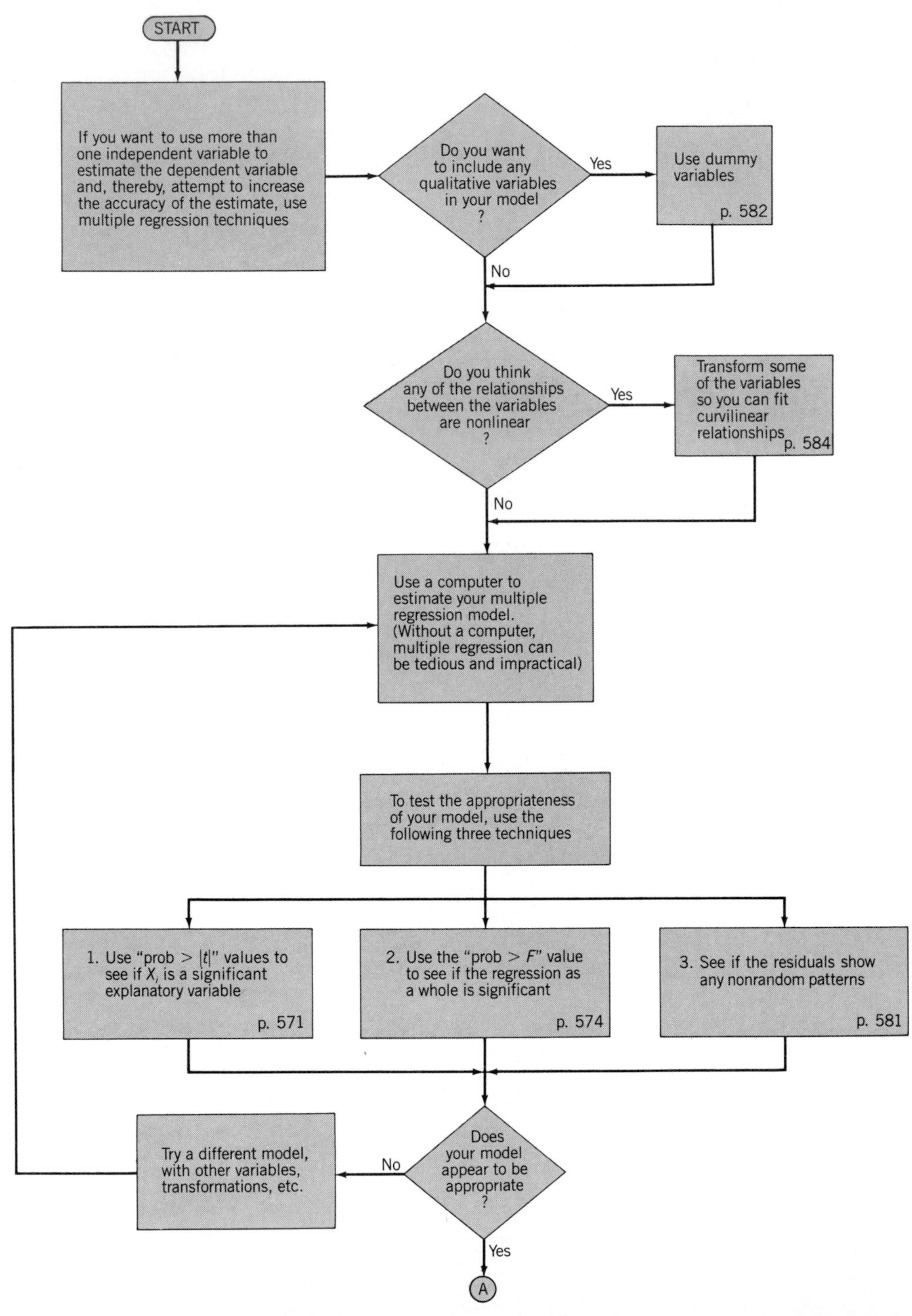

START
If you want to use more than one independent variable to estimate the dependent variable and, thereby, attempt to increase the accuracy of the estimate, use multiple regression techniques
Do you want to include any qualitative variables in your model ?
Yes
Use dummy variables p. 582
No
Do you think any of the relationships between the variables are nonlinear ?
Yes
Transform some of the variables so you can fit curvilinear relationships p. 584
No
Use a computer to estimate your multiple regression model. (Without a computer, multiple regression can be tedious and impractical)
To test the appropriateness of your model, use the following three techniques
1. Use "prob > |t|" values to see if X_i is a significant explanatory variable p. 571
2. Use the "prob > F" value to see if the regression as a whole is significant p. 574
3. See if the residuals show any nonrandom patterns p. 581
Does your model appear to be appropriate ?
No
Try a different model, with other variables, transformations, etc.
Yes
A

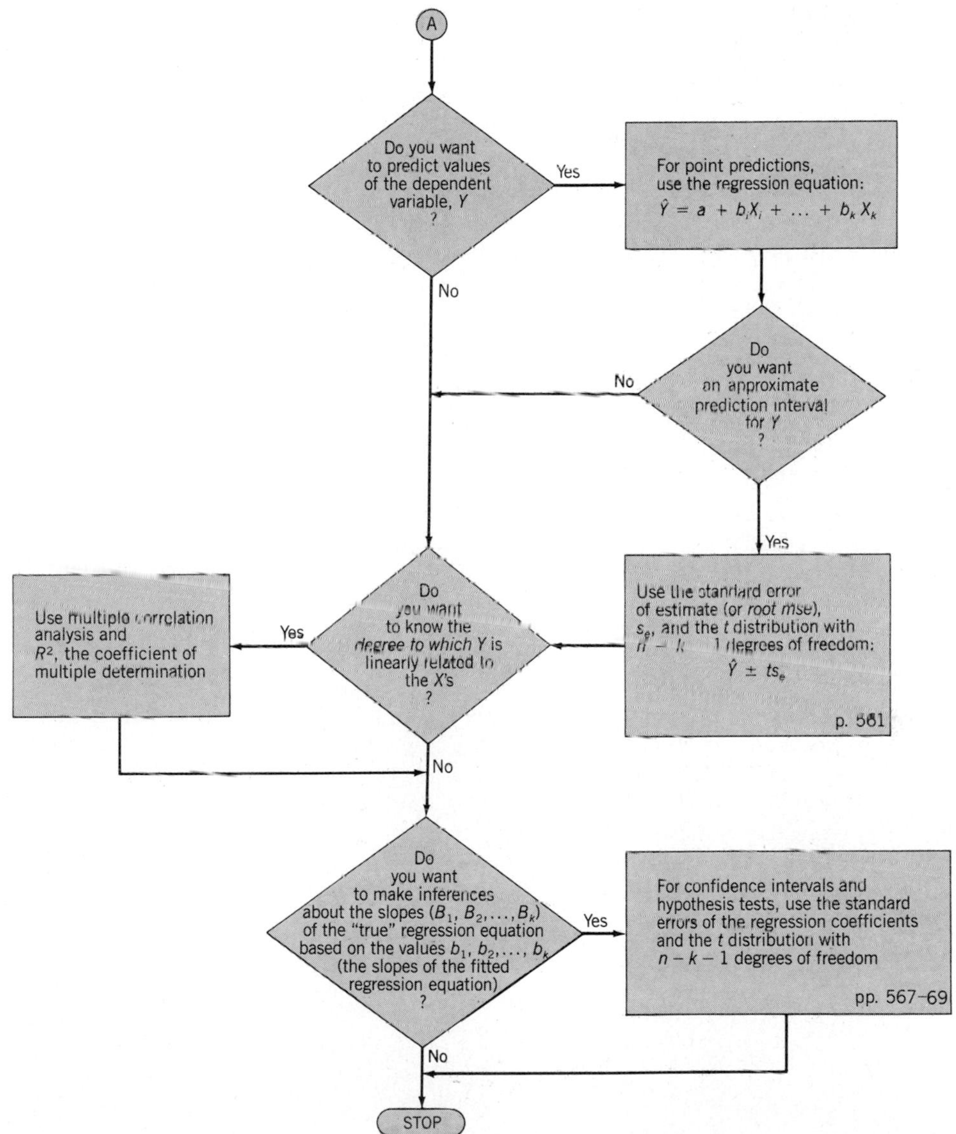

A
Do you want to predict values of the dependent variable, Y ?
Yes
For point predictions, use the regression equation:
$\hat{Y} = a + b_i X_i + \ldots + b_k X_k$
No
Do you want an approximate prediction interval for Y ?
No
Yes
Use the standard error of estimate (or *root mse*), s_e, and the t distribution with $n - k - 1$ degrees of freedom:
$\hat{Y} \pm ts_e$
p. 561
Do you want to know the *degree to which* Y is linearly related to the X's ?
Yes
Use multiple correlation analysis and R^2, the coefficient of multiple determination
No
Do you want to make inferences about the slopes ($B_1, B_2, \ldots, B_k$) of the "true" regression equation based on the values $b_1, b_2, \ldots, b_k$ (the slopes of the fitted regression equation) ?
Yes
For confidence intervals and hypothesis tests, use the standard errors of the regression coefficients and the t distribution with $n - k - 1$ degrees of freedom
pp. 567–69
No
STOP

CHAPTER 13

NONPARAMETRIC METHODS

1. INTRODUCTION TO NONPARAMETRIC STATISTICS, 606
2. THE SIGN TEST FOR PAIRED DATA, 608
3. A RANK SUM TEST: The Mann-Whitney *U* Test, 614
4. ONE-SAMPLE RUNS TESTS, 622
5. RANK CORRELATION, 628
6. THE KOLMOGOROV-SMIRNOV TEST, 638
7. TERMS, 642
8. EQUATIONS, 643
9. REVIEW EXERCISES, 644
10. CONCEPTS TEST, 649
11. CONCEPTUAL CASE, 651
12. COMPUTER DATA BASE EXERCISE, 652
13. FLOW CHART, 658

OBJECTIVES: In Chapters 7 to 12, we learned how statisticians take samples from populations and attempt to reach conclusions from those samples. But how can we handle cases in which we do not know what kind of population we are sampling—that is, when we do not know the shape of the population distribution? In these cases, we can often apply the techniques of *nonparametric statistics* discussed in this chapter.

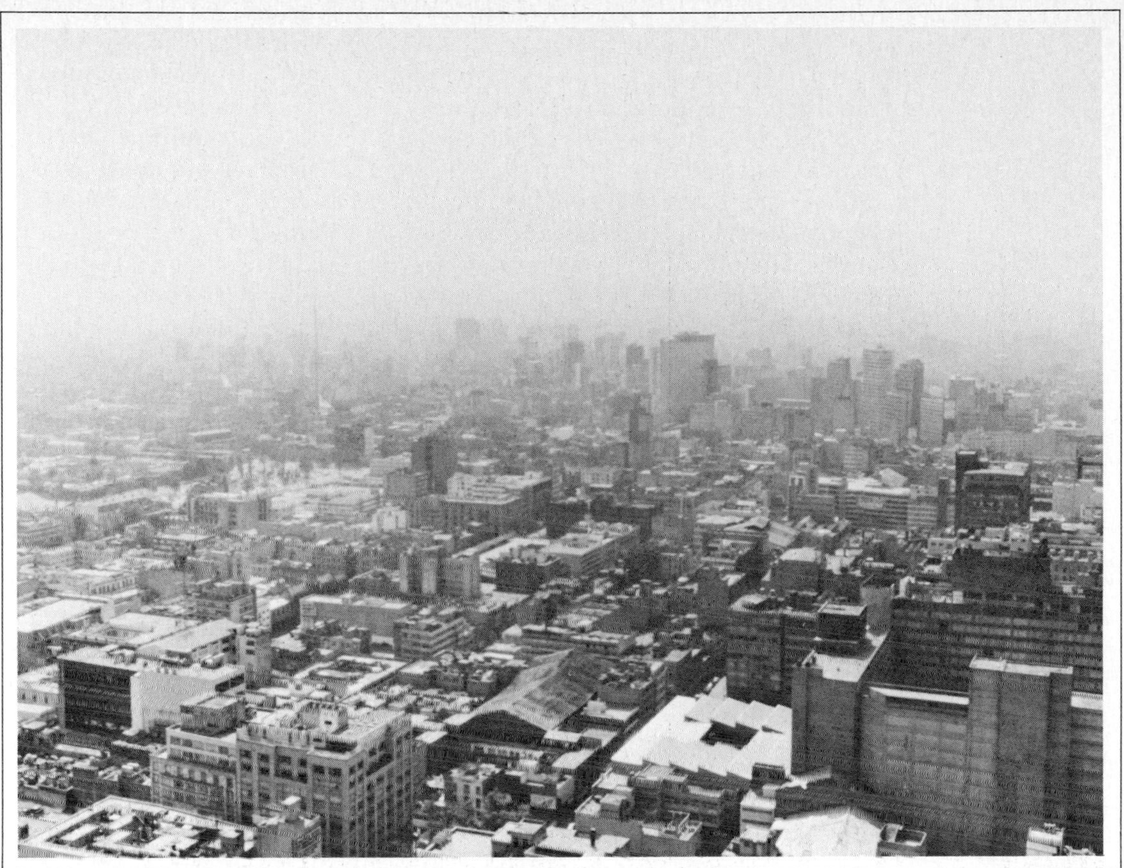

Although the effect of air pollution on health is a complex problem, an international organization has decided to make a preliminary investigation of (1) average year-round quality of air, and (2) the incidence of pulmonary related diseases. A preliminary study ranked 11 of the world's major cities from 1 (worst) to 11 (best) in these two variables.

	CITY										
	A	B	C	D	E	F	G	H	I	J	K
Air-quality rank	4	7	9	1	2	10	3	5	6	8	11
Pulmonary-disease rank	5	4	7	3	1	11	2	10	8	6	9

The health organization's data are different from any we have seen so far in this book: They do not give us the *variable* used to determine these ranks. (We don't know if the rank of pulmonary disease is a result of pneumonia, emphysema, or other illnesses per 100,000 population.) Nor do we know the values (whether City D has twice as much pollution as city K or 20 times as much). If we knew the variables and their values, we could use the regression techniques of Chapter 11. Unfortunately, that is not the case; but even without any knowledge of either variables or values, we can use the techniques in this chapter to help the health organization with its problem.

Parametric statistics

The majority of hypothesis tests discussed so far have made inferences about population *parameters,* such as the mean and the proportion. These parametric tests have used the parametric statistics of samples that came from the population being tested. To formulate these tests, we made restrictive assumptions about the populations from which we drew our samples. In each case in Chapter 9, for example, we assumed that our samples either were large or came from *normally distributed* populations. But populations are not always normal. And even if a goodness-of-fit test (Chapter 10) indicates that a population *is* approximately normal, we cannot always be sure we're right, because the test is not 100 percent reliable. Clearly, there are certain situations in which the use of the normal curve is not appropriate. For these cases, we need alternatives to the parametric statistics and the specific hypothesis tests we've been using so far.

Shortcomings of parametric statistics

13-1 INTRODUCTION TO NONPARAMETRIC STATISTICS

Nonparametric statistics

Fortunately, in recent times statisticians have developed useful techniques that do not make restrictive assumptions about the shape of population distributions. **These are known as *distribution-free* or, more commonly, *nonparametric* tests.** The hypotheses of a nonparametric test are concerned with something other than the value of a population parameter. A large number of these tests exist, but this chapter will examine only a few of the better known and more widely used ones:

1. The sign test for paired data, where positive or negative signs are substituted for quantitative values.
2. A rank sum test, often called the Mann-Whitney *U* Test, which can be used to determine whether two independent samples have been drawn from the same population. It uses more information than the sign test.
3. The one-sample runs test, a method for determining the randomness with which sampled items have been selected.
4. Rank correlation, a method for doing correlation analysis when the data are not available to use in numerical form, but when information is sufficient to rank the data first, second, third, and so forth.
5. The Kolmogorov-Smirnov test, another method for determining the goodness of fit between an observed sample and a theoretical probability distribution.

Advantages of Nonparametric Methods

Nonparametric methods have a number of clear advantages over parametric methods:

1. They do not require us to make the assumption that a population is distributed in the shape of a normal curve or another specific shape.

2. Generally, they are easier to do and to understand. Most nonparametric tests do not demand the kind of laborious computations often required, for example, to calculate a standard deviation. A nonparametric test may ask us to replace numerical values with the order in which those values occur in a list, as has been done in Table 13-1. Obviously, dealing computationally with 1, 2, 3, 4, and 5 takes less effort than working with 13.33, 76.50, 101.79, 113.45, and 189.42.

TABLE 13-1 Converting parametric values to nonparametric ranks

Parametric value	113.45	189.42	76.50	13.33	101.79
Nonparametric value	4	5	2	1	3

3. Sometimes even formal ordering or ranking is not required. Often, all we can do is describe one outcome as "better" than another. When this is the case, or when our measurements are not as accurate as is necessary for parametric tests, we can use nonparametric methods.

Disadvantages of Nonparametric Methods

Two disadvantages accompany the use of nonparametric tests:

1. They ignore a certain amount of information. We have demonstrated how the values 1, 2, 3, 4, and 5 can replace the numbers 13.33, 76.50, 101.79, 113.45, and 189.42. Yet if we represent "189.42" by "5," we lose information that is contained in the value of 189.42. Notice that in our ordering of the values 13.33, 76.50, 101.79, 113.45, and 189.42, the value 189.42 can become 1,189.42 and still be the fifth, or largest, value in the list. But if this list is a data set, we can learn more knowing that the highest value is 1,189.42 instead of 189.42 than we can by representing both these numbers by the value 5.

2. They are often not as efficient or "sharp" as parametric tests. The estimate of an interval at the 95 percent confidence level using a nonparametric test may be twice as large as the estimate using a parametric test such as those in Chapter 8. When we use nonparametric tests, we make a tradeoff: We lose sharpness in estimating intervals, but we gain the ability to use less information and to calculate faster.

EXERCISES

13-1 What is the difference between the kinds of questions answered by parametric tests and those answered by nonparametric tests?

13-2 The null hypothesis most often examined in nonparametric tests:
a) Includes specification of a population's parameters.
b) Is used to evaluate some general population aspect.
c) Is very similar to that used in regression analysis.
d) Simultaneously tests more than 2 population parameters.

13-3 What are the major advantages of nonparametric methods over parametric methods?

13-4 What are the primary shortcomings of nonparametric tests?

13-5 George Shoaf is an interviewer with a large insurance company. George works in the company's home office, and to make the best use of his time, the company requires the receptionist to schedule his interviews according to a precise schedule. There is no 5-minute period unaccounted for, including telephone calls. Unfortunately, the receptionist has been underestimating the amount of time interviews will take, and she has been scheduling too many prospective employees, resulting in long waits in the lobby. Although waiting periods may be short in the morning, as the day progresses and the interviewer gets further behind, the waits become longer. In assessing the problem, should the interviewer assume that the successive waiting times are normally distributed?

13-6 International Communications Corporation is planning to change the benefits package offered to employees. The company is considering different combinations of profit-sharing, health-care, and retirement benefits. Samples of a broad range of benefit combinations were described in a pamphlet and distributed among employees, whose preferences were then recorded. The results follow:

RANK	1	2	3	4	5	6	7	8	9	10	11	12	13	14	15	16	17	18	19
PROFIT-SHARING–HEALTH-CARE–RETIREMENT COMBINATION	15	5	14	4	6	16	7	8	13	3	17	18	12	2	9	1	11	19	10
NUMBER OF PREFERENCES	52	49	39	38	37	36	32	29	26	25	24	18	15	15	14	10	10	10	9

Will the company sacrifice any real information by using the ranking test as its decision criterion? (*Hint:* You might graph the data.)

13-2 THE SIGN TEST FOR PAIRED DATA

One of the easiest nonparametric tests to use is the sign test. Its name comes from the fact that it is based on the direction (or signs for pluses or minuses) of a pair of observations and not on their numerical magnitude.

Use sign test for paired data

Consider the result of a test panel of 40 college juniors evaluating the effectiveness of two types of classes: large lectures by full professors or small sections by graduate assistants. Table 13-2 lists the responses to this request: "Indicate how you rate the effectiveness in transmitting knowledge of these

TABLE 13-2 Evaluation by 40 students of 2 types of classes

Panel-member number	1	2	3	4	5	6	7	8	9	10	11	12	13	14	15	16
Score for large lectures (1)	2	1	4	4	3	3	4	2	4	1	3	3	4	4	4	1
Score for small sections (2)	3	2	2	3	4	2	2	1	3	1	2	3	4	4	3	2
Sign of score 1 minus score 2	−	−	+	+	−	+	+	+	+	0	+	0	0	0	+	−

two types of classes by giving them a number from 4 to 1. A rating of 4 is excellent, and 1 is poor." In this case, the sign test can help us determine whether students feel there is a difference between the effectiveness of the two types of classes.

Converting values to signs

We can begin, as we have in Table 13-2, by converting the evaluations of the two teaching methods into signs. Here a plus sign means the student prefers large lectures; a minus sign indicates a preference for small sections; and a zero represents a tie (no preference). If we count the bottom row of Table 13-2, we get these results:

Number of + signs	19
Number of − signs	11
Number of 0's	10
Total sample size	**40**

Stating the Hypotheses

Finding the sample size

We are using the sign test to determine whether our panel can discern a real difference between the two types of classes. Since we are testing perceived differences, we shall exclude tie evaluations (0s). We can see that we have nineteen plus signs and eleven minus signs, for a total of 30 usable responses. If there is no difference between the two types of classes, p (the probability that the first score exceeds the second score) would be .5, and we would expect to get about fifteen plus signs and fifteen minus signs. We would set up our hypotheses like this:

H_0: $p = .5$ ← null hypothesis: There is no difference between the 2 types of classes.

H_1: $p \neq .5$ ← alternative hypothesis: There is a difference between the 2 types of classes.

Choosing the distribution

If you look carefully at the hypotheses, you will see that the situation is similar to the fair-coin toss that we discussed in Chapter 5. If we tossed a fair coin 30 times, p would be .5, and we would expect about fifteen heads and fifteen tails. In that case, we would use the binomial distribution as the appropriate sampling distribution. You may also remember that when np and nq are each at least 5, we can use the normal distribution to approximate the binomial. This is just the case with the results from our panel of college juniors. Thus, we can apply the normal distribution to our test of the two teaching methods.

17	18	19	20	21	22	23	24	25	26	27	28	29	30	31	32	33	34	35	36	37	38	39	40
1	2	2	4	4	4	4	3	3	2	3	4	3	4	3	1	4	3	2	2	2	1	3	3
3	2	3	3	1	4	3	3	2	2	1	1	1	3	2	2	4	4	3	3	1	1	4	2
−	0	−	+	+	0	+	0	+	0	+	+	+	+	+	−	0	−	−	−	+	0	−	+

$p_{H_0} = .5 \leftarrow$ hypothesized proportion of the population who feel that both types of classes are the same

$q_{H_0} = .5 \leftarrow$ hypothesized proportion of the population who feel the 2 types of classes are different ($q_{H_0} = 1 - p_{H_0}$)

$n = 30 \leftarrow$ sample size

$\bar{p} = .633 \leftarrow$ proportion of successes in the sample (19/30)

$\bar{q} = .367 \leftarrow$ proportion of failures in the sample (11/30)

Testing a Hypothesis of No Difference

Calculating the standard error

Suppose the chancellor's office wants to test the hypothesis that there is no difference between student perception of the two types of classes at the .05 level of significance. We shall conduct this test using the methods we introduced in Chapter 9. The first step is to calculate the standard error of the proportion:

$$\sigma_{\bar{p}} = \sqrt{\frac{pq}{n}} \qquad [8\text{-}4]$$

$$= \sqrt{\frac{(.5)(.5)}{30}}$$

$$= \sqrt{.00833}$$

$$= .091 \leftarrow \text{standard error of the proportion}$$

Illustrating the test

Since we want to know whether the true proportion is larger *or* smaller than the hypothesized proportion, this is a two-tailed test. Figure 13-1 illustrates this hypothesis test graphically. The two colored regions represent the .05 level of significance.

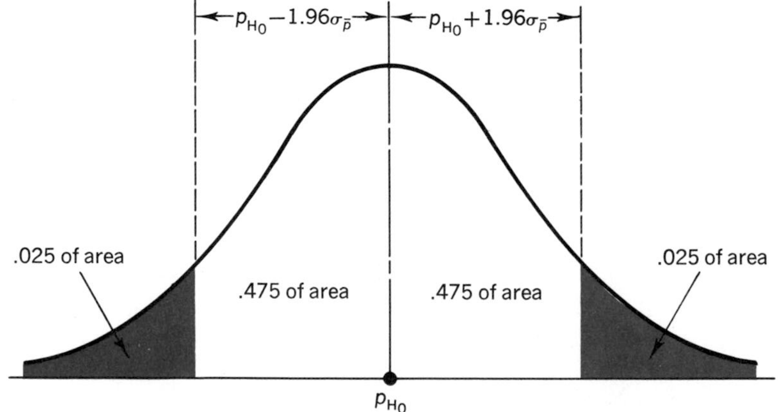

FIGURE 13-1 Two-tailed hypothesis test of a proportion at the .05 level of significance

Finding the limits of the acceptance region

Because we are using the normal distribution in our test, we can determine from Appendix Table 1 that the z value for .475 of the area under the curve is 1.96. Thus, we can calculate the limits of the acceptance region for the null hypothesis as follows:

$$\begin{aligned} p_{H_0} + 1.96\sigma_{\bar{p}} &= .5 + (1.96)(.091) \\ &= .5 + .178 \\ &= .678 \leftarrow \text{upper limit} \end{aligned}$$

and:

$$\begin{aligned} p_{H_0} - 1.96\sigma_{\bar{p}} &= .5 - (1.96)(.091) \\ &= .5 - .178 \\ &= .322 \leftarrow \text{lower limit} \end{aligned}$$

Interpreting the results

Figure 13-2 illustrates these two limits of the acceptance region, .322 and .678, and the sample proportion, .633. We can see that the sample proportion falls within the acceptance region for this hypothesis test. Therefore, the chancellor should accept the null hypothesis that students perceive no difference between the two types of classes.

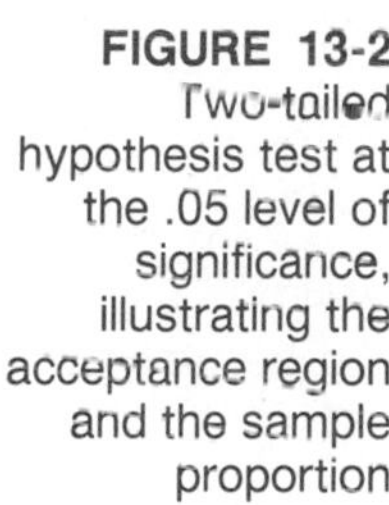

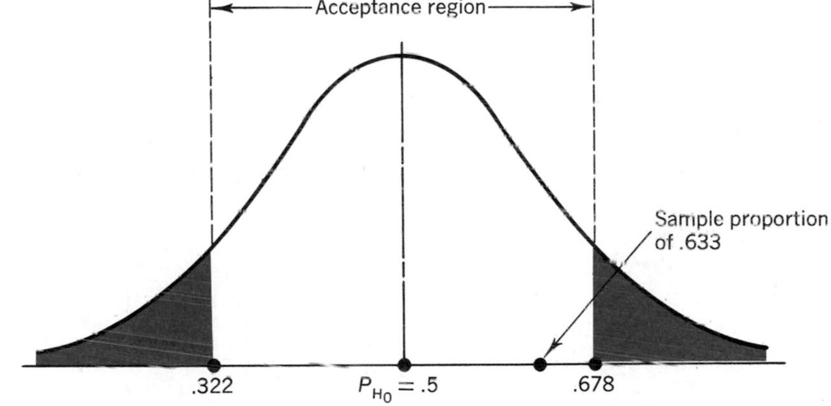

FIGURE 13-2 Two-tailed hypothesis test at the .05 level of significance, illustrating the acceptance region and the sample proportion

A final word about the sign test

A sign test such as this is quite simple to do and applies to both one-tailed and two-tailed tests. It is usually based on the binomial distribution. Remember, however, that we were able to use the normal approximation to the binomial as our sampling distribution because np and nq were both greater than 5. If these conditions are not met, we must use the binomial instead.

EXERCISES

13-7 The following data show employees' rates of defective work before and after a change in the wage incentive plan. Compare the two sets of data below to see if the change lowered the defective units produced. Use the .05 level of significance.

Before	8	7	6	9	11	10	8	6	5	8	9	10
After	6	5	8	6	9	8	10	7	4	6	9	10

13-8 Use the sign test to see if there is a difference between the number of days until the collection of an account receivable before and after a new collection policy. Use the .10 significance level.

Before	32	35	33	36	44	41	32	39	31	47	30	29
After	36	37	34	40	40	42	40	42	33	46	29	35

13-9 A company is considering switching from its straight salary form of payment to a group incentive plan, so that when employees increase output, they will be rewarded for their effort. Management decided to test the new method for its effect on output. Prior to this point, in one assembly department, the day shift's and the night shift's unit output were considered equal. Therefore, to test the new plan, the company put the day shift on the group incentive plan and left the night shift on straight salary for a 34-day period. The output per day for each group during this time is shown below.

DAY SHIFT	NIGHT SHIFT	DAY SHIFT	NIGHT SHIFT
79	76	75	76
84	82	90	92
92	92	79	74
83	81	83	81
75	76	85	80
89	88	86	79
76	74	94	94
94	97	82	81
94	92	91	94
82	80	84	83
70	73	88	89
81	81	98	96
88	86	79	80
77	75	88	85
86	84	93	90
90	86	78	78
85	86	94	92

At a 5 percent significance level, does the wage incentive program used on the day shift lead to an increase in output?

13-10 Because of the severity of recent winters, there has been talk that the earth is slowly progressing toward another ice age. Some scientists hold different views, however, because the summers have brought extreme temperatures as well. One scientist suggested looking at the mean temperature for each month to see if it was lower than in the previous year. Another meteorologist at the government weather service argued that perhaps they should look as well at temperatures in the spring and fall months of the last 2 years, so that their conclusions would be based on other than extreme temperatures. In this way, he said, they could detect whether there appeared to be a general warming or cooling trend or just extreme temperatures in the summer and winter months. So 15 dates in the spring and fall were randomly selected, and the temperatures in the last 2 years were noted for a particular location with generally moderate temperatures. Following are the dates and corresponding temperatures for 1982 and 1983.

a) Is the meteorologist's reasoning as to the method of evaluation sound? Explain.
b) Using a sign test, determine whether the meteorologist can be 95 percent sure that 1983 was cooler than 1982, based on these data.

TEMPERATURE (FAHRENHEIT)

DATE	1982	1983	DATE	1982	1983
Mar. 29	46°	44°	Oct. 12	58°	56°
Apr. 4	51	53	May 31	73	75
Apr. 13	48	48	Sept. 28	68	66
May 22	67	64	June 5	74	71
Oct.1	55	52	June 17	80	82
Mar. 23	46	50	Oct. 5	64	64
Nov. 12	49	49	Nov. 28	53	49
Sept. 30	63	60			

13-11 With the concern over radiation exposure and its relationship to the incidence of cancer, city environmental specialists keep a close eye on the types of industry coming into the area and the degree to which they employ radiation in their production. An index of exposure to radioactive contamination has been developed and is used daily to determine if the levels are increasing or are higher under certain atmospheric conditions.

Environmentalists claim that radioactive contamination has increased in the last year because of new industry in the city. City administrators, however, claim that new, more stringent regulations on industry in the area have made levels lower than last year, even with new industry using radiation. To test their claim, records for 10 randomly selected days of the year have been checked, and the index of exposure to radioactive contamination has been noted. The following results were obtained:

INDEX OF RADIATION EXPOSURE

1982	1.402	1.401	1.400	1.404	1.395	1.402	1.406	1.401	1.404	1.406
1983	1.440	1.395	1.398	1.404	1.393	1.400	1.401	1.402	1.400	1.403

Can the administrators be 92 percent sure that the levels of radioactive contamination have changed—or more specifically, that they have been reduced?

13-12 As part of the recent interest in population growth and the sizes of families, a population researcher examined a number of hypotheses concerning the family size that various people look upon as ideal. She suspected that variables of race, sex, age, and background might account for some of the different views. In one pilot sample, the researcher tested the hypothesis that women today think of an ideal family as being smaller than the ideal held by their mothers. She asked each of the participants in the pilot study to state the number of children she would choose to have or that she considered ideal. Responses were anonymous, to guard against the possibility that people would feel obligated to give a socially desirable answer. In addition, people of different backgrounds were included in the sample. Below are the responses of the mother–daughter pairs.

IDEAL FAMILY SIZE

SAMPLE PAIR	A	B	C	D	E	F	G	H	I	J	K	L	M
Daughter	3	4	2	1	5	4	2	2	3	3	1	4	2
Mother	4	4	4	3	5	3	3	5	3	2	2	3	1

a) Can the researcher be 97 percent sure that the mothers and daughters do not have essentially the same ideal of family size? Use the binomial distribution.
b) Determine if the researcher could conclude that the mothers do not have essentially the same family-size preferences as their daughters by using the normal approximation to the binomial.
c) Assume that for each pair listed, there were 10 more pairs who responded in an identical manner. Calculate the range of the proportion for which the researcher would conclude that there is no difference in the mothers and daughters. Is your conclusion changed?
d) Explain any differences in conclusions obtained in parts *a*, *b*, and *c*.

13-13 After collecting data on the amount of air pollution in Los Angeles, the Environmental Protection Agency decided to issue strict new rules to govern the amount of hydrocarbons in the air. For the next year, they took monthly measurements of this pollutant and compared them to the preceding year's measurements for corresponding months. Based on the following data, does the EPA have enough evidence to conclude with a 90 percent confidence that the new rules were effective in lowering the amount of hydrocarbons in the air? To justify maintaining these laws for another year, they must be 80 percent sure of their effectiveness. Will these laws still be in effect next year?

	LAST YEAR*	THIS YEAR
Jan.	7.0	5.3
Feb.	6.0	6.0
Mar.	5.4	5.6
April	5.9	6.0
May	3.9	3.7
June	5.7	4.7
July	6.9	6.1
Aug.	7.6	7.2
Sept.	6.3	6.4
Oct.	5.8	5.7
Nov.	5.1	4.9
Dec.	5.9	5.8

* Measured in parts per million.

13-3 A RANK SUM TEST: The Mann-Whitney *U* Test

Mann-Whitney *U* test introduced

Rank sum tests are a whole family of tests. We shall concentrate on one member of this family, the Mann-Whitney *U* test, which will enable us to determine whether two independent samples have been drawn from the same population (or from two different populations having the same distribution). It uses *ranking* information rather than pluses and minuses and, therefore, is less wasteful of data than the sign test.

Approaching a Problem Using the Mann-Whitney *U* Test

Suppose that the board of regents of a large eastern state university wants to test the hypothesis that the mean SAT scores of students at two branches of

TABLE 13-3 SAT scores for students at two state university branches

Branch A	1,000	1,100	800	750	1,300	950	1,050	1,250	1,400	850	1,150	1,200	1,500	600	775
Branch S	920	1,120	830	1,360	650	725	890	1,600	900	1,140	1,550	550	1,240	925	500

the state university are equal. The board keeps statistics on all students at all branches of the system. A random sample of fifteen students from each branch has produced the data shown in Table 13-3.

Ranking the items to be tested

To apply the Mann-Whitney U test to this problem, we begin by ranking all the scores in order from lowest to highest, indicating beside each the symbol of the branch. Table 13-4 accomplishes this.

TABLE 13-4 SAT scores ranked from lowest to highest

RANK	SCORE	BRANCH	RANK	SCORE	BRANCH
1	500	S	16	1,000	A
2	550	S	17	1,050	A
3	600	A	18	1,100	A
4	650	S	19	1,120	S
5	725	S	20	1,140	S
6	750	A	21	1,150	A
7	775	A	22	1,200	A
8	800	A	23	1,240	S
9	830	S	24	1,250	A
10	850	A	25	1,300	A
11	890	S	26	1,360	S
12	900	S	27	1,400	A
13	920	S	28	1,500	A
14	925	S	29	1,550	S
15	950	A	30	1,600	S

Next, let's learn the symbols used in a Mann-Whitney U test in the context of this problem:

Symbols for expressing the problem

n_1 = number of items in sample 1; that is, the number of students at Branch A

n_2 = number of items in sample 2; that is, the number of students at Branch S

R_1 = sum of the ranks of the items in sample 1: the sum from Table 13-5 of the ranks of all the Branch A scores

R_2 = sum of the ranks of the items in sample 2: the sum from Table 13-5 of the ranks of all the Branch S scores

In this case, both n_1 and n_2 are equal to 15, but it is *not* necessary for both samples to be of the same size. Now in Table 13-5, we can reproduce the data from Table 13-3, adding the ranks from Table 13-4. Then we can total the ranks for each branch. As a result, we have all the values we need to solve this problem, because we know that:

$$n_1 = 15$$
$$n_2 = 15$$
$$R_1 = 247$$
$$R_2 = 218$$

TABLE 13-5 Raw data and rank for SAT scores

BRANCH A	RANK	BRANCH S	RANK
1,000	16	920	13
1,100	18	1,120	19
800	8	830	9
750	6	1,360	26
1,300	25	650	4
950	15	725	5
1,050	17	890	11
1,250	24	1,600	30
1,400	27	900	12
850	10	1,140	20
1,150	21	1,550	29
1,200	22	550	2
1,500	28	1,240	23
600	3	925	14
775	7	500	1
	247 ← total ranks		**218 ← total ranks**

Calculating the *U* Statistic

Using the values for n_1 and n_2 and the ranked sums of R_1 and R_2, we can determine the *U statistic*, a measurement of the difference between the ranked observations of the two samples of SAT scores:

Defining the *U* statistic

$$U = n_1 n_2 + \frac{n_1(n_1 + 1)}{2} - R_1 \qquad \textbf{[13-1]}$$

$$= 15)(15) + \frac{(15)(16)}{2} - 247$$

$$= 225 + 120 - 247$$

$$= 98 \leftarrow U \textit{ statistic}$$

If the null hypothesis that the $n_1 + n_2$ observations came from identical populations is true, then this *U* statistic has a sampling distribution with a mean of:

Mean of the *U* statistic

$$\mu_U = \frac{n_1 n_2}{2} \qquad \textbf{[13-2]}$$

$$= \frac{(15)(15)}{2}$$

$$= 112.5 \leftarrow \text{mean of the } U \text{ statistic}$$

and a standard error of:

Standard error of the U statistic

$$\text{Standard error of the } U \text{ statistic} \rightarrow \sigma_U = \sqrt{\frac{n_1 n_2(n_1 + n_2 + 1)}{12}} \quad [13\text{-}3]$$

$$= \sqrt{\frac{(15)(15)(15 + 15 + 1)}{12}}$$

$$= \sqrt{\frac{6{,}975}{12}}$$

$$= \sqrt{581.25}$$

$$= 24.1 \leftarrow \text{standard error of the } U \text{ statistic}$$

Testing the Hypotheses

The sampling distribution of the U statistic can be approximated by the normal distribution when both n_1 and n_2 are larger than 10. Because our problem meets this condition, we can use the normal distribution and the z table to make our test. The board of regents wishes to test at the .15 level of significance the hypothesis that these samples were drawn from identical populations.

Stating the hypotheses

$H_0: \mu_1 = \mu_2 \leftarrow$ null hypothesis: There is no difference between the two populations, and so they have the same mean.

$H_1: \mu_1 \neq \mu_2 \leftarrow$ alternative hypothesis: There is a difference between the two populations; in particular, they have different means.

$\alpha = .15 \leftarrow$ level of significance for testing these hypotheses

Illustrating the test

Finding the limits of the acceptance region

The board of regents wants to know whether the mean SAT score for students at either of the two schools is better or worse than the other. Therefore, this is a two-tailed hypothesis test. Figure 13-3 illustrates this test graphically. The two colored areas represent the .15 level of significance. Since we are using the normal distribution as our sampling distribution in this test, we can determine from Appendix Table 1 that the appropriate z value for an area of .425 is 1.44. The two limits of the acceptance region can be calculated like this:

$$\mu_U + 1.44\sigma_U = 112.5 + (1.44)(24.1)$$
$$= 112.5 + 34.7$$
$$= 147.2 \leftarrow \text{upper limit}$$

and:

$$\mu_U - 1.44\sigma_U = 112.5 - (1.44)(24.1)$$
$$= 112.5 - 34.7$$
$$= 77.8 \leftarrow \text{lower limit}$$

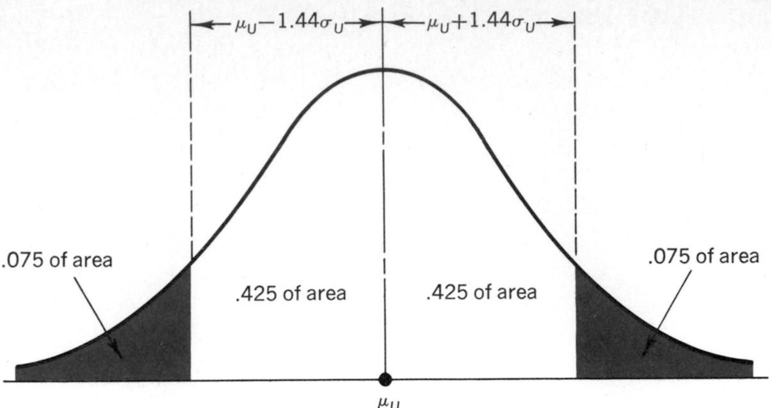

FIGURE 13-3 Two-tailed hypothesis test at the .15 level of significance

Interpreting the results

Figure 13-4 illustrates the limits of the acceptance region, 77.8 and 147.2, and the U value calculated earlier, 98. We can see that the sample U statistic does lie within the acceptance region. Thus, we would accept the null hypothesis of no difference and conclude that the distributions, and hence the mean SAT scores at the two schools, are the same.

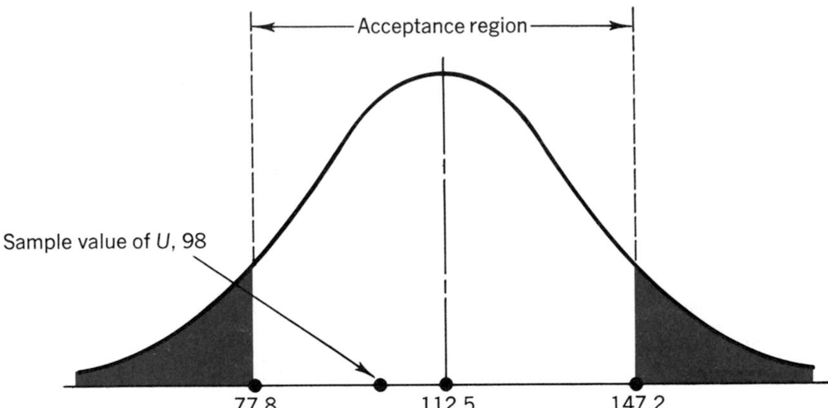

FIGURE 13-4 Two-tailed hypothesis test at the .15 level of significance, showing the acceptance region and the sample U statistic

Special Properties of the *U* Test

Another way to compute the U statistic

The U statistic has a feature that enables users to save calculating time when the two samples under observation are of unequal size. We just computed the value of U using Equation 13-1:

$$U = n_1 n_2 + \frac{n_1(n_1 + 1)}{2} - R_1 \qquad \textbf{[13-1]}$$

But just as easily, we could have computed the U statistic using the R_2 value, like this:

$$U = n_1 n_2 + \frac{n_2(n_2 + 1)}{2} - R_2 \qquad \textbf{[13-4]}$$

The answer would have been 127 (which is just as far *above* the mean of 112.5 as 98 was *below* it). In this problem, we would have spent the same amount of time calculating the value of the U statistic using either Equation 13-1 or Equation 13-4. In other cases, when the number of items is larger in one sample than in the other, choose the equation that will require less work. Regardless of whether you calculate U using Equation 13-1 or 13-4, you will come to the same conclusion. Notice that in this example, the answer 127 falls in the acceptance region just as 98 did.

Handling ties in the data

What about *ties* that may happen when we rank the items for this test? For example, what if the two scores ranked 13 and 14 in Table 13-4 both had the value 920? In this case, we would find the average of their ranks $(13 + 14)/2 = 13.5$, and assign the result to both of them. If there were a three-way tie among the scores ranked 13, 14, and 15, we would average these ranks $(13 + 14 + 15)/3 = 14$, and use that value for all three items.

EXERCISES

13-14 Test the hypothesis of no difference between the ages of male and female employees of a certain company, using the Mann-Whitney U test for the sample data below. Use the .05 level of significance.

Males	26	25	38	33	42	40	44	26	43	35
Females	44	30	34	47	35	46	35	47	48	34

13-15 The following table shows sample retail prices for two brands of manual typewriters. Use the Mann-Whitney U test to determine if there is any difference between the retail prices of the two brands throughout the country. Use the .01 level of significance. (Disregard the fact that we have fewer than 10 observations for n_1 and n_2.)

Typewriter A	$89	90	92	81	76	88	85		
Typewriter B	$70	93	81	87	89	71	90	96	82

13-16 A mail-order gift company has the following sample data on dollar sales, separated according to how the order was paid for. Test the hypothesis that there is no difference in the dollar amount of orders paid for by check and orders paid for by credit card. Use the rank sum test with a level of significance of .05. (Disregard the fact that we have fewer than 10 observations for n_1 and n_2.)

Credit-card orders	78	64	75	45	82	69	60
Check orders	110	70	53	51	61	68	

13-17 The following data show sample unit output per day for employees in two age groups. Use the Mann-Whitney U test to determine if there is any difference between the output of older and younger employees. Use the .05 level of significance. (Disregard the fact that we have fewer than 10 observations for n_1 and n_2.)

Over 40	24	28	15	47	23	25	53	20		
Under 40	22	12	30	16	26	14	18	21	16	18

13-18 A manufacturer of toys changed the type of plastic molding machines it was using, because a new one gave evidence of being more economical. As the Christmas season began, however, inventories looked somewhat smaller than last year. Since production records for the past years were readily available, the production manager decided to compare the monthly output for the 16 months when the old machines were used and the 10 months of production so far this year. Records show these output amounts with the old and new machines.

MONTHLY OUTPUT IN UNITS			
OLD MACHINES	NEW MACHINES	OLD MACHINES	NEW MACHINES
992	965	966	956
945	1,054	889	900
938	912	972	
1,027	850	940	
892	796	873	
983	911	1,015	
1,014	877	1,016	
1,258	902	897	

Can the company be 95 percent sure that the change in machines has reduced output?

13-19 Authorities for the Massachusetts Highway Department were considering purchasing a new ferry for the Martha's Vineyard crossing. The existing ferry held, on the average, 32 vehicles. The ferry under consideration was larger, but authorities doubted whether the additional space was really usable. Because of the many differing sizes of vehicles that typically used any ferry, it was impossible to estimate with accuracy whether the new ferry would be able to carry more vehicles. Relative capacities were particularly important because of a Massachusetts law requiring competitive bidding on all public contracts. The highway department had to know whether the ferry it was considering was compatible in size with a duplicate of the original (for which they had received a lower bid).

To aid in the decision, several tests were conducted on the existing ferry. Another state, which already had one of the new ferries in operation, conducted similar tests in response to the request of the Massachusetts Highway Department. The statistic that was recorded was the lengthwise footage for vehicles that were loaded on board. The data are presented below:

LENGTHWISE FOOTAGE OF VEHICLES LOADED PER TRIP (AT CAPACITY)														
Existing ferry	453	438	447	449	452	450	439	445	446	454	451	448	442	447
Proposed ferry	458	459	450	448	459	457	462	439	448	454				

Use the Mann-Whitney *U* test to draw a conclusion about the capacity differential of the 2 ships. Use the 10 percent significance level.

13-20 To increase sales during heavy shopping days, a chain of stores selling cheese in shopping malls gives away samples at the stores' entrances. The chain's management defines the heavy shopping days and randomly selects the days for sampling. From a sample of days that were considered heavy shopping days, the data below give one store's sales on days when cheese sampling was done and on days when it was not done.

SALES (IN HUNDREDS)

Promotion days	18	21	23	15	19	26	17	18	22	20	18	21
Regular days	22	17	15	23	25	22	26	24	16	17	23	21

Use a Mann-Whitney U test and a 9 percent level of significance to decide whether the storefront sampling produced greater sales.

13-21 A company is interested in knowing whether there is a difference in the output rate for men and women employees in the molding department. Judy Johnson, production manager, was asked to conduct a study in which male and female workers' output was measured for one week. Somehow, one of the office clerks misplaced a portion of the data, and Judy was able to locate only the following information from the records of the tests:

$$\sigma_u = 64.265077$$
$$\mu_u = 420$$
$$R_1 = 830$$

Judy also remembered that the sample size for men, n_2, had been 2 units larger than n_1.

Reconstruct a z value for the test and determine if the weekly output can be assumed, with a 5 percent level of significance, to be the same for both men and women. Indicate also the values for n_1, n_2, and R_2.

13-22 A large hospital hires most of its nurses from the 2 major universities in the area. Over the last year, they have been giving a test to the newly graduated nurses entering the hospital to determine which school, if either, seems to be better educating their nurses. Based on the following scores (out of 100 possible points), help the personnel office of the hospital determine whether the schools differ in quality. Use the Mann-Whitney U test with a 7 percent level of significance.

TEST SCORES

School A	97	69	73	84	76	92	90	88	84	87	93
School B	88	99	65	69	97	84	85	89	91	90	87

13-23 The E-Z-Drive driving school teaches people the fundamentals of handling an automobile in a 4-week course that is offered monthly. All students are normally taught by the same instructor, using the teaching method (Method 1) that E-Z-Drive has used for the past few years. This month, however, the 24 students have been randomly split into 2 classes; one class is being taught by Method 1, and the other is being taught by a newer, more innovative approach (Method 2). The students in each class all seemed to have roughly comparable driving skills at the start of the month, so the management of E-Z-Drive feels that the scores of all the students on the standardized final exam should indicate whether or not both teaching methods prepare students for the final equally well. Test this hypothesis at the .05 significance level, using the scores of the students given below. (40 is the highest possible grade.)

FINAL EXAM SCORES

Method 1	27	36	24	10	11	34	29	17	35	27	29	28	12
Method 2	19	23	18	9	28	19	11	13	16	10	8		

13-4 ONE-SAMPLE RUNS TEST

Concept of randomness

So far, we have assumed that the samples in our problems were randomly selected—that is, chosen without preference or bias. What if you were to notice recurrent patterns in a sample chosen by someone else? Suppose that applicants for advanced job training were to be selected without regard to sex from a large population. Using the notation W = woman and M = man, you find that the first group enters in this order:

W, W, W, W, M, M, M, M, W, W, W, W, M, M, M, M

By inspection, you would conclude that although the total number of applicants is equally divided between the sexes, the order is not random. A random process would rarely list two items in alternating groups of four. Suppose now that the applicants begin to arrive in this order:

W, M, W, M, W, M, W, M, W, M, W, M, W, M, W, M

It is just as unreasonable to think that a random selection process would produce such an orderly pattern of men and women. In this case, too, the *proportion* of women to men is right, but you would be suspicious about the *order* in which they are arriving.

The theory of runs

To allow us to test samples for the randomness of their order, statisticians have developed the *theory of runs*. **A run is a sequence of identical occurrences preceded and followed by different occurrences or by none at all.** If men and women enter as follows, the sequence will contain three runs:

$$\underbrace{W,}_{\text{1st}}\ \underbrace{M,\ M,\ M,\ M,}_{\text{2nd}}\ \underbrace{W}_{\text{3rd}}$$

And this sequence contains six runs:

$$\underbrace{W,\ W,\ W,}_{\text{1st}}\ \underbrace{M,\ M,}_{\text{2nd}}\ \underbrace{W,}_{\text{3rd}}\ \underbrace{M,\ M,\ M,\ M,}_{\text{4th}}\ \underbrace{W,\ W,\ W,\ W,}_{\text{5th}}\ \underbrace{M}_{\text{6th}}$$

Symbols for expressing the problem

A *test of runs* would use the following symbols if it contained just two kinds of occurrences:

n_1 = number of occurrences of type 1

n_2 = number of occurrences of type 2

r = number of runs

Let's apply these symbols to a different pattern for the arrival of applicants:

M, W, W, M, M, M, M, W, W, W, M, M, W, M, W, W, M

In this case, the values of n_1, n_2, and r would be:

$n_1 = 8 \leftarrow$ number of women

$n_2 = 9 \leftarrow$ number of men

$r = 9 \leftarrow$ number of runs

A Problem Using a One-Sample Runs Test

A manufacturer of breakfast cereal uses a machine to insert randomly one of two types of toys in each box. The company wants randomness so that every child in the neighborhood does not get the same toy. Testers choose samples of 60 successive boxes to see if the machine is properly mixing the two types of toys. Using the symbols A and B to represent the two types of toys, a tester reported that one such batch looked like this:

B, A, B, B, B, A, A, A, B, B, A, B, B, B, B, A, A, A, A, B,
A, B, A, A, B, B, B, A, A, B, A, A, A, A, B, B, A, B, B, A,
A, A, A, B, B, A, B, B, B, B, A, A, B, B, A, B, A, A, B, B

Stating the problem symbolically

The values in our test will be:

$n_1 = 29 \leftarrow$ number of boxes containing toy A

$n_2 = 31 \leftarrow$ number of boxes containing toy B

$r = 29 \leftarrow$ number of runs

The Sampling Distribution of the *r* Statistic

The *r* statistic, the basis of a one-sample runs test

The *number of runs,* or *r*, is a statistic with its own special sampling distribution and its own test. Obviously, runs may be of differing lengths, and various numbers of runs can occur in one sample. Statisticians can prove that too many or too few runs in a sample indicate that something other than chance was at work when the items were selected. **A *one-sample runs test,* then, is based on the idea that *too few* or *too many runs* show that the items were not chosen randomly.**

To derive the mean of the sampling distribution of the *r* statistic, use the following formula:

Mean and standard error of the *r* statistic

Mean of the *r* statistic →

$$\mu_r = \frac{2n_1n_2}{n_1 + n_2} + 1 \qquad \textbf{[13-5]}$$

Applying this to the cereal company, the mean of the r statistic would be:

$$\mu_r = \frac{(2)(29)(31)}{29 + 31} + 1$$
$$= \frac{1798}{60} + 1$$
$$= 29.97 + 1$$
$$= 30.97 \leftarrow \text{mean of the } r \text{ statistic}$$

The standard error of the r statistic can be calculated with this formidable-looking formula:

Standard error of the r statistic

$$\sigma_r = \sqrt{\frac{2n_1n_2(2n_1n_2 - n_1 - n_2)}{(n_1 + n_2)^2(n_1 + n_2 - 1)}} \quad \textbf{[13-6]}$$

For our problem, the standard error of the r statistic becomes:

$$\sigma_r = \sqrt{\frac{(2)(29)(31)(2 \times 29 \times 31 - 29 - 31)}{(29 + 31)^2(29 + 31 - 1)}}$$
$$= \sqrt{\frac{(1{,}798)(1{,}738)}{(60)^2(59)}}$$
$$= \sqrt{\frac{3{,}124{,}924}{212{,}400}}$$
$$= \sqrt{14.71}$$
$$= 3.84 \leftarrow \text{standard error of the } r \text{ statistic}$$

Testing the Hypotheses

In the one-sample runs test, the sampling distribution of r can be closely approximated by the normal distribution if *either* n_1 or n_2 is larger than 20. Since our cereal company has a sample of 60 boxes, we can use the normal approximation. Management is interested in testing at the .20 level the hypothesis that the toys are randomly mixed, so the test becomes:

Stating the hypotheses

H_0: H_1: In a one-sample runs test, no symbolic statement of the hypotheses is appropriate.

$\leftarrow$ null hypothesis: The toys are randomly mixed.

$\leftarrow$ alternative hypothesis: The toys are not randomly mixed.

$\alpha = .20$ $\leftarrow$ level of significance for testing these hypotheses

---

Illustrating the test

Since too many *or* two few runs would indicate that the process by which the toys are inserted is not random, a two-tailed test is appropriate. Figure 13-5 illustrates this test graphically.

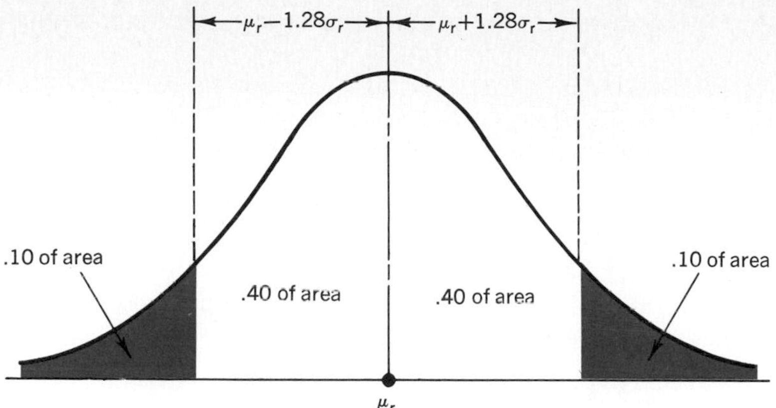

FIGURE 13-5 Two-tailed hypothesis test at the .20 level of significance

Finding the limits of the acceptance region

Because we can use the normal distribution, we can turn to Appendix Table 1 to find the appropriate z value for .40 of the area under the curve. We can then use this value, 1.28, to calculate the limits of the acceptance region:

$$\begin{aligned}\mu_r + 1.28\sigma_r &= 30.97 + (1.28)(3.84)\\ &= 30.97 + 4.92\\ &= 35.89 \leftarrow \text{upper limit}\end{aligned}$$

and:

$$\begin{aligned}\mu_r - 1.28\sigma_r &= 30.97 - (1.28)(3.84)\\ &= 30.97 - 4.92\\ &= 26.05 \leftarrow \text{lower limit}\end{aligned}$$

Interpreting the results

Both these limits to the acceptance region, 26.05 and 35.89, and the number of runs in the sample, 29, are shown in Fig. 13-6. There, we can see that the observed number of runs, 29, falls within the acceptance region. Therefore, management should accept the null hypothesis and conclude from this test that the toys are being inserted in the boxes in random order.

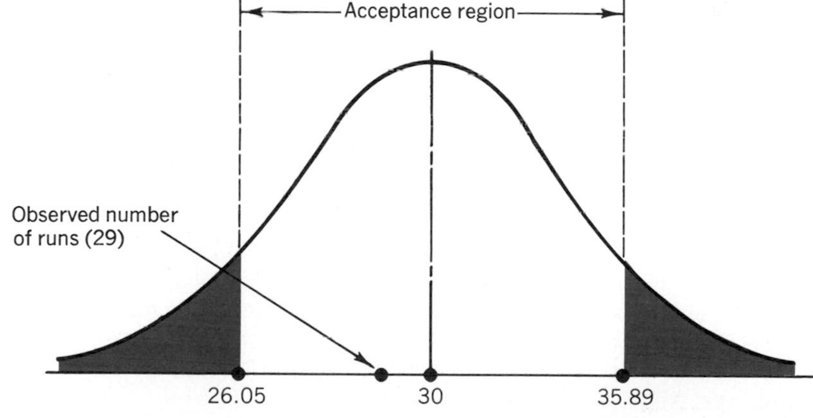

FIGURE 13-6 Two-tailed hypothesis test at the .20 level of significance, showing the acceptance region and the observed number of runs

EXERCISES

13-24 Test for the randomness of the following sample, using the .05 significance level:

A, B, B, B, B, A, B, A, B, B, A, A, B, A, A, A, B, B, B, A,
B, B, A, A, A, A, B, A, B, B, A, A, A, B, A, A, B, A, B, B

13-25 A sequence of small glass sculptures was inspected for shipping damage. The sequence of acceptable and damaged pieces was as follows:

A, A, A, A, D, A, D, D, D, A, A, D, D, A, A, A, A, A, A, A, D, D, D, D, D

Test for the randomness of the damage to the shipment, using the .10 significance level.

13-26 The following data represent the percentage of defective items turned out by a single machine for 25 consecutive days. Test the randomness of this sequence at the .05 level by designating values by whether they are above or below the median.

8.2	9.4	11.1	10.4	8.6
10.3	12.3	12.0	9.3	9.7
8.9	10.0	11.8	9.9	10.9
9.4	8.4	10.1	12.2	11.9
10.3	11.4	8.8	7.4	11.2

13-27 The following is the order of male and female résumés received in answer to an advertisement for a commercial artist at an advertising agency. Test this sequence for randomness. Use the .01 level of significance.

M, F, M, F, M, M, M, F, F, M, F, M, F, M, F, M, M, M, M, F, M, F, M, F, M
M, F, F, F, M, F, M, F, M, F, M, M, F, M, M, F, M, M, M, M, F, M, F, M, M

13-28 A restaurant owner has noticed over the years that older couples appear to eat earlier than young couples at his quiet, romantic restaurant. He suspects that perhaps it is because of children having to be left with babysitters and also because the older couples may retire earlier at night. One night he decided to keep a record of couples' arrivals at the restaurant. He noted whether each couple was over or under 30. His notes are reproduced below. (A = 30 and older; B = younger than 30.)

(5:30 P.M.) A, A, A, A, A, A, B, A, A, A, A, A, A, B, B,
B, A, B, B, B, B, B, B, A, B, B, B, B, B, B, A (10 P.M.)

At a 5 percent level of significance, was the restaurant owner correct in his thought that the age of his customers at different dining hours is less than random?

13-29 Kathy Phillips is in charge of production scheduling for a printing company. The company has 6 large presses, which frequently break down, and one of Kathy's biggest problems is meeting deadlines when there are unexpected breakdowns in presses. She suspects that the older presses break down earlier in the week than the newer presses, since all presses are checked and repaired over the weekend. To test her hypothesis, Kathy recorded the number of all the presses as they broke down during the week. Presses numbered 1, 2, and 3 are the older ones.

NUMBER OF PRESS IN ORDER OF BREAKDOWN
1, 2, 3, 1, 4, 5, 3, 1, 2, 3, 1, 3, 6, 2, 3, 6, 2, 2, 3, 5, 4, 6, 4, 5, 1, 3, 4, 5, 5, 6, 4, 5, 2, 3, 5, 6, 4, 3, 2, 5, 4, 6

a) At a 2 percent level of significance, does Kathy have a valid hypothesis that the breakdowns of presses are not random?
b) Is her hypothesis appropriate for the decision she wishes to make about rescheduling more work earlier in the week on the newer presses?

13-30 Martha Bowen, a department manager working in a large marketing-research firm, is in charge of all the research data analyses done in the firm. Accuracy and thoroughness are her responsibility. The department employs a number of research assistants to do some analyses and uses a computer to analyze some types of data. Typically, each week Martha randomly chooses completed analyses before they are reported and conducts tests to ensure that they have been done correctly and thoroughly. Martha's assistant, Kim Tadlock, randomly chooses 49 analyses per week from those completed and filed each day, and Martha does the re-analyses. Martha wanted to make certain that the selection process was a random one, so she could provide assurances that the computer analyses and those done by hand were both periodically checked. She arranged to have the research assistants place a special mark on the back of the records, so that they could be identified. Since Kim was unaware of the mark, the randomness of the test would not be affected. Kim completed her sample with the following data:

SAMPLES OF DATA ANALYSES FOR ONE WEEK (1: by computer, 2: by hand)
1, 1, 1, 1, 1, 1, 1, 1, 1, 2, 1, 1, 1, 1, 1, 1, 1, 1, 1, 2, 1, 1, 1, 1, 1, 1, 1, 1, 1, 2, 1, 1, 1, 1, 1, 1, 1, 1, 1, 2, 1, 1, 1, 1, 1, 1, 1, 1, 1

a) At a 1 percent significance level, can you conclude that the sample was random?
b) If the sample were distributed as follows, would the sample be random?

1, 1, 1, 1, 1, 1, 1, 1, 1, 1, 1, 1, 1, 1, 1, 1, 1, 1, 1, 1, 1, 1, 1, 1, 1,
1, 1, 1, 1, 1, 1, 1, 1, 1, 1, 1, 1, 1, 1, 1, 1, 1, 1, 1, 1, 2, 2, 2, 2

c) Since computer analyses are much faster than those done by hand, and since a number of the analyses are possible to do by computer, there are about three times as many computer analyses per week as hand analyses. Is there statistical evidence in part *a* to support the belief that somewhere in the sampling process there is something less than randomness occurring? If so, what is the evidence?
d) Does the conclusion you reached in part *c* lead you to any new conclusions about the one-sample runs test, particularly in reference to your answer in part *a*?

13-31 Prof. Ike Newton is interested in determining if his brightest students (those making the best grades) tend to turn in their tests earlier (because they can recall the material faster) or later (because they take longer to write down all they know) than the others in the class. For a particular physics test, he observes that the students make the following grades in order of turning their tests in:

97	65	78	93	88	69	85	80	83
76	89	85	74	94	71	82	83	91
54	32	69	59	51	57	42	90	92

a) If Professor Newton counts those making a grade of 90 and above as his brightest students, then at a 5 percent level of significance, can he conclude the brightest students turned their tests in randomly?
b) If 60 and above is passing in Professor Newton's class, then did those students passing versus those not passing turn their tests in randomly? (Also use the 5 percent significance level.)

13-32 An electric company has flagged certain of its customers as being a risk to the company because they seldom pay their bills on time. Since this concern has become a big problem for the company, management has decided to send a letter with the next bill describing stricter penalties for those who are late. From the time the customer gets the bill until it is past due, there is a span of 2 weeks. In this 2-week period, the electric company plans to monitor when the people send their payment. Those people who have already been determined to be a risk are denoted by an "R" in the following payment sequence, the other customers by a "C."

```
C  C  C  C  C  C  C
R  R  C  C  C  C  C
C  R  R  C  C  R  R
R  R  R  C  C  C  C
R  R  R  R  C  C  R
```

a) Is the sequence above random with respect to the good customers and those who are risks? Use a 15 percent significance level.
b) Can you conclude from the result in part a that the high-risk customers tend to make their payments later than do other customers?
c) If you can't draw that conclusion from part a, what other test might be useful in checking it out?

13-5 RANK CORRELATION

Function of the rank correlation coefficient

Chapters 11 and 12 introduced us to the notion of correlation and to the correlation coefficient, a measure of the closeness of association between two variables. Often in correlation analysis, information is not available in the form of numerical values like those we used in the problems of those chapters. But if we can assign rankings to the items in each of the two variables we are studying, a *rank correlation coefficient* can be calculated. **This is a measure of the correlation that exists between the two sets of ranks, a measure of the degree of association between the variables that we would not have been able to calculate otherwise.**

Advantage of using rank correlation

A second reason for learning the method of rank correlation is to be able to simplify the process of computing a correlation coefficient from a very large set of data for each of two variables. To prove how tedious this can be, try expanding one of the correlation problems in Chapter 11 by a factor of 10 and performing the necessary calculations. Instead of having to do these calculations, we can compute a measure of association that is based on the *ranks* of the observations, *not the numerical values* of the data. This measure is called the Spearman rank correlation coefficient, in honor of the statistician who developed it in the early 1900s.

The Coefficient of Rank Correlation

Listing the ranked variables

By working a couple of examples, we can learn how to calculate and interpret this measure of the association between two ranked variables. First, consider Table 13-6, which lists five persons and compares the academic rank they achieved in college with the level they have attained in a

TABLE 13-6 Comparison of the ranks of 5 students

STUDENT	COLLEGE RANK	COMPANY RANK 10 YEARS LATER
John	4	4
Margaret	3	3
Debbie	1	1
Steve	2	2
Lisa	5	5

certain company 10 years after graduation. The value of 5 represents the highest rank in the group; the rank of 1, the lowest.

Calculating the rank correlation coefficient

Using the information in Table 13-6, we can calculate a coefficient of rank correlation between success in college and company level achieved ten years later. All we need is Equation 13-7 and a few computations.

Coefficient of rank correlation

$$r_s = 1 - \frac{6\Sigma d^2}{n(n^2 - 1)} \quad [13\text{-}7]$$

where:

- r_s = coefficient of rank correlation (Notice that the subscript s, from Spearman, distinguishes this r from the one we calculated in Chapter 11.)
- n = number of paired observations
- Σ = notation meaning "the sum of"
- d = difference between the ranks for each pair of observations

The computations are easily done in tabular form, as we show in Table 13-7. Therefore, we have all the information we need to find the rank correlation coefficient for this problem:

$$\begin{aligned} r_s &= 1 - \frac{6\Sigma d^2}{n(n^2 - 1)} \quad [13\text{-}7] \\ &= 1 - \frac{6(0)}{5(25 - 1)} \\ &= 1 - \frac{0}{120} \\ &= 1 \leftarrow \text{rank correlation coefficient} \end{aligned}$$

Explaining values of the rank correlation coefficient

As we learned in Chapter 11, this correlation coefficient of 1 shows that there is a perfect association or *perfect correlation* between the two variables. This verifies the fact that the college and company ranks for each person were identical.

TABLE 13-7 Generating information to compute the rank correlation coefficient

STUDENT	COLLEGE RANK (1)	COMPANY RANK (2)	DIFFERENCE BETWEEN THE 2 RANKS (1) − (2)	DIFFERENCE SQUARED $[(1) - (2)]^2$
John	4	4	0	0
Margaret	3	3	0	0
Debbie	1	1	0	0
Steve	2	2	0	0
Lisa	5	5	0	0
				$\Sigma d^2 =$ **0** ← **sum of the squared differences**

Computing another rank correlation coefficient

One more example should make us feel comfortable with the coefficient of rank correlation. Table 13-8 illustrates five more people, but this time, the ranks in college and in a company ten years later seem to be extreme opposites. We can compute the difference between the ranks for each pair of observations, find d^2, and then take the sum of all the d^2's. Substituting these values into Equation 13-7, we find a rank correlation coefficient of −1:

$$r_s = 1 - \frac{6\Sigma d^2}{n(n^2 - 1)} \quad \textbf{[13-7]}$$

$$= 1 - \frac{6(40)}{5(25 - 1)}$$

$$= 1 - \frac{240}{120}$$

$$= 1 - 2$$

$$= -1 \leftarrow \text{rank correlation coefficient}$$

TABLE 13-8 Generating data to compute the rank correlation coefficient

STUDENT	COLLEGE RANK (1)	COMPANY RANK (2)	DIFFERENCE BETWEEN THE 2 RANKS (1) − (2)	DIFFERENCE SQUARED $[(1) - (2)]^2$
Roy	5	1	4	16
David	1	5	−4	16
Jay	3	3	0	0
Charlotte	2	4	−2	4
Kathy	4	2	2	4
				$\Sigma d^2 =$ **40** ← **sum of the squared differences**

Interpreting the results

In Chapter 11, we learned that a correlation coefficient of −1 represents *perfect inverse correlation*. And that is just what happened in our case: the people who did the best in college wound up ten years later in the lowest ranks of an organization. Now let's apply these ideas.

Solving a Problem Using Rank Correlation

Rank correlation is a useful technique for looking at the connection between air quality and the evidence of pulmonary-related diseases that we discussed in our chapter-opening problem. Table 13-9 reproduces the data found by the health organization studying the problem. In the same table, we also do some of the calculations needed to find r_s.

TABLE 13-9 Ranking of eleven cities

CITY	AIR-QUALITY RANK (1)	PULMONARY-DISEASE RANK (2)	DIFFERENCE BETWEEN THE 2 RANKS (1) − (2)	DIFFERENCE SQUARED [(1) − (2)]^2
A	4	5	−1	1
B	7	4	3	9
C	9	7	2	4
D	1	3	−2	4
E	2	1	1	1
F	10	11	−1	1
G	3	2	1	1
H	5	10	−5	25
I	6	8	−2	4
J	8	6	2	4
K	11	9	2	4
	Best rank = 11 Worst rank = 1			Σd^2 = **58** ← **sum of the squared differences**

Finding the rank correlation coefficient

Using the data in Table 13-9 and Equation 13-7, we can find the rank correlation coefficient for this problem:

$$r_s = 1 - \frac{6\Sigma d^2}{n(n^2 - 1)} \quad \textbf{[13-7]}$$

$$= 1 - \frac{6(58)}{11(121 - 1)}$$

$$= 1 - \frac{348}{11(120)}$$

$$= 1 - \frac{348}{1{,}320}$$

$$= 1 - .264$$

$$= .736 \leftarrow \text{rank correlation coefficient}$$

Interpreting the results

A correlation coefficient of .736 suggests a substantial positive association between average air quality and the occurrence of pulmonary disease, at least in the eleven cities sampled; that is, high levels of pollution go with high incidence of pulmonary disease.

How can we test this value of .736? We can apply the same methods we used to test hypotheses in Chapter 9. In performing such tests on r_s, we are trying to avoid the error of concluding that an association exists between two variables if, in fact, no such association exists in the population from which these two samples were drawn; that is, if the *population* rank correlation coefficient, ρ_s (*rho-sub-s*), is really equal to zero.

Testing hypotheses about rank correlation

For small values of n (n less than or equal to 30), the distribution of r_s is not normal, and unlike other small sample statistics we have encountered, it is not appropriate to use the t distribution for testing hypotheses about the rank correlation coefficient. Instead, we use Appendix Table 7 to determine the acceptance and rejection regions for such hypotheses. In our current problem, suppose that the health organization wants to test, at the .05 level of significance, the null hypotheses that there is zero correlation in the ranked data of *all* cities in the world. Our problem then becomes:

$H_0: \rho_s = 0$ ← null hypothesis: There is no correlation in the ranked data of the population.

$H_1: \rho_s \neq 0$ ← alternative hypothesis: There is a correlation in the ranked data of the population.

$\alpha = .05$ ← level of significance for testing these hypotheses

---

A two-tailed test is appropriate; so we look at Appendix Table 7 in the row for $n = 11$ (the number of cities) and the column for a significance level of .05. There we find that the critical values for r_s are $\pm.6091$; that is, the upper limit of the acceptance region is .6091, and the lower limit of the acceptance region is $-.6091$.

Figure 13-7 shows the limits of the acceptance region and the rank correlation coefficient we calculated from the air-quality sample. From this figure, we can see that the rank correlation coefficient lies outside the acceptance region. Therefore, we would reject the null hypothesis of no correlation and conclude that there *is* an association between air-quality levels and the incidence of pulmonary disease in the world's cities.

The appropriate distribution for values of n greater than 30

If the sample size is greater than 30, we can no longer use Appendix Table 7. However, when n is greater than 30, the sampling distribution of r_s is approximately normal, with a mean of zero and a standard deviation of $1/\sqrt{n-1}$. Thus, the standard error of r_s is:

Standard error of r_s →
$$\sigma_{r_s} = \frac{1}{\sqrt{n-1}} \quad \textbf{[13-8]}$$

and we can use Appendix Table 1 to find the appropriate z values for testing hypotheses about the population rank correlation.

Example with n greater than 30

As an example of hypothesis testing of rank correlation coefficients when n is greater than 30, consider the case of a social scientist who tries to

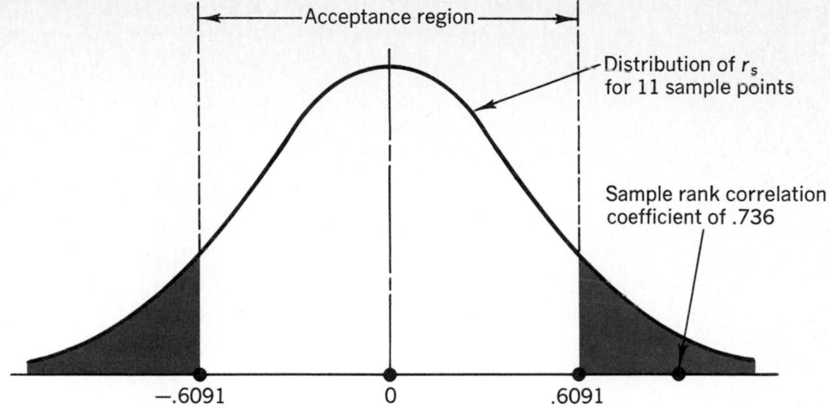

FIGURE 13-7 Two-tailed hypothesis test, using Appendix Table 7 at the .05 level of significance, showing the acceptance region and the sample rank correlation coefficient

determine whether bright people tend to choose spouses who are also bright. He randomly chooses 32 couples and tests to see if there is a significant rank correlation in the IQs of the couples. His data and computations are given in Table 13-10 on the following page.

Using the data in Table 13-10 and Equation 13-7, we can find the rank correlation coefficient for this problem:

$$r_s = 1 - \frac{6\Sigma d^2}{n(n^2 - 1)} \quad \textbf{[13-7]}$$

$$= 1 - \frac{6(1{,}043.5)}{32(1{,}024 - 1)}$$

$$= 1 - \frac{6{,}261}{32{,}736}$$

$$= 1 - .191$$

$$= .809 \leftarrow \text{rank correlation coefficient}$$

If the social scientist wishes to test his hypothesis at the .01 level of significance, his problem can be stated:

Stating the hypotheses

$H_0\colon \rho_s = 0$ ← null hypothesis: There is no rank correlation in the population; that is, husband and wife intelligence is randomly mixed.

$H_1\colon \rho_s > 0$ ← alternative hypothesis: The population rank correlation is positive; that is, bright people choose bright spouses.

$\alpha = .01$ ← level of significance for testing these hypotheses

An upper-tailed test is appropriate. From Appendix Table 1, we find that the appropriate z value for the .01 level of significance is 2.33. Figure 13-8 illustrates this hypothesis test graphically; we show there the colored region in the upper tail of the distribution that corresponds to the .01 level of significance.

TABLE 13-10 Computation of rank correlation of husbands' and wives' IQs

COUPLE (1)	HUSBAND'S IQ (2)	WIFE'S IQ (3)	HUSBAND'S RANK (4)	WIFE'S RANK (5)	DIFFERENCE BETWEEN RANKS (4) − (5)	DIFFERENCE SQUARED $[(4) - (5)]^2$
1	95	95	8	4.5	3.5	12.25
2	103	98	20	8.5	11.5	132.25
3	111	110	26	23	3	9.00
4	92	88	4	2	2	4.00
5	150	106	32	18	14	196.00
6	107	109	24	21.5	2.5	6.25
7	90	96	3	6	−3	9.00
8	108	131	25	32	−7	49.00
9	100	112	17.5	25.5	−8	64.00
10	93	95	5.5	4.5	1	1.00
11	119	112	29	25.5	3.5	12.25
12	115	117	28	30	−2	4.00
13	87	94	1	3	−2	4.00
14	105	109	21	21.5	−0.5	0.25
15	135	114	31	27	4	16.00
16	89	83	2	1	1	1.00
17	99	105	14.5	16.5	−2	4.00
18	106	115	22.5	28	−5.5	30.25
19	126	116	30	29	1	1.00
20	100	107	17.5	19	−1.5	2.25
21	93	111	5.5	24	−18.5	342.25
22	94	98	7	8.5	−1.5	2.25
23	100	105	17.5	16.5	1	1.00
24	96	103	10	15	−5	25.00
25	99	101	14.5	13	1.5	2.25
26	112	123	27	31	−4	16.00
27	106	108	22.5	20	2.5	6.25
28	98	97	12.5	7	5.5	30.25
29	96	100	10	11.5	−1.5	2.25
30	98	99	12.5	10	2.5	6.25
31	100	100	17.5	11.5	6	36.00
32	96	102	10	14	−4	16.00
					Sum of the squared differences → $\Sigma d^2 =$	**1043.50**

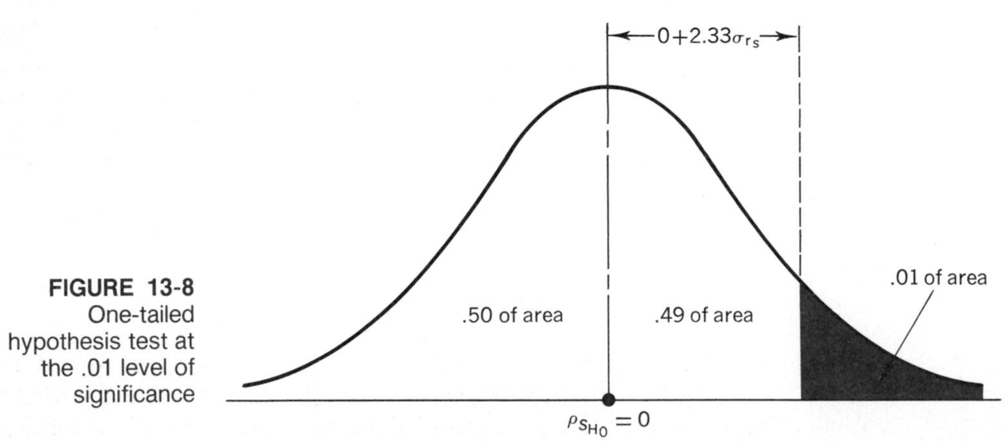

FIGURE 13-8 One-tailed hypothesis test at the .01 level of significance

Calculating the limit of the acceptance region

We can now calculate the limit of our acceptance region:

$$\rho_{s_{H_0}} + 2.33\sigma_{r_s} = 0 + 2.33\left(\frac{1}{\sqrt{n-1}}\right)$$

$$= 0 + \frac{2.33}{\sqrt{31}}$$

$$= 0 + \frac{2.33}{5.568}$$

$$= 0.42 \leftarrow \text{upper limit of acceptance region}$$

Interpreting the results

Figure 13-9 shows the limit of the acceptance region and the rank correlation coefficient we calculated from the IQ data. In Fig. 13-9, we can see that the rank correlation coefficient of .809 lies far outside the acceptance region. Therefore, we would reject the null hypothesis of no correlation and conclude that bright people tend to choose bright spouses.

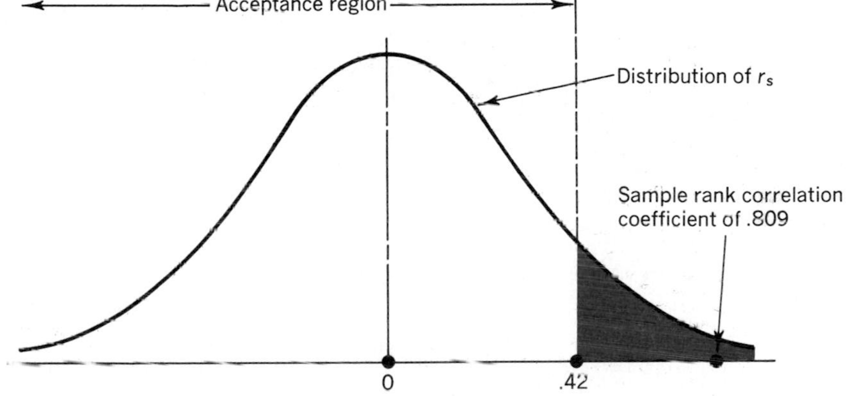

FIGURE 13-9 One-tailed hypothesis test at the .01 level of significance, showing the acceptance region and the sample rank correlation coefficient

A Special Property of Rank Correlation

Advantage of rank correlation

Rank correlation has a useful advantage over the correlation method we discussed in Chapter 11. Suppose we have cases in which one or several very extreme observations exist in the original data. By the use of numerical values as was done in Chapter 11, the correlation coefficient may not be a good description of the association that exists between two variables. Yet extreme observations in a *rank* correlation test will never produce a large rank difference.

Consider the following data array of two variables, X and Y:

X	10	13	16	19	25
Y	34	40	45	51	117

Because of the large value of the fifth Y term, we would get two significantly different answers for r using the conventional and the rank correlation methods. In this case, the rank correlation method would be less sensitive to the extreme value. We would assign a rank order of 5 to the numerical value of 117 and avoid the unduly large effect on the value of the correlation coefficient.

EXERCISES

13-33 Below are ratings of aggressiveness (*X*) and amount of sales in the last year (*Y*) for 8 salespeople. Is there a significant rank correlation between the two measures? Use the .05 significance level.

X	30	17	35	28	42	25	19	34
Y	35	31	40	46	50	32	33	42

13-34 A plant supervisor ranked a sample of 8 workers on the number of hours worked overtime and length of employment. Is the rank correlation between the two measures significant at the .01 level?

Amount of overtime	5.0	8.0	2.0	4.0	3.0	7.0	1.0	6.0
Years employed	1.0	6.0	4.5	2.0	7.0	8.0	4.5	3.0

13-35 Below are ratings of clarity of job definition and job satisfaction for 6 managers. Because of the value 18 lying far from the other values, these data would not be suitable for usual correlation analysis, but a rank correlation might still tell us something. Test the significance of the rank correlation for these data, using the .05 significance level.

Job definition	70	86	93	82	56	84
Job satisfaction	41	52	49	18	51	54

13-36 The Occupational Safety and Health Administration (OSHA) was conducting a study of the relationship of expenditures for plant safety and the accident rate in the plants. OSHA had confined its studies to the synthetic chemical industry. To adjust for the size differential that existed among some of the plants, OSHA had converted its data into expenditures per production employee. The results of the data are listed below.

EXPENDITURE BY CHEMICAL COMPANIES PER PRODUCTION EMPLOYEE IN RELATION TO ACCIDENTS PER YEAR

Company	*A*	*B*	*C*	*D*	*E*	*F*	*G*	*H*	*I*	*J*	*K*
Expenditure	$60	$45	$30	$20	$28	$42	$39	$54	$48	$58	$26
Accidents	3	7	6	9	7	4	8	2	4	3	8

Is there a significant correlation between expenditures and accidents in the chemical-company plants? Use a rank correlation (with 1 representing highest expenditure and accident rate) to support your conclusion. Test at the 5 percent significance level.

13-37 As part of a standards department's training, time-study analysts are tested on their ability to detect differences in work rates. They are not asked to estimate the work rate, only to rank, in order of increasing productivity, the workers who were filmed. Below are the results of one analyst's rankings and the actual ranks as determined by a time study of the film frames.

RANK										
Analyst's	9	1	10	3	5	2	4	6	7	8
Actual	7	2	6	4	3	5	1	10	8	9

Use the rank correlation test at the 5 percent significance level to decide if the analyst is able to detect different work rates.

13-38 The Carolina Lighting Company has 2 trained interviewers to recruit manager trainees for new sales outlets. Although each of the interviewers has a unique style, both are thought to be good preliminary judges of managerial potential. The personnel manager wondered how closely the interviewers would agree, so she had both of them independently evaluate 14 applicants. They ranked the applicants in terms of their degree of potential contribution to the company. The results are given below. Use a rank correlation at the 1 percent significance level, and determine if there is a significant positive correlation between the two interviewers' rankings.

Applicant	1	2	3	4	5	6	7	8	9	10	11	12	13	14
Interviewer 1	1	11	12	2	13	10	3	4	14	5	6	9	7	8
Interviewer 2	4	12	11	2	13	10	1	3	14	8	6	5	9	7

13-39 Nancy McKenzie, foreman for a lithographic camera assembly process, feels that the longer a group of employees work together, the higher the daily output rate. She has gathered the following data for a group of employees who worked together for 10 days.

Daily output	4.0	6.0	5.0	7.0	2.0	8.0	3.0	0.5	9.0	6.0
Days worked together	1	2	3	4	5	6	7	8	9	10

Can Nancy conclude at a 1 percent significance level that there is no correlation between the number of days worked together and the daily output?

13-40 An electronics firm, which recruits many engineers, wonders if the cost of extensive recruiting efforts is worth it. If the firm could be confident (using a 1 percent significance level) that the population rank correlation between applicants' résumés scored by the personnel department and interview scores is positive, it would feel justified in discontinuing recruitment and relying on résumé scores in hiring. The firm has drawn a sample of 35 engineer applications in the last 2 years. On the basis of this sample, shown below, should the firm discontinue recruitment and use résumé scores to hire?

INDIVIDUAL	INTERVIEW SCORE	RÉSUMÉ SCORE	INDIVIDUAL	INTERVIEW SCORE	RÉSUMÉ SCORE
1	81	113	19	81	111
2	88	88	20	84	121
3	55	76	21	82	83
4	83	129	22	90	79
5	78	99	23	63	71
6	93	142	24	78	108
7	65	93	25	73	68
8	87	136	26	79	121
9	95	82	27	72	109
10	76	91	28	95	121
11	60	83	29	81	140
12	85	96	30	87	132
13	93	126	31	93	135
14	66	108	32	85	143
15	90	95	33	91	118
16	69	65	34	94	147
17	87	96	35	94	138
18	68	101			

13-41 A computer-science department was interested in finding out if the salaries of its master's and doctoral students in their first jobs were related to the number of graduate credit hours they had taken. For the graduating class of 1982, they computed the following chart:

STARTING YEARLY SALARY (IN DOLLARS)	NUMBER OF CREDIT HOURS
25,000	40
22,900	34
31,000	45
21,000	31
24,500	33
30,900	47
22,575	32
40,000	60
19,000	30

Calculate a rank correlation for the data above. Interpret this result for the computer-science department using a 2 percent significance level.

13-42 In-Style Fashions, a clothing store in a new mall, has just hired a new manager. With hopes of impressing the company, this new manager wants to conduct a study of the relationship of sales to the amount of time certain outfits are on the mannequins. He hopes to find that there will be a correlation between the number of days an outfit is displayed and the number of outfits of that type sold. He wants to be 90 percent sure of a significant correlation. Use a rank correlation to help the manager.

OUTFIT	DAYS ON DISPLAY	NUMBER SOLD
A	4	20
B	5	19
C	10	30
D	12	4
E	11	3
F	3	10
G	19	39
H	18	35
I	9	16
J	8	25
K	2	5
L	14	33

13-6 THE KOLMOGOROV-SMIRNOV TEST

The K-S test and its advantages

The Kolmogorov-Smirnov test, named for the statisticians A. N. Kolmogorov and N. V. Smirnov, who developed it, is a simple nonparametric method for testing whether there is a significant difference between an observed frequency distribution and a theoretical frequency distribution.

The K-S test is therefore another measure of the *goodness of fit* of a theoretical frequency distribution, as was the chi-square test we studied in Chapter 10. However, the K-S test has several advantages over the χ^2 test: It is a more powerful test, and it is easier to use, since it does not require that data be grouped in any way.

A special advantage

The K-S statistic, D_n, is particularly useful for judging how close the observed frequency distribution is to the expected frequency distribution, because the probability distribution of D_n depends on the sample size n but is independent of the expected frequency distribution (D_n is a "distribution-free" statistic).

A Problem Using the K-S Test

Working a problem

Suppose that the Orange County Telephone Exchange has been keeping track of the number of "senders" (a type of automatic equipment used in telephone exchanges) that were in use at a given instant. Observations were made on 3,754 different occasions. For capital-investment planning purposes, the budget officer of this company thinks that the pattern of usage follows a Poisson distribution with a mean of 8.5. If he wants to test this

TABLE 13-11 Observed and relative cumulative frequencies

NUMBER BUSY	OBSERVED FREQUENCY	CUMULATIVE OBSERVED FREQUENCY	RELATIVE CUMULATIVE OBSERVED FREQUENCY
0	0	0	.0000
1	5	5	.0013
2	14	19	.0051
3	24	43	.0115
4	57	100	.0266
5	111	211	.0562
6	197	408	.1087
7	278	686	.1827
8	378	1,064	.2834
9	418	1,482	.3948
10	461	1,943	.5176
11	433	2,376	.6329
12	413	2,789	.7429
13	358	3,147	.8383
14	219	3,366	.8966
15	145	3,511	.9353
16	109	3,620	.9643
17	57	3,677	.9795
18	43	3,720	.9909
19	16	3,736	.9952
20	7	3,743	.9971
21	8	3,751	.9992
22	3	3,754	1.0000

hypothesis at the .01 level of significance, he can employ the K-S test.

We would set up our hypotheses like this:

Stating the hypotheses

H_0: A Poisson distribution with $\lambda = 8.5$ is a good description of the pattern of usage. ← null hypothesis

H_1: A Poisson distribution with $\lambda = 8.5$ is not a good description of the pattern of usage. ← alternative hypothesis

$\alpha = .01$ ← level of significance for testing these hypotheses

Next, we would list the data that we observed. Table 13-11 lists the observed frequencies and transforms them into relative cumulative observed frequencies.

Computing and comparing expected frequencies

Now we can use the Poisson formula to compute the expected frequencies. From Equation 6-4, this is $e^{-\lambda} \cdot \lambda^x/x!$. By comparing these expected frequencies with our observed frequencies, we can examine the extent of the difference between them: the absolute deviation. Table 13-12

TABLE 13-12 Relative observed cumulative frequencies, expected relative cumulative frequencies, and absolute deviations

NUMBER BUSY	OBSERVED FREQUENCY	CUMULATIVE OBSERVED FREQUENCY	RELATIVE CUMULATIVE OBSERVED FREQUENCY	RELATIVE CUMULATIVE EXPECTED FREQUENCY	$\lvert f_e - f_o \rvert$ ABSOLUTE DEVIATION
0	0	0	.0000	.0002	.0002
1	5	5	.0013	.0019	.0006
2	14	19	.0051	.0093	.0042
3	24	43	.0115	.0301	.0186
4	57	100	.0266	.0743	.0478
5	111	211	.0562	.1496	.0934
6	197	408	.1087	.2562	.1475
7	278	686	.1827	.3856	.2029
8	378	1,064	.2834	.5231	.2397
9	418	1,482	.3948	.6530	.2582
10	461	1,943	.5176	.7634	.2458
11	433	2,376	.6329	.8487	.2157
12	413	2,789	.7429	.9091	.1662
13	358	3,147	.8383	.9486	.1103
14	219	3,366	.8966	.9726	.0760
15	145	3,511	.9353	.9862	.0509
16	109	3,620	.9643	.9934	.0291
17	57	3,677	.9795	.9970	.0175
18	43	3,720	.9909	.9987	.0078
19	16	3,736	.9952	.9995	.0043
20	7	3,743	.9971	.9998	.0027
21	8	3,751	.9992	.9999	.0007
22	3	3,754	1.0000	1.0000	.0000

lists the relative observed cumulative frequencies, the expected relative cumulative frequencies, and the absolute deviations for $x = 0$ to 22.

Calculating the K-S Statistic

To compute the K-S statistic for this problem, you simply pick out D_n, the maximum absolute deviation, of f_e from f_o.

Computing the K-S statistic

K-S statistic: → $$D_n = \max|f_e - f_o \quad [13\text{-}9]$$

In this problem, $D_n = .2582$ at $x = 9$.

Computing the critical value

A K-S test must always be a one-tailed test. The critical values for D_n have been tabulated and can be found in Appendix Table 8. By looking in the row for $n = 3{,}754$ (the sample size) and the column for a significance level of .01, we find that the critical value of D_n must be computed using the formula:

$$\frac{1.63}{\sqrt{n}} = \frac{1.63}{\sqrt{3{,}754}} = \frac{1.63}{61.27} = .0266$$

Our conclusion

The next step is to compare the calculated value of D_n with the critical value of D_n from the table. If the table value for the chosen significance level is greater than the calculated value of D_n, then we will accept the null hypothesis. Obviously, $.0266 < .2582$, so we reject H_0 and conclude that a Poisson distribution with a mean of 8.5 is *not* a good description of the pattern of sender usage at the Orange County Telephone Exchange.

EXERCISES

13-43 At the .10 level of significance, can we conclude that the following distribution follows a Poisson distribution with $\lambda = 2$?

Number of arrivals per day	0	1	2	3	4	5	6 or more
Number of days	10	19	31	26	11	3	7

13-44 Randall Nelson, salesman for the V-Star company, has 7 accounts to visit per week. It is thought that the sales by Mr. Nelson may be described by the binomial distribution, with the probability of selling each account being .45. Examining the observed frequency distribution of Mr. Nelson's number of sales per week, determine whether the distribution does in fact correspond to the suggested distribution. Use the .05 significance level.

Number of sales per week	0	1	2	3	4	5	6	7
Frequency of the number of sales	25	32	61	47	39	21	18	12

13-45 Below is a table of observed frequencies, along with the frequencies to be expected under a normal distribution.
a) Calculate the K-S statistic.
b) Can we conclude that this distribution does in fact follow a normal distribution? Use the .01 level of significance.

	TEST SCORE				
	51–60	61–70	71–80	81–90	91–100
Observed frequency	30	100	440	500	130
Expected frequency	20	170	500	410	100

13-46 A discount-store manager is keeping track of the arrival of customers at checkout counters, to see how many cashiers are needed to handle the flow. In a sample of 400 five-minute intervals, there were 18, 58, 97, 84, 69, 47, and 27 intervals in which 0, 1, 2, 3, 4, 5, or 6 or more customers, respectively, arrived at a checkout counter. Are these data consistent at the .10 level of significance with a Poisson distribution with $\lambda = 3$?

13-47 Below is an observed frequency distribution. Using a normal distribution with $\mu = 2.44$ and $\sigma = .4$:
a) Find the probability of falling in each class.
b) From part *a*, compute the expected frequency of each category.
c) Calculate D_n.
d) At the .15 level of significance, does this distribution seem to be well described by the suggested normal distribution?

Observed value of the variable	<1.9	1.9–2.19	2.2–2.59	2.6–2.99	≥ 3.0
Observed frequency	5	19	35	24	7

13-48 Jackie Denn, an airline food-service administrator, has examined past records from 200 randomly selected cross-country flights to determine the frequency with which low-sodium meals were requested. The number of flights in which 0, 1, 2, 3, or 4 or more low-sodium meals were requested was 25, 45, 67, 43, and 20, respectively. At the .05 level of significance, can she reasonably conclude that these requests follow a Poisson distribution with $\lambda = 1$?

13-7 TERMS INTRODUCED IN CHAPTER 13

KOLMOGOROV-SMIRNOV TEST A nonparametric test, which does not require that data be grouped in any way, for determining whether there is a significant difference between an observed frequency distribution and a theoretical frequency distribution.

MANN-WHITNEY *U* TEST A nonparametric method used to determine whether two independent samples have been drawn from populations with the same distribution.

NONPARAMETRIC TESTS Statistical techniques that do not make restrictive assumptions about the shape of a population distribution when performing a hypothesis test.

ONE-SAMPLE RUNS TEST A nonparametric method for determining the randomness with which sampled items have been selected.

RANK CORRELATION A method for doing correlation analysis when the data are not available to use in numerical form, but when information is sufficient to rank the data.

RANK CORRELATION COEFFICIENT A measure of the degree of association between two variables that is based on the ranks of observations, not their numerical values.

RANK SUM TESTS A family of nonparametric tests that make use of the order information in a set of data.

RUN A sequence of identical occurrences preceded and followed by different occurrences or by none at all.

SIGN TEST A test for the difference between paired observations where + and − signs are substituted for quantitative values.

THEORY OF RUNS A theory developed to allow us to test samples for the randomness of their order.

13-8 EQUATIONS INTRODUCED IN CHAPTER 13

[13-1]

$$U = n_1 n_2 + \frac{n_1(n_1 + 1)}{2} - R_1$$

p. 616

To apply the Mann-Whitney U test, you need this formula to derive the U statistic, a measurement of the difference between the ranked observations of the two variables. R_1 is the sum of the ranks of the observations of variable 1; n_1 and n_2 are the numbers of items in samples 1 and 2, respectively. Both samples need not be of the same size.

[13-2]

$$\mu_U = \frac{n_1 n_2}{2}$$

p. 616

If the null hypothesis of a Mann-Whitney U test is that $n_1 + n_2$ observations came from identical populations, then the U statistic has a sampling distribution with a mean equal to the product of n_1 and n_2 divided by 2.

[13-3]

$$\sigma_U = \sqrt{\frac{n_1 n_2 (n_1 + n_2 + 1)}{12}}$$

p. 617

This formula enables us to derive the *standard error of the U statistic* of a Mann-Whitney U test.

[13-4]

$$U = n_1 n_2 + \frac{n_2(n_2 + 1)}{2} - R_2$$

p. 618

This formula and Equation 13-1 can be used interchangeably to derive the U statistic in a Mann-Whitney U test. Use this formula if the number of observations of variable 2 is significantly smaller than the number of observations of variable 1.

[13-5]
$$\mu_r = \frac{2n_1n_2}{n_1 + n_2} + 1$$
p. 623

When doing a one-sample runs test, use this formula to derive the mean of the sampling distribution of the *r statistic*. This *r* statistic is equal to the *number of runs* in the sample being tested.

[13-6]
$$\sigma_r = \sqrt{\frac{2n_1n_2(2n_1n_2 - n_1 - n_2)}{(n_1 + n_2)^2(n_1 + n_2 - 1)}}$$
p. 624

This formula enables us to derive the *standard error of the r statistic* in a one-sample runs test.

[13-7]
$$r_s = 1 - \frac{6\Sigma d^2}{n(n^2 - 1)}$$
p. 629

The *coefficient of rank correlation,* r_s, is a measure of the closeness of association between two ranked variables.

[13-8]
$$\sigma_{r_s} = \frac{1}{\sqrt{n - 1}}$$
p. 632

This formula enables us to calculate the *standard error of* r_s in a hypothesis test on the coefficient of rank correlation.

[13-9]
$$D_n = \max |f_e - f_o|$$
p. 641

If we compare this computed value to a critical value of D_n in the K-S table, we can test distributional goodness of fit.

13-9 CHAPTER REVIEW EXERCISES

13-49 A college football coach has a theory that in athletics, success feeds on itself. In other words, he feels that winning a championship one year increases the team's motivation to win it the next year. He expressed his theory to a student of statistics, who asked him for the records of the team's wins and losses over the last several years. The coach gave him a list, specifying whether the team had won (W) or lost (L) the championship that year. The results of this tally are presented below.

W, W, W, W, W, W, L, W, W, W, W, W, L, W, W, W, W, L, L, W, W, W, W, W, W

a) At a 10 percent significance level, is the occurrence of wins and losses a random one?
b) Does your answer to question *a*, combined with a sight inspection of the data, tell you anything about the one-sample runs test?

13-50 A small metropolitan airport recently opened a new runway, creating a new flight path over an upper-income residential area. Complaints of excessive noise had deluged the airport authority to the point that the 2 major airlines servicing the city had installed special engine baffles on the turbines of the jets, to reduce noise and help ease the pressure on the authority. Both airlines wanted to see if the baffles had helped to reduce the number of complaints that had been brought against the airport. If they had not, the baffles would be removed, because they increased fuel consumption. Based on the following data, can it be said at the .045 level of significance that installing the baffles has reduced the number of complaints?

COMPLAINTS BEFORE AND AFTER BAFFLES WERE INSTALLED

Before	15	20	24	18	30	46	15	29	17	21	18
After	23	19	12	9	16	12	28	20	16	14	11

13-51 The American Broadcasting System (ABS) had invested a sizable amount of money into a new program for television, *High Times. High Times* was ABS's entry into the situation-comedy market and featured the happy-go-lucky life in a college dormitory. Unfortunately, the program had not done as well as expected, and the sponsor was considering canceling. To beef up the ratings, ABS introduced coed dormitories into the series. Presented below are the results of telephone surveys before and after the change in the series. Surveys were conducted in several major metropolitan areas, so the results are a composite from the cities.

a) Using a *U* test, can you infer at the .05 significance level that the change in the series format helped the ratings?
b) Do the results of your test say anything about the effect of sex on TV program ratings?

SHARE OF AUDIENCE BEFORE AND AFTER CHANGE TO CO-ED DORMITORIES

Before	22	18	19	20	27	22	25	19	22	24	18	16	14	28	30	15	16
After	25	28	18	30	33	25	29	29	19	16	30	33	13	25			

13-52 To determine whether small price differences affect sales, a mail-order sportswear company divided its customers into 2 equal groups in terms of past order amounts. Members of the 2 groups were sent different catalogs, one with higher-priced clothing than the other. Below are the weekly sales (in thousands) for the 2 groups over the 12-week period after the mailing of the catalog.

High prices	20	22	18	15	17	14	8	10	9	12	19	20
Low prices	16	17	20	15	14	13	10	11	7	10	15	16

Test the hypothesis of no difference between the sales from the 2 catalogs. Use the .10 significance level.

13-53 The Ways and Means Committee of the U.S. House of Representatives was attempting to evaluate the results of a tax cut given to individuals during the preceding year. The intended purpose had been to stimulate the economy, the theory being that with a tax reduction, the consumer would spend the tax savings. The committee had employed an independent consumer-research group to select a sample of households and maintain records of consumer spending both before and after the legislation was put into effect. A portion of the data from the research group is listed below.

SCHEDULE OF CONSUMER SPENDING

HOUSE-HOLD	BEFORE LEGISLATION	AFTER LEGISLATION	HOUSE-HOLD	BEFORE LEGISLATION	AFTER LEGISLATION
1	$ 3,578	$ 4,296	17	$11,597	$12,093
2	10,856	9,000	18	9,612	8,375
3	7,450	8,200	19	3,461	3,740
4	9,200	9,200	20	4,500	4,500
5	8,760	8,840	21	8,341	8,500
6	4,500	4,620	22	7,589	7,609
7	15,000	14,500	23	25,750	24,321
8	22,350	22,500	24	14,673	13,500
9	7,346	7,250	25	5,003	6,072
10	10,345	10,673	26	10,940	11,398
11	5,298	5,349	27	8,000	9,007
12	6,950	7,000	28	14,256	14,500
13	34,782	33,892	29	4,322	4,258
14	12,837	12,650	30	6,828	7,204
15	7,926	8,437	31	7,549	7,678
16	5,789	6,006	32	8,129	8,125

13-54 At a significance level of 4 percent, determine if the tax-reduction policy has achieved its desired goals.

John Adams, estimator for an air-conditioning installation service, must be concerned about the weather, since poor weather conditions can cause unnecessary delays and increase labor costs on a job. When establishing bids for installation jobs, should Adams consider inclement weather (rain, snow, too cold, too hot) as a random event?

13-55 Two television weathermen got into a discussion one day about whether years with heavy rainfall tended to occur in spurts. One of them said he thought that there were patterns of annual rainfall amounts, and that several wet years were often followed by a number of drier-than-average years. The other weatherman was skeptical and said he thought that the amount of rainfall for consecutive years was fairly random. To investigate the question, they decided to look at the annual rainfall for several years back. They found the median amount and classified the rainfall as below (B) or above (A) the median annual rainfall. A summary of their results follows:

A, A, B, B, B, B, A, B, A, A, A, B, A, B, A, B, A, A, B, B, B, A, A, B, A,
B, A, A, B, B, B, A, B, B, B, A, B, A, A, A, B, A, A, A, B, A, B, B, A

If the weathermen test at a 5 percent significance level, will they conclude that the annual rainfall amounts do not occur in patterns?

13-56 The Northwest Container Corporation has recently invested in a trade advertising campaign to increase interest in its products. The advertisements list a toll-free number to call for more information. The number and a small advertisement are also displayed in the Yellow Pages of many northwestern cities, and the company credits this advertising for many of the new accounts generated. A receptionist collected the following data on the number of new accounts inquiring about the company through the toll-free line:

NUMBER OF NEW INQUIRIES PER WEEK

Before trade ads	17	26	19	22	11	32	13	15	9	24	26
After trade ads	19	30	14	25	15	29	19	16	6	26	22

Management has let its skepticism be known about the trade advertising, and before it approves further funds for advertising, it wants to be 95 percent sure that a significant increase in inquiries is due to the advertising. Can the company be that sure?

13-57 The National Association of Better Advertising for Children (NABAC), a consumer group for improving children's television, was conducting a study on the effect of Saturday morning advertising. Specifically, the group wanted to know if a significant degree of purchasing was stimulated by advertising directed at children, and if there was a positive correlation between Saturday morning TV advertising time and product sales.

NABAC chose the children's breakfast-cereal market as a sample group. They selected products whose advertising message was aimed entirely at children. The results of the study are presented below. (The highest-selling cereal has sales rank 1).

COMPARISON OF TV ADVERTISING TIME AND PRODUCT SALES

PRODUCT	ADVERTISING TIME IN MINUTES	SALES RANK
Captain Grumbles	0.50	10
Obnoxious Berries	3.00	1
Fruity Hoops	1.25	9
OO La Granola	2.00	5
Sweet Tweets	3.50	2
Chocolate Chumps	1.00	11
Sugar Spots	4.00	3
Count Cavity	2.50	8
Crunchy Munchies	1.75	6
Karamel Kooks	2.25	4
Flakey Flakes	1.50	7

Can the group conclude that there is a *positive* rank correlation between the amount of Saturday morning advertising time and sales volume of breakfast cereals? Test at a 5 percent significance level.

13-58 The following ratings were made by people who used 2 detergents for 3 weeks. Test the hypothesis that the users found no difference in the 2 products. Use the .05 level of significance.

Product 1	4 4 5 5 3 2 5 3 1 2 5 3 4 2 5 5
Product 2	2 3 3 3 3 3 3 4 3 2 3 2 2 3 3 4

13-59 As part of a survey on restaurant quality, a local magazine asked area residents to rank 2 steak houses. On a scale of 1 to 10, subjects were to rate characteristics such as food quality, atmosphere, service, and price.

After data were collected, one of the restaurant owners proposed that various statistical tests be performed. He specifically mentioned that he would like to see a mean and standard deviation for the responses to each question about each restaurant, in order to see which one had scored better. Several of the magazine workers argued against his suggestion, noting that the quality of input data would not justify a detailed statistical analysis. They argued that what was important was the residents' rankings of the two restaurants. Evaluate the arguments presented by the restaurant owner and the magazine employees.

13-60 Senior business students interviewed by Ohio Insurance Company were asked not to discuss their interviews with others in the school until the recruiter left. The recruiter, however, suspected that the later applicants knew more about what she was looking for. Were her suspicions correct? To find out, rank the interview scores received by subjects. Then test the significance of the rank correlation coefficient between the scores and interview number. Use the .05 significance level.

INTERVIEW NUMBER	SCORE	INTERVIEW NUMBER	SCORE	INTERVIEW NUMBER	SCORE	INTERVIEW NUMBER	SCORE
1	25	6	32	11	37	16	43
2	29	7	39	12	41	17	44
3	28	8	34	13	38	18	66
4	33	9	35	14	24	19	47
5	30	10	42	15	45	20	50

13-61 More than 3 years ago, the Occupational Safety and Health Administration (OSHA) required a number of safety measures to be implemented in the Northbridge Aluminum plant. Now OSHA would like to see whether the changes have resulted in fewer accidents in the plant. They have collected these data:

ACCIDENTS AT THE NORTHBRIDGE PLANT

	JAN.	FEB.	MAR.	APR.	MAY	JUNE	JULY	AUG.	SEPT.	OCT.	NOV.	DEC.
1980	5	3	4	2	6	4	3	3	2	4	5	3
1981	4	4	3	3	3	4	0	5	4	2	0	1
1982	3	2	1	1	0	2	4	3	2	1	1	2
1983	2	1	0	0	1	2						

a) Determine the median number of accidents per month. If the safety measures have been effective, we should find early months falling above the median and later months below the median. Accordingly, there will be a small number of runs above and below the median. Conduct a test at the .03 level of significance to see if the accidents are randomly distributed.
b) What can you conclude about the effectiveness of the safety measures?

13-62 A large countywide ambulance service calculates that for any given township it serves, during any given 8-hour shift, there is a 30 percent chance of receiving at least one call for assistance. Here follows a random sampling of 60 days:

Number of shifts during which calls were received	1	2	3
Number of days	27	11	6

At the .05 level of significance, do these calls for assistance follow a binomial distribution?

13-63 A marketing-researcher studying sales per distributor has gathered the following information and has classified 150 distributors by the number of units they sell per month.

Unit sales per month	50 or less	51–100	101–150	150 or more
Number of distributors/group	13	53	62	22

Before the individual distributors were combined into groups, the sample mean and standard deviation were calculated to be 94.5 and 37.2 units per month, respectively.

a) What is the probability (using a normal distribution with $\mu = 94.5$ and $\sigma = 37.2$) that the monthly unit sales of a distributor will be <50.5 units; between 50.5 and 100.5 units; between 100.5 and 150.5 units; >150.5 units?
b) Using the probabilities in part *a*, find the expected frequencies for the 150 distributors' monthly unit sales.
c) At the .10 level of significance, does the observed distribution follow the normal distribution found in part *b*?

13-10 CHAPTER CONCEPTS TEST

Answers are in the back of the book.

T F 1. One advantage of nonparametric methods is that some of the tests do not require us even to rank the observations.

T F 2. The Mann-Whitney *U* test is one of a family of tests known as rank difference tests.

T F 3. A sign test for paired data is based upon the binomial distribution, but can often be approximated by the normal distribution.

T F 4. One disadvantage of nonparametric methods is that they tend to ignore a certain amount of information.

T F 5. In the Mann-Whitney *U* test, two samples of size, n_1 and n_2, are taken to determine the *U* statistic. The sampling distribution of the *U* statistic can be approximated by the normal distribution when either n_1 or n_2 is greater than 10.

T F 6. The Mann-Whitney *U* test tends to waste less data than the sign test.

T F 7. Assume that in a rank test, two elements are tied for the 10th rank position. We assign each of them a rank of 10.5 and the next element after these two receives a rank of 11.

T F 8. In contrast to regression analysis, where one may compute a coefficient of correlation, an equivalent measure may be determined in a ranking of two variables in nonparametric testing. This equivalent measure is called a rank correlation coefficient.

T F 9. In a one-sample runs test, the number of runs is a statistic having its own sampling distribution.

T F 10. One disadvantage in using the rank correlation coefficient is that it is very sensitive to extreme observations in the data set.

T F 11. The Kolmogorov-Smirnov test is a measure of the goodness of fit of a theoretical distribution.

T F 12. Nonparametric methods are more efficient than parametric methods.

T F 13. The one-sample runs test enables us to determine whether two independent samples have been drawn from populations with the same distributions.

T F 14. The sequence A, A, B, A, B contains four runs.

T F 15. A rank correlation coefficient of −1 represents perfect inverse rank correlation.

T F 16. In a one-sample runs test, the alternative hypothesis is that the sequence of observations is not random.

T F 17. In the Mann-Whitney *U* test, it is not necessary that the two samples be of the same size.

18. In a sign test for paired data, 800 students were asked to give ranks (on a scale of 0 to 10) for their attitudes toward true-false and multiple-choice tests. When signs were calculated for the two sets of paired data, 138 of the 800 paired responses received a value of 0. Does this mean that 138 students:
    a) Did not like either type of test?
    b) Did not answer the survey?
    c) Ranked the types equally?
    d) Thought one of the types was perfect and the other was awful?

19. Suppose that, in question 18, the administration felt that true-false tests were liked 3 times as well as multiple-choice tests. Assuming that a preference for true-false tests is a "success," what is the null hypothesis for the administration's sign test for paired data?
    a) $p = .25$ b) $p = .75$ c) $p \neq .25$ d) $p \neq .75$

20. Questions 20 and 21 refer to the following situation. Five former patients are selected at random from Ward A at Trinity Hospital, and 4 former patients are selected at random from Ward B. The

patients stayed the following number of days:

Ward A:	13	4	2	10	6
Ward B:	10	9	7	8	

A Mann-Whitney *U* test is to be performed to determine if there is a significant difference between the lengths of the hospital stays for the 2 wards. If the lengths of stay are ranked from shortest to longest, what is the ranking for the 13-day stay in Ward A?
a) 9 b) 8 c) 9½ d) 7½

21. If the lengths of stay are ranked from shortest to longest, what is the value of $(R_1 - R_2)$?
a) −½ b) 0 c) ½ c) 2½
22. What is the maximum number of runs possible in a sequence of length 5 using 2 symbols?
a) 6 b) 4 c) 3 d) 5
23. The sequence C, D, C, D, C, D, C, D, C, D would probably be rejected by a test of runs as not being truly random because:
a) The pattern C, D occurs only 5 times; this is not often enough to guarantee randomness.
b) The sequence contains too many runs.
c) The sequence contains too few runs.
d) The sequence contains only 2 symbols.
e) None of these.
24. In a Mann-Whitney *U* test, a particular sampling distribution for *U* has a mean of 15. One value of *U* is calculated as $n_1n_2 + \frac{n_1(n_1 + 1)}{2} - R_1$, which equals 22.5. Can we immediately conclude that the value of $n_1n_2 + \frac{n_2(n_2 + 1)}{2} - R_2$ in this situation is:
a) 10? c) 7.5?
b) 12.5? d) Cannot be determined from information given

Questions 25 to 27 refer to the following situation: Seven businessmen (denoted A–G) were ranked from 1 to 7 on a scale of yearly salary level, with 1 being highest. The results were:

A	*B*	*C*	*D*	*E*	*F*	*G*
2	*6*	*4*	*1*	*3*	*5*	*7*

25. Which of the following is correct?
a) E earned more than 4 others.
b) C and F earned the same amount.
c) C's earnings are less than those of 4 others.
d) All of these.
e) a and c but not b.
26. Suppose that, as the second part of this study, the 7 businessmen are ranked according to how happy they seem to be, with 1 being the happiest. If salaries and happiness are perfectly correlated, what must be the happiness ranking for businessman A?
a) 1 b) 2 c) 3 d) 6
27. If, in the happiness ranking of question 26, salaries and happiness were perfectly inversely correlated, what must be the happiness ranking of businessman F?
a) 7 b) 2 c) 5 d) 3
28. When compared to parametric methods, nonparametric methods:
a) Are less accurate c) Are computationally easier
b) Are less efficient d) Require less information

e) All of these
f) b, c, and d, but not a
g) None of these

29. For a perfect inverse correlation, the coefficient of rank correlation r_s would be:
a) equal to 1
b) between 0 and −1
c) equal to 0
d) none of these

30. A sequence of identical occurrences preceded and followed by different occurrences or none at all is a ________________.

31. A nonparametric method used to determine whether two independent samples have been drawn from populations with the same distribution is the ________________.

32. A nonparametric technique for determining the randomness with which sampled items have been selected is the ________________.

33. A ________________ test tests for the difference between paired observations by substituting +, −, and 0 for quantitative values.

34. A ________________ coefficient measures the degree of association between two variables and is based on the ranks of the observations.

35. The U statistic has a special property that enables us to save computational time when ________________.

13-11 CONCEPTUAL CASE (Northern White Metals Company)

Winston Allen, Northern's grizzled chief shipping coordinator, walked briskly across the plant, his rapid pace and the spring in his step belying his advanced years. He was on his way to met with Norma Hasselman, the company's financial officer, to discuss which trucking firm Northern should use as its primary shipper in the coming year.

Northern actually owned only one tractor-trailer truck, and this was used for specialty deliveries, primarily those to other Segue subsidiary companies. All other shipments of Northern products were made by independent trucking firms, with trucks hired on an as-needed basis. The company usually shipped orders that comprised an entire truckload, although occasionally smaller shipments were made. In either case, transportation arrangements were made at least three days in advance, and all freight charges were prepaid by Northern.

Using common carriers, as these truck-for-hire firms are called, had served Northern well for many years. As the size and number of orders grew, however, the system became increasingly cumbersome and difficult to coordinate. Convinced of the need for a change in the company's shipping methods, Norma had undertaken a comprehensive financial study to evaluate the feasibility of running a fleet of company-owned trucks. She had decided that, based on Northern's current requirements, this system would prove too costly and should not be considered further. It was at this point that Winston, who had first worked as a dispatcher for a local trucking firm, suggested using a contract carrier to serve Northern's shipping needs.

Under a contract-carrier arrangement, an agreement is reached with a trucking company whereby the firm provides exclusive service to the hirer but maintains control and management of all trucking equipment and personnel. In Northern's case, this method would cost a bit more than using common carriers but would offer the company a much greater degree of shipping-department flexibility.

Under Winston's recommendation, two firms were selected as possible candidates. Each had served many of Northern's customers at one time or another over the years, and preliminary negotiations indicated that the contract fees would be nearly identical with either firm.

Norma, with her usual penchant for complexity, suggested that in order to make the proper selection, she would need data about delivery-time comparisons, annual dollar losses from damage, accidents per driver-mile and resultant delay-time figures, and numerous other factors. These would be subjected to rigorous analysis, and only then could an intelligent decision be made.

"Hold it, Norma," Winston grumbled. "Even if we could get all these data, which we can't, I don't see that we really need it. Look, these two firms are basically the same," he continued, "and all we want is to provide our customers with the best service we possibly can."

"And . . . ?" Norma prompted him.

"And all we really need to do is simply ask a group of our customers who have experience with both firms which one provides the better service," Winston responded, more patient now. "Then we just choose one."

"Well, I don't believe it's quite as simple as that," she exclaimed, "but I think you may be on to something there, Win!"

Smiling, Winston left the office and hurried back to the loading docks.

Assuming that good service means things like prompt delivery, driver courtesy, neat paperwork, and so forth, how might Northern survey its customers to determine preference between the two trucking firms? What analytical procedures might be employed to determine if one firm is superior to the other? If no difference were detected, how might Norma decide which company to contract with?

13-12 COMPUTER DATA BASE EXERCISE

Laurel and Frank were glad to get back to their test-market analysis for the Menagerie.

"You know," said Frank, "this is an interesting problem to work on, and I'm dying to see the results."

Several months before, Dunlap and Joe had had a serious disagreement about the finish on the Menagerie animals. Dunlap wanted to paint them bright primary colors that would dazzle the preschoolers. Joe, on the other hand, believed the parents would be more attracted to "natural" varnish finish because it looked more wholesome, and they made the purchase decision.

Laurel and Frank had suggested a fifty-store cross-country test market, since Cold River was planning to introduce the line in those markets anyway.

Each store had stocked both painted and unpainted, and now the results were in.

CROSS-COUNTRY TEST MARKET

	Toys Sold			Toys Sold	
STORE	PAINTED	UNPAINTED	STORE	PAINTED	UNPAINTED
1	16	20	26	7	9
2	15	11	27	7	15
3	15	13	28	9	9
4	8	10	29	13	8
5	1	3	30	23	3
6	7	21	31	6	11
7	3	9	32	22	0
8	12	19	33	19	17
9	9	12	34	16	2
10	19	16	35	11	12
11	16	18	36	2	3
12	12	13	37	22	14
13	14	11	38	3	9
14	7	5	39	13	14
15	18	15	40	13	18
16	11	9	41	25	13
17	10	20	42	22	1
18	16	16	43	19	17
19	2	19	44	7	9
20	12	18	45	5	7
21	1	12	46	1	2
22	11	20	47	3	5
23	17	20	48	9	11
24	14	17	49	2	7
25	5	9	50	26	1

QUESTIONS

1. At how many stores were painted toys preferred?
2. Can Frank and Laurel reject the hypothesis that there is no difference in preference between the two types of toys at the 5 percent significance level?
3. What was the average number of painted toys sold per store? The average number of unpainted toys?
4. Discuss the results of your statistical analysis. What should Frank and Laurel recommend? Is there a clear choice?

The next morning Fred and Irene were back in Laurel's and Frank's office.

"Now it's your turn to do something for me besides undermine my effectiveness," yelled Fred.

"But, Fred, it's obvious your sales reps are having too many 3-martini lunches and generally being too free with their expense accounts," accused Irene.

"Irene, you've been giving me too hard a time. Sales are the lifeblood of Cold River, and all of my people are top-notch. You have hamstrung us ever since we got those new detailed expense account sheets. This place is becoming full of red tape just like some kind of super conglomerate. Besides, good sales reps make sales by seeing customers and spending money—NOT by pushing pencils to fill out more silly forms. You're dead wrong this time, and Frank and Laurel will prove it to you."

"We'll be glad to test some hypotheses for you Fred, but we can't promise what the results will show," answered Laurel.

	FIRST WEEK OF OCT. 1979		FIRST WEEK OF OCT. 1980	
SALESPERSON	EXPENSES	SALES	EXPENSES	SALES
1	140	1500	244	1365
2	228	1881	250	1536
3	171	2059	168	1978
4	181	1662	233	1841
5	172	1595	187	1334
6	203	1228	176	1875
7	156	1484	200	1480
8	193	1913	243	1913
9	175	1401	246	1596
10	217	1795	235	1534
11	179	1163	186	1592
12	151	2299	233	2004
13	224	1445	154	1889
14	153	2005	244	1752
15	197	1774	196	1884
16	177	2065	185	1508
17	193	1686	185	1259
18	192	1997	187	2017
19	183	1745	207	2105
20	215	1085	179	1819
21	159	1910	228	1495
22	214	1683	172	1265
23	176	1800	235	2131
24	229	1231	159	2223
25	175	1989	229	1839

QUESTION

5. Test Fred's statement about the sales force. If you rank all of the salespeople according to sales, is there a correlation between this rank and the rank based upon expenses?

"Look who's coming down the hall," said Laurel. "It's Fred."

"Oh, no, not again," whispered Frank. "Everytime he comes here we end up proving somebody's pet theory, usually Fred's, is just a lot of smoke."

"I know. The trouble is they only remember when we prove them wrong. You know, I was thinking, maybe we ought to use a higher confidence level. Then we would reject fewer hypotheses."

"Just what are you two whispering about?" greeted Fred. "Who are you going to get into hot water next?"

Irene followed Fred into the room. "Fred, I always knew you weren't worth the powder it cost to blow you to Jericho, and now I've got the facts and figures to prove it statistically!"

"Irene . . . " Laurel started to say.

"I've looked at the pay scales for your salespersons and found out that women aren't being paid the same as the men. How can you explain your way out of that, you stuffed shirt?"

"Irene, Irene. You know all my staff is paid only on a merit basis. The girls, too. Even though we don't pay on a commission basis, the salary each salesperson receives is an accurate reflection of his or her productivity. The girls just don't produce as much as the men do."

"I knew you'd try to worm out of your predicament like that, Fred. I have data on average monthly sales for both men and women for the past six months, and it looks to me as though there is no difference between the two groups. I'm sure that Laurel and Frank can prove my hunch too."

"Sure we can," Laurel said.

"Oh no, not again," moaned Fred.

"Quit grinning, Frank, and let's get to work," Laurel said.

AVERAGE MONTHLY SALES

WOMEN

2,871	2,774	5,195	3,952	4,031	932
7,963	7,074	4,775	5,542	5,682	6,224
840	3,854	2,595	4,306	3,031	5,971
1,981	6,942	5,853	7,810	1,683	5,457
766	1,627	4,134	6,667	1,006	3,426
5,076	1,954	774	5,609	1,657	2,842
7,157	2,038	5,008	5,423	2,888	2,878

MEN

5,626	5,173	7,991	4,317	5,077	5,132
2,932	5,572	3,950	5,724	869	5,369
2,374	1,297	3,669	8,486	3,659	2,897
8,512	4,800	4,532	5,603	7,437	3,016
2,999	4,101	3,844	4,559	1,164	4,811
5,180	6,545	5,580	6,481	1,577	4,213
3,292	5,512	1,165	4,052	9,107	3,936
5,193	9,149	7,826	3,543	3,995	5,820

PROBLEMS

6. Compute the mean and standard deviation of the average monthly sales for men and women salespersons.

7. Test the assumption that both samples have been drawn from the same population.

A little while later, Nick Pappas approached Frank and Laurel with an awkward problem. Cold River's oak sled slats were cut by eye, without a jig. As a result, they varied in length. If the slats were cut too long, 43.5 inches or more, the slats wouldn't fit in their packing cartons. Fortunately, that didn't happen very often. Sled slats were supposed to be cut 41 inches long, but lengths up to 42.25 inches were perfectly acceptable. Lengths between 42.25 and 43.50 were also acceptable but only marginally. Packing these longer lengths would weaken the cartons, and sometimes they would tear during shipping. If a carton tore, the sled was returned. Past experience showed that returns were not excessive unless significantly more than 10 percent of the sleds were too long.

"For the sample you see here, I tested whether too high a proportion of the sleds were too long," Nick explained. "As you can see, at the 5 percent significance level we're doing all right. But even so, I'd still like to reduce the number of slats that are too long. To do that, I need to find out whether the problem occurs randomly or if it happens in streaks. If it happens in streaks, further study may let us correct it. Can you two help me out?"

QUESTIONS

8. Check Nick's work: At a 5 percent significance level, is the proportion of sleds longer than 42.25 inches significantly greater than 10 percent?
9. What did Frank and Laurel find out about the randomness of the problem?

SLED LENGTHS
(SEQUENCE IS BY ROWS ACROSS)

40.61	38.40	40.19	40.68	41.26	40.32	39.72	42.92	40.42	38.45	42.52	40.71
38.27	39.39	42.08	43.29	40.94	40.43	42.54	41.01	42.39	40.97	40.66	40.51
40.68	41.20	40.30	41.88	38.83	39.93	42.42	40.44	41.99	41.08	40.85	41.61
41.35	39.45	43.69	41.81	40.10	40.02	38.07	39.77	40.86	40.93	41.21	41.16
39.87	41.65	42.85	41.86	41.18	42.30	42.19	40.61	39.86	40.63	42.53	41.24
42.33	40.87	41.22	41.03	40.34	41.50	40.92	41.92	41.80	40.50	43.08	42.31
40.89	40.45	41.47	40.85	39.35	39.73	40.19	40.43	42.30	40.67	41.64	40.57
42.40	40.91	40.56	40.65	38.81	41.84	43.29	41.37	40.64	40.04	39.66	40.43
42.13	41.43	39.77	42.17	40.63	41.26	40.47	41.64	40.66	40.13	40.17	41.49
38.19	40.11	43.22	40.31	42.13	41.45	42.00	39.69	40.51	40.18	40.78	39.84
40.92	41.38	41.69	41.25	40.26	41.13	41.78	40.12	40.43	41.12	42.94	41.70
40.61	40.85	41.35	40.23	41.63	39.76	41.37	41.04	41.33	41.36	39.55	40.68
40.66	40.04	41.98	40.37	41.32	40.21	41.39	42.45	41.04	40.08	40.15	42.25
40.32	40.66	41.23	41.03	40.58	41.17	40.91	39.24	40.22	40.98	42.17	41.07
41.00	40.11	41.72	42.59	41.69	40.34	41.92	39.79	40.89	41.80	41.99	39.99
41.27	41.41	41.02	40.57	42.37	40.29	41.09	40.78	41.99	41.09	40.77	42.42
39.84	40.74	40.41	38.08	40.79	40.32	41.37	39.48	41.84	41.69	40.19	41.62
40.81	41.81	41.14	40.87	40.51	40.81	42.07	42.46	42.19	39.61	38.06	41.47
40.15	40.54	41.57	41.47	39.62	40.03	39.36	40.02	42.48	40.98	40.36	39.60
42.28	40.83	41.66	42.43	41.86	41.13	40.28	41.93	41.20	40.64	39.17	40.65
42.41	42.84	41.00	40.67	42.55	41.06	40.51	39.09	43.50	39.83	40.33	42.73
39.01	41.45	40.76	41.82	40.95	39.45	40.42	42.38	41.04	42.42	40.58	39.32
42.89	41.52	42.10	40.24	42.76	40.73	42.35	39.57	41.89	39.16	39.96	41.99
42.69	42.00	40.87	42.04	40.77	42.66	42.32	42.05	38.88	39.19	41.47	40.88
42.67	39.79	40.71	40.81	42.02	40.32	40.80	40.79	41.28	40.36	39.81	41.68
41.29	42.76	38.57	40.83	41.69	39.86	42.02	40.94	40.47	40.82	41.54	39.83
42.20	39.34	40.46	41.24	41.24	38.79	41.33	41.82	42.07	42.65	40.34	39.82
41.56	40.91	40.13	41.29	38.44	41.48	41.38	42.03	40.98	41.52	42.94	40.59
40.84	38.43	42.31	41.61	40.88	42.85	41.47	40.23	40.47	41.56	40.28	41.00
39.61	42.04	40.18	41.35	39.26	42.27	43.63	42.13	41.85	41.94	41.00	40.92
42.32	43.10	39.21	40.76	39.99	41.92	38.88	41.35	40.56	41.14	40.39	41.29
40.06	41.16	43.47	40.78	41.13	42.37	39.44	41.03	41.99	43.08	41.03	40.75
41.59	41.43	40.79	41.86	40.33	42.65	39.53	41.59	41.05	40.15	43.24	41.91
41.01	42.47	40.18	39.65								

13-13 FLOW CHART

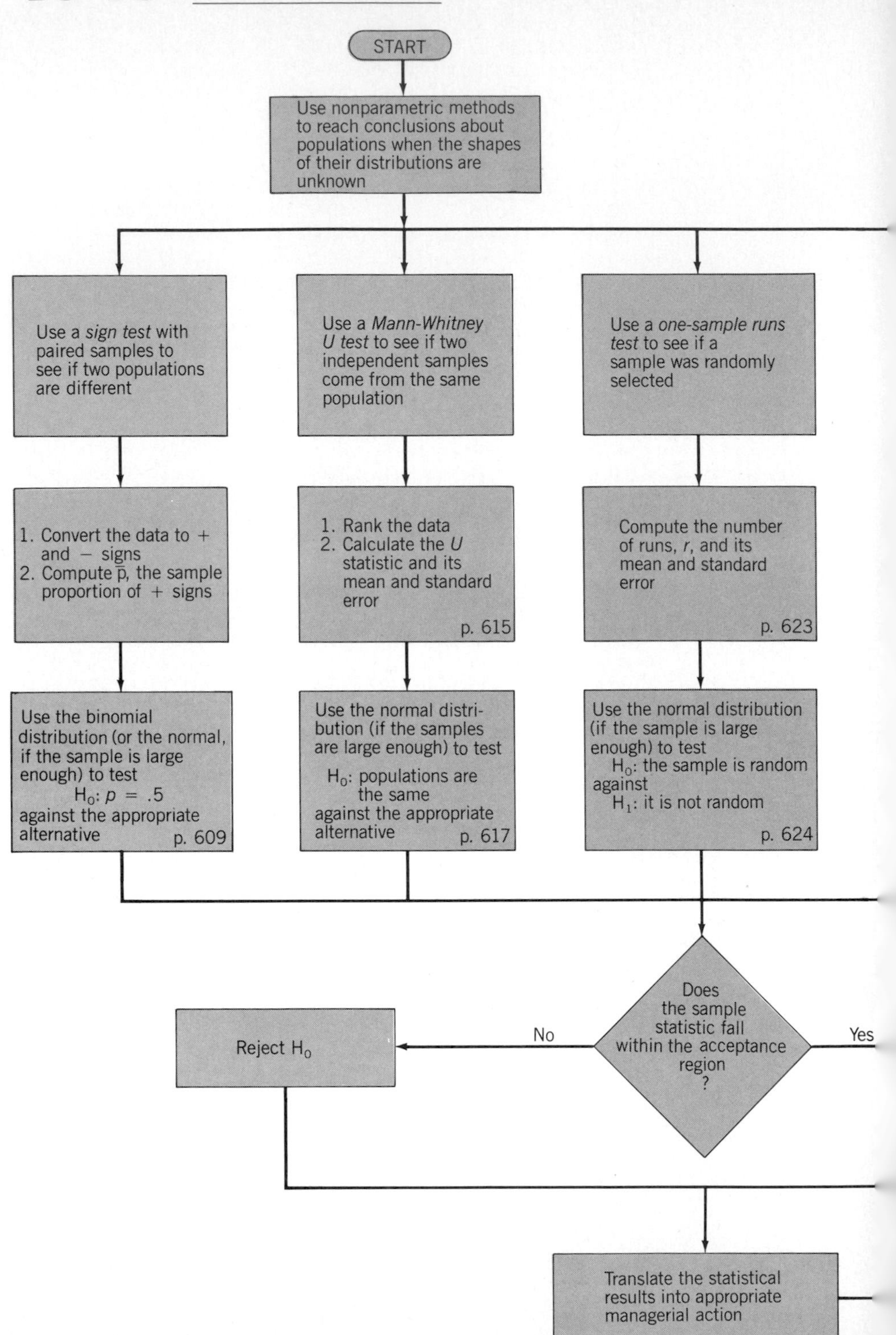

START
Use nonparametric methods to reach conclusions about populations when the shapes of their distributions are unknown
Use a *sign test* with paired samples to see if two populations are different
Use a *Mann-Whitney U test* to see if two independent samples come from the same population
Use a *one-sample runs test* to see if a sample was randomly selected
1. Convert the data to + and − signs
2. Compute $\bar{p}$, the sample proportion of + signs
1. Rank the data
2. Calculate the *U* statistic and its mean and standard error
p. 615
Compute the number of runs, *r*, and its mean and standard error
p. 623
Use the binomial distribution (or the normal, if the sample is large enough) to test
H_0: $p = .5$
against the appropriate alternative
p. 609
Use the normal distribution (if the samples are large enough) to test
H_0: populations are the same
against the appropriate alternative
p. 617
Use the normal distribution (if the sample is large enough) to test
H_0: the sample is random
against
H_1: it is not random
p. 624
Does the sample statistic fall within the acceptance region ?
No
Yes
Reject H_0
Translate the statistical results into appropriate managerial action

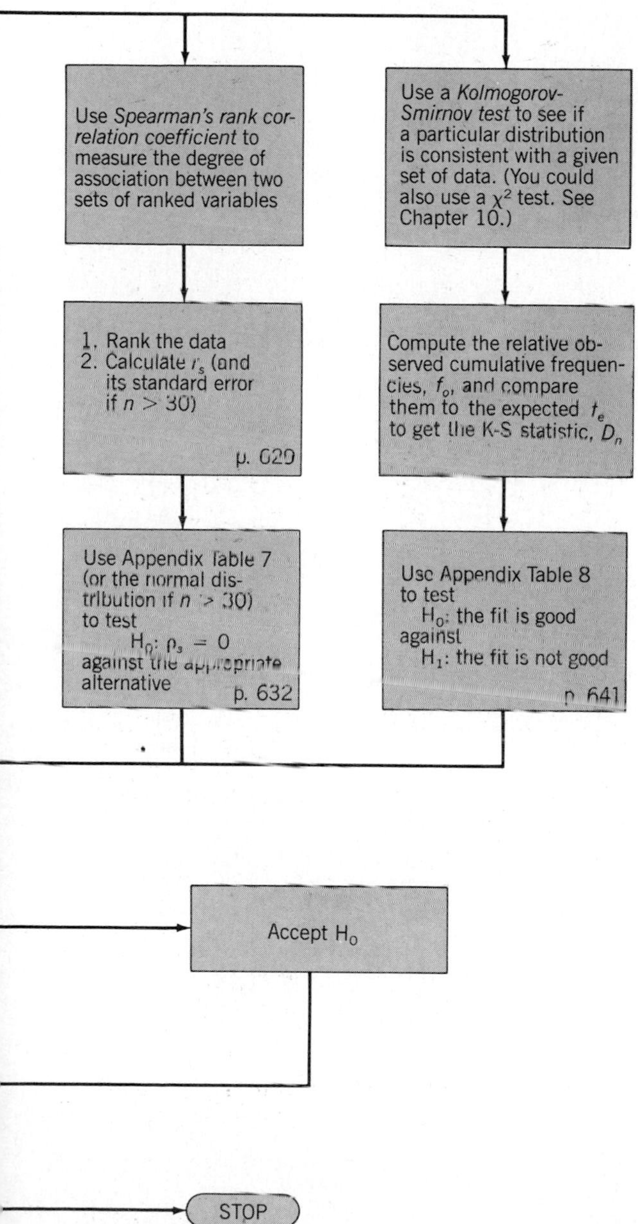

Use *Spearman's rank correlation coefficient* to measure the degree of association between two sets of ranked variables
Use a *Kolmogorov-Smirnov test* to see if a particular distribution is consistent with a given set of data. (You could also use a χ^2 test. See Chapter 10.)
1. Rank the data
2. Calculate r_s (and its standard error if $n > 30$)
p. 629
Compute the relative observed cumulative frequencies, f_o, and compare them to the expected f_e to get the K-S statistic, D_n
Use Appendix Table 7 (or the normal distribution if $n > 30$) to test
H_0: $\rho_s = 0$
against the appropriate alternative
p. 632
Use Appendix Table 8 to test
H_0: the fit is good
against
H_1: the fit is not good
p. 641
Accept H_0
STOP

CHAPTER 14

TIME SERIES

1. INTRODUCTION, 662
2. VARIATIONS IN TIME SERIES, 662
3. TREND ANALYSIS, 665
4. CYCLICAL VARIATION, 676
5. SEASONAL VARIATION, 681
6. IRREGULAR VARIATION, 688
7. A PROBLEM INVOLVING ALL FOUR COMPONENTS OF A TIME SERIES, 689
8. TIME SERIES ANALYSIS IN FORECASTING, 696
9. TERMS, 697
10. EQUATIONS, 697
11. REVIEW EXERCISES, 699
12. CONCEPT TEST, 701
13. CONCEPTUAL CASE, 703
14. COMPUTER DATA BASE EXERCISE, 704
15. FLOW CHART, 705

OBJECTIVES: In Chapter 14 we shall study the behavior of *time series,* data collected over a period of time. Our purpose will be to see what changes take place over time in the event we are observing. Often we may try to predict what the future behavior of that event will be. If you have ever been asked, "Why isn't your grade-point average higher for the last three years?" and you have countered with, "But look what I did last semester," you have invited your questioner to examine the time series of your grades, hoping that the recent behavior of this series will overshadow earlier behavior.

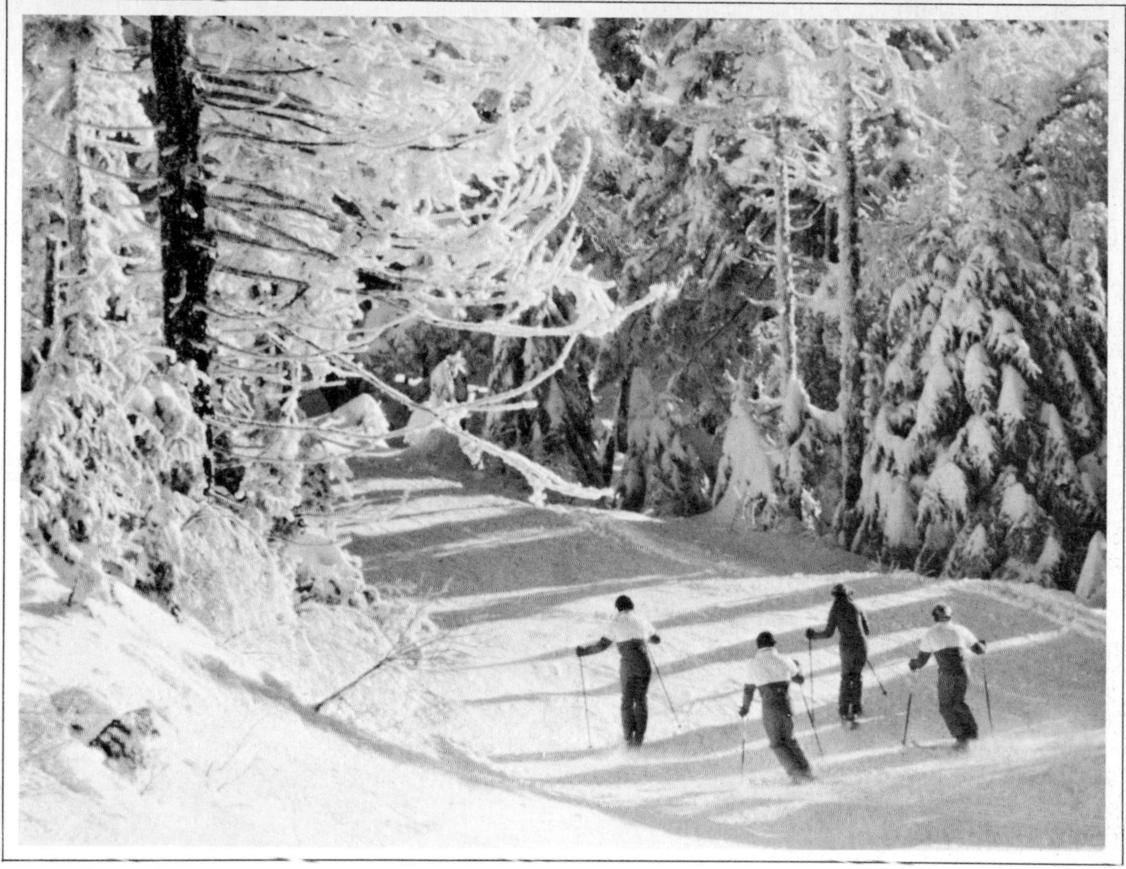

The management of the New England Resort Hotel has these quarterly occupancy data over a 5-year period:

YEAR	1ST QTR.	2ND QTR.	3RD QTR.	4TH QTR.
1979	1,861	2,203	2,415	1,908
1980	1,921	2,343	2,514	1,986
1981	1,834	2,154	2,098	1,799
1982	1,837	2,025	2,304	1,965
1983	2,073	2,414	2,339	1,967

To improve service, management must establish the seasonal pattern of demand for rooms. Using methods covered in this chapter, we shall help the hotel discern such a seasonal pattern, if it exists, and to use it to forecast demand for rooms.

14-1 INTRODUCTION

Forecasting, or predicting, is an essential tool in any decision-making process. Its uses vary from determining inventory requirements for a local shoe store to estimating the annual sales of video games. The quality of the forecasts management can make is strongly related to the information that can be extracted and used from past data. *Time series analysis* is one quantitative method we use to determine patterns in data collected over time. Table 14-1 is an example of time series data.

TABLE 14-1 Time series for the number of ships loaded at Morehead City, N.C.

Year	1976	1977	1978	1979	1980	1981	1982	1983
Number	98	105	116	119	135	156	177	208

Use of time series analysis

Time series analysis is used to detect patterns of change in statistical information over regular intervals of time. We *project* these patterns to arrive at an estimate for the future. Thus, time series analysis helps us cope with uncertainty about the future.

EXERCISES

14-1 Of what value are forecasts in the decision-making process?

14-2 For what purpose do we apply time series analysis to data collected over a period of time?

14-3 How can one benefit from determining past patterns?

14-4 How would errors in forecasts affect a city government?

14-2 VARIATIONS IN TIME SERIES

Four kinds of variation in time series

We use the term *time series* to refer to any group of statistical information accumulated at regular intervals. There are four kinds of change, or variation, involved in time series analysis. They are:

1. Secular trend
2. Cyclical fluctuation
3. Seasonal variation
4. Irregular variation

Secular trend

With the first type of change, secular trend, the value of the variable tends to increase or decrease over a long period of time. The steady increase in the cost of living recorded by the Consumer Price Index is an example of secular trend. From year to individual year, the cost of living varies a great deal; but if we examine a long-term period, we see that the trend is toward a steady increase. Figure 14-1(a) shows a secular trend in an increasing but fluctuating time series.

Cyclical fluctuation

The second type of variation seen in a time series is cyclical fluctuation. The most common example of cyclical fluctuation is the business cycle. Over time, there are years when the business cycle hits a peak above the

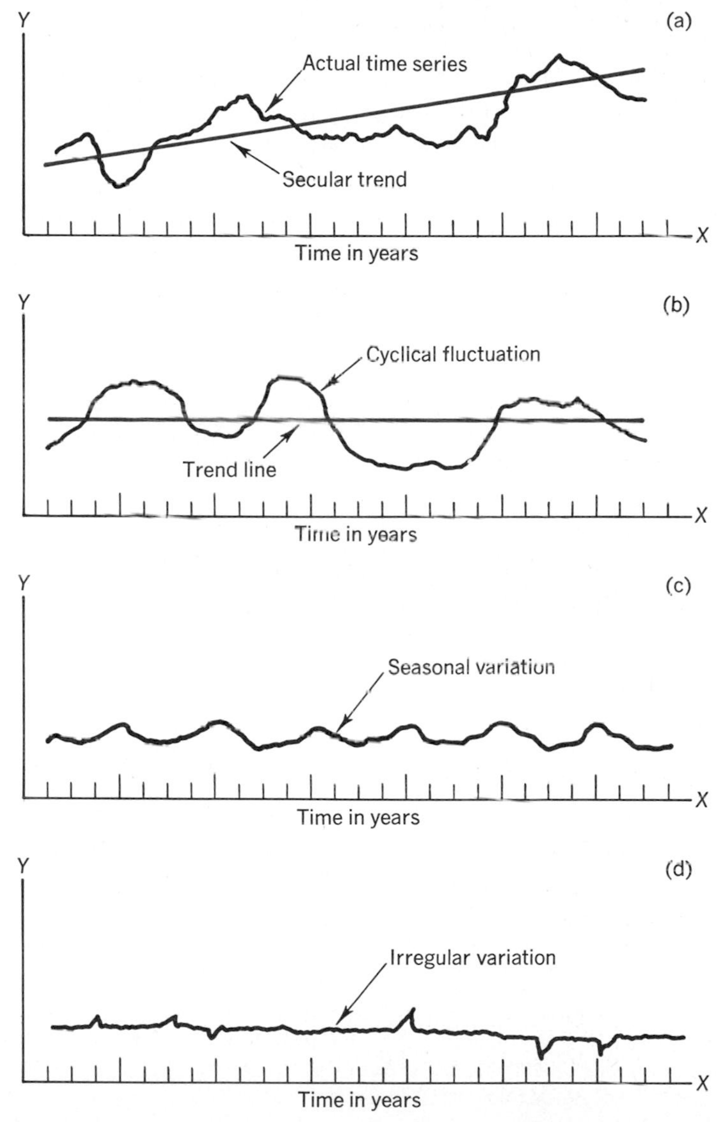

FIGURE 14-1
Time series variations

trend line. At other times, business activity is likely to slump, hitting a low point below the trend line. The time between hitting peaks or falling to low points is at least one year, and it can be as many as fifteen or twenty years. Figure 14-1(b) illustrates a typical pattern of cyclical fluctuation above and below a secular trend line. Note that the cyclical movements do not follow any definite trend but move in a somewhat unpredictable manner.

Seasonal variation

The third kind of change in time series data is seasonal variation. As we might expect from the name, seasonal variation involves patterns of change within a year that tend to be repeated from year to year. For example, a physician can expect a substantial increase in the number of flu cases every winter and of poison ivy every summer. Since these are regular patterns, they are useful in forecasting the future. In Fig. 14-1(c), we see a seasonal variation. Notice how it peaks in the fourth quarter of each year.

Irregular variation

Irregular variation is the fourth type of change discussed in time series analysis. In many situations, the value of a variable may be completely unpredictable, changing in a random manner. Irregular variations describe such movements. The effects of the Middle East conflict in 1973 and the Iranian situation in 1979–1981 on gasoline sales in the United States are examples of irregular variation. Figure 14-1(d) illustrates the characteristics of irregular variation.

Thus far we have referred to a time series as exhibiting one or another of these four types of variation. In most instances, however, a time series will contain several of these components. Thus we can describe the overall variation in a single time series in terms of these four different kinds of variation. In the following sections, we will examine the four components and the ways in which we measure each.

EXERCISES

14-5 Identify the four principal components of a time series and explain the kind of change, over time, to which each applies.

14-6 Which of the four components of a time series would we use to describe the effect of Christmas sales upon a retail department store?

14-7 What is the advantage of reducing a time series into its four components?

14-8 Which of the four components of a time series might the U.S. Department of Agriculture use to describe a 7-year weather pattern?

14-9 How would a war be accounted for in a time series?

14-10 What component of a time series explains the general growth and decline of the steel industry over the last 2 centuries?

14-11 Assume that there are only two political parties in the land of Demagoguery, the Stubborn Mules and the Forgetful Elephants. The Stubborn Mules are currently in power, but as their economic programs have been put into place, all the leading economic indicators have declined. Suppose that this country has developed a Measure of All Developments in the Economy, (MADE), an aggregate index that takes all the economic indicators into consideration. Plotting this MADE index versus time yields a time series, which has recently declined with all the leading economic indicators. Describe the types of variation affecting the MADE time series now, from the point of view of:

a) The Stubborn Mules
b) The Forgetful Elephants

14-3 TREND ANALYSIS

Two methods of fitting a trend line

Of the four components of a time series, secular trend represents the long-term direction of the series. One way to describe the trend component is to fit a line visually to a set of points on a graph. Any given graph, however, is subject to slightly different interpretations by different individuals. We can also fit a trend line by the method of least squares, which we examined in Chapter 11. In our discussion, we will concentrate on the method of least squares, since visually fitting a line to a time series is not a completely dependable process.

Reasons for Studying Trends

There are three reasons why it is useful to study secular trends:

Three reasons for studying secular trends

1. **The study of secular trends allows us to describe a historical pattern.** There are many instances when we can use a past trend to evaluate the success of a previous policy. For example, a university may evaluate the effectiveness of a recruiting program by examining its past enrollment trends.

2. **Studying secular trends permits us to project past patterns, or trends, into the future.** Knowledge of the past can tell us a great deal about the future. Examining the growth rate of the world's population, for example, can help us estimate the population for some future time.

3. **In many situations, studying the secular trend of a time series allows us to eliminate the trend component from the series.** This makes it easier for us to study the other three components of the time series. If we want to determine the seasonal variation in ski sales, for example, eliminating the trend component gives us a more accurate idea of the seasonal component.

Trend lines take different forms

Trends can be linear, or they can be curvilinear. Before we examine the linear, or straight-line, method of describing trends, we should remember that some relationships do not take that form. The increase of pollutants in the environment follows an upward sloping curve similar to that in Fig. 14-2(a). Another common example of a curvilinear relationship is the life cycle of a new business product, illustrated in Fig. 14-2(b). When a new product is introduced, its sales volume is low (I). As the product gains recognition and success, unit sales grow at an increasingly rapid rate (II).

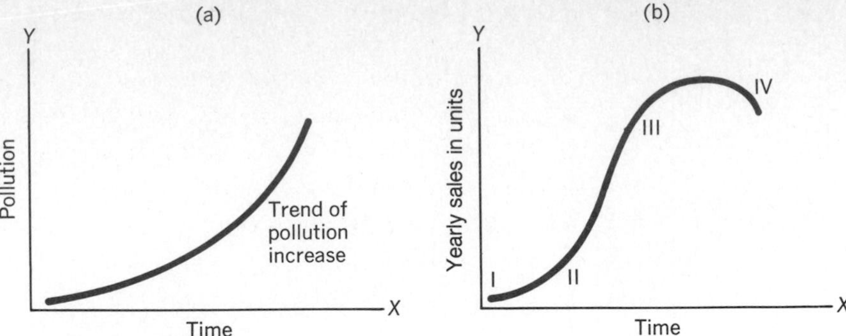

FIGURE 14-2
Curvilinear trend relationships

After the product is firmly established, its unit sales grow at a stable rate (III). Finally, as the product reaches the end of its life cycle, unit sales begin to decrease (IV).

Fitting the Linear Trend by the Least Squares Method

Besides those trends that can be described by a curved line, there are others that are described by a straight line. These are called linear trends. Before developing the equation for a linear trend, we need to review the general equation for estimating a straight line (Equation 11-3):

Equation for estimating a straight line

$$\hat{Y} = a + bX \tag{11-3}$$

where:

- $\hat{Y}$ is the estimated value of the dependent variable
- X is the independent variable (*time* in trend analysis)
- a is the Y-intercept (the value of Y when $X = 0$)
- b is the slope of the trend line

Finding the best-fitting trend line

We can describe the general trend of many time series using a straight line. But we are faced with the problem of finding the best-fitting line. As we did in Chapter 11, we can use the least squares method to calculate the best-fitting line, or equation. There we saw that the best-fitting line was determined by Equations 11-4 and 11-5, which are now renumbered as Equations 14-1 and 14-2.

$$b = \frac{\Sigma XY - n\overline{X}\,\overline{Y}}{\Sigma X^2 - n\overline{X}^2} \tag{14-1}$$

$$a = \overline{Y} - b\overline{X} \tag{14-2}$$

where:

- Y represents the values of the dependent variable.
- X represents the values of the independent variable.
- $\overline{Y}$ is the mean of the values of the dependent variable.
- $\overline{X}$ is the mean of the values of the independent variable.
- n is the number of data points in the time series.
- a is the Y-intercept.
- b is the slope.

With Equations 14-1 and 14-2, we can establish the best-fitting line to describe time series data. However, the regularity of time series data allows us to simplify the calculations in Equations 14-1 and 14-2 through the process we shall now describe.

Translating or Coding Time

Coding the time variable to simplify computation

Normally, we measure the independent variable *time* in terms such as *weeks, months,* and *years.* Fortunately, we can convert these traditional measures of time to a form that simplifies the computation. In Chapter 3, we called this process *coding.* To use coding here, we find the mean time and then subtract that value from each of the sample times. Suppose our time series consists of only three points, 1980, 1981, and 1982. If we had to place these numbers in Equations 14-1 and 14-2, we would find the resultant calculations tedious. Instead, we can transform the values 1980, 1981, and 1982 into corresponding values of -1, 0, and 1, where 0 represents the mean (1981), -1 represents the first year ($1980 - 1981 = -1$), and 1 represents the last year ($1982 - 1981 = 1$).

Treating odd and even numbers of elements

We need to consider two cases when we translate time values. The first is a time series with an *odd number of elements,* as in the previous example. The second is a series with an *even number of elements.* Consider Table 14-2. In part *a,* on the left, we have an odd number of years. Thus, the process is the same as the one we just described, using the years 1980, 1981, and 1982. In part *b,* on the right, we have an *even* number of elements. In cases like this, when we find the mean and subtract it from each element, the fraction ½ becomes part of the answer. To simplify the coding process and to remove the ½, we multiply each time element by 2. We will denote the "coded," or translated, time with a lowercase x.

Why use coding?

We have two reasons for this translation of time. First, it eliminates the need to square numbers as large as 1977, 1978, 1979, and so on. This method also sets the mean year, $\bar{x}$, equal to zero and allows us to simplify Equations 14-1 and 14-2.

Simplifying the calculation of *a* and *b*

Now we can return to our calculations of the slope (Equation 14-1) and the Y-intercept (Equation 14-2) to determine the best-fitting line. Since we are using the coded variable x, we replace X and $\overline{X}$ by x and $\bar{x}$ in Equations

TABLE 14-2 Translating, or coding, time values

(a) When there is an *odd* number of elements in the time series

X (1)	$X - \bar{X}$ (2)	TRANSLATED OR CODED TIME (3)
1977	1977 − 1980 =	−3
1978	1978 − 1980 =	−2
1979	1979 − 1980 =	−1
1980	1980 − 1980 =	0
1981	1981 − 1980 =	1
1982	1982 − 1980 =	2
1983	1983 − 1980 =	3
$\Sigma X =$ **13,860**		$\bar{x}$ (the mean year) = 0

$$\bar{X} = \frac{\Sigma X}{n} = \frac{13{,}860}{7} = 1980$$

(b) When there is an *even* number of elements in the time series

X (1)	$X - \bar{X}$ (2)	$(X - \bar{X}) \times 2$ (3)	TRANSLATED OR CODED TIME (4)
1978	1978 − 1980½ =	−2½ × 2 =	−5
1979	1979 − 1980½ =	−1½ × 2 =	−3
1980	1980 − 1980½ =	− ½ × 2 =	−1
1981	1981 − 1980½ =	½ × 2 =	1
1982	1982 − 1980½ =	1½ × 2 =	3
1983	1983 − 1980½ =	2½ × 2 =	5
$\Sigma X =$ **11,883**			$\bar{x}$ (the mean year) = 0

$$\bar{X} = \frac{\Sigma X}{n} = \frac{11{,}883}{6} = 1980\tfrac{1}{2}$$

14-1 and 14-2. Then, since the mean of our coded time variable $\bar{x}$ is zero, we can substitute 0 for $\bar{x}$ in Equations 14-1 and 14-2, as follows:

$$b = \frac{\Sigma XY - n\bar{X}\bar{Y}}{\Sigma X^2 - n\bar{X}^2} \qquad \textbf{[14-1]}$$

$$= \frac{\Sigma xY - n\bar{x}\bar{Y}}{\Sigma x^2 - n\bar{x}^2} \leftarrow \left\{ \begin{array}{l} \bar{x} \text{ (the coded variable) substituted for } \bar{X} \text{ and} \\ x \text{ substituted for } X \end{array} \right.$$

$$= \frac{\Sigma xY - n0\bar{Y}}{\Sigma x^2 - n0^2} \leftarrow \{\bar{x} \text{ replaced by } 0$$

$$= \frac{\Sigma xY}{\Sigma x^2} \qquad \textbf{[14-3]}$$

Equation 14-2 changes as follows:

$$a = \bar{Y} - b\bar{X} \qquad \textbf{[14-2]}$$

$$= \bar{Y} - b\bar{x} \leftarrow \{\bar{x} \text{ substituted for } \bar{X}$$

$$= \bar{Y} - b0 \leftarrow \{\bar{x} \text{ replaced by } 0$$

$$= \bar{Y} \qquad \textbf{[14-4]}$$

Equations 14-3 and 14-4 represent a substantial improvement over Equations 14-1 and 14-2.

A Problem Using the Least Squares Method (Even Number of Elements) in a Time Series

Using the least squares method

Consider the data in Table 14-1, illustrating the number of ships loaded at Morehead City between 1976 and 1983. In this problem, we want to find the equation that will describe the secular trend of loadings. To calculate the necessary values for Equations 14-3 and 14-4, let us look at Table 14-3.

Finding the slope and Y-intercept

With these values, we can now substitute into Equations 14-3 and 14-4 to find the slope and the Y-intercept for the line describing the trend in ship loadings:

$$\begin{aligned} b &= \frac{\Sigma xY}{\Sigma x^2} \\ &= \frac{1{,}266}{168} \\ &= 7.536 \end{aligned} \qquad \textbf{[14-3]}$$

and:

$$\begin{aligned} a &= \bar{Y} \\ &= 139.25 \end{aligned} \qquad \textbf{[14-4]}$$

Thus, the general linear equation describing the secular trend in ship loadings is:

$$\begin{aligned} \hat{Y} &= a + bx \\ &= 139.25 + 7.536x \end{aligned} \qquad \textbf{[11-3]}$$

TABLE 14-3 Intermediate calculations for computing the trend

X (1)	Y† (2)	$X - \bar{X}$ (3)	x (4)	xY (4) × (2)	x^2 $(4)^2$
1976	98	1976 − 1979½‡	= −3½ × 2 = −7	−686	49
1977	105	1977 − 1979½	= −2½ × 2 = −5	−525	25
1978	116	1978 − 1979½	= −1½ × 2 = −3	−348	9
1979	119	1979 − 1979½	= −½ × 2 = −1	−119	1
1980	135	1980 − 1979½	= ½ × 2 = 1	135	1
1981	156	1981 − 1979½	= 1½ × 2 = 3	468	9
1982	177	1982 − 1979½	= 2½ × 2 = 5	885	25
1983	208	1983 − 1979½	= 3½ × 2 = 7	1,456	49
$\Sigma X =$ **15,836**	$\Sigma Y =$ **1,114**			$\Sigma xY =$ **1,266**	$\Sigma x^2 =$ **168**

$$\bar{X} = \frac{\Sigma X}{n} = \frac{15{,}836}{8} = 1{,}979\tfrac{1}{2}$$

$$\bar{Y} = \frac{\Sigma Y}{n} = \frac{1{,}114}{8} = 139.25$$

† Y is in number of ships.
‡ 1,979½ corresponds to $x = 0$.

where:

- $\hat{Y}$ is the estimated annual number of ships loaded.
- x is the coded time value representing the number of *half-year* intervals. (A minus sign indicates half-year intervals before $1979\frac{1}{2}$; a plus sign indicates half-year intervals after $1979\frac{1}{2}$.)

Projecting with the Trend Equation

Once we have developed the trend equation, we can project it to forecast the variable in question. In the problem of finding the secular trend in ship loadings, for instance, we determined that the appropriate secular trend equation was:

$$\hat{Y} = 139.25 + 7.536x$$

Using our trend line to predict

Now, suppose we want to estimate ship loadings for 1984. First, we must convert 1984 to the value of the coded time (in half-year intervals).

$$\begin{aligned} x &= 1984 - 1979\tfrac{1}{2} \\ &= 4.5 \text{ years} \\ &= 9 \textit{ half}\text{-year intervals} \end{aligned}$$

Substituting this value into the equation for the secular trend, we get:

$$\begin{aligned} \hat{Y} &= 139.25 + 7.536(9) \\ &= 139.25 + 67.82 \\ &= 207 \text{ ships loaded} \end{aligned}$$

Therefore, we have estimated that 207 ships will be loaded in 1984. If the number of elements in our time series had been odd, not even, our procedure would have been the same except that we would have dealt with one-year intervals, not half-year intervals.

Use of the Second-Degree Equation in a Time Series

Handling time series that are described by curves

So far, we have described the method of fitting a straight line to a time series. But many time series are best described by curves, not straight lines. In these instances, the linear model does not adequately describe the change in the variable as time changes. To overcome this problem, we often use a parabolic curve, which is described mathematically by a second-degree equation. Such a curve is illustrated in Fig. 14-3. The general form for an estimated second-degree equation is:

$$\hat{Y} = a + bx + cx^2 \qquad \textbf{[14-5]}$$

where:

- $\hat{Y}$ is the estimate of the dependent variable.
- a, b, and c are numerical constants.
- x represents the coded values of the time variables.

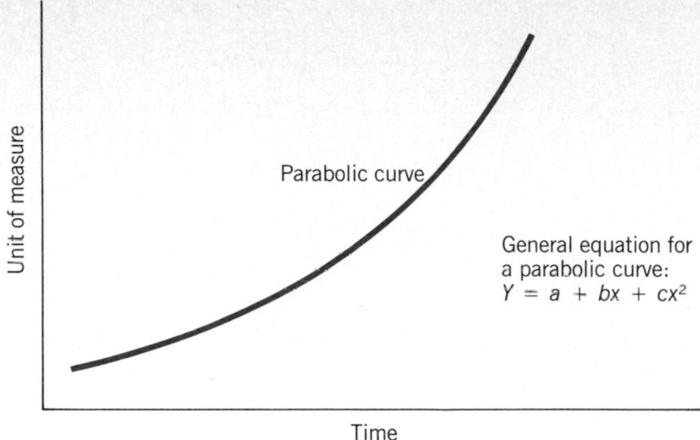

FIGURE 14-3
Form and equation for a parabolic curve

Finding the values for a, b, and c

Again we use the least squares method to determine the second-degree equation to describe the best fit. The derivation of the second-degree equation is beyond the scope of this text. However, we can determine the value of the numerical constants (a, b, and c) from the following three equations:

Equations to find a, b, and c to fit a parabolic curve →

$$\Sigma Y = an + c\Sigma x^2 \quad \textbf{[14-6]}$$

$$\Sigma x^2 Y = a\Sigma x^2 + c\Sigma x^4 \quad \textbf{[14-7]}$$

$$b = \frac{\Sigma xY}{\Sigma x^2} \quad \textbf{[14-3]}$$

When we find the values of a, b, and c by solving Equations 14-6, 14-7, and 14-3, simultaneously, we substitute these values into the second-degree equation, Equation 14-5.

As in describing a linear relationship, we transform the independent variable, time (X), into a coded form (x) to simplify the calculation. We'll now work through a problem in which we fit a parabola to a time series.

A Problem Involving a Parabolic Trend (Odd Number of Elements in the Time Series)

In recent years, the sale of electric quartz watches has increased at a significant rate. Table 14-4 contains sales information that will help us determine the parabolic trend describing watch sales.

TABLE 14-4 Annual sales of electric quartz watches

X (year)	1979	1980	1981	1982	1983
Y (unit sales in millions)	13	24	39	65	106

Coding the time variable

We organize the necessary calculations in Table 14-5. The first step in this process is to translate the independent variable X into a coded time variable x. Note that the coded variable x is listed in one-year intervals

TABLE 14-5 Intermediate calculations for computing the trend

Y (1)	X (2)	$X - \bar{X} = x$ (3)	x^2 $(3)^2$	x^4 $(3)^4$	xY $(3) \times (1)$	x^2Y $(3)^2 \times (1)$
13	1979	$1979 - 1981 = -2$	4	16	−26	52
24	1980	$1980 - 1981 = -1$	1	1	−24	24
39	1981	$1981 - 1981 = 0$	0	0	0	0
65	1982	$1982 - 1981 = 1$	1	1	65	65
106	1983	$1983 - 1981 = 2$	4	16	212	424
$\Sigma Y =$ **247**	$\Sigma X =$ **9,905**		$\Sigma x^2 =$ **10**	$\Sigma x^4 =$ **34**	$\Sigma xY =$ **227**	$\Sigma x^2Y =$ **565**

$$\bar{X} = \frac{\Sigma X}{n} = \frac{9,905}{5} = 1981$$

because there is an odd number of elements in our time series. Thus, it is not necessary to multiply the variable by 2.

Calculating a, b, and c by substitution

Substituting the values from Table 14-5 into equations 14-6, 14-7, and 14-3, we get:

$$247 = a(5) + c(10) \quad ① \qquad \textbf{[14-6]}$$

$$565 = a(10) + c(34) \quad ② \qquad \textbf{[14-7]}$$

$$b = \frac{227}{10} \quad ③ \qquad \textbf{[14-3]}$$

From ③ we see that:

$$b = 22.7$$

Now we must find a and c by solving equations ① and ②.

1. Multiply equation ① by 2 and subtract equation ② from equation ①

$$\begin{array}{rrl} 494 = & 10a + 20c & ① \text{ Equation } 1 \times 2 \\ -565 = & -10a - 34c & ② \\ \hline -\ 71 = & -14c & ④ \end{array}$$

From equation ④ we readily find c:

$$-14c = -71$$

$$c = \frac{-71}{-14}$$

$$= 5.07$$

2. Substitute the value for c into equation ①:

$$247 = 5a + 10c$$
$$247 = 5a + 10(5.07)$$
$$247 = 5a + 50.7$$
$$196.3 = 5a$$
$$a = 39.3$$

This gives us the appropriate values of a, b, and c to describe the time series presented in Table 14-4 by the following equation:

$$\begin{aligned}\hat{Y} &= a + bx + cx^2 \\ &= 39.3 + 22.7x + 5.07x^2\end{aligned} \qquad \textbf{[14-5]}$$

Does our curve fit the data?

In graphing the watch data, our purpose is to see how well the parabola we just derived fits the time series. We've done this in Fig. 14-4.

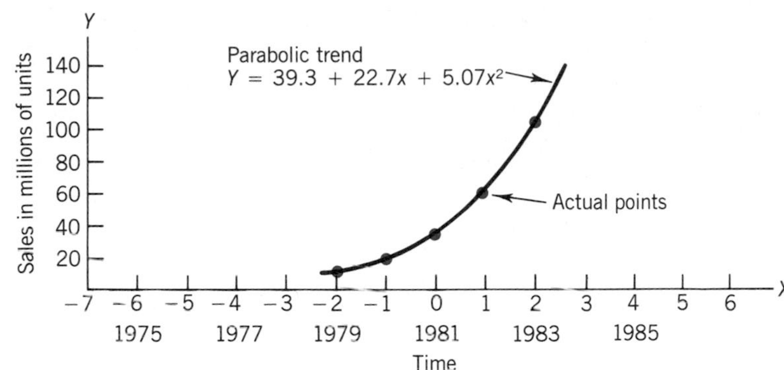

FIGURE 14-4 Parabolic trend fitted to data in Table 14-4

Forecasts Based on a Second-Degree Equation

Suppose we want to forecast watch sales for 1988. To make a prediction, we must first translate 1988 into a coded variable x by subtracting the mean year, 1981:

$$\begin{aligned}X - \bar{X} &= x \\ 1988 - 1981 &= 7\end{aligned}$$

This value ($x = 7$) is then substituted into the second-degree equation describing watch sales:

$$\begin{aligned}\hat{Y} &= 39.3 + 22.7x + 5.07x^2 \\ &= 39.3 + 22.7(7) + 5.07(7)^2 \\ &= 39.3 + 158.9 + 5.07(49) \\ &= 39.3 + 158.9 + 248.4 \\ &= 446.6\end{aligned}$$

Making the forecast

We conclude, based on the past secular trend, that watch sales should be approximately 446,600,000 units by 1988. This extraordinarily large forecast suggests, however, that we must be more careful in forecasting with a parabolic curve than we are when using a linear trend. The slope of the second-degree equation in Fig. 14-4 is continually increasing. Therefore, the parabolic curve may become a poor estimator as we attempt to predict further into the future. In using the second-degree-equation method, we must also take into consideration factors that may be slowing or reversing the growth rate of the variable.

Being careful in interpreting the forecast

In our watch example, we can assume that during the time period under consideration, the product is at a very rapid growth stage in its life cycle. But we must realize that as the cycle approaches a mature stage, sales will probably decelerate and no longer be predicted accurately by our parabolic curve. When we calculate predictions for the future, we need to consider the possibility that the trend line may *change*. Such a situation could cause considerable error. It is therefore necessary to exercise particular care when using a second-degree equation as a forecasting tool.

EXERCISES

14-12 The president of the National Motor Company is studying his compact-car sales over the last 5 years:

Year	1979	1980	1981	1982	1983
Number of compacts sold	794	865	931	1,041	1,150

a) Find the linear equation that describes the trend in the number of compacts sold by National.
b) Estimate the number of compacts that National can expect to sell in 1984.

14-13 The owner of Progressive Builders is examining the number of solar homes started in the region in each of the last 7 months:

Month	June	July	Aug.	Sept.	Oct.	Nov.	Dec.
Number of homes	15	15	26	27	33	41	51

a) Plot these data.
b) Develop the linear estimating equation that best describes these data, and plot the line on the graph from part *a* (let x units equal one month).
c) Develop the second-degree estimating equation that best describes these data and plot this curve on the graph from part *a*.
d) Estimate March sales using both curves you have plotted.

14-14 The Tasty-Smack hamburger chain has significantly increased its investment in inventory over the last 6 years. The information is printed below.

Year	1977	1978	1979	1980	1981	1982
Inventory (×$100,000)	4	4.5	6	8	8.5	10

a) Plot these data
b) Develop the linear estimating equation that best describes these data, and plot this line on the graph from part *a*.
c) Develop the second-degree estimating equation that best describes these data, and plot this curve on the graph from part *a*.
d) Estimate the 1984 inventory using both the curves you have plotted.

14-15 Mike Godfrey, the auditor of a state public school system, has reviewed the inventory records to determine if the current inventory holdings of textbooks are typical. The following inventory amounts are from the previous 5 years:

Year	1979	1980	1981	1982	1983
Inventory (×$1,000)	$4,560	$4,850	$5,430	$5,670	$5,930

a) Find the linear equation that describes the trend in the inventory holdings.
b) Estimate for him the value of the inventory for the year 1984.

14-16 The following table records first-class postal rates from 1968 to 1980:

Year	1968	1970	1972	1974	1976	1978	1980
Postal rate (¢)	5	5	8	8	10	13	15

a) Plot these data.
b) Develop the linear estimating equation that best describes these data, and plot this line on the graph from part *a*. (Let X units = 1 year).
c) Develop the second-degree estimating equation that best describes these data, and plot this curve on the graph from part *a*.
d) What would be wrong with using your answer to estimate rates?

14-17 Environtech Engineering, a company that specializes in the construction of antipollution filtration devices, has recorded the following sales record over the last 9 years:

Year	1975	1976	1977	1978	1979	1980	1981	1982	1983
Sales (×$100,000)	8	9	11	12	15	19	25	26	30

a) Plot these data.
b) Develop the linear estimating equation that best describes these data, and plot this line on the graph from part *a*.
c) Develop the second-degree estimating equation that best describes these data, and plot this curve on the graph from part *a*.
d) Does the market to the best of your knowledge favor *b* or *c* as the more accurate estimating method?

14-18 Bonco Corportion has been selling its automatic Gizmo-Gadget for the past 5 years.

Year	1979	1980	1981	1982	1983
Gizmo-Gadgets Sold (in thousands)	7	9	10	9.5	8

a) Plot these data.
b) Develop the linear estimating equation that best describes these data, and plot this line on the graph from part *a*.
c) Develop the second-degree estimating equation that best describes these data, and plot this curve on the graph from part *a*.
d) Does the second degree appear to be necessary in approximating the data well?
e) Based on your answer to part *d*, estimate the number of Gizmo-Gadgets that Bonco can expect to sell in 1984.

14-19 The State Department of Motor Vehicles is studying the number of traffic fatalities in the state resulting from drunk driving for each of the last 9 years.

Year	1975	1976	1977	1978	1979	1980	1981	1982	1983
Deaths	150	180	170	190	160	200	170	180	210

a) Find the linear equation that describes the trend in the number of traffic fatalities in the state resulting from drunk driving.
b) Estimate the number of traffic fatalities resulting from drunk driving that the state can expect in 1984.

14-4 CYCLICAL VARIATION

Cyclical variation defined

Cyclical variation is the component of a time series that tends to oscillate above and below the secular trend line for periods longer than one year. The procedure used to identify cyclical variation is the residual method.

Residual Method

Justification for disregarding seasonal variation

When we look at a time series consisting of annual data, only the secular-trend, cyclical, and irregular components are considered. (This is true because seasonal variation makes a complete, regular cycle within each year and thus does not affect one year any more than another.) Since we can describe secular trend using a trend line, we can isolate the remaining cyclical and irregular components from the trend. We will assume that the cyclical component explains most of the variation left unexplained by the trend component. (Many real-life time series do not satisfy this assumption. Methods such as Fourier analysis and spectral analysis can analyze the cyclical component for such time series. These, however, are beyond the scope of this book.)

Expressing cyclical variation as a percent of trend

If we use a time series composed of annual data, we can find the fraction of the trend by dividing the actual value (Y) by the corresponding trend value ($\hat{Y}$) for each value in the time series. We then multiply the result of this calculation by 100. This gives us the measure of cyclical variation as a *percent of trend*. We express this process in Equation 14-8:

$$\text{Percent of trend} = \frac{Y}{\hat{Y}} \times 100 \quad [14\text{-}8]$$

where:

- Y is the actual time series value.
- $\hat{Y}$ is the estimated trend value from the same point in the time series.

Now let's apply this procedure.

TABLE 14-6 Grain received by farmers' cooperative over 8 years

X YEAR	Y ACTUAL BUSHELS (×10,000)	$\hat{Y}$ ESTIMATED BUSHELS (×10,000)
1976	7.5	7.6
1977	7.8	7.8
1978	8.2	8.0
1979	8.2	8.2
1980	8.4	8.4
1981	8.5	8.6
1982	8.7	8.8
1983	9.1	9.0

A farmers' marketing cooperative wants to measure the variations in its members' wheat harvest over an 8-year period. Table 14-6 shows the volume harvested in each of the eight years. Column $\hat{Y}$ contains the values of the linear trend for each time period. The trend line has been generated using the methods illustrated in section 3 of this chapter. Note that when we graph the actual (Y) and the trend ($\hat{Y}$) values for the eight years in Fig. 14-5, the actual values move above and below the trend line.

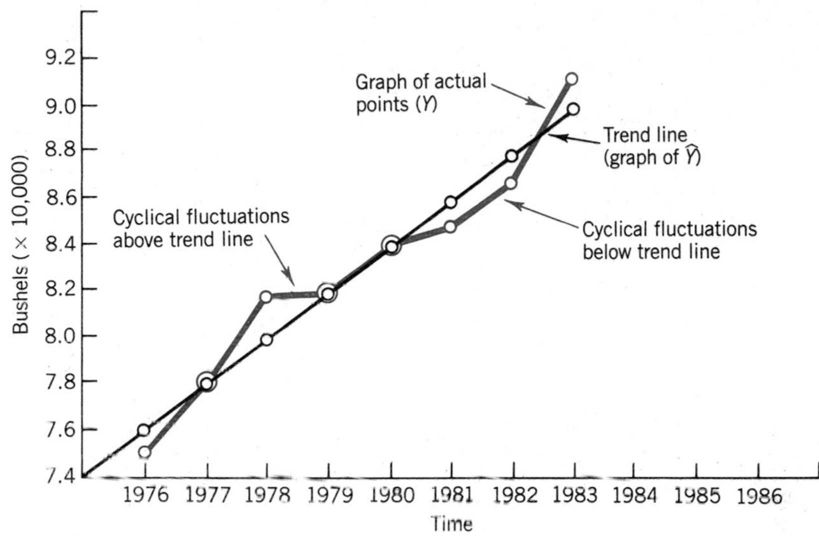

FIGURE 14-5
Cyclical fluctuations around the trend line

Interpreting cyclical variations

Now we can determine the percent of trend for each of the years in the sample (column 4 in Table 14-7). From this column we can see the variation in actual harvests around the estimated trend (98.7 to 102.5). We can attribute these cyclical variations to factors such as rainfall and temperature. However, since these factors are relatively unpredictable, we cannot forecast any specific patterns of variation using the method of residuals.

TABLE 14-7 Calculation of percent of trend

X YEAR (1)	Y ACTUAL BUSHELS (×10,000) (2)	$\hat{Y}$ ESTIMATED BUSHELS (×10,000) (3)	$\frac{Y}{\hat{Y}} \times 100$ PERCENT OF TREND (4) = $\frac{(2)}{(3)} \times 100$
1976	7.5	7.6	98.7
1977	7.8	7.8	100.0
1978	8.2	8.0	102.5
1979	8.2	8.2	100.0
1980	8.4	8.4	100.0
1981	8.5	8.6	98.8
1982	8.7	8.8	98.9
1983	9.1	9.0	101.1

Expressing cyclical variations in terms of relative cyclical residual

The *relative cyclical residual* is another measure of cyclical variation. In this method, the *percentage* deviation from the trend is found for each value. Equation 14-9 presents the mathematical formula for determining the relative cyclical residuals. As with percents of trend, this measure is also a percentage.

$$\text{Relative cyclical residual} = \frac{Y - \hat{Y}}{\hat{Y}} \times 100 \qquad [14\text{-}9]$$

where:

- Y is the actual time series value.
- $\hat{Y}$ is the estimated trend value from the same point in the time series.

Table 14-8 shows the calculation of the relative cyclical residual for the farmers' cooperative problem. Note that the easy way to compute the relative cyclical residual (column 5) is to subtract 100 from the percent of trend (column 4).

TABLE 14-8 Calculation of relative cyclical residuals

YEAR (1)	Y ACTUAL BUSHELS (×10,000) (2)	$\hat{Y}$ ESTIMATED BUSHELS (×10,000) (3)	$\frac{Y}{\hat{Y}} \times 100$ PERCENT OF TREND $(4) = \frac{(2)}{(3)} \times 100$	$\frac{Y - \hat{Y}}{\hat{Y}} \times 100$ RELATIVE CYCLICAL RESIDUAL (5) = (4) − 100
1976	7.5	7.6	98.7	−1.3
1977	7.8	7.8	100.0	0.0
1978	8.2	8.0	102.5	2.5
1979	8.2	8.2	100.0	0.0
1980	8.4	8.4	100.0	0.0
1981	8.5	8.6	98.8	−1.2
1982	8.7	8.8	98.9	−1.1
1983	9.1	9.0	101.1	1.1

Comparing the two measures of cyclical variation

These two measures of cyclical variation, percent of trend and relative cyclical residual, are percentages of the trend. For example, in 1981, the *percent of trend* indicated that the actual harvest was 98.8 percent of the expected harvest for that year. For the same year, the *relative cyclical residual* indicated that the actual harvest was 1.2 percent short of the expected harvest (a relative cyclical residual of −1.2).

Graphing cyclical variation

Frequently, we graph cyclical variation as the percent of trend. Figure 14-6 illustrates how this process eliminates the trend line and isolates the cyclical component of the time series. It must be emphasized that the procedures discussed in this section can be used only for describing past

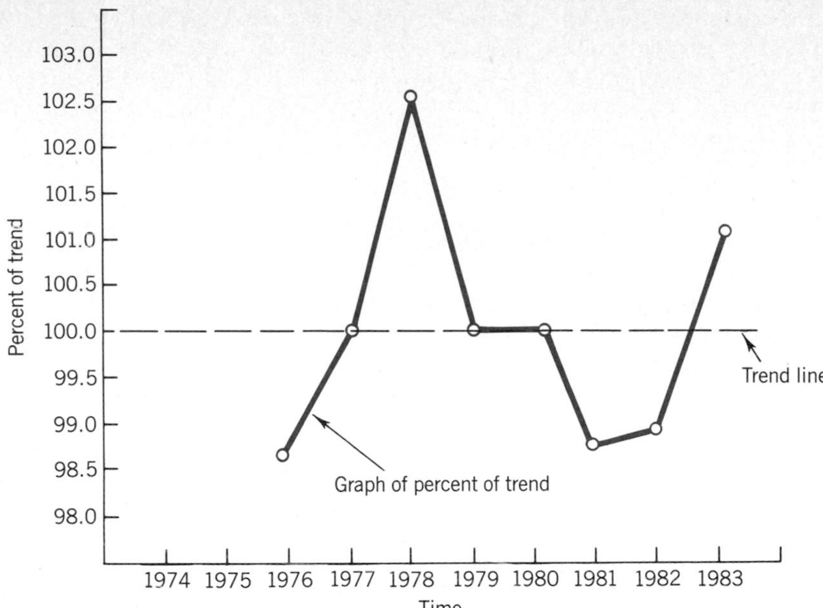

FIGURE 14-6
Graph of percent of trend around trend line for data in Table 14-7

cyclical variations and not for predicting future cyclical variations. Predicting cyclical variation requires the use of techniques beyond the scope of this book.

EXERCISES

14-20 Microprocessing, a computer firm specializing in software engineering, has compiled the following revenue record for the years 1977 to 1983:

Year	1977	1978	1979	1980	1981	1982	1983
Revenue (×$100,000)	1.5	1.6	1.6	1.8	1.9	2.2	2.5

The second-degree equation that best describes the secular trend for these data is:

$$\ddot{Y} = 1.75 + .16x + .03x^2, \text{ where } 1980 = 0 \text{ and } x \text{ units} = 1 \text{ year}$$

a) Calculate the percent of trend for these data.
b) Calculate the relative cyclical residual for these data.
c) Plot the percent of trend from part *a*.
d) In which year does the largest fluctuation from trend occur, and is it the same for both methods?

14-21 The Western Natural Gas Company has supplied 18, 20, 21, 25, and 26 billion cubic feet of gas, respectively, for the years from 1979 to 1983.
a) Find the linear estimating equation that best describes these data.
b) Calculate the percent of trend for these data.
c) Calculate the relative cyclical residual for these data.
d) In which years does the largest fluctuation from trend occur, and is it the same for both methods?

14-22 Joe Honeg, the sales manager responsible for the appliance division of a large consumer-products company, has collected the following data regarding unit sales for his division during the last 5 years:

Year	1979	1980	1981	1982	1983
Units (×$10,000)	36	43	45	53	54

The equation describing the secular trend for appliance sales is:

$$\hat{Y} = 46.2 + 4.6x, \text{ where } 1981 = 0 \text{ and } x \text{ units} = 1 \text{ year}$$

a) Calculate the percent of trend for these data.
b) Calculate the relative cyclical residual for these data.
c) Plot the percent of trend from part *a*.
d) In which year does the largest fluctuation from trend occur, and is it the same for both methods?

14-23 Suppose you are a financial planning executive employed by a major railroad and you have compiled the industry's financing requirements from the past 7 years.

Year	1977	1978	1979	1980	1981	1982	1983
Capital investments (×$100 million)	2.2	2.1	2.4	2.6	2.7	2.9	2.6

The trend equation that describes these data is:

$$\hat{Y} = 2.5 + .11x, \text{ where } 1980 = 0 \text{ and } x \text{ units} = 1 \text{ year}$$

a) Calculate the percent of trend for these data.
b) Calculate the relative cyclical residual for these data.
c) Plot the percent of trend from part *a*.
d) In which year does the largest fluctuation from trend occur, and is it the same for both methods?

14-24 Parallel Breakfast Foods has data on the number of boxes of cereal it has sold in each of the last seven years.

Year	1977	1978	1979	1980	1981	1982	1983
Boxes (×10,000)	20.5	19.7	21.3	24.1	25.2	22.0	22.5

a) Find the linear estimating equation that best describes these data.
b) Calculate the percent of trend for these data.
c) Calculate the relative cyclical residual for these data.
d) In which year does the biggest fluctuation from the trend occur under each measure of cyclical variation? Is this year the same for both measures? Why, or why not?

14-25 Wombat Airlines, an Australian company, has gathered data on the number of passengers who have flown on its planes during each of the past 5 years.

Year	1979	1980	1981	1982	1983
Passengers (in tens of thousands)	3.5	4.2	3.9	3.8	3.6

a) Find the linear estimating equation that best describes these data.
b) Calculate the percent of trend for these data.
c) Calculate the relative cyclical residual for these data.
d) Based on the data and your calculations above, give a one-sentence summary of the position that Wombat Airlines is in.

14-5 SEASONAL VARIATION

Seasonal variation defined

Besides secular trend and cyclical variation, time series also include seasonal variation. Seasonal variation is defined as repetitive and predictable movement around the trend line in *one year or less.* In order to detect seasonal variation, time intervals need to be measured in small units, such as days, weeks, months, or quarters.

We have three main reasons for studying seasonal variation:

Three reasons for studying seasonal variation

1. **We can establish the pattern of past changes.** This gives us a way to compare two time intervals that would otherwise be too dissimilar. If a flight training school wants to know if a slump in business during December is normal, it can examine the seasonal pattern in previous years and find the information it needs.

2. **It is useful to project past patterns into the future.** In the case of long-range decisions, secular trend analysis may be adequate. But for short-run decisions, the ability to predict seasonal fluctuations is often essential. Consider a wholesale food chain that wants to maintain a minimum adequate stock of all items. The ability to predict short-range patterns, such as the demand for turkeys at Thanksgiving, candy at Christmas, or peaches in the summer, is useful to the management of the chain.

3. **Once we have established the seasonal pattern that exists, we can eliminate its effects from the time series.** This adjustment allows us to calculate the cyclical variation that takes place each year. When we eliminate the effect of seasonal variation from a time series, we have *deseasonalized* the time series.

Ratio-to-Moving-Average Method

Using the ratio-to-moving-average method of measuring seasonal variation

In order to measure seasonal variation, we typically use the ratio-to-moving-average method. This technique provides an *index* that describes the degree of seasonal variation. The index is based on a mean of 100, with the degree of seasonality measured by variations away from the base. For example, if we examine the seasonality of canoe rentals at a summer resort, we might find that the spring-quarter index is 142. The value 142 indicates that 142 percent of the average quarterly rentals occur in the spring. If management recorded 2,000 canoe rentals for all of last year, then the average quarterly rental would be 2,000/4 = 500. Since the spring-quarter index is 142, we estimate the number of spring rentals as follows:

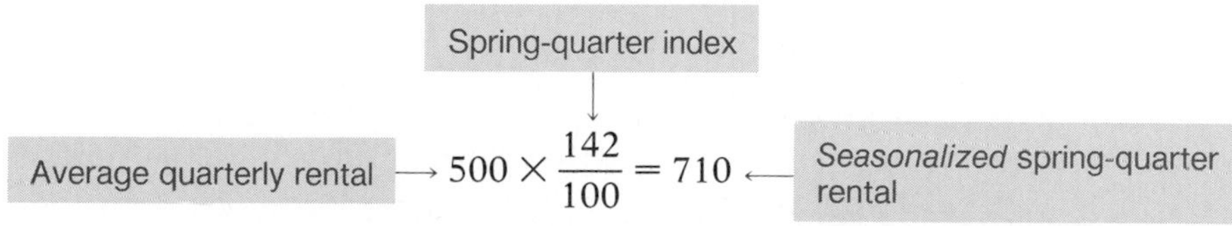

An example of the ratio-to-moving-average method

Our chapter-opening example can illustrate the ratio-to-moving-average method. The resort hotel wanted to establish the seasonal pattern of room demand by its clientele. Hotel management wants to improve customer service and is considering several plans to employ personnel during peak periods to achieve this goal. Table 14-9 contains the quarterly occupancy; that is, the average number of guests during each quarter of the last five years.

TABLE 14-9 Time series for hotel occupancy

	Number of guests per quarter			
YEAR	I	II	III	IV
1979	1,861	2,203	2,415	1,908
1980	1,921	2,343	2,514	1,986
1981	1,834	2,154	2,098	1,799
1982	1,837	2,025	2,304	1,965
1983	2,073	2,414	2,339	1,967

We will refer to Table 14-9 to demonstrate the six steps required to compute a seasonal index.

Step 1: Calculate 4-quarter moving total

1. The first step in computing a seasonal index is to calculate the 4-quarter moving total for the time series. To do this, we total the values for the quarters during the first year, 1979, in Table 14-9: 1,861 + 2,203 + 2,415 + 1,908 = 8,387. A moving total is associated with the middle data point in the set of values from which it was calculated. Since our first total of 8,387 was calculated from four data points, we place it opposite the midpoint of those quarters, so it falls in column 4 of Table 14.10, between the rows for the 1979-II and 1979-III quarters.

We find the next moving total by dropping the 1979-I value, 1,861, and adding the 1980-I value, 1,921. By dropping the first value and adding the fifth, we keep four quarters in the total. The four values added now are 2,203 + 2,415 + 1,908 + 1,921 = 8,447. This total is entered in Table 14-10 directly below the first quarterly total of 8,387. We continue the process of "sliding" the 4-quarter total over the time series until we have included the last value in the series. In this example, it is the 1,967 rooms in the fourth quarter of 1983, the last number in column 3 of Table 14-10. The last entry in the moving total column is 8,793. It is between the rows for the 1983-II and 1983-III quarters, since it was calculated from the data for the four quarters of 1983.

Step 2: Compute the 4-quarter moving average

2. In the second step, we compute the 4-quarter moving average by dividing each of the 4-quarter totals by four. In Table 14-10, we divided the values in column 4 by four, to arrive at the values for column 5.

Step 3: Centering the 4-quarter moving average

3. In the third step, we *center* the 4-quarter moving average. The moving averages in column 5 all fall halfway between the quarters. We would like to have moving averages associated with each quarter. In order to

TABLE 14-10 Calculating the 4-quarter centered moving average

YEAR (1)	QUARTER (2)	OCCUPANCY (3)	STEP 1: 4-QUARTER MOVING TOTAL (4)	STEP 2: 4-QUARTER MOVING AVERAGE (5) = (4) ÷ 4	STEP 3: 4-QUARTER CENTERED MOVING AVERAGE (6)	STEP 4: PERCENTAGE OF ACTUAL TO MOVING-AVERAGE VALUES $(7) = \frac{(3)}{(6)} \times 100$
1979	I	1,861				
	II	2,203				
			8,387	2,096.75		
	III	2,415			2,104.250	114.8
			8,447	2,111.75		
	IV	1,908			2,129.250	89.6
			8,587	2,146.75		
1980	I	1,921			2,159.125	89.0
			8,686	2,171.50		
	II	2,343			2,181.250	107.4
			8,764	2,191.00		
	III	2,514			2,180.125	115.3
			8,677	2,169.25		
	IV	1,986			2,145.625	92.6
			8,488	2,122.00		
1981	I	1,834			2,070.000	88.6
			8,072	2,018.00		
	II	2,154			1,994.625	108.0
			7,885	1,971.25		
	III	2,098			1,971.625	106.4
			7,888	1,972.00		
	IV	1,799			1,955.875	92.0
			7,759	1,939.75		
1982	I	1,837			1,965.500	93.5
			7,965	1,991.25		
	II	2,025			2,012.000	100.6
			8,131	2,032.75		
	III	2,304			2,062.250	111.7
			8,367	2,091.75		
	IV	1,965			2,140.375	91.8
			8,756	2,189.00		
1983	I	2,073			2,193.375	94.5
			8,791	2,197.75		
	II	2,414			2,198.000	109.8
			8,793	2,198.25		
	III	2,339				
	IV	1,967				

center our moving averages, we associate with each quarter the average of the two 4-quarter moving averages falling just above and just below it. For the 1979-III quarter, the resulting **4-quarter centered moving average** is 2104.25; that is, (2096.75 + 2111.75)/2. The other entries in column 6 are calculated the same way. Figure 14-7 illustrates how the moving average has smoothed the peaks and troughs of the original time series. The seasonal and irregular components have been smoothed, and the resulting dotted colored line represents the cyclical and trend components.

Sometimes step 3 can be skipped

Suppose we were working with the admissions data for a hospital emergency room, and we wanted to compute *daily* indices. In steps 1 and 2, we would compute 7-day moving totals and moving averages, **and the moving averages would already be centered** (because the middle of a 7-day period is the fourth of those seven days). In this case, step 3 is unnecessary. Whenever the number of periods for which we want indices is odd (seven days in a week, three shifts in a day), we can skip step 3. However, when the number of periods is even (four quarters, twelve months,

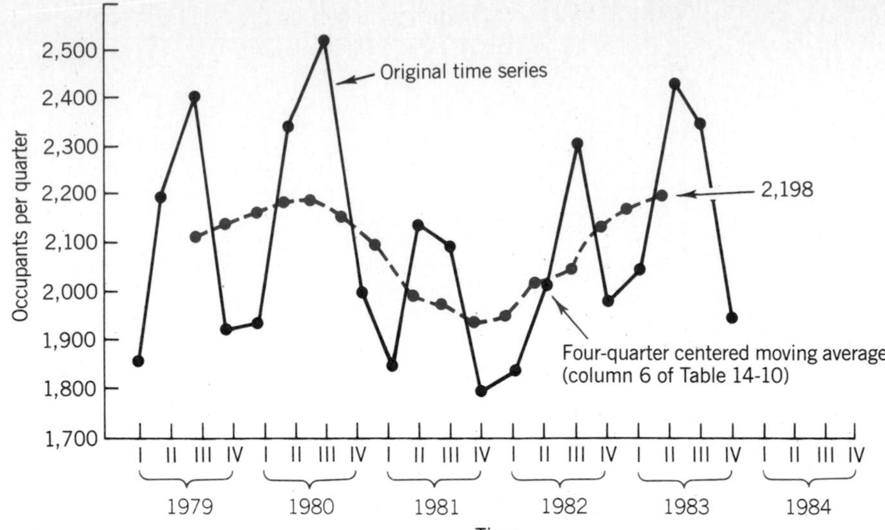

FIGURE 14-7 Using a moving average to smooth the original time series

24 hours), then we must use step 3 to center the moving averages we get with step 2.

Step 4: Calculate percentage of actual value to moving average value

4. Next, we calculate the percentage of the actual value to the moving average value for each quarter in the time series having a 4-quarter moving average entry. This step allows us to recover the seasonal component for the quarters. We determine this percentage by dividing each of the actual quarter values in column 3 of Table 14-10 by the corresponding 4-quarter centered moving-average values in column 6 and then multiplying the result by 100. For example, we find the percentage for 1979-III as follows:

$$\frac{\text{Actual}}{\text{Moving average}} \times 100 = \frac{2{,}415}{2104.250} \times 100$$
$$= 114.8$$

Step 5: Collect answers from step 4 and calculate modified mean

5. To collect all the percentage of actual to moving-average values in column 7 of Table 14-10, arrange them by quarter. Then calculate the "modified mean" for each quarter. The modified mean is calculated by discarding the highest and lowest values for each quarter and averaging the remaining values. In Table 14-11, we present the fifth step and show the process for finding the modified mean.

Reducing extreme cyclical and irregular variations

The seasonal values that we recovered for the quarters in column 7 of Table 14-10 still contain the cyclical and irregular components of variation in the time series. By eliminating the highest and lowest values from each quarter, we *reduce* the extreme cyclical and irregular variations. When we average the remaining values, we further smooth the cyclical and irregular components. Since cyclical and irregular variations tend to be removed by this process, the modified mean is an index of the seasonality component. (Some statisticians prefer to use the median value instead of computing the modified mean to achieve the same outcome.)

TABLE 14-11 Demonstration of step 5 in computing a seasonal index*

YEAR	QUARTER I	QUARTER II	QUARTER III	QUARTER IV
1979	—	—	114.8	~~89.6~~
1980	89.0	107.4	~~115.3~~	~~92.6~~
1981	~~88.6~~	108.0	~~106.4~~	92.0
1982	93.5	~~100.6~~	111.7	91.8
1983	~~94.5~~	~~109.8~~	—	—
	182.5	**215.4**	**226.5**	**183.8**

Modified mean:

Quarter I $\dfrac{182.5}{2} = 91.25$

Quarter II $\dfrac{215.4}{2} = 107.70$

Quarter III $\dfrac{226.5}{2} = 113.25$

Quarter IV $\dfrac{183.8}{2} = 91.90$

Total of indices = **404.1**

* Eliminated values are indicated by a colored slash.

Step 6: Adjust the modified mean

6. The final step, demonstrated in Table 14-12, adjusts the modified mean slightly. Notice that the four indices in Table 14-11 total 404.1. However, the base for an index is 100. Thus, the four quarterly indices should total 400, and their mean should be 100. To correct for this error, we multiply each of the quarterly indices in Table 14-11 by an adjusting constant. This number is found by dividing the desired sum of the indices (400) by the actual sum (404.1). In this case, the result is .9899. Table 14-12 shows that multiplying the indices by the adjusting constant brings the quarterly indices to a total of 400. (Sometimes even after this adjustment, the mean of the seasonal indices is not exactly 100 because of accumulated rounding errors. In this case, it is exactly 100.)

TABLE 14-12 Demonstration of step 6

QUARTER	UNADJUSTED INDICES	×	ADJUSTING CONSTANT	=	SEASONAL INDEX
I	91.25	×	.9899	=	90.3
II	107.70	×	.9899	=	106.6
III	113.25	×	.9899	=	112.1
IV	91.90	×	.9899	=	91.0
			Total of seasonal indices	=	**400.0**

Mean of seasonal indices $= \dfrac{400}{4} = 100.0$

Uses of the Seasonal Index

Deseasonalizing the time series

The ratio-to-moving-average method just explained allows us to identify seasonal variation in a time series. The seasonal indices are used to remove the effects of seasonality from a time series. This is called *deseasonalizing* a time series. Before we can identify either the trend or cyclical components of a time series, we must eliminate seasonal variation. To deseasonalize a time series, we divide each of the actual values in the series by the appropriate seasonal index (expressed as a percent). To demonstrate, we shall deseasonalize the value of the first four quarters in Table 14-9. In Table 14-13, we show the deseasonalizing process using the values for the seasonal indices from Table 14-12. Once the seasonal effect has been eliminated, the deseasonalized values that remain reflect only the trend, cyclical, and irregular components of the time series.

TABLE 14-13 Demonstration of deseasonalizing data

YEAR (1)	QUARTER (2)	ACTUAL OCCUPANCY (3)		$\left(\frac{\text{SEASONAL INDEX}}{100}\right)$ (4)		DESEASONALIZED OCCUPANCY (5) = (3) ÷ (4)
1979	I	1,861	÷	$\left(\frac{90.3}{100}\right)$	=	2,061
1979	II	2,203	÷	$\left(\frac{106.6}{100}\right)$	=	2,067
1979	III	2,415	÷	$\left(\frac{112.1}{100}\right)$	=	2,154
1979	IV	1,908	÷	$\left(\frac{91.0}{100}\right)$	=	2,097

Using seasonality in forecasts

Once we have removed the seasonal variation, we can compute a deseasonalized trend line, which we can then project into the future. Suppose the hotel management in our example estimates from a deseasonalized trend line that the deseasonalized average occupancy for the fourth quarter of the next year will be 2,121. When this prediction has been obtained, management must then take the seasonality into account. To do this, they multiply the deseasonalized predicted average occupancy of 2,121 by the fourth-quarter seasonal index (expressed as a percent) to obtain a seasonalized estimate of 1,930 rooms for the fourth-quarter average occupancy. Here are the calculations:

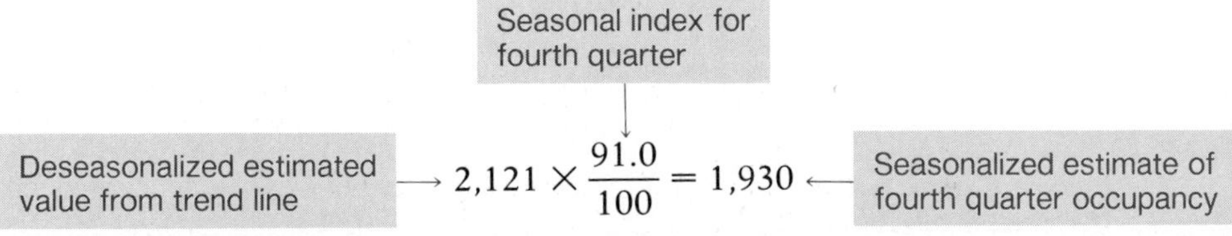

EXERCISES

14-26 The owner of The Pleasure-Glide Boat Company has compiled the following quarterly figures regarding the company's investment in accounts receivable over the last five years (×$1,000):

	SPRING	SUMMER	FALL	WINTER
1979	101	118	90	79
1980	108	123	94	83
1981	109	125	96	86
1982	113	131	102	91
1983	119	140	108	97

a) Calculate a 4-quarter centered moving average.
b) Find the percentage of actual to moving average for each period.
c) Determine the modified seasonal indices and the seasonal indices.

14-27 Bob Buckfelder, personnel manager for an electronic-components production facility, determined the following daily average absentee rates for each quarter over a 4-year period:

	SPRING	SUMMER	FALL	WINTER
1979	6.7	6.1	6.8	7.2
1980	6.9	5.9	6.6	7.0
1981	7.0	6.2	6.7	7.3
1982	7.1	6.3	6.9	7.5

Construct a 4-quarter centered moving average and plot it on a graph along with the original data. What can you conclude from your graph about absenteeism?

14-28 The Federal Reserve released the following percentages of actual to moving average describing the quarterly amount of cash in circulation over a 4-year period:

	SPRING	SUMMER	FALL	WINTER
1980	87	105	86	122
1981	85	108	83	124
1982	84	104	87	125
1983	88	103	88	121

Calculate the seasonal index for each quarter.

14-29 A large manufacturer of automobile springs has determined the following percentages of actual to moving average describing the firm's quarterly cash needs for the last 6 years:

	SPRING	SUMMER	FALL	WINTER
1978	108	128	94	70
1979	112	132	88	68
1980	109	134	84	73
1981	110	131	90	69
1982	108	135	89	68
1983	106	129	93	72

Calculate the seasonal index for each quarter. Comment on how it compares to the indices you calculated for problem 26.

14-30 A university's dean of admissions has compiled the following quarterly enrollment figures for the previous 5 years (×100):

	FALL	WINTER	SPRING	SUMMER
1979	220	203	193	84
1980	235	208	206	76
1981	236	206	209	73
1982	241	215	206	92
1983	239	221	213	115

a) Calculate a 4-quarter centered moving average.
b) Find the percentage of actual to moving average for each period.
c) Determine the modified seasonal indices and the seasonal indices.

14-31 The Ski and Putt Resort, a combination of ski slopes and golf courses, has just recently tabulated its data on the number of customers it has had during each season of the last 5 years. Calculate the seasonal index for each quarter. If 15 people are employed in the summer, what should winter employment be, assuming both sports have equal labor requirements?

	SPRING	SUMMER	FALL	WINTER
1979	150	225	100	250
1980	125	200	125	300
1981	175	250	150	350
1982	150	275	175	300
1983	150	250	150	275

(The table entries are in thousands of customers.)

14-32 McTaggart Soups Incorporated has collected quarterly data on the number of cans of soup (in millions) it has sold during the past 5 years. Calculate the seasonal index for each quarter.

	SPRING	SUMMER	FALL	WINTER
1979	3.5	2.8	3.3	5.1
1980	3.7	2.5	3.2	4.9
1981	3.6	2.9	3.5	5.2
1982	3.2	3.0	3.6	5.3
1983	4.0	3.2	3.9	5.5

If working capital is directly related to sales, by what percentage should it increase between summer and winter?

14-6 IRREGULAR VARIATION

The final component of a time series is irregular variation. After we have eliminated trend, cyclical, and seasonal variations from a time series, we still have an unpredictable factor left. Typically, irregular variation occurs over short intervals and follows a random pattern.

Difficulty of dealing with irregular variation

Because of the unpredictability of irregular variation, we do not attempt to explain it mathematically. However, we can often isolate its causes. New York City's financial crisis of 1975, for example, was an irregular factor that severely depressed the municipal bond market. Not all causes of irregular variation can be identified so easily, however. One factor that allows managers to cope with irregular variation is that over time, these random movements tend to counteract each other.

EXERCISES

14-33 Why don't we project irregular variations into the future?

14-34 Which of the following illustrate irregular variations?

a) An extended drought leading to increasing food prices
b) The effect of snow upon ski slopes
c) A federal tax rebate provision for the purchase of new houses, leading to an increase in housing sales

14-35 Make a list of 5 irregular variations in time series that you deal with as a part of your daily routine.

14-36 What allows management to cope with irregular variation in time series?

14-7 A PROBLEM INVOLVING ALL FOUR COMPONENTS OF A TIME SERIES

For a problem that involves all four components of a time series, we turn to a firm that specializes in producing recreational equipment. To forecast future sales based on an analysis of its past pattern of sales, the firm has collected the information in Table 14-14. Our procedure for describing this time series will consist of three stages:

1. Deseasonalizing the time series
2. Developing the trend line
3. Finding the cyclical variation around the time line

TABLE 14-14 Quarterly sales

	Sales per quarter (×$10,000)			
YEAR	I	II	III	IV
1979	16	21	9	18
1980	15	20	10	18
1981	17	24	13	22
1982	17	25	11	21
1983	18	26	14	25

Step 1: Computing seasonal indices

Since the data are available on a quarterly basis, we must first deseasonalize the time series. The steps to do this are shown in Tables 14-15 and 14-16. These steps are the same as those originally introduced in section 5 of this chapter.

In Table 14-15, we have tabulated the first four steps in computing the seasonal index. In Table 14-16, we complete the process.

Finding the deseasonalized values

Once we have computed the quarterly seasonal indices, we can find the deseasonalized values of the time series by dividing the actual sales (in Table 14-14) by the seasonal indices. Table 14-17 shows the calculation of the deseasonalized time series values.

Step 2: Developing the trend line using the least squares method

The second step in describing the components of the time series is to develop the trend line. We accomplish this by applying the least squares method to the deseasonalized time series (after we have translated the time variable). Table 14-18 presents the calculations to identify the trend component (see page 693).

TABLE 14-15 Calculation of the first 4 steps to compute the seasonal index

YEAR	QUARTER	ACTUAL SALES	STEP 1 4-QUARTER MOVING TOTAL	STEP 2 4-QUARTER MOVING AVERAGE	STEP 3 4-QUARTER CENTERED MOVING AVERAGE	STEP 4 PERCENTAGE OF ACTUAL TO MOVING AVERAGE
(1)	(2)	(3)	(4)	$(5) = \frac{(4)}{4}$	(6)	$(7) = \frac{(3)}{(6)} \times 100$
1979	I	16				
	II	21				
			64	16.00		
	III	9			15.825	56.7
			63	15.75		
	IV	18			15.625	115.2
			62	15.50		
1980	I	15			15.625	96.0
			63	15.75		
	II	20			15.750	127.0
			63	15.75		
	III	10			16.000	62.5
			65	16.25		
	IV	18			16.750	107.5
			69	17.25		
1981	I	17			17.625	96.5
			72	18.00		
	II	24			18.500	129.7
			76	19.00		
	III	13			19.000	68.4
			76	19.00		
	IV	22			19.125	115.0
			77	19.25		
1982	I	17			19.000	89.5
			75	18.75		
	II	25			18.625	134.2
			74	18.50		
	III	11			18.625	59.1
			75	18.75		
	IV	21			18.875	111.3
			76	19.00		
1983	I	18			19.375	92.9
			79	19.75		
	II	26			20.250	128.4
			83	20.75		
	III	14				
	IV	25				

TABLE 14-16 Steps 5 and 6 in computing the seasonal index

Step 5*

YEAR	I	II	III	IV
1979	—	—	~~56.7~~	~~115.2~~
1980	96.0	~~127.0~~	62.5	~~107.5~~
1981	~~96.5~~	129.7	~~68.4~~	115.0
1982	~~89.5~~	~~134.2~~	59.1	111.3
1983	92.9	128.4	—	—
Modified sum =	**188.9**	**258.1**	**121.6**	**226.3**

Modified mean: Quarter I $\frac{188.9}{2} = 94.45$

II $\frac{258.1}{2} = 129.05$

III $\frac{121.6}{2} = 60.80$

IV $\frac{226.3}{2} = 113.15$

397.45

* Arrange percentages from column 7, Table 14-15, by quarter and find the modified mean.

Step 6†

$$\text{Adjusting factor} = \frac{400}{397.45} = 1.0064$$

QUARTER	INDICES	×	ADJUSTING FACTOR	=	SEASONAL INDICES
I	94.45	×	1.0064	=	95.1
II	129.05	×	1.0064	=	129.9
III	60.80	×	1.0064	=	61.2
IV	113.15	×	1.0064	=	113.9
			Sum of seasonal indices	=	**400.1**

† Correcting the indices in step 5.

With the values from Table 14-18, we can now find the equation for the trend. From Equations 14-3 and 14-4 we find the slope and Y-intercept for the trend line as follows:

$$b = \frac{\Sigma xY}{\Sigma x^2} \qquad \textbf{[14-3]}$$

$$= \frac{420.3}{2{,}660}$$

$$= .16$$

$$a = \overline{Y} \qquad \textbf{[14-4]}$$

$$= 18.0$$

TABLE 14-17 Calculation of deseasonalized time series values

YEAR (1)	QUARTER (2)	ACTUAL SALES (3)	SEASONAL INDEX / 100 (4)	DESEASONALIZED SALES (5) = (3) ÷ (4)
1979	I	16	.951	16.8
	II	21	1.299	16.2
	III	9	.612	14.7
	IV	18	1.139	15.8
1980	I	15	.951	15.8
	II	20	1.299	15.4
	III	10	.612	16.3
	IV	18	1.139	15.8
1981	I	17	.951	17.9
	II	24	1.299	18.5
	III	13	.612	21.2
	IV	22	1.139	19.3
1982	I	17	.951	17.9
	II	25	1.299	19.2
	III	11	.612	18.0
	IV	21	1.139	18.4
1983	I	18	.951	18.9
	II	26	1.299	20.0
	III	14	.612	22.9
	IV	25	1.139	21.9

The appropriate trend line is described using the straight-line equation (Equation 11-3), with X replaced by x:

$$\hat{Y} = a + bx \qquad [11\text{-}3]$$
$$= 18 + .16x$$

Step 3: Finding the cyclical variation

We have now identified the seasonal and trend components of the time series. Next we find the cyclical variation around the trend line. This component is identified by measuring deseasonalized variation around the trend line. In this problem, we will calculate cyclical variation in Table 14-19, using the residual method. (See page 694.)

Assumptions about irregular variation

If we assume that irregular variation is generally short-term and relatively insignificant, we have completely described the time series in this problem using the trend, cyclical, and seasonal components. Figure 14-8 (on page 695) illustrates the original time series, its moving average (containing both the trend and cyclical components), and the trend line.

Predicting using time series

Now suppose that the management of the recreation company we have been using as an example wants to estimate the sales volume for the third quarter of 1984. What should the management do?

Step 1: Determining the deseasonalized value for sales for the period desired

1. They have to determine the deseasonalized value for sales in the third quarter of 1984 by using the trend equation, $\hat{Y} = 18 + .16x$. This

TABLE 14-18 Identifying the trend component

YEAR (1)	QUARTER (2)	Y DESEASONALIZED SALES (COLUMN 5 OF TABLE 14-17) (× \$10,000) (3)	($\frac{1}{2}x$) TRANSLATING OR CODING THE TIME VARIABLE (4)	x (5) = (4) × 2	xY (6) = (5) × (3)	x^2 (7) = $(5)^2$
1979	I	16.8	−9½	−19	−319.2	361
	II	16.2	−8½	−17	−275.4	289
	III	14.7	−7½	−15	−220.5	225
	IV	15.8	−6½	−13	−205.4	169
1980	I	15.8	−5½	−11	−173.8	121
	II	15.4	−4½	− 9	−138.6	81
	III	16.3	−3½	− 7	−114.1	49
	IV	15.8	−2½	− 5	− 79.0	25
1981	I	17.9	−1½	− 3	− 53.7	9
	II	18.5	− ½	− 1	− 18.5	1
Mean →			0*			
	III	21.2	½	1	21.2	1
	IV	19.3	1½	3	57.9	9
1982	I	17.9	2½	5	89.5	25
	II	19.2	3½	7	134.4	49
	III	18.0	4½	9	162.0	81
	IV	18.4	5½	11	202.4	121
1983	I	18.9	6½	13	245.7	169
	II	20.0	7½	15	300.0	225
	III	22.9	8½	17	389.3	289
	IV	21.9	9½	19	416.1	361
		$\Sigma Y =$ **360.9**			$\Sigma xY =$ **420.5**	$\Sigma x^2 =$ **2,660**

$$\bar{Y} = \frac{\Sigma Y}{n} = \frac{360.9}{20} = 18.0$$

* We assign the mean of 0 to the middle of the data (1981-II½) and then measure the translated time, x, by ½ quarters because we have an even number of periods.

requires them to code the time, 1984-III. That quarter (1984-III) is three quarters past 1983-IV, which, we see in Table 14-18, has a coded time value of 19. Adding 2 for each quarter, they find $x = 19 + 2(3) = 25$. Substituting this value ($x = 25$) into the trend equation produces the following result:

$$\begin{aligned} \hat{Y} &= a + bx \qquad\qquad [11\text{-}3] \\ &= 18 + .16(25) \\ &= 18 + 4 \\ &= 22 \end{aligned}$$

Thus, the deseasonalized sales estimate for 1984-III is \$220,000. This point is shown on the trend line in Fig. 14-8.

TABLE 14-19 Identifying the cyclical variation

YEAR (1)	QUARTER (2)	Y DESESEASONALIZED SALES (COLUMN 5, TABLE 14-17) (3)	$a + bx = \hat{Y}$* (4)	$\frac{Y}{\hat{Y}} \times 100$ PERCENT OF TREND $(5) = \frac{(3)}{(4)} \times 100$
1979	I	16.8	$18 + .16(-19) = 14.96$	112.3
	II	16.2	$18 + .16(-17) = 15.28$	106.0
	III	14.7	$18 + .16(-15) = 15.60$	94.2
	IV	15.8	$18 + .16(-13) = 15.92$	99.2
1980	I	15.8	$18 + .16(-11) = 16.24$	97.3
	II	15.4	$18 + .16(-9) = 16.56$	93.0
	III	16.3	$18 + .16(-7) = 16.88$	96.6
	IV	15.8	$18 + .16(-5) = 17.20$	91.9
1981	I	17.9	$18 + .16(-3) = 17.52$	102.2
	II	18.5	$18 + .16(-1) = 17.84$	103.7
	III	21.2	$18 + .16(1) = 18.16$	116.7
	IV	19.3	$18 + .16(3) = 18.48$	104.4
1982	I	17.9	$18 + .16(5) = 18.80$	95.2
	II	19.2	$18 + .16(7) = 19.12$	100.4
	III	18.0	$18 + .16(9) = 19.44$	92.6
	IV	18.4	$18 + .16(11) = 19.76$	93.1
1983	I	18.9	$18 + .16(13) = 20.08$	94.1
	II	20.0	$18 + .16(15) = 20.40$	98.0
	III	22.9	$18 + .16(17) = 20.72$	110.5
	IV	21.9	$18 + .16(19) = 21.04$	104.1

* The appropriate value for x in this equation is obtained from column 5 of Table 14-18.

Step 2: seasonalizing the initial estimate

2. Now management must seasonalize this estimate by multiplying it by the third-quarter seasonal index, expressed as a percent:

Seasonal index for quarter III from step 5 of Table 14-16

Trend estimate from Equation 11-3 → $22 \times \frac{61.2}{100} = 13.5$ ← Seasonalized estimate

Caution in using the forecast

On the basis of this analysis, the firm estimates that sales for 1984-III will be $135,000. We must stress, however, that this value is only an estimate and does not take into account the cyclical and irregular components. As we noted earlier, the irregular variation cannot be predicted mathematically. Also, remember that our earlier treatment of cyclical variation was descriptive of past behavior and not predictive of future behavior.

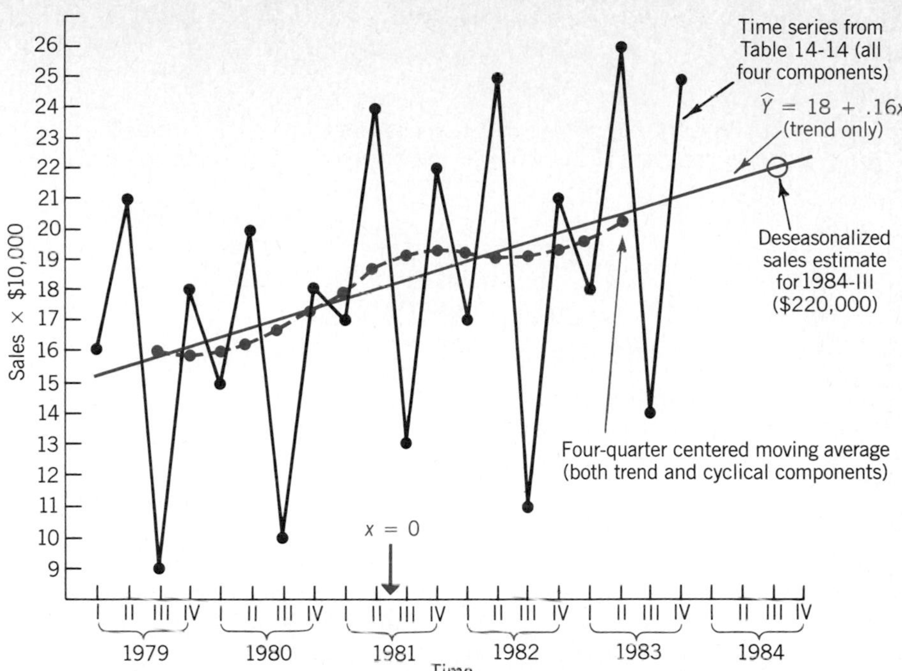

FIGURE 14-8
Time series, trend line, and 4-quarter centered moving average for quarterly sales data in Table 14-14

EXERCISES

14-37 A state commission designed to monitor energy consumption assembled the following seasonal data regarding natural gas consumption, in millions of cubic feet:

	WINTER	SPRING	SUMMER	FALL
1980	291	246	231	280
1981	298	251	228	289
1982	301	258	239	293
1983	303	264	240	297

a) Determine the seasonal indices and deseasonalize these data (using a 4-quarter centered moving average).
b) Calculate the least squares line that best describes these data.
c) Identify the cyclical variation in these data by the relative cyclical residual method.
d) Plot the original data, the deseasonalized data, and the trend.

14-38 The following data describe the marketing performance of a regional beer producer:

YEAR	SALES BY QUARTER (×\$100,000) I	II	III	IV
1979	19	24	38	25
1980	21	28	44	23
1981	23	31	41	23
1982	24	35	48	21

a) Calculate the seasonal indices for these data. (Use a 4-quarter centered moving average.)
b) Deseasonalize these data using the indices from part *a*.

14-39 For problem 38:
a) Find the least squares line that best describes the trend in deseasonalized beer sales.
b) Identify the cyclical component in this time series by computing the percent of trend.

14-8 TIME SERIES ANALYSIS IN FORECASTING

In this chapter, we have examined all four components of a time series. We have described the process of projecting past trend and seasonal variation into the future, while taking into consideration the inherent inaccuracies of this analysis. In addition, we noted that although the irregular and cyclical components do affect the future, they are erratic and difficult to use in forecasting.

Recognizing limitations of time series analysis

We must realize that the mechanical approach of time series analysis is subject to considerable error and change. It is necessary for management to combine these simple procedures with knowledge of other factors in order to develop workable forecasts. Analysts are constantly revising, updating, and discarding their forecasts. If we wish to cope successfully with the future, we must do the same.

When using the procedures described in this chapter, we should pay attention particularly to the two following problems:

1. In forecasting, we project past trend and seasonal variation into the future. We must ask, "How regular and lasting were the past trends? What are the chances that these patterns are changing?"

2. How accurate are the historical data we use in series analysis? If a company has changed from a FIFO (first-in, first-out) to a LIFO (last-in, first-out) inventory accounting system in a period during the time under consideration, the data (such as quarterly profits) before and after the change are not comparable and not very useful for forecasting.

EXERCISES

14-40 List 4 errors that can affect forecasting with time series.

14-41 When using time series to predict the future, what assurances do we need about the historical data on which our forecasts are based?

14-42 What problems would you see developing if we used past college enrollments to predict future college enrollments?

14-43 How would forecasts using time series analysis handle things such as:
a) Changes in the federal tax laws?
b) Changes in accounting systems?
c) Rapid rises in the rate of inflation?
d) Changes in the birthrate?

14-9 TERMS INTRODUCED IN CHAPTER 14

CODING A method of converting traditional measures of time to a form that simplifies computation (often called translating).

CYCLICAL FLUCTUATION A type of variation in time series, in which the value of the variable fluctuates above and below a secular trend line.

DESEASONALIZATION A statistical process used to remove the effects of seasonality from a time series.

IRREGULAR VARIATION A condition in time series when the value of a variable is completely unpredictable.

MODIFIED MEAN A statistical method used in time series. Discards the highest and lowest values when computing a mean.

RATIO-TO-MOVING-AVERAGE METHOD A statistical method used to measure seasonal variation. Employs an index describing the degree of that variation.

RELATIVE CYCLICAL RESIDUAL A measure of cyclical variation, it uses the percentage deviation from the trend for each value in the series.

RESIDUAL METHOD A method of describing the cyclical component of a time series. It assumes that most of the variation in the series not explained by the secular trend is cyclical variation.

SEASONAL VARIATION Patterns of change in a time series within a year, patterns that tend to be repeated from year to year.

SECOND-DEGREE EQUATION A mathematical form used to describe a parabolic curve that may be used in time series analysis.

SECULAR TREND A type of variation in time series, the value of the variable tending to increase or decrease over a long period of time.

TIME SERIES Information accumulated at regular intervals and the statistical methods used to determine patterns in such data.

14-10 EQUATIONS INTRODUCED IN CHAPTER 14

[14-1]

$$b = \frac{\Sigma XY - n\overline{X}\,\overline{Y}}{\Sigma X^2 - n\overline{X}^2}$$ *p. 666*

This formula, originally introduced in Chapter 11 as Equation 11-4, enables us to calculate the *slope of the best-fitting regression line* for any two-variable set of data points. The symbols $\overline{X}$ and $\overline{Y}$ represent the means of the value of the independent variable and dependent variable respectively; n represents the number of data points with which we are fitting the line.

[14-2] $$a = \bar{Y} - b\bar{X}$$ *p. 666*

We met this formula as Equation 11-5. It enables us to compute the *Y-intercept of the best-fitting regression line* for any 2-variable set of data points.

[14-3] $$b = \frac{\Sigma xY}{\Sigma x^2}$$ *p. 668*

When the individual years (X) are changed to coded time values (x) by subtracting out the mean ($x = X - \bar{X}$), Equation 14-1 for the slope of the trend line is simplified and becomes Equation 14-3.

[14-4] $$a = \bar{Y}$$ *p. 668*

In a similar fashion, using coded time values also allows us to simplify Equation 14-2 for the intercept of the trend line.

[14-5] $$\hat{Y} = a + bx + cx^2$$ *p. 670*

Sometimes we wish to fit a trend with a parabolic (or second-degree) curve instead of a straight line ($\hat{Y} = a + bx$). The general form for a fitted second-degree curve is obtained by including the second-degree term (cx^2) in the equation for $\hat{Y}$.

[14-6] $$\Sigma Y = an + c\Sigma x^2$$ *p. 671*

[14-7] $$\Sigma x^2 Y = a\Sigma x^2 + c\Sigma x^4$$ *p. 671*

In order to find the least squares second-degree fitted curve, we must solve Equations 14-6 and 14-7 simultaneously for the values of a and c. The value for b is obtained from Equation 14-3.

[14-8] $$\text{Percent of trend} = \frac{Y}{\hat{Y}} \times 100$$ *p. 676*

We can measure cyclical variation as a *percent of trend* by dividing the actual value (Y) by the trend value ($\hat{Y}$) and then multiplying by 100.

[14-9] $$\text{Relative cyclical residual} = \frac{Y - \hat{Y}}{\hat{Y}} \times 100$$ *p. 678*

Another measure of cyclical variation is the *relative cyclical residual,* obtained by dividing the deviation from the trend ($Y - \hat{Y}$) by the trend value, and multiplying the result by 100. The relative cyclical residual can easily be obtained by subtracting 100 from the percent of trend.

14-11 CHAPTER REVIEW EXERCISES

14-44 The owner of an air-conditioning and heating company is examining data regarding quarterly revenue. He wants to determine the trend in his business (×$1,000).

	SPRING	SUMMER	FALL	WINTER
1980	30	31	40	42
1981	28	34	43	46
1982	33	36	44	48
1983	34	39	45	50

a) Calculate the seasonal indices for these data (use a 4-quarter centered moving average).
b) Deseasonalize these data, using the indices from part *a*.
c) Find the least squares line that best describes these data.

14-45 Wheeler Airline, a regional carrier, has estimated the number of passengers to be 595,000 (deseasonalized) for the month of December. How many passengers should the company anticipate if the December seasonal index is 128?

14-46 An EPA research group has measured the level of mercury contamination in the ocean at a certain point off the East Coast. The following percentages of mercury were found in the water:

	JAN.	FEB.	MAR.	APR.	MAY	JUNE	JULY	AUG.	SEPT.	OCT.	NOV.	DEC.
1981	4	.6	.9	.7	.8	.6	.7	.5	.5	.6	.3	.4
1982	.5	.8	.8	.9	.6	.7	.8	.6	.5	.5	.4	.3
1983	.3	.5	.7	.8	.8	.6	.9	.7	.6	.5	.4	.4

Construct a 4-month centered moving average, and plot it on a graph along with the original data.

14-47 A production manager for a Canadian paper mill has accumulated the following information describing the number of pounds processed quarterly (× 1,000,000 pounds):

	WINTER	SPRING	SUMMER	FALL
1980	2.6	4.1	4.8	3.2
1981	2.9	4.5	5.0	3.4
1982	2.8	4.9	5.5	3.3
1983	3.1	5.1	5.6	3.6

a) Calculate the seasonal indices for these data (percentage of actual to centered moving average).
b) Deseasonalize these data, using the seasonal indices from part *a*.
c) Find the least squares line that best describes these data.
d) Estimate the number of pounds that will be processed during the spring of 1984.

14-48 The number of farm loans approved by a small rural bank during the 7 years from 1977 to 1983 were 975, 1,364, 1,221, 1,575, 1,776, 1,853, and 2,094, respectively.
a) Develop the linear estimating equation that best describes these data.
b) How many farm loans can the bank expect to make in 1984?

14-49 The president of a ski-equipment wholesale house assembled the following information regarding his quarterly revenue (×$10,000).

	I	II	III	IV
1980	70.2	58.4	52.7	77.9
1981	70.4	59.8	54.2	80.3
1982	72.1	57.5	52.0	83.5
1983	73.6	63.5	57.9	88.2

a) Calculate the seasonal indices for these data (percentage of actual to centered moving average).
b) Deseasonalize these data, using the seasonal indices from part *a*.
c) Find the least squares line that best describes these data.
d) Estimate the revenue for the first quarter of 1984.

14-50 John Barry, a hospital administrator planning for a new emergency-room facility, has examined the number of patients who have visited the present facility during each of the last six years.

Year	1978	1979	1980	1981	1982	1983
Number of patients (×100)	398	436	458	513	569	631

a) Find the linear equation that describes the trend in the number of patients visiting the emergency room.
b) Estimate for him the number of patients the hospital's emergency room should be prepared to accommodate in 1985.

14-51 An assistant undersecretary in the U.S. Commerce Department has the following data describing the value of grain exported during the last 15 quarters (in billions):

	I	II	III	IV
1980	1	3	6	4
1981	2	2	7	5
1982	2	4	8	5
1983	1	3	8	6

a) Determine the seasonal indices and deseasonalize these data (using a 4-quarter centered moving average).
b) Calculate the least squares line that best describes these data.
c) Identify the cyclical variation in these data by the relative cyclical residual method.
d) Plot the original data, the deseasonalized data, and the trend.

14-52 Richie Bell's College Bicycle Shop has determined from a previous trend analysis that spring sales should be 156 bicycles (deseasonalized). If the spring seasonal index is 140, how many bicycles should the shop sell this spring?

14-53 An Ohio manufacturer of heavy earth-moving equipment has recorded the following sales records over the past 20 years (in millions of dollars): 25, 28, 27, 29, 31, 29, 32, 34, 30, 32, 29, 26, 28, 33, 32, 36, 35, 37, 39, and 35. Construct a 4-year centered moving average of sales and plot it on a graph along with the original data.

14-54 The publisher of *Track and Road Magazine* is interested in determining the rate at which the number of subscribers has been increasing. The subscription information from the last 8 years is presented below:

Year	1976	1977	1978	1979	1980	1981	1982	1983
Number of subscribers (×1,000,000)	12	11	19	17	19	18	20	23

a) Develop the linear estimating equation that describes the trend of subscriptions.
b) How many subscriptions should the firm anticipate for 1985?

14-55 As part of an investigation being done by a federal agency into the psychology of criminal activity, a survey of the number of homicides and assaults over the course of a year produced the following results:

Season	Spring	Summer	Fall	Winter
Number of homicides and assaults	36,000	58,000	42,000	26,000

a) If the corresponding seasonal indices are 94, 125, 96, and 85, respectively, what are the deseasonalized values for each season?
b) What is the meaning of the seasonal index of 125 for the summer season?

14-12 CHAPTER CONCEPTS TEST

Answers are in the back of the book.

T F 1. Time series analysis is used to detect patterns of change in statistical information over regular intervals of time.

T F 2. Secular trends represent the long-term direction of a time series.

T F 3. When coding time values, we subtract from each value the smallest time value in the series; hence, the code of the smallest value is zero.

T F 4. When using the least squares method to determine a second-degree equation of best fit, the values of 4 numerical constants must be determined.

T F 5. Time series analysis helps us to analyze past trends, but it cannot aid us in future uncertainties.

T F 6. When we are predicting far into the future, a second-degree equation usually gives more accurate predictions than a linear equation.

T F 7. When using the residual method, we assume that the cyclical component explains most of the variation left unexplained by the trend component.

T F 8. The relative cyclical residual can be computed for an entry in a time series by subtracting 10 from the percent of trend for that entry.

T F 9. The repetitive movement around a trend line in a 2-year period is best described as seasonal.

T F 10. Once seasonal indices are computed for a time series, the series can be deseasonalized so that only the trend component remains.

T F 11. The percent of trend should not be used for predicting future cyclical variations.

T F 12. Over time, random movements tend to counteract one another in irregular variation in a time series.

T F 13. Before percent of trend can be calculated, a trend line (graph of $\hat{Y}$) must first be calculated.

T F 14. If a time series contains an odd number of elements, then the coding for some of the entries will be in half-units.

T F 15. To be considered a time series, a group of statistical information must have been accumulated at *regular* intervals.

T F 16. Of the four types of variation, cyclical is the most difficult to predict.

T F 17. Seasonal variation is repetitive and predictable variation around the trend line within a year.

18. A time series of annual data can contain which of the following components?
a) Secular trend
b) Cyclical fluctuation
c) Seasonal variation
d) All of these
e) a and b but not c

19. Suppose you were considering a time series of data for the quarters of 1978 and 1979. The third quarter of 1979 would be coded as:
a) 2 b) 3 c) 5 d) 6

20. Suppose that a particular time series should be fitted with a parabolic curve. The general form for this second-degree equation is $\hat{Y} = a + bx + cx^2$. What do the x's represent in this formula?
a) Coded values of the time variables
b) A numerical constant that is determined by a formula
c) Estimates of the dependent variable
d) None of these

21. Assume that a time series with annual data for the years 1969–1977 is described well by the second-degree equation $\hat{Y} = 5 + 3x + 9x^2$. Based only upon this secular trend, what is the forecast value for 1978?
a) 161 b) 245 c) 347 d) 293.75 e) 200.75

22. Suppose that the linear equation $\hat{Y} = 10 + 3x$ describes well an annual time series for 1975–1981. If the actual value of Y for 1978 is 8, what is the percent of trend for 1978?
a) 125% b) 112.5% c) 90% d) 80%

23. A time series for the years 1970–1981 had the following relative cyclical residuals, in chronological order: −1%, −2%, 1%, 2%, −1%, −2%, 1%, 2%, −1%, −2%, 1%, 2%. The relative cyclical residual for 1982 should be:
a) 3% c) −2%
b) −1% d) Cannot be determined from information given

24. Assume that you have been given quarterly sales data for a 5-year period. To use the ratio-to-moving-average method of computing a seasonal index, your first step would be:
a) Compute the 4-quarter moving average.
b) Discard highest and lowest values for each quarter.
c) Calculate the 4-quarter moving total.
d) None of these.

Questions 25 through 27 deal with a seasonal index being computed, using the ratio-to-moving-average method for quarterly data from 1976–1980. The percentages of actual to moving average for the third quarter of each year are:
1976: 109.0; 1977: 112.8; 1978: 110.0; 1979: 108.0; 1980: 104.6

25. What is the *unadjusted* index for the third quarter?
a) 108.88 b) 109.0 c) 110.23 d) 110.96 e) None of these

26. Assume that the total of the unadjusted indices for the four quarters is 404.04. If the unadjusted index for the first quarter is 97.0, what is the adjusted seasonal index for the first quarter?
a) 96.03 d) 99.00
b) 97.98 e) Cannot be determined from information given
c) 24.01

27. The adjusted seasonal index for the fourth quarter is 95.0. If the deseasonalized trend line that was calculated to estimate quarterly sales is $\hat{Y} = 400 + 9x$, what would be the seasonalized sales estimate for the fourth quarter of 1981?
a) 499.7 b) 643.0 c) 610.85 d) 676.8

28. If a time series has an even number of years, and we use coding, then each coded interval is equal to:
a) A year d) Six months
b) Two years e) None of these
c) A month

29. A method used to deal with cyclical variation when the cyclical component does not explain most of the variation left unexplained by the trend component is:

a) Spearman analysis
b) Specific analysis
c) Second-degree analysis
d) Relative cyclical residual
e) All of these
f) None of these

30. Dividing each actual value in a time series by the corresponding trend value, and multiplying by 100, gives the ____________.
31. Repetitive and predictable movement around the trend line in one year or less is ____________ variation.
32. ____________ variation in time series is characterized by unpredictable, random movement and usually occurs over short intervals.
33. ____________ variation is the time series component that oscillates above and below the trend line for periods longer than one year.
34. Using seasonal indices to remove effects of seasonality from a time series is known as ____________ the time series.
35. The first step in computing a seasonal index is to calculate the ____________.

14-13 CONCEPTUAL CASE (Northern White Metals Company)

"I just wanted to let you know we appreciated your help on that trucking decision," Dick said into the phone.

"Well, thank you, but it was nothing," replied Jody. "How did everything turn out?"

"Turned out fine," Dick answered. "Don Wills and Dave Lillich negotiated a great deal for us. They're a shrewd pair, even for flashy New York lawyers," he chuckled.

"So I hear," Jody replied. "By the way, what did you think of that sales analysis Sarah ran for you? Was it helpful?"

Dick replied that it was indeed helpful and that he especially appreciated the brief explanatory discourse on regression analysis that accompanied it. He further noted that he had nearly completed Northern's 1984 sales plan and was about to begin work formulating his general five-year business plan. This would be submitted to Segue corporate management and would include anticipated new equipment requirements, cost estimates, and financing needs as well as long-run sales projections.

"Which brings to mind a question," he continued. "I think it's safe to state that high-tech applications sales, which we're still rather new in, will continue to increase at the present rate. It's a booming business, and I don't see it fluctuating like building products sales do. The point is, I'm having trouble trying to forecast sales in construction-related products, in spite of our long history of selling to this industry. You've seen the data, Jody; what do you think?" Dick asked.

"I see your problem," Jody replied, thinking. "I agree with your conclusions about high-tech products, at least from what I've seen so far. I'll need some more information on Northern's past building-products sales, but I think we can help you out."

"I also need some idea about trends in aluminum raw material prices," Dick added. "I think they tend to move with the business cycle, a lot like construction does, but I need a better idea of where they might be heading so I can forecast production costs, too."

"No problem, Dick," Jody said reassuringly. "Look forward to hearing from you."

Dick needs some assistance in analyzing historical data to help him make inferences about the future—that is, to aid him in developing a workable five-year plan. What information does he have to provide to Jody, and how will she analyze this information to help Dick formulate his projections? What words of advice about interpreting the analysis should she pass to Dick so he can make the best use of it?

14-14 COMPUTER DATA BASE EXERCISE

"Hey, Frank," said Laurel. "Look what Fred put on my desk—leftover doughnuts from the sales meeting. He's not such a bad guy, just a little reactionary."

"I definitely detect a change of heart over the past couple of weeks. We need to reinforce him by doing something nice."

"You know, Nick was mentioning the other day that we might need a new factory in five years. We could do a time series analysis on ten years of sales and project sales for him and make a pretty graph of deseasonalized sales growth for Fred at the same time. He could put it on his wall and give copies to the sales force."

"Good idea."

PROBLEM

1. Do a time series analysis of Rough Rider sales over 10 years. Deseasonalize sales, using the ratio-to-moving-average method. (Use a 12-month centered moving average.) Then find the least squares line that best describes the deseasonalized data.

YEAR	MONTHLY SALES (1969–1978)											
1969	1,490	1,597	908	437	150	112	87	161	498	1,433	1,793	3,195
1970	1.543	1,529	1,153	503	205	132	89	189	636	1,185	2,358	3,258
1971	2,184	2,221	1,167	522	184	141	106	201	652	1,543	2,434	3,652
1972	2,279	2,256	1,289	649	241	170	115	207	815	1,520	2,825	4,323
1973	2,583	2,303	1,388	772	228	169	131	234	853	1,653	2,841	4,422
1974	2,911	2,786	1,571	770	275	188	152	257	938	1,694	3,269	4,597
1975	2,972	2,841	1,674	947	296	187	160	288	1,015	2,348	3,790	5.816
1976	3,579	3,213	1,978	951	332	212	162	314	993	2,255	3,659	5,909
1977	3,681	3,365	2,265	1,043	336	236	177	322	1,044	2,670	4,405	6,437
1978	3,899	3,217	2,148	1,134	348	256	180	321	1,152	2,681	4,611	6,649

14-15 FLOW CHART

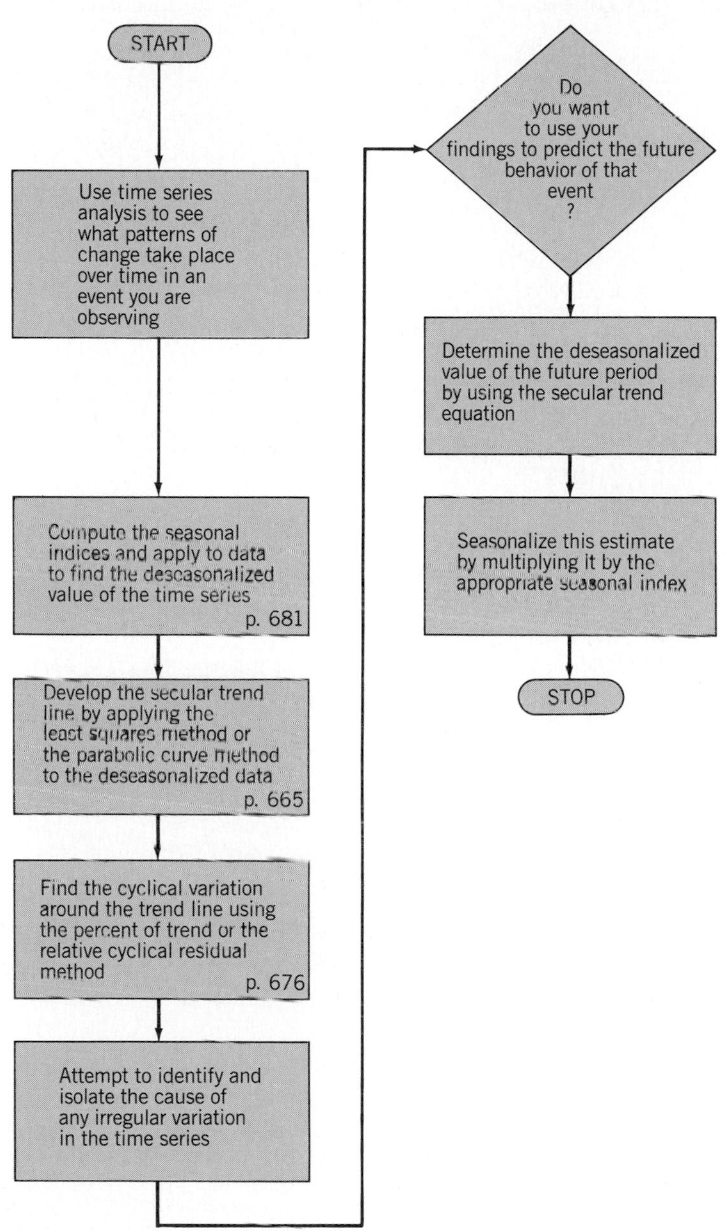

START
Use time series analysis to see what patterns of change take place over time in an event you are observing
Compute the seasonal indices and apply to data to find the deseasonalized value of the time series
p. 681
Develop the secular trend line by applying the least squares method or the parabolic curve method to the deseasonalized data
p. 665
Find the cyclical variation around the trend line using the percent of trend or the relative cyclical residual method
p. 676
Attempt to identify and isolate the cause of any irregular variation in the time series
Do you want to use your findings to predict the future behavior of that event ?
Determine the deseasonalized value of the future period by using the secular trend equation
Seasonalize this estimate by multiplying it by the appropriate seasonal index
STOP

CHAPTER 15

INDEX NUMBERS

1. DEFINING AN INDEX NUMBER, 708
2. UNWEIGHTED AGGREGATES INDEX, 712
3. WEIGHTED AGGREGATES INDEX, 715
4. AVERAGE OF RELATIVES METHODS, 722
5. QUANTITY AND VALUE INDICES, 728
6. ISSUES IN CONSTRUCTING AN INDEX NUMBER, 732
7. TERMS, 734
8. EQUATIONS, 735
9. REVIEW EXERCISES, 736
10. CONCEPTS TEST, 739
11. CONCEPTUAL CASE, 742
12. COMPUTER DATA BASE EXERCISES, 743
13. FLOW CHART, 745

OBJECTIVES: *Index numbers* are shorthand for describing economic variables. Suppose you hear that the cost-of-living index is now 120 when compared with the base year of 1980. This number is a statistician's quick way of saying that the cost of living has risen 20 percent since 1980. We can use index numbers also to measure changes in productivity, unemployment, and wage rates.

Precision Metal Products manufactures high-quality fabrications for use in the production of farm machinery. The company's three principal materials are coal, iron ore, and nickel ore. Management has the following data showing prices of these materials in 1963 and 1983 and quantity data for 1976, a year when purchasing patterns were characteristic of the entire 20-year period.

RAW MATERIAL	QTY. USED 1976 (000 TONS)	PRICE/TON 1963	PRICE/TON 1983
Coal	158	$ 7.56	$19.50
Iron ore	12	9.20	21.40
Nickel ore	5	12.30	36.10

Management would like help in constructing some measure of the change in material prices in the 20-year period. Using the methods in this chapter, we can supply them with such a figure to use in their planning.

Why use an index number?

At some time, everyone faces the question of how much something has changed over a period of time. We may want to know how much the price of groceries has increased, so we can adjust our budgets accordingly. A factory manager may wish to compare this month's per-unit production cost with that of the past six months. Or a medical research team may wish to compare the number of flu cases reported this year with the number reported in previous years. In each of these situations, the degree of change needs to be determined and defined. Typically, we use *index numbers* to measure such differences.

15-1 DEFINING AN INDEX NUMBER

An index number measures how much a variable changes over time. We calculate an index number by finding the ratio of the current value to a base value. Then we multiply the resulting number by 100 to express the index as a percentage. This final value is the *percentage relative*. Note that the index number for the base year is always 100.

Calculating a simple index

The secretary of state of North Carolina has data indicating the number of new businesses incorporated. The data he collects show that 9,300 were started in 1968, 6,500 in 1973, 9,600 in 1978, and 10,100 in 1983. If 1968 is the base year, he can calculate the index numbers reflecting volume changes using the process presented in Table 15-1.

TABLE 15-1 Calculation of index numbers (Base year = 1968)

YEAR (1)	NUMBER OF NEW INCORPORATIONS (000) (2)	RATIO (3) = (2) ÷ (9.3)	INDEX OR PERCENTAGE RELATIVE (4) = (3) × 100
1968	9.3	$\frac{9.3}{9.3} = 1.00$	$1.00 \times 100 = 100$
1973	6.5	$\frac{6.5}{9.3} = 0.70$	$0.70 \times 100 = 70$
1978	9.6	$\frac{9.6}{9.3} = 1.03$	$1.03 \times 100 = 103$
1983	10.1	$\frac{10.1}{9.3} = 1.09$	$1.09 \times 100 = 109$

Using these calculations, the secretary of state finds that incorporations in 1973 had an index of 70 relative to 1968. Another way to state this is to say that the number of incorporations in 1973 was 70 percent of the number of incorporations in 1968.

Types of Index Numbers

Price index

There are three principal types of indices: the price index, the quantity index, and the value index. A *price index* is the one most frequently used. It compares changes in price from one period to another. The familiar Consumer Price Index, tabulated by the Bureau of Labor Statistics, measures overall price changes of a variety of consumer goods and services and is used to define the cost of living.

Quantity index

A *quantity index* measures how much the number or quantity of a variable changes over time. Our example using incorporations determined a quantity index relating the number in 1973, 1978, and 1983 to that in 1968.

Value index

The last type of index, the *value index,* measures changes in total monetary worth. That is, it measures changes in the dollar value of a variable. In effect, the value index combines price and quantity changes to present a more informative index. In our example, we determined only a quantity index. However, we could have included the dollar effect by computing the total capitalized value for the years under consideration. Table 15-2 presents the corresponding value indices for 1973, 1978, and 1983. From this computation, we can say that the *value index* of incorporations in 1983 was 160. Or we can say that the incorporated value of 1983 increased 60 percent relative to the incorporated value of 1968.

TABLE 15-2 Computing a value index (Base year = 1968)

YEAR (1)	INCORPORATED VALUE (MILLIONS) (2)	RATIO (3) = (2) ÷ (18.4)	INDEX OR PERCENTAGE RELATIVE (4) = (3) × 100
1968	$18.4	$\frac{18.4}{18.4} = 1.00$	1.00 × 100 = 100
1973	14.6	$\frac{14.6}{18.4} = 0.79$	0.79 × 100 = 79
1978	26.2	$\frac{26.2}{18.4} = 1.42$	1.42 × 100 = 142
1983	29.4	$\frac{29.4}{18.4} = 1.60$	1.60 × 100 = 160

Usually an index measures change in a variable over a period of time, such as in a time series. However, it can also be used to measure differences in a given variable in different locations. This is done by simultaneously collecting data in different locations and then comparing the data. The comparative cost-of-living index, for example, shows that in terms of the cost of goods and services, it is cheaper to live in Austin, Texas, than in New York City.

Composite index numbers

A single index may reflect a composite, or group, of changing variables. The Consumer Price Index measures the general price level for specific goods and services in the economy. It combines the individual prices of the goods and services to form a composite price index number.

Uses of Index Numbers

Index numbers can be used in several ways. It is most common to use them by themselves, as an end result. Index numbers such as the Consumer Price Index are often cited in news reports as general indicators of the nation's economic condition.

One use of the Consumer Price Index

Management uses index numbers as part of an intermediate computation to understand other information better. In the chapter on time series, seasonal indices were used to modify and improve estimates of the future. The use of the Consumer Price Index to determine the "real" buying power of money is another example of how index numbers help increase knowledge of other factors. Table 15-3 shows the weekly salary paid to a secretary over a period of years, the corresponding Consumer Price Index values, and computation of the secretary's real salary. The secretary's dollar salary increased substantially, but the actual buying power of her income increased less rapidly. This can be attributed to the simultaneous rise in the cost-of-living index from 100 to 192.

TABLE 15-3 Computation of real wages

YEAR (1)	WEEKLY SALARY PAID (2)	CONSUMER PRICE INDEX (3)	$(4) = \frac{(2) \times 100}{(3)}$	REAL OR ADJUSTED SALARY
1970	\$ 76.50	100	$76.50 \times \frac{100}{100} =$	\$76.50
1973	97.00	123	$97.00 \times \frac{100}{123} =$	\$78.86
1983	215.32	192	$215.32 \times \frac{100}{192} =$	\$112.15

Problems Related to Index Numbers

Several things can distort index numbers. The four common causes of distortion are discussed below:

Limited data

1. Sometimes there is **difficulty in finding suitable data** to compute an index. Suppose the sales manager of Colonial Aircraft is interested in computing an index describing seasonal variation in the sale of the company's small planes. If sales are reported only on an annual basis, he would be unable to determine the seasonal sales pattern.

Incomparability

2. Incomparability of indices occurs when attempts are made to compare one index with another after there has been a basic change in what is being measured. If the managers of Phoenix Television Company compare price indices of television sets from 1973 to 1983, they find that prices have increased substantially. However, this comparison does not take into consideration technological advances in the quality of television sets made over the time period in consideration.

Inappropriate weighting

3. Inappropriate weighting of factors can also distort an index. In developing a composite index, such as the Consumer Price Index, we must consider changes in some variables to be more important than changes in others. The effect on the economy of a 50-cent-per-gallon increase in the price of gasoline cannot be counterbalanced by a 50-cent decrease in the price of cars. It must be realized that the 50-cent per gallon increase in gas cost has a much greater effect on consumers. Thus, greater weight has to be assigned to the increased gas price than to the increase in the cost of cars.

Use of an improper base

4. Distortion of index numbers also occurs when **selection of an improper base** occurs. Sometimes a firm selects a base that automatically leads to a result that is in its own interest and proves its initial assumption. If Consumers Against Oil Waste wants to portray oil companies in a bad light, it might measure this year's profits with a recession year as its base for oil profits. This would produce an index that shows oil profits have increased substantially. On the other hand, if Consumers for Unlimited Oil Use wishes to show that this year's profits are minimal, it might select a year with high profits for its base year. Using high profit as a base would probably result in an index indicating a small increase, or maybe even a decline, in oil profits, this year. Therefore, we must always consider how and why the base period was selected before we accept a claim based on the result of comparing index numbers.

Sources of Index Numbers

Sources of data for index numbers

When managers apply index numbers to everyday problems, they use many sources to obtain the necessary information. The source depends on their information requirements. A firm can use monthly sales reports to determine its seasonal sales pattern. In dealing with broad areas of national economy and the general level of business activity, publications such as the *Federal Reserve Bulletin, Moody's, Monthly Labor Review,* and the *Consumer Price Index* provide a wealth of data. Many federal and state publications are listed in the U.S. Department of Commerce pamphlet, *Measuring Markets.* Almost all government agencies distribute data about their activities, from which index numbers can be computed. Many financial newspapers and magazines provide information from which index numbers can be computed. When you read these sources, you will find that many of them use index numbers themselves.

EXERCISES

15-1 What is the index for a base year?

15-2 Explain the differences between the three principal types of indices: *price, quantity,* and *value.*

15-3 What does the Consumer Price Index measure? Is this based on a single variable or a composite of variables?

15-4 What are two basic ways of using index numbers?

15-5 What does an index number measure?

15-6 How is a percentage relative (index) found?

15-2 UNWEIGHTED AGGREGATES INDEX

The simplest form of a composite index is an unweighted aggregates index. *Unweighted* means that all the values considered in calculating the index are of equal importance. *Aggregate* means that we add, or sum, all the values. The principal advantage of an unweighted aggregates index is its simplicity.

Calculating an unweighted aggregates index

An unweighted aggregates index is calculated by adding all the elements in the composite for the given time period and then dividing this result by the sum of the same elements during the base period. Equation 15-1 presents the mathematical formula for computing an unweighted quantity index.

$$\text{Unweighted aggregates quantity index} = \frac{\Sigma Q_1}{\Sigma Q_0} \times 100 \qquad [15\text{-}1]$$

where:

- Q_1 = quantity of each element in the composite for current year
- Q_0 = quantity of each element in the composite for base year

Note that we can substitute *either* prices or values for quantities in Equation 15-1 to find the general equation for a price index or a value index. Since the ratio is multiplied by 100, the resulting index is technically a percentage. However, it is customary to refer only to the value and to omit the percent sign when discussing index numbers.

The example in Table 15-4 demonstrates how we apply an unweighted index. In this case, we want to measure changes in general price levels on the basis of changes in prices of a few items. The 1978 prices are the base values with which we compare the 1983 prices.

Interpreting the index

From these calculations, we determine that the price index describing the change in these items from 1978 to 1983 is 145. If the elements in this composite are representative of the general price level, we can say that prices rose 45 percent from 1978 to 1983. We cannot, however, expect a sample of four items to reflect accurate price changes for all goods and services. Thus, this calculation provides us with only a very rough estimate.

Suppose we now add the change in price of hand-held electronic calculators from 1978 to 1983 to our composite (Table 15-5). Again, 1978 is the base period against which we compare the 1983 prices.

Limitations of an unweighted index

Intuitively we know that the previous index of 145 is a more accurate estimate of general price behavior than 70.6, since more prices rose than fell

TABLE 15-4 Computation of an unweighted index

ELEMENTS IN THE COMPOSITE	Prices 1978 P_0	Prices 1983 P_1
Milk (1 gallon)	$1.48	$1.79
Eggs (1 dozen)	.65	.83
Hamburger (1 pound)	1.09	1.59
Gasoline (1 gallon)	.48	1.17
	$\Sigma P_0 =$ **3.70**	$\Sigma P_1 =$ **5.38**

$$\text{Unweighted aggregates price index} = \frac{\Sigma P_1}{\Sigma P_0} \times 100 \quad \textbf{[15-1]}$$

$$= \frac{5.38}{3.70} \times 100$$

$$= 1.45 \times 100$$

$$= 145$$

between 1978 and 1983. Thus we see **the major disadvantage of an unweighted index. It does not attach greater importance, or weight, to the price change of a high-use item than it does to a low-volume item.** (A family may purchase 50 dozen eggs a year, but it would be unusual for a family to own more than one or two calculators.) A substantial price change for slow-moving items can completely distort an index. For this reason, it is not common to use a simple unweighted index in important analyses.

The deficiencies of an unweighted index suggest that we use a weighted index. There are two ways to calculate more sophisticated indices. Each of these will be discussed in detail in the following sections.

TABLE 15-5 Computation of an unweighted index

ELEMENTS IN THE COMPOSITE	Prices 1978 P_0	Prices 1983 P_1
Milk (1 gallon)	$ 1.48	$ 1.79
Eggs (1 dozen)	.65	.83
Hamburger (1 pound)	1.09	1.59
Gasoline (1 gallon)	.48	1.17
Hand-held electronic calculator (1)	36.50	23.00
	$\Sigma P_0 =$ **40.20**	$\Sigma P_1 =$ **28.38**

$$\text{Unweighted aggregates price index} = \frac{\Sigma P_1}{\Sigma P_0} \times 100 \quad \textbf{[15-1]}$$

$$= \frac{28.38}{40.20} \times 100$$

$$= .706 \times 100$$

$$= 70.6$$

EXERCISES

15-7 In an effort to get a measure of economic hardship, the IMF collected data on the price increases of 5 major products imported by a group of less-developed countries. Using 1980 as the base period, express the 1983 prices in terms of an unweighted aggregates index.

PRODUCT	A	B	C	D	E
1980 price	$ 98	$418	$2,266	$49	$185
1983 price	$127	$532	$2,290	$60	$221

15-8 With union negotiations pending, representatives of the management of a large manufacturing facility are compiling data on wage levels. The following data concern base pay for the different classes of labor within the facility over a 4-year period.

	WAGES PER HOUR			
	1980	1981	1982	1983
Class A	$8.48	$9.32	$10.34	$11.16
Class B	6.90	7.52	8.19	8.76
Class C	4.50	4.99	5.48	5.86
Class D	3.10	3.47	3.85	4.11

Using 1980 as the base period, calculate the unweighted aggregates wage index for 1981, 1982, and 1983.

15-9 The vice-president of sales for the Xenon Computer Corporation is examining the commission rate employed for the last 3 years. Below are the commission earnings of the company's top 5 sales personnel.

	1981	1982	1983
Guy Howell	$48,500	$55,100	$63,800
Skip Ford	41,900	46,200	60,150
Nelson Price	38,750	43,500	46,700
Nina Williams	36,300	45,400	39,900
Ken Johnson	33,850	38,300	50,200

Using 1981 as the base period, express the commission earnings in 1982 and 1983 in terms of an unweighted aggregates index.

15-10 Bill Ivey, the administrator of a small rural hospital, has compiled the information shown below regarding food purchased for the hospital kitchen. For the commodities listed, the corresponding price indicates the average price for that year. Using 1982 as the base period, express the prices in 1981 and 1983 in terms of an unweighted aggregates index.

COMMODITY	1981	1982	1983
Dairy products	$2.34	$2.38	$2.60
Meat products	3.19	3.41	3.36
Vegetable products	.85	.89	.94
Fruit products	1.11	1.19	1.18

15-11 A chemical processing plant utilized 5 materials in the manufacture of an industrial cleaning agent. The following data indicate the final inventory levels for these materials for the years 1981 and 1983.

MATERIAL	A	B	C	D	E
Inventory (tons) 1981	86	395	1,308	430	113
Inventory (tons) 1983	95	380	1,466	469	108

Using 1981 as the base period, express the 1983 inventory levels in terms of an unweighted aggregates index.

15-12 John Dykstra, a management trainee in a bank, has collected information on the bank's transactions for the years 1982 and 1983:

	WITHDRAWALS		DEPOSITS	
TYPE OF TRANSACTION	SAVINGS	CHECKING	SAVINGS	CHECKING
Number of transactions 1982	169,000	21,843,000	293,000	2,684,000
Number of transactions 1983	158,000	23,241,000	303,000	3,361,000

Using 1982 as the base period, express the number of banking transactions in 1983 in terms of an unweighted aggregates index.

15-13 The Bookster Publishing Company began its business of publishing college textbooks in 1980. It is interested in determining how its sales have changed compared to its first year. A summary of the company's records shows how many new books it published in each year in the following areas:

	1981	1982	1983
Biology	20	22	22
Mathematics	15	10	16
History	11	12	19
English	2	3	5
Sociology	5	0	3
Physics	18	11	24
Chemistry	21	24	31
Philosophy	7	10	11

Using 1981 as the base year, calculate the unweighted aggregates quantity index for 1982 and 1983. Interpret the results for the publishing company.

15-3 WEIGHTED AGGREGATES INDEX

Advantages of weighting in an index

As we have said, often we have to attach greater importance to changes in some variables than to others when we compute an index. This weighting allows us to include more information than just the change in price over time. It also lets us improve the accuracy of the general price level estimate based on our sample. The problem is to decide how much weight to attach to each of the variables in the sample.

The general formula for computing a weighted aggregates price index is:

$$\text{Weighted aggregates price index} = \frac{\Sigma P_1 Q}{\Sigma P_0 Q} \times 100 \qquad \textbf{[15-2]}$$

where:

- P_1 = price of each element in the composite in the current year
- P_0 = price of each element in the composite in the base year
- Q = quantity weighting factor chosen

Computing a weighted aggregates index

Consider the example in Table 15-6. Each of the elements in the composite is taken from Table 15-5 and is weighted according to the volume of sales. The process of weighted aggregates confirms our earlier intuitive impression from page 712 that the general price level had risen (index = 200.6).

Typically, management uses the quantity of an item consumed as the measure of its importance in computing a weighted aggregates index. This leads to an important question in applying the process: Which quantities are used?

Three ways to weight an index

In general, there are three ways to weight an index. The first involves using quantities consumed during the base period in computing each index number. This is called the *Laspeyres method,* after the statistician who developed it. The second uses quantities consumed during the period in question for each index. This is the *Paasche method,* in honor of the person who devised it. The third way is called the *fixed weight aggregates method.*

TABLE 15-6 Computation of a weighted aggregates index

ELEMENTS IN THE COMPOSITE	Q VOLUME (BILLIONS) (1)	P_0 1978 PRICES (2)	P_1 1983 PRICES (3)	P_0Q WEIGHTED SALES (4) = (2) × (1)	P_1Q WEIGHTED SALES (5) = (3) × (1)
Milk	20.000 (gal.)	$ 1.48	$ 1.79	1.48 × 20.0 = 29.6	1.79 × 20.00 = 35.800
Eggs	3.500 (doz.)	.65	.83	.65 × 3.5 = 2.275	.83 × 3.5 = 2.905
Hamburger	11.000 (lbs.)	1.09	1.59	1.09 × 11.0 = 11.99	1.59 × 11.00 = 17.490
Gasoline	154.000 (gal.)	.48	1.17	.48 × 154.0 = 73.92	1.17 × 154.00 = 180.180
Calculators	0.002 (units)	36.50	23.00	36.50 × 0.002 = 0.073	23.00 × 0.002 = 0.046
				ΣP_0Q = **117.858**	ΣP_1Q = **236.421**

$$\text{Weighted aggregates index} = \frac{\Sigma P_1 Q}{\Sigma P_0 Q} \times 100 \qquad \textbf{[15-2]}$$

$$= \frac{236.42}{117.86} \times 100$$

$$= 2.006 \times 100$$

$$= 200.6$$

With this method, one period is chosen, and its quantities are used to find *all* indices. (Note that if the chosen period is the base period, the fixed weight aggregates method is the same as the Laspeyres method.)

Laspeyres Method

Using the Laspeyres method

The Laspeyres method, which uses quantities consumed during the base period, is the method most commonly used, because it requires quantity measures for only one period. Since each index number depends upon the same base price and quantity, management can compare the index of one period directly with the index of another. Suppose a steel manufacturer's price index is 103 in 1980 and 125 in 1983, using 1977 base prices and quantities. The company concludes that the general price level has increased 22 percent from 1980 to 1983. To calculate the Laspeyres index, the company first multiplies the current period price by the base period quantity for each element in the composite, then it sums each of the resulting values. Next it multiplies the base period price by the base period quantity for each element, and again it sums the resulting values. By dividing the first sum by the second and multiplying the result by 100, management can convert this value to a percentage relative. Equation 15-3 presents the formula used to determine the Laspeyres index.

$$\text{Laspeyres index} = \frac{\Sigma P_1 Q_0}{\Sigma P_0 Q_0} \times 100 \quad [15\text{-}3]$$

where:

- P_1 = prices in the current year
- P_0 = prices in the base year
- Q_0 = quantities sold in the base year

Example using the Laspeyres method

Let's work an example to demonstrate how the Laspeyres method is used. Suppose we want to determine changes in price level between 1979 and 1983. Table 15-7 contains the pertinent data for 1979 and 1983.

Drawing conclusions from the calculated index

If we have selected a representative sample of goods, we can conclude that the general price index for 1983 is 120, based on the 1979 index of 100. Alternatively, we can say that prices have increased by 20 percent. Notice that we have used the average quantity consumed in 1979 rather than the total quantity consumed. Actually, it does not matter which is used, as long as we apply the same quantity measure throughout the problem. Typically, we select the quantity measure that is easiest to find.

Advantage of the Laspeyres method

One advantage of the Laspeyres method is the comparability of one index with another. If we had the 1980 prices for the previous example, we would be able to find a value for the 1980 general price index. This index could be compared directly with the 1983 index. Using the same base period quantity allows us to make a direct comparison.

Another advantage is that many commonly used quantity measures

TABLE 15-7 Calculation of a Laspeyres index

ELEMENTS IN THE COMPOSITE (1)	P_0 BASE PRICE 1979 (2)	P_1 CURRENT PRICE 1983 (3)	Q_0 AVERAGE QUANTITY CONSUMED IN 1979 BY A FAMILY (4)	P_0Q_0 (5) = (2) × (4)	P_1Q_0 (6) = (3) × (4)
Bread (1 loaf)	$ .52	$ .64	200 loaves	$104	$128
Potatoes (1 lb.)	.12	.18	300 lbs.	36	54
Chicken (3-lb. fryer)	1.19	1.28	100 chickens	119	128
				$\Sigma P_0Q_0 =$ **259**	$\Sigma P_1Q_0 =$ **310**

$$\text{Laspeyres price index} = \frac{\Sigma P_1Q_0}{\Sigma P_0Q_0} \times 100 \qquad \textbf{[15-3]}$$

$$= \frac{310}{259} \times 100$$

$$= 1.20 \times 100$$

$$= 120$$

are not tabulated every year. A firm might be interested in some variable whose quantity measure is computed once every ten years. Since the Laspeyres method uses only one quantity measure, that of the base year, the firm does not need yearly tabulations to measure quantities consumed.

Disadvantage of the Laspeyres method

The primary disadvantage of the Laspeyres method is that it does not take into consideration changes in consumption patterns. Items purchased in large quantities just a few years ago may be relatively unimportant today. Suppose the base quantity of an item differs greatly from the quantity for the period in question. Then the change in that item's price indicates very little about the change in the general price level.

Paasche Method

Difference between Paasche and Laspeyres methods

The second way to compute a weighted aggregates price index is the Paasche method. Finding a Paasche index is similar to finding a Laspeyres index. The difference is that the Paasche method uses quantity measures for the *current* period rather than for the *base* period.

The Paasche index is calculated by multiplying the current period price by the current period quantity for each item in the composite and summing these products. Then the base period price is multiplied by the current period quantity for each item, and the results are summed. The first sum is divided by the second sum, and the resulting value is multiplied by 100 to convert the value into a percentage relative. Equation 15-4 defines the method for calculating a Paasche index.

Calculating a Paasche index

$$\text{Paasche index} = \frac{\Sigma P_1Q_1}{\Sigma P_0Q_1} \times 100 \qquad \textbf{[15-4]}$$

where:

- P_1 = current period prices
- P_0 = base period prices
- Q_1 = current period quantities

With this equation, we can rework the problem in Table 15-7. Notice that we have discarded the quantities consumed in 1979. They have been replaced by the quantities consumed in 1983. Table 15-8 presents the information necessary for this modified problem.

Interpeting the difference between the two methods

In this analysis, we find that the price index for 1983 is 112. As you see from Table 15-7 on page 718, the price index calculated by the Laspeyres method is 120. The difference between these indices reflects the change in consumption patterns of the three variables in the composite.

Advantage of the Paasche method

The Paasche method is particularly helpful because it combines the effects of changes in price and consumption patterns. Thus, it is a better indicator of general changes in the economy than the Laspeyres method. In our examples, the Paasche index shows a trend toward less expensive goods and services, since it indicates a price level increase of 12 percent instead of the 20 percent increase calculated using the Laspeyres method.

Disadvantages of the Paasche method

One of the principal disadvantages of the Paasche method is the need to tabulate quantity measures for each period examined. Frequently, quantity information for each period is either expensive to gather or unavailable. It would be hard, for example, to find reliable sources of data to determine quantity measures of 100 food products consumed in different countries for each of several years.

Each value for a Paasche price index is the result of both price and quantity changes from the base period. **Since the quantity measures used**

TABLE 15-8 Calculation of a Paasche index

ELEMENTS IN THE COMPOSITE (1)	P_1 CURRENT PRICE 1983 (2)	P_0 BASE PRICE 1979 (3)	Q_1 AVERAGE QUANTITY CONSUMED IN 1983 BY A FAMILY (4)	P_1Q_1 (5) = (2) × (4)	P_0Q_1 (6) = (3) × (4)
Bread (1 loaf)	$ .64	$ .52	200 loaves	$128	$104
Potatoes (1 lb.)	.18	.12	100 lbs.	18	12
Chicken (3-lb. fryer)	1.28	1.19	300 chickens	384	357
				ΣP_1Q_1 = **530**	ΣP_0Q_1 = **473**

[15-4] Paasche price index

$$= \frac{\Sigma P_1Q_1}{\Sigma P_0Q_1} \times 100$$

$$= \frac{530}{473} \times 100$$

$$= 1.12 \times 100$$

$$= 112$$

for one index period are usually different from the quantity measures for another index period, it is impossible to attribute the difference between the two indices to price changes only. Thus, it is difficult to compare indices from different periods as calculated by the Paasche method.

Fixed Weight Aggregates Method

Fixed weight aggregates method

The third technique used to assign weights to elements in a composite is the fixed weight aggregates method. It is similar to both the Laspeyres and Paasche methods. However, instead of using base period or current period weights (quantities), it uses weights from a representative period. The representative weights are referred to as fixed weights. The fixed weights and the base prices do not have to come from the same period.

Calculating a fixed weight aggregates index

We calculate a fixed weight aggregates price index by multiplying the current period prices by the fixed weights and summing the results. Then we multiply the base period prices by the fixed weights and sum them. Finally, we divide the first sum by the second and multiply by 100 to convert the ratio to a percentage relative. The formula used to calculate a fixed weight aggregates price index is presented in Equation 15-5.

$$\text{Fixed weight aggregates price index} = \frac{\Sigma P_1 Q_2}{\Sigma P_0 Q_2} \times 100 \qquad \textbf{[15-5]}$$

where:

- P_1 = current period prices
- P_0 = base period prices
- Q_2 = fixed weights

Example of a fixed weight aggregates index

We can demonstrate the process used to calculate a fixed weight aggregates price index by solving our chapter-opening example. Recall that management wants to determine the price level changes of raw materials consumed by the company between 1963 and 1983. It has accumulated the information in Table 15-9. From examination of past purchasing records, management has decided that the quantities purchased in 1976 were characteristic of the purchasing patterns during the 20-year period. The 1963 price level is the base price in this analysis. Calculation of the fixed weight aggregates index is shown in Table 15-9. The company management concludes from this analysis that the general price level has increased 157 percent over the 20-year period.

Advantage of a fixed weight aggregates index

The primary advantage of a fixed weight aggregates price index is the flexibility in selecting the base price and the fixed weight (quantity). In many cases, the period that a company wishes to use as the base price level may have an uncharacteristic consumption level. Therefore, by being able to select a different period for the fixed weight, the company can improve the accuracy of the index. This index also allows a company to

TABLE 15-9 Computation of a fixed weight aggregates index

RAW MATERIALS (1)	Q_2 QUANTITY CONSUMED 1976 (Thousands of tons) (2)	P_0 AVERAGE PRICE 1963 ($ per ton) (3)	P_1 AVERAGE PRICE 1983 ($ per ton) (4)	WEIGHTED AGGREGATE 1963 (5) = (3) × (2)	WEIGHTED AGGREGATE 1983 (6) = (4) × (2)
Coal	158	$ 7.56	$19.50	$1,194.48	$3,081.00
Iron ore	12	9.20	21.40	110.40	256.80
Nickel ore	5	12.30	36.10	61.50	180.50
				ΣP_0Q_2 = **1,366.38**	ΣP_1Q_2 = **3,518.30**

$$\text{Fixed weight aggregates price index} = \frac{\Sigma P_1Q_2}{\Sigma P_0Q_2} \times 100 \qquad \textbf{[15-5]}$$

$$= \frac{3{,}518.30}{1{,}366.38} \times 100$$

$$= 2.57 \times 100$$

$$= 257$$

change the price base without changing the fixed weight. This is useful because quantity measures are often expensive or impossible to obtain for certain periods.

EXERCISES

15-14 Bill Simpson, owner of a California vineyard, has collected the following information describing the prices and quantities of harvested crops for the years 1980, 1981, 1982, and 1983.

TYPE OF GRAPE	PRICE (PER TON) 1980	1981	1982	1983	QUANTITY HARVESTED (TONS) 1980	1981	1982	1983
Ruby Cabernet	$108	$109	$113	$111	1,280	1,150	1,330	1,360
Barber	93	96	96	101	830	860	850	890
Chenin Blanc	97	99	106	107	1,640	1,760	1,630	1,660

Construct a Laspeyres index for each of these 4 years, using 1980 as the base period.

15-15 Use the data from problem 15-14 to calculate a fixed weight index for each year, using 1980 prices as the base and the 1983 quantities as the fixed weights.

15-16 Use the data from problem 15-14 to calculate a Paasche index for each year, using 1981 as the base period.

15-17 Julie Pristash, the marketing manager of Mod-Stereo, a manufacturer of blank cassette tapes, has compiled the following information regarding unit sales for 1981, 1982, and 1983. Using the average quantities sold from 1981 to 1982 as the fixed weights, calculate the fixed weight index for each of the years 1981 to 1983 based on 1981.

LENGTH OF TAPE	RETAIL PRICE 1981	1982	1983	AVERAGE QUANTITY (×100,000) 1981–1983
30 minutes	$2.20	$2.60	$2.85	32
60 minutes	2.60	2.90	3.15	119
90 minutes	3.10	3.20	3.25	75
120 minutes	3.30	3.35	3.40	16

15-18 Gray P. Saeurs owns the corner fruitstand in a small town. After hearing many complaints that his prices constantly change during the summer, he has decided to see if this is true. Based on the following data, help Mr. Saeurs calculate the appropriate weighted aggregate price indices for each month. Use June as the base period. Is your result a Laspeyres index or a Paasche index?

FRUIT	PRICE PER POUND JUNE	JULY	AUG.	NO. OF POUNDS SOLD JUNE
Apples	$ .25	$ .30	$ .40	125
Oranges	.40	.45	.40	200
Peaches	.55	.40	.50	350
Watermelons	.95	1.00	.95	100
Cantaloupes	.90	.95	1.00	150

15-19 Charles Widget is in charge of keeping in stock certain items that his company needs in repairing its machines. Since he started this job three years ago, he has been observing the changes in the prices for the items he keeps in stock. He arranged the data in the following table in order to calculate a fixed weight aggregate price index. Perform the calculations Mr. Widget would do using 1981 as the base year.

ITEM	PRICE PER ITEM 1981	1982	1983	AVERAGE NO. USED DURING 3-YEAR PERIOD
W-gadget	$1.25	$1.50	$2.00	900
X-gadget	6.50	7.00	6.25	50
Y-gadget	5.25	5.90	6.40	175
Z-gadget	.50	.80	1.00	200

15-4 AVERAGE OF RELATIVES METHODS

Unweighted Average of Relatives Method

As an alternative to the aggregates methods, we can use the average of relatives method to construct an index. Once again, we will use a price index to introduce the process.

Actually, we used a form of the average of relatives method in calculating the simple index in Table 15-1 on page 708. In that one-product example, we calculated the percentage relative by dividing the number of incorporations in the current year, Q_1, by the number in the base year, Q_0, and multiplying the result by 100.

Calculating an unweighted average of relatives index

With more than one product (or activity), we first find the ratio of the current price to the base price for each product and multiply each ratio by

100. We then add the resulting percentage relatives and divide by the number of products. (Notice that the aggregates methods discussed in section 3 differ from this method. They sum all the prices *before* finding the ratio.) Equation 15-6 presents the general form for the unweighted average of relatives method.

$$\text{Unweighted average of relatives index} = \frac{\sum\left(\frac{P_1}{P_0} \times 100\right)}{n} \quad [15\text{-}6]$$

where:

- P_1 = current period prices
- P_0 = base period prices
- n = number of elements (or products) in the composite

Comparing the unweighted aggregates index and the unweighted average of relatives index

In Table 15-10, we rework the problem in Table 15-4 on page 713 using the unweighted average of relatives method rather than the unweighted aggregates method.

Based on this analysis, the general price level index for 1983 is 160. In Table 15-4, the unweighted aggregates index for the same problem is 145. Obviously, there is a difference between these two indices. With the unweighted average of relatives method, we compute the average of the ratios of the prices for each product. With the unweighted aggregates method, we compute the ratio of the sums of the prices of each product. Notice that this is not the same as assigning some items more weight than others. Rather, the

TABLE 15-10 Computation of an unweighted average of relatives index

PRODUCT (1)	1978 PRICES (2)	1983 PRICES (3)	RATIO × 100 $(4) = \frac{(3)}{(2)} \times 100$
Milk (1 gal.)	\$1.48	\$1.79	$\frac{1.79}{1.48} \times 100 = 1.21 \times 100 = 121$
Eggs (1 doz.)	.65	.83	$\frac{.83}{.65} \times 100 = 1.28 \times 100 = 128$
Hamburger (1 lb.)	1.09	1.59	$\frac{1.59}{1.09} \times 100 = 1.46 \times 100 = 146$
Gasoline (1 gal.)	.48	1.17	$\frac{1.17}{.48} \times 100 = 2.44 \times 100 = \underline{244}$
			$\sum\left(\frac{P_1}{P_0} \times 100\right) = \mathbf{639}$

$$\text{Unweighted average of relatives index} = \frac{\sum\left(\frac{P_1}{P_0} \times 100\right)}{n} \quad [15\text{-}6]$$

$$= \frac{639}{4}$$

$$= 160$$

average of relatives method converts each element to a relative scale where each element is represented as a *percentage* rather than as an *amount*. Because of this, each of the elements in the composite is measured against a base of 100.

Weighted Average of Relatives Method

Most problems management has to deal with require weighting by *importance*. Thus, it is more common to use the weighted average of relatives method than the unweighted method. When we computed a weighted aggregates price index in section 3 of this chapter, we used the quantity consumed to weight the elements in the composite. To assign weights using the weighted average of relatives, we use the value of each element in the composite. (The value is the total dollar volume obtained by multiplying price by quantity.)

Different ways to determine weights

With the weighted average of relatives method, there are several ways to determine weighted value. As in the Laspeyres method, we can use the base value found by multiplying the base quantity by the base price. Using base value will produce exactly the same result as calculating the index using the Laspeyres method. Since the result is the same, the decision to use the Laspeyres method or the weighted average of relatives method often depends on the availability of data. If value data are more readily available, the weighted average of relatives method is used. We use the Laspeyres method when quantity data are more readily obtained.

Equation 15-7 is used to compute a weighted average of relatives price index. This is a general equation into which we can substitute values from the base period, the current period, or any fixed period.

$$\text{Weighted average of relatives price index (general form)} = \frac{\Sigma\left[\left(\frac{P_1}{P_0} \times 100\right)(P_nQ_n)\right]}{\Sigma P_nQ_n} \qquad [15\text{-}7]$$

where:

- P_nQ_n = the value
- P_0 = prices in the base period
- P_1 = prices in the current period
- P_n = prices for the base, current, or fixed period
- Q_n = quantities for the base, current, or fixed period

If we wish to compute a weighted average of relatives index using base values, P_0Q_0, the equation would be:

$$\text{Weighted average of relatives price index (using base values)} = \frac{\Sigma\left[\left(\frac{P_1}{P_0} \times 100\right)(P_0Q_0)\right]}{\Sigma P_0Q_0} \qquad [15\text{-}8]$$

TABLE 15-11 Computing a weighted average of relatives index

ELEMENTS IN THE COMPOSITE (1)	PRICES 1979 P_0 (2)	PRICES 1983 P_1 (3)	QUANTITY 1979 Q_0 (4)	PERCENTAGE PRICE RELATIVE $\frac{P_1}{P_0} \times 100$ $(5) = \frac{(3)}{(2)} \times 100$	BASE VALUE P_0Q_0 (6) = (2) × (4)	WEIGHTED PERCENTAGE RELATIVE (7) = (5) × (6)
Bread (1 loaf)	$ .52	$ .64	200 loaves	$\frac{.64}{.52} \times 100 = 123$	$104	12,792
Potatoes (1 lb.)	.12	.18	300 lbs.	$\frac{.18}{.12} \times 100 = 150$	36	5,400
Chicken (3-lb. fryer)	1.19	1.28	100 fryers	$\frac{1.28}{1.19} \times 100 = 108$	119	12,852
					$\Sigma P_0Q_0 = \mathbf{259}$	$\Sigma\left[\left(\frac{P_1}{P_0} \times 100\right)(P_0Q_0)\right] = \mathbf{31,044}$

$$\text{Weighted average of relatives index} = \frac{\Sigma\left[\left(\frac{P_1}{P_0} \times 100\right)(P_0Q_0)\right]}{\Sigma P_0Q_0} \qquad \textbf{[15-8]}$$

$$= \frac{31,044}{259}$$

$$= 120$$

Relation of weighted average of relatives to Laspeyres method

Equation 15-8 will produce the same result as the Laspeyres method for any given problem.

In addition to the specific cases of the general form of the weighted average of relatives method, we can use values determined by multiplying the price from one period by the quantity from a different period. Usually, however, we find Equations 15-7 and 15-8 adequate.

Example of weighted average of relatives index

Here is an example. The information in Table 15-11 comes from Table 15-7 on page 718. Since we have base quantities and base prices, we will use Equation 15-8. The price index of 120 is identical to that calculated in Table 15-7 using the Laspeyres method.

Using base values, fixed values, or current values

As was the case for weighted aggregates, when we use base values, P_0Q_0, or fixed values, P_2Q_2, for weighted averages, we can readily compare the price level of one period with that of another. However, when we use current values, P_1Q_1, in computing a weighted average of relatives price index, we *cannot* directly compare values from different periods, since both the prices and the quantities may have changed. Thus, we usually use either base values or fixed values when computing a weighted average of relatives index.

EXERCISES

15-20 F. C. Linley, owner of the San Mateo Seals, collected information regarding the ticket prices and volume for his franchise over the last 4 years.

	AVERAGE ANNUAL PRICE				TICKETS SOLD (×10,000)			
	1980	1981	1982	1983	1980	1981	1982	1983
Box seats	$6.50	$7.25	$7.50	$8.10	26	27	31	28
General admission	3.50	3.85	4.30	4.35	71	80	89	90

Calculate a weighted average of relatives price index for each of the years 1980 through 1982, using 1981 as the base year and for weighting.

15-21 The following table contains information from the raw-material purchase records of a tire manufacturer for the years 1981, 1982, and 1983.

MATERIAL	AVERAGE ANNUAL PURCHASE PRICE/TON 1981	1982	1983	VALUE OF PURCHASE (THOUSANDS) 1983
Butadiene	$ 17	$ 15	$ 11	$ 50
Styrene	85	89	95	210
Rayon cord	348	358	331	1,640
Carbon black	62	58	67	630
Sodium pyrophosphate	49	56	67	90

Calculate a weighted average of relatives price index for each of those 3 years, using 1983 for weighting and for the base year.

15-22 A Tennessee public interest group has surveyed the cost of automobile repairs in 3 major Tennessee cities (Knoxville, Memphis, and Nashville). With the following information, construct an unweighted average of relatives price index using the 1979 prices as a base.

TYPE OF REPAIR	1979	1981	1983
Replacement of water pump	$ 35	$ 37	$ 41
Regrinding of engine valves (6 cyl.)	189	205	216
Wheel balancing	26	29	30
Tune-up (minor)	16	16	18

15-23 Garret Cage, president of a local bank, is interested in the average levels of total savings and checking accounts for each of the last 3 years. He sampled days from each of these years; using the levels on those days, he determined the following yearly averages:

	1981	1982	1983
Savings accounts	$1,845,000	$2,320,000	$2,089,000
Checking accounts	385,000	447,000	491,000

Calculate an unweighted average of relatives index for each year, using 1981 as the base period.

15-24 As a part of the evaluation of a possible acquisition, a New York City conglomerate has collected this sales information:

PRODUCT	AVERAGE ANNUAL PRICE 1981	AVERAGE ANNUAL PRICE 1983	TOTAL DOLLAR VALUE (THOUSANDS) 1981
Calculators	$ 45	$ 20	$ 80
Radios	16	29	700
Portable TVs	114	128	1,140

a) Calculate the unweighted average of relatives price index, using 1981 as the base period.
b) Calculate the weighted average of relatives price index, using the dollar value for each product in 1981 as the appropriate set of weights and 1981 as the base year.

15-25 A survey of transatlantic passenger rates for flights from New York to various European cities produced these results:

DESTINATION	AVERAGE ANNUAL PASSENGER RATES 1974	1975	1976	1977	1978	PASSENGERS (×1,000) 1978
Paris	$230	$238	$244	$259	$261	1,890
London	216	218	225	232	248	3,450
Munich	234	241	251	256	266	1,670
Rome	280	289	301	313	325	1,430

Calculate the weighted average of relatives index for each of the years 1974 through 1977, using 1978 as the base year and for weighting.

15-26 In a study of group health insurance policies, commissioned by the Rhode Island Medical Care Association, the following sample of average individual rates was collected. Using 1982 as the base period, calculate an unweighted average of relatives price index for each year.

INSURANCE GROUP	1980	1981	1982	1983
Physicians	$54	$65	$86	$103
Students	39	41	55	76
Government employees	48	61	76	93
Teachers	46	58	75	96

15-27 A new motel chain hopes to place its first motel in Boomingville, but before it makes a commitment to start construction, it wants to check out the room prices charged nightly by the other motels and hotels. After sending an employee to investigate the prices, the motel chain received data in the following form:

HOTEL	PRICE PER ROOM PER NIGHT 1981	1982	1983	NO. ROOMS RENTED 1981
Happy Hotel	$35	$37	$42	1,250
Room Service Rooms	25	26	28	950
Executive Motel	45	45	51	1,000
Country Inn	37	38	44	600
Family Fun Motel	26	30	31	2,075

Help the company determine the relative prices, using 1981 as the base year, and use an unweighted average of relatives index.

15-28 The Quick-Stop Gas Station has been selling road maps to its customers for the past three years. The maps that are sold are of the nearest city, the county the gas station is in, the state it is in, and the entire United States. From the following table, calculate the weighted average relatives price indices for 1982 and 1983, using 1981 as the base year.

MAPS	PRICE PER MAP 1981	1982	1983	QUANTITY SOLD 1981
City	$ .75	$ .90	$1.10	1,000
County	.75	.90	1.00	400
State	1.00	1.50	1.50	1,000
United States	2.50	2.75	2.75	220

15-5 QUANTITY AND VALUE INDICES

Quantity Indices

Using a quantity index

Our discussion of index numbers up to now has concentrated on price indices so that it would be easier to understand the general concepts. However, we can also use index numbers to describe quantity and value changes. Of these two, we more frequently use quantity indices. The Federal Reserve Board calculates quarterly indices in its monthly publication, *The Index of Industrial Production* (IIP). The IIP measures the quantity of production in the areas of manufacturing, mining, and utilities. It is computed using a weighted average of relatives quantity index in which the fixed weights (prices) and the base quantities are measured from 1967.

Advantages of a quantity index

In times of inflation, a quantity index provides a more reliable measure of actual output of raw materials and finished goods than a corresponding value index does. Similarly, agricultural production is best measured using a quantity index, because it eliminates misleading effects from fluctuating prices. We frequently use a quantity index to measure commodities that are subject to considerable price variation.

Any of the methods discussed in previous sections of this chapter to determine price indices can be used to calculate quantity indices. When we computed price indices, we used quantities or values as weights. Now that we want to compute quantity indices, we use prices or values as weights. Let's consider the construction of a weighted average of relatives quantity index.

The general process for computing a weighted average of relatives quantity index is the same as that used to compute a price index. Equation 15-9 describes the formula for this type of quantity index. In this equation, value is determined by multiplying quantity by price. The value associated with each quantity is used to weight the elements in the composite.

Computing a weighted average of relatives quantity index

$$\text{Weighted average of relatives quantity index} = \frac{\Sigma\left[\left(\frac{Q_1}{Q_0} \times 100\right)(Q_nP_n)\right]}{\Sigma Q_nP_n} \qquad [15\text{-}9]$$

where:

- Q_1 = quantities for the current period
- Q_0 = quantities for the base period
- Q_n and P_n = quantities and prices that determine values we use for weights. In particular, $n = 0$ for the base period, $n = 1$ for the current period, and $n = 2$ for a fixed period that is not a base or current period.

Consider the problem in Table 15-12 on the next page. We use Equation 15-9 to compute a weighted average of relatives quantity index. The value, Q_nP_n, is determined from the base period and is therefore symbolized Q_0P_0.

Value Indices

A disadvantage of a value index

A value index measures general changes in the total value of some variable. Since value is determined both by price and quantity, a value index actually measures the combined effects of price and quantity changes. The principal disadvantage of a value index is that it does not distinguish between the effects of these two components.

Advantages of a value index

Nevertheless, a value index is useful in measuring overall changes. Medical insurance companies, for example, often cite the sharp increase in the *value* of payments awarded in medical malpractice suits as the primary reason for discontinuing malpractice insurance. In this situation, value involves both a greater number of payments and larger cash amounts awarded.

TABLE 15-12 Computation of a weighted average of relatives quantity index

ELEMENTS IN THE COMPOSITE (1)	QUANTITIES (BILLIONS OF BUSHELS) 1979 Q_0 (2)	1983 Q_1 (3)	PRICE (PER BUSHEL) 1979 P_0 (4)	$\frac{Q_1}{Q_0} \times 100$ PERCENTAGE RELATIVES $(5) = \frac{(3)}{(2)} \times 100$	BASE VALUE Q_0P_0 $(6) = (2) \times (4)$	$\frac{Q_1}{Q_0} \times 100 \times Q_0P_0$ WEIGHTED RELATIVES $(7) = (5) \times (6)$
Wheat	29	24	$3.80	$\frac{24.0}{29.0} \times 100 = 83$	$29 \times 3.80 =$ 110.20	9,146.60
Corn	3	2.5	2.91	$\frac{2.5}{3} \times 100 = 83$	$3 \times 2.91 =$ 8.73	724.59
Soybeans	12	14	6.50	$\frac{14.0}{12.0} \times 100 = 17$	$12 \times 6.50 =$ 78.00	9,126.00
					$\Sigma Q_0P_0 =$ **196.93**	
					$\Sigma\left[\left(\frac{Q_1}{Q_0} \times 100\right)(Q_0P_0)\right] =$	**18,997.19**

$$\text{Weighted average of relatives quantity index} = \frac{\Sigma\left[\left(\frac{Q_1}{Q_0} \times 100\right)(Q_0P_0)\right]}{\Sigma Q_0P_0} \qquad [15\text{-}9]$$

$$= \frac{18{,}997.19}{196.93}$$

$$= 96$$

EXERCISES

15-29 The financial vice-president of the American division of Banshee Camera Company is examining the company's cash and credit sales over the last 5 years.

	VALUE OF SALES (×$100,000) 1979	1980	1981	1982	1983
Credit	$5.66	$6.32	$6.53	$6.98	$7.62
Cash	2.18	2.51	2.48	2.41	2.33

Calculate an unweighted average of relatives value index for each year, using 1979 as the base period.

15-30 A Georgia firm manufacturing heavy equipment has collected the following production information about the company's principal products. Calculate a weighted aggregates quantity index using the quantities and prices from 1983 as the bases and the weights.

PRODUCT	QUANTITIES PRODUCED 1981	1982	1983	COST OF PRODUCTION/UNIT (THOUSANDS) 1983
River barges	92	118	85	$ 33
Railroad gondola cars	456	475	480	56
Off-the-road trucks	52	56	59	116

15-31 Arkansas Electronics has marketed 3 basic types of calculators: for the business sector, the scientific sector, and a simple model capable of basic computational functions. The following information describes unit sales for the past 3 years:

MODEL	NUMBER SOLD (×100,000) 1981	1982	1983	PRICE 1983
Business	11.85	13.32	15.75	$34.00
Scientific	10.32	11.09	10.18	69.00
Basic	7.12	7.48	7.89	13.00

Calculate the weighted average of relatives quantity indices using the prices and quantities from 1983 to compute the value weights, with 1981 as the base year.

15-32 Explain the principal disadvantage in using value indices.

15-33 What is the major difference between a weighted aggregates index and a weighted average of relatives index?

15-34 In preparation for an appropriations hearing, the police commissioner of a Maryland town has collected the following information:

TYPE OF CRIME	1980	1981	1982	1983
Assault and rape	110	128	134	129
Murder	30	45	40	48
Robbery	610	720	770	830
Larceny	2,450	2,630	2,910	2,890

Calculate the unweighted average of relatives quantity index for each of these years, using 1983 as the base period.

15-35 William Olsen, owner of a real estate office, has collected the following sales information for each of the firm's sales personnel:

SALESPERSON	VALUE OF SALES (×1,000) 1980	1981	1982	1983
Thompson	$490	$560	$530	$590
Alfred	630	590	540	680
Jackson	760	790	810	840
Blockard	230	250	240	360

Calculate an unweighted average of relatives value index for each year, using 1980 as the base period.

15-36 After encouraging a chemical company to make its employees handle certain dangerous chemicals with protective gloves, the Public Health Agency is now interested in seeing if this rule has had its effect in curbing the number of cancer deaths in that area. Before this rule went into effect, cancer was widespread not only among the workers at the company but also among their families and close friends and neighbors. The following data shows what these numbers were in 1960 before the rule and what they were after the rule in 1980.

AGE GROUP	NO. IN POPULATION FOR 1960	DEATHS IN 1960	DEATHS IN 1980
<4 yrs.	5,000	400	125
4–15 yrs.	4,000	295	200
16–35 yrs.	24,000	1,230	1,000
36–60 yrs.	19,000	700	450
>60 yrs.	7,000	1,100	935

Use a weighted aggregates index of the number of deaths, using the 1960 population size as the weights to help the Public Health Agency understand what has happened to the cancer rate.

15-37 A veterinarian has noticed she has treated a large number of pets this past winter. She wonders whether this amount was spread across the three winter months evenly or whether she treated more pets in any certain month. Using December as the base period, calculate the weighted average of relatives quantity indices for January and February.

	NUMBER TREATED DEC.	JAN.	FEB.	PRICE PER VISIT AVERAGE FOR 3 MONTHS
Cats	100	200	95	$ 55
Dogs	125	75	200	65
Parrots	15	20	15	85
Snakes	10	5	5	100

15-6 ISSUES IN CONSTRUCTING AN INDEX NUMBER

Imperfections in index numbers

In this chapter, we have used examples with small samples and short time spans. Actually, index numbers are computed for composites with many elements, and they cover long periods of time. This produces relatively accurate measures of changes. However, even the best index numbers are imperfect.

Problems in Construction

Although there are many problems in constructing an index number, there are three principal areas of difficulty:

Which items should be included in a composite?

1. Selecting an item to be included in a composite. Almost all indices are constructed to answer a particular question. Thus, the items included in the composite depend upon the question. The Consumer Price Index asks, "How much has the price of a certain group of items purchased by moderate-income urban Americans changed from one period to another?" From this question, we know that only those items that reflect the purchases of moderate-income urban families should be included in the composite. We must realize that the Consumer Price Index will less accurately reflect price changes of goods purchased by low- or high-income on rural families than by moderate-income urban families.

Need for selection of appropriate weights

2. Selecting the appropriate weights. In the previous sections of this chapter, we emphasized that the weights selected should represent the relative importance of the various elements. Unfortunately, what is appropriate in one period may become inappropriate in a short period of time. This must be kept in mind when comparing values of indices computed at different times.

What is a normal base period?

3. Selecting the base period. Typically, the base period selected should be a normal period, preferably a fairly recent period. "Normal" means that the period should not be at either the peak or the trough of a fluctuation. One technique to avoid using an irregular period is to average the values of several consecutive periods to determine a normal value. The U.S. Bureau of Labor Statistics frequently uses the average of 1971 and 1972 consumption patterns to compute the Consumer Price Index. Frequently, management tries to select a base period that coincides with the base period for one or more of the major indices, such as the Index of Industrial Production. Use of a common base allows management to relate its index to the major indices.

Caveats in Interpreting an Index

In addition to these problems in constructing indices, there are several common errors made in interpreting indices:

Problems with generalizing from an index

1. Generalization from a specific index. One of the most common misinterpretations of an index is generalization of the results. The Consumer Price Index measures how prices of a particular combination of goods purchased by moderate-income urban Americans has changed. Despite its specific definition, the Consumer Price Index is frequently described as reflecting the cost of living for all Americans. Although it is related to the cost of living to some degree, to say that it measures the change in the cost of living is incorrect.

Additional knowledge needed

2. Lack of general knowledge regarding published indices. Part of the problem leading to the error above is lack of knowledge of what the various published indices measure. All the well-known indices are accompanied by detailed statements concerning measurement. Management should become familiar with exactly what each index measures.

Time affects an index

3. Effect of time span on an index. Factors related to an index tend to change with time. In particular, the appropriate weights tend to change. Thus, unless the weights are changed accordingly, the index becomes less reliable.

Lack of measurement of quality

4. Quality changes. One frequent criticism of index numbers is that they do not reflect changes in the quality of the items they measure. If the quality has indeed changed, then the index either understates or overstates the price level changes. For example, if we construct an index number to describe price changes in pocket calculators over the last decade, the resulting index would understate the actual change that is due to rapid technological improvements in calculators.

EXERCISES

15-38 What is the effect of time upon the weighting of a composite index?

15-39 List several preferences for the choice of a base period.

15-40 Describe a technique used to avoid the use of an irregular period for a base.

15-41 Is it correct to say that the Consumer Price Index measures the "cost of living"?

15-42 What problems exist with index numbers if the quality of an item changes?

15-7 TERMS INTRODUCED IN CHAPTER 15

CONSUMER PRICE INDEX The U.S. government prepares this index, which measures changes in the prices of a representative set of consumer items.

FIXED WEIGHT AGGREGATES METHOD Used to weight an aggregates index, this method uses as weights quantities consumed during some representative period.

INDEX NUMBER A ratio that measures how much a variable changes over time.

INDEX OF INDUSTRIAL PRODUCTION Prepared monthly by the Federal Reserve Board, the IIP measures the quantity of production in the areas of manufacturing, mining, and utilities.

LASPEYRES METHOD To weight an aggregates index, this method uses as weights the quantities consumed during the base period.

PAASCHE METHOD In weighting an aggregates index, the Paasche method uses as weights the quantities consumed during the current period.

PERCENTAGE RELATIVE Ratio of a current value to a base value with the result multiplied by 100.

PRICE INDEX Compares changes in price from one period to another.

QUANTITY INDEX A measure of how much the number or quantity of a variable changes over time.

UNWEIGHTED AGGREGATES INDEX Uses all the values considered, where each value is of equal importance.

UNWEIGHTED AVERAGE OF RELATIVES METHOD To construct an index number, this method first finds the ratio of the current price to the base price for each product, adds the resulting percentage relatives, and then divides by the number of products.

WEIGHTED AGGREGATES INDEX Using all the values considered, this index assigns weights to these values.

WEIGHTED AVERAGE OF RELATIVES METHOD To construct an index number, this method weights by importance and uses the value of each element in the composite.

15-8 EQUATIONS INTRODUCED IN CHAPTER 15

[15-1] $$\text{Unweighted aggregates quantity index} = \frac{\Sigma Q_1}{\Sigma Q_0} \times 100$$ *p. 712*

To compute an unweighted aggregates quantity index, divide the sum of the current year quantities of the elements in the index by the sum of the base year quantities, and multiply the result by 100.

[15-2] $$\text{Weighted aggregates price index} = \frac{\Sigma P_1 Q}{\Sigma P_0 Q} \times 100$$ *p. 716*

For a weighted aggregates price index using quantities as weights, obtain the weighted sum of the current year prices by multiplying each price in the index by its associated quantity and summing the results. Then divide this weighted sum by the weighted sum of the base year prices, and multiply the result by 100.

[15-3] $$\text{Laspeyres index} = \frac{\Sigma P_1 Q_0}{\Sigma P_0 Q_0} \times 100$$ *p. 717*

The Laspeyres price index is a weighted aggregates price index using the base year quantities as weights.

[15-4] $$\text{Paasche index} = \frac{\Sigma P_1 Q_1}{\Sigma P_0 Q_1} \times 100$$ *p. 718*

To get the Paasche price index, we compute a weighted aggregates price index using the current year quantities for weights.

[15-5] $$\text{Fixed weight aggregates price index} = \frac{\Sigma P_1 Q_2}{\Sigma P_0 Q_2} \times 100$$ *p. 720*

The fixed weight aggregates price index is a weighted aggregates price index whose weights are the quantities from a representative year, not necessarily either the base year or the current year.

[15-6] Unweighted average of relatives price index $= \frac{\sum\left(\frac{P_1}{P_0} \times 100\right)}{n}$ p. 723

We compute an unweighted average of relatives price index by multiplying the ratios of current prices to base prices by 100, summing the results, and then dividing by the number of elements used in the index.

[15-7] Weighted average of relatives price index $= \frac{\sum\left[\left(\frac{P_1}{P_0} \times 100\right)(P_nQ_n)\right]}{\sum P_nQ_n}$ p. 724

With this index, we weight the relative prices by the values for a fixed reference period and divide the weighted sum of relative prices by the sum of the weights. If we use the base year values as weights, we get:

[15-8] $$\frac{\sum\left[\left(\frac{P_1}{P_0} \times 100\right)(P_0Q_0)\right]}{\sum P_0Q_0}$$ p. 724

which is the same as the Laspeyres price index.

[15-9] Weighted average of relatives quantity index $= \frac{\sum\left[\left(\frac{Q_1}{Q_0} \times 100\right)(Q_nP_n)\right]}{\sum Q_nP_n}$ p. 729

In this quantity index, we weight the relative quantities by the values for a fixed reference period and divide the weighted sum by the sum of the weights.

15-9 CHAPTER REVIEW EXERCISES

15-43 Kamischika Motorcycles began producing 3 models of mopeds in 1981. For the 3 years 1981 through 1983, sales were as follows:

	AVERAGE ANNUAL PRICE			UNITS SOLD (×10,000)		
MODEL	1981	1982	1983	1981	1982	1983
I	$139	$155	$149	3.7	4.1	7.6
II	169	189	189	2.3	4.6	8.1
III	199	205	219	1.6	2.1	3.4

a) Calculate the weighted average of relatives price indices using the prices and quantities from 1983 as the bases and weights.

b) Calculate the weighted average of relatives price indices using the total dollar values for each year as the weights and 1983 as the base year.

15-44 These data indicate the value (in millions of dollars) of the principal products exported by a developing country. Determine unweighted aggregate value indices for 1981 and 1983 based on 1979.

COMMODITY	1979	1981	1983
Coffee	$834	$1,436	$1,321
Sugar	96	118	122
Copper	241	258	269
Zinc	142	125	106

15-45 In a survey of U.S. coal production for the previous 4 years, the information below was collected. Using the value of the 1983 production for weighting and 1983 as the base year, calculate the weighted average of relatives quantity index for each of the 4 years.

TYPE OF COAL	PRODUCTION (MILLIONS OF TONS) 1980	1981	1982	1983	VALUE (MILLIONS) 1983
Anthracite	7.4	6.8	7.1	7.2	$ 90
Bituminous	595	580	601	625	5,050

15-46 A survey by the National Dairy Products Association produced the following information. Construct a Laspeyres index where 1979 is the base period; let 1979 = 100.

PRODUCT	AVERAGE PRICE PER-UNIT 1979	1983	TOTAL QUANTITY (BILLIONS) 1979
Cheese (lbs.)	$1.45	$1.49	2.6
Milk (gals.)	1.60	1.61	47.6
Butter (lbs.)	.70	.80	3.1

15-47 Robert Barry, Ltd., a garment consulting firm, has examined the pricing trends of clothing items for a client. This table contains the results of the survey (shown in unit prices):

PRODUCTS	1980	1981	1982	1983
Jeans	$13.00	$13.00	$15.00	$15.00
Jackets	19.00	19.50	22.00	24.00
Shirts	12.00	11.00	12.00	13.00

Calculate an unweighted average of relatives index for each year, using 1980 as the base period.

15-48 What problem would exist in comparing price indices describing computer sales over the past few decades?

15-49 The vice-president of sales for the National Hospital Supply Company conducted a survey of travel expenses incurred by selected salespeople. Of particular interest were data regarding expenditures for gasoline and the price paid per gallon.

SALESPEOPLE	EXPENDITURES ON GASOLINE 1979	1980	1981	AVERAGE PRICE/GALLON 1979
A	$704	$ 985	$1,391	.52
B	635	875	1,306	.55
C	752	1,023	1,523	.59
D	503	696	1,106	.56
E	593	781	1,215	.55

Calculate an unweighted average of relatives index for each year, using 1981 as the base period.

15-50 This information describes the unit sales of a bicycle shop for 3 years:

MODEL	NUMBER SOLD 1981	1982	1983	PRICE 1981
Sport	45	48	56	$ 89
Touring	64	67	71	104
Cross-country	28	35	27	138
Sprint	21	16	28	245

Calculate the weighted average of relatives quantity indices, using the prices and quantities from 1981 to compute the value weights, with 1981 as the base year.

15-51 Denise Alford, accountant for a mass-transit system, has recorded the following per-vehicle expenses for the years 1979, 1981, and 1983. Using 1981 as the base period, express the expenses of 1979 and 1983 in terms of an unweighted aggregates index.

COSTS	1979	1981	1983
Fuel	$24,378	$36,421	$37,613
Wages	1,816	2,019	2,136
Maintenance	638	681	701

15-52 An Ohio consumer protection agency has surveyed the price changes of a meat-packing company. The following table contains the average annual per-pound prices for a sample of the firm's products. Construct an unweighted average of relatives price index using the prices from 1981 as the base period.

PRODUCTS	1981	1982	1983
Sirloin	$1.69	$1.81	$1.85
Chuck	.91	1.15	1.24
Bologna	1.45	1.58	1.53
Hot dogs	.99	1.03	1.01
Rib eyes	2.39	2.61	2.56

15-53 Why must one exercise caution in selecting a base period?

15-54 Harry Wada, a purchasing agent, has compiled the price information presented below. Using 1980 as the base period, calculate the unweighted aggregates price index for 1981, 1982, and 1983.

MATERIAL	1980	1981	1982	1983
Aluminum	$ .96	$ .99	$1.03	$1.06
Steel	1.48	1.54	1.55	1.59
Brass tubing	.21	.25	.26	.31
Copper wire	.06	.08	.07	.09

15-55 A USDA survey of grain production for selected areas in the U.S. yielded this information:

PRODUCT	QUANTITIES PRODUCED (MILLIONS OF BUSHELS) 1979	1980	1981	1982	1983	PRICE PER BUSHEL 1979
Wheat	610	620	640	630	650	$ 4.40
Corn	390	390	410	440	440	3.60
Oats	100	90	120	130	150	1.20
Rye	10	20	10	10	20	24.00
Barley	160	150	120	190	180	2.10
Soybeans	130	140	160	120	130	5.60

Using the prices from 1979 for weights, calculate the weighted aggregates quantity indices for each year.

15-56 John Pringle, an international mineral trader, has collected the following information on prices and quantities of minerals exported by an African country for the years 1982 and 1983. Calculate a Paasche index for 1983, using 1982 as the base period.

MINERAL	QUANTITY (MILLION TONS) 1983	PRICE (PER LB.) 1982	1983
Copper	38.1	$.59	$.63
Lead	53.5	.17	.16
Zinc	86.4	.21	.23

15-57 A large European automobile manufacturer has compiled the following information on car sales of one U.S. manufacturer:

SIZE	AVERAGE ANNUAL PRICE (HUNDREDS) 1975	1977	1979	UNITS SOLD (×1,000) 1975	1977	1979
Subcompact	$31	$34	$35	32	65	86
Compact	38	39	40	45	68	73
Sedan	45	49	53	462	325	386

a) Calculate the weighted average of relatives price indices using the prices and quantities from 1977 as the bases and weights.
b) Calculate the weighted average of relatives price indices using the total dollar values for each year as the weights and 1977 as the base year.

15-10 CHAPTER CONCEPTS TEST

Answers are in the back of the book.

T F 1. The index number for a base year is always zero.
T F 2. Index numbers can be used to measure differences in a given variable in several locations.
T F 3. The simplest form of a composite index is an unweighted aggregates index.
T F 4. A disadvantage of the Laspeyres method is that indices are not comparable to one another.

T F 5. If the fixed weight aggregates method is used, with the chosen value period being the base period, this is the same as the Paasche method.

T F 6. The average of relatives method sums percentages, not amounts.

T F 7. A substantial price change for a slow-moving item can completely distort an unweighted index.

T F 8. In times of inflation, a quantity index provides a better measure of actual output than a corresponding value index.

T F 9. A value index measures the combined effects of price and quantity changes.

T F 10. When using the weighted average of relatives price index, indices from different periods are always comparable.

T F 11. The Laspeyres method is most commonly used because it requires quantity measures for only one period.

T F 12. An index number is always found by taking the ratio of a current value to a base value and multiplying by 100.

T F 13. A chief advantage of index numbers is that selection of an improper base does not distort them.

T F 14. While often used as measurements in and of themselves, index numbers can also be used as part of intermediate computations.

T F 15. Whenever we use the symbol P_1 in one of our index formulas, we are referring to the price in the base year.

T F 16. With the aggregates or average of relatives index, it is more common to weight the elements making up the index.

T F 17. The major disadvantage of an unweighted aggregates index is that it does not allow for changes in price.

T F 18. If an index number calculation over 8 years with a base value of 100 gave an index for 1973 of 110, what would be the percentage relative for 1973?

a) 110
b) 90.9
c) 13.75
d) 880
e) Cannot be determined from information given

19. To measure changes in total monetary worth, one should calculate:

a) A price index
b) A quantity index
c) A value index
d) None of these

20. Suppose that the composite price index for 1 gallon of milk, 2 loaves of bread, and 1 pound of hamburger was 110 in 1976 and 119 in 1977. If both these indices were computed from a 1975 base of 100, how much did the general price level rise between 1976 and 1977?

a) 9%
b) 8.18%
c) 19%
d) 7.56%
e) Cannot be determined from information given

21. Which of the following describes an advantage of using the Laspeyres method?

a) Many commonly used quantity measures are not tabulated for every period.
b) Changes in consumption patterns are taken into account.
c) One index can be easily compared with another.
d) All of these.
e) a and c but not b.

22. Suppose that the weighted aggregates price index for a set of prices was calculated as 106 using the Laspeyres method and as 112 using the Paasche method. What can be concluded from this?

a) The Paasche index is incorrect.
b) There is a trend toward less expensive goods.

c) There is a trend toward more expensive goods.
d) The difference between the two indices can be attributed to a poor estimation of consumer attitudes.
e) a and d only.

23. When computing a weighted average of relatives index, we would be best able to compare indices from various periods if:
a) Base values were used as P_nQ_n.
b) Current values were used as P_nQ_n.
c) Fixed values were used as P_nQ_n.
d) Either base or fixed values were used as P_nQ_n.
e) Either current values or fixed values were used as P_nQ_n.

24. Commodities that are subject to considerable price variations could best be measured by a:
a) Price index
b) Quantity index
c) Value index
d) None of these

25. A base period can be described as a "normal" period if:
a) It is at neither the peak nor trough of a fluctuation.
b) It is the most recent period for which we have data.
c) There was no inflation or deflation of prices during the period.
d) It is the average of several consecutive periods.

26. The weights used in a quantity index are:
a) Percentages of total quantity
b) Prices
c) Average quantities
d) None of these

27. In the unweighted average of relatives method, $\frac{P_1}{P_0} \times 100$ should be calculated for each product in the composite. What is then done with these values to finish the calculation?
a) The values are multiplied together.
b) The largest value is found.
c) The values are averaged.
d) The average difference from the median of the values is found and then squared.

28. If you wanted to measure how much the cost of a particular variable changes over time, you would use:
a) A value index
b) An inflation index
c) A quantity index
d) All of these
e) None of these

29. It is possible to change the base year without changing the quantities weights when using the:
a) Paasche method
b) Laspeyres method
c) Weighted aggregates method
d) None of these

30. If all the values considered in calculating an index are of equal importance, the index is ________________.

31. The weighted index method in which quantities consumed during the base period are used as weights is the ________________ method.

32. If we sum all the values in calculating an index, the index is called ________________.

33. Using weights from a representative period (which is not necessarily the base or current period) to compute a weighted aggregates price index is the ________________ aggregates method.

34. The ________________ method uses quantities consumed in the current period in question when computing a weighted index.

35. We must realize that the mechanical approach of index numbers is subject to considerable ________________ and ________________.

15-11 CONCEPTUAL CASE (Northern White Metals Company)

Dick sat in his office early one cold December evening. "Jody has done her usual thorough job," he thought, as he reviewed the large volume of information that had arrived in the afternoon mail. The analysis was complete, but it was also rather complex. Bleary-eyed at the end of a long day, Dick decided to postpone any further work until the morning.

At 7:30 A.M. the following day, a hot cup of coffee in hand, Dick again began to review the analysis of building-products sales and raw-material price trends Jody had provided. Primary aluminum prices were currently a bit depressed, but had been heading upward for many years. Dick knew the industry had undergone several overcapacity–undercapacity cycles during these years, which led to alternating high and low raw-material prices. Nevertheless, the data seemed to reveal generally increasing costs to NWMC. Turning to the next section of Jody's report, Dick was surprised at what he found. She had compiled some additional data, information he had not requested, with a brief note of explanation. Dick picked up the phone and called New York.

"I knew you'd be calling," Jody answered. "What did you think of that little bonus analysis?"

"I'm not quite sure," Dick replied. "I know you did a lot of work on this, but all I expected was sales and materials cost trends. It's a little hard to relate all these other factors, how they've changed, and whatnot. What prompted you to check all these things out, anyway?"

Impatient that Dick had not yet perceived the full significance of the analysis, Jody explained. "Actually, it was Sarah's idea. We noticed the trends in materials cost, and then she decided to do a little research. We checked out the price trends of raw aluminum production equipment and they've been moving in a different direction—that is, down!"

"Wait a minute," Dick interrupted, "if you're suggesting we start manufacturing our own primary aluminum . . ."

"I know, I know," Jody responded, "that requires a huge investment in mining and other production equipment that Northern could never afford."

"You bet it does," Dick said.

"But," Jody added with emphasis, "you could afford recycling equipment and melt down scrap and waste aluminum. We checked out scrap resale prices and, with the way high-tech applications products are growing," she continued enthusiastically, "well, we think you should add some scrap-smelting capacity."

Dick sat back, amazed.

"You guys don't kid around, do you?" he said with admiration. "I want to review all this in detail, as there are some pretty obvious implications for my long-term planning. But honestly, Jody, isn't there some way you can arrange all this information to make it a little easier to understand

and present? We have all these variables, and they're all changing in all different directions, and . . ."

"Easy, Dick," Jody reassured him. "Sarah has already taken care of that. We sent out the information last night, so you can expect it before noon. Call me if you have any other questions or need any more work done. Things are a little slow around here."

Dick, appreciative of the scope of the analysis Jody and Sarah conducted for him, nevertheless wanted additional help in understanding how these many variables have changed over time. Furthermore, he hopes the implications of these changes, which so interested Sarah and Jody, will be made clearer. Anticipating this in advance, Jody has assured Dick that Sarah has taken the appropriate action. What would Sarah have done to measure and relate the changes in materials prices, equipment costs, scrap prices, and so on, to enable Dick to better understand and utilize the information? What difficulties might she have encountered, and what qualifications might she wish to provide Dick for interpreting the data?

15-12 COMPUTER DATA BASE EXERCISE

Fred, in gratitude for the new graph on his wall, suggested to Frank one day that he might let Frank help him out with a little problem.

"I've been thinking about a price cut on the Rough Rider. It seems like the retail price is awfully high these days, especially with money so tight for most young folks. Nick Pappas says I can't do it, because materials are going up faster than the price. He said he could give you folks materials costs over the last 30 years if you wanted to do a price index on the cost and compare that to the prices I give you."

"Sure, Fred. Laurel can use the weighted aggregates method to whip up some data in no time," answered Frank. "Glad to do it; inflation is always interesting."

PROBLEM

1. Look at the changes in cost of wood, varnish, and labor from year to year with a weighted aggregates price index using 1950 as the base year. Cold River has always used 2.3 board feet of wood, .015 gallons of varnish, and 1.9 hours of labor per sled. Compare that to Cold River's sled price. Would you have recommended a price cut in 1979?

SLED COST AND PRICE DATA (1950–1979)

YEAR	WOOD COST ($/BOARD FOOT)	VARNISH COST ($/GALLON)	LABOR COST ($/HOUR)	SLED PRICE ($/SLED)
1950	0.14	1.75	1.90	7.25
1951	0.14	1.85	1.90	7.25
1952	0.16	1.87	2.00	7.25
1953	0.16	2.05	2.00	7.75
1954	0.17	2.55	2.15	7.75
1955	0.19	2.60	2.25	8.25
1956	0.25	2.85	2.50	8.75
1957	0.25	3.25	2.50	9.25
1958	0.27	3.25	3.15	10.25
1959	0.29	3.29	3.15	10.75
1960	0.34	3.35	3.15	11.00
1961	0.37	3.40	3.65	11.50
1962	0.45	3.65	3.75	12.00
1963	0.45	3.95	3.95	13.25
1964	0.46	4.00	4.25	14.25
1965	0.50	4.10	4.65	15.75
1966	0.51	4.50	4.95	17.00
1967	0.53	4.65	5.15	17.75
1968	0.58	4.68	5.65	19.00
1969	0.66	4.95	5.85	19.75
1970	0.66	5.15	6.15	20.75
1971	0.69	5.20	6.40	21.75
1972	0.74	5.53	6.65	22.75
1973	0.74	5.75	6.95	24.00
1974	0.76	6.85	7.35	25.25
1975	0.79	7.55	7.60	26.25
1976	0.80	8.25	8.00	27.75
1977	0.83	8.65	8.25	29.25
1978	0.93	8.95	8.65	30.75
1979	0.95	9.75	9.15	33.50

15-13 FLOW CHART

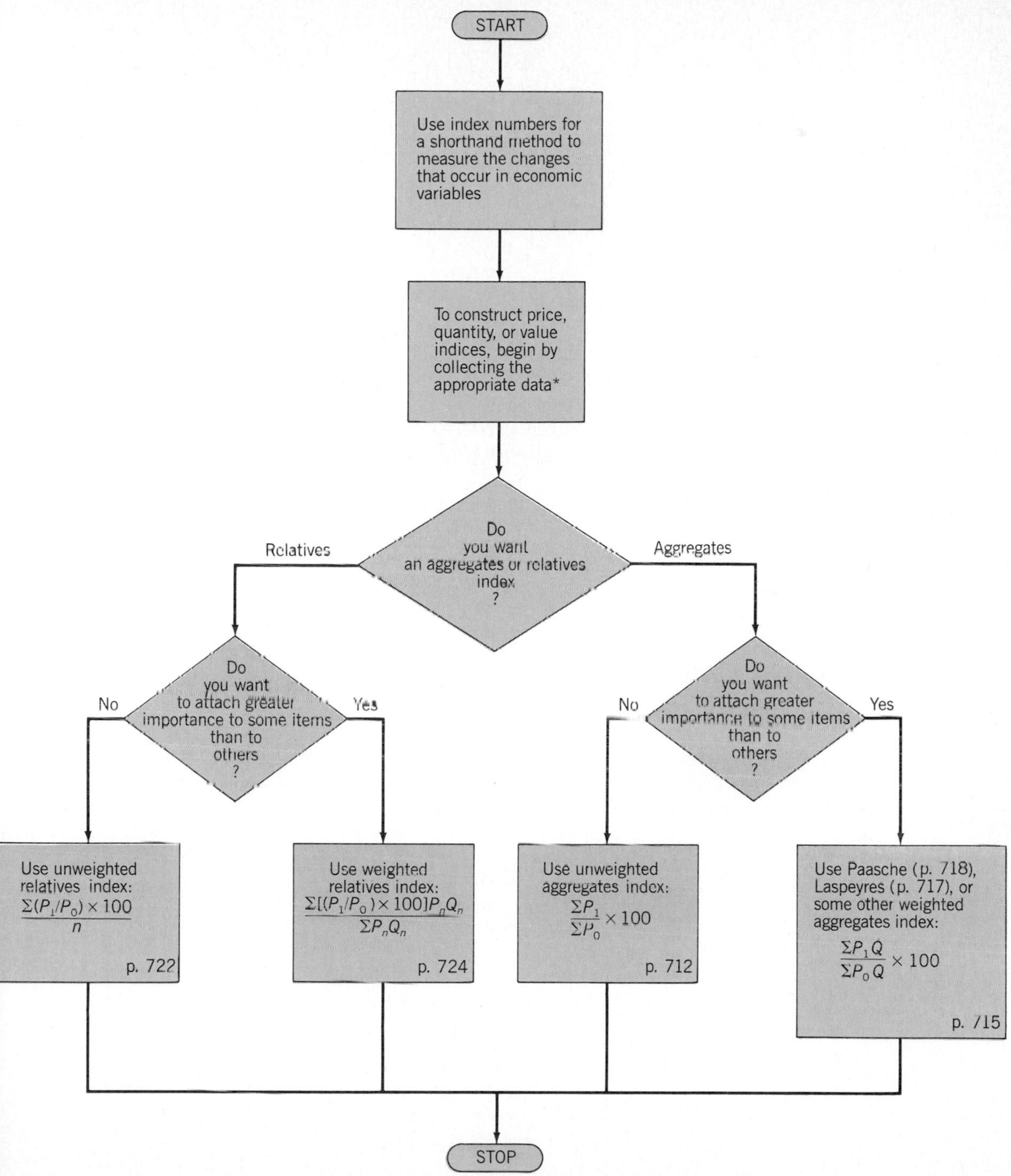

START
Use index numbers for a shorthand method to measure the changes that occur in economic variables
To construct price, quantity, or value indices, begin by collecting the appropriate data*
Do you want an aggregates or relatives index ?
Relatives
Aggregates
Do you want to attach greater importance to some items than to others ?
No
Yes
Do you want to attach greater importance to some items than to others ?
No
Yes
Use unweighted relatives index: $\frac{\Sigma(P_1/P_0) \times 100}{n}$ p. 722
Use weighted relatives index: $\frac{\Sigma[(P_1/P_0) \times 100]P_nQ_n}{\Sigma P_nQ_n}$ p. 724
Use unweighted aggregates index: $\frac{\Sigma P_1}{\Sigma P_0} \times 100$ p. 712
Use Paasche (p. 718), Laspeyres (p. 717), or some other weighted aggregates index: $\frac{\Sigma P_1 Q}{\Sigma P_0 Q} \times 100$ p. 715
STOP

*All formulas in this flow chart are for price indices. Those for quantity or value indices are similar, and many of them are included in the chapter

CHAPTER 16

DECISION THEORY

1. THE DECISION ENVIRONMENT, 748
2. EXPECTED PROFIT UNDER UNCERTAINTY: Assigning Probability Values, 750
3. USING CONTINUOUS DISTRIBUTIONS IN DECISION THEORY: Marginal Analysis, 758
4. UTILITY AS A DECISION CRITERION, 768
5. HELPING DECISION MAKERS SUPPLY THE RIGHT PROBABILITIES, 772
6. DECISION TREE ANALYSIS, 775
7. TERMS, 785
8. EQUATIONS, 786
9. REVIEW EXERCISES, 786
10. CONCEPTS TEST, 789
11. CONCEPTUAL CASE, 792

OBJECTIVES: Most consequential managerial decisions must be made under conditions of uncertainty, because managers seldom have complete information about what the future will bring. In our final chapter, we shall learn methods that are useful when we must decide among alternatives despite uncertain conditions. We shall also investigate how to determine the worth of additional information. As a student, you make complex decisions about which questions are apt to appear on examinations and what study times will be required to earn certain grades in a course. When you do this, you demonstrate intuitive use of some techniques we shall introduce here.

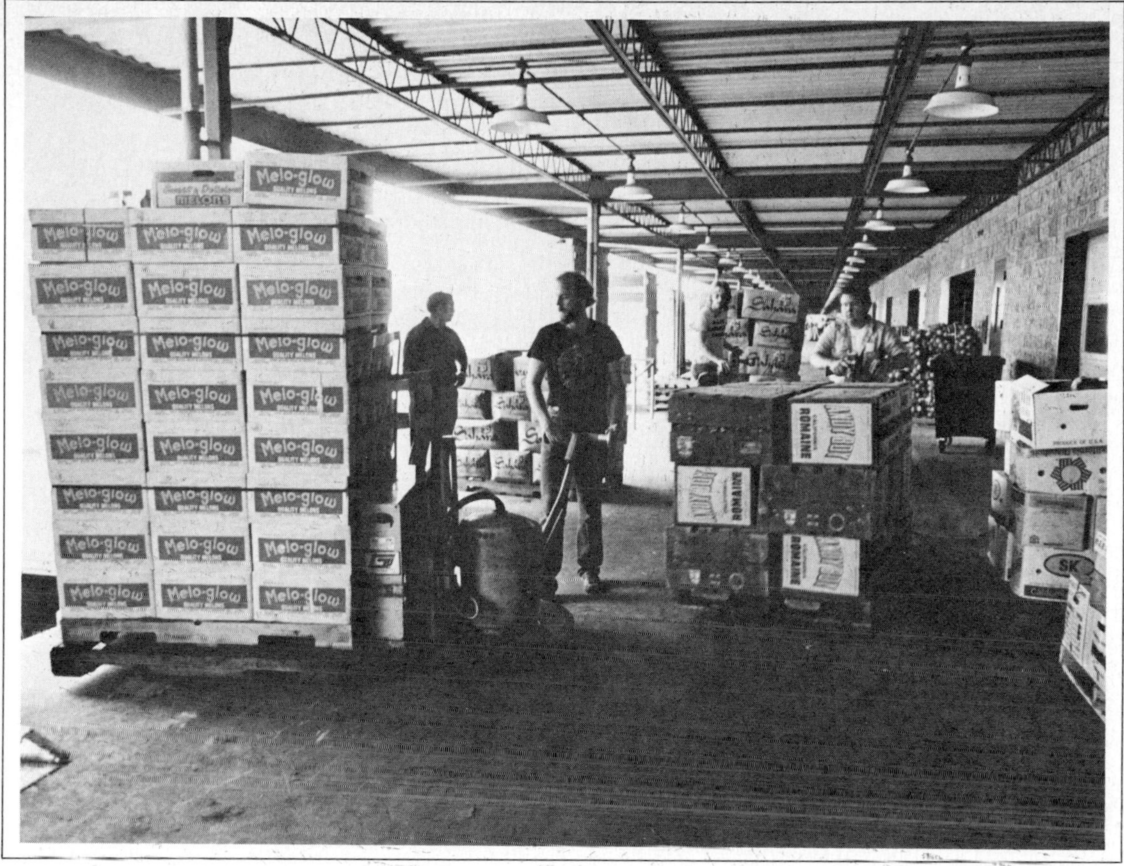

Acme Fruit and Produce wholesalers buys blueberries, then sells them to retailers. Acme currently pays $20 a case. Berries sold on the same day bring $32 a case. Extremely perishable, berries not sold on the first day are worth only $2 a case. Acme has calculated that the mean past daily sales is 60 cases and that the standard deviation of past daily sales is 10 cases. Using the techniques introduced in this chapter, we tell Acme how many cases to order each day to maximize profits.

In section 3 of Chapter 6 (beginning on page 210) we introduced you to the idea of using expected value in decision making. There we worked through a simple problem involving the purchase of strawberries for resale. That kind of problem is part of a set of problems that can be solved using the techniques developed in this chapter.

What is decision theory?

In the last 25 years, managers have used newly developed statistical techniques to solve problems for which information was incomplete, uncertain, or in some cases almost completely lacking. This new area of statistics has a variety of names: *statistical decision theory, Bayesian decision theory* (after the Reverend Thomas Bayes, whom we introduced in Chapter 5), or simply *decision theory*. These names can be used interchangeably.

When we did hypothesis testing, we had to decide whether to accept or to reject the stated hypothesis. In decision theory, we must decide among alternatives by taking into account the *monetary* repercussions of our actions. A manager who must select from among a number of available investments should consider the profit or loss that might result from each alternative. Applying decision theory involves selecting an alternative and having a reasonable idea of the economic consequences of choosing that action.

16-1 THE DECISION ENVIRONMENT

Decision theory may be applied to problems whether the time span is five years or one day, whether it involves financial management or a plant assembly line, and whether it is in the public or private sector. Regardless of the environment, most of these problems have common characteristics. As a result, decision makers approach their solutions in fairly consistent ways. The elements common to most decision theory problems are these:

Elements common to decision theory problems

1. An objective the decision maker is trying to reach. If the objective is to minimize downtime of expensive machinery, the manager may try to find the optimum number of spare motors to be kept on hand for quick repairs. Success in finding that number can be measured by counting downtime each month.

2. Several courses of action. The decision should involve a choice among alternatives (called *acts*). In our example involving spare motors, the various acts open to the decision maker might include stocking one, two, three, four, or five spare motors or choosing not to stock any spare motors.

3. A calculable measure of the benefit or worth of the various alternatives. In general, these costs can be negative or positive and are called *payoffs*. Cost accountants should be able to determine the cost of lost production time resulting from a motor burnout both when a spare is on hand and when one is not available. But sometimes the payoffs involve consequences that are more than solely financial. Imagine trying to decide the optimum number of spare generators a hospital might require in the event of a power failure. Not having enough could cost lives as well as money.

4. Events beyond the control of the decision maker. These uncontrollable occurrences are often called *outcomes* or *states of nature,* and their existence creates difficulties as well as interest in decision making under uncertainty. Such events could be the number of motors in our expensive production machinery that will burn out in a given month. Preventive maintenance will reduce motor burnouts, but they will still happen.

5. Uncertainty concerning which outcome or state of nature will actually happen. In our example, we must be certain about how many motors will burn out. This uncertainty is generally handled by the use of probabilities assigned to the various events that might take place, say a .1 chance of losing five motors a month.

EXERCISES

16-1 Wholesale Lamps has been in contact with Leerie's, a local retail lamp shop, about supplying it with a special chrome tree lamp, which the shop wants to use as a drawing card in an upcoming sale. Wholesale Lamps must order the lamps in 2 days to deliver them by the sale date. Wholesale's cost is $49 for the lamps; it will sell them to Leerie's for $54. Wholesale is uncertain about the number Leerie's desires but guesses that it will be between 15 and 20. One of the managers has assigned probabilities to the various numbers that Leerie's might order. The manager of Wholesale Lamps does not foresee a market for the lamps it does not sell to Leerie's. Leerie's is expected to submit the order tomorrow. Should the manager of Wholesale Lamps use decision theory to order the lamps for Leerie's?

16-2 The Madison County Cougars Club, a large civic organization, will once again operate a cotton-candy booth at the Madison County Fair. The Cougars own the machine and rent the booth, but they must decide how much sugar to buy and how many paper cones to stock. The club treasurer knows the number of cones that were sold in the previous years as well as the amount of sugar that was purchased. The Cougars want to make as much money as possible from the concession stand and plan to sell the cones for 30¢. As yet, the club is uncertain about the price of sugar and whether it will be able to sell the unused portion. Can the Cougars use decision theory to solve their problem?

16-3 The 8th Avenue Book Store relied on the Grambler News Service to supply it with several well-known magazines. Each week, Grambler would deliver a predetermined number of *Today's Romances,* among others, and pick up any unsold copies of the previous week's magazines. The number of copies that the bookstore would sell was never known for sure, but the manager did have past sales data. Grambler charged its bookstands 38¢ for magazines that sold for 50¢. Management of the bookstore wanted to get maximum profitability from the sale of its magazines and was considering the optimum number of *Today's Romances* to order. Should the manager of the bookstore use decision theory to decide the number of magazines to stock?

16-2 EXPECTED PROFIT UNDER UNCERTAINTY: Assigning Probability Values

Buying decision under conditions of uncertainty

Buying and selling strawberries, as in our example in Chapter 6, is only one case in which decisions have to be made under uncertainty. Another involves a newspaper dealer who buys newspapers for 6¢ each and sells them for 10¢ each. Any papers not sold by the end of the day are completely worthless to him. The dealer's problem is to determine the optimum number he should order each day. On days when he stocks more than he sells, his profits are reduced by the cost of the unsold papers. On days when buyers request more copies than he has in stock, he loses sales and makes smaller profits than he could have.

The dealer has kept a record of his sales for the past 100 days (Table 16-1). This information is a distribution of the dealer's past sales. Because sales volume can take on only a limited number of values, the distribution is discrete. We will assume, for purposes of discussion, that the dealer will sell only the number of papers listed—not, say, 412, 525, or 637. Furthermore, the dealer has no reason to believe that sales volume will take on any other value in the future.

TABLE 16-1 Distribution of newspaper sales

DAILY SALES	NUMBER OF DAYS SOLD	PROBABILITY OF EACH NUMBER BEING SOLD
300	15	.15
400	20	.20
500	45	.45
600	15	.15
700	5	.05
	100	**1.00**

This information tells the dealer something about the historical pattern of his sales. Although it does not tell him what quantity the buyers will request tomorrow, it does tell him that there are 45 chances in 100 that the quantity will be 500 papers. Therefore, a probability of .45 is assigned to the sales figure of 500 papers. The probability column in Table 16-1 shows the relationship between the total observations of sales (100 days) and the number of times each possible value of daily sales appeared in the 100 observations. The probability of each sales level occurring is thus derived by dividing the total number of times each value has appeared in the 100 observations by the total number of observations; that is, 15/100, 20/100, 45/100, 15/100, and 5/100.

Maximizing Profits Instead of Minimizing Losses

Back in section 3 of Chapter 6, when we first introduced you to using expected value in decision making, we used an approach that minimized losses and led us to an optimum stocking pattern for our strawberry dealer. It is just as easy to find the optimum stocking pattern by *maximizing profits,* and that's just what we'll do at this point.

A Chapter 6 problem worked another way

Recall that our fruit and vegetable wholesaler in Chapter 6 bought strawberries at $20 a case and resold them at $50 a case. There we assumed that the product had no value if not sold on the first day (a restriction we shall soon lift). If buyers call for more cases tomorrow than the wholesaler has in stock, profits suffer by $30 (selling price minus cost) for each case he cannot sell. On the other hand, costs also result from stocking *too many* units on a given day. If the wholesaler has thirteen cases in stock but sells only ten, he makes a profit of $300, ($30 a case on ten cases). But this profit must be reduced by $60, the cost of the three cases not sold and of no value.

A 100-day observation of past sales gives the information shown in Table 16-2. The probability values there are obtained just as they were in Table 6-6.

TABLE 16-2 Cases sold during 100 days

DAILY SALES	NUMBER OF DAYS SOLD	PROBABILITY OF EACH NUMBER BEING SOLD
10	15	.15
11	20	.20
12	40	.40
13	25	.25
	100	**1.00**

Notice that there are only four discrete values for sales volume, and as far as we know, there is no discernible pattern in the sequence in which these four values occur. We assume that the retailer has no reason to believe sales volume will behave differently in the future.

Calculating Conditional Profits

To illustrate this retailer's problem, we can construct a table showing the results in dollars of all possible combinations of purchases and sales. The only values for purchases and for sales that have meaning to us are ten, eleven, twelve, and thirteen cases, because the retailer has no reason to consider buying fewer than ten or more than thirteen cases.

Conditional profit table

Table 16-3, called a *conditional profit table,* shows the profit resulting from any possible combination of supply and demand. The profits could be either positive or negative (although they are all positive in this example) and are conditional in that a certain profit results from taking a specific stocking action (ordering 10, 11, 12, or 13 cases) and selling a specific number of cases (10, 11, 12, or 13 cases).

TABLE 16-3 Conditional profit table

POSSIBLE DEMAND (SALES) IN CASES	Possible stock action: 10 CASES	11 CASES	12 CASES	13 CASES
10	$300	$280	$260	$240
11	300	330	310	290
12	300	330	360	340
13	300	330	360	390

Table 16-3 also reflects the losses that occur when stock remains unsold at the end of a day. It does not reflect profit denied the retailer because of inability to fill all buyers' requests.

Notice that the stocking of ten cases each day will always result in a profit of $300. Even on those days when buyers want thirteen cases, the retailer can sell only ten. When the retailer stocks eleven cases, his profit will be $330 on days when buyers request eleven, twelve, or thirteen cases. But on days when he has eleven cases in stock and buyers buy only ten cases, profit drops to $280. The $300 profit on the ten cases sold must be reduced by $20, the cost of the unsold case. A stock of twelve cases will increase daily profits to $360, but only on those days when buyers want twelve or thirteen cases. Should buyers want only ten cases, profit is reduced to $260; the $300 profit on the sale of ten cases is reduced by $40, the cost of two unsold cases. Stocking thirteen cases will result in a profit of $390 (a $30 profit on each case sold, with no unsold cases) when there is a market for thirteen cases. When buyers purchase fewer than thirteen cases, such a stock action results in profits of less than $390. For example, with a stock of thirteen cases and sale of only eleven cases, the profit is $290; the profit on eleven cases, $330, is reduced by the cost of two unsold cases ($40).

Function of the conditional profit table

Such a conditional profit table does *not* show the retailer how many cases he should stock each day in order to maximize profits. It reveals the outcome only if a specific number of cases is stocked and a specific number of cases is sold. Under conditions of uncertainty, the retailer does not know in advance the size of any day's market. However, he must still decide which number of cases, stocked consistently, will maximize profits over a long period of time.

Calculating Expected Profits

The next step in determining the best number of cases to stock is assigning probabilities to the possible outcomes or profits. We say in Table 16-2 that the probabilities of the possible values for the retailer's sales are as follows:

Cases	10	11	12	13
Probability	.15	.20	.40	.25

Using these probabilities and the information contained in Table 16-3, we can now compute the expected profit of each possible stock action.

Computing expected profit

We stated in Chapter 6 that **we can compute the expected value of a random variable by weighting each possible value the variable can take by the probability of its taking on that value.** Using this procedure, we can compute the expected daily profit from stocking ten cases each day. See Table 16-4. The figures in column 4 of Table 16-4 are obtained by weighting the conditional profit of each possible sales volume (column 2) by the probability of that conditional profit occurring (column 3). The sum in the last column is the expected daily profit resulting from stocking ten cases each day. It is not surprising that this expected profit is $300, since we saw in Table 16-3 that stocking ten cases each day would always result in a daily profit of $300, regardless of whether buyers wanted ten, eleven, twelve, or thirteen cases.

For 10 units

TABLE 16-4 Expected profit from stocking 10 cases

MARKET SIZE IN CASES	CONDITIONAL PROFIT		PROBABILITY OF MARKET SIZE		EXPECTED PROFIT
10	$300	×	.15	=	$ 45.00
11	300	×	.20	=	60.00
12	300	×	.40	=	120.00
13	300	×	.25	=	75.00
			1.00		**$300.00**

The same computation for a daily stock of eleven units can be made, as we have done in Table 16-5. This tells us that if the retailer stocks eleven cases each day, his expected daily profit over time will be $322.50. Eighty-five percent of the time the daily profit will be $330; on these days, buyers ask for eleven, twelve, or thirteen cases. However, column 3 tells us that 15 percent of the time the market will take only ten cases, resulting in a profit of only $280. It is this fact that reduces the daily expected profit to $322.50.

For 11 units

TABLE 16-5 Expected profit from stocking 11 cases

MARKET SIZE IN CASES	CONDITIONAL PROFIT		PROBABILITY OF MARKET SIZE		EXPECTED PROFIT
10	$280	×	.15	=	$ 42.00
11	330	×	.20	=	66.00
12	330	×	.40	=	132.00
13	330	×	.25	=	82.50
			1.00		**$332.50**

For 12 and 13 units

For twelve and thirteen units, the expected daily profit is computed as shown in Tables 16-6 and 16-7 respectively.

TABLE 16-6 Expected profit from stocking 12 cases

MARKET SIZE IN CASES	CONDITIONAL PROFIT		PROBABILITY OF MARKET SIZE		EXPECTED PROFIT
10	$260	×	.15	=	$ 39.00
11	310	×	.20	=	62.00
12	360	×	.40	=	144.00
13	360	×	.25	=	90.00
			1.00		**$335.00**

optimum stock ← action

TABLE 16-7 Expected profit from stocking 13 cases

MARKET SIZE IN CASES	CONDITIONAL PROFIT		PROBABILITY OF MARKET SIZE		EXPECTED PROFIT
10	$240	×	.15	=	$ 36.00
11	290	×	.20	=	58.00
12	340	×	.40	=	136.00
13	390	×	.25	=	97.50
			1.00		**$327.50**

We have now computed the expected profit of each of the four stock actions open to the retailer. These expected profits are:

- If 10 cases are stocked each day, expected daily profit is $300.00.
- If 11 cases are stocked each day, expected daily profit is $322.50.
- If 12 cases are stocked each day, expected daily profit is $335.00.
- If 13 cases are stocked each day, expected daily profit is $327.50.

Optimum solution

The *optimum stock action* is the one that results in the greatest expected profit—the largest daily average profits and thus the maximum total profits over a period of time. In this illustration, the proper number to stock each day is twelve cases, since that quantity will give the highest possible average daily profits under the conditions given.

What the solution means

We have *not* reduced uncertainty in the problem facing the retailer. Rather, we have used his past experience to determine the best stock action open to him. He still does not know how many cases will be requested on any given day. There is no guarantee that he will make a profit of $335.00 tomorrow. However, if he stocks twelve cases each day under the conditions given, he will have *average* profits of $335.00 per day. This is the best he can do, because the choice of any one of the other three possible stock actions will result in a lower expected daily profit.

Expected Profit with Perfect Information

Definition of perfect information

Now suppose that the retailer in our illustration could remove all uncertainty from his problem by obtaining complete and accurate information about the future, referred to as *perfect* information. This does not mean that sales would not vary from ten to thirteen cases per day. Sales would still be ten cases per day 15 percent of the time, eleven cases 20 percent of the time, twelve cases 40 percent of the time, and thirteen cases 25 percent of the time. However, with perfect information, the retailer would know in advance how many cases were going to be called for each day.

Use of perfect information

Under these circumstances, the retailer would stock today the exact number of cases buyers will want tomorrow. For sales of ten cases, the retailer would stock ten cases and realize a profit of $300. When sales were going to be eleven cases, he would stock exactly eleven cases, thus realizing a profit of $330.00.

TABLE 16-8 Conditional profit table under certainty

POSSIBLE SALES IN CASES	Possible stock actions			
	10 CASES	11 CASES	12 CASES	13 CASES
10	$300	—	—	—
11	—	$330	—	—
12	—	—	$360	—
13	—	—	—	$390

Table 16-8 shows the conditional profit values that are applicable to the retailer's problem if he has perfect information. Knowing the size of the market in advance for a particular day, the retailer chooses the stock action that will maximize his profits. This means he buys and stocks quantities that avoid *all* losses from obsolete stock as well as *all* losses that reflect lost profits on unfilled requests for merchandise.

Expected profit under certainty

We can now compute the expected profit under certainty. This is shown in Table 16-9. The procedure is the same as that already used, but you will notice that the conditional profit figures in column 2 of Table 16-9 are the maximum profits possible for each sales volume. When buyers buy twelve cases, for example, the retailer will always make a profit of $360

TABLE 16-9 Expected profit under certainty

MARKET SIZE IN CASES	CONDITIONAL PROFIT UNDER CERTAINTY		PROBABILITY OF MARKET SIZE		EXPECTED PROFIT UNDER CERTAINTY
10	$300	×	.15	=	$ 45.00
11	330	×	.20	=	66.00
12	360	×	.40	=	144.00
13	390	×	.25	=	97.50
			1.00		**$352.50**

under certainty because he will have stocked exactly twelve cases. With perfect information, then, our retailer could count on making an average profit of $352.50 a day. This is a significant figure because it is the *maximum profit* possible.

Expected Value of Perfect Information

Value of certainty

Assuming that a retailer could obtain a perfect predictor about the future, what would be its value to him? He must compare the cost of that information with the additional profit he would realize as a result of having the information.

The retailer in our example can earn average daily profits of $352.50 if he has perfect information about the future (see Table 16-9). His best expected daily profit without the predictor is only $335.00 (see Tables 16-4 to 16-7). The difference of $17.50 is the maximum amount the retailer would be willing to pay, per day, for a perfect predictor, because that is the maximum amount by which he can increase his expected daily profit. This difference is the *expected value of perfect information* and is referred to as EVPI. There is no sense in paying more than $17.50 for the predictor; to do so would cost more than the knowledge is worth.

Why do we need the value of certainty?

Calculating the value of additional information in the decision-making process is a serious problem for managers. In our illustration, we found that our retailer would pay $17.50 a day for a perfect predictor. Only infrequently, however, can we secure a perfect predictor. In most decision-making situations, managers are really attempting to evaluate the worth of information that will enable them to make better, rather than perfect, decisions.

EXERCISES

16-4 Center City Motor Sales has recently incorporated. Its chief asset is a franchise to sell automobiles of a major American manufacturer. CCMS's general manager is planning the staffing of the dealership's garage facilities. From information provided by the manufacturer and from other nearby dealerships, he has estimated the number of annual mechanic hours that the garage will be likely to need.

Hours	10,000	12,000	14,000	16,000
Probability	.2	.3	.4	.1

The manager plans to pay each mechanic $9.00 per hour and to charge his customers $16.00. Mechanics will work a 40-hour week and get an annual 2-week vacation.

a) Determine how many mechanics Center City should hire.

b) How much should Center City pay to get perfect information about the number of mechanics they need?

16-5 Airport Rent-a-Car is a locally operated business in competition with several major firms. ARC is planning a new deal for prospective customers who want to rent a car for only one day and return it to the airport. For $17.00, the company will rent a small economy car to a customer, whose only other expense is to fill the car with gas at the day's end. ARC is planning to buy a number of small cars from the manufacturer at a reduced price of $4,600. The big question is how many to buy. Company executives have decided on the following probable average demands per day for the service:

Number of cars rented	8	9	10	11	12	13
Probability	.17	.18	.20	.16	.15	.14

The company plans on offering the plan 6 days a week (312 days per year) and anticipates that its variable cost per car per day will be $1.50. After the end of 1 year, the company expects to sell the cars and recapture 50 percent of the original cost. Disregarding the time value of money and any noncash expenses, determine the optimal number of cars for ARC to buy.

16-6 Cynthia Baum, merchandise manager for the Grant Shoe Company, was planning production decisions for the coming year's summer line of shoes. Her chief concern was with estimating the summer sales of a new design of fashion sandals. Fashion sandals had posed problems for 2 reasons: (1) The limited selling season did not provide enough time for the company to produce a second run of a popular item, and (2) the styles changed dramatically from year to year, and unsold sandals became worthless. Cynthia had discussed the new shoe with salespeople and had formulated the following estimate of how the item would sell:

	SANDAL SALES				
Pairs (in thousands)	30	35	40	45	50
Probability	.10	.15	.20	.30	.25

Information from the production department revealed that the shoe would cost $7.50 per pair to manufacture. Marketing had informed Cynthia that the wholesale price would be $14.00 a pair. Using the expected value decision criterion, calculate the number of pairs that Cynthia should recommend the company produce.

16-7 For several years, the Madison Rhodes Department Store had featured personalized pencils as a Christmas special. Madison Rhodes purchased the pencils from its supplier, who provided the embossing machine. The personalizing was done on the department store premises. Despite the success of the pencil sales, Madison Rhodes had received comments that the quality of the lead in the pencils was poor, and the store had found a different supplier. The new supplier would, however, be unable to begin servicing the department store until after the first of January. Madison Rhodes was forced to purchase its pencils one final time from its original supplier, to meet Christmas demand. It was, therefore, important that pencils not be overstocked, and yet the manager was adamant about not losing too many customers because of stockouts. The pencils came packed 15 to the box, 72 boxes to the case. Madison Rhodes paid $60 per case and sold the pencils for $1.50 per box. Labor costs are 37.5¢ per box sold. Based on previous year's sales, management constructed the following schedule:

Expected sales (cases)	15	16	17	18	19	20
Probability	.05	.20	.30	.25	.10	.10

a) How many cases should Madison Rhodes order?
b) What's the expected profit?

16-8 Emily Scott, head of a small business consulting firm, must decide how many M.B.A.s to hire as full-time consultants for the next year. (Emily has decided that she will not bother with any part-time employees.)

Emily knows from experience that the probability distribution on the number of consulting jobs her firm will get each year is represented by the numbers below:

Consulting jobs	24	27	30	33
Probability	.3	.2	.4	.1

Emily also knows that each M.B.A. hired will be able to handle exactly 3 consulting jobs per year. The salary of each M.B.A. is $30,000. Each consulting job is worth $15,000 to Emily's firm. Each consulting job that the firm is awarded but cannot complete costs the firm $5,000 in future business lost.

a) How many M.B.A.s should Emily hire?

b) What is the expected value of perfect information to Emily?

16-9 Balloon Buffoons, a balloon delivery service, is expanding. The company already employs three drivers and would like to know how many more it should hire to maximize daily expected profits. Each driver will earn $60 in daily wages, and the company will incur additional daily costs of $20 per driver. Each driver may deliver at most 20 sets of balloons per day. Each delivery requested but not made owing to lack of drivers costs the company $2.50 in goodwill. The number of deliveries requested per day has the probability distribution given below.

Deliveries requested	60	80	100	120	140
Probability	.2	.2	.3	.1	.2

a) Determine how many drivers Balloon Buffoons should hire.

b) Determine the expected daily value of perfect information to Balloon Buffoons.

16-3 USING CONTINUOUS DISTRIBUTIONS IN DECISION THEORY: Marginal Analysis

Limitations of the discrete method

In many inventory problems, the number of computations required makes the use of conditional profit and expected profit tables difficult. Our previous illustration contained only four possible stock actions and four possible sales levels, resulting in a conditional profit table containing sixteen possibilities for conditional profits. If we had 300 possible values for sales volume and an equal number of calculations for determining conditional and expected profit, we would have to do a great many computations. The marginal approach avoids this problem.

Marginal analysis is based on the fact that when an additional unit of an item is bought, two fates are possible: The unit will be sold, or it will not be sold. The sum of the probabilities of these two events must be 1. (For example, if the probability of selling the additional unit is .6, then the probability of not selling it must be .4).

Derivation of marginal profit

If we let p represent the probability of selling one additional unit, then $1 - p$ must be the probability of not selling it. If the additional unit is sold, we shall realize an increase in our conditional profits as a result of the profit from the additional unit. We refer to this as *marginal profit*, or *MP*. In our previous illustration about the retailer, the marginal profit resulting from the sale of an additional unit is $30, the selling price ($50) minus the cost ($20).

Table 16-10 illustrates this point. If we stock ten units each day and daily demand is for ten or more units, our conditional profit is $300 per day. Now we decide to stock eleven units each day. If the eleventh unit is sold (and this is the case in which demand is for eleven, twelve, or thirteen units), our conditional profit is increased to $330 per day. Notice that the increase in conditional profit does not follow merely from *stocking* the eleventh unit. Under the conditions assumed in the problem, this increase in profit will result only when demand is for eleven or more units. This will be the case 85 percent of the time.

TABLE 16-10 Conditional profit table

POSSIBLE DEMAND (SALES) IN CASES	PROBABILITY OF MARKET SIZE	Possible stock actions			
		10 CASES	11 CASES	12 CASES	13 CASES
10	.15	$300	$280	$260	$240
11	.20	300	330	310	290
12	.40	300	330	360	340
13	.25	300	330	360	390

Derivation of stocking rule

We must also consider how profits would be affected by stocking an additional unit and not selling it. This reduces our conditional profit. The amount of the reduction is referred to as the *marginal loss* (*ML*) resulting from the stocking of an item that is not sold. In our previous example, the marginal loss was $20 per unit, the cost of the item.

Table 16-10 also illustrates marginal loss. Once more we decide to stock eleven units. If the eleventh unit (the marginal unit) is not sold, the conditional profit is $280. The $300 conditional profit when ten units were stocked and ten were sold is reduced by $20, the cost of the unsold unit.

Additional units should be stocked as long as the expected marginal profit from stocking each of them is greater than the expected marginal loss from stocking each. **The size of each day's order should be increased up to the point where the expected marginal profit from stocking one more unit if it sells is just equal to the expected marginal loss from stocking that unit if it remains unsold.**

In our illustration, the probability distribution of demand is:

MARKET SIZE	PROBABILITY OF MARKET SIZE
10	.15
11	.20
12	.40
13	.25
	1.00

This distribution tells us that as we increase our stock, the probability of selling one additional unit (this is p) decreases. If we increase our stock from ten to eleven units, the probability of selling all eleven is .85. This is the probability that demand will be for eleven units or more. Here is the computation:

Probability that demand will be for 11	.20
Probability that demand will be for 12	.40
Probability that demand will be for 13	.25
Probability that demand will be for 11 or more units	**.85**

If we add a twelfth unit, the probability of selling all twelve units is reduced to .65 (the sum of the probabilities of demand for twelve or thirteen units). Finally, the addition of a thirteenth unit carries with it only a .25 probability of our selling all thirteen units, because demand will be for thirteen units only 25 percent of the time.

Deriving the Minimum Probability Equation

Expected marginal profit and loss defined

The *expected marginal profit* from stocking and selling an additional unit is the marginal profit of the unit multiplied by the probability that the unit will be sold; this is $p(MP)$. The *expected marginal loss* from stocking and not selling an additional unit is the marginal loss incurred if the unit is unsold multiplied by the probability that the unit will not be sold; this is $(1 - p)(ML)$. We can generalize that the retailer in this situation would stock up to the point at which:

$$p(MP) = (1 - p)(ML) \quad \textbf{[16-1]}$$

This equation describes the point at which the expected marginal profit from stocking and selling an additional unit, $p(MP)$, is equal to the expected marginal loss from stocking and not selling the unit, $(1 - p)(ML)$. As long as $p(MP)$ is larger than $(1 - p)(ML)$, additional units should be stocked, because the expected profit from such a decision is greater than the expected loss.

Optimum inventory purchase level

In any given inventory problem, there will be only *one* value of p for which the maximizing equation will be true. We must determine that value in order to know the optimum stock action to take. We can do this by taking our maximizing equation and solving it for p in the following manner:

$$p(MP) = (1 - p)(ML) \quad \textbf{[16-1]}$$

Multiplying the two terms on the right side of the equation, we get:

$$p(MP) = ML - p(ML)$$

Collecting terms containing p, we have:

$$p(MP) + p(ML) = ML$$

or:

$$p(MP + ML) = ML$$

Dividing both sides of the equation by $MP + ML$ gives:

Minimum probability equation

Minimum required probability ⟶ $$p = \frac{ML}{MP + ML} \quad [16\text{-}2]$$

The letter p represents the minimum required probability of selling at least one additional unit to justify the stocking of that additional unit. The retailer should stock additional units so long as the probability of selling at least an additional unit is greater than p.

We can now compute p for our illustration. The marginal profit per unit is \$30 (the selling price minus the cost); the marginal loss per unit is \$20 (the cost of each unit); thus:

$$p = \frac{ML}{MP + ML} = \frac{\$20}{\$30 + \$20} = \frac{\$20}{\$50} = .4$$

This value of a .4 for p means that in order to make the stocking of an additional unit justifiable, we must have at least a .4 *cumulative* probability of selling that unit or more. In order to determine the probability of selling each additional unit we consider stocking, we must compute a series of cumulative probabilities as we have done in Table 16-11.

Calculation of cumulative probabilities

The cumulative probabilities in the right-hand column of Table 16-11 represent the probabilities that sales will reach or exceed each of the four sales levels. For example, the 1.00 that appears beside the 10-unit sales level means that we are 100 percent certain of selling ten or more units. This must be true because our problem assumes that one of the four sales levels will *always* occur.

TABLE 16-11 Cumulative probabilities of sales

SALES UNITS	PROBABILITY OF THIS SALES LEVEL	CUMULATIVE PROBABILITY THAT SALES WILL BE AT THIS LEVEL OR GREATER
10	.15	1.00
11	.20	.85
12	.40	.65
13	.25	.25

The .85 probability value beside the 11-unit sales figure means that we are only 85 percent sure of selling eleven or more units. This can be calculated in two ways. First, we could add the chances of selling eleven, twelve, and thirteen units:

11 units	.20	
12 units	.40	
13 units	+.25	
	.85	= probability of selling 11 or more

Or we could reason that sales of eleven or more units include all possible outcomes except sales of ten units, which has a probability of .15.

All possible outcomes	1.00	
Probability of selling 10	−.15	
	.85	= probability of selling 11 or more

The cumulative probability value of .65 assigned to sales of twelve units or more can be established in similar fashion. Sales of twelve or more must mean sales of twelve or of thirteen units; so:

Probability of selling 12	.40	
Probability of selling 13	+.25	
	.65	= probability of selling 12 or more

And, of course, the cumulative probability of selling thirteen units is still .25, because we have assumed that sales will never exceed thirteen.

As we mentioned previously, the value of p decreases as the levels of sales increase. This causes the expected marginal profit to decrease and the expected marginal loss to increase until, at some point, our stocking of an additional unit would not be profitable.

We have said that additional units should be stocked as long as the probability of selling at least an additional unit is greater than p. We can now apply this rule to our probability distribution of sales and determine how many units should be stocked.

In this case, the probability of selling eleven or more units is .85, a figure clearly greater than our p of .40; thus, we should stock an eleventh unit. The expected marginal profit from stocking this unit is greater than the expected marginal loss from stocking it. We can verify this as follows:

$$p(MP) = .85(\$30) = \$25.50 \text{ expected marginal profit}$$
$$(1-p)(ML) = .15(\$20) = \$3.00 \text{ expected marginal loss}$$

Optimum stocking level for this problem

A twelfth unit should be stocked because the probability of selling twelve or more units (.65) is greater than the required p of .40. Such action will result in the following expected marginal profit and expected marginal loss:

$$p(MP) = .65(\$30) = \$19.50 \text{ expected marginal profit}$$
$$(1-p)(ML) = .35(\$20) = \$7.00 \text{ expected marginal loss}$$

Twelve is the *optimum* number of units to stock, because the addition of a thirteenth unit carries with it only a .25 probability that it will be sold, and that is less than our required p of .40. The following figures reveal why the thirteenth unit should not be stocked:

$$p(MP) = .25(\$30) = \$7.50 \text{ expected marginal profit}$$
$$(1 - p)(ML) = .75(\$20) = \$15.00 \text{ expected marginal loss}$$

If we stock a thirteenth unit, we add more to expected loss than we add to expected profit.

Notice that the use of marginal analysis leads us to the same conclusion that we reached with the use of conditional profit and expected profit tables. Both methods of analysis suggest that the retailer should stock twelve units each period.

Adjusting the optimal stocking level

Our strategy, to stock twelve cases every day, assumes that daily sales is a random variable. In actual practice, however, daily sales often take on recognizable patterns depending upon the particular day of the week. In retail sales, Saturday is generally recognized as being a higher-volume day than, say, Tuesday. Similarly, Monday retail sales are typically less than those on Friday. In situations with recognizable patterns in daily sales, we can apply the techniques we have learned by computing an optimal stocking level for *each* day of the week. For Saturday, we would use as our input data past sales experience for Saturdays only. Each of the other six days could be treated in the same fashion. Essentially, this approach represents nothing more than recognition of, and reaction to, discernible patterns in what may at first appear to be a completely random environment.

Using the Standard Normal Probability Distribution

We first learned the concept of the standard normal probability distribution in Chapter 6. We can now use this idea to help us solve a decision theory problem employing a continuous distribution.

Solving a problem using marginal analysis

Assume that a manager sells an article having normally distributed sales with a mean of 50 units daily and a standard deviation in daily sales of 15 units. The manager purchases this article for \$4 per unit and sells it for \$9 per unit. If the article is not sold on the selling day, it is worth nothing. Using the marginal method of calculating optimum inventory purchase levels, we can calculate our required p:

$$p = \frac{ML}{MP + ML} \qquad [16\text{-}2]$$

$$= \frac{\$4}{\$5 + \$4} = .44$$

This means that the manager must be .44 sure of selling at least an additional unit before it would pay to stock that unit. Let us reproduce the curve of past sales and determine how to incorporate the marginal method with continuous distributions of past daily sales.

Standard normal probability distribution combined with marginal analysis

Now refer to Fig. 16-1. If we erect a vertical line b at 50 units, the area under the curve to the right of this line is one-half the total area. This tells us that the probability of selling 50 or more units is .5. *The area to the right of any such vertical line represents the probability of selling that quantity or more.* As the area to the right of any vertical line decreases, so does the probability that we will sell that quantity or more.

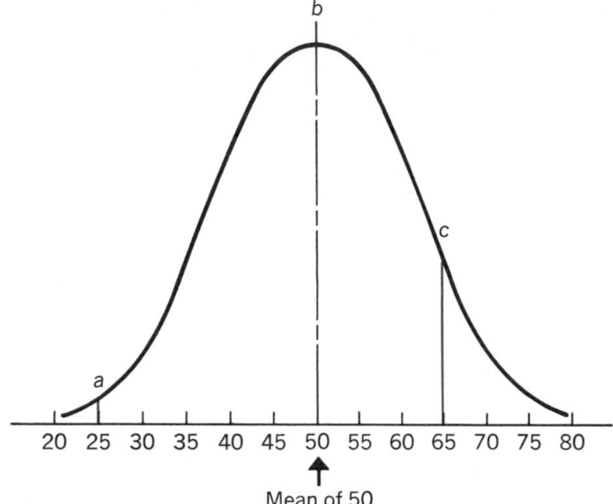

FIGURE 16-1
Normal distribution of past daily sales

Suppose the manager considers stocking 25 units, line a. Most of the entire area under the curve lies to the right of the vertical line drawn at 25; thus, the probability is great that the manager will sell 25 units or more. If he considers stocking 50 units (the mean), one-half the entire area under the curve lies to the right of vertical line b; thus he is .5 sure of selling the 50 units or more. Now, say he considers stocking 65 units. Only a small portion of the entire area under the curve lies to the right of line c; thus the probability of selling 65 or more units is quite small.

Figure 16-2 illustrates the .44 probability that must exist before it pays our manager to stock another unit. He will stock additional units until he reaches point Q. If he stocks a larger quantity, the shaded area under the curve drops below .44 and the probability of selling another unit or more falls below the required .44. How can we locate point Q? As we saw in Chapter 6, we can use Appendix Table 1 to determine how many standard deviations it takes to include any portion of the area under the curve measuring from the mean to any points such as Q. In this particular case, since we know that the shaded area must be .44 of the total area, then the area from the mean to point Q must be .06 (the total area from the mean to the right tail is .50). Looking in the body of the table, we find that .06 of the area under the curve is located between the mean and a point .15 standard deviations to the right of the mean. Thus we know that point Q is .15 standard deviations to the right of the mean (50).

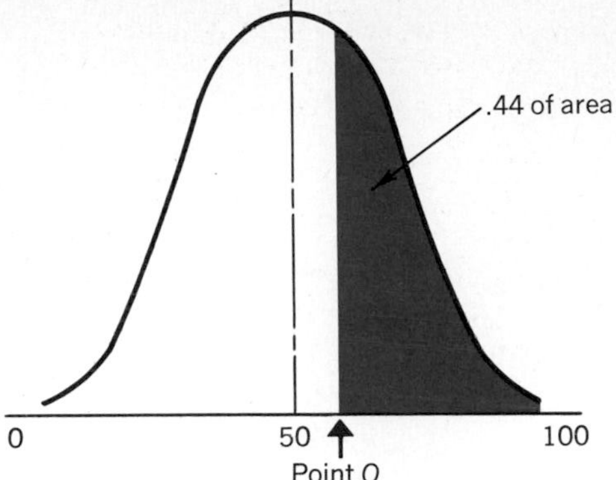

FIGURE 16-2 Normal probability distribution, with .44 of the area under the curve shaded

Optimum solution for this problem

We have been given the information that 1 standard deviation for this distribution is 15 units; so .15 times this would be 2.25 units. Since point Q is 2.25 units to the right of the mean (50), it must be at about 52 units. This is the optimum order for the manager to place: 52 units per day.

Now that we have been through one problem using a continuous probability distribution, we can work our chapter-opening problem involving these data for a normally distributed daily sales record:

Mean of past daily sales	60 cases
Standard deviation of past daily sales distribution	10 cases
Cost per case	$20
Selling price per case	$32
Value if not sold on first day	$ 2

As we did in the previous problem, we first calculate the p that is required to justify the stocking of an additional case. In this instance:

Minimum required probability

$$p = \frac{ML}{MP + ML} \qquad [16\text{-}2]$$

$$= \frac{\$20 - \$2}{\$12 + (\$20 - \$2)}$$

Notice that a salvage value of $2 is deducted from the cost of $20 to obtain the *ML*.

$$= \frac{\$18}{\$12 + \$18}$$

$$= \frac{\$19}{\$30} = .63$$

We can now illustrate the probability on a normal curve by marking off .63 of the area under the curve, starting from the right-hand end of the curve, as in Fig. 16-3.

The manager will want to increase his order size this time until it reaches point Q. Notice that point Q lies to the *left* of the mean, whereas in

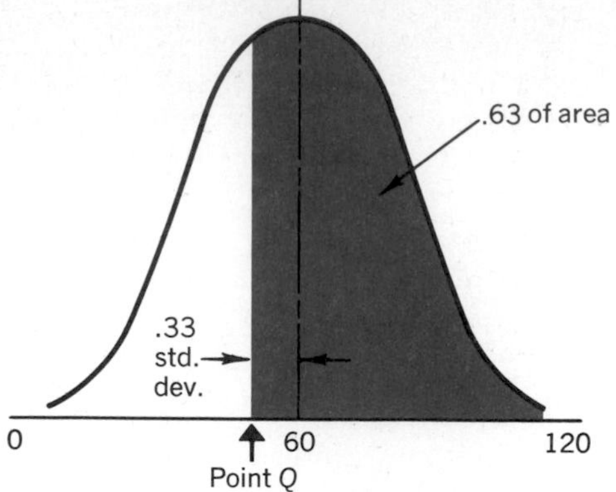

FIGURE 16-3 Normal probability distribution, with .63 of the area under the curve shaded

the preceding problem it lay to the *right* of the mean. How can we locate point Q? Since .5 of the area under the curve is located between the mean and the right-hand tail, .13 of the shaded area must be to the left of the mean, $(.63 - .5 = .13)$. We look for .13 in the body of Appendix Table 1. The nearest value to .13 is .1293, so we want to find a point Q with .1293 of the area under the curve contained between the mean of the curve and that point Q. The table indicates point Q to be .33 standard deviations from the mean. We can now solve for point Q as follows:

$$
\begin{aligned}
.33 \times \text{standard deviation} &= .33 \times 10 \text{ cases} = 3.3 \text{ cases} \\
\text{Point } Q &= \text{mean less } 3.3 \text{ cases} \\
&= 60 - 3.3 \text{ cases} = 56.7, \text{ or } 56 \text{ cases}
\end{aligned}
$$

EXERCISES

16-10 Highway road construction in North Carolina is concentrated in the months from May through September. To provide some measure of protection to the crews at work on the highways, the Department of Transportation (DOT) requires that large, orange MEN WORKING signs be placed well in advance of any construction. Because of vandalism, wear and tear, and theft, each year DOT purchases a number of new signs to be put into service. The signs are actually made under the auspices of the Department of Corrections, but because of interdepartmental budgeting and accounting, DOT is charged a price equivalent to one it might pay were it to buy the signs from an outside source. The interdepartmental charge for the signs is \$11 if more than 30 of the same kind are ordered. Otherwise, the cost per sign is \$15. Because of budget pressures, DOT attempts to minimize its costs both by not buying too many signs and by attempting to buy in sufficiently large quantity to get the \$11 price. In recent years, the department has averaged purchases of 84 signs per year with a standard deviation of 11. Determine the number of signs DOT should purchase.

16-11 The town of Green Lake, Wisconsin, is preparing for the celebration of the 79th Annual Milk and Dairy Day. As a fund-raising device, the city council once again plans to sell souvenir T-shirts. The T-shirts, printed in 6 colors, will have a picture of a cow and the words, "79th Annual Milk and Dairy Day," on the front. The city council purchases heat transfer patches from a supplier for $.75 and plain white cotton T-shirts for $1.50. A local merchant supplies the appropriate heating device and also purchases all unsold white cotton T-shirts. The council plans to set up a booth on Main Street and sell the shirts for $3.25. The transfer of the color to the shirt will be completed when the sale is made. In the past year, similar shirt sales have averaged 200 with a standard deviation of 34. The council knows that there will be no market for the patches after the celebration. How many patches should the city council buy?

16-12 Bike Wholesale Parts was established in the early 1970s in response to demands of several small and newly established bicycle shops that needed access to a wide variety of inventory but were not able to finance it themselves. The company carries a wide variety of replacement parts and accessories but does not maintain any stock of completed bicycles. Management is preparing to order 27″ × 1¼″ rims from the Flexspin Company in anticipation of a business upturn expected in about 2 months. Flexspin makes a superior product, but the lead time required necessitates that wholesalers make only one order, which must last through the critical summer months. In the past, Bike Wholesale Parts has sold an average of 120 rims per summer with a standard deviation of 28. The company expects that its stock of rims will be depleted by the time the new order arrives. Bike Wholesale Parts has been quite successful and plans to move its operations to a larger plant during the winter. Management feels that the combined cost of moving some items such as rims and the existing cost of financing them is at least equal to the firm's purchase cost of $7.30. Accepting management's hypothesis that any unsold rims at the end of the summer season are permanently unsold, determine the number of rims the company should order if the selling price is $8.10.

16-13 The B&G Cafeteria features barbecued chicken each Thursday. The special has become a popular item, and cafeteria manager Patricia Arden wants to ensure that the cafeteria will make money on the special in the long run. Including labor, each portion of chicken costs the cafeteria 95¢ to prepare and sell. The customers pay $1.20 and consider it a good deal. Data taken from last year indicate that barbecued chicken sales are normally distributed, with mean 160 and standard deviation 23. If B&G Cafeteria converts one chicken into two portions of barbecued chicken, how many chickens should be prepared each Thursday?

16-14 Paige's Tire Service stocks two types of radial tires: polyester-belted and steel-belted. The polyester-belted radials cost the company $30 each and sell for $35. The steel-belted radials cost the company $45 and sell for $60. For various reasons, Paige's Tire Service will not be able to reorder any radials from the factory this year, so they must order just once to satisfy customers' demand for the entire year. At the end of the year, owing to new tire models, Paige will have to sell all its inventory of radials for scrap rubber at $5 each. The annual sales of both types of radial tires are normally distributed with mean and standard deviation indicated below.

	ANNUAL MEAN SALES	STANDARD DEVIATION
Polyester-belted	300	50
Steel-belted	200	20

a) How many polyester-belted radials should be ordered?
b) How many steel-belted radials should be ordered?

16-15 Plain Games, a toy and hobby shop, is getting ready to make its final order of toys and games, which will arrive exactly 4 weeks before Christmas. The manager is most concerned about a line of toys produced by the North Pole Company—they are decorated to be very Christmas-oriented and will be worth almost nothing to the store after Christmas. Each such toy sells for $6, but will be sold to a discount retailer for only $1 after the holiday season. Plain Games pays the factory $4 for each toy. The manager knows from past experience that the demand for North Pole toys during the 4 weeks before Christmas is normally distributed, with mean 600 and standard deviation 120. How many North Pole toys should be stocked for the last 4 weeks of the Christmas buying season?

16-4 UTILITY AS A DECISION CRITERION

Different decision criteria

So far in this chapter, we have used expected value (expected profit, for example) as our decision criterion. We assumed that if the expected profit of alternative A was better than that of alternative B, then the decision maker would certainly choose alternative A. Conversely, if the expected loss of alternative C was greater than the expected loss of alternative D, then we assumed that the decision maker would surely choose D as the better course of action.

Shortcomings of Expected Value as a Decision Criterion

There are situations, however, in which the use of expected value as the decision criterion would get a manager into serious trouble. Suppose a businessman owns a new factory worth \$2 million. Suppose further that there is only one chance in 1,000, (.001) that it will burn down this year. From these two figures we can compute the expected loss:

$$.001 \times \$2{,}000{,}000 = \$2{,}000 = \text{expected loss by fire}$$

An insurance representative offers to insure the building for \$2,250 this year. If the businessman applies the notion of minimizing expected losses, he will refuse to insure the building. The expected loss of insuring (\$2,250) is higher than the expected loss by fire. If, however, the businessman feels that a \$2 million uninsured loss would wipe him out, he will probably discard expected value as his decision criterion and buy the insurance at the extra cost of \$250 per year per policy (\$2,250 − 2,000). He would choose *not* to minimize expected loss in this case.

Another example

Take an example closer, perhaps, to student life. You are a student with just enough money to get through the semester. A friend offers to sell you a .9 chance of winning \$10 for just \$1. You would most likely think of the problem in terms of expected values and reason as follows: "Is .9 × \$10 greater than \$1?" Because \$9 (the expected value of the bet) is nine times greater than the cost of the bet (\$1), you might feel inclined to take your friend up on this offer. Even if you lose, the loss of \$1 will not affect your situation materially.

Now your friend offers to sell you a .9 chance at winning \$1,000 for \$100. The question you would now ponder is, "Is .9 × \$1,000 greater than \$100?" Of course, \$900 (the expected value of the bet) is still nine times the cost of the bet (\$100), but you would more than likely think twice before putting up your money. Why? Because even though the pleasure of winning \$1,000 would be high, the pain of losing your hard-earned \$100 might be more than you care to experience.

Say, finally, that your friend offers to sell you a .9 chance at winning \$10,000 for your total assets, which happen to be \$1,000. If you use expected value as your decision criterion, you would ask the question, "Is .9 × $10,000 greater than $1,000?" You would get the same answer as before—yes. The expected value of the bet ($9,000) is still nine times greater than the cost of the bet ($1,000), but now you would probably refuse your friend, not because the expected value of the bet is unattractive, but because the thought of losing all your assets is completely unacceptable as an outcome.

Function of utility

In this example, you changed the decision criterion away from expected value when the thought of losing $1,000 was too painful, despite the pleasure to be gained from $10,000. At this point, you no longer considered the expected value but thought solely of *utility*. In this sense, utility refers to the pleasure or displeasure one would derive from certain outcomes. Your utility curve in Fig. 16-4 is linear around the origin ($1 of gain is as pleasurable as $1 of loss is painful in this region), but it turns down rapidly when the potential loss rises to levels near $1,000. Specifically, this utility curve shows us that from your point of view, the displeasure from losing only $1,000 is about equal to the pleasure from winning nine times that amount. The shape of one's utility curve is a product of one's psychological makeup, one's expectations about the future, and the particular decision or act being evaluated. A person can have one utility curve for one situation and quite a different one for the next situation.

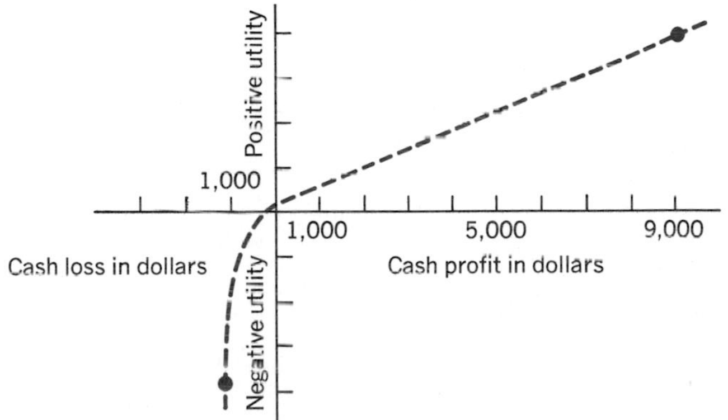

FIGURE 16-4 Utility of various profits and losses

Different Utilities

Attitudes toward risk

The utility curves of three different managers' decisions are shown on the graph in Fig. 16-5. We have arbitrarily named these managers David, Ann, and Jim. Their attitudes are readily apparent from analysis of their utility curves. David is a cautious and conservative businessman. A move to the right of the zero profit point increases his utility only very slightly, whereas a move to the left of the zero profit point decreases his utility rapidly. In terms of numerical values, David's utility curve indicates that going from $0 to $100,000 profit increases his utility by a value of 1 on the vertical scale, while moving into the loss range by only $40,000 decreases his utility by the same value of 1, on the vertical scale. David will avoid situations in which high losses might occur; he is said to be averse to risk.

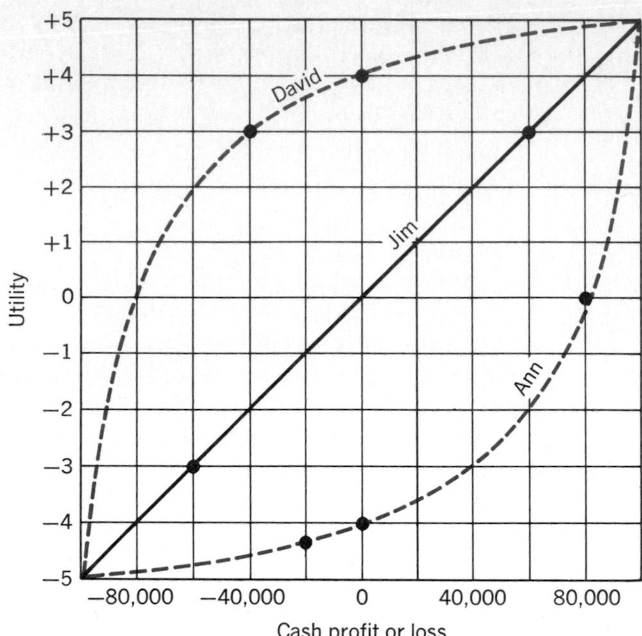

FIGURE 16-5
Three utility curves

Ann is quite another story. We see from her utility curve that a profit increases her utility by much more than a loss of the same amount decreases it. Specifically, increasing her profits $20,000 (from $80,000 to $100,000) raises her utility from 0 to +5 on the vertical scale, but lowering her profits $20,000 (from $0 to −$20,000) decreases her utility by only .25, from −4 to −4.25. Ann is a player of long shots; she feels strongly that a large loss would not make things much worse than they are now but that a big profit would be quite rewarding. She will take large risks to earn even larger gains.

Who would use expected value?

Jim, fairly well off financially, is the kind of businessman who would not suffer greatly from a $60,000 loss nor increase his wealth significantly with a $60,000 gain. Pleasure from making an additional $60,000 or pain from losing it would be of about equal intensity. **Because his utility curve is linear, he can effectively use expected value as his decision criterion, whereas David and Ann must use utility. Jim will act when the expected value is positive, David will demand a high expected value for the outcome, and Ann may act when the expected value is negative.**

EXERCISES

16-16 L. Myron Thurston is a single, wealthy man in the 70 percent tax bracket. Thurston often supplies venture capital to small start-up firms in return for some type of equity position. Recently, Thurston has been approached by Circutronics, a small company entering the microcircuitry industry, which has requested

$600,000 backing. Because of his tax position, Thurston has invested in tax-exempt municipal securities. Currently, he has a very large position in Center City Water and Sewage Authority Bonds, which are returning 4.5 percent. Thurston considers the 4.5 percent after-tax return to be his utility breakeven point. Above that point, his utility rises very rapidly; below, it drops only slightly, since Thurston can well afford to lose the money.

a) What dollar return must Circutronics Company promise before Thurston will consider financing it?
b) Graph L. Myron Thurston's utility curve.

16-17 The Enduro Manufacturing Company is a partnership producing structural-steel building components. Financial manager and partner William Flaherty is examining potential projects that the firm might undertake in the coming fiscal year. The company has a target rate of return of 10 percent on its investment, but because there is no outside financing and interference, the partners have accepted projects with rates of return between 0 and 100 percent. Above 10 percent, the partners' utility rises very rapidly; between 0 and 10 percent, it rises only slightly above 0; below 0, it falls very rapidly. Flaherty is considering several projects that will cause Enduro to invest $250,000. Plot the firm's utility curve.

16-18 An investor is convinced that the price of a share of XYZ stock will rise in the near future. XYZ stock is currently selling for $50 a share. Upon inspecting the latest quotes on the options market, she finds that she can purchase an option at a cost of $4 per share, allowing her to buy XYZ for $48 per share within the next 2 months. She can also purchase an option to buy the stock within a 4-month period; this option, which costs $8 a share, also allows her to exercise the option at $48 per share. She has estimated that the probability values for the stock are as follows:

PRICE PER SHARE	PROBABILITY OF THIS PRICE AT 2 MONTHS	4 MONTHS
$42	.05	0
48	.10	.05
52	.15	10
56	.20	.15
60	.50	.30
64	0	.40

The investor plans to exercise her options just prior to their expiration if the stock is selling for more than $48 and immediately sell it at the current market price. Of course, if the stock is selling for $48 or less when the options expire, she will lose the entire purchase cost of the options. The investor is relatively conservative, with the following utility values for changes in her assets as follows:

CHANGE	UTILITY
+1,200	1.0
+800	.9
+400	.8
0	.7
−400	.1
−800	0.0

The investor is considering one of 3 alternatives: (1) Buy 100 options that expire in 2 months, (2) buy 100 options that expire in 4 months, or (3) don't buy at all. Which of the three alternatives will maximize her expected utility?

16-5 HELPING DECISION MAKERS SUPPLY THE RIGHT PROBABILITIES

Missing information

The two problems we worked using the normal probability distribution required us to know both the mean (μ) and the standard deviation (σ). But how can we make use of a probability distribution when past data are missing or incomplete? By working through a problem, we shall see how we can often generate the required values by using an *intuitive* approach.

Assume that you are thinking about purchasing a machine to replace hand labor on an operation. The machine will cost \$10,000 per year to operate and will save \$8 for each hour it operates. To break even, then, it must operate at least \$10,000/\$8 = 1,250 hours annually. If you are interested in the probability that it will run more than 1,250 hours, you must know something about the distribution of running times, specifically the mean and standard deviation of this distribution. But since you do not have a history of the machine's operation, where would you find these figures?

An Intuitive Approach to Estimating the Mean and Standard Deviation

Estimating the mean

We could ask the foreman of this operation, who has been closely involved with the process, to guess the mean running time of the machine. Let us say that his best estimate is 1,400 hours. But how would he react if you asked him to give you the standard deviation of the distribution? This term may not be meaningful to him, and yet he probably has some intuitive notion of the dispersion of the distribution of running times. Since most people understand betting odds, let us approach him on that basis.

Estimating the standard deviation

We begin by counting off an equal distance on each side of his mean, say 200 hours. This gives us an interval from 1,200 to 1,600 hours. Then we can ask, "What are the odds the number of hours will lie between 1,200 and 1,600 hours?" If he has had any experience with betting, he should be able to reply. Suppose he says, "I think the odds it will run between 1,200 and 1,600 hours are 4 to 3." We show his answer on a probability distribution in Fig. 16-6.

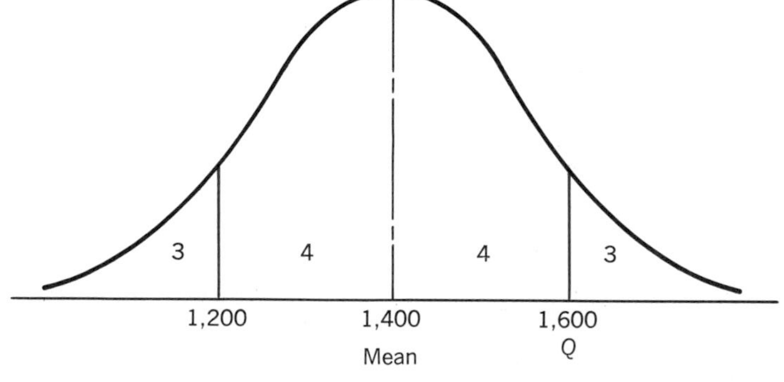

FIGURE 16-6 Foreman's odds intervals for operating times of proposed machines

Figure 16-6 illustrates the foreman's reply that the odds are 4 to 3 the machine will run between 1,200 and 1,600 hours rather than outside those limits. What should we do next? First, we label the 1,600-hour point on the distribution in Fig. 16-6 point Q. Then we can see that the area under the curve between the mean and point Q according to the foreman's estimates is 4/7 of *half* the area under the entire curve, or 4/14 = (.2857) of the *total* area under the curve.

Look at Fig. 16-7. If we turn to Appendix Table 1 for the value .2857, we find that point Q is .79 standard deviations to the right of the mean. Since we know that the distance from the mean to Q is 200 hours, we see that:

$$.79 \text{ standard deviations} = 200 \text{ hours}$$

and thus:

$$\begin{aligned} 1 \text{ standard deviation} &= 200/.79 \\ &= 253 \text{ hours} \end{aligned}$$

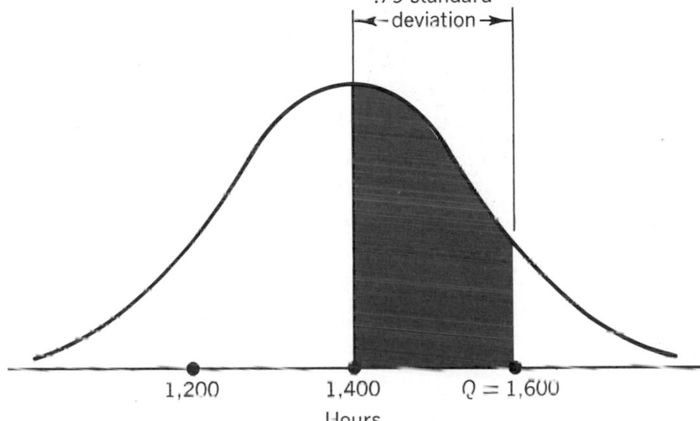

FIGURE 16-7 Determination of standard deviation from foreman's odds

Calculating the breakeven probability

Now that we know the mean and standard deviation of the distribution of running times, we can calculate the probability of the machine's running fewer than its break-even point of 1,250 hours:

$$\begin{aligned} \frac{1{,}400 - 1{,}250}{253} &= \frac{150}{253} \\ &= .59 \text{ standard deviations} \end{aligned}$$

Figure 16-8 illustrates this situation. In Appendix Table 1, we find that the area between the mean of the distribution and a point .59 standard deviations below the mean (1,250 hours) is .2224 of the total area under the curve. To .2224, we add .5, the area from the mean to the right-hand tail. This gives us .7224. Because .7224 is the probability that the machine will operate *more* than 1,250 hours, the chances that it will operate less than 1,250 hours (its

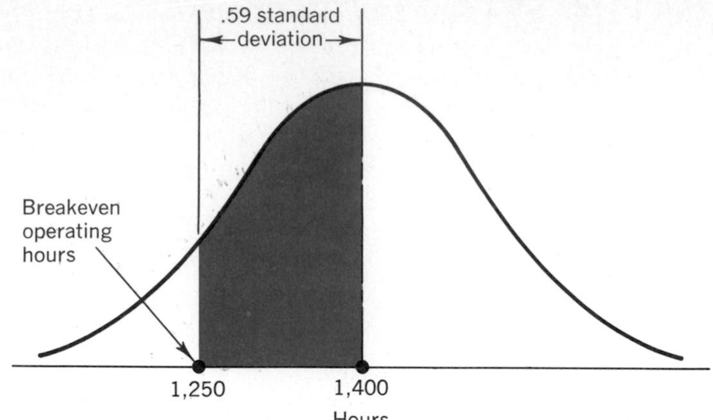

FIGURE 16-8 Probability machine will operate between 1,250 and 1,400 hours

breakeven point) are 1 − .7224, or .2776. Apparently, this is not too risky a situation.

Securing information for models

This problem illustrates how we can make use of other people's knowledge about a situation without requiring them to understand the intricacies of various statistical techniques. Had we expected the foreman to comprehend the theory behind our calculations, or had we even attempted to explain the theory to him, we might never have been able to benefit from his practical wisdom concerning the situation. By using language and terms of reference that he understood, we were able to get the foreman to give us workable estimates of the mean and standard deviation of the distribution of operating times for the machine we contemplated purchasing. In this case (and for that matter, in most others, too), it is wiser to accommodate the ideas and knowledge of other people in your models than to search until you find a situation that will fit a model that has already been developed.

EXERCISES

16-19 Northwestern Industrial Pipe Company is considering purchasing a new electric arc welder for $1,875. The welder is expected to save the firm $4 an hour when it can be used in place of the present, less-efficient welder. Before making the decision, Northwestern's production manager said there were only about 120 hours a year of welding on which the new arc welder could be substituted for the present one. He gave 5 to 3 odds that the actual outcome would be within 30 hours of his estimate. Can Northwestern be 95 percent sure that the new electric arc welder will pay for itself over a 3-year period?

16-20 Natalie Myers, a traveling sales representative for Elremco Products, is considering purchasing a new car for business use. The model she plans to buy is a compact with a sticker price of $5,200. Because her car is used solely for business purposes, Natalie can deduct $.20 a mile for operating expenses. Natalie will buy the car only if the tax savings from purchasing the car will pay for the automobile over its lifetime. Natalie has been in the 25 percent tax bracket for some years, and it appears she will remain there in the foreseeable future. A reputable automotive magazine says that the average life of the car she is considering is 90,000 miles. The article further states that the odds are 4 to 3 that the actual mileage will be within 10,000 miles of the 90,000. What is the probability that the car will last long enough for Natalie to break even?

16-21 Relman Electric Battery Company has felt the effects of a recovering economy as demand for its products has risen in recent months. The company is considering hiring 6 new people for its assembly operation. Plant production manager Mike Casey, whose performance is measured in part by cost efficiency, does not want to hire additional employees unless they can be expected to have jobs for at least 6 months. If the employees are terminated involuntarily before that time, the company is forced by union rules to pay a substantial termination bonus. Additionally, if employees are laid off within 6 months after hiring, the company's unemployment tax rate is raised. Relman's corporate economist expects that the upswing in the economy will last at least 8 months and gives 7 to 2 odds that the length of the upswing will be within a 1-month range of that figure. Casey wants to be 95 percent sure that he will not have to lay of any newly hired employees. Should he hire 6 new people at this time?

16-22 The Newton Pines Police Force is considering purchasing a VASCAR radar unit to be installed on the town's single police cruiser. The town council has balked at the idea, because it is not certain that the unit is worth its price of $2,000. Police Chief Buren Hubbs has stated that he is sure that the unit will pay for itself through the increased number of $20 citations that he and his deputy will give. Buren has been overheard to say that he will give 9 to 1 odds that the increase in citations in the first year will be between 95 and 135 if the unit is purchased. He expects that there will be 115 more tickets given if the cruiser is equipped with VASCAR. Can the town council be 99 percent sure that the unit will be paid for by the increase in revenue from citations in the first year?

16-23 You are planning to invest $10,000 in Warner common stock if it has a 60 percent probability of rising to a price of $60 per share within 6 months. You ask two knowledgeable brokers the following questions: "What is your best estimate of the price of Warner in 6 months?" and, "What are the odds that Warner will sell at a price within plus or minus $5 of your best estimate price?" Their responses are as follows:

BROKER	BEST ESTIMATE	ODDS OF PRICE IN ±$5 RANGE
A	58	2 to 1
B	63	5 to 1

Based on the combined assessment of the two brokers, what decision should you make on the proposed purchase of Warner stock?

16-24 Gryphon Motorcars is contemplating whether or not to upgrade its only existing production facility, which cannot keep up with the overwhelming demand for the sporty Gryphon G-car. Upgrading the production facility will cost $5 million. The plant manager has estimated that with the upgrade, he will expect to produce 1,500 more G-cars per year. He also gave 5 to 2 odds that the actual production will be within 200 G-cars per year of his estimate in any given year. Gryphon makes a profit of $1,000 on each G-car sold. Assuming that the overwhelming consumer demand holds up, so that every G-car produced will be sold, can Gryphon be 99 percent sure that the upgrade will pay for itself in 4 years?

16-6 DECISION TREE ANALYSIS

Decision tree fundamentals

A decision tree is a graphic model of a decision process. With it, we can introduce probabilities into the analysis of complex decisions involving (1) many alternatives and (2) future conditions that are not known but that can be specified in terms of a set of discrete probabilities or a continuous probability distribution. Decision tree analysis is a useful tool in making decisions concerning investments, the acquisition or disposal of physical property, project management, personnel, and new-product strategies.

The term *decision tree* is derived from the physical appearance of the usual graphic representation of this technique. We will use a branch for each alternative and subbranches for each possible outcome or chance event that can occur from that alternative. Because each subbranch can branch again, we eventually build a treelike structure representing all possible outcomes.

A decision tree is like the probability tree we introduced in Chapter 5. But a decision tree contains *both* the probabilities of outcomes *and* the conditional monetary values attached to those outcomes, so that expected values can be computed. Decision trees have standard symbols: Squares symbolize decision points, and circles represent chance events. From each square and circle, branches are drawn. These represent each possible outcome or state of nature that could result.

Decision tree illustrating plant expansion problem

With a decision tree, we can analyze whether the Lakeshore Manufacturing Company should build a large or a small plant to process a new product with an expected market life of ten years.

If Lakeshore builds a large processing plant, it must keep it for ten years. If it builds a small one, it can either expand in two years if demand is high or stay in the small plant making smaller benefits on a small volume of sales. Expanding a small plant after two years would cost $2,200,000.

Demand may be high during the first two years but low for the remaining eight if many users find the product unsatisfactory. On the other hand, high demand during the first two years may indicate high demand for the next eight years. If, within the first two years, demand is high and the company does not expand, competitive products will be introduced and the benefits lowered. Table 16-12 lists the manager's estimates of demand for the next ten years. The manager estimates the financial costs and benefits of the different options available to the company to be:

TABLE 16-12 Estimate of 10-year demand for Lakeshore's new product

PROBABILITY	DEMAND FOR THE FIRST 2 YEARS	DEMAND FOR THE NEXT 8 YEARS
.6	high	high
.1	high	low
.7 ← Probability of high demand during first two years		
.3	low	low
0	low	high
.3 ← Probability of low demand during first two years		

1. A large plant with high demand would yield $1,000,000 annually in benefits.
2. A large plant with low demand would yield $100,000 annually because of production inefficiencies.

3. A small plant, not expanded, with a low demand would yield annual benefits of $200,000 for 10 years.
4. A small plant during a 2-year period of high demand would yield $450,000 annually. If high demand continued and the plant were not expanded, the yield would drop (owing to competition) to $300,000 annually for the next 8 years.
5. A small plant that is expanded after 2 years to meet high demand would yield $700,000 annually for the next 8 years.
6. A small plant that is expanded after 2 years would yield $50,000 annually for 8 years if demand were low during that period.
7. A large plant would cost $3,000,000 to build and put into operation.
8. A small plant would cost $1,300,000 to build and put into operation.

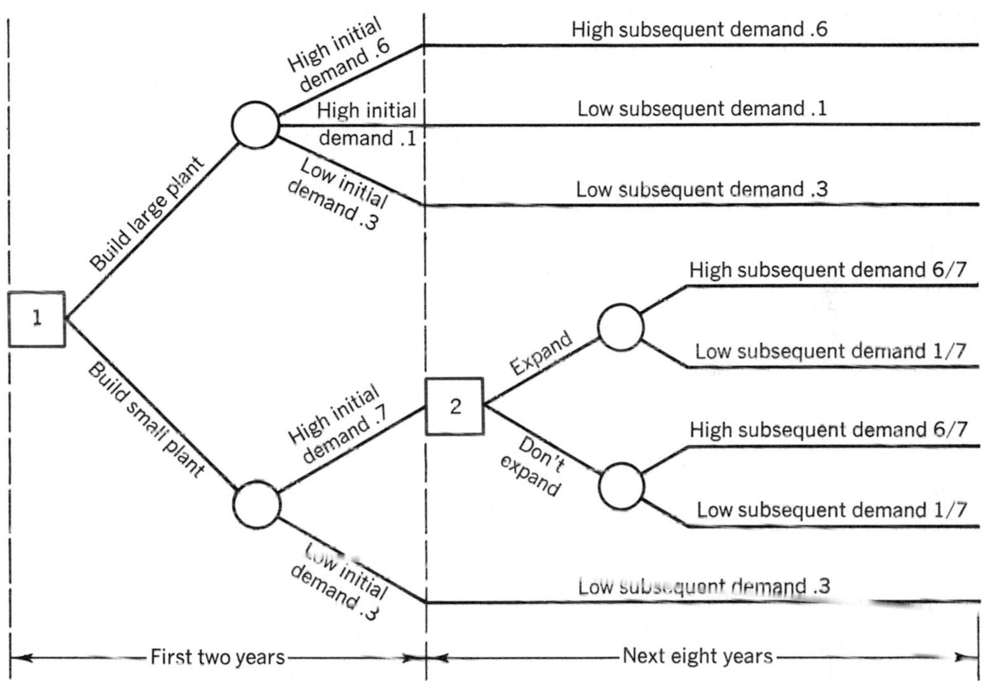

FIGURE 16-9
Decision tree of Lakeshore Manufacturing Company problem, with probabilities of various demand combinations

Figure 16-9 illustrates the Lakeshore size-of-plant problem as a decision tree. The decision horizon is divided into two parts: (1) the first two years and (2) the remaining eight years. The first decision point, [1], is whether to build a large or a small plant; the second decision point comes at the end of year two, [2], and concerns whether to expand the small plant.

The upper branch of the decision tree and the three branches that emanate from it in Fig. 16-9 illustrate the three outcomes possible if the company elects to build a large plant:

1. High initial demand followed by high subsequent demand
2. High initial demand followed by low subsequent demand
3. Low initial demand followed by low subsequent demand

The lower branch of the decision tree and the branches emanating from it illustrate the five outcomes possible if the company decides to build a small plant. These are:

1. High initial demand followed by plant expansion and high subsequent demand
2. High initial demand, plant expansion, and low subsequent demand
3. High initial demand, no plant expansion, and high subsequent demand
4. High initial demand followed by no expansion and low subsequent demand
5. Low initial demand followed by low subsequent demand with no expansion

We can begin to combine probability values with conditional monetary values on the upper branch of the decision tree. This has been done in Fig. 16-10. Thus, if the Lakeshore Company builds a *large* plant, the total expected benefit (net of plant costs) would be \$3,580,000 (the sum of the expected values of all three branches in Fig. 16-10).

FIGURE 16-10
Portion of decision tree showing expected monetary benefit of large plant

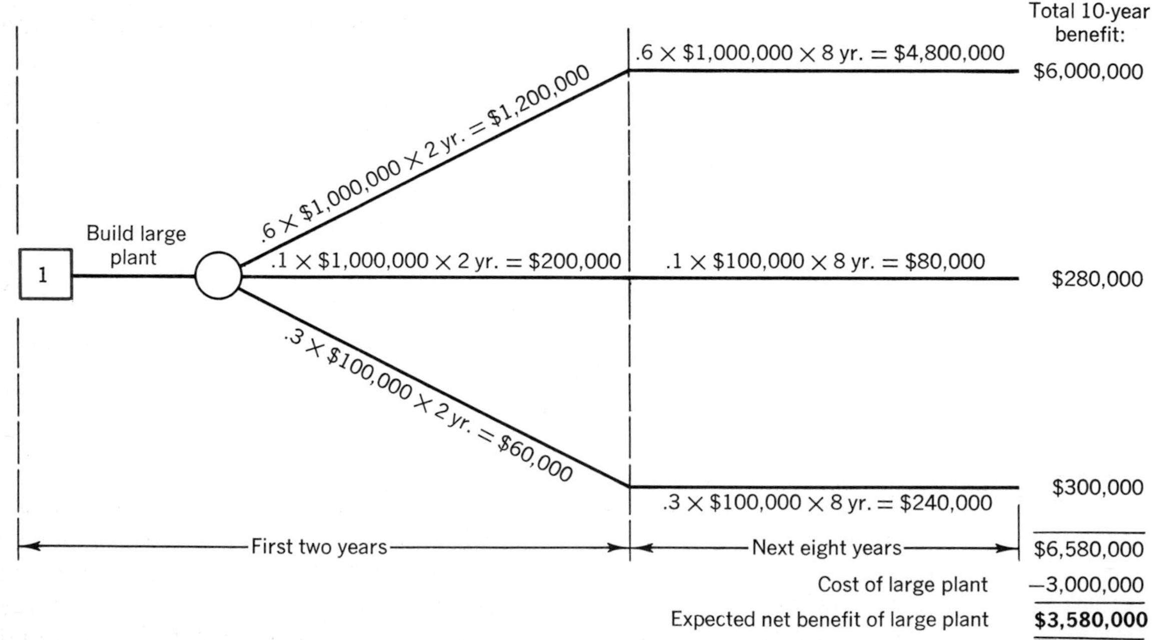

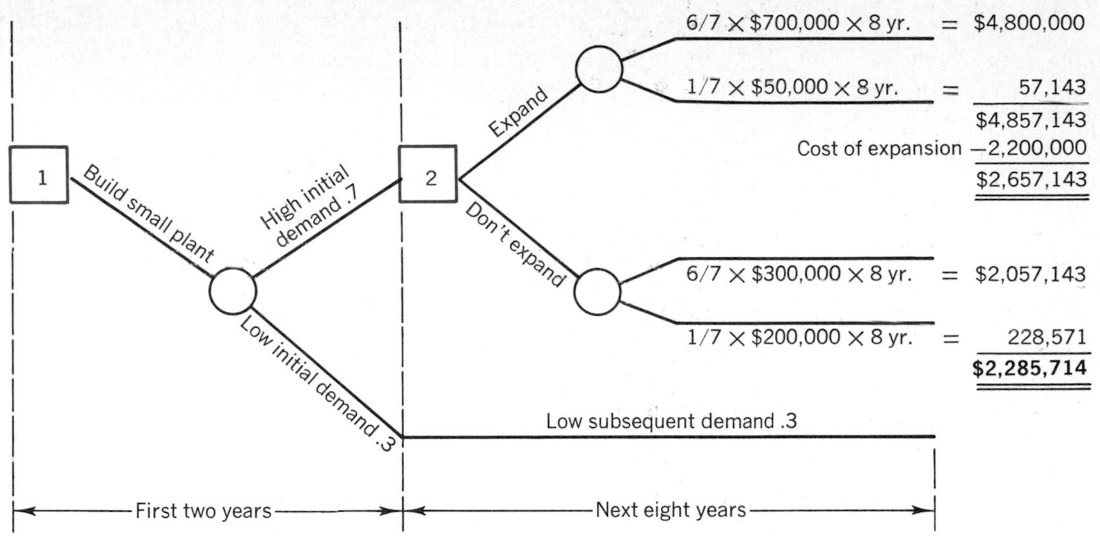

FIGURE 16-11
Portion of decision tree showing expected monetary benefits from expanding or not expanding small plant in two years

Rollback process

Next, consider the financial benefits on the lower branch of the original tree, illustrated in Fig. 16-11. We begin by concerning ourselves *only* with the portion of the tree that comes after the second decision point, [2]. The second decision about the small plant (to expand or not to expand) affects our original decision. Since we cannot wait two years to make the original decision, we must evaluate the second decision *now,* based on the best market information available, and incorporate it into the original decision on plant size. **The process now moves from right to left. We make future decisions first and then roll them back to become part of earlier decisions.** We have two rules concerning *rollback* in decision theory analysis:

1. If the branches emanate from a *circle,* we calculate the total expected benefits by summing all the expected values of the branches.
2. If the branches emanate from a *square,* we calculate the expected benefit for each branch emanating from that square and let the total expected benefit be equal to the value of the branch with the highest expected benefit.

Decision criterion: Total expected benefits

Figure 16-11 shows that after deducting expansion costs, the expected financial benefits of an expanded small plant over an 8-year period are $2,657,143. Over the same 8-year period, the expected financial benefits of an unexpanded small plant are $2,285,714. We can conclude that given the cost and the market information we have now, it would be financially more advantageous (almost $400,000 more expected benefit over eight

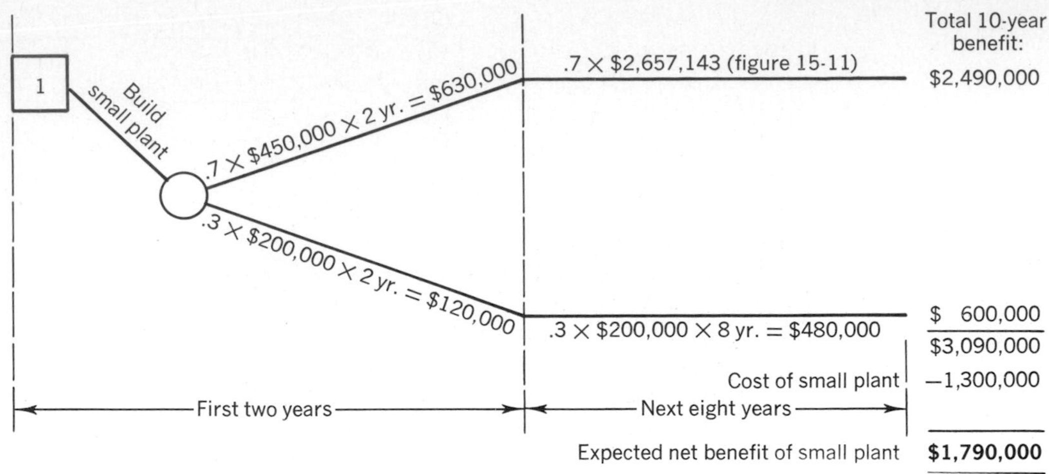

FIGURE 16-12
Portion of decision tree showing expected benefit if small plant is built

years) to expand a small plant after two years *if* it is decided now to build a small plant in the first place and *if* demand is high in the first two years.

Figure 16-12 repeats Fig. 16-11 but indicates that decision [2] would result in expansion of a small plant with an expected 8-year benefit of $2,657,143. Thus, if demand is high in the first two years, our gain from this alternative is $900,000 (in the first two years) + $2,657,143 (in the next eight years). But the chances that demand will be high are only .7. Therefore, we multiply both these figures by .7 and add the results to get $2,490,000.

If demand in the first two years is low, we would not expand the plant. Our gain for the first two years would be $400,000, ($200,000 × 2 years), and for the last eight years it would be $1,600,000, ($200,000 × 8 years). But the chances that demand would be low are only .3. Therefore, we multiply both these figures by .3 and add the results to get $600,000.

Adding $2,490,000 and $600,000, we get a total expected benefit for the small plant of $3,090,000. Subtracting the cost of the small plant from this figure leaves a net benefit of $1,790,000. This figure is substantially smaller than $3,580,000, the net benefit of a large plant. In *this* case and under *these* assumptions, it would be financially wiser for the Lakeshore Manufacturing Company to build a large plant.

Using Decision Tree Analysis

Assumptions about the future

In the solution of the Lakeshore Manufacturing Company problem, we divided the future into two periods, the first two years and the remaining eight. This may or may not be a realistic division. In a case in which it is not, we can easily structure the Lakeshore problem in terms of whatever time periods apply to the individual case, with estimates of demand for each period. The Lakeshore problem, for example, could be divided into ten

1-year periods. Then we could also modify our procedure to allow for expansion in any of the ten future years. We can allow for other financial alternatives, such as leasing additional space, selling and leasing back the existing plant, selling or renting excess space in the existing facilities, or using various combinations of these alternatives. In each of these cases, however, the computational aspects of decision tree analysis become more cumbersome because of the additional rollbacks, branches, and subbranches involved. The problem may become too complex. Remember to stop at a level of complexity that allows you to consider major consequences of future alternatives without becoming bogged down in detail.

Generally, decision tree analysis requires the decision maker to proceed through these six steps:

Decision tree steps

1. **Define the problem in structured terms.** First determine which factors are relevant to the solution. Then estimate probability distributions that are appropriate to describe future behavior of those factors. Collect financial data concerning conditional outcomes.

2. **Model the decision process;** that is, construct a decision tree that illustrates all the alternatives involved in the problem. This step *structures* the problem, in that it allows the entire decision process to be presented schematically and in an organized, step-by-step fashion. In this step, the decision maker chooses the number of periods into which the future is to be divided.

3. **Apply the appropriate probability values and financial data** to each of the branches and subbranches of the decision tree. This will enable you to distinguish the probability value and conditional monetary value associated with each outcome.

4. **"Solve" the decision tree.** Using the methodology we have illustrated, proceed to locate that particular branch of the tree that has the largest expected value or that maximizes the decision criterion, whatever it is.

5. **Perform sensitivity analysis;** that is, determine how the solution reacts to changes in the inputs. Changing probability values and conditional financial values allows the decision maker to test both the magnitude and the direction of the reaction. This step allows experiment without real commitments or real mistakes and without disrupting operations.

6. **List the underlying assumptions.** Explain the estimating techniques used to arrive at the probability distributions. What kinds of accounting and cost-finding assumptions underlie the conditional financial values used to arrive at a solution? Why has the future been divided into a certain number of periods? By making these assumptions explicit, you enable others to know what risks they are taking when they use the results of your decision tree analysis. Use this step to specify limits under which the results obtained will be valid, and especially the conditions under which the decision will not be valid.

Advantages of the decision tree approach

Decision tree analysis is a technique managers use to structure and display alternatives and decision processes. It is popular because it:

- Structures the decision process, guiding managers to approach decision making in an orderly, sequential fashion
- Requires the decision maker to examine all possible outcomes, desirable and undesirable
- Communicates the decision-making process to others; illustrates each assumption about the future
- Allows a group to discuss alternatives by focusing on each financial figure, probability value, and underlying assumption — one at a time; thus, a group can move in orderly steps toward a consensus decision, instead of debating a decision in its entirety
- Can be used with a computer, so that many different sets of assumptions can be simulated and their effects on the final outcome observed

EXERCISES

16-25 The Motor City Auto Company is planning to introduce a new automobile that features a radically new pollution-control system. It has 2 options. The first option is to build a new plant, anticipating full production in 3 years. The second option is to rebuild a small existing pilot plant for limited production for the coming model year. If the results of the limited production show promise at the end of the first year, full-scale production in a newly constructed plant would still be possible 3 years from now. If it is decided to proceed with the pilot plant, and later analysis shows that it is unattractive to go into full production, the pilot plant can still be operated by itself at a small profit. The expected annual profits for various alternatives are as follows:

PRODUCTION FACILITY	CONSUMER ACCEPTANCE	ANNUAL PROFIT (MILLION)
New plant	High	14
New plant	Low	−6
Pilot plant	High	2
Pilot plant	Low	1

Motor City's marketing-research division has estimated that there is a 50 percent probability that consumer acceptance will be high and 50 percent that it will be low. If the pilot plant is put into production, with a correspondingly low-keyed advertising program, the researchers feel that the probabilities are 45 percent for high consumer acceptance and 55 percent for low acceptance. Further, they have estimated that if the pilot plant is built and consumer acceptance is found to be high, there is a 90 percent probability of high acceptance with full production. If consumer acceptance with the pilot models is found to be low, however, there is only a 10 percent probability of high eventual acceptance with full production. Which plant should be built?

16-26 Refer to the Lakeshore Manufacturing problem in the text and in Fig. 16-9. The management of Lakeshore has been advised that in addition to the options currently available (building a large plant, building a small plant and expanding it 2 years later, and building a small plant and not expanding it), another option exists. This option would allow them to construct a plant of a size between the large and small plant they are currently considering. The cost of building this medium-sized plant is estimated to be $2,100,000, but it would not be expandable. The economic benefits estimated by Lakeshore management to accrue from such a plant under differing conditions are these:

DEMAND	BENEFITS/YEAR
High	$750,000
Low	$150,000

a) Will the existence of this third option cause Lakeshore to take an action different from the one it took in the original problem?
b) If your answer to part *a* is no, then state what the cost of a medium-sized plant would have to be for Lakeshore to consider this new option.
c) In the original problem, are there any nonfinancial considerations that would cause Lakeshore management to prefer the smaller plant to the larger one, even though the expected benefit from the larger plant is considerably higher?

16-27 Jiffy-Burger, a fast-food organization, is considering bringing out a new product for one of its restaurants. In this particular location, there is one competing restaurant. The fixed cost of developing the new food item is estimated to be $25,000. The profit this one restaurant will earn on the new product depends on (a) what kind of a promotional campaign Jiffy-Burger uses to introduce its new product, (b) whether the competitor responds with a similar product of his own, and (c) what kind of promotional campaign the competitor uses if he brings out a competing product. Jiffy-Burger thinks that here is a .7 probability the competitor will bring out a competing product if Jiffy introduces one. Jiffy-Burger can choose 4 different promotion schemes, which can be described as (1) minimal, (2) low, (3) moderate, and (4) comprehensive. If the competitor introduces a competing product, probabilities of the competitor's promotional response to these campaigns are estimated by Jiffy to be:

JIFFY-BURGER CAMPAIGN	COMPETITOR'S RESPONSE			
	Minimal	Low	Moderate	Comprehensive
Minimal	.8	.1	.05	.05
Low	.2	.6	.1	.1
Moderate	.1	.1	.5	.3
Comprehensive	.1	.1	.1	.7

If the competitor responds, the conditional profits that Jiffy will earn for each of the possible combinations of Jiffy-Burger promotional actions and competitor responses have been estimated by Jiffy's accounting department to be (net of promotional expense):

JIFFY-BURGER CAMPAIGN	COMPETITOR'S RESPONSE			
	Minimal	Low	Moderate	Comprehensive
Minimal	$ 60,000	$40,000	$20,000	$10,000
Low	70,000	60,000	40,000	20,000
Moderate	90,000	80,000	60,000	30,000
Comprehensive	100,000	90,000	70,000	50,000

If there is no response from the competitor to Jiffy's introduction of a new food product, the conditional profits associated with each possible Jiffy promotional strategy are: minimal ($80,000), low ($95,000), moderate ($120,000), and comprehensive ($150,000). In this particular situation, what should Jiffy's new-product decision be? Draw a decision tree for this problem.

16-28 Sam Sloe, a junior business major at Big. U., lives off campus in Rickshaw Apartments and has just missed the bus that would have taken him to campus for his 9 A.M. test. It is now 8:45 A.M. and Sam has several options available to get him to campus: waiting for the next bus, walking, riding his bike, or driving his car. The bus is scheduled to arrive in 10 minutes, and it will take Sam exactly 20 minutes to get to his test from the time he gets on the bus. However, there is a .2 chance that the bus will be five minutes early, and a .3 chance the bus will be 5 minutes late. If Sam walks, there is a .8 chance he will get to his test in 30 minutes, and a .2 chance he will get there in 35 minutes. If Sam rides his bike, he will get to the test in 25 minutes with probability .5, 30 minutes with probability .4, and there is a .1 chance of a flat tire, causing him to take 45 minutes. If Sam drives his car to campus, he will take 15 minutes to get to campus, but the time needed to park his car and get to his test is given by the following table:

Time to park & arrive (minutes)	10	15	20	25
Probability	.25	.55	.15	.05

a) Assuming that Sam wants to minimize his expected late time in getting to his test, draw the decision tree and determine his best option.
b) Suppose instead that Sam wants to maximize his expected utility as measured by the projected test score given below. Use the same decision tree to determine his optional decision now.

Arrival time	9:10	9:15	9:20	9:25	9:30
Projected test score	90	80	75	60	30

16-29 Speedee Bikes, a motorcycle retailer, has been enjoying considerable success in recent years, and is trying to decide which of three available options it should pursue, if any. The options are to expand the store, open a new smaller store in the next town, or open a new large store in the next town. Store expansion costs $40,000, a new small store $70,000, and a new large store $100,000. If a new small store is opened, there is a .6 chance that it will meet with consumer approval. If a new large store is opened, there is a .8 chance that it will meet with consumer approval. Consumer approval or lack thereof affects the volume of additional business that Speedee does, as shown by the probabilities in this table:

	VOLUME OF ADDITIONAL BUSINESS		
	High	Moderate	Low
Approval	.6	.3	.1
No approval	.2	.5	.3

Speedee knows that expanding the current store will meet with automatic consumer approval. The conditional profits of any option depend on the volume of additional business, as shown below:

	VOLUME OF ADDITIONAL BUSINESS		
	High	Moderate	Low
Store expansion	$ 50,000	$35,000	$20,000
New small store	100,000	70,000	40,000
New large store	130,000	90,000	60,000

If the conditional profits above are for the next 3 years, which option (if any) should Speedee pursue if the goal is to maximize additional company profits? (Draw the decision tree.)

16-7 TERMS INTRODUCED IN CHAPTER 16

CERTAINTY The decision environment in which only one state of nature exists.

CONDITIONAL PROFIT The profit that would result from a given combination of decision alternative and state of nature.

DECISION POINT Branching point that requires a decision.

DECISION TREE Graphic display of the decision environment, indicating decision alternatives, states of nature, probabilities attached to those states of nature, and conditional benefits and losses.

EXPECTED MARGINAL LOSS The marginal loss multiplied by the probability of not selling that unit.

EXPECTED MARGINAL PROFIT The marginal profit multiplied by the probability of selling that unit.

EXPECTED PROFIT The summation of the conditional profits for a given decision alternative, each weighted by the probability that it will happen.

EXPECTED PROFIT WITH PERFECT INFORMATION The expected value of profit with perfect certainty about the occurrence of the states of nature.

EXPECTED VALUE CRITERION A criterion requiring the decision maker to calculate the expected value for each decision alternative (the sum of the weighted payoffs for that alternative in which the weights are the probability values assigned by the decision maker to the states of nature than can happen).

MARGINAL LOSS The loss incurred from stocking a unit that is not sold.

MARGINAL PROFIT The profit earned from selling one additional unit.

MINIMUM PROBABILITY The probability of selling at least an additional unit that must exist to justify stocking that unit.

NODE Point at which a chance event takes place on a decision tree.

OBSOLESCENCE LOSS The loss occasioned by stocking too many units and having to dispose of unsold units.

OPPORTUNITY LOSS The profit that could have been earned if stock had been sufficient to supply a unit that was demanded.

PAYOFF The benefit that accrues from a given combination of decision alternative and state of nature.

ROLLBACK Also called foldback; method of using decision trees to find optimum alternatives. Involves working from right to left in the tree.

SALVAGE VALUE The value of an item after the initial selling period.

STATE OF NATURE Future event not under the control of the decision maker.

THE EXPECTED VALUE OF PERFECT INFORMATION The difference between expected profit (under conditions of risk) and expected profit with perfect information.

UTILITY The value of a certain outcome or payoff to someone; the pleasure or displeasure someone derives from an outcome.

16-8 EQUATIONS INTRODUCED IN CHAPTER 16

[16-1]

$$p(MP) = (1 - p)(ML)$$

p. 760

This equation describes the point at which the *expected profit* from stocking and selling an additional unit, $p(MP)$, is equal to the *expected loss* from stocking and not selling the unit, $(1 - p)(ML)$. As long as $p(MP)$ is larger than $(1 - p)(ML)$, additional units should be stocked, because the expected profit from such a decision is greater than the expected loss.

[16-2]

$$p = \frac{ML}{MP + ML}$$

p. 761

This is the *minimum probability equation*. The letter p represents the minimum required probability of selling at least an additional unit to justify the stocking of that additional unit. As long as the probability of selling one additional unit is greater than p, the retailer should stock that unit. This equation is Equation 16-1 solved for p.

16-9 CHAPTER REVIEW EXERCISES

16-30 The Mountain Manufacturing Company is planning to produce citizen's band radios. One problem they face is a make-or-buy decision for plug-in intermediate frequency (IF) modules. They can buy these modules from an electric vendor for $22 a unit. Alternatively, they may produce them at their own plant for variable costs of $14 a unit. If they produce the modules, they will incur annual fixed costs of $20,000 per year. Each citizen's band radio produced requires 1.05 of these IF modules (this takes into account defective IF modules). The company foresees annual demand for the citizen's band radios to be normally distributed with mean sales of 2,800 units and with a standard deviation of 500 units. What is the probability that the required usage of IF modules will be sufficiently large to justify producing them rather than buying them? If it is company policy to make components only when there is better than a 50 percent probability that usage is 1.5 standard deviations above the make-or-buy breakeven point, what should the decision be on this matter?

16-31 Sarah Peterson is going to open a health-food store, the Boysenberry Farms Organic Food Emporium. In planning for her initial stock, Sarah is trying to decide how many jars of Mrs. Miles' Currant Jelly to purchase. Mrs. Miles makes her currant jelly only once every 2 months, so it is necessary for Sarah to plan in advance how much she will need (there is no chance of reorder in the interim period). Sarah is torn between satisfying her customers and friends and losing money because of spoilage, since the jelly has only a 2-month shelf life. Sarah is sure that she will sell at least 10 jars during the period, and 18 different friends have promised that they will buy the jelly when it comes into stock. Sarah knows that the probability of selling more than 18 jars is practically nil and feels that sales will fall somewhere between 10 and 18 jars—despite what her friends have promised. Sarah has all the cost data and is planning a 50 percent markup. As the problem stands now, can Sarah reach a solution to her problem by using decision theory?

16-32 For the price of $17.50, La Maison de la Langouste offers, as an entree, 2 spiny-shelled lobster tails imported from the waters off the Yucatan Peninsula. Because of federal health regulations, the lobsters cannot enter the United States if they are still alive. Accordingly, only refrigerated tails are sent to the United States. At La Maison de la Langouste, the chef has found that the texture of the lobster is impaired if it is refrigerated for more than 24 hours. To maintain its image as the quintessence of haute cuisine, La Maison employs an agent to place refrigerated lobster tails on a plane leaving from the peninsula each day. The chef is trying to choose the optimum number of tails for the agent to purchase and send. He wants to satisfy the customers, yet he realizes that always carrying enough to satisfy the customers might be too costly. He has calculated the cost of a lobster tail at $4.65, including transportation. Past experience has shown the following distribution of sales of spiny-shelled lobster-tail entrees per day:

Number	22	23	24	25	26	27	28	29
Probability	.08	.09	.10	.15	.18	.16	.13	.11

a) Using expected profit as the decision criterion, how many lobster tails should the chef order?
b) If La Maison de la Langouste adopted a policy that required customers to order spiny-shelled lobster a day in advance, how much could it expect to save?

16-33 Bay Lakes Lawn and Garden Care Company provides services for homeowners and small businesses. The firm is considering purchasing a new fertilizer spreader at a cost of $38.50. The spreader is estimated to save 5 minutes labor for every hour it is in use. Head lawn-care specialist Ralph Medlin estimates that the odds are 6 to 4 that the life of the spreader is within 6 hours of 54 hours. If the company pays its gardening help $9 an hour, what is the probability that the spreader will pay for itself before it has to be scrapped?

16-34 Archdale Stores, a chain of retailers specializing in men's fashions, is considering purchasing a batch of 5,700 neckties from Beau Charm Company. The batch of ties will cost Archdale $16,500, and each tie will sell for $3.50. Archdale's vice-president of sales has stated that he thinks the chain could sell 5,000 ties, and the odds are 2 to 3 that the actual sales will be within 200 of his estimate. Leftover ties are worthless.
a) What is the probability that Archdale will at least break even on the necktie sales?
b) What is the probability that Archdale can earn 10 percent on its inventory investment?

16-35 The luggage department of Madison Rhodes Department Store featured a special Day-After-Christmas Sale of Luggage on unsold Christmas merchandise. The luggage brand on sale was Imagemaker. The manager of the luggage department was planning his order. Because the store did not carry Imagemaker during the year, the manager wanted to avoid overstocking; yet, because of a special price the manufacturer offered on the line, he also wanted to minimize stockouts. He was currently attempting to decide the number of women's tote bags to purchase. His estimate of the probable sales, based in part on past performance, is shown below.

Bags	27	28	29	30	31	32	33
Probability	.11	.13	.17	.20	.15	.14	.10

The store is planning to sell the tote bag for $37.30. His cost is $22.00. How many bags should he order for the sale?

16-36 During a meeting to discuss scheduling plant capacity, production managers for Keystone Foundry and Metalworks were concentrating on planning for the manufacture of castings used by small diesel-engine manufacturers. Because of a recent recession, demand by the engine manufacturers had been sluggish, but there were signs that it might increase in the coming year. The managers had made these estimates on the expected sales of castings:

	POUNDS	PROBABILITY
Weak sales	45,000	.40
Average sales	50,000	.35
Strong sales	55,000	.25

To produce the castings, Keystone had a fixed start-up cost of $30,000 and a variable manufacturing cost of $.50 per pound. On the average, sales prices were $1.50 per pound.

a) What is the total cost of producing to meet average sales?
b) Using expected profit as the decision criterion, at what level should Keystone produce?
c) How much should Keystone pay to find out exactly what sales will be?

16-37 At the Campus Set, a store carrying clothes tailored for the young woman, manager Judy Sommers is ordering the season's collection of bathing suits from the store's traditional supplier, Jamaican Swimwear. As in past years, Sommers is ordering almost entirely 2-piece suits, but she does plan to carry a few 1-piece suits. From past experience, Sommers estimates the sales of 1-piece suits will be as follows:

Sales	9	10	11	12	13	14	15
Probability	.04	.17	.20	.19	.18	.12	.10

There is no market for unsold 1-piece bathing suits, so Sommers wants to be very careful about the number she orders. The suits will retail for $28.75; Campus Set's cost is $19.50. Use marginal analysis to determine the number of 1-piece bathing suits Judy Sommers should order for Campus Set.

16-38 The policy of the Newland Company is not to undertake new business ventures unless annual return on investment has a 60 percent probability of being 13 percent or higher. The managers are contemplating a new venture, the production of dentures. This venture will require an investment of $500,000. They estimate that a set will cost them $80 in variable costs, and their annual fixed costs are expected to be $125,000. Their marketing specialists have analyzed the potential demand for dentures and have found that at a selling price of $130 per set, the expected annual sales would be 4,000 sets, and the standard deviation is estimated to be 450 sets. They further determined that at a price of $140 per set, expected annual demand would be 3,200 sets with a standard deviation of 300 sets annually. Should they proceed with this venture? If so, which selling price would allow a higher probability of returning 13 percent on their investment annually?

16-39 Flint City Appliance Sales was planning for its big Founder's Day Weekend Sale. As a special offer, the store was offering a Royalty Washer and Dryer Combination for only $500. Royalty had recently informed its distributors that a new product innovation would make existing washer-dryer combinations virtually obsolete, and therefore it was offering stores its current first-line washer-dryer combination for only $350. Although the manager of Flint city did not believe all of the marketing department's talk of obsolescence, he did know that any new gadget that Royalty put on its newer machines would make his older machines very difficult to sell. He wanted, therefore, to be very careful about the number of machines he ordered for the Founder's Day Sale. His estimate of the sales for the weekend are presented below.

Expected sales	4	5	6	7	8	9
Probability	.12	.18	.24	.30	.12	.04

Use marginal analysis to determine the number of washer-dryer combinations Flint City should have ordered. Assume the store had 2 in stock.

16-40 A textile mill must decide whether to extend $100,000 credit to a new customer that manufactures dresses. The mill's prior experience with a number of dress manufacturers has led it to classify such customers as follows: 30 percent are poor risks; 50 percent are average risks; and 20 percent are good risks. Expected profits on this order (if credit is extended to the dress manufacturer) are −$15,000 if it turns out to be a poor risk, $10,000 if it turns out to be an average risk, and $20,000 if it turns out to be a good risk. Draw a decision tree to determine whether the mill should extend credit to this manufacturer.

16-41 The textile mill in problem 16-40 can purchase a comprehensive credit analysis and rating (poor, average, or good) on the manufacturer for a cost of $2,000. The credit agency's past reliability is summed up in the following table, whose entries are the probabilities (from past experience) that the agency will correctly rate the dress manufacturer, given the true credit category in which the manufacturer belongs. Draw a decision tree to determine whether the mill should purchase the credit rating.

AGENCY RATING	TRUE CATEGORY Poor	Average	Good
Poor	.6	.3	.2
Average	.3	.6	.4
Good	.1	.1	.4

16-42 Steel-fab Manufacturing is a competitor of the Enduro Company (problem 16-17) in the structural steel components market. Unlike Enduro, Steel-fab is publically held and is also financed in part by a bond issue. Accordingly, the company has adopted a 9 percent cutoff rate of return. Below the 9 percent level, the firm's utility curve steepens as the return moves farther away. Above the 9 percent level, the firm's utility grows at a slower rate because of the accompanying risk involved with higher rates of return. The utility for 15 percent is only slightly higher than for 14 percent. Steel-fab is considering a $300,000 project. Plot the firm's utility curve.

16-43 Meat manager Wayne Runnion of the Big L Supermarket is attempting to determine the number of turkeys to order for the 2 weeks before Thanksgiving. Traditionally, demand has been quite high during that preholiday period, and Runnion wants to take advantage of it. Unfortunately, however, during the two weeks following Thanksgiving, demand for turkeys is very low until it picks up again, somewhat, for Christmas. Even though the turkeys are frozen and spoilage is no problem, Big L simply does not have the space to store unsold turkeys without cutting into other profitable items. Runnion's estimate of the probable sales is given below.

Pounds	12,000	12,500	13,000	13,500	14,000	14,500
Probability	.17	.22	.28	.16	.11	.06

Runnion plans to sell the turkeys at an average of $.59 a pound. His cost is $.50 a pound.

a) What is the maximum Big L could lose on its turkey sales if it purchased in the 12,000- to 14,500-lb range?
b) Calculate the number of pounds of turkey Big L should purchase.

16-44 Robert Ingersoll of Tungsten Products has approached both the Enduro Manufacturing Company and Steel-fab Manufacturing about the possibility of a joint venture with one of them. In this venture, a tungsten alloy is used in place of certain steel alloys. Tungsten Products has the technological expertise but not the production capabilities. The joint venture will be a 50-50 split and will cost each company $500,000 in capital investment.

a) If the expected first-year profit on the project is $80,000, would either or both firms accept the offer?
b) Superimpose the graphs from questions 16-17 and 16-42, adjusting the coordinates, and show the area where Enduro would accept a project and Steel-fab would not.
c) If the expected first-year profit on the project was $110,000, would either of the firms accept it? How much would Steel-fab bid for a 50 percent share of the $110,000?

16-10 CHAPTER CONCEPTS TEST

Answers are in the back of the book.

T F 1. Decision theory assumes that no events are beyond the control of the decision maker.

T F 2. A conditional profit table does not reflect the profit denied a retailer because of inability to fill all buyers' requests.

T F 3. An obsolescence loss occurs when a retailer is out of stock and buyers want to buy.

T F 4. In most stocking actions, several values of p will solve the equation $p(MP) = (1 - p)(ML)$, but only one is the best solution.

T F 5. If stocking 19 units of a good yields an expected daily profit of $51.50, a retailer stocking 19 units can expect average profits of $51.50 per day.

T F 6. A person can have one utility curve for one situation and quite a different one for the next situation.

T F 7. It is always difficult to make use of other people's knowledge about a situation without explaining statistical techniques to them.

T F 8. With perfect information, a retailer would consistently make the maximum profit possible.

T F 9. One advantage of using decision trees is that every outcome, desirable or undesirable, must be investigated.

T F 10. On a decision tree, a circle represents a decision point.

T F 11. If a retailer can earn $100 per day with perfect information, then EVPI = $100.

T F 12. The loss that results from stocking an item that is not sold is denoted *ML*.

T F 13. When rolling back a decision tree, the process moves from right to left.

T F 14. A businessman with a linear utility curve can effectively use expected monetary value as his decision criterion.

T F 15. On the graph of a normal distribution of sales, the area to the right of a vertical line represents the probability of selling that quantity or less.

T F 16. A decision that maximizes expected profits will also minimize expected losses.

T F 17. An individual's utility curve is based on mathematical, not behavioral considerations.

18. From which of the following can a retailer immediately determine how many cases he should stock each day to maximize profits?
    a) Expected profit from each stocking action
    b) Expected loss from each stocking action
    c) Conditional profit table
    d) a, b, and c
    e) a and b but not c

19. Consider a conditional-loss table with possible sales levels listed vertically in the first column and possible stock actions listed horizontally in the first row. Any value in a column below a zero indicates:
    a) An opportunity loss
    b) An obsolescence loss
    c) A profit
    d) None of these

20. Suppose that the only 2 possible stocking actions for a particular product are 10 and 15 bottles. Expected profits are $3.35 for 10 bottles and $3.50 for 15 bottles. If expected loss for 10 bottles is $1.10 and 15 bottles are stocked, we may conclude that expected loss is:
    a) Higher than $1.10
    b) Lower than $1.10
    c) Higher than $2.25
    d) Undeterminable from information given

21. A businessman who is said to be averse to risk:
    a) Prefers to take large risks to earn large gains
    b) Prefers to act anytime expected monetary value is positive
    c) Avoids all situations but those with very high expected values
    d) None of these

22. Suppose that the actual standard deviation of a normal distribution is unknown but that you are told, "The odds are 5 to 3 that a random observation is between 500 and 900." You know that the mean is 700. The area under the normal curve between the values 700 and 900 is:
    a) $8/16$ b) $3/8$ c) $5/8$ d) $5/16$

23. A certain product sells for $25 and is purchased by the retailer for $17. If it is not sold within 2 weeks, the retailer will recoup only $8 of his original $17 investment, because of spoilage. The value of *MP* for this situation is:
    a) $9 b) $17 c) $8 d) $25

24. Assume that, for a particular stocking operation, $ML = \$10$ and $MP = \$30$. Then, $p = .25$. For which of the following situations would you stock the unit in question?
   a) The fifth unit when P(requests for 5 or more units) = .50
   b) The third unit when P(requests for less than 3 units) = .10 and P(requests for exactly 3 units) = .09
   c) The ninth unit when P(requests for more than 9 units) = .16 and P(requests for exactly 9 units) = .05
   d) All of these
   e) a and b but not c
25. A manager is deciding whether to buy a new building or to rent it. If he buys, the cost for the next year will be $5,500, which will include mortgage payments, insurance, and other usual expenses. If he rents, the comparable expense for the next year will be either $6,000, $5,300, or $4,200, depending upon market fluctuations. The manager wishes to make his choice based upon expected monetary values for the next year. The decision tree for this situation would have:
   a) 1 decision point and no chance events
   b) 1 chance event and 1 decision point
   c) 2 decision points and 3 chance events
   d) 1 decision point and 3 chance events
26. For a particular decision, the total benefit of a new plant is $18,200,000. If the expected net benefit of this plant is $11,500,000, what is the cost of the plant?
   a) $6,700,000
   b) $8,400,000
   c) $29,700,000
   d) $11,500,00
   e) Cannot be determined from information given
27. Assume that 3 businesswomen are questioned regarding their utilities in risk situations. It is found that Laura is averse to risk, Lisa plays long shots, and Leslie is so well off financially that the amounts of money in question are negligible when compared to her wealth. For the situations in question, utility could be used as the decision criterion for:
   a) Laura
   b) Lisa
   c) Leslie
   d) All three
   e) a and b but not c
28. A person who is attempting to maximize his expected utility would use the expected value criterion if:
   a) He is risk-averse
   b) He is a risk seeker
   c) He has a nonlinear utility curve
   d) None of these
29. When a problem has a large number of possible actions, we would normally use a:
   a) Conditional table
   b) Marginal table
   c) Utility table
   d) Marginal analysis
   e) None of these
30. Events beyond the control of the decision maker are called ________________ or ________________ of nature.
31. The maximum amount that a retailer will be willing to pay for a perfect predictor is called the ________________.
32. There are two types of losses in a stocking operation: ________________ losses and ________________ losses.
33. The pleasure or displeasure one receives from certain outcomes is one's ________________.
34. The act of calculating expected benefits for each circle and square of a decision tree is called ________________.
35. If a profit increases a person's utility by much more than a loss of the same size would decrease it, that person will often act when the expected value is ________________.

16-11 CONCEPTUAL CASE (Northern White Metals Company)

Dick was hopeful as he completed the presentation of his five-year plan at the December 1983 division presidents' meeting. He had made three principal recommendations, all of which he felt were vital to the long-term success of NWMC.

First, he recommended the purchase of some small-scale scrap-smelting equipment, so that scrap aluminum and waste by-products could be recycled into reusable raw materials. Even if open-market raw-materials prices declined more than 75 percent (a very likely event), the smelter would still provide lower costs and thereby improve Northern's profitability. Segue management had given its unanimous approval for this project.

Dick's second recommendation was to expand Northern's customer base outside the northeastern United States. The company had nearly doubled sales in two years, he had asserted proudly, but growth was now slowing because of market saturation. Corporate management could see the advisability of this recommendation, and Dick appeared to have a well-conceived sales expansion plan. His final recommendation, though, left the CEO strangely reticent.

Dick pointed out that, even without a sales expansion program, Northern's plant would reach its capacity limit within eighteen months. He therefore recommended that an additional plant be built, or an aluminum manufacturing company acquired, to serve new markets.

"That's not a whole lot of lead time, Dick," the CEO said with concern, "and it seems as though there is little point in expanding your market if we don't add more manufacturing facilities, wouldn't you agree?"

"Unfortunately, sir, I can't do one without the other," Dick replied with confidence.

"Well, I'll think about it and let you know my decision next week," the CEO said as he got up to leave.

Dick decided not to stay in New York that evening and caught an afternoon flight back to Boston. On his way home, he stopped off at his office to finish some paperwork. He found, though, that the disappointment of an unenthusiastic response to his expansion plans made it difficult to concentrate. As he got up to leave, the telephone rang.

"I thought you'd be there," the CEO barked. "Listen, Lennox, I'm not entirely in favor of your southern expansion scheme, but everyone else seems to think your plan is rock solid. At any rate, they recommend giving you carte blanche on expanding your operations, and I've decided to go along with it. You find a good deal and we'll do it!" he exclaimed. "Keep me advised along the way, that's all," he added, and hung up. Dick was ecstatic. Not only had his recommendations been approved, he had been given full authority to implement them as well.

The next morning Dick and Norma, the chief financial officer, discussed the available options. Northern's expansion could be brought about by building a new plant or by acquisition. After a quick analysis they determined that, given current construction prices and the small amount of time he had, building a new factory should not be considered a viable option. That afternoon, Dick was on the phone to Segue's investment bankers, the prestigious Wall Street firm of Specker, Stathis, Mallinson & Co. He explained the situation, and a meeting was arranged to discuss plans to acquire an aluminum manufacturing company located in the southern part of the country.

Within two months, the firm had identified three possible acquisition candidates. Each was a different-size operation, offering different levels of production capacity, and all were favorably located.

Dick decided that selection should be based on cost, of course, but more important on the sales volume that could be expected within five years in the new geographic region. If the large plant were purchased, Dick thought, and sales were flat, as in a recession, the company would face tremendous extra costs from the excess capacity. On the other hand, if the small plant were purchased and demand grew rapidly, Northern would lose valuable sales to competitors.

Dick knew that many intermediate situations could occur, and laughed when he realized he had initially imagined two negative scenarios. In any event, the difficulty of this acquisition-based expansion decision was clear, and he thought he knew where he might turn for help.

"Jody," Dick began as she answered the phone, "NWMC is about to begin its pincer-like movement southward, and once again, we require your expert assistance." He proceeded to relate his dilemma. Before long, Jody interrupted him.

"Dick, this is a pretty big problem, and we'll need to talk about a few things in more detail," she explained. "Sarah and I will be on the 8:00 shuttle to Boston on Friday. Have someone meet us at the airport," she requested, "and, by the way, make sure this car has a ski rack on it, ok?"

Before Sarah and Jody enjoy a well-deserved ski weekend in New England, they will endeavor to aid Dick in his rather complex decision problem. What steps will Sarah and Jody take to establish a usable framework for the problem? What information will they require of Dick? How can they assist Dick in providing the most useful information possible? What analysis should Jody and Sarah perform? What qualifications and cautions should they offer Dick in utilizing the results of their analysis?

AFTERWORD

We've come a long way and looked at many techniques that statisticians use to aid decision makers. We always concentrated on *appropriate* uses of the methods, but you will surely encounter *inappropriate* uses. Sometimes, ignorance is to blame, but too often there is a conscious attempt to mislead us. The section below will make you aware of potential abuses.

FALLING OFF THE TRUE PATH

How to lie with statistics

Benjamin Disraeli once made the statement, "There are three kinds of lies: lies, damned lies, and statistics." This rather severe castigation of statistics, made so many years ago, has come to be a rather apt description of many of the statistical deceptions we encounter in our everyday lives. Darrell Huff, in an enjoyable little book, *How to Lie with Statistics,* noted that "the crooks already know these tricks; honest men must learn them in self-defense." The purpose of this section is to review some of the common ways statistics are used incorrectly, whether out of honest lack of knowledge or in an attempt to deceive the user. In either case, users of statistics who do not know how to cope with such deceptive practices cannot derive much real value from this discipline.

Biased Samples

Statistics professors often use classroom demonstrations to prove one point or another. One of the most common ones involves tossing a coin to show that the long-run tendency is for the coin (if it's a fair one) to come up heads half the time and tails the other half the time. Suppose our professor tosses a fair coin ten times and it comes up heads on eight of these tosses. What should he do? One explanation for the class is that this coin is biased (not too likely an explanation, since the work involved in biasing a standard coin so that it will behave this way is rather substantial). Another explanation is that he has not tossed the coin a sufficient number of times. The second explanation is more likely to be the one used by the professor. He will more than likely continue to toss the coin until the proportion of heads and tails that appear becomes more even.

Statistical evidence

But suppose the purpose of such an experiment was to provide "statistical evidence" that was to be used to convince people to change their minds about things other than coins. If you and I interview ten people concerning their political views, we may find that all ten are staunch Democrats. Does this give us the evidence we need to assert publicly, for political purposes, that "all those interviewed supported the Democratic platform"? Of course not. But unless the user of this information understands the sampling issue involved, and unless we are given complete information about the sampling process, how are we to react? How can we be sure that the pollster didn't "start out to find a biased coin" and then stop the polling process when an insufficient sample size "uncovered one for him," instead of making sure the sampling procedure was adequate? The answer is that without more complete information or a previous reputation for statistically accurate polling, we cannot be sure. We can, however, be alert to the risks we take when we do not ask for additional information.

Averages and Comparisons

Problems with averages

One of the oldest stories about improper use of averages is about a recruiter whose job it was to select pilots for the air force. His mandate was to ensure that the average pilot was 6 feet tall. As the story goes, he went out and found two unusual gentlemen, one only 4 feet tall and the other 8 feet tall. Of course, neither qualified, since the smaller one couldn't see over the cockpit dashboard, and the taller one couldn't even fit in the cockpit. In fact, however, they did average 6 feet. In our previous study of variation, we have learned to be sensitive to variation whenever we are using a measure of central tendency to describe data. In many cases, however, the statistical deception employed is much less obvious than that in our pilot example.

One school that trains private pilots for their instrument examination advertised that "our graduates score higher on the instrument written examination than graduates of other schools." To the unsuspecting reader, this seems perfectly clear. If you want to score higher on your instrument written examination, then this school is your best bet.

Problems with tests

In fact, however, whenever we are using tests, we have to deal with standard error. Specifically, we need some measure of the precision of the test instrument, usually represented by standard error. This would tell us how large a difference in one school's grades would have to be for it to be statistically significant. Unfortunately, the advertisement did not offer such data; it merely asserted that "our graduates do better."

Problems with means

People who are sensitive to how tax monies are used often get upset over the seemingly low classroom utilization in public colleges and universities. One sometimes sees statements like, "At Eastern University, the average classroom utilization is only 34 percent." How are we to react to such assertions? The figure that is being quoted is a mean and includes potential scheduling hours that may have little or no value to the educational process. For example, classes held late at night (say, after 9:00) may be unproductive in terms of learning because of fatigue. And then, classes scheduled before 8:00 A.M. may not be feasible because of interruption of the normal sleep period and lack of adequate transportation facilities in these very early hours. Finally, classes scheduled on Saturdays and Sundays may encounter resistance because of religious traditions. When all these factors are considered, classroom utilization may be significantly higher than 34 percent, but until we know the basis for computing the average, we cannot react intelligently to such a published figure.

Making Big Jumps

Projecting too far

College students often see ads for learning aids. One very popular such aid is a combination outline, study guide, and question set for various courses. Advertisements about such items often claim better examination scores with less studying time. Suppose a "study guide" for a basic statistics course is available through an organization that produces such guides for 50 different courses. If this study guide for basic statistics has been tested (and let us assume properly), the firm may advertise that "our study guides have been statistically proven to raise grades and lower study time." Of course their assertion is quite true, but only as it applies to their basic statistics experience. There may be no evidence of statistical significance that establishes the same kind of results for the other 49 guides.

Results in different places

Another product may be advertised as being beneficial in removing crab grass from your lawn and may assert that the product has been "thoroughly tested" on real lawns. Even if we assume that the proper statistical procedures were, in fact, used during the tests, such claims still involve "big jumps." Suppose that the test plot was in Florida, and your lawn problems are in Utah. Differences in rainfall, soil fertility, airborne pollutants, temperature, dormancy hours, and germination conditions may vary widely between these two locations. Claiming results for a statistically valid test under a completely different set of test conditions is invalid. One such test cannot measure effectiveness under a wide variety of environmental conditions.

Double counting

A national association of trucklines claimed in an advetisement that "75 percent of everything you use travels by truck." This might lead us to believe that cars, railroads, airplanes, ships, and other forms of transportation carry only 25 percent of what we use. Reaching such a conclusion is easy but not enlightening. Missing from the trucking assertion is the question of "double counting." What did they do when something was carried to your city by rail and delivered to your house by truck? Or how were packages treated if they went by airmail and then by scooter? When the double-counting issue (a very complex one to treat) is resolved, it turns out that trucks carry a much lower proportion of the goods you use than truckers claimed. Although trucks are involved in *delivering* a relatively high proportion of what you use, railroads and ships still carry more goods for more total miles.

What causes what?

And then, of course, there is always some study purporting to show that one variable causes some change in another variable. Many years ago, Prof. Stanley Jevons demonstrated that changes in sun spots caused business cycles. Even if this assertion were supported by statistically sound regressions, we must still remember that people who apply regression analysis sometimes find a relationship between two variables that have no real common bond. And when they find such a statistical relationship, they may incorrectly assert that one variable "causes" a change in the other. In this regard, if one were to run a large number of regressions between many pairs of variables, it would probably be possible to get some rather interesting suggested "relationships." It might be possible, for example, to find a high statistical relationship between your income and the amount of beer that is consumed in the United States, or even between the length of a freight train (in cars) and the weather. But in neither case is there a factor common to both variables; hence, such "relationships" are meaningless. As in most other statistical "situations," it takes *both* knowledge of the inherent limitations of the technique that is used *and* a large dose of common sense to avoid coming to unwarranted conclusions.

Finding things that do not exist

Graphs and Pictures

Pictures lie, too

How many times have we heard the old aphorism, "One picture is worth a thousand words"? And if that picture (or graph, in the case of statistical presentations) leads us to an invalid conclusion, what is it worth then? Granted, the impact of pictorial displays is high. Glancing at one graph is easier than reading five pages of summary description, but the opportunity to mislead through the use of charts and graphs is perhaps the greatest challenge of all to someone practicing "statistical deception."

Suppose a California community is trying to attract retirees from colder climates. Further suppose that the community competes with Florida communities in this regard. Now, in the minds of potential retirees, the average winter temperature ranks high on the list of criteria affecting their choice of a retirement community. The same graphed data can possibly create two different impressions among those who see it.

When the scales are left off

First, assume that the average winter temperature in the California community is two degrees higher than that of competing Florida communities. How should we illustrate this situation graphically, so that it will be interpreted in our favor? In Fig. A-1, we illustrate average winter temperature graphically, without supplying the numbers for the vertical scale. A quick glance at Fig. A-1 suggests that winter temperatures in the California community are *much* higher than those in Florida communities. This is simply because we have neglected to indicate that each mark on the vertical scale is only one degree; hence, readers will tend to use relative heights on the two graphs in Fig. A-1 to form an opinion (which will probably be wrong).

Turning things around for your benefit

Now suppose that you are employed by the Chamber of Commerce in a Florida community. You realize that your community has a two-degree disadvantage over your California competition, and you want to

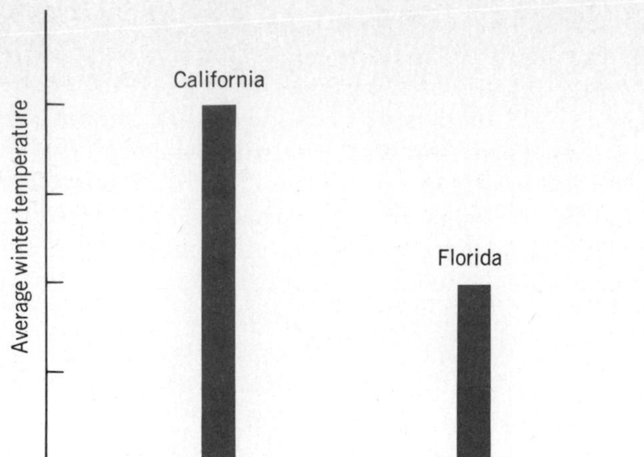

FIGURE A-1 Average winter temperatures in California and Florida communities

minimize that difference in graphical presentations. How to do it? The graph in Fig. A-2, using the same data, minimizes the adverse difference for the Florida community. It does this in two ways: by supplying numbers for the vertical scale and by changing the dimensions of the vertical scale to minimize the visual difference between the two bars. Viewers of the graph in Fig. A-2 would get the impression that winter temperatures are just about the same in both locations, an impression highly desired by the Florida community.

We have included several exercises involving statistical deception, so that you can decide how much to believe of what you read and see.

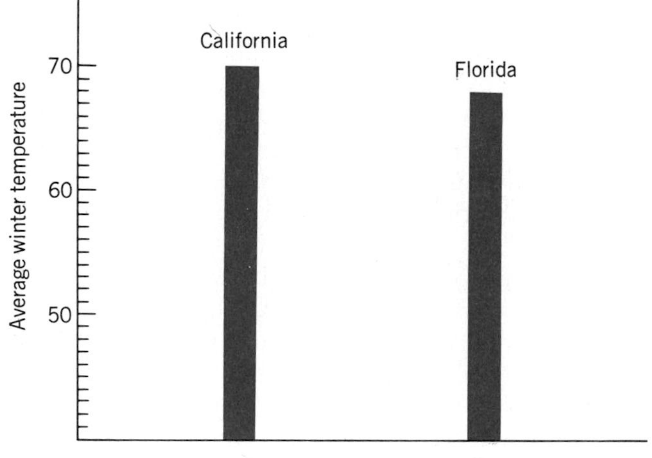

FIGURE A-2 Average winter temperatures in California and Florida communities

EXERCISES

A-1 Recently, a student group surveyed attitudes toward a number of economic, social, and political issues. To obtain their data, they went in groups of two or three to several shopping centers around the city in the afternoons after school. Here they surveyed people for a couple of hours every day, asking them several questions on current topics of interest. Is their sample representative of the population of the city? Why, or why not?

A-2 A private school has been suffering from decreased enrollment in the last two years and has launched a recruiting campaign in newspaper ads. One ad claims, ''Our high school seniors scored 25 points higher on the average on college entrance exams than do seniors in the public schools.'' Should parents rush to enroll their children in the private school, so that they will do well on these exams?

A-3 Research psychologists often remark how much we know about typical college sophomores, because they are the most common subjects in university research. What are some of the shortcomings of using college sophomores in so much of our research?

A-4 An advertisement for a headache and pain remedy claims ''laboratory tests showed that'' this product ''relieves pain twice as fast'' as the leading competitor's product. What questions should occur to us in hearing this statement?

ANSWERS TO CHAPTER CONCEPTS TESTS

CHAPTER 2

1. **T**	13. **T**	25. **b**
2. **T**	14. **T**	26. **e**
3. **F**	15. **F**	27. **d**
4. **F**	16. **F**	28. **e**
5. **T**	17. **T**	29. **e**
6. **T**	18. **d**	30. **population, sample**
7. **T**	19. **b**	31. **frequency**
8. **T**	20. **a**	32. **discrete, continuous**
9. **F**	21. **c**	33. **mark**
10. **F**	22. **c**	34. **ogive**
11. **F**	23. **a**	35. **point**
12. **F**	24. **d**	

CHAPTER 3

1. **F**	13. **T**	25. **b**
2. **T**	14. **F**	26. **c**
3. **F**	15. **F**	27. **e**
4. **F**	16. **F**	28. **f**
5. **F**	17. **F**	29. **e**
6. **T**	18. **c**	30. **symmetrical, skewed**
7. **T**	19. **a**	31. **sample, population**
8. **F**	20. **b**	32. **coding**
9. **T**	21. **a**	33. **geometric, arithmetic**
10. **F**	22. **b**	34. **bimodal**
11. **T**	23. **c**	35. **central tendency**
12. **F**	24. **d**	

CHAPTER 4

1. **T**	13. **F**	25. **d**
2. **T**	14. **T**	26. **d**
3. **F**	15. **T**	27. **e**
4. **T**	16. **F**	28. **f**
5. **T**	17. **F**	29. **e**
6. **F**	18. **d**	30. **fractile**
7. **T**	19. **b**	31. **interquartile**
8. **F**	20. **b**	32. **variance, standard deviation**
9. **T**	21. **c**	
10. **F**	22. **a**	33. **coefficient of variation**
11. **T**	23. **a**	34. **standard score**
12. **T**	24. **c**	35. **percentiles**

CHAPTER 5

1. **F**	13. **F**	25. **c**
2. **F**	14. **T**	26. **c**
3. **T**	15. **T**	27. **e**
4. **T**	16. **F**	28. **e**
5. **T**	17. **T**	29. **d**
6. **F**	18. **b**	30. **event, experiment**
7. **F**	19. **c**	31. **sample space**
8. **T**	20. **b**	32. **Venn diagram**
9. **T**	21. **e**	33. **mutually exclusive**
10. **T**	22. **a**	34. **conditional**
11. **F**	23. **d**	35. **subjective approach**
12. **F**	24. **d**	

CHAPTER 6

1. **F**	13. **T**	25. **e**
2. **F**	14. **F**	26. **e**
3. **T**	15. **F**	27. **c**
4. **F**	16. **F**	28. **d**
5. **T**	17. **F**	29. **f**
6. **T**	18. **e**	30. **expected value**
7. **F**	19. **b**	31. **binomial, Bernoulli**
8. **F**	20. **a**	32. **continuity**
9. **T**	21. **d**	33. np, $\sqrt{npq}$
10. **T**	22. **d**	34. λ
11. **T**	23. **c**	35. **probability distribution**
12. **F**	24. **c**	

CHAPTER 7

1. **T**	13. **T**	25. **c**
2. **F**	14. **F**	26. **b**
3. **F**	15. **F**	27. **d**
4. **F**	16. **T**	28. **e**
5. **T**	17. **T**	29. **d**
6. **T**	18. **d**	30. **sample**
7. **T**	19. **e**	31. **sampling fraction**
8. **F**	20. **e**	32. **systematic**
9. **T**	21. **e**	33. **Precision**
10. **F**	22. **d**	34. **clusters**
11. **T**	23. **b**	35. **sample proportions**
12. **F**	24. **a**	

CHAPTER 8

1. **F**	13. **T**	25. **a**
2. **F**	14. **T**	26. **d**
3. **T**	15. **F**	27. **e**
4. **T**	16. **F**	28. **d**
5. **F**	17. **F**	29. **e**
6. **F**	18. **e**	30. **point**
7. **T**	19. **b**	31. **interval**
8. **T**	20. **a**	32. **degrees of freedom**
9. **T**	21. **c**	33. **Student's *t* distribution**
10. **T**	22. **e**	34. **confidence**
11. **T**	23. **d**	35. **distance, mean**
12. **F**	24. **a**	

CHAPTER 9

1. **F**	13. **F**	25. **c**
2. **T**	14. **F**	26. **a**
3. **F**	15. **T**	27. **a**
4. **T**	16. **F**	28. **a**
5. **T**	17. **F**	29. **f**
6. **F**	18. **d**	30. **hypothesis**
7. **T**	19. **b**	31. **II, β (beta)**
8. **T**	20. **a**	32. **null, alternative**
9. **T**	21. **c**	33. **paired**
10. **F**	22. **c**	34. **tailed**
11. **F**	23. **b**	35. **right-tailed**
12. **F**	24. **b**	

CHAPTER 10

1. **T**	13. **T**	25. **c**
2. **T**	14. **F**	26. **e**
3. **F**	15. **F**	27. **c**
4. **T**	16. **T**	28. **e**
5. **T**	17. **F**	29. **f**
6. **F**	18. **b**	30. **grand**
7. **T**	19. **a**	31. **analysis of variance (ANOVA)**
8. **T**	20. **d**	
9. **T**	21. **e**	32. **independence**
10. **F**	22. **c**	33. ***F***
11. **T**	23. **b**	34. **goodness-of-fit**
12. **F**	24. **d**	35. **between column variance, within column variance, *F***

CHAPTER 11

1. **F**	13. **T**	25. **a**
2. **F**	14. **T**	26. **c**
3. **F**	15. **F**	27. **b**
4. **F**	16. **F**	28. **c**
5. **T**	17. **T**	29. **d**
6. **T**	18. **d**	30. **inverse**
7. **T**	19. **a**	31. **curvilinear**
8. **T**	20. **a**	32. **slope**
9. **F**	21. **e**	33. **standard error of estimate**
10. **T**	22. **b**	
11. **F**	23. **c**	34. **coefficient of determination**
12. **T**	24. **d**	35. **+ or − .866**

CHAPTER 12

1. **T**	13. **F**	25. **b**
2. **F**	14. **F**	26. **a**
3. **T**	15. **T**	27. **b**
4. **F**	16. **F**	28. **d**
5. **F**	17. **F**	29. **e**
6. **T**	18. **c**	30. **modeling techniques**
7. **T**	19. **b**	31. **transformations**
8. **T**	20. **d**	32. **computed *F*-ratio**
9. **F**	21. **b**	33. **dummy**
10. **T**	22. **a**	34. **standard error**
11. **T**	23. **c**	35. **strength of the relationship of the variables**
12. **F**	24. **d**	

CHAPTER 13

1. **T**	13. **F**	25. **a**
2. **F**	14. **T**	26. **b**
3. **T**	15. **T**	27. **d**
4. **T**	16. **T**	28. **f**
5. **F**	17. **T**	29. **d**
6. **T**	18. **c**	30. **run**
7. **F**	19. **b**	31. **Mann-Whitney *U* test**
8. **T**	20. **a**	32. **one-sample runs test**
9. **T**	21. **b**	33. **sign**
10. **F**	22. **d**	34. **rank correlation**
11. **T**	23. **b**	35. **the samples are of unequal size**
12. **F**	24. **c**	

CHAPTER 14

1. **T**	13. **T**	25. **b**
2. **T**	14. **F**	26. **a**
3. **F**	15. **T**	27. **c**
4. **F**	16. **F**	28. **d**
5. **F**	17. **T**	29. **f**
6. **F**	18. **e**	30. **percent of trend**
7. **T**	19. **c**	31. **seasonal**
8. **F**	20. **a**	32. **Irregular**
9. **F**	21. **b**	33. **Cyclical**
10. **F**	22. **d**	34. **deseasonalizing**
11. **T**	23. **d**	35. **four quarter moving total**
12. **T**	24. **c**	

CHAPTER 15

1. **F**	13. **F**	25. **a**
2. **T**	14. **T**	26. **b**
3. **T**	15. **F**	27. **c**
4. **F**	16. **T**	28. **e**
5. **F**	17. **F**	29. **d**
6. **T**	18. **a**	30. **unweighted**
7. **T**	19. **c**	31. **Laspeyres**
8. **T**	20. **e**	32. **aggregate**
9. **T**	21. **e**	33. **fixed weight**
10. **F**	22. **c**	34. **Paasche**
11. **T**	23. **d**	35. **error, change**
12. **T**	24. **b**	

CHAPTER 16

1. **F**	14. **T**	27. **d**
2. **T**	15. **F**	28. **d**
3. **F**	16. **T**	29. **d**
4. **F**	17. **F**	30. **outcomes, states**
5. **T**	18. **e**	31. **expected value of perfect information (EVPI)**
6. **T**	19. **a**	
7. **F**	20. **b**	
8. **T**	21. **c**	32. **obsolescence, opportunity**
9. **T**	22. **d**	
10. **F**	23. **c**	33. **utility**
11. **F**	24. **e**	34. **rollback**
12. **T**	25. **b**	35. **negative**
13. **T**	26. **a**	

APPENDIX TABLE 1

Areas under the Standard Normal Probability Distribution between the Mean and Positive Values of z*

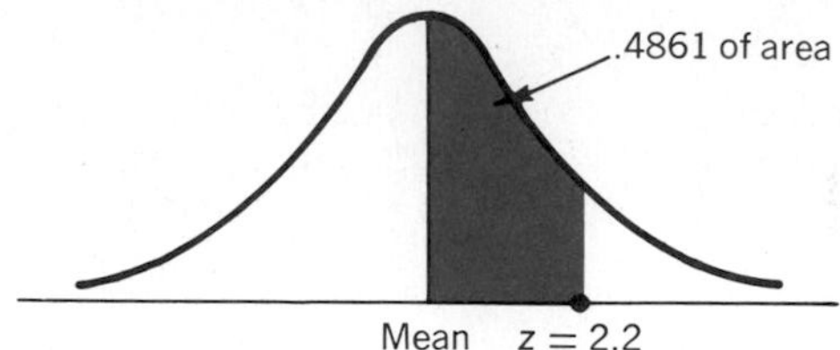

EXAMPLE: To find the area under the curve between the mean and a point 2.2 standard deviations to the right of the mean, look up the value opposite 2.2 in the table; .4861 of the area under the curve lies between the mean and a z value of 2.2.

z	.00	.01	.02	.03	.04	.05	.06	.07	.08	.09
0.0	.0000	.0040	.0080	.0120	.0160	.0199	.0239	.0279	.0319	.0359
0.1	.0398	.0438	.0478	.0517	.0557	.0596	.0636	.0675	.0714	.0753
0.2	.0793	.0832	.0871	.0910	.0948	.0987	.1026	.1064	.1103	.1141
0.3	.1179	.1217	.1255	.1293	.1331	.1368	.1406	.1443	.1480	.1517
0.4	.1554	.1591	.1628	.1664	.1700	.1736	.1772	.1808	.1844	.1879
0.5	.1915	.1950	.1985	.2019	.2054	.2088	.2123	.2157	.2190	.2224
0.6	.2257	.2291	.2324	.2357	.2389	.2422	.2454	.2486	.2517	.2549
0.7	.2580	.2611	.2642	.2673	.2704	.2734	.2764	.2794	.2823	.2852
0.8	.2881	.2910	.2939	.2967	.2995	.3023	.3051	.3078	.3106	.3133
0.9	.3159	.3186	.3212	.3238	.3264	.3289	.3315	.3340	.3365	.3389
1.0	.3413	.3438	.3461	.3485	.3508	.3531	.3554	.3577	.3599	.3621
1.1	.3643	.3665	.3686	.3708	.3729	.3749	.3770	.3790	.3810	.3830
1.2	.3849	.3869	.3888	.3907	.3925	.3944	.3962	.3980	.3997	.4015
1.3	.4032	.4049	.4066	.4082	.4099	.4115	.4131	.4147	.4162	.4177
1.4	.4192	.4207	.4222	.4236	.4251	.4265	.4279	.4292	.4306	.4319
1.5	.4332	.4345	.4357	.4370	.4382	.4394	.4406	.4418	.4429	.4441
1.6	.4452	.4463	.4474	.4484	.4495	.4505	.4515	.4525	.4535	.4545
1.7	.4554	.4564	.4573	.4582	.4591	.4599	.4608	.4616	.4625	.4633
1.8	.4641	.4649	.4656	.4664	.4671	.4678	.4686	.4693	.4699	.4706
1.9	.4713	.4719	.4726	.4732	.4738	.4744	.4750	.4756	.4761	.4767
2.0	.4772	.4778	.4783	.4788	.4793	.4798	.4803	.4808	.4812	.4817
2.1	.4821	.4826	.4830	.4834	.4838	.4842	.4846	.4850	.4854	.4857
2.2	.4861	.4864	.4868	.4871	.4875	.4878	.4881	.4884	.4887	.4890
2.3	.4893	.4896	.4898	.4901	.4904	.4906	.4909	.4911	.4913	.4916
2.4	.4918	.4920	.4922	.4925	.4927	.4929	.4931	.4932	.4934	.4936
2.5	.4938	.4940	.4941	.4943	.4945	.4946	.4948	.4949	.4951	.4952
2.6	.4953	.4955	.4956	.4957	.4959	.4960	.4961	.4962	.4963	.4946
2.7	.4965	.4966	.4967	.4968	.4969	.4970	.4971	.4972	.4973	.4974
2.8	.4974	.4975	.4976	.4977	.4977	.4978	.4979	.4979	.4980	.4981
2.9	.4981	.4982	.4982	.4983	.4984	.4984	.4985	.4985	.4986	.4986
3.0	.4987	.4987	.4987	.4988	.4988	.4989	.4989	.4989	.4990	.4990

* From Robert D. Mason, *Essentials of Statistics,* © 1976, p. 307. Reprinted by permission of Prentice-Hall, Inc., Englewood Cliffs, N.J.

APPENDIX TABLE 2

Areas in Both Tails Combined for Student's t Distribution.*

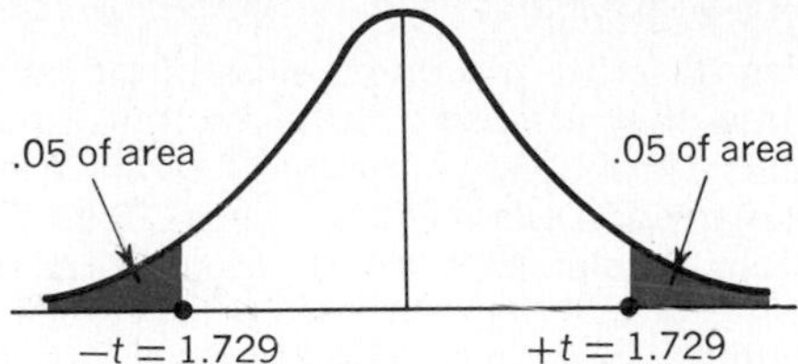

EXAMPLE: To find the value of t which corresponds to an area of .10 in both tails of the distribution combined, when there are 19 degrees of freedom, look under the .10 column, and proceed down to the 19 degrees of freedom row; the appropriate t value there is 1.729.

Degrees of freedom	Area in both tails combined			
	.10	.05	.02	.01
1	6.314	12.706	31.821	63.657
2	2.920	4.303	6.965	9.925
3	2.353	3.182	4.541	5.841
4	2.132	2.776	3.747	4.604
5	2.015	2.571	3.365	4.032
6	1.943	2.447	3.143	3.707
7	1.895	2.365	2.998	3.499
8	1.860	2.306	2.896	3.355
9	1.833	2.262	2.821	3.250
10	1.812	2.228	2.764	3.169
11	1.796	2.201	2.718	3.106
12	1.782	2.179	2.681	3.055
13	1.771	2.160	2.650	3.012
14	1.761	2.145	2.624	2.977
15	1.753	2.131	2.602	2.947
16	1.746	2.120	2.583	2.921
17	1.740	2.110	2.567	2.898
18	1.734	2.101	2.552	2.878
19	1.729	2.093	2.539	2.861
20	1.725	2.086	2.528	2.845
21	1.721	2.080	2.518	2.831
22	1.717	2.074	2.508	2.819
23	1.714	2.069	2.500	2.807
24	1.711	2.064	2.492	2.797
25	1.708	2.060	2.485	2.787
26	1.706	2.056	2.479	2.779
27	1.703	2.052	2.473	2.771
28	1.701	2.048	2.467	2.763
29	1.699	2.045	2.462	2.756
30	1.697	2.042	2.457	2.750
40	1.684	2.021	2.423	2.704
60	1.671	2.000	2.390	2.660
120	1.658	1.980	2.358	2.617
Normal Distribution	1.645	1.960	2.326	2.576

* Taken from Table III of Fisher and Yates, *Statistical Tables for Biological, Agricultural and Medical Research*, published by Longman Group Ltd., London (previously published by Oliver & Boyd, Edinburgh) and by permission of the authors and publishers.

APPENDIX TABLE 3

The Cumulative Binomial Distribution*

EXAMPLE: These tables describe the cumulative binomial distribution; a sample problem will illustrate how they are used. Suppose that we are grading bar examinations and wish to find the probability of finding 7 or more failures in a batch of 15, when the probability that any one exam is a failure is .20.

In binomial notation, the elements in this example can be represented:

n = 15 (number of exams to be graded)
p = .20 (probability that any one exam will be a failure)
r = 7 (number of failures in question)

Steps for solution:

1. Since the problem involves 15 trials or inspections, first find the table for $n = 15$.
2. The probability of a failing examination is .20; therefore, we look through the $n = 15$ table until we find the column where $p = 20$.
3. We then move down the $p = 20$ column until we are opposite the $r = 7$ row.
4. The answer there is found to be 0181; this is interpreted to be a probability of .0181.

This problem asked for the probability of *7 or more* failures. Had it asked for the probability of *more than 7* failures, we would have looked up the probability of *8* or more.

Note that this table only goes up to $p = .50$. When p is *larger* than .50, q $(1 - p)$ is *less* than .50. Therefore the problem is worked in terms of q and the number of passing exams $(n - r)$ rather than in terms of p and r (the number of failures). For example, suppose $p = .60$ and $n = 15$. What is the probability of more than 12 failures? More than 12 failures (13, 14, or 15 failures) is the same as 2 or fewer successes. The probability of 2 or fewer successes is 1 − the probability of 3 or more successes. We look in the $n = 15$ table for the $p = 40$ column and the $r = 3$ row. There we see the number 9729, which we interpret as a probability of .9729; so the answer is 1 − .9729, or .0271.

n = 1

P R	01	02	03	04	05	06	07	08	09	10
1	0100	0200	0300	0400	0500	0600	0700	0800	0900	1000
P R	**11**	**12**	**13**	**14**	**15**	**16**	**17**	**18**	**19**	**20**
1	1100	1200	1300	1400	1500	1600	1700	1800	1900	2000
P R	**21**	**22**	**23**	**24**	**25**	**26**	**27**	**28**	**29**	**30**
1	2100	2200	2300	2400	2500	2600	2700	2800	2900	3000
P R	**31**	**32**	**33**	**34**	**35**	**36**	**37**	**38**	**39**	**40**
1	3100	3200	3300	3400	3500	3600	3700	3800	3900	4000
P R	**41**	**42**	**43**	**44**	**45**	**46**	**47**	**48**	**49**	**50**
1	4100	4200	4300	4400	4500	4600	4700	4800	4900	5000

* Reproduced from Robert Schlaifer, *Introduction to Statistics for Business Decisions*, published by McGraw-Hill Book Company, 1961, by specific permission from the copyright holder, the President and Fellows of Harvard College.

n = 2

R \ P	01	02	03	04	05	06	07	08	09	10
1	0199	0396	0591	0784	0975	1164	1351	1536	1719	1900
2	0001	0004	0009	0016	0025	0036	0049	0064	0081	0100

R \ P	11	12	13	14	15	16	17	18	19	20
1	2079	2256	2431	2604	2775	2944	3111	3276	3439	3600
2	0121	0144	0169	0196	0225	0256	0289	0324	0361	0400

R \ P	21	22	23	24	25	26	27	28	29	30
1	3759	3916	4071	4224	4375	4524	4671	4816	4959	5100
2	0441	0484	0529	0576	0625	0676	0729	0784	0841	0900

R \ P	31	32	33	34	35	36	37	38	39	40
1	5239	5376	5511	5644	5775	5904	6031	6156	6279	6400
2	0961	1024	1089	1156	1225	1296	1369	1444	1521	1600

R \ P	41	42	43	44	45	46	47	48	49	50
1	6519	6636	6751	6864	6975	7084	7191	7296	7399	7500
2	1681	1764	1849	1936	2025	2116	2209	2304	2401	2500

n = 3

R \ P	01	02	03	04	05	06	07	08	09	10
1	0297	0588	0873	1153	1426	1694	1956	2213	2464	2710
2	0003	0012	0026	0047	0073	0104	0140	0182	0228	0280
3				0001	0001	0002	0003	0005	0007	0010

R \ P	11	12	13	14	15	16	17	18	19	20
1	2950	3185	3415	3639	3859	4073	4282	4486	4686	4880
2	0336	0397	0463	0533	0608	0686	0769	0855	0946	1040
3	0013	0017	0022	0027	0034	0041	0049	0058	0069	0080

R \ P	21	22	23	24	25	26	27	28	29	30
1	5070	5254	5435	5610	5781	5948	6110	6268	6421	6570
2	1138	1239	1344	1452	1563	1676	1793	1913	2035	2160
3	0093	0106	0122	0138	0156	0176	0197	0220	0244	0270

R \ P	31	32	33	34	35	36	37	38	39	40
1	6715	6856	6992	7125	7254	7379	7500	7617	7730	7840
2	2287	2417	2548	2682	2818	2955	3094	3235	3377	3520
3	0298	0328	0359	0393	0429	0467	0507	0549	0593	0640

R \ P	41	42	43	44	45	46	47	48	49	50
1	7946	8049	8148	8244	8336	8425	8511	8594	8673	8750
2	3665	3810	3957	4104	4253	4401	4551	4700	4850	5000
3	0689	0741	0795	0852	0911	0973	1038	1106	1176	1250

n = 4

R \ P	01	02	03	04	05	06	07	08	09	10
1	0394	0776	1147	1507	1855	2193	2519	2836	3143	3439
2	0006	0023	0052	0091	0140	0199	0267	0344	0430	0523
3			0001	0002	0005	0008	0013	0019	0027	0037
4									0001	0001

R \ P	11	12	13	14	15	16	17	18	19	20
1	3726	4003	4271	4530	4780	5021	5254	5479	5695	5904
2	0624	0732	0847	0968	1095	1228	1366	1509	1656	1808
3	0049	0063	0079	0098	0120	0144	0171	0202	0235	0272
4	0001	0002	0003	0004	0005	0007	0008	0010	0013	0016

n = 4

R \ P	21	22	23	24	25	26	27	28	29	30
1	6105	6298	6485	6664	6836	7001	7160	7313	7459	7599
2	1963	2122	2285	2450	2617	2787	2959	3132	3307	3483
3	0312	0356	0403	0453	0508	0566	0628	0694	0763	0837
4	0019	0023	0028	0033	0039	0046	0053	0061	0071	0081

R \ P	31	32	33	34	35	36	37	38	39	40
1	7733	7862	7985	8103	8215	8322	8425	8522	8615	8704
2	3660	3837	4015	4193	4370	4547	4724	4900	5075	5248
3	0915	0996	1082	1171	1265	1362	1464	1569	1679	1792
4	0092	0105	0119	0134	0150	0168	0187	0209	0231	0256

R \ P	41	42	43	44	45	46	47	48	49	50
1	8788	8868	8944	9017	9085	9150	9211	9269	9323	9375
2	5420	5590	5759	5926	6090	6252	6412	6569	6724	6875
3	1909	2030	2155	2283	2415	2550	2689	2834	2977	3125
4	0283	0311	0342	0375	0410	0448	0488	0531	0576	0625

n = 5

R \ P	01	02	03	04	05	06	07	08	09	10
1	0490	0961	1413	1846	2262	2661	3043	3409	3760	4095
2	0010	0038	0085	0148	0226	0319	0425	0544	0674	0815
3		0001	0003	0006	0012	0020	0031	0045	0063	0086
4						0001	0001	0002	0003	0005

R \ P	11	12	13	14	15	16	17	18	19	20
1	4416	4723	5016	5296	5563	5818	6061	6293	6513	6723
2	0965	1125	1292	1467	1648	1835	2027	2224	2424	2627
3	0112	0143	0179	0220	0266	0318	0375	0437	0505	0579
4	0007	0009	0013	0017	0022	0029	0036	0045	0055	0067
5				0001	0001	0001	0001	0002	0002	0003

R \ P	21	22	23	24	25	26	27	28	29	30
1	6923	7113	7293	7464	7627	7781	7927	8065	8196	8319
2	2833	3041	3251	3461	3672	3883	4093	4303	4511	4718
3	0659	0744	0836	0933	1035	1143	1257	1376	1501	1631
4	0081	0097	0114	0134	0156	0181	0208	0238	0272	0308
5	0004	0005	0006	0008	0010	0012	0014	0017	0021	0024

R \ P	31	32	33	34	35	36	37	38	39	40
1	8436	8546	8650	8748	8840	8926	9008	9084	9155	9222
2	4923	5125	5325	5522	5716	5906	6093	6276	6455	6630
3	1766	1905	2050	2199	2352	2509	2670	2835	3003	3174
4	0347	0390	0436	0486	0540	0598	0660	0726	0796	0870
5	0029	0034	0039	0045	0053	0060	0069	0079	0090	0102

R \ P	41	42	43	44	45	46	47	48	49	50
1	9285	9344	9398	9449	9497	9541	9582	9620	9655	9688
2	6801	6967	7129	7286	7438	7585	7728	7865	7998	8125
3	3349	3525	3705	3886	4069	4253	4439	4625	4813	5000
4	0949	1033	1121	1214	1312	1415	1522	1635	1753	1875
5	0116	0131	0147	0165	0185	0206	0229	0255	0282	0313

n = 6

R \ P	01	02	03	04	05	06	07	08	09	10
1	0585	1142	1670	2172	2649	3101	3530	3936	4321	4686
2	0015	0057	0125	0216	0328	0459	0608	0773	0952	1143
3		0002	0005	0012	0022	0038	0058	0085	0118	0159
4					0001	0002	0003	0005	0008	0013
5										0001

R \ P	11	12	13	14	15	16	17	18	19	20
1	5030	5356	5664	5954	6229	6487	6731	6960	7176	7379
2	1345	1556	1776	2003	2235	2472	2713	2956	3201	3446
3	0206	0261	0324	0395	0473	0560	0655	0759	0870	0989
4	0018	0025	0034	0045	0059	0075	0094	0116	0141	0170
5	0001	0001	0002	0003	0004	0005	0007	0010	0013	0016
6										0001

R \ P	21	22	23	24	25	26	27	28	29	30
1	7569	7748	7916	8073	8220	8358	8487	8607	8719	8824
2	3692	3937	4180	4422	4661	4896	5128	5356	5580	5798
3	1115	1250	1391	1539	1694	1856	2023	2196	2374	2557
4	0202	0239	0280	0326	0376	0431	0492	0557	0628	0705
5	0020	0025	0031	0038	0046	0056	0067	0079	0093	0109
6	0001	0001	0001	0002	0002	0003	0004	0005	0006	0007

R \ P	31	32	33	34	35	36	37	38	39	40
1	8921	9011	9095	9173	9246	9313	9375	9432	9485	9533
2	6012	6220	6422	6619	6809	6994	7172	7343	7508	7667
3	2744	2936	3130	3328	3529	3732	3937	4143	4350	4557
4	0787	0875	0969	1069	1174	1286	1404	1527	1657	1792
5	0127	0148	0170	0195	0223	0254	0288	0325	0365	0410
6	0009	0011	0013	0015	0018	0022	0026	0030	0035	0041

R \ P	41	42	43	44	45	46	47	48	49	50
1	9578	9619	9657	9692	9723	9752	9778	9802	9824	9844
2	7819	7965	8105	8238	8364	8485	8599	8707	8810	8906
3	4764	4971	5177	5382	5585	5786	5985	6180	6373	6563
4	1933	2080	2232	2390	2553	2721	2893	3070	3252	3438
5	0458	0510	0566	0627	0692	0762	0837	0917	1003	1094
6	0048	0055	0063	0073	0083	0095	0108	0122	0138	0156

n = 7

R \ P	01	02	03	04	05	06	07	08	09	10
1	0679	1319	1920	2486	3017	3515	3983	4422	4832	5217
2	0020	0079	0171	0294	0444	0618	0813	1026	1255	1497
3		0003	0009	0020	0038	0063	0097	0140	0193	0257
4				0001	0002	0004	0007	0012	0018	0027
5								0001	0001	0002

R \ P	11	12	13	14	15	16	17	18	19	20
1	5577	5913	6227	6521	6794	7049	7286	7507	7712	7903
2	1750	2012	2281	2556	2834	3115	3396	3677	3956	4233
3	0331	0416	0513	0620	0738	0866	1005	1154	1313	1480
4	0039	0054	0072	0094	0121	0153	0189	0231	0279	0333
5	0003	0004	0006	0009	0012	0017	0022	0029	0037	0047
6					0001	0001	0001	0002	0003	0004

n = 7

R \ P	21	22	23	24	25	26	27	28	29	30
1	8080	8243	8395	8535	8665	8785	8895	8997	9090	9176
2	4506	4775	5040	5298	5551	5796	6035	6266	6490	6706
3	1657	1841	2033	2231	2436	2646	2861	3081	3304	3529
4	0394	0461	0536	0617	0706	0802	0905	1016	1134	1260
5	0058	0072	0088	0107	0129	0153	0181	0213	0248	0288
6	0005	0006	0008	0011	0013	0017	0021	0026	0031	0038
7					0001	0001	0001	0001	0002	0002

R \ P	31	32	33	34	35	36	37	38	39	40
1	9255	9328	9394	9454	9510	9560	9606	9648	9686	9720
2	6914	7113	7304	7487	7662	7828	7987	8137	8279	8414
3	3757	3987	4217	4447	4677	4906	5134	5359	5581	5801
4	1394	1534	1682	1837	1998	2167	2341	2521	2707	2898
5	0332	0380	0434	0492	0556	0625	0701	0782	0869	0963
6	0046	0055	0065	0077	0090	0105	0123	0142	0164	0188
7	0003	0003	0004	0005	0006	0008	0009	0011	0014	0016

R \ P	41	42	43	44	45	46	47	48	49	50
1	9751	9779	9805	9827	9848	9866	9883	9897	9910	9922
2	8541	8660	8772	8877	8976	9068	9153	9233	9307	9375
3	6017	6229	6436	6638	6836	7027	7213	7393	7567	7734
4	3094	3294	3498	3706	3917	4131	4346	4563	4781	5000
5	1063	1169	1282	1402	1529	1663	1803	1951	2105	2266
6	0216	0246	0279	0316	0357	0402	0451	0504	0562	0625
7	0019	0023	0027	0032	0037	0044	0051	0059	0068	0078

n = 8

R \ P	01	02	03	04	05	06	07	08	09	10
1	0773	1492	2163	2786	3366	3904	4404	4868	5297	5695
2	0027	0103	0223	0381	0572	0792	1035	1298	1577	1869
3	0001	0004	0013	0031	0058	0096	0147	0211	0289	0381
4			0001	0002	0004	0007	0013	0022	0034	0050
5							0001	0001	0003	0004

R \ P	11	12	13	14	15	16	17	18	19	20
1	6063	6404	6718	7008	7275	7521	7748	7956	8147	8322
2	2171	2480	2794	3111	3428	3744	4057	4366	4670	4967
3	0487	0608	0743	0891	1052	1226	1412	1608	1815	2031
4	0071	0097	0129	0168	0214	0267	0328	0397	0476	0563
5	0007	0010	0015	0021	0029	0038	0050	0065	0083	0104
6		0001	0001	0002	0002	0003	0005	0007	0009	0012
7									0001	0001

R \ P	21	22	23	24	25	26	27	28	29	30
1	8483	8630	8764	8887	8999	9101	9194	9278	9354	9424
2	5257	5538	5811	6075	6329	6573	6807	7031	7244	7447
3	2255	2486	2724	2967	3215	3465	3718	3973	4228	4482
4	0659	0765	0880	1004	1138	1281	1433	1594	1763	1941
5	0129	0158	0191	0230	0273	0322	0377	0438	0505	0580
6	0016	0021	0027	0034	0042	0052	0064	0078	0094	0113
7	0001	0002	0002	0003	0004	0005	0006	0008	0010	0013
8									0001	0001

n = 8

R \ P	31	32	33	34	35	36	37	38	39	40
1	9486	9543	9594	9640	9681	9719	9752	9782	9808	9832
2	7640	7822	7994	8156	8309	8452	8586	8711	8828	8936
3	4736	4987	5236	5481	5722	5958	6189	6415	6634	6846
4	2126	2319	2519	2724	2936	3153	3374	3599	3828	4059
5	0661	0750	0846	0949	1061	1180	1307	1443	1586	1737
6	0134	0159	0187	0218	0253	0293	0336	0385	0439	0498
7	0016	0020	0024	0030	0036	0043	0051	0061	0072	0085
8	0001	0001	0001	0002	0002	0003	0004	0004	0005	0007

R \ P	41	42	43	44	45	46	47	48	49	50
1	9853	9872	9889	9903	9916	9928	9938	9947	9954	9961
2	9037	9130	9216	9295	9368	9435	9496	9552	9602	9648
3	7052	7250	7440	7624	7799	7966	8125	8276	8419	8555
4	4292	4527	4762	4996	5230	5463	5694	5922	6146	6367
5	1895	2062	2235	2416	2604	2798	2999	3205	3416	3633
6	0563	0634	0711	0794	0885	0982	1086	1198	1318	1445
7	0100	0117	0136	0157	0181	0208	0239	0272	0310	0352
8	0008	0010	0012	0014	0017	0020	0024	0028	0033	0039

n = 9

R \ P	01	02	03	04	05	06	07	08	09	10
1	0865	1663	2398	3075	3698	4270	4796	5278	5721	6126
2	0034	0131	0282	0478	0712	0978	1271	1583	1912	2252
3	0001	0006	0020	0045	0084	0138	0209	0298	0405	0530
4			0001	0003	0006	0013	0023	0037	0057	0083
5						0001	0002	0003	0005	0009
6										0001

R \ P	11	12	13	14	15	16	17	18	19	20
1	6496	6835	7145	7427	7684	7918	8131	8324	8499	8658
2	2599	2951	3304	3657	4005	4348	4685	5012	5330	5638
3	0672	0833	1009	1202	1409	1629	1861	2105	2357	2618
4	0117	0158	0209	0269	0339	0420	0512	0615	0730	0856
5	0014	0021	0030	0041	0056	0075	0098	0125	0158	0196
6	0001	0002	0003	0004	0006	0009	0013	0017	0023	0031
7						0001	0001	0002	0002	0003

R \ P	21	22	23	24	25	26	27	28	29	30
1	8801	8931	9048	9154	9249	9335	9411	9480	9542	9596
2	5934	6218	6491	6750	6997	7230	7452	7660	7856	8040
3	2885	3158	3434	3713	3993	4273	4552	4829	5102	5372
4	0994	1144	1304	1475	1657	1849	2050	2260	2478	2703
5	0240	0291	0350	0416	0489	0571	0662	0762	0870	0988
6	0040	0051	0065	0081	0100	0122	0149	0179	0213	0253
7	0004	0006	0008	0010	0013	0017	0022	0028	0035	0043
8			0001	0001	0001	0001	0002	0003	0003	0004

R \ P	31	32	33	34	35	36	37	38	39	40
1	9645	9689	9728	9762	9793	9820	9844	9865	9883	9899
2	8212	8372	8522	8661	8789	8908	9017	9118	9210	9295
3	5636	5894	6146	6390	6627	6856	7076	7287	7489	7682
4	2935	3173	3415	3662	3911	4163	4416	4669	4922	5174
5	1115	1252	1398	1553	1717	1890	2072	2262	2460	2666
6	0298	0348	0404	0467	0536	0612	0696	0787	0886	0994
7	0053	0064	0078	0094	0112	0133	0157	0184	0215	0250
8	0006	0007	0009	0011	0014	0017	0021	0026	0031	0038
9				0001	0001	0001	0001	0002	0002	0003

n = 9

R \ P	41	42	43	44	45	46	47	48	49	50
1	9913	9926	9936	9946	9954	9961	9967	9972	9977	9980
2	9372	9442	9505	9563	9615	9662	9704	9741	9775	9805
3	7866	8039	8204	8359	8505	8642	8769	8889	8999	9102
4	5424	5670	5913	6152	6386	6614	6836	7052	7260	7461
5	2878	3097	3322	3551	3786	4024	4265	4509	4754	5000
6	1109	1233	1366	1508	1658	1817	1985	2161	2346	2539
7	0290	0334	0383	0437	0498	0564	0637	0717	0804	0898
8	0046	0055	0065	0077	0091	0107	0125	0145	0169	0195
9	0003	0004	0005	0006	0008	0009	0011	0014	0016	0020

n = 10

R \ P	01	02	03	04	05	06	07	08	09	10
1	0956	1829	2626	3352	4013	4614	5160	5656	6106	6513
2	0043	0162	0345	0582	0861	1176	1517	1879	2254	2639
3	0001	0009	0028	0062	0115	0188	0283	0401	0540	0702
4			0001	0004	0010	0020	0036	0058	0088	0128
5					0001	0002	0003	0006	0010	0016
6									0001	0001

R \ P	11	12	13	14	15	16	17	18	19	20
1	6882	7215	7516	7787	8031	8251	8448	8626	8784	8926
2	3028	3417	3804	4184	4557	4920	5270	5608	5932	6242
3	0884	1087	1308	1545	1798	2064	2341	2628	2922	3222
4	0178	0239	0313	0400	0500	0614	0741	0883	1039	1209
5	0025	0037	0053	0073	0099	0130	0168	0213	0266	0328
6	0003	0004	0006	0010	0014	0020	0027	0037	0049	0064
7			0001	0001	0001	0002	0003	0004	0006	0009
8									0001	0001

R \ P	21	22	23	24	25	26	27	28	29	30
1	9053	9166	9267	9357	9437	9508	9570	9626	9674	9718
2	6536	6815	7079	7327	7560	7778	7981	8170	8345	8507
3	3526	3831	4137	4442	4744	5042	5335	5622	5901	6172
4	1391	1587	1794	2012	2241	2479	2726	2979	3239	3504
5	0399	0479	0569	0670	0781	0904	1037	1181	1337	1503
6	0082	0104	0130	0161	0197	0239	0287	0342	0404	0473
7	0012	0016	0021	0027	0035	0045	0056	0070	0087	0106
8	0001	0002	0002	0003	0004	0006	0007	0010	0012	0016
9							0001	0001	0001	0001

R \ P	31	32	33	34	35	36	37	38	39	40
1	9755	9789	9818	9843	9865	9885	9902	9916	9929	9940
2	8656	8794	8920	9035	9140	9236	9323	9402	9473	9536
3	6434	6687	6930	7162	7384	7595	7794	7983	8160	8327
4	3772	4044	4316	4589	4862	5132	5400	5664	5923	6177
5	1679	1867	2064	2270	2485	2708	2939	3177	3420	3669
6	0551	0637	0732	0836	0949	1072	1205	1348	1500	1662
7	0129	0155	0185	0220	0260	0305	0356	0413	0477	0548
8	0020	0025	0032	0039	0048	0059	0071	0086	0103	0123
9	0002	0003	0003	0004	0005	0007	0009	0011	0014	0017
10								0001	0001	0001

n = 10

R \ P	41	42	43	44	45	46	47	48	49	50
1	9949	9957	9964	9970	9975	9979	9983	9986	9988	9990
2	9594	9645	9691	9731	9767	9799	9827	9852	9874	9893
3	8483	8628	8764	8889	9004	9111	9209	9298	9379	9453
4	6425	6665	6898	7123	7340	7547	7745	7933	8112	8281
5	3922	4178	4436	4696	4956	5216	5474	5730	5982	6230
6	1834	2016	2207	2407	2616	2832	3057	3288	3526	3770
7	0626	0712	0806	0908	1020	1141	1271	1410	1560	1719
8	0146	0172	0202	0236	0274	0317	0366	0420	0480	0547
9	0021	0025	0031	0037	0045	0054	0065	0077	0091	0107
10	0001	0002	0002	0003	0003	0004	0005	0006	0008	0010

n = 11

R \ P	01	02	03	04	05	06	07	08	09	10
1	1047	1993	2847	3618	4312	4937	5499	6004	6456	6862
2	0052	0195	0413	0692	1019	1382	1772	2181	2601	3026
3	0002	0012	0037	0083	0152	0248	0370	0519	0695	0896
4			0002	0007	0016	0030	0053	0085	0129	0185
5					0001	0003	0005	0010	0017	0028
6								0001	0002	0003

R \ P	11	12	13	14	15	16	17	18	19	20
1	7225	7549	7839	8097	8327	8531	8712	8873	9015	9141
2	3452	3873	4286	4689	5078	5453	5811	6151	6474	6779
3	1120	1366	1632	1915	2212	2521	2839	3164	3494	3826
4	0256	0341	0442	0560	0694	0846	1013	1197	1397	1611
5	0042	0061	0087	0119	0159	0207	0266	0334	0413	0504
6	0005	0008	0012	0018	0027	0037	0051	0068	0090	0117
7		0001	0001	0002	0003	0005	0007	0010	0014	0020
8							0001	0001	0002	0002

R \ P	21	22	23	24	25	26	27	28	29	30
1	9252	9350	9436	9511	9578	9636	9686	9730	9769	9802
2	7065	7333	7582	7814	8029	8227	8410	8577	8730	8870
3	4158	4488	4814	5134	5448	5753	6049	6335	6610	6873
4	1840	2081	2333	2596	2867	3146	3430	3719	4011	4304
5	0607	0723	0851	0992	1146	1313	1493	1685	1888	2103
6	0148	0186	0231	0283	0343	0412	0490	0577	0674	0782
7	0027	0035	0046	0059	0076	0095	0119	0146	0179	0216
8	0003	0005	0007	0009	0012	0016	0021	0027	0034	0043
9			0001	0001	0001	0002	0002	0003	0004	0006

R \ P	31	32	33	34	35	36	37	38	39	40
1	9831	9856	9878	9896	9912	9926	9938	9948	9956	9964
2	8997	9112	9216	9310	9394	9470	9537	9597	9650	9698
3	7123	7361	7587	7799	7999	8186	8360	8522	8672	8811
4	4598	4890	5179	5464	5744	6019	6286	6545	6796	7037
5	2328	2563	2807	3059	3317	3581	3850	4122	4397	4672
6	0901	1031	1171	1324	1487	1661	1847	2043	2249	2465
7	0260	0309	0366	0430	0501	0581	0670	0768	0876	0994
8	0054	0067	0082	0101	0122	0148	0177	0210	0249	0293
9	0008	0010	0013	0016	0020	0026	0032	0039	0048	0059
10	0001	0001	0001	0002	0002	0003	0004	0005	0006	0007

n = 11

R \ P	41	42	43	44	45	46	47	48	49	50
1	9970	9975	9979	9983	9986	9989	9991	9992	9994	9995
2	9739	9776	9808	9836	9861	9882	9900	9916	9930	9941
3	8938	9055	9162	9260	9348	9428	9499	9564	9622	9673
4	7269	7490	7700	7900	8089	8266	8433	8588	8733	8867
5	4948	5223	5495	5764	6029	6288	6541	6787	7026	7256
6	2690	2924	3166	3414	3669	3929	4193	4460	4729	5000
7	1121	1260	1408	1568	1738	1919	2110	2312	2523	2744
8	0343	0399	0461	0532	0610	0696	0791	0895	1009	1133
9	0072	0087	0104	0125	0148	0175	0206	0241	0282	0327
10	0009	0012	0014	0018	0022	0027	0033	0040	0049	0059
11	0001	0001	0001	0001	0002	0002	0002	0003	0004	0005

n = 12

R \ P	01	02	03	04	05	06	07	08	09	10
1	1136	2153	3062	3873	4596	5241	5814	6323	6775	7176
2	0062	0231	0486	0809	1184	1595	2033	2487	2948	3410
3	0002	0015	0048	0107	0196	0316	0468	0652	0866	1109
4		0001	0003	0010	0022	0043	0075	0120	0180	0256
5				0001	0002	0004	0009	0016	0027	0043
6							0001	0002	0003	0005
7										0001

R \ P	11	12	13	14	15	16	17	18	19	20
1	7530	7843	8120	8363	8578	8766	8931	9076	9202	9313
2	3867	4314	4748	5166	5565	5945	6304	6641	6957	7251
3	1377	1667	1977	2303	2642	2990	3344	3702	4060	4417
4	0351	0464	0597	0750	0922	1114	1324	1552	1795	2054
5	0065	0095	0133	0181	0239	0310	0393	0489	0600	0726
6	0009	0014	0022	0033	0046	0065	0088	0116	0151	0194
7	0001	0002	0003	0004	0007	0010	0015	0021	0029	0039
8					0001	0001	0002	0003	0004	0006
9										0001

R \ P	21	22	23	24	25	26	27	28	29	30
1	9409	9493	9566	9629	9683	9730	9771	9806	9836	9862
2	7524	7776	8009	8222	8416	8594	8755	8900	9032	9150
3	4768	5114	5450	5778	6093	6397	6687	6963	7225	7472
4	2326	2610	2904	3205	3512	3824	4137	4452	4765	5075
5	0866	1021	1192	1377	1576	1790	2016	2254	2504	2763
6	0245	0304	0374	0453	0544	0646	0760	0887	1026	1178
7	0052	0068	0089	0113	0143	0178	0219	0267	0322	0386
8	0008	0011	0016	0021	0028	0036	0047	0060	0076	0095
9	0001	0001	0002	0003	0004	0005	0007	0010	0013	0017
10						0001	0001	0001	0002	0002

R \ P	31	32	33	34	35	36	37	38	39	40
1	9884	9902	9918	9932	9943	9953	9961	9968	9973	9978
2	9256	9350	9435	9509	9576	9634	9685	9730	9770	9804
3	7704	7922	8124	8313	8487	8648	8795	8931	9054	9166
4	5381	5681	5973	6258	6533	6799	7053	7296	7528	7747
5	3032	3308	3590	3876	4167	4459	4751	5043	5332	5618
6	1343	1521	1711	1913	2127	2352	2588	2833	3087	3348
7	0458	0540	0632	0734	0846	0970	1106	1253	1411	1582
8	0118	0144	0176	0213	0255	0304	0359	0422	0493	0573
9	0022	0028	0036	0045	0056	0070	0086	0104	0127	0153
10	0003	0004	0005	0007	0008	0011	0014	0018	0022	0028
11				0001	0001	0001	0001	0002	0002	0003

n = 12

R \ P	41	42	43	44	45	46	47	48	49	50
1	9982	9986	9988	9990	9992	9994	9995	9996	9997	9998
2	9834	9860	9882	9901	9917	9931	9943	9953	9961	9968
3	9267	9358	9440	9513	9579	9637	9688	9733	9773	9807
4	7953	8147	8329	8498	8655	8801	8934	9057	9168	9270
5	5899	6175	6443	6704	6956	7198	7430	7652	7862	8062
6	3616	3889	4167	4448	4731	5014	5297	5577	5855	6128
7	1765	1959	2164	2380	2607	2843	3089	3343	3604	3872
8	0662	0760	0869	0988	1117	1258	1411	1575	1751	1938
9	0183	0218	0258	0304	0356	0415	0481	0555	0638	0730
10	0035	0043	0053	0065	0079	0095	0114	0137	0163	0193
11	0004	0005	0007	0009	0011	0014	0017	0021	0026	0032
12				0001	0001	0001	0001	0001	0002	0002

n = 13

R \ P	01	02	03	04	05	06	07	08	09	10
1	1225	2310	3270	4118	4867	5526	6107	6617	7065	7458
2	0072	0270	0564	0932	1354	1814	2298	2794	3293	3787
3	0003	0020	0062	0135	0245	0392	0578	0799	1054	1339
4		0001	0005	0014	0031	0060	0103	0163	0242	0342
5				0001	0003	0007	0013	0024	0041	0065
6						0001	0001	0003	0005	0009
7									0001	0001

R \ P	11	12	13	14	15	16	17	18	19	20
1	7802	8102	8364	8592	8791	8963	9113	9242	9354	9450
2	4270	4738	5186	5614	6017	6396	6751	7080	7384	7664
3	1651	1985	2337	2704	3080	3463	3848	4231	4611	4983
4	0464	0609	0776	0967	1180	1414	1667	1939	2226	2527
5	0097	0139	0193	0260	0342	0438	0551	0681	0827	0991
6	0015	0024	0036	0053	0075	0104	0139	0183	0237	0300
7	0002	0003	0005	0008	0013	0019	0027	0038	0052	0070
8			0001	0001	0002	0003	0004	0006	0009	0012
9								0001	0001	0002

R \ P	21	22	23	24	25	26	27	28	29	30
1	9533	9604	9666	9718	9762	9800	9833	9860	9883	9903
2	7920	8154	8367	8559	8733	8889	9029	9154	9265	9363
3	5347	5699	6039	6364	6674	6968	7245	7505	7749	7975
4	2839	3161	3489	3822	4157	4493	4826	5155	5478	5794
5	1173	1371	1585	1816	2060	2319	2589	2870	3160	3457
6	0375	0462	0562	0675	0802	0944	1099	1270	1455	1654
7	0093	0120	0154	0195	0243	0299	0365	0440	0527	0624
8	0017	0024	0032	0043	0056	0073	0093	0118	0147	0182
9	0002	0004	0005	0007	0010	0013	0018	0024	0031	0040
10			0001	0001	0001	0002	0003	0004	0005	0007
11									0001	0001

R \ P	31	32	33	34	35	36	37	38	39	40
1	9920	9934	9945	9955	9963	9970	9975	9980	9984	9987
2	9450	9527	9594	9653	9704	9749	9787	9821	9849	9874
3	8185	8379	8557	8720	8868	9003	9125	9235	9333	9421
4	6101	6398	6683	6957	7217	7464	7698	7917	8123	8314
5	3760	4067	4376	4686	4995	5301	5603	5899	6188	6470
6	1867	2093	2331	2581	2841	3111	3388	3673	3962	4256
7	0733	0854	0988	1135	1295	1468	1654	1853	2065	2288
8	0223	0271	0326	0390	0462	0544	0635	0738	0851	0977
9	0052	0065	0082	0102	0126	0154	0187	0225	0270	0321
10	0009	0012	0015	0020	0025	0032	0040	0051	0063	0078
11	0001	0001	0002	0003	0003	0005	0006	0008	0010	0013
12							0001	0001	0001	0001

n = 13

R \ P	41	42	43	44	45	46	47	48	49	50
1	9990	9992	9993	9995	9996	9997	9997	9998	9998	9999
2	9895	9912	9928	9940	9951	9960	9967	9974	9979	9983
3	9499	9569	9630	9684	9731	9772	9808	9838	9865	9888
4	8492	8656	8807	8945	9071	9185	9288	9381	9464	9539
5	6742	7003	7254	7493	7721	7935	8137	8326	8502	8666
6	4552	4849	5146	5441	5732	6019	6299	6573	6838	7095
7	2524	2770	3025	3290	3563	3842	4127	4415	4707	5000
8	1114	1264	1426	1600	1788	1988	2200	2424	2659	2905
9	0379	0446	0520	0605	0698	0803	0918	1045	1183	1334
10	0096	0117	0141	0170	0203	0242	0287	0338	0396	0461
11	0017	0021	0027	0033	0041	0051	0063	0077	0093	0112
12	0002	0002	0003	0004	0005	0007	0009	0011	0014	0017
13							0001	0001	0001	0001

n = 14

R \ P	01	02	03	04	05	06	07	08	09	10
1	1313	2464	3472	4353	5123	5795	6380	6888	7330	7712
2	0084	0310	0645	1059	1530	2037	2564	3100	3632	4154
3	0003	0025	0077	0167	0301	0478	0698	0958	1255	1584
4		0001	0006	0019	0042	0080	0136	0214	0315	0441
5				0002	0004	0010	0020	0035	0059	0092
6						0001	0002	0004	0008	0015
7									0001	0002

R \ P	11	12	13	14	15	16	17	18	19	20
1	8044	8330	8577	8789	8972	9129	9264	9379	9477	9560
2	4658	5141	5599	6031	6433	6807	7152	7469	7758	8021
3	1939	2315	2708	3111	3521	3932	4341	4744	5138	5519
4	0594	0774	0979	1210	1465	1742	2038	2351	2679	3018
5	0137	0196	0269	0359	0467	0594	0741	0907	1093	1298
6	0024	0038	0057	0082	0115	0157	0209	0273	0349	0439
7	0003	0006	0009	0015	0022	0032	0046	0064	0087	0116
8		0001	0001	0002	0003	0005	0008	0012	0017	0024
9						0001	0001	0002	0003	0004

R \ P	21	22	23	24	25	26	27	28	29	30
1	9631	9691	9742	9786	9822	9852	9878	9899	9917	9932
2	8259	8473	8665	8837	8990	9126	9246	9352	9444	9525
3	5887	6239	6574	6891	7189	7467	7727	7967	8188	8392
4	3366	3719	4076	4432	4787	5136	5479	5813	6137	6448
5	1523	1765	2023	2297	2585	2884	3193	3509	3832	4158
6	0543	0662	0797	0949	1117	1301	1502	1718	1949	2195
7	0152	0196	0248	0310	0383	0467	0563	0673	0796	0933
8	0033	0045	0060	0079	0103	0132	0167	0208	0257	0315
9	0006	0008	0011	0016	0022	0029	0038	0050	0065	0083
10	0001	0001	0002	0002	0003	0005	0007	0009	0012	0017
11						0001	0001	0001	0002	0002

n = 14

R \ P	31	32	33	34	35	36	37	38	39	40
1	9945	9955	9963	9970	9976	9981	9984	9988	9990	9992
2	9596	9657	9710	9756	9795	9828	9857	9881	9902	9919
3	8577	8746	8899	9037	9161	9271	9370	9457	9534	9602
4	6747	7032	7301	7556	7795	8018	8226	8418	8595	8757
5	4486	4813	5138	5458	5773	6080	6378	6666	6943	7207
6	2454	2724	3006	3297	3595	3899	4208	4519	4831	5141
7	1084	1250	1431	1626	1836	2059	2296	2545	2805	3075
8	0381	0458	0545	0643	0753	0876	1012	1162	1325	1501
9	0105	0131	0163	0200	0243	0294	0353	0420	0497	0583
10	0022	0029	0037	0048	0060	0076	0095	0117	0144	0175
11	0003	0005	0006	0008	0011	0014	0019	0024	0031	0039
12		0001	0001	0001	0001	0002	0003	0003	0005	0006
13										0001

R \ P	41	42	43	44	45	46	47	48	49	50
1	9994	9995	9996	9997	9998	9998	9999	9999	9999	9999
2	9934	9946	9956	9964	9971	9977	9981	9985	9988	9991
3	9661	9713	9758	9797	9830	9858	9883	9903	9921	9935
4	8905	9039	9161	9270	9368	9455	9532	9601	9661	9713
5	7459	7697	7922	8132	8328	8510	8678	8833	8974	9102
6	5450	5754	6052	6344	6627	6900	7163	7415	7654	7880
7	3355	3643	3937	4236	4539	4843	5148	5451	5751	6047
8	1692	1896	2113	2344	2586	2840	3105	3380	3663	3953
9	0680	0789	0910	1043	1189	1348	1520	1707	1906	2120
10	0212	0255	0304	0361	0426	0500	0583	0677	0782	0898
11	0049	0061	0076	0093	0114	0139	0168	0202	0241	0287
12	0008	0010	0013	0017	0022	0027	0034	0042	0053	0065
13	0001	0001	0001	0002	0003	0003	0004	0006	0007	0009
14										0001

n = 15

R \ P	01	02	03	04	05	06	07	08	09	10
1	1399	2614	3667	4579	5367	6047	6633	7137	7570	7941
2	0096	0353	0730	1191	1710	2262	2832	3403	3965	4510
3	0004	0030	0094	0203	0362	0571	0829	1130	1469	1841
4		0002	0008	0024	0055	0104	0175	0273	0399	0556
5			0001	0002	0006	0014	0028	0050	0082	0127
6					0001	0001	0003	0007	0013	0022
7								0001	0002	0003

R \ P	11	12	13	14	15	16	17	18	19	20
1	8259	8530	8762	8959	9126	9269	9389	9490	9576	9648
2	5031	5524	5987	6417	6814	7179	7511	7813	8085	8329
3	2238	2654	3084	3520	3958	4392	4819	5234	5635	6020
4	0742	0959	1204	1476	1773	2092	2429	2782	3146	3518
5	0187	0265	0361	0478	0617	0778	0961	1167	1394	1642
6	0037	0057	0084	0121	0168	0227	0300	0387	0490	0611
7	0006	0010	0015	0024	0036	0052	0074	0102	0137	0181
8	0001	0001	0002	0004	0006	0010	0014	0021	0030	0042
9					0001	0001	0002	0003	0005	0008
10									0001	0001

n = 15

R \ P	21	22	23	24	25	26	27	28	29	30
1	9709	9759	9802	9837	9866	9891	9911	9928	9941	9953
2	8547	8741	8913	9065	9198	9315	9417	9505	9581	9647
3	6385	6731	7055	7358	7639	7899	8137	8355	8553	8732
4	3895	4274	4650	5022	5387	5742	6086	6416	6732	7031
5	1910	2195	2495	2810	3135	3469	3810	4154	4500	4845
6	0748	0905	1079	1272	1484	1713	1958	2220	2495	2784
7	0234	0298	0374	0463	0566	0684	0817	0965	1130	1311
8	0058	0078	0104	0135	0173	0219	0274	0338	0413	0500
9	0011	0016	0023	0031	0042	0056	0073	0094	0121	0152
10	0002	0003	0004	0006	0008	0011	0015	0021	0028	0037
11			0001	0001	0001	0002	0002	0003	0005	0007
12									0001	0001

R \ P	31	32	33	34	35	36	37	38	39	40
1	9962	9969	9975	9980	9984	9988	9990	9992	9994	9995
2	9704	9752	9794	9829	9858	9883	9904	9922	9936	9948
3	8893	9038	9167	9281	9383	9472	9550	9618	9678	9729
4	7314	7580	7829	8060	8273	8469	8649	8813	8961	9095
5	5187	5523	5852	6171	6481	6778	7062	7332	7587	7827
6	3084	3393	3709	4032	4357	4684	5011	5335	5654	5968
7	1509	1722	1951	2194	2452	2722	3003	3295	3595	3902
8	0599	0711	0837	0977	1132	1302	1487	1687	1902	2131
9	0190	0236	0289	0351	0422	0504	0597	0702	0820	0950
10	0048	0062	0079	0099	0124	0154	0190	0232	0281	0338
11	0009	0012	0016	0022	0028	0037	0047	0059	0075	0093
12	0001	0002	0003	0004	0005	0006	0009	0011	0015	0019
13					0001	0001	0001	0002	0002	0003

R \ P	41	42	43	44	45	46	47	48	49	50
1	9996	9997	9998	9998	9999	9999	9999	9999	10000	10000
2	9958	9966	9973	9979	9983	9987	9990	9992	9994	9995
3	9773	9811	9843	9870	9893	9913	9929	9943	9954	9963
4	9215	9322	9417	9502	9576	9641	9697	9746	9788	9824
5	8052	8261	8454	8633	8796	8945	9080	9201	9310	9408
6	6274	6570	6856	7131	7392	7641	7875	8095	8301	8491
7	4214	4530	4847	5164	5478	5789	6095	6394	6684	6964
8	2374	2630	2898	3176	3465	3762	4065	4374	4686	5000
9	1095	1254	1427	1615	1818	2034	2265	2510	2767	3036
10	0404	0479	0565	0661	0769	0890	1024	1171	1333	1509
11	0116	0143	0174	0211	0255	0305	0363	0430	0506	0592
12	0025	0032	0040	0051	0063	0079	0097	0119	0145	0176
13	0004	0005	0007	0009	0011	0014	0018	0023	0029	0037
14			0001	0001	0001	0002	0002	0003	0004	0005

APPENDIX TABLE 4

Values of $e^{-\lambda}$ (for computing Poisson probabilities)

λ	$e^{-\lambda}$	λ	$e^{-\lambda}$	λ	$e^{-\lambda}$	λ	$e^{-\lambda}$
0.1	0.90484	2.6	0.07427	5.1	0.00610	7.6	0.00050
0.2	0.81873	2.7	0.06721	5.2	0.00552	7.7	0.00045
0.3	0.74082	2.8	0.06081	5.3	0.00499	7.8	0.00041
0.4	0.67032	2.9	0.05502	5.4	0.00452	7.9	0.00037
0.5	0.60653	3.0	0.04979	5.5	0.00409	8.0	0.00034
0.6	0.54881	3.1	0.04505	5.6	0.00370	8.1	0.00030
0.7	0.49659	3.2	0.04076	5.7	0.00335	8.2	0.00027
0.8	0.44933	3.3	0.03688	5.8	0.00303	8.3	0.00025
0.9	0.40657	3.4	0.03337	5.9	0.00274	8.4	0.00022
1.0	0.36788	3.5	0.03020	6.0	0.00248	8.5	0.00020
1.1	0.33287	3.6	0.02732	6.1	0.00224	8.6	0.00018
1.2	0.30119	3.7	0.02472	6.2	0.00203	8.7	0.00017
1.3	0.27253	3.8	0.02237	6.3	0.00184	8.8	0.00015
1.4	0.24660	3.9	0.02024	6.4	0.00166	8.9	0.00014
1.5	0.22313	4.0	0.01832	6.5	0.00150	9.0	0.00012
1.6	0.20190	4.1	0.01657	6.6	0.00136	9.1	0.00011
1.7	0.18268	4.2	0.01500	6.7	0.00123	9.2	0.00010
1.8	0.16530	4.3	0.01357	6.8	0.00111	9.3	0.00009
1.9	0.14957	4.4	0.01228	6.9	0.00101	9.4	0.00008
2.0	0.13534	4.5	0.01111	7.0	0.00091	9.5	0.00007
2.1	0.12246	4.6	0.01005	7.1	0.00083	9.6	0.00007
2.2	0.11080	4.7	0.00910	7.2	0.00075	9.7	0.00006
2.3	0.10026	4.8	0.00823	7.3	0.00068	9.8	0.00006
2.4	0.09072	4.9	0.00745	7.4	0.00061	9.9	0.00005
2.5	0.08208	5.0	0.00674	7.5	0.00055	10.0	0.00005

APPENDIX TABLE 5

Area in the Right Tail of a Chi-square (χ^2) Distribution.*

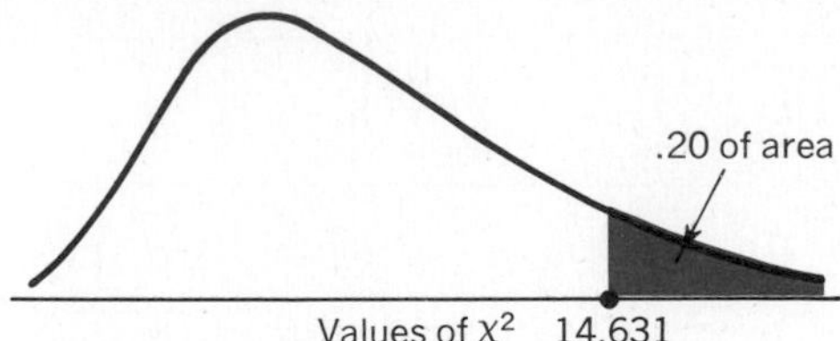

EXAMPLE: In a chi-square distribution with 11 degrees of freedom, if we want to find the appropriate chi-square value for .20 of the area under the curve (the colored area in the right tail) we look under the .20 column in the table and proceed down to the 11 degrees of freedom row; the appropriate chi-square value there is 14.631

Degrees of freedom	Area in right tail .99	.975	.95	.90	.800
1	.00016	.00098	.00398	.0158	.0642
2	.0201	.0506	.103	.211	.446
3	.115	.216	.352	.584	1.005
4	.297	.484	.711	1.064	1.649
5	.554	.831	1.145	1.610	2.343
6	.872	1.237	1.635	2.204	3.070
7	1.239	1.690	2.167	2.833	3.822
8	1.646	2.180	2.733	3.490	4.594
9	2.088	2.700	3.325	4.168	5.380
10	2.558	3.247	3.940	4.865	6.179
11	3.053	3.816	4.575	5.578	6.989
12	3.571	4.404	5.226	6.304	7.807
13	4.107	5.009	5.892	7.042	8.634
14	4.660	5.629	6.571	7.790	9.467
15	5.229	6.262	7.261	8.547	10.307
16	5.812	6.908	7.962	9.312	11.152
17	6.408	7.564	8.672	10.085	12.002
18	7.015	8.231	9.390	10.865	12.857
19	7.633	8.907	10.117	11.651	13.716
20	8.260	9.591	10.851	12.443	14.578
21	8.897	10.283	11.591	13.240	15.445
22	9.542	10.982	12.338	14.041	16.314
23	10.196	11.689	13.091	14.848	17.187
24	10.856	12.401	13.848	15.658	18.062
25	11.524	13.120	14.611	16.473	18.940
26	12.198	13.844	15.379	17.292	19.820
27	12.879	14.573	16.151	18.114	20.703
28	13.565	15.308	16.928	18.939	21.588
29	14.256	16.047	17.708	19.768	22.475
30	14.953	16.791	18.493	20.599	23.364

* Taken from Table IV of Fisher and Yates, *Statistical Tables for Biological, Agricultural and Medical Research,* published by Longman Group Ltd., London (previously published by Oliver & Boyd, Edinburgh) and by permission of the authors and publishers.

.20	.10	.05	.025	.01	Degrees of freedom
		Area in right tail			
1.642	2.706	3.841	5.024	6.635	1
3.219	4.605	5.991	7.378	9.210	2
4.642	6.251	7.815	9.348	11.345	3
5.989	7.779	9.488	11.143	13.277	4
7.289	9.236	11.070	12.833	15.086	5
8.558	10.645	12.592	14.449	16.812	6
9.803	12.017	14.067	16.013	18.475	7
11.030	13.362	15.507	17.535	20.090	8
12.242	14.684	16.919	19.023	21.666	9
13.442	15.987	18.307	20.483	23.209	10
14.631	17.275	19.675	21.920	24.725	11
15.812	18.549	21.026	23.337	26.217	12
16.985	19.812	22.362	24.736	27.688	13
18.151	21.064	23.685	26.119	29.141	14
19.311	22.307	24.996	27.488	30.578	15
20.465	23.542	26.296	28.845	32.000	16
21.615	24.769	27.587	30.191	33.409	17
22.760	25.989	28.869	31.526	34.805	18
23.900	27.204	30.144	32.852	36.191	19
25.038	28.412	31.410	34.170	37.566	20
26.171	29.615	32.671	35.479	38.932	21
27.301	30.813	33.924	36.781	40.289	22
28.429	32.007	35.172	38.076	41.638	23
29.553	33.196	36.415	39.364	42.980	24
30.675	34.382	37.652	40.647	44.314	25
31.795	35.563	38.885	41.923	45.642	26
32.912	36.741	40.113	43.194	46.963	27
34.027	37.916	41.337	44.461	48.278	28
35.139	39.087	42.557	45.722	49.588	29
36.250	40.256	43.773	46.979	50.892	30

APPENDIX TABLE 6

Values of *F* for *F* Distributions with .05 of the Area in the Right Tail.*

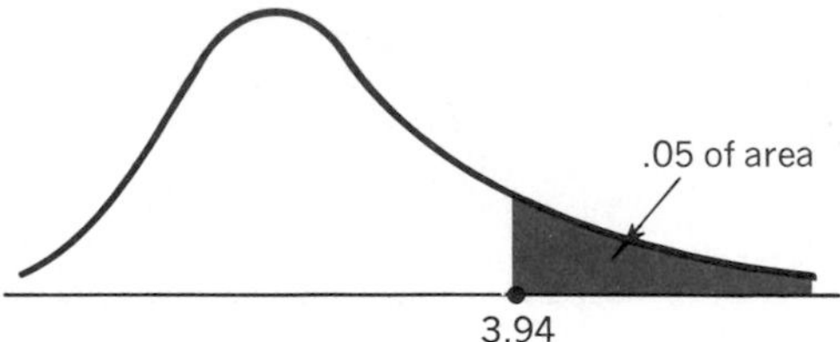

EXAMPLE: For a test at a significance level of .05 where we have 15 degrees of freedom for the numerator and 6 degrees of freedom for the denominator, the appropriate *F* value is found by looking under the 15 degrees of freedom column and proceeding down to the 6 degrees of freedom row; there we find the appropriate *F* value to be 3.94.

Degrees of freedom for denominator	Degrees of freedom for numerator																		
	1	2	3	4	5	6	7	8	9	10	12	15	20	24	30	40	60	120	∞
1	161	200	216	225	230	234	237	239	241	242	244	246	248	249	250	251	252	253	254
2	18.5	19.0	19.2	19.2	19.3	19.3	19.4	19.4	19.4	19.4	19.4	19.4	19.4	19.5	19.5	19.5	19.5	19.5	19.5
3	10.1	9.55	9.28	9.12	9.01	8.94	8.89	8.85	8.81	8.79	8.74	8.70	8.66	8.64	8.62	8.59	8.57	8.55	8.53
4	7.71	6.94	6.59	6.39	6.26	6.16	6.09	6.04	6.00	5.96	5.91	5.86	5.80	5.77	5.75	5.72	5.69	5.66	5.63
5	6.61	5.79	5.41	5.19	5.05	4.95	4.88	4.82	4.77	4.74	4.68	4.62	4.56	4.53	4.50	4.46	4.43	4.40	4.37
6	5.99	5.14	4.76	4.53	4.39	4.28	4.21	4.15	4.10	4.06	4.00	3.94	3.87	3.84	3.81	3.77	3.74	3.70	3.67
7	5.59	4.74	4.35	4.12	3.97	3.87	3.79	3.73	3.68	3.64	3.57	3.51	3.44	3.41	3.38	3.34	3.30	3.27	3.23
8	5.32	4.46	4.07	3.84	3.69	3.58	3.50	3.44	3.39	3.35	3.28	3.22	3.15	3.12	3.08	3.04	3.01	2.97	2.93
9	5.12	4.26	3.86	3.63	3.48	3.37	3.29	3.23	3.18	3.14	3.07	3.01	2.94	2.90	2.86	2.83	2.79	2.75	2.71
10	4.96	4.10	3.71	3.48	3.33	3.22	3.14	3.07	3.02	2.98	2.91	2.85	2.77	2.74	2.70	2.66	2.62	2.58	2.54
11	4.84	3.98	3.59	3.36	3.20	3.09	3.01	2.95	2.90	2.85	2.79	2.72	2.65	2.61	2.57	2.53	2.49	2.45	2.40
12	4.75	3.89	3.49	3.26	3.11	3.00	2.91	2.85	2.80	2.75	2.69	2.62	2.54	2.51	2.47	2.43	2.38	2.34	2.30
13	4.67	3.81	3.41	3.18	3.03	2.92	2.83	2.77	2.71	2.67	2.60	2.53	2.46	2.42	2.38	2.34	2.30	2.25	2.21
14	4.60	3.74	3.34	3.11	2.96	2.85	2.76	2.70	2.65	2.60	2.53	2.46	2.39	2.35	2.31	2.27	2.22	2.18	2.13
15	4.54	3.68	3.29	3.06	2.90	2.79	2.71	2.64	2.59	2.54	2.48	2.40	2.33	2.29	2.25	2.20	2.16	2.11	2.07
16	4.49	3.63	3.24	3.01	2.85	2.74	2.66	2.59	2.54	2.49	2.42	2.35	2.28	2.24	2.19	2.15	2.11	2.06	2.01
17	4.45	3.59	3.20	2.96	2.81	2.70	2.61	2.55	2.49	2.45	2.38	2.31	2.23	2.19	2.15	2.10	2.06	2.01	1.96
18	4.41	3.55	3.16	2.93	2.77	2.66	2.58	2.51	2.46	2.41	2.34	2.27	2.19	2.15	2.11	2.06	2.02	1.97	1.92
19	4.38	3.52	3.13	2.90	2.74	2.63	2.54	2.48	2.42	2.38	2.31	2.23	2.16	2.11	2.07	2.03	1.98	1.93	1.88
20	4.35	3.49	3.10	2.87	2.71	2.60	2.51	2.45	2.39	2.35	2.28	2.20	2.12	2.08	2.04	1.99	1.95	1.90	1.84
21	4.32	3.47	3.07	2.84	2.68	2.57	2.49	2.42	2.37	2.32	2.25	2.18	2.10	2.05	2.01	1.96	1.92	1.87	1.81
22	4.30	3.44	3.05	2.82	2.66	2.55	2.46	2.40	2.34	2.30	2.23	2.15	2.07	2.03	1.98	1.94	1.89	1.84	1.78
23	4.28	3.42	3.03	2.80	2.64	2.53	2.44	2.37	2.32	2.27	2.20	2.13	2.05	2.01	1.96	1.91	1.86	1.81	1.76
24	4.26	3.40	3.01	2.78	2.62	2.51	2.42	2.36	2.30	2.25	2.18	2.11	2.03	1.98	1.94	1.89	1.84	1.79	1.73
25	4.24	3.39	2.99	2.76	2.60	2.49	2.40	2.34	2.28	2.24	2.16	2.09	2.01	1.96	1.92	1.87	1.82	1.77	1.71
30	4.17	3.32	2.92	2.69	2.53	2.42	2.33	2.27	2.21	2.16	2.09	2.01	1.93	1.89	1.84	1.79	1.74	1.68	1.62
40	4.08	3.23	2.84	2.61	2.45	2.34	2.25	2.18	2.12	2.08	2.00	1.92	1.84	1.79	1.74	1.69	1.64	1.58	1.51
60	4.00	3.15	2.76	2.53	2.37	2.25	2.17	2.10	2.04	1.99	1.92	1.84	1.75	1.70	1.65	1.59	1.53	1.47	1.39
120	3.92	3.07	2.68	2.45	2.29	2.18	2.09	2.02	1.96	1.91	1.83	1.75	1.66	1.61	1.55	1.50	1.43	1.35	1.25
∞	3.84	3.00	2.60	2.37	2.21	2.10	2.01	1.94	1.88	1.83	1.75	1.67	1.57	1.52	1.46	1.39	1.32	1.22	1.00

* Source: M. Merrington and C. M. Thompson, *Biometrika,* vol. 33 (1943).

Values of F for F Distributions with .01 of the Area in the Right Tail.

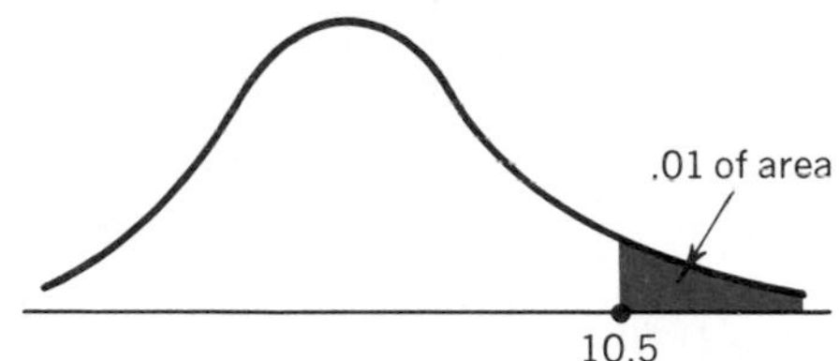

EXAMPLE: For a test at a significance level of .01 where we have 7 degrees of freedom for the numerator and 5 degrees of freedom for the denominator, the appropriate F value is found by looking under the 7 degrees of freedom column and proceeding down to the 5 degrees of freedom row; there we find the appropriate F value to be 10.5.

	Degrees of freedom for numerator																		
	1	2	3	4	5	6	7	8	9	10	12	15	20	24	30	40	60	120	∞
1	4,052	5,000	5,403	5,625	5,764	5,859	5,928	5,982	6,023	6,056	6,106	6,157	6,209	6,235	6,261	6,287	6,313	6,339	6,366
2	98.5	99.0	99.2	99.2	99.3	99.3	99.4	99.4	99.4	99.4	99.4	99.4	99.4	99.5	99.5	99.5	99.5	99.5	99.5
3	34.1	30.8	29.5	28.7	28.2	27.9	27.7	27.5	27.3	27.2	27.1	26.9	26.7	26.6	26.5	26.4	26.3	26.2	26.1
4	21.2	18.0	16.7	16.0	15.5	15.2	15.0	14.8	14.7	14.5	14.4	14.2	14.0	13.9	13.8	13.7	13.7	13.6	13.5
5	16.3	13.3	12.1	11.4	11.0	10.7	10.5	10.3	10.2	10.1	9.89	9.72	9.55	9.47	9.38	9.29	9.20	9.11	9.02
6	13.7	10.9	9.78	9.15	8.75	8.47	8.26	8.10	7.98	7.87	7.72	7.56	7.40	7.31	7.23	7.14	7.06	6.97	6.88
7	12.2	9.55	8.45	7.85	7.46	7.19	6.99	6.84	6.72	6.62	6.47	6.31	6.16	6.07	5.99	5.91	5.82	5.74	5.65
8	11.3	8.65	7.59	7.01	6.63	6.37	6.18	6.03	5.91	5.81	5.67	5.52	5.36	5.28	5.20	5.12	5.03	4.95	4.86
9	10.6	8.02	6.99	6.42	6.06	5.80	5.61	5.47	5.35	5.26	5.11	4.96	4.81	4.73	4.65	4.57	4.48	4.40	4.31
10	10.0	7.56	6.55	5.99	5.64	5.39	5.20	5.06	4.94	4.85	4.71	4.56	4.41	4.33	4.25	4.17	4.08	4.00	3.91
11	9.65	7.21	6.22	5.67	5.32	5.07	4.89	4.74	4.63	4.54	4.40	4.25	4.10	4.02	3.94	3.86	3.78	3.69	3.60
12	9.33	6.93	5.95	5.41	5.06	4.82	4.64	4.50	4.39	4.30	4.16	4.01	3.86	3.78	3.70	3.62	3.54	3.45	3.36
13	9.07	6.70	5.74	5.21	4.86	4.62	4.44	4.30	4.19	4.10	3.96	3.82	3.66	3.59	3.51	3.43	3.34	3.25	3.17
14	8.86	6.51	5.56	5.04	4.70	4.46	4.28	4.14	4.03	3.94	3.80	3.66	3.51	3.43	3.35	3.27	3.18	3.09	3.00
15	8.68	6.36	5.42	4.89	4.56	4.32	4.14	4.00	3.89	3.80	3.67	3.52	3.37	3.29	3.21	3.13	3.05	2.96	2.87
16	8.53	6.23	5.29	4.77	4.44	4.20	4.03	3.89	3.78	3.69	3.55	3.41	3.26	3.18	3.10	3.02	2.93	2.84	2.75
17	8.40	6.11	5.19	4.67	4.34	4.10	3.93	3.79	3.68	3.59	3.46	3.31	3.16	3.08	3.00	2.92	2.83	2.75	2.65
18	8.29	6.01	5.09	4.58	4.25	4.01	3.84	3.71	3.60	3.51	3.37	3.23	3.08	3.00	2.92	2.84	2.75	2.66	2.57
19	8.19	5.93	5.01	4.50	4.17	3.94	3.77	3.63	3.52	3.43	3.30	3.15	3.00	2.92	2.84	2.76	2.67	2.58	2.49
20	8.10	5.85	4.94	4.43	4.10	3.87	3.70	3.56	3.46	3.37	3.23	3.09	2.94	2.86	2.78	2.69	2.61	2.52	2.42
21	8.02	5.78	4.87	4.37	4.04	3.81	3.64	3.51	3.40	3.31	3.17	3.03	2.88	2.80	2.72	2.64	2.55	2.46	2.36
22	7.95	5.72	4.82	4.31	3.99	3.76	3.59	3.45	3.35	3.26	3.12	2.98	2.83	2.75	2.67	2.58	2.50	2.40	2.31
23	7.88	5.66	4.76	4.26	3.94	3.71	3.54	3.41	3.30	3.21	3.07	2.93	2.78	2.70	2.62	2.54	2.45	2.35	2.26
24	7.82	5.61	4.72	4.22	3.90	3.67	3.50	3.36	3.26	3.17	3.03	2.89	2.74	2.66	2.58	2.49	2.40	2.31	2.21
25	7.77	5.57	4.68	4.18	3.86	3.63	3.46	3.32	3.22	3.13	2.99	2.85	2.70	2.62	2.53	2.45	2.36	2.27	2.17
30	7.56	5.39	4.51	4.02	3.70	3.47	3.30	3.17	3.07	2.98	2.84	2.70	2.55	2.47	2.39	2.30	2.21	2.11	2.01
40	7.31	5.18	4.31	3.83	3.51	3.29	3.12	2.99	2.89	2.80	2.66	2.52	2.37	2.29	2.20	2.11	2.02	1.92	1.80
60	7.08	4.98	4.13	3.65	3.34	3.12	2.95	2.82	2.72	2.63	2.50	2.35	2.20	2.12	2.03	1.94	1.84	1.73	1.60
120	6.85	4.79	3.95	3.48	3.17	2.96	2.79	2.66	2.56	2.47	2.34	2.19	2.03	1.95	1.86	1.76	1.66	1.53	1.38
∞	6.63	4.61	3.78	3.32	3.02	2.80	2.64	2.51	2.41	2.32	2.18	2.04	1.88	1.79	1.70	1.59	1.47	1.32	1.00

APPENDIX TABLE 7

Values for Spearman's Rank Correlation (r_s) for Combined Areas in Both Tails.*

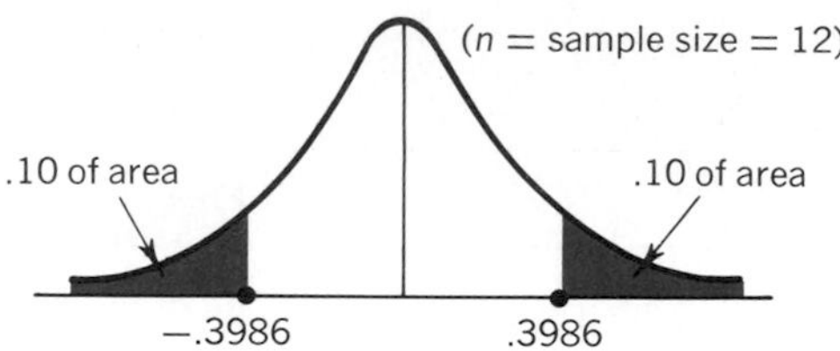

EXAMPLE: For a two-tailed test of significance at the .20 level, with $n = 12$, the appropriate value for r_s can be found by looking under the .20 column and proceeding down to the 12 row; there we find the appropriate r_s value to be .3986.

n	.20	.10	.05	.02	.01	.002
4	.8000	.8000				
5	.7000	.8000	.9000	.9000		
6	.6000	.7714	.8286	.8857	.9429	
7	.5357	.6786	.7450	.8571	.8929	.9643
8	.5000	.6190	.7143	.8095	.8571	.9286
9	.4667	.5833	.6833	.7667	.8167	.9000
10	.4424	.5515	.6364	.7333	.7818	.8667
11	.4182	.5273	.6091	.7000	.7455	.8364
12	.3986	.4965	.5804	.6713	.7273	.8182
13	.3791	.4780	.5549	.6429	.6978	.7912
14	.3626	.4593	.5341	.6220	.6747	.7670
15	.3500	.4429	.5179	.6000	.6536	.7464
16	.3382	.4265	.5000	.5824	.6324	.7265
17	.3260	.4118	.4853	.5637	.6152	.7083
18	.3148	.3994	.4716	.5480	.5975	.6904
19	.3070	.3895	.4579	.5333	.5825	.6737
20	.2977	.3789	.4451	.5203	.5684	.6586
21	.2909	.3688	.4351	.5078	.5545	.6455
22	.2829	.3597	.4241	.4963	.5426	.6318
23	.2767	.3518	.4150	.4852	.5306	.6186
24	.2704	.3435	.4061	.4748	.5200	.6070
25	.2646	.3362	.3977	.4654	.5100	.5962
26	.2588	.3299	.3894	.4564	.5002	.5856
27	.2540	.3236	.3822	.4481	.4915	.5757
28	.2490	.3175	.3749	.4401	.4828	.5660
29	.2443	.3113	.3685	.4320	.4744	.5567
30	.2400	.3059	.3620	.4251	.4665	.5479

* Source: W.J. Conover, *Practical Nonparametric Statistics*, John Wiley & Sons, Inc., New York, 1971.

APPENDIX TABLE 8

Critical Values of D in the Kolmogorov-Smirnov Goodness-of-Fit Test.

Sample size (n)	Level of significance for D = Maximum $\|F(x) - S_n(x)\|$				
	.20	.15	.10	.05	.01
1	.900	.925	.950	.975	.995
2	.684	.726	.776	.842	.929
3	.565	.597	.642	.708	.828
4	.494	.525	.564	.624	.733
5	.446	.474	.510	.565	.669
6	.410	.436	.470	.521	.618
7	.381	.405	.438	.486	.577
8	.358	.381	.411	.457	.543
9	.339	.360	.388	.432	.514
10	.322	.342	.368	.410	.490
11	.307	.326	.352	.391	.468
12	.295	.313	.338	.375	.450
13	.284	.302	.325	.361	.433
14	.274	.292	.314	.349	.418
15	.266	.283	.304	.338	.404
16	.258	.274	.295	.328	.392
17	.250	.266	.286	.318	.381
18	.244	.259	.278	.309	.371
19	.237	.252	.272	.301	.363
20	.231	.246	.264	.294	.356
25	.21	.22	.24	.27	.32
30	.19	.20	.22	.24	.29
35	.18	.19	.21	.23	.27
Over 35	$\frac{1.07}{\sqrt{n}}$	$\frac{1.14}{\sqrt{n}}$	$\frac{1.22}{\sqrt{n}}$	$\frac{1.36}{\sqrt{n}}$	$\frac{1.63}{\sqrt{n}}$

Source: Adapted from F. J. Massey, Jr., "The Kolmogorov-Smirnov test for goodness of fit," *J. Am. Stat. Assoc.* 46:68–78, 1951. By permission of the author and publishers.

Note: The values of D given in the table are critical values associated with selected values of n. Any value of D that is greater than or equal to the tabulated value is significant at the indicated level of significance.

APPENDIX TABLE 9

Square Roots for Numbers from 1 to 400.*

1	1.00	41	6.40	81	9.00	121	11.00	161	12.69
2	1.41	42	6.48	82	9.06	122	11.05	162	12.73
3	1.73	43	6.56	83	9.11	123	11.09	163	12.77
4	2.00	44	6.63	84	9.17	124	11.14	164	12.81
5	2.24	45	6.71	85	9.22	125	11.18	165	12.85
6	2.45	46	6.78	86	9.27	126	11.23	166	12.88
7	2.65	47	6.86	87	9.33	127	11.27	167	12.92
8	2.83	48	6.93	88	9.38	128	11.31	168	12.96
9	3.00	49	7.00	89	9.43	129	11.36	169	13.00
10	3.16	50	7.07	90	9.49	130	11.40	170	13.04
11	3.32	51	7.14	91	9.54	131	11.45	171	13.08
12	3.46	52	7.21	92	9.59	132	11.49	172	13.11
13	3.61	53	7.28	93	9.64	133	11.53	173	13.15
14	3.74	54	7.35	94	9.70	134	11.58	174	13.19
15	3.87	55	7.42	95	9.75	135	11.62	175	13.23
16	4.00	56	7.48	96	9.80	136	11.66	176	13.27
17	4.12	57	7.55	97	9.85	137	11.70	177	13.30
18	4.24	58	7.62	98	9.90	138	11.74	178	13.34
19	4.36	59	7.68	99	9.95	139	11.79	179	13.38
20	4.47	60	7.75	100	10.00	140	11.83	180	13.42
21	4.58	61	7.81	101	10.05	141	11.87	181	13.45
22	4.69	62	7.87	102	10.10	142	11.92	182	13.49
23	4.80	63	7.94	103	10.15	143	11.96	183	13.53
24	4.90	64	8.00	104	10.20	144	12.00	184	13.56
25	5.00	65	8.06	105	10.25	145	12.04	185	13.60
26	5.10	66	8.12	106	10.30	146	12.08	186	13.64
27	5.20	67	8.19	107	10.34	147	12.12	187	13.67
28	5.29	68	8.25	108	10.39	148	12.17	188	13.71
29	5.39	69	8.31	109	10.44	149	12.21	189	13.75
30	5.48	70	8.37	110	10.49	150	12.25	190	13.78
31	5.57	71	8.43	111	10.54	151	12.29	191	13.82
32	5.66	72	8.49	112	10.58	152	12.33	192	13.86
33	5.74	73	8.54	113	10.63	153	12.37	193	13.89
34	5.83	74	8.60	114	10.68	154	12.41	194	13.93
35	5.92	75	8.66	115	10.72	155	12.45	195	13.96
36	6.00	76	8.72	116	10.77	156	12.49	196	14.00
37	6.08	77	8.77	117	10.82	157	12.53	197	14.04
38	6.16	78	8.83	118	10.86	158	12.57	198	14.07
39	6.25	79	8.89	119	10.91	159	12.61	199	14.11
40	6.32	80	8.94	120	10.95	160	12.65	200	14.14

* Source: Levin and Kirkpatrick, *Quantitative Approaches to Management,* 5th ed., New York: McGraw-Hill Book Co., Inc., 1982.

201	14.18	241	15.52	281	16.76	321	17.92	361	19.00
202	14.21	242	15.56	282	16.79	322	17.94	362	19.03
203	14.25	243	15.59	283	16.82	323	17.97	363	19.05
204	14.28	244	15.62	284	16.85	324	18.00	364	19.08
205	14.32	245	15.65	285	16.88	325	18.03	365	19.11
206	14.35	246	15.68	286	16.91	326	18.06	366	19.13
207	14.39	247	15.72	287	16.94	327	18.08	367	19.16
208	14.42	248	15.75	288	16.97	328	18.11	368	19.18
209	14.46	249	15.78	289	17.00	329	18.14	369	19.21
210	14.49	250	15.81	290	17.03	330	18.17	370	19.24
211	14.53	251	15.84	291	17.06	331	18.19	371	19.26
212	14.56	252	15.87	292	17.09	332	18.22	372	19.29
213	14.59	253	15.91	293	17.12	333	18.25	373	19.31
214	14.63	254	15.94	294	17.15	334	18.28	374	19.34
215	14.66	255	15.97	295	17.18	335	18.30	375	19.36
216	14.70	256	16.00	296	17.20	336	18.33	376	19.39
217	14.73	257	16.03	297	17.23	337	18.36	377	19.42
218	14.76	258	16.06	298	17.26	338	18.38	378	19.44
219	14.80	259	16.09	299	17.29	339	18.41	379	19.47
220	14.83	260	16.12	300	17.32	340	18.44	380	19.49
221	14.87	261	16.16	301	17.35	341	18.47	381	19.52
222	14.90	262	16.19	302	17.38	342	18.49	382	19.54
223	14.93	263	16.22	303	17.41	343	18.52	383	19.57
224	14.97	264	16.25	304	17.44	344	18.55	384	19.60
225	15.00	265	16.28	305	17.46	345	18.57	385	19.62
226	15.03	266	16.31	306	17.49	346	18.60	386	19.65
227	15.07	267	16.34	307	17.52	347	18.63	387	19.67
228	15.10	268	16.37	308	17.55	348	18.65	388	19.70
229	15.13	269	16.40	309	17.58	349	18.68	389	19.72
230	15.17	270	16.43	310	17.61	350	18.71	390	19.75
231	15.20	271	16.46	311	17.64	351	18.74	391	19.77
232	15.23	272	16.49	312	17.66	352	18.76	392	19.80
233	15.26	273	16.52	313	17.69	353	18.79	393	19.82
234	15.30	274	16.55	314	17.72	354	18.81	394	19.85
235	15.33	275	16.58	315	17.75	355	18.84	395	19.87
236	15.36	276	16.61	316	17.78	356	18.87	396	19.90
237	15.39	277	16.64	317	17.80	357	18.89	397	19.92
238	15.43	278	16.67	318	17.83	358	18.92	398	19.95
239	15.46	279	16.70	319	17.86	359	18.95	399	19.98
240	15.49	280	16.73	320	17.89	360	18.97	400	20.00

ANSWERS TO SELECTED EVEN-NUMBERED EXERCISES

Some answers or parts of answers have been omitted. When an exercise calls for simple rearrangement or display of data with no computation or interpretation, the resulting answer may not appear.

CHAPTER 2

2-2 The franchises that make up the average are chosen as being representative of the entire collection of franchises from 5 states. They form a *sample* of the larger *population* of franchises. From the sample, an inference is drawn about the population as a whole; when the average goes down, all sales as a whole are considered to have gone down.

2-4 The sample may have contained a greater percentage of conservatives (or liberals) than the actual voting population, a greater percentage of Republicans (or Democrats) than the actual voting population, or maybe a greater percentage of farm persons (or city dwellers) than the actual voting population. The sample could also have been biased. Maybe the questions were slanted toward one candidate, or perhaps the pollsters did not ask the right questions. The sample could also have been too small. (*Note:* Experts have attributed the real cause of the turnabout to the fact that Dewey supporters became so confident of victory that they did not bother to vote, whereas Truman supporters did.)

2-6 We cannot draw any conclusions from these data as they exist. We would first need to do a certain amount of rearranging, such as listing the grades from highest to lowest or determining the most frequent grade pair.

2-8 No. In this case, the raw data would be a list of sample units indicating whether or not they were defective. The quality control section has already performed an analysis on these data to calculate the averages contained in the report.

2-10

450–499.9	1	550–599.9	9	650–699.9	4
500–549.9	10	600–649.9	15	700–749.9	1

2-12 a) 7 equal intervals b) 13 equal intervals

a)

CLASS	FREQUENCY
30–39	.02
40–49	.08
50–59	.20
60–69	.28
70–79	.22
80–89	.12
90–99	.08
	1.00

b)

CLASS	FREQUENCY
35–39	.02
40–44	.04
45–49	.04
50–54	.08
55–59	.12
60–64	.12
65–69	.16
70–74	.12
75–79	.10
80–84	.06
85–89	.06
90–94	.04
95–99	.04
	1.00

2-16 a)

SPREAD	SAT DIFFERENTIAL
1.3	150
0.8	160
0.6	75
0.4	45
0.3	60
0.3	50
0.2	10
0.1	5
0.1	5
0.1	0
0.1	−5

SPREAD	SAT DIFFERENTIAL
0.0	0
−0.1	5
−0.2	−10
−0.2	−10
−0.5	−40
−0.5	−80
−0.6	−110
−0.7	−110
−1.1	−130

b) From the array, we can see that the most common spread is 0.1, which occurs 4 times.
c) For a spread of 0.1, the most common SAT differential is +5 which occurs twice out of the 4 data points.
d) Spread and SAT differential appear to be related.

2-18

CLASSES (LBS./SQ.IN.)	RELATIVE FREQUENCIES
2490.0−2493.9	.150
2494.0−2497.9	.175
2498.0−2501.9	.325
2502.0−2505.9	.225
2506.0−2509.9	.125

The greatest number of the samples (32.5%) fell in the class 2498.0−2501.9 lbs./sq. in. This would have been somewhat difficult to see from the data in the table.

2-20 a)

"BEFORE" CLASSES	FREQUENCY	RELATIVE FREQUENCY
1 to 2	5	.25
3 to 4	8	.40
5 to 6	3	.15
7 to 8	3	.15
9 to 10	1	.05
	20	**1.00**

b)

"AFTER" CLASSES	FREQUENCY	RELATIVE FREQUENCY
1 to 2	4	.20
3 to 4	3	.15
5 to 6	7	.35
7 to 8	2	.10
9 to 10	4	.20
	20	**1.00**

c) In order to be able to make comparisons of the frequency distributions

2-20 d)

CHANGE	CHANGE	CHANGE	CHANGE
3	−1	2	1
−1	5	4	1
5	−1	2	−1
1	2	−3	5
0	2	1	0

"CHANGE" CLASSES	FREQUENCY	RELATIVE FREQUENCIES
−3 to −1	5	.25
0 to 2	10	.50
3 to 5	5	.25
	20	**1.00**

e) Sales appear to have increased, but the apparent increase could be due to other factors we don't know about, so we can't say for sure that the new slogan has helped.

2-22 a) 29.995–34.995
34.995–39.995
39.995–44.995
44.995–49.995
49.995–54.995
54.995–59.995

b) 30.00–34.99
35.00–39.99
40.00–44.99
50.00–54.99
55.00–59.99

c) 32.5, 37.5, 42.5, 47.5, 52.5, 57.5

2-24

CLASS MARKS	STATED LIMITS	REAL LIMITS
8.50	7.0– 9.99	6.995– 9.995
11.50	10.0–12.99	9.995–12.995
14.50	13.0–15.99	12.995–15.995
17.50	16.0–18.99	15.995–18.995
20.50	19.0–21.99	18.995–21.995
23.50	22.0–24.99	21.995–24.995
26.50	25.0–27.99	24.995–27.995
29.50	28.0–30.99	27.995–30.995

2-26

CLOSED	OPEN
Single	Single
Married	Married
Divorced	Other
Separated	
Widowed	

2-28

CLASS MARKS	REAL LIMITS	STATED LIMITS
102.45	99.95–104.95	100.0–104.9
107.45	104.95–109.95	105.0–109.9
112.45	109.95–114.95	110.0–114.9
117.45	114.95–119.95	115.0–119.9
122.45	119.95–124.95	120.0–124.9
127.45	124.95–129.95	125.0–129.9
132.45	129.95–134.95	130.0–134.9
137.45	134.95–139.95	135.0–139.9

2-30 a)

WAITING TIME (DAYS)	FREQUENCY
22-24	2
25-27	2
28-30	7
31-33	10
34-36	9
37-39	9
40-42	5
43-45	4
46-48	1
49-52	1
Total	**50**

b)

WAITING TIME (DAYS)	FREQUENCY
22-27	4
28-33	17
34-39	18
40-45	9
46-24	2
Total	**50**

2-32 a) Discrete, Open
b) Discrete, Closed (0-10 gallons of each flavor per day)
c) Both qualitative (flavor) and quantitative (amount).
d) 0 to 1; 1.5 to 2.5; 3 to 4; 4.5 to 5.5; 6 to 7; 7.5 to 8.5; 9 to 10

2-34

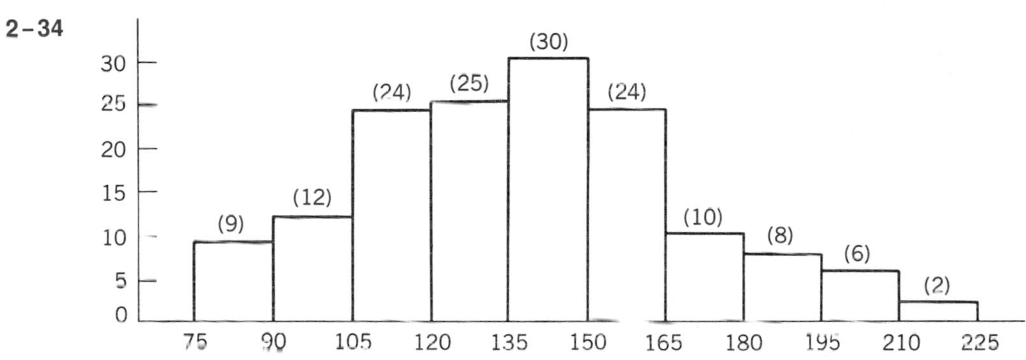

2-36 a)

CLASS	CUMULATIVE FREQUENCY
Less than 3.0	0
Less than 3.2	1
Less than 3.4	5
Less than 3.6	16
Less than 3.8	31
Less than 4.0	43
Less than 4.2	54
Less than 4.4	62
Less than 4.6	69
Less than 4.8	75

b)

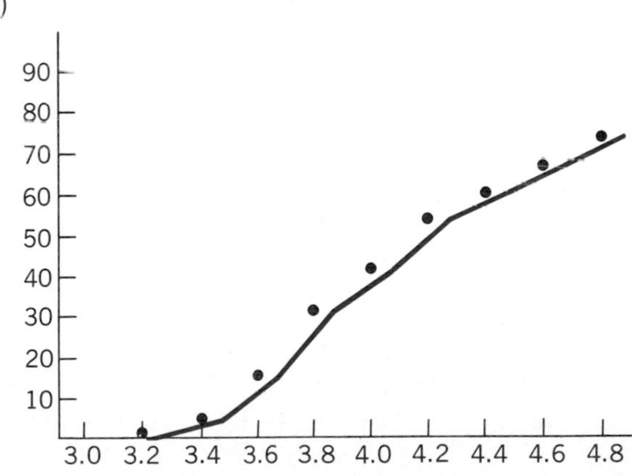

2-36 c)

CLASS	CUMULATIVE FREQUENCY
More than 2.99	75
More than 3.19	74
More than 3.39	70
More than 3.59	59
More than 3.79	44
More than 3.99	32
More than 4.19	21
More than 4.39	13
More than 4.59	6
More than 4.80	0

d)

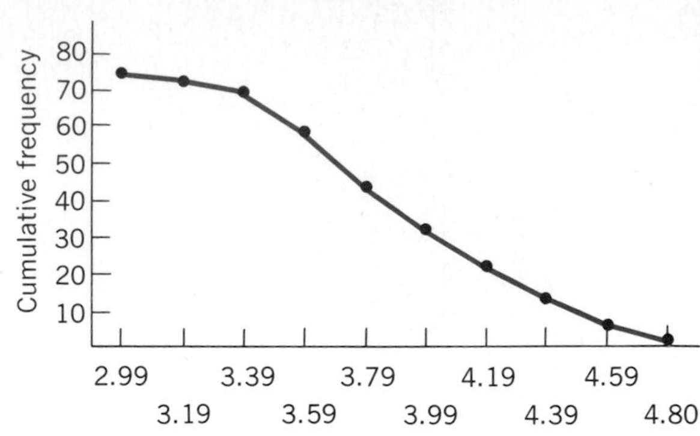

2-38 a)

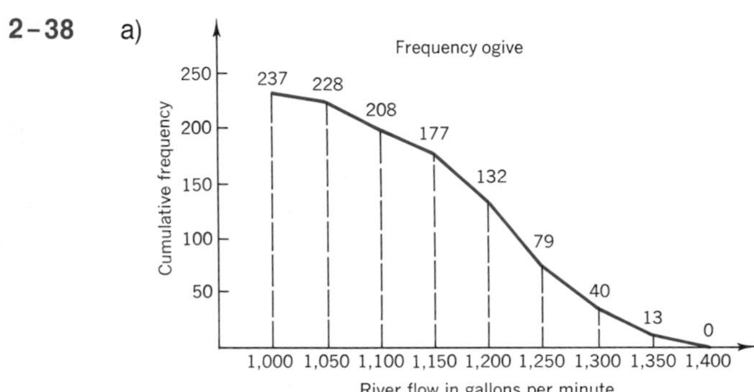

River flow "more than"	1,000	1,050	1,100	1,150	1,200	1,250	1,300	1,350	1,400
Cumulative frequency	237	228	208	177	132	79	40	13	0

b)

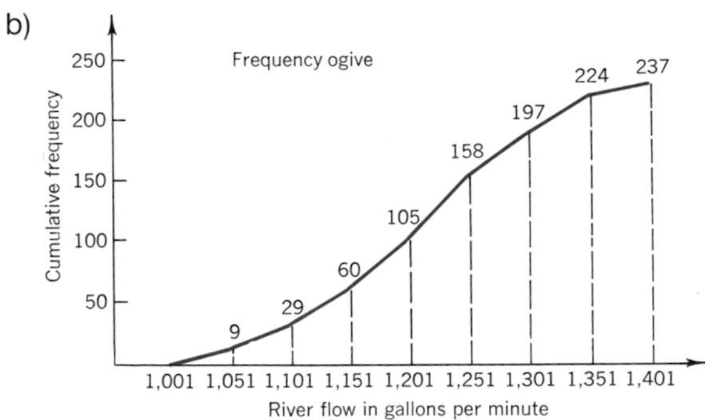

River flow "less than"	1001	1051	1101	1151	1201	1251	1301	1351	1401
Cumulative frequency	0	9	29	60	105	158	197	224	237

c) about 83%

2–40 b)

MINUTES TO SET TYPE	FREQUENCY	MINUTES TO SET TYPE "LESS THAN"	CUMULATIVE FREQUENCY
19.0–19.7	4	19.0	0
19.8–20.5	4	19.8	4
20.6–21.3	10	20.6	8
21.4–22.1	5	21.4	18
22.2–22.9	7	22.2	23
23.0–23.7	5	23.0	30
23.8–24.5	11	23.8	35
24.6–25.3	4	24.6	46
Total	**50**	25.4	50

c)

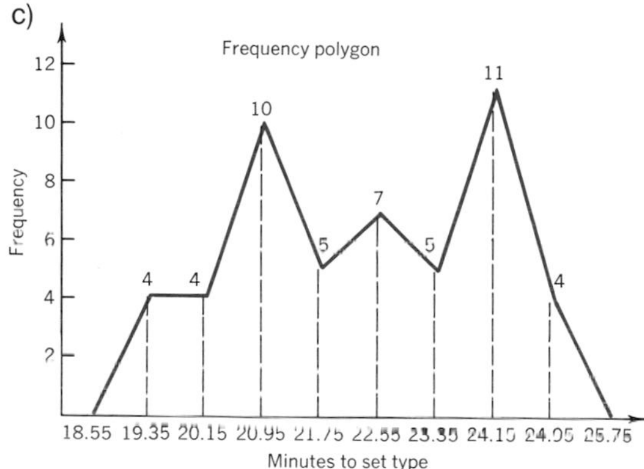

d)

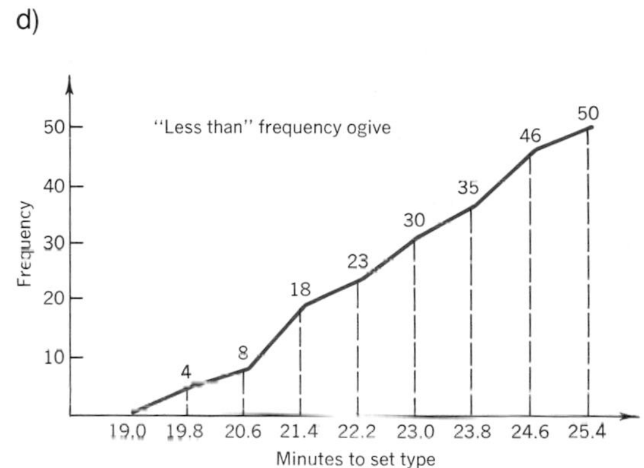

e) about 78% of the time.

2–42 a)

TAXES EVADED	FREQUENCY	RELATIVE FREQUENCY	"LESS THAN" CUMULATIVE RELATIVE FREQUENCY
less than 1	0	.00	.00
1–500	5	.20	.20
501–1000	1	.04	.24
1001–1500	3	.12	.36
1501–2000	4	.16	.52
2001–2500	6	.24	.76
2501–3000	6	.24	1.00
	25	**1.00**	

2-42 b)

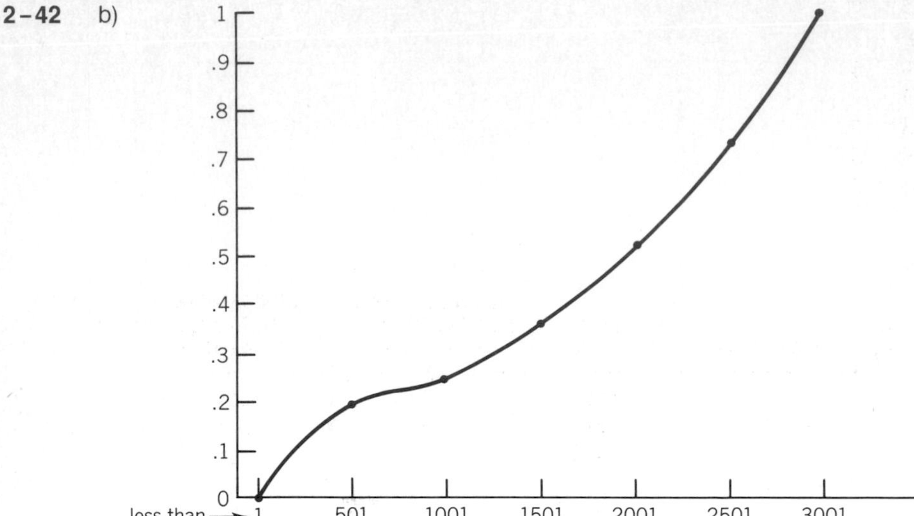

2-44 By grouping those of the same educational level together, we can see group differences associated with educational level more clearly.

10th grade–$7,200 11th grade–$8,800	Did not complete high school
High school– $8,500 High school– $9,500 High school–$15,200 High school–$15,100 High school–$12,900 High school–$13,000	High school graduates
2 years college–$11,200 1 year college –$10,100 2 years college– $8,600 1 year college – $7,200 2 years college– $9,200	One or two years of college
B.S. –$10,400 B.S. –$14,000 B.A.–$12,800 B.A.– $9,800 B.S. –$10,600 B.A.–$17,200 B.S. –$16,400	College degrees
M.A.–$13,500 M.A.–$11,600 M.A.–$18,100	Master's degrees
M.D. –$35,000 M.D. –$50,000 Ph.D.–$14,500 Ph.D.–$22,000 Ph.D.–$32,000 Law Degree–$38,000 Law Degree–$26,000	Professional degrees

2-46 a)

1.8	1.3	.9	.7
1.8	1.2	.9	.7
1.7	1.2	.9	.6
1.6	1.2	.8	.5
1.5	1.1	.8	.5
1.5	1.1	.8	.3
1.5	1.1	.8	.3
1.4	1.0	.7	.2
1.4	1.0	.7	.1
1.3	1.0	.7	.1

b)

SALES INCREASE (PERCENT/WEEK)	FREQUENCY	RELATIVE FREQUENCY	SALES INCREASE (PERCENT/WEEK) MORE THAN	CUMULATIVE RELATIVE FREQUENCY
0– .25	3	.075	0	1.000
.26– .50	4	.100	.25	.925
.51– .75	6	.150	.50	.825
.76–1.00	10	.250	.75	.675
1.01–1.25	6	.150	1.00	.425
1.26–1.50	7	.175	1.25	.275
1.51–1.75	2	.050	1.50	.100
1.76–2.00	2	.050	1.75	.050
Total	**40**	**1.000**	2.00	.000

c)

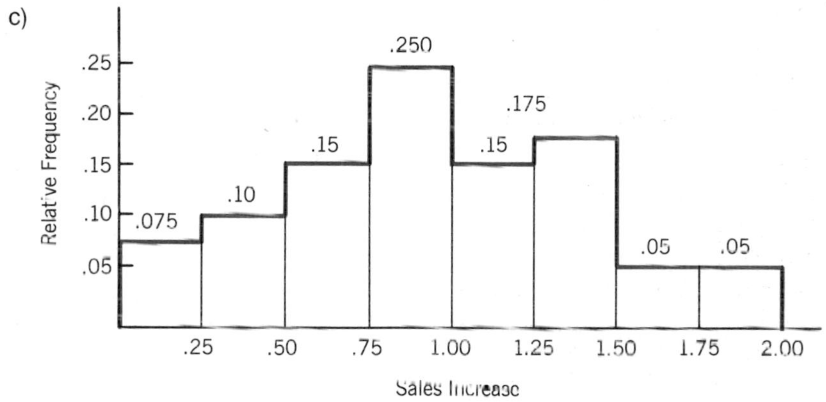

d) and e)

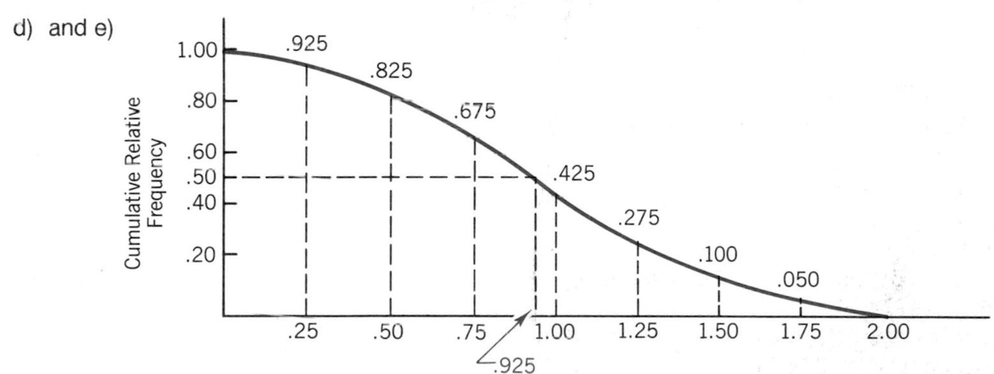

2-48 First construct the data for units produced per day by dividing by 20.

UNITS PRODUCED PER DAY	UNITS PRODUCED PER DAY	UNITS PRODUCED PER DAY
494.9	504.9	506.2
502.6	529.4	525.4
501.4	493.6	495.5
486.1	497.8	499.6
495.4	496.4	511.9

Now, we will construct the distributions starting at 485.0 units per day.

CLASSES (UNITS PER DAY)	FREQUENCY	RELATIVE FREQUENCY
485.0–489.9	1	.067
490.0–494.9	2	.133
495.0–499.9	5	.333
500.0–504.9	3	.200
505.0–509.9	1	.067
510.0–514.9	1	.067
515.0–519.9	0	.000
520.0–524.9	0	.000
525.0–529.9	2	.133
Total	**15**	**1.000**

CLASSES (MINS.)	FREQUENCY
25–27	1
28–30	2
Total	**20**

2-50 The real limits given form the lower and upper boundaries for each interval, and the stated limits are then determined by rounding the lower limit up and the upper limit down. Once the stated limits are determined, the class marks can be calculated using equation 2–2.

REAL LIMITS	STATED LIMITS	CLASS MARK
14.65–15.25	14.7–15.2	14.95
15.85–16.45	15.9–16.4	16.15
16.45–17.05	16.5–17.0	16.75
17.05–17.65	17.1–17.6	17.35
17.65–18.25	17.7–18.2	17.95
18.25–18.85	18.3–18.8	18.55

2-52 $$\frac{2{,}000}{2{,}000 + 8{,}000} = .2 \times 250 = 50$$

2-54 Histogram

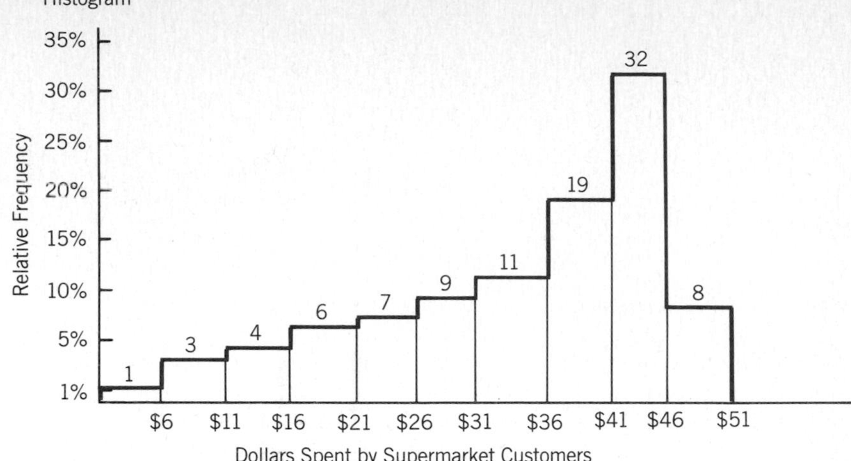

Polygon

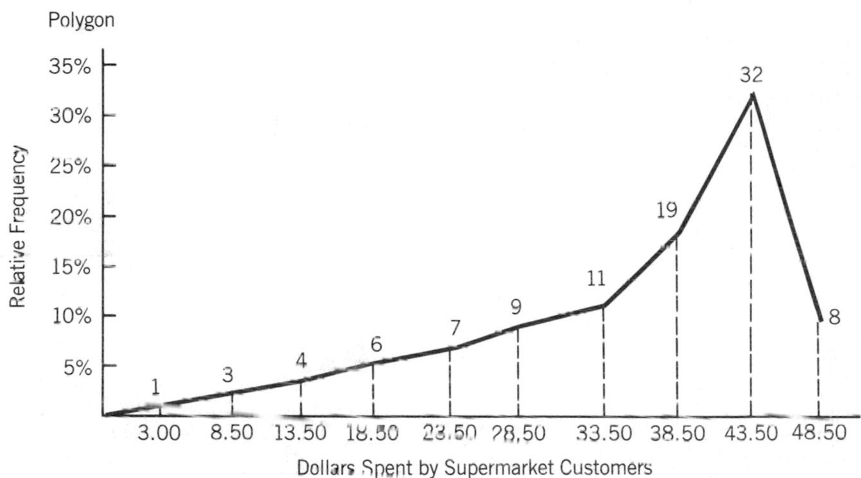

2-56

STATED LIMITS	REAL LIMITS	CLASS MARKS
1.00–1.39	.995–1.395	1.20
1.40–1.79	1.395–1.795	1.60
1.80–2.19	1.795–2.195	2.00
2.20–2.59	2.195–2.595	2.40
2.60–2.99	2.595–2.995	2.80
3.00–3.39	2.995–3.395	3.20
3.40–3.79	3.395–3.795	3.60
3.80–4.19	3.795–4.195	4.00
4.20–4.59	4.195–4.595	4.40
4.60–4.99	4.595–4.995	4.80
5.00–no limit	4.995–no limit	no mark

2-58

AGE GROUP	RELATIVE PROP.		SAMPLE SIZE		# IN SAMPLE
12-17	.15	×	3000	=	450
18-23	.33	×	3000	=	990
24-29	.25	×	3000	=	750
30-35	.17	×	3000	=	510
36 +	.10	×	3000	=	300
					$n = 3000$

2-60 $n = 2000$ 880 returned questionnaires

Tests for data:

1) The source would appear to be possibly biased by the small return rate of only 44 percent of the sample. Those who responded may have more extreme viewpoints.
2) In this situation there is no other evidence available to support or contradict as yet.
3) Yes, the data from the 56 percent who did not respond to the questionnaire is missing.
4) 880. No, they don't represent those groups of individuals who chose not to respond.
5) In this example, no conclusions were drawn.

2-62

CLASS MARK	CLASS MARK
$ 3.00	$28.50
8.50	33.50
13.50	38.50
18.50	43.50
23.50	no mark

2-64 Yes and no. It is not raw data, because the scores are composites of other values. The raw data would be the individual scores on tests, homework and papers. However, if someone were interested in doing some analysis on final grades, it would be raw data for that purpose.

2-66 The distributions must all contain the amounts between $0 and $20,000 as a minimum.

a) The distribution meeting all the requirements is given below:

$ 0-$ 1,999		$ 0-$ 2,000
2,000- 3,999		2,001- 4,000
4,000- 5,999	With $0-$2,000 as	4,001- 6,000
6,000- 7,999	the first interval	6,001- 8,000
8,000- 9,999	the correct distribution is	8,001- 10,000
10,000- 11,999	given on the right.	10,001- 12,000
12,000- 13,999		12,001- 14,000
14,000- 15,999		14,001- 16,000
16,000- 17,999		16,001- 18,000
18,000- 19,999		18,001- 20,000
20,000- 21,999		

b) The distribution which meets all requirements is given below:

\$ 0–\$ 1,999	Again, if you were	\$ 0–\$ 2,000
2,000– 3,999	to use \$2,000 as	2,000– 4,000
4,000– 5,999	the end point of	4,001– 6,000
6,000– 7,999	the first interval,	6,001– 8,000
8,000– 9,999	the distribution would	8,001– 10,000
10,000– 11,999	be as on the right.	10,001– 12,000
12,000– 13,999		12,001– 14,000
14,000– 15,999		14,001– 16,000
16,000– 17,999		16,001– 18,000
18,000 and above		above \$18,000

CHAPTER 3

3–2

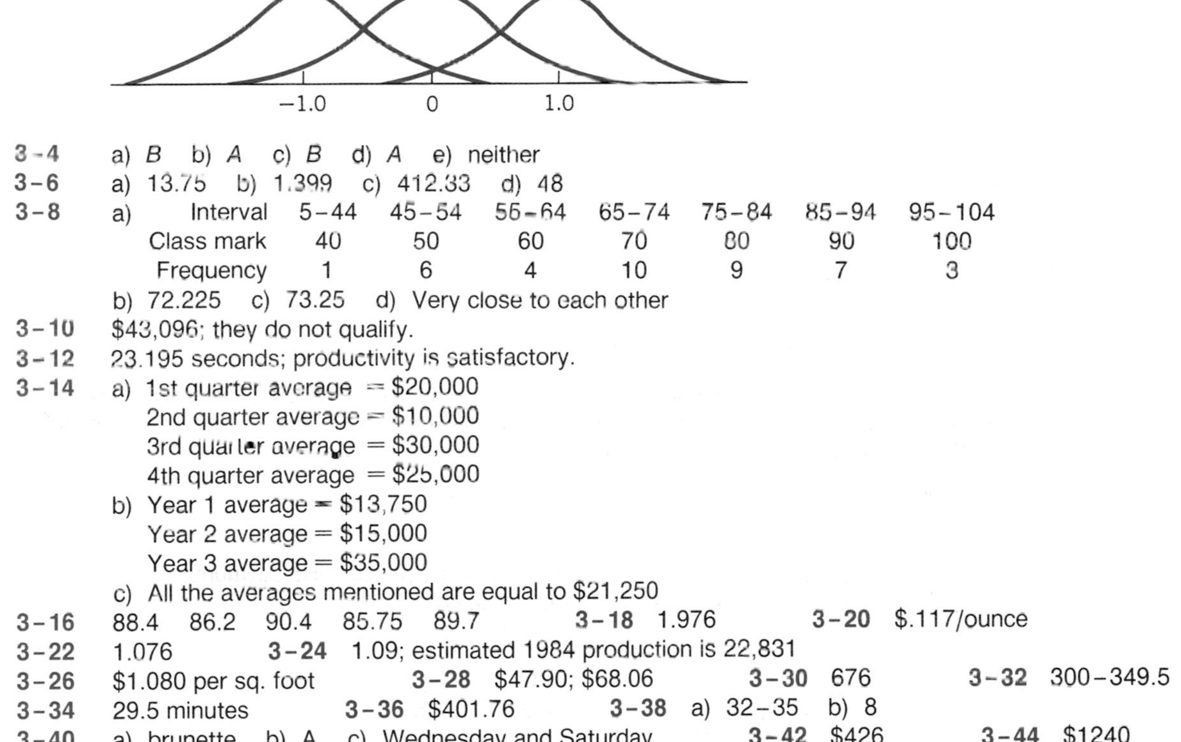

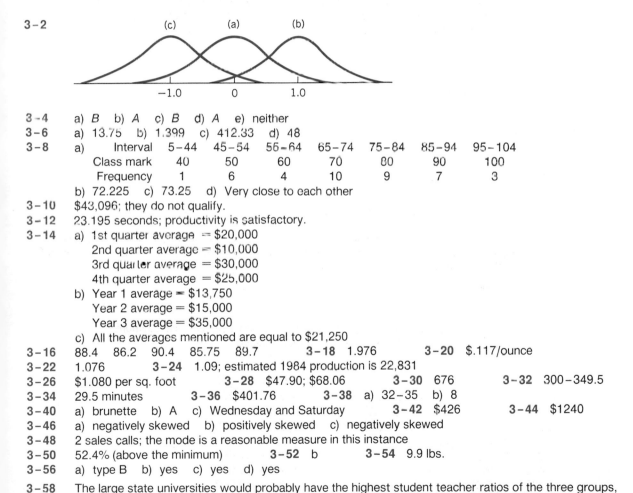

3–4 a) *B* b) *A* c) *B* d) *A* e) neither

3–6 a) 13.75 b) 1.399 c) 412.33 d) 48

3–8 a)

Interval	5–44	45–54	55–64	65–74	75–84	85–94	95–104
Class mark	40	50	60	70	80	90	100
Frequency	1	6	4	10	9	7	3

b) 72.225 c) 73.25 d) Very close to each other

3–10 \$43,096; they do not qualify.

3–12 23.195 seconds; productivity is satisfactory.

3–14 a) 1st quarter average = \$20,000
2nd quarter average = \$10,000
3rd quarter average = \$30,000
4th quarter average = \$25,000

b) Year 1 average = \$13,750
Year 2 average = \$15,000
Year 3 average = \$35,000

c) All the averages mentioned are equal to \$21,250

3–16 88.4 86.2 90.4 85.75 89.7 **3–18** 1.976 **3–20** \$.117/ounce

3–22 1.076 **3–24** 1.09; estimated 1984 production is 22,831

3–26 \$1.080 per sq. foot **3–28** \$47.90; \$68.06 **3–30** 676 **3–32** 300–349.5

3–34 29.5 minutes **3–36** \$401.76 **3–38** a) 32–35 b) 8

3–40 a) brunette b) A c) Wednesday and Saturday **3–42** \$426 **3–44** \$1240

3–46 a) negatively skewed b) positively skewed c) negatively skewed

3–48 2 sales calls; the mode is a reasonable measure in this instance

3–50 52.4% (above the minimum) **3–52** b **3–54** 9.9 lbs.

3–56 a) type B b) yes c) yes d) yes

3–58 The large state universities would probably have the highest student teacher ratios of the three groups, and the private colleges the smallest, with the category "all colleges" falling in the middle. The distribution of "all student teacher ratios" would be skewed to the right since there are many more

colleges than just state universities and since student teacher ratios in large state universities are quite large themselves.
Private colleges would have the most peaked distributions and the large state universities would have the least peaked distributions. Ratios for "all colleges" would be in the middle.

3-60 18.1015 years **3-62** 1.107 **3-64** −7 (unfavorable ratings)

3-66 a) all three are equivalent
b) Median
c) Mode
d) Mean or median

3-68 Ultraviolet

3-70 a) $18.46
b) $1.19 (the average payoff is 6.4%)

CHAPTER 4

4-2 a, because the values tend to cluster more around the mean. **4-4** c

4-6 There are many ways that the concept may be involved. Certainly, the FTC would examine the price variability for the industry and compare the result to that of the suspect companies. The agency might examine price distributions for similar products, for the same products in a city, or for the same products in different cities. If the variability was significantly different in any of these cases, this result might constitute evidence of a conspiracy to set prices at the same levels.

4-8 a) 43 b) 19 c) 8 **4-10** a) 14 b) 7 c) 39 46 57 65 70 1st quartile
72 72 75 77 79 2nd quartile
81 81 84 84 84 3rd quartile
87 93 94 94 97 4th quartile

4-12 Interquartile range .54 minutes; quartile deviation .27 minutes

4-14 Interquartile range 4600 miles; quartile deviation 2300 miles

4-16 a) 410 b) 237 c) 138 **4-18** a) 3.5 b) 22.456 c) 4.74

4-20 56,566.67

4-22 a) 3.87 days
b) 195 should be; 249 actually are
c) 247 should be; 249 are

4-24 5 weeks below; 1 week below

4-26 Product 1 produced the response latency with the largest deviation

4-28 $390,000 $\pm$ 2($10,000) **4-30** Sample 2 has the greater relative dispersion

4-32 Sample 2 has the greater relative variability

4-34 Company 1 pursued the riskier strategy **4-36** Lee

4-38 I has the least relative variation

4-40 a) 6% b) .354 $(\%)^2$ c) .595%
This distribution has very little spread; the mean is a good measure of central tendency.

4-42 Curve A actual officer's salaries; food purchases curve B; curve C aircraft maintenance

4-44 Company may be hiring less experienced sales reps, or hiring more experienced sales reps along with the less experienced ones.

4-46 Later period. **4-48** $29.30; $2.50

4-50 $.03; .001175 $(\$)^2$; $.0343. The variance among states in heating fuel is relatively small.

4-52 a) 5.14
b) 11.25 should be; 14 are

4-54 .286; .132; .363

CHAPTER 5

5-2 The Surgeon General's office undoubtedly studied the incidence of sickness and death among smokers and nonsmokers. Evidence indicated that smokers were more likely to have poor health (or earlier deaths) than nonsmokers. From his samples, the Surgeon General has assigned a higher probability of poor health occurring in the smoking population than in the nonsmoking population.

5-4 This decision involves estimates of demand, costs, physical plant additions required, and new employees necessary. Each of these estimates involves a degree of uncertainty and therefore a probability estimate.

5-6 a, b, and d are mutually exclusive.

5-8 a) 0 b) 1/36 c) 5/36 d) 6/36 e) 4/36 f) 3/36 g) 2/36

5-10 a) They are collectively exhaustive; they are not mutually exclusive.

b)

M only	P only	M, P only	B, P only	P, Wk only
B only	Wk only	M, Wk only	W, P only	M, W, P only
W only	M, W only	B, W only	W, Wk only	W, P, Wk only

c) M, Wk M, W, P B, W W, P, Wk B, P

5-12 a) 1/13 b) 1/4 c) 1/26 d) 1/2 e) 3/13 (These are classical probabilities.)

5-14 a) 1/13, 2/13, 4/13, 2/13 b) Probability of greater than 400,000 or less than 200,000 is zero.

5-16 a) subjective b) relative frequency c) subjective d) relative frequency e) classical

5-18 .30, .40, .62 **5-20** .0001768 **5-22** .145 **5-24** a) 1/2 b) 1/2

5-26 a) 1/4 b) 1/2 c) 1/13 **5-28** a) .05 b) .02 c) .001

5-30 Let R = the event that the Republicans increase their control of the state legislature in the next election
E = the event that the economy improves significantly by November.

Using Equation 5-3,

$$P(R \text{ or } E) = P(R) + P(E) - P(R \text{ and } E)$$

Rearranging,

$$P(R) = P(R \text{ or } E) - P(E) + P(R \text{ and } E)$$

We know that:

$$P(R \text{ or } E) = 0.75$$
$$P(E) = 0.55$$
$$P(R \text{ and } E) = 0.40$$

Thus

$$P(R) = 0.75 - 0.55 + 0.40 = 0.60$$

So

$$P(R) = 0.60$$

5-32 a) P(all three) = P(first)·P(second)·P(third)
= (0.8)·(0.7)·(0.9) = .504

b) P(first & third, not second) = P(first)·P(not second)·P(third)
= (0.8)·(0.3)·(0.9) = .216

c) P(none) = P(not first)·P(not second)·P(not third)
= (0.2)·(0.3)·(0.1) = .006

d) P(at least one) = 1 − P(none) = .994

e) P(first two) = P(first)·P(second)
= (0.8)·(0.7) = .56

5-34 a) .57 b) .15 c) .60 d) .45 **5-36** a) 3/16 b) 1/2 c) 1/9 d) 1/3

5-38 .06 **5-40** a) .1083 b) .5307 c) .2599 d) .1011 **5-42** a) .45 b) .90

5-44 a) .72 b) .19 c) .09 **5-46** .45 **5-48** a) .34 b) .82

5-50 a) .75 b) .0625 c) .1875 d) .353 e) .118 f) .529

5-52 Difference in rates suggest that the risk increases as one gets older (common sense); higher rates for young drivers suggest they have a higher probability of having accidents.

5-54 Using past data on failures, econometricians calculate the relative frequency of failures and use this as an estimate.

5-56 a) 1/7 b) 2/7 c) 3/7 d) Classical probability estimates

5-58 a) Each of the items on the list represents an event in the category "Mistakes made. . . ."
b) No
c) Not collectively exhaustive

5-60 a) .3333
b) Relative frequency of occurrence
c) The calculated probability is an inaccurate estimate

5-62 a) Frequency of past occurrences
b) .102

5-64 .0696 **5-66** .014

5-68 a) .3333; .6897; .9375
b) .6667; .3103; .0625

5-70

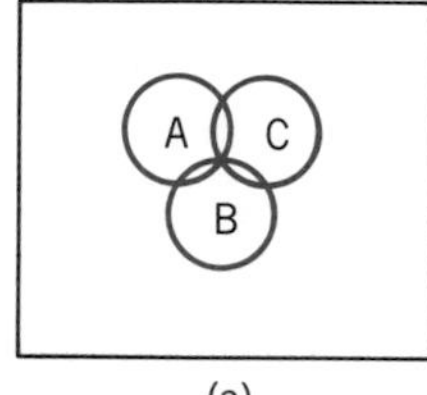

(a)

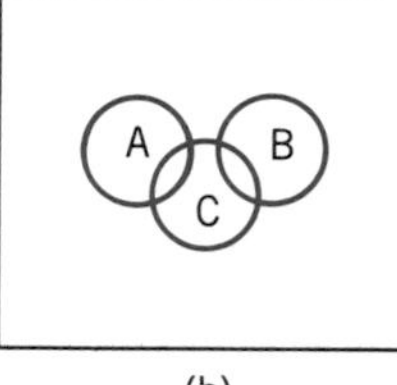

(b)

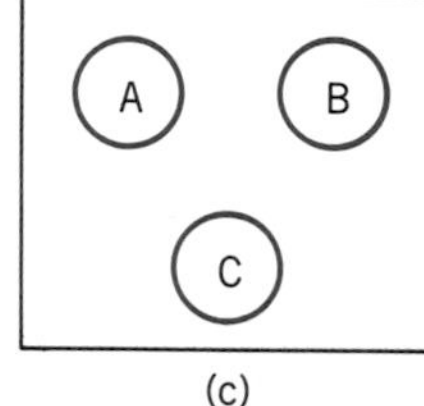

(c)

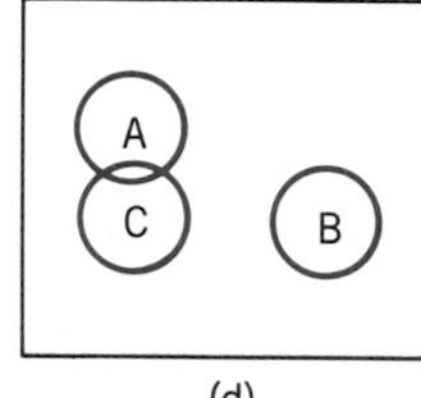

(d)

5-72 a) .0031 b) .475 c) .03

CHAPTER 6

6-2

VALUE	PROBABILITY
2	.05
3	.15
4	.30
5	.10
6	.20
7	.15
8	.05
	1.00

6-4 a), b), and e)

6-6

Probability distribution of sales

Probability: .1 .2 .3 .4 .5 .6

Sales: 12,000 15,000 18,000

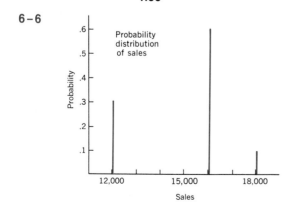

SALES	PROBABILITY
12,000	.3
16,000	.6
18,000	.1
	1.0

6-8 a)

OUTCOME	PROBABILITY
8,000	.05
9,000	.15
10,000	.25
11,000	.30
12,000	.20
13,000	.05
	1.00

b) $10,600

6-10 a)

OUTCOME	PROBABILITY
0	.03
1	.08
2	.30
3	.42
4	.12
5	.05
	1.00

b) $2.67

6-12 14 months

6-14 Expected number of cakes sold = 0(.05) + 1(.10) + 2(.20) + 3(.30) + 4(.25) + 5(.10)
= 0 + .10 + .40 + .90 + 1.00 + .50
= 2.9

Expected revenue = $11 (Expected number of cakes sold)
= $11 (2.9)
= $31.90

Daily costs = (Number of cakes)(Cost per cake)
= (5)($6.50)
= $32.50

Expected daily profits = Expected daily revenue − Daily costs
= $31.90 − $32.50
= −$0.60

Thus Betty expects to lose sixty cents each day as a result of cake sales. This is not profitable unless it brings more customers into her shop, or helps in other more intangible ways.

6-16 10 cars **6-18** a) .0102 b) .0109 c) .4202 d) .2557

6-20 a) $\mu = 3; \sigma = 1.5$ b) $\mu = 15; \sigma = 2.45$ c) $\mu = 50; \sigma = 6.71$ d) $\mu = 2; \sigma = 1.38$
e) $\mu = 2137.5; \sigma = 10.34$ **6-22** a) .3456 b) .1296

6-24 a)

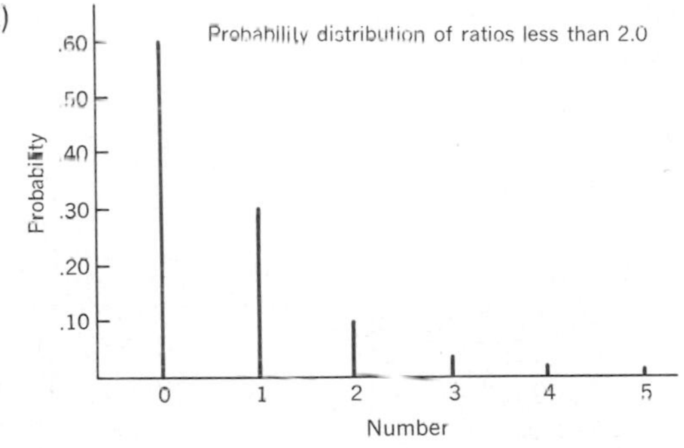

NUMBER OF RATES LESS THAN 2.0	PROBABILITY
0	.5905
1	.3280
2	.0729
3	.0081
4	.0005
5	.0000
	1.0000

b) .1319 decrease

6-26 Let r be a binomial random variable ($n = 15$, $p = 0.3$) representing the number of browsing customers who buy something.

a) $P(r \geqslant 1) = .9953$
b) $P(r \geqslant 4) = .7031$
c) $P(r = 0) = 1 - P(x \geqslant 1) = 1 - .9953 = .0047$
d) $P(r \leqslant 4) = 1 - P(x \geqslant 5) = 1 - .4845 = .5155$

6-28 a) .3209 b) .4633 c) .0771 **6-30** a) .1913 b) .9985 c) .4493

6-32 .5859; move the employee **6-34** a) .8647 b) .1353
6-36 a) .49659 b) .12166 c) .02839 d) .34761 e) .03414
6-38 a) .9306 b) .0262 c) .7157 d) .4212
6-40 a) 9.615 b) 87.7686 **6-42** .5705 **6-44** .0082
6-46 a) −.36 b) .0668 c) .0810 **6-48** Once every 10 days
6-50 a) .0548 b) .0228 **6-52** a) Poisson b) Normal c) Binomial d) Normal
6-54 A random variable is considered discrete if it can assume only a limited number of values. A continuous random variable can assume any value within a given range. Just as there are dicrete and continuous random variables, so also are there discrete and continuous probability functions, each associated with the appropriate type of random variable.
6-56 a) .1637 b) .8187 **6-58** 11 interns
6-60 a) Binomial b) Poisson c) Normal d) Binomial **6-62** a) .1323 b) .0255
6-64 a) .1701 b) .0030 c) .2969 d) .1311
6-66 a) .3080 b) .6482 c) .3518 d) .0181
6-68 b) expected sales 30
c) stockout of 6
6-70 .9192 **6-72** a) A b) B
6-74 a) 25,000 b) 19,000 c) 1,000 d) 17,000 **6-76** a) .5910 b) .0000
6-78 a) .3745; .3980; error 6%
b) .6255; .6482; error 4%
c) .3745; .3518; error 6%
d) .0119; .0181; error 34%

CHAPTER 7

7-2 If we are only generalizing to the same group of observations in making our conclusions, then the set of elements is the population under study. If, however, we wish to draw conclusions about some larger group of which these elements are only a part, then the set of observations would be considered a sample.

7-4 Probability samples involve more statistical analysis and planning at the beginning of a study and usually take more time and money than judgment samples.

7-6 From what we've been told in the problem, Jean's position is apparently quite defensible. Perhaps what makes statistical sampling unique is that it permits statistical inference to be made about a population and its parameters. This is apparently what Jean has done. There are no hard and fast rules as to the size of the sample that must be drawn before inferences can be made. Specifically, there is nothing magic about the 50 percent mark. Common sense would seem to point out that gathering data from 50 percent of some populations might tend to be just as difficult as gathering data from the entire population—for instance, the population of the United States or the world. The defense for Jean's position lies in empirical evidence and some explanation and reasoning with management, educating them about the abilities of statistical inference.

7-8 Situation *b*. The distributions have greater between-group variance and less within-group variance than in *a*.

7-10 Jan. 3, 17, 31; Feb. 14, 28; Mar. 14, 28; Apr. 11, 25; May 9, 23; June 6, 20; July 4, 18; Aug. 1, 15, 29; Sept. 12, 26; Oct. 10, 24; Nov. 7, 21; Dec. 5, 19.

7-12 No.

7-14 One chance in ten for 3, 6, or 8. We would expect to see each number 12.5 times. In actuality, 3 appears 6 times, 6 appears 20 times, and 8 appears 19 times.

7-16 Yes. The accident times during the year are probably randomly distributed, making that a good candidate for systematic sampling.

7-18 Stratified sampling is more appropriate in this case, since there appear to be two very dissimilar groups, which probably have smaller variation *within* each group than *between* groups.

7-20 Sampling error **7-22** No

7-24 The left graph represents the sample distribution of Swinford's sample. The right graph is apparently a frequency distribution of the means of the various samples that were in all of the loan studies.

7-26 Since each of the 50 numbers sent to the Board was itself a mean, the Board received information about the distribution of a sample mean of times for groups of employees.

7-28 a) .8480 b) .9689 **7-30** about 16 **7-32** a) .2776 b) .2033; less

7-34 a) .4681 b) .4168 **7-36** No; the statement can be made only with a .9648 probability.

7-38 a) 100 b) 1.13 c) .0136 d) .9480 **7-40** 256

7-42 a) 1.41 b) .0755 **7-44** .3358 **7-46** .9522 **7-48** .7372

7-50 Random sampling **7-52** Yes **7-54** 100 **7-56** No

7-58 Don't increase the sample size **7-60** .9192 **7-62** 41

CHAPTER 8

8-2 Measuring an entire population may not be feasible because of time and cost considerations. A sample yields only an estimate and is subject to sampling errors.

8-4 An estimator is a sample statistic used to estimate a population parameter. An estimate is a specific numerical value for an estimator.

8-6 It assures us that the estimator becomes more reliable with larger samples. **8-8** 17.45 33.08

8-10 .568 **8-12** a) .15 b) 9.6 ± .15 **8-14** a) 2.0 b) 210 ± 2.0

8-16 6.0 ± .16 inches

8-18 a) 25.1 ± 1.331
b) Since Dee can be 95.5% certain that the true mean lies in the interval above, and since the entire interval lies below 26.9, it seems very likely that Dee has met her goal.

8-20 The confidence interval is the range of an estimate; i.e., the interval between and including the upper confidence limit and the lower confidence limit.

8-22 a) High confidence levels produce large confidence intervals; thus the more confident we are, the less we can be confident of.
b) Narrow confidence intervals produce low confidence levels; thus the more definite our estimate, the less confidence we can have in it.

8-24 No.

8-26 a) 30 ± 3.92
b) 12 ± 11.76
c) 35 ± 2.94
d) 18 ± 5.88

8-28 a) (67.428, 69.372)
b) (67.12, 69.68)

8-30 a) .536 b) (14.551, 17.049) **8-32** 38 ± 1.47 years

8-34 (196,963.419, 203,036.581)

8-36 a) .056
b) 72% ± 9.2%

8-38 a) .0215 b) (.325, .395)

8-40 a) n = 20; t = 1.729 (90%)
b) n = 12; t = 2.201 (95%)
c) n = 7; t = 3.707 (99%)

8-42 80% ± 11.1%

8-44 a) 4.604 b) 2.898 c) 2.056 d) 2.131 e) 2.110 f) 1.771 **8-46** (26.33, 28.27)

8-48 a) 12.15 b) .2 c) (12.016, 12.284)

8-50 (28.299, 41.701) **8-52** 1068 **8-54** 316 **8-56** 78 **8-58** 243 days

8-60 An interval estimate gives an indication of possible error through the extent of its range and through the probability associated with the interval. A point estimate is only a single number and thus one needs additional information to determine its reliability.

8-62 601

8-64 a) .9
b) .098
c) 3.2 ± .582

8-66 $\bar{X}$ is called the "best" estimator of the population mean because it exhibits all the qualities of good estimators (unbiasedness, consistency, efficiency, sufficiency).

8-68 a) 86.64% b) 91.08% c) 97.86% **8-70** 637 **8-72** a) 3.639
b) 3.578 **8-74** a) 3 dollars b) $3 **8-76** $360, $30

8-78 a) .12 mg
b) 5.0 ± .12 mg

8-80 35% ± 9.4%

8-82 a) .05 fl. oz.
b) 128.4 ± .10 fl. oz.

CHAPTER 9

9-2 Theoretically, one could toss a coin a large number of times to see if the proportion of heads was very different from .5. Similarly, by recording the outcomes of many dice rolls, one could see if the proportion of any side was very different from 1/6. A large number of trials would be needed for each of these examples.

9-4 a) Assume a hypothesis about a population.
b) Collect sample data.
c) Calculate a sample statistic.
d) Use the sample statistic to evaluate the hypothesis.

9-6 We mean that we would not have reasonably expected to find that particular sample if in fact the hypothesis had been true.

9-8 There is a 31.74 percent probability of mistakenly rejecting the hypothesis.

9-10 No, we cannot. **9-12** We should accept the claim.

9-14 A null hypothesis represents the hypothesis you are trying to reject; the alternative hypothesis represents all other possibilities.

9-16 Type I: the probability that we will reject the null hypothesis when in fact it is true.
Type II: the probability that we will accept the null hypothesis when in fact it is false.

9-18 The significance level of a test indicates the probability of a type I error.

9-20 a) normal b) normal
c) *t* with 15 d.f. d) normal e) *t* with 24 d.f.

9-22 A one-tailed test would be used when we are testing whether the population mean is lower or higher than some hypothesized value. A two-tailed test will reject the null hypothesis if the sample mean is significantly higher or lower than the hypothesized population mean.

9-24 $H_0: \mu = 10$ tons $H_1: \mu > 10$ tons 9-26 (32.354, 35.646)
9-28 Accept H_0 9-30 Reject H_0; yes they are overestimating the cost
9-32 Reject H_0; the assembly has been significantly sped up
9-34 9.5: $1 - \beta = .0202$; 10.0: $1 - \beta = .0968$; 10.5: $- \beta = .2912$
9-36 9.5: $1 - \beta = .0099$; 10.0: $1 - \beta = .0582$; 10.5: $- \beta = .2061$
9-38 Accept H_0 9-40 a) Reject H_0 b) Reject H_0 9-42 Reject H_0
9-44 Reject H_0 9-46 Accept H_0 9-48 Reject H_0
9-50 Accept H_0; the claim is not in error. 9-52 a) 2.736 b) Reject H_0
9-54 a) 8.75 b) $s = 8.74$; $\hat{\sigma}_{\bar{x}} = 3.09$ c) Reject H_0 9-56 Accept H_0
9-58 Accept H_0 9-60 Reject H_0 9-62 Reject H_0 9-64 Reject H_0
9-66 Accept H_0 9-68 Accept H_0 9-70 .0387 9-72 Recalibrate
9-74 a) $H_0: \mu = 85$ $H_1: \mu > 85$
b) $H_0: \mu = 66$ $H_1: \mu > 66$
c) $H_0: \mu = 12{,}500$ $H_1: \mu \neq 12{,}500$
9-76 No, because each of the sample means is equally distant from the hypothesized mean and, therefore, equally likely to lead to rejection or acceptance of the null hypothesis.
9-78 Reject H_0 9-80 Reject H_0 9-82 a) .1336 b) .0228 c) .1587
9-84 Reject H_0 9-86 Accept H 9-88 Reject H_0 9-90 Reject H_0
9-92 Accept H_0 9-94 Reject H_0 9-96 Reject H_0 9-98 Accept H_0
9-100 Accept H_0 9-102 Accept H_0 9-104 Reject H_0
9-106 a) .0918 b) .3707 c) .7486

CHAPTER 10

10-2 To determine whether or not three or more populations means can be considered equal.
10-4 a) chi-square
b) analysis of variance
c) normal or t distribution
d) F distribution
10-6 a) 4 b) 6 c) 15 d) 16 e) 10
10-8 a) 1.723
b) $H_0: p_A = p_B = p_C = p_D$
$H_1: p_A, p_B, p_C, p_D$ are not equal
c) Accept H_0
10-10 a) $H_0: p_D = p_L = p_B = p_S$
$H_1: p_D, p_L, p_B, p_S$ are not equal
b) 17.475
c) Reject H_0
10-12 Reject H_0 10-14 Accept H_0 10-16 a) 6.98 b) Accept H_0
10-18 Reject H_0 10-20 Accept H_0
10-22 a) .0630; .3734; .4505; .1131
b) 9, 56, 68, 17
c) Accept H_0
10-24 Accept H_0
Reject H_0
10-26 a) 81.95 b) 238.05 c) 21.05 d) 11.31
10-28 Accept H_0
Accept H_0
10-30 a) 33.5 b) 8.333 c) 7.375 d) 1.130
10-32 Reject H_0 10-34 Reject H_0 10-36 Reject H_0 10-38 Accept H_0

10-40 Accept H_0 **10-42** (125.24, 538.58) **10-44** Reject H_0
10-46 Reject H_0 **10-48** Accept H_0 **10-50** Accept H_0 **10-52** Accept H_0
10-54 Reject H_0 **10-56** Accept H_0 **10-58** Reject H_0
10-60 a) Normal b) Chi-square
c) Analysis of variance
d) *t*-test
10-62 Reject H_0 **10-64** Accept H_0
10-66 b) Chi square 9.019
c) H_0: Type of car driven does not depend on age; H_1: Type of car is related to age
d) Accept H_0
10-68 Reject H_0 **10-70** Reject H_0 **10-72** Reject H_0 **10-74** Reject H_0

CHAPTER 11

11-2 An estimating equation is the mathematical relationship describing the association between a dependent variable and one or more independent variables.

11-4 The term *direct relationship* applies to the situation in which the dependent variable increases as the independent variable(s) increases. The term *indirect relationship* describes the situation in which the dependent variable decreases as the independent variable(s) increases.

11-6 A linear relationship describes the situation in which the dependent variable changes a constant amount for equal incremental changes in the independent variable(s). A curvilinear relationship describes the situation in which the dependent variable changes at an increasing (or decreasing) rate with equal incremental changes in the independent variable(s).

11-8 It is the process that determines the relationship between a dependent variable and more than one independent variable.

11-10 a) Yes, direct and linear.
b) Yes, inverse and curvilinear.
c) Yes, inverse and curvilinear.

11-12

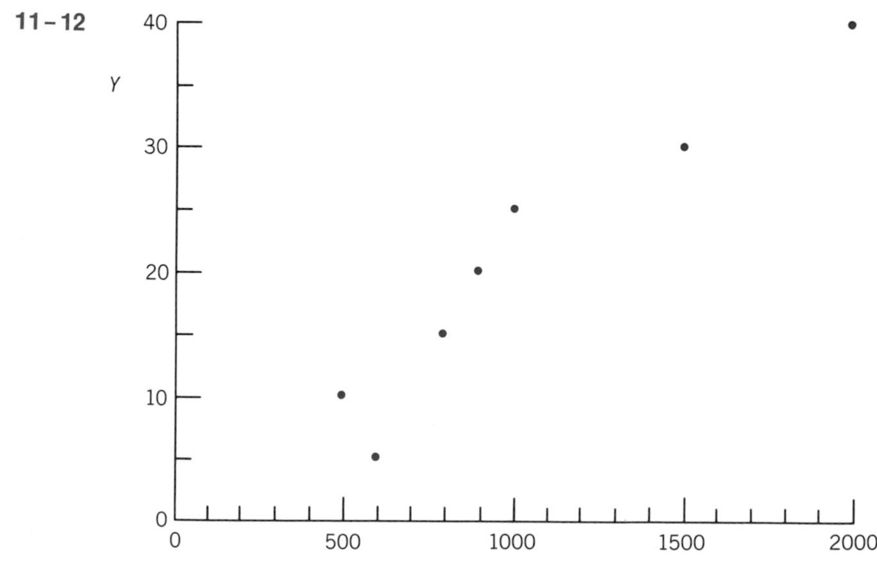

A direct linear relationship seems to exist.
Clearly it is absurd to suggest that use of facial tissues causes the common cold (while the opposite may well be true).

11–14 a)

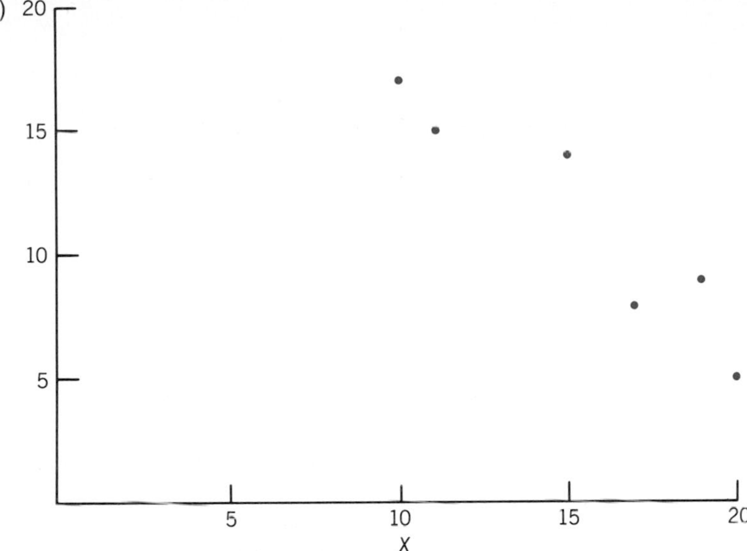

b) $\hat{Y} = 27.6234 - 1.0624\ X$

c) $x = 12, \quad \hat{y} = 14.875$
$x = 14, \quad \hat{y} = 12.75$
$x = 18, \quad \hat{y} = 8.50$

11–16 a) $\hat{Y} = -1.96828 + .81364\ X$
b) 5.59 c) (8.736, 31.264)

11–18 a)

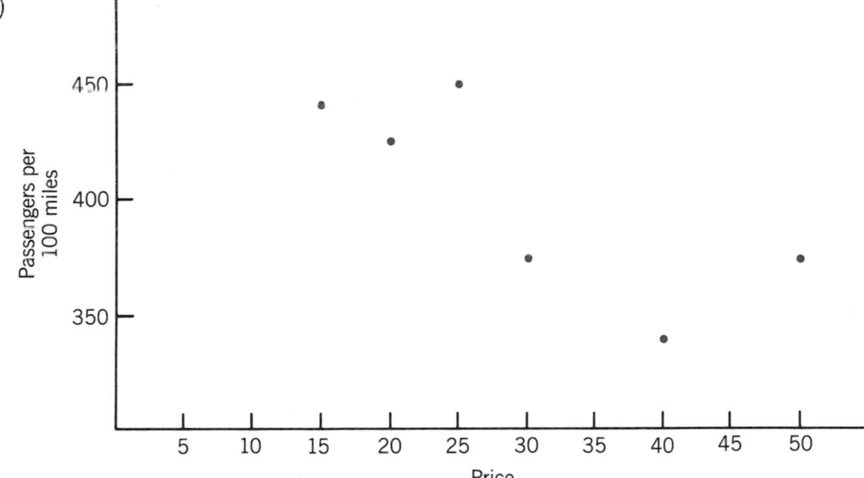

b) $\hat{Y} = 482.9 - 2.765\ X$
c) 386.1

11–20 a)

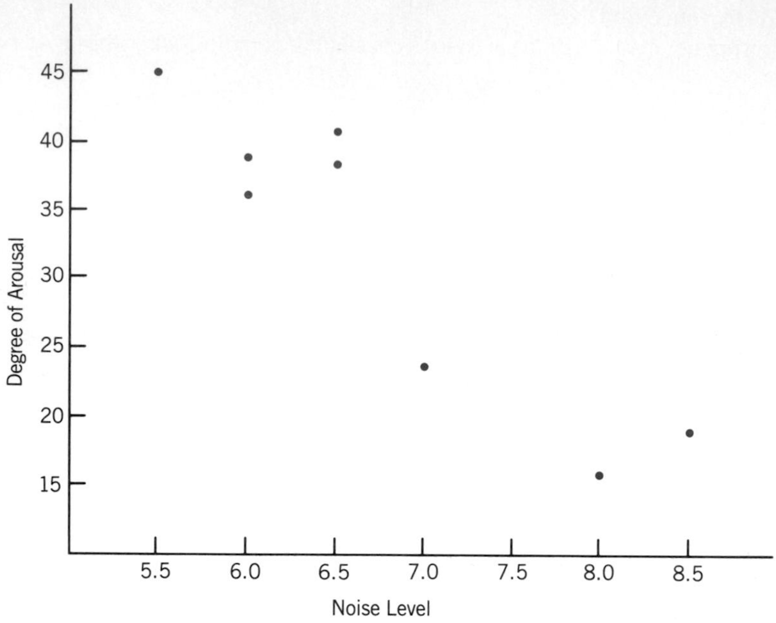

45
40
35
30
25
20
15
Degree of Arousal
5.5
6.0
6.5
7.0
7.5
8.0
8.5
Noise Level

b) $\hat{Y} = 99.5 - 10\,X$
c) 27

11–22 a)

10
8
6
4
2
0
Minor Track Accidents
10
20
30
40
50
Youth Soccer Games

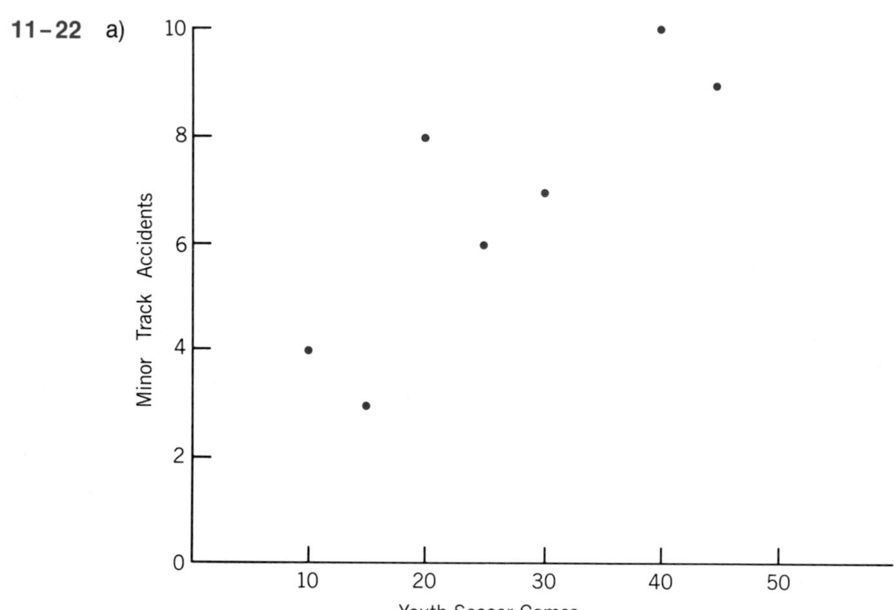

b) $\hat{Y} = 2.22 + .17\,X$
c) 8.17 d) 1.48

11-24 a)

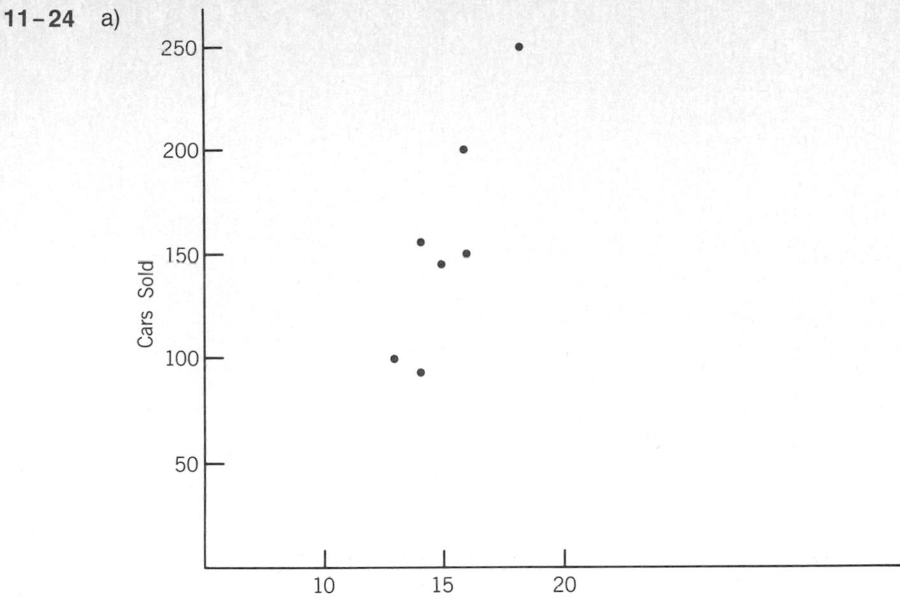

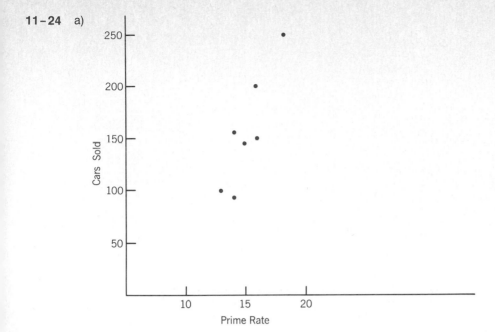

b) $\hat{Y} = -305.337 + 30.832\ X$
c) 126.311

11-26 $r = -.7381$

11-28 $r = -.9211$

11-30 a) Positive b) Positive c) Positive d) Zero

11-32 a) $\hat{Y} = 2.0848 + .8195\ X$
b) .6794

11-34 a) .062 b) (.6178, .8822)

11-36 Accept H_0

11-38 a) Yes, the slope has changed
b) No, the slope has not changed.

11-40 Reject H_0

11-42 The coefficient of determination describes the percent of the change of the dependent variable which is described by the independent variable(s). The coefficient of correlation indicates whether the relationship is direct or inverse; it does not tell how much of the variation in Y is explained by the independent variable(s).

11-44 Correlation does not imply causality because it is simply a statistical technique applied to a set of numbers thought to show a relationship between variables. The relationship between two variables may be due to an external cause affecting them both.

11-46 $r = \pm .8794$

11-48 $r = -.9386$

11-50 a) 1, + b) 2, + c) 2, − d) 2, −

11-52 $r = .953$

11-54 Reject H_0

11-56 a)

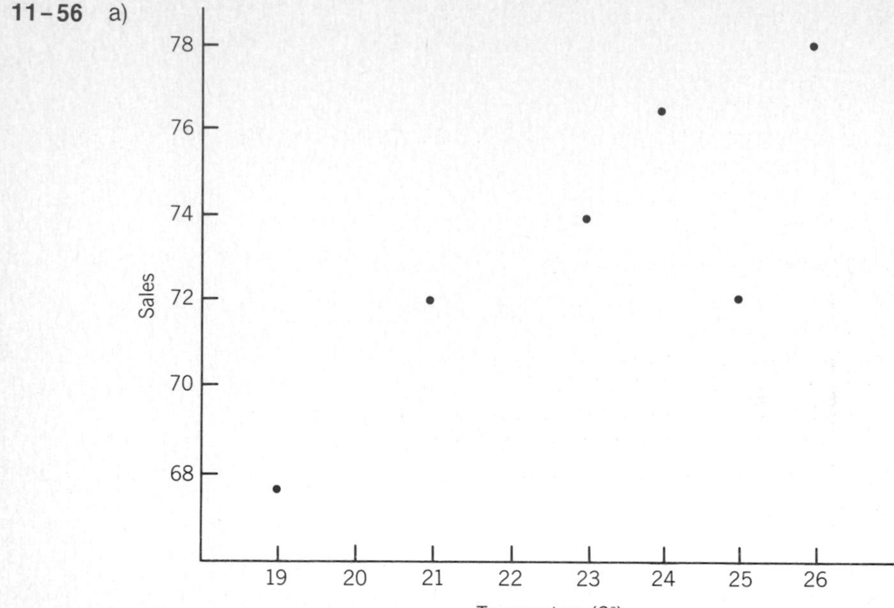

b) $\hat{Y} = 41.95 + 1.35\,X$

11-58 a) $\hat{Y} = 5.94 + .81\,X$
b) 6.99
c) ($1,227,000, $4,821,000)

CHAPTER 12

12-2 To include qualitative factors in our regression.

12-4 More. There is no way that *adding* an additional variable could *decrease* the explained portion of the dependent variable. We are just using more of the information available to us.

12-6 No. Multiple regression is based on the same assumptions and procedures as simple regression.

12-8 a) $\hat{Y} = -2.9961 + .5996X_1 + .9049X_2$
b) $\hat{Y} = 33.0679$

12-10 a) $\hat{Y} = -6.3666 + .1553X_1 + .7262X_2$
b) 7.6236 pounds
c) 5.0007 − 10.2465

12-12 a) $\hat{Y} = 18.01 + .23X_1 + 1.15X_2$
b) $\hat{Y} = 29.625\%$

12-14 a) $\hat{Y} = -19.47 - 3.92\,X_1 + 17.36\,X_2 + 6.68\,X_3$
b) 4.14 c) .9806 d) 71.454

12-16 a) $\hat{Y} = -1140.44 + 12.01\,X_1 + .18\,X_2 - .09\,X_3$
b) .931 c) 2225.16

12-18 a) $\hat{Y} = -49.95 + 1.07\,X_1 + 1.36\,X_2 + 2.04\,X_3 - 1.80\,X_4$
b) .7642 c) 77.40

12-20 a) $\hat{Y} = 30.980426 + .145184\,X_1 + .081609\,X_2 - 2.716856\,X_3$
b) .6176 c) 21

12-22 a) Accept H_0 b) (1.35, .95)

12-24 a) 5.77 b) 7.85

c) The regression is not significant as a whole.

12-26 The regression is significant as a whole.

12-28 Multicollinearity is present because the prime rate at banks is dependent upon the Federal Reserve discount rate which for the most part moves directly with inflation.

12-30 a) $\hat{Y} = -10115.386 - 10.669497\ X_1 + 41.432653\ X_2 + 144.214\ X_3$

b) No c) (61.567, 89.004)

12-32 a) $\hat{Y} = b_0 + b_1X_1 + b_2X_2$ (where $\hat{Y}$ is the failure rate, X_1 is a dummy variable, and X_2 is the number of gears)

12-34 a) No; $\hat{Y} = 13.906 + 3.5\ X_1 - 206\ X_2$

b) Reaction to penicillin is not a significant explanatory variable

12-36 a) Deviations from the line will not be random.

b) The residuals will exhibit the same non random pattern as in (a) above.

12-38 a) The judge has spotted the obvious pattern in the residuals.

b) The most direct model is a second-degree equation; the number of days in court should be squared and added as an additional independent variable.

12-40 a) $\hat{Y} = -13.42 + 1.20\ X_1 + .20\ X_2 + 1.47\ X_3$

b) $R^2 = .9449$

c) X_1 (number of trout) is significant; water temperature and kilograms of food are not.

d) 838 kilograms

12-42 a) $\hat{Y} = 90.03 + 99.49\ X_1 + 21.54\ X_2 - 34.46\ X_3$

b) 446.79, 656.01

c) There is a significant difference between dogs and cats.

d) Yes

CHAPTER 13

13-2 *b*

13-4 They do not use all the information in the data, since they usually rely on ranks or counts.

13-6 Yes, a great deal of information is sacrificed by using a ranking test. If the data were examined, it could be seen that there is a very distinct bi-modal distribution. In this instance, choice of two packages might well be the better alternative.

13-8 Accept H_0

13-10 a) The meteorologist has a bit of a point, but it is not strong. A nonparametric test does not address itself to his concern.

b) Accept H_0

13-12 a) Accept H_0 b) Accept H_0 c) Reject H_0

d) The only change in the computations of *b* and *c* is in the standard error of the mean. With only 13 responses, the reliability of our sample was lessened by the small size of the sample.

13-14 Accept H_0 13-16 Accept H_0 13-18 Reject H_0 13-20 Accept H_0

13-22 Accept H_0 13-24 Accept H_0 13-26 Accept H_0 13-28 Reject H_0

13-30 a) Accept H_0 b) Reject H_0 c) Certainly.

d) The test only looks for randomness in the sample; it does not see if the sample proportion is reasonable.

13-32 a) Reject H_0 b) No. c) The Mann-Whitney *U* Test 13-34 Accept H_0

13–36 There is a significant correlation.
13–38 The rankings are positively correlated.
13–40 The personal interviews should no longer be used.
13–42 Reject H_0 **13–44** Reject H_0 **13–46** Accept H_0 **13–48** Reject H_0
13–50 Reject H_0 **13–52** Accept H_0
13–54 Although historical data enable us to know what sort of weather to expect at any season of the year, the weather conditions that actually occur are quite random.
13–56 They cannot be 95% sure that the inquiries have increased.
13–58 Accept H_0 **13–60** Reject H_0 **13–62** Accept H_0

CHAPTER 14

14–2 To determine what patterns exist within the data over the period examined.
14–4 Demands for services such as water and sewer would perhaps not be met; adjustment of the tax rate to provide for municipal services might lag behind the actual demand for those services. Extra resources would probably be needed to allow a smooth municipal operation in a situation in which forecasting is poor.
14–6 Seasonal. **14–8** Cyclical variation. **14–10** Secular trend.
14–12 a) $\hat{Y} = 956.2 + 88.8x$, where 1981 = 0 and x units = 1 year
b) 1222.6
14–14 a)

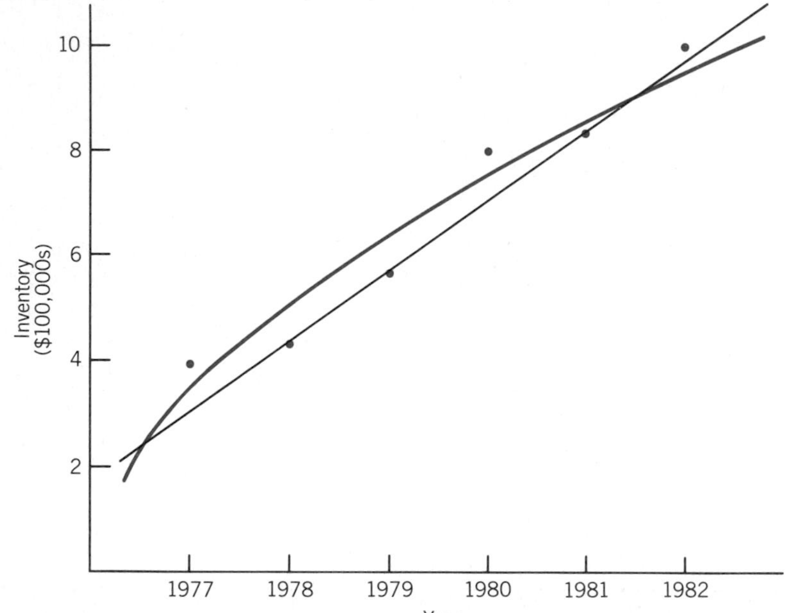

b) $\hat{Y} = 6.8333 + .6286x$, where 1979½ = 0 and x units = ½ year
c) $\hat{Y} = 6.7813 + .6286x + .0045x^2$
d) somewhere between \$1,100,000 and \$1,200,000

14–16 a)

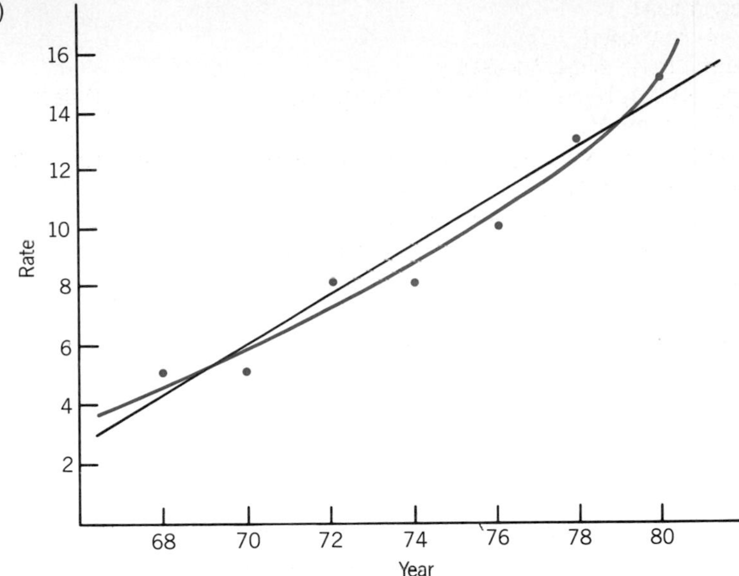

b) $\hat{Y} = 9.1429 + .8571x$, where 1974 = 0 and x units = 1 year

c) $\hat{Y} = 8.4762 + .8571x + .0417x^2$

d) Given the shape of this second degree curve, it would only be a matter of a few years before estimated rates would be so high as to be improbable and thus not useful; also, at those levels competition would be so profitable that there would be a question whether or not the postal service would survive.

14–18 a)

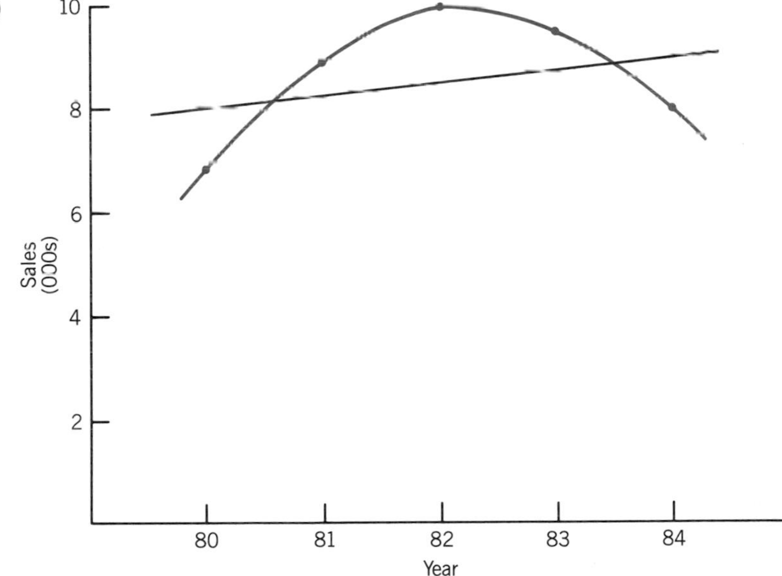

b) x 1980 1981 1982 1983 1984

$\hat{Y} = 8.7 + .25x$

c) x 1980 1981 1982 1983 1984
$\hat{Y} = 9.9143 + .2500x - .6071x^2$
d) Yes e) 5.201 (5201)

14–20 a) 97.4, 103.2, 98.8, 102.9, 97.9, 100.5, 100.0
b) −2.6, 3.2, −1.2, 2.9, −2.1, .5, 0.0
c)

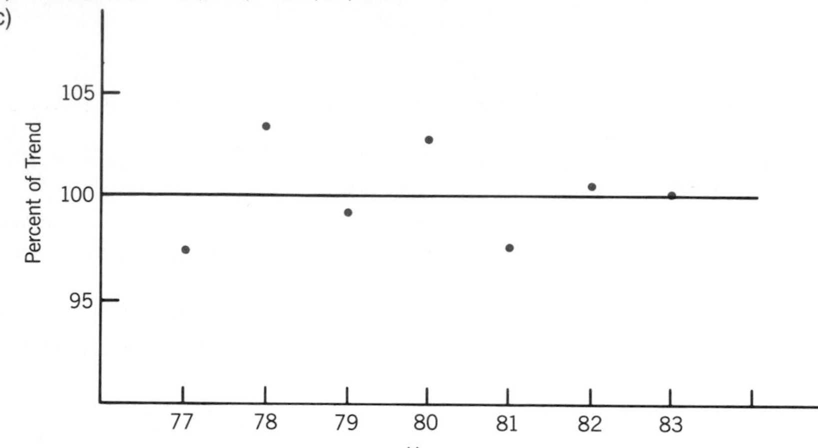

d) 1978; yes, it is the same.

14–22 a) 97.0, 103.0, 97.0, 104.0, 97.0
b) −3.0, 3.0, −3.0, 4.0, −3.0
c)

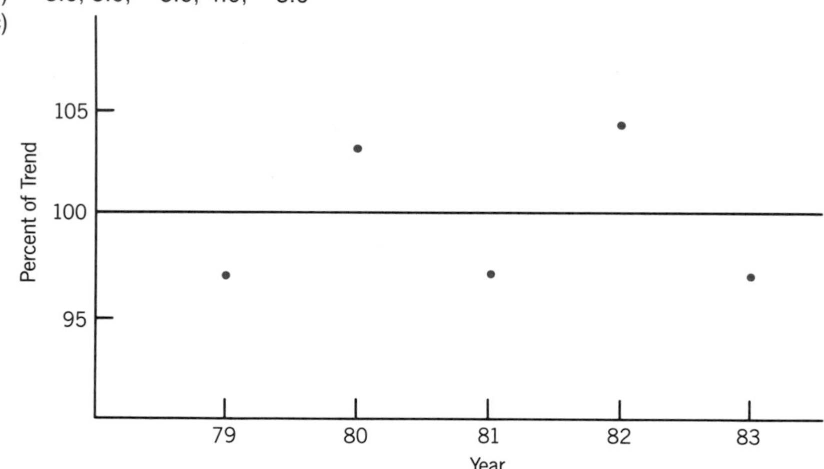

d) 1981; yes, it is the same.

14–24 a) $\hat{Y} = 22.186 + .518x$
b) 99.4, 93.1, 98.3, 108.6, 111.0, 94.7, 94.8
c) −.6, −6.9, −1.7, 8.6, 11.0, −5.3, −5.2
d) 1982 under both measures; relative cyclical residual is percent of trend −100.

14–26 a) 97.875, 99.375, 100.5, 101.5, 102.125, 102.5, 103, 103.625, 104.5, 105.75, 107.25, 108.625, 110, 111.875, 113.75, 115.25
b) 91.954, 79.497, 107.463, 121.182, 92.044, 80.976, 105.825, 120.627, 91.866, 81.324, 105.361, 120.598, 92.727, 81.341, 104.615, 121.475
c) 105.593, 120.905, 91.999, 81.150; 125.687, 121.012, 92.080, 81.222

14–28 86.0, 104.5, 86.5, 123.0

14-30 a) 176.875, 179.375, 181.625, 182.25, 181.375, 181.25, 181.375, 181.375, 181.625, 183.375, 184.125, 186.125, 188.25, 188.75, 190.375, 194.125

b) 109.117, 46.829, 129.387, 114.129, 113.577, 41.931, 130.117, 113.577, 115.272, 39.829, 130.889, 115.514, 109.429, 48.742, 125.542, 113.844

c) 129.752, 113.986, 111.503, 44.380, 129.875, 114.094, 111.608, 44.422

d) 26

14-32 97.088, 76.572, 90.472, 135.869; 77.4%

14-34 a) and c)

14-36 These irregular variations even themselves out over time and they tend to be minor in magnitude.

14-38 a) 75.886, 105.080, 142.050, 76.984

b) 25.038, 22.840, 26.751, 32.474, 27.673, 26.646, 30.975, 29.876, 30.309, 29.501, 28.863, 29.876, 31.626, 33.308, 33.791, 27.278

14-40 A large irregular component; a change in the weather which produces a larger or smaller than expected seasonal index; a change in technology which affects the secular trend; an economic change which alters the time scale of the cyclical component.

14-42 The decline in birth rates which has occurred will no doubt affect future college enrollments; we need to be especially careful about the behavior in birth rates seventeen or eighteen years in the past when estimating college enrollments.

14-44 a) 81.577, 90.611, 111.236, 116.576

b) 36.775, 34.212, 35.959, 36.028, 34.323, 37.523, 38.656, 39.459, 40.453, 39.730, 39.555, 41.175, 41.678, 43.241, 42.454, 42.890.

c) $\hat{Y} = 38.870 + 0.268x$

14-46 .7, .75, .725, .675, .6125, .575, .525, .4625, .45, .475, .5625, .6875, .7625, .7625, .75, .7125, .6625, .625, .55, .4625, .4, .375, .4125, .5125, .6375, .7125, .75, .7625, .725, .6875, .6125, .5125

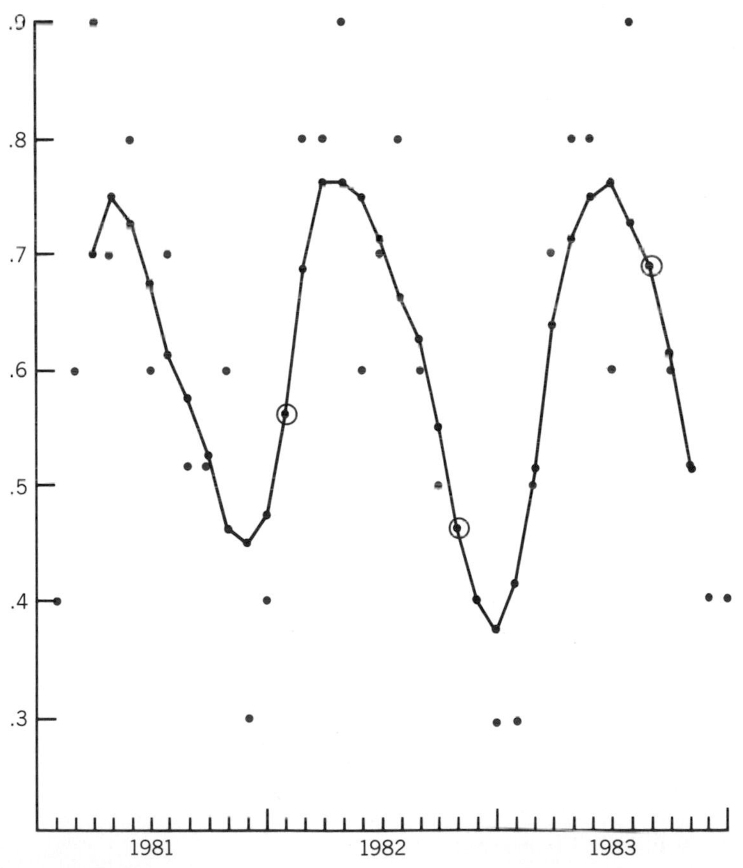

14–48 a) $\hat{Y} = 1551.14 + 174.64x$
b) 2249.7 loans
14–50 a) $\hat{Y} = 500.83 + 23.13x$ b) 70.900 patients
14–52 218 bicycles
14–54 a) $\hat{Y} = 17.375 + .72x$
b) 22.415 or 22,415,000 subscriptions

CHAPTER 15

15–2 Price indices and quantity indices describe the change in a single variable, price and quantity (or number), respectively. A value index describes how the product of two variables, price and quantity, changes over a period of time.

15–4 An index may be used by itself or as a part of an intermediate computation to understand some other information better.

15–6 $\text{Percentage relative} = \dfrac{\text{Current value}}{\text{Base value}} \times 100$

15–8 108, 100.0, 110.1, 121.2, 130.1
15–10 100.0, 95.2, 102.7 **15–12** 108.3
15–14 100.0, 101.9, 106.3, 107.2
15–16 98.2, 100.0, 104.3, 105.1
15–18 July 95.55; August 103.04; Laspeyres
15–20 80.4, 88.9, 96.6, 100.0
15–22 100.0, 106.5, 114.75
15–24 a) 135 b) 117
15–26 64.5, 77.0, 100.0, 127
15–28 100.00, 129.42, 138.65
15–30 94.7, 101.3, 100.0

15–32 A value index depends upon changes in both quantity and prices; as a result, a change in a value index cannot be identified with any single component.

15–34 76.5, 92.7, 95.2, 100.0
15–36 75.456

15–38 Appropriate weighting for one period may become inappropriate in a short time. Unless the weights are changed the index becomes less informative.

15–40 The values from several adjoining periods are averaged.

15–42 An index does not reflect changes in the quality of items and therefore understates or overstates the price level change if the quality changes.

15–44 100.0, 147.5, 138.5
15–46 100.0, 101.1

15–48 The problem of incomparability of indices would be present; there has been a basic change in what is being measured by the indices since computer technology has changed significantly over the past few decades.

15–50 100.0, 101.6, 116.7
15–52 100, 111, 112
15–54 100.0, 105.5, 107.4, 112.5
15–56 100.0, 105.5

CHAPTER 16

16-2 No, not yet. The club's objective—to make money—is apparent. The varying states of nature—how many cones might be sold—are equally apparent, as are the possible actions the Cougars might take—the amount of supplies to stock. Uncertainty is present in two places. The states of nature and the cost of the sugar. Therein lies the problem. Until a price for the sugar is established, the payoffs cannot be determined.

16-4 a) 6
b) $12,000 unpaid vacations; $11,712 paid vacations

16-6 45,000 pairs

16-8 a) Emily should hire either 10 or 11 MBA's and expect her company to make a profit of $112,500 on their consulting work.
b) Expected profit under certainty $139,500; EVPI $27,000.

16-10 77 signs **16-12** 84

16-14 a) Paige's should stock 348 polyester-belted tires for next year.
b) Paige's should stock 212 steel-belted tires for next year.

16-16 a) $90,000
b)

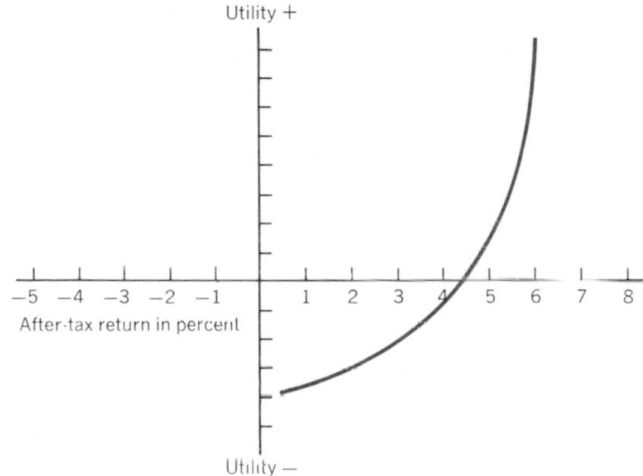

16-18 Buy the four-month option.

16-20 .1335

16-22 No, only 89 percent sure.

16-24 Gryphon can be 99.62% sure that the upgrade will pay for itself within 4 years.

16-26 a) No
b) Less than $1,640,000
c) Although the solution indicates the larger plant is preferred, the management may prefer to avoid the embarrassment of having a plant which is too large (a very visible error) in favor of having to enlarge a plant two years later (a fairly invisible error).

16-28 a) Sam should ride his bike.
b) Sam should drive his car.

16-30 They should buy the modules.

16-32 a) 52 tails (26 entrees)
b) $14.892

16-34 a) .7704 b) .3156

16-36 a) $55,000 b) 50,000 lbs. c) $2250

16-38 Proceed with a price of $130 **16-40** Yes, extend credit.

16-42

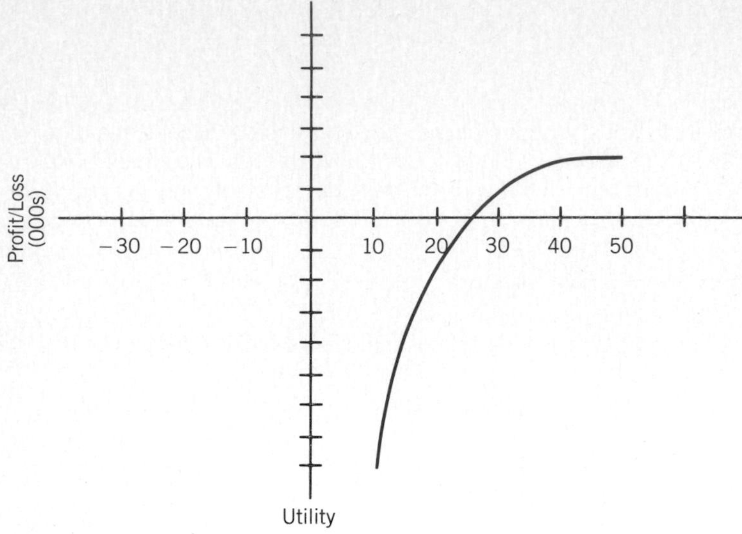

16-44 a) Enduro would accept.

b)

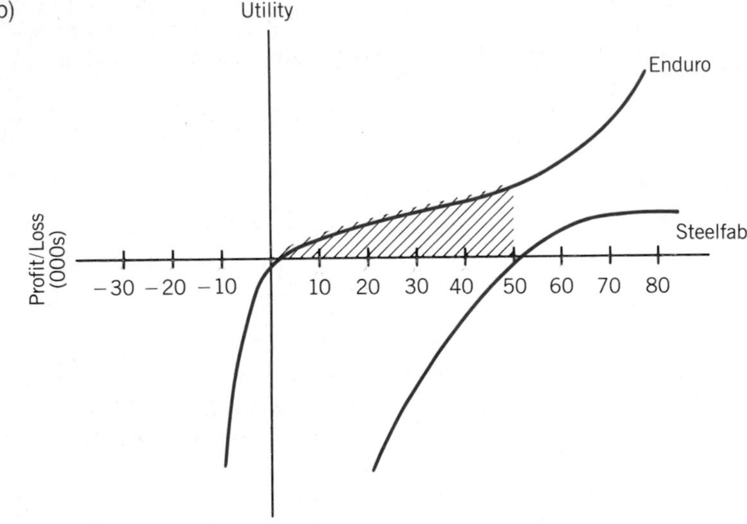

c) Yes, both; Steelfab would bid up to $611,111

BIBLIOGRAPHY

Introductions to Statistics for the Layman

CAMPBELL, S. K., *Flaws and Fallacies in Statistical Thinking*. Englewood Cliffs, N.J.: Prentice-Hall, 1974.

HUFF, D., *How to Lie with Statistics*. New York: Norton, 1954.

LEVIN, R. I., AND D. S. RUBIN, *Applied Elementary Statistics*. Englewood Cliffs, N.J.: Prentice Hall, 1980.

MOSTELLER, F., W. H. KRUSKAL, R. S. PIETERS, G. R. RISING, AND R. F. LINK, *Statistics by Example*. Reading, Mass.: Addison-Wesley, 1973.

REICHMAN, W. J., *Use and Abuse of Statistics*. New York: Oxford Univ. Press, 1963.

TANUR, J. M. et al., *Statistics: A Guide to the Unknown*. San Francisco: Holden-Day, 1972.

Probability

FELLER, W., *An Introduction to Probability Theory and Its Applications*, Vol. 1, 2nd ed. New York: Wiley, 1971.

FREUND, J. E., *Introduction to Probability*. Encino, Calif.: Dickenson, 1973.

MOSTELLER, F. R., E. K. ROURKE, AND G. B. THOMAS, JR., *Probability with Statistical Applications*, 2nd ed. Reading, Mass.: Addison-Wesley, 1970.

Sampling Theory and Techniques

COCHRAN, W. G., *Sampling Techniques*, 2nd ed. New York: Wiley, 1963.

HANSEN, M. H., W. N. HURWITZ, AND W. G. MADOW, *Sample Survey Methods and Theory*, Vol. 1: *Methods and Applications*; Vol. II: *Theory*. New York: Wiley, 1963.

SLONIM, M. J., *Sampling in a Nutshell*. New York: Simon & Schuster, 1973.

Nonparametric Statistics

CONOVER, W. J., *Practical Non-Parametric Statistics*. New York: Wiley, 1971.

GIBBONS, J. D., *Nonparametric Statistical Inference*. New York: McGraw-Hill, 1971.

LEHMANN, E. L., *Nonparametrics: Statistical Methods Based on Ranks*. San Francisco: Holden-Day, 1975.

NOETHER, G. E., *Elements of Nonparametric Statistics*, 2nd ed. New York: Wiley, 1976.

OSTLE, B., AND W. M. RICHARD, *Statistics in Research*. Ames, Iowa: The Iowa State University Press, 1975.

Special Statistical Topics

ANDERSON, V. L., AND R. A. MCLEAN, *Design of Experiments: A Realistic Approach*. New York: Dekker, 1974.

HARRIS, R. J., *A Primer of Multivariate Statistics*. New York: Academic Press, 1974.

MOSTELLER, F., AND J. W. TUKEY, *Data Analysis and Regression*. Reading, Mass.: Addison-Wesley, 1977.

TUKEY, J. W., *Exploratory Data Analysis*. Reading, Mass.: Addison-Wesley, 1971.

U.S. DEPT. OF LABOR, *The Consumer Price Index: History and Techniques*. Bureau of Labor Statistics Bulletin 1517, updated, Washington, D.C.

VELLEMAN, P. F., AND D. C. HOAGLIN, *Applications, Basics, and Computing of Exploratory Data Analysis*. Boston: Duxbury Press, 1981.

Statistical Decision Theory

DEGROOT, M. H., *Optimal Statistical Decisions*. New York: McGraw-Hill, 1970.

LEVIN, R. I., AND C. KIRKPATRICK, *Quantitative Approaches to Management*, 5th ed. New York: McGraw-Hill, 1982.

MORRIS, W. T., *Management Science—A Bayesian Introduction*. Englewood Cliffs, N.J.: Prentice-Hall, 1968.

RAIFFA, H., *Decision Analysis, Introductory Lectures on Choices under Uncertainty*. Reading, Mass.: Addison-Wesley, 1968.

WINKLER, R. L., *Introduction to Bayesian Inference Decision*. New York: Holt, 1972.

Statistical Tables

BURRINGTON, R. S., AND D. C. MAY, *Handbook of Probability and Statistics with Tables*, 2nd ed. New York: McGraw-Hill, 1970.

Handbook of Tables for Probability and Statistics, 2nd ed. Cleveland: Chemical Rubber Co., 1968.

NATIONAL BUREAU OF STANDARDS, *Tables of the Binomial Probability Distribution*. Washington, D.C.: Govt. Printing Office, 1950.

PEARSON, E. S., AND H. O. HARTLEY, *Biometrika Tables for Statisticians*, 2nd ed. Cambridge, Eng.: Cambridge Univ. Press, 1962.

SHELBY, S., *Standard Mathematical Tables*, 17th ed. Cleveland: Chemical Rubber Co., 1969.

Dictionaries and General Reference Works

FREUND, J., AND F. WILLIAMS, *Dictionary/Outline of Basic Statistics*. New York: McGraw-Hill, 1966.

KENDALL, M. G., AND W. R. BUCKLAND, *A Dictionary of Statistical Terms*, 3rd ed. New York: Hafner Press, 1971.

INDEX

Achenwall, Gottfried, 2
Actual mean, 65
Advantages of data array, 13
Advantages of histograms, 30
Advantages of the mode, 88
Advantages of polygons, 30
Advantages of relative frequency, 28
Ali, Muhammad, 144
All-inclusive, 15
Alpha (α), 365, 412
Alternative hypothesis, 412
Analysis of variance (ANOVA), 426-89
Analysis of variance for regression, 573, 591
Approach to statistics, 3
Approximating the data array, 33
A priori probability, 148, 182
Arithmetic mean, 62, 63
  advantages of, 68
  disadvantages of, 68
  population, 63
  sample, 63
Arranging data, 12
Arranging data to convey meaning, 6-55
Assumptions for statistics, 3
Average, 62
Average absolute deviation, 113, 130
  calculating, 114
  characteristics of, 114
Average deviation measures, 113
Average inventory, 14

Bayes, Thomas, 144, 175, 748
Bayesian decision theory, 175, 748
Bayes' theorem, 175, 182
Bernoulli, Jacob, 144, 214
Bernoulli process, 214, 247
  use of, 214, 222
Beta (β), 365, 375, 412
Between-column variance, 451, 475
Bills of Mortality, 2
Bimodal distribution, 87, 91
Binomial distribution, 214, 247, 330
  dispersion for, 221
  illustration of, 216
  measures of central tendency, 221
  shortcomings of, 311
Binomial formula, 215
Binomial table, 219
BMD, 129
Boxplots, 130

Calculating the mean, 64
Calculating the mean from grouped data, 86
Calculating the median from grouped data, 79
Calculating the median from ungrouped data, 78
Census, 268, 299
Central limit theorem, 287, 299
Certainty, 756, 785
Characteristic probability, 214
Characteristics of relative frequency distribution, 15
Charlemagne, 2
Chebyshev, P. L., 117
Chebyshev's theorem, 117, 130
  use of, 119
Chi-square, 426-89
  precautions, 438
Chi-square distribution, 433, 475
Chi-square statistic χ^2, 432
Choosing the correct probability distribution, 246
Classes, 14
  continuous, 17, 37
  discrete, 17
  equal, 20
  intervals, 21
  limits, 23, 37, 38
  marks, 23, 37
  mutually exclusive, 15
  open-ended, 16
  overlapping, 15
  of qualitative data, 15
  unequal, 21
Classical probability, 147, 182
  shortcomings of, 148
Classifying data, 20
Class intervals, 21
  construction of, 24
Class limits, 23, 37, 38
Class marks, 23, 37
Clusters, 274, 299
Cluster sampling, 274, 299
Codes, 66
Coding, 91, 667, 697
Coding the class marks, 66
Coefficient of correlation, 518, 525, 535
Coefficient of determination, 518, 535
Coefficient of multiple determination, 562, 591
Coefficient of variation, 126, 130
  computing, 126
Collecting data, 8
Collectively exhaustive events, 146, 182
Comparing the mean, median and mode, 90

Complete enumeration, 268
Computed *F*-ratio, 573, 591
Computed *t*, 570, 591
Conditional losses, 211
Conditional probability, 164, 167, 182
  formula, 169
Conditional profit, 751, 785
Confidence interval, 323, 324, 326, 345
Confidence level, 324, 345
  shortcomings of, 324
Confidence limits, 324, 345
Consistent estimator, 314, 345
Constructing class intervals, 24
Constructing a frequency distribution, 20
Constructing a relative frequency polygon, 30
Consumer Price Index, 710, 711, 734
Contingency table, 429, 475
Continuity correction factor, 242, 247
Continuous classes, 17
Continuous data, 37
Continuous distributions, 758
Continuous probability distribution, 202, 230, 247
Continuous random variable, 230, 247
Correlation, 490-547
  analysis, 518, 535
  use of, 533
Correlation analysis, 518, 535
Counting frequencies, 22
Cumulative frequency distribution, 31, 37
  "less-than," 31
  "more-than," 31
Curvilinear relationship, 495, 496, 535
Cyclical fluctuation, 662, 663, 697
Cyclical variation, 676

Data, 8, 38
  arranging, 6 55
  array, 12-13, 38
  classifying, 20
  collecting, 8
  discrete, 17, 38
  grouped, 64
  illustrating, 22
  patterns in, 10
  point, 8, 38
  qualitative, 15
  raw, 11, 38
  set, 8, 38
  tests for, 9
  trends in, 22
  ungrouped, 64

Data array, 12, 38
advantages of, 13
approximating, 33
disadvantages of, 13
Data point, 8, 38
sorting, 22
Data set, 8, 38
Deciles, 109, 130
Decision point, 777, 785
Decision theory, 3, 746–93
Decision tree, 775, 785
de Fermat, Pierre, 143
Degrees of freedom, 335, 345
function of, 336
de Laplace, Jarquis, 144
de Moivre, Abraham, 144
Dependent samples, 394, 412
Dependent variable, 492, 535
Descriptive statistics, 3
Deseasonalization, 686, 697
Difference between samples and populations, 9
Direct relationship, 496, 499, 535
Disadvantages of data array, 13
Disadvantages of the mode, 88
Discrete classes, 17
Discrete data, 17, 38
Discrete probability distribution, 202, 247
Dispersion, 58, 106, 130
distance measures, 108
Distance measure, 108, 130
Distribution-free test, 606
Distributions, 198–265
Dividing the range into equal classes, 20
Domesday Book, 2
Dummy variable, 579, 591

Efficient estimator, 314, 345
Equal classes, 20
Estimate, 311, 345
interval, 313–45
point, 313, 316, 345
types, 313
Estimated mean, 65
Estimated regression coefficients, 556
Estimating equation, 499, 535
shortcomings of, 508
Estimating the mean, 64
Estimation, 310–55
determining sample size, 340
Estimator, 313, 345
consistent, 314, 345
criteria of, 314
efficient, 314, 345
sufficient, 315, 345
unbiased, 314, 345
Event, 145, 182, 295
Expected frequencies, 430, 475
Expected losses, 211
Expected marginal loss, 760, 785
Expected marginal profit, 760, 785
Expected profit, 750, 785
calculation of, 752
Expected profit with perfect information, 755, 785
Expected value, 206, 247
use in decision making, 210
Expected value criterion, 768, 785
Expected value of perfect information (EVPI), 756, 785
Expected value of a random variable, 206, 247
Experiment, 145, 182, 295
Exploratory data analysis (E.D.A.), 128, 130

F distribution, 456, 475
F-ratio, 455, 475
F table, 457
precautions of, 459
Factorial experiment, 297, 299
"Federal Reserve Bulletin," 711
FIFO (first-in, first-out), 696
Finite population, 271, 299
Finite population multiplier, 292, 299, 365
Fixed weight aggregates method, 716, 720, 734
Foundation of Mathematics and Other Logical Essays, The, 151
Fractile, 109, 130
Frequencies:
"less-than," 31
"more-than," 31
Frequency curve, 30, 38
creating a, 30
Frequency distribution, 10, 12–14, 38, 200
construction of, 20
cumulative, 31
graphing, 28
relative, 15
table, 13
Frequency polygons, 29, 38
Frequency table, 13
Function of graphs, 28
Function of populations, 9
Function of samples, 9

Gallup Poll, 9
Garbage in, garbage out, 8
Gauss, Karl, 230
Gaussian theory, 230
Geometric mean, 74, 91
calculation of, 75
Geometric mean growth rate, 74, 75
GIGO, 8
Gombauld, Antoine, 143
Good, Richard, 151
Goodness-of-fit test, 375, 443
Gossett, W. S., 334
Gottingen, 2
Grand mean, 450, 475
Graphing frequency distributions, 28
Graphs, 2–55
functions of, 28
Graunt, Captain John, 2
Grouped data, 64

Henry VII, 2
Histogram, 28, 38
advantages of, 30
History of probability theory, 144
History of statistics, 2
Horizontal axis, 28
Hypothesis, 358, 412
formulation of, 359
Hypothesis testing, 356–425

Illustrating the data, 22
Independence, 158
Independent variable, 492, 535
Index of Industrial Production (IIP), 728, 734
Index numbers, 706–45
problems with, 710, 732
sources of, 711
types of, 709
Inferential statistics, 3
Infinite population, 271, 300
Interfractile range, 109, 130
calculating, 109
Interquartile range, 110, 111, 130
Interval estimate, 313, 319, 323, 325, 326, 330, 345
Inverse relationship, 496, 500, 535
Irregular variation, 662, 664, 697

Joint probability, 159, 171, 182
Judgment sampling, 269, 300

Kolmogorov, A. N., 638
Kolmogorov-Smirnov test, 606, 638, 642
Koopman, Bernard, 151
Kurtosis, 59, 91

Lagrange, Joseph, 144
Laspeyres method, 716, 717, 734
Latin square, 299, 300
Least squares method, 501, 535
Left-tailed test, 367
Leptokurtic, 60, 91
"Less-than" frequencies, 31
"Less-than" ogive, 32
LIFO (last-in, first-out), 696
Limits, 23
class, 23, 37
real, 23
stated, 23
Linear relationship, 496, 535
Losses, 210
marginal, 758
obsolescence, 210, 755, 758
opportunity, 210, 758
Lower-tailed test, 367, 412

Mann-Whitney test, 606, 614, 642
Marginal loss (*ML*), 759, 785
Marginal probability, 153, 159, 172, 182
Marginal profit (*MP*), 758, 785
Marlborough, 2
Mean, 60, 91
actual, 65
arithmetic, 68
calculation of, 64
estimation of, 64, 65
geometric, 74
Measure of central tendency, 58, 60, 62, 91
Measure of kurtosis, 59
Measures of dispersion, 58, 91, 106
financial use, 106
quality control use, 106
uses of, 106
Measures of location, 58
Measures of skewness, 58
"Measuring Markets," 711
Measuring variability, 104–39
Median, 60, 77, 91
advantages, 82
calculation of, 78, 79
class, 91
disadvantages, 82
Median class, 91
Mendel, Gregor, 439
Mesokurtic, 60, 91
Midpoints, 24
Minimum probability, 760, 785
MINITAB, 129
Modal class, 84
Mode, 60, 84, 91
advantages of, 88
disadvantages of, 88
location of, 85
Mode in Skewed Distributions, The, 85
Mode in Symmetrical Distributions, The, 85

Modeling techniques, 548–603
Modified mean, 684, 697
"Monthly Labor Review," 711
"Moody's," 711
"More-than" frequencies, 31
"More-than" ogive, 32
Multicollinearity, 574, 591
Multimodal distributions, 87
Multiple regression, 535, 548–603
Mutually exclusive, 15
Mutually exclusive classes, 15
Mutually exclusive events, 145, 182

Natural and Political Observations, 2
Negatively skewed, 59
Node, 785
Nonparametric methods, 604–59
  disadvantages of, 607
Nonparametric statistics, 606
Nonparametric tests, 606, 642
Normal curve, 231
Normal distribution, 230, 247
  characteristics of, 231
  shortcomings of, 242
Null hypothesis, 361, 412

Obsolescence loss, 210, 755, 785
Ogives, 31, 38
  "less-than," 32
  "more-than," 32
  of relative frequencies, 32
  shapes of, 32
  S-shaped, 32
Old Testament, 2
One-sample runs test, 622, 642
One-tailed test, 371, 412
Open-ended classes, 16, 17, 38
Opportunity losses, 210, 211, 785
Overlapping classes, 15

Paasche method, 716, 718, 734
Paired difference test, 394, 412
Parameters, 62, 91, 268, 300
Pascal, Blaise, 143
Patterns, 14
Patterns in data, 10
Payoff, 748, 785
Peakedness, 59
Percentage relative, 708, 734
Percentiles, 109, 131
Platykurtic, 60, 91
Point estimate, 313, 316, 345
Poisson, Simeon Denis, 224
Poisson distribution, 224, 247
  conditions of, 224
  construction, 227
  formula, 225
Polygons, 29
  advantages of, 30
  constructing, 30
  frequency, 29, 38
  relative frequency, 30
Population, 9, 38
  function of, 9
Population arithmetic mean, 63
Population distribution, 280
Population mean, 62, 312
Population parameter, 269
Population proportion, 312, 318
  point estimate of, 318
Population standard deviation, 116, 327
Population variance, 115, 463, 469
Positively skewed, 59

Posterior probability, 175, 182
  calculating, 175
  with inconsistent outcomes, 180
  with more information, 178
Power curve, 375, 412
Power of the hypothesis test, 412
Precision, 300
Price index, 709, 734
Probability, 3, 182
  a priori, 148, 182
  classical, 147, 182
  conditional, 164, 167, 182
  joint, 159, 171, 182
  marginal, 153, 159, 172, 182
  posterior, 175, 182
  rules of, 152
  subjective, 150, 183
  tree, 183
  types, 147
  unconditional, 153
Probability distribution, 200, 247
  finding, 204
  types, 202
Probability I, 142–97
Probability rules, 152
Probability sampling, 300
Probability theory, 144
Probability tree, 160, 183
Probability II, 198–265
Probability value, 409, 412
Problems with unequal classes, 21
Profit:
  conditional, 751, 785
  expected, 750, 785
  marginal, 758, 785

Quadratic regression model, 589
Qualitative data, 15, 579
Quantity index, 709, 728, 734
Quartile deviation, 109, 110, 131
  advantages of, 111
Quartiles, 109, 131

R^2, 262, 591
r statistic, 623
Ramsey, Frank, 151
Random sampling, 269, 270, 272, 300
Random variable, 204, 247
Range, 108, 131
  computing, 108
Rank correlation, 628, 642
  advantage of, 635
Rank correlation coefficient, 628, 643
Rank sum tests, 614, 643
Ratio-to-moving-average method, 681, 697
Raw data, 11, 38
Real limits, 23
Regression, 490–547
  multiple, 535
  use of, 533
Regression line, 497, 535
Relationships:
  curvilinear, 495, 496, 535
  direct, 496, 535
  inverse, 496, 535
  linear, 496, 535
Relative cyclical residual, 678, 697
Relative dispersion, 126
Relative frequency, 15
  advantages of, 28
  characteristics of, 15
  distributions, 15, 38
  histogram, 28
  polygon, 36
Relative frequency distribution, 15, 38

Relative frequency histogram, 28
  function of, 28
Relative frequency of occurrence, 148, 183
  use of, 149
Relative frequency polygon, 30
Relative measure, 126
Relevance of probability theory, 144
Replacement, 271
Representative sample, 10, 38
Residual method, 676, 697
Revised probabilities, 175
Right-tailed test, 367
Robust analysis methods, 128
Rollback, 779, 785
Rules for events that are not mutually exclusive, 155
Rules of probability, 152
Run, 622, 643

Salvage value, 765, 785
Sample, 9, 38, 268, 300
  function of, 9
  precision of the mean, 291
  representative, 10
Sample arithmetic mean, 63
Sample mean, 62
Sample space, 145, 183
Sample standard deviation, 120
  computing, 120
Sample standard score, 123
  computing, 123
Sample statistic, 269
Sampling, 266–309
  cluster, 274, 299
  error, 300
  fraction, 293, 300
  judgment, 269, 300
  nonrandom, 269
  probability, 269, 300
  random, 269, 270, 300
  stratified, 274, 300
  systematic, 270, 273, 300
Sampling distribution of the mean, 282, 300
Sampling distribution of the proportion, 277
Sampling distributions, 266–309
Sampling distribution of a statistic, 300
Sampling error, 300
Sampling fraction, 293, 300
Sampling from non-normal populations, 285
Sampling from normal population, 283
SAS, 129, 440, 459, 560, 591
Savage, Leonard, 151
Scatter diagram, 494, 535
Seasonal variation, 662, 664, 681, 697
Second-degree equation, 670, 697
Second-degree regression model, 589
Secular trend, 662, 663, 665, 697
Shapes of ogives, 32
Significance level, 362, 412
  selection of, 364
Sign test, 608, 643
Simon, Pierre, 144
Simple random sampling, 270, 271, 275, 300
Simple regression, 490–547
Sinclair, Sir John, 2
Skewness, 58, 91
  negative, 59
  positive, 59
Slope, 498, 504, 535
Smirnov, N. V., 638
Sorting the data points, 22
Spinks, Leon, 144
SPSS, 129
S-shaped ogive, 32
Standard deviation, 113, 116, 131
  characteristics of, 123
  computation of, 117, 120
  shortcomings of, 126

Standard error, 278, 300
Standard error of estimate, 509, 536
Standard error of the mean, 278, 300
Standard error of the proportion, 278, 331
Standard error of a regression coefficient, 529, 536, 568, 591
Standard normal probability distribution, 233, 247
  table, 235
Standard score, 119, 131
  calculating, 119
  interpreting, 120
Standard unit, 236
Stated limits, 23
State of nature, 749, 785
Statistical Account of Scotland, 2
Statistical decision theory, 748
Statistical dependence, 167, 183
  types, 167
Statistical independence, 158, 183
  types, 159
Statistical inference, 3, 275, 300
Statistics, 1, 62, 91, 268, 300
  approaches to, 3
  assumption for, 3
  descriptive, 3
  history of, 2
  inferential, 3
  strategy for, 3
  subdivision within, 3
Steps for finding the median of grouped data, 80
Strata, 300
Strategy for statistics, 3
Stratified sample, 274, 300
Student, 334
Student's t distribution, 334, 345
  characteristics of, 334
  condition for use of, 334
Subdivisions within statistics, 3
Subjective probability, 150, 183
  use of, 150
Sufficient estimator, 315, 345
Summary measures of frequency distributions, 56–103
Summary statistics, 58, 91
Symmetrical, 58, 91
Systematic sampling, 270, 273, 300
  characteristics of, 273
  shortcomings of, 273

t distribution, 383, 385
t table, 336
Table of random digits, 272
Tables, 2–55
Tables and graphs, 2–55
Test of independence, 429, 476
Tests for data, 9
Theoretical sampling distribution, 282
Theory of runs, 622, 643
Time series, 660–705
  problems with, 689
  variations of, 662
Transformations, 589, 591
Trend analysis, 665
Trends in data, 22
Tukey, John W., 128
Two-tailed test, 366, 412
Type I error, 365, 412
Type II error, 365, 412
Types of probability, 147

U statistic, 616
Unbiased estimator, 314, 345
Unconditional probability, 153
Unequal classes, 21
  problems with, 21
Ungrouped data, 64
Unweighted aggregates index, 712, 734
Unweighted average of relatives method, 722, 734
Upper-tailed test, 367, 412
Use of the appropriate mean, 75
Utility, 768, 785

Value index, 709, 728, 729
Variable:
  dependent, 492, 535
  dummy, 591
  independent, 492, 535
Variance, 113, 115, 131
  calculating, 120
  formulation of, 115
Venn, John, 153
Venn diagram, 153, 183
Vertical axis, 28

Weighted aggregates index, 715, 735
Weighted average, 72
Weighted average of relatives method, 724, 735
Weighted mean, 71, 91
  calculation of, 72
Width of class intervals, 21
William the Conqueror, 2
Within-column variance, 453, 476

$\hat{Y}$ (y-hat), 501
Y-intercept, 504, 536

z table, 336
Zimmerman, E. A. W., 2